LEADING

Sir Alex Ferguson

Sir Alex Ferguson was born in 1941 in Govan, Scotland. A goal-scoring centre-forward, he was later transferred to Rangers for a Scottish record transfer fee. In 1974, he entered management with East Stirlingshire and St Mirren before joining Aberdeen, where consistent domestic success, followed by victory in the 1983 Cup Winners' Cup over Real Madrid, brought him wider attention.

Arriving at Manchester United in 1986, he went on to accumulate 38 trophies, including five FA Cups, 13 Premier Leagues and two Champions Leagues. He was knighted in 1999, following Manchester United's remarkable Treble campaign, and his overall haul of 49 trophies makes him the most successful British manager of all time.

Sir Alex announced his retirement in 2013, but he continues to serve United as a director and is a Fellow to the Executive Education Program at Harvard Business School.

Sir Michael Moritz

Sir Michael Moritz was born in Cardiff, studied at Oxford and became a journalist at *Time* magazine in the US in the late 1970s. It was during this period that he met the young Steve Jobs and wrote the first book about Apple, *The Little Kingdom: The Private Story of Apple Computer*. Moritz co-authored a second business book, *Going for Broke: The Chrysler Story*, and in 1986 joined Sequoia Capital, in Silicon Valley, California.

Sequoia Capital's close alliances with young founders have been transformed into companies now worth nearly $1.5 trillion – the most of any private investment firm in the world. These include the first investments in companies such as Apple and Cisco and, more recently, YouTube, Airbnb, Dropbox and WhatsApp. Michael Moritz has been a member of the Board of Directors of Google, Yahoo!, PayPal and LinkedIn.

In 2012 he became chairman of Sequoia Capital and was knighted in 2013. His family's philanthropic work includes Europe's largest scholarship programme for low income university students. The son of refugees from Nazi Germany, he lives in San Francisco with his wife, Harriet Heyman.

LEADING

ALEX FERGUSON

WITH MICHAEL MORITZ

EPILOGUE BY MICHAEL MORITZ

HODDER &
STOUGHTON

First published in Great Britain in 2015 by Hodder & Stoughton
An Hachette UK company

First published in trade paperback in 2016

2

The Data Room Infographics by Jack Hagley

A CIP catalogue record for this title is available
from the British Library

ISBN 978 1 473 62165 7

Typeset by Palimpsest Book Production Ltd,
Falkirk, Stirlingshire

Printed and bound by Clays Ltd, St Ives plc

Hodder & Stoughton policy is to use papers that are
natural, renewable and recyclable products and made
from wood grown in sustainable forests. The logging and
manufacturing processes are expected to conform to
the environmental regulations of the country of origin.

Hodder & Stoughton Ltd
Carmelite House
50 Victoria Embankment
London EC4Y 0DZ

www.hodder.co.uk

For my family

I have had a privileged life after being brought up in Govan, a working-class area of Glasgow, where my parents Alex and Lizzie gave me a foundation that has stayed with me to this day. My brother Martin has always been a loyal and great friend, following the same path that was laid out by our parents.

I had the good fortune to meet a wonderful girl who has been my rock for almost 50 years. Cathy has presented me with three great sons who have inherited our work ethic and are a credit to both of us. Those three sons have given us more joy than we could ever have imagined, 11 grandchildren ranging in age from five to 21.

It has been an interesting journey as we have watched their development through the years and it is amazing to see the traits I expect from our family within them. I hope that their futures are lined with the same success that I have been fortunate enough to enjoy. Good luck to all of them.

Alex Ferguson

For the winning teams of Sequoia Capital – with thanks.

Michael Moritz

CONTENTS

INTRODUCTION

When I left Govan High School in Glasgow at the age of 16 to begin my apprenticeship as a tool-maker at Remington Rand and start my life in football at Queen's Park, I could never have imagined that, 55 years later, I would be standing at the front of a lecture theatre at the Harvard Business School, talking to a class of MBA students about myself.

The first class I taught in October 2012 was jammed to the rafters. From my position in the pit at the front of the lecture hall, I could see the students waiting patiently in their tiered rows of seats – each with their own name card in front of them – and yet more crammed in the aisles. It was an intimidating scene, but also a tribute to the fascination exerted by Manchester United. Our club was in very good company, because among the organisations studied during the Strategic Marketing in Creative Industries course at the Business School are Burberry, the fashion retailer; Comcast, the giant American cable television operator; Marvel Enterprises, the Hollywood studio behind the *Spider-Man* and *Iron Man* comic and film franchises; and, of all things, the business activities of the music superstars Beyoncé and Lady Gaga.

When I looked at the students gathered in one of Aldrich Hall's lecture rooms, I was struck by their cosmopolitan nature,

age and intelligence. There were as many nationalities represented in the room as there are on the books of any Premier
League squad. The students were all extremely well schooled,
and would either work, or had already worked, for some of the
most successful companies in the world. All were at the point
where they could look forward to the best years of their lives.
I could not help but think that the quieter ones, who seemed
to be absorbing everything, were the people who would become
the most successful.

I found myself on the campus of Harvard University in
October of 2012 thanks to a collision of circumstances. A year
or so previously I had received an approach from Anita Elberse,
a professor at Harvard Business School. She had been curious
about the way I managed United and the success that the club
had enjoyed, and this resulted in a Harvard case study, *Sir Alex
Ferguson: Managing Manchester United*, which was written
following Anita spending a few days shadowing me at our
training ground in the mornings and interviewing me in the
afternoons. Around the same time, she invited me to come and
speak to her class at their campus in Boston. I was intrigued,
if a little daunted, and accepted the invitation.

Looking back, it's easy to see that this lecture marked the
start of a transitional phase in my career. Although I didn't
know it at the time, we were just a few weeks into what would
turn out to be my final season in charge at Old Trafford, and
there was a lot on my mind. We had lost the title in the previous
season on goal difference to our local rivals, Manchester City,
but were determined to bounce back. And we had started the
new season strongly. Two days before I flew to Boston, we had
come away from St James' Park with a 3–0 win over Newcastle
United. It was our fifth victory in seven games and took us to
second place in the Premier League, four points behind Chelsea.

We had also made a 100 per cent start to our Champions League campaign, UEFA's premier club competition, formerly known as the European Cup.

But for the time being, as I stood at the front of the classroom in Harvard, I put the Premier League and Champions League campaigns to one side and focused on sharing some of the secrets behind Manchester United's recent success.

The class began with Professor Elberse providing an overview of the different constituents I dealt with as manager of Manchester United – the players and the staff, the fans and the media, the board and our owners. I followed this by giving the students my thoughts on the principal elements of leadership. I then took questions from the students. This was the most enjoyable part of the day and it raised topics that I found myself thinking about in the days that followed. The students were all curious about how I became a leader, the individuals who had a major influence on my approach to life, the way I dealt with absurdly gifted and highly paid young men, the manner in which United maintained a thirst for excellence – and a raft of other topics. Understandably they also wanted to know about the daily habits of household names like Cristiano Ronaldo and David Beckham.

It took me a bit of time to adjust to standing in front of a blackboard rather than sitting in a football dugout, but I gradually began to realise that teaching bears some similarities to football management. Perhaps the most important element of each activity is to inspire a group of people to perform at their very best. The best teachers are the unsung heroes and heroines of any society, and in that classroom I could not help but think of Elizabeth Thomson, a teacher at Broomloan Road Primary School, who encouraged me to take my school work seriously and who helped me gain admission to Govan High School.

I have spent much of my life trying to coax the best out of young people and the Harvard classroom presented another such opportunity. As the years have gone by, I have found that my appetite for, and appreciation of, youthful enthusiasm has only grown. Young people will always manage to achieve the impossible – whether that is on the football field or inside a company or other big organisation. If I were running a company, I would always want to listen to the thoughts of its most talented youngsters, because they are the people most in touch with the realities of today and the prospects for tomorrow.

The books I have previously written about my addiction to football are full of details about competitions, games and the composition of teams that I played in and managed. The first, *A Light in the North: Seven Years with Aberdeen*, appeared in 1985, two years after Aberdeen's European Cup Winners' Cup victory. In 1999, after Manchester United won the Treble – the Premier League, the FA Cup and the UEFA Champions League – I published *Managing My Life*, and a few months after my retirement in 2013, *My Autobiography* was released.

This book is different. It's my attempt to sum up what I learned from my life in general and my time as a manager – first in Scotland for 12 years with East Stirlingshire, St Mirren and Aberdeen, and then, south of the border, for 26 years with Manchester United. I have also included some interesting data covering my time in management and some archival material that has not been seen before as a way to illustrate a few of the topics being addressed. The data and archive material can be found at the back of the book.

Figuring out what it takes to win trophies with a round ball differs from the challenges facing the leaders of companies like BP, Marks & Spencer, Vodafone, Toyota or Apple, or the people who run large hospitals, universities or global charities. Yet there are traits that apply to all winners, and to organisations whose leaders aspire to win. This is my attempt to explain how I built, led and managed the organisation at Manchester United, and the sorts of things that worked for me. I don't pretend for a moment that they can be easily transplanted elsewhere, but I hope that readers will find some ideas or suggestions that can be emulated or modified for their own use.

I am not a management expert or business guru, and have little interest in pounding the lecture circuit repeating a canned pitch. So don't expect any academic jargon or formulaic prose. Don't ask me to explain double-entry book-keeping, how to hire 500 people in six months, the challenges of matrix management, the way to get a manufacturing line to churn out 100,000 smartphones a day, or the best approach to developing software. I don't have a clue. That expertise belongs to others because my whole life has revolved around football. This book contains the lessons and observations about how I pursued excellence on and off the football pitch.

Unlike the great American basketball coach John Wooden, whose 'Pyramid of Success' accompanied him throughout most of his career from 1928 to 1975, I never employed a one-page diagram or a massive guide that would be handed out to players at the start of each season and viewed as gospel. Nor did I favour minute instructions written on 3- x 5-inch cards, or copious notes compiled over the years. My approach to leadership and management evolved as the seasons went by. This is my attempt to sum up what I learned and distil it on paper.

This book came to life after I was approached by Michael Moritz, Chairman of Sequoia Capital, the US headquartered private investment firm best known for helping to shape and organise companies such as Apple, Cisco Systems, Google,

PayPal and YouTube and, more recently, WhatsApp and Airbnb. We had first talked about collaborating on a book several years before my retirement, but the timing was not right for either of us. Happily, in the past couple of years, we both had the time to devote our energy towards putting words on paper. It turned out that Michael, who led Sequoia Capital between the mid-1990s and 2012, had always wondered how Manchester United had maintained a high level of performance over several decades. As we talked, it was obvious that Michael's interest stemmed from his desire to ensure that Sequoia Capital did the same. As you might know, Sequoia Capital has been able to collect more than its fair share of silverware. Michael has contributed an epilogue to the book which, though it makes me blush from time to time, explains more fully why and how our paths came to cross.

Leading is the result of many conversations between Michael and me that cover a range of topics – some of which I hadn't pondered previously. The conversations allowed me to collect my thoughts about issues that confront any leader but which, because of the pressure of their daily obligations, I never had time to gather. I hope you find some of them useful.

Alex Ferguson
Manchester
August 2015

1

BECOMING YOURSELF

Listening

How does someone become their true self? When I was young I never gave the topic much thought but, as a player and particularly as a manager, I became increasingly interested in the subject. If you are leading people, it helps to have a sense of who they are – the circumstances in which they were raised, the actions that will draw out the best in them, and the remarks that will cause them to be spooked. The only way to figure this out is by two underrated activities: listening and watching.

Most people don't use their eyes and ears effectively. They aren't very observant and they fail to listen intently. As a result, they miss half of what is going on around them. I can think of some managers who could talk under water. I don't think it helps them. There's a reason that God gave us two ears, two eyes and one mouth. It's so you can listen and watch twice as much as you talk. Best of all, listening costs you nothing.

Two of the best listeners I have met were television interviewers. Before his death in 2013, David Frost had spent nearly five decades interviewing people, including, most famously, the former US president Richard Nixon. I first met Frost in 2005 when we were both investors in a property fund manager. A few years later, after he'd left the BBC, he interviewed me for Sky Sports.

Unlike most television interviewers, David did not feel the need to prove he was smarter than his guest. He did not keep snapping at their heels, or interrupting, but he was definitely no pushover – as he demonstrated with the 28 hours and 45 minutes of conversations he taped with Richard Nixon in 1977. Some of this was because of the format of his shows. He was not doing post-match, 90-second interviews with a producer yelling into his earpiece demanding a sound-bite. And he wasn't swivelling his head, mid-interview, as he tried to catch the eye of his next unsuspecting target. David would look you in the eyes, lock out the rest of the world and demonstrate great interest. He had time on his side – 30 or 60 minutes (an eternity in today's world of instant messaging and Twitter) to gradually make his guest feel at ease. David's greatest gift was his ability to get a guest to relax, and that always seemed to allow him to extract more from an interview. It's little wonder that his nickname was 'The Grand Inquisitor'.

Charlie Rose, the American television interviewer, is similar. I don't know Charlie as well as I knew David, but a couple of years ago I was invited to appear on his show. I was a little apprehensive about appearing on American television, which isn't as familiar to me as all the British talk shows. The day before I went on Charlie's show, he invited me for a drink at Harry Cipriani, an Italian restaurant on Fifth Avenue in New York. Charlie is a big man and has hands the size of dinner plates, so I wondered whether he was going to clamp me in a vice. His opening line was, 'You know I'm half Scottish', and after that, I knew all would be well. Charlie had cleverly put me at my ease and given us something familiar to talk about.

On the following day the taping went fine, with Charlie listening just as intently as David, even though I suspect his producer was wondering about whether she would have to use subtitles to make my Scottish accent comprehensible to viewers in Mississippi and Kansas.

I have never been a television host but I've always valued listening. This doesn't mean I was in the habit of phoning people to ask them what I should do in a particular situation. On the whole I liked to work things out for myself. But I do remember seeking help when, in 1984, I was offered the manager's position at Glasgow Rangers by John Paton, who was one of the club's largest shareholders. It was the second time that there had been overtures from Rangers, so I called Scot Symon, who had managed the club for 13 years, and sought his advice. I already had my doubts about going to Rangers. If I was going to leave Aberdeen I was unsure about going to another Scottish club. When Scot discovered that I had not talked to the ultimate authority at Rangers, vice-chairman Willie Waddell, he urged me to decline the offer, since he felt it was more of a fishing expedition and probably hadn't been officially sanctioned by the board. I did, and I've never regretted that decision.

Many people cannot stop long enough to listen – especially when they become successful and all the people around them are being obsequious and pretending to hang on their every word. They launch into monologues as if suddenly they know everything. Putting these megalomaniacs to one side, it always pays to listen to others. It's like enrolling in a continuous, lifelong free education, with the added benefit that there are no examinations and you can always discard useless comments. A few examples come to mind:

Years ago somebody gave me a set of tapes containing conversations with Bill Shankly, the Liverpool manager between 1959 and 1974. They were reminiscences, and were not designed for broadcast, but I listened to them several times while driving. They contained all sorts of anecdotes, but the inescapable truth of those tapes was the degree of Shankly's complete obsession with football, which must have been in his bone marrow. Even if Shankly verged on the extreme, it reinforced to me the dedication required to succeed.

On another occasion, after a game against Leeds United in 1992, I was in the team bath with the players – which was highly unusual for me – listening to their analysis of the match. Steve Bruce and Gary Pallister were raving about Eric Cantona, the French striker Leeds had signed from Nîmes. Steve Bruce, who was then United's captain, was particularly complimentary about Cantona's abilities. Somehow, those comments planted a seed, which soon afterwards led to us buying Cantona.

Even as we signed Eric Cantona, I sought advice from people I trusted. I chatted with both Gérard Houllier, the French manager, and the French sports journalist, Erik Bielderman, in an attempt to better understand the player I was buying. I also spoke to Michel Platini who said, 'You should sign him, his character is underestimated, he just needs a bit of understanding.' They all provided tips about the best way to handle Eric, who arrived at United with a reputation – which was unfair – for being unmanageable. It proved to be a pivotal decision for United that season – arguably for the whole decade. In the six games we played before Eric arrived we had scored four goals. In the six games following his arrival, we scored 14.

The comment that led us to Cantona was unusual but I made it a practice to listen intently to how the players would predict the probable line-up of our opponents. It was always a guessing game until we got handed the team-sheet and our opponents' line-up could have a big influence on our tactics. During the week before a game, players often talk to their pals around the League, particularly their former team-mates, so they sometimes pick up clues about which players they would be facing in the tunnel. We used to have little competitions to see whether we could guess the line-up. No matter how hard I listened, I could never fully anticipate the 11 characters we would be up against. As the squads expanded, it became even harder to do. Inevitably, after we eventually had the information, the line-up would differ from what I had expected and the players would rib me by saying, 'You're right again, Boss.'

After United got beaten at Norwich in November 2012, out of courtesy I had to show my face in their manager's room. Chris Hughton was gracious enough, but the room was packed with people celebrating their win. I did not want to show any weakness, so I put on a good face and listened to what they had to say – particularly about the players they were singling out for praise. I just remembered all their names and made a mental note to put everyone on our radar screen.

Looking back further, I remember another critical piece of advice. In 1983, when Aberdeen – the team I managed between 1978 and 1986 – were due to play Real Madrid in the final of the European Cup Winners' Cup in Gothenburg, I invited Jock Stein to accompany us. Jock was one of my heroes and was the first British manager to win the European Cup in 1967, when Celtic beat Inter Milan. Jock said two things that I have never forgotten. First, he told me, 'Make sure you are the second team on the ground for training on the day before the game because then your opponents will think you are watching them while they work.' He also advised me to take along a bottle of Macallan whisky for Real Madrid's manager, the great Alfredo

Di Stéfano. When I gave Di Stéfano that bottle, he was really taken aback. It made him think that we were in awe of him – that he was the big guy and that little Aberdeen felt they were beaten already. I'm glad I listened to Jock because both his tips helped.

Later, when I worked for Jock as assistant manager of Scotland, I used to pepper him with questions about tactics and dealing with management issues. He was as close to a managerial mentor as I ever had, and I would soak up almost everything he had to say. Jock used to advise me never to lose my temper with players straight after the game. He kept saying, 'Wait till Monday, when things have calmed down.' It was sound advice; it just didn't happen to suit my style. Nonetheless, it is no coincidence that in my office in Wilmslow the largest photograph on the wall is of Jock Stein and me, before the Wales v Scotland game on 10 September 1985 – the night he died.

There is one final example that comes to mind: Jimmy Sirrel, who was manager of Notts County and an instructor on a coaching course I attended in 1973 at Lilleshall, one of the United Kingdom's National Sports Centres, taught me a crucial lesson. He told me never to let all the players' contracts expire around the same time because it allows them to collude against the manager and the club. I'd never thought about that before Jimmy mentioned it to me but, afterwards, I paid very close attention to making sure we staggered the contracts. I bet Jimmy's advice took him less than a minute to convey, but the benefit of listening to him lasted me a lifetime. It just shows that advice often comes when you least expect it, and listening, which costs nothing, is one of the most valuable things you can do.

Watching

Watching is the other underrated activity, and again, it costs nothing. For me there are two forms of observation: the first is on the detail and the second is on the big picture. Until I was managing Aberdeen and hired Archie Knox as my assistant manager, I had not appreciated the difference between watching for the tiny particulars while also trying to understand the broader landscape. Shortly after he arrived at Aberdeen, Archie sat me down and asked me why I had hired him. The question perplexed me, until he explained that he had nothing to do since I insisted on doing everything. He was very insistent, and was egged on by Teddy Scott, Aberdeen's general factotum, who agreed with him. Archie told me that I shouldn't be conducting the training sessions but, instead, should be on the sidelines watching and supervising. I wasn't sure that I should follow this advice because I thought it would hamper my control of the sessions. But when I told Archie I wanted to mull over his advice, he was insistent. So, somewhat reluctantly, I bowed to his wishes and, though it took me a bit of time to understand you can see a lot more when you are not in the thick of things, it was the most important decision I ever made about the way I managed and led. When you are a step removed from the fray, you see things that come as surprises – and it is important to allow yourself to be surprised. If you are in the middle of a training session with a whistle in your mouth, your entire focus is on the ball. When I stepped back and watched from the sidelines, my field of view was widened and I could absorb the whole session, as well as pick up on players' moods, energy and habits. This was one of the most valuable lessons of my career and I'm glad that I received it more than 30 years ago. Archie's observation was the making of me.

As a player I had tried to do both – paying attention to the ball at my feet whilst being aware of what was happening elsewhere on the field. But until Archie gave me a finger wagging, I had not really understood that, as a manager, I was in danger of losing myself to the details. It only took me a handful of days to understand the merit of Archie's point, and from that moment I was always in a position to be able to zoom in to see the detail and zoom out to see the whole picture.

As a manager you are always watching out for particular things. You might be monitoring a player in training to see if he has shaken off a thigh injury; appraising a promising 12 year old in the youth academy; looking at a hot prospect in a night game at some stadium in Germany; examining the demeanour of a player or coach at the lunch table. You could also be searching for patterns and clues in a video analysis reel, the body language during a negotiation, or the length of the grass on a pitch. Then, on Saturday afternoons or Wednesday evenings, there would be the need for the other, wider lens – the one capable of taking in the whole picture.

It sounds simple to say you should believe what your eyes tell you, but it is very hard to do. It is astonishing how many biases and preconceived notions we carry around, and these influence what we see, or, more precisely, what we think we see. If I was told by a scout that a player had a good left foot, it would be hard for me to forget that observation when I went to watch him in action – and in doing so it would be easy to overlook another quality or, much more painfully, ignore a major fault. I was certainly interested in what other people had to say, but I always wanted to watch with my own eyes without having my judgement swayed by the filters of others.

Here is one observation from which I benefited for decades. In 1969 West Germany were training at Rugby Park in Kilmarnock and I asked Karl-Heinz Heddergot, of the German FA, for permission to watch the practice. The only people in the ground were the German players and staff, a few groundsmen, and me. I watched the training for around an hour and a half. The German squad played without goalkeepers, and just concentrated on possession of the ball, which was unusual during a period when coaches used to emphasise training sessions composed of long-distance running. That one encounter made an enormous impression on me, and thereafter I started to emphasise the importance of possession. As soon as I became a coach at St Mirren, I started doing 'boxes' – where we'd pit four players against two in a confined amount of space. We started with boxes that were 25 yards by 25 yards, which forced the players to perform in a confined space and improve their ball skills. As players' skills improved, we tightened the boxes. It helped with everything: awareness, angles, touch on the ball, and eventually it led to being able to play one-touch football. It was a coaching technique I used right up until my last training session at United on 18 May 2013. Watching that practice for 90 minutes in Kilmarnock back in 1969 furnished me with a lesson I used for half a century.

Observation – sizing up others and measuring situations – is an essential part of preparation, and, at United, we made it a habit to carefully watch opponents before going up against them in big games. This was even more important in the era prior to sophisticated video analysis, when the best we could do was fast forward or rewind through a videotape. One example of this paying off was in United's 1991 European Cup Winners' Cup final against Barcelona. It was the first European final to be played by an English team following the ban from European competition after the Heysel disaster of 1985. I had attended Barcelona's semi-final first leg against Juventus with Steve Archibald, a former Aberdeen player, during which their main striker, Hristo Stoichkov, was hugely impressive and scored two goals. In the second leg in Turin he suffered a hamstring injury that ruled him out of the final. It played havoc with their normal formation. During the final they relied on Michael Laudrup to be their chief offensive weapon, driving forward from midfield which, thanks to watching Barcelona previously, we had anticipated. We had already adjusted our tactics, steadfastly refused to be lured too far forward by Laudrup, and eventually won 2–1.

There were also plenty of times when I saw a player out of the corner of my eye who came as a complete, but pleasant, surprise. In 2003 I had gone to watch a young Petr Čech play in France. Didier Drogba, whom I had not heard of, was playing in the same game. He was a dynamo – a strong, explosive striker with a true instinct for goal – though he ultimately slipped through our fingers. That didn't happen with Ji-sung Park. I had gone to get the measure of Lyon's Michael Essien in the Champions League in 2005 during their quarter-final ties with PSV Eindhoven, and saw this ceaseless bundle of energy buzz about the field like a cocker spaniel. It was Ji-sung Park. The following week I sent my brother, Martin, who was a scout for United, to watch him, to see what his eyes told him. They told him the same thing and we signed him. Ji-sung was one of those rare players who could always create space for himself.

These were very special moments. I always enjoyed stumbling across a new talent when I was least expecting it. Very rarely do you see something so astonishing that you sense it arrived from another world (though Eric Cantona, at his very best, could have done so). These moments – and players – are the reward for a lifetime of careful watching. None of them suddenly dropped into our lap; they were the result of keeping our radar operating 24 hours a day.

Reading

I have picked up a lot from reading books over the years. As a boy I disappointed my parents by not working hard enough at school (largely because I was already besotted by football), so my formal education ended when I was 16. But I've always liked reading. In fact I was in the library in Glasgow on 6 February 1958 when I heard about the Munich air disaster. I've subscribed for many years to the *Daily Express* during the week and the Scottish *Sunday Mail* and *Sunday Post*, the *Sunday Express* and *Independent* on the weekends. I've also been partial to the *Racing Post*, which keeps me up to date on horse racing. But, more importantly, I've always liked books.

My interest in books stretches far beyond football. One of the coaches I read about came from a sport about which I know nothing. He was the great UCLA basketball coach John Wooden, who led his team to ten national championship titles in 12 seasons. He was probably stronger as an inspirational coach than as a master of tactics, but there was no misunderstanding about who was boss. He would not tolerate any waywardness or people straying from the path he mapped out. I also read up on Vince Lombardi, who was a household name in the United States during the time he was the coach of the Green Bay Packers. He was as obsessed about American football as I was about English football. I found him easy to identify with and love his quote, 'We didn't lose the game; we just ran out of time.'

I have dipped into other books about management and leadership but, maybe because I was always so preoccupied with my own job, I never found one that spoke to me. The same goes for sports books and players' biographies. For the most part, a United player's autobiography was an account, albeit from a different angle, of something I had already lived through. I just found I preferred reading books that had little to do with my daily work. From time to time I tripped across other football books such as David Peace's novel, *The Damned Utd*, a fictionalised account of Brian Clough's 44-day spell as manager of Leeds United in 1974, but cannot say I found it captivating. However, I was taken by *Farewell but not Goodbye*, the autobiography of Bobby Robson, a man whom I admired greatly, who started his life down a coal-mine and who, after being fired as England manager after being one step short of the 1990 World Cup final, showed great courage by picking himself up and going to the Netherlands to manage PSV Eindhoven before later heading to Porto and Barcelona and, eventually returning to his hometown, Newcastle. Of the players' autobiographies, the one I would single out is Gary Neville's *Red*, which was published in 2011. It's a thoughtful book and helps the reader understand the pressure on players and their need to succeed.

I don't want to overplay this, but I found some observations in books about military history relevant to football. Every general has to learn the best time to attack and when it is better to be conservative. Oddly, this was reiterated by a training course I attended with the SAS, who explained how they mounted attacks by outflanking and diverting the enemy on either side and then launching a deadly assault down the middle. One year we took the whole United squad to the SAS training grounds in Herefordshire for a couple of days during a break in the season. They gave us a taste of everything – winching descents from helicopters, the shooting range, and simulated break-ups of hostage situations. The players loved it. One lesson I took from the SAS was the effectiveness of a battle formation, where troops attacking on the flanks create softness in the central defences. I took that lesson right to the training pitch where we worked on it for a week before a Liverpool game. I had players attacking the back post and the front post and then Gary Pallister came from right outside the centre of the box to score. In fact Pallister scored twice using precisely the same ploy. It could have been a re-enactment of a battle plan – except none of the TV commentators picked up on that.

I've always been interested in American history – both military and political – and I've read a fair amount about Abraham Lincoln and JFK, especially the value of taking your time before making decisions. I found Doris Kearns Goodwin's book *Team of Rivals: the Political Genius of Abraham Lincoln* absorbing, while JFK's careful approach during the Cuban Missile Crisis of 1962 is as fine an example of deliberate decision-making as you will find. I certainly found more virtue in patiently working towards the right decision as I got older. In my early days as a manager I could be impetuous – always in a hurry to get things done and stamp my authority on a situation. It takes courage to say, 'Let me think about it.' When you're young you want to fly to the moon and you want to get there quickly. I think it's usually enthusiasm that causes this. As you get older you temper your enthusiasm with experience.

I realise that we're shaped by lots of other forces beyond just watching, listening and reading. We're all accidental victims of our parents' DNA; we are shaped by the luck of the draw, the circumstances in which we grew up and the education we received. But we all have two sets of very powerful tools that we completely control: our eyes and our ears. Watching others, listening to their advice and reading about people are three of the best things I ever did.

2

RECOGNISING HUNGER

Discipline

Discipline was drummed into me from an early age. My father was a real disciplinarian. He worked in ship-building, which was a hard and cruel business. He didn't talk much. He could be stubborn and was a man of few words but he was very intelligent. He was self-educated, left school at 14, but read all the time. He wanted my brother and me to be trained in a craft and refused to let me become a professional footballer until after I had finished my apprenticeship as a tool-maker. He drummed discipline into us from an early age. On schooldays he would always shake my leg promptly at 6 a.m. He would also be out of the house at 6.45 a.m. on the dot because he liked to be at the yard when the gates opened. Maybe that's why, a couple of decades later as a manager, I got into the habit of appearing for work before the milkman arrived. After I started being paid for playing football, I used to go out on Saturday nights. My father didn't like that. He thought I was living life too well. I went about six months without talking to him. The two of us were too alike.

When I was 14 I started playing for Drumchapel Amateurs, which was the biggest amateur team in Scotland. It was run by Douglas Smith, a relatively wealthy man whose family owned a shipbreaking yard. He had an arrangement with Reid's Tea Rooms in the centre of Glasgow so that boys could get a free lunch. He ran five teams – Under-18s, Under-17s, Under-16s, Under-15s and Under-14s. Every weekend he would take us down to his estate in Dunbartonshire, just outside Glasgow, walk us through his piggery and then make us play five-a-side games on his bowling green. He tensed up when one of his teams lost and would start sweating and get visibly angry. He had a great sense of discipline and a deep desire to win.

Discipline had been an issue from day one at St Mirren, which I managed between 1974 and 1978. When I first arrived, the local paper, the *Paisley Daily Express,* sent a photographer out to take a picture of the team with their new manager. The next morning I saw the photograph in the paper with Ian Reid, the player who had been the team captain, standing behind me with his fingers making a set of rabbit ears. After we lost our first game to Cowdenbeath, I called Reid into my office on the Monday morning. He said that his rabbit ears were only a joke and I told him, 'It's not the kind of joke I like.' John Mowat was a good, young player who started answering back when I gave him instructions during a game. I put both Reid and Mowat in my black book. There was another player who told me that he couldn't attend a training session because he and his girlfriend had tickets for a pop concert. I asked him whether the concerts were on every night of the year. When he said that wasn't the case, I told him, 'If you want to go to the concert, fine, but don't come back.' I just wanted to make it very clear to all the players that I did not want to be messed about with. They got the message.

When I became a manager, one of my duties was to instil discipline. At St Mirren, the team was composed of part-time players but, nonetheless, we all travelled on the same bus to away games. One player decided to drive himself to East Fife one Saturday. I tore into him in the dressing room before the game for being too big for his boots and I told him he wouldn't be part of the team that day. Then I realised I didn't have a spare player to replace him with, so that piece of discipline went out the window.

When I got to Aberdeen, which is a more sedate place than Glasgow, I realised that I would need to inject a bit of Glaswegian ferocity and discipline into the team. I didn't spare the horses. I was aggressive and demanding and I suspect not everyone enjoyed it, but it made the players into men and increased their profiles.

At Aberdeen there were three players who, in my opinion, were a nuisance. They just did not take training seriously enough. So I would make them work out again each afternoon, dumped them into the reserve team and sent them to play in freezing places like Peterhead on Tuesday and Wednesday nights. Eventually, I just got rid of them all.

Discipline might also have been instilled, decades ago, by the fact that teams rarely seemed to change. It's hard to believe (especially when you see the seven substitutes sitting on the bench during Premier League games) that substitutes were only first allowed in the mid-1960s. When I was a boy a team barely changed for the entire season, and even now I can name the Raith Rovers team from the early 1950s. There was also a large element of economic necessity about staying in the team to ensure you got your bonus money.

From time to time, in my younger days, I was too much of a disciplinarian and did things that I regretted. For example, after Aberdeen returned home from Sweden with the European Cup Winners' Cup in 1983, we had a parade which ended at our stadium, Pittodrie, which was packed to the gills. All the fans wanted to see the players carry the trophy around the field and Mark McGhee, Aberdeen's centre-forward, was eager to show them the trophy. However, I thought he had been celebrating too much and so I tore into him and forbade him from carrying the trophy. Then his mother arrived in the dressing room and, of course, that made me feel rotten. So the next morning I phoned McGhee and apologised and asked him to accompany me down to the harbour where he and I showed the trophy to the fans who had travelled by boat back from Gothenburg. I was not eager to repeat incidents like that.

The issue of discipline accompanied me throughout my career. In the conversations I had with Martin Edwards before accepting Manchester United's offer to join them in November 1986, he alluded to the habit of some of the players to drink too much. He mentioned that one of the reasons United had been interested in me was that I had built a reputation as a manager who was known for maintaining discipline and not tolerating poor behaviour.

When I got to United there was a lax attitude towards lots of things, including the clothes the players wore when travelling to games. They used to wear the tracksuits of whatever clothing company was sponsoring them – Reebok, Puma, adidas. It was a royal mess. I immediately insisted that they travel in flannels, the club blazer and tie. When Fabien Barthez joined us in 2000 as a goalkeeper from Monaco, he had to adjust to our clothing regimen. He did this by changing clothes on the bus on the way to games. After the game he would return his jacket, trousers, shirt and tie to Albert Morgan, our kit man, who would take care of them until Fabien was required to again appear as a representative of our club. Eric Cantona breached the dress code on one occasion when there was a big civic reception in the town hall for the team and he appeared wearing a suede jacket which had long fringes and a picture of an American Indian chief on the back. The next day he swore to me – and I believed him – that he had thought it was going to be a casual occasion, which is how it would have been treated in France.

Players give a manager plenty of opportunities to crack the whip, so it's best to pick and choose the moments. You don't have to mete out punishment very often for everyone to get the message. For example, I never thought it useful to fine players if they were late for training. Around Manchester, especially in the winter, the roads quickly get clogged if there is an accident or maintenance works. Players would sometimes get stuck in traffic jams and arrive late. If it happened once or twice I didn't care. However, if someone was a repeated late offender, I'd suggest to him that he leave his house ten minutes earlier and would point out to him that, by being late, he was letting his team-mates down. No team player wants to do that. I only remember fining one player for tardy appearances at the training ground and that was the goalkeeper, Mark Bosnich, who was repeatedly late.

I wasn't afraid of crossing into what some of the players might have considered their private territory – hairstyles and jewellery. I never understood why players would want to have long hair when they spend so much effort trying to be as fit and quick as possible. Anything, even a few extra locks of hair, just didn't seem sensible. I had my first issue with a player on this topic when Karel Poborský came to Manchester from Slavia Prague in 1996, looking as though he was going to play for Led Zeppelin rather than United. I did manage to persuade him to trim his locks but, even so, they were always too long for my taste. There were other players who would be wearing necklaces carrying crosses that seemed heavier than those the pilgrims carry up the Via Dolorosa in Jerusalem. I banned all those. However, there wasn't much I could do about tattoos since it was hard – even for me – to argue that they added any weight. Eric Cantona started that particular craze when he arrived one morning with the head of an American Indian chief stencilled on to his left breast. Since Eric was venerated by his team-mates, several other players followed suit. I was always struck by the fact that Cristiano Ronaldo never chose to deface his body. It said a lot about his self-discipline.

Leaders can also hand down different sentences. Inexperienced, or insecure, leaders are often tempted to make any infraction a capital offence. That is all well and good except, once you have hung the person, you are plumb out of options. I gradually began to understand the wisdom behind the phrase, 'Let the punishment fit the crime' and, as judge, jury and chief executioner, I had plenty of sentences at my disposal. A simple yet deadly one was silence, and I used it often. It did not require any public humiliation or tongue-lashing, yet because everyone likes to be acknowledged, the recipient of my silent treatment knew that he was in the woodshed. I doled out lots of fines to players as a way to rap their knuckles and try to keep them focused on the team. They would usually be handed out after bookings or red cards received for stupid behaviour, like dissent shown towards the referee or a wild tackle or unsuitable behaviour off the pitch. These numbers grew more consequential in absolute size as pay ballooned in the Premier League, but the nature of the fine – a week's or two weeks' wages – remained constant. After a disastrous Christmas party in 2007, I fined the first and the reserve team a week's wages.

For the youngsters who were hoping to make the squad, I could set their heads spinning by just refusing to let them travel with the first team. For the squad members there were a couple of other ways I used to drive home the price of infractions. One was to leave a player out of the side, but the more severe was to make him sit in the stands dressed in his civvies. That is a footballer's equivalent of a public hanging. Nobody was immune from this.

Finally, there were the severest penalties of all – a suspension and a transfer. You might think that the second was the toughest, but that was not the way I looked at it. Once we had decided a player was going to be transferred, it was because he either no longer fitted into what we needed at United or, in a few cases, like Cristiano Ronaldo, we were honouring promises. From my point of view, the suspension was by far the most painful because the penalty was borne by both the player *and* the club. That happened in January 1995 when Eric Cantona was suspended for the final four months of the season by United and a further four months by the FA.

Every player dislikes being omitted from the first team, and that sense of disappointment only grows as players age and start to come to grips with the fact that their best playing days are behind them. However, I never let sentiment interfere with my team selections and that was particularly true for big games. In 1994 I dropped Bryan Robson from the squad for the FA Cup final. Bryan was at the end of his distinguished 13-year stay at United and I had underestimated how important it was to him to have a crack at winning his fourth FA Cup medal. In retrospect, I would have kept him in the squad and perhaps played him for the last part of the game

Even though, as my players knew too well, I had a tendency to explode, my temper usually did not have a destructive effect. That was not the case for players who abandoned their self-control and self-discipline on the field. If they got a string of yellow cards or, worse still, a red card as a result of some rush of blood to the head, it could have bitter consequences for the team. Not only did we have to play with ten men but we also lost the services of the player while he was suspended. Peter Schmeichel, Paul Ince, Bryan Robson, Roy Keane, Mark Hughes and Eric Cantona could all start a fight in an empty house. That did not help our cause one bit, and I made no secret about my displeasure when they got sent off for committing some act of folly.

There are some people who just seem to be immune to discipline. Juan Sebastián Verón, the Argentinian midfielder, was like that. Try as I might, I could not get him to fit into our system. He was a fantastic player with tremendous ability, but he was just a wild card. If I played him centre midfield he would end up wide right. If I played him wide right, he would wind up wide left. He simply did not have the necessary self-discipline and so we traded him after two years and 82 appearances. You cannot build a team with blithe free spirits.

There are also some players who will follow instructions to the letter. Ji-sung Park, our South Korean midfielder, was one of those. If I gave him an instruction he was like a dog with a bone – he just would not let go. When we played AC Milan in the Champions League in 2010, I asked Ji-sung Park to mark Andrea Pirlo, their midfielder and creative force. Pirlo was used to running the show for Milan but Ji-sung effectively suffocated him.

I placed discipline above all else and it might have cost us several titles. If I had to repeat things, I'd do precisely the same, because once you bid farewell to discipline you say goodbye to success and set the stage for anarchy. Shortly after Christmas in 2011, I discovered that three United players had gone out on the town on Boxing Day and were the worse for wear when they showed up for training the following morning. So I ordered all of them to do extra training, and dropped the three of them from the team we fielded for the following game against Blackburn Rovers. We already had a large number of injuries, and although this decision weakened us further, I felt this was the correct thing to do. We lost the game to Blackburn 3–2, which cost us a precious three points, and eventually we lost the League to Manchester City on goal difference. Many years earlier, in 1995, our decision to suspend Eric Cantona for the remainder of the season, following his fight with a fan after he got sent off at Crystal Palace, cost us both the League and FA Cup. At the time we suspended Eric (a suspension that, subsequently, was made even more severe by the FA) we were just a point off the top of the table and, had he played for the remainder of the season, I am positive we would have won by about ten points, instead of being pipped at the post by one point by Blackburn Rovers. In the long run principles are just more important than expediency.

If you can assemble a team of 11 talented players who concentrate intently during training sessions, take care of their diet and bodies, get enough sleep and show up on time, then you are almost halfway to winning a trophy. It is always astonishing how many clubs are incapable of doing this.

Before we beat Liverpool 1–0 in the 1996 FA Cup final, I sensed we would win the game by the way our opponents appeared for their pre-match inspection of the pitch. The entire Liverpool team, with the exception of the manager and his assistant, appeared in white suits supplied by a fashion designer. For me it signalled a breakdown in discipline and showed that the team was distracted by a frivolous sideshow. I mentioned this to my kit manager, Norman Davies, and the forecast proved correct when Eric Cantona scored a few minutes from the final whistle. A different example occurred years earlier when in September 1985 Aberdeen beat Rangers 3–0 at Ibrox Park after two of our opponents got sent off during the first half. Rangers had just tried to bully us and, with the crowd going nuts, lost control of their senses. It was complete pandemonium and we had to scuttle to the dressing room for safety for a period during the second half while the police cleared the pitch of marauding fans. This was one of those classic cases where our opponents destroyed themselves.

I always felt that our triumphs were an expression of the consistent application of discipline. It may surprise some to learn that much of the success comes from not getting carried away or trying to do the impossible and taking too many risks. I had a habit of sitting down in January and looking at the fixtures for the remainder of the season for both United and our principal opponents, and would tot up the points that I thought each club would obtain. I was never too far off and the exercise helped illuminate how important it was to grind out the unglamorous 1–0 results. During these sorts of games, we would concentrate on maintaining a compact midfield and yielding nothing. One particular game sticks in my mind: in

March 2007 we went to Middlesbrough during a three-month period when we had the Swedish striker, Henrik Larsson, on loan from Helsingborgs. I could not have asked more from him when, under real pressure, he abandoned his attacking position and fell back into midfield just to help dig out the result. When Henrik appeared in the dressing room at the end of the game, all the players and staff stood up and spontaneously broke into applause for the immense effort he had made in his unaccustomed role. At the end of the season we requested an extra Premier League winners' medal for Henrik, even though he had not played the ten games that at the time were required to obtain the award.

Work Rate

My parents always worked. My father worked in the Glasgow shipyards while my mother first worked in a wire factory and then in one that made parts for aeroplanes. My father often worked 60 hours a week and his was a tough, cold, dangerous existence. Glasgow is at about the same latitude as Moscow, so when the winter winds swept up the Clyde, the shipyards were brutal places. He would usually take two weeks off a year. In 1955 he worked 64 hours a week for pay of £7 and 15 shillings, or about £189 in today's money. After he died from cancer in 1979, my mother cleaned houses. My parents' devotion to work was probably accentuated by the fact that there wasn't much of a social safety net. Safety standards were appalling, health benefits were negligible, and the industry of lawyers who specialise in making ridiculous claims for the thinnest of reasons didn't exist. I never knew a time when my parents were not working. For a holiday in the summer we used to take a bus to Saltcoats, where all my brother and I did was play football or draughts or chess.

Since both my parents worked their fingers to the bone, I somehow just absorbed the idea that the only way I was going to improve my life was to work very hard. It was baked into my marrow. I was incapable of coasting and I have always been irritated by people who frittered away natural talents because they were not prepared to put in the hours. There's a lot of satisfaction that comes from knowing you're doing your best, and there's even more that comes when it begins to pay off. I suppose that explains why I played in games on the day that I got married and on the day my first son was born. I only missed three United games out of 1,500 – the first to be in Glasgow with my brother following the death of his wife in 1998, then because of my eldest son's wedding in South Africa in 2000 and finally to scout David de Gea in 2010.

At St Mirren and Aberdeen I used to watch as many games a week as possible. I usually did this with Archie Knox, who was Aberdeen's assistant manager. Archie's parents were farmers and he grew up on a farm outside Dundee. So he had always worked farmers' hours and shared my sort of work ethic. The two of us would travel to the games together and, if we were going to Glasgow, Archie would drive down there and I would sleep, and on the way back I'd do the driving and Archie would be snoring away. The round trip could take six hours. Whenever we got tempted to skip a game and take the night off, we'd always say to each other, 'If we miss one game in Glasgow, we'll miss two.'

In most football clubs, managers work much harder than people imagine. Within the Premier League there is unrelenting pressure, and outside the Premier League there isn't enough money around for managers to employ big staffs. That was certainly true when I was starting out. At St Mirren I had a staff of four, which included the assistant manager, a reserve team coach, the physio and a part-time kit manager. At Aberdeen Teddy Scott was the kit man, coach of the reserves and general oiler of any squeaky wheels. He also did all the laundry and ironed the kits. Occasionally he'd sleep on the snooker table because he'd missed the last bus. Even at United, when I started, we only had a staff of eight.

A few times at Aberdeen the entire staff, the apprentices and even the chairman would be up at six o'clock in the morning to go and clear snow from the ground. In March 1980 we started our run towards my first League championship on a day when we had cleared seven or eight inches of snow off the field. We beat Morton 1–0. It was the only game played that day in Scotland.

All the top managers, Carlo Ancelotti, José Mourinho and Arsène Wenger have a formidable work ethic. But it is the unsung heroes who I always admired the most – the sort of managers who would never give up, even though life and luck had not given them one of the top teams. In Scotland I used to run into Alex Smith and Jim McLean in all sorts of godforsaken places, on nights when the rain was hammering down and it would have been much nicer to be sitting in front of the television. Alex managed clubs north of the border for almost 40 years, and Jim was the manager of Dundee United for 22 seasons. Lennie Lawrence and John Rudge are two men whose names most people outside football probably don't even know but Lennie is one of the few people who has managed over 1,000 games for clubs like Charlton Athletic, Bradford City, Luton Town and Grimsby Town, while John managed Port Vale for 16 seasons before spending another 14 years or so as the director of football at

Stoke City. Neither of them ever gave up. Football consumed them. I would often see them watching our reserve team play in front of a handful of fans.

The relentless perseverance of these men was matched by some players on the pitch. Three for whom I developed great admiration were Tony Adams of Arsenal, Gianfranco Zola when he played for Chelsea and Jamie Carragher of Liverpool. I always thought Adams was a United player in the wrong shirt. Alcohol has ruined the careers and lives of many footballers, and at United the sad legacy of George Best will always loom large in our collective memories, so Tony's brave confrontation with his demons at the end of the 1990s was, in itself, extraordinary. But it was what he made himself on the field that captured my attention. What he lacked in talent and pace, he more than compensated for in attitude. He was an average player who transformed himself into an outstanding leader through sheer hard work and application. He always had a winning attitude, and handsomely repaid both George Graham's and Arsène Wenger's faith in him.

I thought Zola was a fantastic example of workmanship. He always gave us trouble but he just never gave up. Even though he is a small man, he could more than hold his own with defenders who were eight or ten inches taller and far stronger. He was full of guile, inordinately creative and completely relentless. His approach to the game dovetailed with mine.

Jamie Carragher trained with United as a youngster. When he was with us he was a midfielder and a mundane, run-of-the-mill player. After he signed for Liverpool, he somehow transformed himself into the heart and soul of the team and its controlling force. In my last season he came on as a substitute in a game that we controlled and I whispered to him, 'Just a wee word, stop kicking our boys.' He responded, 'I'm going to kick every one of them.' I have spent some time with him since I retired and have been really impressed. I wouldn't be surprised if he becomes Liverpool's manager at some point in the future, but first he has to decide if he wants to leave the TV studio and get back into a more challenging role in football.

At United we have been blessed with many players who have this sort of winning attitude. When winning becomes a way of life, true winners are relentless. Corny though it sounds, the very best footballers were competing against themselves to become as good as they could be. It was no accident that players like Ronaldo, Beckham, the Neville brothers, Cantona, Scholes, Giggs and Rooney would all have to be dragged off the training ground. They all just had a built-in desire to excel and improve. Gary Neville, for example, pushed himself harder because he knew that he did not possess the natural talent of some of his team-mates. I never used to worry about what he was up to on a Friday night because, certainly in his younger years, he would always be in bed by 9.30 p.m.

David Beckham was also extraordinary. When he came to us he lived in digs, and would not just train in the mornings and afternoons, but would then show up in the evening to train with the schoolboys. When, at the start of the season, we gave players what in England is called the 'bleep test', to get a sense of their level of aerobic fitness, Beckham would always be off the scales. The same goes for Ronaldo. He had this desire to become the greatest player in the world and was determined to do so. He also paid tremendous attention to nutrition, which pre-dated his move to England. These days he is religious about taking ice baths after every game so that he can continue to play at the level he demands of himself. He does not touch alcohol, and keeps himself at about three kilograms below his natural weight because, now in his thirties, he has found this helps him maintain his pace.

In a perfect world I would have filled every team-sheet with 11 men who had as much determination as talent. But life is not like that, and if I had to choose between someone who had great talent but was short on grit and desire, and another player who was good but had great determination and drive, I would always prefer the latter. The former might work well for a brief period, but they never have the staying power that gives a great club stability and consistency.

The work ethic I have just described of a handful of managers and players is true of the very best athletes in any sport. They have a formidable appetite for work and extraordinary self-discipline. Look at A. P. McCoy, the jockey who won more than 4,000 races and who, over the course of his career, broke every single rib and numerous other bones. His natural weight is about 75 kg, but for about 25 years he has kept himself at about 63 kg. When he announced his retirement, his wife said she would finally have to learn how to cook potatoes. Novak Djokovic, the tennis champion who is a friend of United's long-time defender, Nemanja Vidić, has a similar intensity. You can only marvel when you hear about his fitness routine and dietary regimen.

The world's best footballers are just as disciplined, even though the occasional photograph of them sunning themselves in Dubai or at a nightclub with a young lady may suggest otherwise. They need to work relentlessly, not just because that's what is required to get to the top, but because there is always someone eager to take their place in the squad. It also explains why almost all football players have working-class roots.

Understandably, middle-class parents want to make sure

their boys go to college or acquire skills which means football never gets as much attention in those households. Around the world, football attracts boys for whom further education is unlikely and who have no choice but to work very hard on acquiring and improving their footballing skills as the path towards a better life. Today the phrase 'working class' does not carry the same connotations as it did decades ago, but most of United's players came from what nowadays are called 'lower-income households'. I don't want to sound like an old fogey, but the overall rise in the standard of living means that today's players grew up with hot water, television, telephones, computers, cars and budget airlines, and in physical surroundings that are far more comfortable than those in which I grew up. I've long had a soft spot for people from a working-class background, because I think it prepares them for the hardness of life.

For almost all the British players who played for me, football was their ticket out of miserable circumstances. Ryan Giggs had a tough start. He was born in Cardiff to a mother who was just 17 and, because his paternal grandfather was from Sierra Leone, Ryan had to deal with racial taunts as a child. As a small boy he was uprooted from Wales when his father, Danny Wilson, left rugby union to become a professional rugby league player in the north of England. His father left the family home, and Ryan was raised by his mother, who was born Lynne Giggs, in Salford, where he developed his footballing touch. Lynne worked two jobs – as a barmaid and auxiliary nurse – though as a single mother never had enough money to be able to afford to buy the best boots for Ryan; but she instilled in him the capacity for hard work. She is a real saint, and Ryan paid perpetual tribute to her when he changed his surname from Wilson.

David Beckham came from a small house in East London and his father worked as a heating engineer. Paul Scholes grew up in a council house in Langley and Nicky Butt hailed from Gorton – both places where you won't see a Bentley parked in the drive. Wayne Rooney comes from a hard neighbourhood in Liverpool and gave serious thought to becoming a professional boxer. Danny Welbeck and Wes Brown both grew up in Longsight, a Manchester neighbourhood known for gang violence. Bryan Robson's dad was a lorry driver. Rio Ferdinand grew up in Peckham, one of the poorest areas of London. The list is endless.

Over the years I became better at judging the influence of background on a British player, because we would know the family backgrounds and the schools that the boys attended. It was more difficult to judge those sorts of nuances, and the character of a player, when we started recruiting from South America or Eastern Europe. Until around the mid-1990s, the youngsters would also understand their place in the pecking order at the club. They would be responsible for removing mud from boots, cleaning the dressing room and doing 'balls and bibs' – collecting the balls and shirt bibs that the players had scattered and dropped on the training ground. The boys would understand that the first-team dressing room was strictly out of bounds. Those sorts of rituals probably just made them yearn for success all the more.

In my last decade as a manager, I often found the traits I had previously found in British players visible in boys who had grown up overseas. Cristiano Ronaldo certainly knew what it was like to struggle. He grew up in a village in Madeira in a family that had very little money and was brought up by his mother. Tim Howard, who made 77 appearances in goal for United, was raised in New Jersey by a single mother who had emigrated to the United States from Hungary, and held down two jobs after Tim's father left the scene. The Da Silva twins were another case. They had grown up in Petrópolis in Brazil, and had an astonishing work ethic. Rafael would show up to our training sessions on the coldest of Manchester days wearing a short-sleeved shirt and shorts, while everyone else, including me, was wrapped in layers. At the end of one season I told the pair of them to make sure they got a good rest over the summer, and discovered that their father built a full-size pitch in their hometown so that they could play every day with their mates.

The majority of the foreign players also made football their ticket to the future. The very best have a deeply ingrained capacity for industry, and intuitively grasp that if you can connect talent and work, you can achieve so much. I came from an era when my father made my Christmas toys, and I suspect some of the foreign players empathise with that. Many of the players we signed came from circumstances every bit as grim, perhaps grimmer, than their British team-mates. Adnan Januzaj, who we signed as a 16 year old in March 2011 was born in Belgium, after his parents fled the brutality of the former Yugoslavia. The Ecudorian Antonio Valencia comes from a very poor background, as did the Brazilian, Anderson. Andrei Kanchelskis, who played for us in the 1990s, grew up in the Soviet Union. Carlos Tévez came from the drug-ridden desolation of the 'Fort Apache' neighbourhood in Buenos Aires. Quinton Fortune was reared in a township in apartheid South Africa.

Sadly, there are examples of players who have similar backgrounds to Giggs or Cristiano Ronaldo, who, despite enormous natural talent, just aren't emotionally or mentally strong enough to overcome the hurts of their childhood and their inner demons. Ravel Morrison might be the saddest case. He possessed as much natural talent as any youngster we ever signed, but kept getting into trouble. It was very painful to sell him to West Ham in 2012 because he could have been a fantastic player. But, over a period of years, the problems off the pitch continued to escalate and we had little option but to cut the cord. There has been little evidence that Ravel has matured and his contract was cancelled by West Ham in 2015.

I have an abiding belief about the virtues of tapping the hunger and drive that can be found in people who have had tough upbringings. Whenever we had a setback at United and everyone needed a bit of a boost, I'd always end team talks before a game by reminding the players that they all came from working-class backgrounds where people didn't have much. I would tell them that it's almost certain that their grandparents or someone in their family used to be working class and worked hard every day just to survive whereas all they had to do was work hard for 90 minutes while getting paid a lot of money. In retrospect the phrase 'working class' might not have meant much to some, especially the foreign players, but I think they all knew people who had been through tough times. We all felt ourselves to be outsiders in some ways, and people who feel like outsiders do one of two things: they either feel rejected, carry a chip on their shoulder and complain that life is unfair, or they use that sense of isolation to push themselves and work like Trojans. I always used to tell the players, 'The minute that we don't work harder than the other team, we'll not be Manchester United.'

Drive

For years I've tried to fathom out why some people possess greater drive than others. I'm not sure I am any closer to solving that riddle today than I was 30 years ago, but I did learn how to harness that power and as I said, I do know that if I had to pick drive or talent as the most potent fuel, it would be the former. For me drive means a combination of a willingness to work hard, emotional fortitude, enormous powers of concentration and a refusal to admit defeat.

At United, there were many players who epitomised the drive required to become successful. At the forefront were the likes of Bryan Robson, Roy Keane, Steve Bruce, Mark Hughes, Brian McClair and Patrice Evra. One player's drive can have an enormous effect on a team – a winning drive is like a magical potion that can spread from one person to another. Bryan Robson was a foreigner to danger. He came from Chester-le-Street, County Durham, a coal-mining area in the north of England, and would plough right into situations that others would avoid. It resulted in him spending a lot of time on the injury list, but it also made him an invaluable leader. Despite dislocating his shoulder several times during his career, he would regularly engage in a daily regime of one thousand press-ups. I used to show players a photograph of Robson defending a corner. His eyes were almost glazed over; he had shut out the rest of the world, and the only thing he was concentrating on was how to make sure that the corner kick was defended properly.

Roy Keane's relentless drive was inspirational. Steve Bruce played 414 games in the centre of our defence, was fearless and a great organiser, but he didn't quite have enough pace. However, like Tony Adams, he made up for his shortcomings with a deeply rooted will to win that was infectious.

David Beckham had a great thirst for victory, as did Nicky Butt, who made 387 appearances for United and was a local lad. The two Neville brothers who came from Bury (just outside Manchester), and Denis Irwin who, like Roy Keane, came from Cork, all had a distinctive drive. They shared similar characteristics: they were entirely dedicated to the club; all were absolutely reliable players who could be counted on to play in 80 per cent of our games; and all could infect others in the team with their will. None of these players relished the sour taste of defeat. Fortunately, as the years went by, we were able to have more players with this sort of edge in the first team.

By singling out these players I don't mean to detract from the others I managed. The reason I mention them is because they did not possess the innate talents of players like Hughes, Cole, Cantona, Verón, Scholes, Giggs and Ronaldo. I use them as examples of drive because, by the application of sheer will-power, undiluted courage and determination, they more than overcame any shortcomings.

Sometimes the drive got out of control and I had to step in. There was an occasion when we played Middlesbrough that a group of players went after the referee like a pack of dogs and I went off my head with them. But I also wanted to be careful that I didn't inadvertently demotivate them. The minute you start intruding too far, you take the drive out of the man. Believe me, it is far easier to do that than to put the drive into someone to whom it does not come naturally. You usually cannot instil an edge in a player if somehow or other he didn't acquire it before he was a teenager. Every now and again there is an example that gives you hope. Ole Gunnar Solskjaer comes to mind. He grew up in a small, quiet Norwegian fishing village, and when he arrived at Old Trafford in 1996 at the age of 23, he looked like a 14-year-old choirboy; there was a certain soft-ness about him. United offered him his first real taste of what victory could be like. He gradually acquired a taste for this and, as a result, became much more aggressive as a player and developed real conviction.

Conviction

Most people don't have inner conviction. Their confidence is easily shaken, they blow with the wind and can be plagued with doubts. I cannot imagine how anyone, without firm convictions and deep inner beliefs, can be an effective leader. As a player my confidence was shaken when Rangers dropped me and wanted me to agree to a transfer as a part-exchange for another player. But I was determined that I wouldn't let them beat me, and before training I used to go and play nine holes of golf to clear my head and get ready to attack the day. I just resolved not to give in and, when they sold me to Falkirk in 1969, it was on my own terms.

When I did waver, or at least was not being true to myself, it sometimes took another person to shake me out of my stupor. There was an occasion during my early time at United in 1991 when Jock Wallace, the former manager of Rangers, phoned me and said he was coming to watch us play Southampton. Jock was suffering from Parkinson's but he was as shrewd as ever and, after the game, we went out for dinner and he said, 'That's not an Alex Ferguson team. Once you get an Alex Ferguson team, you'll be all right.' It was a wonderful piece of advice because I hadn't been entirely true to my own beliefs. I knew some of the players weren't good enough but, instead of selling them, I'd been trying to turn them into something they weren't capable of becoming. John Lyall, the West Ham manager, told me something very similar. He said, 'Make sure you see Alex Ferguson in your team.' Both Jock and John were implicitly telling me to be true to my own beliefs and convictions. Today, I use the same line with other managers I am trying to encourage.

I don't remember many periods of self-doubt, particularly after I left Aberdeen. I had worked hard and served a footballing apprenticeship that, from the time I started playing to the time I left Scotland, had lasted more than 29 years, and I had achieved considerable success at Aberdeen. These experiences helped harden my inner beliefs and strengthened my confidence in my own conviction. When I was offered the United job, I was very proud and felt confident in my own judgement and abilities. But after I arrived at Old Trafford, and I saw what I had to contend with regarding the drinking culture, I got a bit rattled. I wondered, 'What have I got myself into?' There was a time in 1989 and the start of 1990 when things just weren't going right with United. Of our opening 24 League games we had only managed to win six, and from the end of November 1989 until early February 1990, it was bleak. We won none of our 11 League games. In fact, after we beat Nottingham Forest on 12 November 1989, we did not win another home game until we played Luton Town on 3 March 1990. The fans were getting restless and the media were sharpening their knives. Compared to the consistent level of success I had experienced at Aberdeen, it was a shock to find myself in that situation. My son Jason, who was in his teens at the time, remembers sitting in the kitchen in tears during this drought, asking whether we could just move back to Aberdeen. He tells me now that I said, 'No. We're going to crack on. It's going to work.'

It's one thing to have confidence in your own abilities. It's a completely different challenge to instil confidence in others. Every player is always competing for their place in the side. If they emerged from the academy, progressed through the reserves and made it into the first-team squad, there was always the prospect of someone else emerging through the youth system, or from the transfer market, who might be better. At the end of every season there were always members of the squad who went on their summer holidays unsure whether their place would be assured when we played our first League game the following August. Young players are usually intimidated by the veterans, in part because they are playing alongside their boyhood idols, while the older players are always battling with the spectre of age and injury. Even if an injury does not bring a rude end to a career or, worse still, the promise of a career, as happened with young Ben Thornley in 1994, it erodes a player's confidence and spirit.

Many players, particularly the younger ones, take their bodies for granted as reliable allies. Yet after an injury, they immediately enter no man's land, where they stop travelling with the team, work through rehab by themselves, and have to deal with the uncertainty of whether they will recover or if the club will buy a replacement. Some are even plagued with guilt about being paid when, in their own mind, they are not contributing anything. Two examples come to mind: when Fernando Redondo joined AC Milan from Real Madrid, he suffered an awful knee injury in one of his first training sessions, and refused to be paid until he was fit to play. It was two and a half years before he made his debut and he didn't take a penny off his new club in that time. When Martin Buchan left Manchester United in 1983 after 11 years of service, he joined Oldham Athletic and received a hefty signing-on fee in the process. Early in his second season he realised that he no longer had what it took to be playing professional football, so knocked on his manager's door, retired, and returned his signing-on fee. Two class acts from men of honour.

Every player can have his confidence rattled during a game.

They may be having an off day, they don't want the ball to come in their direction and, believe it or not, they may even secretly want to get substituted. I always found that strikers and goalkeepers had the most doubts about themselves and, if their confidence was shaken, they completely changed. When goal-scorers don't score, they are convinced they will never score again, and when they score they cannot imagine they will ever miss another opportunity. All my strikers were like that, including Mark Hughes, Eric Cantona and Ruud van Nistelrooy. Mark Hughes, who in recent years has been a manager, played for United between 1983 and 1986, and 1988 and 1995; he was as tough as nails and a man of great determination. Mark was born to be a big game player and could always be counted on in the most important games, but was deeply affected when he didn't score.

Van Nistelrooy's entire identity as a man was bound up with scoring goals. When he didn't score in a game, even if we won, the storm clouds would gather. He had that Calvinist attitude which meant he felt he hadn't earned his keep and didn't deserve to be paid if he failed to score. Without doubt, of all the strikers I managed, he was the most single-minded. His whole existence revolved around scoring goals. After we beat Everton in 2003 to win the League, Ruud ran straight to the dressing room to see whether he or Thierry Henry had won the Golden Boot, the award given to the Premier League player who has scored the most goals in the season. It turned out that he'd won it that year and could enjoy his summer.

As for goalkeepers, Tim Howard has had a wonderful career at Everton since he left United in 2006. However, though he got off to a good start during his first season at Old Trafford, after we brought him over from America, his confidence never seemed to be the same after he made a mistake in 2004 against FC Porto, which eliminated us from that year's Champions League competition. It rattled him to his core, and though he came back into the side, he never seemed impregnable. I feel for goalkeepers because, after they let in a goal, everyone in the entire stadium is looking at them. It's all too easy to forget about the mistimed tackle, the three bad passes or the botched back pass that caused the goal in the first place.

When David de Gea joined us in 2011, he had the unenviable task of filling a role that had been masterfully occupied by the Dutchman, Edwin van der Sar, for six years. David was just 20 and, though he was tall, he had yet to develop the muscular strength to deal with some of the Premier League's bruisers. His first few months were mixed and both the press and the fans were on his back. After one game, I could see that he was down, so rather than talk to him directly, I chose to make my remarks to the whole team. I told them that David was a perfect example of the character of United and that he had come to England not speaking a word of English, didn't even have a driver's licence, and then gets a weekly hammering from strikers who have been ordered to make his life miserable. I could see when I finished that my little talk had lifted his spirits. He is now among the very best keepers in the world, thanks to the work of Eric Steele, the goalkeeping coach, and others.

The other place where the level of individual confidence is revealed is when penalty kicks are taken in a sudden-death finish. Some players, like Patrice Evra, would be spectacular penalty takers during practice but dreaded the idea of being asked to do the same in a game. Paul Ince was the same, and Wes Brown, our long-time stalwart defender, would sooner have played barefoot than take a penalty. I think Wes prayed that the game would be decided before he had to take his turn. Then there were the guys who just brimmed with confidence. On the rare occasion that Eric Cantona would miss from the spot, he had a look on his face that said to the world, 'How did that happen?' I don't think he thought it conceivable that he could miss a penalty. Denis Irwin, Steve Bruce, Brian McClair, Ruud van Nistelrooy, Robin van Persie, Wayne Rooney: all relished hammering in penalties. Rooney seems to excel when he is under pressure. In May 2011 we were trailing Blackburn Rovers 1–0, needed a point to win the League, and 17 minutes from the end of regular time we got a penalty. Rooney absolutely battered it into the top corner. I'm sure it helps that, even before he has taken the field in any given match, Wayne has decided where he will place the ball if he takes a penalty kick.

From time to time, I'd slide players on in the last few minutes of regular time if I sensed we were heading for a sudden-death finish. I did that in the 2008 Champions League final when I sent on Anderson, the Brazilian midfielder, to take a penalty kick. He was only 20 at the time, but he had all the confidence in the world and scored our sixth penalty, helping us beat Chelsea for our third success in the competition.

Sometimes the occasion would overwhelm even the most experienced of players. You can imagine the tension associated with what might have been the biggest single game of a player's career. It is unrealistic to think that all of them can ignore the press build-up, block out the noise and atmosphere inside a stadium and treat a cup final – particularly a Champions League final – as just another game against 11 mortals. Life does not work that way. When we played Barcelona in Rotterdam in the 1991 European Cup Winners' Cup final, Paul Ince, who was 23 years old at the time, was a bag of nerves. It did not help matters that the kick-off was delayed to allow the crowd to finish entering the stadium. Paul had a rocky first half, during which Bryan Robson had been snapping at him. At half-time I said to him, 'Incey, just concentrate on the game. Forget everything that's happened before the game. Nothing bad is going to happen. Just go and relax and enjoy it.' In the second half he was much better and worked brilliantly with Robson to protect our defence.

We also had peculiar situations when a player might voluntarily make life more difficult for himself and increase his own anxiety level. That happened in 1995 when we were knocked out of the UEFA Cup at Old Trafford by Rotor Volgograd. I had picked John O'Kane, who was a gifted player but had only appeared a few times in the first team, to play right-back. Ten minutes before the kick-off, well after the team-sheets had been submitted, he told me he wanted to play left-back. It was clear that he was rattled by the prospect of the game, but there was nothing I could do. It was a death wish because he was up against a Volgograd winger who was a flying machine. I put Phil Neville at right-back, played O'Kane at left-back and pulled him out of the game before half an hour had gone by, after he had been torn apart.

Every now and again, something beyond our control would rattle the confidence and resolve of the entire club. At those sorts of junctures it's vital to boost the collective confidence. When Manchester City started forking out the biggest sums ever seen in Britain, it was natural that everyone at United would be reading the newspapers with a mixture of shock and awe. This was exacerbated when we gave Manchester City the League championship on goal difference in 2012 after we only got ten points out of a possible 18 in the final six games of the season. I know people will misinterpret this, or take it for sour grapes, but City didn't win that championship; we lost it.

I used City's Premier League title to buttress everyone's confidence later that summer. As we reassembled for the following season, I kept reiterating that United expected to win absolutely every game we played. It didn't matter whether our opponent was the reigning Premier League, or Champions League champions, or a fourth division team we'd drawn in the FA Cup. I was just able to keep reinforcing the ideology that no club was bigger than United – no matter whether their owner controlled all the oil in the Persian Gulf, or every coalmine in Russia.

3

ASSEMBLING THE PIECES

Organisation

I realise that the system within a football club doesn't have the complexity of what is required to design a nuclear submarine, build 50 million mobile phones or organise clinical trials for a new drug. But like every organisation we needed to be well run and had to be sure that our system was deeply ingrained. Our product just happened to be a football team, rather than a car or washing machine, and our whole reason for being was to make sure all the pieces of our product – all the different players – fitted together.

I've always felt that it's impossible to field a great football team if you don't have a great organisation. Most owners and managers mess around with team selection without any underlying purpose. They arrange everything back to front and are too impatient for quick results. Before you can field a great team, you have to build a great organisation, and all the elements have to be assembled properly. That takes time, especially in circumstances which business books call 'turnarounds'. At United my responsibility was for the team, while the club's CEOs – principally Martin Edwards from the time I joined the club until 2000, and thereafter my commercial soul-mate David Gill – worried about everything else.

When I joined United there were four or five departments and about 85 people, including the groundsmen, laundry team, kitchen and administrative staff. The club made money from the sale of season tickets and gate receipts. If we were on television, which was rare in the mid-1980s, we'd get a small four-figure sum for a live game. After I assessed the situation, my aim was to build the club again rather than to build the team. I was confident that if we did the first part properly, and people were patient, we'd eventually be able to have the best team. It was also clear that we were not going to be an overnight success.

These days Manchester City and Liverpool are trying desperately to develop their own talent. Manchester City, which doesn't have Liverpool's lineage or history, and has always operated in United's long shadow, is pulling out all the stops. Manchester City spent £32.5 million, on Robinho, the day after Sheikh Mansour's purchase of the club in 2008 and more than £600 million since, but I am not sure that it has bought them much beyond a squad which, at the end of last season, was showing signs of wear and tear. While you might be able to buy your way to short-term success, it does not work over the long term. That requires patience, and the construction of a complete organisation.

Preparation

The most important aspect of our system was training. Whatever happens on a Saturday afternoon has already occurred on the training ground. If I was starting again as a manager, the thing

I would focus on the most is a player's attitude during training sessions. If they take it seriously and have the necessary talent and determination, good things will happen. If they are inclined to slack off, they will never make it over the long haul. Our training ground was where the real work was done. There was a rhythm to this from which we rarely deviated. The day following a game, all the players would come in for loosening exercises, a massage and Jacuzzi. On Monday we would have a thorough training session and, if we had a midweek fixture, Tuesday would be devoted to pre-match preparation, Thursday would be a recovery day and then the whole cycle would start again. We were very careful to emphasise the need for proper recovery – not just after games but also after big competitions. For example, we gave players who participated in the World Cup a full 28 days to recover from the exertions. I would also sometimes send a few of the older players away for a week's break in December. In the winter of the 1998–99 season, I sent Peter Schmeichel off on holiday to get some sun on his back and rest. From time to time I did the same with younger players. I sent Gary Neville to Malta for a week when, early in the season following the 1998 World Cup, it became apparent that his batteries were low. These breaks helped restore them and ensure they were fit for the rest of the season.

I laid down the ground rules for training and I wanted my ideas to be implemented on the practice field. When Steve McClaren took over training at United in 1999, I was very specific with him. He was going to run the training, but I made sure he understood that I required intensity, concentration and commitment in every training session. I told him that if he was dissatisfied, he either had to start all over again until it was right, or get the players back for an additional session. There had to be no bad sessions.

I just didn't want people tinkering with our training system. When Carlos Queiroz started running training sessions, a couple of the players didn't like the sessions because they were too repetitive. I stopped one training session and told them, 'When I was a player I wished I'd been coached by Carlos. All the repetitive things we are working on will become second nature on Saturday when you have no time to think.' All our planning and preparation was to help guard against a sudden rush of animal instincts in the heat of the moment. When a game starts to go in the wrong direction, it is so easy for players – especially the youngsters – to be controlled by their heart rather than their head. That's the last thing you want. But don't forget that football is an emotional game and there can be bad tackles or refereeing decisions that can affect people. Desire and a ferocious need to win are wonderful attributes, but they have to be tempered by a cool head. Ninety per cent of the time most players are fine, but there can be occasions when raw emotion overtakes the need for discipline. All of our drills on the training grounds, all our tactical talks and assessment of competitors were done as a way to hammer into the heads of the players the need to stick to the plan. It is very hard to persuade extremely competitive spirits to be patient. Yet very often our victories were squeaked out in the last few minutes, after we had drained the life from our opponents. Games – like life – are all about waiting for chances and then pouncing on them.

As the years went by the system became so familiar and so well understood that my assistants didn't need to be reminded. It was helped by the fact that we had players who had been with the club for many years like Vidić, Evra and Ferdinand and, most of all, by the players who had known no other world than United – like Scholes, Giggs and the Neville brothers. The players came to understand my values, and the older players automatically transmitted these values to the younger players or new signings. There was just a consistency of ideas.

It's extraordinary what you can do on the training ground, especially if you have people with receptive minds who are eager to improve. Andy Cole was a standout example. When he joined us as a 23 year old after being at Arsenal, Bristol City and Newcastle United, he just wanted to loiter in the penalty box and score. After about three months of training he had improved immeasurably. He was better on his feet and his overall foot-balling ability had been enhanced. I discovered that this sort of change was not limited to the younger players. One extraordinary example was Henrik Larsson, who was a striker in his mid-thirties when he was loaned to us in 2007 during the Swedish off-season. Everybody kept saying, 'I wish he had been with us when he was a boy.' He just sopped up everything we said to him, but he returned to Sweden because he had made a promise to his family and his club, Helsingborgs. Something similar happened when we signed Michael Owen when he was almost 30. He only made 52 appearances for us but, even though he had played for Liverpool, Real Madrid and Newcastle United, and had been in the England team for a decade, he still had the desire and pride to want to improve while he was at Old Trafford.

When René Meulensteen became our coach after Carlos Queiroz left us for the second time, it was much easier, because he had worked for several years within our system. He'd been on the scene and had helped the players who were then young-sters – Danny Welbeck, Tom Cleverley and Cristiano Ronaldo – develop their technical skills. René inherited all of Carlos's crossing and defending drills, but he also added features of his own. René was also a devotee of Wiel Coerver, the great Dutch coach, who was among the first to emphasise the importance of ankle mobility and its influence on ball control, so he also helped enhance our system. Mick Phelan is another example of the benefits of growing up within a system. He had played for me; I brought him in as a youth coach and he gradually worked his way up the organisation until he became assistant manager in 2008.

I never had a chance to experiment with helping some of United's best players become coaches and – eventually – managers, but I always felt that would have been a great way to ensure the continuity of excellence at Old Trafford. Ryan Giggs, Paul Scholes, Gary Neville and Nicky Butt all had those attributes, but I was never going to suggest to them, 'Quit playing and become a coach.' I had really wanted Neville to be involved with our academy, but he got a contract with Sky and went into the television world. I was disappointed, as Gary's character and attitude would have enhanced the club and Paul is one of the best assessors of a footballer within the game. I feel they were a loss to Manchester United.

I've lost count of the times during my career that I was accused of having a lot of luck, or intimidating referees into providing a lavish amount of extra time, when United were losing at home. There were plenty of times when Lady Luck blew in our direction – it happens all the time in football. Yet preparation had a lot more to do with our success than a few fortunate breaks.

Part of the pursuit of excellence involves eliminating as many surprises as possible because life is full of the unexpected. That's what our scouts, our youth system and the innumerable training sessions were all about. But there were also occasions where we did extra homework because we felt unprepared. For example,

I always wanted to know as much as possible about what we were going to contend with before any game. After I joined United, I had no idea about all the players at the clubs in what was then the First Division. So I asked John Lyall to send me his files and reports on all the teams and players we were up against. He had an experienced eye and reading his material was a great help.

Relentless homework, all of it unglamorous, was a mainstay of United. Here's one example. When we played Bayern Munich in the 1999 Champions League final, we had done our homework. In every game you wanted to have a sense for how the opposing manager might change his tactics during a game. Of course, that is something that is difficult to predict, but thorough preparation can sometimes suggest which players might get substituted. In the 1999 final, the Bayern winger, Mario Basler, who was deadly with free kicks, scored a few minutes into the game. Alexander Zickler, who was a mainstay of the Bayern side for many seasons, played wide left that night. We had predicted that Zickler and Basler would both be substituted. We hadn't rubbed any crystal ball; we had just watched the tapes of Bayern and knew they would take these players off. Zickler came off in the 71st minute and Basler in the 87th. These substitutions deprived Bayern of a lot of their ability to penetrate our defences and, as a result, they were less of a threat and we could throw more bodies forward in search of a goal. Many years later, while we were preparing to meet Barcelona in the 2008 Champions League semi-final, Carlos Queiroz placed mats on the field to show the players exactly where he wanted them – a couple of the mats were almost placed atop one another to emphasise how tightly we wanted Scholes and Carrick to bottle the attacks through our midfield. Barcelona failed to score in either leg.

In the 36 hours before a game there was a rhythm to our preparation. We'd show a short, condensed video of the opponents to the players before we practised and then, at the hotel, on the evening of the game, we'd centre their attention on the things they needed to pay heed to. We kept these videos short because most players, especially the young ones, have limited attention spans. I always liked to dwell on an opponent's weaknesses rather than its strengths. While it was good to look at video of some of the lethal players we would find ourselves up against, ultimately no battles are won by mounting a sterling defence. The way to win battles, wars and games is by attacking and overrunning the opposing side. So I would always dwell on our opponents' weaknesses – partly to exploit them and partly to impart in my players a sense of what was possible. If you overemphasise opponents' strengths, you just plant seeds of doubt in your players.

On the day of the game itself, I'd finalise the team and run through the precise tactics I wanted employed. I paid attention to a couple of other little items. I used to check out which of the players on the opposing team were making their Old Trafford debut. We used to purposefully exert more pressure on these individuals – it was one way we rolled out our red carpet. Another thing I was always mindful about were the talented players we would line up against who were not especially hard workers. These players would always have something left in the last 20 minutes because they had not been busting their guts during the earlier stages. Matthew Le Tissier, who appeared more than 500 times for Southampton, was one of these types. He could be loitering around for a good part of the game and, just when everyone was spent, could ruin our afternoon in the blink of an eye. The others in this category were the so-called 'floaters', the sort of players who would often wear the number 10 shirt in Spain or South America. They drifted around between the midfield and the strikers and you never knew if they would play on the left or right or in the middle of the park. David Silva was one of two or three players who filled this role at Valencia. These type of players are free to roam and would save their energy for when their team had the ball. The fact that they could appear in different parts of the pitch and not operate in restricted areas meant we could not afford a single lapse of concentration.

On our own team, the best players tended to be sticklers for preparation. That's part of the reason why they were good or great. David Beckham, Ryan Giggs, Cristiano Ronaldo and Wayne Rooney would all stay after training to perfect their free kicks. They would not disappear for a long bath, or a massage, or be straight out the door because they had to run down to a car dealership. They would be religious about spending an extra 30 minutes trying to bend balls around a row of mannequins and past the goalkeeper. That's why Beckham became a master of taking free kicks from between 25 and 30 yards from goal; and Giggs from between 18 and 23 yards; while Rooney was better closer to the penalty box. As for Ronaldo, he'd be able to score from free kicks if he took them from behind the moon.

The crowd looked at the goal Beckham scored from the halfway line against Wimbledon in 1996 as if it was some sort of miracle. It was nothing of the sort. He must have practised that same kick hundreds of times so, when opportunity struck in south London, he seized it. The same goes for lots of goals scored by the United players. They had been scored, or certainly practised, for hundreds of hours during training sessions.

I came to admire how some other managers prepared their

teams because the majority of them had the challenge of extracting performance from players who had nowhere near the talent of the Manchester United squad. Sam Allardyce, who played for most of his career at Bolton and Preston before managing Bolton, Newcastle, Blackburn and West Ham in the Premier League, is a prime example. Kevin Davies was a striker who played for Sam at Bolton, but did not move like lightning and was quite cumbersome.

When Sam managed Bolton (between 1999 and 2007) he concentrated on squeezing every drop of advantage from players like Davies, and he did this through preparation and anything extra that technology might have to offer. He would know which sort of ball into the penalty box would be guaranteed to give opponents the most problems and he even went to the extreme of having exercise bikes set up in the dugouts so that the substitutes could be properly warmed up before they took the field. It has rarely been acknowledged, but Sam's belief in the benefits of preparation have paid dividends for him, even if several of the owners he worked for did not have the slightest inkling of how he transformed middling players into decent teams.

There were a couple of times when we suffered setbacks that were so severe, I was forced to re-examine our entire approach. After Chelsea won the 2004–05 Premier League title, I took a fresh look at our pre-season preparation. Chelsea had steamrollered all the other clubs and wound up with 95 points compared to Arsenal with 83 and United with 77. It was humiliating. We spent an entire season chasing their tail, but there was just no way we could catch Chelsea. I did not want that to happen again.

After Chelsea's first triumph, I paid much more attention to the intensity of our pre-season preparation. Chelsea had just been much fitter than United during the 2004–05 season. We redesigned the pre-season fixtures for 2006–07 – as the schedule for 2005–06 was already in place – so that we played higher calibre and more competitive teams. While it was important for the club to wave the flag in countries where we had a big following, it did not make much sense to play fixtures where Fabien Barthez, who was our goalkeeper for three seasons, could play as a striker. So we made sizeable changes. It was much healthier to play more challenging exhibition games than win a walk in the park 10–0 in Thailand. It was a real lesson to me about the risks of clinging to past practices and not moving with the times.

Despite Chelsea's triumph, I did not want to rush things during the following pre-season period. I wanted to ease the players back into the rhythm of the season in a gradual fashion. High-performance athletes have a tendency to push themselves too much or over-train. For some it is an obsession, while others worry about an erosion of fitness levels that could cause them to lose their place in the team. In pre-season, we would work on mobility, but we would steer clear of serious physical encounters or severe interval training. There would never be any serious, long lectures, detailed post-mortems of the previous season, or dozens of hours of video analysis. We would conduct medical tests on the players. We would set up a series of 15 medical stations in the gym that were manned with nurses and doctors and would run a battery of tests on each of the players. This allowed us to have accurate readings on the players' medical and physical conditions. We ran specific cardiac tests and comprehensive blood assessments; scanned tendons with ultrasound machines and checked to make sure all vaccinations were current. We also scrutinised the players' flexibility, mobility and balance; gave them eye examinations and cognitive assessments so that, throughout the season, we had a benchmark against which to test the severity of concussions. These tests were literally from head to toe, since the players had their teeth examined by dentists and their feet by podiatrists. All this allowed us to figure out how vulnerable each player was to injury and we categorised them in three different buckets: high, medium and low. We then designed gym programmes, customised for each player, for the first block of the season.

The change to our pre-season routine took a little time to bear fruit. In 2005–06 Chelsea won the Premier League title again, albeit by a greatly reduced margin of eight points. And by 2006–07 our fitness improved enough to turn the eight-point deficit into a Premier League title of our own – this time by six points from Chelsea.

In football, just like in other activities, the best-laid plans sometimes don't work and improvisation is required. It actually happens on a fairly regular basis. I would often twiddle things during a game or at half-time. One example that comes to mind is a game against West Ham in the closing weeks of the season in April 2011. A few months earlier, West Ham had whipped us 4–0 in a Carling Cup tie where I had fielded a team of young players. Towards the end of that game, Wally Downes, West Ham's first-team coach, asked Wes Brown, as he waited on the sidelines to replace Jonny Evans, 'Are you going on to make a difference?' That got right under my skin, as did the taunts from West Ham's supporters after the game, who were very aggressive towards me in the car park. I told them, 'We're going to be back here in April and we're going to relegate you.' However, when we were 2–0 down at half-time in a match towards the end of the season, I was a long way from fulfilling my promise. So I tossed our game plan out of the window, pulled Patrice Evra, who had played for France in the middle of the week, out of the game, and moved Ryan Giggs to left-back. Eventually we won 4–2 with Rooney scoring a hat-trick. A few weeks later, at the end of the season, West Ham got relegated to the Championship.

Something similar happened at Old Trafford in 2009 when we trailed Tottenham Hotspur 2–0. At half-time I brought on Carlos Tévez, the Argentinian striker, for Nani, and the effect was dramatic. Tévez was like a clockwork mouse, except you never had to wind him up – he was just tireless. He came on to the field, started hurling himself at every Tottenham player, completely changed the pace of the game and stirred up the fans. We won that game 5–2 and went on to win the League by four points. It's odd to think of the effect of that one change to a plan.

Sometimes we were outwitted by opponents who approached a particular game with more finely tuned tactics and were better prepared. In 1996, Newcastle United thrashed us 5–0 at St James' Park. Kevin Keegan, who was Newcastle's manager, fielded a team full of threatening attackers, including Alan Shearer, Les Ferdinand, Peter Beardsley and David Ginola. The savagery of that defeat was apparent in the last goal, which was scored by the Belgian centre-back, Philippe Albert, who managed to chip a ball over the head of our goalkeeper, Peter Schmeichel, from 20 yards. We were humiliated.

We could be outdone by our own ill-discipline too. You can get into real trouble if players ignore plans or don't stick to them. That happened to United in both our Champions League final games against Barcelona. We lost both because two or three players ignored our plans and played their own game. You cannot do that when you play Barcelona, particu-larly when the club was managed by Pep Guardiola, because of their ability to keep control of the ball. United were used to having the ball for three-quarters of a game, so as we prepared to play Barcelona we knew, because of their ability to retain possession, that they would throw us off our normal game.

Every now and again we were also undone by the atmosphere we encountered. There were two grounds that always caused us trouble – when we played Liverpool at Anfield, and Leeds at Elland Road (when they used to be regular opponents). We've been to Anfield with some of our very best teams, but the crowd – who are merciless towards visiting teams and refereeing decisions of which they don't approve – whips up such an atmosphere that it erodes the players' confidence and makes them lose their concentration. It only takes a momentary lapse to upset hours of dedicated preparation, and there's very little you can do to help players with that. While there are elements of chess to a game of football, wingers, goalkeepers and centre-backs – unlike rooks, bishops and knights – are made of flesh and blood and emotions.

One other element of preparation worth mentioning is the way I approached the idea of risk. It would not surprise me if some observers feel that much of United's success was due to our willingness to take unnecessary chances. When the crowd at Old Trafford are chanting, 'Attack! Attack! Attack!', it is easy to think that we automatically threw caution to the wind. I never thought about it like this because part of a leader's job is to eliminate as many risks as possible. Some might think that my fondness for horses or cards means that I am a gambler at heart, but that isn't really true. In my private life I have always been very careful about the amount of money I am prepared to spend on a horse or bet at a race-track, and the same caution applied at Old Trafford. We tried to leave nothing to chance. I cannot tell you how many half-time talks centred on the need to be patient and wait for the right opportunity to occur, rather than to be daredevils. I would only want to take a risk during the last 15 minutes of a game if we were trailing by a goal. At that point, it doesn't matter whether you lose by one or two goals, and it was only then that I was prepared to throw the kitchen sink at things.

Frequently when this happened, the opposition played right into our hands by trying to defend their lead. They would substitute a defensive player for an attacker and it could change the entire balance of the game. Suddenly we could surge around their box without worrying as much about their ability to counter-attack. Our opponents probably thought they were eliminating a risk by falling back into a defensive posture, but it gave us an advantage without us having to, in the grand scheme of things, unduly increase the amount of risk we took. And more often than not, the goal would come. The value of last minute goals was the impact on the dressing room, with everyone celebrating, and for the fans, who couldn't wait to get home or to the pub to talk about it.

Our critics would say this was lucky, or down to the pressure to extend the game into 'Fergie Time', but in truth it came down to careful preparation and having a deliberate and thoughtful approach to risk.

Pipeline

When you run any organisation, you have to look as far down the road as you can. But if your organisation is anything like Manchester United, then your perspective is constantly changing. Sometimes it was possible to look several years ahead, and sometimes it was impossible to see beyond the next challenge; or, in our case, the next game. But prioritising a long-term strategy for the club was crucial, and at United we always had to be thinking about the composition of the team a few seasons ahead. So we had to have a conveyor belt of talent.

Every game requires 11 starting players and seven substitutes, and our whole organisation was designed to produce them. I always wanted to know about what the pipeline of players looked like for the team we would select three years in the future. It is so much easier to produce a consistent level of high performance when you nourish youngsters, help them develop and provide a pathway to success.

This was no easy task, because it meant sifting through all the millions of boys who dream about becoming football players. It means watching tens of thousands of games – many of them in the pouring rain and bleak surrounds. I read recently that Steve Coppell, who played for United between 1975 and 1983 before going on to a career as a manager, said, 'It's like turtles in the South Seas. Thousands are hatched on the beaches, but few of them ever reach the water.' Steve is dead right, except at United we were more interested in the turtles that we thought would be able to survive long journeys in the sea, rather than those who could just reach the water's edge.

When I joined Aberdeen in 1978 we had two scouts; by the time I left we had 17 scouts, who were responsible for identifying promising youngsters who lived in Scotland. The result was fabulous. When Aberdeen played in the European Cup Winners' Cup final in 1983 against Real Madrid, we fielded eight home-grown players who had worked their way through the youth teams and only three players who had been bought (and that number included one, Gordon Strachan, who was at the club when I arrived).

My experience with Gordon only served to strengthen my belief in the benefits of developing youngsters. When I arrived at Aberdeen his head was on the block because my predecessor had decided to sell him. I put the transfer on hold until I had given myself the opportunity to make my own assessment and I liked what I saw. So we kept Gordon, helped him improve his skills – particularly using the entire width of the pitch and getting himself into the right position – and he went on to great things: a sterling career as a player for Manchester United and Scotland and a managerial career which has culminated in him leading his own country.

At United, in the mid-1980s, there were scouts everywhere – all over England and all over Ireland. But there was a gaping hole in the system. There were just four scouts to cope with Greater Manchester and the wider city region, and only two for the whole of Manchester. To combat this weakness we changed the management of the youth system and instilled new energy and leadership under Les Kershaw, who was helped by Nobby Stiles and Brian Kidd, who had both played on the 1968 European Cup-winning team, and who knew the area. Les was a real, and unusual, find. He had taught chemistry at Manchester Metropolitan University, and was scouting part-time for Arsenal when Bobby Charlton mentioned his name. Les brought the detached objectivity of the science laboratory to Old Trafford and had an enormous impact on the way we built the backbone of our youth programme. The scouts were part-timers and we built an incentive compensation scheme. They got a fixed weekly stipend, and bonuses if the boy was signed for the club, made the first team or represented his country. They were also paid extra if the player stayed with the club for multiple years.

In retrospect the greatest evidence of the power of youth was in the United squad that won the Treble in 1999. That squad contained 30 players of whom 15 were under 25 years old. It included David Beckham who was a great advertisement for the youth-team policy. We first heard about David in 1986 when he was 12 years old and he was spotted by our scout Malcolm Fidgeon. The real pull for David came through meeting Bobby Charlton when he attended the Manchester United legend's soccer school. Coincidentally, 1986 was also the year we heard about Ryan Giggs. Ryan and David made their debuts for the first team when they were 17 years old. Nicky Butt and Gary Neville were also 17, Phil Neville was 18 and Paul Scholes was 19 when they first played for the first team.

The full impact of our youth programme became apparent at the start of the 1995–96 season, when six of the 13 players I used during the game against Aston Villa – which we lost – had come through our system. Alan Hansen, the television pundit, surveyed the result and concluded, as he announced to the British public that night, 'You can't win anything with kids.' I have always thought the opposite – you will never win anything without kids.

Youngsters can inject a fantastic spirit in an organisation and a youngster never forgets the person or organisation that gave him his first big chance. He will repay it with a loyalty that lasts a lifetime. For young players, nothing is impossible, and they will try and run through a barbed-wire fence, while older players will try to find the gate. Every generation also raises the level of the game, because they stand atop more shoulders than the previous one. That's truer today than ever before, because of the spread of television and the catchment area of a large club's scouting organisations. Television means that boys all over the world are able to watch Lionel Messi or Cristiano Ronaldo. I am sure there are thousands of them trying to emulate Lionel's feints or Cristiano's moves. Somewhere there are a couple of boys who will be trying to improve upon their heroes' skills, and eventually they too will be inspiring yet another generation to ever more creative heights.

I suspect that the way we approached the young players was a highly magnified, miniature version of the way in which employees are trained to progress through a large organisation. We had distinct layers and a structure, and the road to success was as clear for them as it might be for a graduate from college who joins a company in a trainee scheme and dreams of one day becoming a vice-president, managing director or CEO. At United our layers were the youth academy, the B team, the A team, the reserves and the first-team squad. The FA Youth Cup was important for several reasons. It gave the youngsters a taste for a tough competition, for the sort of preparation that was an echo of life in the first team and a sense of the difference between being a winner and loser.

When we first came across young boys with talent, we were all over them. We gave them endless drills and were not shy about telling them precisely what they needed to do. We wanted to be confident that they had mastered the skills essential for their success, which was why the youth academy was no laughing matter. The boys fell under the gaze of Eric Harrison and they trained with great intensity on Tuesday and Thursday nights, during sessions in which the first-team coaches were also heavily involved. Archie Knox and I made it a point to watch these sessions, and Eric made the boys feel as though these sessions were as important as a cup final. Some of them found their time with Eric far more intimidating than their time with me. As the boys matured, we eased off a bit and, eventually, if they made the first team, we might have demanded that they polish some aspect of their game but, for the most part, the management challenge changed. We knew that they had the skills and trusted in their competence, so our focus started to shift to their emotional and psychological needs. We also shielded them from the press. For example, Ryan Giggs did not give his first interview until he was 20, and then it was with Hugh McIlvanney of the *Sunday Times*, who we knew as trustworthy.

One of the ways we blended youth with experience was out of the sight of the television cameras. Every now and again senior players like Bryan Robson and Darren Fletcher would play with the reserve team. That was a shot in the arm for the players we were counting on for the future. Even if the experienced players just showed up to stand on the side-lines and watch the youth team, the youngsters got a huge boost of confidence. Bryan Robson, Steve Bruce, Brian McClair all did that, and Gary Neville would also help the young players sort out their contracts. They each had their own way of helping the youngsters. Gary would always be rebuking them, but he wanted them to be successful. Oddly, when Gary himself came into the squad, he had been under similar pressure from Peter Schmeichel. When Ryan Giggs made it to the first squad he was really helped by Paul Ince, who took him under his wing. The same thing had happened to me as a youngster at St Johnstone, when three of the older players – Jim Walker, Jimmy Little and Ron McKinven – had looked out for me. At United, Eric Cantona performed one of the most avuncular acts towards younger players when, after the whole squad pooled the pot for FA Cup final media appearances, each individual was given the choice of taking their share or leaving it in for a draw to win the lot. All the young players, like David Beckham and Gary Neville, took their share, but Paul Scholes and Nicky Butt stayed in. When Eric won the draw he gave all his prize money to Paul Scholes and Nicky Butt, who had just entered the first-team squad and for whom, at the time, £7,500 was the equivalent of two months' wages. His reason was typical Eric: 'Because they have balls.'

It is such a tonic for a youngster to feel that he has a mentor whom he can trust and who has his interests at heart. There is more of a natural bond between players than there is between the coaching staff and the players. Some of this is because of the normal organisational gap that exists between an employee and a manager. The other is because of age difference. For example, towards the end of my time at United it would have been much easier for James Wilson to identify with Patrice Evra than with me, since I was old enough to be his grandfather. There is a lot to be said for either picking, or being lucky enough to land, the right mentor. The best ones can change your life.

No matter how hard we worked to blood youngsters, Barcelona is still able to do this better than any club. The way they develop boys into some of the best players in the world is breathtaking. It demonstrates the benefits of long-term investments in people and thorough training in the ways of the organisation. Great teamwork comes from deep familiarity and developing close bonds with others. In a company, people who have worked together for a long time will know how others will react in certain situations, and may even be able to anticipate what their colleagues might say. The same thing holds true on the football pitch. The most magical example was the Messi-Iniesta-Xavi troika at Barcelona. The three of them knew each other so well that the way they passed the ball in a wee circle among themselves made you dizzy. It's like watching a spinning carousel.

At Arsenal, Arsène Wenger has had his own twist on building for the long term. When he arrived in England his policy was based on his knowledge of French football and his method for developing the team was to buy a lot of French players in their mid-teens and early twenties, such as Thierry Henry, Patrick Vieira and Nicolas Anelka. More recently, Arsène has adapted this approach and has spent big sums on Mesut Özil and Alexis Sánchez and also bought young English players like Oxlade-Chamberlain, Walcott and Chambers.

In my last decade at United, we employed a similar tactic. We just cast our net farther afield and bought the Da Silva twins from Brazil when they were 17, Giuseppe Rossi, the Italian centre-forward, whom we later sold to Villarreal, and Gérard Piqué, from Barcelona when he was just 17. In England, players can be offered a professional contract at 16, which can be signed at 17. At the time, Spanish regulations allowed us to offer Piqué a contract at 16, but Spanish clubs could not do this and could not therefore protect their assets. This was also the case when Cesc Fàbregas signed for Arsenal.

Our emphasis on youth strengthened as the years went by, and our system became better tuned. United's global network expanded in relation to identifying the best young players, regardless of which country they were playing in – Macheda (Italy), Possebon (Brazil) and Januzaj (Belgium). During my last few seasons at United we put a whole bevy of youngsters under contract: Tyler Blackett, Paddy McNair, James Wilson, Andreas Pereira and Will Keane. If I had my way I would make sure that any sons of United players with great promise would all be targeted for our youth system. It underlines the import-ance of investing in the sorts of facilities that will attract youngsters and, in particular, help sway their parents. Every parent wants the best for their children, and the clubs that can demonstrate this sort of support will strengthen their negotiating positions. It makes it far tougher to sell the dream of the future if you cannot point to the staff and facilities that will make it come true.

4

ENGAGING OTHERS

Teamwork

Balance is the key to every team. It is impossible to win a football game with 11 goalkeepers or with a group of people with identical talents. I imagine that's true in other organisations too.

We thought a lot about the age composition of our team, and kept close track of how many players were over the age of 30, between 23 and 30, and aged 20 to 23. I never wanted a team that was either too old, where players had lost a yard or took longer to recover from injuries, but I also didn't want one which was too young, inexperienced and impetuous.

I've read some of the stuff that was written about the condition of the United squad when I retired. You would have thought that I had left 11 corpses on the steps of a funeral home. It's hilarious. At the start of the 2012–13 season I had not imagined that I would be retiring, and I was as intent as I had ever been in ensuring we were well equipped for future campaigns. At the end of that season the average/median age of our squad was just under 26 – or about the same as it had been throughout the previous 25 years.

A lot has also been made of the fact that we had some players who were aged 30 or older. That's true, but it also ignores the fact that these days the player who takes good care of himself can expect to perform at a very high level until he is 35 or 36. That was not the case 25 years ago, before we all started paying attention to the benefits of sports science, nutrition, more modern training regimens and better pitches. Juventus didn't sign a two-year contract with Patrice Evra in 2014 when he was 33 because they were daft. Patrice was part of the Juventus team that beat Real Madrid to reach the Champions League final last year, a starting 11 that included six players aged 30 or over. Chelsea signed 36-year-old Didier Drogba in the summer of 2014, and he went on to make 40 appearances in a season that saw them win the Premier League and the League Cup.

When I arrived at United, the average age of the squad was too high for my liking. I tried to figure out whether I could shape them into something stronger, and went about analysing every detail of our set-up: pre-season preparation, training, the way in which we started the season and the reason we lost specific games. Between 1988 and 1991 I concluded that Father Time was the enemy, and told our chairman, Martin Edwards, to conduct a fire sale and get rid of the lot for whatever he could get for them. Today, I probably would do this more quickly but, in the 1980s, before the dawn of the Premier League and the barrel-loads of television money, we did not have the spending power. I also had hoped that, with time, I could get the players, especially the established internationals, to increase the scale of their ambition and boost their performance. By the late 1980s, though, I was determined to wipe the slate clean and keep as many young people as I could. So we sold Jesper Olsen (27) for £400,000, Gordon Strachan (32) for £300,000, Paul McGrath (29) for £450,000, Chris Turner (30) for £175,000

and Norman Whiteside (24) for £600,000, and gave free transfers to Kevin Moran (32) and Frank Stapleton (31). That cleared
the decks and gave me the opportunity to start redressing the
balance of our team. In their place we signed Gary Pallister
(24), Neil Webb (26), Mick Phelan (26) and Danny Wallace
(25). Facing up to the issue, concluding that we had the wrong
people and changing the composition of the team, laid the
foundation for all our subsequent success. It took me time to
confront reality and sell these players and, in retrospect, I was
too hesitant. Afterwards, when the deed had been done, I
remember feeling like I'd almost gone through a cleansing ritual.
It was liberating. I wondered why it had taken me so long.

Getting an organisation into balance doesn't occur once. It
requires perpetual work. I felt I was always re-tuning things
– although, once in a while, we had to do more than just a
simple brake adjustment and oil change. We needed to change
with the times, so we did, and this occurred on a regular
four-year cycle. Our squad in the early 1990s was British and
muscular. By the late 1990s it had become more refined, and
a decade later we had a decidedly continental flair. Players
like Ronaldo, Nani and Evra would have seemed like oddities
in the late 1980s. Whenever we sold popular players who were
past their prime or had lost their place in the team, there
would always be a lot of flak. It wasn't something I enjoyed
doing, but it was just one of those ugly necessities of life.
When we sold Paul Ince to Inter Milan in 1995, I got a raft
of abusive letters. But what the fans did not appreciate was
that I was under considerable pressure to make sure that we
could make room in the side for Nicky Butt, Paul Scholes
and David Beckham. Ben Thornley, another youngster at the
time, also looked as if he would make it, until he was terribly
injured in a reserve game. I did not want these players going

to other clubs and, at the time, we were getting lots of enquiries about whether Butt was for sale. Something similar happened when I decided to sell Jaap Stam, the Dutch centre-back, in 2001. He was 29 at the time, and Lazio offered us over £15 million for him, which I thought was a very good deal, particularly because I knew that I could sign Laurent Blanc for close to nothing. I felt terrible telling Stam of the decision because I could see he was devastated. I met him at a petrol station to break the news – a venue that probably did not make things easier for either of us. It was the right decision for United, even though Jaap continued to play well for several years after he left Old Trafford and, in retrospect, his sale was premature.

Every member of a team has got to understand that they are part of a jigsaw puzzle. If you remove one piece, the picture doesn't look right. Each player has to understand the qualities and strengths of their team-mates. In football eight players, not 11, win games, because everybody has off-days and it's almost impossible to make 11 people play to perfection simultaneously.

Out of the 2,131 games that I managed over nearly 40 years, I can only point to about 20 games where every player was absolutely magnificent. The one game that sticks in my mind as an example of this was when we played Wimbledon in the FA Cup fifth round in 1994. At the time Wimbledon were in the Premiership, and they had a team composed of big, powerful players who would trample you to death. We never seemed to give the ball away, and there was one goal that we scored after a magnificent passing move. It was one of those rare games where our performance could have been set to music. Whilst the Wimbledon game may be an under-the-radar example, most will remember the 7–1 victory over Roma in the 2007 Champions League quarter-finals. It was the perfect illustration of a team ethic, and co-ordination that was as close to perfection as you can get.

The reality is that there are very few highly consistent players. A guy who might score a couple of goals in one game may just fire blanks in the next. Or a defender who tackles flawlessly in one outing may get a red card in the next. The sheer number of games in a season undermines this drive for consistency. In the top flight of European football, the teams play half a dozen pre-season matches, plus – depending on cup runs and European competitions – between 55 and 65 games during a season that stretches over nine months. That's the equivalent of one game every four or five days. Also, for a team at Manchester United's level, almost every player will be playing for their country as well: that's another eight to ten games each season.

No matter how carefully players are trained, or how much they are cosseted, it is difficult to have all of them at peak performance for every match. I was always sparing in my use of the younger players to make sure we didn't play them too much during their first two or three seasons. They were always raring to go but, at that stage, were still developing both physically and mentally. I also did not want them taking it for granted that they had earned a permanent place in the first team. It was good to keep them hungry. Paul Scholes, partly because of injuries, only started 38 League games in his first three seasons as a first-team player. At the other extreme, it's difficult to rely on players reaching the twilight of their careers, because it takes them longer to recover from injury and they sometimes have recurring conditions that can sideline them for weeks at a time. In all my time at United we had a number of players who you could depend upon to be available for selection and play the majority of the games in a season. These included Steve Bruce, Denis Irwin, Brian McClair, Mark Hughes, Gary Pallister,

Dwight Yorke, Eric Cantona, David Beckham, Phil Neville and Patrice Evra, during the peaks of their careers.

The task of building and maintaining a team is never done. Not only are there injuries, or the fatigue that can set in during a very long season, but you also have to deal with Father Time. There are always youngsters, in the full blush of youth, pressing to get into the first team; conversely, there are players in their mid-thirties who might have been mainstays of the club for many years but are approaching their sell-by date. This means that top-flight teams are in a perpetual state of evolution, and woe betide the manager who gets lulled into feeling that particular players can go on for ever. I was always on the lookout for new players for the first-team squad – either those who were home-grown at United (which was my strong preference) or from elsewhere. Whenever we came across a player of unusual ability, the unspoken question was whether he would serve us better than the current incumbent. This goes for a reserve goalkeeper as much as it does for a potent striker. Another exercise that I used to employ to keep myself honest was to ask myself which member of our first-team squad would be able to command a starting place with Real Madrid or AC Milan or whatever team happened to be Champions of Europe that year. That little mental exercise always illuminated our weaker spots.

When I assembled a squad, I would always try to ensure that I had half a dozen multi-purpose players who could play a variety of positions. It provides a manager with so much more flexibility, either during the course of a season if there is a plague of injuries or, for tactical reasons, during a game. Ryan Giggs, Phil Neville, Paul Scholes and John O'Shea are prime examples of that sort of a player. They could play with great distinction in four or five positions. The other virtue I prized was reliability. I wanted players who were fit to play in every game. Nobody would want to run an organisation whose top performers could only appear for work three days a week. The same goes for football teams, which is why I cherished players like Brian McClair or Denis Irwin, who between them played 1,000 games for United. They were great soldiers, although obviously without the profile of some of our household names. Mick Phelan was similar and would do anything that was asked of him. He would play in any position and would, if needs be, mark a man like a limpet mine.

Durability was another key characteristic. Steve Bruce, Gary Pallister, Denis Irwin, David Beckham, Dwight Yorke, Ryan Giggs and Eric Cantona rarely ever spent extended periods out with an injury. In 1990, when Mark Hughes got injured against Liverpool, I genuinely thought he was going to be out for a month. He was back in the team ten days later. That sort of durability was a godsend to me because it widened my options and also meant that I could field teams where all the players were familiar with each other. In the 1992–93 Premier League campaign, eight players started 40 or more games in a 42-match schedule. It should be no surprise to hear that was the first year United won the League while I was manager.

I'm not exactly sure why Premier League players are more prone to injuries than their predecessors, especially since most of them are fitter and stronger than the players of 20 years ago. My suspicion is that the quality of the pitches has a lot to do with the higher injury rate. The fact that most top-notch venues now have pitches that are as smooth as the surface of a snooker table makes the game far quicker and more attractive to watch. But it also allows the players, who gain confidence from a sure footing and even surface, to hold the ball longer and also to tackle quicker and harder. So the velocity with which players collide is far greater than when I played. This makes it all the more important to have a squad that includes a healthy portion of multi-purpose players.

Some people wonder whether any organisation can survive if it is entirely composed of creative players. I suppose they worry that creativity brings its own negatives in the shape of ego and individualism. People with big egos want to win so that was never a problem for me. It is wonderful to dream of fielding 11 spectacularly creative players every Saturday, but that breaks down in practice because you have to deal with the realities of needing a solid defence to withstand attacks. You need to have balance in your team, but I always found myself drawn to the creative, attacking players. They can see things that others cannot. On a football field, they are the players who are able to penetrate opponents, make a decisive run, are equally comfortable hitting a 50-yard laser pass or carving open a defence with a short pass, like Paul Scholes, or switching the course of play like David Beckham. Creative players can change a game and galvanise a club. When Cristiano Ronaldo was playing for United, I kept telling him that his job was to create opportunities. In the 2004 FA Cup semi-final against Arsenal, my instructions to Ronaldo were simple: 'Don't worry about defending – just attack.' We played three central midfielders and that gave Cristiano the platform, and freedom, to terrorise Arsenal. It is players like Ronaldo, Giggs, Cantona and Scholes who decide matches. Teams filled with players like Steve Bruce, Roy Keane, Jaap Stam, Gary Neville, Patrice Evra, Nemanja Vidić and Bryan Robson would be almost unbeatable, but would not be able to split open a competitor – especially important when your opponents will do anything not to lose. The ones who can slice open competitors are the few truly creative sorts.

The 1999 side exemplified this because we had creativity up

front, and in midfield Scholes was the clever one with the piercing passes, Beckham was a spectacular crosser of balls from the sidelines, and Giggs's bolts of electricity would leave opponents flailing. And behind them sat Keane – the indomitable, tireless driver. There were other combinations that worked well too. Dwight Yorke, whom we signed from Aston Villa in 1998, could skewer the opposition, create something out of nothing, beat a man and was deadly in front of the goal. Ole Solskjaer, Teddy Sheringham and Andy Cole could all have played for any of the top European clubs. Ole and Andy were fabulous finishers and Teddy was a clever passer in the last third of the field. But none of them had that extra gift with which Dwight Yorke was blessed. Dwight's arrival also had the unexpected benefit of bringing out the best in Andy Cole, with whom he developed an extraordinary relationship. In 1998–99 (the season United won the Treble), the pair scored 53 goals between them.

One attribute of the exceptional creative type is that you have to keep them from being bored. Usually it isn't a question of arrogance or complacency, they just don't seem to feel sufficiently challenged. This was sometimes the case with Paul Scholes. Things would come so easily to him that, from time to time, when we were leading in a game, he would just tune out. He'd start to flick balls and do little tricks, as if he was at a Christmas party. I'd tell him, 'Scholesy, stop the carrying on.' He would look at me as if he had no idea what I was talking about. But he knew, and when the going was tough and he had to perform, he rarely ever fell short.

I always had a fondness for the kings of creativity who would play for our opponents, even if I might have wished they were wearing United red. Dennis Bergkamp at Arsenal, Gianfranco Zola at Chelsea, Zinedine Zidane and Dejan Savićević in Europe, Glenn Hoddle at Tottenham and Paul Gascoigne at Newcastle and Tottenham are examples of that sort of extraordinary flair. Gascoigne, at his peak, was the best English player I have seen in my time, with the exception of Bobby Charlton. Xavi, Iniesta and Messi at Barcelona have been the master chefs for the past few years. All of them would get three Michelin stars and you would walk 50 miles barefoot to watch them in the kitchen. Speaking of fondness, I never allowed my personal feelings about a particular player to cloud my judgement about what was best for the team. Obviously I found it easier to get on with some players rather than others, but irrespective of any private feelings, I wanted the very best team on the field. I just think a leader has to keep reminding himself to be clinical about these sorts of judgements. You don't have to love your players or your management team, but you do need to respect their abilities.

As I mentioned, at United we effectively rebuilt the team on four-year cycles – even though it may not have seemed apparent to all but the most ardent fan. For example, little more than three years after our 1999 Champions League final, ten members of the 18-man squad had left the club; five years after the victory, only five of those players were still at Old Trafford. It meant being very clinical about the capabilities of each player, which was not always easy when some of them had played hundreds of games for the club and made huge contributions to our success. But there was no choice. At Aberdeen, if we wound up third in the League, nobody beyond the team and the coaching staff would be too bothered because Rangers and Celtic were always supposed to occupy the top two spots. At United it was another matter entirely. The genetic make-up of the club was formed from victory.

One aspect of team-building that often gets overlooked is the need for old-timers to have the necessary patience with newcomers. Football can be brutal and there is nowhere to hide on a pitch. When new players arrived at United, particularly if they were transfers and immediately thrust into the first team, they were often uncomfortable with our style of play and performing in front of 75,000 people. When Patrice Evra, our great left-back, played his first game for United in 2006, it was in a derby against Manchester City. He spent the game walking around in a trance. It was a disaster and we lost 3–1. I signed Evra in the same season that we bought Nemanja Vidić from Spartak Moscow and the pair of them took about six months to settle in.

I always felt it was important to be careful about the way a newcomer was threaded into the side, especially if he was not a product of our youth system. For the newcomer everything was unfamiliar, and I am not alluding to the Manchester weather or driving cars with steering wheels on the right-hand side. I mean our system of play and, in particular, the habits and quirks of other players. The boys who had grown into men at Manchester United, such as Ryan Giggs, Paul Scholes, Nicky Butt and David Beckham, could almost have played together blindfolded. They knew how their team-mates would react, or where they were likely to be in particular situations, and could communicate without speaking. They trusted each other's judgements and had that sense of fellowship which is the glue for any group of people who want to outperform competitors. The newcomer did not have that advantage, which is why I always tried to make sure that I wasn't integrating a lot of new players into the first team at the same time. It was almost like trying to teach each person a new language, while familiarising them with several local dialects.

Players sometimes also coveted particular shirt numbers. The number 7, which had taken on a mythical status, having previously been worn by George Best, Bryan Robson and Eric

Cantona, was a shirt that David Beckham, who had started his United career wearing number 24, was eager to wear. At that stage, after David had just played a couple of seasons in the first-team squad, I would have preferred if Roy Keane had taken the number. But Roy was not fussed about it and so I gave it to David. I quickly realised that, as a United fan, this number really mattered to him. He wore it with distinction. After my last season, the number 7 shirt became available and was worn by Antonio Valencia, who subsequently felt it added a burden to his game. He switched back to his previous number the following season.

I also found that experienced players are honest enough with themselves to know if they aren't quite as good as another player. That's particularly the case with older players. A 35-year-old player knows he doesn't have the pace of a top-notch 20 year old, and all team members were aware of the difference between themselves and the unnatural talent of a Cristiano Ronaldo or Eric Cantona. The older players aren't competing against the youngsters as much as they are contending with the comparisons with their younger selves.

Another thing I had to look out for were character clashes. If people are so selfish that they are only thinking about themselves, it just doesn't work. When people start butting heads it destroys a team. We had a situation at United where Andy Cole and Teddy Sheringham just didn't like each other and they wouldn't work together on the field. During one game they had an argument in the tunnel at half-time. So I called them into the office and told them that if I saw that again, they'd both be gone. The change was immediate and there was never another problem between them. Whilst they were never going to be the best of friends, they were professional about the whole situation. But Andy did not want to play second fiddle to anyone, and after Ruud van Nistelrooy arrived, it was clear he was unhappy. Some years later there was tension between Ruud van Nistelrooy and Cristiano Ronaldo. Ruud was dissatisfied with the number of passes he was receiving from Cristiano, and his very evident irritation exacted a toll on the younger player.

When I appointed Roy Keane as club captain in 1997, it aroused the ire of Peter Schmeichel. Schmeichel admired Keane as a player and, best as I know, there wasn't any particular animosity between them. It was just that Schmeichel's pride was hurt, and he let me know in no uncertain terms by storming into my office and going completely berserk. I refused to back down and he stormed out, but I just reiterated to Peter his importance to the team while telling him that the decision had been made. This, obviously, wasn't the best way to usher in Keane as the club leader.

Working as a team didn't stop at the touchlines, and it was a sensibility that was required everywhere. When I brought René Meulensteen back to United in 2007 after he had a brief, ill-fated spell as manager of Brøndby in Denmark, my coaching staff were unhappy. René isn't shy about telling others what's wrong with them, so the prospect of his return was not greeted with undiluted joy. I told everybody that the reason René was being rehired was because he was a spectacular development coach and it was good for the club.

I used all sorts of ploys to try to emphasise to the players, particularly the younger ones, the benefits of teamwork. In my office at the Carrington training ground, I used to have a large black and white photograph from the 1930s, of 11 workers in New York, eating their lunch while sitting on a steel girder several hundred feet above street level during the construction of Rockefeller Center. It makes the hairs on the back of my neck stand up. These guys are sitting there, wearing their cloth hats, without any safety harnesses, and one of them is lighting a cigarette. I'd explain to the players if one of the workers got into trouble his mates would try to save him. I'd say: 'That's team spirit – when you give your life to someone. No one at the club ever wins a thing without the other ones.' Of course, some of the boys completely missed the point. Once, when I asked a player, 'What can you say about that photograph?' the reply was, 'They've all got hats on.'

We were very careful about trying to make sure the limelight shone on as many players as possible. Inevitably, the press would focus on the goal-scorers, but there were plenty of ways for us to ensure that credit was shared as widely as possible. We would rotate different players in front of the press for post-game inter-view sessions. There were also plenty of opportunities in the match programme or on the website or on MUTV to showcase different personalities. Most were willing to do this, although a few, like Paul Scholes, preferred to stay in the shadows, and some of the foreign players who were unsure about their command of English tended to hold back. If we were playing in Spain, or Portugal, we would be sure to line up a player who spoke Spanish or Portuguese. That was just good business, because those sorts of appearances helped broaden United's appeal.

There is one other lesson I learned regarding teamwork, and it is on an odd topic – nepotism. It does not matter whether you are running a family-managed organisation, or one with more widely distributed stakeholders: a leader is always tempted to look at his own kith and kin, or family friends, through a different lens. Some leaders think that if they bring a close relative into the organisation, it will send the wrong message, destroy teamwork and throw everything out of kilter, because people will assume that a surname, or a personal relationship, is more important than ability. These leaders have a firm rule and refuse to hire family members or friends, even if their credentials suggest they are more than worthy. Others will lurch in the opposite direction and turn a blind eye to the shortcomings of their son or niece.

I encountered this issue when one of my twin sons, Darren, wanted to play as a professional. I never really considered signing him for United because I always thought it was going to be too awkward for both of us. So Cathy and I went to see Brian Clough at Nottingham Forest, and Darren was about to sign for him in 1990 when Archie Knox, my assistant manager, argued that I should not let him go to an opponent. Archie's point was that it was only going to be awkward if Darren made the first team. I talked it over with Cathy, who suggested I let Darren decide. I remember going to his bedroom to pose the question and it was Darren who decided he wanted to play for his old man.

As things would have it, Darren made his debut for the first team in 1990 and played 16 games during 1993, the year United won our first League title under my management. He was very unlucky because he got a hamstring injury in a Scotland Under-21 game against Italy and was out for a couple of months. By the time he was ready to return, Paul Ince and Bryan Robson had recovered from injuries, and the following summer I did what I needed to do as manager and signed Roy Keane, who was then 21, to buttress our midfield. That was a tragedy for Darren, because after that he never really got back into the side; he asked for a transfer because he was keen to play regular first-team football. I helped him land at Wolverhampton Wanderers but then, poor devil, he had to endure four managers in as many seasons. While he was in the first team and in the dressing room, it was a bit difficult for both of us. To Darren's credit, he understood that, at

United, I was the manager not his dad, as I found out when I tried to pump him for information about the lifestyle habits of a couple of players. There was no way that Darren was going to squeal on his team-mates. He played his cards very close to his chest. As for moving Darren along to Wolves, Cathy has never forgiven me. From time to time she will remind me with the words: 'You sold your own son.'

Captains

As hard as I worked on my own leadership skills, and as much as I tried to influence every aspect of United's success on the field, at kick-off on match day things moved beyond my control. On the field, the person responsible for making sure the 11 players acted as a team was the club captain. Even though I imagine some people think this is a ceremonial position, it is far from that. Yes, there are elements of symbolism to the role, because the captain is the man who always gets to lift the trophy – but I only ever wanted a leader, rather than someone who might look good on top of a cake. It is a critical decision. For football managers the club captain is the equivalent of what a business unit leader or a country manager might be in a company. He is the person responsible for making sure the agenda of the organisation is pursued.

I was always a strong personality, and when I selected people to transmit my intentions to others, I looked for the same quality in them. I don't know where it came from, but even when I was playing for my school team and getting into youth-team football, I'd start getting into the players. My dad always used to go to the games and watch and never say a word. But there was one boy whose dad complained to mine and said,

'Could you speak to your son, he's always going on to my boy.'

Every leader has different characteristics and leads in his own manner. I suppose that's true for CEOs of companies as much as it is for football managers or captains. That was certainly the case during my career as a manager when each of our captains had very different personality traits. When I selected the captain I was looking for four principal virtues. The first was a desire to lead on the field. Some of the finest players just did not aspire to do that, even though they commanded immense respect. Paul Scholes is the shining example of this. He was an extraordinary player and an emblem of everything United stood for but, even though he has what it takes to be a winning manager, he never aspired to be our captain. He is a man of few words, doesn't wear his emotions on his sleeve, and has no need for the limelight. However, nobody should be fooled, because deep down he torments himself if he messes up.

The second attribute I wanted was someone I could trust to convey my desires, and the third was a person whom the other players would respect as a leader and whose instructions they would follow. Not every creative person is born to be a leader. They may be incredible members of a team and astonishingly productive individual contributors, but poor leaders. My son Mark tells me this is also true in his line of work, where people who are very gifted as investors often are not the best types to run and lead an investment organisation, simply because the skills required in that role are not their forte. I also wanted captains capable of adapting to changing circumstances. No general is going to win a war unless he has colonels and majors who, in the thick of a fight that is going poorly, can muster the troops, galvanise them into action and help them defy the odds. The same was true for us, even though United's battles were fought on grounds with names such as Anfield, Camp Nou or Stadio delle Alpi rather than Waterloo or El Alamein.

There were a handful of captains of other teams that I came to admire, although I obviously didn't know them as well as the Aberdeen or United skippers. Alan Shearer at Newcastle United, John Terry at Chelsea and Tony Adams at Arsenal are the ones who stick out for me. They were all driven guys who had an edge to their personalities, and their teams were all the better as a result. Johan Cruyff was probably the most influential during my career. The players, whether it was at Ajax or in the Dutch side, probably listened to him more than they did the manager. Cruyff couldn't help himself: he had to direct and control everything.

When I arrived at Aberdeen I didn't have to worry about picking a leader for the team because Willie Miller was the captain – when I got there and when I left – which was a real tribute to his ability and fitness level. At United Bryan Robson was the club skipper when I appeared and there wasn't a player on the field who could match his determination and grit or his ability to read a game. He was a perfect captain and ticked all the boxes. I trusted him to make on-field adjustments to playing positions; he was also someone who would speak his mind, which was something I valued. Robson remained captain until he started getting plagued by injuries, and in 1991 Steve Bruce led the team for most of the season. Bruce was solid, courageous, and stuck his head into all manners of dangerous positions. Not only would he always put his neck on the line, but he also has a natural instinct for taking care of those around him and a great sense of humour. Both Bryan and Steve were invaluable in other ways, particularly when it came to helping young players and their parents understand the possibilities if they elected to cast their lot with United. When Bruce's knees began to give him trouble,

I picked our talisman, Eric Cantona, and subsequently Roy Keane. Eric and Roy were a study in contrasts – one French and the other Irish. Eric was a man of few words, but when he offered praise it had a dramatic effect. It was more meaningful to David Beckham, after he scored his miraculous goal against Wimbledon, on the opening day of the 1996–97 season, that Eric considered it the best goal he had ever witnessed, than the fact that he had pulled off the impossible. Roy, by contrast, was a man whose intensity could intimidate his team-mates, but he was a great leader on the pitch.

Peter Schmeichel became captain when Roy Keane was injured, and was the team leader on the day we beat Bayern Munich to win the Champions League in 1999 when Roy was suspended. Even though there are other examples of goalkeepers who acted as captains, such as Iker Casillas of Real Madrid and Spain and Gianluigi Buffon and Dino Zoff in Italy, there is a natural tendency to select a player who is in the thick of things rather than the one between the posts. So a goalkeeper who becomes a captain has to be a bit larger than life, and Peter certainly was. Not only was he a massive physical presence – taller than many of the defenders who played for United – but he was also able to transmit his confidence, enthusiasm and zest along the entire length of the pitch.

In the downtime between games I would often solicit the opinion of my captains, but they all understood that I was the ultimate decision-maker. I was also keen to hear what they had to say about particular players, but captains tend to toe the line and stay true to their playing comrades rather than tell tales out of school. I remembered this dividing line from my own playing days and respected it. I frequently talked to the captains and other senior players about how we might approach an opponent. In 1996 as we were preparing to meet Liverpool in the FA Cup final, I spent time with Eric Cantona and Peter Schmeichel trying to figure out how we were going to deal with Steve McManaman. Eric suggested that we drop Roy Keane in front of our back four to keep tabs on McManaman, who floated behind their forwards and was a real handful. It was an astute observation, which we followed; as a result, McManaman was silenced and we won what was a tedious, uneventful game when Eric scored the only goal. Eric's advice was crucial. It didn't matter to me that he had come up with the idea rather than a member of the coaching staff or myself. It just made a ton of sense. It wasn't as if I was chasing honours or looking for personal glory or seeking to be the font of all wisdom. I just wanted the team to win.

It was never quite the same in my last decade at United. Some of that was due to the changing nature of the game, the increase in the number of fixtures we played each season and the rise in the number of substitutes used during games which, by the start of the 1995–96 season, had risen to three. A captain simply could not play in each and every game – so the armband tended to move around. These factors led to a spell where Giggs, Ferdinand, Evra and Vidić, whom we all called Vida, wore the armband at different times. Towards the end of my time, when Vida became more prone to injuries, he and Patrice more or less alternated as captain. You could not have found two more different personalities. Vida is dour and uncompromising while Patrice just brimmed with enthusiasm. He came to me once and asked whether he had gone over the top in a tirade in the dressing room. I reassured him and said that he had saved me from having to shout. Patrice's instinctive reaction was great because it showed how deeply he cared and I thought it would goad his team-mates into performing better. It was the mark of a natural leader.

5

SETTING STANDARDS

Excellence

Everyone has a different definition of 'world class', the two words that seem to have taken the place of 'great' or 'excellent'. If you read the papers, or listen to the television commentators, we seem to be awash with 'world-class' footballers. The same thing seems to be happening in the classroom, because I keep hearing about 'grade inflation' – or the way in which an A* gets given to a lot more students than in yesteryear. In my book there are only two world-class players playing today – Lionel Messi and Cristiano Ronaldo. There are a considerable number of great players, and an even larger collection of good ones, but of the thousands of professional footballers playing today, only Cristiano and Lionel have earned the right to be described as 'world class'. Other players can produce 'world-class' moments – a spectacular goal, an extraordinary pass, or an astonishing save – but there are hundreds of moments in a game and thousands in a career. There are a number of subjective and objective criteria that I use as a way to rank players. The subjective ones include their ability with both feet; their sense of balance; the disciplined fashion in which they take care of their fitness; their attitude towards training; the consistency between games and over multiple seasons; their demonstrated mastery in several different positions; and the way they add flair to any team for which they play. The objective ones that are impossible to dispute are: the number of goals they have scored; the games they have played for several of the best club teams in the world; the number of League championship and cup medals they have won, and their appearances in World Cups. When you employ this sort of measurement approach, it becomes far easier to define the very highest levels of performance. The people who are least confused about this are other players.

There are a decent number of great players in the game today – Thomas Müller at Bayern Munich, Luis Suárez and Neymar at Barcelona and Alexis Sánchez at Arsenal – but I'm sure that all four would admit that they are not at the same level as Messi and Ronaldo. I don't mean to demean or criticise any of the great or very good footballers who played for me during my 26-year career at United, but there were only four who were world class: Cantona, Giggs, Ronaldo and Scholes. And, of the four, Cristiano was like an ornament on top of a Christmas tree. He was the one who added that final touch. Roy Keane, Bryan Robson and Steve Bruce were great players, but they earned that distinction from their attitude, ambition, leadership ability and intensity rather than some of the other attributes.

Looking a little further back, Bobby Charlton, who played 758 games for the club and 106 games for England, including appearances in the final stages of four World Cup tournaments, illustrates what I mean by 'world class'. Bobby seemed to float above the field, was two footed, could play on the left, the right or in the centre, and had an inner confidence and steely resolve. Bobby, despite all his accomplishments, has always been a modest, humble man. He is quiet and shy, but on one occasion when United were trailing at half-time he said, 'Give me the ball. I can win this.' He was not boasting or preening, he just knew what he could do and, more importantly, his team-mates recognised this. United went on to win that game and they did so because of Charlton – a player who was world class.

In football, a manager is fortunate if he has one world-class player in a squad; most clubs do not have that luxury. Yet, even for them, it is still possible to field a very good team. Properly harmonised, 11 good players can form a team that is more than the sum of its parts. Yet I cannot think of a team that achieved great things at the highest level without a world-class player.

Part of the way you develop excellence in an organisation is to be careful about the way you define success. I was always careful about setting specific, long-range targets. I would never say, 'We expect to win the League and two pieces of silverware this season.' First, it conveys the wrong message, because it sounds cocky and arrogant. Second, it applies a lot of additional pressure on everyone without any real benefit. Third, it sets everyone up for disappointment. It was much easier to say, 'At United we expect to win every game,' because that was the case from about 1993 and it also conveyed the spirit of the club. Making sure everyone understood that we expected to triumph in every game set an agenda of excellence and allowed me to regularly administer booster-shots of intensity.

There's a balance that needs to be weighed when conveying a sense of what's possible with the reality of the circumstances. You have to set up each individual for success, which requires considered thought. It's so easy to set unrealistic expectations and I learned this early in my career. At one point in my first season at St Mirren, the team had won eight games in a row and were well placed in the second division. I was feeling buoyant and told the press that we would not lose a game for the rest of the season. Instead, we won only one of our remaining fixtures, and the club finished the season in sixth place.

At United the press would always ask me at the start of the season what I hoped to achieve. My canned response was to tell them that we wanted to win one trophy and we didn't care which one it was. I was careful not to build up false expectations or place too much pressure on everyone. It is counterproductive. However, we never went two consecutive seasons without a major trophy between my first piece of silverware at United and the end of my career, a period of 23 years.

I was also lucky that, with one exception, I never had an owner or director tell me that they expected me to bring home a piece of silverware. The only time it happened was just before I got fired from St Mirren, when a director told me (even though we had been promoted the season before and had a very young team) that he expected us to win the League in the following season. It was the only time anyone ever said to me: 'We need you to win a trophy.' What he failed to acknowledge was that to achieve that we needed two or three new players that the club did not want to buy.

Winning anything requires a series of steps. You cannot win the League with one giant leap. So I would be careful to divide everything up into digestible chunks. Nobody is going to take a climbing team to the foot of Everest, point to the summit and say 'Okay, lads, get up there.' At the start of the season I would avoid communicating any particular objective with the players. My comments to the press about wanting to win a trophy were reasonably generic and the squad were used to these expectations anyway. I would only start to become less vague in November as the shape of the season and the form of our rivalries became clear. At that point, as the afternoons shortened, I would say to the players, 'If we're first, second or third, or within three points of the lead, on New Year's Day, we have a fantastic chance.'

In November 2009 René Meulensteen set a specific target for the points we wanted in the bag at the end of December, but over that period we lost to Chelsea, Aston Villa and Fulham and I felt the target actually became counterproductive. I thought it better to have an element of vagueness about the specific goal. If we came out of Christmas week in fifth place, it was not a complete disaster because, over the years, it became folklore within the club that United always performed better in the second half of the season. We would always say, 'The second half will look after itself.' Of course, it was a bit more complicated than this, but it buoyed spirits to have that outlook. The reality of anything that's fiercely competitive is that very often nothing is decided until the bitter end. In all my time at United, the winner of the League title was only decided two weeks or more from the end of the season on four occasions.

Being willing to reappraise your targets during a game is crucial too. If you are in real trouble, it often seems like an impossible task to set things right. That happened to us in 2001 when we were 3–0 down to Tottenham at half-time. At the break I was realistic with the players and told them we were in a royal mess. There was deathly quiet in the dressing room and all I said was, 'Score the next goal and let's see where that takes us.' I didn't say something like, 'We've got forty-five minutes to score four times.' That would have seemed impossible. When we walked into the tunnel to take to the pitch, Teddy Sheringham, a former Manchester United player now playing for Tottenham, was barking at his team-mates, 'Don't let them score early.' Having experienced life inside Old Trafford he knew how dangerous we could be when coming from behind.

However, we did score the one goal, and that led, inconceivable though it sounds, to a further four. We eventually won the game 5–3.

Once United started winning domestic competitions, I began to have higher aspirations. I shared these with the coaching staff and explained that, while we obviously had to pursue the League title with a vengeance, our new target was to win the European Champions League. By 1993, the year that United won its first League title while I was manager, the club had only won the Champions League – or the European Cup as it was known until 1992 – once compared to six victories for Real Madrid, four for AC Milan and Liverpool, three for Bayern Munich and Ajax and two for Benfica and Nottingham Forest.

I employed the same approach to the pursuit of the European Cup as I did for the domestic trophies. We had to do it step by step. The first obvious goal was to emerge from the group stages with at least ten points. We only failed to do this three times – in 1994–95, 2005–06 and 2011–12.

I operated in a similar manner with players. I never told Cristiano Ronaldo or Dimitar Berbatov that we expected them to score a minimum of 25 goals a season, or instructed Paul Scholes or Roy Keane that they had to maintain a pass completion rate of at least 80 per cent. I never had a particular quota that I expected any player to fulfil, but they all knew I expected nothing but the best from them. Signing a player to a new contract always presented a good opportunity to review performance levels and it gave me room to talk about where they needed to improve. Whenever we bought a player I would make a point of sitting down with him and explaining exactly what was expected of him at a club like Manchester United.

As for myself, I never wrote out a series of personal goals. When I was 17, I did not tell myself that I needed to score 100 goals by the time I was 30 or finish my playing career with half a dozen medals and a score of Scottish caps. It was similar when I was a manager; although I did know, after Aberdeen had established itself as a winning club, that I wanted to work in a larger setting. Once I got to United, beyond a few brief flirtations with a handful of other clubs, I never thought much about working elsewhere. From time to time people suggested that I become manager of England, but that post, irrespective of the decade, has always held little appeal to me. Not only would I have had to deal with the guilt of turning my back on Scotland, but I would also have had to contend with all the frustrations of the position. It's a hopeless job because, before any major competition, the press and the public whip themselves into a frenzy. They tend to forget that a national team manager, even though he might be handsomely compensated, is in a part-time role. He only sees the players intermittently, he doesn't conduct daily training sessions, and it is unrealistic for any group of players, no matter how talented, to instinctively sense, in the way that they can do at their club, what one of their national team-mates might do. I had a taste of the frustrations of managing a national team when I stepped in for a short stint as Scottish manager following the death of Jock Stein in 1985. It was definitely not my cup of tea. In my opinion, international management jobs are for experienced men in the later stages of their career who have the patience to deal with the short-comings of the post and carry the reputation needed to command a dressing room full of players with whom they spend little time.

After I got to Manchester, I could not imagine a larger stage than Old Trafford. Obviously I'm very aware of Camp Nou and the Bernabéu, which are both great settings, but for me neither has had the allure of Old Trafford. I never gave myself a quota for the number of League titles or FA Cup trophies I had to win before I retired. If I had said to myself, I cannot go until United has won five Champions League titles, I would still be at Old Trafford, even though, privately, I believe we should have achieved that goal under my watch. I never said to myself that my life would not be complete unless United strikers won a certain number of Ballon d'Or awards or Player of the Year awards. I just don't operate like that. All I ever wanted to do was win more trophies. I just could never get enough.

Inspiring

You don't get the best out of people by hitting them with an iron rod. You do so by gaining their respect, getting them accustomed to triumphs and convincing them that they are capable of improving their performance. I cannot think of any manager who succeeded for any length of time by presiding over a reign of terror. It turns out that the two most powerful words in the English language are, 'Well done'. Much of leadership is about extracting that extra 5 per cent of performance that individuals did not know they possessed.

It was always important that the players erased the memory of the previous season, whether we had won or lost. If we had done well in the previous year, it did not guarantee that we would automatically do so again. And, if we had lost, I had no interest in prolonging any hangover of defeatism. The coaching staff, in particular the sports science crew, would come to me with new ideas before or during the pre-season, but I would never conduct any big post-mortem with the players. I used to gather them around me in a semi-circle at the training ground and re-emphasise my desire to win and use it as an opportunity to set expectations. I used to ask the mature players, who had begun to acquire a taste for United's victory habits, how many medals they had won. I told them that they could not consider themselves to be a United player until they had won ten medals. I remember saying to Rio Ferdinand that he could never think of himself as a United player until he attained the level of Ryan Giggs. Of course, that was mission impossible.

It is much easier to do difficult things if others like you. Though I have never tried to court popularity, I always tried to pay particular attention to people at United – or at the other clubs I was involved with – who worked behind the scenes and were our unsung heroes. It wasn't a false front; it just seemed like the right thing to do. These people weren't getting the multimillion-pound salaries or public acclaim, and didn't wear Patek Philippe watches or drive Bentleys. Some of them – the laundry team, the groundsmen, the hospitality waitresses – took the bus to work. They were the mainstays of the club. At United, some of them have been there even longer than Ryan Giggs. In a way, they are the club's equivalent of the Civil Service – they outlast the governments and, at United, they provided continuity and a connection with our heritage. It was very easy for me to feel affinity towards them, since most had backgrounds much like my own.

Some managers try to be popular with the players and become one of the boys. It never works. As a leader, you don't need to be loved, though it is useful, on occasion, to be feared. But, most of all, you need to be respected. There are just some natural boundaries, and when those get crossed it makes life harder. When I was playing at Rangers, they hired a new manager, David White. He was young and a good man but just out of his depth. He was overawed by the club, while at the same time he was living in the shadow of Jock Stein over at Celtic. The players didn't have much respect for him, and part of the reason was because he was too close to them. The same thing happened at United when Wilf McGuinness succeeded Sir Matt Busby in 1969. Wilf had several things going against him. He was succeeding a legend; he was only 31 years old and had no management experience. But, worst of all, he was managing a group of men with whom he had played. It was an impossible position for him. My immediate predecessor at United, Ron Atkinson, had a similar issue. He had enjoyed much more success as a manager than Wilf, but he too chose to fraternise with the players. It just doesn't work. A leader is not one of the boys.

It is vital to keep some sort of distance. This could be expressed in small but significant ways. For example, I generally rode at the front of the team bus. The players understood the distance, and at the end of the season when they had their parties, I was never invited. They'd invite all the management staff, but they wouldn't invite me. I wasn't offended by this. It was the right thing for them to do. With one exception in Aberdeen, I never attended any of the players' weddings. There was a line that they were not prepared to cross and they respected my position. It also makes things easier because, as a manager, you can't be sentimental about them. Jock Stein told me once, 'Don't fall in love with the players because they'll two-time you.' That may be a bit harsh, but Jock was right that you cannot get too attached to people who work for you. The one time you must have that attachment is when they are in trouble – when they need your advice. I couldn't count the number of times where I helped players with personal matters, and I'm proud of the fact they trusted me and that they knew that discussion would stay private. In these situations I acted as a priest, father or lawyer – whatever it took to make the problem go away. Even to this day, many former players still come to me for advice; this is a reflection of the trust that underpinned our relationship.

When players got too old I couldn't afford to be kind to them at the expense of the club. All the evidence is on the football field. It just doesn't lie. I had to make a lot of horrible decisions and I had to be ruthless. I never expected the players to love me, but neither did I want them to hate me, because that would have made it impossible to extract the most from them. All I wanted was for them to respect me and follow my instructions.

Unless you understand people, it's very hard to motivate them. I learned this years ago in Scotland when I was handed a lesson by a young lad. While I managed Aberdeen, we used to travel down to Glasgow every Thursday night to coach young kids on an AstroTurf field so that we could identify the best young talent. I was down there one night, dressed in my track-suit emblazoned with its 'AF' initials, when I saw this kid, who was about eight, smoking a cigarette. I said, 'Put that cigarette out, son. What would your dad think if he saw you smoking?' The boy looked at me and he said, 'Fuck off!' and walked away. My assistant manager, Archie Knox, who was with me, burst out laughing at the way this kid had chopped my legs off. But when I started thinking about the incident, I realised that I knew nothing about that boy. I had no idea where he came from, what his parents were like, whether he was taunted by his pals and why he harboured such anger. Unless you know those sorts of things and have an understanding of someone's personality, it is impossible to get the best out of them. Before we signed players, especially youngsters, I always tried to under-stand the circumstances in which they had been raised. The first ten or 12 years of anyone's life have such a profound influence on the way they act as adults.

Another crucial ingredient of motivation is consistency. As a leader you can't run from one side of the ship to the other. People need to feel that you have unshakeable confidence in a particular approach. If you can't show this, you'll lose the team very quickly. There is a phrase in football about players 'not playing for the manager', which I have seen happen a thousand times. Once that happens, the manager is as good as dead, because he has failed in his major undertaking – which is to motivate the players to follow him. The time to be inconsistent is when changes need to be made because the world is changing around you. There was always the temptation when things weren't going well to change or to leap to a new lily pad. That doesn't work. Sometimes, if we lost some games, we'd hear that the players thought that our training should be more light-hearted; that our results would improve if, instead of concentrating our training sessions around technical skills, we played mock games. I always refused to bow to those suggestions. Any field on a Sunday is full of people playing park games, work games or pub games, but that doesn't make these people better footballers. I just believe that continual devotion to improving technical skills, and the enhancement of tactics, lead to better results, and I wasn't about to change just to temporarily please others.

Leaders are usually unaware, or at least underestimate, the motivating power of their presence. Nobody sees themselves as others see them. I'd never really understood this until Rio Ferdinand buttonholed me one day because I had missed some training sessions while travelling abroad to scout a player. Rio said, 'Where have you been? It's not the same when you are not here.' It didn't matter that Carlos Queiroz was running the training sessions and the routine and drills were exactly the same as if I had been there. Rio had noticed my absence, and perhaps some of the players had eased off a little because I was missing from the sidelines. I don't know whether that actually happened because I wasn't there – and maybe that's the point.

I took Rio's observation to heart. After that, if I had to go and watch a player or check out a team, we chartered a private plane so I could be at the training ground the next day even if I hadn't got to bed until two in the morning. The lesson I absorbed was that even if I said nothing during the practice (and I rarely said much), my physical presence was a more important motivational tool than I had realised. Anyone who is in charge of a group of people has got to have a strong personality. That doesn't mean dominating every conversation or speaking at the top of your voice. Some quiet people have very strong personalities and rooms fall silent when they have something to say. A strong personality is an expression of inner strength and fortitude.

I always got more out of players by praising them than by scorning them with criticism. Footballers, like all human beings, are plagued by a range of emotions that run all the way from profound insecurity to massive over-confidence. Trying to measure where, along this spectrum, each of these players was on any particular day was very important. If you hope to motivate people, you need to know when to prey on their insecurities and when to bolster their self-confidence. People perform best when they know they have earned the trust of their leader.

My father was a man of few words. He didn't dole out praise. His main desire was for me to keep my feet on the ground and retain my humility. After I scored three goals in one game and got home, he just handed out stick. He said, 'You don't shoot enough. You don't pass enough.' I suppose my dad's remarks made me want to work harder so that I could garner praise from him but, after I had played well, it was always deflating to hear him utter those sorts of remarks. By contrast, my mother and my granny used to be full of compliments and praise, and their joy in my successes was evident. In retrospect I sometimes wonder whether my parents inadvertently supplied me with two engines: one that made me want to try even harder and a second that made me feel I was capable of anything.

I wasn't afraid of criticising a player when I felt I could help him improve, but I always tried to couch this in a positive way. For example, I would tell a young player that he would be far more effective if he passed the ball more. That message is more likely to be absorbed than barking, 'You're never going to be any good if you keep hogging the ball.' After a game I would always try to avoid criticising the players. They had enough pressure, without me piling it on in public. I saved my criticism for the private sessions away from prying eyes. I tried to employ heat shields to deflect criticism from a player who had misplaced a pass that gave away a goal, or another who had missed a sitter that could have won us a game. It was always easy to give the press something else to write about – a couple of decisions that had gone against us, a penalty that should have won us the game, a long injury list or a pile-up of fixtures. I tried to take the pressure off the player who did not need me or anyone else to remind him of his mistake. Most players are mortified when they let down their team. My first inclination was always to defend the player and sort it out afterwards.

Every player is different, and I came to learn that they all required different care and feeding. Some would be at one extreme and need little from me. This was particularly true of players who had made a couple of hundred appearances, had inner confidence, and understood me. The youngsters and those who, for whatever reason, were less assured, needed different handling. I'm sure that, from time to time, I underestimated the degree of intimidation experienced by new players. All the youngsters who had been part of the United system for years were intimidated enough by the first-team dressing room. But imagine what it was like for a player signed from overseas who had never played in England and sometimes could not understand what was being said. I know that Tim Howard, whom we signed from the American team MetroStars, in 2003, and quickly started to employ as our first-team goalkeeper, found a massive contrast between his former team, which had been at the bottom of the MLS, and United. He had to quickly adjust to the notion that men whom he had worshipped from afar were now his team-mates, and to our more direct and confrontational style of management. I'm not sure there is anything that can prepare someone for a dose of Glaswegian bluntness, doled out by a shipyard worker's son, particularly when that man is in ultimate control of your destiny.

You might think that team-mates would resent another player who was treated differently. That would probably be true if he was an everyday character. But, once in a while, someone would appear who required something special. Eric Cantona fits into that category. He had been a bit of a wayward character at his other clubs and had gained a reputation for being unruly and difficult. His disciplinary record was longer than your arm. It was almost as if he was considered some sort of demon. That made no sense to me. When you are dealing with individuals with unusual talent, it makes sense to treat them differently. I just made it a point to ignore what had happened in the past and treat Eric as a new man when he joined United. When Eric was with us I would always make a point of talking to him every day – on the training ground, or in the cafeteria or dressing room. He was a sensitive person who was easily bothered by all sorts of things, but he loved talking about football and that was a way to help restore his spirits. I did things for Eric and for the really special players that I did not do for others, but I don't think this was resented, because the players understood the exceptional talents had qualities they did not possess. My relationship with Eric might also have been helped by the fact that neither of us were English and, to some degree, we considered ourselves outsiders. But even the players I thought I understood well could react in unexpected ways. I did not realise until fairly recently that, when he was far younger, Gary Neville was unable to sleep after I handed him a tongue-lashing. It just emphasises how any leader needs to put himself in the shoes of the listener. For example, I was always very careful when I rested a player to emphasise how I was counting on him for a subsequent, crucial fixture. This helped – but probably didn't completely satisfy – their desire to play in every game, and hopefully prevented them interpreting my decision as a lack of confidence in them.

With most players I did not have to urge them to increase their work rate or expend more energy, but there were a few, like Gary Pallister, who played 437 games for United between 1989 and 1998 who needed the extra poke. The irony of this is that Pallister was probably the best defender I ever managed, but he had a laidback attitude towards life. He did not like training, and in games it always seemed to take him 15 minutes to coax his engine into life. There was a first half in a game against Liverpool in 1990 when he just tortured me. At half-time I said to him, 'You are coming off.' Then I thought better of myself, changed my mind and told him, 'No, I'm not taking you off. You can suffer along with me.'

Paul Ince was another. He was a good player but he had a

tendency to run with the ball rather than pass it. Every now and again I'd have to upbraid him and I did so after a game against Norwich in 1992, which we had to win in order to have a shot at the League title, and he went berserk. He started yelling that I always blamed him, and the other players had to hold him back. I told him, 'I'm not blaming you. You made mistakes. You ran with the ball when you should have passed it.'

When I was younger I was more inclined to be severe. I cringe when I think back to a live TV interview moments after Aberdeen had won the 1983 Scottish Cup final against Rangers – three days after winning the European Cup Winners' Cup final against Real Madrid – when I blasted the team for a 'disgrace of a performance'. Later, after I had tucked more experience under my belt, I took a different approach. There is no benefit in engaging in public hangings. It just doesn't buy you anything. It humiliates the victim and does not do much to encourage those around him. So I tried to stick to a few rules. While not always succeeding in the heat of the moment, I would try to reserve my severest comments for a private session with a player. I would always try to meld criticism with support by saying, 'You know you are capable of better. What were you thinking?' It was also important to make everyone understand that any disciplinary action was not arbitrary: it applied to everyone and it was unchangeable. When Ryan Giggs started arguing with me at half-time during a game against Juventus in the 1996–97 season, I stapled him to the bench for the second half. When Paul Scholes, one of the best players ever to wear United red, committed a few daft tackles that resulted in needless red cards, I would always discipline him. His actions had let the side down; however valuable a player he was, he wasn't above the law.

One other aspect of managing high-achievers that is worth emphasising is the need to restrain them from trying to do the impossible. Every now and again someone would pull off an acrobatic goal or some other exquisite form of mastery, but you can never count on these. There is always a temptation when the chips are down to try and resort to stunts that might have worked in the pages of the old comic magazine *Boy's Own Paper*, but were almost always guaranteed to fail in front of 75,000 desperate fans. Whenever we were in a tight game and trailing by a goal, I would always emphasise to the team that we should not panic, and I would implore them not to try and shoot from outside the box. Instead I would want them to keep their heads, retain possession and get crosses into the penalty box. Gary Neville, who was our indomitable right-back for so many years, had this habit of trying to shoot from 35 yards. It drove me bananas. After the game I would always be asking him, 'How many times have I told you it doesn't work?' Disciplined perseverance pays far more dividends than impetuous attempts at individual heroism.

Part of the way to extract the most out of people is to show genuine loyalty when the rest of the world is baying for blood. Football provides plenty of opportunities to do this. After Eric Cantona's famous kung-fu attack on what appeared to me to be – when I reviewed tapes of the incident after the match – an aggressive, foul-mouthed fan at Crystal Palace in 1995, the club, which gave him a four-month suspension (which was doubled, in a punitive manner, by the FA), did everything we could to support him. Eric had been sent into exile and forbidden from training or travelling on our pre-season tour, so it was natural for him to feel isolated and forgotten. I worked very hard to make sure he understood that we cared about him, and eventually, when he was teetering on the edge of departing to play in Italy, our loyalty towards him caused him to stay in Manchester.

Some years later, in the 1998 World Cup in France, after David Beckham got sent off for lashing out at Argentina's Diego Simeone, now the Atlético Madrid manager, we wanted to be sure we were by his side. The entire press corps was convinced that David's dismissal from the game had cost England the fixture, and the headlines reflected this. They were merciless: '10 Heroic Lions, 1 Stupid Boy' was the headline in the *Daily Mirror*, while the *Daily Star* blared: 'Beck Off'. There were effigies of David hanging from lamp-posts, and it wouldn't have surprised me if an immigration officer had refused him permission to re-enter Britain. After I saw what happened, I immediately phoned David, because I knew he would be devastated. He was. I learned afterwards that he had burst into tears when he saw his parents after the game and was almost inconsolable.

The last thing David needed was criticism from me, because he had already found himself guilty. So I phoned him, tried to bolster his confidence, told him that I understood what had occurred, that these things happen to us all, and that Manchester United, and everyone associated with the club, knew he was a wonderful player and were looking forward to his return, and that we would take care of him. United's first away game of the following season was against West Ham, where an effigy of Beckham was displayed hanging from a noose en route to the stadium, and the United team bus was pelted with stones and pint glasses.

Something similar happened when we went to sign Ruud van Nistelrooy from PSV Eindhoven in 2000. We had agreed on terms and I was stunned when Ruud failed his medical test. PSV claimed that Ruud was fit, and to demonstrate this arranged for a filmed training session. He broke down on camera and you can see the film of the session on YouTube, with Ruud howling in pain on the ground. It turned out that he had torn a cruciate ligament. So we suspended the deal but I immediately flew to the Netherlands to see Ruud, who was bed-ridden. I told him that it was not like the old days; that cruciate ligaments could be repaired; that he would regain his fitness and we would then sign him. I think that helped reassure Ruud, and it was also a way of ensuring that he did not go to another club. Just over a year later he was in United red, scoring on his debut.

Occasionally players can face much bigger challenges. Fortunately it is extremely rare for a top-notch player to come down with a life-threatening illness, but when Darren Fletcher fell sick with ulcerative colitis, it presented an opportunity for United to demonstrate unflinching support, because he was out of the side for a very long time. Darren had tried to muscle his way through this debilitating condition for a couple of years, but eventually it made him housebound and he underwent surgery. Coincidentally my sister-in-law had died of complications from the disease, so I was all too aware of the torture Darren had been silently enduring. It would have been easy for the club to consign him to the wilderness, but we made sure that he understood we wanted him to get well and return to the side and gave him a new contract. He had come to United as a teenager and never let us down, so while he was undergoing treatments we made him a reserve team coach so that he would not feel abandoned. I poked my head into one of his half-time team talks and he was spectacular. He was berating the players and I listened to him tell them, 'If you think that performance is going to get you in the Manchester United first team, you have to be joking. You have no chance.' In due course Darren recovered, felt great personal relief when he publicly revealed his private battle and is now the proud captain of West Bromwich Albion.

Though this sounds odd, I would sometimes protect players by leaving them out of the first team. It happened at both ends of the spectrum. For youngsters (as I have mentioned), I thought it best to gradually introduce them to the rigours of life in the first team. And for players in their thirties, I often rested them to make sure they did not overtax their bodies. When Eric Cantona and Gary Neville came to me to say they wanted to retire, I tried to talk both of them out of doing so. I urged Eric to talk to his father, but that didn't work. Gary, being a proud professional, was also adamant. I had urged him to wait until the end of the 2010–11 season to make his decision but he just said, 'No, Boss, I'm finished. I am just kidding myself on.' On more than one occasion I left Wayne Rooney out of battles on Merseyside with Everton, not because of fitness concerns, but because the Everton fans could be merciless on him. Even though Wayne, particularly as he has got older, can shield himself from most abuse, it just did not seem sensible to expose him, or more particularly the entire team, to the abuse that would have been levelled at him. The abuse is so extreme that even Wayne's father, a diehard Everton fan, skips United's games at Goodison Park.

Football provides plenty of opportunities for a manager to show his support. There may be the times, like with Beckham or Van Nistelrooy, where the players were dealing with ugly situations. But, more often than not, it is the little things – helping youngsters improve their technique, making suggestions like one I made to Cristiano Ronaldo that he shorten his running stride when he was preparing to cross the ball, standing by players when they get injured, blooding a teenager when he makes his way into the first team – that instil a sense of loyalty. I was not doing these things because I was trying to emulate Mother Teresa, I was doing them because they would help

United, but they had the side-effect of demonstrating to the player that we had confidence in him. This instils tremendous loyalty; it also helped them to lift their game. Their way of returning these favours was to give that extra 5 per cent during a match. And so, inadvertently, I gradually came to understand this back-door route to inspiring people.

The criticism of others also provides a way to rally the troops. It is one thing for an individual to be singled out for a press savaging, particularly when some of it may be deserved. It is quite another when a whole organisation is pilloried. I almost used to enjoy it when that happened, because it played right into our hands. It would get under the collective skin, it would bring people closer together, and it offered me a convenient rallying cry. In 1996, after we were clobbered in successive League games by Newcastle and Southampton, we lost our third League game in a row against Chelsea and BBC radio broadcast a programme about our supposed demise. It was a perfect tonic for us, and I am sure helped us go on to win the Premier League. In hindsight, I can see why it was such a big story as in my last 20 years at United it only happened on two other occasions.

Complacency

Complacency is a disease, especially for individuals and organisations that have enjoyed success. I like to think that United's ability to avoid lapsing towards complacency was one of the characteristics that distinguished the club. We were not always successful at doing so, but I was always eager to stamp out the slightest trace of complacency. It's like dry rot or woodworm because, once damp gets into the brickwork or insects into the wood, you don't notice the damage until it is too late. Whenever we played a game I never thought victory was in the bag. People might think of me as a 'winning manager', but just look at the statistics. At United I managed a total of 1,500 games, of which we lost 267, drew 338 and won 895. So overall you could conclude that every time I walked out on to a pitch I only had just under a 60 per cent chance of winning. In the hotel in Moscow in 2008, after we had just won the Champions League and Premier League, I talked to the players about the 2008–09 season and emphasised the need to be prepared for a tough, fresh series of campaigns where nothing was guaranteed.

I received my first high-profile lesson in the curse of complacency in 1968 during my first season as a player for Rangers. We had not lost a game up until the very last match against Aberdeen. We went down 3–2 and lost the League. After the game, thousands of supporters went berserk and were breaking windows and stampeding. It was mayhem. We required a police escort to leave the stadium unscathed. It would not have taken us much to win the League. It was our job to do our job – and we didn't.

Another example of complacency, or over-confidence, sticks in my mind. It comes from tennis. I attended the final of the US Women's Open Championship in 2012, when Victoria Azarenka almost beat Serena Williams. Azarenka was up 5–3 in the final set and gave a little fist-pump to her family and friends in the box. From that point on it was all downhill. She lost the game she was serving to win the championship, and Williams went on to take the trophy. I saw Azarenka's face after she lost. She was devastated. It just shows you should never touch a cup until you have won it.

The same thing happened to the US team in the Ryder Cup tournament at Medinah in 2012, when they were leading the

Europeans by 10 points to 6 and only had to win 4½ points from the remaining 12 in order to win the trophy. I'm sure a degree of complacency had set in – it is just human nature. The moment that happens, things start to go wrong, and it almost always leads down the road to perdition. At Medinah you could see uncertainty start to creep into Team USA after they gave up one point. Then, after the next one went out of the window, confusion started to set in. It wasn't long before they were panicking, and by then the jig was up. Players forget what they are supposed to do, are incapable of calming themselves down and commit mistakes they don't usually make. Eventually they capitulate.

I've seen this happen a million times. It begins with uncertainty which leads to confusion. Then panic starts to set in and, before you know it, the team has capitulated and defeat becomes inevitable. Meantime, the behaviour of their opponents starts to change: their confidence begins to build, their concentration sharpens and they block out all distractions. They can smell the scent of blood and, before you know it, complacency has scored another ugly victory.

We weren't immune to it ourselves at United, and there are a few specific games that I am embarrassed to recall. In November 1998 we played Blackburn Rovers and were coasting towards what looked like a straightforward 3–0 win, made easier by the fact that they were only playing with ten men. Then Blackburn scored two goals in the last 25 minutes and we disintegrated. It was absolute mayhem. We were clearing balls off the line and booting them into the stand and I was saying to myself, 'If we lose, I'm going to kill every single one of them.' We scratched out a narrow victory on that occasion, but it was complacency, perhaps compounded by some substitutions I made, that nearly caused us profound embarrassment.

Without doubt our worst dose of complacency occurred in 2012 when we played Everton at Old Trafford. It was April, we had played 34 games in the Premier League season and were first in the table, five points in front of Manchester City. Goodness knows what happened in that game. Maybe everybody thought it would be a humdrum affair and a routine win. Maybe we all thought we were about to add yet another trophy to our collection, particularly since it had been the best performance of the season. We were 4–2 up with seven minutes to play; one or two of the players got a little lazy running back to their defensive positions and stopped doing their jobs.

I think about that game a lot, and even now I cannot account for what happened. We were 1–0 down after 33 minutes. We got the equaliser just before half-time and the next three goals were unbelievable. We sliced Everton to bits and were leading 4–2. The irony was that we were haunted by Darron Gibson, a strong midfielder we had only just sold to Everton. I kept telling the team to not let Gibson get in a position with the ball in the middle of the pitch. But, for some reason, we didn't, and wound up with Darron Gibson actually running the show. And in the 85th minute Everton dragged the score back to 4–4. One week later we played Manchester City at the Etihad Stadium and lost 1–0 – a result that was partly caused by a couple of mistakes I made with team selection, and by Roberto Mancini's emphasis on defence. Manchester City wound up winning the League.

In my last season as a manager, in March 2013, we were 2–0 up against Chelsea in the FA Cup at Old Trafford and it looked as if we were coasting to victory. That was the trouble – we were coasting. Chelsea made a couple of substitutions that changed the momentum and got a goal back before equalising soon after. By the end of the game we were under extreme pressure and just managed to hang on for a draw. The match went to a replay at Stamford Bridge which we lost; our complacency had turned a comfortable victory into defeat.

I was always careful not to exude any sign of over-confidence. That was not a pantomime show or a false front, it is how I feel about pursuing anything that others also want. You just cannot take anything for granted. If United happened to be at the top of the table and there were five games left to play, I would never say, 'If we get three points here nobody stands a chance of catching up.' Instead I would say, 'Let's get this game out of the way. Just get the job done.' You win by taking one step at a time.

One final exhibition of complacency lodges in my memory and it was the last home game of the 2006–07 season against West Ham. We had already wrapped up the title the previous week, but I had lectured the team before the game that they owed it to everyone to make sure we won. West Ham, for their part, needed to beat us in order to stay in the Premier League. I had left Ronaldo, Giggs and Scholes on the bench because we had the FA Cup final the following week but, right before half-time, Carlos Tévez scored for West Ham. I put our three best players on after half-time but we still lost. The complacency of the United team on that occasion made me furious. I let the players have it full throttle at the end of the game. It was an appalling way to end the season, it was an awful display to our fans of what Manchester United stood for, and it left a terrible taste in my mouth. The players might have thought it was a meaningless game – but I didn't.

Complacency can often start seeping into an organisation that has had a string of triumphs. More money starts flowing around; travel policies are loosened so that people start booking expensive airline seats or five-star hotels. Then plaques and mementos of victories, or important milestones, begin popping up on desks and office shelves. Some organisations, and United certainly is one of those, even have a museum where their old products – or, in our case, trophies – are on display. At United, as the years passed by, the essentials of life certainly got easier. We started chartering planes to ferry the team around, the comfort of our buses increased immeasurably, and it was all too easy for us to take these luxuries for granted.

Nonetheless it is important for all the people associated with an organisation to feel part of a big success. A few days after we secured any of our trophies, I'd gather all the staff at Carrington together and we would toast our success with a glass of champagne before getting to work. I always felt that the trick was to celebrate our triumphs without for a moment losing the edge and depth of desire that had taken us there. I just wanted to be on my guard that victories weren't seen as automatic guarantees of future success, and that celebrations did not sow the seeds of complacency.

People who have given everything to achieve the impossible deserve recognition and praise. However, I have never been a big fan of celebrations. While I was at United and participated in many, the commercial side of the club organised all those sort of events. Whenever one of my players won the Ballon d'Or, or the Professional Footballers' Association Player of the Year award, I would be sure to attend the banquets. But I cannot pretend I enjoyed all the drinking that accompanied them.

I loved celebrating goals, particularly ones like the bicycle kick Wayne Rooney pulled off against Manchester City in 2011. For me the final whistle of a game was always salvation. The final whistle is the greatest moment. It is definitive, and marks the time when you finally achieve something. I only felt in a celebratory mood for a couple of hours after a big victory. It didn't matter if it was a League Championship or Champions League. Celebrations after victories are exhausting. As a manager, after a game, you need to give the press interviews, return to a hotel, freshen up and attend a reception. By the time the day was done it was one o'clock in the morning and I would be dying to get to bed. I'd usually lie in bed for a bit and feel a sense of satisfaction, but by the time I woke up that was gone.

I recognised that a victory or major event had a different meaning if you are a player, or supporter, or director – you can celebrate as long as you want. It was always very rewarding to see the amount of happiness a team can provide – especially to a community that either does not have much of a share of the limelight or has been down on its luck. The victory in the European Cup Winners' Cup in 1983 was a great tonic for Aberdeen – a city which, despite the business brought by North Sea oil, is easily forgotten. Aberdeen is closer to Oslo than London, and in winter there can be fewer than six and a half hours of daylight. Even in May, when we had our homecoming parade, there was a freezing wind howling off the North Sea. The city council declared an official holiday, and all the schools closed except one – the Albyn School which, at the time, was an all-girls' school. However, when we passed the school, all the girls were outside or looking through the windows, cheering the bus.

Even though Manchester is much bigger and better known, the United victories meant a lot to the locals. The whole area had known its share of misery – and I'm not talking about Liverpool's run in the 1970s and 1980s. I'm referring to the local economy, the decimation of almost every manufacturing business, and the enormous hardships this caused for numerous families. For many of these people, United's victories were the best thing that happened in their lives. I'm sure that, for some, our open-topped bus processions through Manchester were better than Christmas.

In 1999, after our Treble, it was extraordinary. In Deansgate, the main road through the centre of Manchester, there was a building that was under construction which had 'DO NOT ENTER' signs plastered all over it. That didn't stop anyone. There were people standing on the open concrete floors and steel beams. Everyone was singing the favourite United songs and throwing scarves and hats at the bus. The same thing happened in 2013, after we won our 20th League title, and the team was taken out on to the balcony of the town hall. For several seasons, when we had won the League, I'd have the staff over to the house for a spread and some drinks.

While I took great pleasure and satisfaction in seeing what we had done for others, I cannot say that I felt as happy. I always felt I had to be in the vanguard of tomorrow. I'd immediately start to think about ways in which we could improve, and players who were coming to the end of their best days. For me, the questions going through the back of my mind during any celebration were, 'How do we top this? How do we get another triumph?' I never wanted us to be torpedoed by complacency.

6

MEASURING PEOPLE

Job Hunting

Unlike a lot of my fellow managers and, more importantly, unlike a lot of the people I grew up with in Scotland, I've never had to contend with the soul-deadening experience of months or years out of work. I can only imagine the devastating effects of being tossed on the ash-heap. Fortunately, I always had a job when I was looking for a fresh challenge, but that did not prepare me for interviews – particularly at the start of my career.

I have done thousands of interviews, but those have been with the press. I've only really done a few job interviews in my life – at Queen's Park in Scotland in 1974, Wolverhampton Wanderers in 1982 and Barcelona in 1983. My interview for the position as manager of Queen's Park was a disaster. I was completely unprepared. I wasn't sure who I was going to meet and I certainly hadn't thought about the questions I would be asked, let alone have a list of topics that I wanted to discuss. So when I arrived, thinking I was just going to see the chairman of the club, I was surprised to find a large interview committee, including men I had played with. There must have been 12 of them in the room. I was nervous. I didn't know how to handle myself. I was shockingly bad. I spent the whole interview trying to justify myself and my record, rather than just being myself. When I came out of the room I knew I had failed and I felt really disappointed. They gave the job to Dave McParland, who later became an assistant to Jock Stein at Celtic.

Over time I discovered that interviews, or meetings, with the principals of other clubs were very revealing. They gave me glimpses of the tone and tenor of each organisation. My encounter at Wolves was astonishing. I had been led to believe that they had already decided to offer me the job, and then I found myself in a hotel, with the whole board, being asked what I would do if I found a player had taken £5,000 from the club's bank account. I thought to myself, 'They don't need a manager, they need an accountant.' I could not get back to Aberdeen quickly enough.

At about the same time, I met Irving Scholar, then the chairman of Tottenham, who offered me the manager's job at White Hart Lane. At the time the club had an incumbent manager, Keith Burkinshaw, and there was no way I was ever going to take anybody's job away from him.

Later in my career, I met with a representative of Massimo Moratti, the long-time owner of Inter Milan. That went out the window the moment he showed me a list of players they were going to buy and sell, which is just as well because I would never have persuaded Cathy to move to Italy.

It's strange to think, looking back, that the job that came to define me – the manager's post at United – was offered to me without a formal interview. Few businesses would think of offering a job to someone they haven't interviewed, or didn't already know pretty well. But that is not always the way it works in football. When I received a telephone call from United, the club was hovering in the first division relegation zone and flirting with disaster. Previously I only had fleeting contact with the Manchester United board when, in 1984, I had helped them buy Gordon Strachan, the midfielder, from Aberdeen, at a time when the player had already agreed to a transfer to a German club. Apart from that, and the briefest of sideline conversations with Bobby Charlton during the 1986 World Cup in Mexico, I had never spoken to any of them about the job. When I finally met them at my sister-in-law's house in Bishopbriggs, just outside Glasgow, it was to discuss the financial realities of the position. They had already decided they wanted me in Manchester, and I was so eager for the job that I moved to Old Trafford for less than I was being paid in Aberdeen.

Over the years I have picked up far more experience of being on the other side of the table – of being the interviewer rather than the interviewee. When I interview someone, I want to know how ambitious they are or whether they are just thinking about a job as a stepping-stone to something else. Apart from their qualities and qualifications, I want to measure the level of their commitment. I always look for enthusiasm, for a positive attitude, for eye contact and for personal courage. As United became more successful, I could see that some job candidates were quite nervous when they came to see me. So I tried to put them at their ease by offering them a cup of tea. I just wanted them to relax enough so that I could get the measure of who they really were.

You can pick up the signs of someone's character in many different ways during an interview – and it's often the little things that make a difference. For example, someone who sits up properly and is leaning forward a little is showing that they are eager to start. That is way better than appearing cocky or over-confident or not seriously interested in the position. Some people are often afraid to ask questions during interviews. That's daft. Interviews should not be a one-way street. You need to know what your employer can offer you. I often get a measure of someone by listening to the questions they pose. It shows how they think; offers a sense of their level of experience and degree of maturity.

In my 26 years at United, the most important interviews I ever did were for the role of my assistant. At United I had seven assistant managers – Archie Knox, Brian Kidd, Steve McClaren, Jim Ryan, Carlos Queiroz, Walter Smith and Mick Phelan. After Brian Kidd left in 1998 I got more serious about interviewing, and the process became more meticulous. We looked at several people but narrowed it down to David Moyes and Steve McClaren.

David was about 35 at the time and was managing Preston North End. He was very tense when I interviewed him and that showed in the seriousness of his face. Steve McClaren was the opposite of David. He was bright, breezy and enthusiastic. He had worked at Oxford United and Derby County, where the players liked him, and he was a voracious consumer of books and videos about football and training techniques. At that point Steve had a lot more experience in the top flight of football than David, and that swung my decision.

The most impressive interview I ever did was with Carlos Queiroz. I'd been looking for a foreign coach who could speak several languages, to help us with the foreign-born players. Andy Roxburgh, the former manager of Scotland, referred me to Carlos, who was coaching South Africa at the time. Quinton Fortune, who is South African and played for United, was also complimentary about Carlos. When Carlos came to the interview he just did everything right. I'd never met him before. He was dressed as if he was going to get married and I could see by the way he sat that he wanted the job. He looked at me intensely – I always watch to see whether people can maintain eye contact because it is a good measure of their confidence. Carlos had good ideas and asked good questions. He was experienced and he was eager and I didn't hesitate in hiring him.

René Meulensteen had a different way of demonstrating his appetite to join United. He had been coaching in Qatar and had been referred to us by Dave Mackay, the great Tottenham Hotspur and Derby County player. In 2001, when he came to seek a job at United, René told us the best way he could advertise his skills was to demonstrate them in action. So we went out on to the training field and he ran a technical session with some younger players and that clinched it for him.

Figuring out whether a coach could do his job was different from taking the measure of a player. The proof of that came when we watched him play. Interviewing a 16-year-old centre-back is not going to tell you very much about his footballing ability, although it will give you some insight into his determination. The only real way to tell whether a player has the toughness and perseverance to flourish for a long time is by the performances he turns in. When you meet new people and try to assess the most vital component – their character – you are only making an educated guess. Sometimes you are right and sometimes you are wrong. The only real test of character comes with the passing of the years and watching them perform – particularly when they are going through a bad spell or recovering from a setback. The ultimate judge of performance is Father Time.

Networking

My 11 grandchildren are the greatest networkers I've ever seen. They're always using Facebook, Instagram, Snapchat or Twitter. I've never been a great networker, in either the new-fangled or old-school manner, but I really believe in what – these days – are called networks.

Decisions are simpler when you are dealing with people you know well. It is far easier to gauge their opinions and weigh their judgements than the observations of strangers. Many of my best appointments – both as coaches and players – stemmed from the referrals and assessments of this informal network, which developed over the years. It wasn't something I consciously sought to assemble. I didn't consciously try to cultivate or ingratiate myself with people because I thought they would do me a favour or be useful to me during my career. A network takes time to develop. Part comes through the passage of time, part from the way you treat others and part from reciprocity. But it all begins at home.

If the people within your organisation feel they are part of a community that has their interests at heart, they will develop great loyalty. And it often starts with what seem like small issues. When we were planning our Carrington training ground in the late 1990s, the architects and the chairman wanted to have two separate dining rooms – one for the players and one for the staff. It was a hangover from our old training ground, The Cliff, where the only people allowed in the dining room were the players and the medical staff. But I disagreed. I wanted everybody together. I wanted the younger players to be able to mingle and eat lunch with the older players and the staff too, including people like the laundry team and groundsmen.

It's great for a young lad to be able to talk to Ryan Giggs, and it was good for all the young players to see and mingle with the first team. It gave them role models and something to aspire to.

Sometimes if I saw a young player, a lad in the academy, eating by himself, I would go and sit beside him. You have to make everyone feel at home. That doesn't mean you're going to be soft on them – but you want them to feel that they belong. I'd been influenced by what I had learned from Marks & Spencer, which, decades ago in harder times, had given their staff free lunches because so many of them were skipping lunch so they could save every penny to help their families. It probably seems a strange thing for a manager to be getting involved in – the layout of a canteen at a new training ground – but when I think about the tone it set within the club and the way it encouraged the staff and players to interact, I can't overstate the importance of this tiny change.

There were, of course, much more high-profile examples of networks in action. The most glittering example must have been the way we uncovered Cristiano Ronaldo. Carlos Queiroz, who had been born in Mozambique, then a Portuguese colony, was my assistant manager for a total of five years. He had encouraged me to strike up a relationship with Sporting Lisbon, because of their ability to develop young players. We liked Carlos, and it seemed like a smart idea, so we started to exchange coaches so they could experience different settings. In 2001 we sent Jim Ryan, who spent 21 years on the coaching staff at United, to Lisbon, and he spotted a 16-year-old striker playing for Sporting's youth team by the name of Cristiano Ronaldo.

Part of the deal with Sporting Lisbon was that we would help open their new stadium with an exhibition match in August 2003, and so we flew directly to Portugal at the end of a summer tour of the United States. The day before the stadium opened, Jorge Mendes, Ronaldo's agent, had told me that both Real Madrid and Arsenal were also in pursuit of his client. It was a brilliantly timed little aside, because the next day Ronaldo played against us and was unbelievable. At half-time I sent Albert Morgan, our kit man, to fetch Peter Kenyon, who was then the club CEO, and told him we were going nowhere until we had that boy signed. We huddled with Cristiano, Jorge Mendes, and the president of Sporting Lisbon, and agreed on a price: £12.24 million. We arranged for a charter plane the following day to fly Ronaldo and his mother and sister, Jorge and Ronaldo's lawyer, to Manchester. So, thanks to the network created by Carlos Queiroz, we got six years of Ronaldo before he fulfilled his lifelong dream to play for Real Madrid, who paid United £80 million for the best player in the world.

Some of our most experienced players formed parts of our intelligence network. I could always count on Ryan Giggs, Paul Scholes, Gary Neville and Rio Ferdinand for sound opinions on players from other top-tier clubs we were scouting or contemplating signing. They all knew what was required of people we would bring to United. They would tend to have very sharp opinions about other English players, and I'd always ask them whether they knew anything I should worry about. I always used to ask the players in the England squad whether they considered any players from other clubs were good enough for United. In 2006 that led us to sign Michael Carrick from Tottenham.

The players would also work hard to try and help me sign prospects with whom they had some tie. Ryan Giggs was relentless in his quest to try and land his fellow Welshman, Aaron Ramsey, from Cardiff City. We flew Aaron up to Manchester but it was too late. I had got word from Dave Jones, the Cardiff manager, that Aaron had originally wanted to play for us, but Arsène Wenger had somehow managed to turn his head and convince him that his future lay at the Emirates. A couple of years later I got my revenge when Roy Hodgson, then the manager of Fulham, was instrumental in helping us snatch his defender, Chris Smalling, away from Arsenal.

Great networks often extended well beyond the current crop of first-team players. It's easy to forget about someone who has left an organisation and assume that because they've retired, or because their most fruitful years are behind them, they are no longer of any use. Quite the contrary. If the organisation has done right by them they will usually have fond memories of it, harbour considerable affection for it and be very happy to help. We tried to do this at United – inspired, in part, by what I saw at Bayern Munich.

In the mid-1990s I approached Martin Edwards and suggested that United take a leaf from Bayern's book and cultivate the talents of some of our best former players. They were familiar with the club, knew what we stood for, appreciated our pursuit of excellence and had the standing and reputation to act as role models. Bayern did this very well, and their greatest players were effectively running the club.

I could never persuade Martin of the benefit of doing this and I think he might have been a bit suspicious that I was trying to rearrange the board of directors. So he just paid lip service to the idea and all we ever did was use former players such as Norman Whiteside, Paddy Crerand and Wilf McGuinness to help entertain supporters during the lunches and dinners that bracketed home games.

When David Gill became the CEO, he embraced the thought because I wanted former players to help with the increased burden of the commercial side. These days we have a number of former players who do a lot of very useful work for the club. Obviously, Sir Bobby Charlton stands in a class by himself, having been a club director since 1984 and who, for 35 years before Ryan Giggs eclipsed his record, had played the most games for the club. But there are others, too, who act as club ambassadors and go on tours or spend time making sure that our commercial sponsors are happy and we retain them. Some of United's all-time greats, like Peter Schmeichel, Andy Cole, Dwight Yorke, Bryan Robson, Denis Law, and, more recently, Ji-sung Park, all do this; it removed a lot of the burden from my shoulders and those of other members of management.

Maybe the most important benefit of our network is the way we threaded former players into the coaching organisation. It's a marvellous way to ensure continuity and excellence, because they know what enormous success tastes like and what is required to achieve it. Over the years we had plenty of other former players sprinkled through the coaching organisation, such as Brian McClair, Tony Whelan, Jim Ryan, Mick Phelan and Paul McGuinness. Ryan Giggs is today's standout, in his role as Louis van Gaal's assistant manager, but Nicky Butt is also assisting in coaching the reserve team and Paul Scholes returned to the club, albeit briefly, to assist Giggs when he was made caretaker manager. We also tried to stand by former players. For example, after Bryan Robson was sacked as the manager of Middlesbrough, I invited him to keep his hand in the game by helping with training sessions at United.

If, as the years go by, some of United's great players have earned their managerial stripes and come back to help run the club, I will have succeeded in bringing a touch of Bayern Munich to Manchester.

I also tried to ensure that our club network extended to the supporters. Just as I was eager to know what was going on in the dressing room, I also liked to know the sentiment of long-time supporters. There were three guys I counted on for this: Norman Williams, Jim Kenway and Bill McGurr. I invited them to watch our training every Monday and Friday because I knew they would be discreet, keep their own counsel and refrain from blabbing to the press. I always used to chat with them while the players were warming up because they struck me as representing the heart and soul of the club and I knew they wouldn't mince words. Every big club has factions among its supporters who are upset about one thing or another, and I just liked keeping my finger on the pulse. In 2011, after we overtook Liverpool's Championship record, Norman Williams turned up to congratulate and thank every player. He was in his eighties and Manchester United was his life – I felt, in hindsight, that this title win completed his life. He certainly said as much to the players when he told them all the same thing: 'You've made my life.' He died the same night.

Oddly enough there was another vital part of our network, and that was my fellow managers. Whenever I called another manager for an assessment about a player I was contemplating signing, I always got a candid assessment. In 1989 I went down to spend a day with John Lyall to get his opinion about Paul Ince, whom he had managed at West Ham. John was glowing in his praise, and Paul made 281 appearances for United and played 53 games for England. In 2010 I briefly flirted with the idea of signing Mario Balotelli, the talented but controversial Italian striker. I did my homework on him, speaking to a few Italian contacts, but the feedback I got confirmed it was too big a risk. I don't know whether this sort of candid, professional courtesy exists in other fields, but for me it was a godsend. And in return I was always careful not to beat about the bush with other managers when they wanted my opinion on a particular player.

Fellow managers steered me away from players but, on occasion, they also stiffened my backbone when I was trying to make a decision. In 1991, I was looking around for additional defensive help, as Steve Bruce – who was then 30 years old – was becoming more prone to injury. We had heard that Everton had made a bid for Paul Parker, who was playing for Queens Park Rangers, and so I phoned their former manager, Jim Smith, to get an opinion. He was unequivocal and said, 'Sign him. He's quick, he can defend, he recovers well. He's like a Rottweiler.' Parker had actually travelled to Everton, but we managed to lure him to Old Trafford the same summer afternoon. I took him out on to the pitch to look around and he was amazed that there were dozens of United supporters in the stands just watching the grass grow. He signed for us that afternoon and went on to make 146 appearances for United – which could have been a lot more had it not been for niggling injuries.

I tried to return these kinds of favours whenever a fellow manager called with a similar question, or to ask my opinion about whether they should take a job at a particular club. In football there's an odd camaraderie between managers. On Saturday afternoons or Wednesday evenings we may be going at each other hammer and tongs and, during negotiations, we're inevitably trying to get the better of one another. Yet, maybe because we have this odd bond, there is always an inclination to extend a helping hand if someone is going through a rough time. I learned about this in Scotland, and when, eventually, I was in the position to continue the tradition, I tried to do so.

When I used to phone Jock Stein to ask for a favour or to see if he could help me get tickets for some game, he always used to say, 'If I can.' That was a great retort. It's easy to forget about the troubles of others but, if you take the time to remember, it goes a very long way. In 1978, when I was coaching St Mirren, we had lost a cup tie to Kilmarnock; the following morning I was feeling pretty despondent when the phone rang. It was Jock Wallace, the manager of Rangers, phoning to cheer me up. So, decades later, when a journalist phoned me to let me know that Chris Wilder, then the manager of Oxford United, was having a lot of problems with the club chairman, it was just second nature to try and help. I gave Chris my phone number and we talked on a number of occasions. I speak to Steve Bruce fairly often, and in the past couple of years have chatted with Alan Pardew, Sean Dyche and Neil Lennon. It is an informal network – full of wisdom and good humour and sympathy – but one I have always valued. Every manager feels lonely when he has to make an important decision. He can consult with his staff but ultimately he needs to make that decision himself. I know what it feels like for these men because as Premier League managers, they are under constant pressure and others keep their distance – either because they see them as damaged goods or because they don't want to intrude. Either way, if I can help some of them when they are in a tough spot, I am more than happy to do so.

Firing

Nobody should look at football for lessons about the way to fire people. It's terrible. I got my first taste of that at Rangers when they fired their manager Scot Symon in 1967. He'd been there 13 years, won 15 trophies and had been incredibly loyal. John Lawrence, the chairman of the club, sent an 80-year-old accountant to tell Symon he was sacked. It was unbelievable. The same thing happened to another pal of mine, John Lyall, who, as both player and manager, devoted 34 years of his life to West Ham United. His reward? When he was fired in 1989, the owner did not even have the grace to thank him for his loyalty. I also never forgot the shabby way in which the board of Celtic treated Jock Stein after his 13 years at the club – in an era where the best teams in Scotland could more than hold their own with their English counterparts – during which he won the European Cup, ten Scottish League championships, eight Scottish Cups and six Scottish League Cups.

Carlo Ancelotti was brutally fired by Roman Abramovich in 2011 after Chelsea lost to Everton, having already lost to United and drawn with Newcastle in the previous two weeks. Carlo had won the 'Double' of the Premier League and the FA Cup for Chelsea the year before and was only the fifth manager ever to do so. Carlo kept his composure, didn't blast Abramovich and behaved perfectly. I don't think I would have been able to do the same if I had been in his shoes.

Most football managers are treated without a shred of dignity. Some owners don't even pay them the courtesy of talking to them in person. They will fire them over the phone or even by text message, or they will use a surrogate, like an accountant, to deliver the message. The reasons for the dismissals are often ludicrous. One manager I know got fired because he banned the chairman's wife from the players' dressing room. Mark Hughes's dismissal from Manchester City in 2009, while he was in the midst of re-fashioning the side, was just a high-profile example of the madness that occurs at clubs every week.

I've always found it hard to get rid of people I liked. Harry McShane was aged about 85 and had been associated with United since the 1950s, first as a player and then as a scout (as well as spending time as the club's stadium announcer). Les Kershaw, our chief scout, wanted me to do the dirty work, so I invited Harry to lunch and tried to talk to him about quitting. He knew exactly what I was doing and didn't make my life easy. He kept saying, 'Aye. Get on with it. What is it you want to say?' And I just couldn't bring myself to fire him and instead copped out. I told him that we'd continue to pay him but wanted to change his roles and he could come to watch the first team and offer me advice about them.

While we sold lots of players and gave others free transfers, I actually did not fire many people. We had one doctor who I agreed could spend time on another job for a limited period. When he decided to extend that period I felt I had to act. I felt let down. He had betrayed my trust, so I got rid of him. But for the most part there were very few dramas among the staff at Old Trafford who fell under my authority. When players leave, especially those who have been pillars of the side, their departure, even if expected, is often tinged with mixed emotions. Sometimes, but not often, the partings were abrupt and took people by surprise. That was the case in 2005 when Roy Keane left after over 12 years with the club. When I broke the news to the players, I was careful to praise all his enormous contributions to United and said that these should be recognised in any comments they might make to others.

By far the hardest conversations were with youngsters who, from the time they had sat on their father's lap watching football on television, had dreamed of playing in the Premier League but were just not good enough to step on to the pitch at Old Trafford. From the moment I started managing, I dreaded these sessions. At St Mirren I decided to make my life a bit easier by delivering the same message to five boys simultaneously. One of them broke down crying and I concluded that, while I was making it easier for myself, I was making it a lot tougher on them. Whether it was at St Mirren, Aberdeen or United, the only message they heard was that I was not hiring them. Conveying that message to teenagers was far harder than selling most first-team players, who had been given an opportunity to demonstrate their value. These boys, and their families, had frequently given up everything to pursue their dreams. Goodness knows how many times the parents had accompanied their boy to practices and games. Lord knows how often they had endured rain and cold to cheer on their son at a game everyone else had forgotten. I felt as bad for the parents as I did for the boy and, quite frequently, all three would break into tears. I would try and console them by explaining that the boy had enough talent to make a life in football and that, just because he wasn't being signed by United, about the hardest club to join, that did not mean his future in the game was closed off.

There were plenty of examples of players who had thrived after being released by Manchester United, and I sometimes used the example of David Platt. He was given a free transfer by United shortly before I arrived, but went on to captain England. Platt had plenty of company. Robbie Savage never played for the first team, but he went to Crewe Alexandra and three years later was playing in the Premier League for Leicester City. There are dozens of Premiership players who have been through the United academy, such as Ryan Shawcross, Phil Bardsley, and Kieran Richardson. It says much about the quality of an organisation if you can help ensure comfortable landings for people who just don't quite have what is required to make it within your own.

If players in the prime of their careers have not been seeking a new club, the news that they are being transferred from Manchester United is akin to hearing that they have been fired.

Sometimes, the arrival of a new player, whether a youngster or a purchase, who begins to command a spot in the first XI can also spell extinction for the lad who once owned the position. Though there were a handful of players whose departures were a relief, for the most part I tried to make sure we engineered a good landing for those we transferred. We tried to do everything we could for all the players we released to help them have a career in the game. My coaches and I were on the phone trying to create opportunities for these boys. We were also regularly contacted by other clubs to see what our plans were for our young players. As a result, many of them already had options on the table by the time they were released by United. I was only too aware of what life was going to be like for these players. They would be going from playing in front of 75,000 people and enjoying some of the best training facilities available anywhere, to a far smaller stage. It's a cruel adjustment to play in front of 15,000 people, disappear from the back pages of the newspapers, have a much smaller pay-cheque and, most of all, know that your dreams of playing at the pinnacle of the game are finished. It can destroy the soul.

Firing people, irrespective of their age, is never easy. I gradually learned that there was no point beating about the bush by taking somebody out for dinner or sending his wife a box of chocolates or flowers to try and soften the news. The gimmicks don't change the message. If you have decided you are going to get rid of someone, nothing beats honesty.

7

FOCUS

Time

My father always said, 'Don't lie, don't steal and always be early.' I cannot stand being late. I've always been early for meetings. I was always the first into work. It just came naturally. I've always been an early riser so it was no great hardship for me to get to work early. I remember talking to Jean-Claude Biver, the CEO of the watchmaker, Hublot, who told me that when he had applied to work at Omega, the person who interviewed him asked him to show up at five o'clock in the morning. During the interview, Jean-Claude enquired about why he'd been asked to appear while it was still dark. The interviewer said, 'I start at five o'clock in the morning so I'm three hours ahead of everyone. I'm working while you are still asleep.' I was a bit like that.

Youngsters think they have all the time in the world. If you are a boy who has just had his tenth birthday, your next one seems an eternity away. That's because the single year that stretches ahead amounts to 10 per cent of the time you have been on earth. It's a different sensation when you turn 50, because the distance to your 51st birthday amounts to just 2 per cent of the time you have been alive. As you get older and more experienced, you start to think about how you allocate time. You gradually come to appreciate that an hour – or weekend – squandered is time you will never recapture.

As a teenager, part of my desire to squeeze the most out of every day was born of necessity because I had to hold down two jobs. I was working as an apprentice tool-maker, which meant leaving home at 6.45 a.m. and putting my card in the punch-clock at 7.40 a.m. After work or at the weekend, instead of going to the pub or snooker halls with the other apprentices, I was playing football. When I was training with St Johnstone I used to have two and a half hours to practise and usually didn't get home until 1 a.m. I did this three times a week and each trip involved multiple bus, train and tram rides.

After players retire and go into management, they often have a series of nasty shocks. One thing that always surprises them is the length of the workday. As a modern player, unless it is on the eve of a game, the day is always done soon after lunch. These days most of them go home, relax, and park themselves in front of some digital device. When you become a manager you discover three things. There is an endless set of tasks to complete and people demanding attention; the day does not stop and there is never enough time.

When I began managing, I had no idea how to budget my time. I was pathetic. I tried to do everything. This was exacerbated by the fact that – when I became manager of St Mirren in 1974 – I was also running two pubs that were three miles apart. Fergie's was in Kinning Park, near Govan, and Shaws was in Bridgeton. I only got into the pub business because playing and managing East Stirlingshire on a part-time contract did not put enough bread on the table for a young family. Although St Mirren paid me, I sometimes wonder whether I would have fared better at the club if I had not been managing the pubs simultaneously.

The combination of managing St Mirren and running my pubs meant that the only time I saw my boys was on the occasional school run, and the only time we would be together as a family would be for a few hours on a Sunday. When I started managing Aberdeen I sold the pubs, because I wanted to concentrate entirely on football. At Aberdeen my workdays were always 12 or 14 hours long, and I didn't stop work when I got home. Then I was on the phone to scouts, coaches or players. I might have put in more hours every week than my father, but I'm not complaining. His work was far tougher than anything I ever did.

In Manchester I continued with a similar daily and weekly rhythm, although the demands were much greater. I'd be at the ground about seven in the morning and would have a stroll around with my cup of tea. I'd always keep eight to nine in the morning wide open so that if anyone wanted to see me – a coach, a doctor, or a player – I was available. At about nine o'clock we'd go to the video analysis room and watch edited footage of previous games or opponents we were about to face. I'd remain at the training ground throughout the day to watch the youth academy work in the gymnasium. I'd get home around nine o'clock in the evening on Monday and Tuesday and sometimes also on Thursday. On Wednesday, if we were playing, I would either be with the team or I would be watching the reserve team, a future opponent or a player we were interested in. When United were based at their old training ground, The Cliff, I used to go to Old Trafford in the afternoon to do some paperwork or make telephone calls. The Carrington training ground included an office for me so, after we moved there, that's where I'd do my paperwork in the morning. Fridays, whether at The Cliff or Carrington, were always a bit different. Every Friday morning David Gill, United's CEO, would come to see me, and after that I would have a pre-game press conference at nine o'clock.

Nights and holidays were not sacred. If I woke up in the middle of the night, I'd usually sneak upstairs to my study and watch a game. I didn't see the point of wasting perfectly good time trying to go back to sleep. I also husbanded my time by never taking the holidays to which I was contractually entitled. From 1995, I was allowed five weeks' holiday a year, but that seemed like an excessive amount of time not to be working. So I always just took two weeks a year and would usually go with the family to mainland Spain or Majorca. It wasn't until I was in my fifties that I started taking three weeks a year. By then our boys were older and starting to live their own lives and Cathy and I made some trips to America. When the two of us started going to the south of France about 15 years ago, I often had meetings with players we wanted to sign in the restaurant of our hotel. It has a fabulous view over the Mediterranean and Cap Ferrat, and I never encountered a player whose contract couldn't be closed at that corner table.

As I got older, two things happened. First I discovered my body slowed down a bit and I found it harder to maintain the energy levels I had when I was much younger. When I was a young manager I could get by on four hours of sleep, but I needed more as I grew older. So I'd often go home and take a nap for an hour before going back to the ground. Then Cathy kept warning me that I was going to kill myself if I kept working so hard. I was painfully aware of how stress had contributed to the heart attack that led to Jock Stein's death during the Scotland–Wales game in Cardiff in 1985, when I was at his side as his assistant manager. So I took Cathy's advice seriously and developed interests outside football – horses, wine, reading. None of these hobbies took up a huge amount of time, but I enjoyed the distraction and the distance they gave me from football. I used to nip down to Newmarket the morning after Champions League games at Old Trafford to watch the horses train. Those early mornings were quiet and peaceful, and I also received an education in some of the nuances of the sport. Not only did I enjoy drinking the wine I bought, but I got interested in monitoring the price fluctuations. It was absorbing and would take my mind off the daily worries. I found that helpful ideas would sometimes pop into my mind from out of nowhere while I was playing cards or reading a book or going through a wine catalogue. I'm sure the same sensation occurs to other leaders when they are riding their bikes, pruning their roses or climbing a mountain. But I didn't find that these pastimes were a miracle cure. I still often found myself unable to sleep or awake in the middle of the night thinking about something concerning United.

Distractions

I have yet to encounter anyone who has achieved massive success without closing themselves off from the demands of others or forgoing pastimes. I'm not suggesting that being completely obsessed with a pursuit leads to a healthy lifestyle or eternal happiness, but I just cannot imagine how, if you aspire to be better than everyone else, you can have balance in your life. If you have two people of equal talent it will be the way in which they marshal their ability that will determine their eventual success. Some people are just better at shutting out the rest of the world than others, and that means they have more time to foster their talent or improve their organisation. One of the most vivid examples of an obsession, mixed with devotion, is the tale of my fellow Glaswegian, Jimmy Sirrel, who managed Notts County. He and his wife were extremely close and, after 40 years of marriage, she suddenly died – early on a Saturday morning – at the age of 60. Jimmy was devastated, phoned his two children to break the news but then, without informing the players of what had happened, managed his Notts County team against West Bromwich Albion to a 1–1 draw that same afternoon.

When you are in your teens or your early twenties, it is fairly easy to concentrate on your obsession – especially if, as a footballer, you steer clear of alcohol and the party scene. A 16-year-old player brimming with talent might have a casual girlfriend and a few mates but, apart from those, the only thing in his life will be football. It will occupy his every waking moment and also enter his dreams and nightmares. All he will dream about is playing for the first team, representing his country, scoring a winning goal or lifting the World Cup. The urge to improve himself dominates everything. Ten years later, everything can be different. He might be mentioned in the newspapers every other day. He might have a wife and young children. He may be a millionaire many times over. He will be unable to walk down a street or enter a restaurant without being asked for a picture or autograph. He may not have a moment's peace unless he is behind the gates of his large house. The same goes for managers of high-profile clubs.

I was fortunate that I had a wife and sons who did not make me feel guilty about spending so little time with them and allowed me to be selfish. I always tried to make sure nothing intruded into the heart of my work life and, unless there was a dire emergency in our family, football always came first. Cathy took care of raising our three sons and I was absent for a lot of the time. For example, I did not watch the boys play in their school games because at weekends my job was to be with Aberdeen or United. For me the Christmas break never really existed, because it falls in the middle of one of the heaviest periods in the top flight of English football. I didn't really appreciate it at the time, but now, with the help of perspective, it's clear that my family gave me the greatest gift that I have ever received: time to concentrate on my obsession with the round ball. I never had to deal with the tension that exists between so many husbands and wives, or parents and children, when the spouse or the young ones feel they are not getting enough attention and that a family member, even when physically present, is emotionally absent.

When I got to United I still hadn't mastered the art of eliminating distractions. I'd automatically accept most invitations to charity dinners or supporters' club events. For my first 12 years at Old Trafford I used to read every letter I received and, during some weeks, I'd get a couple of hundred. I just felt an obligation to take care of these because many of them were from people for whom Manchester United was the most important thing in their lives. We'd get letters from people notifying us of a death in their family and asking us to send a note to the bereaved. We'd hear from parents who had a sick child in the hospital asking for an autograph, or there would be people requesting a message to be read out at a birthday or wedding. I used to dictate answers to all these letters.

I gradually became better about controlling my time. Lyn Laffin, who became my assistant shortly after I joined United, started shielding me from many of the incessant telephone calls, and dealt with some of the fans who used to call with suggestions about players who should be sold or new tactics I should employ.

I never did get used to e-mail, so I didn't have to worry about this perpetual, intrusive distraction that can play havoc with even the most concentrated train of thought. During my last ten years at United Lyn took care of almost all the correspondence, because she knew my prose style, so all I had to do was approve it and add my signature.

There were some other rules that also helped me make the most out of every day. I would never accept a lunch invitation, except for sponsors' lunches at Old Trafford and the annual Football Writers' lunches in Manchester, because before you know it, especially if a drive is involved, those midday breaks can gobble up three hours. I also started to eliminate many of the charity functions. As manager of United you are expected to make some appearances to help the cause. Part of this was just a case of getting older, because the midweek dinners aren't as easy when you are 65 years old as when you are a 35 year old. Some were just rituals like meeting with sponsors, charity events and award ceremonies. I would always attend the annual League Managers Association dinner, United's annual dinner on behalf of UNICEF, and the events for the charity I formed, The Elizabeth Hardie Ferguson Charitable Trust. Whenever one of our players won the Professional Footballers' Association Player of the Year, or the Ballon d'Or, I'd be sure to attend those festivities.

I stopped attending supporters' club dinners about a decade before I retired. They usually made for very long nights, with never-ending queues for autographs and photographs. I don't mean to sound ungrateful or aloof – the supporters at Manchester United are the best in the world – but my job was to win trophies, not sign autographs, and I always felt that I was better off focusing on that. I also became more disciplined about which teams I'd go to watch. In my last decade at United I tried to limit it to teams we'd be pitted against in European fixtures. Mick Phelan, my assistant manager, and I would fly out in a chartered plane, have dinner, watch the game (leaving ten minutes before the end) and be back in Manchester by 1 a.m. That might seem like a long day, but it was an abbreviated version of what I did when I was younger.

Learning to concentrate on the essentials was a skill I gradually acquired, and it was something I was keen to hammer into the skulls of all the players. Young players, being teenagers or 20-somethings, usually have two things on their minds. One is football, the second is the other half of the human race. All the nightclubs in Manchester have always been eager to attract United players because they know that word would soon spread among the young ladies. They used to dole out special passes to the players; these allowed them to jump the queues and gain free admission. I have yet to meet a 15-year-old aspiring footballer who wants to live like a monk. It is impossible to completely remove the boy from the man, particularly the young man.

It's no accident that the best players, and the ones who play at their peak for the longest, tend to be those who can shield themselves from the demands of others. Cristiano Ronaldo was among the very best. He didn't drink and he didn't smoke. When he came to Manchester his mother and his sister lived with him. Every now and again he might appear in a TV advertisement or on a magazine cover or, during the summer break, in a Los Angeles nightclub. But don't be deceived, Cristiano knew how to manage himself and his time.

Apart from his skill and his fame, Cristiano – and players of his generation – have far more distractions than I did as a player. They need far more internal discipline to shut off the outside world than people of 50 years ago. When I was a boy, the biggest distractions were the radio, the newspaper, a book – and church on Sunday. I listened to the great boxing matches on the radio with my dad – Randolph Turpin, Sugar Ray Robinson and the last fights of Joe Louis and Jersey Joe Walcott – and we would also tune in to hear the music hall singer, Ronnie Ronalde, on a Sunday, or the quiz show, *Top of the Form*. The local cinema, The Plaza, was about a hundred yards from our door – so that was always good for *Tarzan* and the *Flash Gordon* films, featuring Buster Crabbe. But beyond that there were only street fights, snooker, games of dice and football. There was no telephone or television, let alone 60-inch colour screens with 300 channels, or mobile phones with millions of apps, e-mail, Facebook and the internet.

I was always alive to pressures on my players and kept an ear cocked for word of distractions they might be facing. The constant worry with the English players is drinking and the bookies. Weakness for the bottle has destroyed many careers, while gambling is a cancer in a dressing room. I usually had a pretty good sense of which players had been out and about because I would get calls from club owners or fans alerting me to the fact. At least for me, these pursuits were less of a concern with the foreign players. We also tried, best as we could, to ensure that they didn't squander their money, although one look at our car park would suggest we weren't that successful. From time to time there were distressing stories in the papers about some players who would blow a king's ransom in the betting shops. We would bring in financial consultants and lawyers to offer advice. We even had one person suggest that players contemplating marriage should exchange vows in Scotland where, according to him, the law is more favourable to husbands than in England. That prompted Cristiano Ronaldo to say that when the time came he would only get married in Scotland.

It is true that few footballers spend a lot of time studying or trying to excel in school examinations. That's one of the reasons why they are successful on the field. When the academy system started, the structure was 12 hours' education and 12 hours' coaching (including matches) per week, which, to me, was an imbalance. My job was to produce footballers. But if any player wanted to pursue qualifications – or if his parents wanted him to do so – we agreed that the club would pay for it. This was a rare occurrence; these boys wanted to be footballers. I understand the benefits of a fine education and how it equips people for their journey in life. I recognise too that many footballers who get injured at the age of 25, or whose careers end in their early thirties (particularly those playing in the lower leagues), don't possess the education, skills or financial cushion required to have a decent life in today's world. Yet the job of a football manager is not to make sure that a boy can become a biologist or geophysicist, or that he is equipped for the 40 or 50 years that will follow his playing career – it is to make sure he will be a great right-back or winger. Eleven Nobel laureates are not going to win the FA Cup.

We faced this issue with my eldest son, Mark, who could probably have carved out a life as a professional footballer. He played for Aberdeen's reserves as a boy, but he had other interests too, and Cathy and I could tell he was ambivalent about a life in football. We were careful not to exert any pressure on him to follow in my footsteps. It's just as well, because he studied at Sheffield Hallam University and at the European University in Paris, became enchanted by the world of investments and, after five years at Goldman Sachs Asset Management, helped form Generation Investment Management, a much-respected fund manager in London.

I'm sure it would be wonderful if one of my young players

had had the grades to gain admission to Cambridge University or Imperial College London, but I can more or less guarantee that, if that were the case, they would not have been able to devote the time required to progress to the first team. There would have been a significant impact on their momentum as footballers. More experienced players are able to deal with this and the example of Vincent Kompany, who combined his studies at Manchester Business School with his role as Manchester City's captain illustrates this. In all my time at United I cannot think of one player who had a degree. Colin Murdock, who did not make the first team but played on our youth team in the early 1990s, got a law degree from Manchester Metropolitan University in the mid-1990s while playing for Preston North End. But Murdock is the exception that proves the rule.

Distractions exact a heavy toll on individuals and organisations and it demands incredible discipline to keep them at bay. At United the players always had demands from the commercial, business side of the club. It was understandable, because the commercial department was responsible for bringing in television and sponsorship revenue, selling executive boxes, staging profitable events and running the hospitality organisation. Without all this revenue we couldn't have done some of the things we did, such as sign some big contracts, pay hefty salaries, improve our training facilities or use private jets for travelling to games.

The sponsors all wanted contact with the players and the demand was insatiable. As the television revenue kept increasing and as United got ever better known around the world, the number of sponsors started to climb. Shielding players from the requests of the commercial team was a big part of my job. Mick Phelan was a dab hand at juggling all this. The commercial guys who, quite naturally, wanted to be able to provide sponsors with behind-the-scenes glimpses of United would produce all these ideas and the stream of requests was endless. Mick would be our intermediary and he'd dole out favours as if he was passing around manhole covers. He made sure that a lot of these were fulfilled during the pre-season, so that we could say with a straight face that our obligations had been satisfied and this allowed us to rebuff demands during the playing season. Some sponsors would want to come and watch the training, which made me queasy because I didn't want others to see who was training and who was injured. So I limited access to a handful of minutes at the start of a session and, otherwise, would make a few appearances at lunchtime and attend one or two dinners during the season.

At United we always wanted to try and support local charities. Every Friday the players would sign around 100 shirts that could be given away to charities or auctioned for a good cause. The one global organisation we supported was UNICEF, and when we were on foreign tours we would take the players to witness some of their work. In Thailand we went by river, in skiffs, to visit a school to see kids who had been rescued from child prostitution, and in South Africa we visited orphanages. These were eye-opening experiences for all of us. But most of our charitable work was done close to home because we wanted to be good citizens and demonstrate that we cared about people all around Manchester. In 2006 we formed a special group, The Manchester United Foundation, to take care of the club's charitable activities – particularly the local schools and hospitals. The players would go and visit schools and the bedsides of seriously ill children. All of these were great things to do, but I kept an eagle eye on them because the most important thing was winning a game on Saturday. The fans aren't going to thank you if you're doing charity work and it costs you three points.

Big games have the most distractions. When I had my first taste of this at Aberdeen after we reached the European Cup Winners' Cup final in 1983, one of the first things I did was make sure that the players' wives and girlfriends understood their role. So, in jest, I wrote a memo to all of them explaining it was their responsibility to pack toothpaste, blankets and other essentials for the trip to Sweden and summoned them to a meeting at Pittodrie where they would hear more of what was required from them. Through the grapevine I very quickly heard that my joke had misfired and gone down like a lead balloon. I walked into the room in Pittodrie where I was greeted by a collection of wives and resounding silence. I apologised for the joke that had backfired and told them that the real purpose of my memo had been to bring them together so that we could prepare for what would be the most important game in their husbands' careers, and perhaps the biggest occasion in which they would ever participate. I made sure the wives understood that their one task was to make sure that their husband was as well prepared as possible for the game and that, under no circumstances, should they do anything that could distract him. After I finished speaking I asked whether they had any questions. There were none. They all understood what I wanted: no distractions.

There are fans that mob you at the airport; the hotel lobby where the team stays can also be teeming with autograph hunters. When United played in the Champions League final against Barcelona in Rome in 2009, I actually asked the hotel management to close off the hotel to fans, because I wanted to eliminate the hubbub. As the years ticked by, I found that I was able to close myself off from the frenzy and tittle-tattle that surrounded United. From time to time I'd notice that the coaching staff were chatting about something and I didn't have a clue what they were discussing because I had been lost in my own thoughts. When we were approaching big games I'd isolate myself in a mental cocoon. Unless somebody brought up an issue relating to the team, I would barely hear anything that was said. I just tried to concentrate on the one big thing – my job. When I was lost in my own thoughts, Cathy would always say, 'You're not listening to me.' She was right.

From time to time there were distractions that could have been avoided. An example was the legal scrap I got into in the late 1970s when I sued St Mirren for wrongful dismissal. I acted emotionally and impulsively and, in retrospect, it would have been better for me to have spent every second thinking about how to turn Aberdeen into a title contender.

Whenever we got caught up in a big match, I always told the players, 'Don't play the occasion, play the game.' There's all the other frippery that doesn't matter: the bands, the pre-game theatrics, the new suits and all the travelling supporters buzzing with anticipation. The first time I took United to a Wembley final in 1990, I was as excited as a teenager on a Saturday night and distracted by the surroundings. I did what I had seen everybody else do and took the team out to inspect the pitch. It was a boiling hot day and we were roasting in our suits and I suddenly realised we were being daft and the players were getting dehydrated. An inspection of the pitch wasn't going to influence the result so I ordered everyone to get to the dressing room. There's only one way to enjoy a final and that's to win it. Nobody ever remembers the losers.

Failing

When you look at a successful person, you cannot imagine that they've ever failed or had a brush with failure. You watch sports stars like Roger Federer, Serena Williams or, in the old days, Muhammad Ali and Stirling Moss, and it's impossible to conceive of them as losers. The same extends to other walks of life, where someone of great accomplishment puts his wares on display. If I look at paintings by L. S. Lowry, the Mancunian best known for his bleak renditions of urban, industrial life, I have a tough time believing that he ever made a bad picture, or if you read one of Robert Caro's books about President Lyndon B. Johnson, you cannot imagine him worrying about writing a paragraph that didn't contain a carefully buffed phrase. But we are all haunted by failure. It paralyses some and motivates others. It was my own inner determination to avoid failure that always provided me with an extra personal incentive to succeed.

After I left Rangers in 1969, it would have been easy for me to feel like a bit of a loser. I had tasted life in the top ranks of football, but I knew I was never a key part of the manager's plans and, when I was transferred after two years at the club, all I had in my silverware drawer was a runners-up medal from a Scottish Cup final. We had got pipped at the post in the final game of the 1967–68 season for the Scottish League when we lost against, of all clubs, Aberdeen. So I could have been overwhelmed by self-pity when I was off-loaded to Falkirk, but I was determined not to be cowed.

I would like to think that, somehow, the people I went on to work with at both Aberdeen and United came to share that same positive attitude towards failure. For me, that whole approach to life could be boiled down to the 101 seconds of injury time that it took United to turn what had looked like a 1–0 defeat by Bayern Munich in the 1999 Champions League final into a 2–1 victory. Bayern Munich's ribbons had already been attached to the Cup in anticipation of the victory ceremony, and the president of UEFA was preparing to present the trophy to them, when our refusal to give up meant those ribbons were changed to red.

As we prepared for the Champions League final nine years later in 2008, I played the DVD of the last three minutes of the 1999 game to emphasise to the players the importance of never, ever capitulating. For me, the only time to give up is when you are dead.

When I started my life as a coach, I never dreamed that I would wind up as the manager of Manchester United. All I thought about was survival. Each time I joined a club – East Stirlingshire, St Mirren and Aberdeen – I just thought to myself, 'I'm not going to fail here.' It was one of the things that drove me. I always had that fear of getting humiliated, and failure was always that wee thing at the back of my mind. I kept silently saying to myself, 'Failure. Don't fail.' When I joined East Stirlingshire as a manager, the only qualifications I had for the job was that I had been a player, had earned my coaching badges and could make a decision. I didn't know anything else. Four weeks earlier I had been a 32-year-old player. Suddenly I was a manager, albeit a part-time manager, who was just hoping to survive long enough to figure things out. After I had been at St Mirren, and got my first wee taste of managerial success, I had a hunch that I would do well when I got to Aberdeen. It was the first time I was a full-time manager and the club had the nucleus of what it took to win – it was a one-town team which had a good owner, decent facilities and a healthy stock of players.

It was only really in my last year at Aberdeen that I started mapping out a path for my future. Prior to that I was just concentrating on surviving and not failing. The complete perfection that Celtic achieved in their 1966–67 season, when they won five competitions, seemed like the stuff of miracles and myth. Even in our strongest seasons at United the fear of failure and the striving for perfection drove me on. Although I helped fill the trophy cabinet at Old Trafford, the club, under my leadership, never managed to go through the entire League season – like Arsenal did in 2003–04 – undefeated. The experience of defeat, or more particularly the manner in which a leader reacts to it, is an essential part of what makes a winner.

Before games I always had a churning in my stomach. It never left me. It was always there. I could never find a way to get rid of it. I remember feeling acutely nervous when I played at Rangers because I never felt that the manager had confidence in me and I always felt I had to justify my place in the team. But in some ways it may actually have got worse as the years went by, no matter how many cups lined the trophy cabinet, because the expectations, and the pressure, increased. Whenever we went to Anfield to play Liverpool I always had butterflies in my stomach.

The worst time was always during the pre-match warm-up. I hated it. If we had a 3 p.m. kick-off, I would give the team talk between 1.15 p.m. and 1.45 p.m. Once I had delivered my piece I would leave the players alone. We had prepared as best we could and last-minute instructions always leave players wondering whether they command the manager's confidence. At 2 p.m. my assistant manager would take our team-sheet to the referee and we would discover what team our opponent had decided to play. Then, after everyone was in their warm-up gear, the dressing room would empty about 2.15 p.m. I detested the next 30 minutes, which always seemed to drag on and on. I was often by myself in our dressing room and the pair of clocks on the wall never seemed to move.

During the pre-match warm-up, when we played at Old Trafford, I used to sit in my office and read the match programme or flip on the television and watch the horse racing. I'd sometimes wander about and try to find someone to talk to. Occasionally a visiting manager would come and have a cup of tea. The loneliness was much worse when we played away games because I had no office to use as a refuge. Then, I would often find myself sitting alone in the dressing room. I don't think this feeling, certainly in my later years as a manager, was caused by worrying about failing. Rather it was prompted by the apprehension, anxiety and uncertainty that always surrounds a big occasion, which might be exacerbated when you depend on others to implement your wishes. I'm sure other leaders experience similar feelings, no matter how worldly and important they may seem to others.

Even now, when I'm watching United from the directors' box or at home on the television, I feel twinges in the pit of my stomach. I never tried to get rid of this feeling. Maybe some people, before a big performance or important encounter, try to calm their nerves with breathing exercises or a dram of whisky, but I never did so. I just accepted that nagging anxiety as part of my job. It accompanied me through life and it would have been a big warning sign that I was no longer up for the task had that anxiety – which really was a sign of how badly I wanted to win – ever disappeared.

The old adage that you learn more from defeats than you do from victories has certainly been true for me. While I am sometimes inclined to say that I never look back, it isn't really true. I wouldn't harp on at the players about defeats, and I would certainly try to mask whatever I was thinking, but privately I always spent more time contemplating games that we lost than the ones we won. It's also true that if, during any season, we failed to win a major competition that we should have won, I found myself stewing on the reasons during the summer so that I could correct whatever was wrong before the start of the next season.

My record is full of defeats. Between 10 August 1974, the day I first managed East Stirlingshire, to 19 May 2013, the day I left the field for the last time as manager of Manchester United, my teams lost about two out of every ten games that they played. There were also plenty of draws that I considered as bad as losses. So I had plenty of opportunities to learn from defeats and setbacks. Though I never got fixated by statistics, my overall win rate as a manager was just under 60 per cent. In United's best season we won nearly 72 per cent of the time.

On occasion we got badly punished and I did not like it one bit – such as the two consecutive League games we lost in the 1996–97 season: 5–0 to Newcastle and 6–3 to Southampton. I don't recall any other times we conceded 11 goals in two consecutive games. In 1995 we lost the League and FA Cup in the space of seven days – one to Blackburn Rovers and the other to Everton. However, I don't ever think I had to contemplate a series of setbacks as severe as those that Bayer Leverkusen suffered in 2002 when they played in a League decider, the German Cup final and the Champions League final – and they lost all three. You would need more than a couple of aspirin to get over that.

At Aberdeen and United, once the squads were properly organised, I always felt our defeats, or disappointing results, were caused by what we failed to do rather than what our opponents did. I found it healthy to approach disappointments in that manner because it meant we were in control and could improve. I was always a better manager after a loss. For whatever reason, it made me sharper. I suppose sometimes I wanted to prove I was not a loser, and at other times I wanted to avenge a defeat. After the 1993–94 season, every year when we did not win the League title seemed like a failure to me. At some point in my life the desire and need to win outstripped my fear of failure. Winning was a matter of pride. It did not matter whether it was the first team or reserves. Losing is a powerful management tool so long as it does not become a habit. I felt that way to the end of my career. After we got pipped at the post for the Premier League by Manchester City in 2012, we were subjected to ugly taunting by some diehard Sunderland fans at the Stadium of Light (which, at that moment, seemed poorly named). Afterwards, in the dressing room, I told all the players – and emphasised it to the younger ones – that they should remember the treatment they had just received every time they returned to play Sunderland. And they did. The following season we returned and beat them 1–0.

Defeats rarely got the better of me, though I am aware that, especially in retirement, it is easy to put a gloss over the past. There is no changing the fact that, beginning in 2008, we reached the Champions League final three times within four years yet only won once. So while I was elated on one occasion, I was disappointed on three. There were some moments of profound despair. In October 1989, as a favour, United had travelled to St Johnstone for a mid-season friendly to help them open their new stadium, McDiarmid Park. We won 1–0 but our performance was worse than pathetic. After the game I went back to my hotel room, eager to escape. Archie Knox, my assistant manager, knocked on the door and told me I had to attend the reception being held for the teams. I was in my bed and told him, 'I'm not going. I can't face those players. They're not good enough.' Archie was right. It took me some time, but eventually I did drag myself downstairs, although I can't say I was good company. A few other defeats stand out because I could not get to sleep after Aberdeen's loss to Dundee United in the 1979–80 Scottish League Cup final, and went home to bed after United's 5–1 defeat to Manchester City in 1989. The two worst defeats were probably both Champions League fixtures – against Borussia Dortmund in 1997 and Real Madrid in 2013. Those defeats were more painful than the humiliations of a 5–0 trouncing by Newcastle in 1996, the 5–0 thumping by Chelsea in 1999 and our League Cup final defeat to Sheffield Wednesday in 1991.

When I knew we were going to be beaten, I always tried to make sure we didn't get smashed to smithereens because of the effect on morale. We played Manchester City at Old Trafford in October 2011 and got beaten 6–1. It was our worst thumping by our crosstown rivals in 22 years, and our biggest home League defeat since 1955 when United were hammered 5–0, also by Manchester City. The irony of it was that for most of the game we outplayed them. City scored two goals either side of half-time, and though we scratched our way back to 3–1, we conceded three goals in the last 13 minutes. In retrospect we should have just bolted the door, prevented City's last three goals, and avoided the embarrassment of the terrible newspaper headlines and the jubilation on the other side of Manchester. More importantly, we lost the League to City that year on goal difference, which made this result even more painful.

Handling the press in the moments after a defeat was really difficult. I might make some general comments about the team but I tried never to single out a player for criticism; though I do recall, to my chagrin, saying something negative about Nani after we lost 5–4 to Chelsea in a League Cup game in 2012. If a striker fluffed a chance, or there was a fatal back-pass or the goalkeeper had a lapse of concentration, the player himself would be more than aware of what he had done. Many of the best players are their own sternest critics and they did not need to read a disparaging comment from me in the Sunday papers. That wasn't going to help. Usually, I tried to deflect the reporters' attention away from both the team and the players, by pointing an accusatory finger at the opponent's tactics, or a refereeing decision. I could always find plenty of reasons for us losing a game that had nothing to do with us, even though I knew in my heart that we had nobody else to blame. I always thought my role was to act as a player's heat deflector in a moment of crisis.

A major loss or pounding can exact a heavy toll on a group of people. It can shake their confidence and, if you aren't careful, the consequences can linger. Whenever we lost an important game in which I knew we had played well, I tried to say very little. Nobody can absorb a message in times like that. You can whisper sweet nothings but the words aren't heard. So I would just go around and pat each of the players on the head. They understood that message – maybe because they felt it too. In football, a whiff of vulnerability is tantamount to giving your competitors an adrenalin shot that would turn a mule into a Derby winner. When you lose, particularly if you get thumped, you carry that loss around. In football it doesn't matter if the team has a lot of changes for the following game, everyone knows the club lost the prior outing. The players know it, the fans know it, and the press are baying like jackals. It adds unwanted pressure that can build on itself. It's like getting a wee tear in your jacket. If you don't get that tear sewn up immediately, it will only get worse. The reverse is also true. Taking to the field when your competitors are concentrating on survival is like having one or two goals in the bag before a boot has touched the ball.

Back at the training ground on the morning after a defeat, I'd gather everyone around me and ask, 'Are we enjoying the headlines this morning?' or, 'Anybody enjoy what happened to our football club last night?' I'd have a scowl on my face and I wouldn't make it easy, but I was also intent on rebuilding the players' confidence. After any defeat I would tend to withdraw and become sullen. The players would be looking to me and muttering between themselves, 'Bloody hell, he's in some mood today.' I am sure most of them did not want to come anywhere close to me in the canteen. I'd say something like, 'If you don't meet people's expectations, you only have yourselves to blame. There's no one else you can blame. We all know we're better than this and we let ourselves down. At our club losing a game is big news, so let's try and avoid the big news. Let's talk about all the good things that we've got – all the good and great performances. I want to come out for the post-game press conference and say, "Fantastic. It was a fantastic performance." I want to be able to say, "Well done Rooney, well done Welbeck, well done Chicharito."' Players who knew me well understood how much I valued winning. They would gradually absorb this sensibility into their own pores and eventually would be transmitting it to newcomers. We had a virus that infected everyone at United. It was called winning.

Manchester City's Premier League victory in 2012 was painful at the time – particularly because it was based on goal difference. It was also something of a tonic because it gave us something to work towards, and the following year we won the League. City finished second, 11 points behind. After my first League win in 1993, every time we finished second, which happened five times during this period, we won it the following season. There's some merit in getting defeated – even though I'd never want it to be a habit. Team members who are hungry for victory and take great pride in their performance will be eager to avenge defeat.

Football is full of setbacks beyond the simple pain of defeat, but it's useless drowning in self-pity. I do not remember a time when every single member of the squad was at peak fitness and ready to play. Somebody was always injured. It was normal for a tenth of the squad to be injured. I also don't remember a time when one of our long-time competitors was not fielding a player we had missed signing. Take December 2009 – it was a horror show. We had 14 of the first-team squad laid up by injury – including two goalkeepers, seven defenders, three midfielders and two strikers. A fit 11 picked from the injured 14 could have beaten any club in Europe. Yet, while they were on the bench, or with the doctors, we lost at home to Aston Villa and away to Fulham. We also occasionally got hammered by viruses that swept through the squad; at the end of 1994 and start of 1995, things were so bad that I even considered closing the training ground. Nine of our players were felled by the flu and, while they were in bed, we dropped points to Nottingham Forest, Leicester City, Southampton, Newcastle United and Crystal Palace. There is nothing I could have done about either the injuries or the flu; we just had to make the best of bad situations.

We made plenty of decisions that we came to regret in the transfer market, but you cannot change history. United probably could have won a couple of League titles with a team composed of players we scouted but did not sign. In 2003 I went to see Petr Čech in goal for Rennes in a game against Auxerre. We thought Petr was a bit young for the bruisers in the Premier

League, but Petr went to Chelsea and in the subsequent decade kept 220 clean sheets for the club. We got our wires crossed on another goalkeeper too, in 1999, after Peter Schmeichel had announced his intention to retire. There had been some preliminary interest in Mark Bosnich, who was playing at Aston Villa, and I was also very interested in Edwin van der Sar who was at Ajax. By the time I informed Martin Edwards, the club chairman, that we had received bad reports on Bosnich, it was too late. Martin had already shaken hands on a deal and Van der Sar went to Juventus.

Didier Drogba was another. He was playing at Olympique de Marseilles and we went to check him out, but the club wanted £25 million for him and Chelsea moved in for the kill before we had made up our minds. Thomas Müller, who scored five goals for Germany in the 2010 and 2014 World Cups, was a ten year old playing for an amateur team several miles from Munich when we first heard about him. We had him watched and the following day he committed himself to Bayern Munich. We wanted to sign Ronaldo, the Brazilian striker, from Cruzeiro in 1994 but we could not get a work permit, and he went to PSV Eindhoven in the Netherlands. We looked at Robin van Persie when he was about 16 and playing for Feyenoord's reserve team, and even then the price on his head was about £6 million. Jim Ryan, who was on our coaching staff for 11 years before becoming United's director of youth football for another decade, watched Van Persie get sent off and subsequently exchange insults with the supporters. Jim wasn't the only person unimpressed by Van Persie's temperament on that occasion, because his club immediately suspended him. There were plenty of other players I would have liked to sign – such as Alan Shearer, the striker who became a thorn in our side while he played for Newcastle, or the Argentinian, Gabriel Batistuta, who spent most of his career playing in Italy, or Samir Nasri who went to Manchester City in 2011. Then, in 2011, I hurtled down on the train from Euston to Lille to sign the young French defender Raphaël Varane. David Gill was getting into the finer points of the contract with Lens, Varane's club, when Zinedine Zidane got wind of this and somehow scooped him up for Real Madrid from under our noses. I don't think José Mourinho, who was then managing Real Madrid, had ever seen Varane play.

I could have let these decisions eat away at me, but I tried to avoid this. We made these choices, nobody else did. You also cannot field a team with players that you don't own, so what's the point of flogging yourself?

As time went by, these missed opportunities and the setbacks and defeats we suffered along the way eventually helped me become a better, or at least more gracious, loser. When I was a young man I was a very bad loser. After any defeat I would go home and sulk. In Aberdeen, after one particularly bad defeat, I ran the players through the town centre so the punters could all give them stick. When we got back to the dressing room I told them, 'Let that be a lesson to you.' Every winner hates to lose. In football all the best players are bad losers, although they display it in different ways.

The most gracious lesson I received about the manner in which to handle defeat was given by Ottmar Hitzfeld, the manager of Bayern Munich between 1998 and 2004, and 2007 and 2008. After we beat Bayern in the Champions League final in 1999 by scoring two goals in the last three minutes (after a campaign that for United had consisted of 63 games and 96 hours of play), I could tell that he was devastated. Within 180 seconds he had gone from thinking the trophy was his to seeing his players either prostrate or holding their heads in their hands. It must have been soul-destroying, but he was most gracious and that was amplified a year later when I went to Munich to watch Rangers, who had a player that interested me, play Bayern. After the game he invited me to have dinner at his table with his two brothers, and they were all so gracious and warm. Then some of the Bayern players came and shook my hand and offered congratulations, even though they must have hated losing. It was a great display of the quality of the club.

Perhaps the most important lesson in how to handle failure was handed down to me by my own dear mother. When I was 21 I'd been playing part-time for St Johnstone and had been in and out of the team, and only played about 50 first-team games in four years. I was really disillusioned. I had broken my nose, cheekbone and eyebrow in a reserve game, and then, after I recovered, the reserve team got destroyed several games in a row. So I went to Canada House on Waterloo Street in Glasgow, and took out papers to emigrate to Canada, because all my dad's family had already moved there. I just didn't want to play another game for the club.

So one day I got my brother's girlfriend to pretend that she was my mother and call Bobby Brown to tell him that I had the flu and couldn't play. He wasn't fooled and sent a telegram to my mother, because we didn't have a phone, telling me to ring him. I went up the road to the phone booth, dialled Stanley 267 (which is a number I suppose I remember because of the embarrassment), and Brown ripped into me. He said, 'You're a disgrace. You think you're kidding me. You got someone to pretend to be your mother. I've got a whole team down with the real flu and you're playing tomorrow and you report to the Buchanan Hotel at twelve o'clock.'

In that game I scored a hat-trick at Ibrox – the first player from a visiting team to do so – and that wee bit of luck changed my life. I had come within a whisker of quitting. My mother had read me the riot act after she'd discovered what had happened. She taught me never to give in and, ever after, one way or another, I have tried to convey the same lesson to others.

Criticism

Football is one of those subjects in which everyone is an expert even if their knowledge of the game couldn't fill a thimble. It's like other forms of entertainment or creative endeavour, where it's easier to be a critic than a practitioner. Everyone has opinions about restaurants, airlines, films, cars and paintings, even if they couldn't cook a boiled egg, fly a kite or draw a square. It's different when you get into more exotic fields and the man on the street is intimidated from passing comment because of ignorance. Only real experts can offer a valuable opinion about the mechanics of a suspension bridge or the best way to set up a laboratory experiment. That's just not the case in football, where managers of top-flight teams have millions of critics – from those closest to them, to fans on the other side of the world.

Some leaders have to contend with criticism from within their own organisation. They might have ambitious underlings vying for their job, or a board of directors muttering between themselves. Whenever someone new assumes a role, there will always be doubts about his capabilities until he has proved himself. If a leader has had a long stint at the helm and encounters a bad patch, he will often have to endure times when people ask whether he is past his sell-by date.

There were only a few times when I had to contend with carping inside the place I worked. At St Mirren, where I was the manager between the ages of 32 and 36, I was politically naïve and got on the wrong side of the owner so, to some extent, I helped stoke his criticism.

There were a few periods when I found the criticism demoralising. Although I don't remember ever being booed by United fans, I do remember a particularly tough time in 1989 when, during the whole of December, we failed to win a game. We had lost or drawn ten out of 15 games. Somebody held a banner high up in the Stretford End that said: '3 YEARS OF EXCUSES AND IT'S STILL CRAP . . . TA RA FERGIE'.

I suppose my confidence was shaken a bit because the day after the game I phoned my brother Martin; I knew he would be objective, give me a fair assessment and tell me where I stood. He said, 'You're just going to have to dig in,' which was a sentiment I found reassuring. Years later, the person who had held up that banner wrote a book titled *Ta Ra Fergie*, and a copy showed up at the house. I mailed it back to the publisher. But on the whole I think I weathered the criticism fairly well. Certainly in 2004 and 2005 when we were not playing well and some fans were on my back, it didn't really bother me.

It is sometimes tricky to put criticism in its proper place when you are under a lot of pressure, haven't had enough sleep and everything is going wrong. It might have been a bit easier for me because growing up in Govan was not for the weak. It was a tough neighbourhood – physically and emotionally. There was no option but to be able to protect yourself from bullies and bruisers, and as boys we would get into fights about everything. My brother, a cousin and I would have fights with the five brothers of the Granger family who lived nearby, and from a fairly young age I had become accustomed to physical pain, the taste of blood in my mouth or bad bruising.

I always found it helpful to put criticism in perspective and these memories of my childhood helped. It's easy for me, decades later, to romanticise aspects of my childhood or my playing career, but both had more than their share of raw moments. Yet physical pain is one thing, mental anguish and emotional pressure are entirely different.

I've seen lots of people crack from the emotional pressure of playing or managing. Obviously I might not have been privy to their personal problems, but there are tremendous pressures. The worst example is Robert Enke, the German international goalkeeper who committed suicide in 2009. He had had a difficult few years playing in Spain before joining the Bundesliga team, Hannover 96, and his personal life had been savaged by the death of an infant daughter. After Enke died, his wife revealed that he had been struggling with depression for many years. Fortunately, we never had to deal with anything as distressing during my time at United.

Everybody has their fears; all footballers want to be in the first team, and many will torture themselves when they are injured or have been dropped, fearful that their playing days are ending. There are plenty of them who have turned to drink or gambling and got sucked into a rat-hole of despair.

Managers, most of whom are on short-term contracts, are not immune to the unrelenting pressure and know that the guillotine blade can descend at any moment. Ralf Rangnick, who managed, among others, Hannover 96 and Schalke 04; Gérard Houllier, who worked at Liverpool and Lyon; and Johan Cruyff, after his stint at Barcelona, stepped away from management because of stress. Pep Guardiola took a sabbatical from football after leaving Barcelona to recharge. You have to wonder whether Kenny Dalglish, the great Celtic and Liverpool player, who later managed Liverpool, was ever the same after the horrors he endured in the aftermath of the Heysel stadium disaster in 1985, where 39 fans died, and the Hillsborough disaster in 1989 that claimed 96 lives. And of course I have always lived with the memory of Jock Stein's collapse and tragic death.

If you're in the public eye, the press coverage creates other issues – especially if you are in the sports business. The press helps inflame irate fans. After we moved to Manchester we used to get so many abusive phone calls that we had to change our home phone number several times.

When things were at their darkest for me at United, I remember my wife Cathy asking me what I'd do if I was sacked, and I told her that we would just have to go back to Scotland. I'm sure I would have been crushed if I had been fired, but I always knew I'd be able to support my family and it wouldn't have been the end of the world.

The press can certainly play their part too. Matt Busby told me, 'I never read the papers when we lost a game. They're not going to write nice things about you. So just don't read those stories.' While Matt Busby's advice made sense, it's impossible to be completely oblivious to what appears in the press. In Scotland I was in the habit of reading the match reports, but after I got to United I would very seldom read the papers. Even if I didn't read the papers or watch the football programmes on television, friends would ask whether I'd heard about what somebody had said or written about me, and United's press officer would brief me on inflammatory stories or rumours that had made it into print. But I learned to deal with it and, during my last ten years or so as a manager, I found the press criticism far less troublesome than when I was younger.

The best protection against attacks from others comes from a few people whose opinions you really care about. The yells of a horde of abusive banshees always fade away when you have the support of a few people that you respect. If we lost a game in Aberdeen I usually had to face the chairman in the boardroom after the game. He would be drinking his Coca-Cola – because he never touched alcohol – and would let off steam by giving me stick about the line-up or a particular player. All his criticism stayed in that room and it usually blew over after ten minutes. Either way, outside the room he was unstintingly loyal. The fact that he never voiced a word of criticism behind my back was probably more helpful to me than pounds of praise or a big hug.

At United, especially in the early years, I found it very reassuring to know that Bobby Charlton was on my side. I never went out of my way to curry favour with him, but he had originally helped advise the board to sign me as a manager and I always felt he was in my corner. During bleak times he often said, 'You'll be all right. You're doing the right thing.' In the months following our 5–1 loss to Manchester City in September 1989, I was feeling a mite vulnerable, and Bobby's backing – particularly during this period – counted for a lot. Not only did his opinion carry a lot of weight through the club, but a few well-chosen words lifted my spirits too. Every leader needs an ally like that.

8

OWNING THE MESSAGE

Speaking

As a manager I communicated with a number of different constituencies and each required special handling: the owner, the coaches and other club staff, the players and the supporters.

Having a healthy, open line of communication with the boss is vital. Few of us don't have a boss. Perhaps the founders of successful companies have designed things in such a way that they don't feel they have anyone they need to please – beyond their inner demons – but the rest of us do. I might have been seen as 'The Boss' by the players, but in football the real boss is the owner, who can hire and fire the manager at will.

I learned this the painful way at St Mirren when I was always arguing with the chairman, Willie Todd, the owner of a painting and decorating company, who had bought the club shortly after I joined. He didn't know much about football and I helped educate him. Before long he began to think he knew a lot about the game and we were soon at loggerheads. It was a very nasty experience, and got to the point where we were not talking to each other. In retrospect, there was only one way it was going to end – and that was badly for me. It did. I was sacked. Managers have to find a way to talk to their bosses, regardless of their differences in character; otherwise it will only end miserably.

At Aberdeen, I wasn't about to repeat the mistake. The personality of Dick Donald, Aberdeen's chairman between 1970 and 1993, was very different from Willie Todd's, and I found him easier to get along with. Though we became close, our conversations were always tinged with formality. I addressed him as 'Mr Chairman', and he always called me 'Mr Ferguson', which helped show I understood the difference between our roles. It was important to establish these boundaries because he was a constant presence around the club, and we would talk almost every day. My other key relationship at Aberdeen was with Archie Knox, my assistant manager. We went everywhere together – working during the day and socialising, when we had time, with our wives in the evening. When I moved to United in 1986 I insisted that he came with me. His last name could have been Ferguson and, while I understood his decision to leave United in 1991 to help Walter Smith at Rangers, it ended a wonderful working relationship.

By the time I got to United I was 44, had experienced success at Aberdeen (where we had won ten trophies and a number of players had earned Scottish caps) and learned that maintaining a healthy relationship with the owner and club chairman was vital. I used to go and see Martin Edwards, United's owner and chairman, in his book- and trophy-filled office at Old Trafford a couple of times a week. No subject was off limits, and I kept him fully informed of everything I was working on and concerned about. We saw eye to eye about most things, with the exception of my own compensation.

This was a time of great change at Old Trafford and in football in general. During the 1990s, the combination of the huge rise in television revenues and the 1995 European Court of Justice's 'Bosman ruling', which lifted many transfer restrictions, gave greater impetus to the business side of the club. After Martin's decision to float United on the Stock Exchange in 1991, the nature of its ownership was altered. The club's stock was no longer concentrated in an individual, but rather distributed among dozens of investment fund managers and hundreds of individuals. For me this meant that, apart from making an appearance at the club's Annual General Meeting, I was no longer in direct contact with all the financial owners of the club, but it was vital that I kept communicating closely with Martin and the board.

The other thing that changed was the gradual increase in authority of the chief executive officer of the club, stemming from the blossoming of United's commercial activities. In 2000 this resulted in the appointment of David Gill. David was responsible for building and running the business activities of United. Over the years David and I became like blood brothers.

After the Glazers took control of United in 2005, the nature of the organisation changed again. Unlike Dick Donald in Aberdeen and Martin Edwards in Manchester, the Glazers did not live near the club they owned. Instead they lived in America and their principal conduit was David Gill. I had talked to Malcolm Glazer after his family bought the club, but I never met him in person. The two family members I saw the most were Joel and Avram who, best as I could tell, were its most enthusiastic football fans. However, it was David who kept the Glazers updated on the health of the club and relayed my requests about purchases of players or upgrades to our training facilities.

After the owner, the next most important constituency I had to talk to was the coaching staff. They were the pipeline for conveying my ideas to players – whether members of the first team or boys coming through the youth system. I am hard pressed to think of a day when I didn't talk to any of the coaches. Even during those very rare times when I was ill in bed, I'd still talk to the staff on the phone. I understood intuitively that if there was a breakdown in communication with my staff, or if instructions were misunderstood or garbled in the re-telling, it would only lead to confusion on the pitch. So, first thing every morning, I would talk to the coaching staff at the training ground and set out my key priorities for the day.

I would talk to the players in one of three settings – during training, on match days, and also by themselves in a one-on-one setting. In some circumstances, especially when I was talking to people I didn't know well, I found it tricky to assess whether I was drilling my message home, so I got into the habit of imagining that I was in the shoes of the listener. I knew from my own experience as a player what it was like to listen to a manager drone on, especially if it was the day before a game, and you were just raring to get on to the training field and blow off some steam. As a result I always tried to keep my team talks short and punchy. I remember once saying this to the players, 'This must be my thousandth team talk,' and Brian McClair, who played 471 games for United between 1987 and 1998, chirped up, 'Yeah, I slept through half of them.' Managers often make things more complicated than they are. The best way to make sure people understand what you expect from them is to be clear and concise, and that was especially true as the number of foreign players increased, since some of them needed subtitles to deal with my Scottish accent. I'm sure there were a few that probably couldn't tell whether I was speaking in English or Welsh.

I took pains to convey to the players that because I was not intimidated by the opposition, neither should they be. I was also careful to remind them of the necessity for us to win all the individual battles that take place during a game. And, more often than not, I would urge the team to be decisive in the final third of the game. At half-time I would relay to the players what I had seen in the first half, make observations about some of the opposing team, and try to tighten everything up. I made a habit of never going around issuing reminders to individual players. It just plants the seeds of doubt in their minds and they are left wondering whether the manager trusts them. Similarly, I never felt it made any sense to be perpetually barking instructions at players during games. If you have to resort to that, it means that you have not prepared or communicated your plan correctly, or you do not trust the players to do what they are supposed to do. Either shortcoming reflects more poorly on the manager than the players.

Bill Shankly, the long-time manager of Liverpool who, like me, came from Scotland, had a reputation for keeping things to the point. I often tried to emulate the effectiveness of one of Bill's favourite lines which was, 'If we get the ball, why don't we pass it to each other? It's a wee bit harder when the other team have got it.' The instructions that I gave most frequently were very short. They were nothing more complicated than 'Keep the ball' or, 'Do not let them score'.

One message that seemed to strike home (at least judging by the number of players who appear to have remembered it) were the words I used at half-time during the 1999 Champions League final when we were trailing Bayern Munich 1–0. I said, 'When that Cup is going to be presented, just remember that you can't even touch it if you're the losers – you'll be walking past it with your losers' medals, knowing someone walking behind you is going to lift the Cup.'

With players, the manner of the delivery of the message could have quite an effect. While I had a reputation for sometimes steam-blasting players, I found that I rarely lost my temper (especially in my later years) in crucial games where we were trailing badly. Then it was vital to stay calm and be very precise with my feedback. Sometimes, Mick Phelan might tell me it was time to give everyone a bit of a roasting, particularly the new players, but tantrums quickly lost their effect. At half-time when we were ahead by a couple of goals, I would frequently put a bit of a bark into my instructions, to ensure that the players did not let their concentration lapse and allow complacency to seep in. I also wanted to notch up as many goals as possible in case an entire season might be decided on goal difference. By contrast, silence can be as effective a way of communicating as anything else. Sometimes, after we had a bad result, I would finish what I had to say to the players and then sit down on the bench and say nothing. The subsequent quietness was probably more effective than anything I said.

Whether the audience is one person or 75,000, you need to assemble your thoughts, know what you want to emphasise and just say it. In team meetings it's important to maintain eye contact and look directly at the players because it adds intensity to the delivery of the message, although I tried to avoid staring at those who I felt might wither under my gaze. There are some managers who will enter a dressing room at half-time with a pack of notes. When they talk to the players they will use their notes as prompts. I cannot imagine how that is an effective way to communicate. If you have command and control of your subject, you don't need notes. No player is going to believe that someone is in control of his material, or is an authority on a subject, if he has to keep resorting to notes. I relied on my memory and my own assessment and, that way, when I was talking to the players, I was able to maintain eye contact. I'm sure I got some stuff wrong. I'd miss a deflection or a foul but, in the grand scheme of things, those tiny details don't count. It's the message, the command of that message and its delivery that pack the punch. Everyone has their own style, but using notes when trying to motivate people is not mine.

If I wanted to convey a particular message, I might summon a player to my office at the Carrington training ground. There was a phone in the dressing room that I used to relay the invitation to come upstairs. I'm sure, when the phone rang, some of the players thought they were being hauled into the headmaster's study for a caning. Some of them were right.

While I was always fixated on both physical and mental freshness, I was careful never to say to a player, 'You look tired', even if I thought that he did. I knew that if I uttered the phrase he would immediately feel tired. Instead I'd say to him, 'You're so strong, nobody is ever going to be able to keep up with you.' Before a game, especially at Old Trafford, I'd emphasise the size of our pitch, which was daunting for most of our opponents, and the need to maintain a high tempo, rhythm and speed. I wanted to plant in their minds that we would have the opponents knackered out by the last 15 minutes of a game.

I used to lie in bed thinking about new themes to talk to the players about, because I never wanted them to feel that I was about to deliver a sermon they had heard the previous week. Once, after I had been to see my very first performance of a classical concert with Carlos Queiroz in Manchester, I talked to the players about the experience. They must have thought I'd gone off my rocker, but I was trying to explain to them how the conductor of the concert, which featured Andrea Bocelli, was trying to obtain the same things from his orchestra as I was doing at United: control, harmony, tempo, timing, rhythm. I knew that the players had never heard this story before because it was brand new, but I'm sure my message was lost on some. There were some stories about teamwork that I'm sure Ryan Giggs or Paul Scholes feel they heard dozens of times, like my tale about large flocks of Canada geese, which can migrate thousands of miles because of the way they work as a team. The birds take turns breaking the air at the front of the flock and, at the back, if one gets injured, a couple drop away from the flock to look after it. I was not asking them to fly for thousands of miles, I was only asking them to play 38 games of football.

Making sure players grasped where they stood was very important. Like all of us they are fragile human beings and it's easy to send unintended messages. If I was not planning to pick a player in a particular game, I'd always try to find a way to explain the reason. They would be worrying that they had fallen out of favour or I had my eye on someone else to fill their boots. Instead I'd try to let them down gently and provide reassurance. Sometimes it was because I was resting them for a more important game. I'd take pains to explain the bigger picture – that the campaign was more important than the game and that we needed to plot out a way of winning every game. In the bigger European games, where we would travel with a squad of 24 players, I would need to explain things to the 13 who were not included in the starting line-up. I tried to make them feel they were part of a squad and that it was the squad – rather than the starting team in any particular game – that would eventually win the League or a cup.

It was all well and good to be chatting with the coaches or the players in quite small groups, but it was another matter to be speaking in front of crowds of people. As you encounter success, more people tend to get interested in what you have to say. I never thought when I first became a manager that I would ever address a crowd of 75,000 people, not to mention the millions more watching on TV – which is what happened after my last ever game at Old Trafford.

Tons of people have told me they are scared witless about speaking in front of others. For some reason it's never bothered me. Even as a boy I was always busy organising other people, and I've long been accustomed to some form of public speaking, even though I am not pretending for a moment that I could deliver a Churchillian speech or the Gettysburg Address. As a teenager I had my stint as a shop steward and, later, when I ran my two pubs, I often had to say something to all the customers. Neither of these settings required great oratorical skill, but I suppose they are one reason why I've never been plagued by the nervous butterflies that afflict many people when they have to stand up and address a group.

I've always marvelled at the way in which some highly skilled public speakers' command of language allows them to convey their thoughts in a powerful fashion. In Scotland in the 1960s and 1970s, everyone paid attention to Jimmy Reid, the trade-union leader and one of the guiding forces of the Communist Party of Great Britain. Love him or loathe him, he knew how to command the attention of a crowd. He was one of the last great political platform speakers – whether it was in the shipyards of Clydebank or in less raucous settings. I spoke at his funeral in 2010 at the Govan Old Parish Church and remember saying that while my education had consisted of football, Jimmy's took place at the Govan library. Words just seemed to flow from him. The speech he made when he was installed as Rector of Glasgow University in 1971, during which he implored the students to reject the rat race, was reprinted in full by the *New*

York Times, which described it as the greatest speech since Abraham Lincoln's Gettysburg Address.

When Nelson Mandela spoke at the Laureus Sports Award dinner in Monaco in 2000, you could have heard a pin drop. He didn't speak for long, but his remarks made the hairs on my neck stand up. Such force; such presence. My pal, Hugh McIlvanney, is no politician, but he is probably the greatest sports writer I have encountered and his control of language is fantastic. I could listen to him all day because he speaks in complete paragraphs.

I don't pretend to command language like a Reid, a Mandela or a McIlvanney, but as a football manager I frequently found myself speaking in public, and sometimes in front of a stadium packed to the gills. Talking to smaller groups is a useful way to practise speaking to bigger audiences. The principles are the same. You need to know what you want to say; you have to contemplate how you are going to deliver the message; and you have to maintain control of the audience. If someone has belief, they can find the words to express it. I've never been one for reading verbatim from a speech written out in longhand, nor have I ever used a Teleprompter. For me it's been more important to plan what I want to say, have a mental road map for the points I want to emphasise, and then try to maintain my train of thought. I'm quite comfortable improvising, particularly when the subject has something to do with football. Usually this works but, on occasion, it's an approach that has failed me.

In 1974, after four months as manager of East Stirlingshire, I became manager of St Mirren, where I was also just relying on instincts. Nobody had given me public-speaking lessons or public-relations tips, so I did what I thought was appropriate. St Mirren was a club located in Paisley, a town that had been hard hit by the closure of the cotton mills and a slump in the automobile industry. Glasgow, which is only ten miles away, cast a long shadow over Paisley, and each weekend bus-loads of men would disappear to watch Celtic or Rangers. The whole town had a major inferiority complex, and I was determined to lift spirits and convince the people there that their football club had a bright future. I decided that some public speaking would do the trick.

St Mirren's crowds were barely larger than a church choir, so one weekend I resorted to communicating with brute force. The club electrician taped a loudspeaker to the roof of a van and, like a politician casting about for votes, I toured Paisley, microphone in hand, imploring people to turn out to support their team. We stopped in the city centre, where I extolled the virtues of the team. It worked, and the crowds began to increase.

I had to do some public speaking when I was managing in Scotland, but the level of activity – and scrutiny – increased when I moved south. Manchester United had charity dinners on the first Monday of every month and I sometimes used to speak at these events. The first one was a fiasco. I tried to make a joke about England and Scotland but it just sailed over the heads of the audience. I had expected a few laughs but all I got was silence. Jokes are tricky things to deliver with any degree of assurance, and I understand why comedians go to small clubs to test out their routines before appearing in big venues or going on television.

As much as it's essential to maintain eye contact when talking to a small group of people, I always found it disconcerting to catch someone's eye when speaking in front of a big room. I tended to look towards the audience because I knew that staring at notes on a lectern is one sure way to lose a crowd's attention.

However, I never looked at any particular individual. Instead, I'd pick a spot at the back of the room slightly above the heads of the audience.

It's easy to get thrown off your horse if you look directly at someone in a crowd of people. Eric Harrison, United's youth coach between 1981 and 1998, discovered the perils of this in 1992. He had asked my advice about public speaking and I'd told him to look at the wall at the back of the room and also to move his head as he spoke so that the entire audience felt included. Instead, he made the fatal mistake of locking eyes with one member of the audience, which was not a smart move, particularly as Eric was speaking in Liverpool, and the crowd consisted of Liverpool and Everton fans. He came scuttling back to Manchester with his tail between his legs because the person he had picked out of the crowd did two things. First, he had slowly crossed his throat with his index finger, and then, when that didn't throw Eric off his stride, he started to wave a white handkerchief. That did the trick and Eric, thoroughly rattled, had to sit down.

When Sir Matt Busby died in 1994, I was asked to speak at his funeral mass at the church of Our Lady and St John in Chorlton-cum-Hardy near Manchester. It was a big event, and thousands of United fans had lined the route of the cortege. The church was packed to the rafters. I was speaking from notes, which I don't usually do, and I got a roasting from my harshest critic, Cathy, my wife. She said, 'You were hopeless. I told you not to use notes. You're useless when you try to speak from notes.'

Speaking without notes is not for the faint of heart, and sometimes it's been my comeuppance. I gave a talk at Goldman Sachs in London some years ago, and I thought it went well enough, but Mark, my son, lambasted me for hopping from point to point and for an overall lack of structure. I discovered that, with or without notes, there's always someone ready to skewer you – one of the perils, I suppose, of opening your mouth in public.

Writing

There were only two ways for me to communicate with the broad base of fans – either via the press or through the notes in the match-day programmes. Every now and again there would be an opportunity at a dinner, or special event, to transmit a message to season-ticket holders or supporters' clubs, but those formats don't offer a way to communicate with 75,000 people, let alone millions of fans scattered all over the world. Communicating through newspapers or on television programmes is fraught with peril. Publishers and broadcasters have their own agendas, so it is very easy for a message to get garbled or taken out of context. However, I knew that I could count on the match-day programme as a vehicle with which to convey messages to the people who came to watch us at Old Trafford.

At St Mirren, Stan Park, a local journalist for the *Paisley Daily Express*, would come in once a week, and I would tell him what I wanted to convey. He ghost-wrote my programme notes, but I would always proof-read them before they went to press to make sure Stan had captured the nuances. That routine seemed to work, so I followed this format at Aberdeen, where I sometimes used the programme notes to exhort the supporters to be more vocal. The running joke, which was a bit harsh, was that the crowd at Pittodrie sometimes made more noise unwrapping their sweetie papers than they did supporting the team.

At United I worked with David Meek, a reporter for the *Manchester Evening News*. Early in my tenure I tried to convey a sense of the possible at United, because when I arrived there was tremendous disaffection, not just with the performance that had the club second from bottom of the old Division One, but also at its ownership.

I used the programme notes to show that, at least on some issues, I sympathised with the supporters. For example, I felt that the ticket prices were too high and had conveyed precisely the same sentiment to Martin Edwards and the rest of the board. I also tried to inject a sense of intimacy, so that the notes weren't just about a recent performance or a new signing, but about the softer side of our club. Every now and again I'd pay tribute to a former player who had died, or to friends, like Douglas Smith, who founded and ran one of my first clubs, Drumchapel Amateurs, or Sean Fallon, Celtic's assistant manager. People don't want mundane recitals of the obvious. They want to read something different and learn about the unexpected.

While I was at Aberdeen I published my first book, *A Light in the North*. I wrote it as a way to supplement my income, but it was more a blow-by-blow description of my time at the club and was written in the wake of our 1985 League victory. The first book I paid real attention to was *Managing My Life*, which came out in 1999 after United won the Treble. I collaborated with Hugh McIlvanney on this work and I found it a cathartic experience. It was a busy period in my life and I found myself scribbling down thoughts and memories during spare moments. Eventually I handed Hugh over 200,000 words of notes, assembled on all sorts of different sheets of paper. He sorted them all out and wove them into prose, but I took great relish in – and derived a lot of consolation from – recounting my childhood years and relaying the tone of the setting and the era in which I was raised.

My most meaningful pieces of writing were probably the shortest – notes or letters written in reply to the correspondence that used to come pouring into the office. Remember, the majority of my managerial time was spent before the era of e-mail and texting, so a personal response came in the form of cards or letters. As the leader of United I felt that it was expected of me, depending on the occasion, to send condolence or congratulatory messages or just to thank people for suggestions they had sent to the office. And every year I send out about 2,000 Christmas cards. Some people might say: why not send that money to charity instead? It's a fair point, but my reason for sending these cards is to let people know that I am thinking of them. I like receiving Christmas cards for precisely the same reason.

Answering

There aren't many areas where I would claim that I've been under more pressure than other leaders, but dealing with the press might be the one. These days it is probably only the leaders of the world's biggest countries who find themselves in front of more microphones and cameras than the football manager of one of Europe's best football teams. It's funny how politicians, particularly when they are campaigning for office, are desperate for press coverage. There were many times when I pined for the opposite and wished that reporters would just leave me alone to concentrate on my job. If United won, we were on the back page of the newspapers. If we lost we wound up on the front pages.

It was one thing to deal with the press in Scotland. At East Stirlingshire in 1974, all I had to do was talk to a young reporter from the *Falkirk Herald*, whose circulation was only about 40,000. The stadium at Aberdeen didn't even have a dedicated press room. I used to have to give my post-game interviews in the foyer of the Pittodrie stadium.

Manchester United was another matter, because it attracted the local and national newspaper, television and radio reporters, and – in the past decade – the growing crowd of internet bloggers who would appear for the regular briefings at United, or the hundreds of international journalists who would come out of the woodwork before major games, and whose reports would almost instantly be transmitted to tens of millions of people all around the world. At Old Trafford they even have cameras, microphones and tape recorders in the players' tunnel, some of which feed the club's own demand for content for its website, TV channel, radio station, magazine and match-day programmes. After a regular game, I'd give three or four television interviews.

During my last few years at United, a comment at a press conference – or even a video taken surreptitiously on a mobile-phone camera at a private function – would quickly be relayed in newspapers and magazines, on Sky Sports News, in innumerable blogs and via an ever increasing number of apps. Here's just one example of how the world cannot get enough of football. Eric Cantona's infamous 'kung-fu' kick at Crystal Palace in 1995 has now garnered over two million views on YouTube. All this for an event that took place 20 years ago – before many of today's football fans were even born! – and ten years before YouTube was even founded.

I've long understood that the press gravitates to what's popular and what will sell newspapers or boost television ratings, even if what is published sometimes isn't closely related to reality. It's easier to get more readers and viewers when writing or talking about popular topics. The press isn't going to spend much time writing about a steelworker who lost his job or a wee guy in a call centre who was fired because of a recession. Those things don't mean a thing to the general public. Football does.

When I joined Rangers, the manager, Scot Symon, had no time for the press. He would not give them the time of day. On one occasion Rangers were playing Sparta Rotterdam in a European Cup tie, when thick fog obscured visibility. A journalist phoned to ask Scot whether the game would be played and he answered, 'No comment'. Imagine if you gave that answer today.

Ron Atkinson, my immediate predecessor at United, had a different approach. I think he spoke to the press every single day of the week, and probably on every single day of the year, because I bet he took telephone calls on Sundays. Ron also allowed the press near the players at the training ground. Ron is a big, outgoing character and he enjoyed the interaction with the press, but his approach was not my cup of tea. First, I would not have known what to talk about if I had met the press every day. I might have been able to say something about the weather or the wine that I had drunk the previous evening, but I would quickly have exhausted my supply of fresh material – at least as it related to United. There was also the bigger issue, which was that I didn't want to have the press in my hair every day, asking me to respond to all sorts of inane questions so that I would blurt out something colourful that they could use to create a story where none existed. I immediately eliminated all the daily briefings and, instead, limited my meetings with the press to the day before a game and immediately after the match. Eventually these sessions just became a waste of time after the more prominent journalists began to skip them as they went in search of the players instead. After a game at Tottenham in the early 2000s, I walked into the press conference and all the main journalists were in the tunnel trying to get hold of the players. There was a smattering of young wire reporters. It was a waste of time.

Encounters with the press, which come in many guises, are all about control. Complete control is easy when you're issuing a press release or a pre-recorded video, when you can edit every word and clip. It's more difficult to retain control during a press conference, or if you get ambushed at an airport when everyone is looking for a chink in your armour. The press are looking for the slightest of slips. The journalists are waiting for a verbal slip while the cameramen are like hunters, ready to snap the shutter as soon as you purse your lips or grimace.

The rulers of North Korea or Cuba may be able to control their press, but it is sheer fantasy to think that anyone in England is going to be able to do the same.

Jock Stein, the manager of Celtic and Scotland, had his own technique. He seemed to know everything about the journalists covering Celtic. He used to know the ones who had drink problems or were gambling too much. He knew all their failings and all their weaknesses. He understood who they were and they knew it. I'm sure that many of them thought twice before writing anything that might embarrass Jock.

While I developed friendships with some of the reporters who covered United – Glenn Gibbons, Bob Cass and Hugh McIlvanney – and came to trust a handful, I never had the easy rapport with the press that Jock developed. They frequently got under my skin, and every now and again I would lash out at one of them in response to something they had written. The reporters would usually blame it on their editors but, if you are the victim of a distorted account, that doesn't matter. I was always determined to communicate with the press on my own terms and, to the best of my ability, control the messages we wanted to disseminate. This revolved around answering questions or, more precisely, not answering questions. If reporters peppered me with questions about injuries or my Saturday line-up, I'd either change the subject or, depending on my mood, tell them it was none of their business. The journalists didn't own the press conferences. I did.

It is important to remember that the reporters are not always asking questions of their own. Frequently, they are planting topics suggested by others. Football reporters have close ties with many of the more important agents. They rely on them for morsels of information that the agents themselves have heard from the players they represent. So when an agent is eager to provoke a bidding war for one of his clients, it's easy for him to plant a question at a press conference by getting a friendly reporter to ask whether we were interested in a particular player.

When journalists or news organisations abused their power, I cut them off. There were always plenty of others eager to take their place. After a series of run-ins with the BBC, I refused to talk to any of their journalists or appear on any of their radio or television programmes for seven years. There were a few reporters who got my goat. Over the years I must have banned over 20 journalists who manufactured stories. I wasn't going to accept it – I would give them the chance to correct it; if they refused to do that, I refused them access. Even though he became a friend and I eventually trusted him, I banned Glenn Gibbons, a Scottish journalist who had grown up in the same area of Glasgow as my father, multiple times. Glenn would always try to appeal to my better instincts by saying, 'What would your dad think of you – banning a boy from the Cowcaddens?' Sometimes I found MUTV, United's own football channel, irritating, and there were some occasions when I just needed a breather and stopped giving interviews to MUTV for a week or two.

It's hard to control your emotions, especially if you've been going through a tough spell, or a player has done something daft that's embarrassed the team. I always tried to be aware of the fact that journalists and photographers would be paying as much attention to my body language as to my words. Paul Doherty, head of sports for Granada Television, told me to always rub my face before I gave a press conference so that I appeared bright and cheery and did not display a hint of tension. He had told me that I was showing too much concern at press conferences and instructed me to, 'Go in there emotionless, with no expression on your face. If you are straight as a die, it will kill them. They are all looking for a weakness.' I took that to heart and, before walking into a press conference, I always used to rub my face. However, to remain emotionless is a lot easier to say than to do, and I remember marvelling at the way President George W. Bush was able to maintain a completely impassive face after he was informed of the 9/11 attacks while sitting in front of a classroom of children and the Washington press corps. I don't think I could have pulled that off. No matter how hard I tried, my emotions and body language changed depending on the circumstances. If things had gone poorly, it was hard not to grimace or have pursed lips and, by contrast, when we had just thumped an opponent it was important not to appear too confident or smug. Either way, I was always aware that a confident air went a long way with the constituency that mattered the most – the players. I also always remembered another piece of advice that Paul Doherty gave me. He said, 'You have to walk out of every press conference unhurt.'

Once in a while I was so upset that I chose not to face the press for fear that I would say something about the referee or assistant referees that would get me into hot water with the authorities. When United lost the second leg of the Round of 16 Champions League tie against Real Madrid in March 2013 because of the bizarre decision of the referee, Cüneyt Çakir, to give Nani a red card for committing a foul on a player he didn't even see, I was beside myself. I knew that the journalists waiting for me in our press room would be like a hundred matadors waving red capes, and I was not about to risk charging at every single one of them. Instead, I sent Mick Phelan to deal with the ridiculous judgement of the referee. I knew on that particular night I would break my own rule and commit the cardinal mistake of actually answering the questions.

It is probably fortunate for me that I did not have to contend with social media for most of my career. The legions of fans following United on Twitter, Facebook or Instagram massively outnumber the fans tracking the club through the *Sun* or *Daily Mirror*. I would wager that younger managers might even start gradually bypassing the major newspapers, skipping the big, formal press conferences and just communicate directly with fans. They say you need a thick skin to deal with some of the abuse on Twitter, but – though it may come from many more quarters – beyond the foul language it isn't any worse than what a manager experiences from newspapers and the television pundits. At least the social networks provide a platform for precise control of the message that you want to communicate, and a way to answer questions, even if they sometimes provoke an unexpected backlash. No matter how savage the treatment in the press, no matter how many questions I didn't answer, I probably was harder on myself after we lost a game than any journalist. If I lost a game it affected me more than anyone else. The journalists could file their column and go to the pub. I had to figure out why we lost and set about fixing the problem.

In retirement, I have found myself watching the way other managers deal with press conferences. I love it, because I want to see where I can help. Every now and again I will phone one of them with some advice. Last season, when Leicester City was lodged at the bottom of the Premier League, I phoned the manager, Nigel Pearson, and told him that he looked too relaxed and over-confident. I told him that he had to show some concern without looking vulnerable. By contrast, when I talked to Sean Dyche, manager of Burnley, who also had a tough season, I tried to reassure him. Sean, who always had a bit of a wee joke with the interviewer, reiterated how hard his team was working, and – while not oblivious to where Burnley stood in the table – he managed to convey a feeling of confidence. Last season, I also took it upon myself to offer Alan Pardew some unsolicited advice before he left Newcastle United to take the helm at Crystal Palace. I asked him, 'What's happened to you? You don't argue with anybody any more. You've given in. You've chucked it. If you want to keep your job, start being Alan Pardew.' He phoned me up a couple of weeks later and said, 'Thanks.' He didn't need to. I know how difficult the job is. I am always happy to help a fellow manager.

9

LEADING NOT MANAGING

Owners

Authority, and the exercise of control, rests on possessing the confidence of those who provide it. No leader stands a chance if the people he is supposedly managing sense that his hold on his job is tenuous. In football the providers of this authority are the club owners. If they are unequivocal about their confidence in – and support of – the manager, they make his job a lot easier. When I applied for my first managerial job, the part-time role at East Stirlingshire, I was so eager to get my foot on the ladder that I didn't pay any attention to the condition of the club or the personalities who controlled the purse-strings. As the years went by, I quickly gained an appreciation of how important it is to understand the person, or people, to whom you have to report and are accountable.

Most of us don't think about the nature of our employer, or boss, or the tone and atmosphere they cultivate inside their organisation. That's really important in football, which is littered with bad owners. I cannot say enough about the benefits of a long-term, stable ownership that's prepared to make the necessary investments to create a vibrant organisation. It's a priceless foundation for management in any walk of life. I've read quite a lot about Warren Buffett and Berkshire Hathaway, and I imagine that the people heading his various companies all think much more about long-term prosperity than the CEO of a publicly listed company who is worried that the investment fund managers will be at his throat if he produces disappointing earnings in the next quarter. If you have owners, or shareholders, who only think about short-term results, it brings about a never-ending cycle of misery for everyone. That's especially true in football.

Football managers should look for their own modified version of Warren Buffett – people who care about the long term; who provide them with the money they need to build their team; who don't meddle in daily management; who are available when needed; and who understand that their job is only to make two decisions. The first is to replace the manager or CEO; the second is to sell the club. Unfortunately, these people are almost impossible to find in football, and the problem only seems to have been exacerbated by the way in which ownership, over the last 50 years, has gradually shifted from local businessmen to foreign oligarchs, sheikhs and hedge-fund managers, chasing their share of the television money that now floods the Premier League.

For their part, owners need to understand that football is different from the businesses they themselves run and where they have enjoyed success. The clubs aren't supermarket chains, banks or electronics wholesalers.

Football is live entertainment, conducted on a scale that has no parallel. You just cannot manufacture wins with the reliability with which you can produce phones or razor blades, because everything hinges on the performance of individuals and the random influences of emotion, chance and injury. Any owner also needs to be realistic. A devoted fan may come to the stadium for every game expecting a victory, but an owner has to be much more grounded.

Between the time I took over at Manchester United and my retirement in 2013, the 48 clubs that have occupied the remaining slots in the Premier League went through 267 permanent managers (not including caretaker roles). It makes you wonder why some clubs even bother to pay managers. At the start of the 2014–15 season, Arsène Wenger had managed almost as many Premier League games as all his fellow managers combined. The real title of the top football man in most Premier League clubs should be 'temporary manager'.

Chelsea ran through 13 full-time managers (not including caretakers) while I was at United, and Manchester City went through 14 (not including caretakers). It would not surprise me if Chelsea has paid as much as £40 million in settlement payments to fired managers. Chelsea and Manchester City have plenty of companions. The Premier League is littered with examples of poor hiring practices. Take Liverpool in 2010 after they sacked Rafael Benítez. The owners looked around and fastened on Roy Hodgson, who had just taken Fulham to the UEFA Cup final. Liverpool hired Roy and within six months they had fired him. I'm not sure it is any better in Europe. Bayern Munich made 14 changes of manager (not including caretakers) while I was at United, although several of the same men held the post on different occasions. It is all so silly, since there is no evidence that frequent sacking of a manager leads to better results.

Years ago there used to be much greater longevity among football managers – perhaps because the owners came from the surrounding communities and were more vested in the long-term success and stability of their club, rather than many of the people who own clubs today. United obviously had Matt Busby for 25 years between 1945 and 1969 (he returned to the club for 1970–71); Joe Harvey was manager of Newcastle for 13 years between 1962 and 1975; Arsenal had Herbert Chapman for 9 years between 1925 and 1934, and his successor, George Allison, was there for 13 years between 1934 and 1947. Scot Symon was at Rangers for 13 years (between 1954 and 1967) while, before him, Bill Struth held the job for an extraordinary 34 years (1920–54).

There's nothing more reassuring for a manager than to feel that he has the support of his boss. It's as true for young people taking their first job, who are at the bottom rung of an organisation, as it is for a leader wanting to know that he is backed by his board of directors. Your boss can make or break you. I learned that while I was at Aberdeen managing under Dick Donald. The greatest gift he gave me was unerring confidence in my capabilities.

This was particularly true in my first year at the club, when we had a bumpy time. I also had to deal with the legacy of the previous manager, Billy McNeill, who had left to manage Celtic and had been popular with the players. In March 1979 I was feeling pretty despondent after Rangers beat Aberdeen 2–1 in the Scottish League Cup final. A couple of the players had made no secret of the fact that they preferred my predecessor, and the local newspaper, *The Press and Journal*, had been questioning my credentials; I said as much to Dick. He just said, 'I hired you because you can do the job. I'm not interested in what the press say. You just get on with your job. Don't moan. Be a man.' It really lifted my spirits.

I received the same sort of support at United, particularly during my early years at the club before the trophies started to appear. In 1990 we travelled to Nottingham Forest in the FA

Cup and the match was billed as do-or-die for my career. The day before the game, Martin Edwards called me with a simple but much appreciated message, 'Whatever happens tomorrow, your job is safe.'

I was fortunate, at both Aberdeen and Manchester United, to have principal owners who had an abiding pride in their ownership of the clubs. At Aberdeen Dick Donald had been involved with the club from 1949, and became its chairman in 1970. He was not about to tolerate any other shareholders meddling in its affairs. His Annual General Meetings were almost always dispatched within three minutes; the longest extended to about seven minutes when a local businessman engaged in a bit of agitation. Even though Dick had played stints of professional football as a young man, he understood the dividing lines that separate owners from managers. I never felt that he wanted to show he knew more about football than me. That was an enormous blessing. The greatest bosses also take great pride in making sure that if employees who have served them well choose to leave, they go on to greater and better things. That was certainly the case with Dick Donald, because when, in 1986, I began to mention to him that I was thinking about leaving Aberdeen for the challenge of a larger club, he was emphatic that I should only contemplate one: Manchester United. This was well before I had any inkling that Manchester United were interested in me, but Dick's allusion to the club was not just characteristic of the man, but also bolstered my confidence. When I finally left Aberdeen, I knew that he didn't want me to go, but I also left with his blessing in my pocket – a priceless benediction.

Today, I tell managers who are casting about for a club to be sure they find a chairman who understands the complexities of their job. The greatest luxury any manager can obtain is sufficient time to either develop a club or turn things around. It takes years to implement your ideas and put your structure in place. If they are fortunate to find an owner who understands the job and is willing to give them time (and those people are rare human beings), they stand a chance. Otherwise, if they don't get results they will be sacked. Every football manager has been sacked. I was sacked – albeit not for football reasons – and José Mourinho, Arsène Wenger and Carlo Ancelotti have all been sacked. The only football manager who has not been sacked is the one who is two minutes into his first job.

There have been some really good owners of clubs but, unfortunately, they are in a distinct minority. The Cobbold family, who controlled Ipswich Town for many years, were gems. They were deeply rooted in the surrounding community and were brewers and pub owners. Both Alf Ramsey and Bobby Robson worked for them as Ipswich managers, for whom they must have been a godsend. Today there is a VIP club at Ipswich Town called the 'Cobbold Club', even though the family hasn't been involved for quite a long time. That speaks volumes. Most clubs would probably like to forget their former owners. Arsenal has also been blessed by owners with a long-term view. For many decades it was owned by a pair of families – the Bracewell-Smiths and Hill-Woods – and then David Dein (a shareholder and vice-chairman), who was responsible for attracting Arsène Wenger to Arsenal and was the club's driving force for a long time.

When I arrived at United, Martin Edwards was the chairman and largest shareholder. He had inherited the position and stake from his father, Louis Edwards, who himself had first bought control in the early 1970s.

As I noted earlier, Martin shared some of Dick Donald's traits. He did not feel impelled to demonstrate his knowledge of football. He was not confused about the difference between an owner and a manager and, on the whole, we got on well.

The Glazer family have taken a lot of flak during the time they have owned United. People have criticised them for paying vast sums in interest payments to the banks that loaned them the money to buy the club, and for the various fees that have been charged. Others have said that the reason United is once more a publicly traded company is so the Glazers can cash in on their investment. I used to get calls from the people running the various supporters' clubs asking for my backing in various campaigns to get rid of the Glazers. Whenever one of these efforts cranked into high gear, somebody would argue that if I announced my resignation as manager, the Glazers would be forced to sell the club. That never made any sense to me. I told the agitators, 'If I quit, do you think United is going to take the field on Saturday without a manager?'

While I was manager, the Glazers caused me no bother. It might surprise people but, from my perspective as a manager, they have been very good owners. A manager wants four things from the owner: no meddling; money when it is needed to buy a player; support; and fair compensation. When they bought the club, the Glazers said it was a long-term investment, and I took some consolation from the fact that, at the time, they had owned the Tampa Bay Buccaneers, the American football team, for a decade. After they took control, they did not come barrelling in with all guns blazing. It was quite the opposite. After they bought the club, nobody got fired. They valued continuity. There was not one change to any of the commercial or coaching staff and they never exerted any pressure on me regarding the squad or our results. That says a lot about their approach.

They never said 'no' or refused to do something that I cared about. I was also probably manna from heaven for them because I never asked for ridiculous amounts of money. When we signed Robin van Persie in 2012 for £24 million which, at the time, was the largest amount we had ever paid for a 29-year-old player, the only question the Glazers asked was about his age. It was a fair question because in 2008 we had bought Dimitar Berbatov from Tottenham for £30.75 million when he was 27 years old. Berbatov's stylish but languid approach did not work out at United, even though he scored 21 goals in 2010–11 and was joint top scorer in the League. In 2012 we sold him to Fulham for £3 million. So I could see why the Glazers had questions about Van Persie. It was entirely reasonable. But when a player of his calibre becomes available, you have to act.

If I was an aspiring football manager, or dreamed about running a big company, I'd take a very careful look at the composition of the ownership before accepting any job. The former chairman of Birmingham City, Carson Yeung, is – as I write – in jail. Former Manchester City owner Thaksin Shinawatra is in self-imposed exile and cannot return to Thailand. There are plenty of inept British owners too. It does not matter where they come from, these people breeze into football. If they buy a club at the bottom of the Premier League, they are all anxious to get a slice of the revenue from European football that accrues to the top sides; if they go fishing for a club in the lower divisions, they all dream of promotion to the Premier League.

Even the dimmest owner knows that if there is a dispute between an individual player and a manager, it is crazy for them to back the player. As soon as they do that, they have let anarchists into the club. Every now and again there will be an example of a manager who antagonises his entire squad, but that's very different. It has been reported that Paolo Di Canio got sacked by Sunderland in 2013 after a group of players marched into the chief executives' office, but there are not many examples like that. I always knew that, even if a player was stirred into a frenzy of self-pity by his agent, the owners would never side with him.

Most former players who decide they want to become managers are like I was when I joined East Stirlingshire. They are too desperate and willing to jump at any offer. They cannot stand waiting at home hoping that the phone will ring, and a period of unemployment can cause anyone to doubt themselves. But managers are invariably too anxious, getting themselves into a position where, on the day they sign their new contract, they are simultaneously signing their own death certificate. The turnover is preposterous. A housefly has a longer life expectancy than the manager of a Premier League team.

Despite this overwhelming evidence, eagerness and ambition often seem to triumph over cold facts. A couple of years ago Ole Gunnar Solskjaer, who was a great striker for United, and scored the winning goal in the 1999 Champions League final against Bayern Munich, was negotiating to become the manager of Cardiff City. After he had retired as a player, Ole had managed United's reserves and then returned to his native Norway to manage Molde, which he did most successfully. After a few seasons in Norway, Ole was pining to manage a Premier League club, and I read in the papers that he was in the finishing stages of discussions with Vincent Tan, the owner of Cardiff City, who had just fired Malky Mackay. I thought to myself, 'Surely he's not thinking about taking that job – it's bound to be a nightmare.' So I texted Ole and gave him some very firm advice. I told him, 'Tomorrow is the strongest you will ever be with the owner. So get everything, down to the smallest detail that could interfere with your management style, written into your contract.' Nine months later, the inevitable occurred and Tan decided that he would pick a new manager. The good news for Ole was that he had a watertight contract and his talent is bound to be recognised by a more appreciative owner.

Then there are victims of misfortune who suddenly find themselves reporting to new owners. That happened to Sam Allardyce at Blackburn Rovers after it was bought by the Rao family, owners of the V. H. Group, a company that operates chicken-processing farms in India. A few weeks after they bought the club, the new owners fired Allardyce, who had managed the club for two years. Even though he was forced to manage on a shoestring, Sam had always ensured Blackburn placed respectably in the Premier League. The Raos had brought in an agent, Jerome Anderson, as a consultant, fired Allardyce, and replaced him with his deputy, Steve Kean. Then, just to demonstrate their complete lack of understanding of football management, the Raos insisted that Kean, towards the end of his time at the club, had to fly out to board meetings in India. They fired Kean two years later and replaced him with a former United player, Henning Berg, who had called me after he had been offered the job. I warned him about the owners, but he was eager to get into the game after being fired by the Norwegian club, Lillestrøm. Fifty-seven days later, they fired him too, and were forced by the courts to pay him £2.2 million to buy out his contract.

There are also too many cases of managers who have contributed sterling service receiving terrible treatment from the owners they have served. Jock Stein served Celtic for 13 years and won 25 trophies for the club before retiring in 1978. It's hard to imagine a better leader than Jock. He didn't drink or smoke, never took any credit for himself and diverted all praise towards his players. After all this, the directors refused to offer him a board seat. Instead, they told him he could work in the Celtic shop. They did the same to his assistant, Sean Fallon, who had spent 28 years with the club. It was a shocking way to treat people who had given their all.

Every now and again I had assistant coaches who wanted to leave United because they knew I wasn't going anywhere – and I always told them to be very careful about where they chose to go. Steve McClaren had replaced Brian Kidd as my assistant at United but, after three years, was chomping at the bit and wanted to leave to manage a club. He had offers from West Ham and Southampton, but elected to go to Middlesbrough because of the reputation of the owner, Steve Gibson. He was young and prepared to invest in the club. Middlesbrough had a fantastic training ground and it all worked out well for McClaren. He picked the employer that was right for him. Steve's decision showed the value of taking time to assess the situation. He did his homework, he spent time assessing the club and, most importantly, he made a judgement about whether he would get the support he desired from the owner. It shows the value of taking sufficient time to make an important decision, rather than quickly hopping on to whatever lily pad happens to float by.

Control

The popular caricature of me is an authoritative tyrant with a lust for power. Not surprisingly, I beg to differ. I'll plead guilty to having a thirst for winning and being fixated on maintaining complete control but – in my book – those are requisites for effective leadership. The skipper of any ship incapable of controlling its course, or altering its speed, is not going to arrive safely in port. The same goes for a football club. A leader who seeks control is very different from one who craves power.

There's a big difference between control and power. The leader of any group usually has considerable power, but it's something that can be easily abused. One of the side-effects of the abuse of power is when someone leads by fear of intimidation. As time went by I learned to control my temper. Some of this was just the passage of the years but, more importantly, I realised that a display of temper is more effective if used sparingly. I just don't believe that you can get the most out of people if they are perpetually afraid of you.

There's nothing wrong with losing your temper for the right reasons but, if you explode at the slightest provocation, it can paralyse an organisation. When I lost my temper, the thunder-clouds would tend to blow over in a day or so. There were some players who wouldn't buckle when I delivered my so-called 'hairdryer treatments', but I'm sure there were plenty of others, particularly the younger ones, who quaked in their boots. Sometimes I didn't realise the effect that a few words from me might have on a player. People used to say that some players would be terrified if I so much as raised an eyebrow or just happened to look at them. I'm sure most leaders are not aware that they scare other people, especially if they rarely raise their voice or have never smashed a teacup on the floor. They probably think of themselves as reasonable and compassionate. Yet anyone who can raise a salary, or fire someone, is almost bound to be seen as intimidating or terrifying – or both. I'll also say, in my defence, that the press sometimes made it appear as if I was in a perpetual bad temper. If you look at all my teams it was evident that they enjoyed playing and they tended to express themselves in an uninhibited fashion. People do not do that if they are quaking in their boots or if their boss has made them afraid of their own shadows. If that had been the case at United, people would have seen a team that concentrated on avoiding defeat rather than winning.

I always thought of myself as tough but fair and found it hard to understand how anyone could view me as a monster but, as the years went by and United became ever more successful, I did gradually come to understood that a wink, a nod or a frown could play havoc with the confidence of a few of the players. In team talks I'd be careful not to single out any of the young players who were new to the squad, and would concentrate on the ones who could look me in the eye. When I knew for certain that a word from me, no matter how carefully phrased, would cause a player to have a sleepless night, I usually got somebody else like Mick Phelan, who eventually became United's assistant manager, to convey the message. Harsh outbursts and temper tantrums can, when used sparingly, have an effect, but it's a negative and corrosive way to run anything. It's far better to give people a belief in themselves, and faith in the direction of their organisation, than to rule like Attila the Hun.

At the same time I was always very careful that my control was not usurped. That explains why I sold players who tried to undermine my control. I hesitate to say this, because it will get wrongly interpreted as callousness, but everyone is disposable. Somebody once said, 'Graveyards are full of indispensable men,' and it's a phrase worth dwelling on.

The truth is, I just could not afford to have our club revolve around either the outlook or health of one or two people. It is just too risky. Let's assume for a moment that I had never had any management issues with a player and they were not causing me the slightest bother. Imagine instead they had sustained a terrible injury, which either sidelined them for a long time or ended their playing career. In that situation I would also have had to figure out a way to prosper without them. Fortunately, in all my time at United, I only had a handful of major issues with players. When we honoured our promise to Cristiano Ronaldo that he could fulfil his lifelong desire to play for Real Madrid, I had to deal with the issue of the loss of the best player in the world, and I had to rebuild and look to a future without him. I hated losing him, and I knew his absence would be noticeable and might make our strike force seem a little gap-toothed for a while, but I also knew that if I made the right decisions then the club would continue to flourish.

It's easy to think that control begins and ends with the person running the organisation. It doesn't. People sometimes talk about me as if I was a control freak, but I don't think of myself that way. It would be impossible to run an organisation like that. I certainly wanted to be in touch and know everything that was going on at the club and that affected my job, such as the observations from training sessions or reserve games, updates from the medical staff, news from the scouting side, the weather forecast for the next game and the condition of the pitch. But I couldn't run everything. I did not need to know what brand of detergent was used in the laundry or the style of font we used in the match-day programmes. Other people had to do that. I was the puppet master, not the control freak.

Delegation

Control and delegation are two sides of the same coin, and in my younger years my instinct was to try and control everything. I must have automatically assumed that if I did something myself it was the quickest and best way to get anything done.

Nobody had ever explained to me that working with, and through, others is by far the most effective way to do things – assuming, of course, that they understand what you want and are keen to follow. I gradually began to understand that this is the difference between management and leadership.

I never had any formal schooling to be a leader. Obviously, I'd paid attention to the way that managers acted during my days as a player but, in any football organisation, there aren't the decades-long programmes designed to produce a CEO like those at big companies such as General Electric or Goldman Sachs. No club is ever going to send an aspiring manager to an Executive MBA Program at Harvard or another business school. So I had to learn on the job and use my wits. I'd never managed a team of people, I didn't understand how working through other people allowed you to do more and amplified your reach.

The world is full of able managers. In life beyond football, corporate training schemes are designed to churn out managers by the thousand. At United we had plenty of people who could manage aspects of our activities far better than I could. The head groundsman knew far more about the technology of soil management and irrigation than I did. The doctors managed a realm whose subtleties I could not pretend to understand. The head of our youth academy knew far more than I about the abilities of each of the lads in the programme. I slowly came to understand that my job was different. It was to set very high standards. It was to help everyone else believe they could do things that they didn't think they were capable of. It was to chart a course that had not been pursued before. It was to make everyone understand that the impossible was possible. That's the difference between leadership and management.

When I started managing, my own naïveté was, to some

extent, exacerbated by the lack of resources at East Stirlingshire and St Mirren, the two Scottish clubs where I cut my teeth. There just wasn't a lot of money available to hire people. So I tried to do everything by myself. I thought I could rule the world. I was ordering the cleaning materials and grass feed, making sure we had the right quantity of pies for the games and fussing over the contents of the match-day programmes. I banned the long-time supporters from coming into the tea room to get free pies and Bovril and there was a real uproar about that. I was just acting on my instincts and what I thought was the right thing to do because I didn't know any better.

As I explained earlier, Archie Knox, my assistant manager at both Aberdeen and United, was the man who educated me about the benefits of delegation. When you're a manager, it's vital to care about the details but it's equally important to understand that there isn't enough time in the day to check on everything. Some managers are fanatics. When Johan Cruyff was managing Barcelona he'd be on the pitch the day before the game with a device to measure the moisture levels. He even insisted that the turf be clipped to a particular height. Later in my career – even when I had become much better at delegating – I would sometimes spot a detail like that. One of the things to which I always paid attention was the width of a pitch. Opponents knew that I liked wide pitches where we could outrun and outpace the competition. Once, when we were playing Manchester City at their former ground at Maine Road, I went to inspect the pitch early one morning and found the groundsman, under orders from management, was narrowing it, which is not something you are allowed to do after you have registered the dimensions with the Premier League at the start of the season. So I complained to the referee, got them to widen the pitch and we thrashed City 3–0.

These are exceptional examples. On the whole it is better to explain to the people around you that you care about little details, but that it's their job to attend to them.

When I hired someone to do something I trusted them to do it. I depended on them to get on with their job and come to me with any problems. At United that might have been the coaches or the scouts, but it was particularly true for the medical staff, sports scientists and video analysis crew. They all had the necessary training and technical background that was beyond me. I am not a doctor, dietician or computer whiz so, while it was up to me to make sure that we hired very capable people to run each of these departments, they had forgotten more about their specialties than I was ever going to know. If the doctor said that a player was not fit to take the field, I would not exert any pressure on them to change their opinion. A good number of the people in these departments started on the bottom rung of their respective ladders, but were promoted as they demonstrated their capabilities. Steve Brown was a young lad who started on a trial basis as a video analyst. He gradually progressed, flourished as he was given more responsibility, got successive pay raises and has become an essential part of that team.

As the business of football has grown, so too have the organisations. This has underlined the need for a football manager to delegate more widely and empower those around him. Nowadays all the big clubs have chief executive officers responsible for all commercial activities and making sure the books are in balance – or, for many clubs, not too far out of control. So I let David Gill worry about television contracts, securing sponsorships, finalising the niceties of player contracts, managing the finance and marketing organisations, dealing with auditors and lawyers, ensuring compliance with health and safety codes and all the laws and regulations that govern any organisation, let alone a place where 75,000 people congregate on a regular basis. I had quite enough on my hands managing the football side of the business.

There's one final example of the power of delegation that I always carried with me from early in my career. In 1972 I went down to Derby to watch a huge end of season game – Liverpool versus Derby County. Jock Stein had set me up with the tickets and Bill Shankly, the Liverpool manager, very kindly gave us a tour of the Derby boardroom. It was about 7.25 p.m. and it was a 7.30 kick-off and I asked Bill whether he should be with his players. He said, 'Son, if I've got to be with my players for the deciding game of the season, there's something wrong with them.'

When we walked into the tunnel all the players were lined up and one, Tommy Smith, the captain, was bouncing a ball on his head. Shankly said, 'Tommy, take them home, son. You know what to do.' That one sentence said everything about Shankly's style of leadership.

Decision-making

Effective delegation depends on the ability of others to make decisions. Some people can make decisions, others cannot. It just doesn't work if you are congenitally hesitant and allow things to linger in a state of suspension. When I was a player I had a couple of managers who always changed their mind. Bobby Brown at St Johnstone would pin a team-sheet on the board and, if somebody complained about the line-up, half an hour later a different team would replace it.

Men like Bobby Brown perhaps lacked the confidence

required to stick to decisions. Others are in a perpetual quest for the last possible morsel of information, using that as an excuse not to make a decision. When you are in the football world, and I suspect in almost every other setting, you have to make decisions with the information at your disposal, rather than what you wish you might have. I never had a problem reaching a decision based on imperfect information. That's just the way the world works.

During my time at United I got rid of several people who could not make decisions. I could never deal with people who were wishy-washy or whose judgement rested on the opinion of the last person they had talked to. They just made my life harder. When I arrived in Manchester in 1986, the chief scout was Tony Collins, who had previously occupied the same position during Don Revie's successful time as manager of Leeds United. Tony was a nice man but he just couldn't give me an opinion about a player. He always used to say, 'Go see him yourself,' or 'You go and watch him.' I replaced him the next summer with Les Kershaw, one of my best ever signings.

Some characters are more suited to being second in command rather than the leader. That isn't a criticism, although it may be interpreted in that manner. I would have been a terrible number two because there is a part of my personality that needs to be the leader. It takes considerable skill to be content as a second fiddle because, even though you may work just as hard as the leader, you will never receive the same praise or financial rewards. Brian Kidd was my assistant manager for seven years, and excelled in that role. He then tried his hand as a manager, which was a taxing experience for him, and has flourished, particularly at Manchester City, as the essential assistant manager.

There is also the question of when you should make a

decision. There are probably only two times to do so – too early and too late. If I was going to err on making one of those mistakes, I far preferred to make the decision earlier rather than later. That's much easier to say than to do. After all, it wasn't until I was approaching 50, in 1990, that I fully appreciated this. I was in my fourth season at United when I finally ripped up the team – something, in retrospect, I should have done several seasons earlier.

If people wobble when making decisions about others, they can be even worse when it comes to making decisions about themselves, because these so often involve emotion and cloudy judgement. In football guys are forever taking jobs that are losing propositions. When Carlos Queiroz left United the second time in 2008 to manage Portugal, I told him he was crazy. I said, 'You're going to be judged on just two things – whether you can win the World Cup or European Championship, and tell me again: when did Portugal win the World Cup?' But Carlos's heart was set on managing his country and so he did so. It was a bad decision and turned into a disaster for him. If he had not returned to his homeland he could well have succeeded me as United's manager.

When I was young I made many more impulsive decisions than in my later years.

At St Mirren I remember taking off Billy Stark, a midfielder, after about seven minutes of play. It was a daft move. Unless he has been booked, injured and about to be arrested for burglary, it is silly to remove a player after less than 10 per cent of a game has been played, given that you obviously thought he was good enough to start a few minutes earlier. It turned out that in that game I badly needed Billy. Decades later, when United trailed West Ham 2–0, I was, as I mentioned previously, much more careful. I had started the game with Patrice Evra at left-back, but he had been on international duty and it showed. I waited until half-time, took off Evra, moved Giggs to left-back and we fought back to win the game 4–2.

I also made some ill-considered decisions when we bought and sold players that I came to regret. As I explained earlier, in 2001 we sold the Dutch defender Jaap Stam to Lazio for several million more than we had paid for him in 1998. Stam was 29 at the time, had just returned from injury and we were being offered a fat packet for him. So I sold him in a blink. Six years later he was still playing for Ajax with a Champions League final appearance for AC Milan along the way. In 2010 we bought the Portuguese winger, Bébé, even though we had not done our normal level of homework. Bébé struggled at United, never became part of the furniture and, after putting him out on loan several times, we eventually sold him.

There were some occasions where hesitancy cost me. After we signed Carlos Tévez, the Argentinian striker, from West Ham on a loan deal in 2007, we started to think about putting him on a long-term contract. Unfortunately, Tévez did not control his own destiny, because his rights – under the perverse system of third-party ownership – were controlled by third parties. This complicated any negotiations, but the real reason he eluded our grasp was because I was unsure whether I wanted him. Before Christmas 2008 we could probably have bought him for around £25.5 million, but I wanted to see how he fared in some more games. By the time I had decided, it was too late, because Manchester City had arrived with an offer for what was said to be £47 million.

I tried not to waste too much energy thinking about why, or how, other managers made decisions. There just was not enough time in the day, and it is hard to second-guess some-body's decision if you haven't been privy to their debates or are unfamiliar with the nuances of their situation. I experienced this myself throughout my career. For example, when I sold Ince, Hughes and Kanchelskis in 1995 I received a lot of criticism from people who were unaware that a hugely talented group of young players were about to emerge. Every now and again I would be perplexed if a top-tier club signed a player we had rejected and, sometimes, while privately cursing, I would admire a smart decision made by a fellow manager, especially if he had beaten us to the punch. Either way, nothing beats the lessons on decision-making imparted by the accounts of the way in which JFK handled the decisions surrounding the Cuban Missile Crisis – his calmness, his refusal to bow to pressure (whether from within or without), his willingness to contend with imperfect information while being under enormous pressure and relentless press coverage – puts everything else in perspective. Making decisions that send 75,000 people home happy at the end of a Saturday afternoon is one thing. Saving hundreds of millions from a nuclear war is another.

10

THE BOTTOM LINE

Buying

A big part of running a successful organisation is being able to convince people to join you, even if they can earn more money elsewhere. That challenge is accentuated in the Premier League because, unlike in other sports such as American football, there is no limit to the salary a club can award a player. This makes it really important for a manager and the scouting organisation to be able to sell the virtues of his club. Even at a club like Manchester United, where eventually we had access to huge transfer sums, we never wanted to get into the position where the size of our chequebook was the only route to success. It is just too risky, since there is always someone who appears with a larger pot of money.

People don't think of a football manager as a salesman. But he is. When we were trying to sign Paul Gascoigne in the summer of 1988, I pitched for my life. I went down to London and met him at his lawyer's house and argued that if he chose to go elsewhere he would be thinking in 20 years that he had made a huge mistake. Since Paul was from Newcastle, I also played up the fact that United teemed with Geordies such as

Bobby Charlton, Steve Bruce and Bryan Robson. I thought these appeals had worked, and then was floored to learn that he had chosen to go to Tottenham after the club bought his mother a house in Gateshead. But Gascoigne was an exception; we usually landed the players we really wanted.

Any leader is a salesman – and he has to sell to the inside of his organisation and to the outside. Anyone who aspires to be a great leader needs to excel at selling his ideas and aspirations to others. Sometimes you have to persuade people to do things they don't want to do, or to sell them on the idea that they can achieve something they had not dreamed about. Usually, this is to people who are already on the payroll. But then there is the challenge of reaching out to people who are not part of the system. In United's case, this meant three main constituencies: potential fans, possible sponsors and potential players – especially youngsters. The commercial side of United took care of the first two, while I was responsible for the third. This meant that part of my job was acting like a sales manager in a company.

Football's version of a field sales team is its scouting system. I built two of these organisations – one at Aberdeen and one at Manchester United. We incentivised the scouts like salesmen: they had a small base stipend and various bonuses if a player they spotted progressed through our system. We gave them specific territories and school teams to cover, and they understood what I was looking for in young players. Like a sales manager, I wanted to approve the terms of each 'sale', because I didn't want them signing players willy-nilly, lest I wound up with six goalkeepers, seven centre-backs and four left-wingers. The first week I was at United, I called a meeting with all the scouts and said, 'I'm not interested in the best boy in your street. I want to know about the best boy in your area. That's who I want.'

Like all sales organisations, our scouting system had people who were better than others. It requires real talent to see something that is unpolished and imagine it as a shiny gem that fits within a tiara. The star scout at Manchester United was Bob Bishop, who was responsible for covering Belfast. He was like a pied piper. He was the scout best known for spotting and signing George Best, but he spotted a raft of good players.

When I was young I picked up some selling tricks from watching other scouts. Bobby Calder was a scout from Aberdeen who I first met when he tried to sign my brother, Martin. He came to our house and brought my mother a box of chocolates, my father a carton of cigarettes and gave me a ten-bob note. Bobby wore a wee pork-pie hat and used to sit like a little, gentle angel. Later, when I was managing Aberdeen, he and I went to try and sign John Hewitt, a boy at a local school whom Manchester United, Celtic and Rangers all wanted to sign. We met with his parents and I went into a big sales pitch about what I was trying to do for Aberdeen and how it was going to be a big club. As we were leaving, Bobby said to the player's mother, 'Mrs Hewitt, I'll come up tomorrow and tell you the true story about the silver city by the sea.' I was furious with him. I thought he was going to screw up our chances. But he was right, and he taught me a very valuable sales lesson. He taught me to identify the decision-makers who influence any sale. In the case of young players, it isn't the player. It also isn't the father because, generally, he only wants to live vicariously through his son. The decision-maker is the mother. The mother wants to know what's going to be best for her son. After that experience, I always told scouts to concentrate on the mothers.

Our pursuit of David Beckham might have demanded a bit more effort than our quest for other youngsters, but, on the whole, it was fairly characteristic. Malcolm Fidgeon, who scouted for us in London, spotted him when he was 12 years old. It helped that David's father had been a diehard United fan and that David had inherited this zeal. But it was also obvious that other clubs would be pursuing him, particularly Tottenham. So we kept very close tabs on him. I got to know David's parents and siblings, partly because it pays to understand someone's background, but also as a way to ensure that they felt we cared about their son. We invited David to Manchester, he attended summer training sessions and we would send him United kit; we invited him into the first-team dressing room when we were playing in London. It made him, and his entire family, feel that we cared – and we did.

If you work for any successful organisation, it's easy to get sloppy and complacent with sales. When I got to United they took it for granted that any young boy in Manchester would migrate towards them, but instead they were going to Manchester City. Even Ryan Giggs was training at Manchester City. You cannot expect to triumph if you expect the world's most gifted to be standing outside your door with a job application form in their hand. The world doesn't work like that. You have to go and hunt for talent. At times, while our scouts would be scouring fields on weekends looking for the most talented young players, I would try to make the first overture to a player, or to his agent, who was part of another club, because the player obviously wants to measure the enthusiasm of his potential manager. When it came time to hammer out terms, I would turn things over to David Gill. This worked well for everyone because it kept me away from some of the tougher conversations that could potentially taint a relationship with a player.

Frugality

Throwing money at a problem has never produced a solution for me. From time to time it might provide a short-term fix – such as the excitement brought by Robin van Persie in 2012 when he was added to our striking line-up, but I cannot think of a single example in football where an open chequebook turned a club into a long-term winner. We also added a lot of fizz to the club with the arrival of Eric Cantona in 1992 – but he only cost us £900,000. Money doesn't suddenly create a club with breadth and depth; it doesn't provide a lineage and history; it doesn't fill stadiums with fans prepared to endure icy rain, and it doesn't make young boys dream.

While I enjoy a flutter on the horses, I have always had an aversion to wasting money. It drove me mad when players got into the habit of regularly exchanging their shirts with opponents or sending them to relatives and friends. Each of those shirts was expensive, and the club had to pay for new ones after exhausting the stock supplied by the sponsor. About six years before I retired, Albert Morgan, our kit man, told me we were going through several hundred strips a season. Most of these shirts wound up in the hands of souvenir traders or, these days, on eBay. I told the players they could keep swapping shirts but that they would have to pay for them out of their own pocket.

The sceptics might point at some of my signings and say that I squandered money. The examples usually trotted out are Dimitar Berbatov, whom we bought for £30.75 million from Tottenham, of which we recouped only about 10 per cent when he was sold to Fulham; Juan Sebastián Verón, bought for £24 million, went for £15 million, and poor Louis Saha, a striker dogged by injuries, was sold for virtually nothing even though we had bought him for £12.4 million. However, if you take a closer look at all of my signings – over many years – the money was well spent. Even the very worst are not in the same postal code as some of the biggest blunders in the Premier League, such as the £50 million that Chelsea impulsively paid for Fernando Torres in 2011, which turned into a handful of dust when they traded him in 2015 to Atlético Madrid.

Some of my churlishness about spending comes from my upbringing. My parents made sure that my brother and I never wanted for anything, but there wasn't a lot of spare money sloshing about our tenement flat in Govan. The same was true when I became a player and a manager. Put it down to my Scottish roots, but I always tried to treat club money as if it were my own.

My first salary as a footballer came at Dunfermline in 1964, as my first club Queen's Park had an amateur status, so there were no wages. During my time at Dunfermline, I was on £28 a week (about £524 in today's money), but because I quit my job as a tool-maker, my guaranteed weekly income dropped from £41, because I lost my £13 a week tool-maker's pay packet, so it was very important to me to get bonus money for wins. When I went to Rangers I was paid £60 (£998) in the summer and £80 (£1,331) during the playing season. When I joined St Mirren as its manager, our first home game was against Hamilton, and we played in front of a crowd of 3,000 in a ground that could house 25,000. Everything about the club was run down. The players, who were part-time, were paid £12 a week during the season and £7 during the summer while the club was in the Scottish second division.

At Aberdeen, the owner, Dick Donald, would keep a close eye on all outlays. He wanted to own a successful club, but was happy with a successful small club, and was always insistent that Aberdeen should operate in the black. He had no tolerance for red ink. He always wore the same tie and he also refused to buy new shoelaces. When one got frayed and snapped he'd just knot it back together. When Aberdeen reached the Scottish League Cup final in 1984, I realised that nobody had ordered any champagne, and so I phoned the club secretary, Ian Taggart, to make sure we took eight cases on the bus (most clubs would order about 20). Taggart panicked and said, 'I can't. Mr Donald will go off his head.' Donald saw the cases and Taggart had to tell him that only two were going on the bus while the rest were going into stores. We ended up hiding the extra champagne in the bus toilet and, on the journey home, after the Cup had been won and the champagne was flowing, Dick turned to me and said: 'Mr Ferguson, how many cups did we win today?'

If I wanted to buy a new left-winger, he'd say, 'Don't we have another left-winger?' And I'd answer, 'Yes, but he's only sixteen and he's barely good enough to play in the reserve team.' He'd always be grumbling about the wages and bonuses I'd award the players and he'd ask, 'Why do you keep giving them raises?' And I'd answer, 'Mr Chairman, we're in the world of football. You don't go down the way, you go up the way, and the only way you're going to keep your best players is by giving them big bonuses when they win things.' Dick was afraid of complacency creeping in and, before the one final, he said, only half-jokingly, 'It wouldn't be a bad idea if we lost this game so the players don't get too big for their boots.' He used to say, 'I never want to see the colour red in this football club's finances.' The most I spent at Aberdeen was £300,000 in 1985 for Jim Bett, and we used the sale of a player to defray part of that cost.

Oddly enough my frugality was part of the reason I got offered the United job. In one of my first sessions with Martin

Edwards, when we were discussing the importance of developing our own pipeline of talented youngsters, I said to him, 'I've never been a buying manager.' He said, 'That's one of the things we thought about when we decided to go for you.' I cannot believe it's attractive to any employer to think he is hiring a big spender.

When I wanted to buy my first player at United, I could only get about £1 million from Martin. All the money had to come from the sale of season tickets or game tickets, or from the transfer of other players. There was no sugar daddy with more money than sense, ploughing money into the club. The very first player I bought was Viv Anderson – a defender. We bought him for £250,000 and then we bought Brian McClair for £850,000. After we did a fire sale of six players – including Jesper Olsen, Gordon Strachan and Paul McGrath – in 1989 I spent about £8 million on five players – the most expensive of whom was the defender, Gary Pallister.

It took about £60 million to build the squad that took United through the 1990s and culminated in our Treble – the League championship, the FA Cup and the Champions League – in 1999. It took just over £320 million in transfer fees to furnish us with the firepower required to compete at the highest of levels for the following decade – but those are only the outlays and do not take into account that over £256 million was received from the sale of players. My largest signing between the time I joined United in 1986 and 2008 was the £29 million we paid for Rio Ferdinand, then aged 23, when we bought him from Leeds United in 2002. Rio then played 12 seasons and 455 games for United and 54 games for England (during his time at United), before moving to Queens Park Rangers a year after I retired. Even though Rio's price was out of the ordinary, it was very good value. Amortised over the time that he was at United, Rio's transfer fee cost the club about £2.5 million per year. But it is also worth bearing in mind his cost was largely offset by the £25 million we received from Real Madrid in 2003 when we sold David Beckham, who had cost us nothing.

Beyond Rio, we built our defence on virtually nothing – £5.5 million for Patrice Evra and £7.5 million for Nemanja Vidić, both of whom we signed in 2006. We signed Rafael da Silva and his brother, Fábio, in 2008, before either of them had turned professional. We solved the goalkeeping problems that had plagued me for six years following the departure of Peter Schmeichel, with the signing of Edwin van der Sar from Fulham in 2005. Van der Sar was 34 years old when we signed him for £2 million. Compare that to the sum spent by Chelsea in the same period. Between the time we signed them and my retirement, Evra, Vidić, the Da Silvas and Van der Sar played a total of 1,049 games for United.

When I was thinking about buying a player, I'd always be assessing his speed, balance and technique. But I also always wanted to know about his reliability. It's one thing to buy a player who is available for selection every week. It's quite another to fork out a king's ransom for someone who is injured every third game. There's no point in buying that player.

Our emphasis on youth produced two things: the pipeline of talent for the first team, and a very healthy sideline business. In my time as United's manager we raised well over £100 million from the sale of players, spotted as youngsters and developed through our youth system. This includes not only the likes of Beckham and Butt but also Gérard Piqué and Giuseppe Rossi who were brought into our academy from overseas. We had spotted them, developed them, and wanted to be paid for our efforts, particularly since most were capable of playing very high

259

quality football for ten to 15 years. Fraizer Campbell, Robbie Brady, Ryan Shawcross, Danny Higginbotham, David Healy and John Curtis are just a few examples of the youngsters who left United to go and play elsewhere. If a lad looked promising at one of our Schools of Excellence, it created little financial risk for us if we signed him. We signed Keith Gillespie as a 16 year old and he played a handful of games at United before we received £1 million for him as part of the deal that brought Andy Cole to Old Trafford. The biggest risk was that we had erred in our assessment of a particular boy and could have used his slot to work with a more talented youngster. We had to wait a little longer to see the real potential in some boys, because not everyone's physique develops at the same rate. If we elected to sell them, we were hard-nosed about negotiations.

If these boys progressed through various levels and eventually got into the youth team or, better still, the reserve team, we had a variety of options. The best players, like Danny Welbeck and Adnan Januzaj, had the talent to make the leap from the youth team to the first-team squad, but the jury usually remained out on the rest of them. It takes until the age of 20 or 21 before you know for certain whether some players will make the grade. If we were still uncertain, we put them out on loan to another club so that they could get blooded in a first team. We did that with Tom Cleverley, lending him to Watford, Wigan, and Leicester City. We lent Jonny Evans to Royal Antwerp and Sunderland twice and Welbeck to Preston and Sunderland. Sometimes it didn't produce the results we hoped for, such as when we lent Giuseppe Rossi to Newcastle and Parma or Federico Macheda to Sampdoria and Queens Park Rangers. They played so few games, their development was halted.

On occasion we might have waited too long before we sold a player who was not going to make the grade yet, or whose value tumbled due to injury. There were only a couple, such as James Chester, on whom we might have lost money. James had a number of knee injuries over a long period, and we ended up selling him to Hull City for £300,000 in 2011. He went on to play over 170 games in the next four and a half seasons and turned out to be an absolute steal.

We were always on the lookout for bargains but, in football, as in life, you get what you pay for. Unless there is an element of luck as there was with Eric Cantona, who we signed after Leeds United had approached us to buy Denis Irwin. The same was true of Peter Schmeichel who was somehow still playing for Brøndby at 28. I still can't believe a big club hadn't bought him. In 2008, a friend of Carlos Queiroz was scouting for us (for free) in Angola and happened upon Manucho. We gave him a try-out and he had a good left foot. We signed him for £250,000, because it was such a small sum, and when it became clear he did not possess the necessary talent, we sold him to Real Valladolid for £2.5 million.

Some clubs – Real Madrid and Manchester City come to mind – have used the chequebook to build a winning team. Real Madrid have long paid big sums to buy wonderfully talented players, the 'Galacticos', at the peak of their careers – Zinedine Zidane, Luís Figo, Kaká, Cristiano Ronaldo, Gareth Bale and James Rodríguez. It has worked for them, which just shows that there is more than one way to go about things. However, my upbringing always inclined me towards building rather than buying. I suppose I was more of what my son Mark, in his line of work, would call a 'value investor'.

I always liked the idea of signing talented players who were in the twilight of their careers. We didn't expect to keep them on the books for a long time, but we knew that, from time to time, we could land a player for a negligible amount of money who could help us fill a need. We signed Laurent Blanc from Inter Milan in 2001 as a free transfer. Blanc was 35 years old, but he was an accomplished and experienced player and we needed a backup in the defensive part of the squad. We used a similar tactic when we signed Michael Owen, the former England striker, in 2009, to add occasional spark to our attack. He had trained as a boy in the United system and was available on a free transfer. So I invited him to my house, made a proposal where he would be paid on a performance basis, and he was over the moon. Even though he was dogged by injuries, it worked out well for Michael because he scored the equalising goal during the first time he appeared at Wembley as a player in a Cup final, when we beat Aston Villa for the League Cup in 2010, and the following year he got a Premier League title medal, his first in 13 years of playing in the top ranks.

We made one exception to our rule about keeping an eye on the bottom line, and that was when it came time to sell players who had done sterling duty for the club. They might have played for ten or more years and reached the point where they were getting injured, unable to maintain a regular place in the first team and could count the seasons that they might still hope to play football on the fingers of one hand. In these cases we leaned over backwards to try and help them on their way by either offering free transfers (so that the acquiring club could justify giving them a larger wage packet), or a testimonial game, or both. The only one that did really well after he left us was Phil Neville, whom we sold to Everton for just over £3 million. In retrospect it was a great deal for Everton because we could clearly have got more for Phil; we also did not antici-pate that he would continue to play for another eight years. Players like Denis Irwin, Steve Bruce, Mick Phelan and Brian McClair were all given free transfers. When Peter Schmeichel wanted to quit we allowed him to go on a free transfer with the one condition that he should not play for an English club. He went off to Sporting Lisbon, but within a couple of years he returned to England to play for Aston Villa and then went to Manchester City. We did not question either move, although we would have been perfectly within our rights to do so. Treating players like this was just the right thing to do.

Compensation

I'm sure nobody thinks of football managers as pricing experts. Pricing is usually considered the realm of brand managers, who decide how much a tube of toothpaste or bottle of vodka should sell for. It's true that, unless I got complaints from fans, I didn't worry about the price of season tickets or merchandise, but I did spend a lot of time dealing with the pricing of players – how much we would be prepared to buy them for and what salaries we'd be prepared to offer.

When you see the large sums paid for players headlined in the newspapers, it's tempting to assume that football clubs spend money willy-nilly. That's only true for a handful – those controlled by owners or ownership groups for whom money is no object. In Europe, that list has been limited to Chelsea, Manchester City and Paris Saint-Germain (PSG). For almost every other club, even in the top leagues, money and budgets matter, and for clubs like Peterborough United, a League One club in the east of England who were managed by my son, Darren, every penny counts. I just don't think you can buy success. You have to earn it.

There's never been as much money in Scottish football as in English; early on in my career I got used to making the most from a little. I happen to think that's a useful discipline for any business or organisation, because it's so easy to waste money. Also, I have always had to answer to owners who wanted to know how their money was going to be spent.

At Aberdeen, I had a cavalcade of players, starting with the captain, Willie Miller, coming into my office demanding pay hikes. The best wages were between £250–£300 a week and Miller wanted £350. Dick Donald, the chairman, wanted to sell him, but I persuaded him that this would only start an exodus. Then his team-mate Alex McLeish showed up with his wife and eventually I got him to accept a £50 rise. Finally, Doug Rougvie appeared, and I told him, 'Doug, I've got this big cake and there's a cherry on the top. Willie Miller is taking three-quarters of it and the cherry. I have a quarter of the cake left for everyone; what do you want me to do?' He was dissatisfied with our offer so we let him go to Chelsea.

As the decades ticked by, pay became more of a topic in football – at least for the press, in the main because of the huge escalation in the gap between an ordinary worker's weekly 'wages' and the salaries amounting to tens of thousands of pounds per week that were now being paid out to top football players.

'Wages', or a 'pay packet' was what we usually called our compensation when I started as a player. This term was not a coincidence because, at the time, almost every player came from a working-class background. The father of Stanley Matthews, then the best-known player in England, was a boxer. Bobby Charlton comes from Ashington, a mining town in the north of England. When I signed for St Johnstone, the fathers of the other players all had working-class jobs. In Britain, football was the sport adopted by the working class, played by young men from working-class families, and this was reflected in the employment terms. If I had not been a footballer, I would probably have been a tool-maker and my team-mates would have worked in the nearby shipyards, steel mills or car factories.

There were more than a few vestiges of *Upstairs, Downstairs* in the way that players were paid. Until 1961, the Football League had put a maximum limit on a player's weekly wage which, at the time, during the playing season, was £20. Understandably the players, who were little more than indentured servants, felt abused and underpaid. There were no negotiations over pay. You took what the manager offered and, frequently, this meant one rate that applied during the season and another – either a lower rate, or no pay whatsoever – during the summer. Any player who took issue with his wages was likely to be sidelined. It was one thing to stage a strike at a factory when the machines would be sitting there on your return, it was quite another to miss a game that would never be played again. Even after the rules, on both wages and the freedom of transfer between clubs, were loosened at the start of the 1960s, some clubs, including Manchester United, tried to enforce an unofficial lid on wages. Eventually, though, market forces prevailed.

I don't mean to suggest that players were indifferent about their pay, or that it was entirely uniform, but in an era that did not include lawyers, agents, accountants, business managers and publicists, it was not the subject of much debate or rancour. Before the Bosman ruling, clubs had all the power. It was primitive. Strikers used to get paid more than defenders and the club captain would usually receive a bit more than everyone else. When I signed for Queen's Park in 1957, it was an amateur club, so I did not receive a wage. At the peak of my playing career between 1967 and 1973, this had risen to £80 a week, and in my last season at Ayr United, I got £60.

Though these days the numbers have more zeroes attached to them than 50 years ago, human nature has not changed much. Like other people, the players of my youth wanted to be paid what they were worth. Throughout my management career I always felt that there was a happy medium. Obviously the club did not want to be taken to the cleaners by some preposterous demand but, on the other hand, I always felt we should be paying players what they deserved. I know it sounds simple, but I found that, if you adhere to that approach, things work out fine.

When I got to Aberdeen the players were being paid £120 a week, which I thought was too low, so I got their wages raised. (Bear in mind the first £100-per-week player was the England and Fulham captain, Johnny Haynes, who had reached that level in 1961.) Beyond the normal haggling, the first time I had to confront serious compensation issues was after Aberdeen won the European Cup Winners' Cup in 1983 by beating Real Madrid. This was, in a way, both the best and worst thing that happened to the club, because it shone a spotlight on the players. The players all wanted more money and every other club wanted to sign them. So within two years we had lost half the team to bigger clubs offering them far more money. We upped the salaries of our best players to £350 a week, adding bonuses for wins or League and Cup victories. Dick Donald was always guarded about using all our money to pay the first team and forgetting about everyone else. He was always eager to make sure we were paying the younger players properly.

I didn't begrudge the players a single penny. In fact, I think the best footballers are underpaid. That might seem ridiculous to someone who is working as a car mechanic or as a nurse, but I look at the topic differently. Players good enough to turn out for any team in the upper echelon of the Champions League have outshone tens of thousands of lads who would give their eyeteeth for the same opportunity. They are talented enough to entertain people all over the world – usually in numbers that dwarf the audiences attracted by music or film stars, and certainly larger than those following other sports.

One by-product of the Premier League compensation system is that bonuses have more or less died out. Top players may get a bonus if they win the League or one of the big European competitions, but the complex, multi-page bonus systems, which used to compensate players for each appearance, or each victory or goals scored, have died out in the upper echelons of the game. While nobody complains about extra money, a financial bonus does not offer the same incentive to top players as it did 25 years ago. The more powerful incentives are to appeal to their competitive instinct, the pride they have in their profession and the prospect of a winner's medal. Bonuses get spent. Medals are for ever.

When lined up against the annual compensation for people who run hedge funds, players like Cristiano Ronaldo and Lionel Messi seem woefully undercompensated. I read recently that the top 25 hedge-fund managers got paid almost £7.5 billion in 2014 – more than the combined payroll of the Premier League, Bundesliga, La Liga and Serie A, and that seems even more preposterous when you learn that many of them recorded worse returns than the stock market.

If a footballer's performance lags for any prolonged period, he finds himself on the bench or put up for transfer. The inequity seems even more pronounced when you consider that, compared to other people, a footballer's peak earning years are very abbreviated – usually about six years and almost always fewer than ten. Don't tell me that some 28 year old who can manipulate a spreadsheet (of which there are hundreds of thousands, maybe millions) deserves to be paid more than a midfielder playing for Swansea City or Southampton.

Every now and again players would get peeved when they read about one of their team-mate's contracts. Some, like Gary Neville or Paul Scholes, didn't pay any attention to what others got paid because they trusted us to compensate them fairly. Even towards the end of their careers, when Gary, Paul and Ryan Giggs were all on one-year contracts, it did not bother them. They were realists and knew we would treat them right. However, others got irked and I understand why. It doesn't matter if the compensation scheme is denominated in hundreds of thousands of pounds per week or in bags of potato crisps. It's all a matter of relative worth, because a lot of people either feel, or want to feel, that they are more valuable than anyone else.

Sometimes a player would be in a particularly strong position and know it. I encountered this with Ruud van Nistelrooy in 2003 after his first couple of spectacular seasons with United. He managed to negotiate a clause in his contract where he would have been allowed to go to Real Madrid if they offered a certain amount of money. This put him in the driver's seat and was not something we repeated. Eventually we let him go to Real Madrid, but he was one of only a tiny number of players who wanted to leave United. When he did leave, after we had enjoyed his services and goals for years, he was 30 and we received most of our initial outlay back.

I had a sharper pencil when negotiating contracts with players than I did for myself. Some leaders don't have much compunction about feathering their own nests at every opportunity. Others are too bashful about pressing to be paid what they are worth. I probably fell between those poles, particularly when the larger sums of money started to flow into football in the

1990s. Perhaps I am wrong, but I have noticed that leaders are sometimes so busy running an organisation that they do not take care of themselves properly. They will invariably not eat, sleep or exercise properly, but they also get into the habit of neglecting the management of their own financial affairs. They will spend tons of time working out remuneration details for others, and just a tiny fraction of that time on their personal arrangements. They are not careful enough about the terms of their own contracts and, if they are lucky enough to salt away some money, they will always have a tough time figuring out how to manage it properly. Maybe it is just because the best leaders tend to be missionaries rather than mercenaries.

When I started at Aberdeen I was paid £12,000 a year, or the equivalent of about £65,000 today, and in my last year in Scotland I was making £25,000, with a good bonus structure. I made a little more money on the side by doing some news-paper columns and public speaking, but it would not have bought many cases of wine. This was at a time when the highest-paid player in the team was on £15,000 a year, and sponsorship deals were tiny by the standards of today's top-echelon Premier League teams. When I started talking to United they actually offered me less than I had made, with bonuses, in my last year at Aberdeen.

After United started to win big competitions on a regular basis, I began to pay more attention to my own compensation. In 1989 Martin Edwards, the club chairman, had tried to sell United for £20 million – laughable by today's standards, but a hefty amount at the time. The deal fell through, however, after the buyer failed to raise the money. After United became a public company in 1991, there was no mystery about the value of Manchester United and I could not help but start to think about the role I had played in that. In 1998 Rupert Murdoch offered £623 million for United, which valued Martin's stake at about £87 million. Perhaps it was my Scottish trade-union heritage that gnawed at me, or maybe I just felt undervalued.

Martin was a good chairman. The club was in his bones and he cared about its welfare, but every time I raised my salary with him it became contentious. I'd go and see him in his office at Old Trafford and he used to punch my requests into this large desk calculator he kept near his phone. Years before, in order to show him I was underpaid, I even handed him the contract of George Graham who, at the time, was manager of Arsenal. I made very little headway and, in a way, I was negotiating from a position of weakness, because Martin knew that there was no football job I wanted more than to be manager of Manchester United. Once David Gill became chief executive, the situation was defused. David was more objective and my salary was adjusted to an appropriate level.

When the Glazers and David Gill agreed to a big increase in Wayne Rooney's salary in 2010, they wanted to know how I felt. I told them I did not think it fair that Rooney should earn twice what I made and Joel Glazer immediately said, 'I totally agree with you but what should we do?' It was simple. We just agreed that no player should be paid more than me. We agreed in less time than it takes to read the previous sentence.

For my last 15 years at United I had a rolling one-year contract and an agreement that if I was sacked I would be entitled to two years' salary, even if I turned up and started managing Manchester City the day after I was fired. That was more than enough for me.

I suspect most football managers get paid less – sometimes far less – than their star players. In the Premier League I imagine that only Arsène Wenger and José Mourinho pull down the amount of money earned by their best players. That probably explains why nothing much is written about a manager's compensation. What message does it send to a team, if most of them are being paid more than their boss?

Negotiation

Buying and selling players provided me with an education in the art of negotiation. I got my first taste of negotiations by watching the trade-union leaders when I worked in the factories. There was a heavy Communist influence at the time, and I always felt they overstepped the mark. They'd go out on strike at the least provocation. They'd refuse to negotiate. It was always head-on confrontation. The last thing you want to do is go out on strike, but they always seemed to do it. What other weapons do you have if you are standing on the picket lines? What happens if someone calls your bluff and you are left warming yourself around braziers for three months? That image stayed with me, and so I always tried not to get myself boxed in during the tussles over players.

It's hard to remain clear-headed during negotiations and not get swept away by the passion of the pursuit or emotions. It's so easy to get over-stretched, and for a football manager it's very easy to feel that one or two new players will change the fortune of a club. If discipline slips during a negotiation it can have all sorts of ramifications. Not only does it drive the price up for a particular transaction, but it has ripple effects. In football, just as in other businesses, it means that people now expect you to pay top dollar. It also has an effect on the rest of the team because it can create unrest if your entire compensation scheme is distorted because of one new arrival or one new contract.

It would be nice to think that everyone behaved in a

gentlemanly manner during negotiations, but unfortunately that is not necessarily the case. You encounter some people with whom a handshake is sufficient to seal an enormously expensive transfer. Then there are others on whom you cannot turn your back for fear that they will try and do something underhanded. Over the years, and with dozens, if not hundreds, of negotiations under my belt, I got better at reading people. But I also learned that, no matter how many times you have been on the verge of signing a contract, there is always room for an ugly surprise.

I tried to stay unemotional and to keep a clear head when we were pursuing a player. When we wanted to sign Phil Neville, we consciously first went after his brother Gary. We knew the pair were very close, but we also knew that Phil had more natural talent and would be more sought after. However, I also knew that once we had bagged Gary, Phil would follow. There were occasions when the sellers tried to use emotion to their advantage. After a game at Old Trafford in August 2004 against Everton, David Gill, Maurice Watkins and I met the club's owner, Bill Kenwright, and their manager, David Moyes, to discuss our offer for the 18-year-old Wayne Rooney. They pulled out all the stops. After we gave them our final offer, Kenwright got his mother on the phone and she told me, 'You are not going to steal my boy.' We ended up by ploughing through the emotion and signing Wayne the following day.

I always tried to tell myself that it wasn't the end of the world if we failed in a particular negotiation and that our success was not going to hinge on the arrival of one player. If you need one person to change your destiny, then you have not built a very solid organisation. We had a chance to buy Sergio Agüero before he went to Manchester City, but eventually his agent was demanding a price we were not prepared to pay. Right towards the end of my time at United, we were pursuing Lucas

Moura, the immensely talented right-winger who, at the time, was playing in his native Brazil for São Paulo. We offered £24 million for him, which we upped to £30 million and then again to £35 million, but PSG signed him for £45 million. David and I were just not prepared to go to those sorts of levels. There were also times when negotiations to get a particular player came to naught but we wound up getting someone better. In 1989 I failed to get Glenn Hysén from Fiorentina, but wound up with Gary Pallister instead. My pursuit of the Dutchman, Patrick Kluivert, who was then playing at AC Milan, was also an exercise in futility, but it turned out all right because a bit later we snared Dwight Yorke.

Negotiations are often irrational. There are all sorts of reasons why people buy and sell things – it doesn't matter whether it is a house, a company, a stock or a football player. I found predicting the outcome of a negotiation was always challenging because, while I tried, I never knew all the cards my opponent was holding or all the pressures to which he was subject. I did know, however, that it is always good to keep as many options open as possible. For example, in 1989, after we lost to Nottingham Forest in the quarter-final of the FA Cup, I told Martin Edwards, our chairman, that we had to sell Gordon Strachan. Sheffield Wednesday had wanted to sign Strachan, but I got a call from Howard Wilkinson, the manager of Leeds United, who had got wind of what was happening. I informed Strachan of the interest from Leeds, but for some reason he was set on moving to Sheffield. I told him that out of courtesy he should tell Wilkinson of his decision, and I also said, 'You never know, he might offer you the moon. You never know what someone's going to offer you.' At the time Leeds were a rising club in what was then the second division, and their chairman, Leslie Silver, was willing to spend. That same night,

Strachan phoned me and said, 'Boss, I just wanted to let you know I've signed for Leeds United. They didn't offer me the moon. They offered me two moons.' Strachan wound up, at the age of 32, with a contract with Leeds that was far better than he was getting at United.

One of my best negotiating lessons came in August 1989 from Colin Henderson, when we wanted to sign Gary Pallister to strengthen United's defence. Henderson was chairman of Middlesbrough and also a senior commercial manager of ICI; he played us for all it was worth. I was eager, perhaps desperate, to sign Pallister so that he could play in a game two days later against Norwich City, and I suspect Henderson detected this. We even had Pallister sitting in the car with his agent outside the hotel in Middlesbrough so that we could get all the documents signed.

I'd told both Martin Edwards and Maurice Watkins, United's solicitor, that the maximum we should pay for Pallister was £1.3 million. In 1989 that was a huge sum, particularly because – prior to that – the largest amount United had ever paid for a player was the £1.8 million we had spent on Mark Hughes in 1988. Maurice and I spent a long night haggling with Henderson and had started the bidding at around £1.3 million. Eventually, we shook hands at £2.3 million, a British transfer record, and no sooner had I breathed a big sigh of relief when Henderson said the payment had to be up front. This was a shocker because, in those days, it was customary to pay big transfer sums in instalments.

I always appreciated the need to strike early during the two annual transfer windows, which were introduced in 2002–03. Other managers would complain about the transfer windows, but I liked their introduction because it meant I did not have to deal with agents for six months of the year. The last thing you want is to have your back up against the wall with the clock ticking while everyone knows that you are on the prowl for a particular type of player. But I would trade that time pressure for the freedom it created for such a large period of the year. In the summer, we would try to make up our minds about who we wanted to pursue before I went on holiday in June, even though the transfer window did not close until the end of August. We would make our intentions known early when David Gill made contact with the chief executive of the club from which we wanted to sign a player. It was just important for us to be in the mix early so that we did not get blindsided. There was a notable occasion in May 2007 when David Gill, accompanied by Carlos Queiroz, who spoke Portuguese, went to Portugal and signed Nani from Sporting Lisbon and Anderson from Porto in the course of 24 hours. That very same month, incidentally, a full ten weeks before the end of the transfer window, we also signed Owen Hargreaves from Bayern Munich.

The setting for negotiations can also play a role and, as I said earlier, I found that the hotel in the south of France where Cathy and I go on holiday was a great spot at which to convince players to cast their lot in with United. It is far away from the madding crowd and, with its view over a sunny Mediterranean, is far more conducive to the notion of a bright future than a small conference room in a stadium or a hotel suite on a rainy day in London. Phil Jones was just one of the players who brought his parents and agent to our hotel; we had a nice little chat in this delightful spot and the deed was done. Sometimes I would also use the aura of Manchester United to help seal a deal by walking a prospect out on to the pitch, or showing him around our Carrington training facility. The players would always be star-struck when they saw the gymnasium.

Contrast that relaxed approach with the problem of negotiating under pressure. Daniel Levy, chairman of Tottenham, nailed us to the flagpole in 2008 when he took us all the way to the last day of the transfer window before agreeing terms for Dimitar Berbatov, Tottenham's talented Bulgarian striker, in whom we had long had an interest. When we got wind of the fact that Levy was trying to sell Berbatov to Manchester City, we stuck in our oar, chartered a plane and flew the player to Manchester, agreeing on terms with the player and, as I thought, a transfer fee with the club. Then Levy came back to us and said he needed Fraizer Campbell, one of our young strikers, as part of the deal. David Gill demurred, so Levy then upped Berbatov's transfer fee a little. Finally, in order to get the deal over the line, and to add insult to injury, we sent Campbell on loan to White Hart Lane and paid the increased fee. We were up until midnight signing and faxing papers to make sure all the paperwork went through before the deadline expired. That whole experience was more painful than my hip replacement.

Brokers

Agents have become like tsetse flies. These days they are everywhere in football, and almost all of them do nothing but feather their own nests and mess up the relationships that players have with their clubs and managers. They have turned many players into merchandise; a conversation with most agents is like trying to arrive at a deal in a souk.

As a result I've developed a pronounced aversion to any middle-man who gets between me and the players with whom I want to have a close relationship. Brokers have their own agendas and both player and club suffer the consequences. I was struck when I read *The Snowball*, the biography of Warren Buffett by Alice Schroeder, to learn of his distrust of investment bankers. I feel about football agents the way Mr Buffett feels about bankers – they are what he calls 'money shufflers'.

Before the introduction of the Bosman ruling, we always used to deal directly with the players and their families. Any boy good enough to play for Manchester United would, almost inevitably, have attracted the attention of other clubs, which meant that our offers would be determined by the forces of the market. Word would always get around and we would usually have a keen sense for what we were up against.

The truth is these days few players have a need for an agent, either because their lives are straightforward or they have little interest in becoming celebrities. If all their income comes from their club contract and they either aren't the type, or don't have the charisma, to attract the interest of sponsors and advertising agencies, all they need is a lawyer and an accountant. A few, and there aren't many of them, have more complicated lives, become mini-business conglomerates and do need someone to take care of all their relationships. Both Gary and Phil Neville signed seven-year contracts in the summer of 1997 in 15 minutes. I loved their father's response to the question of why they had done so – 'Because they wouldn't give us ten years.'

Agents cleverly, and slyly, insert themselves between the player and the club and try to up the ante. They claim to represent the interest of their clients but their ultimate motive is to maximise the amount of money that flows into their own pockets. Players, particularly the youngsters, have been bamboozled into thinking that it is impossible to obtain a fair deal without an agent, and they have also been fooled into thinking that the only route towards a fair deal is to play monkey games during negotiations that can take an eternity. The opposite is true, because few players calculate the amount that they are forking out for these agents over the course of their careers. The sums can be staggering. An agent will expect to receive 5 per cent of his client's basic salary from a contract negotiation. So, in a transfer where a player signs a five-year contract worth £100,000 a week, the agent will receive £1,300,000. Staggering. Harry Swales, who represented Ryan Giggs, Bryan Robson and Kevin Keegan for many years, would always refuse to take a percentage of the player's income from the club. Instead, he just took a percentage of any commercial contracts in which he was involved.

I frequently tried to use a respected player as our contract negotiator. Youngsters and their parents tended to view players as their natural allies, rather than someone like David Gill or myself, who would, inevitably, be viewed as management and, at least when we were in the thick of a negotiation, as their adversaries. I have already mentioned that, in their role as captain, both Bryan Robson and Steve Bruce were very helpful in this regard, as was Brian McClair. The same goes for Gary Neville, although I have to say there were occasions when I dreaded his appearance almost as much as the arrival of an agent. We took to calling him 'Arthur Scargill', the long-time leader of the National Union of Mineworkers, who was known for his uncompromising position on almost everything. Gary was similar. He would come into my office with a player and announce, 'I think your offer is rubbish.' He would be genuinely offended by some of our offers and would let us know that in very colourful language. But Gary was fair and he was good for the player and good for the club. I would rather deal with Gary at any time of day or night than with an agent.

There are some decent agents, but you don't need all the fingers of one hand to count them. Jorge Mendes is one. He represents some of the best players, including Cristiano Ronaldo, Ángel Di María and Diego Costa. In dealing with Jorge, especially when I was working to keep Ronaldo at United for another year in 2008 when he was pining to go to Real Madrid, I always felt that he was trying to represent the player's best interests. But Jorge is a rarity.

Many agents have no qualifications beyond the ability to ingratiate themselves with the player and his family.

I did not have a problem so much with Carlos Tévez as with his advisor, Kia Joorabchian. I always felt he was engineering another move for Tévez and, as a result, never had the feeling that the player belonged to United. It just seemed like we were renting him until Joorabchian could cut a better deal elsewhere.

There are one or two football agents I simply do not like, and Mino Raiola, Paul Pogba's agent, is one of them. I distrusted him from the moment I met him. He became Zlatan Ibrahimović's agent while he was playing for Ajax, and eventually he wound up representing Pogba, who was only 18 years old at the time. We had Paul under a three-year contract, and it had a one-year renewal option which we were eager to sign. Raiola suddenly appeared on the scene and our first meeting was a fiasco. He and I were like oil and water.

From then our goose was cooked because Raiola had been able to ingratiate himself with Paul and his family and the player signed with Juventus.

This sort of atmosphere makes it hard to establish a close relationship with a player and massively complicates life for a manager. If I felt these people genuinely had the players' interests at heart, I might feel differently. Players do not understand that their lives would be better – both financially and emotionally – if they paid a lawyer on an hourly basis to help them with their contracts. Paul Scholes was represented by Grant Thornton, the accounting firm. He paid them a simple fee and the job was done.

Agents have just become an unsavoury part of football life. I wish guys like Paul Scholes and Ryan Giggs, some of the very best players of recent times, would help educate youngsters and their parents that there is no need for them to employ agents. They would be doing the boys and football a tremendous favour.

11

BUSINESS DEVELOPMENT

Innovation

Between 1986 and 2013, the commercial side of United changed almost beyond recognition. In my final year at the club the turnover had risen to £363 million. While success on the field provided the foundation for this growth, I had little involvement in the details associated with making the cash registers ring. The commercial growth was the responsibility of the chairman and CEO. They had to worry about dealing with the sponsors and negotiating the sponsorship contracts; expanding our catering, hospitality and events activities; organ-ising the pre-season tours, and assembling the tools for the media and marketing side, including MUTV, the website, the magazine and, these days, feeding our Twitter, Facebook and Instagram accounts. They also built up the human resources function, because you need it when you are employing 800 people. All this changed as the club grew.

In retrospect, I suppose there was always the risk that I would get diverted from my job by taking on a wider set of respons-ibilities at the club. But there was always a natural division of responsibilities and I cannot think of any top-flight manager who runs the football and commercial activities of a club. The separation of duties in football is somewhat equivalent to what you would find at a newspaper or fashion house or advertising agency. At each you have someone responsible for putting out the product – the editor, designer, or the head of creative. And then you have a CEO who takes care of all commercial activities – selling subscriptions and advertising; opening shops and selling dresses; soliciting clients and making ends meet. Either way, I had enough on my plate keeping the team in contention, and staying one step ahead of all the changes that crept into the game.

In the past 40 years, advances in technology and the amount of information that is available have helped transform football in the same way it has changed other sports. If you compare the Formula One car that Lewis Hamilton drives today with those that Stirling Moss used to guide around circuits in the early 1950s and early 1960s, the bicycles that Chris Froome has used to win the Tour de France with what Eddy Merckx rode in the 1970s, or the tennis rackets used respectively by Rod Laver and Roger Federer, the equipment and training approaches are very different.

Innovations in a variety of fields have been applied by football clubs. Everyone is always looking for the edge that will make them better than their opponents. As soon as you have fastened on that advantage, there's always a desire to keep it under close wraps although, inevitably, word leaks out and others emulate advances. At United, innovation and information have marched side by side for the past 30 years.

Diet has improved; players' careers have lengthened; the pitches – thanks to soil technology – have better drainage, underground heating and stronger varieties of grass that no longer disintegrate into muddy quagmires after the first rainfall;

footballs no longer absorb water the way they used to do; players wear kit made of synthetic materials compared to the cotton and wool of yesteryear. Today's top-flight football game is played at a much higher pace than 30 years ago – helped, in part, by the back-pass rule, which was introduced in 1992, but largely because of the massive improvement in the pitches. These have given today's players spectacular stages on which to perform. As a result, I would wager today's players run 15 per cent more than those who turned out in the 1960s.

Nutrition, sports and medical science, data and video analysis and, of all things, optometry have each played a part in the evolution of football. When people used to approach me and suggest that it was essential we adapt some new technique, I was invariably sceptical. Any number of peddlers used to approach us with the latest gimmick or fad. Some of their sales pitches would make you wonder whether they had bottled healing water from Lourdes. I always wanted someone to prove why a new-fangled idea would help us, and perhaps I sometimes came across as a bit old-fashioned. However, when it made sense and offered United a way to improve, I was eager to embrace it. I didn't want United to get left behind because others had stolen a march on us. I absolutely did not want to miss the future. So we added sports science and nutrition programmes to our repertoire and made massive improvements to the quality of our medical care and staff. We also developed our video analysis systems.

Nobody used to pay any attention to a footballer's diet. The normal lunch before a game consisted of three courses. In Scotland it was usually soup, a pot roast or mince and potatoes, and a treacle sponge for dessert. I don't know who came up with that menu – perhaps it was someone who wanted to guarantee a nice Saturday afternoon nap. It was definitely too heavy for me, so Cathy used to make me two slices of lemon sole followed by toast and honey for dinner on a Friday, and for a pre-game lunch on the Saturday.

Diet was very much on my mind when I took my first job as a manager with East Stirlingshire. We were due to play against Falkirk (a team I was eager to beat because I had played for them) and I wanted to change habits. I informed the board that I would start taking the team to lunch before games as part of our preparation. There was complete uproar because the lunch was going to cost £28, and in those days players were expected to buy their own lunches. I went to the hotel in Falkirk the day before the game, talked to the chef and instructed him to serve each player with two slices of lemon sole and toast and honey. The chef told me the players would be starving and I said, 'Good.' We won 2–0. The same thing happened when I went to Aberdeen, where the team had been in the habit of holing up in a hotel and having a fillet steak before a game. The hotel owner had been friendly with Billy McNeill, Aberdeen's previous manager, and, after hearing about my request for a menu change, predicted to the club chairman that I wouldn't last long as manager. So we changed locations in a hurry and thereafter the team always had lunch at the Ferry Hotel, where the menu consisted of protein, carbohydrates and sugar – or two slices of lemon sole, toast and honey.

Top-flight clubs in England began to take notice of the beneficial effects of diet in the 1990s. Most of the youngsters who came into the game in the early 1990s had just subsisted on a steady diet of pie and chips; for them, the idea of a nutritious regimen was as foreign as a bowl of spaghetti bolognese. The approach to diet has gone through different phases. Bananas were popular for a time, and then somebody thought carbloading, with large helpings of spaghetti, would be helpful. At

United we began to take it seriously in 1990–91 when I hired Trevor Lea, a nutritionist from Sheffield. It was odd, but earlier in his life he had owned a newspaper and magazine shop that sold sweets and chocolates, which was hardly the background you would expect for a nutritionist.

Trevor understood that laying out healthy foods at the training centre only addressed part of the issue. So we called a meeting one evening with the players' wives and girlfriends. Trevor explained to the partners what he was seeking and emphasised the need for the players to reduce their consumption of fatty foods on the days leading up to games. There was a severe aspect to his approach, and he had no time for people who wouldn't comply with his regimen. This even extended to me during one of my attempts to lose weight and lower my fat levels. Every now and again I'd falter until he said, 'Either you do it all the time with me or not at all, because you are wasting my time.' He was right to admonish me. Under his guidance we lowered the players' fat levels from 14–15 per cent of their body weight to about 8 per cent. We also had sunbeds installed at Carrington to help boost the Vitamin D levels of players who had grown up in sunnier climes than the north of England.

Most footballers have very good eyesight and I had never thought much about the issue until Dr Gail Stephenson wrote to me out of the blue in the 1990s. She was a diehard United fan, but she was also a vision expert at Liverpool University. We had adopted a grey strip for away games and lost four of the five games in which we wore them. She wrote and told me that the drab colour made it much harder for the players to pick out their team-mates than our regular kit. We changed the strip and started to win. So Gail had my attention. I invited her in for a meeting, was impressed, and she became a valuable member of our back-room team. She then made the case that players' performance could be enhanced if their peripheral vision was improved. Like lots of others, I had always assumed that peripheral vision was some natural trait, like hair colour or height. Players who spend most of their time roaming one side of the field (a left-back or a right-winger) will have good peripheral vision in one direction and poor in the other. Some of Gail's work was based on research done with ice hockey players who were recovering from concussions, and our players came to benefit from her training.

The same went for sports science. At United we started taking this seriously in 2007 when we hired Tony Strudwick as our first director of sports science. He massively improved our approach to conditioning and the benefits of mobility and flexibility and indoor warm-up sessions. Our gym, which previously had lots of weightlifting equipment, suddenly had rows of exercise bikes and treadmills and big television screens so that the players could watch their favourite shows while exercising. He taught us how to measure the intensity of workouts so we could monitor which players were taxing their cardiovascular and muscular systems. Instead of running for miles, as we did when I played, the emphasis turned to interval training – short, explosive (and gruelling) surges of speed. The furthest the players were made to run was about 200 metres. It amounted to a revolution in the way we approached fitness. Tony also emphasised core body work, and that too was a big help. When it became clear that compression socks helped players recover from games we added this detail to our physical preparation.

It's amazing to think that 40 years ago we'd do a training session and then run 8,000 metres or clamber up and down the endless stadium steps of Hampden Park. It was no wonder we were wiped out for days. When I played for Rangers, the training was pathetic. Every morning was the same. We'd go on to the running track and run a lap and walk a lap. Then we'd go behind the goal and do exercises and finally we'd have a game on the training ground. There was no technical training. The only time you'd see a ball was during the game. There was never any discussion of tactics. Our health checks were also primitive. We did not measure lung capacity, or muscle mass, and there were no stress and blood tests, CT scans or electro-cardiograms and echocardiograms.

In retrospect, even at Aberdeen I was, unwittingly, torturing the players. We'd run them up and down hills and around a golf course. It was all quite old-fashioned but I didn't know any better. At United new training techniques and fresh data allowed us to make sure players didn't burn out. After each training session, Tony used to give me a summary sheet that would show how hard each player had worked. It was quite illuminating. We also started doing this during games – every now and again the reports were quite damning. All of these elements, and more, brought Manchester United into the 21st century.

Data Overload

Today there is so much information available that it can drown you. When I started in football I had the opposite problem – too little information. The clubs didn't employ statisticians and data scientists; the players didn't wear heart-rate monitors to measure their intensity during training, or GPS devices to track the distance covered in games. There were no televised record-ings of opponents, let alone tightly edited clips. As a young manager the way I gathered information on players and teams was to go and watch dozens of games every season. I'd travel throughout Scotland, in all sorts of weather, every day of the week, to watch teams like Partick Thistle, Motherwell, Hibernian and Heart of Midlothian. In an average year I would put tens of thousands of miles on my car.

When I sought information on players, I'd always try and keep it simple. I was very interested in understanding the character of the player and the sort of upbringing he had received. Apart from that I wanted to watch his speed, his balance, his ball technique, and get a sense for his enthusiasm. We never used stopwatches to see how quickly a player could cover 50 or 100 yards. We could just tell whether they were quick or slow, and for me quickness was vital. It is easy to make things too complicated. If you looked at Brian McClair and Carlos Tévez in training you would never guess that, during a game, they would run all day. If some computer had relied on data from their training sessions to predict their performance, it would have reached the wrong conclusion. With Ruud van Nistelrooy we knew he excelled at short sprints and that was his forte. So we sought to improve that, rather than his overall stamina.

There have always been data hounds in football, just as there are in any sport. However, everything changed after Sky started blanketing the airwaves with football games. Prior to that, the only information a viewer would receive would be the result, the names of the goal-scorers and the times of the goals. These days the television coverage is drenched with possession percentages, assists, shots on goal – and what your dog had for lunch on Easter Sunday ten years ago. A manager receives all that information and a whole lot more. The statistical information was always important and I always looked at the data, but this did not determine how I picked a team. The data was more of a tool to ensure that standards were being maintained.

The coaching staff, in particular the goalkeeping coaches, tend to get fixated on analysing the way in which opponents take penalties, particularly if a game heads towards a sudden-death finish. They will be poring over this data for hours and will be full of predictions about whether the ball will be struck to the left or right or into one of the top corners. I always thought this was useless, and kept telling our goalkeepers to stay in the middle rather than go sprawling to one side. I had no idea until recently, when a friend pointed it out to me, that in 2005 some Israeli economic psychologists, after analysing 286 penalties, had published a paper titled, 'Action bias among elite soccer goalkeepers', which arrived at the same conclusion: the best way to save a penalty is to stay in the centre of the goal.

Television coverage spawned another speciality: video analysis. These days every club worth its salt has a video analysis room and a team of people responsible for compiling clips from games. Maybe because I had managed for years without video analysis, I never used it as a crutch. It was a helpful aid, but it's easy to spend too much time watching hour after hour of footage. For the most part I relied on my eyes. No machine is going to tell you whether a player is lazy or has the right attitude. The evidence was always right in front of me: not on a screen but on the football pitch. I would always glance at the data, but it almost never told me anything I hadn't already concluded. Sometimes I completely disagreed with the data. In 1987, the United chairman, Martin Edwards, came to see me while I was watching a reserve game to tell me that Steve Bruce had failed his medical as we were concluding his purchase from Norwich City. I said, 'He's hardly missed a game for about five years, so how can there be a problem?' And we went ahead with the deal.

One piece of information that I did find useful crept into use during the 1980s. This was the data gathered during pre-season 'bleep tests' – a series of short, 20-metre sprints used to gauge the players' fitness. The bleep tests were brutal but accurate – and always useful for me and my staff. We used to measure a player's fitness level at the end of one season and then, when we regrouped for pre-season training, we would test them again, so that we immediately had a sense for whether they had taken care of themselves during the summer break.

Years ago, the only way you could take a look at a player or team was by travelling to watch him play. There's still nothing that beats that sort of inspection, but today's video coverage is coming closer. At Aberdeen we had primitive video analysis. It consisted of VHS tapes of the handful of televised games that were usually shot with a couple of cameras. These tapes were of a low quality and we had no equipment and no people to edit the tapes. They were better than nothing – but not by much. Nowadays they seem to have cameras at every game, filming from all sorts of angles. At United our video analysis team reduced endless hours of tape to their essence.

We first installed specialised video analysis systems at United in the early 2000s. These allowed us to show players what they needed to improve and changed the way we planned for the future. It also gave us a lot more information and data about opposing teams and players. It's a very important part of the planning process, and really shines when the calendar gets packed and Premier League games start to pile up, with Champions League, FA Cup and League Cup fixtures.

The videos illuminated the system of play employed by an opponent, the substitutes they were likely to use in particular situations, and their approach to corners and free kicks. It helped me pick the right teams because I always had to be planning several games ahead – knowing that I had to field our strongest XI for a particular fixture. In my later years at United I worked even harder to do this and would rest players for two games so that they were primed for the most important.

The sports science and video analysis crews would forever be coming up with new ways to measure things, which was fine by me since I was always curious about fresh insights. However, I had grown up in an age before computers could generate heat maps of a player's performance or tell you how many yards he ran during a game, so I always relied more on the accumulated expertise garnered from watching tens of thousands of players compete in thousands of games, rather than on a computer printout.

As time went by we were sitting on top of a heap of information that kept growing in size. The immediate and natural impulse of any competitive person is to keep information private. However, I always thought of information in two buckets: what I was willing to disclose and nuggets I wouldn't tell my grandmother.

One mark of a leader is his willingness to share information. A great leader is happy to share his knowledge – or, at least, a portion of his knowledge. Bobby Robson, when he was the manager of Ipswich, introduced me to the notion of sharing information before Aberdeen played his team in a UEFA Cup match. Bobby invited me to watch the Ipswich training drill and I actually picked up a wee passing drill that I used for a while. I'm sure Bobby knew that I was already familiar with all his players, because I'd either seen them play or watched them on television, and all I was doing was watching a training session. I thought this was a generous gesture and a mark of the man and it is something I took away with me.

People used to be surprised how willing I was to let coaches from all over the world come to our training ground and take notes. Maybe they thought I was teaching them how to make an atom bomb using cornflakes, ketchup and two cups of flour. Once Ernst Künnecke, the manager of Waterschei, had come to watch Aberdeen play before the 1983 semi-final of the European Cup Winners' Cup. He was staying over a few days and I invited him to come and watch us train. He was flabbergasted but all we were doing was running a normal session emphasising possession, crossing and finishing. Nonetheless, I'm sure he went away thinking, 'Bloody hell. That's some club. They let you watch the training.'

In 2011 Bayern Munich let us check out their medical centre when we were thinking about improving our own. Steve McNally, United's senior doctor, and I nipped across to Germany to take a look. They let us inspect everything. They ran their medical centre like a hospital; we were massively impressed and borrowed a lot of their ideas. They also had a video analysis centre with amphitheatre seating, where the videos came up with subtitles for foreign players who didn't have a good command of German. I would have loved to have that at United for the players like Carlos Tévez and Juan Sebastián Verón who didn't understand English.

We did the same when we built the medical centre at Carrington. Word got round that it was the best in England and immediately all the other Premier League clubs wanted to inspect it. I just didn't see what the fuss was about. Everyone knew that we had a sizeable medical staff with physiotherapists, doctors, dentists and chiropodists. They knew the sorts of machines we had bought and I'm sure the various manufacturers would have been happy to send them the brochures.

I'm sometimes amazed by how people get fixated on information. It's like standing in a hospital room staring at the numbers on the bedside monitors while the patient chokes to death on a chicken sandwich. You have to consider the human element of life and the way that circumstances and chance can upset everything – even the most accurate and clearly reported data. Knowing the heart-rate of a player and doing all the video analysis in the world of his opposite number isn't going to help you if he loses control and gets sent off in the first minute.

Confidentiality

While I like to think that I'm quite open and willing to share experiences, there are some things I've always been very careful about because in any intensely competitive pursuit, maintaining secrecy and confidentiality is a potent weapon. There is no benefit to be gained by telegraphing your moves or declaring your intentions to competitors. I would always try to keep a cloak of secrecy over anything we considered important – the amount of money we had at our disposal for new signings, the players we fancied, or injuries. My mantra was, 'Tell them nothing.' I'd never give anyone any inkling of who I wanted to sign and I had no interest in letting my fellow managers know the fitness levels of my players.

In the 2009–10 season, after Wayne Rooney got injured during the first leg of the Champions League quarter-final, I ordered him to keep wearing his rehab boot so that Bayern Munich would not expect him to turn out for the second leg. The subterfuge worked well enough, but unfortunately we failed to make the semi-finals. Stealth and secrecy are two valuable weapons for any organisation.

I used to announce the complete team line-up to the players a day before the game, but then it kept getting leaked to the newspapers. So I changed my approach and told each individual whether they would be playing but I was careful to ensure that I didn't disclose the complete team-sheet to anyone until the morning of the match. When Paul Scholes returned from his first experience with retirement to play against Manchester City in an FA Cup game in 2012, even the other players were unaware of his pending appearance until he removed his tie and jacket and put on his strip.

Agents always badgered their players for this sort of information, which they would then leak in order to curry favour with journalists. They would sit in their cars outside the training ground, waiting for their clients to emerge. They would phone the players and barrage them with questions such as, 'How are things today? How was training? Who is injured? Are you playing tomorrow? What did the manager say?' A minute later they would be distributing this feed to their favourite journalists.

There was a period during which United's secrets kept popping up in one newspaper written by the same journalist. It drove me bonkers. I couldn't figure out how this was happening, and then I discovered that the reporter lived in Alderley Edge, a village on the outskirts of Manchester, as did some of our players. It turned out that he would have drinks with some of the players on Saturday nights and, being a good reporter, he had a knack for getting them to say things that they should have kept secret. As soon as I cottoned on to what was happening, I gathered all the players who lived in Alderley Edge and told them in no uncertain terms, 'If I see one more story that includes facts I don't want to read, all of you are done. I don't care who leaked the information, you are all going to be fined.' That did the trick.

Graeme Hogg, a defender at United in the mid-1980s, was

another player who struggled to understand the concept of secrecy. We were due to play Everton in 1987, the season they won the League, and had spent the entire week working on an approach where I played with just three defenders to counter their two strikers. On the morning of the game I picked up the newspaper and Graeme Hogg had helped fashion a column titled, 'How we will beat Everton'. I couldn't believe it. I told myself I had to wait to calm down so that when I got hold of Hogg I would only commit serious assault rather than premeditated murder. Hogg started that game, but he only played a handful more games before we sold him to Portsmouth in 1988.

All things considered, I had it easy compared to anyone in politics. I had dinner with Tony Blair in Manchester before the 1997 election, and we talked about how hard it would be to keep his Cabinet ministers on the straight and narrow because they were all after his job and would leak nuggets to their favourite journalists in order to gain favourable coverage. I said to him, 'If you can keep them all in the same room, every day, you won't have a problem. But they will want to fly the nest.' He laughed and said, 'You're probably right.' I said, 'I am right. Don't worry about it.'

My circle of confidants was very small. I would confide my real feelings to Cathy and my brother, Martin, and Bridget and John Robertson, my in-laws. Beyond my family members, I knew that close pals from my boyhood and two from our time in Aberdeen, our lawyer Les Dalgarno, and our family friend, Gordon Campbell, could be relied upon to be discreet.

After Archie Knox headed back to Scotland, I gradually developed close relationships with Carlos Queiroz and Mick Phelan. But, much as I trusted them implicitly, I never was as close to Carlos and to Mick as I was to Archie. But then again, Archie and I had spent hundreds of hours together when we were earning our stripes, and that forms a different, deeper sort of bond. Among managers, I always felt close to John Lyall, and to Bobby Robson, the former England manager, whom I admired greatly, and Sam Allardyce.

But as I say, the inner circle of confidants is really quite small. Perhaps it is just very difficult to have more than a few close friends because these sorts of relationships build over a long time and lots of shared experiences. As my father always said, you only need six people to carry your coffin and, as I have got older, I have become ever more appreciative of that remark.

12

THE RELEVANCE OF OTHERS

Rivalries

Football is littered with great rivalries. Many of them are rooted in parochialism and are the outcome of times when travel was far more difficult than it is today. Remember, it was not until the 1950s that British clubs began to venture into Europe, and so in those days everything tended to be far more local. Newspaper journalists got into the habit of headlining local derbies and that remains true. It does not matter whether the game is between Celtic and Rangers, Everton and Liverpool, Tottenham and Arsenal, or Manchester United and Manchester City. A rivalry, particularly a local one, adds spice and bite.

Some fans, for whom football is bigger than religion, even inherit family rivalries. Their father, or grandfather, might have supported a particular team and those are the colours they will root for until their dying day. I cannot tell you how many photographs we used to receive of a newborn baby, clad in a Manchester United strip and named after a player. These babies were born into tribes, whether they liked it or not.

I don't remember a time when I was not thinking about

rivalry and competition. In Glasgow the great divide was – and still is – between Celtic and Rangers (the Old Firm). For many decades this had a deeply sectarian edge because Celtic tended to field players who had Irish Catholic roots, while Rangers drew their teams from Protestant Scotland. At Aberdeen our longest rivalry was with Rangers, but during my time at the club a new rivalry developed with Dundee United.

At United I inherited rivalries that had accumulated over decades. These varied a little, depending on the era, but a few were perennial. For United the tussles with the Merseysiders, Liverpool – whose stadium is only 32 miles from Old Trafford – and Manchester City always loomed large. The same applied to Leeds United, during the era when they were playing in the top flight. From time to time this had a vicious edge, such as the time a Leeds fan attacked Eric Harrison, our youth coach, thinking he was me. In the past 15 years, the dates of fixtures against Chelsea and Arsenal have also tended to be circled in diaries months ahead of the actual game.

Football was tailored for my personality because winning and losing is so clearly defined and measured so often. Ever since I was a boy, I've never wanted anyone to beat me. It might be because of my Glasgow upbringing, or because of my working-class roots (that's for the psychoanalysts to decide), but in Govan there were always kids who wanted to pick a fight and were natural enemies.

The spectre of contending with a rival helped goad teams towards higher performance. In Aberdeen I'd portray a visit from one of the big Glasgow clubs as an assault on our manhood. I would tell the players, 'Rangers and Celtic come up here and think they're going to walk all over us.' The implication is obvious.

Early on during my time at United, I was quoted as saying that my greatest challenge was knocking Liverpool off their perch. Somehow this quote became folklore and it was repeated endlessly. The odd thing is that I don't remember ever uttering the phrase. Either way, it was helpful, because it captured the century-long rivalry between United and Liverpool and, of course, during the 1970s and 1980s, Anfield was always a furnace. In the 26-year gap of United's League titles between 1967 and 1993, Liverpool won the League 11 times, the FA Cup three times and, most gallingly, the European Cup four times. Liverpool's success during this era was unprecedented because no other club had ever dominated English football in a similar manner. I am not sure whether United's players ever consciously thought about topping Liverpool's victory record, but I certainly always thought of it as the bogey I had to beat. The spectre of all that silverware heading to Liverpool was an intolerable prospect.

Once, in 1988, we left Anfield after a 3–3 draw marked by some appalling decisions by the referee. I said to a radio interviewer, 'It's no surprise managers have to leave Anfield choking on their own vomit, biting their tongue, afraid to tell the truth.'

There were obviously some theatrics associated with the way I stirred the competitive juices of our players when we were due to meet a long-time foe, but there were very few examples of either occasions or people (other than referees or linesmen) that made me livid for months. It is healthy for football clubs to have rivals and foes because it spurs them to perform to the best of their abilities, but I'm not so sure it pays to have bitter feuds or real enemies. I cannot think of a manager – even in the midst of our fiercest battles – with whom I would refuse to dine. I just tried to keep my thoughts to myself because the secret is not to put your own weaknesses on display. The best way to get even is to make sure you beat them. I had some well publicised spats with other managers such as Arsène Wenger but these disputes don't last for ever and he has been very helpful with our work at UEFA.

You cannot define yourself by your rivals and competitors or change your strategy and approach because of something they do. For years Manchester City, the other club in Manchester, tried to define themselves by what we did. Their chairman, Peter Swales, regularly referred to us as 'Them across the road'. He couldn't get Manchester United out of his head. Instead of seeking to improve Manchester City, and concentrate on what was under his control, he worried about us. It made no sense. On the other hand, we had one supporter, Norman Williams, who watched every home game and travelled to many away games. However, in a lifetime of supporting United, he never went to City's stadium. I asked him once why he refused to do so. His answer: 'I'm afraid of what I might catch.'

Nonetheless, you can learn from your competitors and, more importantly, you can raise your standards by trying to match or outperform them. Between 1994 and 1999 Juventus, the Italian club, served that role for United, when they were managed by Marcello Lippi and played at the level I wanted to attain. I greatly admired Lippi. He had such a sense of style and, with his silver hair, leather coat and small cigar, reminded me of Paul Newman. Eventually, I enjoyed one of my greatest nights as a manager there in the 1999 Champions League semi-final. We went two goals down after 11 minutes and came back to win 3–2, to knock them out and reach the final in Barcelona.

It's hard to keep your head when competitors do irrational things. In business, if a competitor lowers prices or splurges on an expensive television advertising campaign, it's easy to auto-matically assume that's the correct course. I suspect it requires a steely nerve to avoid following suit. In football, while I was managing, there was a similar phenomenon when other clubs and owners were prepared to pay a king's ransom to buy their way to success. In Scotland, that was Rangers. In retrospect I might have been a bit fortunate with the timing of my departure from Aberdeen, because it coincided with the arrival of Graeme Souness at Rangers, and the start of a big spending spree as they imported players from England and the Continent. Yet, if I had stayed at Aberdeen, I would not have been tempted to chase Rangers and to resort to spending willy-nilly. I would have stuck to my guns.

In England, the kings of spending were Chelsea and, in more recent years, Manchester City. Obviously, United have spent heavily since I retired, but that's over a shorter period. The success that José Mourinho achieved in his first season at Chelsea in 2004–05, when he won the Premier League and League Cup, was mainly due to his stubbornness, the determined manner he scratched out victories and draws and the fact that he had his players believing he was the Messiah. It also did not hurt that he spent almost £100 million during his first season at the club. However, he is a great leader and spectacular manager who has achieved major triumphs in four different countries. It's hard to think of anyone else who has done that.

When Manchester City was bought by Mansour bin Zayed Al Nahyan in 2008, I never for a moment thought, 'This is going to make it hard for us.' I just considered it another in a long line of challenges with which we had to contend. I didn't expect City to do the things that they've done in the last few years – some of which have been directly aimed at challenging United, but some of which have also been good for the economy of Manchester. Who could have imagined that they would build 6,000 new homes in some of Manchester's more rundown areas as part of their development plans? However, my attitude remains the same, despite the fact that they have spent in excess of £700 million from 2008 until my retirement. It's completely in United's power to beat them, no matter how much money they spend. There's no doubt that City's spending spree and their effort to create an instant history has caused jealousy around the Premier League, but I always tried to reinforce the message that, no matter how many players they bought for huge amounts of money, they could only start a game on a Saturday with 11 men.

Global Markets

I have never studied economics, but football gave me a bit of an education in the subject. Though I've always been sympathetic towards trade unions, mainly because of what my father and his generation endured in the Scottish shipyards, I have become a big believer in free markets that provide everyone an equal opportunity to compete. Immigration may cause all sorts of social and political issues, but it has transformed the standard of play in the Premier League.

When I started in football, the sport was parochial. The British clubs had all been brewed in neighbourhoods, towns and cities. Many of the players could walk from their homes to the grounds and this continued for a long time. In 1967, when Celtic became the first British club to win the European Cup, it did so with a team entirely composed of players born within 30 miles of Glasgow. When United won the European Cup under Matt Busby in 1968, it was with a team of seven Englishmen, one Scotsman, one Northern Irishman and two who represented the Republic of Ireland. There had only been one or two foreign players in England prior to the late 1970s, when Tottenham bought Ossie Ardiles and Ricky Villa after the 1978 World Cup.

When I arrived at Aberdeen, there were no foreign players (and in this case 'foreign' includes English, Welsh and Irish). Every player was Scottish. When I went to United we had just two foreign players – John Sivebaek and Jesper Olsen – and both came from Denmark. Half a generation later, everything had changed. Chelsea were the first top-division side to field a starting XI without a British player when, in December 1999, they selected two Frenchmen, two Italians, and one Uruguayan, a Dutchman, a Nigerian, a Romanian, a Brazilian, a Norwegian and a Spaniard. In 2005 Arsenal, in a game against Crystal Palace, became the first team in the Premier League to select a complete match-day squad without a British player. The first time I fielded a team without a single English player was on 10 May 2009, at Old Trafford, in a 2–0 win against Manchester City, when we had players from the Netherlands, Brazil, Serbia, Northern Ireland, France, Portugal, Scotland, Wales, South Korea, Argentina and Bulgaria.

The arrival of overseas players occurred in two phases. Prior to 1995, when the European Court of Justice rendered its 'Bosman ruling', European players were still partially imprisoned by their clubs. In England, tribunals run by the FA had been used from the early 1980s to settle disputes about transfer prices. Once the European Court of Justice ruled that clubs no longer had to pay transfer fees after the expiration of a player's contract, all hell broke loose. Suddenly it was a free-for-all. There was increased pressure on the clubs to renegotiate contracts long before they expired, and the players – or at least the good ones – had much more negotiating power.

In Britain the trend towards foreign players accelerated in

311

the 1980s, when we gradually stopped producing a disproportionate share of the best players in the world. One simple
measure is the way that British teams have stopped qualifying
for the World Cup. Wales hasn't qualified since 1958, Northern
Ireland since 1986, Scotland since 1998 and the Republic of
Ireland last qualified in 2002. This happened for two reasons
– Margaret Thatcher and BSkyB.

I don't know whether Margaret Thatcher consciously sought
to destroy British football, because obviously (and correctly)
she was vocal about her disdain for hooliganism and crowd
violence, but that's what she managed to do. Following an
industrial dispute with the government, many teachers stopped
organising extra-curricular sports activities. It had disastrous
consequences. My experience was that young boys paid careful
attention to their schoolteachers, and many of them became
acquainted with the need to train and acquired substantial skills,
discipline and youthful experience playing in front of critical
and demanding eyes. Much of that evaporated, as schoolteachers
were replaced by fathers, uncles and grannies. I'm sure they
were all well meaning, but gradually, under their tutelage, the
level of high-school football started to deteriorate. Competitive
school football, which was the spawning ground of footballers
for so many generations, was replaced by boys' club football,
where there was far too much emphasis on playing a very high
number of games each season. For example, Ryan Giggs, as a
14 year old in his last year as a boys' club footballer for Salford
Boys and Deans FC, played well over 100 games.

This trend was exacerbated by rules introduced as part of
the new academy system by the Football Association that forbade
clubs from coaching boys in their youth academies for more
than an hour and a half per week. It was absolute nonsense.
This was the equivalent of telling a child who liked to play the

violin or piano that they could still aspire to join one of the world's best symphony orchestras but they could only practise for 90 minutes a week. Great footballers and great artists aren't made on 90 minutes a week. As a boy, prior to the Second World War, Stanley Matthews used to play with a ball for six to eight hours a day. George Best perfected his skills in Belfast during the 1950s by spending a childhood with a ball never far from his feet, and the same went for Cristiano Ronaldo when he was growing up in Madeira during the 1990s. Then we had to face the restrictive changes to the rules that meant we were only permitted to sign players to our academy who lived within one hour's travel of Old Trafford. Had this been in place in 1991, we could never have signed David Beckham. The change in the law had a pronounced effect on our ability to develop players born throughout Britain and immediately forced us to look overseas for players who were not covered by this regulation. This has been a boon to fans because it means that all the best European clubs have widened their scouting funnels and the global competition for talent has led to a rise in the quality of the game.

In 1992, at the beginning of the Premier League era, an avalanche of money began to pour into the game, with the signing of BSkyB's television five-year contract, which was worth £304 million. (By contrast the latest TV contract, signed in 2015, is valued at £5.13 billion.) The foreign players arrived in several waves. The first came from northern Europe, and were followed by several superb players, in the twilights of their careers, who were attracted by the wages offered by Premier League clubs. Then there were the French speakers recruited by Arsène Wenger at Arsenal. Roman Abramovich's purchase of Chelsea in 2003 marked the beginning of an unprecedented spending spree. The lengths to which clubs would go in order to sign players was exemplified by the case of Benito Carbone, who played for Sheffield Wednesday and Aston Villa before going to Bradford City. When Carbone moved to Bradford, he joined a team fighting for its life in the Premier League. In 2002 the club eventually claimed that continuing to pay Carbone's wages of £40,000 a week would force it into bankruptcy. So Carbone forfeited £3.32 million and returned to Italy.

The first non-British player I signed for United was Andrei Kanchelskis from Shakhtar Donetsk in March 1991. Peter Schmeichel followed in August 1991 from Brøndby in Denmark. The man who made the most waves was Eric Cantona. Eric was born in Marseilles, had played for Marseille, Bordeaux, Montpellier and Nîmes before crossing the Channel; he spoke little English when he joined us. Cantona had a huge impact on United, most of which emanated from his talent and drive, but some from his attitude towards training and fitness. The young players thought of him as the king and hung on his every word and he captained the team in 1996 and 1997. As Cantona started to blossom at United, other clubs all wanted their own version of Cantona. By the time Eric retired in 1997, foreign players had become the backbone of top-flight football in England.

Gradually the complexion of United started to change. We were as avid as ever about identifying boys from Manchester or elsewhere in England, but our scouting system had expanded. We now trawled for players in many more places, and our scouting system became truly global. In the latter part of the 1990s we put scouts in Italy, Spain, France, Germany, the Netherlands and Portugal to supplement our network of contacts in those countries. Then in 2000 we began hiring scouts in South America, notably John Calvert-Toulmin in Brazil and Jose Mayorga in Argentina. Now United has also got a good base of contacts in Mexico and Chile. This gradually started to pay off with the signing of Diego Forlán, the Da Silva twins from Brazil and Chicharito, who became our first player from Mexico.

The arrival of the foreign players presented new challenges. They were catapulted into a strange country where everything was different: food, weather and language. We did our best to make sure they settled in by finding them houses and arranging for schooling. We also tried to ensure they could eat their favourite foods. Barry Moorhouse, who was United's player liaison officer, was responsible for this. Many of the English players had trouble with my Scottish accent, but that was nothing compared to the trouble it created for the foreign players. Anderson, a Brazilian, and Nani, a Portuguese player, who both arrived in 2007, were two for whom language, at first, was a formidable barrier. To their credit both players took the time to improve their English, and it became easier to communicate with them.

Some players had an enviable ear for language. Patrice Evra speaks several, Nemanja Vidić picked up English within weeks, and Chicharito, who grew up in Mexico, and the Da Silva twins, who were born in Brazil, understood that their football would improve if they brushed up on their English. The standout was Diego Forlán. He had a great ear for language and could have been a translator at the United Nations because he could shift with ease between Spanish, Portuguese, Italian and French. When, in 2014, he signed for the Japanese club, Cerezo Osaka, he astonished his hosts by speaking in Japanese during his inaugural press conference.

Beyond the language barrier, I think too much is made of the difficulties of integrating foreign players. I came to welcome what they brought to the club, and the multiculturalism enriched everything. Dwight Yorke, for example, who was born in Tobago, brought a lovely warmth and carefree sense of joy to the club after we bought him from Aston Villa in 1998, and that was good for morale. The gap between the home and foreign players was most evident at dinner at The Lowry, the hotel where we stayed prior to home games and where we always always had a buffet dinner. The staff would tend to congregate at one table and the British players at another, where they would all be solemn and speaking to each other in low voices. The table that was always the most raucous and alive with laughter was where the Serbs, Dutch, French and Portuguese sat.

The foreign players also set an example for some of the English players. For one thing, they tended to stay away from alcohol. Some did this for religious reasons but it mainly stemmed from the fact that they had grown up in places where getting drunk on Friday and Saturday nights is not a matter of habit. They did not feel compelled to explore their body's capacity for alcohol at Christmas parties or after we brought home a trophy. The majority of them would be very careful about their diet and dedicated about training. One of the other traits that distinguished the foreign players was their physique. The medical scans of the players who hailed from climates warmer than Britain tended to reveal much healthier joints. Their knees and hips didn't have the telltale signs of early arthritis that you would tend to find in the British players who had grown up in the damp and the cold. They also tended to be wiser about listening to their bodies. Unlike the British players, they would not try to play through injuries and risk turning a bad knock into a recurring aggravation. They just do not try to prove they can beat the pain.

About the only issue I had with the foreign players was when they got homesick or had gone to play international games and wanted to extend their stays in their homelands. Eric Djemba-Djemba, the Cameroonian midfielder, who played for United between 2003 and 2005, often returned late from leave.

For United there were only positives about extending our reach, mining new countries for talent and importing these players. When we won the Champions League in 1999, we did so with five players from outside Britain on the field – if you excuse the Irishmen – but our successes in the ensuing 14 years were only made possible because we travelled beyond our pre-existing borders.

Commentators frequently remark on the number of foreign players in the Premier League, but they often ignore the nationality of managers. In the 2014–15 season, there were eight foreign-born managers at the helm of Premier League clubs. Like the foreign-born players, they have enriched the game, although the first to arrive from outside the United Kingdom or Ireland, the Czechoslovak, Dr Josef Venglöš, did not appear until 1990 and only had a brief stint at Aston Villa. But, since then, foreign-born managers have become a staple of the Premier League, and the fact that many played for, or managed, first-rate European clubs, where they were schooled differently, has added layers to the game. (I'm referring to more than just the style of dress you see on the sidelines, though they look mighty dapper. Just look at the turnout of managers like Roberto Mancini, Roberto Di Matteo – during his brief time at the helm of Chelsea – or Roberto Martínez. Fortunately, José Mourinho proves that style is not just the preserve of managers named Roberto.)

Injecting these foreign sensibilities into the Premier League has made it a better sport for the fans, even if, from time to time, I might have objected to some of the tactics. The only managers who ever took the Premier League away from me have been from outside England: Arsène Wenger (France), Roberto Mancini and Carlo Ancelotti (Italy) and Kenny Dalglish, who was managing Blackburn Rovers at the time (Scotland). One small, yet startling, point: the last time an English manager won the English League was in 1992, when Howard Wilkinson was at Leeds.

It's actually remarkable how many Scotsmen have done well as Premier League managers – it's one of those rare statistics to which I do pay attention. Believe it or not, when Paul Lambert was sacked by Aston Villa in 2015 it was the first time since 1984 that there had been no Scottish manager in the Premier League. Just four years before that, seven of the 20 teams in the Premier League were headed by managers who had been raised in the Glasgow area. I know I am hopelessly biased, but I think managers like Kenny Dalglish, David Moyes, Paul Lambert, Owen Coyle, Bill Shankly, George Graham and, of course, Matt Busby just have, or had, a dour grit, stubbornness and determination about them that equips them well and is part of their heritage.

13

TRANSITIONS

Arriving

Leaders who are new to an organisation are often far too eager to stamp their imprint on everything. I know there's a widely held belief that a leader only has a chance to make his presence felt during his first 100 days, but it is not something to which I subscribe. There is a right and wrong way to arrive in a fresh setting – especially when you are the new sheriff in town. It is very tempting to appear with a fresh posse of trusted lieutenants and all guns blazing. In football, some of this behaviour occurs because of the inordinate emphasis on short-term results. A new manager knows that he has a limited lifespan if he does not generate quick results, even with a multi-year contract in his pocket and an owner promising to be patient.

I made this mistake when I became the manager of St Mirren. I was 32 years old, with all of four months of management experience, a bit too cocky for my own good and determined to shake things up. Instead of taking time to get my bearings and assess everything, I arrived with too many preconceived ideas. I was hot-headed, very passionate about my job, and did not want anyone to make me look like a fool. I'm sure some of that had to do with my own insecurity and inexperience. I was wondering to myself, 'What are they all thinking? What are they going to do? How are they going to react?' Then, of course, there are the periods of self-doubt when you are wondering whether you are making the right decisions. I was too eager to show that I was the boss and too quick to make decisions. Quite frequently I made decisions that I regretted.

Steve Archibald, a fantastic striker at Aberdeen, drove me nuts shortly after I arrived. He had an opinion on every subject, and was not bashful about sharing them. He should have been a professor and he did not make my arrival at Aberdeen easy. He was constantly questioning everything. But he was stubborn, wanted to win, and I just found a way to deal with his personality.

When I arrived at United in November 1986, I was only accompanied by Archie Knox. Cathy stayed in Aberdeen with the boys so that they did not interrupt their schooling which, in a way, was a blessing for me, because all I had on my plate was work. Archie and I had been together for three years at Aberdeen and I wanted him with me at United because we looked at the world in a similar manner, which gave us a unified consistency. He excelled at his job and was hard-working and trustworthy. I did not consider it a handicap to work with the United staff that had worked for my predecessor, Ron Atkinson. I actually thought it was helpful because, unlike me, they knew the club and were familiar with the players and our competitors in what was then the first division. In a way it is a little bit similar to what happens when a new prime minister arrives in Downing Street. He does not change the people who run all the Civil Service departments, but he does set out his own agenda and make his priorities clear.

I was more than happy with the backroom staff and coaching

team that I had inherited at Old Trafford, with the exception of the chief scout, whom I asked to leave at the end of my first season. All of them were good, solid characters, and they had an interest in seeing that the new manager did well. Not only was it in their self-interest, but it was also a matter of professional pride.

I knew that it would take time for me to take stock of everything at United, and I also wasn't about to make foolish promises about what was possible. I knew there was a lot to address, but I knew too that I couldn't do everything immediately. I immersed myself in the club; looked carefully at their performance history; examined the way they approached the pre-season; investigated their youth and scouting system; and gradually started to understand each of the players. I developed a keener sense for how much the club's heritage relied on attack. United had embraced an attacking style of football from its earliest years as a club, and this was a tradition that threaded its way back through the eras before and, of course, after the Second World War. Today's generation still knows the names of Bobby Charlton, George Best and Denis Law, but others such as Willie Morgan, David Pegg, who died in the Munich air crash, Charlie Mitten, who played in the early 1950s, and Billy Meredith, who played at the start of the 20th century, are only known to the diehards. This heritage, which had worked so well for Sir Matt Busby, fitted me like a glove, since attacking was my natural instinct.

All this took time. And then there were the surprises. For example, I would never have guessed that the undersoil heating at Old Trafford did not work. It had gone on the blink during our first FA Cup third-round tie against Manchester City, and we discovered that rats had chewed through the underground cables. It had been repaired in time for the fourth-round tie, three weeks later, against Coventry City but, again, on the morning of the match, we found out that half the ground was frozen and the other half was a swamp. You cannot anticipate things like that; it just shows that, when you are trying to build the pyramids, some guys will always drop or break some stones. I'd wager that no winning organisation has ever been built in the first 100 days. If you want to build a winning organisation, you have to be prepared to carry on building every day. You never stop building – if you do, you stagnate. I always used to say, 'The bus is moving; make sure you're on it, don't be left behind.' Manchester United was always a bus on the move.

There is no point suddenly changing routines that players are comfortable with. It is counterproductive, saps morale and immediately provokes players to question the new man's motives. A leader who arrives in a new setting, or inherits a big role, needs to curb the impulse to display his manhood.

If I were given the chance to replay my arrival at United, I would do two things differently, because in one respect I moved too quickly, and in another too slowly. Before I arrived at Old Trafford, I had been alerted to the fondness that some players had for the pub, and I was well aware of the fact that alcohol is one of the enemies of high performance. I wasn't about to let it fester, and so I tried to stamp out the drinking immediately. The Monday after my first game in charge of United, I gathered everyone in the club into the gymnasium. There were around 40 people in the place – players, coaches and backroom staff. I just told everyone plain and simple, 'Look, all these stories I'm hearing about your drinking habits have got to change. You have got to change because I'm not going to change.' I'm sure that a lot of the audience were thinking to themselves that they had heard it all before. It was not as if any binges had occurred in the few days that I had been in charge, or that I had any firm evidence that a player had crossed the line. I was just working from hearsay, and that's not wise.

Knowing what I know today, I would not have held that meeting but, instead, made an example of one or two players after they had crossed the line, rather than cast aspersions on everyone. It was too early for me to force a confrontation on an issue, but in the long run it didn't hurt. It is all well and good, as a new arrival, to feel the impulse to issue your own version of the Ten Commandments, but actions speak so much louder than words. My message about alcohol would have been more effective if I had just quietly gone about getting rid of one of the players who had the wrong priorities. In the end it took a long time to eradicate the drinking habit at United, but after I sold some of the main culprits, people could see I was not just full of hot air and things slowly started to improve. Eventually, the drinking stopped, apart from the occasional outings.

The second mistake I made was to wait too long to reshape the team. Some of this was out of my hands, because we had a limited budget for transfers and our pool of talented young players was thin. Nonetheless, I let the prospect of what was possible, rather than what was probable, cloud my judgement. In my heart I knew that I would never be able to turn some of the players into the sort of performers required to consistently win trophies. I gave some of them too much benefit of the doubt and, had I moved a bit more quickly, I suspect we could have become a winning club a couple of years earlier.

If you are a new boss, there is always a fine line to walk when you first appear. You want to eliminate as much uncertainty as possible because that can paralyse an organisation. Yet you also do not want to make promises you know you might not keep. At United, I hope I made it clear to people – particularly the non-playing staff – that they were secure and I wasn't about to put them in front of a firing squad. All I sought was performance and, as long as they performed, they were going to be part of the journey ahead.

When a former player, who is new to management, asks me for advice, I usually tell him not to seek confrontation. Whenever you show up in a new role, it will not be long before you have to face trouble and a clash over something. There is nothing to be gained by stirring it up yourself. Trouble will find you quick enough.

Leaving

Leaving is complicated, and almost impossible to get right. Gallons of ink have been spilled on how David Moyes became my successor as manager of United. I understand why critics, particularly in light of the results of the 2013–14 season, say we should have handled the transition better. That season was a real disappointment, which culminated in the failure to qualify for the Champions League for the first time since 1995. It was not a happy time. But not much has been said about the challenge of picking a manager at a top-tier football club. It is not an easy undertaking.

At United the issue was complicated by the length of my tenure. I do not want to sound vainglorious, but no manager in the post-Second World War era has led a team for as long as I led United. Sir Matt Busby managed United (in two spells) for 24 seasons, Bill Shankly was at the helm of Liverpool for 15 seasons, and Arsène Wenger has been at Arsenal since 1996.

I'm sure the length of time I had been in the role made things trickier. I know it did not make them easier. Picking a successor was never going to be a piece of cake.

I'm sure football clubs could learn a lesson or two from companies that have a successful history of navigating management transitions. For example, I was never asked the question that I have since learned is commonly posed to the CEOs of many companies: 'If you get hit by a bus, who takes your place?' It is a good question, because it forces people to pay attention to the issue. However, I am not sure that it would have changed anything at United because, without trying to make any excuses, there are peculiarities associated with picking a Premier League manager.

Like other organisations on the prowl for a leader, United's board of directors had the freedom to survey the field. We had the opportunity to look within the club or cast our net further afield. Either way, we had far fewer candidates than a normal company. The trouble with football clubs, particularly those in the top tier of the Premier League, Bundesliga, La Liga or Serie A, is that there are not many candidates qualified to become their manager, and owners and boards of directors invariably find that their choices are further limited by the men who are available and not bound to another commitment from which they cannot extricate themselves.

It's not as if any of the clubs in these leagues have hundreds, let alone thousands, of employees in their coaching ranks. If the criterion for the search for a successor to a United manager is limited to those who have managed a Premier League club in the previous five years, there are probably around 50 candidates; if the desire is to find someone who has managed a club that's finished in the top six, then the number dwindles to 12; and if you add the hardest criterion of all – a consistent history of winning – then you are left with about 3 who are already at top clubs. Managers just have a very tough time maintaining a winning record. David O'Leary was manager of Leeds from 1998 till 2002, when he reached the semi-finals of both the UEFA Cup and Champions League and secured a fourth-place finish in the Premiership. For a brief time he was on the top of every club's list. Then Leeds faded, O'Leary's lustre was tarnished, and he hasn't managed a top-tier team since 2006.

We obviously had a preference for a manager with experience of top-flight football, who had persevered through hard times and demonstrated that he could handle the pressure of the press coverage and the relentless trickery of agents. Personally, I have a bias that favours managers who have been solid players. Even though there are a handful of examples of managers who either did not play much professional football or did so at mediocre clubs (José Mourinho and Gérard Houllier being the two prime examples), I have a bias towards candidates who have done well on the pitch. They just have more experience and greater credibility with players.

At United we didn't have an obvious internal successor, though it was not for want of trying. Even before the Glazer family arrived in Manchester, I had been thinking a lot about potential successors. During my entire time at United, the only real internal candidate for the manager's role was Carlos Queiroz. Unfortunately, he spoiled his chances by leaving United twice – first for Real Madrid and then by going to manage Portugal. I was always encouraging some of the best United players – Ryan Giggs, Gary Neville, Darren Fletcher, Nicky Butt, Dwight Yorke and Andy Cole – to earn their coaching credentials, yet it was unrealistic to expect any of them to switch from being a player to immediately becoming manager of the club for which they had just finished playing.

United tried that once when Wilf McGuinness succeeded Matt Busby in 1969, having retired from playing in 1959. It was a disaster. Forget about the tensions caused by the fact that Sir Matt kept his office and was a daily presence at the club, McGuinness – or anyone else for that matter – was always going to have a tough time managing his former team-mates. Ryan Giggs is eventually going to be a great manager – he has intelligence, presence and knowledge – but there was no chance that I would ever have asked him, or any other player, to consider being my successor while he was still fortunate enough to be playing. A footballer needs to squeeze every last possible moment out of his playing career. There is more than enough time for management later in life. Had Ryan Giggs retired in his mid-thirties, rather than when he was 40, there is every chance that he would have been my assistant in my final five years at Manchester United, alongside Mick Phelan. He would have had to start at a lower coaching level, but he would definitely have been alongside me and Mick, learning the trade.

But, assistant managers can get itchy feet. It is very hard to keep them, particularly if they know their boss has no intention of retiring. Former Manchester United coaches and players are all over the place. Mark Hughes has flourished, although – because he is such a retiring and quiet man – I had always wondered whether he had the personality to pull it off. He did a good job as the Wales manager, followed that with a stint at Blackburn before going to Manchester City, where I thought the new owners treated him unfairly when they sacked him. Now he is at Stoke City and in his element.

Assistant managers who stay in the role for a long time do so because they aren't cut out for the top job. René Meulensteen, who was United's technical skills coach for the youth academy between 2001 and 2006, wanted to manage a club; against my advice he departed for Brøndby in Denmark. After about six months it wasn't working out for him, so I brought him back to United as a first-team coach. He then left again, but he had bad experiences as a manager at Anzhi Makhachkala and Fulham. I think he now understands his forte is as a wonderful first-team coach.

We also always kept track of what was happening in management circles elsewhere. For example, I had dinner with Pep Guardiola in New York in 2012, but couldn't make him any direct proposal because retirement was not on my agenda at that point. He had already won an enviable number of trophies with Barcelona – two Champions Leagues, three La Liga titles, two Copa del Reys (Spanish Cup), two UEFA Super Cups and two FIFA Club World Cups – and I admired him greatly. I asked Pep to phone me before he accepted an offer from another club, but he didn't and wound up joining Bayern Munich in July 2013.

Life is such that the best of theories, or the best of intentions, sometimes don't translate into practice. Believe me, the United board wanted nothing more than to select a manager who would be with the club for a long time. All of us knew the history of the club and the success and benefits that come from stable leadership. When we started the process of looking for my replacement, we established that several very desirable candidates were unavailable. It became apparent that José Mourinho had given his word to Roman Abramovich that he would return to Chelsea, and that Carlo Ancelotti would succeed him at Real Madrid. We also knew that Jürgen Klopp was happy at Borussia Dortmund, and would be signing a new contract. Meantime, Louis van Gaal had undertaken to lead the Dutch attempt to win the 2014 World Cup.

We could obviously have taken the risk on a young manager who had not been tested, but eventually, as everyone knows, we selected David Moyes. Many people seem to have forgotten his performance at Everton where, despite being under severe financial constraints, he achieved strong League performances.

Sadly, things did not turn out for David as he and we all wished. Despite what people might think, the board of directors at United wants nothing more than for its manager to succeed. If the manager succeeds, the club succeeds, and the virtuous cycle is renewed. When David was appointed to a six-year contract, it was done with the best of intentions. Everyone hoped he would have a very long run at United. But it did not work out like that. I also know the Glazers well enough to understand that removing David was the last thing they wanted to do.

I'm sure there are some things that David would do differently if he had the opportunity to relive his time at Old Trafford, such as keeping Mick Phelan, who would have been the invaluable guide to the many layers of the club that Ryan Giggs is to Louis van Gaal today. The results were obviously disappointing, but it is difficult to imagine what it is like to walk out of the tunnel into a packed stadium knowing that every person is wondering about your future. I had experienced that feeling once or twice and it is very lonely. It is obviously fair to ask whether the transition at United could have been managed better. But the club did a good job, working through a discreet process in a professional manner. Right now, I hope that Louis van Gaal stays for a long time and, obviously, with Ryan Giggs at his side, there is a path towards a healthy, long-term succession plan.

About the only manager transition in top-flight English football that has gone well for the club was when Bob Paisley succeeded Bill Shankly at Liverpool. Shankly had rebuilt the club, gaining promotion back to the top division, winning three top division titles, two FA Cups and a UEFA Cup during his tenure, and Paisley, who managed the club between 1974 and 1983, topped it by winning three European Cups. As an outsider, I would never have guessed that Paisley would pull off what he eventually accomplished. In fact, when Shankly recommended Paisley, he initially refused the job. He had been the physiotherapist and then first-team coach prior to assuming the role; he was as quiet as Shankly was ebullient. He kept Shankly's team intact, understood the system, and gradually improved his squad by adding quality players and continuing the principles put in place by Shankly. Whoever selected Paisley deserves a lot of credit.

I had two attempts at retirement as a manager. I botched the first one – which is, perhaps, why I did a better job of it the second time around. My first run at retirement was a textbook case for how not to do it. I was turning 60, which in my father's time was a watershed age, but these days has far less significance. Nonetheless, I found myself contemplating my age. I was also irritated with the club who, in response to questions from the press, had announced that there would be no position for me in the organisation after retirement, lest there be a repeat of what happened after Matt Busby retired.

I could not help but think of what happened to Jock Stein and Bill Shankly after they had retired from Celtic and Liverpool, and I was determined that would not happen to me. I made matters worse by not having a plan for what I would do after I retired and by announcing my intention prior to the start of the 2001–02 season, which made the players go to sleep. It was as if I had put chloroform over their mouths. I knew when I made the decision and announced it to the players that I had made a mistake.

By Christmas 2001, Cathy and my boys persuaded me to change my mind. I was relieved they did so because, left to my own devices, I'm not sure that I would have summoned up the courage to phone Maurice Watkins, the club's solicitor, and announce my change of heart. He just said, 'I told you that you were stupid.' In retrospect, it all worked out well enough. It was as if I had inadvertently given myself a half-time breather. After 15 minutes, I was raring to get back on the field.

Had it not been for the death of Bridget Robertson, Cathy's sister, in October 2012, I would have continued managing United. I really wanted to win another Champions League and I had been planning for the future. In my last summer as manager of Manchester United, when I met Robin van Persie during the process of signing him from Arsenal, one of the questions he asked me was, 'How long are you going to carry on for?' I told him the truth. Retirement was not on my agenda. We'd tied down a number of our squad to new deals and, with an eye on the future of the club, signed Powell (18), Henríquez (18), and Zaha (20), as well as agreeing contracts with some of the most promising youngsters. It was business as usual. Also, I had already started work on a couple of new signings for the following summer. It would have been interesting, if I had stayed on, to see if we could have got those deals over the line. But Bridget's death was the watershed moment. It is hard to conjure up a more tangible reminder of mortality, and I felt that, after all those years during which Cathy had put me first, it was time that I took care of her needs. Bridget had not just been Cathy's sister but also her closest friend. When I decided to really retire, I just went with my instincts.

There were no demons in my mind about the horrors of not going to work. I also had a list of things that I wanted to do, so I could not imagine that I was going to be bored. Maybe things had just run their course and 39 years of management had been enough. I just sensed it was time to go. I knew that I would miss the players and the staff, and I was not quite sure how I would adjust to not going at full tilt, but I also felt a great sense of relief about not having to do certain things – particularly contending with the press and dealing with agents. Once I made the decision, I found myself looking forward to retirement.

I was fortunate because I got to retire as a football manager. Most football managers do not have that opportunity. Some lose a few games, get fired and never find another management job. They just disappear and are never heard from again. Or there are people like Bill Shankly who, after his retirement from Liverpool, discovered that the audience that used to lap up his stories had vanished. He was a lost soul. He used to go and watch the training sessions at Tranmere Rovers and Everton. He was only 68 when he died.

I imagine that some people thought I would have trouble letting go and ceding the authority that I had enjoyed for so long to others. But I was not confused about the difference between the role of being a United director and ambassador and the club's manager. After anyone retires from a position of responsibility and remains associated with the same organisation, it is unfair to your successor to try and retain the authority you once possessed. You have to let go and let the new man and the new regime do what they think is best.

I had heard the stories of what happened after Matt Busby had retired. He stayed in his office at Old Trafford, continued to show up at the club most days and was the power behind the throne. That was all a bit far-fetched, but I did not want to intimidate my successor with my presence in his day-to-day working environment. This is why I cleared out my office at Carrington straight away and, apart from attending games, and activities with sponsors, I maintained my distance. Carrington was off-limits and I chose not to join the other directors when they went to the dressing room after games; that remains the case today. I was not about to meddle in somebody else's business. I realised that when I watched a United game, the television directors kept a camera trained on me to gauge my reaction. I think they hoped they would catch me acting like Statler or Waldorf, the two curmudgeons in *The Muppets*, who are always criticising what is happening on the stage. I just wanted David and United to win – just as I do these days with Louis van Gaal. When the club made the decision to remove David, there were some who wanted me to return to the sidelines. But I was not tempted for a moment. I had made my decision to retire. My time was over.

Obviously I had a great run at United and accumulated a lovely set of trophies. But when I look at my name on the stand that's opposite my seat at Old Trafford, I wonder, from time to time, whether I deserve that recognition. This is not an attempt at false modesty, but sometimes I think that, with the teams and players I had at my disposal, we should have done more.

My most acute disappointment is with the Champions League. We lost three Champions League semi-finals and two finals. When I retired, United had won the trophy three times, but we really should have won it five times. Real Madrid has won it ten times (including five in a row), Bayern Munich has won it five times (including three in a row) and Barcelona, AC Milan and Ajax have taken it home more often than United. But the comparison that really hurts is with Liverpool, who have won the Cup five times. It is not much consolation that they only won it once during my time at United. It still stings.

I could argue that for three years the regulations were stacked against us, but every club faced the same restrictions about the number of foreign players that were permitted. After we won the Double in 1994, we had a strong squad, but the rules – until they were changed in late 1995 – allowed teams to field only three players born outside the country in which they were employed, plus two 'assimilated' players who had come through their youth set-up. Unfortunately our squad included Brian McClair (from Scotland), Denis Irwin and Roy Keane (from Ireland), Peter Schmeichel (from Denmark), Andrei Kanchelskis (from Ukraine/Russia/Soviet Union), Eric Cantona (from France), and Mark Hughes and Ryan Giggs (from Wales).

We were also unlucky on a couple of occasions – but that's football (and life). We should have won when we played Borussia Dortmund in the Champions League semi-finals in 1997 but we lost our goalkeeper the night before the game and against Bayer Leverkusen in 2002 we went out on the away goals rule at the semi-final stage of the Champions League, having drawn 2–2 at Old Trafford and 1–1 in Germany. We could have won both the 2009 and 2011 finals against Barcelona. The first was played in Rome and, through poor planning, we stayed in a lousy hotel and several players felt groggy after uncomfortable nights. At Wembley in 2011, Barcelona were very clever and rattled us by maintaining a lot of possession. Instead of staying patient and sticking to our plan, a bit of panic set in and our attacking impulse became our undoing. We were overcome by primal instincts.

Fresh Challenges

But those are the yesterdays and now, after a lifetime of getting ready for work at six in the morning, I like waking up at eight, having breakfast with Cathy (which I had not done for 30 years), reading the paper, and going to have lunch in the village. I suppose retirement, for some people, can be like bereavement.

Immediately after you retire, there are lots of things to do and plenty of people around. Normally, after the players had disappeared at the end of the season, I would be in my office at Carrington every day until we left for our annual holiday in France in early June. In 2013 I found there were other things that filled my time. There was a fair amount of press attention after I retired, and I was helping to put the finishing touches to my autobiography. After that the summer got chewed up, with a pair of notable firsts, one more pleasurable than the other: a boat trip up the coast of Western Scotland, and a stint in hospital for a hip replacement.

The first reminder that I had retired came when we were on holiday in France that June. In previous years I would be on the telephone several times a day, usually dealing with players we wanted to buy or were willing to sell. David Gill would make frequent visits, and the club was never far from my mind. I would also have to meet players, and sometimes their parents, when we wanted to convince them to stake their futures to United. It was always the arrival of the fixture list for the upcoming season that would jolt me out of any propensity to put all cares aside. In 2013, for the first time in my life, my most pressing need, as I relaxed by the Mediterranean, was to beat my brother-in-law, John Robertson, at Kaluki.

When I recovered from the hip surgery and started going to games at Old Trafford, it felt a little odd. I had never had lunch in the directors' lounge before a game, and for the first time I also really noticed the noise of the crowd. While I had been managing, I had usually been able to block out the sound from the stands, and it rarely ever registered with me.

It is only now, a couple of years into this new chapter of my life, that I really have come to appreciate the change in circumstances. While I was working I had never fully appreciated that I was not in control of my life. I know this will seem peculiar, given how much I value the virtues of control and discipline, but when you sit atop any organisation, you are imprisoned by the calendar and the relentless needs of others. It doesn't matter if you work 24 hours a day, there will always be something or someone that demands your attention.

It was no wonder I always sensed – though I am not complaining – that the hamster wheel never stopped spinning. I was always looking at my watch – and not just in the closing minutes of games. So after I retired, for the first time in my life, I was in charge of my life in a way that I had not been since the school holidays of my childhood, when the only thing I needed to do was be home for lunch and dinner. It was a liberating and refreshing experience and has allowed me to do things that I could never have done while I was at the helm of United.

I have tried to balance things so that I stay vital and engaged, while also leading my life at a different pace. Apart from Manchester United games, the regular fixtures in my diary are appearances for the club in my role as a board member and club ambassador; the classes that I teach at Harvard; and the work I do as a UEFA coaching ambassador. In the UEFA role, I chair the annual Elite Coaches Forum in Geneva. In advance I will meet Ioan Lupescu from UEFA and we will structure the agenda. The forum itself is attended by the coaches of the teams competing in the Champions League and Europa League, as well as experienced coaches like Gérard Houllier, Roy Hodgson and UEFA president Michel Platini and his committee. The retired Italian referee, Pierluigi Collina, also attends, and we discuss with him the performance of referees but, in general, we cover the issues related to the previous season's competitions and look at ways we can continue to improve the game. I'm also a member of the technical study group of the Champions League and the Europa League; we meet the day after the finals to analyse the trends and tactics from the previous night's game.

During the horse-racing season, barely a week goes by without some kind of activity. Together with a few pals, I have ownership interests in a number of horses. We buy them usually when they are two year olds. I have enjoyed watching What A Friend winning two Group One races, or going to race meetings at York or Doncaster, and being able to linger at the track without feeling the need to bolt back to Manchester.

I like going through the sales catalogues and trying to understand the bloodlines and pedigree of the horses. Every now and again, when one of these horses turns into a winner, we have made some decent money – although this is the exception. I don't kid myself: horse racing is a pastime; it is not a way to build a durable investment. I always try to either watch or listen to a race when one of our horses is running, and invariably get a chuckle when the phone rings, or the texts arrive, at the end of the races.

I found myself getting absorbed by *The Brothers*, Stephen Kinzer's account of the lives of the Dulles brothers who were the US Secretary of State and head of the CIA in the 1950s. This was not a subject I knew much about, and the litany of their endless interference in countries all around the world during the Cold War kept me riveted. Coincidentally, at about the same time, I also picked up Ben Macintyre's *A Spy Among Friends*, another study of the Cold War era, which explains the way the double-agent, Kim Philby, betrayed his closest friends, as he spent decades leading a treacherous life in broad daylight. I'm glad the Dulles boys and Philby weren't working for United. Though I don't read many books about football, I have found myself going back to my roots and enjoyed two works about the sport north of the border. The first, *Black Diamonds and the Blue Brazil*, is an affectionate portrait of Cowdenbeath FC written by a long-time fan, Ron Ferguson, who, despite the name, is not a relative. The second is a biography of Sean Fallon, *Celtic's Iron Man*, by Stephen Sullivan. Fallon was Jock Stein's right-hand man at Celtic for many years, and this book is a detailed account of the life that, to all intents and purposes, they led together.

Retirement has presented the opportunity to indulge myself in trips and excursions that I would not have taken while at United. I fulfilled one ambition in 2014 when I attended the Oscars in Los Angeles. The Kentucky Derby horse race and the US Masters golf are also on the wish-list.

There have also been some really special experiences, like the tour I received of the vast State Hermitage museum in St Petersburg, which has the largest collection of paintings anywhere in the world. Mikaël Silvestre, who was a stalwart of United's defence for many seasons, was kind enough to line up a dinner, while Cathy and I were visiting Paris, at Le Taillevent, one of Europe's gastronomic treasures. Mikaël ensured that we were spoiled rotten, but he also couldn't resist playing a practical joke; he had instructed the sommelier to tell me that, unfortunately, he could not serve us any wine, because we had chosen to dine on Tuesday – the one day in the week when the restaurant did not offer alcohol. I also spent a couple of pleasurable days at Notre Dame, the university just west of Chicago, where Bobby Clark, the former Aberdeen and Scotland goalkeeper, is the football coach. Bobby gave me a tour of the Notre Dame campus, which has a staggering collection of stadiums and gyms that are better than those of most Premier League sides.

Sharing stories and memories with Mikaël or Bobby reminds me of what I miss about my old life. It isn't the open-top bus tours, the pleasure of spotting a youngster with great talent or the thrill of a closely fought game. Rather, it is all those shared experiences and the camaraderie that emerges between people who live and work together for a long time. I miss talking to Mick Phelan; seeing Albert Morgan, our kit man, every day; giving stick to Tony Sinclair and Joe Pemberton, our head groundsmen at Old Trafford and Carrington. I also used to relish the daily exchanges with the laundry team and Carol Williams and Rita Gaskell from the canteen. But most of all I miss being around the company of young people eager to take on impossible challenges – whether they were the players or the eager crew of video analysts. Just thinking about all these people and the scenes inside a winning dressing room makes me chuckle. But, as I said, those are the yesterdays and right now I keep remembering a short piece of advice about tomorrow that I was given before I retired. It was, 'Don't put your slippers on.' The line has stuck with me. It's why I put my shoes on right after breakfast.

EPILOGUE

SIR ALEX FERGUSON – THROUGH ANOTHER LENS

Since his retirement, match days for Sir Alex Ferguson have brought a fresh ritual. Gone are the times when he would leave The Lowry Hotel, where the Manchester United squad often stay on the night before home games, for the ride in the team bus to Old Trafford. Instead he arrives in one of the Chevrolet SUVs supplied by United's largest sponsor, and makes his way to the executive suite for a pre-game lunch.

These days, when Sir Alex watches a game, it's no longer from the manager's seat but rather from the directors' box – a perch that would have seemed inconceivable to a child growing up, as he did, in 1940s Govan. At kick-off he takes his seat – among the eight inscribed with 'Reserved for Sir Alex Ferguson' – opposite the triple-decker North Stand, the largest football stand in the United Kingdom, which, since 2011, has borne his name in large red letters. He no longer chews gum throughout the game, but instead repeatedly clears his throat. He keeps his thoughts to himself, particularly on days when United are not at their best, but every now and again, when a player in red is on the attack, he will mutter, 'Take him on, son. Take him on.'

After the game, he will retreat to his own suite, which has few of the trappings of the luxury boxes found at American stadiums or new football grounds like the Emirates, Arsenal's London home. It is the size of a windowless railway carriage: three black couches line the wall, a small bar stands at one end, a television is mounted near the ceiling and, occasionally, after the end of a game, the door opens and a security guard ushers in a new visitor.

Sometimes the door opens and a familiar face appears – a talk-show host, a film star or a former player. There might be a couple of people, dressed smartly in suits and ties, who have won a prize at a charity auction to watch a game with Sir Alex. People come to obtain an autograph, shake his hand or pose for a photograph. Drinks are passed around, glasses are raised and Sir Alex genially introduces everyone – urging them all to try the steak pies.

Eventually, the crowd thins down to a smaller group, most of whom have known Sir Alex – or Alec, as his Scottish relatives and friends call him – for the better part of a lifetime, and are now in their sunset years. At this point in the proceedings, it is hard to believe that the man on the receiving end of much good-natured teasing managed Manchester United for 26 years – first as Alex Ferguson OBE, then as Alex Ferguson CBE and, finally, as Sir Alex Ferguson, during which time he won 38 trophies, including 13 Premier League and two Champions League titles.

For those in the suite, the facts that, under his leadership, United won their 20th League championship, eclipsing the record set by Liverpool, or that, by the end of a truly remarkable career (although he would be the last person to mention this fact), he had become the most successful manager in the history of football, are beside the point. His career, an extraordinary mix of personal stamina, willpower and leadership, is not what draws these people to Old Trafford. There may be a friend, who tells how, when he was lying despondently in a hospital bed receiving life-saving treatment, Sir Alex came and spent several hours lifting him out of his gloom. There might be the wife of a former player, glowing with the satisfaction that comes from knowing she and her husband are sitting there because Sir Alex answered her letter and invited them to spend the afternoon with him.

Manchester United's long-time kit man, Albert Morgan, proudly wearing his club blazer, will sit quietly and act as the occasional straight-man. Ferguson's brother, Martin, invariably introduced as 'the greatest scout in history', might be there, along with one or two of Sir Alex's grandchildren. John Robertson, Sir Alex's wry brother-in-law, who was a compositor for the *Glasgow Herald*, will be muttering amusing and sardonic asides. Then the good-natured jousting begins and the conversation enters familiar stomping grounds, with stories, the comfort of recycled jokes and past embarrassments plucked out of the air. There will be prolonged discussion over whether St Patrick was Welsh. Somebody will try to remember the starting line-up for St Mirren in the early 1970s, and soon everyone is pitching in until the faded team-card is complete.

It's hard to imagine anyone less qualified than me to fill out a musty team-card or to write a book about football with Sir Alex Ferguson. As a ten year old in Wales in the 1960s, my peak footballing accomplishment was to stand on the touchline as the 'physio', holding a sponge and a bottle of water, lest any of my schoolmates might get injured, and to guard the Thermos and slices of oranges that served for their half-time refreshments.

Though I had followed Manchester United since the team

won the European Cup for the first time in 1968, and, like every British schoolboy, knew the names of its troupe of players, I don't qualify as a diehard fan. Manchester United's former captain, the blunt and confrontational Roy Keane, would dismiss me as a member of the 'prawn sandwich' crowd. When I moved to the US in 1980 to become a journalist at *Time* magazine, I kept half an eye on the team, but it wasn't until the late 1990s that I began to follow the club more closely – partly, no doubt, because more games were being broadcast in the United States. The other reason I was drawn back to the game was because of a fondness for the theatre and gossip that surrounds the Premier League: the big-ticket transfers, the rash managerial sackings, the intensity of the local derbies and, more often than not through this period, another trophy for Sir Alex Ferguson's United team.

As a journalist at *Time*, before, in 1986, joining Sequoia Capital, the California-based private investment partnership, I wrote two books about companies dominated by strong leaders. The first was an account (written with Barry Seaman) of Lee Iacocca's turnaround of Chrysler almost 40 years ago. The second, published in 1984, was a study of the very early years of Apple and the influence of its co-founder, Steve Jobs.

As the years slid by, I became increasingly interested in the ways one person can shape and influence an organisation, particularly the handful who maintain their hunger for success and can coax others to perform at high levels for prolonged periods. When, in the mid-1990s, I found myself *primus inter pares* among Sequoia's partners, I became even more aware of the challenge. Like any organisation, Sequoia Capital has to constantly fight for its place in the world. While we have an affinity for winning, I don't pretend for a moment that we resemble Manchester United. For a start, our lineage is nowhere near as long. We only came into being in 1974 when Don Valentine, a veteran of Silicon Valley's semiconductor industry, organised our first investment partnership. We operate beyond the glare of public scrutiny, although that has changed to a modest degree in the past few years, since Silicon Valley is now awash with journalists and bloggers. There is now even a popular HBO series titled *Silicon Valley*.

While few know the names of Sequoia's principals, that is not the case for some of the founders or companies with whom we have been involved since their inception. The most successful of these – Apple, Cisco, Google, Yahoo! and PayPal – have become every bit as visible in the business pages as United is on the sports pages. The same is true for some of our more recent investments, such as LinkedIn, Airbnb and Dropbox or, in China, VIPShop and JD.com. The combined market capitalisation of companies that received their first investment from Sequoia Capital is about $1.5 trillion.

After the Premier League arrived on American television and I was able to watch Manchester United regularly, my curiosity about the skill it takes to become a successful leader eventually led me to Sir Alex. I was intrigued to know how he had accumulated more trophies than any other manager in the world's most competitive and popular sport. Thanks to the good offices of Charlie Stillitano, one of the founding members of the US Soccer Foundation, I was introduced to the man himself. In a London hotel room, on the eve of a United game against Arsenal seven years ago, we polished off a bottle of wine and – interrupted a couple of times by players who needed some private words with Sir Alex – began the first of many conversations that eventually helped form this book.

The list of leadership topics that Sir Alex and I started to chew over soon stretched the length of a football field. How had he been able to inculcate the benefits of teamwork above the role of an individual – particularly among young, highly paid, intensely competitive characters? How had he managed to instil hope of a better tomorrow and the desire to win in a club that, prior to his arrival in 1986, had failed to win an English League championship for almost 20 years? How did he find and develop talent? How did he retain them? How did he set targets? How did he make people aspire to achieve the impossible? When did he give up on young players? How did he balance different levels of compensation? How did he cope with distractions, mete out punishment and instil discipline? How did he bounce back from setbacks or deal with press criticism or maintain balance in his life? How did he think about competitors and deal with changes? How did he set aside his personal feelings for particular individuals? How did he prevent complacency from setting in? How did he prepare, plan and communicate? How did he maintain his enthusiasm and hunger?

Many of the habits and approaches that hold true for the best football teams are also germane for any organisation that seeks to excel – even an investment partnership housing multiple businesses and active on several continents. There are plenty of parallels between life in the English Premier League, the most fiercely contested sporting competition in the world, and the stretch of land that lies between San Francisco and San Jose – which is little farther than the distance between Old Trafford and Anfield. Yet it is also easy to make too many trite analogies between Manchester United, an organisation that, 50 to 60 times a year, confronts a worldwide television audience, most of whom consider themselves qualified experts, and the world of large companies and government agencies, or of local hospitals, boy-scout troops and community centres.

For Sequoia Capital, lessons drawn from leaders in other fields or organisations can be applied in two ways. The first is to our own, internal investment partnership, where we deal with many of the organisational challenges that bedevil any company or institution seeking to perform at the highest possible level. Like any other organization, we contend with issues around recruitment, team-building, setting of standards, questions of inspiration and motivation, avoiding complacency, the arrival of new competitors and the continual need to refresh ourselves and purge under-performers. The second is towards the companies in which we invest, and where we are often the first, serious business partner for talented entrepreneurs, frequently still in their early or mid-twenties, setting out on a path that, sometimes, turns an entire industry upside down. In the first case, after internal wrangling and jawboning, we can usually apply what seems relevant. In the second, where we are minority shareholders in companies started and run by people of great wit, imagination, drive and, often, emotional fragility and temperamental dispositions, we need to rely on powers of persuasion, motivation, sensible counsel and, more often than not, good humour, to help someone do something, or make a decision, the wisdom of which might not be immediately apparent.

There is no other place in the world where companies wreak so much havoc on existing industries as Silicon Valley, the world I have inhabited since the early 1980s. Here new technology companies are formed almost every day. Most of them either fail or are quickly subsumed by others. Only a handful, far fewer than all the Silicon Valley spin-masters would have you believe, are great in the way in which Manchester United, Bayern Munich, Real Madrid or Barcelona are great and have dominated football since the Second World War. In the past

40 years, the list of technology giants is surprisingly short; the only qualifiers, at least in my book, are Apple, Cisco, Oracle, Google, Facebook, Intel, Microsoft, Amazon, Qualcomm, Alibaba and Tencent (though the last five are based in Seattle, San Diego and China rather than Silicon Valley proper).

Any student of business, management or economics knows there are very few groups capable of excelling for a long time. Just think of all the restaurants, hotels, bars, bakeries and toy shops on the High Street that once commanded a devoted following, only to founder as their standards fell or tastes changed. The same is true in the corporate world, and in the United States a quick look at the Dow Jones 30 index shows the vicissitudes of time. Only seven companies that were in the index in 1976 are still present. Some, like steel mills and ship-builders, were slaughtered by offshore competition; retailers, like Sears, clung too much to their heritage; while once powerful companies in a wide range of industries – newspapers, cinema, radio and television broadcasting, advertising, real-estate brokerage, printing – have been upset, transformed or gutted by advances in technology. Many, of course, were felled by managers who made the wrong choices, thought themselves invulnerable and were undone by a combination of ineptitude and vanity.

For firms like Sequoia Capital, this cycle of growth and decay is of keen interest because our business depends on it. The technology world is far less forgiving of leadership failures than other industries, because a sudden, underlying change can quickly catapult a young company into a position of prominence and spell trouble for an industry leader. The floor of the technology world is littered with the butchered carcasses of high flyers that once could do no wrong: Digital Equipment, Compaq, Data General, Cray Computer Corporation, Silicon

Graphics, Lotus Development, PeopleSoft, Novell, Sun Microsystems, Wang Laboratories, Siebel Systems, BlackBerry, Nokia – the list is endless. So we've always been eager to learn about what leadership characteristics differentiate the so-called 'academy' companies from the true giants, particularly since I have always felt that a vast gulf separates a great leader from a very good manager. Accomplished and skilful managers can be hired by the truckload. Leaders are the rarest of commodities. So, here is what I learned about the character of one leader – the man who used to wear a jacket bearing the initials 'AF'.

When the teenager, later identified as 'AF', started as a professional footballer, he and his fellow players were treated little better than oddly gifted manual workers, employed by local business people who, in addition to a football club, also owned steel mills, shipyards, a chain of shops or, in the case of Louis Edwards, Manchester United's chairman and principal shareholder between 1965 and 1980, a meat distribution business. The class barriers, reinforced by archaic structures laid down by the Football Association's rule-makers in their London headquarters, reinforced this divide.

Sir Alex played his first League game in 1957 – when, despite the date, the game was still lodged in its interwar mode. Players selected for international teams would often only discover they had been picked after seeing their name on a team-sheet in the newspapers. Floodlights were just starting to appear; the handful of fixtures that received television coverage were broadcast in black and white; commercial hoardings were absent from most British stadiums; fans stood on terraces (with the seats reserved for VIPs and season-ticket holders); the footballs were made of leather and became painfully heavy when wet; boots covered the ankles; players' shirts and shorts were made of cotton and the pitches quickly turned to mud. It was still an intensely local game. In the United Kingdom international fixtures were often interpreted to mean games between England, Scotland, Wales and Ireland. European football – the European champion-ship and the European Cup Winners' Cup – had yet to be launched and the European Cup was only two years old; the majority of players were born within a couple of bus rides of their club ground, and a salary cap that existed until 1961 meant that football workers were paid like factory hands. It was also a game played by white men; it was not until 1978 that a black footballer first appeared in the English national side.

Sir Alex himself attributes much of his success to his working-class roots on the banks of the River Clyde. The memory of the grit and perseverance his father displayed as a shipyard worker – working 60-hour weeks in cold, dangerous conditions – looms large. Beyond this ingrained disposition for hard work, and a touching inclination to appear early for appointments, Sir Alex has always seen himself as something of an outsider, a rebel without being a firebrand, irritated by pompous people in positions of authority and happiest when surrounded by family and the friends he has known since childhood. While he is intensely competitive and doesn't easily forget past slights, he is not a man who harbours malice. He has a natural sympathy for those who are struggling and an affinity with his fellow managers, partly because all of them had a common challenge: the unpredictable behaviour of club owners who could dismiss them at a moment's notice. It was entirely characteristic of him, in remarks to a packed Old Trafford following his final game as a manager, to mention the United midfielder, Darren Fletcher, who for the previous five years had been battling ulcerative colitis, and the retirement of the midfielder, Paul Scholes, after more than 700 appearances for the club, whose dislike of the spotlight was inversely related to the influence he wielded on the pitch.

He might blanch at the label, but Sir Alex, a lifelong supporter of the British Labour Party, is, at heart, a conservative – with a small 'c'. He is self-made, keenly appreciates loyalty (which is returned in spades), doesn't tolerate slackers, poseurs and braggarts, and cannot hide his disdain for high-profile free-loaders who show up with an entourage for an important game and demand a clutch of free tickets for the best seats in the ground. Even though he's worked hard all his life, Sir Alex feels he's had it easy compared to miners, farmers, fishermen, oil-field workers, steelworkers and shipbuilders – manual labourers who have often faced difficult and dangerous conditions at work. He is, by nature, an optimist, and though he has the jovial characteristics of the pub owner he once was, he is not inclined to embrace complete strangers with bear hugs as his brother, Martin, is prone to do.

Though he is fond of the good things in life and is wealthy by most people's standards, Sir Alex isn't avaricious, and has never felt the need to own the largest house (or collection of homes) or a stable of exotic cars. Compared to today's footballing stars, he and his wife Cathy live quietly and modestly. Though she never attended games at Old Trafford, Cathy – whose instinct is to protect her husband from the overtures of strangers – has always been keenly aware of whatever duel is being fought on the field.

Sir Alex has a chess master's memory for numbers, deals and people, which lends additional authority to his observations. Ask him the score of football games played decades ago, and he'll remember not just the final score and most names on the starting team-sheets but also the critical substitutions and the build-up to many of the goals. He will reel off the entire Premier

League fixture list for the weekend that lies ahead with the same quiet confidence with which other people complete *The Times* crossword in ten minutes. He will remember with precision what price he paid and gained for a player (wincing when recalling occasions on which the latter was less than the former); the amount he contributed for his share of a horse – like Harry the Viking or Chapter and Verse – and how much he paid for a 1986 Pétrus or 1993 Sassicaia, though his face will suddenly harden and his lips will purse when recounting an investment over which he feels he was duped. It is easy to see how, if destiny and circumstances had been different, he probably would have succeeded at whatever he had turned towards: leading a trade union, operating a chain of retailers, commanding an aircraft carrier, or – if for some reason Silicon Valley had developed between Glasgow and Edinburgh in the 1940s and 1950s – founding a company.

Unnervingly he can recite the names of the hotels that he and Cathy have visited and, without guile and almost reflexively, will name each of the children of their friends. He is reticent about asking others for special treatment and will cringe when recounting an experience or pleasure that came his way due to the kindness of others. Long-time football fans might remember his emotional outbursts on the sidelines, and journalists who covered him throughout his career might recall being subjected to the occasional stream of profanities and abuse, but most people aren't aware of his patience and innumerable acts of kindness: the good-natured way he will pose for photographs or sign autographs, politely say a few words to someone who interrupts his dinner at a restaurant or who stops him in the street. Little wonder that, for years, he has welcomed the relative anonymity of New York, where he has an apartment.

He likes winning whatever card game (such as Kaluki) or

snooker challenge he plays. He prefers red wine and has never drunk whisky, the pride of his homeland. For the past 15 years, his summers have been spent in the same hotel in the south of France, where he knows all the staff by name, and thoroughly admires the way the owner is up at dawn meticulously inspecting his property.

Sir Alex is a card-carrying member of several tribes – his own family, the memory of the tenements of Govan, Glasgow, Scotland and Manchester United. Most of all he still feels he belongs to the working-class tribe, and remembers, with a shiver, the cold Scottish mornings when, as an apprentice tool-maker, he had to tie rags around the end of the lathes to keep his hands warm.

Sir Alex Ferguson was United's manager from 1986 to 2013, but never held the title that, in the business world, applies to the most senior person in the organisation: chief executive officer. From 1980 to 2000 that role belonged to Martin Edwards, at the time the club's principal shareholder, from 2000 to 2003 to Peter Kenyon and from 2003 to 2013 to David Gill, whom Sir Alex came to view as a blood brother.

This may sound odd, but Sir Alex, unlike so many other people who experience success at the head of an organisation, was not confused about his position. He knew he was a hired hand. He did not delude himself into thinking that he was the man who built Manchester United; he was well aware of the fact that he had come to a club with a rich heritage that had enjoyed much success due to the work, sacrifices and perform-ance of those who had preceded him. Sir Alex never imagined when he joined United that his image would one day be cast in bronze and be placed, for all to see, outside the stadium. I would be surprised if he ever thought, even in his most private moments, that he was bigger than the club. He has the sort of moral compass that is not found among leaders who award themselves a disproportionate share of the spoils; talk about themselves and their accomplishments in the third person; don't have the humility and inner decency to recognise that they are standing on the shoulders of those who came before; or understand that they are merely custodians, charged with leaving the organisation in better condition than it was when they arrived.

Ferguson ruled everything that occurred on the pitch, was responsible for the lion's share of the club's spending and was in charge of the majority of the club's payroll. Generation of revenue (negotiation of television rights, sales of sponsorships, setting of ticket prices, international tours) and management of advertising, promotions, stewardship of financial systems and human relations were the preserve of the club's 'commercial side', which fell under the purview of the CEO. But of course the 'commercial side' hinged on a first-rate performance on the field, and the growth in the value of the club – from £20 million in 1989, when Martin Edwards first thought about selling his stake, to £1.93 billion today – is irrevocably associated with Sir Alex. While he had plenty of frustrations during his managerial life, his control over what is colloquially called the 'dressing room' – the players, coaches, groundsmen and the medical and sports science staff – was as complete as that of any absolute monarch. The way that former players, now in their fifties or sixties, still address him as 'Boss' is freighted with meaning. In the words of Reggie Jackson, one of the kings of American baseball during the 1970s and 1980s, Sir Alex was the straw that stirred the drink.

Other business organisations split executive responsibilities in a similar way to Manchester United. Think of an advertising agency or fashion house, whose inspiration and following comes from the inventiveness and imagination of a creative director, but where the commercial affairs are run by a CEO. Consider the newspapers and magazines of yesteryear, where the editorial coverage was the preserve of the editor and the sale of subscriptions and advertising of the publisher or the CEO. Look at movie companies where directors are always at war with the men (and now women) who used to be called 'suits'. In the arts there are orchestra conductors, museum and theatre directors responsible for artistic repertoires, shadowed by a CEO, whose name is usually unknown to the public but who is responsible for maintaining a going concern. If Manchester United were a Silicon Valley company, Sir Alex's title would probably have been chief product architect or chief designer, and David Gill's would have been chief commercial officer.

Some – particularly from the business world, large public agencies or the military – will look at Manchester United and conclude that this footballing enterprise would be straightforward to run. If so, they are underestimating the challenge of constantly buffing a global entertainment brand that relies on the unpredictable physical condition and mental state of a changing collection of absurdly talented live performers. While United's reputation is vast (and, thanks to the explosion of satellite television and mobile computing, it now has fans in faraway places such as Bhutan, Djibouti or Belize), its business and payroll, measured alongside some of Silicon Valley's companies or some of the world's larger companies, is surprisingly small and pedestrian. The club's revenues in its last fiscal year were £433 million, which is what Apple and Google do in 30 hours and four days respectively. It only operates one line of business and it does this in one time zone rather than in separate locations scattered across different continents. The club's expansion opportunities are circumscribed. The Old Trafford stadium has 75,731 seats and is already the largest club ground in Britain. It is hard to squeeze more games into a year when, in a busy season, the most heavily worked players already take the field 38 times for Premier League games as well as FA Cup, League Cup and European competition fixtures, not to mention the pre-season exhibitions, friendlies, international matches, testimonial and charitable games that find their way into the calendar. United's share of television revenue, which was non-existent before the formation of the English Premier League, fluctuates with the team's performance, as do its other sources of revenue: ticket sales, rental of luxury boxes, and sponsorship and merchandising opportunities. Like most sports franchises, Manchester United would not meet any of Warren Buffett's investment criteria – its performance is unpredictable, it requires large capital outlays and there is no lid on costs.

And yet a huge gulf exists between Manchester United, and the other top-ranked clubs in the Premier League, and every other football team in Britain. The vast difference in crowd size is illustrative of the way that in football, as in almost every other organised activity, the fruits of triumph are concentrated in a few hands. Manchester United might fill their stands with 75,000 people for every game (as befits a stadium that is as much an international house of worship as a 'theatre of dreams'), but drop down 15 teams to West Bromwich Albion, and average attendance is 25,000; drop down to the league below, the Championship, and the crowds can dwindle to under 15,000. So, while Manchester United may appear easy to operate, it is, as with other organisations, another matter entirely to operate it well. It is even more of a challenge to keep it operating at a very high standard for a protracted period. Maintaining that standard of excellence is no fluke.

That same disparity, between the winners and the also-rans, exists in the technology world. Here, the market-leading company will sweep up the lion's share of the spoils – measured in customers, profits, free cash flow and market value. Think of IBM at the peak of the mainframe business; Intel, when the demand for microprocessors was unstoppable; Microsoft, as personal computer software spread into every business and home; eBay, when online auctions were all the vogue; Google, as it became synonymous with 'search' and Facebook with its hammer-lock on social networking. Then of course there is Apple which, without the monopoly characteristics of these other companies (making its accomplishment even more staggering), has outstripped them all.

The rivalries that exist in the English Premier League, while heated and often profane, seem quaint and gentlemanly compared to the competition that exists between the founders of technology companies where vicious barbs, lawsuits, theft of trade secrets and targeted assaults on one another's payroll are the order of the day. Perhaps this is only natural since the winner in technology races (where so often the leaders are monopolies in all but the eye of the law) mops up not just a share but the equivalent of all of the Premier League's television, ticket, merchandising, beer and hot dog money (including the ketchup and mustard). Microsoft, Intel, Amazon, Bloomberg, Google, Apple, Facebook, Oracle, Qualcomm, Alibaba, Baidu, Tencent, Cisco and eBay all illustrate this point, and if anyone thinks the competitive atmosphere in California is hot, they should go to China to sample the invective with which technology CEOs greet a rival's move. The founders of many of these technology companies would sooner share a pint of turpentine with one of their arch-rivals than sit down and mend fences with a glass of Tignanello, one of Sir Alex's favourite red wines. Larry Ellison, the founder of Oracle, was probably only half joking when he said he wanted to shoot the CEO of PeopleSoft, a company he acquired after a bitter two-year takeover battle in 2005.

Despite the difference in tone that exists between our two worlds, writing *Leading* with Sir Alex made two things apparent. The first is that a manager of a professional football team, and someone who works in an investment partnership with a fondness for the venture capital business, share the same pursuit – they are both transfixed by the possibilities of eternal youth. While both need to make sure their own house is always in order, their pursuit of success and market leadership is not constricted by the straitjacket that eventually fells every technology company – a slowing growth rate, some caused by sheer size, but most by a massive market change. We also have another enormous advantage which for a football club means fielding young players and, in the case of a venture capitalist, constantly striking up partnerships with young founders eager to make a mark with a new idea. Both manager and investor are largely insulated from the challenges posed by old products or ageing workforces. We have the wonderful luxury of always being able to stay on the young side of life.

The second point that became clear was that the principles of leadership are timeless, and that the opaque jargon found in so many management books is little more than a marketing ruse. The trick lies not in memorising some list of the rudiments of leadership (which any intelligent 14 year old can do) but, rather, having the stamina, knowledge and skill to consistently implement them. Press Sir Alex to choose three words to summarise his approach to leadership and he would pick three that begin with the same letter – preparation, perseverance and patience. Compel him to select one word and he would fasten on – consistency.

There are plenty of attributes that separate the great leader from the good manager. Both may put their work before family and friends, survive on little sleep, endure a lifetime of red-eye flights. Look more closely and you will find that the great leader possesses an unusual, and essential, characteristic – he will think and operate like an owner, or a person who owns a substantial stake of the business, even if, in a financial or legal sense, he is neither. It is extremely rare to find this trait among people like Sir Alex who are hired into a company, although in Silicon Valley this sense of long-term proprietorship is the distinctive hallmark of the best company founders. These sorts of people will never be oblivious to the pressing exigencies of their business, but they will always have a larger purpose in mind. Their attitude and approach is a world removed from that of most of the handsomely paid retainers who find themselves at the helm of an enterprise.

The great leader will embrace audacity and the unthinkable, will not shirk from making controversial and unpopular decisions, and will have unshakeable confidence in his convictions. He will have a clear sense of his ultimate goal and will be able to communicate that articulately to others. While his business may be complicated, he will be able to strip things down to their essence. The great leader will not compile endless lists of marching orders but, rather, will have a preference for keeping his followers' eyes on no more than two or three objectives. He will have the patience required to assemble something superlative while simultaneously curbing his own impatience. He will survey his colleagues with a clinical detachment and, regardless of their past contributions, will not hesitate about bidding them farewell if they miss too many beats. The great leader is prepared to trust the judgement of others, is unafraid of delegating authority, refrains from micromanagement, and will not be impelled to dominate every conversation or insist upon always having the last word in a debate. The great leader knows that most success comes from making a few large decisions correctly rather than trying to be involved in making lots of small choices. He will understand that there are others in the organisation capable of doing things that he himself cannot do or would not do as well. He will derive more satisfaction from the achievements of his organisation than from his own accomplishments, will not demand outlandish compensation for himself, will treat the organisation's money as if it were his own and will have no particular need to be singled out by the spotlight. He will probably watch and listen more than he talks, will not radiate anxiety when the chips are down, will have a keen understanding of what he doesn't know and a fetching sense of humility. If he does his job well, people will see him as being tough but fair rather than capricious and mercurial. He will definitely not feel the need to be universally loved. At the end of his tenure, knowing that his time has ended, he will relinquish authority with grace and will not sour the life of his successor.

Compare this with the capable manager who has attained his position by virtue of attrition, by being politically acceptable or by being a faithful, long-suffering servant. Having achieved the position that he has sought for many years he will concentrate on making sure that nothing goes wrong on his watch, will be wary about offending others, will shy away from making difficult decisions, will be at ease with the imperfections of compromise, will allow his strategy to be dictated by others, will find refuge in appeasement and court the affection of those around him. When he eventually retires, his organisation will be little different from the one he inherited. It will definitely not have achieved anything remarkable.

The great leader has two other traits that separate him from other helmsmen. The first is an obsession. Obsessives, those who cannot imagine doing anything else with their lives, always find their work more fulfilling than those who find themselves in a profession because it was expected of them or because they did not have a calling that tugged at their emotions. For people, like Sir Alex, who are obsessed by a pursuit, there is no separation between life and work. They are leading their life, rather than feeling compelled to seek respectability from their work.

The obsessives will find it far easier to maintain their enthusiasm for their calling than the person who clambers up an organisation and survives the Darwinism of the workplace. It is much more natural for the obsessive to achieve the consistency – of effort, determination, drive and ambition – that is the foundation of leadership. It is much easier to endure all the setbacks, reversals and frustrations of management when you deeply enjoy your work – a sense that most ordinary managers rarely, if ever, experience.

The second trait of the distinctive leader is his capacity for dealing with people. These leaders will be able to extract extraordinary levels of performance and commitment from their employees and colleagues. Some of that will just be by setting a personal example, but the bulk will come from having a keen understanding for the character of their employees and an empathy for them when they are weathering difficult circumstances. They will be able to blend intimacy with ambition.

Listening to Sir Alex, and watching him with others, made it clear that there is an uncommon resilience about him and the mainstays of his United teams. The need to succeed ran deep. This is the inner fortitude born of adversity, shaped by setbacks, reversals and the fear of failure, burnished by the sense of social inequity common to outsiders, underdogs and immigrants, by the stubborn refusal never, ever, to give up, and the personal

367

shame associated with disappointing colleagues. These are the same constitutional underpinnings required of entrepreneurs, and have been the characteristics of the sort of people I have always admired. About ten years ago I added a piece of copy to the Sequoia website that tried to summarise the character of the people with whom we seek to work. It reads: 'The creative spirits. The underdogs. The resolute. The determined. The indefatigable. The defiant. The outsiders. The independent thinkers. The fighters. The true believers.' Reading it now makes me think it could also serve as instructions for Sir Alex's United scouts.

Silicon Valley teems with examples of these types. Jerry Yang, the co-founder of Yahoo!, is one. His father died when he was a toddler and Jerry arrived in the United States from Taiwan, with his mother and younger brother, at the age of ten unable to understand English. Sergey Brin, the co-founder of Google, and Jan Koum, the co-founder of WhatsApp, share some of the same lineage as Jerry, though they arrived from the east. Sergey and his family fled religious persecution in the Soviet Union, as did Jan and his mother when they left Ukraine in 1992. There was much poignancy to the symbolism associated with the spot where, in February 2014, Jan signed the papers to sell his company to Facebook for $19 billion. It was outside the former welfare office in Mountain View where he and his mother had queued to collect their weekly food stamps. I'm not saying that childhood privation is a prerequisite for entre-preneurial success, but the children of middle-class parents – Microsoft's Bill Gates, Facebook's Mark Zuckerberg and Snapchat's Evan Spiegel – are among the minority of successful technology entrepreneurs. The most successful start-ups will, almost inevitably, have an immigrant or first-generation American or someone who has emerged from tough circum-stances in their starting line-up.

Most entrepreneurs, especially in Silicon Valley, are self-made. They are not the product of business schools, and the majority of them have not spent any time working inside a large company being fashioned by others. They are what they have made themselves. Nobody has trained them to be what they become but they are, like Sir Alex, the products of their obsessions. The reason baby-faced leaders emerge in Silicon Valley is because they trip upon their obsession before the rest of the world wakes up to its potential. For these teenagers, or 20-somethings, their areas of interest develop wickedly fast, and either have not hit the radar screens of the big companies or are dismissed as fads. That's been true of personal computer software, short-form messaging, file-sharing software, music streaming, the use of black cars in place of taxis and the rental of spare bedrooms. Like Sir Alex, these founders were learning to be leaders on the job – which, in most cases, was their very first, full-time occupation.

By contrast Sir Alex, who happened on his calling before he was old enough to wear long trousers to school, chose a field – football – where changes occur slowly and the tricks of the trade are well known. This meant that, for him (and all the top-flight managers), it took far longer to accumulate the experience and knowledge required to lead than it does for a young Silicon Valley founder who has leapt on a new breakthrough before it has aroused notice elsewhere. By the time he arrived at United, Sir Alex had already served a long apprenticeship as a professional footballer, and had earned his coaching 'badges' before going on to manage Scottish clubs for 12 years. He had spent 30 years preparing for the opportunity that he earned at Old Trafford. Yet, whether it is in Manchester or Cupertino, mastery of a particular field remains a prerequisite for leadership, because it is the breeding ground for inner conviction and the foundation on which authority, and ultimately the respect of others, comes to rest.

Like Sir Alex, the Silicon Valley founders rely on their eyes, ears and instincts. For them it tends to lead to a desire to figure things out from first principles and a disdain for all conventions. They will harbour contempt for the structure and hierarchy of larger companies though, eventually, their own companies will take on these same habits. Early on, these founders will fire a relentless barrage of questions aimed at those who know a lot about a particular topic. They will also tear through piles of books or, these days, delve into the nooks and crannies of the web and late at night fall asleep listening to TED talks. As these small companies become larger and attract attention, the boundaries of the worlds of the founders expand. Accomplished and experienced people will take their calls or meet them. Warren Buffett is famous for entertaining the founders of some of Silicon Valley's younger companies at his favourite lunch spot in Omaha. Retired CEOs are usually happy to welcome these adventurers to their vacation homes in Florida or Palm Springs. Whatever form it takes, the underlying propellant is an inexhaustible thirst for knowledge.

These characters aren't afraid of adopting what makes sense for them and ignoring everything else, which is why their companies become the corporate expression (like United under Sir Alex) of themselves: Apple a product of a ruthless, poetic perfection; Oracle of a ferocious competitor with a tendency to vacuum up assets; Google an extension of Stanford University writ large; Intel, in its heyday, a triumph of engineering precision, and Amazon an expression of mathematical prowess. Along the way, there are usually lots of mistakes, much confusion, considerable management turnover, failed products and close encounters of the worst kind.

Growing up, while simultaneously building a company and trying to develop as a leader, is a tall order. Bill Gates, Mark Zuckerberg, Larry Page, Jeff Bezos, Larry Ellison, Elon Musk – and plenty more – all became chief executive officers when they were a decade younger than Sir Alex was when he took his first managerial position at East Stirlingshire. They are the products of their childhood and the hobby that turned into an obsession and became the seed of a business. None of them had built a management team, called on customers, dealt with suppliers or negotiated contracts. Their first customer is often themselves (since many of them build a product to satisfy a personal need); their initial hires are usually friends or school-mates (since nobody with a well-polished CV is inclined to risk going to work for somebody whose voice has barely broken); their early suppliers will be wary; their landlord will demand cash up front.

For these founders, the challenge of becoming their own person is exacerbated by the demands of a young company, which will only become more taxing as it grows. Since they are rowing against the tide, these people are suspicious of those who don't share their interests, or are of a different generation. Their task is made no easier by the fact that many of them do not share Sir Alex's gregarious disposition and ease in the company of others. On Myers-Briggs personality tests, plenty will be classified as either introverts, or extreme introverts. For this cadre of founders, eye contact, public speaking and small talk are painful activities. They will prefer the companionship of a computer, a technical paper or a book to that of a fellow human being. For them, overcoming their natural reticence is the first of many accomplishments.

Like United, the distinctive Silicon Valley companies will be shaped by leaders for whom working on products is the activity they most enjoy. For Sir Alex, that meant working with the United players and shaping their style of play. In California it might mean a founder who is fixated on the elegance of a chunk of code, the speed at which bytes are transmitted, the chemical and physical properties of a piece of silicon, the space in which data is stored or the size of a typeface. Like Sir Alex they will tend to leave to others the activities that don't interest them. Hence the manner in which Steve Jobs ceded logistics and operations to Tim Cook, or the way Bill Gates spent little time worrying about the design of marketing campaigns.

The best of these corporate leaders will also shun distractions and apportion their time with great care. Not for them incessant speeches at conferences, television interviews, meetings with politicians or attendances at charity functions. For them, every moment not spent dealing with business (or, when they get a bit older, family) is a wasted opportunity. Look at the old photographs of a younger Alex Ferguson, appearing bleary-eyed after surviving on four or five hours of sleep a night, and you see the face of every young entrepreneur. The most extreme example of this blistering desire to concentrate on his business that I ever encountered was the young Bill Gates. After he had bought a television set so he could watch educational videotapes, he eliminated the temptation to watch shows or movies by disconnecting the tuner. He also removed the radio from his car, lest news bulletins or music prevented him thinking about Microsoft during his brief commutes or on trips to and from the airport. For Bill and for Microsoft, the ability to shut off the outside world paid enormous dividends. The helicopter rides that he took to save time when forced to attend social engagements, or the enforced solitary confinement when he decamped twice a year to pore over technical papers and books, both helped eliminate the noise. It took Bill until 1994, when he was 39, to partially abandon his first true love, Microsoft, and marry Melinda French.

Profiles of successful leaders invariably dwell on what is visible – the result of careful handling by publicists, staged appearances or simply the reticence of the individuals themselves. Success depends on what happens behind the scenes where the hard work – the 17- or 18-hour-long days and the seven-days-a-week ritual – is conducted. Sir Alex is a great believer in the virtues of industry and set the example with his own actions – not asking anyone to apply themselves with more resolve than he demanded of himself. Sir Alex's world was visible for millions of viewers to see, and might have seemed effortless and spontaneous from the comfort of an armchair, but it was the result of relentless preparation. Behind every trophy there were dozens of Saturday mornings standing in driving rain scouting teenagers; behind every League trophy were thousands of training sessions; behind every triumph was a large, increasingly global network of individuals, whose sole task was to funnel youngsters into a system that ten, 15 or even 20 years later would have them making a critical pass or an important tackle.

I know Sir Alex would applaud the work ethic found among California's younger companies, not to mention their counterparts in China, who sometimes make me feel that Silicon Valley is a retirement community. It's why, in their formative years, companies like Google and Facebook had 'war rooms', where tiger teams of programmers were sequestered until they had solved a particular crisis, or 'lockdowns' where coders were forbidden to leave the premises until some calamity had been averted.

Sir Alex will be the first to say that much of the success he enjoyed was made possible by the setting in which he found himself – which, I suspect, is also responsible for the good fortune of many people in Silicon Valley. Sir Alex is not referring to United's history and earlier association with success, as much as he is to the support he received from the club's owners and board of directors, the ultimate arbiters of his fate – and, to a lesser extent, to the growth in the television market.

At both Aberdeen and United, Sir Alex did not have to deal with owners or directors who wanted to meddle in football affairs, or assistant managers who usurped his authority. Sir Alex was given what every leader deserves – control to shape his own destiny and that of his organisation. Having the time to establish a solid foundation and to, gradually, build towards long-term prosperity, is not a luxury afforded most football managers or business leaders, where the pressure to win or the need to produce quarterly earnings makes the quick fix almost irresistible. This freedom from the tyranny of immediate results enabled Sir Alex to constantly work on the composition of the club several years into the future, without worrying whether he would still be there if United had a bad losing streak. He was also granted the freedom to control his own realm. In Silicon Valley the founders of companies are also fixated on the importance of control. Today, they try to enshrine their position with all sorts of legal protections, which, for the weaker ones, means that they are doing themselves and their companies a disfavour. Nonetheless, the underlying impulse remains the same as Sir Alex's – the conviction that, come hell or high water, their way is the best.

Undoubtedly some of United's success during this period rests on the way technological breakthroughs transformed the television coverage of football. United, and for that matter the rest of the Premier League, have reaped enormous dividends from a huge decline in the price of computing and communication. Satellite transmission, remote-controlled cameras, high-definition displays, flatscreen televisions, the proliferation of the internet, the rise of social networking and instant communications are what have allowed United to perform on a global stage. Sir Alex readily admits that he vastly underestimated the impact of satellite and cable transmission of football games, and the container-loads of money that trailed in their wake. Yet the crowds that began to gather in living rooms and pubs to watch United did so because of the entertainment that he helped orchestrate. Any time United slipped, or were eliminated from the final throes of the European Cup competition, it had an immediate effect on the club's revenues. The revenues that flowed to United from the expanded television coverage were inextricably linked to the team's performance. The results lifted United's share of broadcast rights from an insignificant amount in 1985–86 to £60.8 million in Sir Alex's final season.

Yet for all the tailwinds propelling technology start-ups, they too, like the Premier League teams, have to deal with cruel blows and rude reversals of fortune. I cannot think of one successful company that Sequoia has been involved with that did not, at some point, face the threat of extinction. Newspaper headlines and television anchors love to proclaim the arrival of yet another Silicon Valley 'overnight success' or announce the baptism of a young, newly minted billionaire. Set aside the fact that a good number of what today are known as 'unicorns' will fall by the wayside, the more noteworthy examples of the companies that have eventually beaten all odds have been started by people blessed (and, in many cases, haunted) by the same sort of inner drive, discipline and hunger that propelled Sir Alex and his most successful players. Look at Pixar, where it took 16 years of experimentation, corporate convulsions, dead-ends and lay-offs before the release of the company's first full-length movie, *Toy*

Story. Or there is Nvidia, a chip company, formed in 1993, which now underpins the video-game industry, but whose first product was an abject failure and nearly consigned the company to oblivion. Today, as each rides high, it is easy to forget that, at the dawn of this century, Amazon was running on fumes and Blockbuster refused to purchase Netflix for pennies on the dollar. LinkedIn, now known around the world for its 364 million strong online professional network, required one year to reach its first 100,000 members. In each of these cases it required extraordinary drive, self-discipline and conviction to stay true to the course.

These triumphs of force and conviction are not limited to small companies. In the mid-1980s Intel, whose original business in computer memory devices had been destroyed by Japanese competitors, was reinvented by Bob Noyce, Gordon Moore and Andy Grove as a designer of microprocessors. Lou Gerstner's astonishing turnaround of IBM in the 1990s demonstrates what an extraordinary leader can do to a company given up for dead. The greatest example of the power of conviction is the minutely chronicled turnaround of Apple by Steve Jobs – a mission given the longest of odds by people such as Michael Dell who, in 1997, famously announced that he would shut the company down and return the proceeds to shareholders.

For each of these examples, the technology industry is littered with examples of companies that did not fulfil their original destiny, because those at the helm either lacked the combination of drive, discipline and conviction that is required to build anything great or because they were started by people who did not understand the vast gulf that separates theory from reality. For me, three examples loom large. The first, by a long measure, is Webvan, an online grocer that became our worst investment because we abandoned common sense in a haphazard pursuit of mindless growth. Another is Zappos, the online shoe retailer, which, though acquired by Amazon in 2008 for just under $1 billion (now worth over $6 billion), did not fulfil its promise because, try as we might, we failed to persuade its founder of all the things that are required to build a great, enduring company. Finally, there is PayPal, which was bought by eBay in 2002 for $1.5 billion, even though Elon Musk and I had implored the rest of the board not to sell the company. Sadly, PayPal is now worth about $40 billion – proof that conviction and patience, as Sir Alex says, are precious commodities.

Understanding what is possible, setting realistic expectations and communicating them clearly enough to bring a team along with you, especially in a setting where everyone wants quick results, is one of the hardest leadership skills. It is easy to brim with enthusiasm, establish unattainable goals and leave everyone feeling deflated if the targets aren't achieved. While at St Mirren Sir Alex learned about the consequences of making bold predictions of future triumphs, and thereafter was careful to build success one step at a time. The purposeful cadence of a relentless, disciplined march is difficult to maintain, but a long record of success is built one trophy (or one sales record, engineering release, or financial result) at a time. The consistent application of a well-tuned approach that does not shift with every passing fancy, but is supple enough to absorb and accommodate useful advances, is one of the distinctive characteristics of Sir Alex's style. It is not an accident that Manchester United (without, under Sir Alex, ever resorting to the power of an overwhelming chequebook) was quick to change the composition of its squad as the Premier League made it possible for the best footballers in the world to ply their trade in Britain.

The goals designed for a young company to serve as a rallying cry tend to be more audacious than the ones Sir Alex so carefully set for United. The more inexperienced Silicon Valley founders are unable to trot out anything beyond the limp and oft-used cries that 'We're going to change the world' or, 'We're going to make a difference'. The more thoughtful, conversely, offer something that, at first hearing, sounds completely implausible. That was certainly my reaction when I first heard Google's co-founder, Larry Page, explain that he wanted to put the internet on a hard drive. It took me a long time to figure out the depth and subtlety of his remark.

Communicating what he wanted from staff and players always seems to have come naturally to Sir Alex. Part of this was born of inner confidence, part from the gradual accumulation of victories, but much came from the absence of any confusion in his own mind about what he wanted. Listen to any of his former players and they will tell you that, once they began to master Sir Alex's heavy Scottish accent, there was no mistaking what he sought. His directions tended to be short and concise because barely anyone, whether they work in a hospital or steel mill or are part of a boy-scout troop, can remember more than three instructions. Long-winded monologues do not strike the target in the way that brief talks relaying precise and concise instructions do. I cannot begin to describe the number of presentations I have sat through where the words of the CEO have been hard to fathom, or where the message was so glib it had no credence. The best summary I ever heard of a business was from Sandy Lerner, the co-founder of Cisco Systems, who, in 1986, when the company had just eight employees, was asked to communicate her company's purpose. Her answer was as terse as a Glaswegian's: 'We network networks.' It sounded deceptively simple, but it served as the company's north star for the ensuing 25 years. Sir Alex's counter might well have been the message that he burned between the ears of every newcomer to the club, 'At United we expect to win every game.' In Silicon Valley they would call that a mission statement.

Plenty of organisations achieve one success, some notch up several, but few make it a habit of a lifetime. Manchester United, under Sir Alex, demonstrates how the taste of success gives people confidence that they can repeat the accomplishment; sets a standard that, at a minimum, needs to be matched; and, as an ever-expanding cadre of people experience triumph, begins to become self-perpetuating. Winners want to be around winners. That same formula applies in Silicon Valley, albeit with a local twist. Here it is most pertinent when young companies, during their early days, try to recruit engineers. If these fledgling enterprises attract the right calibre of engineers, the after-effects can last for ten years. Engineers tend to have a particularly acerbic view of the credentials of others and only want to make job offers to those who meet their standards. (It's an attitude faintly reminiscent of the way Sir Alex views a person on whom he bestows the ultimate compliment, 'a true professional'.) When this works, the prospects for the business explode dramatically – particularly today when well-written software can quickly touch hundreds of millions of people. If the recruiting machines sputter, or hiring standards are lowered, it is almost impossible for the company to meet the leader's original aspiration.

On the other side of the same coin is staff retention. I don't mean to belittle the way Sir Alex inspired his teams to achieve more than they thought they were capable of doing; of building tremendous bonds of loyalty with players, many of whom he first came to know as young teenagers; and of perpetually needing to ensure that he had the best goalkeeper or midfielder on his team-sheet. At United it was very rare, at least while Sir

Alex was at the helm, for an agent to convince one of his clients to try his chances at another club, and much of that was due to the fact that most of the squad, if they were appearing regularly, could not have imagined a better stage on which to perform. From time to time, there might have been posturing about a move elsewhere, as there was with Wayne Rooney in 2010 when the end of his contract loomed; but, for the most part, the last thing on the mind of a United player was a job with another club.

That is not the case in California, where people tend to work for Silicon Valley rather than for a particular company. Here there is a similar need to ensure that any business has the best possible management or engineering line-up, but the task is made significantly harder because of the hordes of recruiters who spend all their waking hours trying to prise alluring candidates from their perches. A lot of this is due to the richness of the job opportunities, since there are many more interesting slots in which top-flight people can ply their trade in Silicon Valley than there are for a star striker employed by one of the best six or seven European football clubs. The main reasons for the job-hopping tendencies in Silicon Valley are, for a minority, the dream of striking out on their own, or frustration with the ballooning size of their employer and, for the majority, the way in which stock compensation programmes are designed. At a young company an early employee is usually given a grant of stock that vests after four years. If the company is flourishing and the stock has enjoyed massive appreciation, many employees will feel that they are better off repeating the cycle by obtaining a new slug of stock granted at a low price. For the best Silicon Valley companies, it is often harder to retain people than to recruit them.

I marvel at what I learned about the way Sir Alex dealt with his players and inspired and cajoled his teams – a habit he refined as the years went by. Not many Silicon Valley CEOs, perhaps because many of them are so young, can modulate their tones with comparable dexterity. Sir Alex could simultaneously play cheerleader, motivational speaker, shrink, confessor, piano-tuner, puppet-master, choreographer, teacher, judge and lord high executioner. As he grew older he became increasingly adroit at modulating the application of these skills and figuring out how to extract that extra 5 per cent – the difference between gold and silver – from individuals and groups of individuals. He learned to bolster players' confidence when their spirits were down; he was quick to bring them down a peg or two when they were getting too big for their boots; he was bemused by some of their habits (like Eric Cantona putting salt in his socks before games, or Cristiano Ronaldo specially tailoring two pairs of socks to get the leg-coverings he desired); he stoked their hunger for repeated success and, most importantly, he made each understand (no matter how much they were getting paid or how often they appeared in advertisements or magazines) that the team was bigger, and much more important, than any individual – a cruel truth that many, in both companies and investment firms, have a habit of forgetting.

While Sir Alex, like most people, enjoys being liked, he never sought affection from his players, though neither did he want to paralyse them with fear. So while he tended to know most of them very well, particularly those that stayed at United for many years, he maintained his distance. Respect was all he sought because, once earned, it makes it so much easier for a leader to control an organisation and bend it to his will.

He also understood that one of the keys to an enduring organisation is to build from within, by helping youngsters gain their footing and become successful, rather than recruiting expensive guns for hire, like the leader of a band of mercenaries.

It is a less risky and more predictable way to build an enduring organisation. This in-house development programme requires great patience, and takes a long time, but it is a process that breeds the sorts of bonds that only years of shared experiences can provide – stability, familiarity, trust and, eventually, life-long loyalty. Some will say that this is impossible in a world attuned to immediate results. I beg to differ. Every great organisation has the ability to adopt this approach if they have the right governance structure and leadership team. It's a style of management for which I have great affection since, at Sequoia, I was the fortunate beneficiary of the same approach, and it is the one that we continue to embrace. We also have tried to do what Sir Alex did, after he fell into his stride at United, when he kept tuning his squad, making sure it was nicely balanced between the enthusiasm of youth, the strength of players in their prime, and the experience of those in the twilight of their careers. Sir Alex was careful to make gradual shifts to the composition of these squads, since wholesale change can confuse, disrupt and demoralise.

Many leaders allow habit, affection, happily shared experiences or sentiment to cloud their judgement. It is easy to fall into a comfortable routine and assume that the people who contributed yesterday will continue to make contributions tomorrow. It is easier to be tolerant or to compromise than to confront ugly situations, deliver painful news or demand changes. Partly because of his nature and partly because it is very difficult to hide shortcomings on a football field (compared to the way mediocre bumblers can survive in large companies for decades), Sir Alex never blanched at putting the team before the man, or the future before past accomplishments. Some saw this as a ruthless display of cold-blooded behaviour, particularly fans ruing the exile of one of their favourites. Sir Alex, rightly, saw it as a necessity. One of the challenges for young founders is to understand that, if their company is ever going to be hugely successful, it will – almost certainly – outstrip the capabilities of the people they first hire to manage sales, or marketing or engineering.

Leaders usually spend far too much time worrying about their competitors. That's especially true in football, where the owners in particular are prone to coveting a competitor's success. I do not mean to imply that Sir Alex paid no attention to his competitors, because he spent as much time as any manager making sure he was staying in touch with their line-ups and tactics and was perfectly willing to borrow ploys that made sense. However, he refused to allow Manchester United to be defined by its competitors, and always felt that the destiny of his club was shaped by what went on inside Old Trafford rather than elsewhere. Hence, his phlegmatic reaction to the arrival of the oligarchs, Middle Eastern princes and other well-heeled foreign owners. For Sir Alex, money never bought success, although the occasional big-ticket signing could bring a frisson to proceedings.

Precisely the same phenomenon occurs in Silicon Valley. While it is foolish to ignore developments elsewhere, no organisation ever achieved greatness by perpetually reacting to its competitors. You cannot lead by following. The businesses that are consigned to eternal mediocrity are those led by people who do not know what they want. By contrast, the few companies destined for greatness tend to be led by people with an idea of what they want, even if, at the outset, this might be outshone by far greater clarity about what they do not like. That was certainly the case for Larry Page and Sergey Brin at the outset of Google. Neither of them cared a whit for the search services provided by Yahoo!, Excite, Lycos, Infoseek or AltaVista, so they sought to produce something superior. The same was true for Apple's senior design team, when they set about trying to imagine an mp3 player they could tolerate (the iPod) or a mobile phone they would like (the iPhone).

Silicon Valley winners emerge by concentrating on what they control and by making sure that, for as long as possible, they stay off the radar screen of foes that have the firepower to blow them to smithereens. Stealth is one of a start-up's most potent weapons. It does not pay to arouse either the ire or the scrutiny of the beast – especially when those beasts are quasi monopolists capable of mounting withering attacks. Any number of companies – such as Novell, Lotus Development, AOL, Adobe, Barland, Netscape and Symantec – discovered the perils of arousing the attention of Microsoft at the height of its powers. A big part of the reason that Google became successful was the way its management maintained a low profile until it was too late for Microsoft – by then also hamstrung by government enquiries – to react and torpedo the business.

When a business or a service firm changes leader, the consequences are usually messy. The sad truth is that, irrespective of the field, there are few examples of companies pulling off smooth management successions. The best examples are organisations that just do it less poorly than others. In settings like large oil companies, airline and hotel businesses or the big consumer brands, the change at the top is invisible for several years because the product catalogue, existing clients or long-held investments don't change overnight. That's less true in the world of technology, where it is so rare for companies to successfully adapt themselves to changing circumstances and brand-new market opportunities. It is even less the case in football, where the effect of a leadership change on team performance – especially a negative one – is laid bare fairly quickly.

Just as employees and shareholders in Silicon Valley companies speculate about the implications of a change in helmsmen, so too did the fans of United when Sir Alex announced his retirement. The British newspapers accorded the changing of the guard at Old Trafford, and the arrival of David Moyes from Everton, with the coverage that usually accompanies the arrival of a new government, a signal event for a member of the royal family, or a state funeral. Yet the United team that took to the field at the start of the 2013–14 season was almost identical to the one that had played, 89 days earlier, for Sir Alex in the last game of his management career.

United's followers might console themselves with the knowledge that leadership changes in Silicon Valley are rarely flawless. Yahoo! for example, which had two CEOs during its first 12 years, riffled through a further six in the subsequent eight years. Something similar has occurred at Hewlett-Packard, which was run by its founders from 1939 to 1978, but which in the last 16 years has run through seven CEOs. As I write, the board of Twitter has found itself with the unenviable task of finding a fourth CEO and considering a sale, even though the company is not yet ten years old. About the only Silicon Valley company I can think of that grew from strength to strength as it swapped CEOs was Intel during its first 30 years. There was a special reason for this. The company's first three CEOs, the third of whom was the utterly remarkable Andy Grove (the person I most admire in Silicon Valley), also happened to be the threesome who showed up for work on the day Intel was formed in 1968. Intel's founding spirit did not get diluted by bureaucrats, chief financial officers, activist shareholders, meddlesome directors or, most importantly, people at the helm who did not have the keenest appreciation for the company's products and a deeply ingrained sense of ownership.

There's one final character trait that all great leaders share – from Intel's first three CEOs to Sir Alex Ferguson himself. It's an attribute that few leaders will readily observe in themselves and few management books will single out. In fact, this impulse is often easier for outsiders to spot and, in the case of Sir Alex, was something I gradually gleaned from our conversations and the outings that provide the backbone for this book. Great leaders are competing – not with others – but with the idea of perfection itself. It does not matter how many sales records they have broken, how many competitors they have extinguished, or how many breathtaking products they have introduced – a greater, more perfect version of their success always beckons. For them greatness is just never good enough. In retirement, Sir Alex, who is not prone to melancholy, is wise enough to relish the triumphs of his life and derive satisfaction from his accomplishments rather than allow himself to dwell on whatever trophies eluded his grasp. For the most successful leader in the history of professional sports, the 38 trophies he added to Manchester United's collection – including those that accompanied the Treble-winning year of 1999 – were milestones on a journey whose ultimate, and maddeningly elusive, destination was the seductive and tantalising notion of perfection itself.

Michael Moritz
San Francisco
September 2015

ACKNOWLEDGEMENTS

It always takes a team, and the one fielded for this book featured Nick Davies, managing director of John Murray Press, whose shrewd eye and keen judgement sharpened the manuscript, as well as Roddy Bloomfield and Kate Miles. Other members of Hodder & Stoughton – Jamie Hodder-Williams, Lucy Hale, Karen Geary and Vickie Boff – were always available at a moment's notice. Alasdair Oliver designed the cover and Amanda Jones managed production. In the United States, Mauro diPreta, the publisher of Hachette Books, and Michelle Aielli helped make sure we received good care in a country where footballs are not round.

From his perch in Aberdeen, Colin Dalgarno provided steadfast and reliable research. In London, Jack Hagley turned numbers into pictures, and is the person responsible for the graphical illustrations in the book, while Sean Pollock shot the cover photograph.

Our literary, legal, financial and publicity squad consisted of Chris Parris-Lamb and David Gernert at The Gernert Company; Sue Knight and the team at Grant Thornton and Les Dalgarno, Ken Gordon and the team at Burness Paull in the United Kingdom and Andrew Kovacs, Sandi Mendleson, David Kass, Karen Valladao, Pete Laboskey and Joe McNulty in the United States.

Mark Damazer, Walter Isaacson, Michael Lewis, Michael Lynton, Jane Sarkin, Doug Stumpf and Judith Thurman provided advice and guidance as we gradually turned an idea into a book. Lyn Laffin and Zoe Diompy in Manchester and Tanya Schillage in California made sure that we always appeared on time. Harriet Heyman helped with the epilogue.

Jason Ferguson in Manchester and Martin O'Connor in New York prompted and nudged us at every turn. They both deserve to have their names in very large fonts on the cover. The man, without whom this would not have happened, is the irrepressible and lovable Charlie Stillitano.

PICTURE ACKNOWLEDGEMENTS

Introduction, Sir Alex Ferguson at Harvard Business School © Anita Elberse; Chapter 1, Scotland manager Jock Stein (right) with his assistant Alex Ferguson (left) in 1985 © EMPICS Sport/PAI; Chapter 2, Manchester United youth team player David Beckham, February 1992 © Mirrorpix; Chapter 3, Sir Alex Ferguson (right) and assistant manager Carlos Queiroz (left) at Carrington training ground, 25 July 2006 © Matthew Peters/ Manchester United via Getty Images; Chapter 4, Steve Bruce and Bryan Robson after Manchester United beat Blackburn to win the FA Premier League in 1993 © David Cannon/ALLSPORT/Getty Images; Chapter 5, Alex Ferguson talks to Eric Cantona during Manchester City vs. Manchester United in 1996 © Mark Leech/Getty Images; Chapter 6, Sporting Lisbon's player Cristiano Ronaldo (right) fights for the ball during a friendly match, August 2003 © Andre Kosters/AFP/Getty Images; Chapter 7, Sir Alex Ferguson during a Champions League match against Real Madrid, 2013 © Back Page Images/Rex Shutterstock; Chapter 8, Sir Alex Ferguson at a press conference in Manchester, 2009 © John Peters/Manchester United via Getty Images; Chapter 9, Aberdeen chairman (centre) Dick Donald with Alex Ferguson (right), pre-season friendly Aberdeen vs. Arsenal, 1980 © SNS Group/Alamy; Chapter 10, Sir Alex Ferguson and David Gill © Ian Hodgson/ANL/Rex Shutterstock © PA Archive/PAI; Chapter 11, Sir Alex Ferguson in the dressing room © Sean Pollock; Chapter 12, Arsenal manager Arsène Wenger and Sir Alex Ferguson during a Premiership match between Arsenal and Manchester United, 2005 © Ben Radford/Getty Images; Chapter 13, Former Manchester United manager, Sir Alex Ferguson waves to the crowd from the directors' box at Old Trafford, October 2013 © epa european pressphoto agency b.v./Alamy; Epilogue, Sir Alex Ferguson being interviewed by Sir Michael Moritz © author collection.

The Data Room, Sir Alex Ferguson lifting the Premier League trophy at Old Trafford, 2013 ©Alex Livesey/Getty Images
The Archive, Sir Alex Ferguson at his desk in Carrington © Sean Pollock

Every reasonable effort has been made to trace copyright holders, but if there are any errors or omissions, Hodder & Stoughton will be pleased to insert the appropriate acknowledgement in any subsequent printings or editions.

THE DATA ROOM

SIR ALEX FERGUSON AT MANCHESTER UNITED 1986–2013

Matches	Won	Drawn	Lost
1,500	895	338	267
	59.7%	22.5%	17.8%

	86/87	87/88	88/89	89/90	90/91	91/92	92/93	93/94	94/95	95/96	96/97	97/98	98/99	99/00	00/01	01/02	02/03	03/04	04/05	05/06	06/07	07/08	08/09	09/10	10/11	11/12	12/13
Winning %																											
League	11	2	11	13	6	2	🏆	🏆	2	🏆	🏆	2	🏆	🏆	🏆	3	🏆	3	3	2	🏆	🏆	🏆	2	🏆	2	🏆
FA Cup	4R	5R	6R	🏆	5R	4R	5R	🏆	F	🏆	4R	5R	🏆		4R	4R	5R	🏆	F	5R	F	6R	SF	3R	SF	4R	6R
League Cup		QF	3R	3R	F	🏆	3R	F	3R	2R	4R	3R	QF	3R	4R	3R	F	4R	SF	🏆	4R	3R	🏆	🏆	QF	QF	4R
Charity Shield / Community Shield				🏆			🏆	🏆		🏆	🏆	F	F	F	F		🏆	F				🏆	🏆	F	🏆	🏆	
Champions League							2R	GR		SF	QF	🏆	QF	QF	SF	QF	16	16	GR	SF	🏆	F	QF	F	GR	16	
Cup Winners' Cup				🏆	2R																						
UEFA Cup / Europa League						1R				1R																16	
Super Cup				🏆									F									F					
Intercontinental Cup													🏆														
Club World Cup														GR									🏆				

Goal Distribution by Minute

Games won or drawn by a Manchester United goal after 85 mins
101

Games lost or drawn by an opposition goal after 85 mins
51

Goals scored **2,769**

Clean sheets **625**

Goals conceded **1,365**

Failed to score **263**

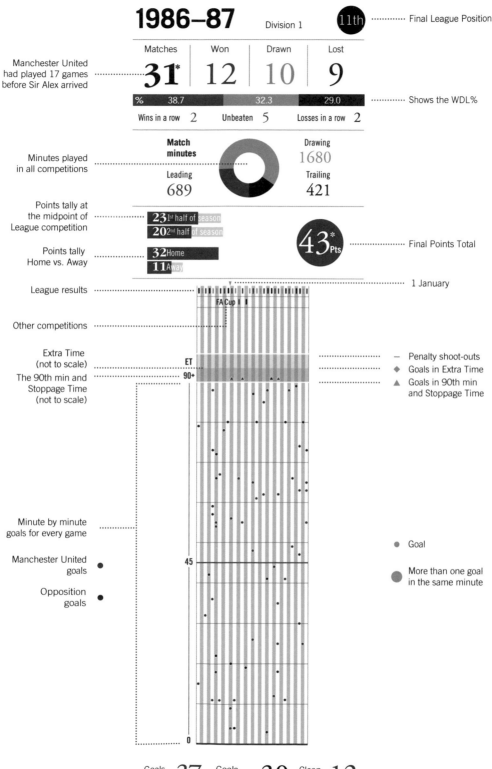

1986–87

Division 1

11th ·········· Final League Position

	Matches	Won	Drawn	Lost
	31*	12	10	9

Manchester United had played 17 games before Sir Alex arrived ··········

| % | 38.7 | 32.3 | 29.0 | ·········· Shows the WDL% |

Wins in a row 2   Unbeaten 5   Losses in a row 2

Match minutes   Drawing 1680 ·········· Minutes played in all competitions

Leading 689   Trailing 421

Points tally at the midpoint of League competition ·········· **23** 1st half of season
20 2nd half of season

43* Pts ·········· Final Points Total

Points tally Home vs. Away ·········· **32** Home
11 Away

League results ·········· 1 January

FA Cup

Other competitions ··········

Extra Time (not to scale) ·········· ET   — Penalty shoot-outs

The 90th min and Stoppage Time (not to scale) ·········· 90+   ◆ Goals in Extra Time
▲ Goals in 90th min and Stoppage Time

Minute by minute goals for every game ··········

Manchester United goals ●   ● Goal

45

Opposition goals ●   ● More than one goal in the same minute

0

Goals scored **37**   Goals conceded **30**   Clean sheets **12**

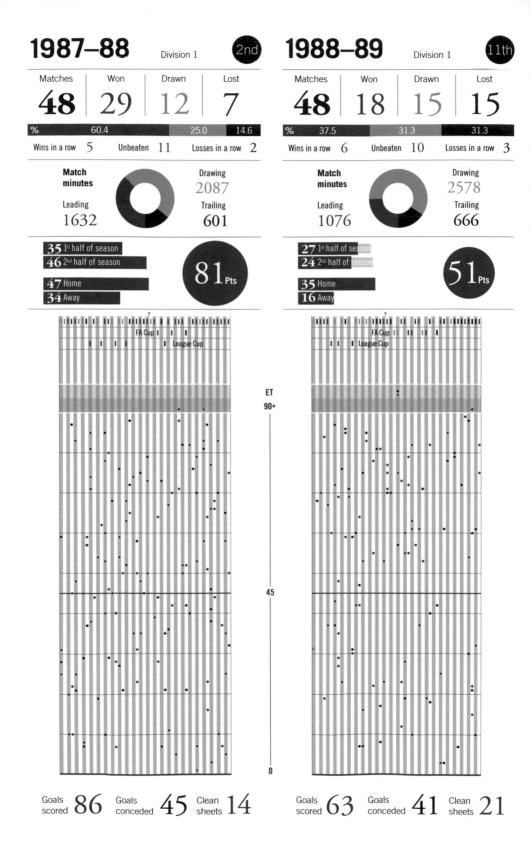

1987–88
Division 1 — **2nd**

Matches	Won	Drawn	Lost
48	29	12	7

%	60.4	25.0	14.6

Wins in a row **5** Unbeaten **11** Losses in a row **2**

Match minutes

Drawing 2087
Leading 1632
Trailing 601

35 1st half of season
46 2nd half of season
47 Home
34 Away

81 Pts

FA Cup
League Cup

ET 90+
45
0

Goals scored **86** Goals conceded **45** Clean sheets **14**

1988–89
Division 1 — **11th**

Matches	Won	Drawn	Lost
48	18	15	15

%	37.5	31.3	31.3

Wins in a row **6** Unbeaten **10** Losses in a row **3**

Match minutes

Drawing 2578
Leading 1076
Trailing 666

27 1st half of season
24 2nd half of season
35 Home
16 Away

51 Pts

FA Cup
League Cup

Goals scored **63** Goals conceded **41** Clean sheets **21**

1989–90

Division 1 • 13th

Matches	Won	Drawn	Lost
49	20	12	17

%	40.8	24.5	34.7

Wins in a row	3	Unbeaten	6	Losses in a row	3

Match minutes

Drawing 2222

Leading 1071

Trailing 1117

22 1st half of season
26 2nd half of season

30 Home
18 Away

48 Pts

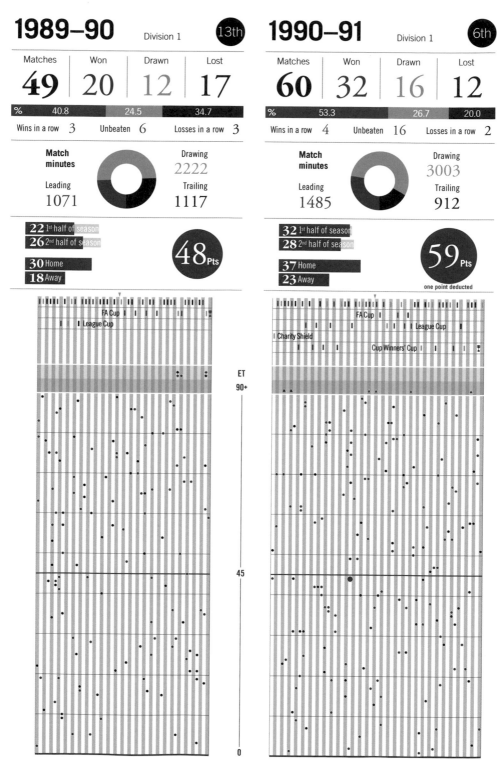

ET 90+

45

0

Goals scored	64	Goals conceded	61	Clean sheets	16

1990–91

Division 1 • 6th

Matches	Won	Drawn	Lost
60	32	16	12

%	53.3	26.7	20.0

Wins in a row	4	Unbeaten	16	Losses in a row	2

Match minutes

Drawing 3003

Leading 1485

Trailing 912

32 1st half of season
28 2nd half of season

37 Home
23 Away

59 Pts

one point deducted

Goals scored	101	Goals conceded	63	Clean sheets	18

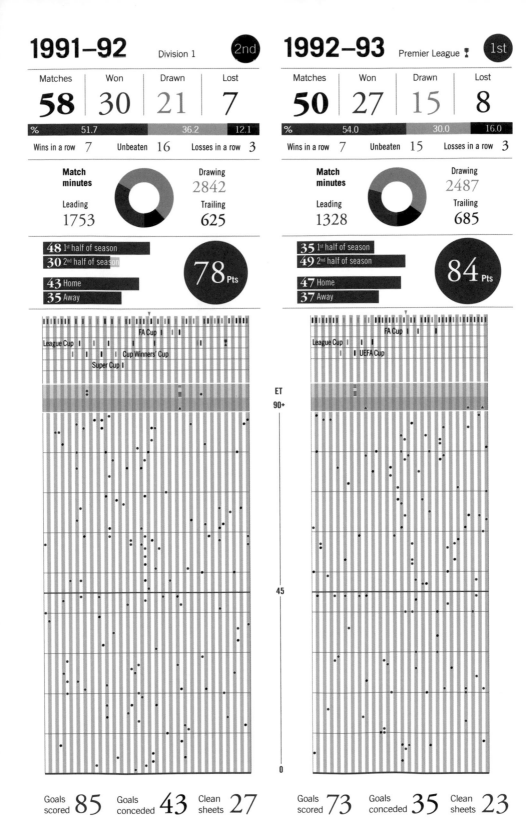

1991–92
Division 1 — 2nd

Matches	Won	Drawn	Lost
58	30	21	7

% 51.7 — 36.2 — 12.1

| Wins in a row 7 | Unbeaten 16 | Losses in a row 3 |

Match minutes

Leading 1753 — Drawing 2842 — Trailing 625

48 1st half of season
30 2nd half of season
43 Home
35 Away

78 Pts

League Cup
FA Cup
Cup Winners' Cup
Super Cup

| Goals scored 85 | Goals conceded 43 | Clean sheets 27 |

1992–93
Premier League — 1st

Matches	Won	Drawn	Lost
50	27	15	8

% 54.0 — 30.0 — 16.0

| Wins in a row 7 | Unbeaten 15 | Losses in a row 3 |

Match minutes

Leading 1328 — Drawing 2487 — Trailing 685

35 1st half of season
49 2nd half of season
47 Home
37 Away

84 Pts

League Cup
FA Cup
UEFA Cup

| Goals scored 73 | Goals conceded 35 | Clean sheets 23 |

ET
90+
45
0

1993–94

Premiership 🏆 (1st)

Matches	Won	Drawn	Lost
63	41	16	6

%	65.1	25.4	9.5

Wins in a row	7	Unbeaten	34	Losses in a row	1

Match minutes

Leading 2610

Drawing 2505

Trailing 555

52 1st half of season
40 2nd half of season
48 Home
44 Away

92 Pts

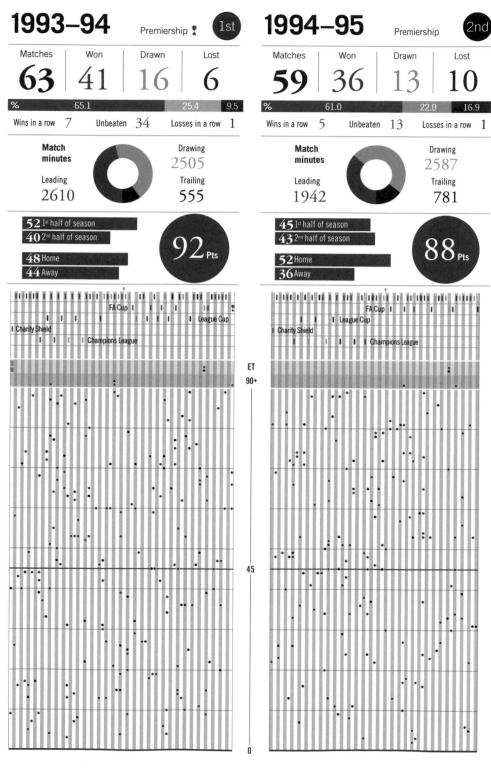

FA Cup
League Cup
Charity Shield
Champions League

ET 90+

45

0

Goals scored	**126**	Goals conceded	**57**	Clean sheets	**26**

1994–95

Premiership (2nd)

Matches	Won	Drawn	Lost
59	36	13	10

%	61.0	22.0	16.9

Wins in a row	5	Unbeaten	13	Losses in a row	1

Match minutes

Leading 1942

Drawing 2587

Trailing 781

45 1st half of season
43 2nd half of season
52 Home
36 Away

88 Pts

FA Cup
League Cup
Charity Shield
Champions League

Goals scored	**110**	Goals conceded	**48**	Clean sheets	**31**

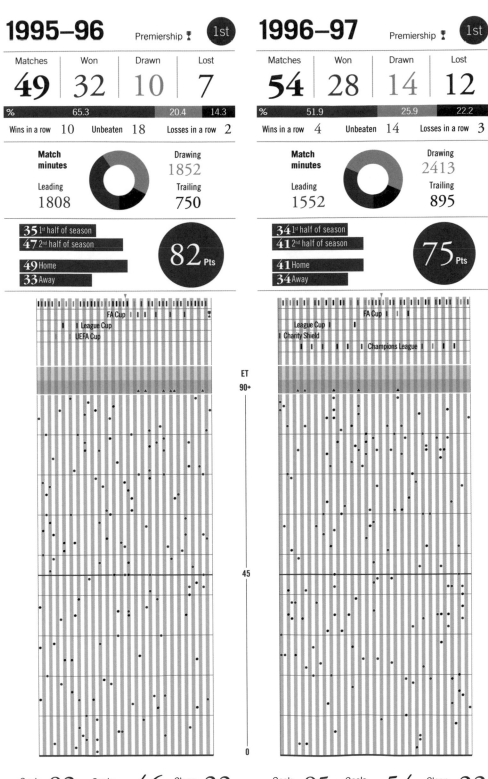

1995–96

Premiership 🏆 — 1st

Matches	Won	Drawn	Lost
49	32	10	7

% — 65.3 — 20.4 — 14.3

Wins in a row 10 — Unbeaten 18 — Losses in a row 2

Match minutes

Drawing 1852

Leading 1808

Trailing 750

35 1st half of season
47 2nd half of season
49 Home
33 Away

82 Pts

FA Cup
League Cup
UEFA Cup

ET 90+
45
0

Goals scored **92** — Goals conceded **46** — Clean sheets **22**

1996–97

Premiership 🏆 — 1st

Matches	Won	Drawn	Lost
54	28	14	12

% — 51.9 — 25.9 — 22.2

Wins in a row 4 — Unbeaten 14 — Losses in a row 3

Match minutes

Drawing 2413

Leading 1552

Trailing 895

34 1st half of season
41 2nd half of season
41 Home
34 Away

75 Pts

FA Cup
League Cup
Charity Shield
Champions League

Goals scored **95** — Goals conceded **54** — Clean sheets **22**

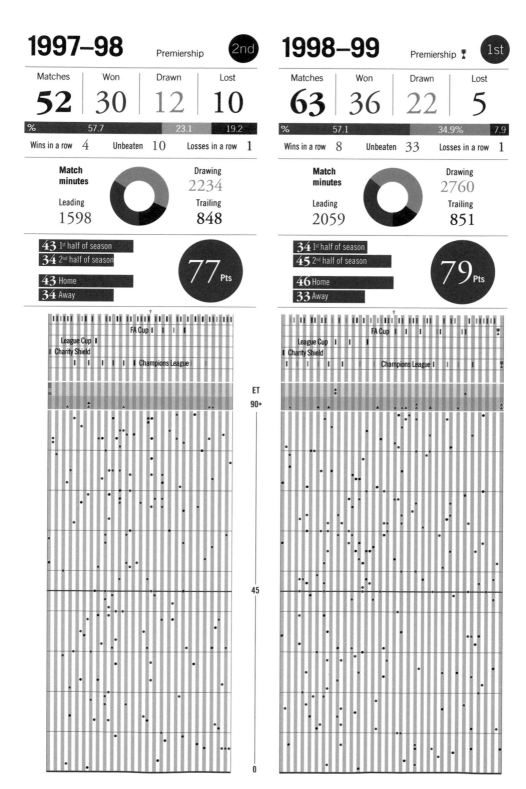

1997–98 — Premiership — 2nd

Matches	Won	Drawn	Lost
52	30	12	10

% 57.7 | 23.1 | 19.2

Wins in a row 4 Unbeaten 10 Losses in a row 1

Match minutes

Drawing 2234
Leading 1598
Trailing 848

43 1st half of season
34 2nd half of season
43 Home
34 Away

77 Pts

FA Cup
League Cup
Charity Shield
Champions League

ET
90+
45
0

Goals scored **102** Goals conceded **43** Clean sheets **23**

1998–99 — Premiership — 1st

Matches	Won	Drawn	Lost
63	36	22	5

% 57.1 | 34.9% | 7.9

Wins in a row 8 Unbeaten 33 Losses in a row 1

Match minutes

Drawing 2760
Leading 2059
Trailing 851

34 1st half of season
45 2nd half of season
46 Home
33 Away

79 Pts

FA Cup
League Cup
Charity Shield
Champions League

Goals scored **128** Goals conceded **63** Clean sheets **23**

1999–2000 Premiership 🏆 1st

Matches	Won	Drawn	Lost
59	38	11	10

| % | 64.4 | 18.6 | 16.9 |

Wins in a row 5   Unbeaten 14   Losses in a row 2

Match minutes

Leading 1932   Drawing 2277   Trailing 1101

43 1st half of season
48 2nd half of season
49 Home
42 Away

91 Pts

Charity Shield
Super Cup
League Cup
Champions League
Intercontinental Cup
Club World Cup

ET 90+
45
0

Goals scored **124**   Goals conceded **66**   Clean sheets **20**

2000–01 Premiership 🏆 1st

Matches	Won	Drawn	Lost
57	32	12	13

| % | 56.1 | 21.1 | 22.8 |

Wins in a row 8   Unbeaten 10   Losses in a row 3

Match minutes

Leading 2096   Drawing 2181   Trailing 853

43 1st half of season
37 2nd half of season
47 Home
33 Away

80 Pts

Charity Shield
League Cup
Champions League
FA Cup

Goals scored **107**   Goals conceded **50**   Clean sheets **23**

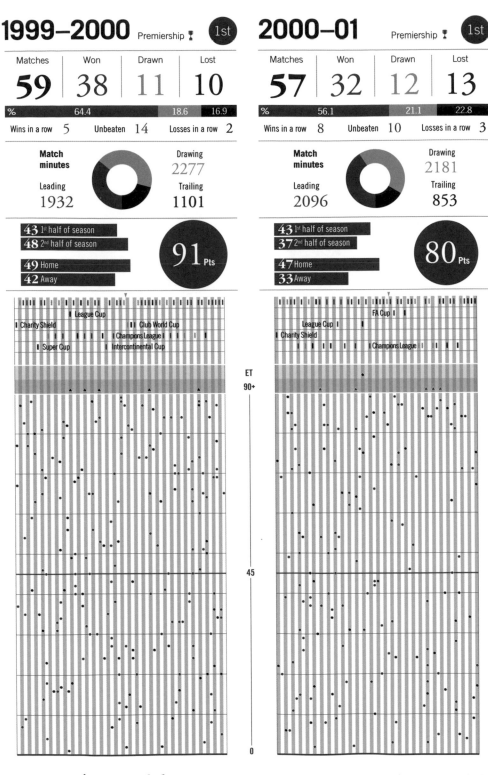

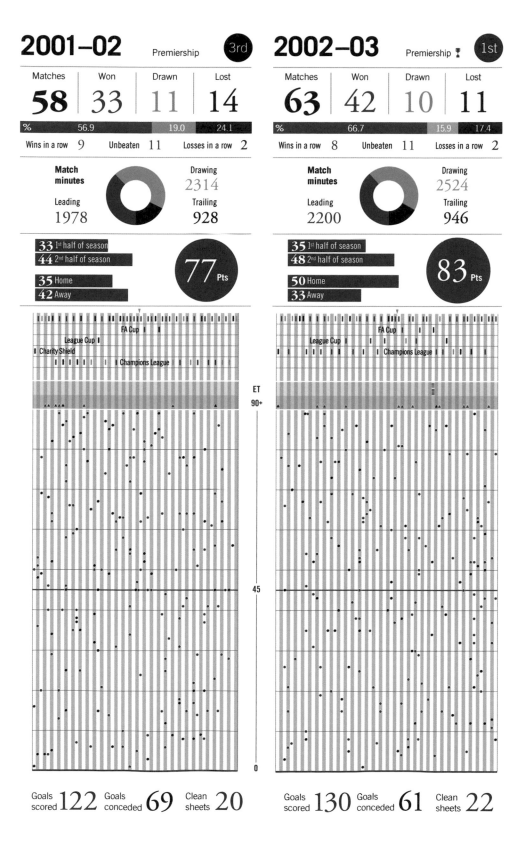

2001–02

Premiership · 3rd

Matches	Won	Drawn	Lost
58	33	11	14

%	56.9	19.0	24.1

Wins in a row 9 · Unbeaten 11 · Losses in a row 2

Match minutes

Drawing 2314

Leading 1978 · Trailing 928

33 1st half of season
44 2nd half of season
35 Home
42 Away

77 Pts

FA Cup
League Cup
Charity Shield
Champions League

ET
90+
45
0

Goals scored **122** · Goals conceded **69** · Clean sheets **20**

2002–03

Premiership ♛ · 1st

Matches	Won	Drawn	Lost
63	42	10	11

%	66.7	15.9	17.4

Wins in a row 8 · Unbeaten 11 · Losses in a row 2

Match minutes

Drawing 2524

Leading 2200 · Trailing 946

35 1st half of season
48 2nd half of season
50 Home
33 Away

83 Pts

FA Cup
League Cup
Champions League

Goals scored **130** · Goals conceded **61** · Clean sheets **22**

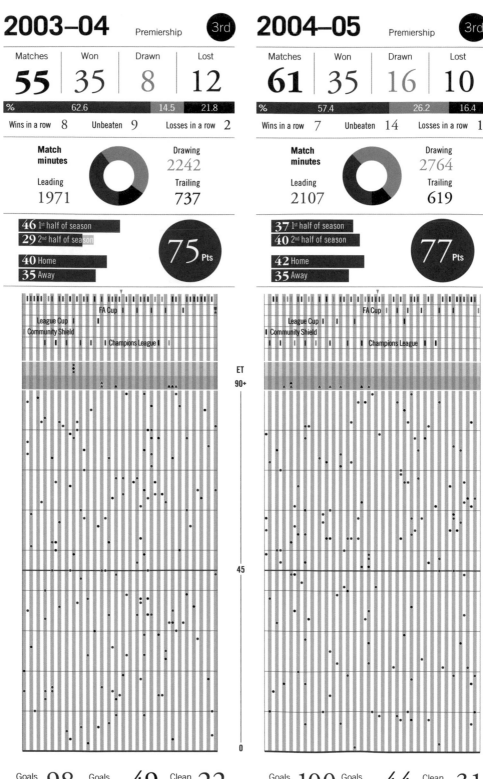

2003–04　Premiership　3rd

Matches	Won	Drawn	Lost
55	35	8	12

%			
62.6	14.5	21.8	

Wins in a row 8　　Unbeaten 9　　Losses in a row 2

Match minutes

Leading 1971　　Drawing 2242　　Trailing 737

46 1st half of season
29 2nd half of season
40 Home
35 Away

75 Pts

FA Cup
League Cup
Community Shield
Champions League

ET
90+
45
0

Goals scored **98**　　Goals conceded **49**　　Clean sheets **22**

2004–05　Premiership　3rd

Matches	Won	Drawn	Lost
61	35	16	10

%			
57.4	26.2	16.4	

Wins in a row 7　　Unbeaten 14　　Losses in a row 1

Match minutes

Leading 2107　　Drawing 2764　　Trailing 619

37 1st half of season
40 2nd half of season
42 Home
35 Away

77 Pts

FA Cup
League Cup
Community Shield
Champions League

Goals scored **100**　　Goals conceded **44**　　Clean sheets **31**

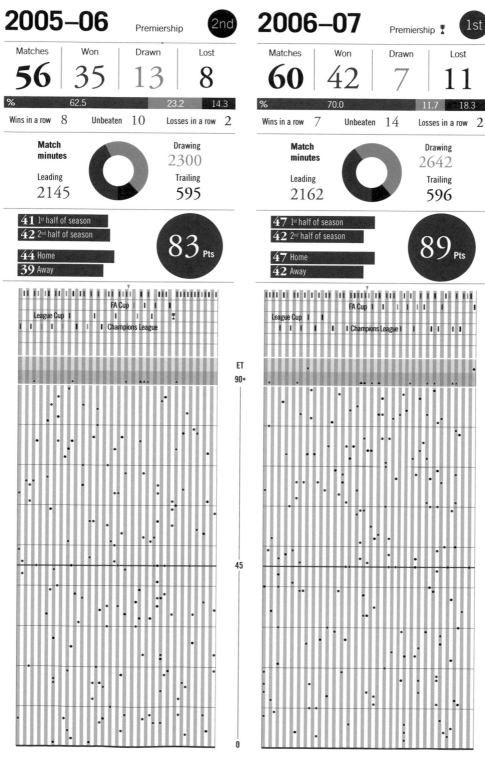

2005–06
Premiership · 2nd

Matches	Won	Drawn	Lost
56	35	13	8

| % | 62.5 | 23.2 | 14.3 |

Wins in a row 8 · Unbeaten 10 · Losses in a row 2

Match minutes
Drawing 2300
Leading 2145
Trailing 595

41 1st half of season
42 2nd half of season
44 Home
39 Away

83 Pts

League Cup · FA Cup · Champions League

ET 90+ · 45 · 0

Goals scored **106** · Goals conceded **44** · Clean sheets **27**

2006–07
Premiership · 1st

Matches	Won	Drawn	Lost
60	42	7	11

| % | 70.0 | 11.7 | 18.3 |

Wins in a row 7 · Unbeaten 14 · Losses in a row 2

Match minutes
Drawing 2642
Leading 2162
Trailing 596

47 1st half of season
42 2nd half of season
47 Home
42 Away

89 Pts

League Cup · FA Cup · Champions League

Goals scored **123** · Goals conceded **51** · Clean sheets **21**

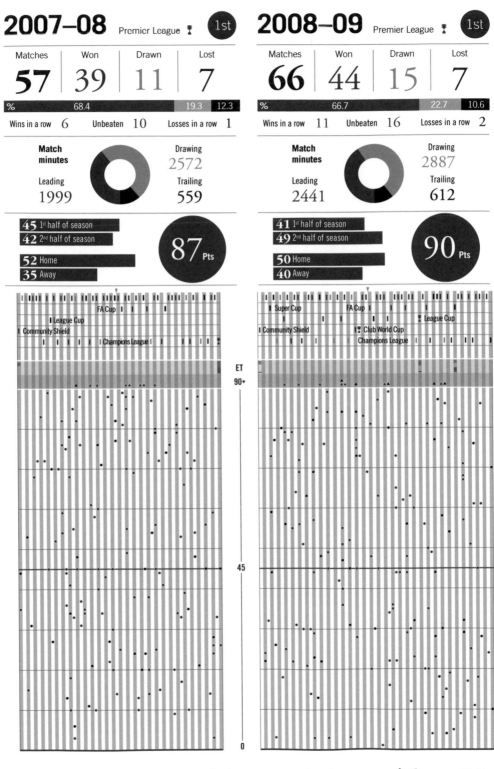

2007–08
Premier League 🏆 1st

Matches	Won	Drawn	Lost
57	39	11	7

| % | 68.4 | 19.3 | 12.3 |

Wins in a row 6 · Unbeaten 10 · Losses in a row 1

Match minutes

Drawing 2572
Leading 1999
Trailing 559

45 1st half of season
42 2nd half of season
52 Home
35 Away

87 Pts

Community Shield · League Cup · FA Cup · Champions League

ET
90+
45
0

Goals scored **110** · Goals conceded **33** · Clean sheets **31**

2008–09
Premier League 🏆 1st

Matches	Won	Drawn	Lost
66	44	15	7

| % | 66.7 | 22.7 | 10.6 |

Wins in a row 11 · Unbeaten 16 · Losses in a row 2

Match minutes

Drawing 2887
Leading 2441
Trailing 612

41 1st half of season
49 2nd half of season
50 Home
40 Away

90 Pts

Community Shield · Super Cup · Club World Cup · FA Cup · Champions League · League Cup

Goals scored **119** · Goals conceded **46** · Clean sheets **39**

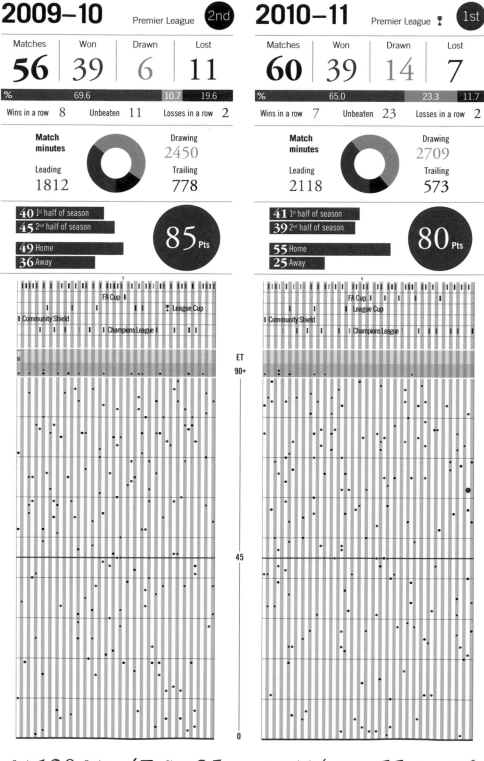

2009–10

Premier League **2nd**

Matches	Won	Drawn	Lost
56	39	6	11

%			
	69.6	10.7	19.6

Wins in a row 8   Unbeaten 11   Losses in a row 2

Match minutes

Drawing 2450
Leading 1812
Trailing 778

40 1st half of season
45 2nd half of season
49 Home
36 Away

85 Pts

FA Cup
League Cup
Community Shield
Champions League

ET
90+
45
0

Goals scored **120**   Goals conceded **47**   Clean sheets **25**

2010–11

Premier League **1st**

Matches	Won	Drawn	Lost
60	39	14	7

%			
	65.0	23.3	11.7

Wins in a row 7   Unbeaten 23   Losses in a row 2

Match minutes

Drawing 2709
Leading 2118
Trailing 573

41 1st half of season
39 2nd half of season
55 Home
25 Away

80 Pts

FA Cup
League Cup
Community Shield
Champions League

Goals scored **114**   Goals conceded **55**   Clean sheets **26**

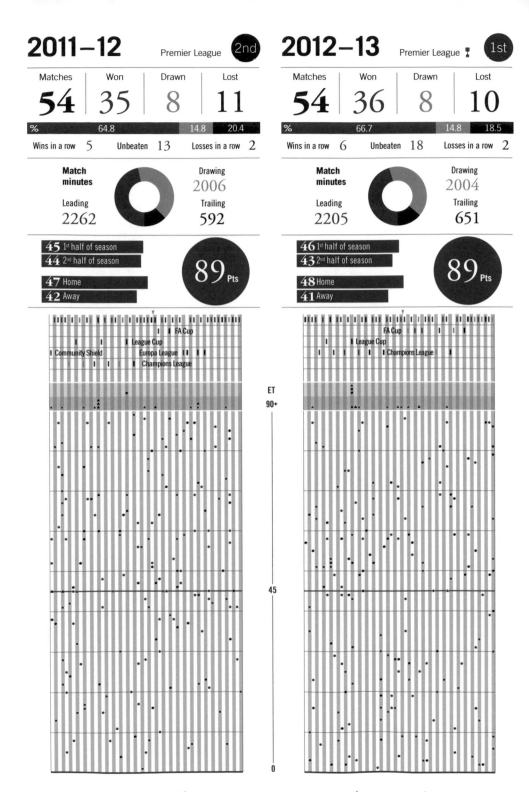

2011–12
Premier League — 2nd

Matches	Won	Drawn	Lost
54	35	8	11

| % | 64.8 | 14.8 | 20.4 |

Wins in a row 5   Unbeaten 13   Losses in a row 2

Match minutes
Drawing 2006
Leading 2262
Trailing 592

45 1st half of season
44 2nd half of season
47 Home
42 Away

89 Pts

Goals scored **120**   Goals conceded **56**   Clean sheets **25**

2012–13
Premier League — 1st

Matches	Won	Drawn	Lost
54	36	8	10

| % | 66.7 | 14.8 | 18.5 |

Wins in a row 6   Unbeaten 18   Losses in a row 2

Match minutes
Drawing 2004
Leading 2205
Trailing 651

46 1st half of season
43 2nd half of season
48 Home
41 Away

89 Pts

Goals scored **114**   Goals conceded **65**   Clean sheets **15**

FA Cup
League Cup
Community Shield
Europa League
Champions League

ET
90+
45
0

Academy Players by first-team debut season

During Sir Alex's time at Manchester United

1986–87
Tony Gill 14/2
Gary Walsh 63/0

1987–88
Deiniol Graham 4/1
Lee Martin 109/2

1988–89
Russell Beardsmore 73/4
Derek Brazil 2/0
Mark Robins 70/17
David Wilson 6/0

1992–93
David Beckham 394/85
Nicky Butt 387/26
Keith Gillespie 14/2
Gary Neville 602/7

1991–92
Ian Wilkinson 1/0

1990–91
Darren Ferguson 30/0
Ryan Giggs 963/168
Paul Wratten 2/0

1989–90

1993–94
Colin McKee 1/0
Ben Thornley 14/0

1994–95
Kevin Pilkington 8/0
Simon Davies 20/1
Chris Casper 7/0
John O'Kane 7/0
Paul Scholes 718/155
Phil Neville 386/8

1995–96
Terry Cooke 8/1

1996–97
Michael Appleton 2/0
Michael Clegg 24/0

2000–01
Bojan Djordjic 2/0
Michael Stewart 14/0
Danny Webber 3/0

1999–2000
Luke Chadwick 39/2
David Healy 3/0
Paul Rachubka 3/0
Richie Wellens 1/0

1998–99
Alex Notman 1/0
Mark Wilson 10/0

1997–98
Danny Higginbotham 7/0
Ronnie Wallwork 28/0
Michael Twiss 2/0
Phil Mulryne 5/0
Wes Brown 362/5
John Curtis 19/0

2001–02
Jimmy Davis 1/0
Daniel Nardiello 4/0
Lee Roche 3/0

2002–03
Darren Fletcher 342/24
Mark Lynch 1/0
Danny Pugh 7/0
Kieran Richardson 81/11
Mads Timm 1/0

2003–04
Phil Bardsley 18/0
Chris Eagles 17/1
Eddie Johnson 1/0
Paul Tierney 1/0

2004–05
Sylvan Ebanks-Blake 2/1
David Jones 4/0
Gérard Piqué 23/2
Giuseppe Rossi 14/4
Jonathan Spector 8/0

2008–09
Ben Amos 7/0
James Chester 1/0
Richard Eckersley 4/0
Federico Macheda 36/5
Danny Welbeck 103/19

2007–08
Fraizer Campbell 4/0
Jonny Evans 156/5
Danny Simpson 8/0

2006–07
Michael Barnes 1/0
David Gray 1/0
Kieran Lee 3/1
Phil Marsh 1/0
Ryan Shawcross 2/0

2005–06
Adam Eckersley 1/0
Darron Gibson 60/10
Ritchie Jones 5/0
Lee Martin 3/0

2009–10
Joshua King 2/0

2010–11
Ravel Morrison 3/0

2011–12
Tom Cleverley 47/4
Larnell Cole 1/0
Zeki Fryers 6/0
Michael Keane 3/0
Will Keane 1/0
Paul Pogba 7/0

2012–13
Robbie Brady 1/0
Ryan Tunnicliffe 2/0
Scott Wootton 4/0

50+ appearances   appearances/goals   **Total appearances:** 5,429 **Total goals:** 573

MANCHESTER UNITED SQUAD MEMBERS, BY NATIONALITY (1986–2013)

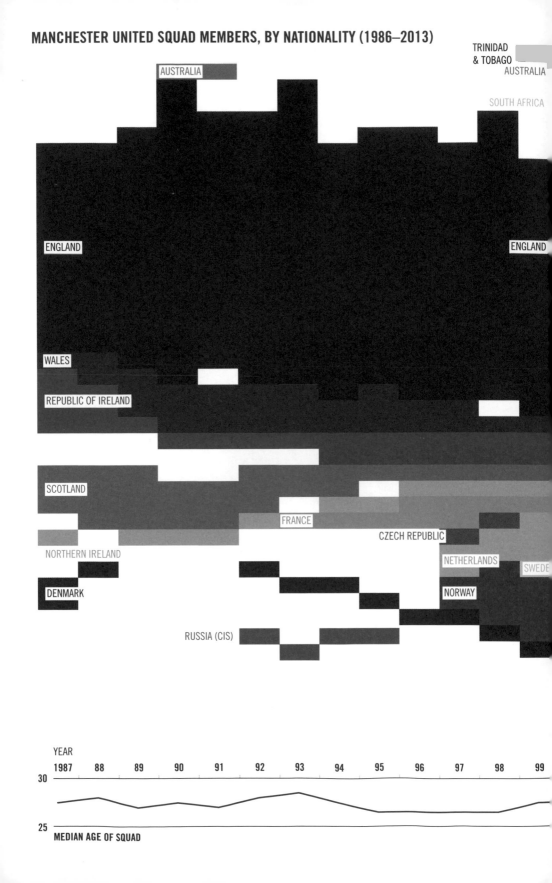

TRINIDAD
& TOBAGO

AUSTRALIA

SOUTH AFRICA

AUSTRALIA

ENGLAND

ENGLAND

WALES

REPUBLIC OF IRELAND

SCOTLAND

FRANCE

CZECH REPUBLIC

NETHERLANDS

SWEDE

NORTHERN IRELAND

DENMARK

NORWAY

RUSSIA (CIS)

YEAR

1987   88   89   90   91   92   93   94   95   96   97   98   99

30

25

MEDIAN AGE OF SQUAD

MEXICO

ARGENTINA

CHINA ANGOLA ECUADOR
SENEGAL JAPAN

CAMEROON SOUTH KOREA

URUGUAY

USA

BRAZIL

WALES

REPUBLIC OF IRELAND

SCOTLAND
NORTHERN IRELAND

FRANCE

BULGARIA

SWEDEN

NORWAY POLAND

PORTUGAL

SPAIN

ITALY

DENMARK

SERBIA

BELGIUM

YEAR
01   02   03   04   05   06   07   08   09   10   11   12   13

MOST SUCCESSFUL EUROPEAN CUP-WINNING MANAGERS 1974–2013

Carlo Ancelotti (ITA)

Champions League: 3   Domestic League Titles: 3   Domestic Cups: 3

Rafa Benítez (SPA)

Champions League: 1   Other European Trophies: 2   Domestic League Titles: 2   Domestic Cups: 2

Vicente del Bosque (SPA)

Champions League: 2   Domestic League Titles: 2

Fabio Capello (ITA)

Champions League: 1   Domestic League Titles: 7

Johan Cruyff (NED)

Champions League: 1   Other European Trophies: 2   Domestic League Titles: 4   Domestic Cups: 3

Sir Alex Ferguson (SCO)

Champions League: 2   Other European Trophies: 2

Domestic League Titles: 17

Domestic Cups: 14

Louis van Gaal (NED)

Champions League: 1   Other European Trophies: 1

Domestic Cups: 3   Domestic League Titles: 7

Raymond Goethals (BEL)

Champions League: 1   Other European Trophies: 1   Domestic League Titles: 4   Domestic Cups: 1

Pep Guardiola (SPA)

Champions League: 2   Domestic League Titles: 6   Domestic Cups: 3

Jupp Heynckes (GER)

Champions League: 2   Domestic League Titles: 3   Domestic Cups: 1

Guus Hiddink (NED)

Champions League: 1   Domestic League Titles: 6   Domestic Cups: 5

Ottmar Hitzfeld (GER)

Champions League: 2

Domestic League Titles: 9   Domestic Cups: 6

Marcello Lippi (ITA)

Champions League: 1   Domestic League Titles: 5   Domestic Cups: 1

José Mourinho (POR)

Champions League: 2   Other European Trophies: 1

Domestic League Titles: 8   Domestic Cups: 7

Bob Paisley (ENG)

Champions League: 3   Other European Trophies: 1

Domestic League Titles: 6   Domestic Cups: 3

Arrigo Sacchi (ITA)

Champions League: 2   Domestic League Titles: 2

Giovanni Trapattoni (ITA)

Champions League: 1   Other European Trophies: 4

Domestic League Titles: 10   Domestic Cups: 3

THE ARCHIVE

The Manchester United Football Club plc

18 August 1997

Dear Eric

Some months have passed since we last spoke and I felt that I should write to you as a mark of respect and esteem in which I hold you.

When we re-started training, I kept waiting for you to turn up as normal but I think that was in hope not realism and I knew in your eyes when we met at Mottram your time at Manchester United was over. Although, I still feel you should have taken both your Father's and my advice and taken a holiday before making such a major decision.

One thing, I would like you to remember is to remain active and fit. I always remember when I finished at 32 and I started management, I was more concerned about organising training and the coaching of players that I forgot about my own fitness and then when I realised about six years later what was happening, I started to train again to recapture my fitness and it was murder, so you do need to keep your fitness.

I am sure you have been keeping an eye on our results and as you can see we are doing quite well as you know we have signed Teddy Sheringham to replace you but at the moment he is finding it difficult to find the space he got at Tottenham and is playing deep so we have some adjusting to do. Players sometimes don't realise how difficult it is to play at our level as every game is a Cup Final for our opponents so I just hope he can do it for us.

Our pre-season tour wasn't too bad. The Far East tour was better than expected and our games against Inter Milan were very good. The Charity Shield wasn't a great performance but we were better than Chelsea and deserved to win, even though it went to penalties.

I still feel as we discussed at the end of the season that a top class striker is what is needed and that is always going to be the problem at our club as the financial restraints will always stop us getting the best because of our wage structure and it is such a pity because when you are at the top you should buy the best to stop the others getting to you. If I was younger, I suppose I would look at it differently, but from a personal point of view, I have not won the European Cup and it does get to me at times. However, I just have to carry on and not put up a mental barrier and I have always had that belief and trust in my players and wish to continue to do so. I keep hoping that I will discover a young Cantona! It is a dream!

As I close this letter, I would like to hope that we will have a chat, a drink, or a meal together soon. I know the club has written to you about the forthcoming dinner and I hope you will manage it, but that is not the most important thing, for me it is to remind you how good a player you were for Manchester United and how grateful I am for the service you gave me. I will never forget that and I hope you won't either.

You are always welcome here and if you just pop in unexpectedly for a cup of tea, no fanfare, just for a chat as friends, that would mean more to me than anything. Eric you know where I am if you need me and now that you are no longer one of my players, I hope you know you have a friend.

Good luck and God bless.

Yours sincerely

Alex Ferguson CBE
MANAGER

A letter acknowledging one of Manchester United's true greats.

IMcL/EO'N

Celtic

14 March 2002

Celtic plc
Celtic Park
Glasgow G40 3RE
Tel: 0141 556 2611
Fax: 0141 551 8106
http://www.celticfc.co.uk

Sir Alex Ferguson
Manchester United plc
Sir Matt Busby Way
Old Trafford
MANCHESTER
M16 ORA

Dear Sir Alex

This is just a brief note to thank you for your time and attention on Wednesday, when you showed me around Carrington with Willie Haughey.

Youth development and quality training facilities have been lower on the Celtic agenda than I believe they should have been and I wish to take steps to address our shortfalls.

Your own personal insights, opinion and advice were not only welcome but very much appreciated.

Thank you very much for your time, once again, particularly at such an important time for Manchester United.

Finally, congratulations on reaching the Champions League Quarter Finals.

Kind regards,

Yours sincerely

Ian McLeod
Chief Executive

A letter from Ian McLeod, Celtic's Chief Executive, following
a visit to Carrington training ground, 2002.

the
MANCHESTER UNITED
FOOTBALL CLUB plc
OLD TRAFFORD
MANCHESTER M16 0RA

Registered Office: Old Trafford, Manchester, M16 0RA

Registered No. 95489 England
Telephone:
061-872 1661 (Office)
061-872 0199 (Ticket and
Match Enquiries)
061-872 3488 (Commercial
Direct Line Mgr.
Fax No. 061-873 7210
Telex: 666564 United G

Chief Executive	Manager	Secretary	Commercial Manager
C. Martin Edwards	Alex Ferguson	Kenneth R. Merrett	D. A. McGregor

£   per week basic wage.

When playing in the First Team, or being nominated as a substitute for Football League Championship matches you will receive:

a.   A bonus of £100 per point.

     For the purpose of assessing the bonus payments contained in Clause 2(a), points will be awarded on the basis of 3 points for a Win and 1 point for a Draw.

b.   In addition a sum of £100,000 will be distributed among the First Team Pool of players if the Club wins the First Division Championship.

     This bonus calculation will be based on the number of League games played by each individual.

     <u>Example:</u> If a player appears in all 38 matches, he will receive 1/13 of £100,000 which equals £7,692.

c.   In addition a sum of £25,000 will be distributed among the First Team Pool of players if the Club finishes in the top four of the First Division or qualifies for the UEFA Cup Competition through its final League position. This payment will not be made in the event of the Club winning the First Division League Championship.

d.   A bonus of £100 for a Win and £50 for a Draw for First Team Friendly matches.

e.   The above payments only relate to First Division matches. In the event of the Club being relegated then the above payments will be reduced by half.

When playing or being nominated as a substitute in the Football Association Cup Competition a win bonus will be paid as follows:

a.   Third Round: £400.
     Fourth Round: £500.
     Fifth Round: £600.
     Sixth Round: £750.
     Semi Final: £1,500.
     Final: £2,500.

b.   Any player selected or being nominated as a substitute for the Final will be paid appearance money of £1,000.

c.   In the event of any round in the Competition ending in a Draw half bonus will be paid.

d.   In addition a sum of £40,000 will be distributed among the First Team Pool of players, based on the number of appearances made by each individual, if the Club wins the Competition.

When playing or being nominated as a substitute in the Littlewoods Cup Competition, a win bonus will be paid as follows:

a.   Second Round: £400.
     Third Round: £400.
     Fourth Round: £500.
     Fifth Round: £600.
     Semi Final: £2,000.
     Final: £2,500.

b.   Any player selected or being nominated as a substitute for the Final will be paid appearance money of £1,000.

c.   In the event of any round in the Competition ending in a Draw half bonus will be paid.

d.   Where a round is played over two legs, a player playing in one game only will be paid full win bonus.

The official bonus structure for the Manchester United squad, late 1980s.

the
MANCHESTER UNITED
FOOTBALL CLUB plc
OLD TRAFFORD
MANCHESTER M16 0RA
Registered Office: Old Trafford, Manchester, M16 0RA

Registered No. 95489 England
Telephone:
061-872 1661 (Office)
061-872 0199 (Ticket and
Match Enquiries)
061-872 3488 (Commercial
Direct Line Mgr.
Fax No. 061-873 7210
Telex: 666564 United G

Chief Executive   Manager   Secretary   Commercial Manager
C. Martin Edwards   Alex Ferguson   Kenneth R. Merrett   D. A. McGregor

    e.   In addition a sum of £40,000 will be distributed among the First Team Pool of players, based on the number of appearances made by each individual, if the Club wins the Competition.

5.   When playing or being nominated as a substitute in the European Champions Cup Competition, a win bonus will be paid as follows:

    a.   First Round: £1,000.
         Second Round: £1,500.
         Third Round: £2,000.
         Semi Final: £3,000.
         Final: £4,000..

    b.   Any player selected or being called on to play as a substitute in the Final will be paid appearance money of £1,000.

    c.   A player playing in only one-leg in any round will be paid Full Win Bonus.

    d.   In addition a sum of £40,000 will be distributed among the First Team Pool of players, based on the number of appearances made by each individual, if the Club wins the Competition.

6.   When playing or being nominated as substitute in the European Cup Winners Cup Competition, a win bonus will be paid as follows:

    a.   First Round: £1,000.
         Second Round: £1,250.
         Third Round: £1,500.
         Semi Final: £2,500.
         Final: £3,000.

    b.   Any player selected or being called on to play as a substitute in the Final will be paid appearance money of £1,000.

    c.   A player playing only one-leg in any round will be paid Full Win Bonus.

    d.   In addition a sum of £30,000 will be distributed among the First Team Pool of players, based on the number of appearances made by each individual, if the Club wins the Competition.

7.   When playing or being nominated as substitute in the UEFA Cup Competition, a win bonus will be paid as follows:

    a.   First Round: £1,000.
         Second Round: £1,250.
         Third Round: £1,500.
         Fourth Round: £2,000.
         Semi Final: £2,500.
         Final: £3,000.

    b.   Any player selected or being called on to play as a substitute in the Final will be paid appearance money of £500 for each game.

    c.   A player playing in only one-leg in any round will be paid Full Win Bonus.

    d.   In addition a sum of £30,000 will be distributed among the First Team Pool of players, based on the number of appearances made by each individual, if the Club wins the Competition.

8.   If you are injured whilst playing in the First Team, you will receive your basic wage and full bonus payments for a period to be decided at the Manager's discretion.

9.   If you are not selected to play but are named on the First Team Sheet you will receive your basic wage and half of any points bonus payment made to the members of the Team for Football League games, or half bonus paid in respect of any Cup ties in Competitions organised by UEFA, The Football Association or The Football League.

10.	Other Competions:	In the event of the Club playing in any other FIRST TEAM Competition apart from those listed above, the Directors undertake to make available a sum of money, the amount to be decided at their discretion for distribution pro-rata to the number of appeatances.
11.	Friendly Matches:	A bonus of £100 for a win and £50 for a Draw for First Team Friendly matches.
12.	Reserve Team:	A bonus of £10 for a win and £5 for a Draw.

LIVERPOOL FOOTBALL CLUB

AND ATHLETIC GROUNDS P.L.C.

ANFIELD ROAD, LIVERPOOL L4 0TH

051-263 2361/2

Official Sponsor
Candy

Telex 627661 LFC G   Fax 051-260 8813

Registered No. 35668, England

Match Information Service Only   Match Ticket Office, Enquiries Only
051-260 9999   051-260 8680

KD:SW   29th August, 1989

Mr. Alex Ferguson,
Manchester United Football Club,
Trafford Park,
Manchester, M16 0RA.

Dear Alex,

    Just a note to thank you most sincerely, albeit belatedly, for your kindness at the time of the Disaster. We needed all the help we could get at that time and we greatly appreciated the co-operation and kindness of you and the lads in attending Colin Ashcroft's funeral. We know that seeing you all there was a great comfort to his family.

    Thanks again Alex to you and the lads.

    Good luck,

                         Yours sincerely,

                         Kenny Dalglish.

L.F.C.
Registered Trade Marks

K.M. DALGLISH, M.B.E.   P.B. ROBINSON
PLAYER/TEAM MANAGER   CHIEF EXECUTIVE/GENERAL SECRETARY

A letter from Kenny Dalglish in the wake of the Hillsborough disaster.

PLAYER ANALYSIS

	CURRENT		YOUTH	TRANSFER
	SQUAD	**EXCESS**	**POTENTIAL**	**TARGETS/POSSIBILITIES**
GOALKEEPERS	3 HOWARD CARROLL STEELE	RICARDO	HEATON LEE	
DEFENDERS	6 NEVILLE, G SILVESTRE BROWN FERDINAND O'SHEA FORTUNE (1)		SPECTOR (3) MCSHANE BARDSLEY	→ HEINZE (PSG) MEXES (AUXERRE) KOMPANY (ANDERLECHT) → PIQUE (YOUTH - BARCELONA)
MIDFIELD	9 GIGGS KEANE SCHOLES RONALDO NEVILLE, P KLERBERSON DJEMBA DJEMBA FLETCHER MILLER	(BUTT) CHADWICK STEWART	RICHARDSON EAGLES (4) N'GALULA D JONES	
ATTACK	4 VAN NISTELROOY SAHA SOLKSJAER (2) BELLION	(FORLAN)	FANGZHOU (5) TIMMS	→ SMITH (LEEDS)
TOTAL	22	5		

Notes of discussion with AF:

(1) Injury issue – may not be available until 2005
(2) Injury issue – further specialist advice being sought
(3) Possibility of promotion to 1st team squad
(4) Reviewing a season long loan option
(5) Unkown quanlity – work permit issues

Discussion document from a board meeting about squad composition, 2004.

SIR ALEX FERGUSON

The euphoria from Tuesday's demolition of the Gunners needs to be set aside today; with City the visitors, the priority is on maintaining the momentum from last week's slick showing at the Riverside

Terrific, tremendous ...the whole place is buzzing! We're going to Rome in a bid to achieve what has never been done before – and that of course is to successfully defend our Champions League crown. The statistics tell you how difficult it is, as we know to our personal cost after failing in Europe following our victory in Barcelona 10 years ago. We are ready for another crack at it, though, after a great semi-final win against Arsenal at the Emirates on Tuesday.

We went through on the back of our first-leg 1-0 win at Old Trafford and then a dominating 3-1 success this week in London. Now we look forward to a fantastic final against Barcelona. But of course Europe is only part of our story this season. We also have a domestic title to defend, so we have to get our Premier League heads on again as we welcome Manchester City to Old Trafford today. We have to put Europe out of our minds, because although we are in a strong position in the league, we must make sure we are completely focused on our remaining games if we are to come out on top.

So enough of Europe for now, especially this afternoon, because

Maturing nicely: Giggs marked game number 801 with another cracking strike

4 Manchester United v Manchester City

a derby poses particular problems as we also know to our cost, especially now that Mark Hughes is in charge. I know him too well to expect anything but a full-on challenge. Mark was a warrior as a player; it's a quality still in him and one that he's trying strenuously to imbue in his players.

Management is not an easy task at the best of times, and Mark is managing City at a vital and transitional stage following the Middle East takeover that put great financial resources at their disposal.

"Mark will be only too aware that signing players, however good they are, is only the start of the process"

They made a startling impact at the start of the season with a £32 million signing, a transfer which put down a big marker of intent. City became the centre of a media storm – in fact I can't remember a time when we were so much squeezed off the back pages!

That kind of media situation does not sit easily with Mark, whose qualities made him one of our great players, but who nevertheless was never one for over-the-top hype, either concerning himself or the team. He was always a constant and consistent trainer, but he enjoyed his family life too and wouldn't hang around before heading for home. He preferred a low-profile life, so what he is experiencing now is something new for him.

He was able to keep his head down when he was manager at Blackburn where, incidentally, he did an outstanding job with a limited budget. Now he is firmly in the media spotlight, and there is no escaping it with all manner of speculation ranging from transfers both in to and out of his club, to chatter about his own future. It's always good to be the manager of a club with money available for new players, but how you spend it is what matters. I am sure there will be all kinds of possibilities turning over in his head as we draw towards the end of the season.

A message to the fans from the official match-day programme, *United Review*, 10 May 2009, Manchester United vs. Manchester City.

The lads head for the away end at the Emirates after an imperious display

Like every manager, Mark will be only too aware that signing players, however good they are individually, is only the start of the process. Building a team is what counts, and this can take years. The nature of the media beast is not one of patience, though, and Mark has already come in for a lot of unfair and hasty criticism.

What he needs is time, and I hope the City owners are prepared to give him a fair share of that precious commodity. He will need the patience of City supporters, too, and I think the whole club must have been cheered by the recent results that suggest the Blues are going to finish the season on a high.

It's certainly something we have noted, and which adds to the challenge we meet today as we seek to maintain our momentum. I thought our 2-0 win at Middlesbrough last Sunday was a big step forward. We have had some tricky moments at the Riverside, and I was worried about having a Saturday-lunchtime start after playing in the Champions League on the Wednesday with obviously not

> "Against the Gunners there was a real maturity to the team that is going to be invaluable in Rome"

a lot of recovery time. Happily I have a squad that enables me to make changes, and I was delighted with the way Ryan Giggs and Paul Scholes in particular returned to the starting line-up. They gave such masterly displays in midfield that we ran the game and got an excellent result.

The win topped a great week for Ryan, voted the PFA Player of the Year and then celebrating 801 appearances for Manchester United by scoring! I have run out of ways of praising his contribution in a fabulous career in a red shirt, and can only congratulate him on another fine effort!

Now we go into today's game after a decent break. Playing at Arsenal on the Tuesday gave us four clear days before taking on City. And maybe I will make another change to keep us

fresh. Certainly we are approaching it in good shape after a brilliant display against the Gunners who started extremely well, only to give us a break when their young full-back slipped at a vital moment.

Ji-sung Park scored to set the scene for two fabulous goals from Cristiano Ronaldo and a performance that I believe would have prevailed even without our fortunate opening. There was a real maturity to the team that is going to be invaluable in Rome. The only disappointment was the red card for Darren Fletcher ruling him out of the final, which made it a bitter-sweet occasion.

Now though, we must put all those issues to one side, to make sure we maintain the energy and drive that's vital if we are to get over the line for the championship.

Alex Ferguson

11-05-13

IAN SETTLE
GUNTERSMLAG.

Dear Sir Alex,

I came in from work today and turned on Match Of The Day. Your speech to the crowd had me beaming, what a wonderful way to bring the curtain down. My dad was a Govan man of your fathers generation, he had connections with Summerston Church way back, and the 129th BB, if I remember. I believe this is where he introduced me to yourself when you were at Ibrox. Lost him in 76, but know he'd have loved your journey. At 52 it's a bit late in the day to start writing to personalitys, but I dare say like others felt this was a once in a lifetime moment.

This was also a big day for my family, as it started with the birth of my third grandchild. At moments like that you think of your oldman. So to turn on the telly at the end of the day and see a Govan lad holding them all spellbound was a bit special.

All the very best for the future.

That was wonderful.

Ian Settle.

A fan responds to Sir Alex Ferguson's retirement.

INDEX

INTRODUCTION TO
INFORMATION
SYSTEMS

INTRODUCTION TO INFORMATION SYSTEMS

Fifteenth Edition

James A. O'Brien

College of Business Administration
Northern Arizona University

George M. Marakas

KU School of Business
University of Kansas

McGraw-Hill
Irwin

INTRODUCTION TO INFORMATION SYSTEMS

Published by McGraw-Hill/Irwin, a business unit of The McGraw-Hill Companies, Inc., 1221 Avenue of the Americas, New York, NY, 10020. Copyright © 2010, 2008, 2007, 2005, 2003, 2001, 2000, 1997, 1994, 1991, 1988, 1985, 1982, 1978, 1975 by The McGraw-Hill Companies, Inc. All rights reserved. No part of this publication may be reproduced or distributed in any form or by any means, or stored in a database or retrieval system, without the prior written consent of The McGraw-Hill Companies, Inc., including, but not limited to, in any network or other electronic storage or transmission, or broadcast for distance learning.

Some ancillaries, including electronic and print components, may not be available to customers outside the United States.

This book is printed on acid-free paper.

1 2 3 4 5 6 7 8 9 0 DOW/DOW 0 9

ISBN 978-0-07-016708-7
MHID 0-07-016708-7

To your love, happiness, and success.

The world of information systems presents new and exciting challenges each and every day. Creating a textbook to capture this world is a formidable task, to be sure. This, the 15th edition of *Introduction to Information Systems*, represents the best we have to offer. We take pride in delivering this new edition to you and we thank all of you for your loyalty to the book and the input you provided that was instrumental in its development. Your continued support fills us with joy and a sense of both accomplishment and contribution.

We are also pleased and excited to welcome a new member to our writing family. Miguel Aguirre-Urreta has joined us in the creation of the materials contained herein. His work and effort on the Real World Cases and blue boxes will be apparent as we bring you new cases in every chapter of the book. Please join us in welcoming Miguel to our family.

On behalf of Jim, Miguel, and myself, please accept our sincere appreciation for your support and loyalty. As always, we hope you enjoy and benefit from this book.

James A. O'Brien was an adjunct professor of Computer Information Systems in the College of Business Administration at Northern Arizona University. He completed his undergraduate studies at the University of Hawaii and Gonzaga University and earned an MS and PhD in Business Administration from the University of Oregon. He has been professor and coordinator of the CIS area at Northern Arizona University, professor of Finance and Management Information Systems and chairman of the Department of Management at Eastern Washington University, and a visiting professor at the University of Alberta, the University of Hawaii, and Central Washington University.

Dr. O'Brien's business experience includes working in the Marketing Management Program of the IBM Corporation, as well as serving as a financial analyst for the General Electric Company. He is a graduate of General Electric's Financial Management Program. He also has served as an information systems consultant to several banks and computer services firms.

Jim's research interests lie in developing and testing basic conceptual frameworks used in information systems development and management. He has written eight books, including several that have been published in multiple editions, as well as in Chinese, Dutch, French, Japanese, and Spanish translations. He has also contributed to the field of information systems through the publication of many articles in business and academic journals, as well as through his participation in academic and industry associations in the field of information systems.

George M. Marakas is a professor of Information Systems at the School of Business at the University of Kansas. His teaching expertise includes Systems Analysis and Design, Technology-Assisted Decision Making, Electronic Commerce, Management of IS Resources, Behavioral IS Research Methods, and Data Visualization and Decision Support. In addition, George is an active researcher in the area of Systems Analysis Methods, Data Mining and Visualization, Creativity Enhancement, Conceptual Data Modeling, and Computer Self-Efficacy.

George received his PhD in Information Systems from Florida International University in Miami and his MBA from Colorado State University. Prior to his position at the University of Kansas, he was a member of the faculties at the University of Maryland, Indiana University, and Helsinki School of Economics. Preceding his academic career, he enjoyed a highly successful career in the banking and real estate industries. His corporate experience includes senior management positions with Continental Illinois National Bank and the Federal Deposit Insurance Corporation. In addition, George served as president and CEO for CMC Group Inc., a major RTC management contractor in Miami, Florida, for three years. Throughout his academic career, George has distinguished himself both through his research and in the classroom. He has received numerous national teaching awards, and his research has appeared in the top journals in his field. In addition to this text, he is the author of three best-selling textbooks on information systems: *Decision Support Systems for the 21st Century, Systems Analysis and Design: An Active Approach, and Data Warehousing, Mining, and Visualization: Core Concepts.*

Beyond his academic endeavors, George is also an active consultant and has served as an advisor to a number of organizations, including the Central Intelligence Agency, Brown & Williamson, the Department of the Treasury, the Department of Defense, Xavier University, Citibank Asia-Pacific, Nokia Corporation, Professional Records Storage Inc., and United Information Systems. His consulting activities are concentrated primarily on electronic commerce strategy, the design and deployment of global IT strategy, workflow reengineering, e-business strategy, and ERP and CASE tool integration.

George is also an active member of a number of professional IS organizations and an avid golfer, second-degree Black Belt in Tae Kwon Do, a PADI master scuba diver trainer and IDC staff instructor, and a member of Pi Kappa Alpha fraternity.

The O'Brien and Marakas Approach

The first thing you probably noticed about this new edition is the new, loose-leaf format. The 15th edition was produced this way in order to deliver a couple of important benefits for instructors and students.

- Lower cost to students—the loose-leaf format allows us to substantially lower the price that your campus bookstore pays for each copy, which should translate to a substantially lower price for each student.
- Less frequent course prep for faculty—We expect that, by providing students with this cost-competitive alternative to a used book, we won't need to revise the book as frequently. So instructors will get additional semesters out of their prep with this edition.
- Improved portability—Students and instructors need only carry the chapter required for today's lecture, leaving the rest in a three ring binder.

If for any reason you need a bound book for your class, simply contact your McGraw-Hill representative. They will arrange to have bound copies of *Introduction to Information Systems*, 15th edition produced for your adoption.

A Business and Managerial Perspective

The Fifteenth Edition is designed for business students who are or who will soon become business professionals in the fast-changing business world of today. The goal of this text is to help business students learn how to use and manage information technologies to revitalize business processes, improve business decision making, and gain competitive advantage. Thus, it places a major emphasis on up-to-date coverage of the essential role of Internet technologies in providing a platform for business, commerce, and collaboration processes among all business stakeholders in today's networked enterprises and global markets. This is the business and managerial perspective that this text brings to the study of information systems. Of course, as in all O'Brien texts, this edition:

- Loads the text with **Real World Cases,** in-depth examples **(Blue Boxes),** and opportunities to learn about real people and companies in the business world **(Real World Activities, Case Study Questions, Discussion Questions**, and **Analysis Exercises).**
- Organizes the text around a simple **Five-Area Information Systems Framework** that emphasizes the IS knowledge a business professional needs to know.
- Places a **major emphasis on the strategic role of information technology** in providing business professionals with tools and resources for managing business operations, supporting decision making, enabling enterprise collaboration, and gaining competitive advantage.

Modular Structure of the Text

The text is organized into modules that reflect the five major areas of the framework for information systems knowledge. Each chapter is then organized into two or more distinct sections to provide the best possible conceptual organization of the text and each chapter. This organization increases instructor flexibility in as-

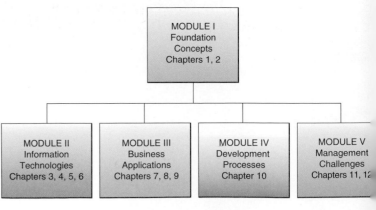

signing course material because it structures the text into modular levels (i.e., modules, chapters, and sections) while reducing the number of chapters that need to be covered.

An Information Systems Framework

Business Applications

How businesses use the Internet and other information technologies to support their business processes, e-business and e-commerce initiatives, and business decision making (Chapters 7, 8, and 9).

Management Challenges

The challenges of business/IT technologies and strategies, including security and ethical challenges and global IT management (Chapters 11 and 12).

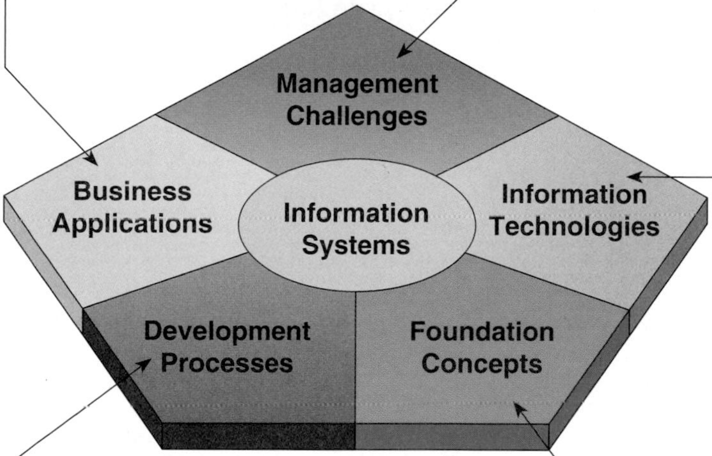

Information Technologies

Includes major concepts, developments, and managerial issues involved in computer hardware, software, telecommunications networks, data resource management technologies, and other technologies (Chapters 3, 4, 5, and 6).

Development Processes

Developing and implementing business/IT strategies and systems using several strategic planning and application development approaches (Chapter 10).

Foundation Concepts

Fundamental business information systems concepts, including trends, components, and roles of information systems (Chapter 1) and competitive advantage concepts and applications (Chapter 2). Selective coverage of relevant behavioral, managerial, and technical concepts.

Diagram labels:
- Management Challenges
- Business Applications
- Information Systems
- Information Technologies
- Development Processes
- Foundation Concepts

Real World Examples

Real World Cases

Each chapter provides three Real World Cases—in-depth examples that illustrate how prominent businesses and organizations have attempted to implement the theoretical concepts students have just learned.

REAL WORLD CASE 1

Cogent Communications, Intel, and Others: Mergers Go More Smoothly When Your Data Are Ready

When Cogent Communications eyes a company to acquire, it goes into battle mode. Two miles north of the Pentagon, across the Potomac in Washington, Cogent sets up what it calls the War Room, where it marshals eight top executives to evaluate the target company. Among those on the due diligence squad are the IS director and IT infrastructure manager.

Cogent, a midsize Internet service provider, understands what far too many companies don't: Its ability to integrate and, in some cases, adopt an acquired company's IT systems and operations can determine whether a merger flourishes or founders. For one thing, unanticipated IT integration costs can offset merger savings. Imagine the business lost when orders vanish, accounts payable go uncollected, and customer information goes AWOL because the acquiring company gave short shrift to the IT challenge ahead.

As 2006 came to a close, it broke records for the number of mergers and acquisitions, but now IT managers have to step up and make sure their data centers can help make those deals a reality. "A well-run data center with reduced complexity makes mergers and acquisitions much easier," says Andi Mann, senior analyst at Enterprise Management Associates (EMA).

More than 11,700 deals were done. As the dust clears, experts and IT managers agree that companies will feel the full impact of this merger and acquisition (M&A) frenzy directly in their data centers. So they advise organizations to prep now or risk experiencing downtime if they have to merge mission-critical assets. "Today, the most downtime companies can afford for critical data center infrastructure is

measured in minutes." Merged and acquired infrastructure "has to be available right away," says Ryan Osborn of AFCOM, a data center industry group.

Observers agree that the key to M&A success from a data center perspective is to focus on virtualization, documentation, and logistics. Osborn says these three areas will help companies get ahead of the game and turn a time of crisis into one of opportunity. "You won't spend your time just moving infrastructure from one data center to another. You can actually do a technology refresh, get newer equipment and come out ahead," he says.

For John Musilli, data center operations manager at Intel in Santa Clara, California, the most critical piece is knowing about basic logistics. "I don't always have to know what a server does, but I do have to know how to keep it alive," he says. "It's getting something moved from Point A to Point B and it doesn't matter whether the logistics deals with putting servers on a truck or transferring data over a line."

Musilli has been through a handful of acquisitions in his eight years at Intel, and he says that he has it down to a science. "As part of the acquiring company, it's my job to provide the skeletal environment to accept any company's assets that come to us," he says. As such, he keeps a healthy amount of generic racking, generic cabling, extra bandwidth on the network, and generic power. "I go generic because I probably won't know what servers, how many slots, or what type of power we'll need beforehand. With generic, I can configure whatever I need in minutes," he says.

For instance, he uses a universal busway for power so that he doesn't have to be concerned about the particular electrical needs of the acquired equipment. "We acquired a company and needed to integrate them in a short period of time because their building lease was up and they had to get out of there," Musilli says. One team was sent ahead of time and spent a year trying to identify each server on 30–40 racks. "None of their applications matched our operating systems," he says. As time dwindled, Musilli told them to pack up all the servers and send them to him. "In the end, it took two man-days to move them intact and get them up and running in our data center," he says.

As companies begin to contemplate future mergers or acquisitions, they must look inward at their own processes and procedures. "Just as important as technology is documentation of processes—you have to know what people are doing with the systems," says EMA's Mann. He warns that one of the first obstacles to having a successful merger or acquisition is the reliance on what he refers to as *tribal knowledge*. Companies that have data centers where the employees hold all the knowledge suffer greatly when, after a merger or acquisition, those people are let go.

"You have to document the knowledge from those people and figure out how to make the processes work with only a handful of employees," he says. Mann recommends

FIGURE 5.1

IT integration and adoption issues can make or break merger and acquisition activities.

Source: McGraw-Hill Companies, Inc./John Flournoy, photographer.

Real Life Lessons

Use Your Brain

Traditional case study questions promote and provide opportunity for critical thinking and classroom discussion.

Use Your Hands

The Real World Activities section offers possibilities for hands-on exploration and learning.

creating a workflow chart that outlines who's responsible for each part of the data center. He suggests considering who handles network management, systems management, application management, and storage. "This will also help you spot redundancies in skill sets or areas where you are lacking in the event of a merger," he says. John Burke, senior analyst at Nemertes Research in Minneapolis, says that in addition to knowing who is responsible, IT groups must know which systems perform which processes.

"You have to have really good information about what goes on in your data center in terms of systems and how they interact with each other and how they interface with the business. You should always know what services you offer and how much it costs to offer them," Burke says. As part of this effort, many organizations employ a configuration management database and asset management tool to help track elements within the data center. "You need a clear and concise view of the data flow within the data center. If you don't know what has to move together, you might disrupt business during a merger or acquisition," he says.

Companies must also develop guidelines for governance to be referenced during a merger. For instance, if two law firms are merging and have competing clients, then IT groups must ensure that data are protected and there is sufficient access control. AFCOM's Osborn says that good documentation helps the discovery process that companies go through before a merger or acquisition. "If the company you are acquiring has good documentation and good processes in place, the acquisition goes much more smoothly," he says.

"In some cases, you might be able to lower your software costs if you use a more robust server with fewer processors, but if the application license doesn't allow for that, then you can't," Osborn says, and adds: "How much money you're going to have to spend to merge technology can weigh heavily on the decision to acquire a company." Nemertes' Burke suggests that one major step to M&A success is to make sure your data center has virtualization tools running on both servers and storage.

Virtualization is important not only for scaling the data center but also for creating a standardized execution environment. "With a well-virtualized data center, you can hide the fact that things are moving around multiple servers and storage devices," Burke says. Rob Laurie, CEO at virtualization-software provider Dunes Technologies in Stamford, Connecticut, says that virtualization is useful for companies that want to test application and infrastructure integration before they put their merged or acquired assets into production. It's also helpful for companies that must integrate assets that can't be physically moved, he says. He warns, however, that for virtualization to be most effective, merging companies must decide on a uniform platform for their virtual environment. "That way, whatever is virtualized in one company could run in the other company's data center without problems," he says. If they don't have the same environment, they must at least have a compatible data format to gain any benefit.

Intel's Musilli suggests that IT's natural attention to detail can sometimes overcomplicate matters. "Mergers and acquisitions aren't always as difficult as people make them. They're simply about the ability to assimilate any two environments," he says. M&As create stress for both acquirer and acquiree, but early involvement by IT can minimize the trauma. Otherwise, you'll need to do too much in too little time. As software engineering guru Frederick Brooks once said, "You can't make a baby in a month using nine women. Plan ahead."

Source: Adapted from Sandra Gittlen, "Mergers Go Smoother with a Well-Prepped Data Center," *Computerworld*, July 28, 2007, and Eric Chabrow, "IT Plays Linchpin Role in High-Stake M&As," *InformationWeek*, June 26, 2006.

CASE STUDY QUESTIONS

1. Place yourself in the role of a manager at a company undergoing a merger or acquisition. What would be the most important things customers would expect from you while still in that process? What role would IT play in meeting those expectations? Provide at least three examples.

2. Focus on what Andi Mann in the case calls "tribal knowledge." What do you think he means by that, and why is it so important to this process? What strategies would you suggest for companies that are faced with the extensive presence of this issue in an acquired organization? Develop some specific recommendations.

3. Most of the discussion on the case focused on hardware and software issues. However, these are essentially enablers for underlying business processes developed by each of the companies involved. What different alternatives do companies have for merging their business processes, and what role would IT play in supporting those activities? Pay particular attention to data management and governance issues.

REAL WORLD ACTIVITIES

1. The case extensively discusses the idea of "virtualization" and the role it plays in the merger process. Go online to research this concept and prepare a report about what it entails, how it works, what are its advantages and disadvantages, and other applications in addition to those noted in the case.

2. Search the Internet for reports of merger and acquisition cases where IT issues played an important role, either positive or negative. How did different organizations handle IT-related matters in the situations you found? What was the ultimate outcome of the process? Prepare a presentation to share your findings with the class.

Strategy, Ethics . . .

Competitive Advantage

Chapter 2 focuses on the use of IT as a way to surpass your competitor's performance.

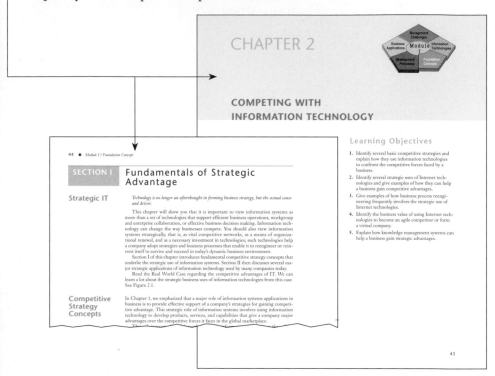

CHAPTER 2

COMPETING WITH INFORMATION TECHNOLOGY

43

44 • Module I / Foundation Concept

SECTION I Fundamentals of Strategic Advantage

Strategic IT

Technology is no longer an afterthought in forming business strategy, but the actual cause and driver.

This chapter will show you that it is important to view information systems as more than a set of technologies that support efficient business operations, workgroup and enterprise collaboration, or effective business decision making. Information technology can change the way businesses compete. You should also view information systems strategically, that is, as vital competitive networks, as a means of organizational renewal, and as a necessary investment in technologies; such technologies help a company adopt strategies and business processes that enable it to reengineer or reinvent itself to survive and succeed in today's dynamic business environment.

Section I of this chapter introduces fundamental competitive strategy concepts that underlie the strategic use of information systems. Section II then discusses several major strategic applications of information technology used by many companies today.

Read the Real World Case regarding the competitive advantages of IT. We can learn a lot about the strategic business uses of information technologies from this case. See Figure 2.1.

Competitive Strategy Concepts

In Chapter 1, we emphasized that a major role of information systems applications in business is to provide effective support of a company's strategies for gaining competitive advantage. This strategic role of information systems involves using information technology to develop products, services, and capabilities that give a company major advantages over the competitive forces it faces in the global marketplace.

Learning Objectives

1. Identify several basic competitive strategies and explain how they use information technologies to confront the competitive forces faced by a business.
2. Identify several strategic uses of Internet technologies and give examples of how they can help a business gain competitive advantages.
3. Give examples of how business process reengineering frequently involves the strategic use of Internet technologies.
4. Identify the business value of using Internet technologies to become an agile competitor or form a virtual company.
5. Explain how knowledge management systems can help a business gain strategic advantages.

Ethics & Security

Chapter 11 discusses the issues surrounding these topics and the challenges IT faces.

Chapter 11 / Security and Ethical Challenges • 455

REAL WORLD CASE 1 Ethics, Moral Dilemmas, and Tough Decisions: The Many Challenges of Working in IT

What Bryan found on an executive's computer six years ago still weighs heavily on his mind. He's particularly troubled that the man he discovered using a company PC to view pornography of Asian women and of children was subsequently promoted and moved to China to run a manufacturing plant. "To this day, I regret not taking that stuff to the FBI." It happened when Bryan, who asked that his last name not be published, was IT dire...

and professional, throughout the company; and they have the technical prowess to manipulate that information. That gives them both the power and responsibility to monitor and report employees who break company rules. IT professionals may also uncover evidence that a coworker is, say, embezzling funds, or they could be tempted to peek at private salary information or personal e-mails. There's little guidance, however, on what to do in these uncomfortable situations...

FIGURE 11.1

The pervasive use of information technology in organizations and society presents individuals with new ethical challenges and dilemmas.

Source: ©Courtesy of Punchstock.

454 • Module V / Management Challenges

SECTION I Security, Ethical, and Societal Challenges of IT

Introduction

There is no question that the use of information technology in business presents major security challenges, poses serious ethical questions, and affects society in significant ways. Therefore, in this section, we explore the threats to businesses and individuals as a result of many types of computer crime and unethical behavior. In Section II, we will examine a variety of methods that companies use to manage the security and integrity of their business systems. Now let's look at a real-world example.

Read the Real World Case on the next page. We can learn a lot from this case about the security and ethical issues that result from the pervasive use of IT in organizations and society today. See Figure 11.1.

Business/IT Security, Ethics, and Society

The use of information technologies in business has had a major impact on society and thus raises ethical issues in the areas of crime, privacy, individuality, employment, health, and working conditions. See Figure 11.2.

It is important to understand that information technology has had beneficial results, as well as detrimental effects, on society and people in each of these areas. For example, computerizing a manufacturing process may have the beneficial result of improving working conditions and producing products of higher quality at lower cost, but it also has the adverse effect of eliminating people's jobs. So your job as a manager or business professional should involve managing your work activities and those of others to minimize the detrimental effects of business applications of information technology and optimize its beneficial effects. That would represent an ethically responsible use of information technology.

. . . and Beyond

(text continues on page 525)

Go Global with IT

This text closes with Chapter 12, an in-depth look at IT across borders.

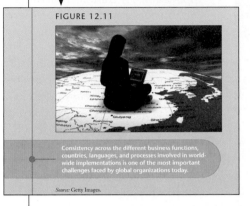

FIGURE 12.11

Consistency across the different business functions, countries, languages, and processes involved in worldwide implementations is one of the most important challenges faced by global organizations today.

Source: Getty Images.

Expand Your Knowledge

Blue boxes in each chapter provide brief, in-depth examples of how corporations apply IS concepts and theories.

Expand Your Horizons

Globe icons indicate examples with an international focus so that your knowledge makes you truly worldly.

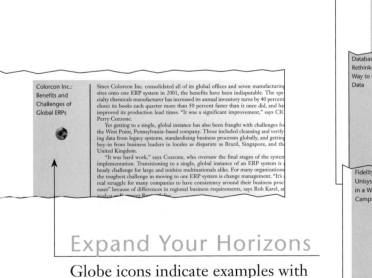

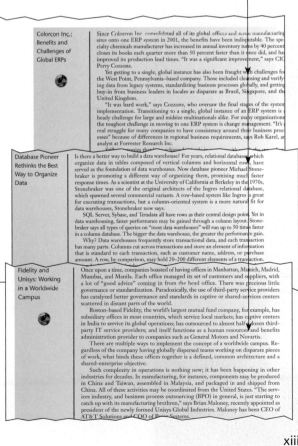

What's New?

The Fifteenth Edition includes significant changes to the Fourteenth Edition's content that update and improve its coverage, many of them suggested by an extensive faculty review process. Highlights of key changes for this edition include the following:

- Real World Cases provide current, relevant, and in-depth examples of IS theory applications. A combination of *Case Study Questions* and *Real World Activities* allows you to engage students on a variety of levels.
- More new Real World Cases: More than two-thirds of the cases are new to the Fifteenth Edition. These up-to-date cases provide students with in-depth business examples of the successes and challenges companies are experiencing in implementing the information technology concepts covered in each chapter.
- *Chapter 3: Computer Hardware* includes updated coverage of Moore's law, in addition to increased and updated coverage of information appliances, Grid computing, and voice recognition, as well as RFID technology and privacy challenges.
- *Chapter 4: Computer Software* provides additional information about OpenOffice Suite and XML.
- *Chapter 5: Data Resource Management* expands the discussion on records and primary keys.
- *Chapter 7: Electronic Business Systems* includes a new discussion on the relationship between SCM, CRM, and ERP with regard to supporting corporate strategy. It also provides an expanded discussion of SCM as a top strategic objective of modern enterprises and a new discussion on the use of digital billboards in targeted marketing.
- *Chapter 8: Electronic Commerce Systems* provides increased coverage and discussion of e-commerce success factors, a new section and discussion of search engine optimization, and new data relating to top retail web sites and online sales volume.
- *Chapter 9: Decision Support Systems* includes an additional discussion with regard to the strategic value of business intelligence activities in the modern organization, added coverage of CAPTCHA tests to prevent machine intervention in online environments, and expanded coverage of both OLAP and the modern use of expert system engines.
- *Chapter 10: Developing Business/IT Solutions* has added coverage of system implementation challenges, user resistance, and end-user development, and logical versus physical models.
- *Chapter 11: Security and Ethical Challenges* includes a new section on cyberterrorism. Additionally, it provides updated coverage of software piracy economic impacts, increased coverage of HIPAA, and a significant increase in discussion of current state of cyber law.
- *Chapter 12: Enterprise and Global Management of Information Technology* provides expanded in-depth coverage of COBIT and IT governance structures in organizations as well as an added section on trends in outsourcing and offshoring.

Student Support

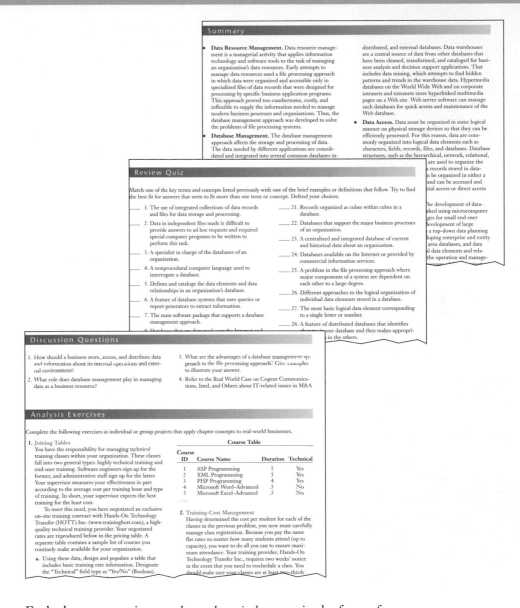

Each chapter contains *complete pedagogical support* in the form of:

- **Summary.** Revisiting key chapter concepts in a bullet-point summary.
- **Key Terms and Concepts.** Using page numbers to reference where terms are discussed in the text.
- **Review Quiz.** Providing a self-assessment for your students. Great for review before an important exam.
- **Discussion Questions.** Whether assigned as homework or used for in-class discussion, these complex questions will help your students develop critical thinking skills.
- **Analysis Exercises.** Each innovative scenario presents a business problem and asks students to use and test their IS knowledge through analytical, Web-based, spreadsheet, and/or database skills.
- **Closing Case Studies.** Reinforcing important concepts with prominent examples from businesses and organizations. Discussion questions follow each case study.

Instructor Support

Online Learning Center

Available to adopting faculty, the Online Learning Center provides one convenient place to access the Instructor's Manual, PowerPoint slides, and videos.

Instructor's Manual (IM)
To help ease your teaching burden, each chapter is supported by solutions to Real World Case questions, Discussion Questions, and Analysis Exercises.

Test Bank
Choose from over 1,200 true/false, multiple-choice, and fill-in-the-blank questions of varying levels of difficulty. Complete answers are provided for all test questions. By using the **EZ Test Computerized Test Bank** instructors can design, save, and generate custom tests. EZ Test also enables instructors to edit, add, or delete questions from the test bank; analyze test results; and organize a database of tests and student results.

PowerPoint Slides
A set of visually stimulating PowerPoint slides accompanies each chapter, providing a lecture outline and key figures and tables from the text. Slides can be edited to fit the needs of your course.

Videos
Videos will be downloadable from the instructor side of the OLC.

MBA MIS Cases

Developed by Richard Perle of Loyola Marymount University, these 14 cases allow you to add MBA-level analysis to your course. See your McGraw-Hill Irwin sales representative for more information.

Online Course Formats

Content for the Fifteenth Edition is available in WebCT, Blackboard, and PageOut formats to accommodate virtually any online delivery platform.

Online Learning Center

Visit www.mhhe.com/obrien for additional instructor and student resources.

Use our EZ Test Online to help your students prepare to succeed with Apple iPod® iQuiz.

Using our EZ Test Online you can make test and quiz content available for a student's Apple iPod®.

Students must purchase the iQuiz game application from Apple for 99¢ in order to use the iQuiz content. It works on fifth-generation iPods and better.

Instructors only need EZ Test Online to produce iQuiz ready content. Instructors take their existing tests and quizzes and export them to a file that can then be made available to the student to take as a self-quiz on their iPods. It's as simple as that.

Empower Your Students

Mastery of Skills and Concepts

This student supplement provides animated tutorials and simulated practice of the core skills in Microsoft Office 2007 Excel, Access, and PowerPoint, as well as animation of 47 important computer concepts.

With MISource's three-pronged **Teach Me–Show Me–Let Me Try** approach, students of all learning styles can quickly master core MS Office skills—leaving you more classroom time to cover more important and more complex topics.

For those students who need it, MISource for Office 2007 is delivered online at www.mhhe.com/misource.

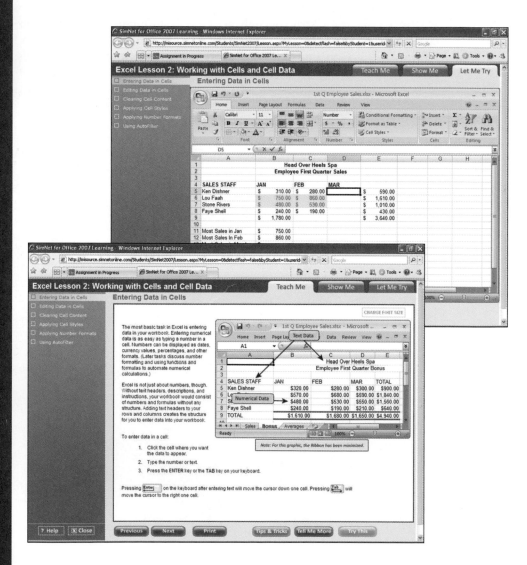

Empower Your Classroom

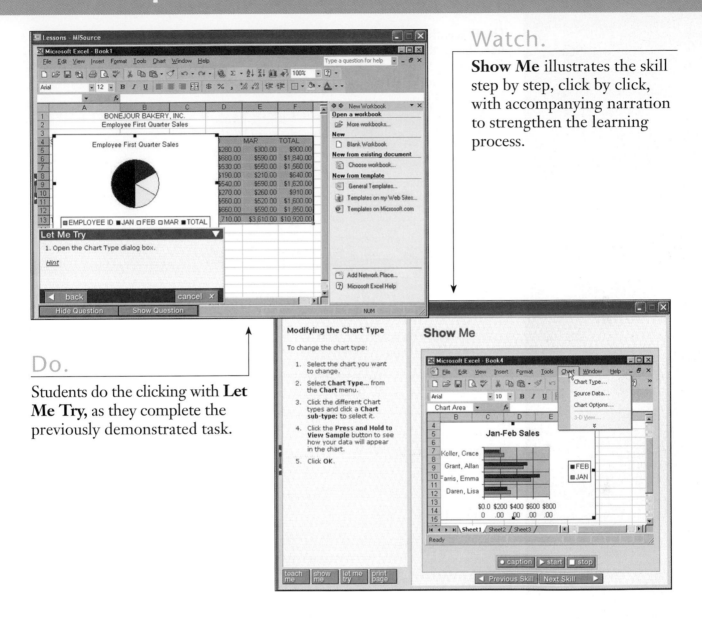

Watch.

Show Me illustrates the skill step by step, click by click, with accompanying narration to strengthen the learning process.

Do.

Students do the clicking with **Let Me Try,** as they complete the previously demonstrated task.

Acknowledgments

The Fifteenth Edition represents an ongoing effort to improve and adapt this text to meet the needs of students and instructors. For this revision, we received the guidance of more than 50 reviewers over the course of several months of review work. We thank all of them for their insight and advice.

Adeyemi A. Adekoya, *Virginia State University*

Hans-Joachim Adler, *University of Texas—Dallas*

Noushin Ashrafi, *University of Massachusetts—Boston*

Bruce Bellak, *New Jersey Institute of Technology*

Jongbok Byun, *Point Loma Nazarene University*

Ralph J. Caputo, *Manhattan College*

Kala Chand Seal, *Loyola Marymount University*

Yong S. Choi, *California State University—Bakersfield*

Carey Cole, *James Madison University*

Susan Cooper, *Sam Houston State University*

Jeffrey P. Corcoran, *Lasell College*

Subhankar Dhar, *San Jose State University*

Thomas W. Dillon, *James Madison University*

David Dischiave, *Syracuse University*

Roland Eichelberger, *Baylor University*

Ray Eldridge, *Freed-Hardeman University*

Dr. Juan Esteva, *Eastern Michigan University*

Warren W. Fisher, *Stephen F. Austin State University*

Janos T. Fustos, *Metropolitan State College of Denver*

Gerald Gonsalves, *College of Charleston*

Phillip Gordon, *Mills College*

Dr. Vipul Gupta, *Saint Joseph's University*

Dr. Arie Halachmi, *Tennessee State University*

Mary Carole Hollingsworth, *Georgia Perimeter College*

Dr. Judy D. Holmes, *Middle Tennessee State University*

Susan Hudgins, *East Central University*

Paramjit Kahai, *The University of Akron*

Betty Kleen, *Nicholls State University*

Kapil Ladha, *Drexel University*

Dr. Dick Larkin, *Central Washington University*

Robert Lawton, *Western Illinois University*

Diane Lending, *James Madison University*

David Lewis, *University of Massachusetts—Lowell*

Dr. Stan Lewis, *The University of Southern Mississippi*

Liping Liu, *The University of Akron*

Celia Romm Livermore, *Wayne State University*

Ronald Mashburn, *West Texas A&M University*

Richard McAndrew, *California Lutheran University*

Robert J. Mills, *Utah State University*

Cleamon Moorer, *Trinity Christian College*

Luvai F. Motiwalla, *University of Massachusetts—Lowell*

Fawzi Noman, *Sam Houston State University*

Magnus Nystedt, *Francis Marion University*

Sandra O. Obilade, *Brescia University*

Denise Padavano, *Pierce College*

Dr. Richard G. Platt, *University of West Florida*

Ram Raghuraman, *Joliet Junior College*

Steve Rau, *Marquette University*

Randy Ryker, *Nicholls State University*

William Saad, *University of Houston—Clear Lake*

Dolly Samson, *Hawai'i Pacific University*

Matthew P. Schigur, *DeVry University—Milwaukee*

Morgan M. Shepherd, *University of Colorado at Colorado Springs*

John Smiley, *Penn State University—Abington*

Toni M. Somers, *Wayne State University*

Cheickna Sylla, *New Jersey Institute of Technology*

Joseph Tan, *Wayne State University*

Nilmini Wickramasinghe, *Cleveland State University*

Jennifer Clark Williams, *University of Southern Indiana*

Mario Yanez, Jr., *University of Miami*

James E. Yao, *Montclair State University*

Vincent Yen, *Wright State University*

Our thanks also go to Robert Lawton of Western Illinois University for his contribution to the analysis exercises and Richard Perle of Loyola Marymount University for his MBA cases that so many instructors use in conjunction with this text.

Much credit should go to several individuals who played significant roles in this project. Thus, special thanks go to the editorial and production team at McGraw-Hill/Irwin: Paul Ducham, publisher; Trina Hauger, developmental editor; Natalie Zook, marketing manager; Bruce Gin, project manager; Lori Kramer, photo coordinator; and Mary Sander, designer. Their ideas and hard work were invaluable contributions to the successful completion of the project. The contributions of many authors, publishers, and firms in the computer industry that contributed case material, ideas, illustrations, and photographs used in this text are also thankfully acknowledged.

Acknowledging the Real World of Business

The unique contribution of the hundreds of business firms and other computer-using organizations that are the subjects of the Real World Cases, exercises, and examples in this text is gratefully acknowledged. The real-life situations faced by these firms and organizations provide readers of this text with valuable demonstrations of the benefits and limitations of using the Internet and other information technologies to enable electronic business and commerce, as well as enterprise communications and collaboration in support of the business processes, managerial decision making, and strategic advantage of the modern business enterprise.

George M. Marakas
James A. O'Brien
Miguel Aguirre-Urreta

Assurance of Learning Ready

Many educational institutions today are focused on the notion of assurance of learning, an important element of some accreditation standards. *Introduction to Information Systems* is designed specifically to support your assurance of learning initiatives with a simple yet powerful solution.

Each test bank question for *Introduction to Information Systems* maps to a specific chapter learning outcome/objective listed in the text. You can use our test bank software, *EZ Test*, to query about learning outcomes/objectives that directly relate to the learning objectives for your course. You can then use the reporting features of *EZ Test* to aggregate student results in similar fashion, making the collection and presentation of assurance of learning data simple and easy.

AACSB Statement

McGraw-Hill Companies is a proud corporate member of AACSB International. Recognizing the importance and value of AACSB accreditation, the authors of *Introduction to Information Systems* 15e have sought to recognize the curricula guidelines detailed in AACSB standards for business accreditation by connecting selected questions in *Introduction to Information Systems* or its test bank with the general knowledge and skill guidelines found in the AACSB standards. It is important to note that the statements contained in *Introduction to Information Systems* 15e are provided only as a guide for the users of this text.

The statements contained in *Introduction to Information Systems* 15e are provided only as a guide for the users of this text. The AACSB leaves content coverage and assessment clearly within the realm and control of individual schools, the mission of the school, and the faculty. The AACSB charges schools with the obligation of doing assessment against their own content and learning goals. While *Introduction to Information Systems* 15e and its teaching package make no claim of any specific AACSB qualification or evaluation, we have, within *Introduction to Information Systems* 15e, labeled selected questions according to the six general knowledge and skills areas. The labels or tags within *Introduction to Information Systems* 15e are as indicated. There are of course many more within the test bank, the text, and the teaching package, which might be used as a "standard" for your course. However, the labeled questions are suggested for your consideration.

Brief Contents

Contents

Module II Information Technologies

Module III   Business Applications

Chapter 7

Electronic Business Systems   259

Chapter 8

Electronic Commerce Systems   311

Chapter 9

Decision Support Systems 349

Chapter 12

Enterprise and Global Management of Information Technology 503

MODULE I

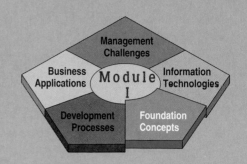

Management Challenges

Business Applications

Module I

Information Technologies

Development Processes

Foundation Concepts

FOUNDATION CONCEPTS

Why study information systems? Why do businesses need information technology? What do you need to know about the use and management of information technologies in business? The introductory chapters of Module I are designed to answer these fundamental questions about the role of information systems in business.

- **Chapter 1: Foundations of Information Systems in Business** presents an overview of the five basic areas of information systems knowledge needed by business professionals, including the conceptual system components and major types of information systems. In addition, trends in information systems and an overview of the managerial challenges associated with information systems are presented.

- **Chapter 2: Competing with Information Technology** introduces fundamental concepts of competitive advantage through information technology and illustrates major strategic applications of information systems.

Completing these chapters will prepare you to move on to study chapters on information technologies (Module II), business applications (Module III), systems development processes (Module IV), and the management challenges of information systems (Module V).

CHAPTER 1

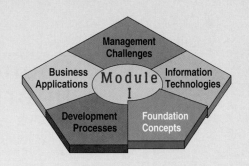

FOUNDATIONS OF INFORMATION SYSTEMS IN BUSINESS

Chapter Highlights

Learning Objectives

1. Understand the concept of a system and how it relates to information systems.

2. Explain why knowledge of information systems is important for business professionals, and identify five areas of information systems knowledge that they need.

3. Give examples to illustrate how the business applications of information systems can support a firm's business processes, managerial decision making, and strategies for competitive advantage.

4. Provide examples of several major types of information systems from your experiences with business organizations in the real world.

5. Identify several challenges that a business manager might face in managing the successful and ethical development and use of information technology in a business.

6. Provide examples of the components of real world information systems. Illustrate that in an information system, people use hardware, software, data, and networks as resources to perform input, processing, output, storage, and control activities that transform data resources into information products.

7. Demonstrate familiarity with the myriad of career opportunities in information systems.

3

SECTION I

Foundation Concepts: Information Systems in Business

The question of why we need to study information systems and information technology has evolved into a moot issue. Information systems have become as integrated into our daily business activities as accounting, finance, operations management, marketing, human resource management, or any other major business function. Information systems and technologies are vital components of successful businesses and organizations—some would say they are business imperatives. They thus constitute an essential field of study in business administration and management, which is why most business majors include a course in information systems. Since you probably intend to be a manager, entrepreneur, or business professional, it is just as important to have a basic understanding of information systems as it is to understand any other functional area in business.

Information technologies, including Internet-based information systems, are playing vital and expanding roles in business. Information technology can help all kinds of businesses improve the efficiency and effectiveness of their business processes, managerial decision making, and workgroup collaboration, which strengthens their competitive positions in rapidly changing marketplaces. This benefit occurs irrespective of whether the information technology is used to support product development teams, customer support processes, e-commerce transactions, or any other business activity. Information technologies and systems are, quite simply, an essential ingredient for business success in today's dynamic global environment.

The Real World of Information Systems

Let's take a moment to bring the real world into our discussion of the importance of information systems (IS) and information technology (IT). See Figure 1.1, and read the Real World Case about using information technology to better understand and satisfy customer needs.

If we are to understand information systems and their functions, we first need to be clear on the concept of a system. In its simplest form, a system is a set of interrelated components, with a clearly defined boundary, working together to achieve a common set of objectives. Using this definition, it becomes easy to see that virtually everything you can think of is a system, and one system can be made up of other systems or be part of a bigger system. We will expand on this concept later in the next section, but for now, this definition gives us a good foundation for understanding the focus of this textbook: information systems.

What Is an Information System?

We begin with a simple definition that we can expand upon later in the chapter. An information system (IS) can be any organized combination of people, hardware, software, communications networks, data resources, and policies and procedures that stores, retrieves, transforms, and disseminates information in an organization. People rely on modern information systems to communicate with one another using a variety of physical devices (*hardware*), information processing instructions and procedures (*software*), communications channels (*networks*), and stored data (*data resources*). Although today's information systems are typically thought of as having something to do with computers, we have been using information systems since the dawn of civilization. Even today we make regular use of information systems that have nothing to do with a computer. Consider some of the following examples of information systems:

- **Smoke signals for communication** were used as early as recorded history and can account for the human discovery of fire. The pattern of smoke transmitted valuable information to others who were too far to see or hear the sender.

- **Card catalogs in a library** are designed to store data about the books in an organized manner that allows readers to locate a particular book by its title, author name, subject, or a variety of other approaches.

REAL WORLD CASE 1

eCourier, Cablecom, and Bryan Cave: Delivering Value through Business Intelligence

Visitors to the eCourier Web site are greeted with the words "*How happy are you?* Take the eCourier happy test today!" Those words and the playful purple Web site represent the company's customer satisfaction focus. And a key for the company in achieving that happiness is through its focus on operational business intelligence.

Business intelligence is moving out of the ivory tower of specialized analysts and is being brought to the front lines. In the case of eCourier, whose couriers carry 2,000 packages around London each day, operational business intelligence allows the company to keep real-time tabs on customer satisfaction. "This is a crucial differentiator in London's competitive same-day courier market, where clients are far more likely to take their business elsewhere than they are to report a problem to their current courier," says the company's chief technology officer and cofounder Jay Bregman.

Online directory London Online alone shows about 350 listings for courier services.

Before implementing operational business intelligence, eCourier sought to define IT as a crucial differentiator. Co-founders Tom Allason, eCourier's CEO, and Bregman ditched the idea of phone dispatchers and instead gave their couriers GPS-enabled handhelds so that couriers can be tracked and orders can be communicated electronically. They also focused on making online booking easy and rewarding; and much was invested in user-friendly applications: Customers can track online exactly where their courier is, eliminating the package delivery guesswork.

Today, 95 percent of deliveries are booked online, meaning that eCourier needs a much smaller staff for monitoring, tracking, and placing orders, which in turn makes the company more scalable. Bregman says this is notable in

a market where many courier companies use telephone dispatchers and guesswork about package whereabouts. Booking and tracking automation—while innovative—did not complete the customer happiness puzzle. Without leading-edge business intelligence, account managers could miss the same issues that plagued other courier services—late deliveries, surly couriers, or even an unnoticed ramp-up in deliveries. "We're only one delivery away from someone deciding to use a different delivery firm," says Bregman.

So eCourier started using software from a company called SeeWhy to try and generate customer data more quickly. "What's unique about SeeWhy," says Bregman, "is its ability to report what's happening with customers instantly." When a new booking enters eCourier's database, the information is duplicated and saved into a repository within SeeWhy. The software then interprets the data by comparing it with previous information and trends, and if it notices an anomaly, it takes action. If a customer typically places an eCourier order every Thursday morning between 9:30 and 10:00 and there's been no contact during that time, eCourier's CRM team will receive an alert shortly after 10:00 that includes the client's history and the number of bookings it typically places in a day. Bregman says there's a fair amount of tuning to get the metrics right. For example, the company had to tweak the system to recognize expected shifts in activity so that it doesn't send a slew of alerts once the after-Christmas drop in business occurs. Getting that perfect balance of when to send alerts and how best to optimize the system is an ongoing process, he says.

The SeeWhy software is designed to establish a "normal" client booking pattern from the first use, which is deepened with each subsequent booking. A sharp drop-off in bookings, an increase in bookings, or a change in dormant account activity generates an alert that is sent to that client's account manager, who then uses the opportunity to problem-solve or, in the case of increased activity, upsell, for example, to overnight or international services. "These capabilities have provided a big payoff," says Bregman. He also believes the system saves his company the expense of having to hire people to monitor for "who's happy and who's not—we're able to do a lot more on our customer team with a lot less."

There are other approaches to judging customer dissatisfaction, however. Cablecom, a Swiss telecom company, used SPSS's statistical software to mine customer data, primarily from trouble tickets—such as the average duration of a ticket, or how many tickets had been opened for a customer over a specific time period—to build a model that could flag when a customer was at a high risk of leaving. "But the model proved to be only about 70% accurate," says Federico Cesconi, director of customer insight and retention.

So Cesconi used SPSS's Dimensions survey research software to create an online customer survey, and from that he was able to determine that customer dissatisfaction usually begins around the ninth month of service, with the bulk of the customer losses occurring between months 12 and 14. Cesconi then created another survey that he now offers to

FIGURE 1.1

Access to quality information about customers helps companies succeed at delivering value to shareholders.

customers in the seventh month of service, and which includes an area where they can type in specific complaints and problems. "Cablecom calls customers within 24 hours of completing the survey," says Cesconi. "The two approaches together provide the best view of customers ready to bolt, and the best chance at retaining them."

In 2002, global law firm Bryan Cave faced the million-dollar question: How do you make the most money with your resources while simultaneously delivering the highest customer value? The problem was pressing. Clients of the firm, which now has 800 lawyers in 15 offices worldwide, were demanding alternatives to the traditional hourly fee structure. They wanted new models such as fixed pricing and pricing that was adjusted during a project.

But making money off these new billing strategies required the complicated balance of staffing and pricing.

Projects weighted too heavily with a law partner's time would be expensive (for the law firm) and not optimized for profit. Devoting too little of a partner's time would leave clients feeling undervalued. Optimizing profit and perceived value had to be achieved by spreading partners' time throughout a number of cases and balancing the remaining resources needed for a case with the less-expensive fees of associates and paralegals. "Clients are most likely to stay with you if you deliver just the right mix," says Bryan Cave's CIO John Alber.

The law firm's traditional method of analyzing collected fees and profit used a spreadsheet that was complicated and took too long. "Spreadsheets provide a level of detail that can be valuable for analysts," says Alber, "but the information in a spreadsheet can be confusing and difficult to work with." Alber says he decided it was better to build an easy-to-understand interface using business intelligence tools; although the company will not release specific figures, Alber says since the company implemented its first BI tool in 2004, both profitability and hours leveraged—the hours worked by equity partners and all other fee earners at the firm—have increased substantially.

The tools also allow lawyers to track budgets in real time so that they can quickly make adjustments. The BI tools even provide a diversity dashboard, which tracks the hourly mix of women and minorities working on the firm's cases, a feature the company will license to Redwood Analytics for sale to other law firms. The firm developed this diversity tool to bring transparency to the diversity reporting process required by many clients. In other words, the tools provide Bryan Cave with a method of customizing its fees and helping clients better understand what they get for their money.

As an illustration, Alber points to the customized pricing one lawyer gave to his real estate client. "Developers think in terms of square feet," says Alber, "and this client couldn't understand why legal fees for a 400,000-square-foot building might be the same as for a 4,000-square-foot building, though it required the same amount of the lawyer's time." So the lawyer used the pricing and staffing modeling tools and historical analysis tools to determine whether it made sense for the law firm to charge clients based on the size of their projects.

He found that while there was risk of underpricing large buildings, the deal volume in small buildings offset that risk for the law firm. The result made per-square-foot pricing possible.

"It may be possible that someone with enough willpower or manpower could do that using traditional analysis," says Alber, "but this lawyer had the information right at his fingertips." Business intelligence enables "us to be in touch with clients and shift things around in response to what customers are asking," says Alber. Adopting new and improved project management, pricing, and customer service capabilities required planning, appropriate pacing, and user buy-in.

"In today's environment, you can't do value innovation without being in touch with the economics of your business, without really understanding where you make money and where you don't, and that's what business intelligence tools do," says Alber. "Our goal," he says, "is to build the best long-term relationships in the world."

Source: Adapted from Diann Daniel, "Delivering Customer Happiness Through Operational Business Intelligence," *CIO Magazine*, December 6, 2007; Diann Daniel, "How a Global Law Firm Used Business Intelligence to Fix Customer Billing Woes," *CIO Magazine*, January 8, 2008; and Mary Weier, "Dear Customer: Please Don't Leave," *InformationWeek*, June 18, 2007.

CASE STUDY QUESTIONS

1. How do information technologies contribute to the business success of the companies depicted in the case? Provide an example from each company explaining how the technology implemented led to improved performance.

2. In the case of law firm Bryan Cave discussed above, the use of BI technology to improve the availability, access, and presentation of existing information allowed them to provide tailored and innovative services to their customers. What other professions could benefit from a similar use of these technologies, and how? Develop two different possibilities.

3. Cablecom developed a prediction model to better identify those customers at risk of switching to other company in the near future. In addition to those noted in the case, what other actions could be taken if that information were available? Give some examples of these. Would you consider letting some customers leave anyway? Why?

REAL WORLD ACTIVITIES

1. Use the Internet to research the latest offerings in business intelligence technologies and their uses by companies. What differences can you find with those reviewed in the case? Prepare a report to summarize your findings and highlight new and innovative uses of these technologies.

2. Why do some companies in a given industry, like eCourier above, adopt and deploy innovative technologies while others in the same line of business do not? Break into small groups with your classmates to discuss what characteristics of companies could influence their decision to innovate with the use of information technologies.

FIGURE 1.2

A framework that outlines the major areas of information systems knowledge needed by business professionals.

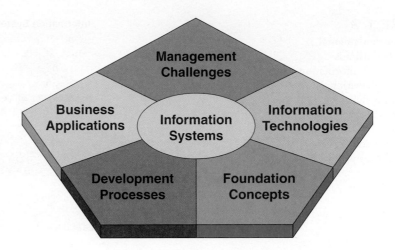

- **Your book bag, day planner, notebooks, and file folders** are all part of an information system designed to help you organize the inputs provided to you via handouts, lectures, presentations, and discussions. They also help you process these inputs into useful outputs: homework and good exam grades.

- **The cash register at your favorite fast-food restaurant** is part of a large information system that tracks the products sold, the time of a sale, inventory levels, and the amount of money in the cash drawer; it also contributes to the analysis of product sales in any combination of locations anywhere in the world.

- **A paper-based accounting ledger** as used before the advent of computer-based accounting systems is an iconic example of an information system. Businesses used this type of system for centuries to record the daily transactions and to keep a record of the balances in their various business and customer accounts.

Figure 1.2 illustrates a useful conceptual framework that organizes the knowledge presented in this text and outlines areas of knowledge you need about information systems. It emphasizes that you should concentrate your efforts in the following five areas of IS knowledge:

- **Foundation Concepts.** Fundamental behavioral, technical, business, and managerial concepts about the components and roles of information systems. Examples include basic information system concepts derived from general systems theory or competitive strategy concepts used to develop business applications of information technology for competitive advantage. Chapters 1 and 2 and other chapters of the text support this area of IS knowledge.

- **Information Technologies.** Major concepts, developments, and management issues in information technology—that is, hardware, software, networks, data management, and many Internet-based technologies. Chapters 3 and 4 provide an overview of computer hardware and software technologies, and Chapters 5 and 6 cover key data resource management and telecommunications network technologies for business.

- **Business Applications.** The major uses of information systems for the operations, management, and competitive advantage of a business. Chapter 7 covers applications of information technology in functional areas of business such as marketing, manufacturing, and accounting. Chapter 8 focuses on e-commerce applications that most companies use to buy and sell products on the Internet, and Chapter 9 covers the use of information systems and technologies to support decision making in business.

- **Development Processes.** How business professionals and information specialists plan, develop, and implement information systems to meet business opportunities. Several developmental methodologies are explored in Chapter 10, including the

FIGURE 1.3

The three fundamental roles of the business applications of information systems. Information systems provide an organization with support for business processes and operations, decision making, and competitive advantage.

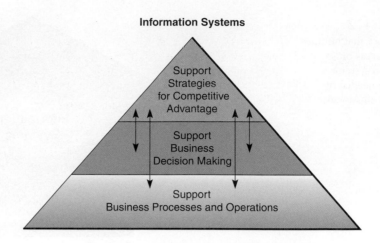

Information Systems

Support Strategies for Competitive Advantage

Support Business Decision Making

Support Business Processes and Operations

systems development life cycle and prototyping approaches to business application development.

- **Management Challenges.** The challenges of effectively and ethically managing information technology at the end-user, enterprise, and global levels of a business. Thus, Chapter 11 focuses on security challenges and security management issues in the use of information technology, while Chapter 12 covers some of the key methods business managers can use to manage the information systems function in a company with global business operations.

The Fundamental Roles of IS in Business

While there are a seemingly endless number of software applications, there are three fundamental reasons for all business applications of information technology. They are found in the three vital roles that information systems can perform for a business enterprise:

- Support of business processes and operations.
- Support of decision making by employees and managers.
- Support of strategies for competitive advantage.

Figure 1.3 illustrates how the fundamental roles interact in a typical organization. At any moment, information systems designed to support business processes and operations may also be providing data to, or accepting data from, systems focused on business decision making or achieving competitive advantage. The same is true for the other two fundamental roles of IS. Today's organizations are constantly striving to achieve integration of their systems to allow information to flow freely through them, which adds even greater flexibility and business support than any of the individual system roles could provide.

Let's look at a typical retail store as a good example of how these roles of IS in business can be implemented.

The Fundamental Roles of IS in Business

Support of Business Processes and Operations. As a consumer, you regularly encounter information systems that support the business processes and operations at the many retail stores where you shop. For example, most retail stores now use computer-based information systems to help their employees record customer purchases, keep track of inventory, pay employees, buy new merchandise, and evaluate sales trends. Store operations would grind to a halt without the support of such information systems.

Support of Business Decision Making. Information systems also help store managers and other business professionals make better decisions. For example, decisions about what lines of merchandise need to be added or discontinued and what kind of investments they require are typically made after an analysis provided by computer-based information systems. This function not only supports the decision making of store managers, buyers, and others, but also helps them look for ways to gain an advantage over other retailers in the competition for customers.

Support of Strategies for Competitive Advantage. Gaining a strategic advantage over competitors requires the innovative application of information technologies. For example, store management might make a decision to install touch-screen kiosks in all stores, with links to the e-commerce Web site for online shopping. This offering might attract new customers and build customer loyalty because of the ease of shopping and buying merchandise provided by such information systems. Thus, strategic information systems can help provide products and services that give a business a comparative advantage over its competitors.

Welch's: Balancing Truckloads with Business Intelligence

Given dramatic fluctuations in gas prices, it's no surprise that companies want to find ways to rein in transportation costs. One company finding success in that endeavor is Welch's, a well-known purveyor of food and packaged consumer goods. The company is tapping the power of business intelligence for better insight into its supply-chain operations, which in turn can help keep transportation expenses lower. Welch's, the $654 million manufacturer known for its jams, jellies, and juices, recently installed an on-demand BI application from Oco.

One way Welch's is leveraging the Oco BI application is to ensure truckloads delivered by its carriers go out full.

The idea is that customers are already paying for the full truck when it delivers goods, even if it's only halfway or three-quarters loaded. With the BI system, Welch's can tell if a buyer's shipment is coming up short of full capacity and help them figure out what else they can order to max it out, thus saving on future shipping costs.

"Welch's can go to the customer and say, 'You're only ordering this much. Why not round out the load with other things you need? It will be a lot cheaper for you,'" says Bill Copacino, president and CEO of Oco. "If you're able to put 4,000 more pounds on the 36,000-pound shipment, you're getting a 10 percent discount on transportation costs," he adds.

"We're essentially capturing every element—from the customer orders we receive, to bills of lading on every shipment we make, as well as every data element on every freight bill we pay," says Bill Coyne, director of purchasing and logistics for Welch's. "We dump them all into one data warehouse [maintained by Oco], and we can mix-and-match and slice-and-dice any way we want." Coyne says that Welch's tries to ship its products five days a week out of its distribution center. "But we found ourselves just totally overwhelmed on Fridays," he says. "We would complain, 'How come there are so many orders on Friday?'"

Now, the new system helps Welch's balance its daily deliveries so that it uses approximately the same number of trucks, rather than hiring for seven trucks on a Monday, five on a Tuesday, eight on a Wednesday, and so forth.

The company reaps transportation savings by using a stable number of trucks daily—"as capacity is not jumping all over the place," Copacino says.

"We are gaining greater visibility into cost-savings opportunities, which is especially important in light of rising fuel and transportation costs," says Coyne. Welch's spends more than $50 million each year on transportation expenses, and the Oco BI application and reporting features have become critical in a very short period of time. "We literally can't go any amount of time without knowing this stuff," Coyne says.

Source: Adapted from Ted Samson, "Welch's Leverages BI to Reduce Transport Costs," *InfoWorld*, October 16, 2008; and Thomas Wailgum, "Business Intelligence and On-Demand: The Perfect Marriage?" *CIO Magazine*, March 27, 2008.

Trends in Information Systems

The business applications of information systems have expanded significantly over the years. Figure 1.4 summarizes these changes.

Until the 1960s, the role of most information systems was simple: transaction processing, record keeping, accounting, and other *electronic data processing* (EDP) applications. Then another role was added, namely, the processing of all these data into useful, informative reports. Thus, the concept of *management information systems* (MIS) was born. This new role focused on developing business applications that provided managerial end users with predefined management reports that would give managers the information they needed for decision-making purposes.

By the 1970s, it was evident that the prespecified information products produced by such management information systems were not adequately meeting the decision-making needs of management, so the concept of *decision support systems* (DSS) was born. The new role for information systems was to provide managerial end users with ad hoc, interactive support of their decision-making processes. This support would be tailored to the unique decisions and decision-making styles of managers as they confronted specific types of problems in the real world.

In the 1980s, several new roles for information systems appeared. First, the rapid development of microcomputer processing power, application software packages, and telecommunications networks gave birth to the phenomenon of *end-user computing*. End users could now use their own computing resources to support their job requirements instead of waiting for the indirect support of centralized corporate information services departments.

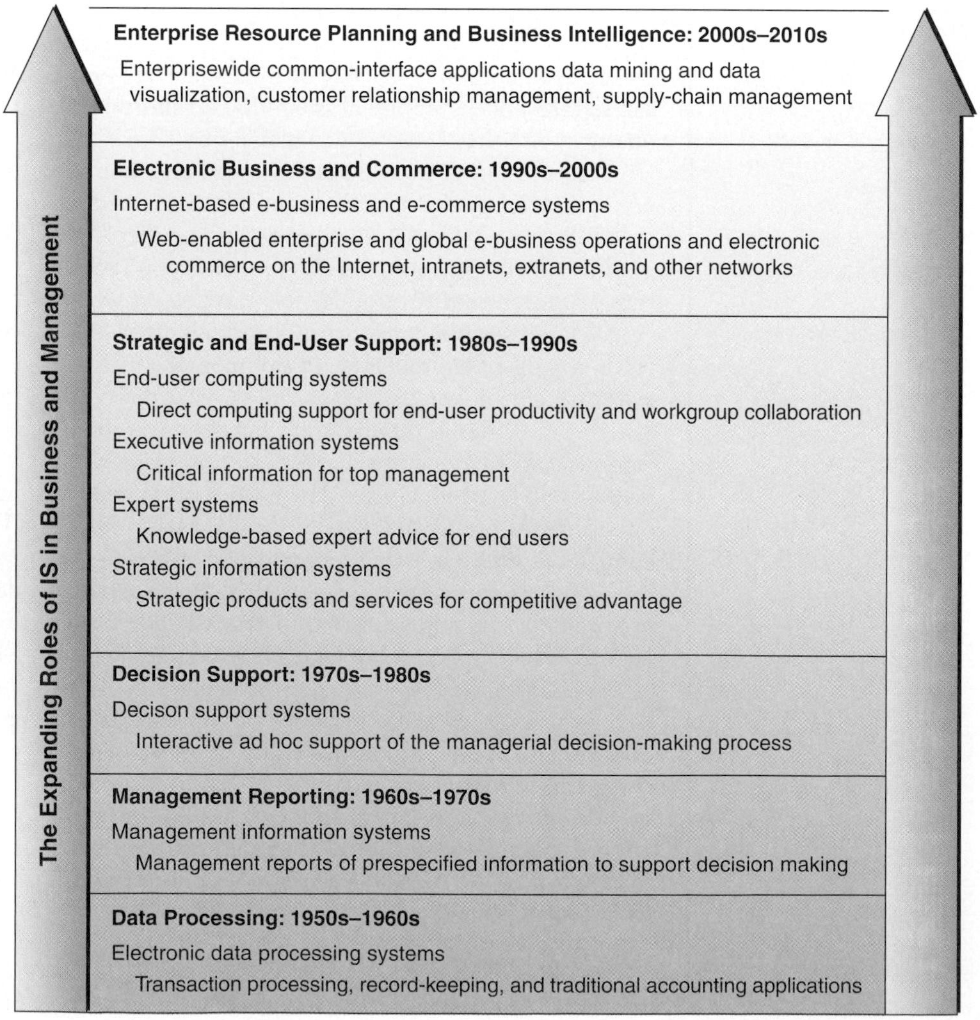

FIGURE 1.4

The expanding roles of the business applications of information systems. Note how the roles of computer-based information systems have expanded over time. Also, note the impact of these changes on the end users and managers of an organization.

The Expanding Roles of IS in Business and Management

Enterprise Resource Planning and Business Intelligence: 2000s–2010s
Enterprisewide common-interface applications data mining and data visualization, customer relationship management, supply-chain management

Electronic Business and Commerce: 1990s–2000s
Internet-based e-business and e-commerce systems
Web-enabled enterprise and global e-business operations and electronic commerce on the Internet, intranets, extranets, and other networks

Strategic and End-User Support: 1980s–1990s
End-user computing systems
Direct computing support for end-user productivity and workgroup collaboration
Executive information systems
Critical information for top management
Expert systems
Knowledge-based expert advice for end users
Strategic information systems
Strategic products and services for competitive advantage

Decision Support: 1970s–1980s
Decison support systems
Interactive ad hoc support of the managerial decision-making process

Management Reporting: 1960s–1970s
Management information systems
Management reports of prespecified information to support decision making

Data Processing: 1950s–1960s
Electronic data processing systems
Transaction processing, record-keeping, and traditional accounting applications

Second, it became evident that most top corporate executives did not directly use either the reports of management information systems or the analytical modeling capabilities of decision support systems, so the concept of *executive information systems* (EIS) developed. These information systems were created to give top executives an easy way to get the critical information they wanted, when they wanted it, and tailored to the formats they preferred.

Third, breakthroughs occurred in the development and application of artificial intelligence (AI) techniques to business information systems. Today's systems include intelligent software agents that can be programmed and deployed inside a system to act on behalf of their owner, system functions that can adapt themselves on the basis of the immediate needs of the user, virtual reality applications, advanced robotics, natural language processing, and a variety of applications for which artificial intelligence can replace the need for human intervention, thus freeing up knowledge workers for more complex tasks. *Expert systems* (ES) and other *knowledge-based systems* also forged a new role for information systems. Today, expert systems can serve as consultants to users by providing expert advice in limited subject areas.

An important new role for information systems appeared in the 1980s and continued through the 1990s: the concept of a strategic role for information systems, sometimes called *strategic information systems* (SIS). In this concept, information technology becomes an integral component of business processes, products, and services that help a company gain a competitive advantage in the global marketplace.

The mid- to late 1990s saw the revolutionary emergence of *enterprise resource planning* (ERP) systems. This organization-specific form of a strategic information system integrates all facets of a firm, including its planning, manufacturing, sales, resource management, customer relations, inventory control, order tracking, financial management, human resources, and marketing—virtually every business function. The primary advantage of these ERP systems lies in their common interface for all computer-based organizational functions and their tight integration and data sharing, necessary for flexible strategic decision making. We explore ERP and its associated functions in greater detail in Chapter 8.

We are also entering an era where a fundamental role for IS is *business intelligence* (BI). BI refers to all applications and technologies in the organization that are focused on the gathering and analysis of data and information that can be used to drive strategic business decisions. Through the use of BI technologies and processes, organizations can gain valuable insight into the key elements and factors—both internal and external—that affect their business and competitiveness in the marketplace. BI relies on sophisticated metrics and analytics to "see into the data" and find relationships and opportunities that can be turned into profits. We'll look closer at BI in Chapter 9.

Finally, the rapid growth of the Internet, intranets, extranets, and other interconnected global networks in the 1990s dramatically changed the capabilities of information systems in business at the beginning of the 21st century. Further, a fundamental shift in the role of information systems occurred. Internet-based and Web-enabled enterprises and global e-business and e-commerce systems are becoming commonplace in the operations and management of today's business enterprises. Information systems is now solidly entrenched as a strategic resource in the modern organization.

A closer look at Figure 1.4 suggests that though we have expanded our abilities with regard to using information systems for conducting business, today's information systems are still doing the same basic things that they began doing more than 50 years ago. We still need to process transactions, keep records, provide management with useful and informative reports, and support the foundational accounting systems and processes of the organization. What has changed, however, is that we now enjoy a much higher level of integration of system functions across applications, greater connectivity across both similar and dissimilar system components, and the ability to

FIGURE 1.5

Businesses today depend on the Internet, intranets, and extranets to implement and manage innovative e-business applications.

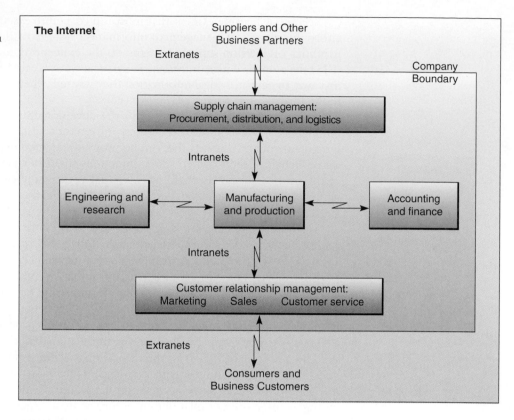

The Role of e-Business in Business

reallocate critical computing tasks such as data storage, processing, and presentation to take maximum advantage of business and strategic opportunities. Because of these increased capabilities, the systems of tomorrow will be focused on increasing both the speed and reach of our systems to provide even tighter integration, combined with greater flexibility.

The Internet and related technologies and applications have changed the ways businesses operate and people work, as well as how information systems support business processes, decision making, and competitive advantage. Thus, many businesses today are using Internet technologies to Web-enable their business processes and create innovative **e-business applications**. See Figure 1.5.

In this text, we define **e-business** as the use of Internet technologies to work and empower business processes, e-commerce, and enterprise collaboration within a company and with its customers, suppliers, and other business stakeholders. In essence, e-business can be more generally considered an *online exchange of value*. Any online exchange of information, money, resources, services, or any combination thereof falls under the e-business umbrella. The Internet and Internet-like networks—those inside the enterprise **(intranet)** and between an enterprise and its trading partners **(extranet)**—have become the primary information technology infrastructure that supports the e-business applications of many companies. These companies rely on e-business applications to (1) reengineer internal business processes, (2) implement e-commerce systems with their customers and suppliers, and (3) promote enterprise collaboration among business teams and workgroups.

Enterprise collaboration systems involve the use of software tools to support communication, coordination, and collaboration among the members of networked teams and workgroups. A business may use intranets, the Internet, extranets, and other networks to implement such systems. For example, employees and external consultants may form a *virtual team* that uses a corporate intranet and the Internet for e-mail,

FIGURE 1.6 Operations and management classifications of information systems. Note how this conceptual overview emphasizes the main purposes of information systems that support business operations and managerial decision making.

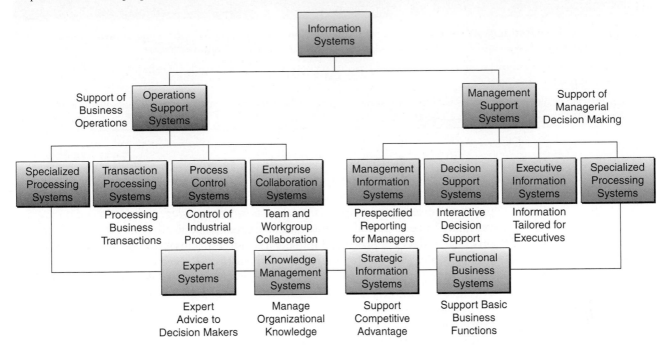

videoconferencing, e-discussion groups, and Web pages of work-in-progress information to collaborate on business projects.

E-commerce is the buying, selling, marketing, and servicing of products, services, and information over a variety of computer networks. Many businesses now use the Internet, intranets, extranets, and other networks to support every step of the commercial process, including everything from advertising, sales, and customer support on the World Wide Web to Internet security and payment mechanisms that ensure completion of delivery and payment processes. For example, e-commerce systems include Internet Web sites for online sales, extranet access to inventory databases by large customers, and the use of corporate intranets by sales reps to access customer records for customer relationship management.

Types of Information Systems

Conceptually, the applications of information systems that are implemented in today's business world can be classified in several different ways. For example, several types of information systems can be classified as either operations or management information systems. Figure 1.6 illustrates this conceptual classification of information systems applications. Information systems are categorized this way to spotlight the major roles each plays in the operations and management of a business. Let's look briefly at some examples of such information systems categories.

Operations Support Systems

Information systems have always been needed to process data generated by, and used in, business operations. Such operations support systems produce a variety of information products for internal and external use; however, they do not emphasize the specific information products that can best be used by managers. Further processing by management information systems is usually required. The role of a business firm's operations support systems is to process business transactions, control industrial processes, support enterprise communications and collaborations, and update corporate databases efficiently. See Figure 1.7.

FIGURE 1.7   A summary of operations support systems with examples.

Operations Support Systems
• **Transaction processing systems.** Process data resulting from business transactions, update operational databases, and produce business documents. Examples: sales and inventory processing and accounting systems.
• **Process control systems.** Monitor and control industrial processes. Examples: petroleum refining, power generation, and steel production systems.
• **Enterprise collaboration systems.** Support team, workgroup, and enterprise communications and collaborations. Examples: e-mail, chat, and videoconferencing groupware systems.

Transaction processing systems are important examples of operations support systems that record and process the data resulting from business transactions. They process transactions in two basic ways. In *batch processing*, transactions data are accumulated over a period of time and processed periodically. In *real-time* (or *online*) processing, data are processed immediately after a transaction occurs. For example, point-of-sale (POS) systems at many retail stores use electronic cash register terminals to capture and transmit sales data electronically over telecommunications links to regional computer centers for immediate (real-time) or nightly (batch) processing. Figure 1.8 is an example of software that automates accounting transaction processing.

Process control systems monitor and control physical processes. For example, a petroleum refinery uses electronic sensors linked to computers to monitor chemical processes continually and make instant (real-time) adjustments that control the refinery process. Enterprise collaboration systems enhance team and workgroup communications and productivity and include applications that are sometimes called *office automation systems*. For example, knowledge workers in a project team may use e-mail to send and receive e-messages or use videoconferencing to hold electronic meetings to coordinate their activities.

Management Support Systems

When information system applications focus on providing information and support for effective decision making by managers, they are called management support systems. Providing information and support for decision making by all types of managers and business professionals is a complex task. Conceptually, several major types of information systems support a variety of decision-making responsibilities: (1) management information systems, (2) decision support systems, and (3) executive information systems. See Figure 1.9.

FIGURE 1.8

QuickBooks is a popular accounting package that automates small office or home office (SOHO) accounting transaction processing while providing business owners with management reports.

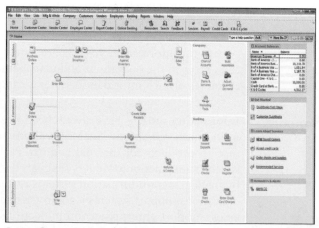

Source: Courtesy of Quickbooks.

FIGURE 1.9 A summary of management support systems with examples.

Management Support Systems

- **Management information systems.** Provide information in the form of prespecified reports and displays to support business decision making. Examples: sales analysis, production performance, and cost trend reporting systems.
- **Decision support systems.** Provide interactive ad hoc support for the decision-making processes of managers and other business professionals. Examples: product pricing, profitability forecasting, and risk analysis systems.
- **Executive information systems.** Provide critical information from MIS, DSS, and other sources tailored to the information needs of executives. Examples: systems for easy access to analyses of business performance, actions of competitors, and economic developments to support strategic planning.

Management information systems (MIS) provide information in the form of reports and displays to managers and many business professionals. For example, sales managers may use their networked computers and Web browsers to receive instantaneous displays about the sales results of their products and access their corporate intranet for daily sales analysis reports that evaluate sales made by each salesperson. **Decision support systems** (DSS) give direct computer support to managers during the decision-making process. For example, an advertising manager may use a DSS to perform a what-if analysis as part of the decision to determine how to spend advertising dollars. A production manager may use a DSS to decide how much product to manufacture, based on the expected sales associated with a future promotion and the location and availability of the raw materials necessary to manufacture the product. **Executive information systems** (EIS) provide critical information from a wide variety of internal and external sources in easy-to-use displays to executives and managers. For example, top executives may use touch-screen terminals to view instantly text and graphics displays that highlight key areas of organizational and competitive performance. Figure 1.10 is an example of an MIS report display.

FIGURE 1.10

Management information systems provide information to business professionals in a variety of easy-to-use formats.

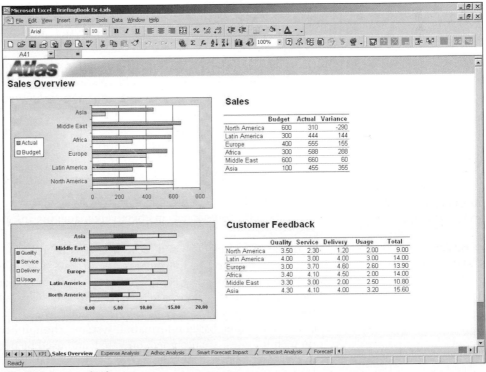

Source: Courtesy of Infor.

FIGURE 1.11   A summary of other categories of information systems with examples.

Other Categories of Information Systems

- **Expert systems.** Knowledge-based systems that provide expert advice and act as expert consultants to users. Examples: credit application advisor, process monitor, and diagnostic maintenance systems.
- **Knowledge management systems.** Knowledge-based systems that support the creation, organization, and dissemination of business knowledge within the enterprise. Examples: intranet access to best business practices, sales proposal strategies, and customer problem resolution systems.
- **Strategic information systems.** Support operations or management processes that provide a firm with strategic products, services, and capabilities for competitive advantage. Examples: online stock trading, shipment tracking, and e-commerce Web systems.
- **Functional business systems.** Support a variety of operational and managerial applications of the basic business functions of a company. Examples: information systems that support applications in accounting, finance, marketing, operations management, and human resource management.

Other Classifications of Information Systems

Several other categories of information systems can support either operations or management applications. For example, **expert systems** can provide expert advice for operational chores like equipment diagnostics or managerial decisions such as loan portfolio management. **Knowledge management systems** are knowledge-based information systems that support the creation, organization, and dissemination of business knowledge to employees and managers throughout a company. Information systems that focus on operational and managerial applications in support of basic business functions such as accounting or marketing are known as functional business systems. Finally, **strategic information systems** apply information technology to a firm's products, services, or business processes to help it gain a strategic advantage over its competitors. See Figure 1.11.

It is also important to realize that business applications of information systems in the real world are typically integrated combinations of the several types of information systems just mentioned. That is because conceptual classifications of information systems are designed to emphasize the many different roles of information systems. In practice, these roles are combined into integrated or cross-functional informational systems that provide a variety of functions. Thus, most information systems are designed to produce information and support decision making for various levels of management and business functions, as well as perform record-keeping and transaction-processing chores. Whenever you analyze an information system, you probably see that it provides information for a variety of managerial levels and business functions.

Managerial Challenges of Information Technology

Figure 1.12 illustrates the scope of the challenges and opportunities facing business managers and professionals in effectively managing information systems and technologies. Success in today's dynamic business environment depends heavily on maximizing the use of Internet-based technologies and Web-enabled information systems to meet the competitive requirements of customers, suppliers, and other business partners in a global marketplace. Figure 1.12 also emphasizes that information systems and their technologies must be managed to support the business strategies, business processes, and organizational structures and culture of a business enterprise. That is because computer-based information systems, though heavily dependent on information technologies, are designed, operated, and used by people in a variety of organizational settings and business environments. The goal of many companies today is to

FIGURE 1.12   Examples of the challenges and opportunities that business managers face in managing information systems and technologies to meet business goals.

The Business Enterprise

Strategies/Processes/Structure/Culture

Information Technology

Customer Value Business Value

Business / IT Challenges

- Speed and flexibility requirements of product development, manufacturing, and delivery cycles.
- Reengineering and cross-functional integration of business processes using Internet technologies.
- Integration of e-business and e-commerce into the organization's strategies, processes, structure, and culture.

Business / IT Developments

- Use of the Internet, intranets, extranets, and the Web as the primary IT infrastructure.
- Diffusion of Web technology to internetwork employees, customers, and suppliers.
- Global networked computing, collaboration, and decision support systems.

Business / IT Goals

- Give customers what they want, when and how they want it, at the lowest cost.
- Coordination of manufacturing and business processes with suppliers and customers.
- Marketing channel partnerships with suppliers and distributors.

maximize their customer and business value by using information technology to help their employees implement cooperative business processes with customers, suppliers, and others.

Success and Failure with IT

By now you should be able to see that the success of an information system should not be measured only by its *efficiency* in terms of minimizing costs, time, and the use of information resources. Success should also be measured by the *effectiveness* of the information technology in supporting an organization's business strategies, enabling its business processes, enhancing its organizational structures and culture, and increasing the customer and business value of the enterprise.

It is important to realize, however, that information technology and information systems can be mismanaged and misapplied in such a way that IS performance problems create both technological and business failures. Let's look at an example of how information technology contributed to business failure and success at some major corporations.

Large-Scale Projects: Failure and Success with IT

Certain IT initiatives fall into the "bet the company" category. Setting up an ERP[1] system from SAP[2] is one such choice. These complex undertakings carry both greater opportunities and greater risks than other enterprise software projects. Done right, an SAP deployment can transform an organization by streamlining operations, cutting costs, and opening up new business opportunities. Done wrong, it can become a multiyear nightmare.

For BWXT Y-12, which manages the U.S. Department of Energy's Y-12 National Security Complex outside of Oak Ridge, Tennessee, converting legacy systems to

---

[1]Recall that ERP stands for *enterprise resource planning*. This type of information system allows an organization to perform essentially all of its business functions by using a common interface, common data, and total connectivity across functions. We focus more on ERP in Chapter 8.
[2]SAP is a German company that specializes in the development of ERP software.

SAP has been a decade-long project. The project began in 1996 as a means of addressing Y2k issues, and parts of the organization are still being moved over to the ERP system, yet each step along the way has delivered a tangible benefit.

Not all implementations, however, have gone as smoothly, and SAP has developed a reputation for being difficult to implement. Several failed deployments have made the news over the past few years. The Hershey Co. began a $115 million deployment of SAP, Siebel Systems, and Manugistics software in 1997. Two years later, the company experienced massive distribution problems that cut into its profits. In August 2004, Hewlett-Packard reported that backlogs and lost revenue resulting from an SAP rollout for its enterprise servers cost $160 million. Whirlpool Corp. and Nike had similar experiences. What does not make the news is that these projects wind up working in the end.

Nevertheless, even if the projects do finally return a result, it takes a lot of work to get to that point. Companies have found that SAP seems to take more investment in customization, more investment in training, and more time and cost to get off the ground than a lot of other solutions. The key, according to analysts, is not to overbuy. Many companies will buy three solutions and try to implement them at the same time; buying one module at a time seems to be a better strategy.

The biggest part of deploying SAP, or any other ERP system for that matter, is not the software itself but the data and processes. Data conversion, in particular, can make or break any project. "Data conversion has been a big technical challenge," says Brian Barton at BWXT. At his company, systems needed to be cleaned so that bad data were not moved into the new systems. Much of the work had to be done manually. "It's easy to accumulate a lot of bad data over the years, particularly with the home-grown systems that have a looser data architecture and less-stringent validity checks."

Once the initial goals have been achieved, further features can be added, or the system can be used in new ways; SAP also has a number of capabilities than can be rolled out one at a time. The key is to look at ERPs as an ongoing investment strategy rather than a one-time implementation.

Source: Adapted from Drew Robb, "SAP Deployments: Pain for Gain," *Computerworld*, September 4, 2006.

Developing IS Solutions

Developing successful information system solutions to business problems is a major challenge for business managers and professionals today. As a business professional, you will be responsible for proposing or developing new or improved uses of information technologies for your company. As a business manager, you will frequently manage the development efforts of information systems specialists and other business end users.

Most computer-based information systems are conceived, designed, and implemented using some form of systematic development process. Figure 1.13 shows that several major activities must be accomplished and managed in a complete IS development cycle. In this development process, end users and information specialists *design* information system applications on the basis of an *analysis* of the business requirements of an organization. Examples of other activities include *investigating* the economic or technical feasibility of a proposed application, acquiring and learning how to use any software necessary to *implement* the new system, and making improvements to *maintain* the business value of a system.

We discuss the details of the information systems development process in Chapter 10. We will explore many of the business and managerial challenges that arise in developing and implementing new uses of information technology in Chapters 11 and 12. Now let's look at how a company changed its development practices to deliver the

FIGURE 1.13

Developing information systems solutions to business problems can be implemented and managed as a multistep process or cycle.

right functionality to users and become more responsive to their needs. This example emphasizes the importance of tailoring systems development practices to the needs of a business.

Agile Systems Development at Con-Way, Inc.

In the old days, companies could spend months planning a technology project and then months or even years implementing it. Not anymore. Strategies are far more dynamic these days, especially as companies respond to challenging economic times.

When someone has a good idea, they want to see it come to fruition right away. At transportation company Con-Way—founded in 1929, with more than 26,000 employees and 2008 revenue over $5 billion—almost all good ideas require technology to implement. Yet historically, ideas would become cold by the time they made it through IT steering committees, project planning, and design reviews. Then, Con-Way became agile—that is, it adopted Agile development practices.

Using Agile, software development is no longer accomplished through lengthy projects.

Instead, the overall concept of the desired system is defined at a high level up front and then developed in short iterations. An iteration is typically no longer than one month, and the software is released for use after each iteration. As people use the software, they determine which features should be built next, providing a feedback loop that results in the highest priority functionality being built. One big change for IT is that with Agile, there is always an impending implementation date: There is never a feeling of being able to relax on a project. Meanwhile, developers, used to having private space, can feel that space is violated due to "pair programming," which has two developers constructing the same piece of code at the same time, and to colocation, which has team members sitting as close together as humanly possible. As for the business users, Agile requires them to take a much more active role through the entire process. They must work jointly with IT to determine the priorities for each iteration, and they must provide daily direction to IT on the needs for the functionality being built.

"I made the case for change in IT by explaining how the business would benefit if we delivered the highest priority functionality faster. I also kept reiterating what was in it for them—and there was a lot," says Jackie Barretta, vice president and CIO of Con-Way, Inc. "At the same time, I made the case for change to the business by preparing a solid ROI that quantified the benefits of increasing the efficiency of development processes, delivering the right functionality more quickly and reducing the overall amount of work in progress."

The change effort has been worth it: After nine months, Agile is delivering on its promises. The iterative approach to software development is providing a feedback loop that results in building the right functionality. "We no longer have the waste problem that was inherent in the old waterfall method. Agile is creating greater alignment between IT and the business because of the constant, daily interaction and because Agile techniques help IT personnel understand the business better," says Barretta. "However, like anything that's really going to pay off, Agile is a huge change for IT and the user community."

Source: Adapted from Jackie Barretta, "How to Instill Agile Development Practices Among Your IT Team," *CIO Magazine*, January 14, 2009.

Challenges and Ethics of IT

As a prospective manager, business professional, or knowledge worker, you will be challenged by the **ethical responsibilities** generated by the use of information technology. For example, what uses of information technology might be considered improper, irresponsible, or harmful to other people or to society? What is the proper business use of the Internet and an organization's IT resources? What does it take to be a **responsible end user** of information technology? How can you protect yourself from computer crime and other risks of information technology? These are some of the questions that outline the ethical dimensions of information systems that we will discuss and illustrate with real world cases throughout this text. Figure 1.14 outlines some of the ethical risks that may arise in the use of several major applications of information technology. The following example illustrates some of the security challenges associated with conducting business over the Internet.

Hannaford Bros.: The Importance of Securing Customer Data

Hannaford Bros. may have started as a fruit and vegetable stand in 1883, but it has expanded from its Maine roots to become an upscale grocer with more than 160 stores throughout Maine, Massachusetts, New Hampshire, upstate New York, and Vermont. In March 2008, the supermarket chain disclosed a data security breach; Hannaford said in a notice to customers posted on its Web site that unknown intruders had accessed its systems and stolen about 4.2 million credit and debit card numbers between December 7 and March 10. The breach affected all of Hannaford's

FIGURE 1.14 Examples of some of the ethical challenges that must be faced by business managers who implement major applications of information technology.

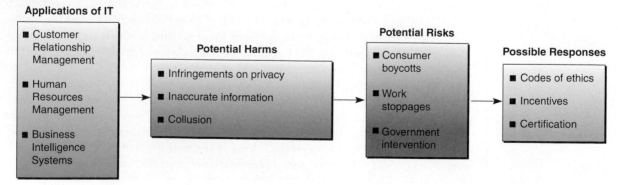

165 supermarkets in New England and New York, as well as 106 stores operated under the Sweetbay name in Florida and 23 independently owned markets that sell Hannaford products.

In a likely precursor of what was yet to come, two class-action lawsuits were filed against the company within the week. The filers argued that inadequate data security at Hannaford had resulted in the compromise of the personal financial data of consumers, thereby exposing them to the risk of fraud. They also claimed the grocer also appeared not to have disclosed the breach to the public quickly enough after discovering it.

Even though the Hannaford breach is relatively small compared with some other corporate security problems, it is likely to result in renewed calls for stricter regulations to be imposed on companies that fail to protect consumer data. In addition to facing the likelihood of consumer lawsuits, retailers who suffer breaches have to deal with banks and credit unions, which are getting increasingly antsy about having to shell out tens of thousands of dollars to pay for the cost of notifying their customers and reissuing credit and debit cards.

Retailers, on the other hand, have argued that the commissions they pay to card companies on each transaction are supposed to cover fraud-related costs, making any additional payments a double penalty. They also have said that the only reason they store payment card data is because of requirements imposed on them by the major credit card companies.

While the ultimate impact of these and other security breaches may be hard to quantify, it represents one of the most important challenges resulting from the ubiquitous use of electronic transaction processing and telecommunication networks in the modern networked enterprise, and one that is likely to keep growing every day. The security of customer and other sensitive data also represents one of the primary concerns of IT professionals.

Source: Adapted from Jaikumar Vijayan, "Hannaford Hit by Class-Action Lawsuits in Wake of Data-Breach Disclosure," *Computerworld*, March 20, 2008.

Challenges of IT Careers

Both information technology and the myriad of information systems it supports have created interesting, challenging, and lucrative career opportunities for millions of men and women all over the globe. At this point in your life you may still be uncertain about the career path you wish to follow, so learning more about information technology may help you decide if you want to pursue an IT-related career. In recent years, economic downturns have affected all job sectors, including IT. Further, rising labor costs in North America, Canada, and Europe have resulted in a large-scale movement to outsource basic software programming functions to India, the Middle East, and Asia-Pacific countries. Despite this move, employment opportunities in the information systems field are strong, with more new and exciting jobs emerging each day as organizations continue to expand their use of information technology. In addition, these new jobs pose constant human resource management challenges to all organizations because shortages of qualified information systems personnel frequently occur. Dynamic developments in business and information technologies cause constantly changing job requirements in information systems, which will ensure that the long-term job outlook in IT remains both positive and exciting.

Along with the myth that there are no jobs for IS professionals (we will dispel this one below!), another common myth is that IS professionals are computer geeks who live in a cubicle. Once again, nothing could be further from the truth! Today's IS professional must be highly skilled in communication, dealing with people, and, most of all, articulate in the fundamentals of business. The marketplace is demanding a *business technologist* with a big "B" and a big "T." The world of the IS professional is filled with constant challenge, variety, social interaction, and cutting-edge decision making. No desks and cubicles here. If action is what you are after, then you have found it here.

One major recruiter of IS professionals is the IT industry itself. Thousands of companies develop, manufacture, market, and service computer hardware, software, data, and network products and services. The industry can also provide e-business and e-commerce applications and services, end-user training, or business systems consulting. The biggest need for qualified people, however, comes from the millions of businesses, government agencies, and other organizations that use information technology. They need many types of IS professionals, such as systems analysts, software developers, and network managers to help them plan, develop, implement, and manage today's Internet-based and Web-enabled business/IT applications.

The accounting industry is a more recent major recruiter of IS professionals. Recent legislation, entitled the Sarbanes-Oxley Act of 2002, required major changes with regard to auditing practices by public accounting firms and internal control processes within publicly held organizations of all sizes and industries. Many of these changes directly affect the IT/IS practices of all parties involved. To facilitate the execution of the covenants of Sarbanes-Oxley, the accounting industry is actively recruiting graduates from accounting programs that have a significant emphasis on IS education. In addition, they are spending equal energy to recruit IS/IT professionals to work within the accounting industry. In either case, the result is a significant increase in demand for graduates with an IS/IT background or emphasis. Figure 1.15 lists just a few of the many career roles available to the modern IT professional.

According to recent reports by the U.S. Department of Labor, computer systems analysts, database administrators, and other managerial-level IS positions are expected to be among the fastest-growing occupations through 2012. Employment of IS professionals is expected to grow more than 36 percent (much higher than average) for all occupations as organizations continue to adopt and integrate increasingly sophisticated technologies. Job increases will be driven by very rapid growth in computer

FIGURE 1.15

Careers in IS are as diverse and exciting as the technologies used in them; IS professionals have career opportunities in every business environment and activity throughout the world.

Systems Analyst	System Consultant	Business Applications Consultant
Chief Information Officer	Computer Operator	Computer Serviceperson
Network Administrator	Data Dictionary Specialist	Network Manager
Database Administrator	Database Analyst	Documentation Specialist
IS Auditor	End-User Computer Manager	Equipment Manufacturer Representative
PC Sales Representative	Programmer	Program Librarian
Project Manager	Records Manager	Hardware Sales Representative
Scheduling and Control Person	Security Officer	Office Automation Specialist
Senior Project Leader	Service Sales Representative	Software Sales Representative
Technical Analyst	Software Quality Evaluator	Technical Writer
Telecommunications Specialist	Training & Standards Manager	User Interface Specialist

system design and related services, which is projected to be one of the fastest-growing industries in the U.S. economy. In addition, many job openings will arise annually from the need to replace workers who move into managerial positions or other occupations or who leave the labor force.

Despite the recent economic downturn among information technology firms, IS professionals still enjoy favorable job prospects. The demand for networking to facilitate sharing information, expanding client/server environments, and the need for specialists to use their knowledge and skills in a problem-solving capacity will be major factors in the rising demand for computer systems analysts, database administrators, and other IS professionals. Moreover, falling prices of computer hardware and software should continue to induce more businesses to expand their computerized operations and integrate new technologies. To maintain a competitive edge and operate more efficiently, firms will keep demanding the services of professionals who are knowledgeable about the latest technologies and can apply them to meet the needs of businesses.

Perhaps, the time has come to put a sharper edge on this message: *the field of information systems is growing at an increasingly rapid pace and there is no risk of being unemployed upon graduation!* It is this author's belief that the concern of over a lack of IT/IS-related jobs was fueled by the news media and is now, quite simply, unfounded. There were headlines proclaiming the death of IS and the lack of jobs in the United States due to massive outsourcing and offshoring. The jobs that were being sent overseas were real ones, to be sure. They were, however, not the jobs that you or your fellow students were ever going to train for during your stay in college—unless, of course, you aspire to being a faceless voice in a call center. These jobs are service-related jobs that, while vital to the big picture, are not the management level, creative business technologist positions that colleges and universities typically train their students to obtain. The real problem facing the IS field today is the *lack of graduates!* Students are opting for other professions because of fear of low pay and unemployment while recruiters are simultaneously begging for more graduates to feed their voracious appetites for more IS professionals. If you choose to avoid a career in information systems, it should not be because there are no jobs, it does not have to do with people, and it is no fun. Over the course of this book, we will dispel, with strong evidence, all of these rumors and myths. Let's start with some facts related to the first one.

The Bureau of Labor Statistics makes for some compelling evidence in favor of a career in information systems:

> *Prospects for qualified computer and information systems managers should be* **excellent.** Fast-paced occupational growth and the limited supply of technical workers will lead to a wealth of opportunities for qualified individuals. While technical workers remain relatively scarce in the United States, the demand for them continues to rise. This situation was exacerbated by the economic downturn in the early 2000s, when many technical professionals lost their jobs. Since then, many workers have chosen to avoid this work since it is **perceived** to have poor prospects.
>
> *People with management skills and an understanding of business practices and principles will have excellent opportunities, as companies are increasingly looking to technology to drive their revenue. (Bureau of Labor Statistics Occupational Outlook Handbook, 2008–2009)*

Increasingly, more sophisticated and complex technology is being implemented across all organizations, which will continue to fuel the demand for these computer occupations. The demand for systems analysts continues to grow to help firms maximize their efficiency with available technology. Expansion of e-commerce—doing business on the Internet—and the continuing need to build and maintain databases that store critical information about customers, inventory, and projects are fueling demand for database administrators familiar with the latest technology. Finally, the increasing importance placed on "cybersecurity"—the protection of electronic information—will result in a need for workers skilled in information security. Let's take a look at the emerging role of business analysts as liasions between IT specialists and their business customers.

The Critical Role of Business Analysts

For two decades, the CIO has been viewed as the ultimate broker between the business and technology functions. But while that may be an accurate perception in the executive boardroom, down in the trenches, business analysts (BA) have been the ones tasked with developing business cases for IT application development, in the process smoothing relations among competing parties and moving projects along.

The 21st century business analyst is a liaison, bridge, and diplomat who balances the oftentimes incongruous supply of IT resources and demands of the business. A recent Forrester Research report found that those business analysts who were most successful were the ones who could "communicate, facilitate and analyze." The business analyst is a hot commodity right now due to business reliance on technology, according to Jim McAssey, a principal at The W Group, a consulting firm. "The global delivery capabilities of technology today make the challenges of successfully bridging the gap between business and IT even harder," he says.

"Companies typically don't invest in an IT project without a solid business case," says Jeff Miller, senior vice president of Aetea, an IT staffing and consulting firm.

A good business analyst is able to create a solution to a particular business problem and act as a bridge to the technologists who can make it happen. "Without the BA role, CIOs are at significant risk that their projects will not solve the business problem for which they were intended," says Miller.

The ideal candidate will have five to ten or more years of experience (preferably in a specific industry), a technical undergraduate degree, and an MBA.

Strong risk assessment, negotiation, and problem resolution skills are key, and hands-on experience is critical. Business analysts must be process-driven and able to see a project through conflict and change, from start to finish. "The BA also must have the ability to learn new processes," says Miller. "A good BA learns business concepts and can quickly relate them to the specific needs of the project."

In the end, the more business technology analysts that are working in the business, the better off the CIO and IT function will be—no matter if the business technology analysts are reporting into IT or the business side. That's because those IT-savvy analysts, who will have a more in-depth understanding of and more expertise in technologies, will "ultimately help the business make better decisions when it comes to its interactions with IT," contend the Forrester analysts. And "CIOs have new allies in the business." Salaries range from $45,000 (entry level) to $100,000 (senior business analyst) per year.

Source: Adapted from Thomas Wailgum, "Why Business Analysts Are So Important for IT and CIOs," *CIO Magazine*, April 16, 2008; and Katherine Walsh, "Hot Jobs: Business Analyst," *CIO Magazine*, June 19, 2007.

The IS Function

The successful management of information systems and technologies presents major challenges to business managers and professionals. Thus, the information systems function represents:

- A major functional area of business equally as important to business success as the functions of accounting, finance, operations management, marketing, and human resource management.

- An important contributor to operational efficiency, employee productivity and morale, and customer service and satisfaction.
- A recognized source of value to the firm.
- A major source of information and support needed to promote effective decision making by managers and business professionals.
- A vital ingredient in developing competitive products and services that give an organization a strategic advantage in the global marketplace.
- A dynamic, rewarding, and challenging career opportunity for millions of men and women.
- A key component of the resources, infrastructure, and capabilities of today's networked business enterprises.
- A strategic resource.

Foundation Concepts: The Components of Information Systems

System Concepts: A Foundation

System concepts underlie all business processes, as well as our understanding of information systems and technologies. That's why we need to discuss how generic system concepts apply to business firms and the components and activities of information systems. Understanding system concepts will help you understand many other concepts in the technology, applications, development, and management of information systems that we cover in this text. For example, system concepts help us understand:

- **Technology.** Computer networks are systems of information processing components that use a variety of hardware, software, data management, and telecommunications network technologies.

- **Applications.** E-business and e-commerce applications involve interconnected business information systems.

- **Development.** Developing ways to use information technology in business includes designing the basic components of information systems.

- **Management.** Managing information technology emphasizes the quality, strategic business value, and security of an organization's information systems.

Read the Real World Case about large-scale problems involving information systems. We can learn a lot from this case regarding the critical role of good IT processes. See Figure 1.16.

What Is a System?

We have used the term *system* well over 100 times already and will use it thousands more before we are done. It therefore seems reasonable that we focus our attention on exactly what a system is. As we discussed at the beginning of the chapter, a system is defined as *a set of interrelated components, with a clearly defined boundary, working together to achieve a common set of objectives by accepting inputs and producing outputs in an organized transformation process.* Many examples of systems can be found in the physical and biological sciences, in modern technology, and in human society. Thus, we can talk of the physical system of the sun and its planets, the biological system of the human body, the technological system of an oil refinery, and the socioeconomic system of a business organization.

Systems have three basic functions:

- **Input** involves capturing and assembling elements that enter the system to be processed. For example, raw materials, energy, data, and human effort must be secured and organized for processing.

- **Processing** involves transformation processes that convert input into output. Examples are manufacturing processes, the human breathing process, or mathematical calculations.

- **Output** involves transferring elements that have been produced by a transformation process to their ultimate destination. For example, finished products, human services, and management information must be transmitted to their human users.

Example. A manufacturing system accepts raw materials as input and produces finished goods as output. An information system is a system that accepts resources (data) as input and processes them into products (information) as output. A business organization is a system in which human and economic resources are transformed by various business processes into goods and services.

REAL WORLD CASE 2

JetBlue and the Veterans Administration: The Critical Importance of IT Processes

When most people think of information technology, software and hardware immediately come to mind. While these are certainly important, good IT processes, particularly those that need to kick in during a disaster situation, are also critical. Most important, these need to be in place before, and not after, they are needed. For an example, go back to February 2007, when JetBlue Airways was forced to cancel more than 1,000 flights after an ice storm.

"For one, we didn't have enough of our home-office employees or crew members trained on our reservation system, so while we were dispatching people to the airports to help, which was great, they weren't trained to actually use the computer system. So we're going through a process now where we're actively training those crew members," says spokesman Eric Brinker. The discount airline is also in the process of expanding the capabilities of its reservation crew members so they can accept more inbound calls. "We basically maxed out," Brinker said. "We're working on a system to be able to automatically notify them better to take phone calls."

In the middle of the crisis, JetBlue's IT department developed a database that allowed the airline's scheduling team to improve multitasking. "They were receiving tons of phone calls from our crew members, and we created a database to enter in the whereabouts of our crew members. Then that information would sync up with the information about the crew members that was in the main system," Brinker said. "Now, during a weather situation, our flight crews and flight hands can call us and give us the location of where they are, and we can start to rebuild the airline immediately using this tool. We do that by cross-referencing where the crew

members say they are versus where the computer says they are, which weren't always in sync."

Brinker said the airline had never experienced a full meltdown before, so it hadn't needed to use this type of database. "The system, which was developed in 24 hours and implemented in the middle of JetBlue's crisis, has now been implemented as a full-time system," he said. "It's a real behind-the-scenes improvement for both our crew members and customers," he said. JetBlue is also improving the way it communicates with its customers, including pushing out automated flight alerts to customers via e-mail and mobile devices.

Even seemingly smaller and less critical processes can have ramifications of a large magnitude in the interconnected world in which we live. In September 2007, during a hearing by the House Committee on Veterans' Affairs, lawmakers learned about an unscheduled system failure that took down key applications in 17 Veterans Administration (VA) medical facilities for a day. Dr. Ben Davoren, the director of clinical informatics for the San Francisco VA Medical Center, characterized the outage as "the most significant technological threat to patient safety the VA has ever had." Yet the shutdown grew from a simple change in management procedure that wasn't properly followed. The small, undocumented change ended up bringing down the primary patient applications at 17 VA medical centers in northern California.

The breakdown exposed just how challenging it is to effect substantial change in a complex organization the size of the VA Office of Information & Technology (OI&T). Begun in October 2005 and originally scheduled to be completed by October 2008, the "reforming" of the IT organization at the VA involved several substantial goals. As part of the reform effort, the VA was to shift local control of IT infrastructure operations to regional data-processing centers.

Historically, each of the 150 or so medical centers run by the VA had its own IT service, its own budget authority, and its own staff, as well as independence with regard to how the IT infrastructure evolved. All of the decisions regarding IT were made between a local IT leadership official and the director of that particular medical center. While that made on-site IT staff responsive to local needs, it made standardization across sites nearly impossible in areas such as security, infrastructure administration and maintenance, and disaster recovery.

On the morning of August 31, 2007, staffers in medical centers around northern California starting their workday quickly discovered that they couldn't log onto their patient systems. The primary patient applications, Vista and CPRS, had suddenly become unavailable. Vista, which stands for Veterans Health Information Systems and Technology Architecture, is the VA's system for maintaining electronic health records. CPRS, the Computerized Patient Record System, is a suite of clinical applications that provides an across-the-board view of each veteran's health record. It includes a real-time order-checking system, a notification

FIGURE 1.16

Good IT processes are as important as hardware and software when it comes to creating business value through the use of technology.

Source: Getty Images.

system to alert clinicians of significant events, and a clinical reminder system. Without access to Vista, doctors, nurses, and others were unable to pull up patient records.

"There was a lot of attention on the signs and symptoms of the problem and very little attention on what is very often the first step you have in triaging an IT incident, which is, 'What was the last thing that got changed in this environment?'" Director Eric Raffin said.

The affected medical facilities immediately implemented their local contingency plans, which consist of three levels: the first of those is a fail-over from the Sacramento Data Center to the Denver Data Center, according to Bryan D. Volpp, associate chief of staff and clinical informatics. Volpp assumed that the data center in Sacramento would move into the first level of backup—switching over to the Denver data center. It didn't happen.

On that day, the Denver site wasn't touched by the outage at all. The 11 sites running in that region maintained their normal operations throughout the day. So why didn't Raffin's team make the decision to fail over to Denver? "What the team in Sacramento wanted to avoid was putting at risk the remaining 11 sites in the Denver environment, facilities that were still operating with no glitches. The problem could have been software-related," Raffin says. In that case, the problem may have spread to the VA's Denver facilities, as well. Since the Sacramento group couldn't pinpoint the problem, they made a decision not to fail over.

Greg Schulz, senior analyst at The Storage I/O Group, said the main vulnerability with mirroring is exactly what Raffin feared. "If I corrupt my primary copy, then my mirror is corrupted. If I have a copy in St. Louis and a copy in Chicago and they're replicating in real time, they're both corrupted, they're both deleted." That's why a point-in-time copy is necessary, Schulz continued. "I have everything I need to get back to that known state."

According to Volpp, "the disruption severely interfered with our normal operation, particularly with inpatient and outpatient care and pharmacy." The lack of electronic records prevented residents on their rounds from accessing patient charts to review the prior day's results or add orders. Nurses couldn't hand off from one shift to another through Vista, as they were accustomed. Discharges had to be written out by hand, so patients didn't receive the normal lists of instructions or medications, which were usually produced electronically.

Volpp said that within a couple of hours of the outage, "most users began to record their documentation on paper," including prescriptions, lab orders, consent forms, and vital signs and screenings. Cardiologists couldn't read EKGs, since those were usually reviewed online, nor could they order, update, or respond to consultations.

In Sacramento, the group finally got a handle on what had transpired to cause the outage. "One team asked for a change to be made by the other team, and the other team made the change," said Raffin. It involved a network port configuration, but only a small number of people knew about it. More important, said Raffin, "the appropriate change request wasn't completed." A procedural issue was at the heart of the problem. "We didn't have the documentation we should have had," he said. If that documentation for the port change had existed, Raffin noted, "that would have led us to very quickly provide some event correlation: Look at the clock, look at when the system began to degrade, and then stop and realize what we really needed to do was back those changes out, and the system would have likely restored itself in short order."

According to Evelyn Hubbert, an analyst at Forrester Research Inc., the outage that struck the VA isn't uncommon. "They don't make the front page news because it's embarrassing." Then, when something happens, she says, "it's a complete domino effect. Something goes down, something else goes down. That's unfortunately typical for many organizations." Schulz concurred. "You can have all the best software, all the best hardware, the highest availability, you can have the best people," Schulz said. "However, if you don't follow best practices, you can render all of that useless."

Source: Adapted from Linda Rosencrance, "Overwhelmed IT Systems Partly to Blame for JetBlue Meltdown," *Computerworld*, February 20, 2007; and Dian Schaffhauser, "The VA's Computer Systems Meltdown: What Happened and Why," *Computerworld*, November 20, 2007.

CASE STUDY QUESTIONS

1. Eric Brinker of JetBlue noted that the database developed during the crisis had not been needed before because the company had never experienced a meltdown. What are the risks and benefits associated with this approach to IT planning? Provide some examples of each.

2. With hindsight, we now know that the decision made by Eric Raffin of the VA not to fail over to the Denver site was the correct one. However, it involved failing to follow established backup procedures. With the information he had at the time, what other alternatives could he have considered? Develop at least two of them.

3. A small, undocumented change resulted in the collapse of the VA system, largely because of the high interrelationship between its applications. What is the positive side of this high degree of interconnection, and how does this benefit patients? Provide examples from the case to justify your answer.

REAL WORLD ACTIVITIES

1. Go online and search for reports on the aftermath of these two incidents. What consequences, financial and otherwise, did the two organizations face? What changes, if any, were implemented as a result of these problems? Prepare a report and present your findings to the class.

2. Search the Internet for examples of problems that companies have had with their IT processes. Break into small groups with your classmates to discuss your findings and what solutions you can propose to help organizations avoid the problems you discovered.

FIGURE 1.17   A common cybernetic system is a home temperature control system. The thermostat accepts the desired room temperature as input and sends voltage to open the gas valve, which fires the furnace. The resulting hot air goes into the room, and the thermometer in the thermostat provides feedback to shut the system down when the desired temperature is reached.

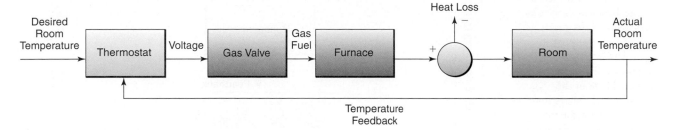

Feedback and Control

The system concept becomes even more useful by including two additional elements: feedback and control. A system with feedback and control functions is sometimes called a *cybernetic* system, that is, a self-monitoring, self-regulating system.

- **Feedback** is data about the performance of a system. For example, data about sales performance are feedback to a sales manager. Data about the speed, altitude, attitude, and direction of an aircraft are feedback to the aircraft's pilot or autopilot.

- **Control** involves monitoring and evaluating feedback to determine whether a system is moving toward the achievement of its goal. The control function then makes the necessary adjustments to a system's input and processing components to ensure that it produces proper output. For example, a sales manager exercises control when reassigning salespersons to new sales territories after evaluating feedback about their sales performance. An airline pilot, or the aircraft's autopilot, makes minute adjustments after evaluating the feedback from the instruments to ensure the plane is exactly where the pilot wants it to be.

Example. Figure 1.17 illustrates a familiar example of a self-monitoring, self-regulating, thermostat-controlled heating system found in many homes; it automatically monitors and regulates itself to maintain a desired temperature. Another example is the human body, which can be regarded as a cybernetic system that automatically monitors and adjusts many of its functions, such as temperature, heartbeat, and breathing. A business also has many control activities. For example, computers may monitor and control manufacturing processes, accounting procedures help control financial systems, data entry displays provide control of data entry activities, and sales quotas and sales bonuses attempt to control sales performance.

Other System Characteristics

Figure 1.18 uses a business organization to illustrate the fundamental components of a system, as well as several other system characteristics. Note that a system does not exist in a vacuum; rather, it exists and functions in an *environment* containing other systems. If a system is one of the components of a larger system, it is a *subsystem*, and the larger system is its environment.

Several systems may share the same environment. Some of these systems may be connected to one another by means of a shared boundary, or *interface*. Figure 1.18 also illustrates the concept of an *open system*, that is, a system that interacts with other systems in its environment. In this diagram, the system exchanges inputs and outputs with its environment. Thus, we could say that it is connected to its environment by input and output interfaces. Finally, a system that has the ability to change itself or its environment to survive is an *adaptive system*.

FIGURE 1.18

A business is an example of an organizational system in which economic resources (input) are transformed by various business processes (processing) into goods and services (output). Information systems provide information (feedback) about the operations of the system to management for the direction and maintenance of the system (control) as it exchanges inputs and outputs with its environment.

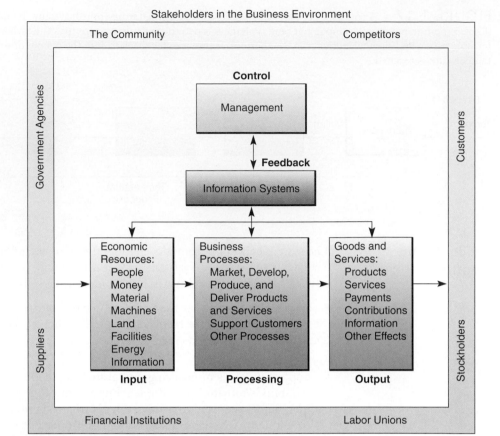

Example. Organizations such as businesses and government agencies are good examples of the systems in society, which is their environment. Society contains a multitude of such systems, including individuals and their social, political, and economic institutions. Organizations themselves consist of many subsystems, such as departments, divisions, process teams, and other workgroups. Organizations are examples of open systems because they interface and interact with other systems in their environment. Finally, organizations are examples of adaptive systems because they can modify themselves to meet the demands of a changing environment.

If we apply our understanding of general system concepts to information systems, it should be easy to see the parallels.

Information systems are made up of interrelated components:

- People, hardware, software, peripherals, and networks.

  They have clearly defined boundaries:

- Functions, modules, type of application, department, or end-user group.

  All the interrelated components work together to achieve a common goal by accepting inputs and producing outputs in an organized transformation process:

- Using raw materials, hiring new people, manufacturing products for sale, and disseminating information to others.

  Information systems make extensive use of feedback and control to improve their effectiveness:

- Error messages, dialog boxes, passwords, and user rights management.

Many information systems are designed to change in relation to their environments and are adaptive:

● Intelligent software agents, expert systems, and highly specialized decision support systems.

Information systems are systems just like any other system. Their value to the modern organization, however, is unlike any other system ever created.

Components of an Information System

We have noted that an information system is a system that accepts data resources as input and processes them into information products as output. How does an information system accomplish this task? What system components and activities are involved?

Figure 1.19 illustrates an **information system model** that expresses a fundamental conceptual framework for the major components and activities of information systems. An information system depends on the resources of people (end users and IS specialists), hardware (machines and media), software (programs and procedures), data (data and knowledge bases), and networks (communications media and network support) to perform input, processing, output, storage, and control activities that transform data resources into information products.

This information system model highlights the relationships among the components and activities of information systems. It also provides a framework that emphasizes four major concepts that can be applied to all types of information systems:

● People, hardware, software, data, and networks are the five basic resources of information systems.

● People resources include end users and IS specialists, hardware resources consist of machines and media, software resources include both programs and procedures, data resources include data and knowledge bases, and network resources include communications media and networks.

FIGURE 1.19

The components of an information system. All information systems use people, hardware, software, data, and network resources to perform input, processing, output, storage, and control activities that transform data resources into information products.

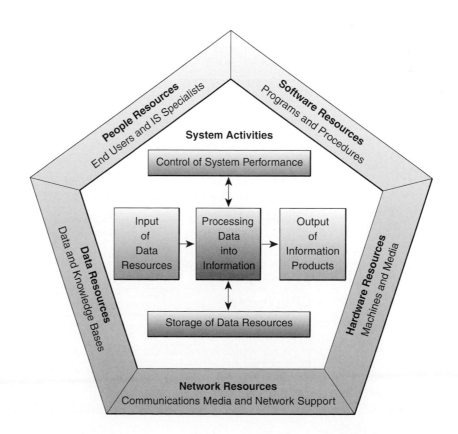

- Data resources are transformed by information processing activities into a variety of information products for end users.
- Information processing consists of the system activities of input, processing, output, storage, and control.

Information System Resources

Our basic IS model shows that an information system consists of five major resources: people, hardware, software, data, and networks. Let's briefly discuss several basic concepts and examples of the roles these resources play as the fundamental components of information systems. You should be able to recognize these five components at work in any type of information system you encounter in the real world. Figure 1.20 outlines several examples of typical information system resources and products.

People Resources

People are the essential ingredient for the successful operation of all information systems. These people resources include end users and IS specialists.

- End users (also called users or clients) are people who use an information system or the information it produces. They can be customers, salespersons, engineers, clerks, accountants, or managers and are found at all levels of an organization. In fact, most of us are information system end users. Most end users in business are knowledge workers, that is, people who spend most of their time communicating and collaborating in teams and workgroups and creating, using, and distributing information.
- IS specialists are people who develop and operate information systems. They include systems analysts, software developers, system operators, and other managerial, technical, and clerical IS personnel. Briefly, systems analysts design information systems based on the information requirements of end users, software developers create computer programs based on the specifications of systems analysts, and system operators help monitor and operate large computer systems and networks.

Hardware Resources

The concept of hardware resources includes all physical devices and materials used in information processing. Specifically, it includes not only machines, such as computers

FIGURE 1.20

Examples of information system resources and products.

Information System Resources and Products
People Resources
Specialists—systems analysts, software developers, systems operators.
End Users—anyone else who uses information systems.
Hardware Resources
Machines—computers, video monitors, magnetic disk drives, printers, optical scanners.
Media—floppy disks, magnetic tape, optical disks, plastic cards, paper forms.
Software Resources
Programs—operating system programs, spreadsheet programs, word processing programs, payroll programs.
Procedures—data entry procedures, error correction procedures, paycheck distribution procedures.
Data Resources
Product descriptions, customer records, employee files, inventory databases.
Network Resources
Communications media, communications processors, network access, control software.
Information Products
Management reports and business documents using text and graphics displays, audio responses, and paper forms.

and other equipment, but also all data media, that is, tangible objects on which data are recorded, from sheets of paper to magnetic or optical disks. Examples of hardware in computer-based information systems are:

- **Computer systems,** which consist of central processing units containing microprocessors and a variety of interconnected peripheral devices such as printers, scanners, monitors, and so on. Examples are handheld, laptop, tablet, or desktop microcomputer systems, midrange computer systems, and large mainframe computer systems.

- **Computer peripherals,** which are devices such as a keyboard, electronic mouse, trackball, or stylus for the input of data and commands, a video screen or printer for the output of information, and magnetic or optical disk drives for the storage of data resources.

Software Resources

The concept of software resources includes all sets of information processing instructions. This generic concept of software includes not only the sets of operating instructions called programs, which direct and control computer hardware, but also the sets of information processing instructions called procedures that people need.

It is important to understand that even information systems that do not use computers have a software resource component. This claim is true even for the information systems of ancient times or the manual and machine-supported information systems still used in the world today. They all require software resources in the form of information processing instructions and procedures to properly capture, process, and disseminate information to their users.

The following are examples of software resources:

- **System software,** such as an operating system program, which controls and supports the operations of a computer system. Microsoft Windows and Unix are two examples of popular computer operating systems.

- **Application software,** which are programs that direct processing for a particular use of computers by end users. Examples are sales analysis, payroll, and word processing programs.

- **Procedures,** which are operating instructions for the people who will use an information system. Examples are instructions for filling out a paper form or using a software package.

Data Resources

Data are more than the raw material of information systems. The concept of data resources has been broadened by managers and information systems professionals. They realize that data constitute valuable organizational resources. Thus, you should view data just as you would any organizational resource that must be managed effectively to benefit all stakeholders in an organization.

The concept of data as an organizational resource has resulted in a variety of changes in the modern organization. Data that previously were captured as a result of a common transaction are now stored, processed, and analyzed using sophisticated software applications that can reveal complex relationships among sales, customers, competitors, and markets. In today's wired world, the data to create a simple list of an organization's customers are protected with the same energy as the cash in a bank vault. Data are the lifeblood of today's organizations, and the effective and efficient management of data is considered an integral part of organizational strategy.

Data can take many forms, including traditional alphanumeric data, composed of numbers, letters, and other characters that describe business transactions and other events and entities; text data, consisting of sentences and paragraphs used in written communications; image data, such as graphic shapes and figures or photographic and video images; and audio data, including the human voice and other sounds.

The data resources of information systems are typically organized, stored, and accessed by a variety of data resource management technologies into:

- Databases that hold processed and organized data.
- Knowledge bases that hold knowledge in a variety of forms, such as facts, rules, and case examples about successful business practices.

For example, data about sales transactions may be accumulated, processed, and stored in a Web-enabled sales database that can be accessed for sales analysis reports by managers and marketing professionals. Knowledge bases are used by knowledge management systems and expert systems to share knowledge or give expert advice on specific subjects. We explore these concepts further in subsequent chapters.

Data versus Information. The word data is the plural of *datum*, though *data* commonly represents both singular and plural forms. Data are raw facts or observations, typically about physical phenomena or business transactions. For example, a spacecraft launch or the sale of an automobile would generate a lot of data describing those events. More specifically, data are objective measurements of the *attributes* (the characteristics) of *entities* (e.g., people, places, things, events).

Example. Business transactions, such as buying a car or an airline ticket, can produce a lot of data. Just think of the hundreds of facts needed to describe the characteristics of the car you want and its financing or the intricate details for even the simplest airline reservation.

People often use the terms *data* and *information* interchangeably. However, it is better to view data as raw material resources that are processed into finished information products. Then we can define information as data that have been converted into a meaningful and useful context for specific end users. Thus, data are usually subjected to a value-added process (*data processing* or *information processing*) during which (1) their form is aggregated, manipulated, and organized; (2) their content is analyzed and evaluated; and (3) they are placed in a proper context for a human user.

The issue of context is really at the heart of understanding the difference between information and data. Data can be thought of as context independent: A list of numbers or names, by itself, does not provide any understanding of the context in which it was recorded. In fact, the same list could be recorded in a variety of contexts. In contrast, for data to become information, both the context of the data and the perspective of the person accessing the data become essential. The same data may be considered valuable information to one person and completely irrelevant to the next. Just think of data as potentially valuable to all and information as valuable relative to its user.

Example. Names, quantities, and dollar amounts recorded on sales forms represent data about sales transactions. However, a sales manager may not regard these as information. Only after such facts are properly organized and manipulated can meaningful sales information be furnished and specify, for example, the amount of sales by product type, sales territory, or salesperson.

Network Resources

Telecommunications technologies and networks like the Internet, intranets, and extranets are essential to the successful e-business and e-commerce operations of all types of organizations and their computer-based information systems. Telecommunications networks consist of computers, communications processors, and other devices interconnected by communications media and controlled by communications software. The concept of network resources emphasizes that communications technologies and networks are fundamental resource components of all information systems. Network resources include:

- **Communications media.** Examples include twisted-pair wire, coaxial and fiber-optic cables, and microwave, cellular, and satellite wireless technologies.

FIGURE 1.21
Business examples of the
basic activities of
information systems.

Information System Activities
● **Input.** Optical scanning of bar-coded tags on merchandise.
● **Processing.** Calculating employee pay, taxes, and other payroll deductions.
● **Output.** Producing reports and displays about sales performance.
● **Storage.** Maintaining records on customers, employees, and products.
● **Control.** Generating audible signals to indicate proper entry of sales data.

● **Network infrastructure.** This generic category emphasizes that many hardware, software, and data technologies are needed to support the operation and use of a communications network. Examples include communications processors, such as modems and internetwork processors, and communications control software, such as network operating systems and Internet browser packages.

Information System Activities

Regardless of the type of information system, the same basic information system activities occur. Let's take a closer look now at each of the basic data or information processing activities. You should be able to recognize input, processing, output, storage, and control activities taking place in any information system you are studying. Figure 1.21 lists business examples that illustrate each of these information system activities.

Input of Data Resources

Data about business transactions and other events must be captured and prepared for processing by the input activity. Input typically takes the form of *data entry* activities such as recording and editing. End users usually enter data directly into a computer system or record data about transactions on some type of physical medium such as a paper form. This entry includes a variety of editing activities to ensure that they have recorded the data correctly. Once entered, data may be transferred onto a machine-readable medium, such as a magnetic disk, until needed for processing.

For example, data about sales transactions may be recorded on source documents such as paper order forms. (A **source document** is the original, formal record of a transaction.) Alternatively, salespersons might capture sales data using computer keyboards or optical scanning devices; they are visually prompted to enter data correctly by video displays. This method provides them with a more convenient and efficient **user interface,** that is, methods of end-user input and output with a computer system. Methods such as optical scanning and displays of menus, prompts, and fill-in-the-blank formats make it easier for end users to enter data correctly into an information system.

Processing of Data into Information

Data are typically subjected to processing activities, such as calculating, comparing, sorting, classifying, and summarizing. These activities organize, analyze, and manipulate data, thus converting them into information for end users. The quality of any data stored in an information system also must be maintained by a continual process of correcting and updating activities.

Example. Data received about a purchase can be (1) *added* to a running total of sales results, (2) *compared* to a standard to determine eligibility for a sales discount, (3) *sorted* in numerical order based on product identification numbers, (4) *classified* into product categories (e.g., food and nonfood items), (5) *summarized* to provide a sales manager with information about various product categories, and finally (6) used to *update* sales records.

Output of Information Products

Information in various forms is transmitted to end users and made available to them in the output activity. The goal of information systems is the production of appropriate information products for end users. Common information products include messages, reports, forms, and graphic images, which may be provided by video displays, audio responses, paper products, and multimedia. We routinely use the information provided by these products as we work in organizations and live in society. For example, a sales manager may view a video display to check on the performance of a salesperson, accept a computer-produced voice message by telephone, and receive a printout of monthly sales results.

Storage of Data Resources

Storage is a basic system component of information systems. Storage is the information system activity in which data are retained in an organized manner for later use. For example, just as written text material gets organized into words, sentences, paragraphs, and documents, stored data are commonly organized into a variety of data elements and databases. This organization facilitates their later use in processing or retrieval as output when needed by users of a system. Such data elements and databases are discussed further in Chapter 5, Data Resource Management.

Control of System Performance

An important information system activity is the **control** of system performance. An information system should produce feedback about its input, processing, output, and storage activities. This feedback must be monitored and evaluated to determine if the system is meeting established performance standards. Then appropriate system activities must be adjusted so that proper information products are produced for end users.

For example, a manager may discover that subtotals of sales amounts in a sales report do not add up to total sales. This conflict might mean that data entry or processing procedures need to be corrected. Then changes would have to be made to ensure that all sales transactions would be properly captured and processed by a sales information system.

Recognizing Information Systems

As a business professional, you should be able to recognize the fundamental components of information systems you encounter in the real world. This demand means that you should be able to identify:

- The people, hardware, software, data, and network resources they use.
- The types of information products they produce.
- The way they perform input, processing, output, storage, and control activities.

This kind of understanding will help you be a better user, developer, and manager of information systems. As we have pointed out in this chapter, this is important to your future success as a manager, entrepreneur, business professional, or modern business technologist.

Summary

- **IS Framework for Business Professionals.** The IS knowledge that a business manager or professional needs to know is illustrated in Figure 1.2 and covered in this chapter and text. This knowledge includes (1) *foundation concepts:* fundamental behavioral, technical, business, and managerial concepts like system components and functions, or competitive strategies; (2) *information technologies:* concepts, developments, or management issues regarding hardware, software, data management, networks, and other technologies; (3) *business applications:* major uses of IT for business processes, operations, decision making, and strategic/competitive advantage; (4) *development processes:* how end users and IS specialists develop and implement business/IT solutions to problems and opportunities arising in business; and (5) *management challenges:* how to manage the IS function and IT resources effectively and ethically to achieve top performance and business value in support of the business strategies of the enterprise.

● **Business Roles of Information Systems.** Information systems perform three vital roles in business firms. Business applications of IS support an organization's business processes and operations, business decision making, and strategic competitive advantage. Major application categories of information systems include operations support systems, such as transaction processing systems, process control systems, and enterprise collaboration systems; and management support systems, such as management information systems, decision support systems, and executive information systems. Other major categories are expert systems, knowledge management systems, strategic information systems, and functional business systems. However, in the real world, most application categories are combined into cross-functional information systems that provide information and support for decision making and also performing operational information processing activities. Refer to Figures 1.7, 1.9, and 1.11 for summaries of the major application categories of information systems.

● **System Concepts.** A system is a group of interrelated components, with a clearly defined boundary, working toward the attainment of a common goal by accepting inputs and producing outputs in an organized transformation process. Feedback is data about the performance of a system. Control is the component that monitors and evaluates feedback and makes any necessary adjustments to the input and processing components to ensure that proper output is produced.

● **Information System Model.** An information system uses the resources of people, hardware, software, data, and networks to perform input, processing, output, storage, and control activities that convert data resources into information products. Data are first collected and converted to a form that is suitable for processing (input). Then the data are manipulated and converted into information (processing), stored for future use (storage), or communicated to their ultimate user (output) according to correct processing procedures (control).

● **IS Resources and Products.** Hardware resources include machines and media used in information processing. Software resources include computerized instructions (programs) and instructions for people (procedures). People resources include information systems specialists and users. Data resources include alphanumeric, text, image, video, audio, and other forms of data. Network resources include communications media and network support. Information products produced by an information system can take a variety of forms, including paper reports, visual displays, multimedia documents, e-messages, graphics images, and audio responses.

Key Terms and Concepts

These are the key terms and concepts of this chapter. The page number of their first explanation appears in parentheses.

1. Computer-based information system (8)
2. Control (36)
3. Data (34)
4. Data or information processing (35)
5. Data resources (33)
6. Developing successful information system solutions (18)
7. E-business (12)
8. E-business applications (12)
9. E-commerce (13)
10. Enterprise collaboration systems (12)
11. Extranet (12)
12. Feedback (29)
13. Hardware resources (32)
    a. Machines (32)
    b. Media (33)

14. Information (34)
    a. Information products (35)
15. Information system (4)
16. Information system activities (35)
    a. Input (26)
    b. Processing (26)
    c. Output (26)
    d. Storage (36)
    e. Control (29)
17. Information system model (31)
18. Intranet (12)
19. Knowledge workers (32)
20. Management information systems (15)
21. Network resources (34)
22. People resources (32)
    a. IS specialists (32)
    b. End users (32)

23. Roles of IS in business (8)
    a. Support of business processes and operations (8)
    b. Support of business decision making (8)
    c. Support of strategies for competitive advantage (9)
24. Software resources (33)
    a. Programs (33)
    b. Procedures (33)
25. System (26)
26. Types of information systems (13)
    a. Cross-functional informational systems (16)
    b. Management support systems (14)
    c. Operations support systems (13)
    d. Functional business systems (16)
    e. Transaction processing systems (14)
    f. Process control systems (14)
    g. Enterprise collaboration systems (14)

Review Quiz

Match one of the previous key terms and concepts with one of the following brief examples or definitions. Look for the best fit for answers that seem to fit more than one key term or concept. Defend your choices.

_____ 1. People who spend most of their workday creating, using, and distributing information.

_____ 2. Computer hardware and software, networks, data management, and other technologies.

_____ 3. Information systems support an organization's business processes, operations, decision making, and strategies for competitive advantage.

_____ 4. Using IT to reengineer business processes to support e-business operations.

_____ 5. Using Web-based decision support systems to support sales managers.

_____ 6. Using information technology for e-commerce to gain a strategic advantage over competitors.

_____ 7. A system that uses people, hardware, software, and network resources to collect, transform, and disseminate information within an organization.

_____ 8. An information system that uses computers and their hardware and software.

_____ 9. Anyone who uses an information system or the information it produces.

_____ 10. Applications using the Internet, corporate intranets, and interorganizational extranets for e-business operations, e-commerce, and enterprise collaboration.

_____ 11. The buying, selling, marketing, and servicing of products over the Internet and other networks.

_____ 12. Groupware tools to support collaboration among networked teams.

_____ 13. A group of interrelated components with a clearly defined boundary working together toward the attainment of a common goal.

_____ 14. Data about a system's performance.

_____ 15. Making adjustments to a system's components so that it operates properly.

_____ 16. Facts or observations.

_____ 17. Data that have been placed into a meaningful context for an end user.

_____ 18. Converting data into information is a type of this kind of activity.

_____ 19. An information system uses people, hardware, software, network, and data resources to perform input, processing, output, storage, and control activities that transform data resources into information products.

_____ 20. Machines and media.

_____ 21. Computers, disk drives, video monitors, and printers are examples.

_____ 22. Magnetic disks, optical disks, and paper forms are examples.

_____ 23. Programs and procedures.

_____ 24. A set of instructions for a computer.

_____ 25. A set of instructions for people.

_____ 26. End users and information systems professionals.

_____ 27. Using the keyboard of a computer to enter data.

_____ 28. Computing loan payments.

_____ 29. Printing a letter you wrote using a computer.

_____ 30. Saving a copy of the letter on a magnetic disk.

_____ 31. Having a sales receipt as proof of a purchase.

_____ 32. Information systems can be classified into operations, management, and other categories.

_____ 33. Includes transaction processing, process control, and end-user collaboration systems.

_____ 34. Includes management information, decision support, and executive information systems.

_____ 35. Information systems that perform transaction processing and provide information to managers across the boundaries of functional business areas.

_____ 36. Internet-like networks and Web sites inside a company.

_____ 37. Interorganizational Internet-like networks among trading partners.

_____ 38. Using the Internet, intranets, and extranets to empower internal business operations, e-commerce, and enterprise collaboration.

_____ 39. Information systems that focus on operational and managerial applications in support of basic business functions such as accounting or marketing.

_____ 40. Data should be viewed the same way as any organizational resource that must be managed effectively to benefit all stakeholders in an organization.

_____ 41. A major challenge for business managers and professionals today in solving business problems.

_____ 42. Examples include messages, reports, forms, and graphic images, which may be provided by video displays, audio responses, paper products, and multimedia.

_____ 43. These include communications media and network infrastructure.

_____ 44. People who develop and operate information systems.

_____ 45. The execution of a set of activities in order to convert data into information.

_____ 46. Those systems implemented in order to direct physical conversion processes, such as oil refinement.

_____ 47. The second stage of information systems evolution, focused on providing managerial users with information relevant to decision making in the form of predefined reports.

_____ 48. A type of operation support systems geared toward the recording and processing of data captured as a result of business transactions.

_____ 49. A type of operation support systems that enhance team and workgroup communication and productivity.

Discussion Questions

1. How can information technology support a company's business processes and decision making and give it a competitive advantage? Give examples to illustrate your answer.

2. How does the use of the Internet, intranets, and extranets by companies today support their business processes and activities?

3. Refer to the Real Word Case on eCourier, Cablecom, and Bryan Cave in the chapter. Jay Bregman, CTO and cofounder of eCourier, notes the company hopes their innovative use of technology will become a differentiator in their competitive market. More generally, to what extent do specific technologies help companies gain an edge over their competitors? How easy or difficult would be to imitate such advantages?

4. Why do big companies still fail in their use of information technology? What should they be doing differently?

5. How can a manager demonstrate that he or she is a responsible end user of information systems? Give several examples.

6. Refer to the Real World Case on JetBlue and the VA in the chapter. How could a process be designed such that these domino effects can be avoided or to some extent controlled? Defend your proposal.

7. What are some of the toughest management challenges in developing IT solutions to solve business problems and meet new business opportunities?

8. Why are there so many conceptual classifications of information systems? Why are they typically integrated in the information systems found in the real world?

9. In what major ways have information systems in business changed during the last 40 years? What is one major change you think will happen in the next 10 years? Refer to Figure 1.4 to help you answer.

10. Refer to the real world example about ERPs in the chapter. Are the failures and successes described due to managerial or technological challenges? Explain.

Analysis Exercises

Complete the following exercises as individual or group projects that apply chapter concepts to real world business situations.

1. **Understanding the Information System**
   The Library as an Information System
   A library makes an excellent information systems model. It serves as a very large information storage facility with text, audio, and video data archives. Look up the definitions for each term listed below and briefly explain a library's equivalents.

   a. Input
   b. Processing
   c. Output
   d. Storage
   e. Control
   f. Feedback

2. **Career Research on the Web**
   Comparing Information Sources
   Select a job title for a career you would like to pursue as a summer intern or new graduate. Provide a real-world example of each element in Figure 1.19. You may need to interview someone familiar with this position to find the information you require.

3. **Skydive Chicago: Efficiency and Feedback**
   Digital Data
   Skydive Chicago (www.SkydiveChicago.com) is one of the United States' premier skydiving resorts, serving skydivers ranging in skills from first-time jumpers to internationally competitive freefly teams.

   Each student in Skydive Chicago's training program makes a series of progressive training jumps under the direct supervision of a United States Parachute Association–rated jumpmaster. The training program gears each jump in the series toward teaching one or two new skills. Jumpmasters video their students' jumps. Students use the feedback these videos provide to identify mistakes. They often copy their videos onto a personal tape for future reference.

   Jumpmasters may also copy well-executed student skydives to the facility's tape library. All students are given access to the dropzone's training room and are encouraged to watch video clips in preparation for their next training jump. This step saves jumpmasters, who are paid per jump, considerable time. Jumpmasters also use these videos to evaluate their training method's effectiveness.

a. How can this information system benefit the skydiving student?

b. How can this information system benefit Skydive Chicago?

c. Draw an information systems model (Figure 1.19). Fill in your diagram with the information about people, hardware, software, and other resources from this exercise.

4. Are Textbooks History?
Trends in Information Systems
The wealth of free information available via the Internet continues to grow at incredible rates. Search engines such as Google make locating useful information practical. This textbook often explores the Internet's impact on various industries, and the textbook industry is no exception. Is it possible that free Internet content might one day replace textbooks?

a. Go to www.google.com and use the search box to look up "End user." Were any of Google's first five search results useful with respect to this course?

b. Go to www.wikipedia.com and use the search box to look up "Knowledge worker." Compare Wikipedia's article with the information provided within this textbook. Which source did you find easiest to use?

What advantages did Wikipedia provide? What advantages did this textbook provide?

c. Did Google, Wikipedia, or this textbook provide the most useful information about "Intranets"? Why?

5. Careers in IS
Disaster Recovery
"How important are your data to you?" "What would happen if . . . ?" While business managers focus on solving business problems and determining what their information systems should do, disaster recovery consultants ask what would happen if things go wrong.

With careful advance planning, disaster recovery specialists help their clients prevent calamity. Although this topic covers a wide variety of software issues, installation configuration issues, and security threats, examining common end-user mistakes may also prove enlightening. Common end-user mistakes include:

- Failure to save work in progress frequently.
- Failure to make a backup copy.
- Failure to store original and backup copies in different locations.

For each of the common end-user mistakes listed above, answer the following questions:

a. How might this mistake result in data loss?

b. What procedures could you follow to prevent this risk?

REAL WORLD CASE 3

Sew What? Inc.: The Role of Information Technology in Small Business Success

What do Sting, Elton John, and Madonna have in common? Besides being international rock stars, they all use theatrical backdrops designed and manufactured by custom drapery maker Sew What? Inc. Based in Rancho Dominguez, California, Sew What? provides custom theatrical draperies and fabrics for stages, concerts, fashion shows, and special events worldwide and has become an industry leader in rock-and-roll staging.

Founded in 1992 by Australian-born Megan Duckett, Sew What? has grown from a tiny kitchen-and-garage operation to a multimillion-dollar enterprise, thanks to Duckett's never-say-no approach to customer satisfaction. "When I see a problem, I just don't back down. I find a way to overcome it and I use everybody I know to help me," she says.

What made it possible for a one-woman business that started in a kitchen to evolve and grow into a multimillion-dollar company with 35 employees? Megan Duckett attributes her success to hard work, quality workmanship, and especially information technology.

Sew What? has enjoyed explosive growth in recent years, reaching $4 million per year in sales by the end of 2006. Company president Duckett credits much of her firm's rapid growth to its ability to leverage information technology and the Internet to drive sales. "Before we put up our Web site, sewwhatinc.com, our business was almost all local," says Duckett. "But after launching the Web site three years ago, we now have clients all over the world. In fact, last year our revenue grew 45% on the previous year's sales, and this year we are on target to enjoy a 65% increase on 2005 sales. And nearly all that growth came from Web-driven sales."

Although the company's Web site may take center stage, managing all the business the site brings in requires a lot of effort behind the scenes. In particular, Duckett relies on a solid IT infrastructure to help keep the company running smoothly. "We are a customer-centric company," notes Duckett. "It's critical that we have excellent back-office information technology to manage the business and deliver outstanding service to our customers."

Sew What? runs most of its business with Intuit's Quick-Books Enterprise Solutions Manufacturing and Wholesale Edition software and Microsoft's Windows Server operating system installed on a Dell PowerEdge 860 server, sporting an Intel Xeon processor and 146 gigabytes of disk storage. According to Duckett, "Running our business requires a lot of storage. In addition to customer information and vital operational and financial QuickBooks files, we need to store thousands of drapery and fabric image files, customer instruction document files, and other types of data." Sew What?'s additional computer support includes an older Dell PowerEdge 500 server dedicated to a few smaller applications and a variety of Dell desktop PC systems for employees.

Sew What? started in 1992 as a part-time endeavor, with Duckett cutting and sewing fabric on her kitchen table. She went full time in 1997 and incorporated in 1998. The important role technology plays in running a successful small business hit home when she lost a big contract. The potential client said that without a Web site, her company "lacked credibility." "Before losing that contract, I thought, 'I run a sewing business, a cottage craft. I don't need a Web site,'" she says. Duckett admits she was rather cocky, mainly because she had grown her business "quite well" by word of mouth alone. "I quickly learned the error of that thought process. You can't have that attitude and stick around," she acknowledges.

Losing the contract also coincided with a period of low growth between 2001 and 2002. That's when Duckett decided to embrace technology. Using Microsoft Publisher, she designed and built her own Web site. "You figure things out and learn how to do it yourself when budgets are thin," she admits.

Duckett kept working to improve the site and make it better for her customers. A year later, feeling that the site needed refreshing, she signed up for a 10-week course in Dreamweaver and again completely rebuilt the site. Yet another Web site reconstruction helped Sew What? grow into a company with customers around the world and a clientele list that includes international rock stars, Gucci, and *Rolling Stone* magazine.

In 2005, Duckett decided she needed to improve the site's navigation because "I wanted it to be sleek and to provide a really good customer experience. That was beyond my abilities, so we hired a Web marketing consulting company to build a custom navigation system for the site."

She worked with the hired guns on branding, search engine optimization, overall design, and site layout. Duckett still provides all the content, including text and images. There's also a Spanish version of the site, and the professionals tuned up the main site's search features to include spelling variants for different English-speaking countries. For example, you can search for the American spelling of theater or the British and Australian version, theatre.

The site also lets potential customers review all kinds of color swatches and teaches them how to calculate accurate measurements for their projects; the differences between a scrim, a tormentor, and a traveler curtain; the proper care and feeding of a variety of drapery materials; and a lot more.

While perusing the Dell Web site one day, Duckett saw a news article about the Dell/NFIB Small Business Excellence Award. The National Federation of Independent Businesses (NFIB) and Dell Inc. present this annual prize to one small business in recognition of its innovative use of technology to improve its customers' experience. The winner receives $30,000 worth of Dell products and services, a lifetime membership to the NFIB, and a day at Dell's headquarters with Michael Dell and other senior executives.

"The description of the kinds of businesses they were looking for perfectly described Sew What?" Duckett realized. "Everything they were looking for, we'd done, so I decided to enter. My husband [and business partner] laughed and reminded me that I never win anything." Writing the essay for the contest caused Duckett to reflect on everything she and her employees had achieved over the years: "We got to sit back and feel really proud of ourselves. Just that process was enough to invigorate everyone in our weekly production meetings."

The contest judges also recognized Megan Duckett's passionate commitment to customer satisfaction and use of information technology for business success, so they awarded Sew What? the Small Business Excellence Award. Winning the award proved to be a very emotional experience. Looking at the caliber and achievements of the nine other finalists, Duckett figured Sew What? would remain just a top-10 finalist: "I could not believe that a big company like Dell—so entrepreneurial and advanced in every way—would look at our little company and recognize it."

Like other small business owners, Duckett puts an enormous amount of physical and emotional energy into her work. "Winning this award is so flattering on a personal level," she says. "This business is ingrained in every cell of my body, and to have someone saying, 'Good job,' well, in small business, nobody ever says that to you."

That may have been true previously, but Sew What?'s technology leadership and business success continue to earn recognition. In March 2007, the company received a Stevie Award for Women in Business for "most innovative company

of the year" among those with up to 100 employees. A few months earlier, Sew What? had received an SMB 20 Award from *PC Magazine*, which honors 20 of the most technologically innovative small- and medium-sized businesses (SMBs) each year. "Small and medium businesses drive today's economy. However, they often don't get the attention and recognition they deserve," said *PC Magazine*'s Editor-in-Chief, Jim Louderback. "We want to highlight the hard work, technological leadership, and innovative spirit of thousands of SMB companies throughout the world."

Duckett plans to use her prize winnings to add a bar code system that can track the manufacturing process at the company's warehouse. In the drapery business, fabric is stored on a roll in the warehouse and then moves through different stages: receiving, cutting, sewing, shipping, and so forth. The scanning process will enable Duckett's team to track how long the fabric stays in any given stage. These data will give them a better idea of their costs, which will then help them produce more accurate price lists.

"We don't need to charge an hour and a half for labor if the cutting only takes an hour and 15 minutes," Duckett notes. Currently, the company uses a handwritten system of sign-in and sign-out sheets that, she says, takes too long and introduces too many errors. "The new system will also let us track the progress of individual orders," she promises. "We'll be able to provide better service by keeping the customer updated."

Source: Adapted from Lauren Simonds, "Pay Attention to the Woman Behind the Curtain," *Small BusinessComputing.com*, July 21, 2006.

CASE STUDY QUESTIONS

1. How do information technologies contribute to the business success of Sew What? Inc.? Give several examples from the case regarding the business value of information technology that demonstrate this conclusion.

2. If you were a management consultant to Sew What? Inc., what would you advise Megan Duckett to do at this point to be even more successful in her business? What role would information technology play in your proposals? Provide several specific recommendations.

3. How could the use of information technology help a small business you know be more successful? Provide several examples to support your answer.

REAL WORLD ACTIVITIES

1. Search the Internet to help you evaluate the business performance of Sew What? Inc. and its competitors at the present time. What conclusions can you draw from your research about Sew What?'s prospects for the future? Report your findings and recommendations for Sew What?'s continued business success to the class.

2. Small businesses have been slower to integrate information technology into their operations than larger companies. Break into small groups with your classmates to discuss the reasons for this state of affairs, identifying several possible IT solutions and their business benefits that could help small businesses become more successful.

CHAPTER 2

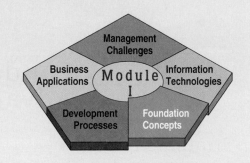

COMPETING WITH INFORMATION TECHNOLOGY

Chapter Highlights

Learning Objectives

1. Identify several basic competitive strategies and explain how they use information technologies to confront the competitive forces faced by a business.

2. Identify several strategic uses of Internet technologies and give examples of how they can help a business gain competitive advantages.

3. Give examples of how business process reengineering frequently involves the strategic use of Internet technologies.

4. Identify the business value of using Internet technologies to become an agile competitor or form a virtual company.

5. Explain how knowledge management systems can help a business gain strategic advantages.

SECTION I	# Fundamentals of Strategic Advantage

Strategic IT

Technology is no longer an afterthought in forming business strategy, but the actual cause and driver.

This chapter will show you that it is important to view information systems as more than a set of technologies that support efficient business operations, workgroup and enterprise collaboration, or effective business decision making. Information technology can change the way businesses compete. You should also view information systems strategically, that is, as vital competitive networks, as a means of organizational renewal, and as a necessary investment in technologies; such technologies help a company adopt strategies and business processes that enable it to reengineer or reinvent itself to survive and succeed in today's dynamic business environment.

Section I of this chapter introduces fundamental competitive strategy concepts that underlie the strategic use of information systems. Section II then discusses several major strategic applications of information technology used by many companies today.

Read the Real World Case regarding the competitive advantages of IT. We can learn a lot about the strategic business uses of information technologies from this case. See Figure 2.1.

Competitive Strategy Concepts

In Chapter 1, we emphasized that a major role of information systems applications in business is to provide effective support of a company's strategies for gaining competitive advantage. This strategic role of information systems involves using information technology to develop products, services, and capabilities that give a company major advantages over the competitive forces it faces in the global marketplace.

This role is accomplished through a strategic information architecture: the collection of strategic information systems that supports or shapes the competitive position and strategies of a business enterprise. So a strategic information system can be any kind of information system (e.g., TPS, MIS, and DSS) that uses information technology to help an organization gain a competitive advantage, reduce a competitive disadvantage, or meet other strategic enterprise objectives.

Figure 2.2 illustrates the various competitive forces a business might encounter, as well as the competitive strategies that can be adopted to counteract such forces. It is important to note that the figure suggests that any of the major strategies may be deemed useful against any of the common competitive forces. Although it is rare and unlikely that a single firm would use all strategies simultaneously, each has value in certain circumstances. For now, it is only important that you become familiar with the available strategic approaches. Let us look at several basic concepts that define the role of competitive strategy as it applies to information systems.

Competitive Forces and Strategies

How should a business professional think about competitive strategies? How can a business use information systems to apply competitive strategies? Figure 2.2 illustrates an important conceptual framework for understanding forces of competition and the various competitive strategies employed to balance them.

A company can survive and succeed in the long run only if it successfully develops strategies to confront five competitive forces that shape the structure of competition in its industry. In Michael Porter's classic model of competition, any business that wants to survive and succeed must effectively develop and implement strategies to counter (1) *the rivalry of competitors within its industry*, (2) *the threat of new entrants into an industry and its markets*, (3) *the threat posed by substitute products that might capture market share*, (4) *the bargaining power of customers*, and (5) *the bargaining power of suppliers*.

REAL WORLD CASE 1

IT Leaders: Reinventing IT as a Strategic Business Partner

CIO Steve Olive isn't handing out any gold stars to IT for providing good PC support or networking service at Raytheon Integrated Defense Systems. "Consistently reliable and excellent IT service should be a given," he says. "What businesses need and IT should be providing are innovative solutions to business challenges." That means creatively applying technology to produce goods more efficiently and at a lower cost, to sell and service more of them, and to do so at the highest possible profit margins.

It also means using IT to create new products and services and even whole new business models, says Darryl Lemecha, CIO at ChoicePoint Inc. Because technology is embedded in just about everything a company does, "technology strategy and business strategy are now one." Kathleen McNulty, CIO at The Schwan Food Co., puts it this way: "It's not about IT automating the business anymore. It's about innovating it, improving it." So forget about IT supporting the business. IT leaders are focused on reinventing the business, starting with the IT organization.

Their timing couldn't be better. According to Gartner Inc., within five years, 60 percent of chief executives will make their CIOs responsible for using information as a strategic (read: revenue-generating) asset. Gartner also predicts that 40 percent of CEOs will make CIOs responsible for business model innovation.

IT executives such as John Hinkle at Trans World Entertainment Corp., Patrick Bennett at E! Entertainment Television Inc., and Filippo Passerini at the Procter & Gamble Co. are all over this trend already. They are completely transforming their IT organizations, and everything is up for radical change, from how and where IT is housed within their companies to IT job titles. IT duties increasingly involve responsibility for business processes as well as the technology that supports them. Also up for reinvention is how IT value is measured.

FIGURE 2.1

IT organizations are being called in to innovate and improve business processes as equal partners.

Source: Getty Images.

"If you want to drive a significant amount of behavioral change in an organization, it takes some big swings," says Hinkle. "Maybe that means dramatic structural change or changing what people do." At Trans World, it involved all of the above.

One of the first things Hinkle did when he came to Trans World from General Electric was abolish the title of analyst and move people in that role into the project management office (PMO), which oversees all technology and business projects, as well as all business process changes for the company's 800 music stores. Project managers have developed expertise and a special rapport with the specific business functions to which they are dedicated. New projects and even systems changes go through the PMO, which uses Six Sigma project management processes.

As CIO, Hinkle oversees the PMO, is a member of the company's executive board, and is deeply entrenched in all business decisions. "I'm involved in merchandising, store planning and in every other core strategic meeting at the company," Hinkle says. "I'm expected to be very well versed in these things, and I'm also expected to answer more than the IT questions. I'm part of the strategy brainstorming."

Hinkle expects his IT team to be equally well versed in business processes, which is why every IT staffer spends a minimum of three days in the field every year, working in a store, a warehouse, or a department such as finance or payroll. "That way, they know what the business really needs and how to help," he says. "You don't have a supply chain system or financial system that works in a box or a point-of-sale system that just takes money. Now we have highly integrated data flows, so every project requires an understanding of all systems and all business areas." By knowing the business, "they better understand why they might get a call for support at 1:00 in the morning," he adds.

At ChoicePoint, Lemecha created a federated structure with two bands of IT positions: one for technical workers, who hold the title of IT architect; and one for managers, who hold the title of business information officer (BPO). "We believe in two independent career paths. Just because you don't manage people doesn't mean you should be limited in how far you go in the company," he says.

The BIOs are embedded in each of ChoicePoint's businesses and act as local CIOs. "They understand the operational issues, they know all of the people, and they spend 100% of their time in the business units," where they can directly affect business–IT alignment, Lemecha says. "They know and understand the business because they live in the business," he says. The chief benefit of this arrangement is "when you fix the alignment problems, you do the right IT projects and, ultimately, impact revenue and get better customer service," Lemecha says. ChoicePoint's consistent revenue growth, ranging between 5 percent and 15 percent annually for the past several years, is no coincidence.

At Cincinnati-based Procter & Gamble (P&G), the company's top IT project over the past three years has been to reinvent IT itself according to a four-year strategic alignment plan. "In the last year, we reshaped, renamed, refocused and began retraining our 2,500-person IT team," says Passerini, who is global business services officer in addition to CIO. The IT department was renamed Information & Decision Solutions (IDS). The new IDS group was then merged into P&G's Global Business Services shared-services organization, which is also home to the human resources, finance, strategic planning, and relocation functions. IDS staffers focus on high-level, IT-enabled business projects exclusively; routine IT tasks are outsourced to Hewlett-Packard Co. under a 10-year, $3 billion agreement signed in 2003.

Passerini has charged IDS with the same three business goals of every other P&G business unit: to increase profits, market share, and volume. To accomplish this, IDS focuses on three key tactics: getting and distributing data faster, innovating and speeding the ways in which P&G gets products to market, and applying "consumer-friendly" techniques to delivering new IT products and services to P&G's internal user base. For example, IDS has developed a virtual modeling process and simulation techniques that allow package design, consumer testing, product testing, and even new manufacturing techniques to be developed and tested in a fully virtual environment, dramatically accelerating the cycle time for new products.

"When we have new products, we can build virtual retail shelves and even show our competitors' products on them. More importantly, we can build our products to the scale of different retailers' shelves. This is all about building business capabilities for P&G," Passerini says. "The whole idea is running IT as a business, but not necessarily using [traditional return-on-investment] financial measures to quantify IT's value," he says. "In the end, no one believes those numbers anyhow. The numbers you want are higher profits, market share, and volumes. In reality, it's all about the relevancy of IT's contribution to the business," Passerini adds. That is how IT's value is measured at P&G.

E! Entertainment Television in Los Angeles has radically departed from its traditional model of separate IT and television broadcast operations. The change coincides with the broadcast side's shift from tape to digital technology. Before, separate vice presidents oversaw online, television network, and IT operations. Now there is a single senior vice president of technology and operations, and ideas, designs, technology, and projects are shared among all three operations.

For example, IT personnel were involved in the design of E! Online content from the time the site was first launched in October 2006, notes Bennett, executive director of business applications. "Before, we would have gotten the specs and built it much like a contractor," he says. "But now, IT was in on branding discussions and audience focus groups from the beginning. "What we've done is flatten the more formal [software development] processes and made them more person-to-person" as a way to develop products and services faster across all media, Bennett says. "As we interact with executives and users and release software iteratively, we're also gaining greater domain knowledge about the business," he notes.

Just recently, IT participated in a discussion about offering an online feature that would let Web viewers of E! Online vote on whether celebrities on the red carpet at the Golden Globe and Oscar celebrations are hot or not. "Now that's not a traditional discussion or conversation you would have in IT," Bennett notes wryly, "but now we're thinking about these kinds of things across all media." Under the new organizational structure, "there's constant interaction and exchange of information and ideas through human contact. As opposed to being assigned to a user department, IT is constantly interacting across media," he says. "You're more of a partner with the business. You're creating products together. IT is definitely stepping out from behind the shadows of backoffice corporate systems."

"It's very much a different mind-set," says Raytheon's Olive, whose overhauled IT organization now includes customer relationship managers who are embedded in the business, plus 10 teams of technical workers who support IT frameworks such as infrastructure, application support, and desktop services. The vast majority of those technical workers are "home-roomed" in cross-business teams that work on projects that the customer relationship managers bring to them, he notes.

"It took two years for this model to really jell. At first, there was a little bit of tension while the clarity of roles and responsibilities was a little confusing," Olive acknowledges. "But once we defined roles and responsibilities, it improved morale and worked to create a highly motivated workforce because we were making higher-level contributions to the business."

Source: Adapted from Julia King, "How IT Is Reinventing Itself as a Strategic Business Partner," *Computerworld*, February 19, 2007.

CASE STUDY QUESTIONS

1. What are the business and political challenges that are likely to occur as a result of the transformation of IT from a support activity to a partner role? Use examples from the case to illustrate your answer.

2. What implications does this shift in the strategic outlook of IT have for traditional IT workers and for the educational institutions that train them? How does this change the emphasis on what knowledge and skills the IT person of the future should have?

3. To what extent do you agree with the idea that technology is embedded in just about everything a company does? Provide examples, other than those included in the case, of recent product introductions that could not have been possible without heavy reliance on IT.

REAL WORLD ACTIVITIES

1. Search the Internet to find information about other firms that have transformed their IT organizations and the role that the CIO plays in the governance structure of the organization. What benefits have they been able to derive from these changes? Prepare a report and present your findings to your class.

2. Consider the virtual reality technologies employed by Procter & Gamble and described in this case. Break into small groups and brainstorm applications of these types of technologies for companies in industries other than those reviewed in the case.

FIGURE 2.2

Businesses can develop competitive strategies to counter the actions of the competitive forces they confront in the marketplace.

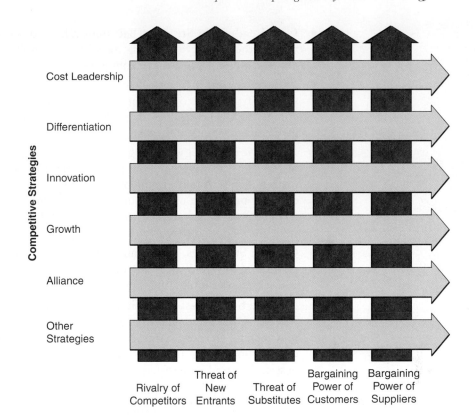

Competition is a positive characteristic in business, and competitors share a natural, and often healthy, rivalry. This rivalry encourages and sometimes requires a constant effort to gain competitive advantage in the marketplace. This ever-present competitive force requires significant resources on the part of a firm.

Guarding against the threat of new entrants also requires the expenditure of significant organizational resources. Not only do firms need to compete with other firms in the marketplace, but they must also work to create significant barriers to the entry of new competition. This competitive force has always been difficult to manage, but it is even more so today. The Internet has created many ways to enter the marketplace quickly and with relatively low cost. In the Internet world, a firm's biggest potential competitor may be one that is not yet in the marketplace but could emerge almost overnight.

The threat of substitutes is another competitive force that confronts a business. The effect of this force is apparent almost daily in a wide variety of industries, often at its strongest during periods of rising costs or inflation. When airline prices get too high, people substitute car travel for their vacations. When the cost of steak gets too high, people eat more hamburger and fish. Most products or services have some sort of substitute available to the consumer.

Finally, a business must guard against the often opposing forces of customer and supplier bargaining powers. If customers' bargaining power gets too strong, they can drive prices to unmanageably low levels or just refuse to buy the product or service. If a key supplier's bargaining power gets too strong, it can force the price of goods and services to unmanageably high levels or just starve a business by controlling the flow of parts or raw materials essential to the manufacture of a product.

Figure 2.2 also illustrates that businesses can counter the threats of competitive forces that they face by implementing one or more of the five basic competitive strategies.

- **Cost Leadership Strategy.** Becoming a low-cost producer of products and services in the industry or finding ways to help suppliers or customers reduce their costs or increase the costs of competitors.

- **Differentiation Strategy.** Developing ways to differentiate a firm's products and services from those of its competitors or reduce the differentiation advantages of competitors. This strategy may allow a firm to focus its products or services to give it an advantage in particular segments or niches of a market.

- **Innovation Strategy.** Finding new ways of doing business. This strategy may involve developing unique products and services or entering unique markets or market niches. It may also involve making radical changes to the business processes for producing or distributing products and services that are so different from the way a business has been conducted that they alter the fundamental structure of an industry.

- **Growth Strategies.** Significantly expanding a company's capacity to produce goods and services, expanding into global markets, diversifying into new products and services, or integrating into related products and services.

- **Alliance Strategies.** Establishing new business linkages and alliances with customers, suppliers, competitors, consultants, and other companies. These linkages may include mergers, acquisitions, joint ventures, forming of "virtual companies," or other marketing, manufacturing, or distribution agreements between a business and its trading partners.

One additional point regarding these strategies is that they are not mutually exclusive. An organization may make use of one, some, or all of the strategies in varying degrees to manage the forces of competition. Therefore, a given activity could fall into one or more of the categories of competitive strategy. For example, implementing a system that allows customers to track their order or shipment online could be considered a form of differentiation if the other competitors in the marketplace do not offer this service. If they do offer the service, however, online order tracking would not serve to differentiate one organization from another.

If an organization offers its online package tracking system in a manner that allows its customers to access shipment information via not only a computer but a mobile phone as well, then such an action could fall into both the differentiation and innovation strategy categories. Think of it this way: Not everything innovative will serve to differentiate one organization from another. Likewise, not everything that serves to differentiate organizations is necessarily viewed as innovative. These types of observations are true for any combination of the competitive strategies, thus making them complementary to each other rather than mutually exclusive.

Strategic Uses of Information Technology

How can business managers use investments in information technology to support a firm's competitive strategies? Figure 2.3 answers this question with a summary of the many ways that information technology can help a business implement the five basic competitive strategies. Figure 2.4 provides examples of how specific companies have used strategic information systems to implement each of these five basic strategies for competitive advantage. Note the major use of Internet technologies for e-business and e-commerce applications. In the rest of this chapter, we discuss and provide examples of many strategic uses of information technology.

Other Strategic Initiatives

There are many strategic initiatives available to a firm in addition to the five basic strategies of cost leadership, differentiation, innovation, growth, and alliance. Let's look at several key strategies that also can be implemented with information technology. They include locking in customers or suppliers, building switching costs, raising barriers to entry, and leveraging investment in information technology.

FIGURE 2.3

A summary of how information technology can be used to implement the five basic competitive strategies. Many companies are using Internet technologies as the foundation for such strategies.

Basic Strategies in the Business Use of Information Technology
Lower Costs   ● Use IT to substantially reduce the cost of business processes.   ● Use IT to lower the costs of customers or suppliers.
Differentiate   ● Develop new IT features to differentiate products and services.   ● Use IT features to reduce the differentiation advantages of competitors.   ● Use IT features to focus products and services at selected market niches.
Innovate   ● Create new products and services that include IT components.   ● Develop unique new markets or market niches with the help of IT.   ● Make radical changes to business processes with IT that dramatically cut costs; improve quality, efficiency, or customer service; or shorten time to market.
Promote Growth   ● Use IT to manage regional and global business expansion.   ● Use IT to diversify and integrate into other products and services.
Develop Alliances   ● Use IT to create virtual organizations of business partners.   ● Develop interenterprise information systems linked by the Internet and extranets that support strategic business relationships with customers, suppliers, subcontractors, and others.

FIGURE 2.4 Examples of how, over time, companies have used information technology to implement five competitive strategies for strategic advantage.

Strategy	Company	Strategic Use of Information Technology	Business Benefit
Cost Leadership	Dell Computer Priceline.com eBay.com	Online build to order Online seller bidding Online auctions	Lowest-cost producer Buyer-set pricing Auction-set prices
Differentiation	AVNET Marshall Moen Inc. Consolidated Freightways	Customer/supplier of e-commerce Online customer design Customer online shipment tracking	Increase in market share Increase in market share Increase in market share
Innovation	Charles Schwab & Co. Federal Express Amazon.com	Online discount stock trading Online package tracking and flight management Online full-service customer systems	Market leadership Market leadership Market leadership
Growth	Citicorp Wal-Mart Toys 'R' Us Inc.	Global intranet Merchandise ordering by global satellite network POS inventory tracking	Increase in global market Market leadership Market leadership
Alliance	Wal-Mart/Procter & Gamble Cisco Systems Staples Inc. and Partners	Automatic inventory replenishment by supplier Virtual manufacturing alliances Online one-stop shopping with partners	Reduced inventory cost/increased sales Agile market leadership Increase in market share

FIGURE 2.5   Additional ways that information technology can be used to implement competitive strategies.

Other Strategic Uses of Information Technology
• Develop interenterprise information systems whose convenience and efficiency create switching costs that lock in customers or suppliers.
• Make major investments in advanced IT applications that build barriers to entry against industry competitors or outsiders.
• Include IT components in products and services to make substitution of competing products or services more difficult.
• Leverage investment in IS people, hardware, software, databases, and networks from operational uses into strategic applications.

Investments in information technology can allow a business to lock in customers and suppliers (and lock out competitors) by building valuable new relationships with them. These business relationships can become so valuable to customers or suppliers that they deter them from abandoning a company for its competitors or intimidate them into accepting less profitable business arrangements. Early attempts to use information systems technology in these relationships focused on significantly improving the quality of service to customers and suppliers in a firm's distribution, marketing, sales, and service activities. More recent projects characterize a move toward more innovative uses of information technology.

A major emphasis in strategic information systems has been to find ways to create switching costs in the relationships between a firm and its customers or suppliers. In other words, investments in information systems technology, such as those mentioned in the Timex example, can make customers or suppliers dependent on the continued use of innovative, mutually beneficial interenterprise information systems. They then become reluctant to pay the costs in time, money, effort, and inconvenience that it would take to switch to a company's competitors.

By making investments in information technology to improve its operations or promote innovation, a firm could also raise barriers to entry that would discourage or delay other companies from entering a market. Typically, these barriers increase the amount of investment or the complexity of the technology required to compete in an industry or a market segment. Such actions tend to discourage firms already in the industry and deter external firms from entering the industry.

Investing in information technology enables a firm to build strategic IT capabilities so that they can take advantage of opportunities when they arise. In many cases, this happens when a company invests in advanced computer-based information systems to improve the efficiency of its own business processes. Then, armed with this strategic technology platform, the firm can leverage investment in IT by developing new products and services that would not be possible without a strong IT capability. An important current example is the development of corporate intranets and extranets by many companies, which enables them to leverage their previous investments in Internet browsers, PCs, servers, and client/server networks. Figure 2.5 summarizes the additional strategic uses of IT we have just discussed.

Timex: Ticking with Product Innovation Software	To keep itself ticking, Timex Corp. has revamped the way it develops wristwatches with product innovation software that can help it quickly tailor new products for a rapidly changing market. For much of the company's 152 years, the watch industry was more about style than engineering, said Bernd Becker, vice president of product development at Timex. But in the "last 10 years, innovation has become the industry buzzword as consumers demand new features in their watches." Keeping track of those innovations and making them easier to build into products is now a key to staying competitive.

To that end, the company adopted a "stage-gate" approach from software vendor Sopheon PLC that uses milestones or "gates" at each step of the innovation process. It allows discussions, reviews, planning, and decisions to be analyzed by everyone from designers and engineers to product marketing staffers. The chosen product, Accolade, brings together cross-functional team members, from brand managers to engineers to manufacturing staff and finance specialists, on a global design project. The software helps organize information in a central database so that decisions can be made on whether to grow or kill a project. This kind of decision-making aspect of the software is one of the key ways by which Timex increases returns on innovation.

"In product development, you always have a large dose of uncertainty to manage," says development analyst Vasco Drecun. "The problem is that most companies use methods all developed from the Industrial Age, when things were more predictable. Those things are gone."

Better knowledge about products, market demand, production requirements, and other variables are essential for a company to remain competitive. "Knowledge will help you manage the risk," says Drecun. Using applications like Accolade helps companies maintain a high innovation level in their portfolio.

Source: Adapted from Todd Weiss, "Timex Ticking with New Product Innovation Software," *Computerworld*, June 20, 2006.

Competitive Advantage and Competitive Necessity

The constant struggle to achieve a measurable competitive advantage in an industry or marketplace occupies a significant portion of an organization's time and money. Creative and innovative marketing, research and development, and process reengineering, among many other activities, are used to gain that elusive and sometimes indescribable competitive advantage over rival firms.

The term *competitive advantage* is often used when referring to a firm that is leading an industry in some identifiable way such as sales, revenues, or new products. In fact, the definition of the term suggests a single condition under which competitive advantage can exist: *when a firm sustains profits that exceed the average for its industry, the firm is said to possess competitive advantage over its rivals*. In other words, competitive advantage is all about profits. Granted, sales, revenues, cost management, and new products all contribute in some way to profits, but unless the contribution results in sustained profits above the average for the industry, no measurable competitive advantage has been achieved. The real problem with a competitive advantage, however, is that it normally doesn't last very long and is generally not sustainable over the long term. Figure 2.6 illustrates this cycle. Once a firm figures out how to gain an advantage over its competitors (normally through some form of innovation), the competitors figure out how it was done through a process referred to as organizational learning. To combat the competitive advantage, they adopt the same, or some similar, innovation. Once this occurs, everyone in the industry is doing what everyone else is doing; what was once a competitive advantage is now a competitive necessity. Once a strategy or action becomes a competitive necessity, instead of creating an advantage, the strategy or action becomes necessary to compete and do business in the industry. When this happens, someone has to figure out a new way to gain a competitive edge, and the cycle starts all over again.

Every organization is looking for a way to gain competitive advantage, and many have successfully used strategic information systems to help them achieve it. The important point to remember is that no matter how it is achieved, competitive advantage doesn't last forever. Arie de Geus, head of strategic planning for Royal Dutch Shell, thinks there may be one way to sustain it: "The ability to learn faster than your competitors may be the only sustainable competitive advantage in the future."

FIGURE 2.6

The move from innovation to competitive advantage quickly becomes competitive necessity when other firms learn how to respond strategically.

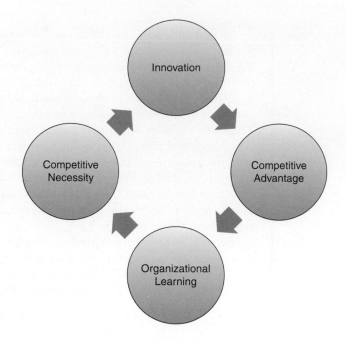

Building a Customer-Focused Business

The driving force behind world economic growth has changed from manufacturing volume to improving customer value. As a result, the key success factor for many firms is maximizing customer value.

For many companies, the chief business value of becoming a customer-focused business lies in its ability to help them keep customers loyal, anticipate their future needs, respond to customer concerns, and provide top-quality customer service. This strategic focus on customer value recognizes that quality, rather than price, has become the primary determinant in a customer's perception of value. Companies that consistently offer the best value from the customer's perspective are those that keep track of their customers' individual preferences; keep up with market trends; supply products, services, and information anytime and anywhere; and provide customer services tailored to individual needs. Thus, Internet technologies have created a strategic opportunity for companies, large and small, to offer fast, responsive, high-quality products and services tailored to individual customer preferences.

Internet technologies can make customers the focal point of customer relationship management (CRM) and other e-business applications. In combination, CRM systems and Internet, intranet, and extranet Web sites create new channels for interactive communications within a company, as well as communication with customers, suppliers, business partners, and others in the external environment. Such communications enable continual interaction with customers by most business functions and encourage cross-functional collaboration with customers in product development, marketing, delivery, service, and technical support. We will discuss CRM systems in Chapter 8.

Typically, customers use the Internet to ask questions, lodge complaints, evaluate products, request support, and make and track their purchases. Using the Internet and corporate intranets, specialists in business functions throughout the enterprise can contribute to an effective response. This ability encourages the creation of cross-functional discussion groups and problem-solving teams dedicated to customer involvement, service, and support. Even the Internet and extranet links to suppliers and business partners can be used to enlist them in a way of doing business that ensures the prompt delivery of quality components and services to meet a company's commitments to its customers. This process is how a business demonstrates its focus on customer value.

Figure 2.7 illustrates the interrelationships in a customer-focused business. Intranets, extranets, e-commerce Web sites, and Web-enabled internal business processes

FIGURE 2.7 How a customer-focused business builds customer value and loyalty using Internet technologies.

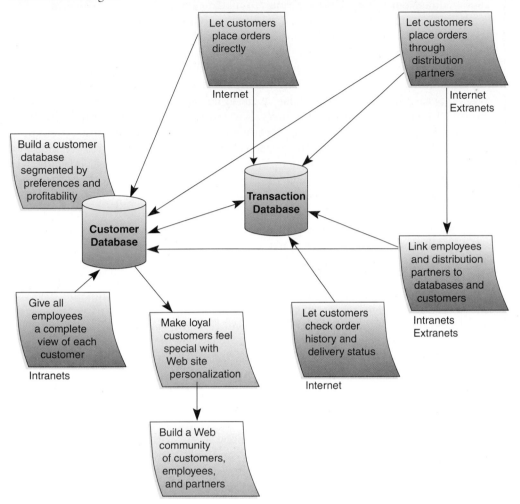

form the invisible IT platform that supports this e-business model. The platform enables the business to focus on targeting the kinds of customers it really wants and "owning" the customer's total business experience with the company. A successful business streamlines all business processes that affect its customers and develops CRM systems that provide its employees with a complete view of each customer, so they have the information they need to offer their customers top-quality personalized service. A customer-focused business helps its e-commerce customers help themselves while also helping them do their jobs. Finally, a successful business nurtures an online community of customers, employees, and business partners that builds great customer loyalty as it fosters cooperation to provide an outstanding customer experience. Let's review a real-world example.

Universal Orlando: IT Decisions Driven by Customer Data	Michelle McKenna is the CIO of Universal Orlando Resort, but also a mother of two and the planner of family vacations. In fact, she thinks of herself first as a theme park customer, second as a senior leader at Universal, and finally as the company's CIO. "Recently we were brainstorming new events that would bring more Florida residents to our theme parks during off-peak tourist periods. Our in-house marketing group was pitching proposals, and

I offered the idea of a Guitar Hero competition. Everyone loved it. But that idea didn't come from being a CIO—it came from being a mother of two," she says.

"Thinking like our customers and focusing on our company's markets are among the most important ways we can fulfill our responsibility to contribute to informed decision making," says McKenna. Moving forward, it's more critical than ever for CIOs to study market trends and find ways to maximize business opportunities.

Universal Orlando is one of many brands in the travel and entertainment industry competing for discretionary dollars spent by consumers on leisure time and vacations. Of course, the competition boils down to a market of one—the individual consumer. People often assume that because of the high volume of guests, the experience at Universal Orlando has to be geared for the masses. But digital technology now enables guests to customize their experience. For example, the new Hollywood Rip Ride RockIt Roller Coaster will allow guests to customize their ride experience by choosing the music that plays around them while on the roller coaster. When the ride ends, guests will be able to edit video footage of that experience into a music video to keep, share with friends, or post online.

Any CIO can take a few steps to get market savvy. Management gets weekly data about what happened in the park and what the spending trends are per guest. CIOs should get copied on any reports like that. They should study them and look for patterns. "Don't be afraid to ask questions about it; give yourself permission to be a smart (and inquisitive) businessperson. When I first joined the company and asked about market issues, people looked at me and thought, 'Why did she ask that? It doesn't have anything to do with technology.' Over time they realized that I needed to understand our data in order to do my job," says McKenna.

Knowledge of market data helps Universal Orlando drill down to understand what is really happening in business. For example, trends indicated that annual pass holders—Florida residents, primarily—spend less on food, merchandise, and other items than day-pass guests.

It turned out that some pass holders do spend on par with day guests, particularly when they attend special events, Mardi Gras and Halloween Horror Nights. "This analysis showed that we needed to segment those annual pass holders more deeply in order to better understand them and market to them. So we are building a new data warehouse and business intelligence tools that will calculate spending by hour and by pass type. The initiative started in IT, and we can find many similar opportunities if we look at market details and ask questions," McKenna says.

Source: Adapted from Michelle McKenna, "Customer Data Should Drive IT Decisions," *CIO Magazine*, June 2, 2008.

The Value Chain and Strategic IS

Let's look at another important concept that can help you identify opportunities for strategic information systems. The **value chain** concept, developed by Michael Porter, is illustrated in Figure 2.8. It views a firm as a series, chain, or network of basic activities that add value to its products and services and thus add a margin of value to both the firm and its customers. In the value chain conceptual framework, some business activities are primary processes; others are support processes. *Primary processes* are those business activities that are directly related to the manufacture of products or the delivery of services to the customer. In contrast, *support processes* are those business activities that help support the day-to-day operation of the business and that indirectly contribute to the products or services of the organization. This framework can highlight where competitive strategies can best be applied in a business. So managers and business professionals should try to develop a variety of strategic uses of the Internet and other technologies for those basic processes that add the most value to a company's products or services and thus to the overall business value of the company.

FIGURE 2.8 The value chain of a firm. Note the examples of the variety of strategic information systems that can be applied to a firm's basic business processes for competitive advantage.

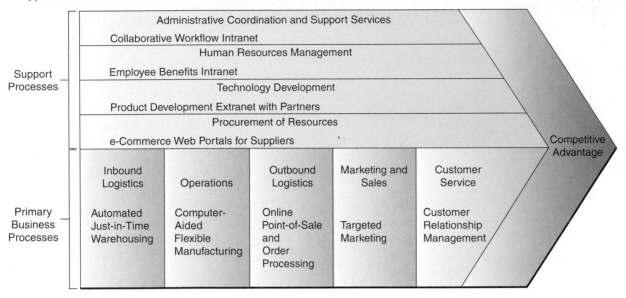

Value Chain Examples

Figure 2.8 provides examples of how and where information technologies can be applied to basic business processes using the value chain framework. For example, the figure illustrates that collaborative workflow intranets can increase the communications and collaboration required to improve administrative coordination and support services dramatically. An employee benefits intranet can help the human resources management function provide employees with easy, self-service access to their benefits information. Extranets enable a company and its global business partners to use the Web to design products and processes jointly. Finally, e-commerce Web portals can dramatically improve procurement of resources by providing online marketplaces for a firm's suppliers.

The value chain model in Figure 2.8 also identifies examples of strategic applications of information systems technology to primary business processes. These include automated just-in-time warehousing systems to support inbound logistic processes that involve inventory storage, computer-aided flexible manufacturing systems, as well as online point-of-sale and order processing systems to improve the outbound logistics processes that handle customer orders. Information systems can also support marketing and sales processes by developing an interactive targeted marketing capability on the Internet and the Web. Finally, a coordinated and integrated customer relationship management system can dramatically improve customer service.

Thus, the value chain concept can help you identify where and how to apply the strategic capabilities of information technology. It shows how various types of information technologies might be applied to specific business processes to help a firm gain competitive advantages in the marketplace.

SECTION II   Using Information Technology for Strategic Advantage

Strategic Uses of IT

Organizations may view and use information technology in many ways. For example, companies may choose to use information systems strategically, or they may be content to use IT to support efficient everyday operations. If a company emphasized strategic business uses of information technology, its management would view IT as a major competitive differentiator. They would then devise business strategies that use IT to develop products, services, and capabilities that give the company major advantages in the markets in which it competes. In this section, we provide many examples of such strategic business applications of information technology. See Figure 2.9.

Read the Real World Case 2 about using information technology to redesign how a business works. We can learn a lot about the advantages gained through the appropriate use of information technology and mobile communications from this case.

Reengineering Business Processes

One of the most important implementations of competitive strategies is business process reengineering (BPR), often simply called *reengineering*. Reengineering is a fundamental rethinking and radical redesign of business processes to achieve dramatic improvements in cost, quality, speed, and service. BPR combines a strategy of promoting business innovation with a strategy of making major improvements to business processes so that a company can become a much stronger and more successful competitor in the marketplace.

However, Figure 2.10 points out that although the potential payback of reengineering is high, so too is its risk of failure and level of disruption to the organizational environment. Making radical changes to business processes to dramatically improve efficiency and effectiveness is not an easy task. For example, many companies have used cross-functional enterprise resource planning (ERP) software to reengineer, automate, and integrate their manufacturing, distribution, finance, and human resource business processes. Although many companies have reported impressive gains with such ERP reengineering projects, many others either have experienced dramatic failures or did not achieve the improvements they sought.

Many companies have found that *organizational redesign* approaches are an important enabler of reengineering, along with the use of information technology. For example, one common approach is the use of self-directed cross-functional or multi-disciplinary *process teams*. Employees from several departments or specialties, including engineering, marketing, customer service, and manufacturing, may work as a team on the product development process. Another example is the use of *case managers*, who handle almost all tasks in a business process instead of splitting tasks among many different specialists.

The Role of Information Technology

Information technology plays a major role in reengineering most business processes. The speed, information-processing capabilities, and connectivity of computers and Internet technologies can substantially increase the efficiency of business processes, as well as communications and collaboration among the people responsible for their operation and management. For example, the order management process illustrated in Figure 2.11 is vital to the success of most companies. Many of them are reengineering this process with ERP software and Web-enabled e-business and e-commerce systems, as outlined in Figure 2.12. Let's take a look at an example.

REAL WORLD CASE 2

For Companies Both Big and Small: Running a Business on Smartphones

In early 2006, San-Antonio, Texas-based CPS Energy, the nation's largest municipally owned energy provider, was by all accounts riding the road to riches. The company had the highest bond ratings of any such utility provider. Its workforce and customer base in general expressed satisfaction. And most important, it was profitable. In other words, there were no external signs that the company was about to launch a technology program that would redefine the way it did business and reshape its workforce of roughly 4,000.

There weren't external signs, but for those in the know, including Christopher Barron, CPS Energy's VP and CIO, it couldn't have been more clear that a change was imminent—and that the future of the company might depend on it.

"We had a much larger workforce than a business our size maybe should have," Barron says.

Barron looked at other companies with large mobile workforces like its own, companies like UPS and FedEx, and saw a huge disparity in the way his business was operating. For instance, specific CPS workers had little or no access to IT systems and resources while away from the office or warehouse. They were often required to visit work sites or customer locations to diagnose issues or suggest fixes before reporting back to the appropriate departments or parties, which would then initiate the next step of the resolution process. That could mean dispatching additional workers, and the whole ordeal could take days.

"If we kept with the amount of manual labor that it took for us to accomplish that work, we would not be in the position to be competitive in the future," Barron says. From this realization, the company's Magellan Program was born.

FIGURE 2.9

Companies of all sizes can benefit from using smartphones to improve their business processes.

The Magellan Program was envisioned by Barron and his colleagues as a way to better mobilize and connect its traditionally siloed workforce to the people and systems they needed to do their jobs. The goals of the program: extend CPS's networking infrastructure, build its own secure Wi-Fi networks in offices and warehouses, and deploy smartphones and custom mobile applications to all CPS staffers who didn't currently have a laptop or other mobile device. For Barron, the first and most significant challenge in deploying smartphones to such a large user base was getting executive buy-in.

"One of our biggest headaches has been, and continues to be, the perception that the technology brings little to the table other than e-mail, and it costs a lot," Barron says.

"For a CIO to try to eliminate all the resistance from a senior executive might take forever," Barron says. "So rather than try to get to the execs and mollify all their fears about cost, usage and safety, we've gone to specific groups, engineers, line workers, office workers, and because it's so cheap we've been able to give the devices out on 'experimental basis.' There's so much value in these handheld devices and two or three applications that they prove themselves," he says. "You just have to get them into the hands of the people that actually need to use them in order to demonstrate that."

Three innovative ways CPS staffers employ their smartphones are as digital cameras at work sites, as GPS tracking mechanisms, and as emergency notification receivers. In the past, CPS might have had to dispatch a small group of "generalist" workers to a service call to make sure the correct person was there. Today, a single worker can visit a site, take a photo of a damaged piece of equipment or infrastructure, and then send it back to headquarters or the office.

Then an expert diagnoses the issue and sends along instructions to fix the problem or dispatches the appropriate worker—who's available immediately via voice e-mail and SMS text via smartphone.

"The Magellan Program, through the use of smartphones and other technology, has or will empower all employees, no matter what work they perform, to become part of the greater company's 'thought network,'" Barron says. "Each person is now like a node in our network." The company is also seeing significant gains in supply chain efficiency related to Magellan and the smartphone deployment, he says. For instance, smartphones help speed up the purchase order process, because in the past a specific person or group of people needed to be on-site to approve orders. Now the approvers can be practically anywhere with cellular coverage. The company's supply chain buyers can also visit warehouses to work with the people who actually order parts, leading to faster order times and more proactive supply chain management overall. In just one year, the time it took to close purchasing and procurement deals decreased by more than 65 percent. Also, inventory levels were reduced by more than $8 million since the Magellan Program began.

In addition, both employee and customer satisfaction levels are up, Barron notes, because staffers now have more access to corporate systems and information and feel closer to the business. Because CPS can now resolve more customer issues with fewer processes, they've reduced the time it takes to complete most service calls, leading to happier customers. In fact, the company received the highest score in J.D. Power and Associates 2007 Gas Utility Residential Customer Satisfaction Survey.

The technology, however, is no longer the exclusive purview of large companies with significant IT budgets, at least not anymore. Lloyd's Construction in Eagan, Minnesota, might not seem as if it needs flashy phone software. The $9-million-a-year demolition and carting company has been run by the same family for the past 24 years. Lloyd's takes down commercial and residential buildings, and then hauls them away. What could be more simple? That is, if wrangling 100 employees, 30 trucks, and more than 400 dumpsters can be called simple. Coordinating those moving parts is crucial to growing the business—and to saving the sanity of Stephanie Lloyd, 41, who has run the company for the past four years. Until recently, Lloyd's used a hodgepodge of spreadsheets, paper ledgers, and accounting software on company PCs to keep track of its workers and equipment. To make matters worse, the company used radios to coordinate with its workers on the job—and the more cell phone towers that came online in Minnesota, the worse Lloyd's radio reception got. It was time, the Lloyds decided, to drag their company into the 21st-century world of smartphones.

Lloyd's considered a half-dozen mobile-productivity software suites before settling on eTrace, which happened to come from a company called GearWorks based just across town. Not only was GearWorks local, but its software worked on Sprint Nextel's i560 and i850 phones, which are aimed at the construction industry. Lloyd's had already started buying these push-to-talk phones to wean workers from their dying radios. Immediately, there were troubles with technophobic staff. Employees had to be guided up a steep learning curve in order to master even basic features on their new phones.

For 18 months the two systems ran side by side: eTrace as it was phased in, and the old paper-and-pencil system as it was phased out. Accounting inconsistencies quickly crept in.

And eTrace gave rise to a delicate labor problem. The software featured integrated mapping and travel data that showed the real-time locations of all company assets. To their chagrin, the Lloyds discovered that those assets were spending too much time parked outside the same lunch spots—ones that were not on prescribed routes. Lloyd was sympathetic to workers' needs for breaks—"we've all worked demolition here," she says—but quickly clamped down on unauthorized ones.

GearWorks' CEO says the challenges Lloyd's faced are to be expected. "All these products operate under the ominous pendulum of challenge and opportunity," says Todd Krautkremer, 47. "But our software does a good job of letting the customer control that rate of change in the business."

Once the deployment dust had settled, the savings became clear. The company employs 12 drivers, 22 foremen, and 7 office workers who use 41 phones running eTrace. The company buys an unlimited data package for each phone, which totals about $4,000 a month. Add other networking charges and Lloyd's spends about $50,000 a year for a complete business, accounting, and communications solution.

Before eTrace, the company paid an accountant 40 hours a week to do the books. Now that person comes in one day a week for 6 hours, saving roughly $1,000 a week.

Data entry and job logging by the dispatcher and foremen, Lloyd says, is roughly 1½ times faster than paper and radio. More efficient routing has cut fuel costs by about 30%. And employees have stopped making unauthorized stops. Lloyd estimates a net improvement in performance of 10–12 percent, or roughly $1 million for 2007—not a bad return on $50,000.

"It really does work," she says.

Source: Adapted from Jonathan Blum, "Running an Entire Business from Smartphones," *FORTUNE Small Business*, March 12, 2008; and Al Sacco, "How Smartphones Help CPS Energy Innovate and Boost the Bottom Line," *CIO Magazine*, July 11, 2008.

CASE STUDY QUESTIONS

1. In which ways do smartphones help these companies be more profitable? To what extent are improvements in performance coming from revenue increases or cost reductions? Provide several examples from the case.

2. The companies described in the case encountered a fair amount of resistance from employees when introducing smartphone technologies. Why do you think this happened? What could companies do to improve the reception of these initiatives? Develop two alternative propositions.

3. CPS Energy and Lloyd's Construction used smartphones to make existing processes more efficient. How could they have used the technology to create new products and services for their customers? Include at least one recommendation for each organization.

REAL WORLD ACTIVITIES

1. In addition to the companies featured in the case, others like FedEx and UPS, which have large mobile workforces, heavily use mobile communication technologies. What other companies could benefit from these innovations?

2. Go online and research uses of smartphones in industries different from the ones reviewed here. Prepare a report to share your findings.

3. Use the Internet to research the latest technological developments in smartphones, and discuss how those could be used by companies to deliver value to customers and shareholders.

FIGURE 2.10

Some of the key ways that business process reengineering differs from business improvement.

	Business Improvement	Business Process Reengineering
Level of Change	Incremental	Radical
Process Change	Improved new version of process	Brand-new process
Starting Point	Existing processes	Clean slate
Frequency of Change	One-time or continuous	Periodic one-time change
Time Required	Short	Long
Typical Scope	Narrow, within functions	Broad, cross-functional
Horizon	Past and present	Future
Participation	Bottom-up	Top-down
Path to Execution	Cultural	Cultural, structural
Primary Enabler	Statistical control	Information technology
Risk	Moderate	High

Source: Adapted from Howard Smith and Peter Fingar, *Business Process Management: The Third Wave* (Tampa, FL: Meghan-Kiffer Press, 2003), p. 118.

FIGURE 2.11   The order management process consists of several business processes and crosses the boundaries of traditional business functions.

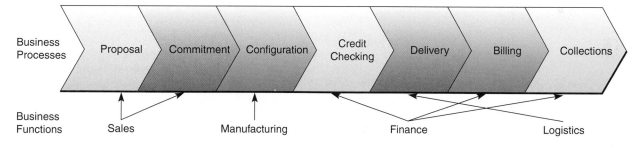

FIGURE 2.12

Examples of information technologies that support reengineering the order management processes.

Reengineering Order Management
● Customer relationship management systems using corporate intranets and the Internet.
● Supplier-managed inventory systems using the Internet and extranets.
● Cross-functional ERP software for integrating manufacturing, distribution, finance, and human resource processes.
● Customer-accessible e-commerce Web sites for order entry, status checking, payment, and service.
● Customer, product, and order status databases accessed via intranets and extranets by employees and suppliers.

Making Workflow Work and Flow: Not Entirely Rocket Science

From a business perspective, workflow is a way to make people, information, and computers work together consistently and efficiently to produce the results the business needs. In effect, workflow applies the equivalent of systems analysis to the entire process, not just to the part done on a machine. From a bottom line perspective, adding workflow to a process saves money, increases customer satisfaction, gets results quicker, and largely eliminates things getting lost in the shuffle. From a manager's perspective, the most important benefits to workflow are saving cost and saving time.

As an example of a typical workflow, Wilhelm Ederyd, a technical project manager at Bonver, a major Scandinavian distributor of home entertainment products, cites building support for individuals and businesses ordering broadband services via the Internet, postal mail, and e-mail. "This can be a rather complex process, with the need for the systems and personnel to interact efficiently in order to make the process slim and pleasant to the customer," Ederyd explains. You can think of workflow as systems analysis that mixes humans, machines, documents, and other information.

In Ederyd's case, he designed the process for ordering and installing the broadband connection for the customer. Typically that means—given a whole raft of business requirements generated by others—working out how the process would flow from the customer's initial contact to the actual installation.

Ederyd's example is a classic case: a fairly complex, multistep process where computers and people have to interact as smoothly and efficiently as possible. It's also a process that is exposed to the customer, and delays or mistakes can damage customer relationships. An advantage of a well-designed workflow process is that it can serve as a template that can be applied quickly to similar processes. "Once you're comfortable with workflow in your organization, it will allow you to implement new business models much faster than your competitors," says Ederyd. "The cost and complexity of doing so is now manageable."

Craig Cameron, a workflow consultant based in Melbourne, cites the example of a major Australian bank that wanted to apply workflow to the process used to order large amounts of hardware. "They needed to go through all these checks and make sure that the right people had signed off on it," Cameron says. "So we implemented a system to do that." This was fine until the other divisions of the bank found out about the new process. "We found out later we'd only created a system for three or so of their teams and suddenly another 15 or so teams wanted to be involved," Cameron says. "Instead of having to do a complete restart, we're extracting what we've already done and cutting and pasting it into a new system. Then we hit a button to create the end user interface."

Workflow isn't rocket science, but it isn't magic either. While workflow can make major improvements in the way an organization runs, it can only do so if the principles are applied correctly. Fundamentally making workflow work for you comes down to understanding the processes that make your business work.

Source: Adapted from Rick Cook, "Making Workflow Work and Flow for You," *CIO Magazine*, October 23, 2007.

Becoming an Agile Company

We are changing from a competitive environment in which mass-market products and services were standardized, long-lived, information-poor, and exchanged in one-time transactions, to an environment in which companies compete globally with niche market products and services that are individualized, short-lived, information-rich, and exchanged on an ongoing basis with customers.

Agility in business performance means the ability of a company to prosper in rapidly changing, continually fragmenting global markets for high-quality, high-performance, customer-configured products and services. An agile company can make a profit in markets with broad product ranges and short model lifetimes and can produce orders individually and in arbitrary lot sizes. It supports *mass customization* by offering individualized products while maintaining high volumes of production. Agile companies depend heavily on Internet technologies to integrate and manage their business processes while they provide the information-processing power to treat their many customers as individuals.

To be an agile company, a business must use four basic strategies. First, the business must ensure that customers perceive the products or services of an agile company as solutions to their individual problems. Thus, it can price products on the basis of their value as solutions, rather than their cost to produce. Second, an agile company cooperates with customers, suppliers, other companies, and even with its competitors. This cooperation allows a business to bring products to market as rapidly and cost-effectively as possible, no matter where resources are located or who owns them. Third, an agile company organizes so that it thrives on change and uncertainty. It uses flexible organizational structures keyed to the requirements of different and constantly changing customer opportunities. Fourth, an agile company leverages the impact of its people and the knowledge they possess. By nurturing an entrepreneurial spirit, an agile company provides powerful incentives for employee responsibility, adaptability, and innovation.

Figure 2.13 summarizes another useful way to think about agility in business. This framework emphasizes the roles customers, business partners, and information technology can play in developing and maintaining the strategic agility of a company.

FIGURE 2.13 How information technology can help a company be an agile competitor, with the help of customers and business partners.

Type of Agility	Description	Role of IT	Example
Customer	Ability to co-opt customers in the exploitation of innovation opportunities • As sources of innovation ideas • As cocreators of innovation • As users in testing ideas or helping other users learn about the idea	Technologies for building and enhancing virtual customer communities for product design, feedback, and testing	eBay customers are its de facto product development team because they post an average of 10,000 messages each week to share tips, point out glitches, and lobby for changes
Partnering	Ability to leverage assets, knowledge, and competencies of suppliers, distributors, contract manufacturers, and logistics providers in the exploration and exploitation of innovation opportunities	Technologies facilitating interfirm collaboration, such as collaborative platforms and portals, supply chain systems	Yahoo! has accomplished a significant transformation of its service from a search engine into a portal by initiating numerous partnerships to provide content and other media-related services from its Web site
Operational	Ability to accomplish speed, accuracy, and cost economy in the exploitation of innovation opportunities	Technologies for modularization and integration of business processes	Ingram Micro, a global wholesaler, has deployed an integrated trading system allowing its customers and suppliers to connect directly to its procurement and ERP systems

Source: Adapted from V. Sambamurthy, Anandhi Bhaharadwaj, and Varun Grover, "Shaping Agility Through Digital Options: Reconceptualizing the Role of Information Technology in Contemporary Firms," *MIS Quarterly*, June 2003, p. 246.

FIGURE 2.14 A virtual company uses the Internet, intranets, and extranets to form virtual workgroups and support alliances with business partners.

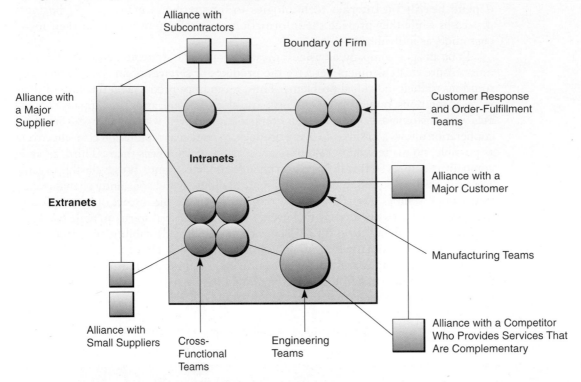

Notice how information technology can enable a company to develop relationships with its customers in virtual communities that help it be an agile innovator. As we will see repeatedly throughout this textbook, information technologies enable a company to partner with its suppliers, distributors, contract manufacturers, and others via collaborative portals and other Web-based supply chain systems that significantly improve its agility in exploiting innovative business opportunities.

Creating a Virtual Company

In today's dynamic global business environment, forming a virtual company can be one of the most important strategic uses of information technology. A virtual company (also called a *virtual corporation* or *virtual organization*) is an organization that uses information technology to link people, organizations, assets, and ideas.

Figure 2.14 illustrates that virtual companies typically form virtual workgroups and alliances with business partners that are interlinked by the Internet, intranets, and extranets. Notice that this company has organized internally into clusters of process and cross-functional teams linked by intranets. It has also developed alliances and extranet links that form interenterprise information systems with suppliers, customers, subcontractors, and competitors. Thus, virtual companies create flexible and adaptable virtual workgroups and alliances keyed to exploit fast-changing business opportunities.

Virtual Company Strategies

Why do people form virtual companies? It is the best way to implement key business strategies and alliances that promise to ensure success in today's turbulent business climate. Several major reasons for virtual companies stand out and are summarized in Figure 2.15.

For example, a business may not have the time or resources to develop the necessary manufacturing and distribution infrastructure, personnel competencies, and information technologies to take full advantage of a new market opportunity in a timely

FIGURE 2.15

The basic business strategies of virtual companies.

Strategies of Virtual Companies
● Share infrastructure and risk with alliance partners.
● Link complementary core competencies.
● Reduce concept-to-cash time through sharing.
● Increase facilities and market coverage.
● Gain access to new markets and share market or customer loyalty.
● Migrate from selling products to selling solutions.

manner. It can assemble the components it needs to provide a world-class solution for customers and capture the market opportunity only by quickly forming a virtual company through a strategic alliance of all-star partners. Today, of course, the Internet, intranets, extranets, and a variety of other Internet technologies are vital components in creating such successful solutions.

United Kingdom's National Rail Enquiries: Everything They Do Is Outsourced

In-house technology is no longer an operational prerequisite, thanks to outsourcing. Software, servers, Internet connectivity, and even whole operations like payroll and HR can be sourced from third parties and branded, so neither the customers nor employees of the business need ever know these mechanisms reside outside the company headquarters.

That being said, the fact that the United Kingdom's rail information service, National Rail Enquiries (NRE), served 55 million customers online last year alone and relies on extensive self-service and contact center service channels but has a core staff of only 21 people—which is no small achievement. "NRE has about 22 suppliers of various services. Everything we do is outsourced. We have 1,500 people in call centers alone, who all work for NRE," says Chris Scoggins, NRE's CEO. The NRE's telephone information service was born of the creation of the organization in 1996 with the privatization of British Rail. Since then, it has expanded to include automated telephone services and a very successful real-time online train time and journey planning service.

Scoggins says NRE has a strategy of maintaining a number of suppliers to effectively play them off against each other and raise the stakes in terms of demonstrating service excellence. "We have the maximum number of suppliers we can manage effectively. But also, and perhaps more importantly, we need the right number of suppliers to maintain a competitive market for the services they run. In some areas, we have a strategy to build up a number of niche players in the market, otherwise we are relying on one supplier."

"What we're trying to do is move toward a number of long-term relationships with partners we trust and give more work to them," Scoggins says. "Contracts are aligned to incentives related to achieving our business objectives and it's up to the supplier to outperform the minimum standard. If they demonstrate they can deliver over and above that then they get more work." Despite heading up a vast, virtual company, Scoggins says there is still pressure to drive business improvement and success. "When I joined there was no real self-service provision for the customer. NRE was a very big, outsourced call center with virtually no other provision for finding information. I saw this as a huge opportunity driven by two things. The first was that customer needs should be met by whichever channel is most convenient for them; the second was our call centers, which have the most volatile volumes in Europe."

NRE is always seeking to be proactive and do new things, like the speech recognition technology they use with their telephone TrainTracker service. "It is the most sophisticated mass-market speech recognition service in the world," notes Scoggins. And adds: "I regard our outsourcing suppliers as part of our team, and my job is getting my team excited and encouraged to do the job in hand."

Source: Adapted from Miya Knights, "Everything We Do Is Outsourced," *CIO Magazine*, June 13, 2007.

Building a Knowledge-Creating Company

In an economy where the only certainty is uncertainty, the one sure source of lasting competitive advantage is knowledge. When markets shift, technologies proliferate, competitors multiply, and products become obsolete almost overnight, successful companies are those that consistently create new knowledge, disseminate it widely throughout the organization, and quickly embody it in new technologies and products. These activities define the "knowledge-creating" company, whose sole business is continuous innovation.

Many companies today can only realize lasting competitive advantage if they become knowledge-creating companies or learning organizations. That means consistently creating new business knowledge, disseminating it widely throughout the company, and quickly building the new knowledge into their products and services.

Knowledge-creating companies exploit two kinds of knowledge. One is *explicit knowledge*, which is the data, documents, and things written down or stored on computers. The other kind is *tacit knowledge*, or the "how-tos" of knowledge, which resides in workers. Tacit knowledge can often represent some of the most important information within an organization. Long-time employees of a company often "know" many things about how to manufacture a product, deliver the service, deal with a particular vendor, or operate an essential piece of equipment. This tacit knowledge is not recorded or codified anywhere because it has evolved in the employee's mind through years of experience. Furthermore, much of this tacit knowledge is never shared with anyone who might be in a position to record it in a more formal way because there is often little incentive to do so or simply, "Nobody ever asked."

As illustrated in Figure 2.16, successful knowledge management creates techniques, technologies, systems, and rewards for getting employees to share what they know and make better use of accumulated workplace and enterprise knowledge. In that way, employees of a company are leveraging knowledge as they do their jobs.

FIGURE 2.16

Knowledge management can be viewed as three levels of techniques, technologies, and systems that promote the collection, organization, access, sharing, and use of workplace and enterprise knowledge.

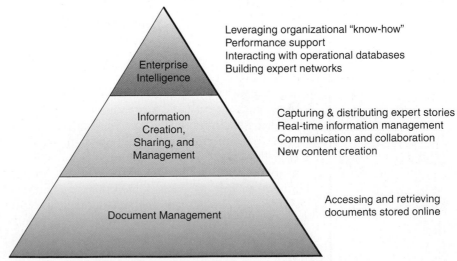

Source: Adapted from Marc Rosenberg, *e-Learning: Strategies for Delivering Knowledge in the Digital Age* (New York: McGraw-Hill, 2001), p. 70.

Knowledge Management Systems

Making personal knowledge available to others is the central activity of the knowledge-creating company. It takes place continuously and at all levels of the organization.

Knowledge management has thus become one of the major strategic uses of information technology. Many companies are building knowledge management systems (KMS) to manage organizational learning and business know-how. The goal of such systems is to help knowledge workers create, organize, and make available important business knowledge, wherever and whenever it's needed in an organization. This information includes processes, procedures, patents, reference works, formulas, "best practices," forecasts, and fixes. As you will see in Chapter 10, Internet and intranet Web sites, groupware, data mining, knowledge bases, and online discussion groups are some of the key technologies that may be used by a KMS.

Knowledge management systems also facilitate organizational learning and knowledge creation. They are designed to provide rapid feedback to knowledge workers, encourage behavior changes by employees, and significantly improve business performance. As the organizational learning process continues and its knowledge base expands, the knowledge-creating company works to integrate its knowledge into its business processes, products, and services. This integration helps the company become a more innovative and agile provider of high-quality products and customer services, as well as a formidable competitor in the marketplace. Now let's close this chapter with an example of knowledge management strategies from the real world.

Intec Engineering: Smarter by the Hour

It's hard to place a value on knowledge management systems. Their ability to generate income is often measured indirectly; their links to cost savings frequently seem tenuous. The return on investment is hard to quantify. Too often, the case for implementing a system to leverage intellectual capital and expertise rests mainly on intuition: It seems like a good idea. But intuition wasn't nearly enough to sell executives at Intec Engineering Partnership Ltd., a company whose dedication to thrift is exceeded only by its passion for sharing knowledge.

An engineering firm serving the oil and gas industry, Intec is headquartered in Houston with offices throughout the world. As Intec grew through expansion and international acquisitions, it became more difficult to keep track of and access information. In fact, according to KPMG International, 6 out of 10 employees say difficulty in accessing undocumented knowledge is a major problem. A group of Intec engineers volunteered to work on the problem of how to better capture lessons learned and share knowledge among them. They diagrammed how they solved engineering problems and envisioned an ideal process: An engineer with a question would go to a knowledge database that would either provide an answer or refer him to an expert. All new knowledge would be automatically captured and stored in the database. Intec shopped around and selected software from AskMe Corp. as the product most likely to facilitate Intec's problem-solving model.

The pilot, called AskIntec, began in May 2002. Three months later, it had exceeded all of the performance and user metrics, and ROI calculations projected an annual return of 133 percent. After nearly a year, the system is paying off almost exactly as projected. "Our numbers were pretty spot-on, but they're going up," says CIO Fran Steele, noting that the company estimates payback of 50 percent more next year as nonengineering employees are added and the system becomes embedded in the culture.

"Some of the return on information is not quantified just by how quickly you can do something, but by the fact that you can do it at all," says Steele. In the end, customers profit from Intec's knowledge management investment. "If we can cut weeks off a project and help them get their facility ready earlier, they can get to market sooner and get that revenue earlier," she says. That's the ultimate value.

Source: Adapted from Kathleen Melymuka, "Knowledge Management Helps Intec Get Smarter by the Hour," *Computerworld*, June 23, 2003.

Summary

- **Strategic Uses of Information Technology.** Information technologies can support many competitive strategies. They can help a business cut costs, differentiate and innovate in its products and services, promote growth, develop alliances, lock in customers and suppliers, create switching costs, raise barriers to entry, and leverage its investment in IT resources. Thus, information technology can help a business gain a competitive advantage in its relationships with customers, suppliers, competitors, new entrants, and producers of substitute products. Refer to Figures 2.3 and 2.5 for summaries of the uses of information technology for strategic advantage.

- **Building a Customer-Focused Business.** A key strategic use of Internet technologies is to build a company that develops its business value by making customer value its strategic focus. Customer-focused companies use Internet, intranet, and extranet e-commerce Web sites and services to keep track of their customers' preferences; to supply products, services, and information anytime, anywhere; and to provide services tailored to the individual needs of the customers.

- **Reengineering Business Processes.** Information technology is a key ingredient in reengineering business operations because it enables radical changes to business processes that dramatically improve their efficiency and effectiveness. Internet technologies can play a major role in supporting innovative changes in the design of workflows, job requirements, and organizational structures in a company.

- **Becoming an Agile Company.** A business can use information technology to help it become an agile

company. Then it can prosper in rapidly changing markets with broad product ranges and short model lifetimes in which it must process orders in arbitrary lot sizes; it can also offer its customers customized products while it maintains high volumes of production. An agile company depends heavily on Internet technologies to help it respond to its customers with customized solutions, and to cooperate with its customers, suppliers, and other businesses to bring products to market as rapidly and cost-effectively as possible.

- **Creating a Virtual Company.** Forming virtual companies has become an important competitive strategy in today's dynamic global markets. Internet and other information technologies play a key role in providing computing and telecommunications resources to support the communications, coordination, and information flows needed. Managers of a virtual company depend on IT to help them manage a network of people, knowledge, financial, and physical resources provided by many business partners to take advantage of rapidly changing market opportunities.

- **Building a Knowledge-Creating Company.** Lasting competitive advantage today can only come from the innovative use and management of organizational knowledge by knowledge-creating companies and learning organizations. Internet technologies are widely used in knowledge management systems to support the creation and dissemination of business knowledge and its integration into new products, services, and business processes.

Key Terms and Concepts

These are the key terms and concepts of this chapter. The page number of their first explanation is in parentheses.

1. Agile company (60)
2. Business process reengineering (56)
3. Competitive forces (44)
4. Competitive strategies (47)
5. Create switching costs (50)
6. Customer value (52)
7. Interenterprise information systems (62)
8. Knowledge-creating company (64)
9. Knowledge management system (65)
10. Leverage investment in IT (50)
11. Lock in customers and suppliers (50)
12. Raise barriers to entry (50)
13. Strategic information systems (44)
14. Value chain (54)
15. Virtual company (62)

Review Quiz

Match one of the key terms and concepts listed previously with one of the brief examples or definitions that follow. Try to find the best fit for answers that seem to fit more than one term or concept. Defend your choices.

_____ 1. A business must deal with customers, suppliers, competitors, new entrants, and substitutes.

_____ 2. Cost leadership, differentiation of products, and new product innovation are examples.

_____ 3. Using investments in technology to keep firms out of an industry.

_____ 4. Making it unattractive for a firm's customers or suppliers to switch to its competitors.

_____ 5. Strategies designed to increase the time, money, and effort needed for customers or suppliers to change to a firm's competitors.

_____ 6. Information systems that reengineer business processes or promote business innovation are examples.

_____ 7. This strategic focus recognizes that quality, rather than price, has become the primary determinant in customers choosing a product or service.

_____ 8. Highlights how strategic information systems can be applied to a firm's business processes and support activities for competitive advantage.

_____ 9. A business finding strategic uses for the computing and telecommunications capabilities it has developed to run its operations.

_____ 10. Information technology helping a business make radical improvements in business processes.

_____ 11. A business can prosper in rapidly changing markets while offering its customers individualized solutions to their needs.

_____ 12. A network of business partners formed to take advantage of rapidly changing market opportunities.

_____ 13. Learning organizations that focus on creating, disseminating, and managing business knowledge.

_____ 14. Information systems that manage the creation and dissemination of organizational knowledge.

_____ 15. Using the Internet and extranets to link a company's information systems to those of its customers and suppliers.

Discussion Questions

1. Suppose you are a manager being asked to develop computer-based applications to gain a competitive advantage in an important market for your company. What reservations might you have about doing so? Why?

2. How could a business use information technology to increase switching costs and lock in its customers and suppliers? Use business examples to support your answers.

3. How could a business leverage its investment in information technology to build strategic IT capabilities that serve as a barrier to new entrants into its markets?

4. Refer to the Real World Case on IT leaders and reinventing IT in the chapter. How would these ideas about the strategic positioning of IT apply to a small company? Do you think a small business would have a harder or an easier time aligning its business and IT organizations? Use an example to illustrate your answer.

5. What strategic role can information play in business process reengineering?

6. How can Internet technologies help a business form strategic alliances with its customers, suppliers, and others?

7. How could a business use Internet technologies to form a virtual company or become an agile competitor?

8. Refer to the Real World Case on companies using smartphones in the chapter. Do you think smaller companies like Lloyds Construction are ready for large-scale implementations of technology in their business? What could they do to prepare for those implementations? Use examples to illustrate your answer.

9. Information technology can't really give a company a strategic advantage because most competitive advantages don't last more than a few years and soon become strategic necessities that just raise the stakes of the game. Discuss.

10. MIS author and consultant Peter Keen says: "We have learned that it is not technology that creates a competitive edge, but the management process that exploits technology." What does he mean? Do you agree or disagree? Why?

Analysis Exercises

1. End-User Computing
Skill Assessment
Not all programs are written by dedicated programmers. Many knowledge workers write their own software using familiar word processing, spreadsheet, presentation, and database tools. This textbook contains end-user computing exercises representing a real-world programming challenge. This first exercise will allow your course instructor to assess the class. Assess your skills in each of the following areas:

a. Word processing: Approximately how many words per minute can you type? Do you use styles to manage document formatting? Have you ever set up your own mail merge template and data source? Have you created your own macros to handle repetitive tasks? Have you ever added branching or looping logic in your macro programs?

b. Spreadsheets: Do you know the order of operations your spreadsheet program uses (what does "=5*2^2-10" equal)? Do you know how to automatically sort data in a spreadsheet? Do you know how to create graphs and charts from spreadsheet data? Can you build pivot tables from spreadsheet data? Do you know the difference between a relative and a fixed cell reference? Do you know how to use functions in your spreadsheet equations? Do you know how to use the IF function? Have you created your own macros to handle repetitive tasks? Have you ever added branching or looping logic in your macro programs?

c. Presentations: Have you ever used presentation software to create presentation outlines? Have you added your own multimedia content to a presentation? Do you know how to add charts and graphs from spreadsheet software into your presentations so that they automatically update when the spreadsheet data change?

d. Database: Have you ever imported data into a database from a text file? Have you ever written queries to sort or filter data stored in a database table? Have you built reports to format your data for output? Have you built forms to aid in manual data entry? Have you built functions or programs to manipulate data stored in database tables?

2. Marketing: Competitive Intelligence
Strategic Marketing
Marketing professionals use information systems to gather and analyze information about their competitors. They use this information to assess their product's position relative to the competition and make strategic marketing decisions about their product, its price, its distribution (place), and how to best manage its promotion. Michael Bloomberg, founder of Bloomberg (www.bloomberg.com), and others have made their fortunes gathering and selling data about businesses. Marketing professionals find information about a business's industry, location, employees, products, technologies, revenues, and market share useful when planning marketing initiatives.

During your senior year, you will find yourself in close competition for jobs. You can take the same intelligence-gathering approach used by professional marketers when planning how to sell your own skills. Use the following questions to help you prepare for your job search:

a. Product: Which business majors are presently in greatest demand by employers? Use entry-level salaries as the primary indicator for demand.

b. Product: Which colleges or universities in your region pose the greatest competitive threat to students with your major?

c. Price: What is the average salary for entry-level employees in your major and geographic region? Is salary your top concern? Why or why not?

d. Place: What areas of the country are currently experiencing the greatest employment growth?

e. Promotion: What is your marketing plan? Describe how you plan to get your name and qualifications in front of prospective employers. How can the Internet help you get noticed?

3. Competing against Free
Wikipedia Faces Down Encyclopedia Britannica
The record and movie industries are not the only industries to find themselves affected by free access to their products. Encyclopedia Britannica faces challenges by a nonprofit competitor that provides its services without charge or advertising, Wikipedia.org. Wikipedia depends on volunteers to create and edit original content under the condition that contributors provide their work without copyright.

Who would work for free? During the creation of the *Oxford English Dictionary* in the 19th century, the editors solicited word articles and references from the general public. In the 20th century, AOL.com found thousands of volunteers to monitor its chat rooms. Amazon.com coaxed more than 100,000 readers to post book reviews on its retail Web site. Outdoing them all in the 21st century, Wikipedia published its one-millionth English language article in March 2006. Wikipedia includes more than two million articles in more than 200 languages, all created and edited by more than one million users.

Can Wikipedia compete on quality? Wikipedia provides its users both editing and monitoring tools, which allows users to self-police. Wikipedia also uses voluntary administrators who block vandals, temporarily protect articles, and manage arbitration processes when disputes arise. A paper published by *Nature* in December 2005 evaluated 50 Wikipedia articles and found an average of four factual errors per Wikipedia article compared with an average of three errors per article in the Encyclopedia Britannica. More significantly, Wikipedians (as the volunteers call themselves) corrected each error by January 2006. Alexa.com rated Wikipedia.org as the 17th most visited Web site on the Internet, while Britannica.com came in 2,858th place (Yahoo and Google ranked in the 1st and 2nd places).

Wikipedia has already built on its success. In addition to offering foreign language encyclopedias, it also provides a common media archive (commons.wikimedia.org), a multilingual dictionary (www.wiktionary.org), and a news service (www.wikinews.org).

a. How does the Wikimedia Foundation meet the criteria for an "agile" company?

b. How does the Wikimedia Foundation meet the criteria for a "virtual" company?

c. How does the Wikimedia Foundation meet the criteria for a "knowledge-creating" organization?

d. How would you recommend that Encyclopedia Britannica adapt to this new threat?

4. Knowledge Management
Knowing What You Know
Employees often receive a great deal of unstructured information in the form of e-mails. For example, employees may receive policies, announcements, and daily operational information via e-mail. However, e-mail systems typically make poor enterprisewide knowledge

management systems. New employees don't have access to e-mails predating their start date. Employees typically aren't permitted to search others' e-mail files for needed information. Organizations lose productivity when each employee spends time reviewing and organizing his or her e-mail files. Lastly, the same information may find itself saved across thousands of different e-mail files, thereby ballooning e-mail file storage space requirements.

Microsoft's Exchange server, IBM's Domino server, and Interwoven's WorkSite, along with a wide variety of open-standard Web-based products, aim to address an organization's need to share unstructured information. These products provide common repositories for various categories of information. For example, management may use a "Policy" folder in Microsoft Exchange to store all their policy decisions. Likewise, sales representatives may use a "Competitive Intelligence" database in IBM's Domino server to store information obtained during the sales process about competing products, prices, or marketplace rumors. WorkSite users categorize and store all their electronic documents in a large, searchable, secured common repository. Organizations using these systems can secure

them, manage them, and make them available to the appropriate personnel. Managers can also appoint a few specific employees requiring little technical experience to manage the content.

However, these systems cannot benefit an organization if its employees fail to contribute their knowledge, if they fail to use the system to retrieve information, or if the system simply isn't available where and when needed. To help managers better understand how employees use these systems, knowledge management systems include usage statistics such as date/time, user name, reads, writes, and even specific document access information.

Research each of the products mentioned above and answer the following questions:

a. What steps might a manager take to encourage his or her employees to use their organization's knowledge management system?

b. Should managers set minimum quotas for system usage for each employee? Why or why not?

c. Aside from setting employee usage quotas, how might an organization benefit from knowledge management system usage statistics?

REAL WORLD CASE 3

Wachovia and Others: Trading Securities at the Speed of Light

Securities trading is one of the few business activities where a one-second processing delay can cost a company big bucks. Wachovia Corporate and Investment Bank is addressing the growing competitive push toward instantaneous trading with a comprehensive systems overhaul. In a project that has cost more than $10 million so far, Wachovia is tearing down its systems silos and replacing them with an infrastructure that stretches seamlessly across the firm's many investment products and business functions.

"Competitive advantage comes from your math, your workflow and your processes through your systems. Straight-through processing is the utopian challenge for Wall Street firms," says Tony Bishop, senior vice president and head of architecture and engineering. The first step in the project, according to Bishop, was to prepare a matrix that cross-referenced every major function (such as research, risk management, selling, trading, clearing, settlement, payment, and reporting) to each major product (debt and equity products, asset-backed finance, derivatives, and so on). The project team then had to take a hard look at the existing systems in each cell. "We looked at the current systems and said, 'Where can we build standardized frameworks, components and services that would allow us to, instead of building it four different times in silos, build it once and extend it into one common sales platform, one common trading platform and so on?'"

The resulting Service Oriented Enterprise Platform is connected to a 10,000-processor grid using GridServer and FabricServer from DataSynapse Inc.

In its data centers, Wachovia brought in Verari Systems Inc.'s BladeRacks with quad-core Intel processors. Bishop says he's creating a "data center in a box" because Verari also makes storage blades that can be tightly coupled with processing blades in the same rack. The processing load at the bank involves a great deal of reading and writing to temporary files, and the intimate linkage of computing and storage nodes makes that extremely efficient.

"We now do pricing in milliseconds, not seconds, for either revenue protection or revenue gain," says Bishop. The advanced infrastructure has tripled processing capacity at one-third the cost, for a ninefold financial return, Bishop adds. Report generation that used to take 16 hours is now done in 15 minutes. "This is where IT becomes the enabler to new business capabilities," he says.

Executing complex strategies based on arcane mathematical formulas, algorithmic trading systems generate thousands of buy and sell orders every second, many of which are canceled and overridden by subsequent orders, sometimes only a few seconds apart. The goal of these computer traders is to profit from minute, fleeting price anomalies and to mask their intentions via "time slicing," or carving huge orders into smaller batches so as not to move the market. A one-millisecond advantage in trading applications can be worth $100 million a year to a major brokerage firm, by one estimate.

The fastest systems, running from traders' desks to exchange data centers, can execute transactions in a few milliseconds—so fast, in fact, that the physical distance between two computers processing a transaction can slow down how fast it happens. This problem is called data latency—delays measured in split seconds. To overcome it, many high-frequency algorithmic traders are moving their systems as close to the Wall Street exchanges as possible.

Wall Street's quest for speed is not only putting floor traders out of work but also opening up space for new alternative exchanges and e-communications networks that compete with the established stock markets. E-trading has reduced overall volatility in the equities markets, because volatility is a product of herd buying or selling, and e-trading—responding instantaneously to tiny price fluctuations—tends to smooth out such mass behavior. It has also provided established exchanges with new revenue opportunities, such as co-location services for companies that wish to place their servers in direct physical proximity to the exchanges' systems. E-trading has also created opportunities for a new class of vendors—execution services firms and systems integrators promising the fastest possible transaction times.

At its most abstract level, the data-latency race represents the spear point of the global movement to eradicate barriers—geographic, technical, psychological—to fair and transparent markets. "Any fair market is going to select the best price from the buyer or seller who gets their [sic] order in there first," says Alistair Brown, founder of Lime Brokerage, one of the new-school broker-dealers, which uses customized Linux servers to trade some 200 million shares a day. "At that point, speed definitely becomes an issue. If everyone has access to the same information, when the market moves, you want to be first. The people who are too slow are going to get left behind."

Value in Milliseconds

On the New Jersey side of the Lincoln Tunnel, in an anonymous three-story building, is one of the financial world's most important data centers. Pushing the doorbell at the unmarked main entrance won't get you inside. It's merely a facade; the real entrance is harder to find.

The servers for five electronic exchanges are located in this data center, along with computers belonging to dozens of trading firms. Run by hosting company Savvis, the Weehawken facility is home to some of the most advanced trading technology anywhere. Much of Savvis's growth can be traced to the spread of what's known as direct market access. In the past, traders used consolidated feeds, which are market data updates such as those provided by Reuters and Thomson. Distributing those feeds, however, could take up to 500 milliseconds, far too long for today's automated trading.

"Now you're seeing a lot of the market data providers and vendors who have direct exchange-feed connectivity," says Varghese Thomas, Savvis's vice president of financial markets. Savvis provides connectivity from the exchange directly to the client without having to go through a consolidated system. The exchanges themselves are also profiting from the demand for server space in physical proximity to the markets. Even on the fastest networks, it takes 7 milliseconds for data to travel between the New York markets and Chicago-based servers and 35 milliseconds between the West and East coasts.

Many broker-dealers and execution-services firms are paying premiums to place their servers inside the data centers of the National Association of Securities Dealers (NASDAQ) and the New York Stock Exchange (NYSE).

About 100 firms now co-locate their servers with NASDAQ's, says Brian Hyndman, NASDAQ's senior vice president of transaction services, at a going rate of about $3,500 per rack per month. NASDAQ has seen 25 percent annual increases in co-location in the last two years.

Physical co-location eliminates the unavoidable time lags inherent in even the fastest wide-area networks. Servers in shared data centers typically are connected via Gigabit Ethernet, with the ultra-highspeed switching fabric called InfiniBand increasingly used for the same purpose, says Yaron Haviv, CTO at Voltaire, a supplier of systems that can achieve latencies of less than a microsecond, or one-millionth of a second. Later this year, NASDAQ will shut down its data center in Trumbull, Connecticut, and move all operations to one opened last year in New Jersey, with a backup in the mid-Atlantic region, Hyndman says. (Trading firms and exchanges are reluctant to disclose the exact locations of their data centers.)

The NYSE will begin to reduce its 10 data centers to 2 in the next couple of years, says CTO Steve Rubinow. Co-location, Rubinow says, not only guarantees fast transactions, but also predictable ones. "If you've got some trades going through at 10 milliseconds and some at 1 millisecond, that's a problem" he says. "Our customers don't like variance."

One of the biggest co-location customers is Credit Suisse, which handles about 10 percent of all U.S. equity trades daily and which helped pioneer black-box trading systems with exotic algorithms that go by monikers like Sniper, Guerrilla, and Inline. Credit Suisse maintains Sun and Egenera blade servers, some running Linux and some Windows, in all the major U.S. markets, says Guy Cirillo, manager of global sales channels for Credit Suisse's Advanced Execution Services (AES) unit, which serves major hedge funds and other buy-side clients.

The AES trading engine in Credit Suisse's Manhattan headquarters is replicated in London, Hong Kong, and Tokyo.

Guaranteed transaction times for AES clients—from the time the order is received on the Credit Suisse system until it gets an acknowledgment from the exchange, e-communications network or "crossing network"—has dropped from 15 milliseconds to 8 in the last year, Cirillo says. Total execution time also includes any delays within the exchange or "liquidity point" itself, a latency variable over which Credit Suisse has no control.

"That response time is something the ECNs [electronic communications networks] and the exchanges compete on as well," Cirillo says. "Their latency, their turnaround time, and their infrastructure are all part of the electronic game."

Source: Adapted from Gary Anthes, "Split Second Securities Trading at Wachovia," *Computerworld*, May 21, 2007; and Richard Martin, "Wall Street's Quest to Process Data at the Speed of Light," *Information Week*, April 21, 2007.

CASE STUDY QUESTIONS

1. What competitive advantages can the companies described in the case derive from the use of faster technology and co-location of servers with the exchanges? Which would you say are sustainable, and which ones temporary or easily imitable? Justify your answer.

2. Tony Bishop of Wachovia stated that "Competitive advantage comes from your math, your workflow and your processes through your systems." Referring to what you have learned in this chapter, develop opposing viewpoints as to the role of IT, if any, in the development of competitive advantage. Use examples from the case to support your positions.

3. What companies in industries other than securities trading could benefit from technologies that focus on reducing transaction processing times? Provide several examples.

REAL WORLD ACTIVITIES

1. Most of the discussion in the case was done from the perspective of the trading firms and the value that these technologies add to them and their customer. However, the case also mentions actions taken by stock exchanges to improve their transaction processing and turn these needs into a revenue-generating asset. Research what recent technologies have been implemented by major stock exchanges such as NYSE and NASDAQ and prepare a report detailing what benefits have occurred as a result.

2. The technologies described in the case represent an example of how different barriers to the flow of goods and information are being overcome by the use of IT. Break into small groups and select an industry other than the one described in the case and brainstorm what barriers to commerce you see there and how IT may help to do away with them.

MODULE II

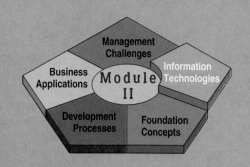

INFORMATION TECHNOLOGIES

What challenges do information system technologies pose for business professionals? What basic knowledge should you possess about information technology? The four chapters of this module give you an overview of the hardware, software, and data resource management and telecommunications network technologies used in information systems and their implications for business managers and professionals.

- **Chapter 3: Computer Hardware** reviews history, trends, and developments in microcomputer, midrange, and mainframe computer systems; basic computer system concepts; and the major types of technologies used in peripheral devices for computer input, output, and storage.

- **Chapter 4: Computer Software** reviews the basic features and trends in the major types of application software and system software used to support enterprise and end-user computing.

- **Chapter 5: Data Resource Management** emphasizes management of the data resources of computer-using organizations. This chapter reviews key database management concepts and applications in business information systems.

- **Chapter 6: Telecommunications and Networks** presents an overview of the Internet and other telecommunication networks, business applications, and trends and reviews technical telecommunications alternatives.

CHAPTER 3

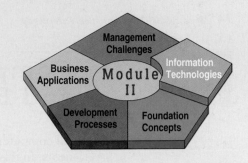

COMPUTER HARDWARE

Chapter Highlights

Learning Objectives

1. Understand the history and evolution of computer hardware.

2. Identify the major types and uses of microcomputer, midrange, and mainframe computer systems.

3. Outline the major technologies and uses of computer peripherals for input, output, and storage.

4. Identify and give examples of the components and functions of a computer system.

5. Identify the computer systems and peripherals you would acquire or recommend for a business of your choice, and explain the reasons for your selections.

Computer Systems: End User and Enterprise Computing

Introduction

All computers are systems of input, processing, output, storage, and control components. In this section, we discuss the history, trends, applications, and some basic concepts of the many types of computer systems in use today. In Section II, we will cover the changing technologies for input, output, and storage that are provided by the peripheral devices that are part of modern computer systems.

Read the Real World Case regarding the business benefits and challenges of grid computing systems. We can learn a lot about how different organizations use large-scale applications of grid computing from this case. See Figure 3.1.

A Brief History of Computer Hardware

Today we are witnessing rapid technological changes on a broad scale. However, many centuries elapsed before technology was sufficiently advanced to develop computers. Without computers, many technological achievements of the past would not have been possible. To fully appreciate their contribution, however, we must understand their history and evolution. Whereas a thorough discussion of computing history is beyond the scope of this text, a brief consideration of the development of the computer is possible. Let's look quickly into the development of computers.

At the dawn of the human concept of numbers, humans used their fingers and toes to perform basic mathematical activities. Then our ancestors realized that by using some objects to represent digits, they could perform computations beyond the limited scope of their own fingers and toes. Can't you just see in your mind a cave full of cavemen performing some group accounting function using their fingers, toes, sticks, and rocks? It creates a comical, yet accurate picture to be sure.

Shells, chicken bones, or any number of objects could have been used, but the fact that the word *calculate* is derived from *calculus*, the Latin word for "small stone," suggests that pebbles or beads were arranged to form the familiar abacus, arguably the first human-made computing device. By manipulating the beads, it was possible with some skill and practice to make rapid calculations.

Blaise Pascal, a French mathematician, invented what is believed to be the first mechanical adding machine in 1642. The machine partially adopted the principles of the abacus but did away with the use of the hand to move the beads or counters. Instead, Pascal used wheels to move counters. The principle of Pascal's machine is still being used today, such as in the counters of tape recorders and odometers. In 1674, Gottfried Wilhelm von Leibniz improved Pascal's machine so that the machine could divide and multiply as easily as it could add and subtract.

When the age of industrialization spread throughout Europe, machines became fixtures in agricultural and production sites. An invention that made profound changes in the history of industrialization, as well as in the history of computing, was the mechanical loom, invented by a Frenchman named Joseph Jacquard. With the use of cards punched with holes, it was possible for the Jacquard loom to weave fabrics in a variety of patterns. Jacquard's loom was controlled by a program encoded into the punched cards. The operator created the program once, and was able to duplicate it many times over with consistency and accuracy.

The idea of using punched cards to store a predetermined pattern to be woven by the loom clicked in the mind of Charles Babbage, an English mathematician who lived in the 19th century. He foresaw a machine that could perform all mathematical calculations, store values in its memory, and perform logical comparisons among values. He called it the *Analytical Engine*. Babbage's analytical engine, however, was never built. It lacked one thing: electronics. Herman Hollerith eventually adapted Jacquard's

REAL WORLD CASE 1

IBM, Wachovia, and PayPal: Grid Computing Makes It Easier and Cheaper

IBM researchers and a team of doctors are building a database of digital images they hope will enable oncologists to diagnose and treat cancer patients faster and with more success. Researchers at the Cancer Institute of New Jersey have digitized CAT scans, MRIs, and other images using a high-performance system and computational time on the World Community Grid, also known as the world's largest public computing grid.

"Digitizing images should enable doctors to diagnose cancers earlier and detect their growth or shrinkage more accurately during treatment," says Robin Willner, vice president of the global community initiatives at IBM. "Right now, the doctor is basically eyeballing it when he's analyzing tissues and biopsies. They're trying to figure out what type of cancer it is and if there's been progress during treatment. If you digitize the image, you're able to compare numbers because you've turned an image into bits and bytes. Now it's a much more accurate comparison."

Researchers have been using the grid to convert hundreds of thousands of images of cancerous tissues and cells into digital images. Once the images are digitized, the grid can check the accuracy of the digital information to ensure that the bits and bytes are translating into real diagnoses. The World Community Grid acts as a virtual supercomputer that is based on thousands of volunteers donating their unused computer time. "If we can improve treatment and diagnosis for cancer, that's great for everybody," said Willner. "There couldn't be a better use for the grid."

The next phase of the project is to build a database that will hold hundreds of thousands, if not millions, of these images. A \$2.5 million grant from the National Institutes of Health (NIH) will enable the Cancer Institute of New Jersey, Rutgers University, and cancer centers around the country to pool their digital images in the database. Willner said the database will enable doctors to compare patients' new images to ones already in the database to help them diagnose the cancer and figure out the best way to treat it. Doctors should be able to use the database to personalize treatments for cancer patients based on how other patients with similar protein expression signatures and cancers have reacted to various treatments.

"The overarching goal of the new NIH grant is to expand the library to include signatures for a wider range of disorders and make it, along with the decision-support technology, available to the research and clinical communities as grid-enabled deployable software," said David J. Foran, a director of the Cancer Institute of New Jersey. "We hope to deploy these technologies to other cancer research centers around the nation."

This isn't IBM's first foray into the medical arena by any means. IBM has also teamed up with the Mayo Clinic to develop a research facility to advance medical imaging. Researchers from both the Mayo Clinic and IBM are working at the new Medical Imaging Informatics Innovation Center in Rochester, Minnesota. Bradley Erickson, chairman of radiology at the Mayo Clinic, said a joint team is already working to find ways to use the Cell chip, mostly known for running inside the PlayStation 3 video-game console, in a medical imaging system. Erickson said that the technology could either reduce work that now takes minutes to a matter of seconds, or work that now takes hours to only minutes.

Grid computing, however, is not limited to nonprofit institutions. Financial services firm Wachovia Corp. has freed some of its Java-based applications from dedicated servers and is allowing these transaction applications to draw computing power from a 10,000-CPU resource pool on servers spread across cities in the United States and in London. Wachovia is tapping into computing power that's available on other systems to perform work. That capability allows companies to avoid dedicated hardware costs and make better use of underutilized hardware.

Tony Bishop, a Wachovia senior vice president and director of product management, said that to use dedicated systems as an alternative would be "three times the cost in terms of capital and people to support it otherwise." Wachovia has eight applications running on its grid that are used in internal transactions, such as order management. The servers are in New York, Philadelphia, London, and at the company's corporate headquarters in Charlotte, North Carolina. Jamie Bernardin, chief technology officer at DataSynapse, the company that developed the technology, said that to improve transaction speeds, the transaction application running on it can grow and contract as needed.

FIGURE 3.1

Grid computing technologies avoid the need for expensive, dedicated hardware by distributing the processing load among commodity-priced equipment.

Because the system can provide resources as needed for the applications, Bishop said performance has improved on some transactions fivefold. "This ability to speed processing means decisions and services can be made and delivered more rapidly. As things get more and more automated and more and more real time, it will be IT in this business that differentiates," says Bishop.

A Linux grid is the power behind the payment system at PayPal, and it has converted a mainframe believer. Scott Thompson, the former executive VP of technology solutions at Inovant, ran the Visa subsidiary responsible for executing Visa credit card transactions worldwide. The VisaNet system was strictly based on IBM mainframes.

In February 2005, Thompson became chief technology officer at the eBay payments company, PayPal, where he confronted a young Internet organization building its entire transaction processing infrastructure on open-source Linux and low-cost servers. Hmmmm, he thought at the time. "I came from Visa, where I had responsibility for VisaNet. It was a fabulous processing system, very big and very global. I was intrigued by PayPal. How would you use Linux for processing payments and never be wrong, never lose messages, never fall behind the pace of transactions?" he wondered.

He now supervises the PayPal electronic payment processing system, which is smaller than VisaNet in volume and total dollar value of transactions, but it's growing fast. It is currently processing $1,571 worth of transactions per second in 17 different currencies. In 2006, the online payments firm, which started out over a bakery in Palo Alto, processed a total of $37.6 billion in transactions. It's headed toward $50 billion very soon.

Now located in San Jose, PayPal grants its consumer members options in payment methods: credit cards, debit cards, or directly from a bank account. It has 165 million account holders worldwide, and it has recently added such businesses as Northwest Airlines, Southwest Airlines, U.S. Airways, and Overstock.com, which now permit PayPal payments on their Web sites.

Thompson supervises a payment system that operates on about 4,000 servers running Red Hat Linux in the same manner that eBay and Google conduct their business on top of a grid of Linux servers. "I have been pleasantly surprised at how much we've been able to do with this approach. It operates like a mainframe," he says.

As PayPal grows, it's much easier to grow the grid with Intel-based servers than it would be to upgrade a mainframe, according to Thompson. "The cost to increase capacity a planned 15 or 20 percent in a mainframe environment is enormous. It could be in the tens of millions to do a step increase. In PayPal's world, we add hundreds of servers in the course of a couple of nights and the cost is in the thousands, not millions."

PayPal takes Red Hat Enterprise Linux and strips out all features unnecessary to its business, and then adds proprietary extensions around security. Another virtue of the grid is that PayPal's 800 engineers can all get a copy of that customized system on their development desktops, run tests on their raw software as they work, and develop to PayPal's needs faster because they're working in the target environment. That's harder to do when the core of the data center consists of large boxes or mainframes. It's not cheap in either case to install duplicates for developers, says Thompson.

Source: Adapted from Sharon Gaudin, "IBM Uses Grid to Advance Cancer Diagnosis and Treatment," *Computerworld*, January 28, 2008; Patrick Thibodeau, "Wachovia Uses Grid Technology to Speed Up Transaction Apps," *Computerworld*, May 15, 2006; and Charles Babcock, "PayPal Says Linux Grid Can Replace Mainframes," *Information Week*, November 28, 2007.

CASE STUDY QUESTIONS

1. Applications for grid computing in this case include medical diagnosis and financial transaction processing. What other areas do you think would be well suited to the use of grid computing and why? Provide several examples from organizations other than those included in the case.

2. The joint effort by IBM and the Cancer Institute of New Jersey works by digitalizing medical diagnoses on the World Community Grid (WCG). What are the advantages and disadvantages of relying on a volunteer-based network such as this? Provide examples of both. Visit the Web site of the WCG to inform your answer.

3. IBM, Wachovia, and PayPal are arguably large organizations. However, several vendors have started offering computing power for rent to smaller companies, using the principles underlying grid computing. How could small and medium companies benefit from these technologies? Search the Internet for these offerings to help you research your answer.

REAL WORLD ACTIVITIES

1. Grid computing technology is becoming increasingly popular and has recently received support from giants such as IBM, Sun, and Oracle. Visit their Web sites (www.ibm.com, www.sun.com, and www.oracle.com) and review their current offerings in this regard. How do their products compare to each other? Prepare a presentation to share your findings with the class.

2. One of the main benefits of grid computing arises from the possibility of replacing expensive hardware, such as mainframes or supercomputers, with commodity-priced servers and even personal computers. What about the cost of administering so many different servers and the power consumption associated with them? Go online to search for information that would allow you to compare grid computing to more traditional, mainframe-based alternatives. Write a report to present your findings.

concept of the punched card to record census data in the late 1880s. Census data were translated into a series of holes in a punched card to represent the digits and the letters of the alphabet. The card was then passed through a machine with a series of electrical contacts that were either turned off or on, depending on the existence of holes in the punched cards. These different combinations of off/on situations were recorded by the machine and represented a way of tabulating the result of the census. Hollerith's machine was highly successful. It cut the time it took to tabulate the result of the census by two-thirds, and it made money for the company that manufactured Hollerith's machine. In 1911, this company merged with its competitor to form International Business Machines (IBM).

The ENIAC (Electronic Numerical Integrator and Computer) was the first electronic digital computer. It was completed in 1946 at the Moore School of Electrical Engineering of the University of Pennsylvania. With no moving parts, ENIAC was programmable and had the capability to store problem calculations using vacuum tubes (about 18,000).

A computer that uses vacuum tube technology is called a first-generation computer. The ENIAC could add in 0.2 of a millisecond, or about 5,000 computations per second. The principal drawback of ENIAC was its size and processing ability. It occupied more than 1,500 square feet of floor space and could process only one program or problem at a time. As an aside, the power requirements for ENIAC were such that adjacent common area lighting dimmed during the power up and calculation cycles. Figure 3.2 shows the ENIAC complex.

In the 1950s, Remington Rand manufactured the UNIVAC I (Universal Automatic Calculator). It could calculate at the rate of 10,000 additions per second. In 1957, IBM developed the IBM 704, which could perform 100,000 calculations per second.

In the late 1950s, transistors were invented and quickly replaced the thousands of vacuum tubes used in electronic computers. A transistor-based computer could perform 200,000–250,000 calculations per second. The transistorized computer represents the second generation of computer. It was not until the mid-1960s that the third generation of computers came into being. These were characterized by solid state technology and integrated circuitry coupled with extreme miniaturization.

No history of electronic computing would be complete without acknowledging Jack Kilby. Kilby was a Nobel Prize laureate in physics in 2000 for his invention of the integrated circuit in 1958 while working at Texas Instruments (TI). He is also the inventor of the handheld calculator and thermal printer. Without his work that generated a patent for a "Solid Circuit made of Germanium," our worlds, and most certainly our computers, would be much different and less productive than we enjoy today.

FIGURE 3.2
ENIAC was the first digital computer. It is easy to see how far we have come in the evolution of computers.

Source: Photo courtesy of United States Army.

In 1971, the fourth generation of computers was characterized by further miniaturization of circuits, increased multiprogramming, and virtual storage memory. In the 1980s, the fifth generation of computers operated at speeds of 3–5 million calculations per second (for small-scale computers) and 10–15 million instructions per second (for large-scale computers).

The age of microcomputers began in 1975 when a company called MITS introduced the ALTAIR 8800. The computer was programmed by flicking switches on the front. It came as a kit and had to be soldered together. It had no software programs, but it was a personal computer available to the consumer for a few thousand dollars when most computer companies were charging tens of thousands of dollars. In 1977 both Commodore and Radio Shack announced that they were going to make personal computers. They did, and trotting along right beside them were Steve Jobs and Steve Wozniak, who invented their computer in a garage while in college. Mass production of the Apple began in 1979, and by the end of 1981, it was the fastest selling of all the personal computers. In August 1982 the IBM PC was born, and many would argue that the world changed forever as a result.

Following the introduction of the personal computer in the early 1980s, we used our knowledge of computer networks gained in the early days of computing and combined it with new and innovative technologies to create massive networks of people, computers, and data on which anyone can find almost anything: the Internet. Today we continue to see amazing advancements in computing technologies.

Okay, it's time to slow down a bit and begin our discussion of today's computer hardware.

Types of Computer Systems

Today's computer systems come in a variety of sizes, shapes, and computing capabilities. Rapid hardware and software developments and changing end-user needs continue to drive the emergence of new models of computers, from the smallest handheld personal digital assistant/cell phone combinations to the largest multiple-CPU mainframes for enterprises. See Figure 3.3.

FIGURE 3.3 Examples of computer system categories.

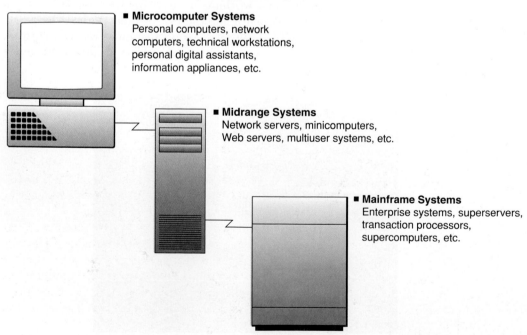

■ **Microcomputer Systems**
Personal computers, network computers, technical workstations, personal digital assistants, information appliances, etc.

■ **Midrange Systems**
Network servers, minicomputers, Web servers, multiuser systems, etc.

■ **Mainframe Systems**
Enterprise systems, superservers, transaction processors, supercomputers, etc.

Categories such as *mainframe, midrange*, and *microcomputer* systems are still used to help us express the relative processing power and number of end users that can be supported by different types of computers. These are not precise classifications, and they do overlap each other. Thus, other names are commonly given to highlight the major uses of particular types of computers. Examples include personal computers, network servers, network computers, and technical workstations.

In addition, experts continue to predict the merging or disappearance of several computer categories. They feel, for example, that many midrange and mainframe systems have been made obsolete by the power and versatility of networks composed of microcomputers and servers. Other industry experts have predicted that the emergence of network computers and *information appliances* for applications on the Internet and corporate intranets will replace many personal computers, especially in large organizations and in the home computer market. Still others suggest that the concept of *nanocomputers* (computing devices that are smaller than micro) will eventually pervade our entire understanding of personal computing. Only time will tell whether such predictions will equal the expectations of industry forecasters.

Microcomputer Systems

The entire center of gravity in computing has shifted. For millions of consumers and business users, the main function of desktop PCs is as a window to the Internet. Computers are now communications devices, and consumers want them to be as cheap as possible.

Microcomputers are the most important category of computer systems for both businesspeople and consumers. Although usually called a *personal computer*, or PC, a microcomputer is much more than a small computer for use by an individual as a communication device. The computing power of microcomputers now exceeds that of the mainframes of previous computer generations, at a fraction of their cost. Thus, they have become powerful networked *professional workstations* for business professionals.

Consider the computing power on the *Apollo 11* spacecraft. Most certainly, landing men on the moon and returning them safely to earth was an extraordinary feat. The computer that assisted them in everything from navigation to systems monitoring was equally extraordinary. *Apollo 11* had a 2.048 MHz CPU that was built by MIT. Today's standards can be measured in the 4 GHz in many home PCs (MHz is 1 million computing cycles per second and GHz is 1 billion computing cycles per second). Further, the *Apollo 11* computer weighed 70 pounds versus today's powerful laptops weighing in as little as 1 pound. This is progress, for sure.

Microcomputers come in a variety of sizes and shapes for a variety of purposes, as Figure 3.4 illustrates. For example, PCs are available as handheld, notebook, laptop, tablet, portable, desktop, and floor-standing models. Or, based on their use, they include home, personal, professional, workstation, and multiuser systems. Most microcomputers are *desktops* designed to fit on an office desk or laptops for those who want a small, portable PC. Figure 3.5 offers advice on some of the key features you should consider when acquiring a high-end professional workstation, multimedia PC, or beginner's system. This breakdown should give you some idea of the range of features available in today's microcomputers.

Some microcomputers are powerful workstation computers (technical workstations) that support applications with heavy mathematical computing and graphics display demands, such as computer-aided design (CAD) in engineering or investment and portfolio analysis in the securities industry. Other microcomputers are used as network servers. These are usually more powerful microcomputers that coordinate telecommunications and resource sharing in small local area networks (LANs) and in Internet and intranet Web sites.

FIGURE 3.4 Examples of microcomputer systems:

a. A notebook microcomputer.
Source: Courtesy of Hewlett-Packard.

b. The microcomputer as a professional workstation.
Source: © Royalty Free/Corbis.

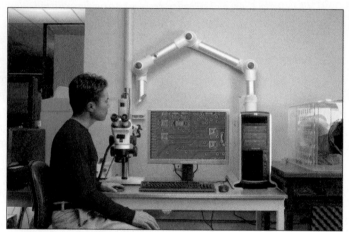

c. The microcomputer as a technical workstation.
Source: Courtesy of Hewlett-Packard.

FIGURE 3.5 Examples of recommended features for the three types of PC users. Note: www.dell.com and www.gateway.com are good sources for the latest PC features available.

Business Pro	Multimedia Heavy or Gamer	Newcomer
To track products, customers, and firm performance, more than just a fast machine is necessary:	Media pros and dedicated gamers will want at least a Mac G4 or a 2–3 GHz Intel dual-core chip, and	Save some money with a Celeron processor in the 2–3 GHz range while looking for
• 3–4 GHz dual-core processor	• 4–8 GB RAM	• 2 GB RAM
• 4–8 GB RAM	• 250+ GB hard drive	• 120–160 GB hard drive
• 500 GB hard drive	• 19-inch or better flat-panel display	• 15- to 17-inch flat panel or wide screen
• Up to 19-inch flat-panel display	• 16× or better DVD+RW	• CD-RW/DVD
• CD-RW/DVD+RW	• Video cards (as fast and as powerful as budget permits)	• USB port
• Network interface card	• Sound cards	• Inkjet printer
• Color laser printer	• Laser printer (color or B&W)	

Corporate PC Criteria

What do you look for in a new PC system? A big, bright screen? Zippy new processor? Capacious hard drive? Acres of RAM? Sorry, none of these is a top concern for corporate PC buyers. Numerous studies have shown that the price of a new computer is only a small part of the total cost of ownership (TCO). Support, maintenance, and other intangibles contribute far more heavily to the sum. Let's take a look at three top criteria.

Solid Performance at a Reasonable Price. Corporate buyers know that their users probably aren't mapping the human genome or plotting trajectories to Saturn. They're doing word processing, order entry, sales contact management, and other essential business tasks. They need a solid, competent machine at a reasonable price, not the latest whizbang.

Many organizations are adopting a laptop, rather than desktop, strategy. Using this approach, the employee uses his or her laptop while in the office and out in the field. With the proliferation of wireless Internet access, this strategy allows employees to take the desktop with them wherever they may be—at their desk, in a conference room, at a meeting offsite, or in a hotel room in another country.

One outcome of this strategy is the development and acquisition of more powerful laptops with larger and higher-quality screens. This demand presents a challenge to laptop manufacturers to provide higher quality while continuing to make the laptop lightweight and portable.

Operating System Ready. A change in the operating system of a computer is the most disruptive upgrade an enterprise has to face. That's why many corporate buyers want their machines to be able to handle current operating systems and anticipated new ones. Although most organizations have adopted Windows XP or Vista, some enterprises still use operating systems of an earlier vintage. Ultimately, they must be able to make the transition to Windows 7 (the newest OS from Microsoft) and even to OS versions expected three to five years from now. Primarily, that demand means deciding what hard disk space and RAM will be sufficient.

Connectivity. Networked machines are a given in corporate life, and Internet-ready machines are becoming a given. Buyers need machines equipped with reliable wireless capabilities. With fewer cables to worry about, wireless networks, especially when combined with laptop PCs, contribute to the flexibility of the workplace and the simplicity of PC deployment. Many organizations are planning for Internet-based applications and need machines ready to make fast, reliable, and secure connections.

Security-Equipped. Most of the data that is processed by networked workstations in a modern corporate environment can be considered proprietary, if not mission-critical. A major criterion for corporate purchase is the degree to which the device can accept or conform to the myriad of security measures in use in that organization. Can it accept a USB dongle, smartcard reader, biometric access device, and so forth? We will cover this aspect in greater detail in Chapter 13.

Computer Terminals

Computer terminals, essentially any device that allows access to a computer, are undergoing a major conversion to networked computer devices. *Dumb terminals*, which are keyboard/video monitor devices with limited processing capabilities, are being replaced by *intelligent terminals*, which are modified networked PCs or network computers. Also included are network terminals, which may be *Windows terminals* that depend on network servers for Windows software, processing power, and storage, or *Internet terminals*, which depend on Internet or intranet Web site servers for their operating systems and application software.

Intelligent terminals take many forms and can perform data entry and some information processing tasks independently. These tasks include the widespread use of **transaction terminals** in banks, retail stores, factories, and other work sites. Examples are automated teller machines (ATMs), factory production recorders, airport check-in kiosks, and retail point-of-sale (POS) terminals. These intelligent terminals use keypads, touch screens, bar code scanners, and other input methods to capture data and interact with end users during a transaction, while relying on servers or other computers in the network for further transaction processing.

Network Computers

Network computers (NCs) are a microcomputer category designed primarily for use with the Internet and corporate intranets by clerical workers, operational employees, and knowledge workers with specialized or limited computing applications. These NCs are low-cost, sealed microcomputers with no or minimal disk storage that are linked to the network. Users of NCs depend primarily on network servers for their operating system and Web browser, application software, and data access and storage.

One of the main attractions of network computers is their lower TCO (total cost of ownership), that is, the total of all costs associated with purchasing, installing, operating, and maintaining a computer. Purchase upgrades, maintenance, and support cost much less than for full-featured PCs. Other benefits to business include the ease of software distribution and licensing, computing platform standardization, reduced end-user support requirements, and improved manageability through centralized management and enterprisewide control of computer network resources.

Information Appliances

PCs aren't the only option: A host of smart gadgets and information appliances—from cellular phones and pagers to handheld PCs and Web-based game machines—promise Internet access and the ability to perform basic computational chores.

Handheld microcomputer devices known as **personal digital assistants** (PDAs) are some of the most popular devices in the information appliance category. Web-enabled PDAs use touch screens, pen-based handwriting recognition, or keypads so that mobile workers can send and receive e-mail, access the Web, and exchange information such as appointments, to-do lists, and sales contacts with their desktop PCs or Web servers.

Now a mainstay of PDA technology is the RIM BlackBerry, a small, pager-sized device that can perform all of the common PDA functions, plus act as a fully functional mobile telephone. What sets this device apart from other wireless PDA solutions is that it is always on and connected. A BlackBerry user doesn't need to retrieve e-mail; the e-mail finds the BlackBerry user. Because of this functionality, there is no need to dial in or initiate a connection. The BlackBerry doesn't even have a visible antenna. When a user wishes to send or reply to an e-mail, the small keyboard on the device allows text entry. Just like a mobile telephone, the BlackBerry is designed to remain on and continuously connected to the wireless network, allowing near real-time transfer of e-mail. Furthermore, because the BlackBerry uses the same network as most mobile telephone services, the unit can be used anywhere that a mobile phone can be used.

A relatively new entrant to this field (although gaining favor in leaps and bounds) is the Apple iPhone (Figure 3.6). iPhone essentially combines three products—a revolutionary mobile phone, a wide-screen iPod music and video player with touch controls, and a breakthrough Internet communications device with desktop-class e-mail, Web browsing, maps, and searching—into one small and lightweight handheld device. iPhone also introduces an entirely new user interface based on a large, multitouch display and pioneering new software, letting users control everything with just their fingers.

The genesis of the iPhone began with Apple CEO Steve Jobs' direction that Apple engineers investigate touch screens. Apple created the device during a secretive and unprecedented collaboration with AT&T Mobility—called Cingular Wireless at the time of the phone's inception—at a development cost of $150 million, by one

FIGURE 3.6

The Apple iPhone—a revolutionary player in the information appliance and PDA marketplace.

Source: Laurens Smak/Alamy.

estimate. During development, the iPhone was code-named "Purple 2." The company rejected an early "design by committee" built with Motorola in favor of engineering a custom operating system, interface, and hardware.

The iPhone went on sale on June 29, 2007. Apple closed its stores at 2:00 p.m. local time to prepare for the 6:00 p.m. iPhone launch, while hundreds of customers lined up at stores nationwide. They sold 270,000 iPhones in the first 30 hours on launch weekend.

In Germany, Deutsche Telekom signed up 70,000 iPhone customers during the 11-week period of November 9, 2007, to January 26, 2008. In the United Kingdom, it has been estimated that 190,000 customers signed with O2 during an 8-week period from the November 9, 2007 launch date to January 9, 2008.

The newest generation of iPhone is the 3G. This version accesses data from the much faster 3G network and provides for the download of literally thousands of applications that allow the iPhone to perform tasks ranging from accessing online banking services to acting as a sophisticated leveling device and everything in between.

The iPhone has truly ushered in an era of software power and sophistication never before seen in a mobile device, completely redefining what people can do on a mobile phone. We can expect to see even more sophisticated mobile PDA-type devices in the future as Moore's law continues to prevail and the marketplace continues to demand more functionality (see the discussion on Moore's law at the end of Section I for more details on this concept).

Information appliances may also take the form of video-game consoles and other devices that connect to your home television set. These devices enable people to surf the World Wide Web, send and receive e-mail, and watch television programs, or play video games, at the same time. Other information appliances include wireless PDAs and Internet-enabled cellular and PCS phones, as well as wired, telephone-based home appliances that can send and receive e-mail and access the Web.

Midrange Systems

Midrange systems are primarily high-end network servers and other types of servers that can handle the large-scale processing of many business applications. Although not as powerful as mainframe computers, they are less costly to buy, operate, and maintain than mainframe systems and thus meet the computing needs of many organizations. See Figure 3.7.

FIGURE 3.7

Midrange computer systems can handle large-scale processing without the high cost or space considerations of a large-scale mainframe.

Source: China Foto Press/Getty Images.

> *Burgeoning data warehouses and related applications such as data mining and online analytical processing are forcing IT shops into higher and higher levels of server configurations. Similarly, Internet-based applications, such as Web servers and electronic commerce, are forcing IT managers to push the envelope of processing speed and storage capacity and other [business] applications, fueling the growth of high-end servers.*

Midrange systems have become popular as powerful network servers (computers used to coordinate communications and manage resource sharing in network settings) to help manage large Internet Web sites, corporate intranets and extranets, and other networks. Internet functions and other applications are popular high-end server applications, as are integrated enterprisewide manufacturing, distribution, and financial applications. Other applications, like data warehouse management, data mining, and online analytical processing (which we will discuss in Chapters 5 and 10), are contributing to the demand for high-end server systems.

Midrange systems first became popular as minicomputers for scientific research, instrumentation systems, engineering analysis, and industrial process monitoring and control. Minicomputers could easily handle such uses because these applications are narrow in scope and do not demand the processing versatility of mainframe systems. Today, midrange systems include servers used in industrial process-control and manufacturing plants and play major roles in computer-aided manufacturing (CAM). They can also take the form of powerful technical workstations for computer-aided design (CAD) and other computation and graphics-intensive applications. Midrange systems are also used as *front-end servers* to assist mainframe computers in telecommunications processing and network management.

| And the Oscar Goes to . . . Penguins and 2,000 Blade Servers | An initial implementation of 500 blade servers soon grew to 2,000 to meet the processing capacity requirements for creating the Oscar-winning animated film *Happy Feet*. The 108-minute computer-generated animated feature, which won an Academy Award in 2006, was put together by digital production company The Animal Logic Group.

"We needed huge numbers of processors in a form factor and price level that would work for our business," says Xavier Desdoigts, director of technical |

operations. "We had to render 140,000 frames, and each frame could take many hours to render. The photorealistic look of the movie made our computational requirements soar to new heights."

For example, Mumble, the main character in the movie, had up to 6 million feathers. "There were six shots in the movie that had more than 400,000 penguins in them," Desdoigts explained. This added up to over 17 million CPU hours used throughout the last nine months of *Happy Feet* production. "We were initially concerned about our ability to build and manage a processing capacity of that scale."

Animal Logic and IBM built a rendering server farm using BladeCenter HS20 blade servers, each with two Intel Xeon servers. Rendering was completed in October 2006, and the film was released the following month in the United States. Management tools to deploy and control the servers while in production included an open-source package for administering computing clusters. For Animal Logic, the biggest sign of success from an IT perspective was that the entire server farm was managed by a single person.

"We have to make sure we choose solutions that aren't overly complex to set up or manage, so our focus can stay on realizing the creative visions of our clients," Desdoigts said. *Happy Feet* quickly became one of the Australian film industry's greatest box-office successes, taking the No. 1 spot in the United States for three consecutive weeks. It made more than $41 million (U.S.) on its opening weekend and showed on 3,800 cinema screens.

Source: Adapted from Sandra Rossi, "And the Oscar Goes to . . . Jovial Penguins and 2,000 Blade Servers," *Computerworld Australia*, March 6, 2007.

Mainframe Computer Systems

Several years after dire pronouncements that the mainframe was dead, quite the opposite is true: Mainframe usage is actually on the rise. And it's not just a short-term blip. One factor that's been driving mainframe sales is cost reductions [of 35 percent or more]. Price reductions aren't the only factor fueling mainframe acquisitions. IS organizations are teaching the old dog new tricks by putting mainframes at the center stage of emerging applications such as data mining and warehousing, decision support, and a variety of Internet-based applications, most notably electronic commerce.

Mainframe systems are large, fast, and powerful computer systems. For example, mainframes can process thousands of million instructions per second (MIPS). Mainframes can also have large primary storage capacities. Their main memory capacity can range from hundreds of gigabytes to many terabytes of primary storage. Mainframes have slimmed down drastically in the last few years, dramatically reducing their air-conditioning needs, electrical power consumption, and floor space requirements—and thus their acquisition and operating costs. Most of these improvements are the result of a move from cumbersome water-cooled mainframes to a newer air-cooled technology for mainframe systems. See Figure 3.8.

Thus, mainframe computers continue to handle the information processing needs of major corporations and government agencies with high transaction processing volumes or complex computational problems. For example, major international banks, airlines, oil companies, and other large corporations process millions of sales transactions and customer inquiries each day with the help of large mainframe systems. Mainframes are still used for computation-intensive applications, such as analyzing seismic data from oil field explorations or simulating flight conditions in designing aircraft. Mainframes are also widely used as *superservers* for the large client/server networks and high-volume Internet Web sites of large companies. As previously mentioned, mainframes are becoming a popular business computing platform for data mining and warehousing, as well as electronic commerce applications.

FIGURE 3.8
Mainframe computer systems are the heavy lifters of corporate computing.

Source: © Royalty Free/Corbis.

Supercomputer Systems

Supercomputers have now become "scalable servers" at the top end of the product lines that start with desktop workstations. Market-driven companies, like Silicon Graphics, Hewlett-Packard, and IBM, have a much broader focus than just building the world's fastest computer, and the software of the desktop computer has a much greater overlap with that of the supercomputer than it used to, because both are built from the same cache-based microprocessors.

The term **supercomputer** describes a category of extremely powerful computer systems specifically designed for scientific, engineering, and business applications requiring extremely high speeds for massive numeric computations. The market for supercomputers includes government research agencies, large universities, and major corporations. They use supercomputers for applications such as global weather forecasting, military defense systems, computational cosmology and astronomy, microprocessor research and design, and large-scale data mining.

Supercomputers use *parallel processing* architectures of interconnected microprocessors (which can execute many instructions at the same time in parallel). They can easily perform arithmetic calculations at speeds of billions of floating-point operations per second (*gigaflops*). Supercomputers that can calculate in *teraflops* (trillions of floating-point operations per second), which use massive parallel processing (MPP) designs of thousands of microprocessors, are now in use. Purchase prices for large supercomputers are in the $5 million to $50 million range.

The use of symmetric multiprocessing (SMP) and distributed shared memory (DSM) designs of smaller numbers of interconnected microprocessors has spawned a breed of *minisupercomputers* with prices that start in the hundreds of thousands of dollars. For example, IBM's RS/6000 SP system starts at $150,000 for a one-processing-node SMP computer. However, it can be expanded to hundreds of processing nodes, which drives its price into the tens of millions of dollars.

The ASCI White supercomputer system, shown in Figure 3.9, consists of three IBM RS/6000 SP systems: White, Frost, and Ice. White, the largest of these systems, is a 512-node, 16-way SMP supercomputer with a peak performance of 12.3 teraflops. Frost is a 68-node, 16-way SMP system; and Ice is a 28-node, 16-way SMP system. Supercomputers like these continue to advance the state of the art for the entire computer industry.

FIGURE 3.9

The ASCI White supercomputer system at Lawrence Livermore National Laboratory in Livermore, California.

Source: Image courtesy of Silicon Graphics, Inc.

Supercomputers Aid Satellite Launches

Satellite launches are a noisy affair, especially for the satellite atop the rocket. Vibration and noise, unless compensated, could render it useless before it reaches orbit, so researchers spend a lot of time on complex computer simulations that help them insulate the delicate craft. Now those simulations are about to get much more accurate, thanks to a new supercomputer that recently began work in Japan.

The Fujitsu FX1 computer was inaugurated in 2009 by the Japan Aerospace Explorations Agency (JAXA). It has 3,008 nodes, each of which has a 4-core Sparc64 VII microprocessor. The machine has 94 terabytes of memory and a theoretical peak performance of 120 teraflops. Running standard benchmarks, it achieved a peak performance of 110.6 teraflops, which ranks it not only the most powerful machine in Japan but also the most efficient supercomputer in the world. Its peak performance represents 91.2 percent of its theoretical performance and outranks the previous record holder, a machine at the Leibniz Rechenzentrum in Munich. Ranked below the German computer is another JAXA machine. "Performance is about 15 times higher than the system we had before," said Kozo Fujii, director of JAXA's Engineering Digital Innovation Center.

Two rows of computer racks make up the main system and a third row alongside is a second less powerful FX1 machine. In an adjoining room sits an NEC SX-9 vector computer for running specialized tasks and the storage that augments the entire system. Altogether a petabyte of disk storage space and 10 petabytes of tape storage are connected to the system (a petabyte is a million gigabytes). And between the lot there are lots of big, industrial air conditioners to keep the room cool and extract the heat generated by this mass of hardware.

JAXA intends to put it to work on simulations such as the acoustic noise experienced by a satellite at launch, said Fujii. "There is a wide band of frequencies and usually the peak frequencies are located between 60 and 100 Hertz and we can capture at that level of frequencies. But hopefully with the new computer we can capture frequencies of 150 or 200 Hz that are difficult for the current computer."

Source: Adapted from Martyn Williams, "World's Most Efficient Supercomputer Gets to Work," *CIO Magazine,* April 2, 2009.

The Next Wave of Computing

Interconnecting microprocessors to create minisupercomputers is a reality, as discussed in the previous section. The next wave is looking at harnessing the virtually infinite amount of unused computing power that exists in the myriad of desktops and laptops within the boundaries of a modern organization.

Distributed or *grid computing* in general is a special type of parallel computing that relies on complete computers (with onboard CPU, storage, power supply, network interface, and so forth) connected to a network (private, public, or the Internet) by a conventional network interface. This is in contrast to the traditional notion of a supercomputer, which has many processors connected together in a single machine. The grid could be formed by harnessing the unused CPU power in all of the desktops and laptops in a single division of a company (or in the entire company, for that matter).

The primary advantage of distributed computing is that each node can be purchased as commodity hardware; when combined, it can produce similar computing resources to a multiprocessor supercomputer, but at a significantly lower cost. This is due to the economies of scale of producing desktops and laptops, compared with the lower efficiency of designing and constructing a small number of custom supercomputers.

One feature of distributed grids is that they can be formed from computing resources belonging to multiple individuals or organizations (known as multiple administrative domains). This can facilitate commercial transactions or make it easier to assemble volunteer computing networks.

A disadvantage of this feature is that the computers that are actually performing the calculations might not be entirely trustworthy. The designers of the system must thus introduce measures to prevent malfunctions or malicious participants from producing false, misleading, or erroneous results, and from using the system as a platform for a hacking attempt. This often involves assigning work randomly to different nodes (presumably with different owners) and checking that at least two different nodes report the same answer for a given work unit. Discrepancies would identify malfunctioning and malicious nodes.

Another challenge is that because of the lack of central control over the hardware, there is no way to guarantee that computers will not drop out of the network at random times. Some nodes (like laptops or dial-up Internet customers) may also be available for computation but not for network communications for unpredictable periods. These variations can be accommodated by assigning large work units (thus reducing the need for continuous network connectivity) and reassigning work units when a given node fails to report its results as expected.

Despite these challenges, grid computing is becoming a popular method of getting the most out of the computing resources of an organization.

Technical Note: The Computer System Concept

As a business professional, you do not need detailed technical knowledge of computers. However, you do need to understand some basic concepts about computer systems, which should help you be an informed and productive user of computer system resources.

A computer is more than a high-powered collection of electronic devices performing a variety of information processing chores. A computer is a *system*, an interrelated combination of components that performs the basic system functions of input, processing, output, storage, and control, thus providing end users with a powerful information processing tool. Understanding the computer as a computer system is vital to the effective use and management of computers. You should be able to visualize any computer this way, from the smallest microcomputer device to the largest computer networks whose components are interconnected by telecommunications network links throughout a building complex or geographic area.

FIGURE 3.10 The computer system concept. A computer is a system of hardware components and functions.

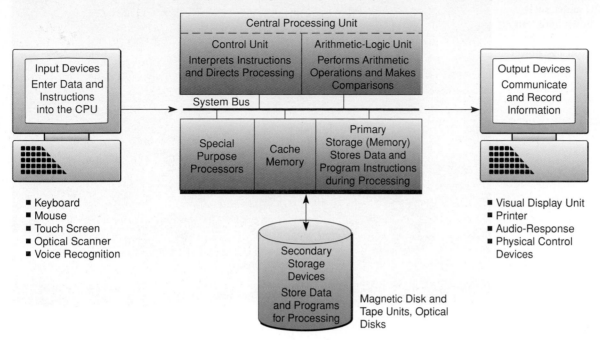

- Keyboard
- Mouse
- Touch Screen
- Optical Scanner
- Voice Recognition

- Visual Display Unit
- Printer
- Audio-Response
- Physical Control Devices

Figure 3.10 illustrates that a computer is a system of hardware devices organized according to the following system functions:

- **Input.** The input devices of a computer system include computer keyboards, touch screens, pens, electronic mice, and optical scanners. They convert data into electronic form for direct entry or through a telecommunications network into a computer system.

- **Processing.** The central processing unit (CPU) is the main processing component of a computer system. (In microcomputers, it is the main *microprocessor*. See Figure 3.11.) Conceptually, the circuitry of a CPU can be subdivided into two major subunits: the arithmetic-logic unit and the control unit. The electronic circuits (known as *registers*) of the *arithmetic-logic unit* perform the arithmetic and logic functions required to execute software instructions.

- **Output.** The output devices of a computer system include video display units, printers, and audio response units. They convert electronic information produced by the computer system into human-intelligible form for presentation to end users.

- **Storage.** The storage function of a computer system takes place in the storage circuits of the computer's primary storage unit, or *memory*, supported by secondary storage devices such as magnetic disk and optical disk drives. These devices store data and software instructions needed for processing. Computer processors may also include storage circuitry called *cache memory* for high-speed, temporary storage of instruction and data elements.

- **Control.** The control unit of a CPU is the control component of a computer system. Its registers and other circuits interpret software instructions and transmit directions that control the activities of the other components of the computer system.

We will explore the various hardware devices associated with each of these system functions in the next section of this chapter.

FIGURE 3.11

Mobile CPU chips, such as the one shown here, can reach speeds up to 3 Ghz to bring desktop-like power to a mobile setting.

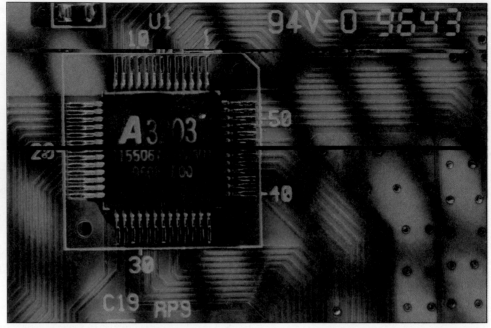

Source: © Getty Images.

Computer Processing Speeds

How fast are computer systems? Early computer processing speeds were measured in milliseconds (thousandths of a second) and microseconds (millionths of a second). Now computers operate in the nanosecond (billionth of a second) range, with picosecond (trillionth of a second) speed being attained by some computers. Such speeds seem almost incomprehensible. For example, an average person taking one step each nanosecond would circle the earth about 20 times in one second!

We have already mentioned the *teraflop* speeds of some supercomputers. However, most computers can now process program instructions at million instructions per second (MIPS) speeds. Another measure of processing speed is *megahertz* (MHz), or millions of cycles per second, and *gigahertz* (GHz), or billions of cycles per second. This rating is commonly called the *clock speed* of a microprocessor because it is used to rate microprocessors by the speed of their timing circuits or internal clock rather than by the number of specific instructions they can process in one second.

However, such ratings can be misleading indicators of the effective processing speed of microprocessors and their *throughput*, or ability to perform useful computation or data processing assignments during a given period. That's because processing speed depends on a variety of factors, including the size of circuitry paths, or *buses*, that interconnect microprocessor components; the capacity of instruction-processing *registers*; the use of high-speed cache memory; and the use of specialized microprocessors such as a math coprocessor to do arithmetic calculations faster.

Moore's Law: Where Do We Go from Here?

Can computers get any faster? Can we afford the computers of the future? Both of these questions can be answered by understanding Moore's law. Gordon Moore, cofounder of Intel Corporation, made his famous observation in 1965, just four years after the first integrated circuit was commercialized. The press called it "Moore's law," and the name has stuck. In its form, Moore observed an exponential growth (doubling every 18 to 24 months) in the number of transistors per integrated circuit and predicted that this trend would continue. Through a number of advances in technology, Moore's law, the doubling of transistors every couple of years, has been maintained and still holds true today. Figure 3.12 illustrates Moore's law as it relates to the evolution of computing power.

FIGURE 3.12

Moore's law suggests that computer power will double every 18 to 24 months. So far, it has.

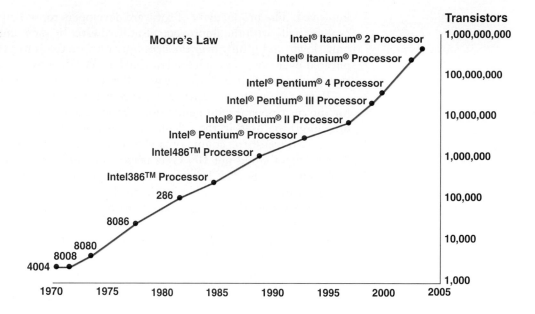

Despite our regular use of exponential growth when predicting the future, particularly the future of technology, humans are often not very good at realizing what exponential growth really looks like. To understand this issue better, let's take a moment to reflect on what Moore's law would mean to us if it applied beyond the number of transistors on a computer chip:

- According to Moore's law, the estimated number of transistors shipped in 2003 was 10^{18}. That's just about 100 times the estimated number of ants in the world.

- In 1978, a commercial flight between New York and Paris cost about $900 and took about seven hours. If Moore's law could be applied to commercial aviation, that same flight today would cost about a penny and would take less than one second.

Over the years, Moore's law has been interpreted and reinterpreted such that it is commonly defined in a much broader sense than it was originally offered. Nonetheless, its application, and its relative accuracy, is useful in understanding where we have been and in predicting where we are going. For example, one common corollary of Moore's law is that the price of a given level of computing power will be cut in half approximately every 18 to 24 months. Moore didn't specifically predict this effect, but it has been shown to be rather consistently accurate as well. This trend is also true for the cost of storage (we will explore this further in the next section).

Although Moore's law was initially made in the form of an observation and prediction, the more widely it became accepted, the more it served as a goal for an entire industry. This caused both marketing and engineering departments of semiconductor manufacturers to focus enormous energy on the specified increase in processing power that it was presumed one or more of their competitors would soon actually attain. Expressed as "a doubling every 18 to 24 months," Moore's law suggests the phenomenal progress of technology in recent years. Expressed on a shorter timescale, however, Moore's law equates to an average performance improvement in the industry as a whole of more than 1 percent *per week*. For a manufacturer competing in the processor, storage, or memory markets, a new product that is expected to take three years to develop and is just two or three months late is 10–15 percent slower or larger than the directly competing products, thus rendering it harder to sell.

A sometimes misunderstood point is that exponentially improved hardware does not necessarily imply that the performance of the software is also exponentially improved. The productivity of software developers most assuredly does not increase exponentially with the improvement in hardware; by most measures, it has increased only slowly and fitfully over the decades. Software tends to get larger and more complicated over time, and Wirth's law (Niklaus Wirth, a Swiss computer scientist) even states humorously that "Software gets slower faster than hardware gets faster."

Recent computer industry studies predict that Moore's law will continue to hold for the next several chip generations (at least another decade). Depending on the doubling time used in the calculations, this progress could mean up to a 100-fold increase in transistor counts on a chip in the next 10 years. This rapid exponential improvement could put 100 GHz personal computers in every home and 20 GHz devices in every pocket. It seems reasonable to expect that sooner or later computers will meet or exceed any conceivable need for computation. Intel, however, suggests that it can sustain development in line with Moore's law for the next 20 years *without* any significant technological breakthroughs. Given the frequency of such breakthroughs in today's marketplace, it is conceivable that Moore's law can be sustained indefinitely. Regardless of what the end of Moore's law may look like, or when it may arrive, we are still moving along at a phenomenal rate of evolution, and the best may be yet to come.

SECTION II Computer Peripherals: Input, Output, and Storage Technologies

The right peripherals can make all the difference in your computing experience. A top-quality monitor will be easier on your eyes—and may change the way you work. A scanner can edge you closer to that ever-elusive goal: the paperless office. Backup-storage systems can offer bank-vault security against losing your work. CD and DVD drives have become essential for many applications. Thus, the right choice of peripherals can make a big difference.

Read the Real World Case 2 about touch screens. We can learn a lot about the future of the human–computer interface and its business applications from this case. See Figure 3.13.

Peripherals

Peripherals is the generic name given to all input, output, and secondary storage devices that are part of a computer system but are not part of the CPU. Peripherals depend on direct connections or telecommunications links to the central processing unit of a computer system. Thus, all peripherals are online devices; that is, they are separate from, but can be electronically connected to and controlled by, a CPU. (This is the opposite of off-line devices that are separate from and not under the control of the CPU.) The major types of peripherals and media that can be part of a computer system are discussed in this section. See Figure 3.14.

Input Technologies

Input technologies now provide a more **natural user interface** for computer users. You can enter data and commands directly and easily into a computer system through pointing devices like electronic mice and touch pads and with technologies like optical scanning, handwriting recognition, and voice recognition. These developments have made it unnecessary to record data on paper *source documents* (e.g., sales order forms) and then keyboard the data into a computer in an additional data-entry step. Further improvements in voice recognition and other technologies should enable an even more natural user interface in the future.

Pointing Devices

Keyboards are still the most widely used devices for entering data and text into computer systems. However, pointing devices are a better alternative for issuing commands, making choices, and responding to prompts displayed on your video screen. They work with your operating system's graphical user interface (GUI), which presents you with icons, menus, windows, buttons, and bars for your selection. For example, pointing devices such as an electronic mouse, trackball, and touch pads allow you to choose easily from menu selections and icon displays using point-and-click or point-and-drag methods. See Figure 3.15.

The **electronic mouse** is the most popular pointing device used to move the cursor on the screen, as well as issue commands and make icon and menu selections. By moving the mouse on a desktop or pad, you can move the cursor onto an icon displayed on the screen. Pressing buttons on the mouse initiates various activities represented by the icon selected.

The trackball, pointing stick, and touch pad are other pointing devices most often used in place of the mouse. A **trackball** is a stationary device related to the mouse. You turn a roller ball with only its top exposed outside its case to move the cursor on the screen. A **pointing stick** (also called a *trackpoint*) is a small button-like device, sometimes likened to the eraser head of a pencil. It is usually centered one row above the space bar of a keyboard. The cursor moves in the direction of the pressure you place on the stick. The **touch pad** is a small rectangular touch-sensitive surface usually placed below the keyboard. The cursor moves in the direction your finger moves on the pad.

REAL WORLD CASE 2

Apple, Microsoft, IBM, and Others: The Touch Screen Comes of Age

The WIMP human–computer interface may have an uninspiring name, but Windows, Icons, Menus, and Pointing (WIMP) devices have dominated computing for some 15 years. The keyboard, mouse, and display screen have served users extraordinarily well.

Now the hegemony of WIMP may be coming to an end, say developers of technologies based on human touch and gesture. For evidence, look no further than Apple's iPhone. From a human-interface point of view, the combined display and input capabilities of the iPhone's screen, which can be manipulated by multiple fingers in a variety of intuitive touches and gestures, is nothing short of revolutionary.

The iPhone isn't the only commercial device to take the human–computer interface to a new level. The Microsoft Surface computer puts input and output devices in a large, tabletop device that can accommodate touches and gestures and even recognize physical objects laid on it. In addition, the DiamondTouch Table from Mitsubishi is a touch- and gesture-activated display that supports small-group collaboration. It can even tell who is touching it.

These devices point the way toward an upcoming era of more natural and intuitive interaction between human and machine. Robert Jacob, a computer science professor at Tufts University, says touch is just one component of a booming field of research on post-WIMP interfaces, a broad coalition of technologies he calls reality-based interaction. Those technologies include virtual reality, context-aware computing, perceptual and affective computing, and tangible interaction, in which physical objects are recognized directly by a computer.

FIGURE 3.13

New human interface technologies promise to revolutionize the way we interact with computers.

Source: McGraw-Hill Companies, Inc./John Flournoy, photographer.

"What's similar about all these interfaces is that they are more like the real world," Jacob says. For example, the iPhone "uses gestures you know how to do right away, such as touching two fingers to an image or application, then pulling them apart to zoom in or pinching them together to zoom out." These actions have also found their way into the iPod Touch and the track pad of the new MacBook Air. "Just think of the brain cells you don't have to devote to remembering the syntax of the user interface! You can devote those brain cells to the job you are trying to do." In particular, he says, the ability of the iPhone to handle multiple touches at once is a huge leap past the single-touch technology that dominates in traditional touch applications such as ATMs.

Although they have not gotten much traction in the marketplace yet, advanced touch technologies from IBM may point a way to the future. In its Everywhere Displays Project, IBM mounts projectors in one or more parts of an ordinary room and projects images of touch screens onto ordinary surfaces, such as tables, walls, or the floor. Video cameras capture images of users touching various parts of the surfaces and send that information for interpretation by a computer. The touch screens contain no electronics—indeed, no computer parts at all—so they can be easily moved and reconfigured.

A variation on that concept has been deployed by a wine store in Germany, says Claudio Pinhanez at IBM Research. The METRO Future Store in Rheinberg has a kiosk that enables customers to get information about the wines the store stocks. "But the store's inventory was so vast customers often had trouble finding the particular wine they wanted on the shelf. They often ended up buying a low-margin wine in a nearby bin of sales specials," Pinhanez says. Now the kiosk contains a "show me" button that, when pressed, shines a spotlight on the floor in front of the chosen item.

IBM is also working on a prototype system for grocery stores that might, for example, illuminate a circle on the floor that asks, "Do you want to take the first steps toward more fiber in your diet?" If the customer touches "yes" with his foot, the system projects footsteps to the appropriate products, such as high-fiber cereal. "Then you could make the cereal box itself interactive," says Pinhanez. "You touch it, and the system would project information about that box on a panel above the shelf." Asked if interactive cereal boxes might be a solution in search of a problem, Pinhanez says, "The point is, with projection and camera technology you can transform any everyday object into a touch screen." He says alternatives that are often discussed (e.g., a store system that talks to customers through their handheld devices) are hard to implement because of a lack of standards for the technology.

Microsoft is working with several commercial partners, including Starwood Hotels & Resorts, which owns the prestigious Sheraton, W, Westin, and Méridien brands, among others, to introduce Surface. It will initially target leisure, entertainment, and retail applications, says Mark Bolger, director of marketing for Surface Computing. For example, he says, one could imagine a hotel guest using a virtual concierge in a Surface computer in the lobby to manipulate maps, photos, restaurant menus, and theater information.

Some researchers say that a logical extension of touch technology is gesture recognition, by which a system recognizes hand or finger movements across a screen or close to it without requiring an actual touch. "Our technology is halfway there," IBM's Pinhanez says, "because we recognize the gesture of touching rather than the occlusion of a particular area. You can go over buttons without triggering them."

Patrick Baudisch at Microsoft Research says the Microsoft prototypes can already act on finger gestures, with the system recognizing finger motions, as well as positions, and understanding the meaning of different numbers of fingers. For example, the motion of one finger is seen as equivalent to a mouse movement, a finger touch is interpreted as a click, and two fingers touching and moving is seen as a scroll command.

Touch technology in its many variations is an idea whose time has come. "It's been around a long time, but traditionally in niche markets. The technology was more expensive, and there were ergonomic problems," he says. "But it's all kind of coming together right now." The rise of mobile devices is a big catalyst, because the devices are getting smaller and their screens are getting bigger. When a screen covers the entire device, there is no room for conventional buttons, which makes it necessary to have other types of interaction (e.g., voice).

Of course, researchers and inventors have envisioned even larger touch displays, including whole interactive walls. A quick YouTube search for "multitouch wall" shows that a number of these fascinating devices have reached the prototype stage, causing multitudes at technology conferences to be entranced. Experts predict, however, that this is just the beginning.

Pradeep Khosla, professor of electrical and computer engineering and robotics at Carnegie Mellon University in Pittsburgh, says touch technology will proliferate, but not by itself. "When we talk face to face, I make eye gestures, face gestures, hand gestures, and somehow you interpret them all to understand what I am saying. I think that's where we are headed," he says. "There is room for all these things, and multimodal gestures will be the future."

Bill Buxton, a researcher at Microsoft, also anticipates a fusion of different interaction technologies. "Touch now may be where the mouse was in about 1983," Buxton says. "People now understand there is something interesting here that's different. But I don't think we yet know what that difference could lead to. Until just one or two years ago there was a real separation between input devices and output devices. A display was a display and a mouse was a mouse."

"There's been this notion that less is more—you try to get less and less stuff to reduce complexity," he says. "But there's this other view that more is actually less—more of the right stuff in the right place, and complexity disappears." In the office of the future, Buxton predicts, desktop computers might be much the same as they are today. "But you can just throw stuff, with the mouse or a gesture, up onto a wall or whiteboard and then work with it with your hands by touch and gesture standing up. Then you'll just pull things into your mobile and have this surface in your hand. The mobile, the wall, the desktop—they are all suitable for different purposes."

Will that be the end of the WIMP interface? Tufts University's Jacob advises users not to discard their keyboards and mice anytime soon. "They really are extremely good," he says. "WIMP almost completely dislodged the command-line interface. The WIMP interface was such a good invention that people just kind of stopped there, but I can't believe it's the end of the road forever."

Buxton agrees. "WIMP is the standard interface going back 20-plus years, and all the applications have been built around that," he says. "The challenge is, without throwing the baby out with the bath, how do we reap the benefits of these new approaches while preserving the best parts of the things that exist?"

Source: Adapted from Gary Anthes, "Give Your Computer the Finger: Touch-Screen Tech Comes of Age," *Computerworld*, February 1, 2008.

CASE STUDY QUESTIONS

1. What benefits may Starwood Hotels derive from the introduction of touch-screen technology, as noted in the case? What possible disruptions may occur as a result? Provide several examples of each.

2. Bill Buxton of Microsoft stated that "[t]ouch now may be where the mouse was in about 1983." What do you make of his comments, and what do you think it would take for touch technology to displace the WIMP interface? Justify your answer.

3. Is advanced touch-screen technology really a solution in search of a problem? Do you agree with this statement? Why or why not?

REAL WORLD ACTIVITIES

1. Most of the fame attached to the iPhone has resulted from individual, end-user applications. How could companies use the iPhone as a platform for commercial use? Break into small groups and brainstorm some possible uses of the technology, as well as what benefits organizations can derive from them. Then prepare a presentation to share your ideas with the class.

2. Information technology advances rapidly, and touch screen is no exception. Go online and search for developments more recent than those mentioned in the case. What new large-scale (i.e., wall-sized) applications could you find? Prepare a report comparing new developments with the examples mentioned here.

FIGURE 3.14

Some advice about peripherals for a business PC.

Peripherals Checklist
● **Monitors.** Bigger is better for computer screens. Consider a high-definition 19-inch or 21-inch flat screen CRT monitor, or LCD flat-panel display. That gives you much more room to display spreadsheets, Web pages, lines of text, open windows, and so on. An increasingly popular setup uses two monitors that allow multiple applications to be used simultaneously.
● **Printers.** Your choice is between laser printers and color inkjet printers. Lasers are better suited for high-volume business use. Moderately priced color inkjets provide high-quality images and are well suited for reproducing photographs; per-page costs are higher than for laser printers.
● **Scanners.** You'll have to decide between a compact, sheet-fed scanner and a flatbed model. Sheet-fed scanners will save desktop space, while bulkier flatbed models provide higher speed and resolution.
● **Hard Disk Drives.** Bigger is better; as with closet space, you can always use the extra capacity. So go for 80 gigabytes at the minimum to 160 gigabytes and more.
● **CD and DVD Drives.** CD and DVD drives are a necessity for software installation and multimedia applications. Common today is a built-in CD-RW/DVD drive that both reads and writes CDs and plays DVDs.
● **Backup Systems.** Essential. Don't compute without them. Removable mag disk drives and even CD-RW and DVD-RW drives are convenient and versatile for backing up your hard drive's contents.

Trackballs, pointing sticks, and touch pads are easier to use than a mouse for portable computer users and are thus built into most notebook computer keyboards.

Touch screens are devices that allow you to use a computer by touching the surface of its video display screen. Some touch screens emit a grid of infrared beams, sound waves, or a slight electric current that is broken when the screen is touched. The computer senses the point in the grid where the break occurs and responds with an appropriate action. For example, you can indicate your selection on a menu display just by touching the screen next to that menu item.

Pen-Based Computing

Handwriting-recognition systems convert script into text quickly and are friendly to shaky hands as well as those of block-printing draftsmen. The pen is more powerful than the keyboard in many vertical markets, as evidenced by the popularity of pen-based devices in the utilities, service, and medical trades.

FIGURE 3.15 Many choices exist for pointing devices including the trackball, mouse, pointing stick, and touch screen.

Source: (left to right) Courtesy of Logitech, Microsoft®, IBM, and © AP/Wide World Photos.

FIGURE 3.16
Many PDAs accept pen-based input.

Source: ©Comstock/PunchStock.

Pen-based computing technologies are still being used in many handheld computers and personal digital assistants. Despite the popularity of touch-screen technologies, many still prefer the use of a stylus rather than their fingertip. *Tablet* PCs and PDAs contain fast processors and software that recognizes and digitizes handwriting, handprinting, and hand drawing. They have a pressure-sensitive layer, similar to that of a touch screen, under their slate-like liquid crystal display (LCD) screen. Instead of writing on a paper form fastened to a clipboard or using a keyboard device, you can use a pen to make selections, send e-mail, and enter handwritten data directly into a computer. See Figure 3.16.

Various pen-like devices are available. One example is the *digitizer pen* and *graphics tablet*. You can use the digitizer pen as a pointing device or to draw or write on the pressure-sensitive surface of the graphics tablet. Your handwriting or drawing is digitized by the computer, accepted as input, displayed on its video screen, and entered into your application.

Speech Recognition Systems

Speech recognition is gaining popularity in the corporate world among nontypists, people with disabilities, and business travelers, and is most frequently used for dictation, screen navigation, and Web browsing.

Speech recognition may be the future of data entry and certainly promises to be the easiest method for word processing, application navigation, and conversational computing because speech is the easiest, most natural means of human communication. Speech input has now become technologically and economically feasible for a variety of applications. Early speech recognition products used *discrete speech recognition*, where you had to pause between each spoken word. New *continuous speech recognition* software recognizes continuous, conversationally paced speech. See Figure 3.17.

Speech recognition systems digitize, analyze, and classify your speech and its sound patterns. The software compares your speech patterns to a database of sound patterns in its vocabulary and passes recognized words to your application software. Typically, speech recognition systems require training the computer to recognize your voice and its unique sound patterns to achieve a high degree of accuracy. Training such systems involves repeating a variety of words and phrases in a training session, as well as using the system extensively.

FIGURE 3.17
Using speech recognition technology for word processing.

Source: © Tim Pennell/Corbis.

Continuous speech recognition software products like Dragon NaturallySpeaking and ViaVoice by IBM have up to 300,000-word vocabularies. Training to 95 percent accuracy may take several hours. Longer use, faster processors, and more memory make 99 percent accuracy possible. In addition, Microsoft Office Suite 2007 has built-in speech recognition for dictation and voice commands of a variety of software processes.

Speech recognition devices in work situations allow operators to perform data entry without using their hands to key in data or instructions and to provide faster and more accurate input. For example, manufacturers use speech recognition systems for the inspection, inventory, and quality control of a variety of products; airlines and parcel delivery companies use them for voice-directed sorting of baggage and parcels. Speech recognition can also help you operate your computer's operating systems and software packages through voice input of data and commands. For example, such software can be voice-enabled so you can send e-mail and surf the World Wide Web.

Speaker-independent voice recognition systems, which allow a computer to understand a few words from a voice it has never heard before, are being built into products and used in a growing number of applications. Examples include *voice-messaging computers*, which use speech recognition and voice response software to guide an end user verbally through the steps of a task in many kinds of activities. Typically, they enable computers to respond to verbal and Touch-Tone input over the telephone. Examples of applications include computerized telephone call switching, telemarketing surveys, bank pay-by-phone bill-paying services, stock quotation services, university registration systems, and customer credit and account balance inquiries.

One of the newest examples of this technology is Ford SYNC. SYNC is a factory-installed, in-car communications and entertainment system jointly developed by Ford Motor Company and Microsoft. The system was offered on 12 different Ford, Lincoln, and Mercury vehicles in North America for the 2008 model year and is available on most 2009 Ford offerings.

Ford SYNC allows a driver to bring almost any mobile phone or digital media player into a vehicle and operate it using voice commands, the vehicle's steering wheel, or manual radio controls. The system can even receive text messages and read them aloud using a digitized female voice named "Samantha." SYNC can interpret a hundred or so shorthand messages, such as LOL for "laughing out loud," and it will read swear words; it won't, however, decipher obscene acronyms. Speech recognition is now common in your car, home, and workplace.

Optical Scanning

Few people understand how much scanners can improve a computer system and make your work easier. Their function is to get documents into your computer with a minimum of time and hassle, transforming just about anything on paper—a letter, a logo, or a photograph—into the digital format that your PC can read. Scanners can be a big help in getting loads of paper off your desk and into your PC.

Optical scanning devices read text or graphics and convert them into digital input for your computer. Thus, optical scanning enables the direct entry of data from source documents into a computer system. For example, you can use a compact desktop scanner to scan pages of text and graphics into your computer for desktop publishing and Web publishing applications. You can scan documents of all kinds into your system and organize them into folders as part of a *document management* library system for easy reference or retrieval. See Figure 3.18.

There are many types of optical scanners, but all employ photoelectric devices to scan the characters being read. Reflected light patterns of the data are converted into electronic impulses that are then accepted as input to the computer system. Compact desktop scanners have become very popular due to their low cost and ease of use with personal computer systems. However, larger, more expensive *flatbed scanners* are faster and provide higher-resolution color scanning.

FIGURE 3.18

A modern document management system can serve as an optical scanner, copier, fax, and printer.

Source: Courtesy of Xerox.

FIGURE 3.19

Using an optical scanning
wand to read bar coding of
inventory data.

Source: © Jeff Smith/The Image Bank/Getty Images.

Another optical scanning technology is called **optical character recognition** (OCR). The OCR scanners can read the characters and codes on merchandise tags, product labels, credit card receipts, utility bills, insurance premiums, airline tickets, and other documents. In addition, OCR scanners are used to automatically sort mail, score tests, and process a wide variety of forms in business and government.

Devices such as handheld optical scanning **wands** are frequently used to read *bar codes*, codes that use bars to represent characters. One common example is the Universal Product Code (UPC) bar coding that you see on just about every product sold. For example, the automated checkout scanners found in supermarkets read UPC bar coding. Supermarket scanners emit laser beams that are reflected off a code. The reflected image is converted to electronic impulses that are sent to the in-store computer, where they are matched with pricing information. Pricing information is returned to the terminal, visually displayed, and printed on a receipt for the customer. See Figure 3.19.

CSK Auto Replaces Paper Forms with Digital Data	CSK Auto Corp. is reaping the benefits of a new proof-of-delivery system it deployed in 2005 to help the $1.6 billion automotive-parts retailer boost its performance. CSK Auto owns more than 1,100 retail outlets in 22 states that operate under the names Checker Auto Parts, Schuck's Auto Supply, and Kragen Auto Parts stores, as well as a wholesale business. CSK Auto, which carries almost 20,000 automotive products, was printing hundreds of thousands of multipart forms as drivers delivered auto parts to their wholesale customers. The forms needed to be stored at several locations and sometimes would get misplaced, resulting in costly overhead. To solve the problem, the company developed and deployed a proof-of-delivery application that runs on an HHP Dolphin 2D handheld computer, which includes an integrated digital camera. When a driver completes a delivery, the receipt information is electronically captured from a bar code, and the driver takes a digital snapshot of the signature at the time of delivery. When drivers return to their offices and dock the handheld units, the data are transmitted to a store server. Customers can view delivery information on CSK Auto's secure Web site.

CSK Auto invested about $1 million into the proof-of-delivery system, but it expects big returns, as it was spending about $500,000 annually on the paper-based system. "One of the interesting and unexpected benefits of the system is that the accounts-payable departments at our larger companies now pay us more quickly because the information is more readily available to them," says Larry Buresh, senior VP and CIO.

Source: Adapted from George Hulme, "CSK Auto Replaces Paper Forms with Digital Data," *Information Week*, April 26, 2005.

Other Input Technologies

Magnetic stripe technology is a familiar form of data entry that helps computers read credit cards. The coating of the magnetic stripe on the back of such cards can hold about 200 bytes of information. Customer account numbers can be recorded on the magnetic stripe so that it can be read by bank ATMs, credit card authorization terminals, and many other types of magnetic stripe readers.

Smart cards that embed a microprocessor chip and several kilobytes of memory into debit, credit, and other cards are popular in Europe and becoming available in the United States. One example is in the Netherlands, where millions of smart debit cards have been issued by Dutch banks. Smart debit cards enable you to store a cash balance on the card and electronically transfer some of it to others to pay for small items and services. The balance on the card can be replenished in ATMs or other terminals. The smart debit cards used in the Netherlands feature a microprocessor and either 8 or 16 kilobytes of memory, plus the usual magnetic stripe. The smart cards are widely used to make payments in parking meters, vending machines, newsstands, pay telephones, and retail stores.

Digital cameras represent another fast-growing set of input technologies. Digital still cameras and digital video cameras (digital camcorders) enable you to shoot, store, and download still photos or full-motion video with audio into your PC. Then you can use image-editing software to edit and enhance the digitized images and include them in newsletters, reports, multimedia presentations, and Web pages. Today's typical mobile phone includes digital camera capabilities as well.

The computer systems of the banking industry can magnetically read checks and deposit slips using **magnetic ink character recognition** (MICR) technology. Computers can thus sort and post checks to the proper checking accounts. Such processing is possible because the identification numbers of the bank and the customer's account are preprinted on the bottom of the checks with an iron oxide–based ink. The first bank receiving a check after it has been written must encode the amount of the check in magnetic ink on the check's lower-right corner. The MICR system uses 14 characters (the 10 decimal digits and 4 special symbols) of a standardized design. *Reader-sorter* equipment reads a check by first magnetizing the magnetic ink characters and then sensing the signal induced by each character as it passes a reading head. In this way, data are electronically captured by the bank's computer systems.

Output Technologies

Computers provide information in a variety of forms. Video displays and printed documents have been, and still are, the most common forms of output from computer systems. Yet other natural and attractive output technologies such as **voice response** systems and multimedia output are increasingly found along with video displays in business applications.

For example, you have probably experienced the voice and audio output generated by speech and audio microprocessors in a variety of consumer products. Voice messaging software enables PCs and servers in voice mail and messaging systems to interact with you through voice responses. Of course, multimedia output is common on the Web sites of the Internet and corporate intranets.

FIGURE 3.20
The flat-panel LCD video monitor is becoming the de facto standard for a desktop PC system.

Source: Courtesy of Hewlett-Packard.

Video Output

Video displays are the most common type of computer output. Many desktop computers still rely on **video monitors** that use a *cathode ray tube* (CRT) technology similar to the picture tubes used in home television sets. Usually, the clarity of the video display depends on the type of video monitor you use and the graphics circuit board installed in your computer. These can provide a variety of graphics modes of increasing capability. A high-resolution, flicker-free monitor is especially important if you spend a lot of time viewing multimedia on CDs, or on the Web, or the complex graphical displays of many software packages.

The biggest use of **liquid crystal displays** (LCDs) has been to provide a visual display capability for portable microcomputers and PDAs. However, the use of "flat panel" LCD video monitors for desktop PC systems has become common as their cost becomes more affordable. See Figure 3.20. These LCD displays need significantly less electric current and provide a thin, flat display. Advances in technology such as *active matrix* and *dual scan* capabilities have improved the color and clarity of LCD displays. In addition, high-clarity flat panel televisions and monitors using *plasma* display technologies are becoming popular for large-screen (42- to 80-inch) viewing.

Printed Output

Printing information on paper is still the most common form of output after video displays. Thus, most personal computer systems rely on an inkjet or laser printer to produce permanent (hard-copy) output in high-quality printed form. Printed output is still a common form of business communications and is frequently required for legal documentation. Computers can produce printed reports and correspondence, documents such as sales invoices, payroll checks, bank statements, and printed versions of graphic displays. See Figure 3.21.

Inkjet printers, which spray ink onto a page, have become the most popular, low-cost printers for microcomputer systems. They are quiet, produce several pages per minute of high-quality output, and can print both black-and-white and high-quality color graphics. **Laser printers** use an electrostatic process similar to a photocopying machine to produce many pages per minute of high-quality black-and-white output.

FIGURE 3.21
Modern laser printers produce high-quality color output with high speed.

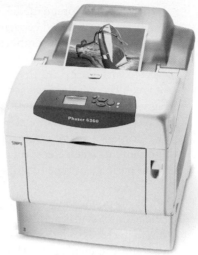

Source: Courtesy of Xerox.

More expensive color laser printers and multifunction inkjet and laser models that print, fax, scan, and copy are other popular choices for business offices.

Storage Trade-Offs

Data and information must be stored until needed using a variety of storage methods. For example, many people and organizations still rely on paper documents stored in filing cabinets as a major form of storage media. However, you and other computer users are more likely to depend on the memory circuits and secondary storage devices of computer systems to meet your storage requirements. Progress in very-large-scale integration (VLSI), which packs millions of memory circuit elements on tiny semiconductor memory chips, is responsible for continuing increases in the main-memory capacity of computers. Secondary storage capacities are also escalating into the billions and trillions of characters, due to advances in magnetic and optical media.

There are many types of storage media and devices. Figure 3.22 illustrates the speed, capacity, and cost relationships of several alternative primary and secondary storage media. Note the cost/speed/capacity trade-offs as you move from semiconductor memories to magnetic disks to optical disks and to magnetic tape. High-speed storage media cost more per byte and provide lower capacities. Large-capacity storage media cost less per byte but are slower. These trade-offs are why we have different kinds of storage media.

FIGURE 3.22
Storage media cost, speed, and capacity trade-offs. Note how cost increases with faster access speeds but decreases with the increased capacity of storage media.

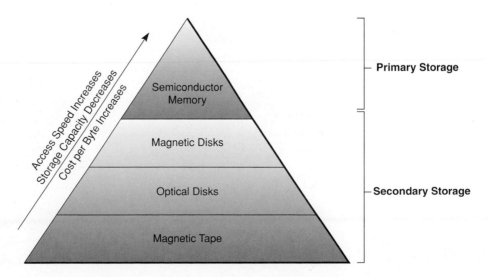

However, all storage media, especially memory chips and magnetic disks, continue to increase in speed and capacity and decrease in cost. Developments like automated high-speed cartridge assemblies have given faster access times to magnetic tape, and the speed of optical disk drives continues to increase.

Note in Figure 3.22 that semiconductor memories are used mainly for primary storage, although they are sometimes used as high-speed secondary storage devices. Magnetic disk and tape and optical disk devices, in contrast, are used as secondary storage devices to enlarge the storage capacity of computer systems. Also, because most primary storage circuits use RAM (random-access memory) chips, which lose their contents when electrical power is interrupted, secondary storage devices provide a more permanent type of storage media.

Computer Storage Fundamentals

Data are processed and stored in a computer system through the presence or absence of electronic or magnetic signals in the computer's circuitry or in the media it uses. This character is called "two-state" or binary representation of data because the computer and the media can exhibit only two possible states or conditions, similar to a common light switch: "on" or "off." For example, transistors and other semiconductor circuits are in either a conducting or a nonconducting state. Media such as magnetic disks and tapes indicate these two states by having magnetized spots whose magnetic fields have one of two different directions, or polarities. This binary characteristic of computer circuitry and media is what makes the binary number system the basis for representing data in computers. Thus, for electronic circuits, the conducting ("on") state represents the number 1, whereas the nonconducting ("off") state represents the number 0. For magnetic media, the magnetic field of a magnetized spot in one direction represents a 1, while magnetism in the other direction represents a 0.

The smallest element of data is called a bit, short for *binary digit*, which can have a value of either 0 or 1. The capacity of memory chips is usually expressed in terms of bits. A byte is a basic grouping of bits that the computer operates as a single unit. Typically, it consists of eight bits and represents one character of data in most computer coding schemes. Thus, the capacity of a computer's memory and secondary storage devices is usually expressed in terms of bytes. Computer codes such as ASCII (American Standard Code for Information Interchange) use various arrangements of bits to form bytes that represent the numbers 0 through 9, the letters of the alphabet, and many other characters. See Figure 3.23.

FIGURE 3.23

Examples of the ASCII computer code that computers use to represent numbers and the letters of the alphabet.

Character	ASCII Code	Character	ASCII Code	Character	ASCII Code
0	00110000	A	01000001	N	01001110
1	00110001	B	01000010	O	01001111
2	00110010	C	01000011	P	01010000
3	00110011	D	01000100	Q	01010001
4	00110100	E	01000101	R	01010010
5	00110101	F	01000110	S	01010011
6	00110110	G	01000111	T	01010100
7	00110111	H	01001000	U	01010101
8	00111000	I	01001001	V	01010110
9	00111001	J	01001010	W	01010111
		K	01001011	X	01011000
		L	01001100	Y	01011001
		M	01001101	Z	01011010

FIGURE 3.24

Computers use the binary system to store and compute numbers.

2^7	2^6	2^5	2^4	2^3	2^2	2^1	2^0
128	64	32	16	8	4	2	1
0 or 1	0 or 1	0 or 1	0 or 1	0 or 1	0 or 1	0 or 1	0 or 1

To represent any decimal number using the binary system, each place is simply assigned a value of either 0 or 1. To convert binary to decimal, simply add up the value of each place.

Example:

2^7	2^6	2^5	2^4	2^3	2^2	2^1	2^0
1	0	0	1	1	0	0	1
128	0	0	16	8	0	0	1

128 + 0 + 0 + 16 + 8 + 0 + 0 + 1 = 153

10011001 = 153

Since childhood, we have learned to do our computations using the numbers 0 through 9, the digits of the decimal number system. Although it is fine for us to use 10 digits for our computations, computers do not have this luxury. Every computer processor is made of millions of tiny switches that can be turned off or on. Because these switches have only two states, it makes sense for a computer to perform its computations with a number system that has only two digits: the **binary number system.** These digits (0 and 1) correspond to the off/on positions of the switches in the computer processor. With only these two digits, a computer can perform all the arithmetic that we can with 10 digits. Figure 3.24 illustrates the basic concepts of the binary system.

The binary system is built on an understanding of exponentiation (raising a number to a power). In contrast to the more familiar decimal system, in which each place represents the number 10 raised to a power (ones, tens, hundreds, thousands, and so on), each place in the binary system represents the number 2 raised to successive powers (2^0, 2^1, 2^2, and so on). As shown in Figure 3.24, the binary system can be used to express any integer number by using only 0 and 1.

Storage capacities are frequently measured in kilobytes (KB), megabytes (MB), gigabytes (GB), or terabytes (TB). Although *kilo* means 1,000 in the metric system, the computer industry uses *K* to represent 1,024 (or 2^{10}) storage positions. For example, a capacity of 10 megabytes is really 10,485,760 storage positions, rather than 10 million positions. However, such differences are frequently disregarded to simplify descriptions of storage capacity. Thus, a megabyte is roughly 1 million bytes of storage, a gigabyte is roughly 1 billion bytes, and a terabyte represents about 1 trillion bytes, while a petabyte is more than 1 quadrillion bytes.

To put these storage capacities in perspective, consider the following: A terabyte is equivalent to approximately 20 million typed pages, and it has been estimated that the total size of all the books, photographs, video and sound recordings, and maps in the U.S. Library of Congress approximates 3 petabytes (3,000 terabytes).

Direct and Sequential Access

Primary storage media such as semiconductor memory chips are called direct access memory or random-access memory (RAM). Magnetic disk devices are frequently called direct access storage devices (DASDs). In contrast, media such as magnetic tape cartridges are known as sequential access devices.

The terms *direct access* and *random access* describe the same concept. They mean that an element of data or instructions (such as a byte or word) can be directly stored and retrieved by selecting and using any of the locations on the storage media. They also mean that each storage position (1) has a unique address and (2) can be individually accessed in approximately the same length of time without having to search

FIGURE 3.25 Sequential versus direct access storage. Magnetic tape is a typical sequential access medium. Magnetic disks are typical direct access storage devices.

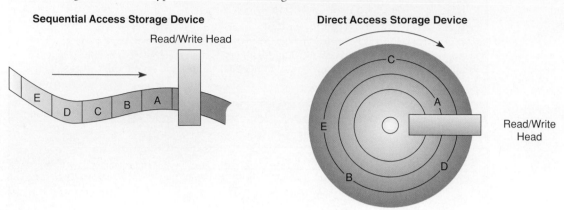

through other storage positions. For example, each memory cell on a microelectronic semiconductor RAM chip can be individually sensed or changed in the same length of time. Also, any data record stored on a magnetic or optical disk can be accessed directly in approximately the same period. See Figure 3.25.

Sequential access storage media such as magnetic tape do not have unique storage addresses that can be directly addressed. Instead, data must be stored and retrieved using a sequential or serial process. Data are recorded one after another in a predetermined sequence (e.g., numeric order) on a storage medium. Locating an individual item of data requires searching the recorded data on the tape until the desired item is located.

Semiconductor Memory

Memory is the coalman to the CPU's locomotive: For maximum PC performance, it must keep the processor constantly stoked with instructions. Faster CPUs call for larger and faster memories, both in the cache where data and instructions are stored temporarily and in the main memory.

The primary storage (main memory) of your computer consists of microelectronic semiconductor memory chips. It provides you with the working storage your computer needs to process your applications. Plug-in memory circuit boards containing 256 megabytes or more of memory chips can be added to your PC to increase its memory capacity. Specialized memory can help improve your computer's performance. Examples include external cache memory of 512 kilobytes to help your microprocessor work faster or a video graphics accelerator card with 64 megabytes or more of RAM for faster and clearer video performance. Removable credit-card-size and smaller "flash memory" RAM devices like a jump drive or a memory stick can also provide hundreds of megabytes of erasable direct access storage for PCs, PDAs, or digital cameras.

Some of the major attractions of semiconductor memory are its small size, great speed, and shock and temperature resistance. One major disadvantage of most semiconductor memory is its volatility. Uninterrupted electric power must be supplied, or the contents of memory will be lost. Therefore, either emergency transfer to other devices or standby electrical power (through battery packs or emergency generators) is required if data are to be saved. Another alternative is to permanently "burn in" the contents of semiconductor devices so that they cannot be erased by a loss of power.

Thus, there are two basic types of semiconductor memory: random-access memory (RAM) and read-only memory (ROM).

● **RAM, random-access memory.** These memory chips are the most widely used primary storage medium. Each memory position can be both sensed (read) and changed (written), so it is also called read/write memory. This is a volatile memory.

FIGURE 3.26
A USB flash memory drive.

Source: Courtesy of Lexar Media.

- **ROM, read-only memory.** Nonvolatile random-access memory chips are used for permanent storage; ROM can be read but not erased or overwritten. Frequently used control instructions in the control unit and programs in primary storage (such as parts of the operating system) can be permanently burned into the storage cells during manufacture, sometimes called *firmware*. Variations include PROM (programmable read-only memory) and EPROM (erasable programmable read-only memory), which can be permanently or temporarily programmed after manufacture.

One of the newest and most innovative forms of storage that uses semiconductor memory is the *flash drive* (sometimes referred to as a *JumpDrive*). Figure 3.26 shows a common flash memory drive.

Flash memory uses a small chip containing thousands of transistors that can be programmed to store data for virtually unlimited periods without power. The small drives can be easily transported in your pocket and are highly durable. Storage capacities currently range as high as 20 gigabytes, but newer flash technologies are making even higher storage capacities a reality. The advent of credit-card-like memory cards and ever-smaller storage technologies puts more data into the user's pocket every day.

Nanochip Inc.: New Memory Process May Overcome Traditional Barriers

A new kind of flash memory technology with potentially greater capacity and durability, lower power requirements, and the same design as flash memory is primed to challenge today's solid-state disk products. Nanochip Inc., based in Fremont, California, said it has made breakthroughs in its array-based memory research that will enable it to deliver working prototypes to potential manufacturing partners by 2009.

Current thinking is that flash memory could hit its limit at around 32–45 nanometers. That describes the smallest possible width of a metal line on the circuit or the amount of space between that line and the next line. The capacity of an integrated circuit is restricted by the ability to print to a smaller and smaller two-dimensional plane, otherwise known as the lithography. That's exactly where Nanochip's technology shines.

"Every two years, you need to buy this new machine that allows you to print something that's smaller and finer," says Stefan Lai of Nanochip. Array-based memory uses a grid of microscopic probes to read and write to a storage material. The storage area isn't defined by the lithography but by the movement of the probes. "If Nanochip can move the probes one-tenth the distance, for example, they can get 100 times the density with no change in the lithography," says Lai. "You don't have to buy all these new machines." IBM has been working on a similar technology for years.

Lai believes that the new memory could herald breakthroughs in mobile devices and biotechnology. "You now need your whole life history stored in your mobile device," he says. "If you want something to store your genome in, it may take a lot of memory, and you'll want to carry it with you." The big question that remains for Nanochip is whether the company can create working prototypes with the cost advantages that array-based technology is supposed to offer over conventional forms of memory.

The challenge for adoption of any new type of memory is that flash itself isn't standing still. "In 2010, it's going to be $1 per gigabyte . . . so hopefully the cost per gigabyte [of probe-based arrays] is going to be low."

Source: Adapted from Dian Schaffhauser, "A Storage Technology That Breaks Moore's Law," *Computerworld*, March 19, 2008.

Magnetic Disks

Multigigabyte magnetic disk drives aren't extravagant, considering that full-motion video files, sound tracks, and photo-quality images can consume colossal amounts of disk space in a blink.

Magnetic disks are the most common form of secondary storage for your computer system. That's because they provide fast access and high storage capacities at a reasonable cost. Magnetic disk drives contain metal disks that are coated on both sides with an iron oxide recording material. Several disks are mounted together on a vertical shaft, which typically rotates the disks at speeds of 3,600 to 7,600 revolutions per minute (rpm). Electromagnetic read/write heads are positioned by access arms between the slightly separated disks to read and write data on concentric, circular tracks. Data are recorded on tracks in the form of tiny magnetized spots to form the binary digits of common computer codes. Thousands of bytes can be recorded on each track, and there are several hundred data tracks on each disk surface, thus providing you with billions of storage positions for your software and data. See Figure 3.27.

Types of Magnetic Disks

There are several types of magnetic disk arrangements, including removable disk cartridges as well as fixed disk units. Removable disk devices are popular because they are transportable and can be used to store backup copies of your data off-line for convenience and security.

- Floppy disks, or magnetic diskettes, consist of polyester film disks covered with an iron oxide compound. A single disk is mounted and rotates freely inside a protective flexible or hard plastic jacket, which has access openings to accommodate the read/write head of a disk drive unit. The 3½-inch floppy disk, with capacities of 1.44 megabytes, was the most widely used version, with a Superdisk technology offering 120 megabytes of storage. Zip drives use a floppy-like technology to provide up to 750 MB of portable disk storage. Today's computers have all but eliminated inclusion of a drive to read floppy disks, but they can be found if necessary.

FIGURE 3.27 Magnetic disk media: a hard magnetic disk drive and a 3½-inch floppy disk.

Source: © Royalty Free/Corbis.

Source: © Stockbyte/PunchStock.

- **Hard disk drives** combine magnetic disks, access arms, and read/write heads into a sealed module. This combination allows higher speeds, greater data recording densities, and closer tolerances within a sealed, more stable environment. Fixed or removable disk cartridge versions are available. Capacities of hard drives range from several hundred megabytes to hundreds of gigabytes of storage.

RAID Storage

RAID computer storage equipment—big, refrigerator-size boxes full of dozens of interlinked magnetic disk drives that can store the equivalent of 100 million tax returns—hardly gets the blood rushing. But it should. Just as speedy and reliable networking opened the floodgates to cyberspace and e-commerce, ever-more-turbocharged data storage is a key building block of the Internet.

Disk arrays of interconnected microcomputer hard disk drives have replaced large-capacity mainframe disk drives to provide virtually unlimited online storage. Known as **RAID (redundant arrays of independent disks)**, they combine from 6 to more than 100 small hard disk drives and their control microprocessors into a single unit. These RAID units provide large capacities (as high as 1–2 terabytes or more) with high access speeds because data are accessed in parallel over multiple paths from many disks. Also, RAID units provide a *fault-tolerant* capacity, in that their redundant design offers multiple copies of data on several disks. If one disk fails, data can be recovered from backup copies automatically stored on other disks. Storage area networks (SANs) are high-speed *fiber channel* local area networks that can interconnect many RAID units and thus share their combined capacity through network servers with many users.

There are a variety of classifications of RAID, and newer implementations include not only hardware versions, but also software methods. The technical aspects of RAID are beyond the scope of this text and probably beyond the needs of the modern business technologist as well. It is sufficient to note that the storage mechanisms in the modern organization are probably using some type of RAID technology. If you are interested in drilling deeper into this technology and how it works, a wide variety of Internet resources are available.

Magnetic Tape

Tape storage is moving beyond backup. Although disk subsystems provide the fastest response time for mission-critical data, the sheer amount of data that users need to access these days as part of huge enterprise applications, such as data warehouses, requires affordable [magnetic tape] storage.

Magnetic tape is still being used as a secondary storage medium in business applications. The read/write heads of magnetic tape drives record data in the form of magnetized spots on the iron oxide coating of the plastic tape. Magnetic tape devices include tape reels and cartridges in mainframes and midrange systems and small cassettes or cartridges for PCs. Magnetic tape cartridges have replaced tape reels in many applications and can hold more than 200 megabytes.

One growing business application of magnetic tape involves the use of high-speed 36-track magnetic tape cartridges in robotic automated drive assemblies that can directly access hundreds of cartridges. These devices provide lower-cost storage to supplement magnetic disks to meet massive data warehouse and other online business storage requirements. Other major applications for magnetic tape include long-term *archival* storage and backup storage for PCs and other systems.

Optical Disks

Optical disk technology has become a necessity. Most software companies now distribute their elephantine programs on CD-ROMs. Many corporations are now rolling their own CDs to distribute product and corporate information that once filled bookshelves.

Optical disks, a fast-growing type of storage media, use several major alternative technologies. See Figure 3.28. One version is called **CD-ROM** (compact disk–read-only

FIGURE 3.28

Comparing the capabilities of optical disk drives.

Optical Disk Drive Capabilities
● **CD-ROM** A CD-ROM drive provides a low-cost way to read data files and load software onto your computer, as well as play music CDs.
● **CD-RW** A CD-RW drive allows you to easily create your own custom data CDs for data backup or data transfer purposes. It will also allow you to store and share video files, large data files, digital photos, and other large files with other people that have access to a CD-ROM drive. This drive will also do anything your CD-ROM drive will do. It reads all your existing CD-ROMs, Audio CDs, and CDs that you have created with your CD burner.
● **CD-RW/DVD** A CD-RW/DVD combination drive brings all the advantages of CD-RW, CD-ROM, and DVD-ROM to a single drive. With a CD-RW/DVD combo drive, you can read DVD-ROM disks, read CD-ROM disks, and create your own custom CDs.
● **DVD-ROM** A DVD-ROM drive allows you to enjoy the crystal-clear color, picture, and sound clarity of DVD video on your PC. It will also prepare you for future software and large data files that will be released on DVD-ROM. A DVD-ROM drive can also read CD-ROM disks, effectively providing users with full optical read capability in one device.
● **DVD+RW/+R with CD-RW** A DVD+RW/+R with CD-RW drive is a great all-in-one drive, allowing you to burn DVD+RW or DVD+R disks, burn CDs, and read DVDs and CDs. It enables you to create DVDs to back up and archive up to 4.7GB of data files (that's up to 7 times the capacity of a standard 650MB CD) and store up to to 2 hours of MPEG2 digital video.

Source: Adapted from "Learn More—Optical Drives," www.dell.com.

memory). CD-ROM technology uses 12-centimeter (4.7-inch) compact disks (CDs) similar to those used in stereo music systems. Each disk can store more than 600 megabytes. That's the equivalent of more than 400 1.44-megabyte floppy disks or more than 300,000 double-spaced pages of text. A laser records data by burning permanent microscopic pits in a spiral track on a master disk from which compact disks can be mass produced. Then CD-ROM disk drives use a laser device to read the binary codes formed by those pits.

CD-R (compact disk–recordable) is another popular optical disk technology. CD-R drives or CD *burners* are commonly used to record data permanently on CDs. The major limitation of CD-ROM and CD-R disks is that recorded data cannot be erased. However, **CD-RW** (CD-rewritable) drives record and erase data by using a laser to heat a microscopic point on the disk's surface. In CD-RW versions using magneto-optical technology, a magnetic coil changes the spot's reflective properties from one direction to another, thus recording a binary 1 or 0. A laser device can then read the binary codes on the disk by sensing the direction of reflected light.

DVD technologies have dramatically increased optical disk capacities and capabilities. DVD (digital video disk or digital versatile disk) optical disks can hold from 3.0 to 8.5 gigabytes of multimedia data on each side. The large capacities and high-quality images and sound of DVD technology are expected to replace CD technologies for data storage and promise to accelerate the use of DVD drives for multimedia products that can be used in both computers and home entertainment systems. Thus, **DVD-ROM** disks are increasingly replacing magnetic tape videocassettes for movies and other multimedia products, while **DVD+RW** disks are being used for backup and archival storage of large data and multimedia files. See Figure 3.29.

FIGURE 3.29
Optical disk storage
includes CD and DVD
technologies.

Source: Photodisc/Getty Images.

**Business
Applications**

One of the major uses of optical disks in mainframe and midrange systems is in **image processing,** where long-term archival storage of historical files of document images must be maintained. Financial institutions, among others, are using optical scanners to capture digitized document images and store them on optical disks as an alternative to microfilm media.

One of the major business uses of CD-ROM disks for personal computers is to provide a publishing medium for fast access to reference materials in a convenient, compact form. This material includes catalogs, directories, manuals, periodical abstracts, part listings, and statistical databases of business and economic activity. Interactive multimedia applications in business, education, and entertainment are another major use of optical disks. The large storage capacities of CD and DVD disks are a natural choice for computer video games, educational videos, multimedia encyclopedias, and advertising presentations.

Radio Frequency Identification

One of the newest and most rapidly growing storage technologies is radio frequency identification (RFID), a system for tagging and identifying mobile objects such as store merchandise, postal packages, and sometimes even living organisms (like pets). Using a special device called an **RFID reader,** RFID allows objects to be labeled and tracked as they move from place to place.

The RFID technology works using small (sometimes smaller than a grain of sand) pieces of hardware called **RFID chips.** These chips feature an antenna to transmit and receive radio signals. Currently, there are two general types of RFID chips: *passive* and *active*. **Passive RFID** chips do not have a power source and must derive their power from the signal sent from the reader. **Active RFID** chips are self-powered and do not need to be close to the reader to transmit their signal. Any RFID chips may be attached to objects or, in the case of some passive RFID systems, injected into objects. A recent use for RFID chips is the identification of pets such as dogs or cats. By having a tiny RFID chip injected just under their skin, they can be easily identified if they become lost. The RFID chip contains contact information about the owner of the pet. Taking this a step further, the Transportation Security Administration is considering using RFID tags embedded in airline boarding passes to keep track of passengers.

Whenever a reader within range sends appropriate signals to an object, the associated RFID chip responds with the requested information, such as an identification number or product date. The reader, in turn, displays the response data to an operator. Readers may also forward data to a networked central computer system. Such RFID systems generally support storing information on the chips as well as simply reading data.

The RFID systems were created as an alternative to common bar codes. Relative to bar codes, RFID allows objects to be scanned from a greater distance, supports storing of data, and allows more information to be tracked per object.

Recently (as discussed in the next section), RFID has raised some privacy concerns as a result of the invisible nature of the system and its capability to transmit fairly sophisticated messages. As these types of issues are resolved, we can expect to see RFID technology used in just about every way imaginable.

RFID Privacy Issues

How would you like it if, for instance, one day you realized your underwear was reporting on your whereabouts?—California State Senator Debra Bowen, at a 2003 hearing on RFID privacy concerns.

The use of RFID technology has caused considerable controversy and even product boycotts by consumer privacy advocates who refer to RFID tags as *spychips*. The two main privacy concerns regarding RFID are:

- Since the owner of an item will not necessarily be aware of the presence of an RFID tag, and the tag can be read at a distance without the knowledge of the individual, it becomes possible to gather sensitive data about an individual without consent.

- If a customer pays for a tagged item by credit card or in conjunction with a loyalty card, then it would be possible to deduce the identity of the purchaser indirectly by reading the globally unique ID of that item (contained in the RFID tag).

Most concerns revolve around the fact that RFID tags affixed to products remain functional even after the products have been purchased and taken home; thus, they can be used for surveillance and other purposes unrelated to their supply chain inventory functions.

Read range, however, is a function of both the reader and the tag itself. Improvements in technology may increase read ranges for tags. Having readers very close to the tags makes short-range tags readable. Generally, the read range of a tag is limited to the distance from the reader over which the tag can draw enough energy from the reader field to power the tag. Tags may be read at longer ranges by increasing reader power. The limit on read distance then becomes the signal-to-noise ratio of the signal reflected from the tag back to the reader. Researchers at two security conferences have demonstrated that passive UHF RFID tags (not the HF-type used in U.S. passports), normally read at ranges of up to 30 feet, can be read at ranges of 50–69 feet using suitable equipment. Many other types of tag signals can be intercepted from 30 to 35 feet away under good conditions, and the reader signal can be detected from miles away if there are no obstructions.

The potential for privacy violations with RFID was demonstrated by its use in a pilot program by the Gillette Company, which conducted a "smart shelf" test at a Tesco in Cambridge, England. They automatically photographed shoppers taking RFID-tagged safety razors off the shelf to see if the technology could be used to deter shoplifting. This trial resulted in consumer boycott against Gillette and Tesco. In another incident, uncovered by the *Chicago Sun-Times*, shelves in a Wal-Mart in Broken Arrow, Oklahoma, were equipped with readers to track the Max Factor Lipfinity lipstick containers stacked on them. Webcam images of the shelves were viewed 750 miles away by Procter & Gamble researchers in Cincinnati, Ohio, who could tell when lipsticks were removed from the shelves and observe the shoppers in action.

The controversy surrounding the use of RFID technologies was furthered by the accidental exposure of a proposed Auto-ID consortium public relations campaign that was designed to "neutralize opposition" and get consumers to "resign themselves to the inevitability of it" while merely pretending to address their concerns. During the U.N. World Summit on the Information Society (WSIS) on November 16–18, 2005,

Richard Stallman, founder of the free software movement, protested the use of RFID security cards. During the first meeting, it was agreed that future meetings would no longer use RFID cards; upon finding out this assurance was broken, he covered his card in tin foil and would uncover it only at the security stations. This protest caused the security personnel considerable concern. Some did not allow him to leave a conference room in which he had been the main speaker, and then prevented him from entering another conference room, where he was due to speak.

The Food and Drug Administration in the United States has approved the use of RFID chips in humans. Some business establishments have also started to "chip" customers, such as the Baja Beach Nightclub in Barcelona. This has provoked concerns into privacy of individuals, as they can potentially be tracked wherever they go by an identifier unique to them. There are concerns that this could lead to abuse by an authoritarian government or lead to removal of other freedoms.

In July 2006, Reuters reported that Newitz and Westhues, two hackers, showed at a conference in New York City that they could clone the RFID signal from a human-implanted RFID chip, which proved that the chip is not hack-proof as was previously believed.

All of these examples share a common thread, and show that whatever can be encoded can also be decoded. RFID presents the potential for enormous efficiencies and cost savings. It also presents significant challenges to privacy and security. Until these issues are worked through, much controversy will continue to surround RFID technologies.

RFID-Enabled Magazines: Tracking Reading Patterns

One of the most vexing problems for magazine publishers is trying to figure out just how many people read printed copies of magazines, rather than letting them languish in stacks of unread mail. Other questions have been raging since the dawn of the printing press, such as How long and often do readers spend reading the pages? Do readers skip around among the articles? Do they read from front to back or from back to front? And does anybody look at the advertisements? Historically, these have been mostly unanswerable questions, left to estimates and guesswork. But a marketing research company, Mediamark Research & Intelligence (MRI) is testing radio frequency identification (RFID) technology to measure magazine readership in public waiting rooms.

The real-world testing follows up a year of laboratory testing. Jay Mattlin, senior vice president of new ventures at MRI, points out that the system needs to be tested "in a non-laboratory setting to determine how well it holds up in this important reading environment."

The project's objectives are to determine whether the RFID-driven passive print monitoring system "can reliably measure—in a waiting room setting—the total time spent with a specific magazine issue, the number of individual reading occasions and potentially, reader exposure to individual magazine pages," according to an MRI statement.

For the lab testing, MRI created an "intelligent" magazine prototype—containing the passive print measuring system—that keeps track of reader activity with designated pages. "Essentially, an RFID tag attached to the magazine sends a signal to a tag reader each time the test subjects turn to one of the designated magazine pages," notes MRI. "The system records the times of the openings and closings of designated pages, as well as the opening/closings of the magazine itself."

Mattlin reported that the system correctly identified magazine openings and closings an average of 95 percent of the time in internal tests.

"We've learned a lot so far in our controlled environment," he noted. "But considering the complexity of trying to measure a non-electronic medium, like magazines, with electronic signals, it's going to take a while before we have a firm grip on the full potential of RFID with regard to magazine audience measurement."

Of course, the most interesting thing to note about this story is the timing: How much value is there in solving the age-old viewership problem as print magazine readership continues to decline, and publishers have shifted most of their focus and content online?

Source: Adapted from Thomas Wailgum, "RFID Chips in Your Magazines," *CIO Magazine*, December 12, 2007.

Predictions for the Future

If Moore's law prevails and technology advancement continues, we can expect to see our lives change in remarkable and unimaginable ways. Although we cannot really predict the future, it is interesting and fun to read the predictions of futurists—people whose job is to think about what the future might bring. Here's one man's perspective on what computing technology might do to change our lives in the decades to come.

Computers Will Enable People to Live Forever

In just 15 years, we'll begin to see the merger of human and computer intelligence that ultimately will enable people to live forever. At least that's the prediction of author and futurist Ray Kurzweil.

Kurzweil suggests that nanobots will roam our bloodstreams, fixing diseased or aging organs, while computers will back up our human memories and rejuvenate our bodies by keeping us young in appearance and health.

The author of the book *The Singularity Is Near*, Kurzweil says that within a quarter of a century, nonbiological intelligence will match the range and subtlety of human intelligence. He predicts that it will then soar past human ability because of the continuing acceleration of information-based technologies, as well as the ability of machines to share their knowledge instantly.

Kurzweil predicts people and computers will intermix with nanobots, blood cell-sized robots, that will be integrated into everything from our clothing to our bodies and brains. People simply need to live long enough—another 15–30 years—to live forever. Think of it as replacing everyone's "human body version 1.0" *with nanotechnology* that will repair or replace ailing or aging tissue, he says. Parts will become easily replaceable.

"A $1,000 worth of computation in the 2020s will be 1,000 times more powerful than the human brain," says Kurzweil, adding that in 25 years we'll have multiplied our computational power by a billion. "Fifteen years from now, it'll be a very different world. We'll have cured cancer and heart disease, or at least rendered them to manageable chronic conditions that aren't life threatening. We'll get to the point where we can stop the aging process and stave off death."

Actually, we'll hit a point where human intelligence simply can't keep up with, or even follow, the progress that computers will make, according to Kurzweil. He expects that nonbiological intelligence will have access to its own design plans and be able to improve itself rapidly. Computer, or nonbiological, intelligence created in the year 2045 will be one billion times more powerful than all human intelligence today.

"Supercomputing is behind the progress in all of these areas," says Kurzweil, adding that a prerequisite for nonbiological intelligence is to reverse-engineer biology and the human brain. That will give scientists a "toolkit of techniques" to apply when developing intelligent computers. In a written report, he said, "We won't experience 100 years of technological advance in the 21st century; we will witness on the order of 20,000 years of progress, or about 1,000 times greater than what was achieved in the 20th century."

According to Kurzweil, here's what we can expect in the not-so-distant future:

- Doctors will be doing a backup of our memories by the late 2030s.
- By the late 2020s, doctors will be sending intelligent bots, or nanobots, into our bloodstreams to keep us healthy, and into our brains to keep us young.

- In 15 years, human longevity will be greatly extended. By the 2020s, we'll be adding a year of longevity or more for every year that passes.

- In the same time frame, we'll routinely be in virtual reality environments. Instead of making a cell call, we could "meet" someone in a virtual world and take a walk on a virtual beach and chat. Business meetings and conference calls will be held in calming or inspiring virtual locations.

- When you're walking down the street and see someone you've met before, background information about that person will pop up on your glasses or in the periphery of your vision.

- Instead of spending hours in front of a desktop machine, computers will be more ingrained in our environment. For instance, computer monitors could be replaced by projections onto our retinas or on a virtual screen hovering in the air.

- Scientists will be able to rejuvenate all of someone's body tissues and organs by transforming their skin cells into youthful versions of other cell types.

- Need a little boost? Kurzweil says scientists will be able to regrow our own cells, tissues, and even whole organs, and then introduce them into our bodies, all without surgery. As part of what he calls the "emerging field of rejuvenation medicine," new tissue and organs will be built out of cells that have been made younger.

- Got heart trouble? No problem, says Kurzweil. "We'll be able to create new heart cells from your skin cells and introduce them into your system through the bloodstream. Over time, your heart cells get replaced with these new cells, and the result is a rejuvenated, young heart with your own DNA."

- One trick we'll have to master is staying ahead of the game. Kurzweil warns that terrorists could obviously use this same technology against us. For example, they could build and spread a bioengineered biological virus that's highly powerful and stealthy.

According to Kurzweil, we're not that far away from solving a medical problem that has plagued scientists and doctors for quite some time now: the common cold. He notes that though nanotechnology could go into our bloodstreams and knock it out, before we even get to that stage, biotechnology should be able to cure the cold in just 10 years.

Source: Adapted from Sharon Gaudin, "Kurzweil: Computers Will Enable People to Live Forever," *InformationWeek*, November 21, 2006.

Summary

- **Computer Systems.** Major types of computer systems are summarized in Figure 3.3. Microcomputers are used as personal computers, network computers, personal digital assistants, technical workstations, and information appliances. Midrange systems are increasingly used as powerful network servers and for many multiuser business data processing and scientific applications. Mainframe computers are larger and more powerful than most midsize systems. They are usually faster, have more memory capacity, and can support more network users and peripheral devices. They are designed to handle the information processing needs of large organizations with high volumes of transaction processing or with complex computational problems. Supercomputers are a special category of extremely powerful mainframe computer systems designed for massive computational assignments.

- **The Computer Systems Concept.** A computer is a system of information processing components that perform input, processing, output, storage, and control functions. Its hardware components include input and output devices, a central processing unit (CPU), and primary and secondary storage devices. The major functions and hardware in a computer system are summarized in Figure 3.10.

- **Peripheral Devices.** Refer to Figures 3.14 and 3.22 to review the capabilities of peripheral devices for input, output, and storage discussed in this chapter.

Key Terms and Concepts

These are the key terms and concepts of this chapter. The page number of their first explanation is given in parentheses.

1. Binary representation (104)
2. Central processing unit (89)
3. Computer system (88)
4. Computer terminal (81)
5. Cycles per second (90)
6. Direct access (105)
7. Graphical user interface (93)
8. Information appliance (82)
9. Magnetic disks (108)
   a. Floppy disk (108)
   b. Hard disk (109)
   c. RAID (redundant array of independent disks) (109)
10. Magnetic stripe (101)
11. Magnetic tape (109)
12. Mainframe system (85)
13. Microcomputer (79)
14. Midrange system (83)
15. Minicomputer (84)

16. MIPS (million instructions per second) (90)
17. Moore's law (90)
18. Network computer (82)
19. Network server (79)
20. Network terminal (81)
21. Off-line (93)
22. Online (93)
23. Optical disks (109)
24. Optical scanning (99)
25. Peripherals (93)
26. Pointing devices (93)
27. Primary storage unit (89)
28. Processing speed (90)
   a. Millisecond (90)
   b. Microsecond (90)
   c. Nanosecond (90)
   d. Picosecond (90)

29. RFID (radio frequency identification) (111)
30. Secondary storage (89)
31. Semiconductor memory (106)
   a. RAM (random-access memory) (106)
   b. ROM (read-only memory) (106)
32. Sequential access (105)
33. Speech recognition (97)
34. Storage capacity (105)
   a. Bit (104)
   b. Byte (104)
   c. Kilobyte (105)
   d. Megabyte (105)
   e. Gigabyte (105)
   f. Terabyte (105)
   g. Petabyte (105)
35. Supercomputer (86)
36. Volatility (106)
37. Workstation computer (79)

Review Quiz

Match one of the previous key terms and concepts with one of the following brief examples or definitions. Try to find the best fit for answers that seem to fit more than one term or concept. Defend your choices.

_____ 1. A computer is a combination of components that perform input, processing, output, storage, and control functions.

_____ 2. The main processing component of a computer system.

_____ 3. A measure of computer speed in terms of processor cycles.

_____ 4. Devices for consumers to access the Internet.

_____ 5. The memory of a computer.

_____ 6. Magnetic disks and tape and optical disks perform this function.

_____ 7. Input/output and secondary storage devices for a computer system.

_____ 8. Connected to and controlled by a CPU.

_____ 9. Separate from and not controlled by a CPU.

_____ 10. Results from the presence or absence or change in direction of electric current, magnetic fields, or light rays in computer circuits and media.

_____ 11. A common computer interface using a desktop metaphor and icons.

_____ 12. Can be a desktop/laptop or handheld computer.

_____ 13. A computer category between microcomputers and mainframes.

_____ 14. A small, portable magnetic disk encased in a thin plastic shell.

_____ 15. A large-capacity disk typically found in computer systems.

_____ 16. Low-cost microcomputers for use with the Internet and corporate intranets.

_____ 17. A redundant array of inexpensive hard drives.

_____ 18. A terminal that depends on network servers for its software and processing power.

_____ 19. A computer that manages network communications and resources.

_____ 20. The most powerful type of computer.

_____ 21. A magnetic tape technology for credit cards.

_____ 22. One-billionth of a second.

_____ 23. Roughly 1 billion characters of storage.

_____ 24. Includes electronic mice, trackballs, pointing sticks, and touch pads.

_____ 25. Early midrange systems used for processing-intensive applications such as scientific research and engineering analysis.

_____ 26. The largest of the three main types of computers.

_____ 27. Processor power measured in terms of number of instructions processed.

_____ 28. Prediction that computer power will double approximately every 18 to 24 months.

_____ 29. Promises to be the easiest, most natural way to communicate with computers.

_____ 30. Capturing data by processing light reflected from images.

_____ 31. The speed of a computer.

_____ 32. One one-thousandth of a second.

_____ 33. 1,024 bytes.

_____ 34. A device with a keyboard and a video display networked to a computer is a typical example.

_____ 35. The amount of data a storage device can hold.

_____ 36. A personal computer used as a technical workstation.

_____ 37. The smallest unit of data storage.

_____ 38. One trillion bytes.

_____ 39. You cannot erase the contents of these storage circuits.

_____ 40. The memory of most computers consists of these storage circuits.

_____ 41. The property that determines whether data are lost or retained when power fails.

_____ 42. Each position of storage can be accessed in approximately the same time.

_____ 43. Each position of storage can be accessed according to a predetermined order.

_____ 44. Microelectronic storage circuits on silicon chips.

_____ 45. Uses magnetic spots on metal or plastic disks.

_____ 46. Uses magnetic spots on plastic tape.

_____ 47. Uses a laser to read microscopic points on plastic disks.

_____ 48. A millionth of a second.

_____ 49. A trillionth of a second.

_____ 50. A grouping of eight bits that represents one alphabetic or special character.

_____ 51. A short-range wireless technology most commonly used to tag, track, and identify objects.

_____ 52. Around a million bytes; more precisely, 2 to the 20th power.

_____ 53. A unit of information or computer storage equal to one quadrillion bytes, or 1,024 terabytes.

Discussion Questions

1. What trends are occurring in the development and use of the major types of computer systems?

2. Will the convergence of PDAs, subnotebook PCs, and cell phones produce an information appliance that will make all of those categories obsolete? Why or why not?

3. Refer to the Real World Case on grid computing at the beginning of the chapter. Given the increasingly ubiquitous presence of computers on every desk, do you think that grid computing approaches will eventually replace more centralized (e.g., mainframe-based) alternatives? Would security considerations play a role in that decision? Provide examples to justify your answer.

4. Do you think that information appliances like PDAs will replace personal computers (PCs) in business applications? Explain.

5. Are networks of PCs and servers making mainframe computers obsolete? Explain.

6. Refer to the Real World Case on touch-screen technology in the chapter. What other applications of this technology could you envision? What do you think will be the next step in communicating with computers? Illustrate your answer with examples.

7. What are several trends that are occurring in computer peripheral devices? How do these trends affect business uses of computers?

8. What are several important computer hardware developments that you expect to happen in the next 10 years? How will these affect the business use of computers?

9. What processor, memory, magnetic disk storage, and video display capabilities would you require for a personal computer that you would use for business purposes? Explain your choices.

10. What other peripheral devices and capabilities would you want to have for your business PC? Explain your choices.

Analysis Exercises

1. Hardware Costs
Purchasing Computer Systems for Your Workgroup
You have been asked to get pricing information for a potential purchase of PCs for the members of your workgroup. Go to the Internet to get prices for these units from Dell and Hewlett-Packard. Look for a high-end office desktop model.

The table below shows the specifications for the basic system you have been asked to price and potential upgrades to each feature. You will want to get a price for the basic system described below and a separate price for each of the upgrades shown.

Component	Basic Unit	Upgrade
CPU (gigahertz)	2.8	3.4
Hard drive (gigabytes)	160	500
RAM (gigabytes)	1	2
Removable media	16× DVD+R/W	48× DVD+R/W
Monitor	17-inch flat screen	19-inch flat screen

Select the standard software licenses; your IT department will install the necessary software for your workgroup. Take a two-year warranty and servicing coverage offered by each supplier. If a two-year warranty is not available, simply note any differences in the coverage with the closest match.

a. Prepare a spreadsheet summarizing this pricing information and showing the cost from each supplier of the following options: (1) units with the basic configuration, (2) the incremental cost of each upgrade separately, and (3) the cost of a fully upgraded unit. If you cannot find features that exactly match the requirements, then use the next higher standard for comparison and make a note of the difference.

b. Prepare a set of PowerPoint slides summarizing your results. Include a discussion of the warranty and servicing contract options offered by each supplier.

2. Price and Performance Trends for Computer Hardware
Hardware Analysis
The table below details price and capacity figures for common components of personal computers. Typical prices for microprocessors, random-access memory (RAM), and hard disk storage are displayed.

The performance of typical components has increased substantially over time, so the speed (for the microprocessor) or the capacity (for the storage devices) is also listed for comparison purposes. Although not all improvements in these components are reflected in these capacity measures, it is interesting to examine trends in these measurable characteristics.

a. Create a spreadsheet based on the figures above and include a new row for each component, showing the price per unit of capacity (cost per megahertz of speed for microprocessors and cost per megabyte of storage for RAM and hard disk devices).

b. Create a set of graphs highlighting your results and illustrating trends in price per unit of performance (speed) or capacity.

c. Write a short paper discussing the trends you found. How long do you expect these trends to continue? Why?

d. Prepare a summary presentation outlining the points from your paper (above). Be sure to *link* your Excel chart into the PowerPoint presentation so that it automatically updates when any data change in the spreadsheet.

3. Can Computers Think Like People?
The Turing Test
The Turing test is a hypothetical test to determine whether a computer system has reached the level of "artificial intelligence." If the computer can fool a person into thinking it is another person, then it has artificial intelligence. Except in very narrow areas, no computer has passed the Turing test.

Free e-mail account providers such as Hotmail or Yahoo take advantage of this fact. They need to distinguish between new account registrations generated by a person and registrations generated by spammers' software. Why? Spammers burn through thousands of e-mail accounts to send millions of e-mails. To help them, spammers need automated tools to generate these accounts. Hotmail fights this practice by requiring registrants to enter correctly an alphanumeric code hidden within an image. Spammers' programs have trouble correctly reading the code, but most humans do not. With this reverse Turing test, also called a "captcha," Hotmail can distinguish between a person and a program and allow only humans to register. As a result, spammers must look elsewhere for free accounts.

a. Aside from those mentioned above, in what applications might businesses find it useful to distinguish between a human and a computer?

	1991	1993	1995	1997	1999	2001	2003	2005
Processor: Speed, MHz	25	33	100	125	350	1000	3,000	3,800
Cost	$180	$125	$275	$250	$300	$251	$395	$549
RAM chip: MB per chip	1	4	4	16	64	256	512	2,000
Cost	$55	$140	$120	$97	$125	$90	$59	$149
Hard drive: GB per drive	0.105	0.250	0.540	2.0	8.0	40.0	160.0	320
Cost	$480	$375	$220	$250	$220	$138	$114	$115

b. Describe a Turing test that a visually impaired person, but not a computer, might pass.

c. Search the Internet for the term "captcha" and describe its strengths and weaknesses.

4. Radio Frequency Identification

Input Device or Invasion of Privacy?

Punch cards, keyboards, bar code scanners—the trend is clear. Input devices have continued to promote faster and more accurate data entry. Key to this advance is capturing data at their source, and no tool does this better than radio frequency identification (RFID) systems. An RFID transmitter sends out a coded radio signal. An RFID tag changes and "reflects" this signal back to an antenna. The RFID system can read the reflection's unique pattern and record it in a database. Depending on the system, this pattern may be associated with a product line, shipping palette, or even a person. Although an RFID system's range is limited to a few dozen feet, this approach enables remarkable inventory tracking that doesn't rely on a human to keyboard in teraction or scan. Except for the presence of a 1-inch-square (5-cm-square) RFID tag, humans may have no idea an RFID system is in operation.

Indeed, that may be part of the problem. Consumers have expressed concern that RFID chips attached to products they purchase may be used to track them. Others fear their government may require embedded RFID chips as a form of personal identification and tracking. What started as a new and improved input device has devolved into a matter of public policy.

a. How would you feel if your university used RFID tags embedded in student IDs to replace the magnetic swipe strip? On a campus, RFID tags might be used to control building access, manage computer access, or even automatically track class attendance.

b. Enter "RFID" into an Internet search engine and summarize the search results. Of the top 20 results, how many were positive, negative, or neutral?

c. Enter "RFID" and "privacy" into an Internet search engine, select a page expressing privacy concerns, and summarize them in a brief essay. Do you find these concerns compelling?

REAL WORLD
CASE 3

Kimberly-Clark and Daisy Brands: Secrets to RFID Success

K imberly-Clark has been around for many years—135 to be exact. And while it may not be a household name, Kimberly-Clark's roster of products and brands certainly are: Kleenex, Scott, Huggies, and Pull-Ups, just to name a few. According to the company, 1.3 billion people use its products every day, contributing to $19.42 billion in sales in 2008.

Behind the nurturing and homey images of those powerhouse brands is a company with operations in 37 countries and a global supply chain that enables Kimberly-Clark to sell its wares in 150 countries.

As one of Wal-Mart's top suppliers, Kimberly-Clark got onboard the RFID revolution early and has been one of the technology's most ardent supporters. "Our goal is to evolve the capabilities of our supply chain to a demand-driven supply network. One of the keys to achieving that vision is to have a highly integrated suite of supply chain systems that provide end-to-end visibility and as close to real-time information as possible," says Mark Jamison, vice president of customer supply chain management at Kimberly-Clark.

About four years ago, Kimberly-Clark started redesigning its supply chain business processes and integrating its systems to that end. The first business process it redesigned was forecast-to-stock. Following that was the redesign of the order-to-cash business processes; the company has chosen a SAP solution for both of these systems.

"When we implement our new order-to-cash system, we will have an integrated suite of systems, and all of our users will be working with the same information as close to real time as possible. In addition, we are developing strategies to better leverage downstream data in our business processes for supply chain, category management and consumer insights," says Jamison.

For many companies, supply chain integration with other enterprise systems is the holy grail of making these initiatives pay off. Kimberly-Clark was no exception. "It was a key driver, but it wasn't the only driver. Historically, our business processes were managed with what I described as a 'patch-quilt' of systems. There was a lot of handing off of information up and down the supply chain," says Jamison. "Not everyone was working with the same information—and not even close to real-time information. And what that tends to drive in the supply chain is surprises, variability and waste. We believe that getting to the end state of high-level integration will allow us to have a more finite supply chain and also helps to manage that variability down and helps to take the waste out."

Real-time data improves the ability to see what's going on in the marketplace and to understand, in a very timely manner, what's happening with the promotions and what's happening with a product in production. And it enables companies to respond, from a supply chain perspective, in a more cost-effective manner, and in a manner that helps increase stock levels and keep things on the shelf. Now that doesn't mean that companies need real-time data at an hour level. But at Kimberly-Clark, managers want to look at it in 8- to 16-hour buckets so that they do get a very timely read as to what's happening in the marketplace.

"Our strategy around RFID has been to focus on business processes and develop repeatable, scalable business processes that are enabled by the technology. The technology in and of itself is not going to bring value to the supply chain. The value to the supply chain comes from reengineering your business processes and enabling those new business processes to work with the technology," notes Jamison.

Kimberly-Clark has focused on redesigning business processes and finding a way for the technology to support those processes. A perfect example of that is in what they have done in the area of promotional execution. Managers found that only 55 percent of the time did their promotional displays move to the floor in time to meet promotion or advertising dates. And that was missing a real opportunity to get that product out to the customers along with retail partners. "So we redesigned the business process that tracks execution of our retail displays on sales floors. We developed daily reports, based on real-time data, and we included our retail operations people in the process so that on a daily basis we can identify those stores which have not executed the promotions," says Jamison.

The retail operations people can then be dispatched to go into the stores of retail partners, and they can get that display and product immediately on the floor. Shortly after the implementation of the new process that was enabled by the technology, Kimberly-Clark saw its execution of promotional displays improve from 55 percent to over 75 percent. The company also saw a corresponding increase in point of sale. "So while we saw the execution improve, we also saw sales increase at a corresponding rate. And I just think that's an excellent example of how RFID, in combination with redesigning a business process, can have big effect on the supply chain," notes Jamison. Another area where they are starting to pilot is trailer management. In its large distribution center, the company has some 500–700 trailers parked in the yard. They are looking at a process where they can track the location and the identity of those trailers. When a trailer comes in the yard, an RFID tag will be applied. The company believes it will be able to improve the accuracy of information and cut down on the amount of time it takes to track trailers in the yard.

"In the supply chain, potentially, we could bring RFIDs back into the manufacturing environments, and trace raw materials. We've found that the bigger payback in the short term for us has been reducing out-of-stocks on the shelf. But we believe there are a lot more opportunities with RFID," says Jamison.

Daisy Brands, which sells its sour cream and cottage cheese through retail stores worldwide, joined Wal-Mart's RFID mandate early on to avoid the rush of companies clamoring for help with RFID products, certification, and services.

While others have hesitated, Daisy says its investment in RFID has been a boon, helping Daisy better manage the flow of its perishable products through Wal-Mart stores and ensure marketing promotions proceed as planned, according to Kevin Brown, Daisy's information systems manager. It also lets Daisy's other customers—including those who don't use RFID—better track their orders.

In 2003, Wal-Mart announced 100 top suppliers would launch its initial RFID effort. Daisy was among another 30-some companies that also volunteered. "We wanted a relationship with the appropriate partners and providers to get this done," says Brown. "Quite frankly, I didn't want to be in line."

"It was never really an ROI project for us," he says. "It's all about being a good partner." That includes not just working more closely with Wal-Mart, but improving tracking services for its other customers. "It's just like going to FedEx to track a package," says Brown. "Our customers can log on to our portal and see what was picked up and by whom." Brown adds that Daisy is beginning to work more closely with Sam's Club on that retailer's RFID ramp-up efforts.

Using Wal-Mart's Retail Link Web site for suppliers, Brown can track, by lot number, how quickly pallets of product make it to stores and when they're unpacked (Wal-Mart has readers at its dock entrances and on its cardboard case compactors) and when products pass through a store's point-of-sale system based on their bar codes. Daisy's own ERP systems contain production and expiration information on all cases and pallets shipped. If product is moving too slowly, indicating a potential issue with freshness, Daisy can dispatch someone to a store to investigate. The information also provides Daisy with insight about trends and behaviors among different types of stores. RFID is far superior to bar codes, Brown says, because it doesn't require a line of sight from a reader.

Brown is also using the information to track promotion success. If a Wal-Mart store, for example, is scheduled to run a two-for-one promotion on sour cream, the items are usually loaded up in an easily accessible, waist-level "coffin cooler." If Daisy doesn't see a proportionately large number of cardboard cases getting destroyed via the compactor—which happens when a store loads up a coffin cooler—it knows the promo may not be taking place as planned. "We need to know the product is going to make it out of the warehouse and into coolers," Brown says. "Is the store ready, and when the coupon breaks, is the product going to be there? We just went through promotions with the holidays, when lots of cooking happens, and we wanted to make sure inventory in warehouses is actually getting put into stores."

"There's more benefit in the long run, using RFID internally, than just compliance," says Brown. "It's one thing to give a customer a purchase order and an invoice, and another to give them insight into how you proceed with all of that."

Source: Adapted from Thomas Wailgum, "Kimberly-Clark's Secrets to RFID Success," *CIO Magazine*, July 30, 2007; and Mary Hayes Weier, "Dairy Company Lends Insight into Wal-Mart's RFID Mandate," *InformationWeek*, January 14, 2008.

CASE STUDY QUESTIONS

1. Mark Jamison of Kimberly-Clark notes that it is business processes, and not the technology (e.g., RFID) itself, what brings value to the supply chain. What does he mean by that? What are the implications for companies seeking to learn from the likes of Kimberly-Clark and Daisy Brands?

2. Both companies reviewed in the case noted they are only starting with RFID. What other uses of the technology would be appropriate for these organizations? How would they benefit from them? Develop several alternatives.

3. While RFID-tagging appears to be very attractive to many companies, barcodes have been around for a long time and are a very efficient, simple, and well-understood technology. Do you expect RFID to completely replace barcodes anytime soon—for some industries or products, but not for others? Justify your answer.

REAL WORLD ACTIVITIES

1. Kimberly-Clark and Daisy Brands were two of the earliest adopters of RFID through their relationship with Wal-Mart. How has that initiative fared since it was announced? Go online and research the most recent developments. Prepare a report to highlight any successes and failures in the advancement toward a fully RFID-enabled supply chain for the giant retailer.

2. What is the value of having access to real-time (or near real-time) information about sales and inventory? Are there any dangers to having this capability, such as overreacting to short-term trends? Break into small groups with your classmates to discuss this issue.

CHAPTER 4

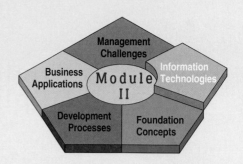

COMPUTER SOFTWARE

Chapter Highlights

Section I
Application Software: End-User Applications

Introduction to Software

Real World Case: GE, H.B. Fuller Co., and Others: Successful Implementations of Software-as-a-Service

Business Application Software

Software Suites and Integrated Packages

Web Browsers and More

Electronic Mail, Instant Messaging, and Weblogs

Word Processing and Desktop Publishing

Electronic Spreadsheets

Presentation Graphics

Personal Information Managers

Groupware

Software Alternatives

Section II
System Software: Computer System Management

System Software Overview

Operating Systems

Real World Case: Power Distribution and Law Enforcement: Reaping the Benefits of Sharing Data through XML

Other System Management Programs

Programming Languages

Web Languages and Services

Programming Software

Real World Case: Wolf Peak International: Failure and Success in Application Software for the Small-to-Medium Enterprise

Learning Objectives

1. Describe several important trends occurring in computer software.

2. Give examples of several major types of application and system software.

3. Explain the purpose of several popular software packages for end-user productivity and collaborative computing.

4. Define and describe the functions of an operating system.

5. Describe the main uses of computer programming software, tools, and languages.

6. Describe the issues associated with open source software.

<table>
<tr><td>SECTION I</td></tr>
</table>

Application Software: End-User Applications

Introduction to Software

This chapter provides an overview of the major types of software you depend on as you work with computers and access computer networks. It discusses their characteristics and purposes and gives examples of their uses. Before we begin, let's look at an example of the changing world of software in business.

Read the Real World Case discussing some innovative and successful implementations of Software-as-a-Service (SaaS). We can learn a lot about the promise of this approach to technology use from this example. See Figure 4.1.

What Is Software?

To fully appreciate the need for and value of the wide variety of software available, we should be sure we understand what software is. **Software** is the general term for various kinds of programs used to operate and manipulate computers and their peripheral devices. One common way of describing hardware and software is to say that software can be thought of as the variable part of a computer and hardware as the invariable part. There are many types and categories of software. We will focus our attention on the different types of software and its uses in this chapter.

Types of Software

Let's begin our analysis of software by looking at an overview of the major types and functions of **application software** and **system software** available to computer users, shown in Figure 4.2. This figure summarizes the major categories of system and application software we will discuss in this chapter. Of course, this figure is a conceptual illustration. The types of software you will encounter depend primarily on the types of computers and networks you use and on the specific tasks you want to accomplish. We will discuss application software in this section and the major types of system software in Section II.

Application Software for End Users

Figure 4.2 shows that application software includes a variety of programs that can be subdivided into general-purpose and function-specific application categories. General-purpose application programs are programs that perform common information processing jobs for end users. For example, word processing, spreadsheet, database management, and graphics programs are popular with microcomputer users for home, education, business, scientific, and many other purposes. Because they significantly increase the productivity of end users, they are sometimes known as *productivity packages*. Other examples include Web browsers, e-mail, and groupware, which help support communication and collaboration among workgroups and teams.

An additional common way of classifying software is based on how the software was developed. Custom software is the term used to identify software applications that are developed within an organization for use by that organization. In other words, the organization that writes the program code is also the organization that uses the final software application. In contrast, COTS software (an acronym that stands for *commercial off-the-shelf*) is developed with the intention of selling the software in multiple copies (and usually for a profit). In this case, the organization that writes the software is not the intended target audience for its use.

Several characteristics are important when describing COTS software. First, as stated in our definition, COTS software products are sold in many copies with minimal changes beyond scheduled upgrade releases. Purchasers of COTS software generally have no control over the specification, schedule, evolution, or access to either the source code or the internal documentation. A COTS product is sold, leased, or licensed to the general public, but in virtually all cases, the vendor of the product retains the intellectual property rights of the software. Custom software, in contrast, is generally owned by the organization that developed it (or that paid to have it

REAL WORLD CASE 1

GE, H.B. Fuller Co., and Others: Successful Implementations of Software-as-a-Service

General Electric's supply chain is not simply enormous. It's a Byzantine web of sourcing partners, touching all corners of the globe: 500,000 suppliers in more than 100 countries that cut across 14 different languages. Each year, GE spends some $55 billion among its vast supplier base.

Long-time GE CIO Gary Reiner knows this problem all too well, since, among his other duties, he is responsible for how the $173 billion conglomerate spends that $55 billion, utilizing GE's Six Sigma practices and taking advantage of its hefty purchasing power. GE, for instance, buys $150 million in desktops and laptops each year from a single supplier, Dell—"at a very low price," says Reiner.

For years, GE's Global Procurement Group faced a challenging reality: trying to accurately track and make sense of all of the supply chain interactions with half a million suppliers—contracts, compliance initiatives, certifications, and other critical data, which needed to be centrally stored, managed, and made accessible to thousands across the globe. GE was using what it called a Global Supplier Library, a homegrown system that, Reiner says, had a "rudimentary capability." Reiner and his staff knew that GE needed something better, but they

FIGURE 4.1

Software-as-a-Service enables one of the largest and most impressive supply chains in the world.

Source: ©Chuck Savage/Corbis.

didn't want to build it. They wanted a supplier information system that was easy to use and install, could unite GE's sourcing empire into one central repository, had multilanguage capabilities, and also offered "self-service" functionality so that each of its suppliers could manage its own data.

The destination was obvious: To achieve one common view of its supplier base, and one version of the truth in all that data, a goal which torments nearly every company today. But to get there, Reiner and his IT and procurement teams took a different route. In 2008, GE bought the application of a little-known Software-as-a-Service (SaaS) vendor that would ultimately become the largest SaaS deployment to date.

"When we judge a solution, we are indifferent to whether it's hosted by a supplier or by us," Reiner says. "We look for the functionality of the solution and at the price." And that, he claims, has been the way they've always operated. Reiner says that his group doesn't see a big difference in cost and in capabilities between on-premise and SaaS products. "And let me emphasize," he adds, "we don't see a big difference in cost either from the point of view of the ongoing operating costs, or the transition costs." Furthermore, when looking at implementation costs, "they're largely around interfacing with existing systems, process changes and data cleansing," he says. "Those three costs exist regardless of whether GE hosts that application or whether the supplier hosts that application."

The Aravo technology platform, which was untested at GE's level of requirements, and with just 20 or so customers, coupled with the sheer scale of GE's needs did not really concern Reiner. "We could have been concerned about that," he concedes. "But that would have also been a concern if we had hosted the software on our own servers. We knew Aravo could handle it." Plus, Reiner says that no other supply chain vendor offered the type of functionality that Aravo's SIM product offered, and Reiner and his team reasoned that it was much cheaper to buy than build. "We'd much rather work with them," he says, "than build it on our own." One GE sourcing manager told Aravo that GE's ROI on the project is not just positive, "it's massively positive."

"They're using SaaS for 100,000 users and 500,000 suppliers in six languages: that's a major technology deployment shift," says Mickey North Rizza, research director at AMR Research. She says that the sheer volume of transactions, combined with the fact that GE supply chain and procurement employees around the world can now access the same sourcing partner information, all from the same central spot, is significant not only for the supply chain management space but also for the SaaS and cloud computing world. "Finally we have a very large company tackling the data transparency issue by using a SaaS product," North Rizza says. "It's a huge deal."

So far, the thorny issue of data quality in GE's supplier data has been improved, because suppliers now use the self-service capabilities in the SaaS system to manage their own data.

GE has 327,000 employees worldwide, and its sourcing systems have more than 100,000 users. There is still more work to do to the SIM platform—for example, GE sourcing employees will add more workflows and new queries to the system; more languages might be added as well (six are operational now).

Reiner says that GE is committed to working with Aravo for the long term and that the system has performed well so far. And SaaS, as an application delivery mechanism, appears to have a bright future at GE.

When Steven John took over as CIO at specialty chemical manufacturer H.B. Fuller Co., he inherited a North American payroll system implementation that was expensive and going nowhere. The business units hadn't participated in the technology decision, and the project was bogged down with customization issues and other concerns. John chose to relinquish control of payroll software and switched to SaaS.

"I wanted to do an implementation that was simple and straightforward—to configure but not customize—and see the benefits of a standard, global platform," John says. "This was a way to teach, save money and outsource a noncore system." Giving up control was an easy trade-off compared with the headaches he would face trying to fix the existing software.

"You're getting a lot more innovation," says Ray Wang, an analyst at Forrester Research Inc. "The products are a lot more configurable than what most people have in their own applications. You can change fields, rename things, and move attributes and workflows. So there's a good level of control there."

What's more, the configuration choices are more refined and well thoughtout, giving users a few good choices instead of myriad options. John found that configuration rather than customization allows H.B. Fuller to maintain its "lean core." "I believe that more standardization leads to more agility," John says. "SaaS allows us to say, 'This is good enough . . . for what we need.' So you don't end up with these horrible situations where you have these highly customized systems. We go with configuration option A, B or C. If one of those three doesn't meet our need, we can try to influence the next release. But in most cases, A, B or C is going to meet the need."

At H.B. Fuller, the move to SaaS for human resources tools allowed the company to empower its people. "I can do a reorganization and have it reflected within minutes, and I don't have to call someone in HR to update everything," John says. "I can also pull up other people's organization charts and see where they are and what they're doing and better understand the organization."

When it comes to managing SaaS, neither the IT department nor the business unit using the software should be eager to relinquish control. "The buying decisions are shifting from IT to the business leaders," who often opt to charge the software as an expense rather than wait for approval through the capital budget committee, Wang says. Still, he adds, "it's very important to engage IT in these SaaS decisions because there are overall IT architectures and blueprints to consider." It becomes very costly when applications don't integrate or interoperate well with one another.

"It's good to at least have some parameters and policies in place so that people understand what type of apps will work better within the environment, what will be cheaper to share information and data with," says Wang.

One of the problems with SaaS is that if your vendor were to go bankrupt, everything would shut down. You don't own the software. It's on lease. The question is, what do you own? If the vendor doesn't have a separate on-premises deployment option, "you need the ability to take out transactional data, master file information, any kind of migration programs, just in case, so you can convert it to an on-premises alternative if they were to go down," Wang says.

In the long term, Wang envisions an IT culture where software as a service is commonplace. "We may live in a world where everything is provisioned. All our applications don't stay on premises, and business leaders are out procuring applications," he says. "IT teams are testing them to make sure they work well in the environment and there are no bugs or viruses and things integrate well, and basically the IT staff will spend a lot of time provisioning services and implementing, integrating, doing installs. That's where we envision the market in 2020."

Source: Adapted from Thomas Wailgum, "GE CIO Gets His Head in the Cloud for New SaaS Supply Chain App," *CIO Magazine*, January 22, 2009; and Stacy Collett, "SaaS Puts Focus on Functionality," *Computerworld*, March 23, 2009.

CASE STUDY QUESTIONS

1. What factors should companies take into consideration when making the decision between developing their own applications, purchasing them from a vendor, or taking the SaaS route, as discussed here? Make a list of factors and discuss their importance to this decision.

2. What risks did GE take on when they contracted with a small and less experienced vendor? What contingencies could have been put in place to prevent any problems from arising? Provide several examples.

3. What should companies do if none of the "configuration options" perfectly fits with their needs? Should they attempt to customize, or select the least-worst alternative? When would they do each?

REAL WORLD ACTIVITIES

1. The case mentions that GE's implementation of SaaS was, at the time, the largest rollout of the technology in the world. What other companies have started using SaaS extensively since? Go online and research recent implementations. How are those different from GE's experience? Prepare a report to share your findings.

2. By implementing systems based on SaaS, companies are relinquishing control over ownership of the technology and are putting access to valuable data on the hands of a third party. What are the perils of taking this approach? How could companies guard against them? Break into small groups to discuss these issues and provide some suggestions and recommendations.

FIGURE 4.2   An overview of computer software. Note the major types and examples of application and system software.

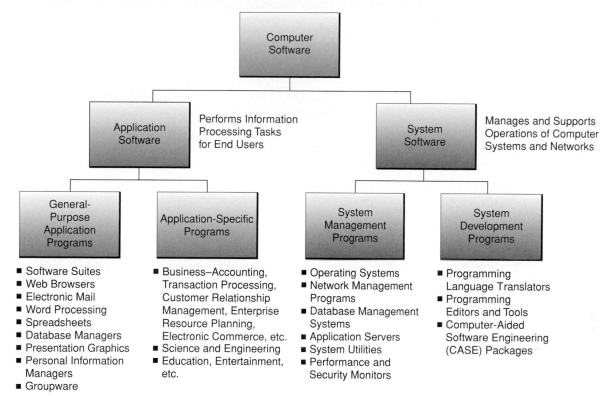

developed), and the specifications, functionality, and ownership of the final product are controlled or retained by the developing organization.

The newest innovation in software development is called **open-source software.** In this approach, developers collaborate on the development of an application using programming standards that allow for anyone to contribute to the software. Furthermore, as each developer completes his or her project, the code for the application becomes available and free to anyone else who wishes to use it. We will discuss this new approach to software development in greater detail in Section II of this chapter.

Visa International: Implementing an e-Business Suite	Visa International is well known and respected all over the world for the innovations it has brought to global commerce with its sophisticated consumer payments processing system. Until recently, however, Visa had many outdated systems managing some of its most critical internal business processes. After an analysis by KPMG in 1999, it was determined that many of Visa's internal systems were becoming a risk to the organization.

The KPMG analysis found that Visa's internal systems were unnecessarily complex and used few of the advantages that technology can bring to an enterprise. For example, Visa's financial management infrastructure was fragmented, complex, and costly to maintain. Often, data were not standardized, resulting in many different databases generating disparate interpretations of business data. Even more surprisingly, Visa's corporate purchasing, accounts payable, and asset management functions were still being managed manually, resulting in time-consuming delays and discrepancies.

Fragmented internal systems are not unusual in a company like Visa that has had rapid double-digit growth for 11 consecutive years. After a careful review of available |

software solutions, Visa chose the Oracle E-Business Suite of business application software to remedy the problems that come with a complex and inefficient back office.

The results of conversion to the new software suite were spectacular. The modern financial applications in the Oracle product turned Visa's cumbersome, outdated desktop procedures into Web-based e-business solutions that met Visa's demands for all roles and processes. For example, Oracle Financials automated Visa's old organization and created a more agile system capable of accounting for the impact of financial activities on a global scale. Accounts payable was transformed from a cumbersome manual process into a streamlined system that automatically checks invoices against outgoing payments and requests reviews of any discrepancies via e-mail. Oracle iProcurement also helped automate Visa's requisitioning and purchasing system by streamlining the entire purchasing process and implementing a self-service model to increase processing efficiency.

Source: Adapted from Oracle Corporation, "Visa to Save Millions a Year by Automating Back-Office Processes with Oracle E-Business Suite," Customer Profile, www.oracle.com, September 13, 2002.

Business Application Software

Thousands of function-specific application software packages are available to support specific applications of end users in business and other fields. For example, business application software supports the reengineering and automation of business processes with strategic e-business applications like customer relationship management, enterprise resource planning, and supply chain management. Other examples are software packages that Web-enable electronic commerce applications or apply to the functional areas of business like human resource management and accounting and finance. Still other software empowers managers and business professionals with decision support tools like data mining, enterprise information portals, or knowledge management systems.

We will discuss these applications in upcoming chapters that go into more detail about these business software tools and applications. For example, data warehousing and data mining are discussed in Chapters 5 and 9; accounting, marketing, manufacturing, human resource management, and financial management applications are covered in Chapters 7 and 8. Customer relationship management, enterprise resource planning, and supply chain management are also covered in Chapter 7. Electronic commerce is the focus of Chapter 8, and decision support and data analysis applications are explored in Chapter 9. Figure 4.3 illustrates some of the many types of business application software that are available today. These particular applications are integrated in the Oracle E-Business Suite software product of Oracle Corp.

FIGURE 4.3 The business applications in Oracle's E-Business Suite software illustrate some of the many types of business application software being used today.

ORACLE E-BUSINESS SUITE

Advanced Planning	Business Intelligence	Contracts
e-Commerce	Enterprise Asset Management	Exchanges
Financials	Human Resources	Interaction Center
Manufacturing	Marketing	Order Fulfillment
Procurement	Product Development	Professional Services Automation
Projects	Sales	Service
Training	Treasury	

Source: Adapted from Oracle Corp., "E-Business Suite: Manage by Fact with Complete Automation and Complete Information," Oracle.com, 2002.

Software Suites and Integrated Packages

Let's begin our discussion of popular general-purpose application software by looking at software suites. The most widely used productivity packages come bundled together as software suites, such as Microsoft Office, Lotus SmartSuite, Corel WordPerfect Office, Sun's StarOffice, and their open-source product, OpenOffice. Examining their components gives us an overview of the important software tools that you can use to increase your productivity.

Figure 4.4 compares the basic programs that make up the top four software suites. Notice that each suite integrates software packages for word processing, spreadsheets, presentation graphics, database management, and personal information management. Microsoft, Lotus, Corel, and Sun bundle several other programs in each suite, depending on the version you select. Examples include programs for Internet access, e-mail, Web publishing, desktop publishing, voice recognition, financial management, and electronic encyclopedias.

A software suite costs a lot less than the total cost of buying its individual packages separately. Another advantage is that all programs use a similar *graphical user interface* (GUI) of icons, tool and status bars, menus, and so on, which gives them the same look and feel and makes them easier to learn and use. Software suites also share common tools such as spell checkers and help wizards to increase their efficiency. Another big advantage of suites is that their programs are designed to work together seamlessly and import each other's files easily, no matter which program you are using at the time. These capabilities make them more efficient and easier to use than a variety of individual package versions.

Of course, putting so many programs and features together in one supersize package does have some disadvantages. Industry critics argue that many software suite features are never used by most end users. The suites take up a lot of disk space (often upward of 250 megabytes), depending on which version or functions you install. Because of their size, software suites are sometimes derisively called *bloatware* by their critics. The cost of suites can vary from as low as $100 for a competitive upgrade to more than $700 for a full version of some editions of the suites.

These drawbacks are one reason for the continued use of integrated packages like Microsoft Works, Lotus eSuite WorkPlace, and AppleWorks. Integrated packages combine some of the functions of several programs—word processing, spreadsheets, presentation graphics, database management, and so on—into one software package.

Because integrated packages leave out many features and functions that are in individual packages and software suites, they are considered less powerful. Their limited functionality, however, requires a lot less disk space (often less than 10 megabytes), costs less than $100, and is frequently preinstalled on many low-end microcomputer systems. Integrated packages offer enough functions and features for many computer users while providing some of the advantages of software suites in a smaller package.

FIGURE 4.4 The basic program components of the top four software suites. Other programs may be included, depending on the suite edition selected.

Programs	Microsoft Office	Lotus SmartSuite	Corel WordPerfect Office	Sun Open Office
Word Processor	Word	WordPro	WordPerfect	Writer
Spreadsheet	Excel	1–2–3	Quattro Pro	Calc
Presentation Graphics	PowerPoint	Freelance	Presentations	Impress
Database Manager	Access	Approach	Paradox	Base
Personal Information Manager	Outlook	Organizer	Corel Central	Schedule

FIGURE 4.5

Using the Microsoft Internet Explorer browser to access Google and other search engines on the Netscape.com Web site.

Source: Netscape content © 2009. Used with permission.

Web Browsers and More

The most important software component for many computer users today is the once simple and limited, but now powerful and feature-rich, Web browser. Browsers such as Microsoft Explorer, Netscape Navigator, Firefox, Opera, or Mozilla are software applications designed to support navigation through the point-and-click hyperlinked resources of the World Wide Web and the rest of the Internet, as well as corporate intranets and extranets. Once limited to surfing the Web, browsers are becoming the universal software platform from which end users launch information searches, e-mail, multimedia file transfers, discussion groups, and many other Internet-based applications.

Figure 4.5 illustrates the use of the Microsoft Internet Explorer browser to access search engines on the Netscape.com Web site. Netscape uses top-rated Google as its default search engine but also provides links to other popular search tools including Ask Jeeves, Look Smart, Lycos, and Overture. Using search engines to find information has become an indispensable part of business and personal Internet, intranet, and extranet applications.

Industry experts predict the Web browser will be the model for how most people use networked computers in the future. Even today, whether you want to watch a video, make a phone call, download some software, hold a videoconference, check your e-mail, or work on a spreadsheet of your team's business plan, you can use your browser to launch and host such applications. That's why browsers are sometimes called the *universal client*, that is, the software component installed on all of the networked computing and communications devices of the clients (users) throughout an enterprise. As an aside, this entire book was revised and edited in a browser-based authoring program called PowerXEditor (we will learn more about PowerXEditor later in this chapter).

Electronic Mail, Instant Messaging, and Weblogs

The first thing many people do at work, all over the world, is check their electronic mail. E-mail has changed the way people work and communicate. Millions of end users now depend on e-mail software to communicate with one another by sending and receiving electronic messages and file attachments via the Internet or their organizations' intranets or extranets. E-mail is stored on networked mail servers until you are ready. Whenever you want to, you can read your e-mail by displaying it on your workstation.

So, with only a few minutes of effort (and a few microseconds of transmission time), a message to one or many individuals can be composed, sent, and received.

As we mentioned previously, e-mail software is now a mainstay component of top software suites and Web browsers. Free e-mail packages such as Microsoft HotMail, Yahoo! Mail, and Netscape WebMail are available to Internet users from online services and Internet service providers. Most e-mail software like Microsoft Outlook Express, Windows Mail, or Netscape Messenger can route messages to multiple end users based on predefined mailing lists and provide password security, automatic message forwarding, and remote user access. They also allow you to store messages in folders and make it easy to add documents and Web file attachments to e-mail messages. E-mail packages enable you to edit and send graphics and multimedia files, as well as text, and provide computer conferencing capabilities. In addition, your e-mail software may automatically filter and sort incoming messages (even news items from online services) and route them to appropriate user mailboxes and folders. Finally, many e-mail clients also include calendaring and contact management functions.

Instant messaging (IM) is an e-mail/computer-conferencing hybrid technology that has grown so rapidly that it has become a standard method of electronic messaging for millions of Internet users worldwide. By using instant messaging, groups of business professionals or friends and associates can send and receive electronic messages instantly and thus communicate and collaborate in real time in a near-conversational mode. Messages pop up instantly in an IM window on the computer screens of everyone in your business workgroup or friends on your IM "buddy list," as long as they are online, no matter what other tasks they are working on at that moment. Instant messaging software can be downloaded and IM services implemented by subscribing to many popular IM systems, including AOL's Instant Messenger and ICQ, MSN Messenger, and Yahoo Messenger. See Figure 4.6.

A **Weblog** (usually shortened to **blog** or written as "Web log" or "weblog") is a **Web site** of personal or noncommercial origin that uses a dated log format updated daily or very frequently with new information about a particular subject or range of

FIGURE 4.6

Using the e-mail features of the Yahoo! instant messaging system.

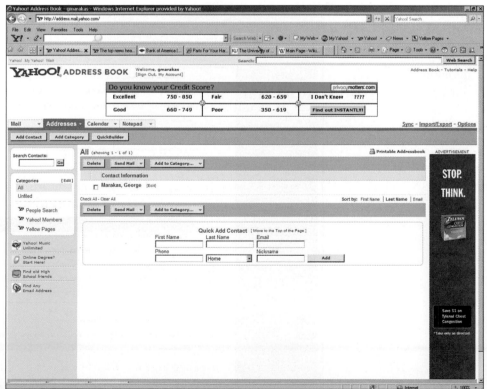

Source: ©Reproduced with permission of Yahoo! Inc.

subjects. The information can be written by the site owner, gleaned from other Web sites or other sources, or contributed by users via e-mail.

A Weblog often has the quality of being a kind of "log of our times" from a particular point of view. Generally, Weblogs are devoted to one or several subjects or themes, usually of topical interest. In general, Weblogs can be thought of as developing commentaries, individual or collective, on their particular themes. A Weblog may consist of the recorded ideas of an individual (a sort of diary) or be a complex collaboration open to anyone. Most of the latter are *moderated discussions*.

Because there are a number of variations on this idea and new variations can easily be invented, the meaning of this term is apt to gather additional connotations with time. As a formatting and content approach for a Web site, the Weblog seems popular because the viewer knows that something changes every day, there is a personal (rather than bland commercial) point of view, and, on some sites, there is an opportunity to collaborate with or respond to the Web site and its participants.

Word Processing and Desktop Publishing

Software for **word processing** has transformed the process of writing just about anything. Word processing packages computerize the creation, editing, revision, and printing of *documents* (e.g., letters, memos, reports) by electronically processing *text data* (words, phrases, sentences, and paragraphs). Top word processing packages like Microsoft Word, Lotus WordPro, Corel WordPerfect, and OpenOffice Writer can provide a wide variety of attractively printed documents with their desktop publishing capabilities. These packages can also convert documents to HTML format for publication as Web pages on corporate intranets or the World Wide Web.

Word processing packages also provide other helpful features. For example, a *spelling checker* capability can identify and correct spelling errors, and a *thesaurus* feature helps you find a better choice of words to express ideas. You can also identify and correct grammar and punctuation errors, as well as suggest possible improvements in your writing style, with grammar and style checker functions. In addition to converting documents to HTML format, you can use the top packages to design and create Web pages from scratch for an Internet or intranet Web site. See Figure 4.7.

FIGURE 4.7

Using the Microsoft Word word processing package. Note the insertion of a table in the document.

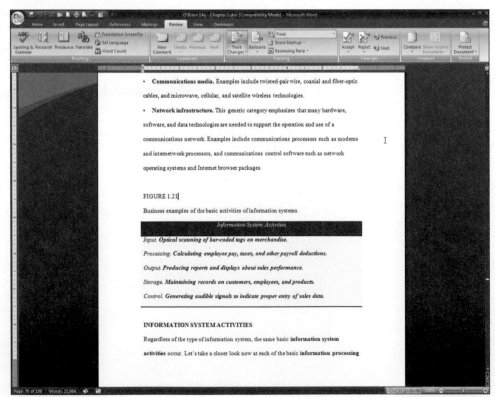

Source: Courtesy of Microsoft®.

End users and organizations can use **desktop publishing** (DTP) software to produce their own printed materials that look professionally published. That is, they can design and print their own newsletters, brochures, manuals, and books with several type styles, graphics, photos, and colors on each page. Word processing packages and desktop publishing packages like Adobe InDesign, Microsoft Publisher, and QuarkXPress are used for desktop publishing. Typically, text material and graphics can be generated by word processing and graphics packages and imported as text and graphics files. Optical scanners may be used to input text and graphics from printed material. You can also use files of *clip art*, which are predrawn graphic illustrations provided by the software package or available from other sources.

Electronic Spreadsheets

Spreadsheet packages like Lotus 1-2-3, Microsoft Excel, OpenOffice Calc, and Corel QuattroPro are used by virtually every business for analysis, planning, and modeling. They help you develop an *electronic spreadsheet*, which is a worksheet of rows and columns that can be stored on your PC or on a network server, or converted to HTML format and stored as a Web page or Web sheet on the World Wide Web. Developing a spreadsheet involves designing its format and developing the relationships (formulas) that will be used in the worksheet. In response to your input, the computer performs necessary calculations according to the formulas you defined in the spreadsheet and displays the results immediately, whether on your workstation or Web site. Most packages also help you develop charts and graphic displays of spreadsheet results. See Figure 4.8.

For example, you could develop a spreadsheet to record and analyze past and present advertising performance for a business. You could also develop hyperlinks to a similar Web sheet on your marketing team's intranet Web site. Now you have a decision support tool to help you answer *what-if questions* you may have about advertising. For example, "What would happen to market share if advertising expenses were to increase by 10 percent?" To answer this question, you would simply change

FIGURE 4.8

Using an electronic spreadsheet package, Microsoft Excel. Note the use of graphics.

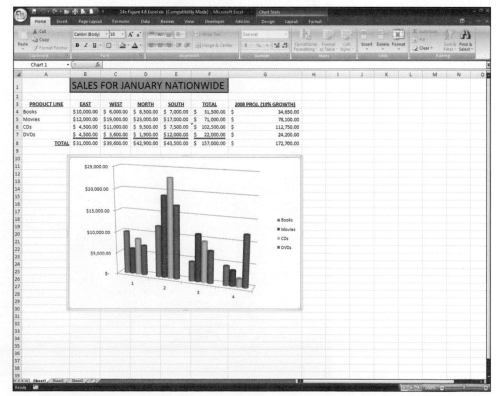

Source: Courtesy of Microsoft®.

the advertising expense formula on the advertising performance worksheet you developed. The computer would recalculate the affected figures, producing new market share figures and graphics. You would then have better insight into the effect of advertising decisions on market share. Then you could share this insight with a note on the Web sheet on your team's intranet Web site.

Presentation Graphics

Presentation graphics software packages help you convert numeric data into graphics displays such as line charts, bar graphs, pie charts, and many other types of graphics. Most of the top packages also help you prepare multimedia presentations of graphics, photos, animation, and video clips, including publishing to the World Wide Web. Not only are graphics and multimedia displays easier to comprehend and communicate than numeric data, but multiple-color and multiple-media displays can more easily emphasize key points, strategic differences, and important trends in the data. Presentation graphics have proved to be much more effective than tabular presentations of numeric data for reporting and communicating in advertising media, management reports, or other business presentations. See Figure 4.9.

Presentation graphics software packages like Microsoft PowerPoint, OpenOffice Impress, Lotus Freelance, or Corel Presentations give you many easy-to-use capabilities that encourage the use of graphics presentations. For example, most packages help you design and manage computer-generated and orchestrated *slide shows* containing many integrated graphics and multimedia displays. You can select from a variety of predesigned *templates* of business presentations, prepare and edit the outline and notes for a presentation, and manage the use of multimedia files of graphics, photos, sounds, and video clips. Of course, the top packages help you tailor your graphics and multimedia presentation for transfer in HTML format to Web sites on corporate intranets or the World Wide Web.

FIGURE 4.9

Using the slide preview feature of a presentation graphics package, Microsoft PowerPoint.

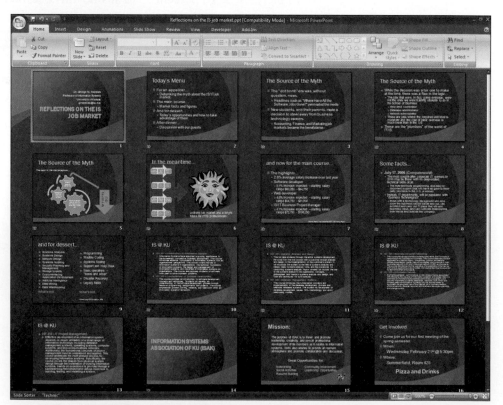

Source: Courtesy of Microsoft®.

FIGURE 4.10
Using a personal information manager (PIM): Microsoft Outlook.

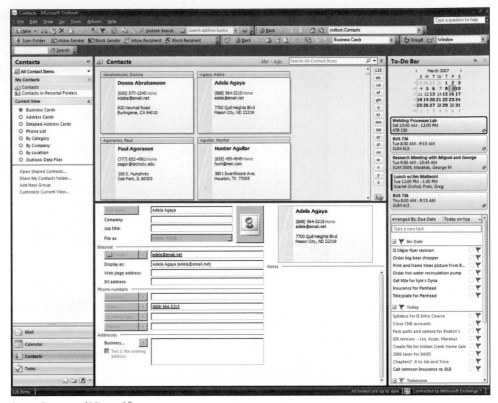

Source: Courtesy of Microsoft®.

Personal Information Managers

The **personal information manager** (PIM) is a popular software package for end-user productivity and collaboration, as well as a popular application for personal digital assistant (PDA) handheld devices. Various PIMs such as Lotus Organizer and Microsoft Outlook help end users store, organize, and retrieve information about customers, clients, and prospects or schedule and manage appointments, meetings, and tasks. A PIM package will organize data you enter and retrieve information in a variety of forms, depending on the style and structure of the PIM and the information you want. For example, information can be retrieved as an electronic calendar or list of appointments, meetings, or other things to do; as the timetable for a project; or as a display of key facts and financial data about customers, clients, or sales prospects. Most PIMs now include the ability to access the World Wide Web and provide e-mail capability. Also, some PIMs use Internet and e-mail features to support team collaboration by sharing information such as contact lists, task lists, and schedules with other networked PIM users. See Figure 4.10.

Groupware

Groupware is software that helps workgroups and teams collaborate to accomplish group assignments. Groupware is a category of general-purpose application software that combines a variety of software features and functions to facilitate collaboration. For example, groupware products like Lotus Notes, Novell GroupWise, and Microsoft Exchange support collaboration through e-mail, discussion groups and databases, scheduling, task management, data, audio and videoconferencing, and so on.

Groupware products rely on the Internet and corporate intranets and extranets to make collaboration possible on a global scale by *virtual teams* located anywhere in the world. For example, team members might use the Internet for global e-mail, project discussion forums, and joint Web page development. Or they might use corporate intranets to publish project news and progress reports and work jointly on documents stored on Web servers. See Figure 4.11.

FIGURE 4.11

Lotus Sametime enables workgroups and project teams to share spreadsheets and other work documents in an interactive online collaboration process.

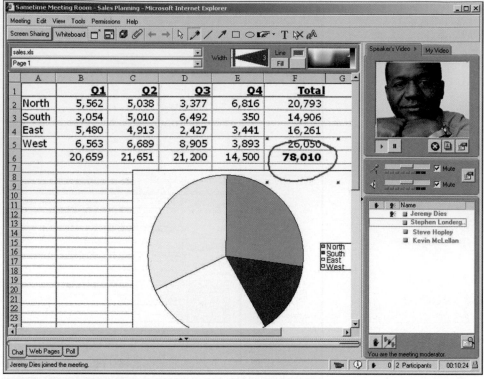

Source: Courtesy of IBM.

Collaborative capabilities are also being added to other software to give it groupware-like features. For example, in the Microsoft Office software suite, Microsoft Word keeps track of who made revisions to each document, Excel tracks all changes made to a spreadsheet, and Outlook lets you keep track of tasks you delegate to other team members. Recently, the Microsoft Office suite has included functions that allow multiple people to work on and edit the same document at the same time. Using this feature, any changes made by one team member will become visible to all team members as they are being made.

Two recent additions to the collaborative software marketplace are Microsoft's Windows SharePoint Services and IBM's WebSphere. Both products allow teams to create sophisticated Web sites for information sharing and document collaboration quickly. Furthermore, businesses can use these products as a platform for application development to facilitate the efficient creation of Web-based business portals and transaction processing applications. Web sites built with collaborative development tools can integrate a wide variety of individual applications that can help increase both individual and team productivity.

Software Alternatives

Many businesses are finding alternatives to acquiring, installing, and maintaining business application software purchased from software vendors or developing and maintaining their own software in-house with their own software developer employees. For example, as we will discuss further in Chapter 12, many large companies are *outsourcing* the development and maintenance of software they need to *contract programming* firms and other software development companies, including the use of *offshore* software developers in foreign countries, and employing the Internet to communicate, collaborate, and manage their software development projects.

Application Service Providers

A large and fast-growing number of companies are turning to application service providers (ASPs), instead of developing or purchasing the application software they need to run their businesses. Application service providers are companies that

FIGURE 4.12

Salesforce.com is a leading application service provider of Web-based sales management and customer relationship management services to both large and small businesses.

Source: Courtesy of Salesforce.com.

own, operate, and maintain application software and the computer system resources (servers, system software, networks, and IT personnel) required to offer the use of the application software for a fee as a service over the Internet. The ASP can bill their customers on a per-use basis or on a monthly or annual fee basis.

Businesses are using an ASP instead of owning and maintaining their own software for many reasons. One of the biggest advantages is the low cost of initial investment, and in many cases, the short time needed to get the Web-based application set up and running. The ASP's pay-as-you-go fee structure is usually significantly less expensive than the cost of developing or purchasing, as well as running and maintaining, application software. In addition, using an ASP eliminates or drastically reduces the need for much of the IT infrastructure (servers, system software, and IT personnel) that would be needed to acquire and support application software, including the continual challenges of distributing and managing companywide software patches and upgrades. Consequently, the use of ASPs by businesses and other organizations is expected to accelerate in the coming years. See Figure 4.12.

| Salesforce.com Big Bet: Software as a Service | Salesforce.com CEO Marc Benioff cast his company as the impetus behind a new era in application development, removing any lingering doubt that he's shooting to replace today's dominant application vendors with Salesforce's software-as-a-service model. "If we're not, then I've been doing the wrong thing for the last 5 1/2 years," Benioff says. "We want to be the ones that replace SAP and Siebel and PeopleSoft. Someone needs to, and it might as well be us."

To that extent, the company introduced two offerings: a customization toolkit called *Customforce*, spun off from its *sforce* application-development platform, and On-Demand Marketplace, a collection of third-party applications, tools, and services built by more than 60 certified partners using the company's *sforce* Web-services

APIs. Customers can either use the combination of *sforce* and *Customforce* to rejigger their Salesforce applications to suit their needs, or, if those capabilities already have been built by one of Salesforce's partners, they can buy them from the On-Demand Marketplace, which boasts tools for everything from data warehousing and enterprise resource planning to project management and wireless extensions.

Salesforce's software-as-a-service model is getting companies to reexamine how they acquire and use applications. It's frequently imitated, most notably by archrival Siebel Systems, which all but created the customer-relationship-management market and now sometimes appears to react to what Salesforce does more than the other way around.

Benioff's approach could boost the application-service-provider (ASP) model in general. ASPs of the late 1990s offered applications that couldn't be customized, but advances such as beefed-up HTML, pervasive broadband connectivity, and the rise of Web services have let services providers—Salesforce in particular—build applications specifically as hosted services and provide for substantial customization of those applications. Salesforce's on-demand model allows those customizations to be transferred when a hosted application is upgraded, overcoming a major reason business-technology managers hesitate to upgrade critical on-premises business applications.

It's too early to tell how widely Benioff's vision will resonate, especially with large companies. Some, like Cisco Systems and payroll-processor Automatic Data Processing Inc., have licensed thousands of seats of Salesforce applications, but most of Salesforce's customers are small and midsize businesses that can't afford on-premises deployments of CRM software packages. Still, Salesforce has influenced the software industry disproportionately to its size and will continue to do so. "This is the kick-off of a major inflection point," says Denis Pombriant, an analyst at Beagle Research Group. "They were a disruptive application. Now they're a disruptive service and a disruptive platform."

Benioff is doggedly committed to his vision, betting that although his idea of "no software" is quaint now, it will ultimately prove to be an accurate forecast of a future in which the service quality, not programming sophistication, will determine which vendors thrive. "What we provide customers is not technology," Benioff says. "We provide customers success."

Source: Adapted from Tony Kontzer, "Benioff's Big Bet," *InformationWeek*, November 8, 2004.

Cloud Computing

One of the most recent advances in computing and software delivery is called cloud computing. Cloud computing is a style of computing in which software and, in some cases, virtualized hardware resources are provided as a service over the Internet. Users need not have knowledge of, expertise in, or control over the technology infrastructure "in the cloud" that supports them. The term cloud is used as a metaphor for the Internet, based on how the Internet is often depicted in computer network diagrams.

The concept incorporates technology trends that have the common theme of reliance on the Internet for satisfying the computing needs of the users. Examples of vendors providing cloud services include SAP Business ByDesign, MidlandHR's "iTrent as a Service," Salesforce.com, and Google Apps, which provide common business applications online that are accessed from a Web browser, while the software and data are stored on the servers.

Cloud computing is often confused with grid computing (recall the concept from Chapter 3 where the CPU power of multiple computers is harnessed to act like one big computer when necessary). Indeed, many cloud computing deployments depend on grids, but cloud computing can be seen as a natural next step from the grid model. The majority of cloud computing infrastructure consists of reliable services delivered through data centers and built on servers with different levels of virtualization technologies. The services are accessible anywhere that has access to networking infrastructure. The cloud appears as a single point of access for all the computing needs of consumers.

As many computer software users generally do not own the infrastructure around them, they can avoid capital expenditure and consume resources as a service, paying instead for what they use. If this sounds alot like how you pay for your electricity or natural gas, it is because the same basic model has been adopted. Many cloud computing offerings have adopted the utility computing model, which is analogous to how traditional utilities like electricity are consumed, while others are billed on a subscription basis. Sharing "perishable and intangible" computing power among multiple users or enterprises can improve utilization rates, as servers are left idle less often because more people are accessing and using the computing resources. Through this approach, significant reductions in costs can be realized while increasing the overall speed of application development. A side effect of this approach is that a given user's or enterprise's computing capacity can be scaled upward almost instantly as needed without having to own an infrastructure that is engineered to be ready for short-term peak loads. Cloud computing has been enabled by large increases in available commercial bandwidth which makes it possible to receive the same response times from centralized infrastructure at other sites.

The real benefit to the organization comes from the cost savings. Cloud computing users can avoid capital expenditure on hardware, software, and services, by simply paying a provider only for what they use. As stated above, consumption is billed on a utility (e.g. resources consumed, like electricity) or subscription (e.g., time based, like a newspaper) basis, with little or no upfront cost. Other benefits of this time-sharing style approach are low barriers to entry, shared infrastructure and costs, low management overhead and immediate access to a broad range of applications. Users can generally terminate the contract at any time and the services are often covered by service level agreements with financial penalties in the event the agreed-upon service levels are not delivered. It is predicted that someday, everyone will compute "in the cloud."

Software Licensing

Regardless of whether a software application is purchased COTS or accessed via an ASP, the software must be licensed for use. Software licensing is a complex topic that involves considerations of the special characteristics of software in the context of the underlying intellectual property rights, including copyright, trademark, and trade secrets, as well as traditional contract law, including the Uniform Commercial Code (UCC).

Contrary to what many believe, when an individual or company buys a software application, they have not purchased rights of ownership. Rather, they have purchased a license to use the software under the terms of the software licensing agreement. Software is generally licensed to better protect the vendor's intellectual property rights. The license often prohibits reverse engineering, modifying, disclosing, or transferring the software. In most cases, the license also gives the purchaser permission to sell or dispose of the rights provided by the license but not to duplicate or resell multiple copies of the software.

The requirement for licensing does not disappear when use of the software is obtained through an ASP. In this case, the license to dispense use of the software is granted to the ASP by the various software vendors, and in return, the ASP agrees to pay the software vendor a royalty based on the number of user accounts to which the ASP resells the rights.

Software vendors are working hard to provide easy licensing and access to their products while simultaneously preventing software piracy, which serves only to raise the ultimate cost of the product.

In the next section, we will learn about an entirely new approach to software licensing: open-source code.

SECTION II | System Software: Computer System Management

System Software Overview

System software consists of programs that manage and support a computer system and its information processing activities. For example, operating systems and network management programs serve as a vital *software interface* between computer networks and hardware and the application programs of end users.

Read the Real World Case on the use of XML by large organizations. We can learn a lot about the business value of using software to share data from this example. See Figure 4.13.

Overview

We can group system software into two major categories (see Figure 4.14):

- **System Management Programs.** Programs that manage the hardware, software, network, and data resources of computer systems during the execution of the various information processing jobs of users. Examples of important system management programs are operating systems, network management programs, database management systems, and system utilities.

- **System Development Programs.** Programs that help users develop information system programs and procedures and prepare user programs for computer processing. Major software development programs are programming language translators and editors, and a variety of CASE (computer-aided software engineering) and other programming tools. We will take a closer look at CASE tools later in this chapter.

Operating Systems

The most important system software package for any computer is its operating system. An operating system is an integrated system of programs that manages the operations of the CPU, controls the input/output and storage resources and activities of the computer system, and provides various support services as the computer executes the application programs of users.

The primary purpose of an operating system is to maximize the productivity of a computer system by operating it in the most efficient manner. An operating system minimizes the amount of human intervention required during processing. It helps your application programs perform common operations such as accessing a network, entering data, saving and retrieving files, and printing or displaying output. If you have any hands-on experience with a computer, you know that the operating system must be loaded and activated before you can accomplish other tasks. This requirement emphasizes that operating systems are the most indispensable components of the software interface between users and the hardware of their computer systems.

Operating Systems Functions

An operating system performs five basic functions in the operation of a computer system: providing a user interface, resource management, task management, file management, and utilities and support services. See Figure 4.15.

The User Interface. The user interface is the part of the operating system that allows you to communicate with it so you can load programs, access files, and accomplish other tasks. Three main types of user interfaces are the *command-driven, menu-driven,* and *graphical user interfaces.* The trend in user interfaces for operating systems and other software is moving away from the entry of brief end-user commands, or even the selection of choices from menus of options. Instead, most software provides an easy-to-use graphical user interface (GUI) that uses icons, bars, buttons, boxes, and other images. These GUIs rely on pointing devices like the electronic mouse or touch pad to make selections that help you get things done. Currently, the most common and widely recognized GUI is the Microsoft Windows desktop.

REAL WORLD CASE 2

Power Distribution and Law Enforcement: Reaping the Benefits of Sharing Data through XML

A power consortium that distributes a mix of "green" and conventional electricity is implementing an XML-based settlements system that drives costs out of power distribution. The Northern California Power Agency (NCPA) is one of several state-chartered coordinators in California that schedules the delivery of power to the California power grid and then settles the payment due to suppliers. NCPA sells the power generated by the cities of Palo Alto and Santa Clara, as well as hydro- and geothermal sources farther north.

Power settlements are a highly regulated and complicated process. Each settlement statement contains how much power a particular supplier delivered and how much was used by commercial vs. residential customers, and the two have different rates of payment. The settlements are complicated by the fact that electricity meters are read only once every 90 days; many settlements must be based on an estimate of consumption that gets revised as meter readings come in.

On behalf of a supplier, NCPA can protest that fees for transmission usage weren't calculated correctly, and the dispute requires a review of all relevant data. Getting one or more of these factors wrong is commonplace. "Power settlements are never completely settled," says Bob Caracristi, manager of power settlements for NCPA. "Negotiations over details may still be going on a year or two after the power has been delivered."

Furthermore, "the enormity of the data" has in the past required a specialist vendor that creates software to analyze the massive settlement statements produced by the grid's manager, the California Independent System Operator. NCPA sought these vendor bids three years ago and received quotes that were "several hundred thousand dollars a year in licensing fees and ongoing maintenance," remarks Caracristi. The need for services from these customized systems adds to the cost of power consumption for every California consumer.

Faced with such a large annual expense, NCPA sought instead to develop the in-house expertise to deal with the statements. Senior programmer analyst Carlo Tiu and his team at NCPA used Oracle's XML-handling capabilities to develop a schema to handle the data and a configuration file that contained the rules for determining supplier payment from the data. That file can be regularly updated, without needing to modify the XML data themselves. In doing so, the NCPA gained a step on the rest of the industry, as the California Independent System Operator started requiring all of its vendors to provide power distribution and billing data as XML files. NCPA has already tested its ability to process XML settlement statements automatically and has scaled out its Oracle system to 10 times its needs "without seeing any bottlenecks," says Tiu.

Being able to process the Independent System Operator statements automatically will represent huge cost savings to NCPA, according to IS manager Tom Breckon. "When settlement statements come in," Breckon says, "NCPA has eight working days to determine where mistakes may have been made. If we fail to get back to [the California Independent System Operator], we lose our chance to reclaim the monies from corrections." Yet, he acknowledges, "we can't inspect that volume of data on a manual basis."

Gaining the expertise to deal with settlements as XML data over the past three years has cost NCPA the equivalent of one year's expense of a manager's salary. Meanwhile, NCPA has positioned itself to become its own statement processor and analyzer, submit disputes to the California Independent System Operator for corrections, and collect more of those corrected payments for members on a timely basis. "In my opinion," says Breckon, "everybody will be doing it this way five years from now. It would reduce costs for all rate payers."

In the state of Ohio, almost 1,000 police departments have found critical new crime-fighting tools by gaining access to the digital records kept by neighboring law enforcement agencies. The Ohio Law Enforcement Gateway Search Engine is an Internet-based tool that can securely comb through numerous crime databases using a single log-in and query, making it easier to use than separate crime databases. For police officers, searching for information on a suspect or a rash of crimes used to require manually logging into several separate crime databases, which could take hours. Now, officers in even the smallest communities can log in just once and quickly gain access to criminal information.

FIGURE 4.13

XML is becoming increasingly popular as an open standard for sharing data across organizations.

Source: © BananaStock/PictureQuest.

The project, which began in 2003, faced a major hurdle: finding a way to get the disparate crime information systems to interoperate with each other. "Everybody wants to share, but nobody wants to use the same product," says Chief Gary Vest of the Powell, Ohio, Police Department, near Columbus. In a major metropolitan area in Ohio, there can be 30 different police departments, each using different products that aren't linked, he says. "That made it difficult for local departments to link suspects and crimes in neighboring jurisdictions."

To make the systems compatible, crime records management vendors rewrote their software so that data from participating departments could be converted into the gateway format for easier data sharing. The vendors used a special object-oriented Global Justice XML Data Model and interoperability standards developed by the U.S. Department of Justice for such purposes. What makes this project different from other fledgling police interoperability programs in the United States is that it's a standards-based system. "You don't have to throw out your vendor to play," notes Vest.

So far, Ohio police can't search on criminal "M.O.'s," but that capability is being worked on. By combing local police records, officers can search for a suspect's name even before it's in the national databases or other larger data repositories, says Vest. "You're a step earlier." Other regional police interoperability projects are in progress around the nation, but this is believed to be the first statewide effort.

In San Diego County, police agencies have been sharing crime data for 25 years using a custom program called the Automated Regional Justice Information System (ARJIS). Barbara Montgomery, project manager for ARJIS, says it differs from the Ohio initiative because it is mainframe-based and all police agencies have to use the same software to access information. Such data-sharing programs are not widespread in the United States because of their cost, especially for smaller police departments, she says. In fact, ARJIS was made possible only after a number of departments pooled their money.

"No single police department could afford to buy [the hardware and the skills of] a bunch of computer programmers so it was truly a 'united we stand, divided we fall' approach," Montgomery says. "The next generation of ARJIS is being planned now, with the system likely to evolve over the next few years from its mainframe roots to a server-based enterprise architecture for more flexibility," says Montgomery.

Along the same lines, the Florida Department of Law Enforcement will begin work on a $15 million project to integrate the back-end systems of 500 law enforcement organizations across the state. In many cases, investigators in Florida law enforcement offices now gather information from other departments in the state via telephone or e-mail. The Florida Law Enforcement Exchange project promises to provide access to statewide law enforcement data with a single query, says state's CIO Brenda Owens, whose IT unit is overseeing the project.

"Our goal is to provide seamless access to data across the state," says Owens. "An operator sitting at a PC in a police department doesn't know or care what the data look like; they can put the inquiry in and get the information back."

Large integration projects such as this often derail because it's difficult to get different groups to agree on metadata types. "The metadata management or understanding the common elements is a huge part of [an integration project]," notes Ken Vollmer, an analyst at Forrester Research. "Trying to combine information from two agencies—that is hard enough. In Florida, you're talking 500 agencies, and they have to have some software to help them determine what the common data elements are."

Source: Adapted from Charles Babcok, "Electricity Costs Attacked through XML," *InformationWeek*, December 26, 2007; Todd Weiss, "Ohio Police Use Specialized Software to Track Data (and Bad Guys)," *Computerworld*, June 23, 2006; and Heather Havenstein, "Florida Begins Linking Its Law Enforcement Agencies," *Computerworld*, February 13, 2006.

CASE STUDY QUESTIONS

1. What is the business value of XML to the organizations described in the case? How are they able to achieve such large returns on investment?

2. What are other ways in which XML could be used by organizations to create value and share data? Look for examples involving for-profit organizations to gain a more complete perspective on the issue.

3. What seem to be important elements in the success of projects relying on extensive use of XML across organizations, and why? Research the concept of metadata to inform your answer.

REAL WORLD ACTIVITIES

1. XBRL stands for eXtensible Business Reporting Language, and it is one of the family of XML languages that is becoming standard for business communication across companies. Among other uses, the Securities and Exchange Commission has run a voluntary XBRL filing program since 2005. Go online and research the current status of XBRL implementation and adoption, including examples of companies that are already using it for business purposes. Prepare a report to share your findings.

2. Investigate other large-scale, systemwide implementations of XML such as the one described in the case involving the California Independent System Operator. Prepare a presentation with the proposed or realized costs and benefits of those efforts and share your findings with the class.

FIGURE 4.14

The system and application software interface between end users and computer hardware.

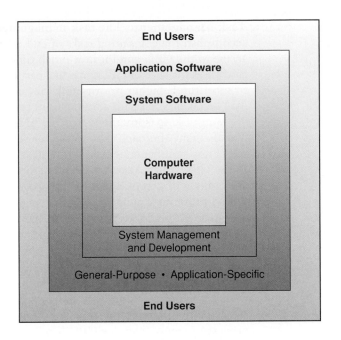

Resource Management. An operating system uses a variety of resource management programs to manage the hardware and networking resources of a computer system, including its CPU, memory, secondary storage devices, telecommunications processors, and input/output peripherals. For example, memory management programs keep track of where data and programs are stored. They may also subdivide memory into a number of sections and swap parts of programs and data between memory and magnetic disks or other secondary storage devices. This process can provide a computer system with a virtual memory capability that is significantly larger than the real memory capacity of its primary storage circuits. So, a computer with a virtual memory capability can process large programs and greater amounts of data than the capacity of its memory chips would normally allow.

File Management. An operating system contains **file management** programs that control the creation, deletion, and access of files of data and programs. File management also involves keeping track of the physical location of files on magnetic disks and other secondary storage devices. So operating systems maintain directories of information about the location and characteristics of files stored on a computer system's secondary storage devices.

FIGURE 4.15

The basic functions of an operating system include a user interface, resource management, task management, file management, and utilities and other functions.

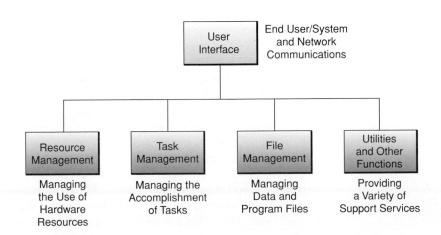

Task Management. The **task management** programs of an operating system help accomplish the computing tasks of end users. The programs control which task gets access to the CPU and for how much time. The task management functions can allocate a specific slice of CPU time to a particular task and interrupt the CPU at any time to substitute a higher priority task. Several different approaches to task management may be taken, each with advantages in certain situations.

Multitasking (sometimes referred to as *multiprogramming* or *time-sharing*) is a task management approach that allows for several computing tasks to be performed in a seemingly simultaneous fashion. In reality, multitasking assigns only one task at a time to the CPU, but it switches from one program to another so quickly that it gives the appearance of executing all of the programs at the same time. There are two basic types of multitasking: *preemptive* and *cooperative*. In preemptive multitasking, the task management functions parcel out CPU *time slices* to each program. In contrast, cooperative multitasking allows each program to control the CPU for as long as it needs it. If a program is not using the CPU, however, it can allow another program to use it temporarily. Most Windows and UNIX-based operating systems use the preemptive approach, whereas most Macintosh-style platforms use cooperative multitasking. Although the terms *multitasking* and *multiprocessing* are often used interchangeably, they are actually different concepts based on the number of CPUs being used. In multiprocessing, more than one CPU is being accessed, but in multitasking, only one CPU is in operation.

Most computers make use of some sort of multitasking. On modern microcomputers, multitasking is made possible by the development of powerful processors and their ability to address much larger memory capacities directly. This capability allows primary storage to be subdivided into several large partitions, each of which is used by a different software application.

In effect, a single computer can act as if it were several computers, or *virtual machines*, because each application program runs independently at the same time. The number of programs that can be run concurrently depends on the amount of memory that is available and the amount of processing each job demands. That's because a microprocessor (or CPU) can become overloaded with too many jobs and provide unacceptably slow response times. However, if memory and processing capacities are adequate, multitasking allows end users to switch easily from one application to another, share data files among applications, and process some applications in a *background* mode. Typically, background tasks include large printing jobs, extensive mathematical computations, or unattended telecommunications sessions.

Microsoft Windows

For many years, MS-DOS (Microsoft Disk Operating System) was the most widely used microcomputer operating system. It is a single-user, single-tasking operating system but was given a graphical user interface and limited multitasking capabilities by combining it with Microsoft **Windows.** Microsoft began replacing its DOS/Windows combination in 1995 with the Windows 95 operating system, featuring a graphical user interface, true multitasking, networking, multimedia, and many other capabilities. Microsoft introduced an enhanced Windows 98 version during 1998, and a Windows Me (Millennium Edition) consumer PC system in 2000.

Microsoft introduced its **Windows NT** (New Technology) operating system in 1995. Windows NT is a powerful, multitasking, multiuser operating system that was installed on many network servers to manage PCs with high-performance computing requirements. New Server and Workstation versions were introduced in 1997. Microsoft substantially enhanced its Windows NT products with the **Windows 2000** operating system during the year 2000.

Late in 2001, Microsoft introduced **Windows XP** Home Edition and Professional versions, and thus formally merged its two Windows operating system lines for consumer and business users, uniting them around the Windows NT and Windows 2000 code base. With Windows XP, consumers and home users finally received an enhanced

FIGURE 4.16   Comparing the purposes of the four versions of the Microsoft Windows Server 2008 operating system.

Microsoft Windows Server 2008 Comparisons
● **Windows Server 2008, Standard Edition**   For smaller server applications, including file and print sharing, Internet and intranet connectivity, and centralized desktop application deployment.
● **Windows Server 2008, Enterprise Edition**   For larger business applications, XML Web services, enterprise collaboration, and enterprise network support.
● **Windows Server 2008, Datacenter Edition**   For business-critical and mission-critical applications demanding the highest levels of scalability and availability.
● **Windows Server 2008, Web Edition**   For Web serving and hosting, providing a platform for developing and deploying Web services and applications.

Windows operating system with the performance and stability features that business users had in Windows 2000 and continue to have in Windows XP Professional. Microsoft also introduced four new **Windows Server 2003** versions in 2008, which are summarized and compared in Figure 4.16.

In 2006, Microsoft released their newest operating system called Vista. Vista contains hundreds of new features; some of the most significant include an updated graphical user interface and visual style dubbed Windows Aero, improved search features, new multimedia creation tools such as Windows DVD Maker, and completely redesigned networking, audio, print, and display subsystems. Vista also aims to increase the level of communication between machines on a home network using peer-to-peer technology, making it easier to share files and digital media between computers and devices.

For developers, Vista introduced version 3.0 of the .NET Framework, which aims to make it significantly easier for developers to write high-quality applications than with the previous versions of Windows.

Microsoft's primary stated objective with Vista, however, has been to improve the state of security in the Windows operating system. One of the most common criticisms of Windows XP and its predecessors has been their commonly exploited security vulnerabilities and overall susceptibility to malware, viruses, and buffer overflows. In light of these complaints, then-Microsoft chairman Bill Gates announced in early 2002 a companywide "Trustworthy Computing Initiative" to incorporate security work into every aspect of software development at the company. Microsoft claimed that it prioritized improving the security of Windows XP and Windows Server 2003 rather than finishing Windows Vista, significantly delaying its completion.

During 2008, a new server product, entitled (appropriately enough) Windows Server 2008, has emerged. Windows Server 2008 is built from the same code base as Windows Vista; therefore, it shares much of the same architecture and functionality. Since the code base is common, it automatically comes with most of the technical, security, management, and administrative features new to Windows Vista such as the rewritten networking processes (native IPv6, native wireless, speed, and security improvements); improved image-based installation, deployment, and recovery; improved diagnostics, monitoring, event logging, and reporting tools; new security features; improved Windows Firewall with secure default configuration; .NET Framework 3.0 technologies; and the core kernel, memory and file system improvements. Processors and memory devices are modeled as Plug and Play devices, to allow hot-plugging of these devices.

Windows Server 2008 is already in release 2 as several performance and security enhancements required a major upgrade.

UNIX   Originally developed by AT&T, **UNIX** now is also offered by other vendors, including Solaris by Sun Microsystems and AIX by IBM. UNIX is a multitasking, multiuser, network-managing operating system whose portability allows it to run on mainframes, midrange computers, and microcomputers. UNIX is still a popular choice for Web and other network servers.

Linux

Linux is a low-cost, powerful, and reliable UNIX-like operating system that is rapidly gaining market share from UNIX and Windows servers as a high-performance operating system for network servers and Web servers in both small and large networks. Linux was developed as free or low-cost *shareware* or *open-source software* over the Internet in the 1990s by Linus Torvald of Finland and millions of programmers around the world. Linux is still being enhanced in this way but is sold with extra features and support services by software vendors such as Red Hat, Caldera, and SUSE Linux. PC versions, which support office software suites, Web browsers, and other application software, are also available.

Open-Source Software

The concept of **open-source software** (OSS) is growing far beyond the Linux operating system. The basic idea behind open source is very simple: When programmers can read, redistribute, and modify the source code for a piece of software, the software evolves. People improve it, people adapt it, people fix bugs. This development can happen at a speed that, if one is accustomed to the slow pace of conventional software development, seems astonishing. The open-source community of software developers has learned that this rapid evolutionary process produces better software than the traditional commercial (closed) model, in which only a very few programmers can see the source. The concept of open source, admittedly, runs counter to the highly commercial (and proprietary) world of traditional software development. Nonetheless, an increasingly large number of developers have embraced the open-source concept and come to realize that the proprietary approach to software development has hidden costs that can often outweigh its benefits.

Since 1998, the OSS movement has become a revolution in software development. This revolution, however, can actually trace its roots back more than 30 years. Typically, in the PC era, computer software had been sold only as a finished product, otherwise called a *precompiled binary*, which is installed on a user's computer by copying files to appropriate directories or folders. Moving to a new computer platform (Windows to Macintosh, for example) usually required the purchase of a new license. If the company went out of business or discontinued support of a product, users of that product had no recourse. Bug fixes were completely dependent on the organization that sold the software. In contrast, OSS is software that is licensed to guarantee free access to the programming behind the precompiled binary, otherwise called the *source code*. This access allows the user to install the software on a new platform without an additional purchase and to get support (or create a support consortium with other like-minded users) for a product whose creator no longer supports it. Those who are technically inclined can fix bugs themselves rather than waiting for someone else to do so. Generally, there is a central distribution mechanism that allows users to obtain the source code, as well as precompiled binaries in some cases. There are also mechanisms by which users may pay a fee to obtain the software, such as on a CD-ROM or DVD, which may also include some technical support. A variety of licenses are used to ensure that the source code will remain available, wherever the code is actually used.

To be clear, there are several things open source is not: It is not shareware, public-domain software, freeware, or software viewers and readers made freely available without access to source code. Shareware, whether or not the user registers it and pays the registration fee, typically allows no access to the underlying source code. Unlike freeware and public-domain software, OSS is copyrighted and distributed with license terms designed to ensure that the source code will always be available. While a fee may be charged for the software's packaging, distribution, or support, the complete package needed to create files is included, not simply a portion needed to view files created elsewhere.

The philosophy of open source is based on a variety of models that sometimes conflict; indeed, it often seems there are as many philosophies and models for developing and managing OSS as there are major products. In 1998, a small group of open-source enthusiasts decided it was time to formalize some things about open source. The newly formed group registered themselves on the Internet as www.open-source.org and began the process of defining exactly what is, and what is not, open-source software. As it stands today, open-source licensing is defined by the following characteristics:

- The license shall not restrict any party from selling or giving away the software as a component of an aggregate software distribution containing programs from several different sources.

- The program must include source code and must allow distribution in source code, as well as compiled form.

- The license must allow modifications and derived works and must allow them to be distributed under the same terms as the license of the original software.

- The license may restrict source code from being distributed in modified form only if the license allows the distribution of patch files with the source code for the purpose of modifying the program at build time.

- The license must not discriminate against any person or group of persons.

- The license must not restrict anyone from making use of the program in a specific field of endeavor.

- The rights attached to the program must apply to all to whom the program is redistributed without the need for execution of an additional license by those parties.

- The license must not be specific to a product.

- The license must not contaminate other software by placing restrictions on any software distributed along with the licensed software.

This radical approach to software development and distribution is not without its detractors—most notably Microsoft. Nonetheless, the open-source movement is flourishing and stands to continue to revolutionize the way we think about software development.

OpenOffice.org 3

A relative newcomer to the open-source arena is an entire office suite offered by Sun Microsystems called OpenOffice.org 3. This product, built under the open-source standards described above, is a complete integrated office suite that provides all the common applications including word processing, spreadsheet, presentation graphics, and database management. It can store and retrieve files in a wide variety of data formats, including all of the file formats associated with the other major office suite applications on the market.

Best of all, OpenOffice.org 3 can be downloaded and used *entirely free of any license fees*. OpenOffice.org 3 is released under the LGPL license. This means you may use it for any purpose: domestic, commercial, educational, or public administration. You may install it on as many computers as you like, and you may make copies and give them away to family, friends, students, employees—anyone you like.

Mac OS X

Actually based on a form of UNIX, the **Mac OS X** (pronounced MAC OS 10) is the latest operating system from Apple for the iMac and other Macintosh microcomputers. The Mac OS X version 10.2 Jaguar has an advanced graphical user interface and multi-tasking and multimedia capabilities, along with an integrated Web browser, e-mail, instant messaging, search engine, digital media player, and many other features.

Mac OS X was a radical departure from previous Macintosh operating systems; its underlying code base is completely different from previous versions. Its core, named Darwin, is an open source, UNIX-like operating system. Apple layered over Darwin a number of proprietary components, including the Aqua interface and the Finder, to complete the GUI-based operating system that is Mac OS X.

Mac OS X also included a number of features intended to make the operating system more stable and reliable than Apple's previous operating systems. Preemptive multitasking and memory protection, for example, improved the ability of the operating system to run multiple applications simultaneously that don't interrupt or corrupt each other.

The most visible change was the Aqua theme. The use of soft edges, translucent colors, and pinstripes—similar to the hardware design of the first iMacs—brought more texture and color to the interface than OS 9's "Platinum" appearance had offered. Numerous users of the older versions of the operating system decried the new look as "cutesy" and lacking in professional polish. However, Aqua also has been called a bold and innovative step forward at a time when user interfaces were seen as "dull and boring." Despite the controversy, the look was instantly recognizable, and even before the first version of Mac OS X was released, third-party developers started producing skins (look and feel colors and styles for application interfaces) for customizable applications that mimicked the Aqua appearance.

Mac OS X also includes its own software development tools, most prominently an integrated development environment called Xcode. Xcode provides interfaces to compilers that support several programming languages including C, C++, Objective-C, and Java. For the Apple Intel Transition, it was modified so that developers could easily create an operating system to remain compatible with both the Intel-based and PowerPC-based Macintosh.

Application Virtualization

Consider all of the various types of software applications we discussed in the first section of this chapter along with the multiple operating systems we just discussed. What happens when a user who has a machine running Windows needs to run an application designed specifically for a machine running Mac OS X? The answer used to be "Borrow someone's Mac." Through the development of application virtualization, a much more useful and productive answer exists. *Application virtualization* is an umbrella term that describes software technologies that improve portability, manageability, and compatibility of applications by insulating them from the underlying operating system on which they are executed. A fully virtualized application is not installed in the traditional sense; it is just executed as if it is. The application is fooled into believing that it is directly interfacing with the original operating system and all the resources managed by it, when in reality it is not. Application virtualization is just an extension of operating system virtualization where the same basic concepts fool the whole operating system into thinking it is running on a particular type of hardware when it is, in fact, not.

The concept of virtualization is not a recent development. The use of a virtual machine was a common practice during the mainframe era where extremely large machines were partitioned into smaller, separate virtual machines or domains to allow multiple users to run unique sets of applications and processes simultaneously. Each user constituency used a portion of the total available machine resources and the virtualization approach made it appear that each domain was an entirely separate machine from all the rest. If you have ever set up a new PC and created a partition on the hard drive, you have taken advantage of virtualization. You have taken one physical drive and created two virtual drives—one for each partition.

Application virtualization is a logical next step from these early roots. The benefits to the enterprise range from the cost savings associated with not having to have multiple platforms for multiple applications, to the energy savings associated with not having a multitude of servers running at low capacity while eating up electricity and generating heat.

A thorough discussion of virtualization is well beyond the scope of this text but suffice to say it is rapidly blurring the boundaries between machines and operating systems and operating systems and applications. Add this to the cloud computing concept and we have the makings of an anytime, anywhere, any machine, any application world.

Asia, Europe, and Latin America: Linux Goes Global

The fact that Linux is an international phenomenon isn't too surprising, since the kernel was invented by Finnish student Linus Torvalds at the University of Helsinki. What began as a modest programming effort—just a hobby, Torvalds once said—has grown beyond the stage of a few maverick users thumbing their noses at Microsoft. In Asia, for example, shipments of Linux server licenses grew by 36 percent in 2004, while shipments of client licenses rose 49 percent.

Some of the deployments are quite substantial: The Industrial and Commercial Bank of China plans to use Linux for all front-end banking operations, Banca Popolare di Milano in Italy is rolling out 4,500 Linux desktops, and LVM Insurance in Germany has Linux on 7,700 desktops and 30 servers, for example.

The reasons for Linux deployments vary, but increasingly they're based less on zealotry and more on practicalities. Much of this demand is coming from China, where the government has backed Linux as an alternative to Microsoft's continued dominance of the operating system market. Government support isn't the only reason a growing number of Chinese companies are using Linux. Practical business demands are playing a role too, particularly in the country's financial industry. In April 2005, the Industrial and Commercial Bank of China (ICBC), the country's largest bank, announced plans to deploy Turbolinux Inc.'s Turbolinux 7 DataServer operating system for all of its front-end banking operations over a three–year period.

In 2003, MercadoLibre.com SA, a Buenos Aires–based online marketplace with operations in multiple countries in the region, outgrew its server infrastructure, which was made up entirely of Sun Microsystems Inc. boxes running Solaris. It opted to migrate to HP Itanium machines running a Linux operating system from Red Hat, instead of adding Sun servers to its existing setup. "With a single shot, we had to solve three issues: availability, scalability, and performance. And we had to do it at a low cost," says Edgardo Sokolowicz, chief technology officer.

An IT executive in Europe says he made the switch to save money on hardware: "Linux in and of itself as an operating system was not the driver. The fact is, Linux enabled us to use a commodity platform. There's nothing we wouldn't run on it." Private corporations and public-sector users in Europe typically cite pragmatic reasons for taking up the open-source operating system. They point to price and performance benefits. They want freedom to swap out hardware. They find the operating system reliable. They like its flexibility.

"It was not that we just wanted to do open-source. We had to find a way to protect our investment in network computing," says Matthias Strelow, a technical project manager at LVM Insurance in Munster, Germany. "I'm not sure it would have been possible with any other operating system."

Source: Adapted from Juan Perez, "Global Linux: Latin America," *Computerworld*, July 18, 2005; Carol Sliwa, "Europe: Financial Services Companies Lead the Charge to Linux," *Computerworld*, July 18, 2005; and Sumner Lemon and Dan Nystedt, "Global Linux: Asia," *Computerworld*, July 18, 2005.

Other System Management Programs

There are many other types of important system management software besides operating systems. These include *database management systems*, which we will cover in Chapter 5, and *network management programs*, which we will cover in Chapter 6. Figure 4.17 compares several types of system software offered by IBM and its competitors.

Several other types of system management software are marketed as separate programs or included as part of an operating system. Utility programs, or utilities, are an important example. Programs like Norton Utilities perform miscellaneous housekeeping and file conversion functions. Examples include data backup, data recovery, virus protection, data compression, and file defragmentation. Most operating systems also provide many utilities that perform a variety of helpful chores for computer users.

FIGURE 4.17   Comparing system software offered by IBM and its main competitors.

Software Category	What It Does	IBM Product	Customers	Main Competitor	Customers
Network management	Monitors networks to keep them up and running.	**Tivoli**	T. Rowe Price uses it to safeguard customer records.	**HP OpenView**	Amazon.com uses it to monitor its servers.
Application server	Shuttles data between business apps and the Web.	**WebSphere**	REI uses it to serve up its Web site and distribute data.	**BEA WebLogic**	Washingtonpost.com builds news pages with it.
Database manager	Provides digital storehouses for business data.	**DB2**	Mikasa uses it to help customers find its products online.	**Oracle 11g**	It runs Southwest Airlines' frequent-flyer program.
Collaboration tools	Powers everything from e-mail to electronic calendars.	**Lotus**	Retailer Sephora uses it to coordinate store maintenance.	**Microsoft Exchange**	Time Inc. uses it to provide e-mail to its employees.
Development tools	Allows programmers to craft software code quickly.	**Rational**	Merrill Lynch used it to build code for online trading.	**Microsoft Visual Studio .NET**	Used to develop management system.

Other examples of system support programs include performance monitors and security monitors. **Performance monitors** are programs that monitor and adjust the performance and usage of one or more computer systems to keep them running efficiently. **Security monitors** are packages that monitor and control the use of computer systems and provide warning messages and record evidence of unauthorized use of computer resources. A recent trend is to merge both types of programs into operating systems like Microsoft's Windows 2008 Datacenter Server or into system management software like Computer Associates' CA-Unicenter, which can manage both mainframe systems and servers in a data center.

Another important software trend is the use of system software known as **application servers,** which provide a *middleware* interface between an operating system and the application programs of users. Middleware is software that helps diverse software applications and networked computer systems exchange data and work together more efficiently. Examples include application servers, Web servers, and enterprise application integration (EAI) software. Thus, for example, application servers like BEA's WebLogic and IBM's WebSphere help Web-based e-business and e-commerce applications run much faster and more efficiently on computers using Windows, UNIX, and other operating systems.

Programming Languages

To understand computer software, you need a basic knowledge of the role that programming languages play in the development of computer programs. A programming language allows a programmer to develop the sets of instructions that constitute a computer program. Many different programming languages have been developed, each with its own unique vocabulary, grammar, and uses.

Machine Languages

Machine languages (or *first-generation languages*) are the most basic level of programming languages. In the early stages of computer development, all program instructions had to be written using binary codes unique to each computer. This type of programming involves the difficult task of writing instructions in the form of strings of binary digits (ones and zeros) or other number systems. Programmers must have a detailed knowledge of the internal operations of the specific type of CPU they are using. They must write long series of detailed instructions to accomplish even simple processing tasks. Programming in machine language requires specifying the storage

FIGURE 4.18

Examples of four levels of programming languages. These programming language instructions might be used to compute the sum of two numbers as expressed by the formula X = Y + Z.

Four Levels of Programming Languages	
● **Machine Languages:** Use binary coded instructions 1010 11001 1011 11010 1100 11011	● **High-Level Languages:** Use brief statements or arithmetic notations BASIC: X = Y + Z COBOL: COMPUTE X = Y + Z
● **Assembler Languages:** Use symbolic coded instructions LOD Y ADD Z STR X	● **Fourth-Generation Languages:** Use natural and nonprocedural statements SUM THE FOLLOWING NUMBERS

locations for every instruction and item of data used. Instructions must be included for every switch and indicator used by the program. These requirements make machine language programming a difficult and error-prone task. A machine language program to add two numbers together in the CPU of a specific computer and store the result might take the form shown in Figure 4.18.

Assembler Languages

Assembler languages (or *second-generation languages*) are the next level of programming languages. They were developed to reduce the difficulties in writing machine language programs. The use of assembler languages requires language translator programs called *assemblers* that allow a computer to convert the instructions of such language into machine instructions. Assembler languages are frequently called symbolic languages because symbols are used to represent operation codes and storage locations. Convenient alphabetic abbreviations called *mnemonics* (memory aids) and other symbols represent operation codes, storage locations, and data elements. For example, the computation X = Y + Z in an assembler language might take the form shown in Figure 4.18.

Assembler languages are still used as a method of programming a computer in a machine-oriented language. Most computer manufacturers provide an assembler language that reflects the unique machine language instruction set of a particular line of computers. This feature is particularly desirable to *system programmers*, who program system software (as opposed to application programmers, who program application software), because it provides them with greater control and flexibility in designing a program for a particular computer. They can then produce more efficient software—that is, programs that require a minimum of instructions, storage, and CPU time to perform a specific processing assignment.

High-Level Languages

High-level languages (or *third-generation languages*) use instructions, which are called *statements*, that include brief statements or arithmetic expressions. Individual high-level language statements are actually *macroinstructions*; that is, each individual statement generates several machine instructions when translated into machine language by high-level language translator programs called *compilers* or *interpreters*. High-level language statements resemble the phrases or mathematical expressions required to express the problem or procedure being programmed. The *syntax* (vocabulary, punctuation, and grammatical rules) and *semantics* (meanings) of such statements do not reflect the internal code of any particular computer. For example, the computation X = Y + Z would be programmed in the high-level languages of BASIC and COBOL as shown in Figure 4.18.

High-level languages like BASIC, COBOL, and FORTRAN are easier to learn and program than an assembler language because they have less rigid rules, forms, and syntaxes. However, high-level language programs are usually less efficient than assembler language programs and require a greater amount of computer time for translation into machine instructions. Because most high-level languages are machine-independent, programs written in a high-level language do not have to be reprogrammed when a new computer is installed, and programmers do not have to learn a different language for each type of computer.

Fourth-Generation Languages

The term fourth-generation language describes a variety of programming languages that are more nonprocedural and *conversational* than prior languages. These languages are called fourth-generation languages (4GLs) to differentiate them from machine languages (first generation), assembler languages (second generation), and high-level languages (third generation).

Most fourth-generation languages are *nonprocedural languages* that encourage users and programmers to specify the results they want, while the computer determines the sequence of instructions that will accomplish those results. Thus, fourth-generation languages have helped simplify the programming process. Natural languages are sometimes considered *fifth-generation* languages (5GLs) and are very close to English or other human languages. Research and development activity in artificial intelligence (AI) is developing programming languages that are as easy to use as ordinary conversation in one's native tongue. For example, INTELLECT, a natural language, would use a statement like, "What are the average exam scores in MIS 200?" to program a simple average exam score task.

In the early days of 4GLs, results suggested that high-volume transaction processing environments were not in the range of a 4GL's capabilities. Although 4GLs were characterized by their ease of use, they were also viewed as less flexible than their predecessors, primarily due to their increased storage and processing speed requirements. In today's large data volume environment, 4GLs are widely used and no longer viewed as a trade-off between ease of use and flexibility.

Modern (and Automatic?) Code Generation

Twenty years ago, software engineer Fred Brooks famously observed that there was no silver bullet that could slay "the monster of missed schedules, blown budgets and flawed products." Today, the creation of software might seem as expensive, trouble-prone, and difficult as ever. And yet progress is being made. While there is still no silver bullet in sight, an array of new techniques promises to further boost a programmer's productivity, at least in some application domains.

The techniques span a broad spectrum of methods and results, but all are aimed at generating software automatically. Typically, they generate code from high-level, machine-readable designs or from domain-specific languages—assisted by advanced compilers—that sometimes can be used by nonprogrammers.

Gordon Novak, a computer science professor at the University of Texas at Austin and a member of the school's Laboratory for Artificial Intelligence, is working on "automatic programming"—using libraries of generic versions of programs, such as algorithms—to sort or find items in a list. But unlike traditional subroutines, which have simple but rigid interfaces and are invoked by other lines of program code, his technique works at a higher level and is therefore more flexible and easier to use.

Novak's users construct "views" that describe application data and principles and then connect the views by arrows in diagrams that show the relationships among the data. The diagrams are, in essence, very high-level flowcharts of the desired program. They get compiled in a way that customizes the stored generic algorithms for the user's specific problem, and the result is ordinary source code such as C, C++, or Java.

Novak says he was able to generate 250 lines of source code for an indexing program in 90 seconds with his system. That's equivalent to a week of productivity for an average programmer using a traditional language. "You are describing your program at a higher level," he says. "And what my program is saying is, 'I can tailor the algorithm for your application for free.'"

Douglas Smith, principal scientist at Kestrel Institute, a nonprofit computer science research firm in Palo Alto, California, is developing tools to "automate knowledge and get it into the computer." A programmer starts with Kestrel's Specware, which is a general-purpose, fifth-generation language that specifies a program's functions without regard to the ultimate programming language, system architecture, algorithms, data structures, and so on. Specware draws on a library of components, but the components aren't code. They are at a higher level and include design knowledge and principles about algorithms, data structures, and so on. Smith calls them "abstract templates."

In addition, Specware can produce proofs that the working code is "correct"— that is, that it conforms to the requirements put in by the user (which, of course, may contain errors). "Some customers want that for very-high-assurance applications, with no security flaws," Smith says. Kestrel does work for NASA and U.S. military and security agencies.

"It's a language for writing down problem requirements, a high-level statement of what a solution should be, without saying how to solve the problem," Smith says. "We think it's the ultimate frontier in software engineering. It's what systems analysts do."

Source: Adapted from Gary Anthes, "In the Labs: Automatic Code Generators," *Computerworld*, March 20, 2006.

Object-Oriented Languages

Object-oriented languages like Visual Basic, C++, and Java are also considered fifth-generation languages and have become major tools of software development. Briefly, whereas most programming languages separate data elements from the procedures or actions that will be performed on them, object-oriented languages tie them together into **objects.** Thus, an object consists of data and the actions that can be performed on the data. For example, an object could be a set of data about a bank customer's savings account and the operations (e.g., interest calculations) that might be performed on the data. An object also could be data in graphic form, such as a video display window plus the display actions that might be used on it. See Figure 4.19.

In procedural languages, a program consists of procedures to perform actions on each data element. However, in object-oriented systems, objects tell other objects to perform actions on themselves. For example, to open a window on a computer video display, a beginning menu object could send a window object a message to open, and

FIGURE 4.19

An example of a bank savings account object. This object consists of data about a customer's account balance and the basic operations that can be performed on those data.

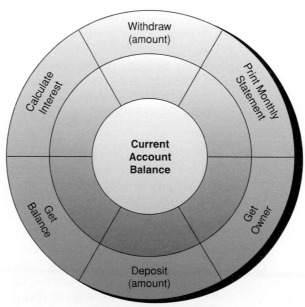

Savings Account Object

FIGURE 4.20   The Visual Basic object-oriented programming environment.

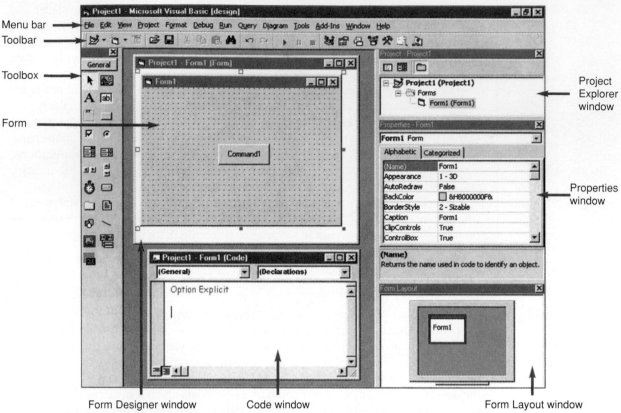

Menu bar

Toolbar

Toolbox

Form

Project Explorer window

Properties window

Form Designer window

Code window

Form Layout window

Source: Courtesy of Microsoft®.

a window would appear on the screen. That's because the window object contains the program code for opening itself.

Object-oriented languages are easier to use and more efficient for programming the graphics-oriented user interfaces required by many applications. Therefore, they are the most widely used programming languages for software development today. Also, once objects are programmed, they are reusable. Therefore, reusability of objects is a major benefit of object-oriented programming. For example, programmers can construct a user interface for a new program by assembling standard objects such as windows, bars, boxes, buttons, and icons. Therefore, most object-oriented programming packages provide a GUI that supports a point-and-click, drag-and-drop visual assembly of objects known as *visual programming*. Figure 4.20 shows a display of the Visual Basic object-oriented programming environment. Object-oriented technology is discussed further in the coverage of object-oriented databases in Chapter 5.

Web Languages and Services

HTML, XML, and Java are three programming languages that are important tools for building multimedia Web pages, Web sites, and Web-based applications. In addition, XML and Java have become strategic components of the software technologies that support many Web services initiatives in business.

HTML

HTML (Hypertext Markup Language) is a page description language that creates hypertext or hypermedia documents. HTML inserts control codes within a document at points you can specify that create links (*hyperlinks*) to other parts of the document or to other documents anywhere on the World Wide Web. HTML embeds control codes in the ASCII text of a document that designate titles, headings, graphics, and multimedia components, as well as hyperlinks within the document.

As we mentioned previously, several of the programs in the top software suites automatically convert documents into HTML formats. These include Web browsers, word processing and spreadsheet programs, database managers, and presentation graphics packages. These and other specialized *Web publishing* programs like Microsoft FrontPage, Lotus FastSite, and Macromedia's DreamWeaver provide a range of features to help you design and create multimedia Web pages without formal HTML programming.

XML

XML (eXtensible Markup Language) is not a Web page format description language like HTML. Instead, XML describes the contents of Web pages (including business documents designed for use on the Web) by applying identifying tags or *contextual labels* to the data in Web documents. For example, a travel agency Web page with airline names and flight times would use hidden XML tags like "airline name" and "flight time" to categorize each of the airline flight times on that page. Or product inventory data available at a Web site could be labeled with tags like "brand," "price," and "size." By classifying data in this way, XML makes Web site information much more searchable, easier to sort, and easier to analyze.

For example, XML-enabled search software could easily find the exact product you specify if the product data on the Web site had been labeled with identifying XML tags. A Web site that uses XML could also more easily determine which Web page features its customers use and which products they investigate. Thus, XML promises to make electronic business and commerce processes a lot easier and more efficient by supporting the automatic electronic exchange of business data between companies and their customers, suppliers, and other business partners.

As mentioned at the beginning of the chapter, this entire textbook was revised and edited for the current edition using an XML-based application called PowerXEditor by Aptara. Let's focus our attention on this unique application of XML intended to create efficiencies in the publishing industry.

Aptara, Inc.: Revolutionizing the Publishing Industry through XML

The publishing industry has experienced an upheaval in the past decade or so. The "long tail" of sales of existing books via Web sellers such as Amazon and the improvement in software and hardware technologies that can replicate the experience of reading a book or magazine means publishing houses are printing and selling fewer new books. As a result, many of these companies are venturing into digital publishing.

"All the publishers are shifting from print to digital," said Dev Ganesan, president and CEO of Aptara, which specializes in content transformation. "That's a huge change. What that means for software companies is that they need to develop platforms for content creation that meet the needs of every customer. At the same time, customers are looking at publishing in terms of handling content in terms of authors, editors, and production employees. On top of that, they're trying to automate parts of the production process. And companies must be willing to market products using traditional and new media to reach the widest possible audience. So there are a lot of challenges, but a lot of opportunities, too."

The upshot of all this is that learning professionals now can deliver content more flexibly and at a lower cost. They can make static content dynamic by taking a body of knowledge in print—such as a book—and converting it to a digital format. They can then chunk that content into smaller sizes and organize those nuggets of information according to learners' needs. Moreover, they can get content published and distributed much more quickly via digital, online media. This is critical in an industry such as health care that faces rapid changes due to technological innovation and regulation, said another Aptara source.

"In addition to the cost savings, they want to turn it around much faster," he said. "Time to market is becoming paramount because there's so much innovation going on. If they don't have their print products out faster, they fall behind."

A breakthrough product from Aptara is called PowerXEditor (PXE). An XML-based application, PXE allows a publisher to upload an existing book layout; edit or revise all elements of the book, including text look and feel, figures, tables, and other elements unique to that book; and output the book to a paging program that sets the book up for final printing. The important issue is that all of this is done in a digital format instead of the previously common method of tear pages and cut and paste of figures and tables. Because the PXE content is XML-based, the application can be accessed via the Internet using any conventional Web browser. This means all of the contributors to a textbook can have access to the various chapters and elements no matter where they are. Add in the workflow management aspects of PXE, and all phases of the textbook revising, copyediting, and proofing processes can be handled with ease.

Figure 4.21 shows a typical PXE screen. You might notice that it is in the process of editing the page you are currently reading. Figure 4.22 shows the XML code for the same page.

Source: Adapted from Brian Summerfield, "Executive Briefings: Balancing Print and Digital Media," *Chief Learning Officer*, March 2008. http://www.clomedia.com/includes/printcontent.php?aid=2133

FIGURE 4.21

The XML-based PowerXEditor allows all the collaborators on a book project to access the elements of the book via a common Web browser. Here is a screenshot of PXE on the page you are currently reading.

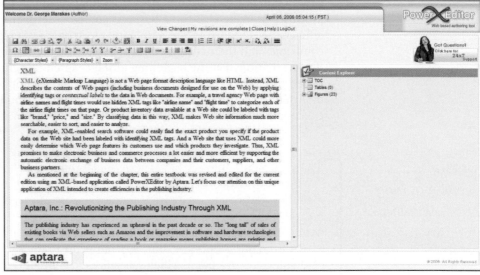

Source: Courtesy of Aptara.

FIGURE 4.22

This is a section of the XML code from the page you are currently reading. While XML looks similar to HTML source code, it is far more powerful and complex.

```
        features to help you design and create multimedia Web pages without formal HTML programming.
      </p>
      <p class="Head3" id="head3_19">XML</p>
    - <p class="Para_FL">
      - <span class="Def_term">
          <b>XML</b>
      </span>
        (eXtensible Markup Language) is not a Web page format description language like HTML. Instead, XML
        describes the contents of Web pages (including business documents designed for use on the Web) by
        applying identifying tags or
        <i>contextual labels</i>
        to the data in Web documents. For example, a travel agency Web page with airline names and flight
        times would use hidden XML tags like "airline name" and "flight time" to categorize each of the airline
        flight times on that page. Or product inventory data available at a Web site could be labeled with tags
        like "brand," "price," and "size." By classifying data in this way, XML makes Web site information much
        more searchable, easier to sort, and easier to analyze.
      </p>
      <p class="Para_indented">For example, XML-enabled search software could easily find the exact product
        you specify if the product data on the Web site had been labeled with identifying XML tags. And a Web
        site that uses XML could more easily determine which Web page features its customers use and which
        products they investigate. Thus, XML promises to make electronic business and commerce processes a
        lot easier and more efficient by supporting the automatic electronic exchange of business data between
        companies and their customers, suppliers, and other business partners.</p>
      <p class="Head3" id="head3_20">Java and .NET</p>
    - <p class="Para_FL">
      - <span class="Def_term">
```

Source: Courtesy of Aptara.

Java and .NET

Java is an object-oriented programming language created by Sun Microsystems that is revolutionizing the programming of applications for the World Wide Web and corporate intranets and extranets. Java is related to the C++ and Objective C programming languages but is much simpler and more secure and is computing-platform independent. Java is also specifically designed for real-time, interactive, Web-based network applications. Java applications consisting of small application programs, called *applets*, can be executed by any computer and any operating system anywhere in a network.

The ease of creating Java applets and distributing them from network servers to client PCs and network computers is one of the major reasons for Java's popularity. Applets can be small, special-purpose application programs or small modules of larger Java application programs. Java programs are platform-independent, too—they can run on Windows, UNIX, and Macintosh systems without modification.

Microsoft's **.NET** is a collection of programming support for what are known as Web services, the ability to use the Web rather than your own computer for various services (see below). .NET is intended to provide individual and business users with a seamlessly interoperable and Web-enabled interface for applications and computing devices and to make computing activities increasingly Web browser–oriented. The .NET platform includes servers, building-block services such as Web-based data storage, and device software. It also includes Passport, Microsoft's fill-in-the-form-only-once identity verification service.

The .NET platform is expected to enable the entire range of computing devices to work together and have user information automatically updated and synchronized on all of them. In addition, it will provide a premium online subscription service. The service will feature customized access to and delivery of products and services from a central starting point for the management of various applications (e.g., e-mail) or software (e.g., Office .NET). For developers, .NET offers the ability to create reusable modules, which should increase productivity and reduce the number of programming errors.

The full release of .NET is expected to take several years to complete, with intermittent releases of products such as a personal security service and new versions of Windows and Office that implement the .NET strategy coming on the market separately. Visual Studio .NET is a development environment that is now available, and Windows XP supports certain .NET capabilities.

The latest version of Java is Java Enterprise Edition 5 (Java EE 5), which has become the primary alternative to Microsoft's .NET software development platform for many organizations intent on capitalizing on the business potential of Web-based applications and Web services. Figure 4.23 compares the pros and cons of using Java EE 5 and .NET for software development.

Web Services

Web services are software components that are based on a framework of Web and object-oriented standards and technologies for using the Web that electronically link the applications of different users and different computing platforms. Thus, Web services can link key business functions for the exchange of data in real time within the Web-based applications that a business might share with its customers, suppliers, and other business partners. For example, Web services would enable the purchasing application of a business to use the Web to check the inventory of a supplier before placing a large order, while the sales application of the supplier could use Web services to automatically check the credit rating of the business with a credit-reporting agency before approving the purchase. Therefore, among both business and IT professionals, the term *Web services* is commonly used to describe the Web-based business and computing functions or services accomplished by Web services software technologies and standards.

Figure 4.24 illustrates how Web services work and identifies some of the key technologies and standards that are involved. The XML language is one of the key technologies that enable Web services to make applications work between different computing

FIGURE 4.23 The benefits and limitations of the Java Enterprise Edition 5 (Java EE 5) and Microsoft .NET software development platforms.

| Java EE 5 | | .NET | |
PROS	CONS	PROS	CONS
• Runs on any operating system and application server (may need adjustments). • Handles complex, high-volume, high-transaction applications. • Has more enterprise features for session management, fail-over, load balancing, and application integration. • Is favored by experienced enterprise vendors such as IBM, BEA, SAP, and Oracle. • Offers a wide range of vendor choices for tools and application servers. • Has a proven track record.	• Has a complex application development environment. • Tools can be difficult to use. • Java Swing environment's ability to build graphical user interfaces has limitations. • May cost more to build, deploy, and manage applications. • Lacks built-in support for Web services standards. • Is difficult to use for quick-turnaround, low-cost, and mass-market projects.	• Easy-to-use tools may increase programmer productivity. • Has a strong framework for building rich graphical user interfaces. • Gives developers choice of working in more than 20 programming languages. • Is tightly integrated with Microsoft's operating system and enterprise server software. • May cost less, due in part to built-in application server in Windows, unified management, and less-expensive tools. • Has built-in support for Web service standards.	• Framework runs only on Windows, restricting vendor choice. • Users of prior Microsoft tools and technology face a potentially steep learning curve. • New runtime infrastructure lacks maturity. • Questions persist about the scalability and transaction capability of the Windows platform. • Choice of integrated development environments is limited. • Getting older applications to run in new .NET environment may require effort.

Source: Carol Silwa, ".NET vs. Java," *Computerworld*, May 20, 2002, p. 31.

FIGURE 4.24

The basic steps in accomplishing a Web services application.

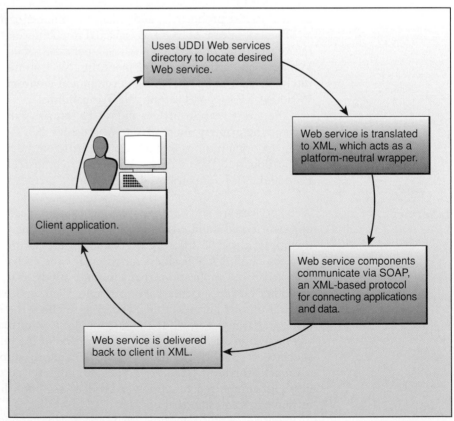

Source: Adapted from Bala Iyer, Jim Freedman, Mark Gaynor, and George Wyner, "Web Services: Enabling Dynamic Business Networks," *Communications of the Association for Information Systems* 11 (2003), p. 543.

platforms. Also important are **UDDI** (Universal Description, Discovery, and Integration), the "yellow pages" directory of all Web services and how to locate and use them, and **SOAP** (Simple Object Access Protocol), an XML-based protocol of specifications for connecting applications to the data that they need.

Web services promise to be the key software technology for automating access to data and application functions between a business and its trading partners. As companies increasingly move to doing business over the Web, Web services will become essential for the development of the easy and efficient e-business and e-commerce applications that will be required. The flexibility and interoperability of Web services will also be essential for coping with the fast-changing relationships between a company and its business partners that are commonplace in today's dynamic global business environment.

Airbus: Flying on SAP and Web Services

European aircraft builder Airbus has implemented a Web services–based travel management application from SAP as a first step in a planned groupwide migration to a service-oriented architecture (SOA). The airplane manufacturer is installing the travel management component of SAP's ERP software, mySAP, which uses SOA technology. "The new system replaces a homegrown system at the company's plant in France, a Lotus-based system in its Spanish operations, and earlier SAP versions at facilities in Germany and the United Kingdom," says James Westgarth, manager of travel technology procurement at Airbus.

"We like the idea of an open architecture, which SOA enables," Westgarth says. "We like the idea of being able to manage everything internally and to cherry-pick for the best solution in every class." "Additional components, such as online booking, could also come from SAP—if the software vendor has a superior product for that application," says Westgarth.

The decision to deploy a new Web services–based travel management system was driven in large part by a need to reduce administration costs and improve business processes.

Airbus has a travel budget of 250 million euros, which is used to help pay for more than 180,000 trips annually. The company aims to reduce costs by eliminating the current paper-based reimbursement process, which consumes time and labor, with a system that enables employees to process their own travel expenses online from their desktops or mobile devices.

A key benefit for employees: Reimbursement time will be reduced to three days from about ten. In addition, the new system allows Airbus to integrate new service providers more easily into its operations, notes Westgarth. The manufacturer has outsourced its valued-added tax reclaim activities to a third party specialized in this service. With the help of application link enablers, Westgarth and his team are able to link their travel management system into the company's other SAP applications, including finance and human resources. Airbus has a strategy to eventually migrate to the mySAP ERP across multiple systems and countries over a number of years.

"The company chose travel management to pilot mySAP ERP," says Westgarth. There have been some issues with the rollout of the travel management application, Westgarth concedes. "Because we're the first big company to implement this technology, we've had difficulty finding enough skilled people on the market," he said. "And some work was required to integrate the Web interface into our portal."

But Airbus employees, Westgarth said, like the Web-based application's new user interface, the single sign-on and the step-by-step guidance. And the company likes the flexibility. "No one was talking about low-cost carriers five years ago," he said. "We need to adapt to the market and to changing needs."

Source: Adapted from John Blau, "Airbus Flies on Web Services With SAP," *IDG News Service/CIO Magazine*, June 8, 2006.

Programming Software

Various software packages are available to help programmers develop computer programs. For example, *programming language translators* are programs that translate other programs into machine language instruction codes that computers can execute. Other software packages, such as programming language editors, are called *programming tools* because they help programmers write programs by providing a variety of program creation and editing capabilities. See Figure 4.25.

Language Translator Programs

Computer programs consist of sets of instructions written in programming languages that must be translated by a language translator into the computer's own machine language before they can be processed, or executed, by the CPU. Programming language translator programs (or *language processors*) are known by a variety of names. An **assembler** translates the symbolic instruction codes of programs written in an assembler language into machine language instructions, whereas a **compiler** translates high-level language statements.

An **interpreter** is a special type of compiler that translates and executes each statement in a program one at a time, instead of first producing a complete machine language program, as compilers and assemblers do. Java is an example of an interpreted language. Thus, the program instructions in Java applets are interpreted and executed *on the fly* as the applet is being executed by a client PC.

Programming Tools

Software development and the computer programming process have been enhanced by adding *graphical programming interfaces* and a variety of built-in development capabilities. Language translators have always provided some editing and diagnostic capabilities to identify programming errors or *bugs*. However, most software development programs now include powerful graphics-oriented *programming editors* and *debuggers*. These **programming tools** help programmers identify and minimize errors while they are programming. Such programming tools provide a computer-aided programming environment, which decreases the drudgery of programming while increasing the efficiency and productivity of software developers. Other programming tools include diagramming packages, code generators, libraries of reusable objects and program code, and prototyping tools. All of these programming tools are an essential part of widely used programming languages like Visual Basic, C++, and Java.

FIGURE 4.25

Using the graphical programming interface of a Java programming tool, Forte for Java, by Sun Microsystems.

Source: Courtesy of Sun Microsystems.

CASE Tools

Since the early days of programming, software developers have needed automated tools. Initially the concentration was on program support tools such as translators, compilers, assemblers, macroprocessors, and linkers and loaders. However, as computers became more powerful and the software that ran on them grew larger and more complex, the range of support tools began to expand. In particular, the use of interactive time-sharing systems for software development encouraged the development of program editors, debuggers, and code analyzers.

As the range of support tools expanded, manufacturers began to integrate them into a single application using a common interface. Such tools were referred to as CASE tools (computer-aided software engineering).

CASE tools can take a number of forms and be applied at different stages of the software development process. Those CASE tools that support activities early in the life cycle of a software project (e.g., requirements, design support tools) are sometimes called *front-end* or *upper* CASE tools. Those that are used later in the life cycle (e.g., compilers, test support tools) are called *back-end* or *lower* CASE tools.

Exploring the details of CASE tools is beyond the scope of this text, and you will encounter them again when you study systems analysis and design. For now, remember that CASE is an important part of resolving the problems of complex application development and maintenance of software applications.

Summary

- **Software.** Computer software consists of two major types of programs: (1) application software that directs the performance of a particular use, or application, of computers to meet the information processing needs of users and (2) system software that controls and supports the operations of a computer system as it performs various information processing tasks. Refer to Figure 4.2 for an overview of the major types of software.

- **Application Software.** Application software includes a variety of programs that can be segregated into general-purpose and application-specific categories. General-purpose application programs perform common information processing jobs for end users. Examples are word processing, electronic spreadsheet, and presentation graphics programs. Application-specific programs accomplish information processing tasks that support specific business functions or processes, scientific or engineering applications, and other computer applications in society.

- **System Software.** System software can be subdivided into system management programs and system development programs. System management programs manage the hardware, software, network, and data resources of a computer system during its execution of information processing jobs. Examples of system management programs are operating systems, network management programs, database management systems, system utilities, application servers, and performance and security monitors. Network management programs support

and manage telecommunications activities and network performance telecommunications networks. Database management systems control the development, integration, and maintenance of databases. Utilities are programs that perform routine computing functions, such as backing up data or copying files, as part of an operating system or as a separate package. System development programs like language translators and programming editors help IS specialists develop computer programs to support business processes.

- **Operating Systems.** An operating system is an integrated system of programs that supervises the operation of the CPU, controls the input/output storage functions of the computer system, and provides various support services. An operating system performs five basic functions: (1) a user interface for system and network communications with users, (2) resource management for managing the hardware resources of a computer system, (3) file management for managing files of data and programs, (4) task management for managing the tasks a computer must accomplish, and (5) utilities and other functions that provide miscellaneous support services.

- **Programming Languages.** Programming languages are a major category of system software. They require the use of a variety of programming packages to help programmers develop computer programs and language translator programs to convert programming language instructions into machine language instruction codes. The five major levels of programming languages are machine languages, assembler languages, high-level languages, fourth-generation languages, and object-oriented languages. Object-oriented languages like Java and special-purpose languages like HTML and XML are being widely used for Web-based business applications and services.

Key Terms and Concepts

These are the key terms and concepts of this chapter. The page number of their first explanation is given in parentheses.

1. Application service provider (ASP) (136)
2. Application software (124)
3. Assembler language (151)
4. CASE tools (161)
5. Cloud computing (138)
6. COTS software (124)
7. Custom software (124)
8. Desktop publishing (DTP) (133)
9. E-mail (130)
10. Fourth-generation language (152)
11. Function-specific application programs (128)
12. General-purpose application programs (124)
13. Groupware (135)
14. High-level language (151)
15. HTML (154)
16. Instant messaging (IM) (131)
17. Integrated package (129)
18. Java (157)
19. Language translator (160)
20. Machine language (150)
21. Middleware (150)
22. Multitasking (144)
23. Natural language (152)
24. Object-oriented language (153)
25. Operating system (140)
26. Personal information manager (PIM) (135)
27. Presentation graphics software (134)
28. Programming language (150)
29. Software suites (129)
30. Spreadsheet package (133)
31. System software (140)
32. User interface (140)
33. Utilities (149)
34. Virtual memory (143)
35. Web browser (130)
36. Web services (157)
37. Word processing software (132)
38. XML (155)

Review Quiz

Match one of the previous key terms and concepts with one of the brief examples or definitions that follow. Try to find the best fit for answers that seem to fit more than one term or concept. Defend your choices.

_____ 1. An approach to computing where tasks are assigned to a combination of connections, software, and services accessed over a network.

_____ 2. Programs that direct the performance of a specific use of computers.

_____ 3. A system of programs that manages the operations of a computer system.

_____ 4. Companies that own, operate, and maintain application software for a fee as a service over the Internet.

_____ 5. Integrated software tool that supports the development of software applications.

_____ 6. Software designed in-house for use by a specific organization or set of users.

_____ 7. The function that provides a means of communication between end users and an operating system.

_____ 8. Acronym meaning commercial off-the-shelf.

_____ 9. Provides a greater memory capability than a computer's actual memory capacity.

_____ 10. The ability to do several computing tasks concurrently.

_____ 11. Converts numeric data into graphic displays.

_____ 12. Translates high-level instructions into machine language instructions.

_____ 13. Performs housekeeping chores for a computer system.

_____ 14. A category of application software that performs common information processing tasks for end users.

_____ 15. Software available for the specific applications of end users in business, science, and other fields.

_____ 16. Helps you surf the Web.

_____ 17. Uses your networked computer to send and receive messages.

_____ 18. Creates and displays a worksheet for analysis.

_____ 19. Allows you to create and edit documents.

_____ 20. Enables you to produce your own brochures and newsletters.

_____ 21. Helps you keep track of appointments and tasks.

_____ 22. A program that performs several general-purpose applications.

_____ 23. A combination of individual general-purpose application packages that work easily together.

_____ 24. Software to support the collaboration of teams and workgroups.

_____ 25. Uses instructions in the form of coded strings of ones and zeros.

_____ 26. Uses instructions consisting of symbols representing operation codes and storage locations.

_____ 27. Uses instructions in the form of brief statements or the standard notation of mathematics.

_____ 28. Might take the form of query languages and report generators.

_____ 29. Languages that tie together data and the actions that will be performed on the data.

_____ 30. As easy to use as one's native tongue.

_____ 31. Includes programming editors, debuggers, and code generators.

_____ 32. Produces hyperlinked multimedia documents for the Web.

_____ 33. A Web document content description language.

_____ 34. A popular object-oriented language for Web-based applications.

_____ 35. Windows, Linux, and Mac OS are common examples.

_____ 36. Software that helps diverse applications work together.

_____ 37. Enables you to communicate and collaborate in real time with the online associates in your workgroup.

_____ 38. Links business functions within applications for the exchange of data between companies via the Web.

Discussion Questions

1. What major trends are occurring in software? What capabilities do you expect to see in future software packages?

2. How do the different roles of system software and application software affect you as a business end user? How do you see this changing in the future?

3. Refer to the Real World Case on Software-as-a-Service (SaaS) in the chapter. Do you think GE would have been better off developing a system specifically customized to their needs, given that GE's supply chain is like nothing else in the world?

4. Why is an operating system necessary? That is, why can't an end user just load an application program into a computer and start computing?

5. Should a Web browser be integrated into an operating system? Why or why not?

6. Refer to the Real World Case on data sharing and XML in the chapter. As noted above, XML needs to be customized with tags or labels that are tied to the business domain for which it will be used. How do companies manage the need to create schemas that are specific to their organizations versus the ideal of sharing data with their partners? Is there a risk of ending up with a bunch of proprietary XML specifications?

7. Are software suites, Web browsers, and groupware merging together? What are the implications for a business and its end users?

8. How are HTML, XML, and Java affecting business applications on the Web?

9. Do you think Linux will surpass, in adoption and use, other operating systems for network and Web servers? Why or why not?

10. Which application software packages are the most important for a business end user to know how to use? Explain the reasons for your choices.

Analysis Exercises

Complete the following exercises as individual or group projects that apply chapter concepts to real-world business situations.

1. **Desktop Application Recognition**
   Tool Selection
   ABC Department Stores would like to acquire software to do the following tasks. Identify which software packages they need.

   a. Surf the Web and their intranets and extranets.

   b. Send messages to one another's computer workstations.

   c. Help employees work together in teams.

d. Use a group of productivity packages that work together easily.

e. Help sales reps keep track of meetings and sales calls.

f. Type correspondence and reports.

g. Analyze rows and columns of sales figures.

h. Develop a variety of graphical presentations.

2. Y2K Revisited
The End of Time

Decades ago, programmers trying to conserve valuable storage space shortened year values to two digits. This shortcut created what became known as the "Y2K" problem or "millennium bug" at the turn of the century. Programmers needed to review billions of lines of code to ensure important programs would continue to operate correctly. The Y2K problem merged with the dot-com boom and created a tremendous demand for information technology employees. Information system users spent billions of dollars fixing or replacing old software. The IT industry is only now beginning to recover from the postboom slump. Could such hysteria happen again? It can and, very likely, it will.

Today, most programs use several different schemes to record dates. One scheme, POSIX time, widely employed on UNIX-based systems, requires a signed 32-bit integer to store a number representing the number of seconds since January 1, 1970. "0" represents midnight on January 1, "10" represents 10 seconds after midnight, and "−10" represents 10 seconds before midnight. A simple program then converts these data into any number of international date formats for display. This scheme works well because it allows programmers to subtract one date/time from another date/time and directly determine the interval between them. It also requires only 4 bytes of storage space. But 32 bits still calculates to a finite number, whereas time is infinite. As a business manager, you will need to be aware of this new threat and steer your organization away from repeating history. The following questions will help you evaluate the situation and learn from history.

a. If 1 represents 1 second and 2 represents 2 seconds, how many seconds can be represented in a binary number 32 bits long? Use a spreadsheet to show your calculations.

b. Given that POSIX time starts at midnight, January 1, 1970, in what year will time "run out"? Remember that half the available numbers represent dates before 1970. Use a spreadsheet to show your calculations.

c. As a business manager, what can you do to minimize this problem for your organization?

3. Tracking Project Work
Queries and Reports

You are responsible for managing information systems development projects at AAA Systems. To better track progress in completing projects, you have decided to maintain a simple database table to track the time your employees spend on various tasks and the projects with which they are associated. It will also allow you to keep track of employees' billable hours each week. The table below provides a sample data set.

a. Build a database table to store the data shown and enter the records as a set of sample data.

b. Create a query that will list the hours worked for all workers who worked more than 40 hours during production week 20.

c. Create a report grouped by project that will show the number of hours devoted to each task on the project and the subtotal number of hours devoted to each project, as well as a grand total of all hours worked.

d. Create a report grouped by employee that will show each employee's hours worked on each task and total hours worked. The user should be able to select a production week and find data for just that week presented.

4. Matching Training to Software Use
3-D Graphing

You have the responsibility to manage software training for Sales, Accounting, and Operations Department workers in your organization. You have surveyed the workers to get a feel for the amounts of time spent using various packages, and the results are shown below. The values shown are the total number of workers in each department and the total weekly hours the department's workers spend using each software package. You have been asked to prepare a spreadsheet summarizing these data and comparing the use of the various packages across departments.

Department	Employees	Spreadsheet	Database	Presentations
Sales	225	410	1,100	650
Operations	75	710	520	405
Accounting	30	310	405	50

a. Create a spreadsheet illustrating each application's average use per department. To do this, you will first enter the data shown above. Then compute the average weekly spreadsheet use by dividing spreadsheet hours by the number of Sales workers. Do this for each department. Repeat these three calculations for both database and presentation use. Round results to the nearest 1/100th.

b. Create a three-dimensional bar graph illustrating the averages by department and software package.

c. A committee has been formed to plan software training classes at your company. Prepare a slide presentation with four slides illustrating your findings. The first slide should serve as an introduction to the data; the second slide should contain a copy of the original data table (without the averages); the third slide should contain a copy of the three-dimensional bar graph from the previous answer; and the fourth slide should contain your conclusions regarding key applications per department. Use professional labels, formatting, and backgrounds.

Project_Name	Task_Name	Employee_ID	Production_Week	Hours_Worked
Fin-Goods-Inv	App. Devel.	456	21	42
Fin-Goods-Inv	DB Design	345	20	20
Fin-Goods-Inv	UI Design	234	20	16
HR	Analysis	234	21	24
HR	Analysis	456	20	48
HR	UI Design	123	20	8
HR	UI Design	123	21	40
HR	UI Design	234	21	32
Shipmt-Tracking	DB Design	345	20	24
Shipmt-Tracking	DB Design	345	21	16
Shipmt-Tracking	DB Development	345	21	20
Shipmt-Tracking	UI Design	123	20	32
Shipmt-Tracking	UI Design	234	20	24

Wolf Peak International: Failure and Success in Application Software for the Small-to-Medium Enterprise

One of the hazards of a growing small business is a software upgrade. If you pick the wrong horse, you may find yourself riding in the wrong direction. Correcting your course may mean not only writing off your first upgrade selection but then going through the agonizing process of finding a better software solution for your company. That's what happened to Wolf Peak International of Layton, Utah, which designs and manufactures eyewear for the safety, sporting, driving, and fashion industries. Founded in 1998, the privately held small to midsize enterprise (SME) also specializes in overseas production, sourcing, importing, and promotional distribution services.

In Wolf Peak's early days, founder-owner Kurt Daems was happy using QuickBooks to handle accounting chores. The package is user friendly and allowed him to drill down to view transaction details or combine data in a variety of ways to create desired reports. As the company prospered, however, it quickly outgrew the capabilities of QuickBooks.

"As Wolf Peak got bigger, the owner felt the need to get into a more sophisticated accounting system," says Ron Schwab, CFO at Wolf Peak International. "There were no financial people in-house at the time the decision was made to purchase a replacement for QuickBooks, and the decision was made without a finance person in place to review it."

Wolf Peak selected one of several accounting software packages promoted to growing SMEs. By the time Schwab joined the company, the package had been installed for six months, following an implementation period that lasted a full year. "The biggest difficulty for QuickBooks users is to go from a very friendly user interface and the ability to find information easily to a more sophisticated, secured, batch-oriented accounting system that became an absolute nightmare to get data out of," notes Schwab. "So the company paid a lot of money to have this new accounting system, but nobody knew how to go in and extract financial or operational data used to make critical business decisions."

There were other problems. Developing reusable reports was difficult, time-consuming, and expensive. The company paid IT consultants to develop reports for specific needs, some of which still had not been delivered, months after they were commissioned. Ad hoc reporting was similarly intractable. Furthermore, the company's prior-year history in QuickBooks could not be converted into the new accounting package. A situation like this creates serious problems. Accustomed to keeping close tabs on the company's operations, Daems found that he simply could not get the information he wanted. He began to lose track of his business. "He got so fed up he finally came to me and said he was ready to look at a SAP software alternative he'd heard about," Schwab recalls. "He wasn't ready to buy it, though, because he'd just sunk a lot of money into the new accounting package."

One year after Wolf Peak had switched over to the new accounting software, Schwab called the offices of JourneyTEAM, a local SAP services partner, and asked their software consultants to demonstrate the SAP Business One software suite.

SAP Business One is an integrated business management software package designed specifically for SMEs like Wolf Peak: The application automates critical operations including sales, finance, purchasing, inventory, and manufacturing and delivers an accurate, up-to-the-minute view of the business. Its relative affordability promises a rapid return on investment, and its simplicity means users have a consistent, intuitive environment that they can learn quickly and use effectively.

"We had a wish list from various company employees asking for a variety of capabilities," recalls Schwab. "The JourneyTEAM people came in and demonstrated all those functionalities and more. They even generated four or five reports that we had spent several thousand dollars and several months trying to get from our other software consultants and had not yet received. Based on our data that they had input into Business One, JourneyTEAM put those reports together in an afternoon."

Daems still had a few reservations: He needed the buy-in of his VP of sales and was concerned about cost. He still wasn't ready to write off the recently installed accounting software.

JourneyTEAM came in and gave another presentation for the Wolf Peak sales team and, following that, came back with an acceptable quote. With some pain, but also considerable relief, Daems wrote off the existing accounting package. "We felt the benefits of SAP Business One far outweighed the costs and time already invested in that software system," Daems says.

Implementation of Business One took just seven weeks from the day of the initial sales presentation. "We implemented SAP Business One during our busiest period of the year with no disruptions," notes Schwab. "It went better than I expected, in particular the cutover and conversion to Business One. JourneyTEAM did an amazing job of getting all our old records converted with no real problems at all. We met our June 30 deadline and cutover during the succeeding long weekend without incident."

Schwab's enthusiasm for SAP Business One is high. "This is the best accounting program I've ever worked with," he says. "I can drill down to anything I want. And with the XL Reporter tool, I can build reports on the fly."

Business One includes a seamlessly integrated reporting and financial analysis tool called XL Reporter that works with Microsoft Excel to provide instant access to financial and operational data. It reports on live data drawn from a variety of sources including general ledger, receivables, payables, sales, purchasing, and inventory software. "Now we're building the reports we want," says Schwab. "To have a program like XL Reporter that lets us build custom reports, preset regular updates, and then work within Microsoft Excel—that's hugely valuable to us. Nobody else offers the ability to do ad hoc queries so easily. Even people who aren't serious programmers can go in and create the documents they need within the limits of their authorizations. So I highly recommend it."

For years, Daems had been running an open receivables report that presents, for example, all the invoices that are 15 days past due and greater than $450. Unfortunately, he simply could not run a report like that with the software package he bought to replace his old QuickBooks program. That situation has now changed.

"With SAP Business One, we can go in there and ask for those parameters and then sort it by oldest, biggest amount, or customer," says Schwab. "And it's paperless. The accounts receivable person doesn't have to print anything out and then write a bunch of notes on it and type them into the system for someone else to find. It's all right there."

Wolf Peak also requires a very complicated commissions report, used to generate the checks that go out to the company's commissioned sales representatives, who receive individualized reports as well. The previous consultants were unable to deliver this set of reports. JourneyTEAM was able to develop it on Business One in an afternoon.

Wolf Peak is already expanding its use of SAP Business One into other areas. The company has applied the software to warehouse management, where it enables Wolf Peak to manage inventory, receiving, warehouse delivery, shipping, and all the other aspects of the warehousing task. Inventory is one of the company's biggest assets, and it has to be managed well. "We have an audit report that lists all of the inventory, the current on-hand quantity, and the demands on it through sales orders or outstanding purchase orders," Schwab says.

This report then lists the value of that inventory and allows Schwab to look at the activity against any inventory item during any period. Beyond that, it enables him to drill down to the actual invoices that affect that inventory item. "We want to minimize what we have on hand," he says, "but we always have to be sure we have enough to meet our customers' needs. Business One lets us do that."

Wolf Peak's management has also begun using the customer relationship management (CRM) functionality within Business One to assist with its collection of receivables. The company's plan is to extend its use of the software to develop and track sales opportunities as well. Three months following its installation, Wolf Peak is quite happy with its decision to go with SAP's Business One software. "Reports that used to take months to create—if we could get them at all—can now be created in minutes," says Schwab.

A less tangible but no less important benefit is the renewed confidence Business One brings to management "A company's greatest untapped asset is its own financial information," says Schwab. "SAP Business One creates an environment where the decision makers get the information they want on a timely basis, in a format they can use. It's amazing what happens when management begins to see what is really happening inside the enterprise. Business One delivers useful information to help make good business decisions—and that's really the bottom line. This is a business management tool."

Source: Adapted from SAP America, "Wolf Peak: Making the Best Choice to Support Growth," *SAP BusinessInsights*, March 2007; JourneyTEAM, "Wolf Peak Success Story—SAP Business One," ABComputer.com, March 2007.

CASE STUDY QUESTIONS

1. What problems occurred when Wolf Peak upgraded from QuickBooks to a new accounting software package? How could these problems have been avoided?

2. Why did SAP's Business One prove to be a better choice for Wolf Peak's management than the new accounting software? Give several examples to illustrate your answer.

3. Should most SMEs use an integrated business software suite like SAP Business One instead of specialized accounting and other business software packages? Why or why not?

REAL WORLD ACTIVITIES

1. This case demonstrates failure and success in the software research, selection, and installation process, as well as some major differences among business application software packages in capabilities, such as ease of use and information access for employees and management. Search the Internet to find several more examples of such success and failure for software suites like SAP Business One or Oracle E-Business Suite and specialized business packages like QuickBooks or Great Plains Accounting.

2. Break into small groups with your classmates to discuss several key differences you have found on the basis of your Internet research. Then make recommendations to the class for how these differences should shape the business application software selection decision for an SME.

CHAPTER 5

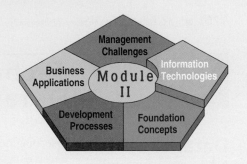

DATA RESOURCE MANAGEMENT

Chapter Highlights

Learning Objectives

1. Explain the business value of implementing data resource management processes and technologies in an organization.

2. Outline the advantages of a database management approach to managing the data resources of a business, compared with a file processing approach.

3. Explain how database management software helps business professionals and supports the operations and management of a business.

4. Provide examples to illustrate each of the following concepts:

   a. Major types of databases.

   b. Data warehouses and data mining.

   c. Logical data elements.

   d. Fundamental database structures.

   e. Database development.

Technical Foundations of Database Management

Database Management

Just imagine how difficult it would be to get any information from an information system if data were stored in an unorganized way or if there were no systematic way to retrieve them. Therefore, in all information systems, data resources must be organized and structured in some logical manner so that they can be accessed easily, processed efficiently, retrieved quickly, and managed effectively. Data structures and access methods ranging from simple to complex have been devised to organize and access data stored by information systems efficiently. In this chapter, we will explore these concepts, as well as the managerial implications and value of data resource management. See Figure 5.1.

It is important to appreciate from the beginning the value of understanding databases and database management. In today's world, just about every piece of data you would ever want to access is organized and stored in some type of database. The question is not so much "Should I use a database?" but rather "What database should I use?" Although many of you will not choose a career in the design of databases, all of you will spend a large portion of your time—whatever job you choose—accessing data in a myriad of databases. Most database developers consider accessing the data to be the business end of the database world, and understanding how data are structured, stored, and accessed can help business professionals gain greater strategic value from their organization's data resources.

Read the Real World Case 1 on the role of data issues in merger and acquistions. We can learn a lot about the importance of careful data planning and documentation from this case.

Fundamental Data Concepts

Before we go any further, let's discuss some fundamental concepts about how data are organized in information systems. A conceptual framework of several levels of data has been devised that differentiates among different groupings, or elements, of data. Thus, data may be logically organized into *characters*, *fields*, *records*, *files*, and *databases*, just as writing can be organized into letters, words, sentences, paragraphs, and documents. Examples of these logical data elements are shown in Figure 5.2.

Character

The most basic logical data element is the character, which consists of a single alphabetic, numeric, or other symbol. You might argue that the bit or byte is a more elementary data element, but remember that those terms refer to the physical storage elements provided by the computer hardware, as discussed in Chapter 3. Using that understanding, one way to think of a character is that it is a byte used to represent a particular character. From a user's point of view (i.e., from a *logical* as opposed to a physical or hardware view of data), a character is the most basic element of data that can be observed and manipulated.

Field

The next higher level of data is the field, or data item. A field consists of a grouping of related characters. For example, the grouping of alphabetic characters in a person's name may form a name field (or typically, last name, first name, and middle initial fields), and the grouping of numbers in a sales amount forms a sales amount field. Specifically, a data field represents an attribute (a characteristic or quality) of some entity (object, person, place, or event). For example, an employee's salary is an attribute that is a typical data field used to describe an entity who is an employee of a business. Generally speaking, fields are organized such that they represent some logical order, for example, last_name, first_name, address, city, state, and zip code.

Record

All of the fields used to describe the attributes of an entity are grouped to form a record. Thus, a record represents a collection of *attributes* that describe a single instance of an *entity*. An example is a person's payroll record, which consists of data

REAL WORLD CASE 1

Cogent Communications, Intel, and Others: Mergers Go More Smoothly When Your Data Are Ready

When Cogent Communications eyes a company to acquire, it goes into battle mode. Two miles north of the Pentagon, across the Potomac in Washington, Cogent sets up what it calls the War Room, where it marshals eight top executives to evaluate the target company. Among those on the due diligence squad are the IS director and IT infrastructure manager.

Cogent, a midsize Internet service provider, understands what far too many companies don't: Its ability to integrate and, in some cases, adopt an acquired company's IT systems and operations can determine whether a merger flourishes or founders. For one thing, unanticipated IT integration costs can offset merger savings. Imagine the business lost when orders vanish, accounts payable go uncollected, and customer information goes AWOL because the acquiring company gave short shrift to the IT challenge ahead.

As 2006 came to a close, it broke records for the number of mergers and acquisitions, but now IT managers have to step up and make sure their data centers can help make those deals a reality. "A well-run data center with reduced complexity makes mergers and acquisitions much easier," says Andi Mann, senior analyst at Enterprise Management Associates (EMA).

More than 11,700 deals were done. As the dust clears, experts and IT managers agree that companies will feel the full impact of this merger and acquisition (M&A) frenzy directly in their data centers. So they advise organizations to prep now or risk experiencing downtime if they have to merge mission-critical assets. "Today, the most downtime companies can afford for critical data center infrastructure is

FIGURE 5.1

IT integration and adoption issues can make or break merger and acquisition activities.

Source: McGraw-Hill Companies, Inc./John Flournoy, photographer.

measured in minutes." Merged and acquired infrastructure "has to be available right away," says Ryan Osborn of AFCOM, a data center industry group.

Observers agree that the key to M&A success from a data center perspective is to focus on virtualization, documentation, and logistics. Osborn says these three areas will help companies get ahead of the game and turn a time of crisis into one of opportunity. "You won't spend your time just moving infrastructure from one data center to another. You can actually do a technology refresh, get newer equipment and come out ahead," he says.

For John Musilli, data center operations manager at Intel in Santa Clara, California, the most critical piece is knowing about basic logistics. "I don't always have to know what a server does, but I do have to know how to keep it alive," he says. "It's getting something moved from Point A to Point B and it doesn't matter whether the logistics deals with putting servers on a truck or transferring data over a line."

Musilli has been through a handful of acquisitions in his eight years at Intel, and he says that he has it down to a science. "As part of the acquiring company, it's my job to provide the skeletal environment to accept any company's assets that come to us," he says. As such, he keeps a healthy amount of generic racking, generic cabling, extra bandwidth on the network, and generic power. "I go generic because I probably won't know what servers, how many slots, or what type of power we'll need beforehand. With generic, I can configure whatever I need in minutes," he says.

For instance, he uses a universal busway for power so that he doesn't have to be concerned about the particular electrical needs of the acquired equipment. "We acquired a company and needed to integrate them in a short period of time because their building lease was up and they had to get out of there," Musilli says. One team was sent ahead of time and spent a year trying to identify each server on 30–40 racks. "None of their applications matched our operating systems," he says. As time dwindled, Musilli told them to pack up all the servers and send them to him. "In the end, it took two man-days to move them intact and get them up and running in our data center," he says.

As companies begin to contemplate future mergers or acquisitions, they must look inward at their own processes and procedures. "Just as important as technology is documentation of processes—you have to know what people are doing with the systems," says EMA's Mann. He warns that one of the first obstacles to having a successful merger or acquisition is the reliance on what he refers to as *tribal knowledge*. Companies that have data centers where the employees hold all the knowledge suffer greatly when, after a merger or acquisition, those people are let go.

"You have to document the knowledge from those people and figure out how to make the processes work with only a handful of employees," he says. Mann recommends creating a workflow chart that outlines who's responsible for each part of the data center. He suggests considering who handles network management, systems management, application management, and storage. "This will also help you spot redundancies in skill sets or areas where you are lacking in the event of a merger," he says. John Burke, senior analyst at Nemertes Research in Minneapolis, says that in addition to knowing who is responsible, IT groups must know which systems perform which processes.

"You have to have really good information about what goes on in your data center in terms of systems and how they interact with each other and how they interface with the business. You should always know what services you offer and how much it costs to offer them," Burke says. As part of this effort, many organizations employ a configuration management database and asset management tool to help track elements within the data center. "You need a clear and concise view of the data flow within the data center. If you don't know what has to move together, you might disrupt business during a merger or acquisition," he says.

Companies must also develop guidelines for governance to be referenced during a merger. For instance, if two law firms are merging and have competing clients, then IT groups must ensure that data are protected and there is sufficient access control. AFCOM's Osborn says that good documentation helps the discovery process that companies go through before a merger or acquisition. "If the company you are acquiring has good documentation and good processes in place, the acquisition goes much more smoothly," he says.

"In some cases, you might be able to lower your software costs if you use a more robust server with fewer processors, but if the application license doesn't allow for that, then you can't," Osborn says, and adds: "How much money you're going to have to spend to merge technology can weigh heavily on the decision to acquire a company." Nemertes' Burke suggests that one major step to M&A success is to make sure your data center has virtualization tools running on both servers and storage.

Virtualization is important not only for scaling the data center but also for creating a standardized execution environment. "With a well-virtualized data center, you can hide the fact that things are moving around multiple servers and storage devices," Burke says. Rob Laurie, CEO at virtualization-software provider Dunes Technologies in Stamford, Connecticutt, says that virtualization is useful for companies that want to test application and infrastructure integration before they put their merged or acquired assets into production. It's also helpful for companies that must integrate assets that can't be physically moved, he says. He warns, however, that for virtualization to be most effective, merging companies must decide on a uniform platform for their virtual environment. "That way, whatever is virtualized in one company could run in the other company's data center without problems," he says. If they don't have the same environment, they must at least have a compatible data format to gain any benefit.

Intel's Musilli suggests that IT's natural attention to detail can sometimes overcomplicate matters. "Mergers and acquisitions aren't always as difficult as people make them. They're simply about the ability to assimilate any two environments," he says. M&As create stress for both acquirer and acquiree, but early involvement by IT can minimize the trauma. Otherwise, you'll need to do too much in too little time. As software engineering guru Frederick Brooks once said, "You can't make a baby in a month using nine women. Plan ahead."

Source: Adapted from Sandra Gittien, "Mergers Go Smoother with a Well-Prepped Data Center," *Computerworld*, July 28, 2007, and Eric Chabrow, "IT Plays Linchpin Role in High-Stake M&As," *InformationWeek*, June 26, 2006.

CASE STUDY QUESTIONS

1. Place yourself in the role of a manager at a company undergoing a merger or acquisition. What would be the most important things customers would expect from you while still in that process? What role would IT play in meeting those expectations? Provide at least three examples.

2. Focus on what Andi Mann in the case calls "tribal knowledge." What do you think is meant by that, and why is it so important to this process? What strategies would you suggest for companies that are faced with the extensive presence of this issue in an acquired organization? Develop some specific recommendations.

3. Most of the discussion on the case focused on hardware and software issues. However, these are essentially enablers for underlying business processes developed by each of the companies involved. What different alternatives do companies have for merging their business processes, and what role would IT play in supporting those activities? Pay particular attention to data management and governance issues.

REAL WORLD ACTIVITIES

1. The case extensively discusses the idea of "virtualization" and the role it plays in the merger process. Go online to research this concept and prepare a report about what it entails, how it works, what are its advantages and disadvantages, and other applications in addition to those noted in the case.

2. Search the Internet for reports of merger and acquisition cases where IT issues played an important role, either positive or negative. How did different organizations handle IT-related matters in the situations you found? What was the ultimate outcome of the process? Prepare a presentation to share your findings with the class.

FIGURE 5.2 Examples of the logical data elements in information systems. Note especially the examples of how data fields, records, files, and databases relate.

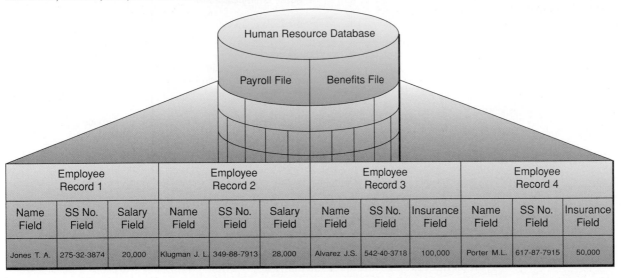

fields describing attributes such as the person's name, Social Security number, and rate of pay. *Fixed-length* records contain a fixed number of fixed-length data fields. *Variable-length* records contain a variable number of fields and field lengths. Another way of looking at a record is that it represents a single *instance* of an entity. Each record in an employee file describes one specific employee.

Normally, the first field in a record is used to store some type of unique identifier for the record. This unique identifier is called the **primary key.** The value of a primary key can be anything that will serve to uniquely identify one instance of an entity, and distinguish it from another. For example, if we wanted to uniquely identify a single student from a group of related students, we could use a student ID number as a primary key. As long as no one shared the same student ID number, we would always be able to identify the record of that student. If no specific data can be found to serve as a primary key for a record, the database designer can simply assign a record a unique sequential number so that no two records will ever have the same primary key.

File

A group of related records is a data file (sometimes referred to as a *table* or *flat file*). When it is independent of any other files related to it, a single *table* may be referred to as a *flat file*. As a point of accuracy, the term *flat file* may be defined either narrowly or more broadly. Strictly speaking, a flat file database should consist of nothing but data and delimiters. More broadly, the term refers to any database that exists in a single file in the form of rows and columns, with no relationships or links between records and fields except the table structure. Regardless of the name used, any grouping of related records in tabular (row-and-column form) is called a *file*. Thus, an employee file would contain the records of the employees of a firm. Files are frequently classified by the application for which they are primarily used, such as a *payroll file* or an *inventory file*, or the type of data they contain, such as a *document file* or a *graphical image file*. Files are also classified by their permanence, for example, a payroll *master file* versus a payroll weekly *transaction file*. A transaction file, therefore, would contain records of all transactions occurring during a period and might be used periodically to update the permanent records contained in a master file. A *history file* is an obsolete transaction or master file retained for backup purposes or for long-term historical storage, called *archival storage*.

Database

A database is an integrated collection of logically related data elements. A database consolidates records previously stored in separate files into a common pool of data

FIGURE 5.3

Some of the entities and relationships in a simplified electric utility database. Note a few of the business applications that access the data in the database.

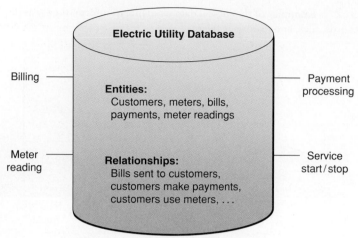

Electric Utility Database

Billing

Payment processing

Entities:
Customers, meters, bills, payments, meter readings

Meter reading

Service start/stop

Relationships:
Bills sent to customers, customers make payments, customers use meters, . . .

Source: Adapted from Michael V. Mannino, *Database Application Development and Design* (Burr Ridge, IL: McGraw-Hill/Irwin, 2001), p. 6.

elements that provides data for many applications. The data stored in a database are independent of the application programs using them and of the type of storage devices on which they are stored.

Thus, databases contain data elements describing entities and relationships among entities. For example, Figure 5.3 outlines some of the entities and relationships in a database for an electric utility. Also shown are some of the business applications (billing, payment processing) that depend on access to the data elements in the database.

As stated in the beginning of the chapter, just about all the data we use are stored in some type of database. A database doesn't need to look complex or technical to be a database; it just needs to provide a logical organization method and easy access to the data stored in it. You probably use one or two rapidly growing databases just about every day: How about Facebook, MySpace, or YouTube?

All of the pictures, videos, songs, messages, chats, icons, e-mail addresses, and everything else stored on each of these popular social networking Web sites are stored as fields, records, files, or objects in large databases. The data are stored in such a way to ensure that there is easy access to it, it can be shared by its respective owners, and it can be protected from unauthorized access or use. When you stop to think about how simple it is to use and enjoy these databases, it is easy to forget how large and complex they are.

For example, in July 2006, YouTube reported that viewers watched more than 100 million videos every day, with 2.5 billion videos in June 2006 alone. In May 2006, users added 50,000 videos per day, and this increased to 65,000 videos by July. In January 2008 alone, almost 79 million users watched more than 3 billion videos on YouTube. In August 2006, *The Wall Street Journal* published an article revealing that YouTube was hosting approximately 6.1 million videos (requiring about 45 terabytes of storage space), and had approximately 500 accounts. As of March 2008, a YouTube search turned up approximately 77.3 million videos and 2.89 million user channels.

Perhaps an even more compelling example of ease of access versus complexity is found in the popular social networking Web site Facebook. Some of the basic statistics are nothing short of amazing! Facebook reports more than 200 million users with more than 100 million logging in at least once each day. The average user has 120 friend relationships established. More than 850 million photos, 8 million videos, 1 billion pieces of content, and 2.5 million events are uploaded or created each month. More than 40 language translations are currently available on the site, with more than 50 more in development. More than 52,000 software applications exist in the Facebook Application Directory and over 30 million active users access Facebook through their mobile devices. The size of their databases is best measured in petabytes, which is equal to one quadrillion bytes. All of this from a database and a simple access method launched in 2004 from a dorm room at Harvard University.

The important point here is that all of these videos, user accounts, and information are easily accessed because the data are stored in a database system that organizes it so that a particular item can be found on demand.

Database Structures

The relationships among the many individual data elements stored in databases are based on one of several logical data structures, or models. Database management system (DBMS) packages are designed to use a specific data structure to provide end users with quick, easy access to information stored in databases. Five fundamental database structures are the *hierarchical, network, relational, object-oriented,* and *multidimensional* models. Simplified illustrations of the first three database structures are shown in Figure 5.4.

FIGURE 5.4

Example of three fundamental database structures. They represent three basic ways to develop and express the relationships among the data elements in a database.

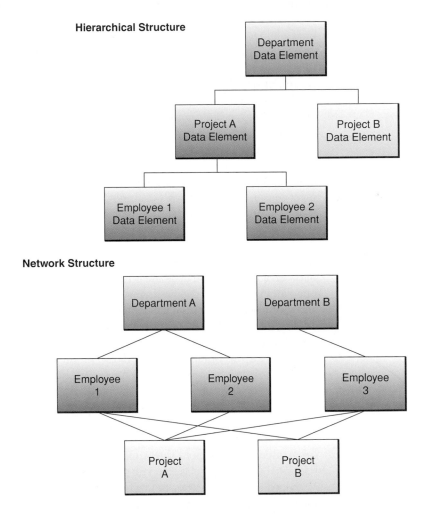

Source: Adapted from Michael V. Mannino, *Database Application Development and Design* (Burr Ridge, IL: McGraw-Hill/Irwin, 2001), p. 6.

Hierarchical Structure

Early mainframe DBMS packages used the hierarchical structure, in which the relationships between records form a hierarchy or treelike structure. In the traditional hierarchical model, all records are dependent and arranged in multilevel structures, consisting of one *root* record and any number of subordinate levels. Thus, all of the relationships among records are *one-to-many* because each data element is related to only one element above it. The data element or record at the highest level of the hierarchy (the department data element in this illustration) is called the root element. Any data element can be accessed by moving progressively downward from a root and along the branches of the tree until the desired record (e.g., the employee data element) is located.

Network Structure

The network structure can represent more complex logical relationships and is still used by some mainframe DBMS packages. It allows *many-to-many* relationships among records; that is, the network model can access a data element by following one of several paths because any data element or record can be related to any number of other data elements. For example, in Figure 5.4, departmental records can be related to more than one employee record, and employee records can be related to more than one project record. Thus, you could locate all employee records for a particular department or all project records related to a particular employee.

It should be noted that neither the hierarchical nor the network data structures are commonly found in the modern organization. The next data structure we discuss, the relational data structure, is the most common of all and serves as the foundation for most modern databases in organizations.

Relational Structure

The relational model is the most widely used of the three database structures. It is used by most microcomputer DBMS packages, as well as by most midrange and mainframe systems. In the relational model, all data elements within the database are viewed as being stored in the form of simple two-dimensional **tables,** sometimes referred to as *relations*. The tables in a relational database are *flat files* that have rows and columns. Each row represents a single record in the file, and each column represents a field. The major difference between a flat file and a database is that a flat file can only have data attributes specified for one file. In contrast, a database can specify data attributes for multiple files simultaneously and can relate the various data elements in one file to those in one or more other files.

Figure 5.4 illustrates the relational database model with two tables representing some of the relationships among departmental and employee records. Other tables, or relations, for this organization's database might represent the data element relationships among projects, divisions, product lines, and so on. Database management system packages based on the relational model can link data elements from various tables to provide information to users. For example, a manager might want to retrieve and display an employee's name and salary from the employee table in Figure 5.4, as well as the name of the employee's department from the department table, by using their common department number field (Deptno) to link or join the two tables. See Figure 5.5. The relational model can relate data in any one file with data in another file if both files share a common data element or field. Because of this, information can be created by retrieving data from multiple files even if they are not all stored in the same physical location.

FIGURE 5.5

Joining the employee and department tables in a relational database enables you to access data selectively in both tables at the same time.

Department Table

Deptno	Dname	Dloc	Dmgr
Dept A			
Dept B			
Dept C			

Employee Table

Empno	Ename	Etitle	Esalary	Deptno
Emp 1				Dept A
Emp 2				Dept A
Emp 3				Dept B
Emp 4				Dept B
Emp 5				Dept C
Emp 6				Dept B

Relational Operations

Three basic operations can be performed on a relational database to create useful sets of data. The *select* operation is used to create a subset of records that meet a stated criterion. For example, a select operation might be used on an employee database to create a subset of records that contain all employees who make more than $30,000 per year and who have been with the company more than three years. Another way to think of the select operation is that it temporarily creates a table whose rows have records that meet the selection criteria.

The *join* operation can be used to combine two or more tables temporarily so that a user can see relevant data in a form that looks like it is all in one big table. Using this operation, a user can ask for data to be retrieved from multiple files or databases without having to go to each one separately.

Finally, the *project* operation is used to create a subset of the columns contained in the temporary tables created by the select and join operations. Just as the select operation creates a subset of records that meet stated criteria, the project operation creates a subset of the columns, or fields, that the user wants to see. Using a project operation, the user can decide not to view all of the columns in the table but instead only those that have the data necessary to answer a particular question or construct a specific report.

Because of the widespread use of relational models, an abundance of commercial products exist to create and manage them. Leading mainframe relational database applications include Oracle 10g from Oracle Corp. and DB2 from IBM. A very popular midrange database application is SQL Server from Microsoft. The most commonly used database application for the PC is Microsoft Access.

Multidimensional Structure

The multidimensional model is a variation of the relational model that uses multidimensional structures to organize data and express the relationships between data. You can visualize multidimensional structures as cubes of data and cubes within cubes of data. Each side of the cube is considered a dimension of the data. Figure 5.6 is an example that shows that each dimension can represent a different category, such as product type, region, sales channel, and time.

Each cell within a multidimensional structure contains aggregated data related to elements along each of its dimensions. For example, a single cell may contain the total sales for a product in a region for a specific sales channel in a single month. A major benefit of multidimensional databases is that they provide a compact and easy-to-understand way to visualize and manipulate data elements that have many interrelationships. So multidimensional databases have become the most popular database structure for the analytical databases that support *online analytical processing* (OLAP) applications, in which fast answers to complex business queries are expected. We discuss OLAP applications in Chapter 10.

Objected-Oriented Structure

The object-oriented model is considered one of the key technologies of a new generation of multimedia Web-based applications. As Figure 5.7 illustrates, an **object** consists of data values describing the attributes of an entity, plus the operations that can be performed upon the data. This *encapsulation* capability allows the object-oriented model to handle complex types of data (graphics, pictures, voice, and text) more easily than other database structures.

The object-oriented model also supports *inheritance*; that is, new objects can be automatically created by replicating some or all of the characteristics of one or more *parent* objects. Thus, in Figure 5.7, the checking and savings account objects can inherit both the common attributes and operations of the parent bank account object. Such capabilities have made *object-oriented database management systems* (OODBMS) popular in computer-aided design (CAD) and a growing number of applications. For example, object technology allows designers to develop product designs, store them as objects in an object-oriented database, and replicate and modify them to create new product designs. In addition, multimedia Web-based applications for the Internet and corporate intranets and extranets have become a major application area for object technology.

FIGURE 5.6   An example of the different dimensions of a multidimensional database.

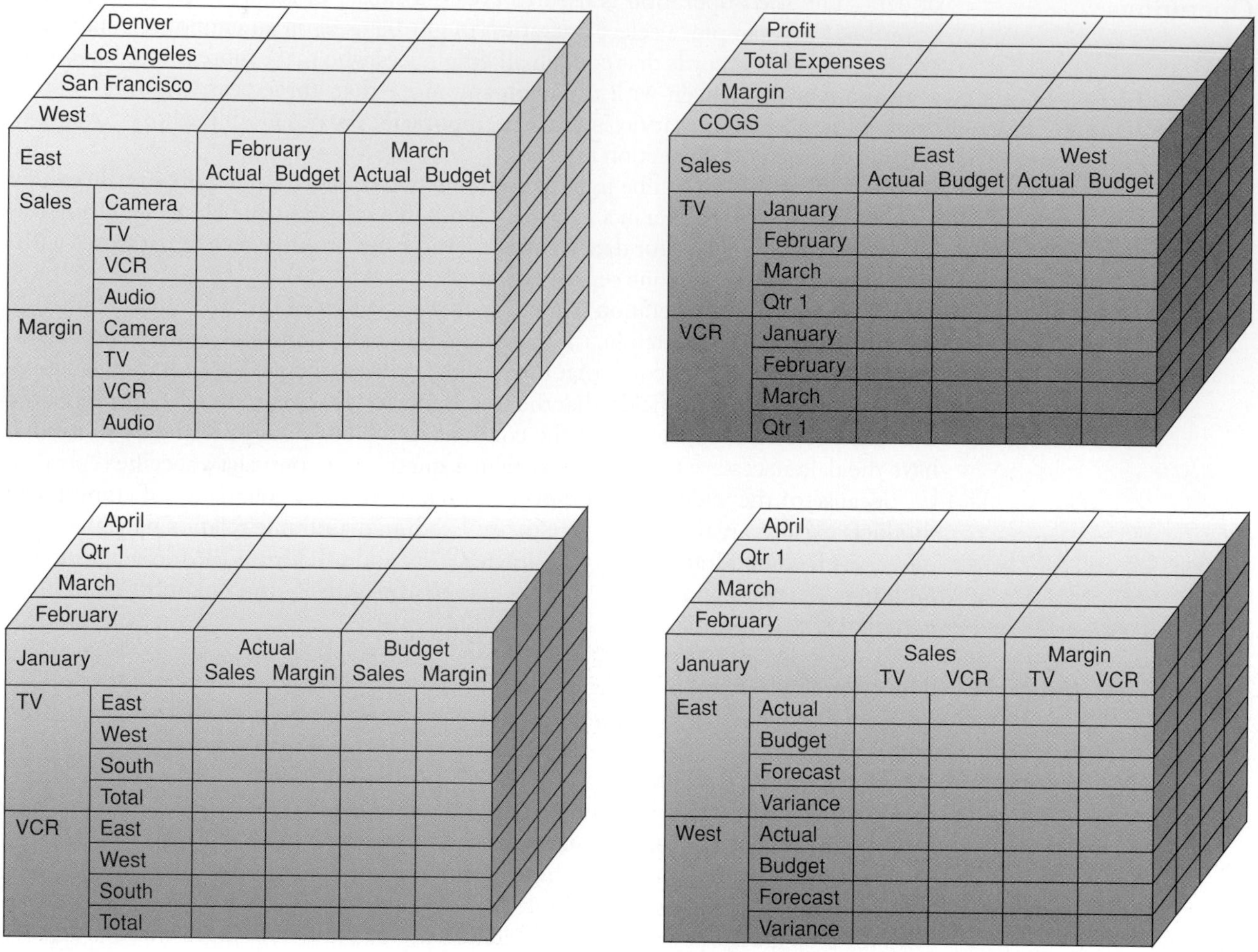

FIGURE 5.7

The checking and savings account objects can inherit common attributes and operations from the bank account object.

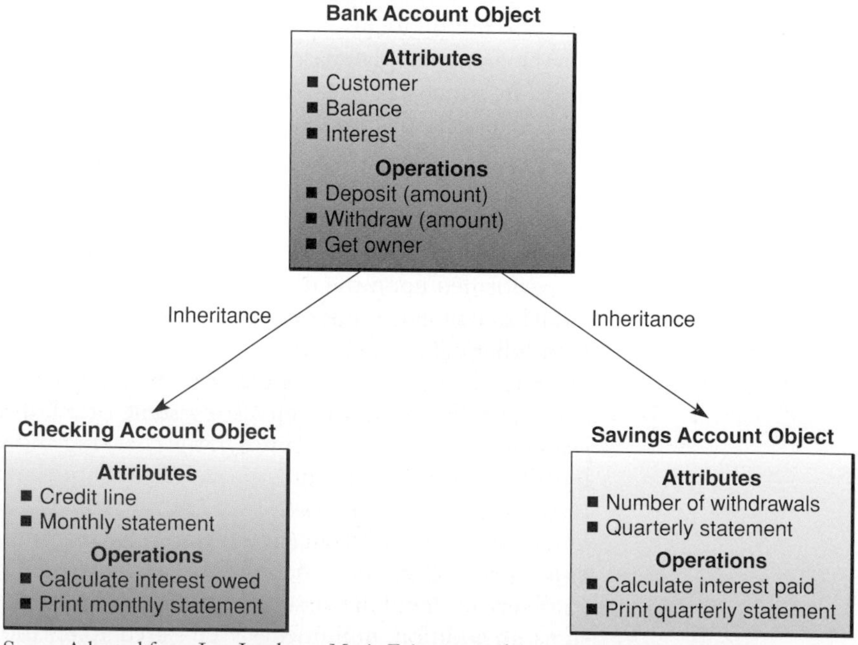

Source: Adapted from Ivar Jacobsen, Maria Ericsson, and Ageneta Jacobsen, *The Object Advantage: Business Process Reengineering with Object Technology* (New York: ACM Press, 1995), p. 65. Copyright © 1995, Association for Computing Machinery. Used by permission.

FIGURE 5.8

Databases can supply data to a wide variety of analysis packages, allowing for data to be displayed in graphical form.

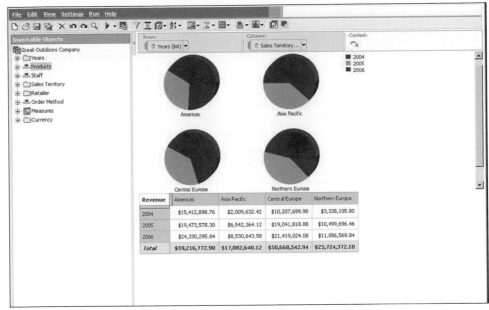

Source: Courtesy of Microsoft®.

Object technology proponents argue that an object-oriented DBMS can work with *complex data types* such as document and graphic images, video clips, audio segments, and other subsets of Web pages much more efficiently than relational database management systems. However, major relational DBMS vendors have countered by adding object-oriented modules to their relational software. Examples include multimedia object extensions to IBM's DB2 and Oracle's object-based "cartridges" for Oracle 10g. See Figure 5.8.

Evaluation of Database Structures

The hierarchical data structure was a natural model for the databases used for the structured, routine types of transaction processing characteristic of many business operations in the early years of data processing and computing. Data for these operations can easily be represented by groups of records in a hierarchical relationship. However, as time progressed, there were many cases in which information was needed about records that did not have hierarchical relationships. For example, in some organizations, employees from more than one department can work on more than one project (refer to Figure 5.4). A network data structure could easily handle this many-to-many relationship, whereas a hierarchical model could not. As such, the more flexible network structure became popular for these types of business operations. Like the hierarchical structure, the network model was unable to handle ad hoc requests for information easily because its relationships must be specified in advance, which pointed to the need for the relational model.

Relational databases enable an end user to receive information easily in response to ad hoc requests. That's because not all of the relationships among the data elements in a relationally organized database need to be specified when the database is created. Database management software (such as Oracle 11g, DB2, Access, and Approach) creates new tables of data relationships by using parts of the data from several tables. Thus, relational databases are easier for programmers to work with and easier to maintain than the hierarchical and network models.

The major limitation of the relational model is that relational database management systems cannot process large amounts of business transactions as quickly and efficiently as those based on the hierarchical and network models; they also cannot process complex, high-volume applications as well as the object-oriented model. This performance gap has narrowed with the development of advanced relational database software with object-oriented extensions. The use of database management software based on the object-oriented and multidimensional models is growing steadily, as these technologies are playing a greater role for OLAP and Web-based applications.

Database Pioneer Rethinks the Best Way to Organize Data

Is there a better way to build a data warehouse? For years, relational databases, which organize data in tables composed of vertical columns and horizontal rows, have served as the foundation of data warehouses. Now database pioneer Michael Stonebraker is promoting a different way of organizing them, promising much faster response times. As a scientist at the University of California at Berkeley in the 1970s, Stonebraker was one of the original architects of the Ingres relational database, which spawned several commercial variants. A row-based system like Ingres is great for executing transactions, but a column-oriented system is a more natural fit for data warehouses, Stonebraker now says.

SQL Server, Sybase, and Teradata all have rows as their central design point. Yet in data warehousing, faster performance may be gained through a column layout. Stonebraker says all types of queries on "most data warehouses" will run up to 50 times faster in a column database. The bigger the data warehouse, the greater the performance gain.

Why? Data warehouses frequently store transactional data, and each transaction has many parts. Columns cut across transactions and store an element of information that is standard to each transaction, such as customer name, address, or purchase amount. A row, by comparison, may hold 20–200 different elements of a transaction. A standard relational database would retrieve all the rows that reflect, say, sales for a month, load the data into system memory, and then find all sales records and generate an average from them. The ability to focus on just the "sales" column leads to improved query performance.

There is a second performance benefit in the column approach. Because columns contain similar information from each transaction, it's possible to derive a compression scheme for the data type and then apply it throughout the column. Rows cannot be compressed as easily because the nature of the data (e.g., name, zip code, and account balance) varies from record to record. Each row would require a different compression scheme.

Compressing data in columns makes for faster storage and retrieval and reduces the amount of disk required. "In every data warehouse I see, compression is a good thing," Stonebraker says. "I expect the data warehouse market to become completely column-store based."

Source: Adapted from Charles Babcock, "Database Pioneer Rethinks the Best Way to Organize Data," *InformationWeek*, February 23, 2008.

Database Development

Database management packages like Microsoft Access or Lotus Approach allow end users to develop the databases they need easily. See Figure 5.9. However, large organizations usually place control of enterprisewide database development in the hands of database administrators (DBAs) and other database specialists. This delegation improves the integrity and security of organizational databases. Database developers use the *data definition language* (DDL) in database management systems like Oracle 11g or IBM's DB2 to develop and specify the data contents, relationships, and structure of each database, as well as to modify these database specifications when necessary. Such information is cataloged and stored in a database of data definitions and specifications called a *data dictionary*, or *metadata repository*, which is managed by the database management software and maintained by the DBA.

A data dictionary is a database management catalog or directory containing metadata (i.e., data about data). A data dictionary relies on a specialized database software component to manage a database of data definitions, which is metadata about the structure, data elements, and other characteristics of an organization's databases. For example, it contains the names and descriptions of all types of data records and their interrelationships; information outlining requirements for end users' access and use of application programs; and database maintenance and security.

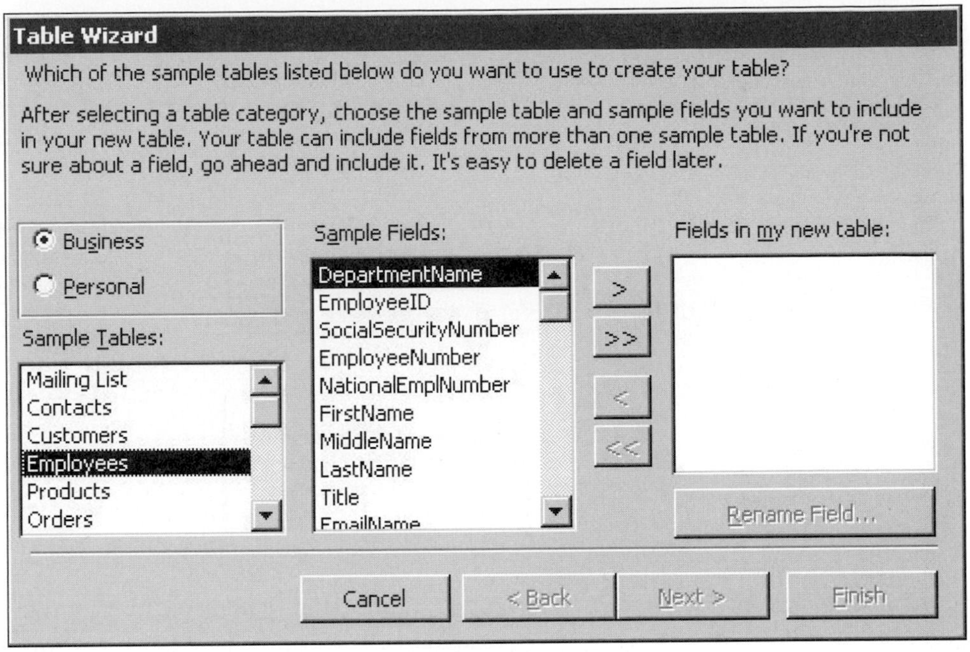

FIGURE 5.9

Creating a database table using the Table Wizard of Microsoft Access.

Table Wizard

Which of the sample tables listed below do you want to use to create your table?

After selecting a table category, choose the sample table and sample fields you want to include in your new table. Your table can include fields from more than one sample table. If you're not sure about a field, go ahead and include it. It's easy to delete a field later.

● Business
○ Personal

Sample Tables:
- Mailing List
- Contacts
- Customers
- Employees
- Products
- Orders

Sample Fields:
- DepartmentName
- EmployeeID
- SocialSecurityNumber
- EmployeeNumber
- NationalEmplNumber
- FirstName
- MiddleName
- LastName
- Title
- EmailName

Fields in my new table:

[>] [>>] [<] [<<]

Rename Field...

[Cancel] [< Back] [Next >] [Finish]

Source: Courtesy of Microsoft®.

The database administrator can query data dictionaries to report the status of any aspect of a firm's metadata. The administrator can then make changes to the definitions of selected data elements. Some *active* (versus *passive*) data dictionaries automatically enforce standard data element definitions whenever end users and application programs access an organization's databases. For example, an active data dictionary would not allow a data entry program to use a nonstandard definition of a customer record, nor would it allow an employee to enter a name of a customer that exceeded the defined size of that data element.

Developing a large database of complex data types can be a complicated task. Database administrators and database design analysts work with end users and systems analysts to model business processes and the data they require. Then they determine (1) what data definitions should be included in the database and (2) what structures or relationships should exist among the data elements.

Data Planning and Database Design

As Figure 5.10 illustrates, database development may start with a top-down **data planning process.** Database administrators and designers work with corporate and end-user management to develop an *enterprise model* that defines the basic business process of the enterprise. They then define the information needs of end users in a business process, such as the purchasing/receiving process that all businesses have.

Next, end users must identify the key data elements that are needed to perform their specific business activities. This step frequently involves developing *entity relationship diagrams* (ERDs) that model the relationships among the many entities involved in business processes. For example, Figure 5.11 illustrates some of the relationships in a purchasing/receiving process. The ERDs are simply graphical models of the various files and their relationships, contained within a database system. End users and database designers could use database management or business modeling software to help them develop ERD models for the purchasing/receiving process. This would help identify the supplier and product data that are required to automate their purchasing/receiving and other business processes using enterprise resource management (ERM) or supply chain management (SCM) software. You will learn about ERDs and other data modeling tools in much greater detail if you ever take a course in systems analysis and design.

FIGURE 5.10

Database development involves data planning and database design activities. Data models that support business processes are used to develop databases that meet the information needs of users.

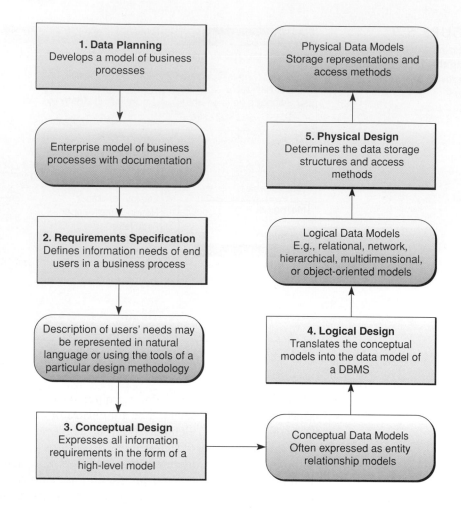

1. Data Planning
Develops a model of business processes

Enterprise model of business processes with documentation

2. Requirements Specification
Defines information needs of end users in a business process

Description of users' needs may be represented in natural language or using the tools of a particular design methodology

3. Conceptual Design
Expresses all information requirements in the form of a high-level model

Conceptual Data Models
Often expressed as entity relationship models

4. Logical Design
Translates the conceptual models into the data model of a DBMS

Logical Data Models
E.g., relational, network, hierarchical, multidimensional, or object-oriented models

5. Physical Design
Determines the data storage structures and access methods

Physical Data Models
Storage representations and access methods

Such user views are a major part of a **data modeling** process, during which the relationships among data elements are identified. Each data model defines the logical relationships among the data elements needed to support a basic business process. For example, can a supplier provide more than one type of product to us? Can a customer have more than one type of account with us? Can an employee have several pay rates or be assigned to several project workgroups?

Answering such questions will identify data relationships that must be represented in a data model that supports business processes of an organization. These data models then serve as *logical design* frameworks (called *schema* and *subschema*). These frameworks determine the *physical design* of databases and the development of application programs to support the business processes of the organization. A schema is an overall logical view of the relationships among the data elements in a database, whereas the

FIGURE 5.11

This entity relationship diagram illustrates some of the relationships among the entities (product, supplier, warehouse, etc.) in a purchasing/receiving business process.

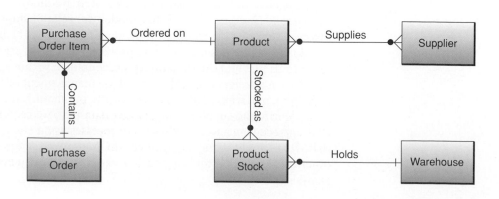

Purchase Order Item — Ordered on — Product — Supplies — Supplier

Contains

Purchase Order

Stocked as

Product Stock — Holds — Warehouse

FIGURE 5.12 Example of the logical and physical database views and the software interface of a banking services information system.

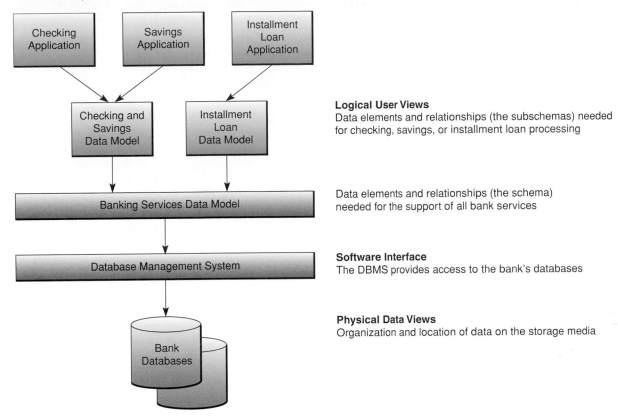

Logical User Views
Data elements and relationships (the subschemas) needed for checking, savings, or installment loan processing

Data elements and relationships (the schema) needed for the support of all bank services

Software Interface
The DBMS provides access to the bank's databases

Physical Data Views
Organization and location of data on the storage media

subschema is a logical view of the data relationships needed to support specific end-user application programs that will access that database.

Remember that data models represent logical views of the data and relationships of the database. Physical database design takes a physical view of the data (also called the *internal view*) that describes how data are to be physically stored and accessed on the storage devices of a computer system. For example, Figure 5.12 illustrates these different database views and the software interface of a bank database processing system. This figure focuses on the business processes of checking, savings, and installment lending, which are part of a banking services data model that serves as a logical data framework for all bank services.

Large-Scale Data Sets: The Sky Is the Limit

In early 2004, the computers at the Minor Planet Center (MPC) sorted through approximately 10,000 observations of astronomic phenomena. They deemed a handful of these observations to deserve follow-up because they were either newly discovered or on a path in Earth's general vicinity. Although the preliminary trajectories that the MPC plotted were not based on enough observation to be accurate, unbeknownst to center officials, the computer had found one object on a collision path with Earth. The discovery was posted on the Web late in the day on January 13, 2004.

Alan Harris, a senior research scientist at the Space Science Institute in Boulder, Colorado, ran some calculations and found that the object was "heading straight for us at around 11 miles per second" and would hit in 26 hours. The near-Earth object (NEO) was estimated to be about 98 feet in diameter. Depending on its composition, it could have disintegrated in the atmosphere or hit the Earth. (The mile-wide, 570-foot Barringer Meteorite Crater in Arizona was created by a 148-foot iron object.) Harris was nonetheless skeptical about the object's preliminary path. The MPC trajectory was based on only a few observations—enough to help astronomers find it, but not accurate enough to determine its actual course.

At 8:30 p.m., Brian Marsden, director of the MPC, got a call from NASA's Jet Propulsion Laboratory. The NASA official "sort of was wondering" about the path of the object, Marsden recalls. Marsden ordered further observations, and the bogey was determined not to be on a threatening path after all.

In some ways, scientists were lucky to have found this potential threat, because finding NEOs today is literally a hit-or-miss activity. The first warning of an asteroid or comet impact may come from calculations performed by some old workstations clustered together at the MPC at the Smithsonian Astrophysical Observatory at Harvard University. These systems aren't large enough to map the sky and provide scientists with a comprehensive view of everything that could do serious damage, but that's changing.

One ambitious project is the Large Synoptic Survey Telescope (LSST) in Tucson, Arizona. The telescope being built for the LSST project will collect data at a rate of about 6 GB (equivalent to the amount of data on one DVD) per 10 seconds, generating many petabytes of data over time. *One petabyte equals roughly 100 times the printed contents of the Library of Congress.* The LSST database will probably be the largest known nonproprietary database in the world. Because operation of the telescope lies some seven to eight years from now, the scientists working on it are hopeful that processing capabilities and storage densities will increase enough to handle these data, but they can still imagine a supercomputer system of 1,000 or so systems networked together.

Scientists hope that LSST and other parallel efforts will help them identify most of the NEOs that may threaten Earth, locating those on a dangerous path long before they strike. They hope that information will give them time to develop ways to deflect the NEO. These system developments will happen, of course, only if the Earth isn't first destroyed by a comet or asteroid.

Source: Adapted from Patrick Thibodeau, "IT to Help Avoid Astronomical Armageddon," *Computerworld*, September 6, 2004.

SECTION II Managing Data Resources

Data Resource Management

Data are a vital organizational resource that need to be managed like other important business assets. Today's business enterprises cannot survive or succeed without quality data about their internal operations and external environment.

> *With each online mouse click, either a fresh bit of data is created or already-stored data are retrieved from all those business Web sites. All that's on top of the heavy demand for industrial-strength data storage already in use by scores of big corporations. What's driving the growth is a crushing imperative for corporations to analyze every bit of information they can extract from their huge data warehouses for competitive advantage. That has turned the data storage and management function into a key strategic role of the information age.*

That's why organizations and their managers need to practice data resource management, a managerial activity that applies information systems technologies like *database management, data warehousing*, and other data management tools to the task of managing an organization's data resources to meet the information needs of their business stakeholders. This section will show you the managerial implications of using data resource management technologies and methods to manage an organization's data assets to meet business information requirements.

Read the Real World Case 2 on Applebee's, Travelocity, and Others. We can learn a lot from this case about the business value of mining data for decision making. See Figure 5.13.

Types of Databases

Continuing developments in information technology and its business applications have resulted in the evolution of several major types of databases. Figure 5.14 illustrates several major conceptual categories of databases that may be found in many organizations. Let's take a brief look at some of them now.

Operational Databases

Operational databases store detailed data needed to support the business processes and operations of a company. They are also called *subject area databases* (SADB), *transaction databases*, and *production databases*. Examples are a customer database, human resource database, inventory database, and other databases containing data generated by business operations. For example, a human resource database like that shown in Figure 5.2 would include data identifying each employee and his or her time worked, compensation, benefits, performance appraisals, training and development status, and other related human resource data. Figure 5.15 illustrates some of the common operational databases that can be created and managed for a small business using Microsoft Access database management software.

Distributed Databases

Many organizations replicate and distribute copies or parts of databases to network servers at a variety of sites. These distributed databases can reside on network servers on the World Wide Web, on corporate intranets or extranets, or on other company networks. Distributed databases may be copies of operational or analytical databases, hypermedia or discussion databases, or any other type of database. Replication and distribution of databases improve database performance at end-user worksites. Ensuring that the data in an organization's distributed databases are consistently and concurrently updated is a major challenge of distributed database management.

Distributed databases have both advantages and disadvantages. One primary advantage of a distributed database lies with the protection of valuable data. If all of an

REAL WORLD CASE 2

Applebee's, Travelocity, and Others: Data Mining for Business Decisions

Randall Parman, database architect at restaurant chain Applebee's International and head of Teradata's user group, opened Teradata's annual user conference in Las Vegas with a warning to those who aren't making the best use of their data. "Data are like gold," Parman noted. "If you don't use the gold, you will have someone else who will come along and take the opportunity," speaking to a room packed with almost 3,900 attendees.

Parman drew an analogy to the story about Isaac Newton's discovery of gravity after he was hit on the head with an apple. "What if Newton had just eaten the apple?" he asked. "What if we failed to use the technology available, or failed to use these insights to take action?" Applebee's, which has 1,900 casual dining restaurants worldwide and grossed $1.34 billion in revenue last year, has a four-node, 4TB data warehouse system. Although the company has a staff of only three database administrators working with the system, "we have leveraged our information to gain insight into the business," he said. "Some of those insights were unexpected, coming out of the blue while we were looking in a completely different direction."

For example, Applebee's had been using the data warehouse to analyze the "back-of-house performance" of restaurants, including how long it took employees to prepare food in the kitchens. "Someone had the unanticipated insight to use back-of-house performance to gauge front-of-house performance," he said. "From looking at the time the order was placed to when it was paid for by credit card and subtracting preparation meal time, we could figure out how long servers were spending time with customers." Parman

added that the information is being used to help the company improve customer experiences.

Applebee's has also advanced beyond basic business decisions based on data—such as replenishing food supplies according to how much finished product was sold daily—to developing more sophisticated analyses. His department, for example, came up with a "menu optimization quadrant" that looks at how well items are selling so that the company can make better decisions about not only what to order, but about what products to promote.

Meanwhile, technology vendors see untapped potential for businesses to spend money on software and hardware that lets them use data to make more sophisticated business decisions. "Companies who operate with the greatest speed and intelligence will win," says Teradata CEO Michael Koehler.

Like many companies, Travelocity.com has lots of unstructured data contained in e-mails from customers, call center representative notes, and other sources that contain critical nuggets of information about how customers feel about the travel site. To offset the inability of business intelligence tools to search for unstructured data, Travelocity has launched a new project to help it mine almost 600,000 unstructured comments so that it can better monitor and respond to customer service issues.

The online travel site has begun to install new text analytics software that will be used to scour some 40,000 verbatim comments from customer satisfaction surveys, 40,000 e-mails from customers, and 500,000 interactions with the call center that result in comments to surface potential customer service issues. "The truth is that it is very laborious and extremely expensive to go through all that verbatim customer feedback to try to extract the information we need to have to make business decisions," notes Don Hill, Travelocity's director of customer advocacy.

"The text mining capability . . . gives us the ability to go through all that verbatim feedback from customers and extract meaningful information. We get information on the nature of the comments and if the comments are positive or negative."

Travelocity will use text analytics software from Attensity to automatically identify facts, opinions, requests, trends, and trouble spots from the unstructured data. Travelocity will then link that analysis with structured data from its Teradata data warehouse so the company can identify trends. "We get to take unstructured data and put it into structured data so we can track trends over time," adds Hill. "We can know the frequency of customer comments on issue 'x' and if comments on that topic are going up, going down, or staying the same."

Unlike other text analytics technology, which requires manual tagging, sorting, and classifying of terms before analysis of unstructured data, Attensity's technology has a

FIGURE 5.13

Modern organizations are extensively aggregating and mining their data to make better decisions.

Source: ©Digital Vision/Getty Images.

natural language engine that automatically pulls out important data without a lot of predefining terms, notes Michelle de Haaff, vice president of marketing at the vendor. This allows companies to have an early warning system to tackle issues that need to be addressed, she added.

VistaPrint Ltd., an online retailer based in Lexington, Massachusetts, which provides graphic design services and custom-printed products, has boosted its customer conversion rate with Web analytics technology that drills down into the most minute details about the 22,000 transactions it processes daily at 18 Web sites.

Like many companies that have invested heavily in online sales, VistaPrint found itself drowning, more than a year ago, in Web log data tracked from its online operations. Analyzing online customer behavior and how a new feature might affect that behavior is important, but the retrieval and analysis of those data were taking hours or even days using an old custom-built application, says Dan Malone, senior manager of business intelligence at VistaPrint.

"It wasn't sustainable, and it wasn't scalable," Malone says. "We realized that improving conversion rates by even a few percentage points can have a big impact on the bottom line." So VistaPrint set out to find a Web analytics package that could test new user interfaces to see whether they could increase conversion rates (the percentage of online visitors who become customers), find out why visitors left the site, and determine the exact point where users were dropping off.

The search first identified two vendor camps. One group offered tools that analyzed all available data, without any upfront aggregation. The other offered tools that aggregated everything upfront but required users to foresee all the queries they wanted to run, Malone says. "If you have a question that falls outside the set of questions you aggregated the data for, you have to reprocess the entire data set."

The company finally turned to a third option, selecting the Visual Site application from Visual Sciences Inc. Visual Site uses a sampling method, which means VistaPrint can still query the detailed data, but "it is also fast because you're getting responses as soon as you ask a question. It queries through 1% of the data you have, and based on that . . . it gives you an answer back. It assumes the rest of the 99% [of the data] looks like that. Because the data has been randomized, that is a valid assumption," notes Malone.

VistaPrint, which has been using the tool for just over a year, runs it alongside the 30–40 new features it tests every three weeks. For example, the company was testing a four-page path for a user to upload data to be printed on a business card. The test showed that the new upload path had the same conversion rate as the control version. "We were a little disappointed because we put in a lot of time to improve this flow," he adds.

When the company added Visual Site to the operation, it found that although the test version was better than the control in three out of four pages, the last page had a big drop-off rate. "We were able to tell the usability team where the problem was," Malone says. VistaPrint also reduced the drop-offs from its sign-in page after the Visual Site tool showed that returning customers were using the new customer-registration process and getting an error notice. The company fixed the problem, and "the sign-in rate improved significantly and led to higher conversions," he says. While Malone concedes that it is hard to measure an exact return on the investment, the company estimates that the tool paid for itself several months after installation.

Source: Adapted from Heather Havenstein, "Use Web Analytics to Turn Online Visitors into Paying Customers," *Computerworld*, September 17, 2007; Mary Hayes Weier, "Applebee's Exec Preaches Data Mining for Business Decisions," *InformationWeek*, October 8, 2007; and Heather Havenstein, "Travelocity.com Dives into Text Analytics to Boost Customer Service," *Computerworld*, November 14, 2007.

CASE STUDY QUESTIONS

1. What are the business benefits of taking the time and effort required to create and operate data warehouses such as those described in the case? Do you see any disadvantages? Is there any reason why all companies shouldn't use data warehousing technology?

2. Applebee's noted some of the unexpected insights obtained from analyzing data about "back-of-house" performance. Using your knowledge of how a restaurant works, what other interesting questions would you suggest to the company? Provide several specific examples.

3. Data mining and warehousing technologies use data about past events to inform better decision making in the future. Do you believe this stifles innovative thinking, causing companies to become too constrained by the data they are already collecting to think about unexplored opportunities? Compare and contrast both viewpoints in your answer.

REAL WORLD ACTIVITIES

1. Go online to the Web site of Attensity (www.attensity.com) and research what other products are offered by the company that complement those discussed in the case. What other examples can you find of companies that have benefited from using these technologies? Prepare a report to summarize your findings.

2. In the opening of the case, Randall Parman of Applebee's International compared data to gold. Although it is easy to figure out the value of gold at any time, valuing data has always been subject to controversy. Search the Internet for alternative methodologies to putting a price tag on the data assets of a company. Contrast different approaches and share your findings with the class.

FIGURE 5.14 Examples of some of the major types of databases used by organizations and end users.

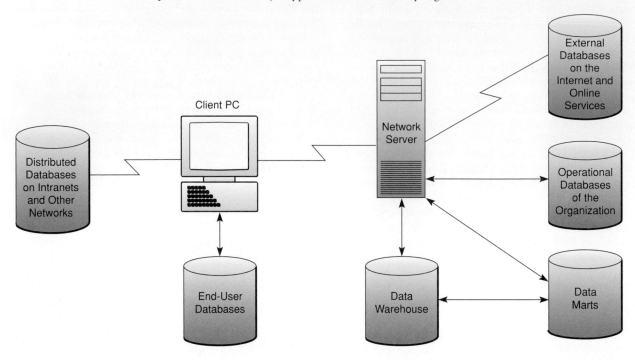

organization's data reside in a single physical location, any catastrophic event like a fire or damage to the media holding the data would result in an equally catastrophic loss of use of that data. By having databases distributed in multiple locations, the negative impact of such an event can be minimized.

Another advantage of distributed databases is found in their storage requirements. Often, a large database system may be distributed into smaller databases based on some logical relationship between the data and the location. For example, a company with several branch operations may distribute its data so that each

FIGURE 5.15

Examples of operational databases that can be created and managed for a small business by microcomputer database management software like Microsoft Access.

Source: Courtesy of Microsoft®.

branch operation location is also the location of its branch database. Because multiple databases in a distributed system can be joined together, each location has control of its local data while all other locations can access any database in the company if so desired.

Distributed databases are not without some challenges, however. The primary challenge is the maintenance of data accuracy. If a company distributes its database to multiple locations, any change to the data in one location must somehow be updated in all other locations. This updating can be accomplished in one of two ways: *replication* or *duplication*.

Updating a distributed database using replication involves using a specialized software application that looks at each distributed database and then finds the changes made to it. Once these changes have been identified, the replication process makes all of the distributed databases look the same by making the appropriate changes to each one. The replication process is very complex and, depending on the number and size of the distributed databases, can consume a lot of time and computer resources.

The duplication process, in contrast, is much less complicated. It basically identifies one database as a master and then duplicates that database at a prescribed time after hours so that each distributed location has the same data. One drawback to the duplication process is that no changes can ever be made to any database other than the master to avoid having local changes overwritten during the duplication process. Nonetheless, properly used, duplication and replication can keep all distributed locations current with the latest data.

One additional challenge associated with distributed databases is the extra computing power and bandwidth necessary to access multiple databases in multiple locations. We will look more closely at the issue of bandwidth in Chapter 6 when we focus on telecommunications and networks.

External Databases

Access to a wealth of information from external databases is available for a fee from commercial online services and with or without charge from many sources on the World Wide Web. Web sites provide an endless variety of hyperlinked pages of multimedia documents in *hypermedia databases* for you to access. Data are available in the form of statistics on economic and demographic activity from *statistical* databanks, or you can view or download abstracts or complete copies of hundreds of newspapers, magazines, newsletters, research papers, and other published material and periodicals from *bibliographic* and *full-text* databases. Whenever you use a search engine like Google or Yahoo to look up something on the Internet, you are using an external database—a very, very large one! Also, if you are using Google, you are using one that averages 112 million searches per day.

Hypermedia Databases

The rapid growth of Web sites on the Internet and corporate intranets and extranets has dramatically increased the use of databases of hypertext and hypermedia documents. A Web site stores such information in a hypermedia database consisting of hyperlinked pages of multimedia (text, graphic and photographic images, video clips, audio segments, and so on). That is, from a database management point of view, the set of interconnected multimedia pages on a Web site is a database of interrelated hypermedia page elements, rather than interrelated data records.

Figure 5.16 shows how you might use a Web browser on your client PC to connect with a Web network server. This server runs Web server software to access and transfer the Web pages you request. The Web site illustrated in Figure 5.16 uses a hypermedia database consisting of Web page content described by HTML (Hypertext Markup Language) code or XML (Extensible Markup Language) labels, image files, video files, and audio. The Web server software acts as a database management system to manage the transfer of hypermedia files for downloading by the multimedia plug-ins of your Web browser.

FIGURE 5.16 The components of a Web-based information system include Web browsers, servers, and hypermedia databases.

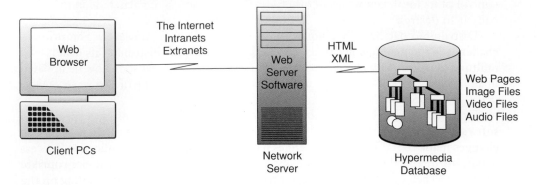

Coty: Using Real-Time Analytics to Track Demand

In the perfume business, it is new products, like the recent launch of Kate, a fragrance Coty branded for supermodel Kate Moss, that can make or break a company's year. But big hits can also lead to big problems. When a product takes off, Coty must respond quickly to keep shelves full. But its ability to ramp up is dependent on glass, packaging, and other suppliers. "If we can't meet demand . . . it annoys the retailers, the consumers lose interest, and we lose sales," says Dave Berry, CIO at Coty, whose other brands include Jennifer Lopez, Kenneth Cole, and Vera Wang.

Empty shelves are the scourge of manufacturing and retail. Just look at the annual shortages of the Christmas season's hottest toys or the rain checks stores must write regularly on sale items. At any given time, 7 percent all U.S. retail products are out of stock; goods on promotion are out of stock more than 15 percent of the time. That's why manufacturers and retailers are pushing for the next breakthroughs in demand forecasting, what has emerged as the discipline of "demand-signal management." Instead of just relying on internal data such as order and shipment records, manufacturers are analyzing weekly and even daily point-of-sale data from retailers so that they can better see what's selling where. This sort of timely, detailed data lets manufacturers spot trends much sooner by region, product, retailer, and even individual store.

Handling demand-signal data presents the same problems real-time data causes in any industry: How to access and integrate high volumes of data, and then combine and analyze it alongside historical information. With the advent of highly scalable data warehouses, low-latency integration techniques, and faster, deeper query and analysis capabilities, the technology is finally here, at a price most can afford. And with easier-to-use business intelligence tools, manufacturers and retailers are pushing analytic tools into the hands of front-line decision makers, most often field sales and marketing people involved in planning, merchandising, and supply chain management.

Over the last two years, Coty has pushed the responsibility for developing accurate forecasts down to its salespeople. Field-level forecasting makes for more accurate and responsive planning, says CIO Berry, who credits an analytics application from vendor CAS with making it easier for salespeople who are new to business intelligence to analyze point-of-sale data and develop forecasts.

An important obstacle to broad adoption of demand-signal analysis has been the lack of standardization in the data supplied by retailers. Coty gets point-of-sale data from the likes of CVS, Target, and Walgreens, but each uses a different format. "The timeliness, accuracy, and depth of the data also varies from retailer to retailer, so it's tough to bring it into a data warehouse," says Berry.

That being said, the payoff from early efforts by Coty has been more accurate forecasting, higher on-shelf availability, and more effective promotions. With faster and more detailed insight into demand, manufacturers can ratchet up revenue by 2 percent to 7 percent, which more than justifies any data-related headaches.

Source: Adapted from Doug Henschen, "In A Down Economy, Companies Turn to Real-Time Analytics to Track Demand," *InformationWeek*, February 28, 2009.

Data Warehouses and Data Mining

A **data warehouse** stores data that have been extracted from the various operational, external, and other databases of an organization. It is a central source of the data that have been cleaned, transformed, and cataloged so that they can be used by managers and other business professionals for data mining, online analytical processing, and other forms of business analysis, market research, and decision support. (We'll talk in-depth about all of these activities in Chapter 9.) Data warehouses may be subdivided into **data marts,** which hold subsets of data from the warehouse that focus on specific aspects of a company, such as a department or a business process.

Figure 5.17 illustrates the components of a complete data warehouse system. Notice how data from various operational and external databases are captured, cleaned, and transformed into data that can be better used for analysis. This acquisition process might include activities like consolidating data from several sources, filtering out unwanted data, correcting incorrect data, converting data to new data elements, or aggregating data into new data subsets.

These data are then stored in the enterprise data warehouse, from which they can be moved into data marts or to an *analytical data store* that holds data in a more useful form for certain types of analysis. *Metadata* (data that define the data in the data warehouse) are stored in a metadata repository and cataloged by a metadata directory. Finally, a variety of analytical software tools can be provided to query, report, mine, and analyze the data for delivery via Internet and intranet Web systems to business end users. See Figure 5.18.

One important characteristic about the data in a data warehouse is that, unlike a typical database in which changes can occur constantly, data in a data warehouse are

FIGURE 5.17   The components of a complete data warehouse system.

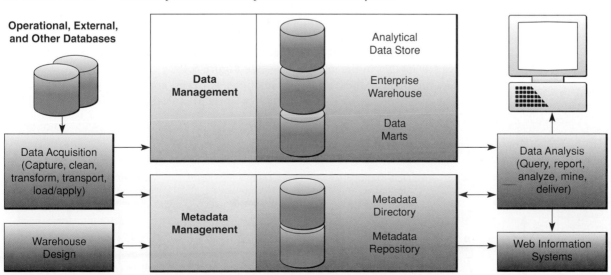

Source: Courtesy of Hewlett-Packard.

FIGURE 5.18

A data warehouse and its data mart subsets hold data that have been extracted from various operational databases for business analysis, market research, decision support, and data mining applications.

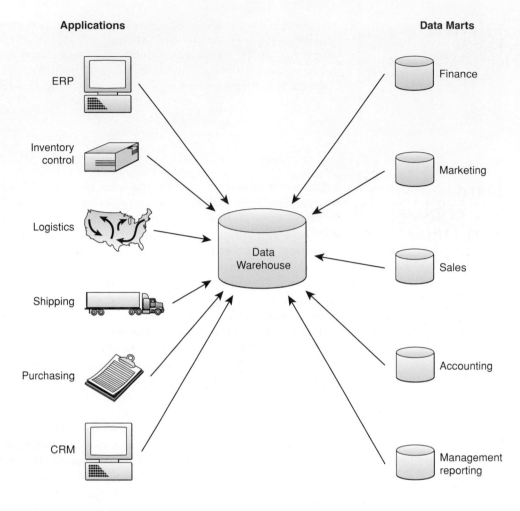

static, which means that once the data are gathered up, formatted for storage, and stored in the data warehouse, they will never change. This restriction is so that queries can be made on the data to look for complex patterns or historical trends that might otherwise go unnoticed with dynamic data that change constantly as a result of new transactions and updates.

Data Mining

Data mining is a major use of data warehouse databases and the static data they contain. In data mining, the data in a data warehouse are analyzed to reveal hidden patterns and trends in historical business activity. This analysis can be used to help managers make decisions about strategic changes in business operations to gain competitive advantages in the marketplace. See Figure 5.19.

Data mining can discover new correlations, patterns, and trends in vast amounts of business data (frequently several terabytes of data) stored in data warehouses. Data

FIGURE 5.19   How data mining extracts business knowledge from a data warehouse.

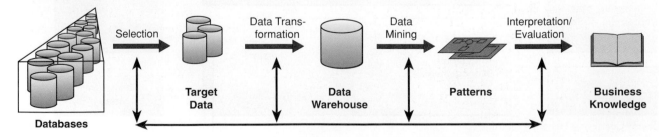

mining software uses advanced pattern recognition algorithms, as well as a variety of mathematical and statistical techniques, to sift through mountains of data to extract previously unknown strategic business information. For example, many companies use data mining to:

- Perform market-basket analysis to identify new product bundles.
- Find root causes of quality or manufacturing problems.
- Prevent customer attrition and acquire new customers.
- Cross-sell to existing customers.
- Profile customers with more accuracy.

We will discuss data mining further, as well as online analytical processing (OLAP) and other technologies that analyze the data in databases and data warehouses to provide vital support for business decisions, in Chapter 9.

R.L. Polk & Co.: Cars Are a Gold Mine of Information

Like a muscle car driving 55 mph on the freeway, R.L. Polk & Co.'s new grid-based data warehouse boasts gobs of untapped power under the hood. In 2006, the Southfield, Michigan–based automotive industry market research company finished moving its main 4TB customer-facing data warehouse to an Oracle 10g grid comprising Dell PowerEdge servers running Linux. The move has helped R.L. Polk save money and improve data redundancy, availability, and access time. It also supports Polk's new service-oriented architecture, which is improving customer service.

"We are getting more bang for our buck," notes Kevin Vasconi, the company's CIO. The data warehouse is doing 10 million transactions a day "without any issues." Encouraged by the experience so far, R.L. Polk is bringing onto the grid other databases, both domestic and overseas, that total 2.5 petabytes of actively managed data.

Founded in 1870—the same year the automobile's predecessor, a motorized handcart, was invented in Germany—R.L. Polk started as a publisher of business directories. It became a car information supplier in 1921 and began to use computer punch cards in 1951. The company is best known to consumers for its Carfax database of car histories.

Only a tiny portion of the grid is apportioned now to the data warehouse. Much of it is devoted to running R.L. Polk's new Web-based applications, which both import data into the data warehouse from 260 discrete sources, such as car dealers or state licensing boards, and stream it out to paying customers, such as carmakers, car dealers, and parts suppliers. The data warehouse serves as R.L. Polk's "single source of truth" on a massive database that includes 500 million individual cars, or almost 85 percent of all cars in the world as of 2002. It also includes data on 250 million households and 3 billion transactions.

R.L. Polk cleanses the names and addresses of all incoming records, adds location data such as latitude and longitude, and, in the case of the 17-digit vehicle identification numbers unique to every car, extrapolates each car's individual features and styling. Looking forward, Vasconi says data already stored on vehicles' on-board computers—such as engine-trouble history, GPS-based location history, and average speeds—will soon also be imported into the data warehouse if privacy issues can be resolved. It's a complicated process, but as his team continues to tweak the Oracle grid engine, he expects to be able to shorten the importation time to less than 24 hours.

"The car is a gold mine of consumer information," notes Vasconi.

Source: Adapted from Eric Lai, "Auto Market Researcher Revs Up Oracle Grid for Massive Data Warehouse," *Computerworld*, October 19, 2006.

Traditional File Processing

How would you feel if you were an executive of a company and were told that some information you wanted about your employees was too difficult and too costly to obtain? Suppose the vice president of information services gave you the following reasons:

- The information you want is in several different files, each organized in a different way.
- Each file has been organized to be used by a different application program, none of which produces the information you want in the form you need.
- No application program is available to help get the information you want from these files.

That's how end users can be frustrated when an organization relies on **file processing** systems in which data are organized, stored, and processed in independent files of data records. In the traditional file processing approach that was used in business data processing for many years, each business application was designed to use one or more specialized data files containing only specific types of data records. For example, a bank's checking account processing application was designed to access and update a data file containing specialized data records for the bank's checking account customers. Similarly, the bank's installment loan processing application needed to access and update a specialized data file containing data records about the bank's installment loan customers. See Figure 5.20.

FIGURE 5.20

Examples of file processing systems in banking. Note the use of separate computer programs and independent data files in a file processing approach to the savings, installment loan, and checking account applications.

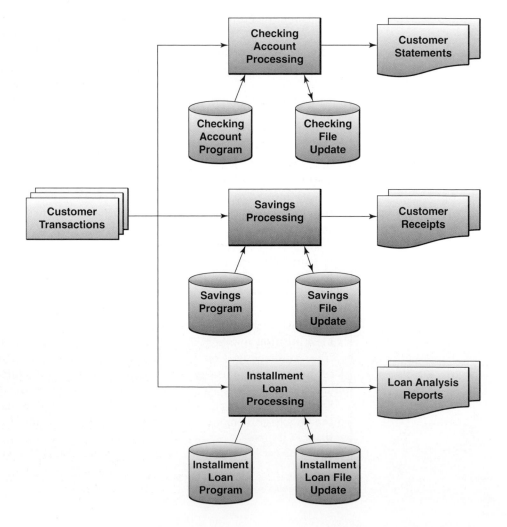

Problems of File Processing

The file processing approach finally became too cumbersome, costly, and inflexible to supply the information needed to manage modern business and, as we shall soon see, was replaced by the *database management approach*. Despite their apparent logic and simplicity, file processing systems had the following major problems:

Data Redundancy. Independent data files included a lot of duplicated data; the same data (such as a customer's name and address) were recorded and stored in several files. This data redundancy caused problems when data had to be updated. Separate *file maintenance* programs had to be developed and coordinated to ensure that each file was properly updated. Of course, this coordination proved difficult in practice, so a lot of inconsistency occurred among data stored in separate files.

Lack of Data Integration. Having data in independent files made it difficult to provide end users with information for ad hoc requests that required accessing data stored in several different files. Special computer programs had to be written to retrieve data from each independent file. This retrieval was so difficult, time-consuming, and costly for some organizations that it was impossible to provide end users or management with such information. End users had to extract the required information manually from the various reports produced by each separate application and then prepare customized reports for management.

Data Dependence. In file processing systems, major components of a system—the organization of files, their physical locations on storage hardware, and the application software used to access those files—depended on one another in significant ways. For example, application programs typically contained references to the specific *format* of the data stored in the files they used. Thus, changes in the format and structure of data and records in a file required that changes be made to all of the programs that used that file. This *program maintenance* effort was a major burden of file processing systems. It proved difficult to do properly, and it resulted in a lot of inconsistency in the data files.

Lack of Data Integrity or Standardization. In file processing systems, it was easy for data elements such as stock numbers and customer addresses to be defined differently by different end users and applications. This divergence caused serious inconsistency problems in the development of programs to access such data. In addition, the *integrity* (i.e., the accuracy and completeness) of the data was suspect because there was no control over their use and maintenance by authorized end users. Thus, a lack of standards caused major problems in application program development and maintenance, as well as in the security and integrity of the data files needed by the organization.

Online Dating: The Technology Behind Finding Love

When Joe wanted to find love, he turned to science.

Rather than hang out in bars or hope that random dates worked out, the 34-year-old aerospace engineer signed up for eHarmony.com, an online dating service that uses detailed profiles, proprietary matching algorithms, and a tightly controlled communications process to help people find their perfect soul mate. Over a three-month period, Joe found 500 people who appeared to fit his criteria. He initiated contact with 100 of them, corresponded with 50, and dated 3 before finding the right match.

The "scientific" matching services, such as eHarmony, PerfectMatch, and Chemistry.com, attempt to identify the most compatible matches for the user by asking anywhere from a few dozen to several hundred questions. The services then assemble a personality profile and use that against an algorithm that ranks users within a set of predefined categories; from there, the system produces a list of appropriate matches.

The technology that powers these dating sites ranges from incredibly simple to incredibly complicated. Unsurprisingly, eHarmony has one of the most sophisticated data centers. "The company stores 4 terabytes of data on some 20 million registered users, each of whom has filled out a 400-question psychological profile," says Joseph Essas, vice president of technology at eHarmony. The company uses proprietary algorithms to score that data against 29 "dimensions of compatibility"—such as values, personality styles, attitudes, and interests—and match up customers with the best possible prospects for a long-term relationship.

A giant Oracle 10g database spits out a few preliminary candidates immediately after a user signs up, to prime the pump, but the real matching work happens later, after eHarmony's system scores and matches up answers to hundreds of questions from thousands of users. The process requires just under 1 billion calculations that are processed in a giant batch operation each day. These operations execute in parallel on hundreds of computers and are orchestrated using software written to the open-source Hadoop software platform.

Once matches are sent to users, the users' actions and outcomes are fed back into the model for the next day's calculations. For example, if a customer clicked on many matches that were at the outset of his or her geographical range—say, 25 miles away—the system would assume distance wasn't a deal-breaker and next offer more matches that were just a bit farther away.

"Our biggest challenge is the amount of data that we have to constantly score, move, apply, and serve to people, and that is fluid," Essas says. To that end, the architecture is designed to scale quickly to meet growth and demand peaks around major holidays. The highest demand comes just before Valentine's Day. "Our demand doubles, if not quadruples."

Source: Adapted from Robert L. Mitchell, "Online Dating: The Technology Behind the Attraction," *Computerworld*, February 13, 2009.

The Database Management Approach

To solve the problems encountered with the file processing approach, the database management approach was conceived as the foundation of modern methods for managing organizational data. The database management approach consolidates data records, formerly held in separate files, into databases that can be accessed by many different application programs. In addition, a *database management system* (DBMS) serves as a software interface between users and databases, which helps users easily access the data in a database. Thus, database management involves the use of database management software to control how databases are created, interrogated, and maintained to provide information that end users need.

For example, customer records and other common types of data are needed for several different applications in banking, such as check processing, automated teller systems, bank credit cards, savings accounts, and installment loan accounting. These data can be consolidated into a common *customer database*, rather than being kept in separate files for each of those applications. See Figure 5.21.

Database Management System

A database management system (DBMS) is the main software tool of the database management approach because it controls the creation, maintenance, and use of the databases of an organization and its end users. As we saw in Figure 5.16, microcomputer database management packages such as Microsoft Access, Lotus Approach, or Corel Paradox allow you to set up and manage databases on your PC, network server, or the World Wide Web. In mainframe and server computer systems, the database management system is an important system software package that controls the

FIGURE 5.21

An example of a database management approach in a banking information system. Note how the savings, checking, and installment loan programs use a database management system to share a customer database. Note also that the DBMS allows a user to make direct, ad hoc interrogations of the database without using application programs.

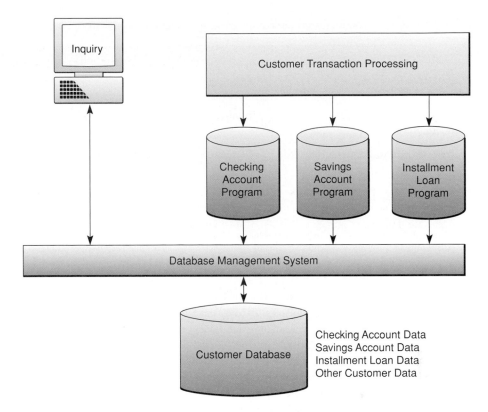

development, use, and maintenance of the databases of computer-using organizations. Examples of popular mainframe and server versions of DBMS software are IBM's DB2 Universal Database, Oracle 10g by Oracle Corp., and MySQL, a popular open-source DBMS. See Figure 5.22. Common DBMS components and functions are summarized in Figure 5.23.

FIGURE 5.22

Database management software like MySQL, a popular open-source DBMS, supports the development, maintenance, and use of the databases of an organization.

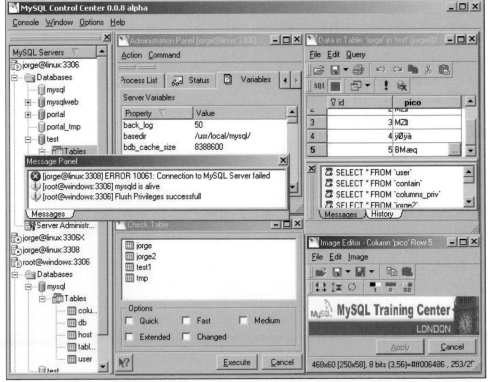

Source: Courtesy of MySQL.com.

FIGURE 5.23   Common software components and functions of a database management system.

Common DBMS Software Components	
● **Database Definition**	Language and graphical tools to define entities, relationships, integrity constraints, and authorization rights.
● **Nonprocedural Access**	Language and graphical tools to access data without complicated coding.
● **Application Development**	Graphical tools to develop menus, data entry forms, and reports.
● **Procedural Language Interface**	Language that combines nonprocedural access with full capabilities of a programming language.
● **Transaction Processing**	Control mechanisms to prevent interference from simultaneous users and recover lost data after a failure.
● **Database Tuning**	Tools to monitor and improve database performance.

Source: Adapted from Michael V. Mannino, *Database Application Development and Design* (Burr Ridge, IL: McGraw-Hill/Irwin, 2001), p. 7.

The three major functions of a database management system are (1) to *create* new databases and database applications, (2) to *maintain* the quality of the data in an organization's databases, and (3) to *use* the databases of an organization to provide the information that its end users need. See Figure 5.24.

Database development involves defining and organizing the content, relationships, and structure of the data needed to build a database. **Database application development** involves using a DBMS to develop prototypes of queries, forms, reports, and Web pages for a proposed business application. **Database maintenance** involves using transaction processing systems and other tools to add, delete, update, and correct the data in a database. The primary use of a database by end users involves employing the *database interrogation* capabilities of a DBMS to access the data in a database to selectively retrieve and display information and produce reports, forms, and other documents.

Database Interrogation

A database interrogation capability is a major benefit of the database management approach. End users can use a DBMS by asking for information from a database using a *query* feature or a *report generator*. They can receive an immediate response in the form of video displays or printed reports. No difficult programming is required. The **query language** feature lets you easily obtain immediate responses to ad hoc data requests: You merely key in a few short inquiries—in some cases, using common sentence structures just like you would use to ask a question. The **report generator** feature allows you to specify a report format for information you want presented as a report. Figure 5.25 illustrates the use of a DBMS report generator.

SQL Queries. SQL (pronounced "see quill"), or Structured Query Language, is an international standard query language found in many DBMS packages. In most cases,

FIGURE 5.24
The three major uses of DBMS software are to create, maintain, and use the databases of an organization.

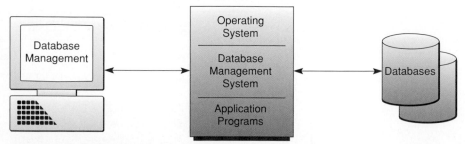

- Create: Database and Application Development
- Maintain: Database Maintenance
- Use: Database Interrogation

FIGURE 5.25

Using the report generator of Microsoft Access to create an employee report.

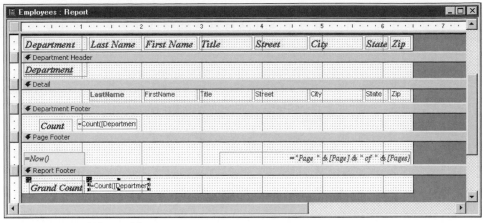

Source: Courtesy of Microsoft®.

SQL is the language structure used to "ask a question" that the DBMS will retrieve the data to answer. The basic form of a SQL query is:

SELECT . . . FROM . . . WHERE . . .

After SELECT, you list the data fields you want retrieved. After FROM, you list the files or tables from which the data must be retrieved. After WHERE, you specify conditions that limit the search to only those data records in which you are interested. Figure 5.26 compares a SQL query to a natural language query for information on customer orders.

Boolean Logic. To fully access the power of SQL, a database user needs to have a basic understanding of the concepts behind **Boolean logic.** Developed by George Boole in the mid-1800s, Boolean logic allows us to refine our searches for specific information such that only the desired information is obtained.

Boolean logic consists of three logical operators: (1) AND, (2) OR, and (3) NOT. Using these operators in conjunction with the syntax of a SQL query, a database user can refine a search to ensure that only the desired data are retrieved. This same set of logical operators can be used to refine searches for information from the Internet (which is really nothing more than the world's largest database). Let's look at an example of how the three logical operators work.

Suppose we are interested in obtaining information about cats from the Internet. We could just search on the word *cats*, and a large number of potentially useful Web sites would be retrieved. The problem is that in addition to the Web sites about cats, we would also retrieve Web sites about cats and dogs, pets in general (if the site includes the word *cats*), and probably even sites about the Broadway musical titled *Cats*.

FIGURE 5.26

Comparing a natural language query with a SQL query.

A Sample Natural Language-to-SQL Translation for Microsoft Access
Natural Language
What Customers had no orders last month?
SQL
SELECT [Customers].[Company Name],[Customers].[Contact Name]
FROM [Customers]
WHERE not Exists {SELECT [Ship Name] FROM [Orders]
WHERE Month {[Order Date]}=1 and Year {[Order Date]}=2004 and [Customers].[Customer ID]=[Orders].[Customer ID]}

To avoid having to sift through all the sites to find what we want, we could use Boolean logic to form a more refined query:

Cats OR felines AND NOT dogs OR Broadway

By using this search query, we would retrieve any Web site with the word *cats* or *felines* but exclude any site that also has the words *dogs* or *Broadway*. Using this approach, we would eliminate any reference to cats and dogs or to the Broadway musical titled *Cats*. This query therefore would result in a more refined search and eliminate the need to look at Web sites that do not pertain to our specific interest.

Graphical and Natural Queries. Many end users (and IS professionals) have difficulty correctly phrasing SQL and other database language search queries. So most end-user database management packages offer GUI (graphical user interface) point-and-click methods, which are easier to use and are translated by the software into SQL commands. See Figure 5.27. Other packages are available that use *natural language* query statements similar to conversational English (or other languages), as illustrated in Figure 5.26.

Database Maintenance

The **database maintenance** process is accomplished by *transaction processing systems* and other end-user applications, with the support of the DBMS. End users and information specialists can also employ various utilities provided by a DBMS for database maintenance. The databases of an organization need to be updated continually to reflect new business transactions (e.g., sales made, products produced, inventory shipped) and other events. Other miscellaneous changes also must be made to update and correct data (e.g., customer or employee name and address changes) to ensure the accuracy of the data in the databases. We introduced transaction processing systems in Chapter 1 and will discuss them in more detail in Chapter 7.

Application Development

In addition, DBMS packages play a major role in **application development.** End users, systems analysts, and other application developers can use the internal 4GL programming language and built-in software development tools provided by many DBMS packages to develop custom application programs. For example, you can use a DBMS to develop the data entry screens, forms, reports, or Web pages of a business application that accesses a company database to find and update the data it needs. A DBMS also makes the job of application software developers easier, because they do not have to develop detailed data-handling procedures using conventional programming languages every time they write a program. Instead, they can include features such as *data manipulation language* (DML) statements in their software that call on the DBMS to perform necessary data-handling activities.

FIGURE 5.27

Using the Query Wizard of the Microsoft Access database management package to develop a query about employee health plan choices.

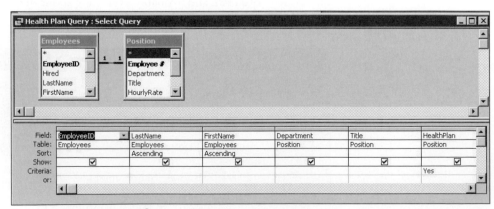

Source: Courtesy of Microsoft®.

Summary

- **Data Resource Management.** Data resource management is a managerial activity that applies information technology and software tools to the task of managing an organization's data resources. Early attempts to manage data resources used a file processing approach in which data were organized and accessible only in specialized files of data records that were designed for processing by specific business application programs. This approach proved too cumbersome, costly, and inflexible to supply the information needed to manage modern business processes and organizations. Thus, the database management approach was developed to solve the problems of file processing systems.

- **Database Management.** The database management approach affects the storage and processing of data. The data needed by different applications are consolidated and integrated into several common databases instead of being stored in many independent data files. Also, the database management approach emphasizes updating and maintaining common databases, having users' application programs share the data in the database, and providing a reporting and an inquiry/response capability so that end users can easily receive reports and quick responses to requests for information.

- **Database Software.** Database management systems are software packages that simplify the creation, use, and maintenance of databases. They provide software tools so that end users, programmers, and database administrators can create and modify databases; interrogate a database; generate reports; do application development; and perform database maintenance.

- **Types of Databases.** Several types of databases are used by business organizations, including operational, distributed, and external databases. Data warehouses are a central source of data from other databases that have been cleaned, transformed, and cataloged for business analysis and decision support applications. That includes data mining, which attempts to find hidden patterns and trends in the warehouse data. Hypermedia databases on the World Wide Web and on corporate intranets and extranets store hyperlinked multimedia pages on a Web site. Web server software can manage such databases for quick access and maintenance of the Web database.

- **Data Access.** Data must be organized in some logical manner on physical storage devices so that they can be efficiently processed. For this reason, data are commonly organized into logical data elements such as characters, fields, records, files, and databases. Database structures, such as the hierarchical, network, relational, and object-oriented models, are used to organize the relationships among the data records stored in databases. Databases and files can be organized in either a sequential or direct manner and can be accessed and maintained by either sequential access or direct access processing methods.

- **Database Development.** The development of databases can be easily accomplished using microcomputer database management packages for small end-user applications. However, the development of large corporate databases requires a top-down data planning effort that may involve developing enterprise and entity relationship models, subject area databases, and data models that reflect the logical data elements and relationships needed to support the operation and management of the basic business processes of the organization.

Key Terms and Concepts

These are the key terms and concepts of this chapter. The page number of their first explanation is in parentheses.

1. Data dependence (195)
2. Data dictionary (180)
3. Data integration (195)
4. Data integrity (195)
5. Data mining (192)
6. Data modeling (182)
7. Data redundancy (195)
8. Data resource management (185)
9. Database administrator (DBA) (180)
10. Database interrogation (198)
11. Database management approach (196)
12. Database management system (DBMS) (196)
13. Database structures (175)
    a. Hierarchical structure (176)
    b. Multidimensional model (177)
    c. Network structure (176)
    d. Object-oriented model (177)
    e. Relational model (176)
14. Duplication (189)
15. File processing (194)
16. Logical data elements (170)
    a. Attribute (170)
    b. Character (170)
    c. Database (173)
    d. Entity (170)
    e. Field (170)
    f. File (173)
    g. Record (170)
17. Metadata (180)
18. Replication (189)
19. Structured Query Language (SQL) (198)
20. Types of databases (185)
    a. Data warehouse (191)
    b. Distributed (185)
    c. External (189)
    d. Hypermedia (189)
    e. Operational (185)

Review Quiz

Match one of the key terms and concepts listed previously with one of the brief examples or definitions that follow. Try to find the best fit for answers that seem to fit more than one term or concept. Defend your choices.

_____ 1. The use of integrated collections of data records and files for data storage and processing.

_____ 2. Data in independent files made it difficult to provide answers to ad hoc requests and required special computer programs to be written to perform this task.

_____ 3. A specialist in charge of the databases of an organization.

_____ 4. A nonprocedural computer language used to interrogate a database.

_____ 5. Defines and catalogs the data elements and data relationships in an organization's database.

_____ 6. A feature of database systems that uses queries or report generators to extract information.

_____ 7. The main software package that supports a database management approach.

_____ 8. Databases that are dispersed over the Internet and corporate intranets and extranets.

_____ 9. Databases that organize and store data as objects.

_____ 10. Databases of hyperlinked multimedia documents on the Web.

_____ 11. The management of all the data resources of an organization.

_____ 12. Processing data in a data warehouse to discover key business factors and trends.

_____ 13. Developing conceptual views of the relationships among data in a database.

_____ 14. A customer's name.

_____ 15. A customer's name, address, and account balance.

_____ 16. The names, addresses, and account balances of all of your customers.

_____ 17. An integrated collection of all of the data about your customers.

_____ 18. Business application programs that use specialized data files.

_____ 19. A treelike structure of records in a database.

_____ 20. A tabular structure of records in a database.

_____ 21. Records organized as cubes within cubes in a database.

_____ 22. Databases that support the major business processes of an organization.

_____ 23. A centralized and integrated database of current and historical data about an organization.

_____ 24. Databases available on the Internet or provided by commercial information services.

_____ 25. A problem in the file processing approach where major components of a system are dependent on each other to a large degree.

_____ 26. Different approaches to the logical organization of individual data elements stored in a database.

_____ 27. The most basic logical data element corresponding to a single letter or number.

_____ 28. A feature of distributed databases that identifies changes in one database and then makes appropriate changes in the others.

_____ 29. A characteristic of data that refers to their accuracy and completeness.

_____ 30. Data that describe the structure and characteristics of databases.

_____ 31. A characteristic or quality of some entity used to describe that entity.

_____ 32. Includes, among others, operational, distributed, and hypermedia databases.

_____ 33. The existence of duplicate data among different files in an organization.

_____ 34. An approach to distributed databases that copies the complete content of a master database to others at a prescribed time of the day.

_____ 35. An object, person, place, event, and so on that is of interest to an organization and thus included in a database.

_____ 36. An approach to database structure that improves on the hierarchical model by allowing many-to-many relationships.

_____ 37. Different levels of data groupings that exist in a database.

Discussion Questions

1. How should a business store, access, and distribute data and information about its internal operations and external environment?

2. What role does database management play in managing data as a business resource?

3. What are the advantages of a database management approach to the file processing approach? Give examples to illustrate your answer.

4. Refer to the Real World Case on Cogent Communications, Intel, and Others about IT-related issues in M&A

situations. Although keeping extra infrastructure and network capacity allows for an easier transition, it is also costly to do so. How can companies balance these two sides of the issue? To what extent can organizations plan their M&A activity in order to justify keeping this extra capacity?

5. What is the role of a database management system in a business information system?

6. In the past, databases of information about a firm's internal operations were the only databases that were considered important to a business. What other kinds of databases are important for a business today?

7. Refer to the Real World Case on Applebee's, Traveloc-ity, and Others in the chapter. What would be the appropriate set of skills that a user of these technologies would possess, as opposed to those that operate on the IT side of the issue? How should these technologies be designed so that users can focus on getting answers to their pressing questions?

8. What are the benefits and limitations of the relational database model for business applications today?

9. Why is the object-oriented database model gaining acceptance for developing applications and managing the hypermedia databases on business Web sites?

10. How have the Internet, intranets, and extranets affected the types and uses of data resources available to business professionals? What other database trends are also affecting data resource management in business?

Analysis Exercises

Complete the following exercises as individual or group projects that apply chapter concepts to real-world businesses.

1. Joining Tables

You have the responsibility for managing technical training classes within your organization. These classes fall into two general types: highly technical training and end-user training. Software engineers sign up for the former, and administrative staff sign up for the latter. Your supervisor measures your effectiveness in part according to the average cost per training hour and type of training. In short, your supervisor expects the best training for the least cost.

   To meet this need, you have negotiated an exclusive on-site training contract with Hands-On Technology Transfer (HOTT) Inc. (www.traininghott.com), a high-quality technical training provider. Your negotiated rates are reproduced below in the pricing table. A separate table contains a sample list of courses you routinely make available for your organization.

   a. Using these data, design and populate a table that includes basic training rate information. Designate the "Technical" field type as "Yes/No" (Boolean).

   b. Using these data, design and populate a course table. Designate the CourseID field as a "Primary Key" and allow your database to automatically generate a value for this field. Designate the "Technical" field type as "Yes/No" (Boolean).

   c. Prepare a query that lists each course name and its cost per day of training.

   d. Prepare a query that lists the cost per student for each class. Assume maximum capacity and that you will schedule two half-day classes on the same day to take full advantage of HOTT's per-day pricing schedule.

Pricing Table

Technical	Price per Day	Capacity
Yes	$2,680	15
No	$2,144	30

Course Table

Course ID	Course Name	Duration	Technical
1	ASP Programming	5	Yes
2	XML Programming	5	Yes
3	PHP Programming	4	Yes
4	Microsoft Word–Advanced	.5	No
5	Microsoft Excel–Advanced	.5	No
...			

2. Training-Cost Management

Having determined the cost per student for each of the classes in the previous problem, you now must carefully manage class registration. Because you pay the same flat rates no matter how many students attend (up to capacity), you want to do all you can to ensure maximum attendance. Your training provider, Hands-On Technology Transfer Inc., requires two weeks' notice in the event that you need to reschedule a class. You should make sure your classes are at least two-thirds full before this deadline. You should also make sure you send timely reminders to all attendees so that they do not forget to show up. Use the database you created in Problem 1 to perform the following activities:

   a. Using the information provided in the sample below, add a course schedule table to your training database. Designate the ScheduleID field as a "Primary Key" and allow your database program to generate a value for this field automatically. Make the CourseID field a number field and the StartDate field a date field.

   b. Using the information provided in the sample below, add a class roster table to your training database. Make the ScheduleID field a number field. Make the Reminder and Confirmed fields both "Yes/No" (Boolean) fields.

c. Because the Class Schedule table relates to the Course Table and the Course Table relates to the Pricing Table, why is it appropriate to record the Price per Day information in the Class Schedule table too?

d. What are the advantages and disadvantages of using the participant's name and e-mail address in the Class Roster table? What other database design might you use to record this information?

e. Write a query that shows how many people have registered for each scheduled class. Include the class name, capacity, date, and count of attendees.

Class Schedule

Schedule ID	Course ID	Location	Start Date	Price per Day
1	1	101-A	7/12/2008	$2,680
2	1	101-A	7/19/2008	$2,680
3	1	101-B	7/19/2008	$2,680
4	4	101-A&B	7/26/2008	$2,144
5	5	101-A...B	8/2/2008	$2,144
...				

Class Roster

Schedule ID	Participant	e-mail	Reminder	Confirmed
1	Linda Adams	adams.l@...	Yes	Yes
1	Fatima Ahmad	ahmad.f@...	Yes	No
1	Adam Alba	alba.a@...	Yes	Yes
4	Denys Alyea	alyea.d@...	No	No
4	Kathy Bara	bara.k@...	Yes	No
...				

3. Selling the Sawdust

Selling Information By-Products

Sawmill operators are in the business of turning trees into lumber. Products include boards, plywood, and veneer. For as long as there have been sawmills, there have been sawmill operators who have tried to solve the problem of what to do with their principal by-product: sawdust. Numerous creative examples abound.

Likewise, businesses often generate tremendous amounts of data. The challenge then becomes what to do with this by-product. Can a little additional effort turn it into a valuable product? Research the following:

a. What are your college's or university's policies regarding student directory data?

b. Does your college or university sell any of its student data? If your institution sells student data, what data do they sell, to whom, and for how much?

c. If your institution sells data, calculate the revenue earned per student. Would you be willing to pay this amount per year in exchange for maintaining your privacy?

4. Data Formats and Manipulation

Importing Formatted Data into Excel

Ms. Sapper, a marketing manager in a global accounting firm, was this year's coordinator for her firm's annual partner meeting. With 400 partners from around the world, Sapper faced daunting communications tasks that she wanted to automate as much as possible. Sapper received a file containing all partners' names, as well as additional personal information, from her IT department. The file ended with the extension "CSV." She wondered to herself what to do next.

The CSV, or *comma separated values* format, is a very basic data format that most database applications use to import or export data. As a minimum, the CSV format groups all fields in a record into a single line of text. It then separates each field within a line with a comma or other delimiter. When the text information contains commas, the format requires this text information to be placed within quotes. Sapper needed to get these data into Excel. Given how busy the IT guys appeared, she decided to do this herself.

a. Download and save "partners.csv" from the MIS 9e OLC. Open the file using Microsoft Word. Remember to look for the "csv" file type when searching for the file to open. Describe the data's appearance.

b. Import the "partner.csv" file into Excel. Remember to look for the "csv" file type when searching for the file to open. Does Excel automatically format the data correctly? Save your file as "partner.xls."

c. Describe in your own words why you think database manufacturers use common formats to import and export data from their systems.

REAL WORLD CASE 3

Amazon, eBay, and Google: Unlocking and Sharing Business Databases

The meeting had dragged on for more than an hour that rainy day in Seattle, and Jeff Bezos had heard enough. The CEO had rounded up 15 or so senior engineers and managers in one of Amazon's offices to tackle a question buzzing inside the company: Should Amazon bust open the doors of its most prized data warehouse, containing its myriad databases, and let an eager world of entrepreneurs scavenge through its data jewels?

For several years, scores of outsiders had been knocking on Amazon's door to gain access to the underlying data that power the $7 billion retailer: product descriptions, prices, sales rankings, customer reviews, inventory figures, and countless other layers of content. In all, it was a data vault that Amazon had spent more than 10 years and a billion dollars to build, organize, and safeguard.

So why on earth would Bezos suddenly hand over the keys? In the hands of top Web innovators, some at the meeting argued, Amazon's data could be the dynamo of new Web sites and businesses that would expand the company's already gigantic online footprint and ultimately drive more sales. Others worried about the risks. A free-for-all, one manager warned, would "change our business in ways we don't understand."

Bezos ended the debate with characteristic gusto. He leaped from his seat, aping a flasher opening a trench coat. "We're going to aggressively expose ourselves!" he declared.

Today, there's considerable reason to cheer Bezos's exhibitionist move. Since the company opened up its data vaults in 2002, under the auspices of a project first called Amazon Web Services, more than 65,000 developers, businesses, and other entrepreneurs have tapped into the data. With it, they're building moneymaking Web sites, new online shopping interfaces, and innovative services for thousands of Amazon's independent sellers. Many have become Bezos's most ambitious business partners overnight. "Two years ago this was an experiment," says Amazon's engineering chief, Al Vermeulen. "Now it's a core part of our strategy."

And that's just at Amazon. A year after Bezos's decision to open Amazon's databases to developers and business partners, eBay's chief executive Meg Whitman answered a similar cry from eBay's developer community, opening the $3 billion company's database of 33 million weekly auction items to the technorati. Some 15,000 developers and others have since registered to use that prized database and access other software features. Already, 41 percent of eBay's listings are uploaded to the site using software that takes advantage of these newly accessible resources.

At Google too, the concept is finding its legs: The company parcels out some of its search-results data and recently unlocked access to its desktop and paid-search products. Now dozens of Google-driven services are cropping up, from custom Web browsers to graphical search engines. Compared with Amazon and eBay, however, Google is taking baby steps. Developers can grab 1,000 search results a day for free, but anything more than that requires special permission. In January 2005, Google finally opened up its Ad-Words paid-search service to outside applications, allowing marketers to automate their Google ad campaigns.

What's behind the open-door policies? True to their pioneering roots, Bezos, Whitman, and the Google boys are pushing their companies into what they believe is the Web's great new beyond: an era in which online businesses operate as open-ended software platforms that can accommodate thousands of other businesses selling symbiotic products and services. Says longtime tech-book publisher Tim O'Reilly, "We can finally rip, mix, and burn each other's Web sites."

Most people think of Amazon as the world's largest retailer, or "earth's biggest bookstore," as Bezos called it in its start-up days. Inside the company, those perceptions are decidedly old school. "We are at heart a technology company," Vermeulen says. He and Bezos have begun to view Amazon as just a big piece of software available over the Web. "Amazon.com is just another application on the platform," Vermeulen asserts.

Eric von Hippel, a business professor at MIT's Sloan School of Management, explains the old rules: "We come from a culture where if you invested in it, you kept it. That was your competitive advantage." The rise of open-source software certainly challenged that notion. The rise of open databases and Web services goes even further, holding out the promise of automating the links between online businesses by applications that depend on companies sharing their vital data.

As Vermeulen says, "Those that succeed have to think about removing walls instead of putting them up." For Amazon, there's some evidence to support that logic. Of the 65,000 people and companies that have signed up to use Amazon's free goodies, about one-third have been tinkering with software tools that help Amazon's 800,000 or so active sellers.

One of the most clever is ScoutPal, a service that turns cell phones into mobile bar-code scanners. "It's like a Geiger counter for books," founder Dave Anderson says. He came up with the idea a couple of years ago when his wife, Barbara, who sells books on Amazon, would lug home 50 pounds of titles from garage sales, only to discover that she'd paid too much for many of them to make any money. Anderson wrote an application that works in tandem with an attachable bar-code scanner. Barbara either scans in books' bar codes or punches in their 10-digit ID numbers. Then she can pull down the latest Amazon prices for the books and calculate her likely profit margin before she pays for the inventory. Anderson says his wife's sales have since tripled to about $100,000 a year, and her profit margins have jumped from 50 percent to 85 percent. He's now bringing in six figures too: ScoutPal has more than 1,000 subscribers, each paying $10 a month.

Other tools are also gaining traction. Software programs like SellerEngine help merchants on the main site upload their inventory, check prices, and automate interactions such as adding new listings. Meanwhile, software from Associates Shop.com lets thousands of other Web site operators—there are more than 900,000 of these so-called Amazon associates—create customized storefronts that link back to Amazon, generating new sales for Bezos and commission revenue for the associates.

For the near term, maybe the biggest benefit to Amazon of letting folks like Anderson tinker with its platform is that it gets experimental research and development (R&D) for free. "We can try to build all the applications for sellers ourselves," Vermeulen says, "or we can build a platform and let others build them." Adds Bezos, "Right now we just want to get people to use the guts of Amazon in ways that surprise us."

The experimentation at eBay has been just as ambitious. The company says that more than 1,000 new applications have emerged from its 15,000 or so registered developers. As with Amazon, the most popular are applications that help sellers automate the process of listing items on eBay or displaying them on other sites. Many of these outfits, such as Channel Advisor (itself a multimillion-dollar business), Marketworks, and Vendio, offer auction-listing software or services to eBay sellers. Jeff McManus, eBay's chief of platform evangelism, marvels at the benefits. "Sellers who use our APIs [application programming interfaces] become at least 50 percent more productive than those who use the Web site itself."

The data links also let companies create storefronts filled with their inventory while making transactions over eBay's network. One example is Las Vegas–based SuperPawn, which runs a chain of 46 pawnshops in Arizona, California, Nevada, Texas, and Washington. The company (recently acquired by the larger pawnshop operator Cash America International) uses eBay's APIs to automatically upload the latest pawned items from its physical stores to eBay. The system already generates more than 5 percent of SuperPawn's $40 million in annual sales and thousands more transactions for eBay.

Source: Erik Schonfeld, "The Great Giveaway," *Business 2.0*, April 2005, pp. 81–86.

CASE STUDY QUESTIONS

1. What are the business benefits to Amazon and eBay of opening up some of their databases to developers and entrepreneurs? Do you agree with this strategy? Why or why not?

2. What business factors are causing Google to move slowly in opening up its databases? Do you agree with its go-slow strategy? Why or why not?

3. Should other companies follow Amazon's and eBay's lead and open up some of their databases to developers and others? Defend your position with examples of the risks and benefits to an actual company.

REAL WORLD ACTIVITIES

1. The concept of opening up a company's product, inventory, and other databases to developers and entrepreneurs is a relatively new one. Use the Internet to find examples of companies that have adopted this strategy and the benefits they claim for doing so.

2. Opening up selective databases to outsiders is not a risk-free strategy for a company. What risks are involved? What safeguards should be put in place to guard against loss or misuse of a company's data? Break into small groups with your classmates to discuss and take a stand on these issues.

CHAPTER 6

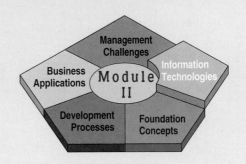

TELECOMMUNICATIONS AND NETWORKS

Chapter Highlights

Learning Objectives

1. Understand the concept of a network.

2. Apply Metcalfe's law in understanding the value of a network.

3. Identify several major developments and trends in the industries, technologies, and business applications of telecommunications and Internet technologies.

4. Provide examples of the business value of Internet, intranet, and extranet applications.

5. Identify the basic components, functions, and types of telecommunications networks used in business.

6. Explain the functions of major components of telecommunications network hardware, software, media, and services.

7. Explain the concept of client/server networking.

8. Understand the two forms of peer-to-peer networking.

9. Explain the difference between digital and analog signals.

10. Identify the various transmission media and topologies used in telecommunications networks.

11. Understand the fundamentals of wireless network technologies.

12. Explain the concepts behind TCP/IP.

13. Understand the seven layers of the OSI network model.

SECTION I	# The Networked Enterprise

The Networked Enterprise

When computers are networked, two industries—computing and communications—converge, and the result is vastly more than the sum of the parts. Suddenly, computing applications become available for business-to-business coordination and commerce, and for small as well as large organizations. The global Internet creates a public place without geographic boundaries—cyberspace—where ordinary citizens can interact, publish their ideas, and engage in the purchase of goods and services. In short, the impact of both computing and communications on our society and organizational structures is greatly magnified.

Telecommunications and network technologies are internetworking and revolutionizing business and society. Businesses have become networked enterprises. The Internet, the Web, and intranets and extranets are networking business processes and employees together and connecting them to their customers, suppliers, and other business stakeholders. Companies and workgroups can thus collaborate more creatively, manage their business operations and resources more effectively, and compete successfully in today's fast-changing global economy. This chapter presents the telecommunications and network foundations for these developments.

Read the Real World Case 1 on the future of public-access Wi-Fi. We can learn a lot about new business models for the provision of this almost ubiquitous service from this case. See Figure 6.1.

The Concept of a Network

Because of our focus on information systems and technologies, it is easy for us to think of networks in terms of connected computers. To understand the value of connecting computers fully, however, it is important to understand the concept of a network in its broader sense.

By definition, the term network means an interconnected or interrelated chain, group, or system. Using this definition, we can begin to identify all kinds of networks: a chain of hotels, the road system, the names in a person's address book or PDA, the railroad system, the members of a church, club, or organization. The examples of networks in our world are virtually endless, and computer networks, though both valuable and powerful, are just one example of the concept.

The concept of networks can be expressed as a mathematical formula that calculates the number of possible connections or interactions in a one-way communication environment: $N(N - 1)$, or $N^2 - N$. In the formula, N refers to the number of *nodes* (points of connection) on the network. If only a few nodes exist on a network, the number of possible connections is quite small. Using the formula, we see that three nodes result in only 6 possible connections. A network of 10 nodes results in a somewhat larger number—90 connections. It's when a large number of nodes are connected that the possible number of connections grows to significant proportions. A network with 100 nodes has 9,900 possible connections, and a network with 1,000 nodes has 999,000 possible connections. This type of mathematical growth is called *exponential*. This term just means that the growth in number of connections is many times greater than the number of nodes. Adding only one more node to a network makes the number of connections grow many times greater. Think of the effect of adding a new entry and exit ramp on a highway system that connects 30,000 cities and towns. How many more connections does that one new ramp create? Maybe more relevant is the effect of adding one additional person as a friend to your Facebook, MySpace, or Plaxo account. If you have 100 unique friends who each have 100 unique friends and the the new friend has 100 unique friends—well, you get the picture. That's what the next section is all about.

Metcalfe's Law

Robert Metcalfe founded 3Com Corp. and designed the Ethernet protocol for computer networks. He used his understanding of the concept of networks to express the exponential growth in terms of potential business value. Metcalfe's law states that *the usefulness, or utility, of a network equals the square of the number of users.*

REAL WORLD CASE 1

Starbucks and Others: The Future of Public Wi-Fi

Public Wi-Fi hot spots have been popular for about eight years. During that time, companies providing the service have been groping about, trying to figure out how to monetize it. The dominant model to date has been just to charge for it. Pay us $20 a month, and you can log in at any of our many locations. Recently, however, a kind of tipping point has been reached; now, instead of being rented for a fee, Wi-Fi will increasingly be given away to motivate customers to buy other goods and services. Now Wi-Fi is just like the free toaster that banks used to hand out for opening a new account.

Starbucks is leading a transition from Wi-Fi-for-money to Wi-Fi as a lure to get people to spend money on other things. It probably has to do with the strong competition Starbucks is facing for the morning breakfast crowd from the likes of McDonald's, which is also being more aggressive with Wi-Fi access.

The Starbucks offer may be a stroke of genius. Starbucks and AT&T will give you two hours of free Wi-Fi per day, but only if you use a Starbucks card. If you want more than two hours, you can pay $19.99 per month, which also entitles you to unlimited Wi-Fi offered by AT&T at some 70,000 hot spots in 89 countries. Starbucks not only trumps other sellers of sugar and caffeine by offering free Wi-Fi, but also pushes its lucrative Starbucks card and provides an upgrade path for people eager to hand over money in exchange for unlimited access.

Starbucks cards benefit Starbucks in three ways. First, people with Starbucks cards in their pockets are probably more likely to choose Starbucks when there are other nearby

FIGURE 6.1

Public wireless access may be at a crossroad with recent moves toward free and advertising-based provision of this service.

Source: Getty Images.

alternatives. Second, by getting millions of customers to pay in advance, Starbucks gets more cash upfront (rather than waiting until people actually get their coffee). Last and best is that cards get lost, stolen, or forgotten. When that happens, Starbucks gets to keep the money without supplying anything.

Like many indie cafes, Seattle's Bauhaus Books and Coffee has long relied on free Wi-Fi to help bring in customers. "In the evenings, the whole bar along the window will be lined with people using their computers," says Grace Heinze, a 13-year manager at Bauhaus, located between downtown Seattle and the trendy neighborhood of Capitol Hill. Bauhaus has thrived despite all of the Starbucks shops that have popped up around it: 15 within half a mile and 38 within one mile.

So is Heinze worried that the fiercely artsy cafe, named for the 1920's German art movement and replete with memorabilia, might lose customers to Starbucks now that it is dumping its high Wi-Fi rate in favor of two free hours of Wi-Fi a day to any customer? Not really.

"People come here because they like our atmosphere and because they like our coffee," Heinze said. "We're not feeling very uptight about this." Wi-Fi hot spots began to emerge around the beginning of the millennium. Propelled by the fast-growing popularity of laptops, Wi-Fi-enabled coffee shops quickly supplanted the older-style cybercafes, which relied on the expensive purchase and upkeep of PCs.

Still, until several years ago, many cafes were granting access to their Wi-Fi hot spots through codes given only to paying customers, according to Jack Kelley, president of Seattle regional chain Caffe Ladro. There was the fear "that if public Wi-Fi was free, you'd fill your place up with 'campers,'" Kelley said, referring to patrons who linger all day without buying anything. But that didn't happen after Ladro's 12 Seattle-area cafes switched to free Wi-Fi several years ago. Nowadays, "we don't even care if you sit in the parking lot and use it," Kelley said. Asked about the impact of Starbucks's move on his business, Kelley retorted, "Wi-Fi is free everywhere these days. Isn't Starbucks a little behind the times?"

As pressure mounts to make more Wi-Fi hot spots free, some operators are turning to Web advertising to offset costs or make money. Those ads are delivered during log-in or at the user's landing page. JiWire serves up ads to more than 8 million users per month on various Wi-Fi networks, including Boingo, at rates far higher than ones on typical Web pages. That kind of advertising "sounds gross" to Ladro's Kelley, though. "It's just like all of those ads in the movie theatre," he said. "I say, enough is enough."

"Many patrons of the smaller coffeehouses will continue to support their local shop due to loyalty, unique surroundings versus corporate giant, community support, convenience of location, etc.," he said. "Any customer losses may also be offset simply because there continues to be so much more demand for Wi-Fi access in general."

Bauhaus's Heinze seconds that. "We're close to two colleges, and we are in a neighborhood with a lot of apartment buildings," she said. Although Bauhaus competes in Starbucks's backyard, according to Heinze, Bauhaus has never "done anything reactive. And isn't that the whole point of being an indie coffeehouse, being your own self? If that happens to be similar to what Starbucks does, that's fine."

Like television, Wi-Fi is increasingly given away in exchange for ads. It's an unproven model; nobody is making huge profits on this approach yet. JiWire's "Ads for Access" program gives some users free Wi-Fi access at hot spots normally paid for by others in exchange for viewing ads over those connections. The company has recently (and wisely) started to target iPhone users. Wi-Fi is free at some airports. One of the largest is Denver International. In addition to advertising, the FreeFi Networks Wi-Fi access is subsidized by Disney-ABC television show rentals, which users can download over the connection. A company called HypeWifi funds its free Wi-Fi access through advertising, but also by doing "market research" for advertisers for a fee. Users logging onto a HypeWifi access point may earn their access by answering a question or two, which is aggregated and presented to the sponsor, along with demographic information about the users.

There's no industry where all players universally provide free Wi-Fi as a matter of course; for example, some hotels offer free Wi-Fi, and some don't. Some airports have it, and some don't. It's also interesting to note that Wi-Fi works as an incentive even when it's not free.

After a few fits and starts, Wi-Fi in the transportation industry is suddenly taking off. A solid majority of major airlines in both the United States and Europe either have or are planning to offer in-flight Wi-Fi. Most will charge for the service. Within two years, all major carriers will offer in-flight Wi-Fi.

Airline Wi-Fi, in turn, has triggered a rush to install Wi-Fi service in trains across Europe. These rail service companies see the airlines as a competitor for the lucrative business traveler market. Commuter trains and even taxis are getting Wi-Fi;

in fact, wherever you find a concentration of businesspeople with expense accounts and time to kill, expect to find Wi-Fi there. Everyone wants these customers because they spend money on other things.

Pricing runs the gamut from no-strings-attached free access, to conspicuously overpriced, to creative or selective pricing à la Starbucks or Boingo. Yet the trend is clear: Wi-Fi is transitioning gradually to always free everywhere. There's just no downside to these trends. Everybody loves Wi-Fi—the freer the better.

Some, however, do not think Wi-Fi has a future. "As mobile broadband takes off, Wi-Fi hot spots will become as irrelevant as telephone booths," says Ericsson Telephone Co. chief marketing officer Johan Bergendahl. "Mobile broadband is growing faster than mobile or fixed telephony ever did." In Austria, they are saying that mobile broadband will pass fixed broadband this year. "It's already growing faster, and in Sweden, the most popular phone is a USB modem," says Bergendahl.

As more people start to use mobile broadband, hot spots will no longer be needed. Also, support for high-speed packet access (HSPA), favored by Ericsson, is being built into more and more laptops. Ericsson recently signed a deal to put HSPA technology in some Lenovo notebooks. "In a few years, [HSPA] will be as common as Wi-Fi is today," says Bergendahl.

Challenges still remain. Coverage, availability, and price—especially when someone is roaming on other networks—are all key factors for success. "Industry will have to solve the international roaming issue," Bergendahl says. "Carriers need to work together. It can be as simple as paying 10 per day when you are abroad." Not knowing how high the bill will be after a business trip is not acceptable for professional users. Coverage will also have to improve.

Source: Adapted from Eric Lai, "Indie Coffeehouses Tell Starbucks: Bring on Your Free Wi-Fi," *Computerworld*, February 14, 2008; Mikael Ricknäs, "Ericsson Predicts Demise of Wi-Fi Hotspots," *Computerworld*, March 10, 2008; and Mike Elgan, "Wi-Fi Wants to Be Free," *Computerworld*, February 15, 2008.

CASE STUDY QUESTIONS

1. Do you agree with the plans by Starbucks to offer time-limited free Wi-Fi to customers? Do you think free Wi-Fi would be enough to instill that kind of loyalty? Based on the experiences of the other coffee houses reported above, do you think free access was a critical factor in developing a loyal customer base?

2. Part of the reason for Starbucks's move had to do with increased competition from chains like McDonald's for the morning breakfast crowd. Do you think that free wireless access by such a competitor would have moved a significant portion of Starbucks's customers away? Why or why not?

3. The case notes some companies that offer free Wi-Fi in exchange for viewing advertisements or answering questions for market research studies. Would you be willing to do so in order to get free wireless access, say, at an airport? Would your answer change if you were using a corporate laptop versus your own, because of security concerns?

REAL WORLD ACTIVITIES

1. Johan Bergendahl of Ericsson believes the demise of Wi-Fi is rather imminent and that mobile broadband will replace hot spots for wireless access. Search the Internet for current commercial offerings of mobile broadband and compare their features with Wi-Fi hotspots. Which one would you choose? Which factors would affect your decision?

2. Go online and look at different companies in one of the industries mentioned in the case, noting which companies offer free wireless access and which ones do not. Break into small groups and brainstorm potential explanations for these differences. Do you see any patterns in the type of companies that charge for access versus those that offer it for free?

Metcalfe's law becomes easy to understand if you think of a common piece of technology we all use every day: the telephone. The telephone is of very limited use if only you and your best friend have one. If a whole town is on the system, it becomes much more useful. If the whole world is wired, the utility of the system is phenomenal. Add the number of wireless telephone connections, and you have a massive potential for value. To reach this value, however, many people had to have access to a telephone—and they had to have used it. In other words, telephone use had to reach a critical mass of users. So it is with any technology.

Until a critical mass of users is reached, a change in technology affects only the technology. Once critical mass is attained, however, social, political, and economic systems change. The same is true of **digital network technologies.** Consider the Internet. It reached critical mass in 1993, when there were roughly 2.5 million host computers on the network; by November 1997, the vast network contained an estimated 25 million host computers. According to Internet World Stats, the number of users on the Internet in March 2009 topped 1.6 billion! More important, that represents only about 24 percent of the estimated world population. With computing costs continuing to drop rapidly (remember Moore's law from Chapter 3) and the Internet growing exponentially (Metcalfe's law), we can expect to see more and more value—conceivably for less cost—virtually every time we log on.

Trends in Telecommunications

Telecommunications is the exchange of information in any form (voice, data, text, images, audio, video) over networks. Early telecommunications networks did not use computers to route traffic and, as such, were much slower than today's computer-based networks. Major trends occurring in the field of telecommunications have a significant impact on management decisions in this area. You should thus be aware of major trends in telecommunications industries, technologies, and applications that significantly increase the decision alternatives confronting business managers and professionals. See Figure 6.2.

Industry Trends

The competitive arena for telecommunications service has changed dramatically in recent years. The telecommunications industry has changed from government-regulated monopolies to a deregulated market with fiercely competitive suppliers of telecommunications services. Numerous companies now offer businesses and consumers a choice of everything from local and global telephone services to communications

FIGURE 6.2

Major trends in business telecommunications.

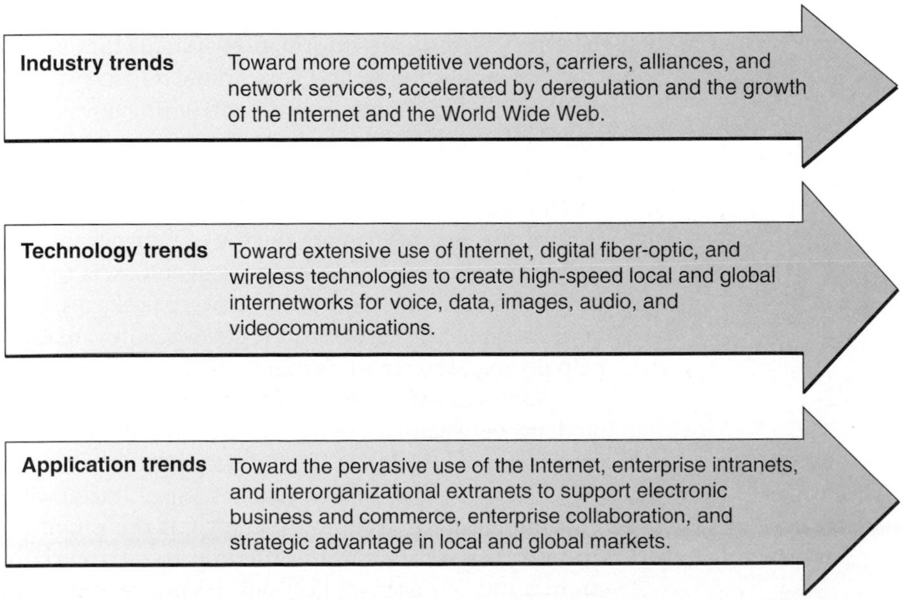

Industry trends Toward more competitive vendors, carriers, alliances, and network services, accelerated by deregulation and the growth of the Internet and the World Wide Web.

Technology trends Toward extensive use of Internet, digital fiber-optic, and wireless technologies to create high-speed local and global internetworks for voice, data, images, audio, and videocommunications.

Application trends Toward the pervasive use of the Internet, enterprise intranets, and interorganizational extranets to support electronic business and commerce, enterprise collaboration, and strategic advantage in local and global markets.

FIGURE 6.3

The spectrum of telecommunications-based services available today.

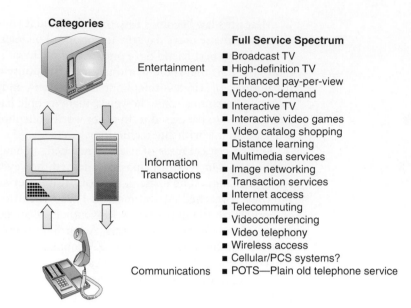

Categories

Entertainment

Information Transactions

Communications

Full Service Spectrum
- Broadcast TV
- High-definition TV
- Enhanced pay-per-view
- Video-on-demand
- Interactive TV
- Interactive video games
- Video catalog shopping
- Distance learning
- Multimedia services
- Image networking
- Transaction services
- Internet access
- Telecommuting
- Videoconferencing
- Video telephony
- Wireless access
- Cellular/PCS systems?
- POTS—Plain old telephone service

satellite channels, mobile radio, cable television, cellular phone services, and Internet access. See Figure 6.3.

The explosive growth of the Internet and the World Wide Web has spawned a host of new telecommunications products, services, and providers. Driving and responding to this growth, business firms have dramatically increased their use of the Internet and the Web for electronic commerce and collaboration. Thus, the service and vendor options available to meet a company's telecommunications needs have increased significantly, as have a business manager's decision-making alternatives.

Technology Trends

Open systems with unrestricted connectivity, using Internet networking technologies as their technology platform, are today's primary telecommunications technology drivers. Web browser suites, HTML Web page editors, Internet and intranet servers and network management software, TCP/IP Internet networking products, and network security firewalls are just a few examples. These technologies are being applied in Internet, intranet, and extranet applications, especially those for electronic commerce and collaboration. This trend has reinforced previous industry and technical moves toward building client/server networks based on an open-systems architecture.

Open systems are information systems that use common standards for hardware, software, applications, and networking. Open systems, like the Internet and corporate intranets and extranets, create a computing environment that is open to easy access by end users and their networked computer systems. Open systems provide greater connectivity, that is, the ability of networked computers and other devices to access and communicate with one another easily and share information. Any open-systems architecture also provides a high degree of network interoperability. That is, open systems enable the many different activities of end users to be accomplished using the different varieties of computer systems, software packages, and databases provided by a variety of interconnected networks. Frequently, software known as *middleware* may be used to help diverse systems work together.

Middleware is a general term for any programming that serves to glue together or mediate between two separate, and usually already existing, programs. A common application of middleware is to allow programs written for access to a particular database (e.g., DB2) to access other databases (e.g., Oracle) without the need for custom coding.

Middleware is commonly known as the plumbing of an information system because it routes data and information transparently between different back-end data sources and end-user applications. It's not very interesting to look at—it usually doesn't have much, if any, visible "front end" of its own—but it is an essential component of any IT infrastructure because it allows disparate systems to be joined together in a common framework.

Telecommunications is also being revolutionized by the rapid change from analog to digital network technologies. Telecommunications systems have always depended on voice-oriented analog transmission systems designed to transmit the variable electrical frequencies generated by the sound waves of the human voice. However, local and global telecommunications networks are rapidly converting to digital transmission technologies that transmit information in the form of discrete pulses, as computers do. This conversion provides (1) significantly higher transmission speeds, (2) the movement of larger amounts of information, (3) greater economy, and (4) much lower error rates than with analog systems. In addition, digital technologies allow telecommunications networks to carry multiple types of communications (data, voice, video) on the same circuits.

Another major trend in telecommunications technology is a change from reliance on copper wire–based media and land-based microwave relay systems to fiber-optic lines and cellular, communications satellite, and other wireless technologies. Fiber-optic transmission, which uses pulses of laser-generated light, offers significant advantages in terms of reduced size and installation effort, vastly greater communication capacity, much faster transmission speeds, and freedom from electrical interference. Satellite transmission offers significant advantages for organizations that need to transmit massive quantities of data, audio, and video over global networks, especially to isolated areas. Cellular, mobile radio, and other wireless systems are connecting cellular phones, PDAs, and other wireless appliances to the Internet and corporate networks.

Business Application Trends

The changes in telecommunications industries and technologies just mentioned are causing a significant change in the business use of telecommunications. The trend toward more vendors, services, Internet technologies, and open systems, and the rapid growth of the Internet, the World Wide Web, and corporate intranets and extranets, dramatically increases the number of feasible telecommunications applications. Thus, telecommunications networks are now playing vital and pervasive roles in Web-enabled e-business processes, e-commerce, enterprise collaboration, and other business applications that support the operations, management, and strategic objectives of both large and small business enterprises.

Internet2

We cannot leave our overview of trends in telecommunications without reiterating that the Internet sits firmly in the center of the action. Despite its importance and seemingly unexplored boundaries, we are already embarking on the next generation of the "network of networks." Internet2 is a high-performance network that uses an entirely different infrastructure than the public Internet we know today. Already, more than 200 universities and scientific institutions and 70 communications corporations are part of the Internet2 network. One big misconception about Internet2 is that it's a sequel to the original Internet and will replace it someday. It never will, because it was never intended to replace the Internet. Rather, its purpose is to build a road map that can be followed during the next stage of innovation for the current Internet. The ideas being honed, such as new addressing protocols and satellite-quality streaming video, will likely be deployed to the Internet, but it might take close to 10 years before we see them.

Furthermore, the Internet2 network may never become totally open; it might remain solely in the domain of universities, research centers, and governments. To be sure, the lightning-fast technologies in use by Internet2 right now must eventually be turned over to the public Internet. For now, the Internet2 project lives for the purpose of sharing, collaborating, and trying new high-speed communication ideas—interestingly, many of the same goals that shaped the early history of today's Internet.

Most of the institutions and commercial partners on the Internet2 network are connected via *Abilene*, a network backbone that will soon support throughput of 10 gigabits per second (Gbps). Several international networks are also plugged into Abilene's infrastructure, and as the project grows, more and more networks will be able to connect to the current framework. The one common denominator among all of the Internet2 partners is their active participation in the development and testing of new applications and Internet protocols with an emphasis on research and collaboration, focusing on things such as videoconferencing, multicasting, remote applications, and new protocols that take advantage of the many opportunities megabandwidth provides. In short, Internet2 is all about high-speed telecommunications and infinite bandwidth.

To give you an idea of exactly how fast this network of the future is, an international team of researchers has already used it to set a new land speed record. At the end of 2002, the team sent 6.7 gigabytes of data across 6,821 miles of fiber-optic network in less than one minute. That's roughly two full-length DVD-quality movies traveling a quarter of the way around the earth in less than one minute at an average speed of 923 million bits per second! It's also approximately 410,000 miles per hour. The same team is already hard at work, attempting to break its own record.

As we are exploring new ways to gain business advantage through the Internet, a significant effort is being made to make the Internet bigger and faster. In 2009, Internet2 celebrated its thirteenth anniversary and has significantly expanded in breadth, speed, and storage capacity since its inception in 1996. We'll look at Internet2 again later in this chapter when we discuss Internet-addressing protocols.

The Business Value of Telecommunications Networks

What *business value* is created when a company capitalizes on the trends in telecommunications we have just identified? Use of the Internet, intranets, extranets, and other telecommunications networks can dramatically cut costs, shorten business lead times and response times, support e-commerce, improve the collaboration of workgroups, develop online operational processes, share resources, lock in customers and suppliers, and develop new products and services. These benefits make applications of telecommunications more strategic and vital for businesses that must increasingly find new ways to compete in both domestic and global markets.

Figure 6.4 illustrates how telecommunications-based business applications can help a company overcome geographic, time, cost, and structural barriers to business

FIGURE 6.4 Examples of the business value of business applications of telecommunications networks.

Strategic Capabilities	e-Business Examples	Business Value
Overcome geographic barriers: Capture information about business transactions from remote locations.	Use the Internet and extranets to transmit customer orders from traveling salespeople to a corporate data center for order processing and inventory control.	Provides better customer service by reducing delay in filling orders and improves cash flow by speeding up the billing of customers.
Overcome time barriers: Provide information to remote locations immediately after it is requested.	Credit authorization at the point of sale using online POS networks.	Credit inquiries can be made and answered in seconds.
Overcome cost barriers: Reduce the cost of more traditional means of communication.	Desktop videoconferencing between a company and its business partners using the Internet, intranets, and extranets.	Reduces expensive business trips; allows customers, suppliers, and employees to collaborate, thus improving the quality of decisions reached.
Overcome structural barriers: Support linkages for competitive advantage.	Business-to-business electronic commerce Web sites for transactions with suppliers and customers using the Internet and extranets.	Fast, convenient services lock in customers and suppliers.

success. Note the examples of the business value of these four strategic capabilities of telecommunications networks. This figure emphasizes how several e-business applications can help a firm capture and provide information quickly to end users at remote geographic locations at reduced costs, as well as support its strategic organizational objectives.

For example, traveling salespeople and those at regional sales offices can use the Internet, extranets, and other networks to transmit customer orders from their laptops or desktop PCs, thus breaking geographic barriers. Point-of-sale terminals and an online sales transaction processing network can break time barriers by supporting immediate credit authorization and sales processing. Teleconferencing can be used to cut costs by reducing the need for expensive business trips, allowing customers, suppliers, and employees to participate in meetings and collaborate on joint projects without traveling. Finally, business-to-business e-commerce Web sites are used by businesses to establish strategic relationships with their customers and suppliers by making business transactions fast, convenient, and tailored to the needs of the business partners involved.

The Internet Revolution

The explosive growth of the Internet is a revolutionary phenomenon in computing and telecommunications. The Internet has become the largest and most important network of networks today and has evolved into a global *information superhighway*. We can think of the Internet as a network made up of millions of smaller private networks, each with the ability to operate independent of, or in harmony with, all the other millions of networks connected to the Internet. When this network of networks began to grow in December 1991, it had about 10 servers. In January 2004, the Internet was estimated to have more than 46 million connected servers with a sustained growth rate in excess of 1 million servers per month. In January 2007, the Internet was estimated to have more than 1 billion users with Web sites in 34 languages from English to Icelandic. Now that is some growth!

The Internet is constantly expanding as more and more businesses and other organizations and their users, computers, and networks join its global Web. Thousands of business, educational, and research networks now connect millions of computer systems and users in more than 200 countries. Internet users projected for 2010 are expected to top the 2 billion user mark, which still only represents approximately one-third of the worldwide population. Apply these numbers to Metcalfe's law, and you can see that the number of possible connections is extraordinary.

The Net doesn't have a central computer system or telecommunications center. There are, however, 13 servers called *root servers* that are used to handle the bulk of the routing of traffic from one computer to another. Each message sent has a unique address code, so any Internet server in the network can forward it to its destination. Also, the Internet does not have a headquarters or governing body. International advisory and standards groups of individual and corporate members, such as the Internet Society (www.isoc.org) and the World Wide Web Consortium (www.w3.org), promote use of the Internet and the development of new communications standards. These common standards are the key to the free flow of messages among the widely different computers and networks of the many organizations and *Internet service providers* (ISPs) in the system.

Internet Service Providers

One of the unique aspects of the Internet is that nobody really owns it. Anyone who can access the Internet can use it and the services it offers. Because the Internet cannot be accessed directly by individuals, we need to use the services of a company that specializes in providing easy access. An **ISP**, or Internet service provider, is a company that provides access to the Internet to individuals and organizations. For a monthly fee, the service provider gives you a software package, user name, password, and access phone number or access protocol. With this information (and some specialized hardware), you can then log onto the Internet, browse the World Wide Web, and send and receive e-mail.

In addition to serving individuals, ISPs serve large companies, providing a direct connection from the company's networks to the Internet. These ISPs themselves are connected to one another through *network access points*. Through these connections, one ISP can easily connect to another ISP to obtain information about the address of a Web site or user node.

Internet Applications

The most popular Internet applications are e-mail, instant messaging, browsing the sites on the World Wide Web, and participating in *newsgroups* and *chat rooms*. Internet e-mail messages usually arrive in seconds or a few minutes anywhere in the world and can take the form of data, text, fax, and video files. Internet browser software like Netscape Navigator and Internet Explorer enables millions of users to surf the World Wide Web by clicking their way to the multimedia information resources stored on the hyperlinked pages of businesses, government, and other Web sites. Web sites offer information and entertainment and are the launch sites for e-commerce transactions between businesses and their suppliers and customers. As we will discuss in Chapter 8, e-commerce Web sites offer all manner of products and services via online retailers, wholesalers, service providers, and online auctions. See Figure 6.5.

The Internet provides electronic discussion forums and bulletin board systems formed and managed by thousands of special-interest newsgroups. You can participate in discussions or post messages on a myriad of topics for other users with the same interests. Other popular applications include downloading software and information files and accessing databases provided by a variety of business, government, and other organizations. You can conduct online searches for information on Web sites in a variety of ways by using search sites and search engines such as Yahoo!, Google, and Fast Search. Logging on to other computers on the Internet and holding real-time conversations with other Internet users in *chat rooms* are also popular uses of the Internet.

FIGURE 6.5
Popular uses of the Internet.

● **Surf.** Point-and-click your way to thousands of hyperlinked Web sites and resources for multimedia information, entertainment, or electronic commerce.
● **e-Mail.** Use e-mail and instant messaging to exchange electronic messages with colleagues, friends, and other Internet users.
● **Discuss.** Participate in discussion forums of special-interest newsgroups, or hold real-time text conversations in Web site chat rooms.
● **Publish.** Post your opinion, subject matter, or creative work to a Web site or Weblog for others to read.
● **Buy and Sell.** Buy and sell practically anything via e-commerce retailers, wholesalers, service providers, and online auctions.
● **Download.** Transfer data files, software, reports, articles, pictures, music, videos, and other types of files to your computer system.
● **Compute.** Log onto and use thousands of Internet computer systems around the world.
● **Connect.** Find out what friends, acquaintances, and business associates are up to.
● **Other Uses.** Make long-distance phone calls, hold desktop videoconferences, listen to radio programs, watch television, play video games, explore virtual worlds, etc.

VF Corporation: Designing Clothes While Sharing Information

If you're in the business of making a few million pairs of blue jeans a year, not much is more important than getting "blue" exactly right. It's why a jeans designer at VF Corp. will express mail swatches dipped in dye back and forth with factories around the world as many times as necessary to make sure designers and manufacturers agree on just the right shade. And it's part of the reason it takes as long as nine months to design a new pair of jeans and get them on the shelves.

VF, the world's largest apparel maker with brands such as Lee Jeans, Vanity Fair lingerie, and North Face outdoor gear, expects that getting new styles to shoppers faster will make it more competitive. To do that, it's creating an IT platform of collaborative design tools that can draw on a database of information such as material characteristics, costs, colors, and templates of past designs. The company has deployed the tools across its five U.S. divisions and built real-time ties to its manufacturers around the world, since 90% of its manufacturing is outside the United States. The ability to share the information via the Internet makes it feasible for the company to collaborate in real time with offshore factories and other supply-chain partners in fairly remote regions.

VF believes finding a more efficient way to agree on blue, and other technology-enabled improvements in how it designs new products and manages logistics, could save it $100 million a year and cut months off the time to get a new design to market. "If you look at the cycle times from design to retail shelf, about two-thirds is spent in product development," says Boyd Rogers, VF's VP of supply chain and technology. "The new system has the potential to remove months from the production cycle, depending how many iterations are made to get the correct color."

Two key elements are the color-technology software from GretagMacbeth LLC to speed electronic collaborating on color choices and the custom-built Strategic Interaction Development Environment, or Stride, which contains graphic tools to manage garment details, a raw-materials database to house garment specifications, and more.

Using the integrated systems, a design team will be able to input product ideas and attach a sketch or set of design specifications. If a similar design exists, the designer can save time by copying the information from another product line and reusing the template. The color-technology system will tie into the Stride system. And the two will let information be shared more easily—for example, in real time with VF's sourcing office in Hong Kong, which contracts with third-party manufacturers throughout Asia to sew the clothes that VF designs. In the future, VF will let raw-material suppliers and manufacturers connect to the Stride system for real-time interaction on issues related to materials and specifications.

"We think $100 million annually over the next five years is absolutely doable," Rogers says. "It's becoming increasingly important to collaborate tightly with our divisions and partners around the world to cut cycle times."

Source: Adapted from Laurie Sullivan, "Designed to Cut Time," *InformationWeek*, February 28, 2005.

Business Use of the Internet

As Figure 6.6 illustrates, business use of the Internet has expanded from an electronic information exchange to a broad platform for strategic business applications. Notice how applications such as collaboration among business partners, providing customer and vendor support, and e-commerce have become major business uses of the Internet. Companies are also using Internet technologies for marketing, sales, and customer relationship management applications, as well as for cross-functional business applications, and applications in engineering, manufacturing, human resources, and accounting. Let's look at a real-world example.

FIGURE 6.6   Examples of how a company can use the Internet for business.

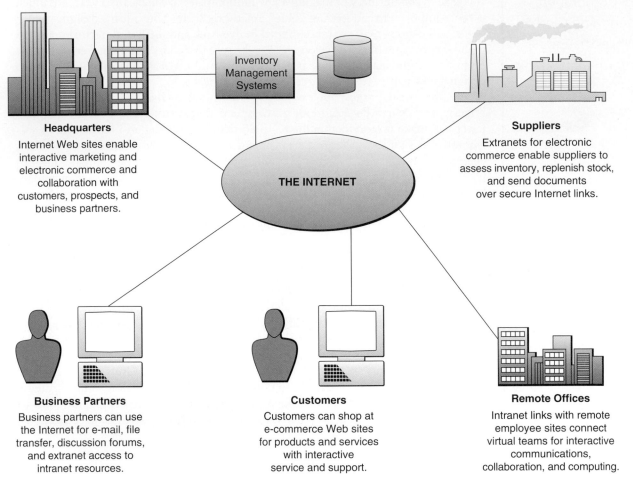

Headquarters
Internet Web sites enable interactive marketing and electronic commerce and collaboration with customers, prospects, and business partners.

Inventory Management Systems

THE INTERNET

Suppliers
Extranets for electronic commerce enable suppliers to assess inventory, replenish stock, and send documents over secure Internet links.

Business Partners
Business partners can use the Internet for e-mail, file transfer, discussion forums, and extranet access to intranet resources.

Customers
Customers can shop at e-commerce Web sites for products and services with interactive service and support.

Remote Offices
Intranet links with remote employee sites connect virtual teams for interactive communications, collaboration, and computing.

The Business Value of the Internet

The Internet provides a synthesis of computing and communication capabilities that adds value to every part of the business cycle.

What business value do companies derive from their business applications on the Internet? Figure 6.7 summarizes how many companies perceive the business value of the Internet for e-commerce. Substantial cost savings can arise because applications that use the Internet and Internet-based technologies (like intranets and extranets) are typically less expensive to develop, operate, and maintain than traditional systems. For example, an airline saves money every time customers use its Web site instead of its customer support telephone system.

It is estimated that for certain types of transactions, the transaction cost savings are significant for online versus more traditional channels. For example, booking a reservation over the Internet costs about 90 percent less for the airline than booking the same reservation over the telephone. The banking industry has also found significant cost savings via the Internet. A typical online banking transaction (payments, balance inquiry, check payment) is estimated to cost anywhere from 50 percent to 95 percent less than its bricks-and-mortar counterpart.

Other primary sources of business value include attracting new customers with innovative marketing and products, as well as retaining present customers with improved customer service and support. Of course, generating revenue through e-commerce applications is a major source of business value, which we will discuss in Chapter 8. To

FIGURE 6.7

How companies are deriving business value from their e-business and e-commerce applications.

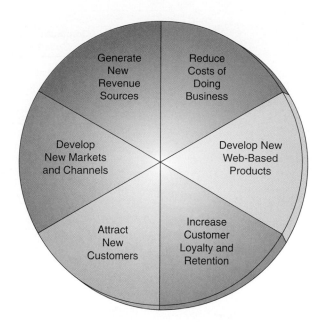

summarize, most companies are building e-business and e-commerce Web sites to achieve six major business values:

- Generate new revenue from online sales.
- Reduce transaction costs through online sales and customer support.
- Attract new customers via Web marketing and advertising and online sales.
- Increase the loyalty of existing customers via improved Web customer service and support.
- Develop new Web-based markets and distribution channels for existing products.
- Develop new information-based products accessible on the Web.

The Role of Intranets

Many companies have sophisticated and widespread intranets, offering detailed data retrieval, collaboration tools, personalized customer profiles, and links to the Internet. Investing in the intranet, they feel, is as fundamental as supplying employees with a telephone.

Before we go any further, let's redefine the concept of an intranet, to emphasize specifically how intranets are related to the Internet and extranets. An **intranet** is a network inside an organization that uses Internet technologies (such as Web browsers and servers, TCP/IP network protocols, HTML hypermedia document publishing and databases, and so on) to provide an Internet-like environment within the enterprise for information sharing, communications, collaboration, and the support of business processes. An intranet is protected by security measures such as passwords, encryption, and firewalls, and thus can be accessed by authorized users through the Internet. A company's intranet can also be accessed through the intranets of customers, suppliers, and other business partners via *extranet* links.

The Business Value of Intranets

Organizations of all kinds are implementing a broad range of intranet uses. One way that companies organize intranet applications is to group them conceptually into a few user services categories that reflect the basic services that intranets offer to their users. These services are provided by the intranet's portal, browser, and server software, as well as by other system and application software and groupware that are part of a company's intranet software environment. Figure 6.8 illustrates how intranets provide an *enterprise information portal* that supports communication and collaboration, Web

FIGURE 6.8

Intranets can provide an
enterprise information
portal for applications in
communication and
collaboration, business
operations and
management, Web
publishing, and intranet
portal management.

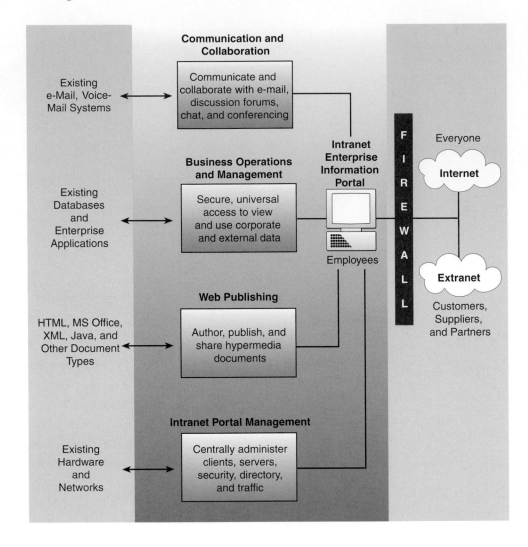

publishing, business operations and management, and intranet portal management.
Notice also how these applications can be integrated with existing IS resources and
applications and extended to customers, suppliers, and business partners via the Internet and extranets.

Communications and Collaboration. Intranets can significantly improve communications and collaboration within an enterprise. For example, you can use your intranet browser and your PC or NC workstation to send and receive e-mail, voice mail,
pages, and faxes to communicate with others within your organization, as well as externally through the Internet and extranets. You can also use intranet groupware features to improve team and project collaboration with services such as discussion
groups, chat rooms, and audio and videoconferencing.

Web Publishing. The advantage of developing and publishing hyperlinked multimedia documents to hypermedia databases accessible on World Wide Web servers has
moved to corporate intranets. The comparative ease, attractiveness, and lower cost of
publishing and accessing multimedia business information internally via intranet Web
sites have been the primary reasons for the explosive growth in the use of intranets in
business. For example, information products as varied as company newsletters, technical drawings, and product catalogs can be published in a variety of ways, including
hypermedia Web pages, e-mail, and net broadcasting, and as part of in-house business

applications. Intranet software browsers, servers, and search engines can help you easily navigate and locate the business information you need.

Business Operations and Management. Intranets have moved beyond merely making hypermedia information available on Web servers or pushing it to users via net broadcasting. Intranets are also being used as the platform for developing and deploying critical business applications to support business operations and managerial decision making across the internetworked enterprise. For example, many companies are developing custom applications like order processing, inventory control, sales management, and enterprise information portals that can be implemented on intranets, extranets, and the Internet. Many of these applications are designed to interface with and access existing company databases and legacy systems. The software for such business uses is then installed on intranet Web servers. Employees within the company or external business partners can access and run such applications using Web browsers from anywhere on the network whenever needed.

Intranet Portal Management. Organizations must employ IT and IS professionals to manage the functions of the intranet along with maintaining the various hardware and software components necessary for successful operations. For example, a network administrator must manage the access of users via passwords and other security mechanisms to ensure that each user is able to use the intranet productively while simultaneously protecting the integrity of the data resources. Included in this job are issues related to protection against unauthorized access, computer viruses, directory management, and other highly important functions.

Now let's look at one company's use of an intranet in more detail to get a better idea of how intranets are used in business.

Constellation Energy: Using an Intranet to Get Employees Working Together and More Productively	When Beth Perlman joined Constellation Energy as its CIO in 2002, employees of the company's four major divisions didn't do much communicating. "It was like four separate companies that never talked," she says.

Perlman herself had offices in two buildings, two Windows 95–based PCs that couldn't access the other's e-mail, and a BlackBerry that couldn't sync with them. Constellation Energy began to standardize its 10,000 employees' desktops in 2005, but that still didn't solve a lot of its information-sharing problems. "I got sick of seeing people e-mail these enormous documents" because there was no other way to electronically share ideas and information, Perlman laments. "It was hard to track versions of documents, such as when staff in different parts of the company needed to provide data for analyst presentations," she says.

What a difference a year makes! Constellation Energy in 2006 rolled out a suite of standardized, common collaboration tools throughout the company, installed wireless networks at 22 of its campuses, and redesigned its myConstellation Intranet portal.

The company's "Connect. Interact. Transform." initiative already has tremendously boosted productivity and collaboration. "It was a very quick ROI [return on investment]," Perlman notes. A big part of the payback has come from an enterprise software license with Microsoft that Perlman says costs "a few hundred thousand dollars," which, along with the redesigned intranet portal, has contributed significantly to Constellation Energy's $90 million in pretax productivity savings in 2005 and 2006.

As part of the "Connect. Interact. Transform." initiative, Perlman's IT organization deployed Microsoft Live Meeting Web conferencing software; SharePoint, an information-sharing and document collaboration tool; and Windows Messenger instant messaging for use on the intranet. To date, Live Meeting has had the biggest |

impact on productivity across the company, according to Perlman. More than 10,000 hours of meetings were logged in 2005 and 2006, saving the company $41 per attendee in expenses and gaining an average of 98 minutes in productivity per employee.

Now, instead of traveling to central offices for training, employees can take classes via their PCs or at kiosks with portal access that are set up in Constellation Energy's service centers for the company's 2,500 field, utility, and other workers who don't have PCs. Through Live Meeting, everyone can see the same information at the same time, Perlman says, including PowerPoint presentations. The IT organization has found this incredibly useful in its own work. "During a meeting, IT staff can look at changes to code in a program and all see the same thing," she notes.

"We thought only a few people would use SharePoint, but now it's being used by everyone. It's really ballooned," she comments. SharePoint provides a central location for documents, such as Word and Excel files, to be viewed and changed. SharePoint also provides version control.

SharePoint's deployment has allowed Kevin Hadlock, Constellation Energy's director of investor relations, to spend more time analyzing data for the company's earnings releases and analyst presentations, as well as hundreds of fewer hours collecting the paperwork that goes into those presentations from the company's four divisions. A presentation was often revised 30–50 times before all changes were made manually in the final version. With SharePoint, all the information is collected electronically.

"I always know what changes have been made," says Hadlock, who says the final presentation material was completed at least one week earlier than in the past and that "the quality and accuracy of the information is greatly improved."

Source: Adapted from Marianne McGee, "Constellation Energy Uses IT to Get Employees Working Together and More Productively," *InformationWeek*, September 12, 2006; and Martin Garevy, "Threats Bring IT and Operations Together," *InformationWeek*, September 19, 2005.

The Role of Extranets

As businesses continue to use open Internet technologies [extranets] to improve communication with customers and partners, they can gain many competitive advantages along the way—in product development, cost savings, marketing, distribution, and leveraging their partnerships.

As we explained previously, extranets are network links that use Internet technologies to interconnect the intranet of a business with the intranets of its customers, suppliers, or other business partners. Companies can establish direct private network links among themselves or create private, secure Internet links called *virtual private networks* (VPNs). (We'll look more closely at VPNs later in this chapter.) Or a company can use the unsecured Internet as the extranet link between its intranet and consumers and others but rely on the encryption of sensitive data and its own firewall systems to provide adequate security. Thus, extranets enable customers, suppliers, consultants, subcontractors, business prospects, and others to access selected intranet Web sites and other company databases. See Figure 6.9.

As shown in the figure, an organization's extranet can simultaneously link the organization to a wide variety of external partners. Consultants and contractors can use the extranet to facilitate the design of new systems or provide outsourcing services. The suppliers of the organization can use the extranet to ensure that the raw materials necessary for the organization to function are in stock or delivered in a timely fashion. The customers of an organization can use the extranet to access self-service functions such as ordering, order status checking, and payment. The extranet links the organization to the outside world in a manner that improves the way it does business.

The business value of extranets is derived from several factors. First, the Web browser technology of extranets makes customer and supplier access of intranet

FIGURE 6.9 Extranets connect the internetworked enterprise to consumers, business customers, suppliers, and other business partners.

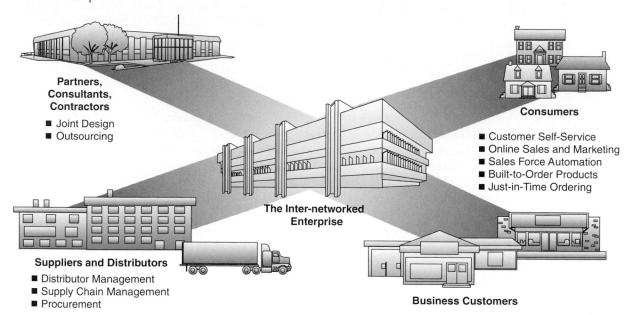

Partners, Consultants, Contractors
- Joint Design
- Outsourcing

The Inter-networked Enterprise

Consumers
- Customer Self-Service
- Online Sales and Marketing
- Sales Force Automation
- Built-to-Order Products
- Just-in-Time Ordering

Suppliers and Distributors
- Distributor Management
- Supply Chain Management
- Procurement

Business Customers

resources a lot easier and faster than previous business methods. Second, as you will see in two upcoming examples, extranets enable a company to offer new kinds of interactive Web-enabled services to their business partners. Thus, extranets are another way that a business can build and strengthen strategic relationships with its customers and suppliers. Also, extranets can enable and improve collaboration by a business with its customers and other business partners. Extranets facilitate an online, interactive product development, marketing, and customer-focused process that can bring better-designed products to market faster.

Extranets: Collaboration Speeds Information	Highway engineers around the sprawling state of Texas want all the accident data they can get. With 800,000 crashes a year in the state, lives can be saved with a new left-turn lane here or a guardrail there, or perhaps a traffic light over a once-quiet rural intersection. Engineers need to analyze accident patterns to know where to spend limited highway-safety funds. Until 2005, however, engineers in the Department of Transportation's 25 district offices could not get the data. To view accident records, they had to go to Austin and pore through reels of microfilm in the state archives, trying to find reports relevant to particular stretches of highway. Even if they found what they were looking for, the information was at least three years out of date because of the backlog of accident reports awaiting microfilming.

That all changed in May 2005 when the state fired up its new Crash Records Information System with digitized police and highway patrol accident reports available through a business intelligence extranet. Traffic engineers around the state are now able to access and analyze the data from their offices, equipped with nothing more than a browser and a password. Making reports available over the Web "will help us save lives," says Carol Rawson, deputy director for traffic operations.

Supersol, a 160-store Israeli supermarket chain, has found that sharing business intelligence with suppliers means fresher goods and fewer products sitting in warehouses. Previously, suppliers had to visit stores and eyeball what was sitting on the shelves or call a Supersol purchasing manager to find out what to deliver.

Now 10 key suppliers check stocks by tapping into Supersol's inventory data warehouse to learn what the supermarket chain has in its Tel Aviv distribution center. The data warehouse is built on NCR's Teradata system with Panorama Software's business intelligence software for accessing and analyzing information. When suppliers can see inventory data, it's easier to eliminate out-of-stocks and overstocking. "The transparency of information is good for both sides," CIO Isaac Shefer says.

Similarly, ArvinMeritor Inc., which manufactures car parts for automakers, service companies such as Midas and Meinke, and retailers like AutoZone, has used an extranet for about 18 months to make production schedules and inventory data available to its suppliers. They check inventory levels of the materials they supply to ArvinMeritor and consult production schedules to anticipate needs.

"They have access to weekly and monthly data on what we plan to produce," says CIO and senior VP Perry Lipe. "That information is extremely key to them. It's one reason why our plants are on schedule and able to meet production forecasts. In addition to helping the just-in-time manufacturing model succeed, making data available to suppliers takes excess inventory out of the supply chain and reduces costs."

"Back in Texas, the Department of Transportation is planning to make the Crash Records Information System available to the public and insurance company representatives who want copies of accident reports," says Catherine Cioffi, Crash Records Information System's project manager. The extranet also will be used to alert local law-enforcement agencies where speeding and drunken-driving offenses occur with greater frequency. Business intelligence extranets, says deputy director for traffic operations Rawson, "help us all do our jobs better."

Source: Adapted from Charles Babcock, "Collaboration Speeds Information," *InformationWeek*, January 24, 2005.

SECTION II	# Telecommunications Network Alternatives

Telecommunications Alternatives

Telecommunications is a highly technical, rapidly changing field of information systems technology. Most business professionals do not need a detailed knowledge of its technical characteristics. However, it is necessary that you understand some of the important characteristics of the basic components of telecommunications networks. This understanding will help you participate effectively in decision making regarding telecommunications alternatives.

Read the Real World Case 2 about the impacts of videoconferencing applications on healthcare. We can learn a lot about the value of network-enabled applications from this case. See Figure 6.10.

A Telecommunications Network Model

Figure 6.11 outlines key telecommunications component categories and examples. Remember, a basic understanding and appreciation, not a detailed knowledge, is sufficient for most business professionals.

Before we begin our discussion of telecommunications network alternatives, we should understand the basic components of a telecommunications network. Generally, a *communications network* is any arrangement in which a *sender* transmits a message to a *receiver* over a *channel* consisting of some type of *medium*. Figure 6.12 illustrates a simple conceptual model of a telecommunications network, which shows that it consists of five basic categories of components:

- **Terminals,** such as networked personal computers, network computers, or information appliances. Any input/output device that uses telecommunications networks to transmit or receive data is a terminal, including telephones and the various computer terminals that were discussed in Chapter 3.

- **Telecommunications processors,** which support data transmission and reception between terminals and computers. These devices, such as modems, switches, and routers, perform a variety of control and support functions in a telecommunications network. For example, they convert data from digital to analog and back, code and decode data, and control the speed, accuracy, and efficiency of the communications flow between computers and terminals in a network.

- **Telecommunications channels** over which data are transmitted and received. Telecommunications channels may use combinations of **media,** such as copper wires, coaxial cables, or fiber-optic cables, or use wireless systems like microwave, communications satellite, radio, and cellular systems to interconnect the other components of a telecommunications network.

- **Computers** of all sizes and types are interconnected by telecommunications networks so that they can carry out their information processing assignments. For example, a mainframe computer may serve as a *host computer* for a large network, assisted by a midrange computer serving as a *front-end processor,* while a microcomputer may act as a *network server* in a small network.

- **Telecommunications control software** consists of programs that control telecommunications activities and manage the functions of telecommunications networks. Examples include network management programs of all kinds, such as *telecommunications monitors* for mainframe host computers, *network operating systems* for network servers, and *Web browsers* for microcomputers.

No matter how large and complex real-world telecommunications networks may appear to be, these five basic categories of network components must be at work to support an organization's telecommunications activities. This is the conceptual framework you can use to help you understand the various types of telecommunications networks in use today.

REAL WORLD CASE 2

Brain Saving Technologies, Inc. and the T-Health Institute: Medicine through Videoconferencing

On average, every 45 seconds, someone in the United States suffers a stroke, the third-leading cause of death as well as the leading cause of permanent disability in the nation, according to the American Heart Association.

The first three hours after a stroke are critical to a patient's survival and recovery. For instance, depending on the type of stroke suffered by a patient, certain drugs can vastly improve the patient's survival and chances for full rehabilitation. Those same drugs, however, can be deadly if given to a patient suffering another type of stroke. Due in part to a shortage of specialty physicians trained to accurately diagnose and treat stroke victims, not all U.S. hospitals have the expertise and equipment to optimally care for stroke patients, particularly in the critical early hours.

The new Neuro Critical Care Center, operated by Brain Saving Technologies Inc. in Wellesley Hills, Massachusetts, will begin to connect emergency-room doctors at a number of suburban hospitals in the state with a remote university hospital that will act as a 'hub' with on-call critical-care neurologists who can assist in making remote diagnoses and treatment recommendations for suspected stroke patients, says Stuart Bernstein, CEO and chief operating officer at Brain Saving Technologies. The connection occurs through a visual-communication workstation that can connect via IP, high-bandwidth communications, or private leased line. The workstation allows the remote specialists to examine and talk to patients, and collaborate with on-site doctors to improve timely diagnosis of strokes and optimize treatment options, Bernstein says.

FIGURE 6.10

Information technology is changing the way medicine works by bringing remote patients and doctors together.

Source: Kevin Maloney/*The New York Times*/Redux.

"Our purpose is to provide member hospitals with a major hospital stroke center, 24 by 7," Bernstein says. CT scans—digital images of patient's brains—can also be transmitted from the member hospitals to the Neuro Critical Care Center specialists to improve diagnosis of the patients, he says. The images are seen simultaneously by doctors at both locations so that they can collaborate. The technology can also help train emergency-room doctors about what characteristics to look for on the CT scans of stroke patients.

A key component of the Neuro Critical Care Center's offering is the Intern Tele-HealthCare Solution from Tandberg, which provides simultaneous audio and video transmission and bidirectional videoconferencing and image-display capabilities to hub and member hospital doctors. Emergency-room doctors can wheel the mobile Tandberg system to patients' bedsides, Bernstein says.

Tandberg's medical video-communication products are also used in other telehealth applications, including situations where doctors need an expert in sign language or a foreign language to communicate with patients or their family members, says Joe D'Iorio, Tandberg's manager of telehealth. "The technology provides real-time visibility and collaboration to help assess patients' well-being and facilitate real-time interaction," he notes.

Doctors have long had a tradition of holding "grand rounds" to discuss patient cases and educate aspiring physicians. The centuries-old practice certainly has its merits, but medical leaders in Arizona want to improve, update, and broaden it to include a larger list of health care practitioners, such as nurses and social workers, regardless of their locations. So the Arizona Telemedicine Program (ATP) drew on its extensive use of videoconferencing equipment to develop the Institute for Advanced Telemedicine and Telehealth, or the T-Health Institute, to facilitate a 21st-century way of teaching and collaborating across disciplines and professions.

"Its specific mission is to use technology to permit interdisciplinary team training," explains Dr. Ronald Weinstein, cofounder and director of the ATP. "Now we're opening it up to a far broader range of participants and patients." The T-Health Institute is a division of the ATP, which Arizona lawmakers established in 1996 as a semiautonomous entity. The ATP operates the Arizona Telemedicine Network, a statewide broadband health care telecommunications network that links 55 independent health care organizations in 71 communities.

Through this network, telemedicine services are provided in 60 subspecialties, including internal medicine, surgery, psychiatry, radiology, and pathology, by dozens of service providers. More than 600,000 patients have received services over the network.

Project leaders say the goal is to create much-needed discussion and collaboration among professionals in multiple health care disciplines so that they can deliver the best care to patients.

"It's the effort to be inclusive," Weinstein says. "Medicine is quite closed and quite limited, but we're counting on telecommunications to bridge some of those communication gaps." The institute is essentially a teleconferencing hub that enables students, professors, and working professionals to participate in live meetings. Its technology also allows them to switch nearly instantly between different discussion groups as easily as they could if they were meeting in person and merely switching chairs.

Gail Barker has noticed that participants who don't speak up during in-person meetings often become much more active in discussions held via videoconferencing. Perhaps it's because they feel less intimidated when they're not physically surrounded by others or because the videoconferencing screen provides a buffer against criticism, says Barker, who is director of the T-Health Institute and a teacher at the University of Arizona's College of Public Health.

When used poorly, videoconferencing can be stiff and dull, just a talking head beaming out across cyberspace without any chance to engage the audience. But Barker and others are finding that when the technology is used in a thoughtful and deliberate manner, it has some advantages over real-life sessions because of its ability to draw more participants into the fray.

"It's literally a new method of teaching medical students. It's a novel approach," says Jim Mauger, director of engineering at Audio Video Resources Inc., a Phoenix-based company hired to design and install the videoconferencing equipment for the T-Health Institute.

The T-Health Institute uses a Tandberg 1500 videoconferencing system, and its video wall has 12 50-inch Toshiba P503DL DLP Datawall RPU Video Cubes. The video wall itself is controlled by a Jupiter Fusion 960 Display Wall Processor utilizing dual Intel Xeon processors. The Fusion 960 allows the wall to display fully movable and scalable images from multiple PC, video, and network sources.

Although Weinstein was able to articulate this vision of interprofessional interaction—that is, he could clearly lay out the user requirements—implementing the technology to support it brought challenges, IT workers say.

Mauger says creating a videoconferencing system that linked multiple sites in one video wall wasn't the challenging part. The real challenge was developing the technology that allows facilitators to move participants into separate virtual groups and then seamlessly switch them around.

"The biggest challenges to making this work were the audio isolation among the separate conference participants as well as fast dynamics of switching video and moving participants to meetings," he explains. He says his team also encountered other challenges—ones that affect more typical IT projects, such as budget constraints, the need to get staffers in different cities to collaborate, and the task of translating user requirements into actionable items. "It's necessary to have someone there on-site who understands all the complex parts of the project," he says. "Someone who is not just meeting with people every now and then, but someone who works with them on a daily basis."

Barker, who teaches in the College of Public Health at the University of Arizona and is a user of the system, led a trial-run training session at the T-Health amphitheater. She met with 13 people, including a clinical pharmacist, two family nurse practitioners, a senior business developer, two program coordinators, a diabetes program case manager, and an A/V telemedicine specialist. For that event, Barker says the biggest benefit was the time saved by having the facility in place; without the T-Health Institute, some participants would have had to make a four-hour round trip to attend in person.

Now the system is opening up to others in Arizona's health care and medical education communities. T-Health Institute officials say they see this as the first step toward a health care system that truly teaches its practitioners to work together across professional disciplines so that they can deliver the best, most efficient care possible.

"We think," Weinstein says, "that this is the only way you're going to create coordinated health care."

Source: Adapted from Marianne Kolbasuk McGee, "Telemedicine Improving Stroke Patients' Survival and Recovery Rates," *InformationWeek*, May 11, 2005; and Mary K. Pratt, "Audiovisual Technology Enhances Physician Education," *Computerworld*, February 16, 2009.

CASE STUDY QUESTIONS

1. From the perspective of a patient, how would you feel about being diagnosed by a doctor who could be hundreds or thousands of miles away from you? What kind of expectations or concerns would you have about that kind of experience?

2. What other professions, aside from health care and education, could benefit from application of some of the technologies discussed in the case? How would they derive business value from these projects? Develop two proposals.

3. The deployment of IT in the health professions is still very much in its infancy. What other uses of technology could potentially improve the quality of health care? Brainstorm several alternatives.

REAL WORLD ACTIVITIES

1. Technology enhances the ability of educational institutes to reach students across geographic boundaries. One recent development in this area is YouTube EDU. Go online to check out the site and prepare a report summarizing its objectives, the kind of content available there, and how it could be used to support traditional modes of education delivery, such as lectures.

2. If widely adopted, these technologies could conceivably lead to a concentration of specialists in a small number of "hub" institutions, essentially creating a two-tier health care system. Do you believe this would lead to an increase or decrease in the availability of these professionals for patients? What could be the positive and negative consequences of this development? Break into small groups with your classmates to discuss these issues.

FIGURE 6.11
Key telecommunications network component categories and examples.

Network Alternative	Examples of Alternatives
Networks	Internet, intranet, extranet, wide area, local area, client/server, network computing, peer-to-peer
Media	Twisted-pair wire, coaxial cable, fiber optics, microwave radio, communications satellites, cellular and PCS systems, wireless mobile and LAN systems
Processors	Modems, multiplexers, switches, routers, hubs, gateways, front-end processors, private branch exchanges
Software	Network operating systems, telecommunications monitors, Web browsers, middleware
Channels	Analog/digital, switched/nonswitched, circuit/message/packet/cell switching, bandwidth alternatives
Topology/Architecture	Star, ring, and bus topologies, OSI and TCP/IP architectures and protocols

Types of Telecommunications Networks

Many different types of networks serve as the telecommunications infrastructure for the Internet and the intranets and extranets of internetworked enterprises. However, from an end user's point of view, there are only a few basic types, such as wide area and local area networks and client/server, network computing, and peer-to-peer networks.

Wide Area Networks

Telecommunications networks covering a large geographic area are called wide area networks (WANs). Networks that cover a large city or metropolitan area (*metropolitan area networks*) can also be included in this category. Such large networks have become a necessity for carrying out the day-to-day activities of many business and government organizations and their end users. For example, WANs are used by many multinational companies to transmit and receive information among their employees, customers, suppliers, and other organizations across cities, regions, countries, and the world. Figure 6.13 illustrates an example of a global wide area network for a major multinational corporation.

Metropolitan Area Networks

When a wide area network optimized a specific geographical area, it is referred to as a **metropolitan area network** (MAN). Such networks can range from several blocks of buildings to entire cities. MANs can also depend on communications channels of moderate-to-high data rates. A MAN might be owned and operated by a single organization, but it usually will be used by many individuals and organizations. MANs might also be owned and operated as public utilities. Your local cable provider or a

FIGURE 6.12
The five basic components in a telecommunications network: (1) terminals, (2) telecommunications processors, (3) telecommunications channels, (4) computers, and (5) telecommunications software.

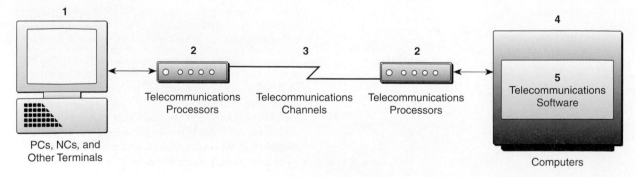

| 1 | 2 | 3 | 2 | 4 |
| PCs, NCs, and Other Terminals | Telecommunications Processors | Telecommunications Channels | Telecommunications Processors | 5 Telecommunications Software / Computers |

FIGURE 6.13   A global wide area network (WAN): the Chevron MPI (Multi-Protocol Internetwork).

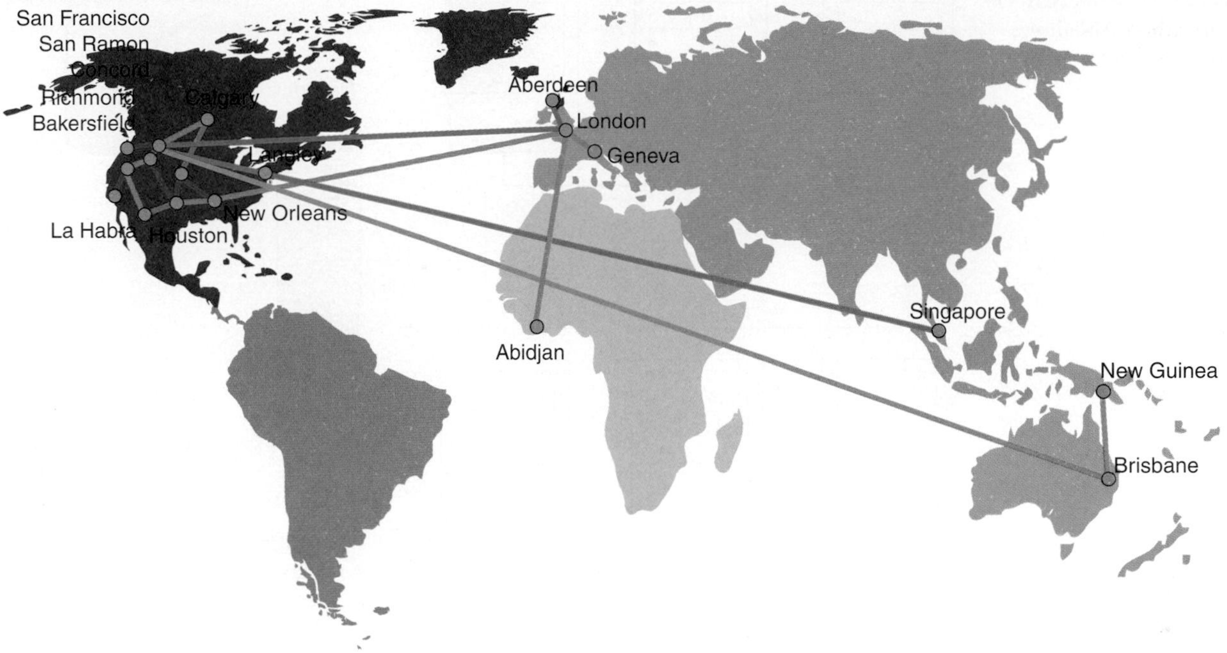

Source: Courtesy of Cisco Systems Inc.

local telephone company is probably operating on a MAN. MANs will often provide means for internetworking of local area networks.

Local Area Networks

Local area networks (LANs) connect computers and other information processing devices within a limited physical area, such as an office, classroom, building, manufacturing plant, or other worksite. LANs have become commonplace in many organizations for providing telecommunications network capabilities that link end users in offices, departments, and other workgroups.

LANs use a variety of telecommunications media, such as ordinary telephone wiring, coaxial cable, or even wireless radio and infrared systems, to interconnect microcomputer workstations and computer peripherals. To communicate over the network, each PC usually has a circuit board called a *network interface card*. Most LANs use a more powerful microcomputer with a large hard disk capacity, called a *file server* or **network server,** that contains a **network operating system** program that controls telecommunications and the use and sharing of network resources. For example, it distributes copies of common data files and software packages to the other microcomputers in the network and controls access to shared laser printers and other network peripherals. See Figure 6.14.

Virtual Private Networks

Many organizations use virtual private networks (VPNs) to establish secure intranets and extranets. A virtual private network is a secure network that uses the Internet as its main *backbone network* but relies on network firewalls, encryption, and other security features of its Internet and intranet connections and those of participating organizations. Thus, for example, VPNs would enable a company to use the Internet to establish secure intranets between its distant branch offices and manufacturing plants and secure extranets between itself and its business customers and suppliers. Figure 6.15 illustrates a VPN in which network routers serve as firewalls to screen Internet traffic between two companies. We will discuss firewalls, encryption, and other network security features in Chapter 13. For the time being, we can think of a VPN as a pipe

FIGURE 6.14

A local area network (LAN). Note how the LAN allows users to share hardware, software, and data resources.

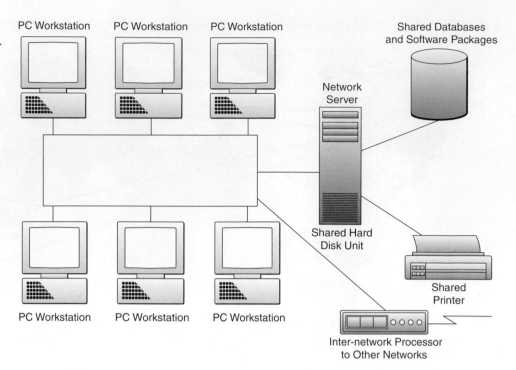

traveling through the Internet. Through this pipe, we can send and receive our data without anyone outside the pipe being able to see or access our transmissions. Using this approach, we can "create" a private network without incurring the high cost of a separate proprietary connection scheme. Let's look at a real-world example about the use of VPN to secure remote and wireless access to sensitive data.

FIGURE 6.15

An example of a virtual private network protected by network firewalls.

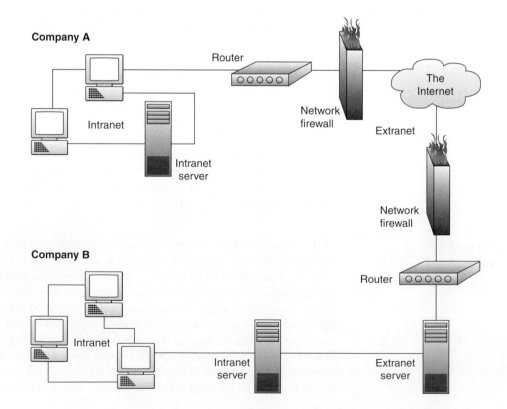

Wireless VPNs: Alternatives for Secure Remote Access

Road warriors wirelessly connect to the corporate network from hot spots at airports or coffee outlets. Just a few years ago, nightmare stories were common of even casual bystanders being able to eavesdrop on corporate communications made in such circumstances. As a result, there's a widespread acceptance that VPNs are pretty much de rigueur for wireless use on the road.

Fast-growing, New York–based Castle Brands uses a PPTP-based VPN—having first weighed open-source and proprietary VPNs. "We tried to keep the cost down, without compromising security," says director of IT Andre Preoteasa. "Throw in the up-front cost of some VPNs, the additional hardware, license fees and yearly support costs, and costs soon climb. With PPTP, if you've got Windows XP, you pretty much have it."

Initial access to the network is password-based, explains Preoteasa, with subsequent access control following role-based rules maintained on the server in the form of Microsoft Active Directory. "People can't just go anywhere and open up anything; the accounting guys get accounting access while the sales guys don't," he says.

At London-based law firm Lawrence Graham, a combination of tokenless, two-factor authentication techniques help ensure secure remote VPN wireless access, says the firm's IT director Jason Petrucci.

"When lawyers log on to the system remotely from a laptop, they are presented with three authentication boxes: one for their username, one for their log-on password and the last for their combined personal PIN code and passcode," he says. "SecurEnvoy is used to manage and deliver this passcode by preloading three one-time passcodes within a text message, which is delivered to the user's BlackBerry."

As passcodes are used, replacements are automatically sent to each lawyer's BlackBerry. "Our lawyers carry BlackBerrys with them wherever they go. A physical token inevitably runs the risk of being left behind or lost altogether."

Meanwhile, at Fortune 50 insurance company MetLife, protecting against data leakage—especially in respect of client information—is of paramount importance when enabling remote wireless access, says Jesus Montano, assistant vice president of enterprise security.

"The challenge is balancing people's access requirements with our overall security requirements, and then working with them to find ways of creating an effective solution without compromising security," he says.

For wireless access from airports and coffee outlets, he explains, these days that means access via VPN vendor Check Point, solely from MetLife-owned laptops, with logons protected by RSA "hard token"–based, two-factor authentication. In addition to the encryption built into the VPN, all the data on the laptop is protected, he adds.

"All wireless traffic is encrypted; the devices are encrypted and wrapped around with a firewall," stresses Montano. "We think we've addressed the most obvious pitfalls in remote access, and think we've got a robust, highly engineered solution."

Source: Adapted from Malcolm Wheatley, "Wireless VPNs Protecting the Wireless Wanderer," *CSO Magazine*, December 15, 2008.

Client/Server Networks

Client/server networks have become the predominant information architecture of enterprisewide computing. In a client/server network, end-user PC or NC workstations are the **clients.** They are interconnected by local area networks and share application processing with network **servers,** which also manage the networks. (This arrangement of clients and servers is sometimes called a *two-tier* client/server architecture.) Local area networks (LANs) are also interconnected to other LANs and wide area networks (WANs) of client workstations and servers. Figure 6.16 illustrates the functions of the computer systems that may be in client/server networks, including optional host systems and superservers.

FIGURE 6.16

The functions of the computer systems in client/server networks.

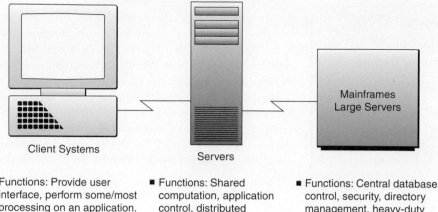

Client Systems

Servers

Mainframes Large Servers

- Functions: Provide user interface, perform some/most processing on an application.

- Functions: Shared computation, application control, distributed databases.

- Functions: Central database control, security, directory management, heavy-duty processing.

A continuing trend is the **downsizing** of larger computer systems by replacing them with client/server networks. For example, a client/server network of several interconnected local area networks may replace a large mainframe-based network with many end-user terminals. This shift typically involves a complex and costly effort to install new application software that replaces the software of older, traditional mainframe-based business information systems, now called legacy systems. Client/server networks are seen as more economical and flexible than legacy systems in meeting end-user, workgroup, and business unit needs and more adaptable in adjusting to a diverse range of computing workloads.

Network Computing

The growing reliance on the computer hardware, software, and data resources of the Internet, intranets, extranets, and other networks has emphasized that, for many users, "the network is the computer." This network computing or *network-centric* concept views networks as the central computing resource of any computing environment.

Figure 6.17 illustrates that in network computing, **network computers** and other *thin clients* provide a browser-based user interface for processing small application programs called *applets*. Thin clients include network computers, Net PCs, and other low-cost network devices or information appliances. Application and database servers provide the operating system, application software, applets, databases, and database

FIGURE 6.17

The functions of the computer systems in network computing.

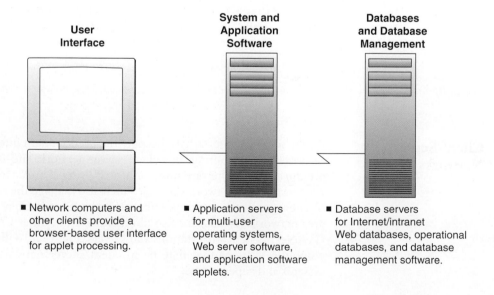

User Interface

System and Application Software

Databases and Database Management

- Network computers and other clients provide a browser-based user interface for applet processing.

- Application servers for multi-user operating systems, Web server software, and application software applets.

- Database servers for Internet/intranet Web databases, operational databases, and database management software.

FIGURE 6.18   The two major forms of peer-to-peer networks.

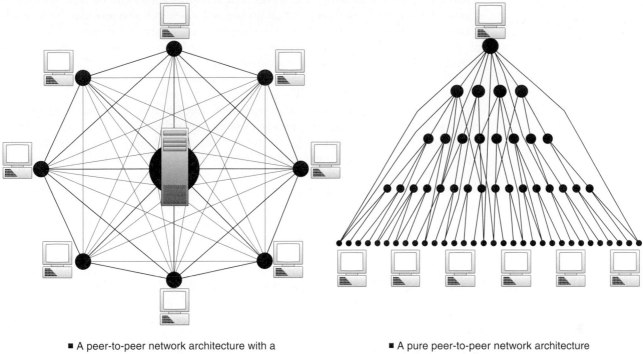

■ A peer-to-peer network architecture with a
directory of all peers on a central server

■ A pure peer-to-peer network architecture
with no central directory server

management software needed by the end users in the network. Network computing is sometimes called a *three-tier* client/server model because it consists of thin clients, application servers, and database servers.

Peer-to-Peer Networks

The emergence of peer-to-peer (P2P) networking technologies and applications for the Internet is being hailed as a development that will have a major impact on e-business and e-commerce and the Internet itself. Whatever the merits of such claims, it is clear that peer-to-peer networks are a powerful telecommunications networking tool for many business applications.

Figure 6.18 illustrates two major models of peer-to-peer networking technology. In the central server architecture, P2P file-sharing software connects your PC to a central server that contains a directory of all of the other users (*peers*) in the network. When you request a file, the software searches the directory for any other users who have that file and are online at that moment. It then sends you a list of user names that are active links to all such users. Clicking on one of these user names prompts the software to connect your PC to that user's PC (making a *peer-to-peer* connection) and automatically transfers the file you want from his or her hard drive to yours.

The *pure* peer-to-peer network architecture has no central directory or server. First, the file-sharing software in the P2P network connects your PC with one of the online users in the network. Then an active link to your user name is transmitted from peer to peer to all the online users in the network that the first user (and the other online users) encountered in previous sessions. In this way, active links to more and more peers spread throughout the network the more it is used. When you request a file, the software searches every online user and sends you a list of active file names related to your request. Clicking on one of these automatically transfers the file from that user's hard drive to yours.

One of the major advantages and limitations of the central server architecture is its reliance on a central directory and server. The directory server can be slowed or overwhelmed by too many users or technical problems. However, it also provides the network with a platform that can better protect the integrity and security of the content and users of the network. Some applications of pure P2P networks, in contrast, have been plagued by slow response times and bogus and corrupted files.

The Internet, as originally conceived in the late 1960s, was a peer-to-peer system. The goal of the original ARPANET (the name of the early version of today's Internet) was to share computing resources around the United States. The challenge for this effort was to integrate different kinds of existing networks, as well as future technologies, with one common network architecture that would allow every host to be an equal player. The first few hosts on the ARPANET (e.g., UCLA and the University of Utah) were already independent computing sites with equal status. The ARPANET connected them together not in a master/slave or client/server relationship, but rather as equal computing peers.

One common use for peer-to-peer networks today is the downloading and trading of files. When the term *peer-to-peer* was used to describe the *Napster* network, it implied that the peer protocol nature was important, but in reality the unique achievement of Napster was the empowerment of the peers (i.e., the fringes of the network) in association with a central index that made it fast and efficient to locate available content. The peer protocol was just a common way to achieve this.

Although much media attention has focused on copyright-infringing uses of file trading networks, there are vast numbers of entirely noninfringing uses. *BitTorrent* was originally designed to keep sites from getting overwhelmed by "flash crowds" and heavy traffic. That makes it very suitable for many situations in which there are massive peaks of demand. Most Linux distributions are released via BitTorrent to help with their bandwidth needs. Another example is *Blizzard Entertainment* (http://www.blizzard.com), which uses a modified version of BitTorrent to distribute patches to its game World of Warcraft (http://www.worldofwarcraft.com). Users have often complained about BitTorrent due to a bandwidth cap that almost defeats its purpose.

Other peer-to-peer networks are emerging as well, such as *PeerCast*, which allows someone to broadcast an Internet radio or television station with very little upstream bandwidth due to its distributed nature. Other peer-to-peer broadcast tools, sometimes called *peer-casting*, include the *IceShare* project and *FreeCast*.

Digital and Analog Signals

We regularly hear the words *analog* and *digital* associated with computers, telephones, and other hardware devices. To be sure you understand exactly what these terms mean, a short discussion may be helpful.

Basically, analog or digital refers to the method used to convert information into an electrical signal. Telephones, microphones, measuring instruments, vinyl record players, CD players, tape decks, computers, fax machines, and so on must convert information into an electrical signal in some manner so that it can be transmitted or processed. For example, a microphone must convert the pressure waves that we call *sound* into a corresponding electrical voltage or current, which can be sent down a telephone line, amplified in a sound system, broadcast on the radio, and/or recorded on some medium.

In an analog system, an electrical voltage or current is generated that is proportional to the quantity being observed. In a digital system, the quantity being observed is expressed as a number. This is really all there is to it, but a few details must still be discussed.

For example, in an electronic analog thermometer, if the temperature being measured is 83 degrees, then the analog system would put out, for example, 83 volts. This level could just as well be 8.3 volts or any other voltage proportional to the temperature. Thus, if the temperature doubled to 166 degrees, the output voltage would double to 166 volts (or perhaps 16.6 volts if the instrument were so scaled). The output voltage is, therefore, "analogous" to the temperature—thus the use of the term *analog*.

In the case of an electronic digital thermometer, however, the output would be the number 83 if the temperature were 83 degrees. Hence it is based on "digits." The only thing wrong with this example is that 83 is a decimal number constructed from the 10 symbols 0, 1, 2, . . ., 8, 9. We commonly use 10 symbols in our numbers for historical reasons; it is probably because we have 10 fingers. It is inconvenient, however, to use 10 symbols to express the output as an electrical voltage. It is much more convenient to have only 2 symbols, 0 and 1. In this case, for example, 0 could be represented by 0 volts, and 1 by 5 volts. Recall from Chapter 3 that this system is known as a binary (only two symbols) number system, but the principle is still the same: The output of the digital thermometer is a number, that is, "digits."

For the thermometer example above, 83 is the binary number 1010011. The electronic thermometer would send the sequence 5 volts, 0 volts, 5 volts, 0 volts, 0 volts, 5 volts, and 5 volts to express the number 83 in binary.

A digital system may seem more complicated than an analog system, but it has a number of advantages. The principal advantage is that once the measurement is expressed in digital form, it can be entered into a computer or a microprocessor and manipulated as desired. If we worked with only analog devices, we would eventually have to convert the output of the analog device into digital form if we wanted to input it into a computer. Because computer networks work primarily with digital signals, most of the hardware used by a computer network is digital.

Telecommunications Media

Telecommunications channels make use of a variety of telecommunications media. These include twisted-pair wire, coaxial cables, and fiber-optic cables, all of which physically link the devices in a network. Also included are terrestrial microwave, communications satellites, cellular phone systems, and packet and LAN radio, all of which use microwave and other radio waves. In addition, there are infrared systems, which use infrared light to transmit and receive data. See Figure 6.19.

FIGURE 6.19 Common telecommunications guided media: (a) twisted-pair wire, (b) coaxial cable, and (c) fiber-optic cable.

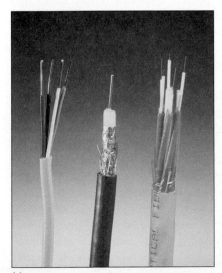

(c)
Source: © Photodisc/PunchStock.

(a)
Source: Phil Degginger/Getty Images.

(b)
Source: Ryan McVay/Getty Images.

Wired Technologies

Twisted-Pair Wire

Ordinary telephone wire, consisting of copper wire twisted into pairs (twisted-pair wire), is the most widely used medium for telecommunications. These lines are used in established communications networks throughout the world for both voice and data transmission. Twisted-pair wiring is wrapped or shielded in a variety of forms and used extensively in home and office telephone systems and many local area networks and wide area networks. Transmission speeds can range from 2 million bits per second (unshielded) to 100 million bits per second (shielded).

Coaxial Cable

Coaxial cable consists of a sturdy copper or aluminum wire wrapped with spacers to insulate and protect it. The cable's cover and insulation minimize interference and distortion of the signals the cable carries. Groups of coaxial cables may be bundled together in a big cable for ease of installation. These high-quality lines can be placed underground and laid on the floors of lakes and oceans. They allow high-speed data transmission (from 200 million to more than 500 million bits per second—200–500 Mbps) and are used instead of twisted-pair wire lines in high-service metropolitan areas, for cable television systems, and for short-distance connections of computers and peripheral devices. Coaxial cables are also used in many office buildings and other worksites for local area networks.

Fiber Optics

Fiber optics uses cables consisting of one or more hair-thin filaments of glass fiber wrapped in a protective jacket. They can conduct pulses of visible light elements (*photons*) generated by lasers at transmission rates as high as trillions of bits per second (terabits per second, or Tbps). This speed is hundreds of times faster than coaxial cable and thousands of times better than twisted-pair wire lines. Fiber-optic cables provide substantial size and weight reductions as well as increased speed and greater carrying capacity. A half-inch-diameter fiber-optic cable can carry more than 500,000 channels, compared with about 5,500 channels for a standard coaxial cable.

Fiber-optic cables are not affected by and do not generate electromagnetic radiation; therefore, multiple fibers can be placed in the same cable. Fiber-optic cables have less need for repeaters for signal retransmissions than copper wire media. Fiber optics also has a much lower data error rate than other media and is harder to tap than electrical wire and cable. Fiber-optic cables have already been installed in many parts of the world, and they are expected to replace other communications media in many applications.

New optical technologies such as *dense wave division multiplexing* (DWDM) can split a strand of glass fiber into 40 channels, which enables each strand to carry 5 million calls. In the future, DWDM technology is expected to split each fiber into 1,000 channels, enabling each strand to carry up to 122 million calls. In addition, newly developed *optical routers* will be able to send optical signals up to 2,500 miles without needing regeneration, thus eliminating the need for repeaters every 370 miles to regenerate signals.

The Problem of "The Last Mile"

While on the subject of telecommunication media, we need to understand a pervasive problem in the telecommunications industry: the problem of the last mile. The last-mile problem, while simple to understand, is still one of the greatest challenges faced by telecommunications providers.

The basic problem goes something like this: The telecommunications provider adopts a new, faster, better technology that can provide higher bandwidths and faster telecommunication speeds to consumers. A good example of this type of situation is the invention of fiber-optic cable and its related optical technologies. Fiber can move data at lightning speed and handle a much larger volume of data than the more typical twisted-pair wiring commonly found in households. So the telecommunications provider completely reengineers the network and begins laying fiber instead of copper wire in trenches. The fiber, costing $500,000 to $1 million per mile, begins bringing all of its faster, better, and cheaper benefits to the front door of the consumer. This is where the last-mile problem begins. Out in front of the house lies enough bandwidth to handle more than 100 million telephone calls or download entire movies in a few seconds. The problem is that the house it is connecting to is wired with twisted-pair wiring that just cannot handle the bandwidth provided by fiber. This situation is analogous to hooking up a garden hose to the water volume generated by Niagara Falls. At the end of the day, the amount of water you get is whatever will come out of the garden hose and nothing more. Therefore, the problem is more than just the cost. In many cases, the wiring in a structure cannot be upgraded and the bandwidth right outside the door just cannot be accessed.

Many methods have been offered to solve the last-mile problem. Cable companies are providing a single-wire solution to many modern households. By using sophisticated technologies, they can bring cable television, Internet access, and telephone services into a home using only the coaxial wire originally put there for cable television. Other solutions include bypassing the old wired network completely and providing high-speed services via a satellite or other wireless approach. Regardless of the solution, the problem of the last mile is still very much an issue to consider when designing a telecommunications network.

Although still in the developmental stages, one solution to the last mile problem may be **WiMax.** Defined as *Worldwide Interoperability for Microwave Access*, WiMax is intended to provide high-speed, mobile telecommunications services to diverse Internet connections and locations. There are still many issues to work out regarding WiMax, but it looks like we may be able to solve the problem of last mile connectivity somewhere in the near future.

Wireless Technologies

Wireless telecommunications technologies rely on radio wave, microwave, infrared, and visible light pulses to transport digital communications without wires between communications devices. Wireless technologies include terrestrial microwave, communications satellites, cellular and PCS telephone and pager systems, mobile data radio, wireless LANs, and various wireless Internet technologies. Each technology utilizes specific ranges within the electromagnetic spectrum (in megahertz) of electromagnetic frequencies that are specified by national regulatory agencies to minimize interference and encourage efficient telecommunications. Let's briefly review some of these major wireless communications technologies.

Terrestrial Microwave

Terrestrial microwave involves earthbound microwave systems that transmit high-speed radio signals in a line-of-sight path between relay stations spaced approximately 30 miles apart. Microwave antennas are usually placed on top of buildings, towers, hills, and mountain peaks, and they are a familiar sight in many sections of the country. They are still a popular medium for both long-distance and metropolitan area networks.

Communications Satellites

Communications satellites also use microwave radio as their telecommunications medium. Typically, high-earth orbit (HEO) communications satellites are placed in stationary geosynchronous orbits approximately 22,000 miles above the equator. Satellites are powered by solar panels and can transmit microwave signals at a rate of several hundred million bits per second. They serve as relay stations for communications signals transmitted from earth stations. Earth stations use dish antennas to beam microwave signals to the satellites that amplify and retransmit the signals to other earth stations thousands of miles away.

Whereas communications satellites were used initially for voice and video transmission, they are now also used for high-speed transmission of large volumes of data. Because of time delays caused by the great distances involved, they are not suitable for interactive, real-time processing. Communications satellite systems are operated by several firms, including Comsat, American Mobile Satellite, and Intellsat.

Various other satellite technologies are being implemented to improve global business communications. For example, many companies use networks of small satellite dish antennas known as VSAT (very small aperture terminal) to connect their stores and distant worksites via satellite. Other satellite networks use many low-earth orbit (LEO) satellites orbiting at an altitude of only 500 miles above the earth. Companies like Globalstar offer wireless phone, paging, and messaging services to users anywhere on the globe. Let's look at a real-world example.

Nevada Department of Corrections: The Case for Satellite Networks

Faced with extremely remote desert locations and a complete lack of network infrastructure across the stark landscape, IT workers with the Nevada Department of Corrections needed to connect 24 prison facilities around the state.

Their initial plan seemed simple: Deploy a new, Web-based prison management application to all 24 prison facilities to replace a 20-year-old DOS screen application. After researching options, the IT team eventually settled on a satellite-based network combined with a key add-on: WAN acceleration appliances from Blue Coat Systems Inc. that could drastically reduce debilitating delays in transmitting data to a satellite and then back to Earth.

Once the system is up and running, inmate information can be kept up to date around the clock. With the old system, data could be as much as 72 hours old, a potential security issue. The hard part was cobbling together a network that allowed NOTIS (the Nevada Offender Tracking Information System) to function properly. With an almost one-second delay in each direction for every single element on a Web page, load times were unacceptable. Opening a Web page "could take you minutes," says Dan O'Barr, infrastructure architect for the corrections department. "With a real-time application, it would completely break it—it will fall apart. It was essentially unusable." The satellite system was the only workable option, but data transmission delays threw a wrench into the rollout. "They're extremely remote areas—there's a whole lot of nothing in every direction there," O'Barr says of the state's prisons. "T1 was not a possibility, regardless of money. There was no other technology available to link them."

IT workers in the department began to search the Internet for answers and discovered WAN acceleration vendors, including Blue Coat in Seattle. The Blue Coat SG appliances, which securely accelerate the delivery of corporate applications while reducing bandwidth usage, initially dropped the satellite delay to under eight seconds for each Web page, O'Barr says.

The Blue Coat technology also gives the Nevada prison system another option in the future: the ability to enable acceleration for mobile devices without added expenses, says Robert Whiteley of Forrester Research. "The killer in satellite networks is latency, the delay it takes to transfer data," he says. "Blue Coat accelerates it and makes it work."

Source: Adapted from Todd Weiss, "Nevada Prison Looks to WAN Acceleration for IT Upgrade," *Computerworld*, May 29, 2007.

Cellular and PCS Systems

Cellular and PCS telephone and pager systems use several radio communications technologies. However, all of them divide a geographic area into small areas, or *cells*, typically from one to several square miles in area. Each cell has its own low-power transmitter or radio relay antenna device to relay calls from one cell to another. Computers and other communications processors coordinate and control the transmissions to and from mobile users as they move from one area to another.

Cellular phone systems have long used analog communications technologies operating at frequencies in the 800–900 MHz cellular band. Newer cellular systems use digital technologies, which provide greater capacity and security, and additional services such as voice mail, paging, messaging, and caller ID. These capabilities are also available with PCS (personal communications services) phone systems. PCS operates at 1,900 MHz frequencies using digital technologies that are related to digital cellular. However, PCS phone systems cost substantially less to operate and use than cellular systems and have lower power consumption requirements.

Wireless LANs

Wiring an office or a building for a local area network is often a difficult and costly task. Older buildings frequently do not have conduits for coaxial cables or additional twisted-pair wire, and the conduits in newer buildings may not have enough room to pull additional wiring through. Repairing mistakes in and damage to wiring is often difficult and costly, as are major relocations of LAN workstations and other components. One solution to such problems is installing a wireless LAN using one of several wireless technologies. Examples include a high-frequency radio technology similar to digital cellular and a low-frequency radio technology called *spread spectrum*.

The use of wireless LANs is growing rapidly as new high-speed technologies are implemented. A prime example is a new open-standard wireless radio-wave technology technically known as IEEE 802.11b, or more popularly as Wi-Fi (for wireless fidelity). Wi-Fi is faster (11 Mbps) and less expensive than standard Ethernet and other common wire-based LAN technologies. Thus, Wi-Fi wireless LANs enable laptop PCs, PDAs, and other devices with Wi-Fi modems to connect easily to the Internet and other networks in a rapidly increasing number of business, public, and home environments. A faster version (802.11g) with speeds of 54 Mbps promises to make this technology even more widely used. By December 2009, the newest version 802.11n is expected to be finalized. This new standard offers speeds of up to 108 Mbps.

Bluetooth

A short-range wireless technology called Bluetooth is rapidly being built into computers and other devices. Bluetooth serves as a cable-free wireless connection to peripheral devices such as computer printers and scanners. Operating at approximately 1 Mbps with an effective range from 10 to 100 meters, Bluetooth promises to change significantly the way we use computers and other telecommunication devices.

To appreciate fully the potential value of Bluetooth, look around the space where you have your computer. You have your keyboard connected to the computer, as well as a printer, pointing device, monitor, and so on. What joins these together are their associated cables. Cables have become the bane of many offices and homes. Many of us have experienced trying to figure out what cable goes where and getting tangled up in the details. Bluetooth essentially aims to fix this; it is a cable-replacement technology.

Conceived initially by Ericsson and later adopted by a myriad of other companies, Bluetooth is a standard for a small, cheap radio chip to be plugged into computers, printers, mobile phones, and so forth. A Bluetooth chip is designed to replace cables by taking the information normally carried by the cable and transmitting it at a special frequency to a receiver Bluetooth chip, which will then give the information received to the computer, telephone, printer, or other Bluetooth device. Given its fairly low cost to implement, Bluetooth is set to revolutionize telecommunications.

The Wireless Web

Wireless access to the Internet, intranets, and extranets is growing as more Web-enabled information appliances proliferate. Smart telephones, pagers, PDAs, and other portable communications devices have become *very thin clients* in wireless networks. Agreement on a standard *wireless application protocol* (WAP) has encouraged the development of many wireless Web applications and services. The telecommunications industry continues to work on *third-generation* (3G) wireless technologies whose goal is to raise wireless transmission speeds to enable streaming video and multimedia applications on mobile devices.

For example, the Smartphone, a PCS phone, can send and receive e-mail and provide Web access via a "Web clipping" technology that generates custom-designed Web pages from many popular financial, securities, travel, sport, entertainment, and e-commerce

FIGURE 6.20 The Wireless Application Protocol (WAP) architecture for wireless Internet services to mobile information appliances.

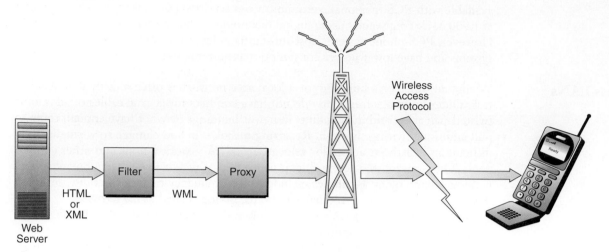

Web sites. Another example is the Sprint PCS Wireless Web phone, which delivers similar Web content and e-mail services via a Web-enabled PCS phone.

Figure 6.20 illustrates the wireless application protocol that is the foundation of wireless mobile Internet and Web applications. The WAP standard specifies how Web pages in HTML or XML are translated into a *wireless markup language* (WML) by *filter* software and preprocessed by *proxy* software to prepare the Web pages for wireless transmission from a Web server to a Web-enabled wireless device.

UPS: Wireless LANs and M-Commerce

UPS is a global company with one of the most recognized and admired brand names in the world. It has become the world's largest package delivery company and a leading global provider of specialized transportation and logistics services. Every day UPS manages the flow of goods, funds, and information in more than 200 countries and territories worldwide. A technology-driven company, UPS has more than 260,000 PCs, 6,200 servers, 2,700 midrange computers, and 14 mainframes. This technology infrastructure is in place to handle the delivery and pickup of more than 3.4 billion packages and documents per year, as well as the 115 million hits per day on its Web site, of which more than 9 million hits are tracking requests.

To manage all this mobile commerce (m-commerce) information, Atlanta-based UPS uses wireless as part of UPScan, a companywide, global initiative to streamline and standardize all scanning hardware and software used in its package distribution centers. For package tracking, UPScan consolidates multiple scanning applications into one wireless LAN application while it maintains interfaces with critical control and repository systems.

UPScan uses Bluetooth, a short-range wireless networking protocol for communications with cordless peripherals (such as ring-mounted wireless manual scanners) linked to wireless LANs, which communicate with corporate systems. UPS has also developed application programming interfaces (APIs) in-house to link its legacy tracking systems to business customers, such as retailers who want to provide order status information on their Web sites from UPS to their customers.

Source: Adapted from UPS Corporate Web Site, "About UPS," http://www.ups.com/content/us/en/about/index.html, n.d.; and Dan Farber, "UPS Takes Wireless to the Next Level," ZDNet Tech Update, http://techupdate.zdnet.com/techupdate/stories/main/0,14179,2913461,00.html, February 19, 2007.

Telecommunications Processors

Telecommunications processors such as modems, multiplexers, switches, and routers perform a variety of support functions between the computers and other devices in a telecommunications network. Let's take a look at some of these processors and their functions. See Figure 6.21.

Modems

Modems are the most common type of communications processor. They convert the digital signals from a computer or transmission terminal at one end of a communications link into analog frequencies that can be transmitted over ordinary telephone lines. A modem at the other end of the communications line converts the transmitted data back into digital form at a receiving terminal. This process is known as *modulation* and *demodulation*, and the word *modem* is a combined abbreviation of those two words. Modems come in several forms, including small stand-alone units, plug-in circuit boards, and removable modem cards for laptop PCs. Most modems also support a variety of telecommunications functions, such as transmission error control, automatic dialing and answering, and a faxing capability. As shown in Figure 6.21, a modem is used in the private-home setting to accept the data from the Internet provider and convert it to input for a PC.

Modems are used because ordinary telephone networks were first designed to handle continuous analog signals (electromagnetic frequencies), such as those generated by the human voice over the telephone. Because data from computers are in digital form (voltage pulses), devices are necessary to convert digital signals into appropriate analog transmission frequencies and vice versa. However, digital communications networks that use only digital signals and do not need analog/digital conversion are becoming commonplace. Because most modems also perform a variety of telecommunications support functions, devices called digital modems are still used in digital networks.

FIGURE 6.21   Examples of some of the communications processors involved in an Internet connection.

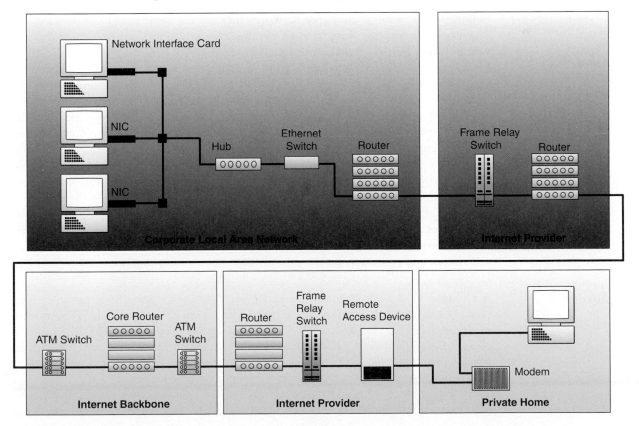

FIGURE 6.22

Comparing modem and telecommunications technologies for Internet and other network access.

Modem (56 Kbps)	DSL (Digital Subscriber Line) Modem
• Receives at 56 Kbps	• Receives at 1.5 Mbps to 5.0 Mbps
• Sends at 33.6 Kbps	• Sends at 128 Kbps to 640 Kbps
• Slowest technology	• Users must be near switching centers
ISDN (Integrated Services Digital Network)	**Cable Modem**
• Sends and receives at 128 Kbps	• Receives at 1.5 Mbps to 20 Mbps
• Users need extra lines	• Sends at 128 Kbps to 2.5 Mbps
• Becoming obsolete	• Speed degrades with many local users
Home Satellite	**Local Microwave**
• Receives at 400 Kbps	• Sends and receives at 512 Kbps to 1.4 Mbps
• Sends via phone modem	• Higher cost
• Slow sending, higher cost	• May require line of sight to base antenna

Figure 6.22 compares several modem and telecommunications technologies for access to the Internet and other networks by home and business users.

Internetwork Processors

Telecommunications networks are interconnected by special-purpose communications processors called internetwork processors, such as switches, routers, hubs, and gateways. A *switch* is a communications processor that makes connections between telecommunications circuits in a network. Switches are now available in managed versions with network management capabilities. A bridge is a device that connects two or more local area networks that use the same communications rules or *protocol*. In contrast, a *router* is an intelligent communications processor that interconnects networks based on different rules or *protocols*, so a telecommunications message can be routed to its destination. A *hub* is a port-switching communications processor. Advanced versions of both hubs and switches provide automatic switching among connections called *ports* for shared access to a network's resources. Workstations, servers, printers, and other network resources are typically connected to ports. Networks that use different communications architectures are interconnected by using a communications processor called a *gateway*. All these devices are essential to providing connectivity and easy access between the multiple LANs and wide area networks that are part of the intranets and client/server networks in many organizations.

Again referring to Figure 6.21, we can see examples of all of these elements. The corporate local area network in the upper left of the figure uses a hub to connect its multiple workstations to the network switch. The switch sends the signals to a series of switches and routers to get the data to their intended destination.

Multiplexers

A multiplexer is a communications processor that allows a single communications channel to carry simultaneous data transmissions from many terminals. This process is accomplished in two basic ways. In *frequency division multiplexing* (FDM), a multiplexer effectively divides a high-speed channel into multiple slow-speed channels. In *time division multiplexing* (TDM), the multiplexer divides the time each terminal can use the high-speed line into very short time slots, or time frames.

For example, if we need to have eight telephone numbers for a small business, we could have eight individual lines come into the building—one for each telephone number. Using a digital multiplexer, however, we can have one line handle all eight telephone numbers (assuming we have an eight-channel multiplexer). Mutliplexers work to increase the number of transmissions possible without increasing the number of physical data channels.

Telecommunications Software

Telecommunications software is a vital component of all telecommunications networks. Telecommunications and network management software may reside in PCs, servers, mainframes, and communications processors like multiplexers and routers. Network servers and other computers in a network use these programs to manage network performance. Network management programs perform functions such as automatically checking client PCs for input/output activity, assigning priorities to data communications requests from clients and terminals, and detecting and correcting transmission errors and other network problems.

For example, mainframe-based wide area networks frequently use *telecommunications monitors* or *teleprocessing* (TP) monitors. The CICS (Customer Identification Control System) for IBM mainframes is a typical example. Servers in local area and other networks frequently rely on *network operating systems* like Novell NetWare or operating systems like UNIX, Linux, or Microsoft Windows 2008 Servers for network management. Many software vendors also offer telecommunications software as *middleware*, which can help diverse networks communicate with one another.

Telecommunications functions built into Microsoft Windows and other operating systems provide a variety of communications support services. For example, they work with a communications processor (such as a modem) to connect and disconnect communications links and to establish communications parameters such as transmission speed, mode, and direction.

Network Management

Network management packages such as network operating systems and telecommunications monitors determine transmission priorities, route (switch) messages, poll terminals in the network, and form waiting lines (queues) of transmission requests. They also detect and correct transmission errors, log statistics of network activity, and protect network resources from unauthorized access. See Figure 6.23.

FIGURE 6.23

Network management software monitors and manages network performance.

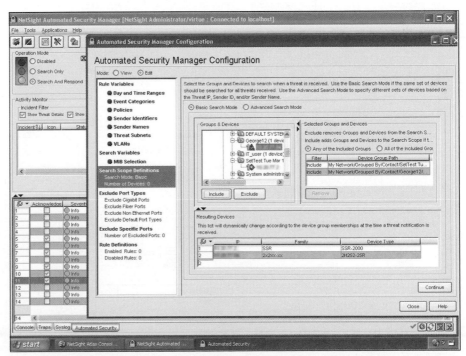

Examples of major **network management** functions include the following:

- **Traffic Management.** Manage network resources and traffic to avoid congestion and optimize telecommunications service levels to users.
- **Security.** Provide security as one of the top concerns of network management today. Telecommunications software must provide authentication, encryption, firewall, and auditing functions, and enforce security policies. Encryption, firewalls, and other network security defenses are covered in Chapter 11.
- **Network Monitoring.** Troubleshoot and watch over the network, informing network administrators of potential problems before they occur.
- **Capacity Planning.** Survey network resources and traffic patterns and users' needs to determine how best to accommodate the needs of the network as it grows and changes.

Network Topologies

There are several basic types of network topologies, or structures, in telecommunications networks. Figure 6.24 illustrates three basic topologies used in wide area and local area telecommunications networks. A *star* network ties end-user computers to a central computer. A *ring* network ties local computer processors together in a ring on a more equal basis. A *bus* network is a network in which local processors share the same bus, or communications channel. A variation of the ring network is the *mesh* network. It uses direct communications lines to connect some or all of the computers in the ring to one another.

Wired networks may use a combination of star, ring, and bus approaches. Obviously, the star network is more centralized, whereas ring and bus networks have a more decentralized approach. However, this is not always the case. For example, the central computer in a star configuration may be acting only as a *switch*, or message-switching computer that handles the data communications between autonomous local

FIGURE 6.24 The ring, star, and bus network topologies.

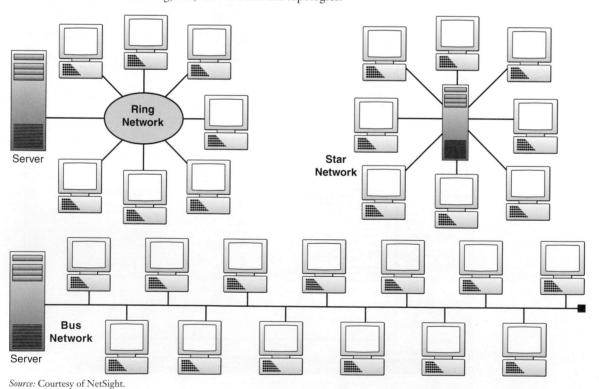

Source: Courtesy of NetSight.

computers. Star, ring, and bus networks differ in their performance, reliability, and cost. A pure star network is considered less reliable than a ring network, because the other computers in the star are heavily dependent on the central host computer. If it fails, there is no backup processing and communications capability, and the local computers are cut off from one another. Therefore, it is essential that the host computer be highly reliable. Having some type of multiprocessor architecture to provide a fault-tolerant capability is a common solution.

Network Architectures and Protocols

Until quite recently, sufficient standards were lacking for the interfaces among the hardware, software, and communications channels of telecommunications networks. This situation hampered the use of telecommunications, increased its costs, and reduced its efficiency and effectiveness. In response, telecommunications manufacturers and national and international organizations have developed standards called *protocols* and master plans called *network architectures* to support the development of advanced data communications networks.

Protocols

A protocol is a standard set of rules and procedures for the control of communications in a network. However, these standards may be limited to just one manufacturer's equipment or just one type of data communications. Part of the goal of communications network architectures is to create more standardization and compatibility among communications protocols. One example of a protocol is a standard for the physical characteristics of the cables and connectors between terminals, computers, modems, and communications lines. Other examples are the protocols that establish the communications control information needed for *handshaking*, which is the process of exchanging predetermined signals and characters to establish a telecommunications session between terminals and computers. Other protocols deal with control of data transmission reception in a network, switching techniques, internetwork connections, and so on.

Network Architectures

The goal of network architectures is to promote an open, simple, flexible, and efficient telecommunications environment, accomplished by the use of standard protocols, standard communications hardware and software interfaces, and the design of a standard multilevel interface between end users and computer systems.

The OSI Model

The Open Systems Interconnection (OSI) model is a standard description or "reference model" for how messages should be transmitted between any two points in a telecommunications network. Its purpose is to guide product implementers so that their products will consistently work with other products. The reference model defines seven layers of functions that take place at each end of a communication. Although OSI is not always strictly adhered to in terms of keeping related functions together in a well-defined layer, many, if not most, products involved in telecommunications make an attempt to describe themselves in relation to the OSI model. It is also valuable as a view of communication that furnishes a common ground for education and discussion.

Developed by representatives of major computer and telecommunication companies beginning in 1983, OSI was originally intended to be a detailed specification of interfaces. Instead, the committee decided to establish a common reference model for which others could develop detailed interfaces that in turn could become standards. OSI was officially adopted as an international standard by the International Organization of Standards (ISO).

The main idea in OSI is that the process of communication between two endpoints in a telecommunication network can be divided into layers, with each layer adding its own set of special, related functions. Each communicating user or program is at a computer equipped with these seven layers of functions. So in a given message between users, there will be a flow of data through each layer at one end down through the layers in that computer; at the other end, when the message arrives, there will be another flow of data up through the layers in the receiving computer and ultimately to the end user or program. The actual programming and hardware that furnishes these seven layers of functions is usually a combination of the computer operating system, applications (e.g., your Web browser), TCP/IP or alternative transport and network protocols, and the software and hardware that enable you to put a signal on one of the lines attached to your computer.

OSI divides telecommunication into seven layers. Figure 6.25 illustrates the functions of the seven layers of the OSI model architecture.

The layers consist of two groups. The upper four layers are used whenever a message passes to or from a user. The lower three layers (up to the network layer) are used when any message passes through the host computer. Messages intended for this computer pass to the upper layers. Messages destined for some other host are not passed to the upper layers but are forwarded to another host. The seven layers are:

> **Layer 1: The physical layer.** This layer conveys the bit stream through the network at the electrical and mechanical level. It provides the hardware means of sending and receiving data on a carrier.
>
> **Layer 2: The data link layer.** This layer provides synchronization for the physical level and does bit-stuffing for strings of 1's in excess of 5. It furnishes transmission protocol knowledge and management.
>
> **Layer 3: The network layer.** This layer handles the routing of the data (sending it in the right direction to the right destination on outgoing transmissions and

FIGURE 6.25 The seven layers of the OSI communications network architecture, and the five layers of the Internet's TCP/IP protocol suite.

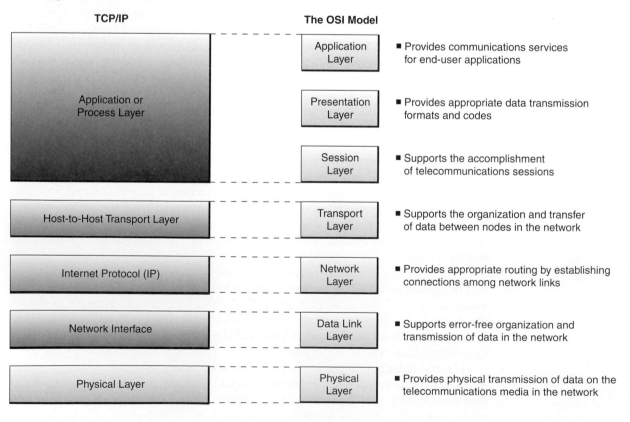

TCP/IP		The OSI Model	
Application or Process Layer		Application Layer	■ Provides communications services for end-user applications
		Presentation Layer	■ Provides appropriate data transmission formats and codes
		Session Layer	■ Supports the accomplishment of telecommunications sessions
Host-to-Host Transport Layer		Transport Layer	■ Supports the organization and transfer of data between nodes in the network
Internet Protocol (IP)		Network Layer	■ Provides appropriate routing by establishing connections among network links
Network Interface		Data Link Layer	■ Supports error-free organization and transmission of data in the network
Physical Layer		Physical Layer	■ Provides physical transmission of data on the telecommunications media in the network

receiving incoming transmissions at the packet level). The network layer does routing and forwarding.

Layer 4: The transport layer. This layer manages the end-to-end control (e.g., determining whether all packets have arrived) and error-checking. It ensures complete data transfer.

Layer 5: The session layer. This layer sets up, coordinates, and terminates conversations, exchanges, and dialogues between the applications at each end. It deals with session and connection coordination.

Layer 6: The presentation layer. This layer, usually part of an operating system, converts incoming and outgoing data from one presentation format to another (e.g., from a text stream into a pop-up window with the newly arrived text). It's sometimes called the syntax layer.

Layer 7: The application layer. At this layer, communication partners are identified, quality of service is identified, user authentication and privacy are considered, and any constraints on data syntax are identified. (This layer is *not* the application itself, although some applications may perform application layer functions.)

The Internet's TCP/IP

The Internet uses a system of telecommunications protocols that has become so widely used that it is now accepted as a network architecture. The Internet's protocol suite is called **Transmission Control Protocol/Internet Protocol** and is known as TCP/IP. As Figure 6.25 shows, TCP/IP consists of five layers of protocols that can be related to the seven layers of the OSI architecture. TCP/IP is used by the Internet and by all intranets and extranets. Many companies and other organizations are thus converting their client/server and wide area networks to TCP/IP technology, which are now commonly called IP networks.

Although many of the technical aspects of the Internet can appear quite complex, the addressing, routing, and transport protocols, which make sure you get to the right Web site or your e-mail is delivered to the right place, are actually elegantly simple. TCP/IP can be thought of as analogous to how the postal system finds your house and delivers your mail. In this analogy, TCP represents the postal system and the various processes and protocols used to move the mail, while IP represents the zip code and address.

The current IP addressing protocol is called IPv4. When IP was first standardized in September 1981, the specification required that each system attached to the Internet be assigned a unique, 32-bit Internet address value. Systems that have interfaces to more than one network require a unique IP address for each network interface. The first part of an Internet address identifies the network on which the host resides, while the second part identifies the particular host on the given network. Keeping with our postal system analogy, the network address can be thought of as the zip code, and the host address represents the street address. By convention, an IP address is expressed as four decimal numbers separated by periods, such as "127.154.95.6." Valid addresses can range from 0.0.0.0 to 255.255.255.255, creating a total of about 4.3 billion addresses (4,294,967,296 to be exact). Using this two-level addressing hierarchy, any computer connected to the Internet can be located.

IP addressing can identify a specific network connected to the Internet. To provide the flexibility required to support networks of varying sizes, the Internet designers decided that the IP address space should be divided into three address classes—Classes A, B, and C. Each class fixes the boundary between the network prefix and the host number at a different point within the 32-bit address.

Class A networks are defined by the first number in an IP address. The value can range from 000 to 127, creating theoretically 128 unique networks. In reality, however, there are only 126 Class A addresses because both 0.0.0.0 and 127.0.0.0 are reserved for special use. Each Class A network address can support a total of 16,777,214 hosts per network, and they represent 50 percent of the total IPv4 address space. The Class A addresses are normally owned by large Internet service providers or well-established major corporations. For example, General Electric owns 3.0.0.0, IBM owns 9.0.0.0, Ford Motor Co. owns 19.0.0.0, and the U.S. Postal Service owns 56.0.0.0.

Class B network addresses range from 128.0 to 255.254. Using a Class B address, 16,384 networks can be identified with up to 65,534 hosts per network. Because the Class B address allocation contains slightly more than 1 million addresses, it represents 25 percent of the IPv4 address space. Class B addresses are also normally owned by very large service providers and global organizations—AOL uses 205.188.0.0.

Class C addresses range from 192.0.0 to 233.255.255 and represent 12.5 percent of the available IPv4 address space. Slightly less than 2.1 million networks can be identified with a Class C address allowing approximately 537 million hosts. The remaining 12.5 percent of the IPv4 address space is reserved for special use.

You would think that 4.3 billion addresses would be sufficient for quite a while, but the Internet is running out of space. During the early days of the Internet, the seemingly unlimited address space allowed IP addresses to be allocated to an organization based on a simple request rather than on actual need. As a result, addresses were freely assigned to those who asked for them without concerns about the eventual depletion of the IP address space. Now many of the Class A and Class B host addresses are not even in use. To make matters worse, new technologies are extending IP addresses beyond computers to televisions, toasters, and coffeemakers.

This is where IPv6 comes to the rescue. Developed to work with Internet2, IPv6 increases the IP address size from 32 bits to 128 bits to support more levels of the address hierarchy and a much greater number of nodes. IPv6 supports more than 340 trillion trillion trillion addresses, enough for each person in the world to be allocated 1 billion personal IP addresses! That should last for a while.

Voice over IP

One of the newest uses for Internet protocol (IP) is *Internet telephony*—the practice of using an Internet connection to pass voice data using IP instead of using the standard public switched telephone network. Often referred to as **voice over IP** or VoIP, this approach makes use of a packet-based (or switched) network to carry voice calls, instead of the traditional circuit-switched network. In simpler terms, VoIP allows a person to function as if he or she were directly connected to a regular telephone network even when at home or in a remote office. It also skips standard long-distance charges because the only connection is through an ISP. VoIP is being used more and more to keep corporate telephone costs down, as you can just run two network cables to a desk instead of separate network and data cables. VoIP runs right over a standard network infrastructure, but it also demands a very well-configured network to run smoothly.

For those of us who love to talk (and not to pay for it), there is *Skype* (www.skype.com). Skype was founded in 2002 to develop the first peer-to-peer (P2P) telephony network. Today, Skype software allows telephone conversation through a PC and over the Internet instead of a separate phone connection. This proprietary freeware uses a messenger-like client and offers inbound and outbound PSTN (public switched telephone network) facilities.

Skype users can call to any non-computer–based landline or mobile telephone in the world and call other Skype users for free. The calls made to or received from traditional telephones are charged a fee, as are the voice-mail messages.

Skype software also provides features like voice mail, instant messaging, call forwarding, and conference calling. Skype users are not billed according to the distance between the two countries. Instead, the users are charged according to the prosperity of the country, the volume of calls made to and from the country, and the access charges. The latest statistical figures show that Skype is one of the fastest-growing companies on the Internet:

- Skype has 54 million members in 225 countries and territories, and the number is swelling—just through word-of-mouth marketing by satisfied users!
- Skype is adding approximately 150,000 users a day, and there are 3 million simultaneous users on the network at any given time.
- Skype has been downloaded 163 million times in 225 countries and territories.
- Skype is available in 27 languages.
- Skype has more users and serves more voice minutes than any other Internet voice communications provider.

Skype continues to grow in the consumer sector and is now offering business-specific services designed to reduce business telecommunication costs while offering more flexible alternatives to current landline or mobile approaches. Skype also demonstrates how VoIP is fast becoming part of the telecommunications infrastructure as shown in the following example.

For those of us to love to talk (and want to pay less than the telephone company wants us to pay), there is *Vonage* (www.vonage.com). The name is a play on their motto: Voice-Over-Net-Age—Vonage. Using VoIP technologies, Vonage offers local and long distance telephone service to homes and businesses for a single low monthly price.

Seaport Hotel In-Room Portal Converges Voice and Web Services

The Seaport Hotel in Boston is testing an in-room portal that enables guests to make telephone calls and access hotel services and the Internet from a touch screen.

Geared toward business travelers, the so-called SeaPortal is unique because it combines telephone and Web services over a service-oriented architecture. In addition, the new technology makes use of the hotel's existing PBX system, a less-expensive approach than replacing the in-house telephone switching system.

When a call is made in-house, a server routes it through the PBX system. If the call is outside the hotel, then the server sends it over Seaport's high-speed Internet provider as a voice over IP (VoIP) call, similar to services provided by Skype or Vonage.

For hotel guests, the system appears on the touch screen as a portal similar to a Web site. There's a welcome section that introduces the service; a destination guide for sports and entertainment, dining, news and weather, and other information; and a section for guest services that include hotel features and Web browsing.

The system is attached to the in-room phone, which rings when a guest presses an icon to make an in-hotel call to housecleaning, the concierge, or another service. Picking up the phone automatically makes the connection. To call outside the hotel, the guest presses on a phone link that calls up a keypad.

The portal provides Web mail access and includes a viewer for reading attachments. In addition, there are USB ports for storing messages or documents on a portable flash drive, or a guest can choose to have a document printed in the hotel's business center. All the services are available at no additional charge, including local and long-distance calls made in the continental United States.

Source: Adapted from Antone Gonsalves, "Seaport Hotel In-Room Portal Converges Voice, Web Services," *InformationWeek*, January 24, 2007.

Bandwidth Alternatives

The communications speed and capacity of telecommunications networks can be classified by bandwidth. The frequency range of a telecommunications channel, it determines the channel's maximum transmission rate. The speed and capacity of data transmission rates are typically measured in bits per second (bps). This level is

FIGURE 6.26

Examples of the
telecommunications
transmission speeds of
various network
technologies.

Network Technologies	Typical–Maximum bps
Wi-Fi: wireless fidelity	11–54M
Standard Ethernet or token ring	10–16M
High-speed Ethernet	100M–1G
FDDI: fiber distributed data interface	100M
DDN: digital data network	2.4K–2M
PSN: packet switching network–X.25	64K–1.5M
Frame relay network	1.5M–45M
ISDN: integrated services digital network	64K/128K–2M
ATM: asynchronous transfer mode	25/155M–2.4G
SONET: synchronous optical network	45M–40G
Kbps = thousand bps or kilobits per second	Gbps = billion bps or gigabits per second
Mbps = million bps or megabits per second	

sometimes referred to as the *baud* rate, though baud is more correctly a measure of signal changes in a transmission line.

Bandwidth represents the capacity of the connection. The greater the capacity, the more likely that greater performance will follow. Thus, greater bandwidth allows greater amounts of data to move from one point to another with greater speed. Although the relationship among bandwidth, data volume, and speed is theoretically sound, in practice, this is not always the case. A common analogy is to think of bandwidth as a pipe with water in it. The larger the pipe, the more water that can flow through it. If, however, the big pipe is connected to a small pipe, the effective amount of water that can be moved in a given time becomes severely restricted by the small pipe. The same problem occurs with network bandwidth. If a large bandwidth connection tries to move a large amount of data to a network with less bandwidth, the speed of the transmission will be determined by the speed of the smaller bandwidth.

Narrow-band channels typically provide low-speed transmission rates up to 64 Kbps but can now handle up to 2 Mbps. They are usually unshielded twisted-pair lines commonly used for telephone voice communications and for data communications by the modems of PCs and other devices. Medium-speed channels (*medium-band*) use shielded twisted-pair lines for transmission speeds up to 100 Mbps.

Broadband channels provide high-speed transmission rates at intervals from 256 Kbps to several billion bps. Typically, they use microwave, fiber optics, or satellite transmission. Examples are 1.54 Mbps for T1 and 45 Mbps for T3 communications channels, up to 100 Mbps for communications satellite channels, and between 52 Mbps and 10 Gbps for fiber-optic lines. See Figure 6.26.

Switching Alternatives

Regular telephone service relies on *circuit switching*, in which a switch opens a circuit to establish a link between a sender and a receiver; it remains open until the communication session is completed. In message switching, a message is transmitted a block at a time from one switching device to another.

Packet switching involves subdividing communications messages into fixed or variable-length groups called packets. For example, in the X.25 protocol, packets are 128 characters long, while in the *frame relay* technology, they are of variable length. Packet switching networks are frequently operated by *value-added carriers* who use computers and other communications processors to control the packet switching process and transmit the packets of various users over their networks.

Early packet switching networks were X.25 networks. The X.25 protocol is an international set of standards governing the operations of widely used, but relatively slow, packet switching networks. *Frame relay* is another popular packet switching protocol and is used by many large companies for their wide area networks. Frame relay is considerably faster than X.25 and is better able to handle the heavy telecommunications traffic of interconnected local area networks within a company's wide area client/ server network. ATM (*asynchronous transfer mode*) is an emerging high-capacity *cell*

FIGURE 6.27

Why four large retail chains chose different network technologies to connect their stores.

Company	Technology	Why
Sears	Frame relay	Reliable, inexpensive, and accommodates mainframe and Internet protocols
Rack Room	VSAT (very small aperture terminal)	Very inexpensive way to reach small markets and shared satellite dishes at malls
Hannaford	ATM (asynchronous transfer mode)	Very high bandwidth; combines voice, video, and data
7-Eleven	ISDN (integrated services digital network)	Can use multiple channels to partition traffic among different uses

switching technology. An ATM switch breaks voice, video, and other data into fixed cells of 53 bytes (48 bytes of data and 5 bytes of control information) and routes them to their next destination in the network. ATM networks are being developed by many companies needing their fast, high-capacity multimedia capabilities for voice, video, and data communications. See Figure 6.27.

Network Interoperability

Section 256 of the Communications Act, enacted in February 1996, states two key purposes: (1) "to promote nondiscriminatory accessibility by the broadest number of users and vendors of communications products and services to public telecommunications networks used to provide telecommunications service" and (2) "to ensure the ability of users and information providers to seamlessly and transparently transmit and receive information between and across telecommunications networks." To accomplish these purposes, the Federal Communications Commission (FCC) is required to establish procedures to oversee coordinated network planning by providers of telecommunications services. It is also authorized to participate in the development, by appropriate industry standards-setting organizations of public telecommunications, of network interconnectivity standards that promote access.

As you can see, the FCC is a key regulatory agency with regard to telecommunications. Although we tend to think of the FCC as the oversight body for radio and television, it is equally involved in all aspects of data and voice communications. If you reread the first paragraph of this section, it becomes clear that there is an important underlying reason for the FCC to be so involved with telecommunications. The answer lies in the importance of a concept called network interoperability.

This interoperability ensures that anyone anywhere on one network can communicate with anyone anywhere on another network without having to worry about speaking a common language from a telecommunications perspective. All that we have discussed in this chapter with regard to business value would not be possible without complete accessibility, transparency, and seamless interoperability across all networks. Without these things, the Internet would not be possible, nor would e-mail, instant messaging, or even common file sharing.

Fortunately for us, everyone in the telecommunications field understands the importance of network interoperability, and as such, they work together to ensure that all networks remain interoperable.

Summary

● **Telecommunications Trends.** Organizations are becoming networked enterprises that use the Internet, intranets, and other telecommunications networks to support business operations and collaboration within the enterprise and with their customers, suppliers, and other business partners. Telecommunications has entered a deregulated and fiercely competitive environment with many vendors, carriers, and services. Telecommunications technology is moving toward open, internetworked digital networks for voice, data, video, and multimedia. A major trend is the pervasive use of the Internet and its technologies to build interconnected enterprise and global networks, like intranets and extranets, to support enterprise collaboration, e-commerce, and other e-business applications.

- **The Internet Revolution.** The explosive growth of the Internet and the use of its enabling technologies have revolutionized computing and telecommunications. The Internet has become the key platform for a rapidly expanding list of information and entertainment services and business applications, including enterprise collaboration, electronic commerce, and other e-business systems. Open systems with unrestricted connectivity using Internet technologies are the primary telecommunications technology drivers in e-business systems. Their primary goal is to promote easy and secure access by business professionals and consumers to the resources of the Internet, enterprise intranets, and interorganizational extranets.

- **The Business Value of the Internet.** Companies are deriving strategic business value from the Internet, which enables them to disseminate information globally, communicate and trade interactively with customized information and services for individual customers, and foster collaboration of people and integration of business processes within the enterprise and with business partners. These capabilities allow them to generate cost savings from using Internet technologies, revenue increases from electronic commerce, and better customer service and relationships through better supply chain management and customer relationship management.

- **The Role of Intranets.** Businesses are installing and extending intranets throughout their organizations to (1) improve communications and collaboration among individuals and teams within the enterprise; (2) publish and share valuable business information easily, inexpensively, and effectively via enterprise information portals and intranet Web sites and other intranet services; and (3) develop and deploy critical applications to support business operations and decision making.

- **The Role of Extranets.** The primary role of extranets is to link the intranet resources of a company to the intranets of its customers, suppliers, and other business partners. Extranets can also provide access to operational company databases and legacy systems to business partners. Thus, extranets provide significant business value by facilitating and strengthening the business relationships of a company with customers and suppliers, improving collaboration with its business partners, and enabling the development of new kinds of Web-based services for its customers, suppliers, and others.

- **Telecommunications Networks.** The major generic components of any telecommunications network are (1) terminals, (2) telecommunications processors, (3) communications channels, (4) computers, and (5) telecommunications software. There are several basic types of telecommunications networks, including wide area networks (WANs) and local area networks (LANs). Most WANs and LANs are interconnected using client/server, network computing, peer-to-peer, and Internet networking technologies.

- **Network Alternatives.** Key telecommunications network alternatives and components are summarized in Figure 6.11 for telecommunications media, processors, software, channels, and network architectures. A basic understanding of these major alternatives will help business end users participate effectively in decisions involving telecommunications issues. Telecommunications processors include modems, multiplexers, internetwork processors, and various devices to help interconnect and enhance the capacity and efficiency of telecommunications channels. Telecommunications networks use such media as twisted-pair wire, coaxial cables, fiber-optic cables, terrestrial microwave, communications satellites, cellular and PCS systems, wireless LANs, and other wireless technologies.

- Telecommunications software, such as network operating systems and telecommunications monitors, controls and manages the communications activity in a telecommunications network.

Key Terms and Concepts

These are the key terms and concepts of this chapter. The page number of their first explanation is in parentheses.

1. Analog (234)
2. Bandwidth (249)
3. Bluetooth (239)
4. Client/server networks (231)
5. Coaxial cable (236)
6. Communications satellites (237)
7. Digital (234)
8. Extranets (222)
9. Fiber optics (236)
10. Internet service provider (ISP) (215)
11. Internet networking technologies (212)
12. Internetwork processors (242)
13. Intranets (219)
14. Legacy systems (232)
15. Local area networks (LAN) (229)
16. Metcalfe's law (208)
17. Middleware (212)
18. Modems (241)
19. Multiplexer (242)
20. Network (208)

21. Network architectures (245)
    a. Open Systems Interconnection (OSI) (245)
    b. TCP/IP (247)
22. Network computing (232)
23. Network interoperability (251)
24. Network topologies (244)
25. Open systems (212)

26. Peer-to-peer networks (233)
27. Protocol (245)
28. Telecommunications (211)
29. Telecommunications media (235)
30. Telecommunications network (225)
31. Telecommunications processors (241)

32. Telecommunications software (243)
33. Virtual private network (VPN) (229)
34. VoIP (248)
35. Wide area networks (WAN) (228)
36. Wireless LAN (239)
37. Wireless technologies (213)

Review Quiz

Match one of the key terms and concepts listed previously with one of the brief examples or definitions that follow. Try to find the best fit for answers that seem to fit more than one term or concept. Defend your choices.

_____ 1. Technique for making telephone calls over the Internet.

_____ 2. The ability for all networks to connect to one another.

_____ 3. An interconnected or interrelated chain, group, or system.

_____ 4. Software that serves to "glue together" separate programs.

_____ 5. The usefulness, or utility, of a network equals the square of the number of users.

_____ 6. Internet-like networks that improve communications and collaboration, publish and share information, and develop applications to support business operations and decision making within an organization.

_____ 7. Provide Internet-like access to a company's operational databases and legacy systems by its customers and suppliers.

_____ 8. Company that provides individuals and organizations access to the Internet.

_____ 9. A communications network covering a large geographic area.

_____ 10. A communications network in an office, a building, or other worksite.

_____ 11. Representation of an electrical signal using binary numbers.

_____ 12. Coaxial cable, microwave, and fiber optics are examples.

_____ 13. A communications medium that uses pulses of laser light in glass fibers.

_____ 14. A short range cable replacement technology for digital devices.

_____ 15. Includes modems, multiplexers, and internetwork processors.

_____ 16. Includes programs such as network operating systems and Web browsers.

_____ 17. A common communications processor for microcomputers.

_____ 18. Helps a communications channel carry simultaneous data transmissions from many terminals.

_____ 19. Star, ring, and bus networks are examples.

_____ 20. Representation of an electrical signal that is analogous to the signal itself.

_____ 21. The communications speed and capacity of telecommunications networks.

_____ 22. Intranets and extranets can use their network firewalls and other security features to establish secure Internet links within an enterprise or its trading partners.

_____ 23. Sturdy cable that provides high bandwidth on a single conductor.

_____ 24. Standard rules or procedures for control of communications in a network.

_____ 25. An international standard, multilevel set of protocols to promote compatibility among telecommunications networks.

_____ 26. The standard suite of protocols used by the Internet, intranets, extranets, and some other networks.

_____ 27. Information systems with common hardware, software, and network standards that provide easy access for end users and their networked computer systems.

_____ 28. Interconnected networks need communications processors such as switches, routers, hubs, and gateways.

_____ 29. Web sites, Web browsers, HTML documents, hypermedia databases, and TCP/IP networks are examples.

_____ 30. Networks in which end-user PCs are tied to network servers to share resources and application processing.

_____ 31. Network computers provide a browser-based interface for software and databases provided by servers.

_____ 32. End-user computers connect directly with each other to exchange files.

_____ 33. Orbiting devices that provide multiple communication channels over a large geographical area.

_____ 34. Older, traditional mainframe-based business information systems.

_____ 35. Any arrangement in which a sender transmits a message to a receiver over a channel consisting of some type of medium.

_____ 36. Provides wireless network access for laptop PCs in business settings.

_____ 37. Their goal is to improve the telecommunications environment by fostering standardized protocols, communications hardware and software, and the design of standard interfaces, among other things.

_____ 38. A type of communications network consisting of terminals, processors, channels, computers, and control software.

_____ 39. Telecommunications technologies that do not rely on physical media such as cables or fiber optics.

Discussion Questions

1. The Internet is the driving force behind developments in telecommunications, networks, and other information technologies. Do you agree or disagree? Why?

2. How is the trend toward open systems, connectivity, and interoperability related to business use of the Internet, intranets, and extranets?

3. Refer to the Real World Case on on telemedicine and videoconferencing in the chapter. Not mentioned in the case are the implications for both privacy and data security arising from the use of these technologies. Which specific ones could arise as a result, and to what extent do you believe those would inhibit the deployment of these advances?

4. How will wireless information appliances and services affect the business use of the Internet and the Web? Explain.

5. What are some of the business benefits and management challenges of client/server networks? Network computing? Peer-to-peer networks?

6. What is the business value driving so many companies to install and extend intranets rapidly throughout their organizations?

7. What strategic competitive benefits do you see in a company's use of extranets?

8. Refer to the Real World Case on Starbucks and others on the future of free, public Wi-Fi. New start-ups are offering free access in exchange for serving advertising while browsing the Web. What do you think about this business model? Would you expect to see any competition between these companies, say, two different providers covering the same airport, or rather some degree of exclusivity?

9. Do you think that business use of the Internet, intranets, and extranets has changed what businesspeople expect from information technology in their jobs? Explain.

10. The insatiable demand for everything wireless, video, and Web-enabled everywhere will be the driving force behind developments in telecommunications, networking, and computing technologies for the foreseeable future. Do you agree or disagree? Why?

Analysis Exercises

1. **How many addresses are enough?**
   The Internet Protocol version 4 assigns each connected computer a 4-byte address known as an IP address. Each message, or packet, includes this address so that routers know where to forward it. This is the Internet's version of mailing addresses.

   Each region of the world has been given a range of IP addresses to administer locally, with America taking the largest share. Asia, with a significantly larger population, received a disproportionately small range of numbers and is afraid of running out.

   Anticipating this problem, the Internet Engineering Task Force adopted IPv6, which uses addresses 16 bytes long. Although slow to be adopted, all Internet root servers now support IPv6, and Internet service providers are rolling it out as needed while maintaining backward compatibility for IPv4. The U.S. federal

   government had mandated the change to IPv6 for all federal agencies by 2008.

   a. Express as a power of 2 the number of nodes that can exist using IPv4.
   b. Express as a power of 2 the number of nodes that can exist using IPv6.

2. **MNO Incorporated Communications Network**
   Calculating Bandwidth
   MNO Incorporated is considering acquiring its own leased lines to handle voice and data communications among its 14 distribution sites in three regions around the country. The peak load of communications for each site is expected to be a function of the number of phone links and the number of computers at that site. Communications data are available below. You have been asked to analyze this information.

a. Create a database table with an appropriate structure to store the data below. Enter the records shown below and get a printed listing of your table.

b. Survey results suggest that the peak traffic to and from a site will be approximately 2 kilobits per second for each phone line plus 10 kilobits per second for each computer. Create a report showing the estimated peak demand for the telecommunications system at each site in kilobits. Create a second report grouped by region and showing regional subtotals and a total for the system as a whole.

Site Location	Region	Phone Lines	Computers
Boston	East	228	95
New York	East	468	205
Richmond	East	189	84
Atlanta	East	192	88
Detroit	East	243	97
Cincinnati	East	156	62
New Orleans	Central	217	58
Chicago	Central	383	160
Saint Louis	Central	212	91
Houston	Central	238	88
Denver	West	202	77
Los Angeles	West	364	132
San Francisco	West	222	101
Seattle	West	144	54

3. **Wireless Radiation**
Frying Your Brains?
Radio waves, microwaves, and infrared all belong to the electromagnetic radiation spectrum. These terms reference ranges of radiation frequencies we use every day in our wireless networking environments. However, the very word *radiation* strikes fear in many people. Cell towers have sprouted from fields all along highways. Tall rooftops harbor many more cell stations in cities. Millions of cell phone users place microwave transmitters/receivers next to their heads each time they make a call. Computer network wireless access points have become ubiquitous. Even McDonald's customers can use their machines to browse the Internet as they eat burgers. With all this radiation zapping about, should we be concerned?

The electromagnetic spectrum ranges from ultralow frequencies to radio waves, microwaves, infrared, visible light, ultraviolet, x-ray, and up to gamma-ray radiation. Is radiation dangerous? The threat appears to come from two different directions, the frequency and the intensity. A preponderance of research has demonstrated the dangers of radiation at frequencies just higher than those of visible light, even including the ultraviolet light used in tanning beds, x-rays, and gamma-rays. These frequencies are high (the wavelengths are small enough) to penetrate and disrupt molecules and even atoms. The results range from burns to damaged DNA that might lead to cancer or birth defects.

However, radiation's lower frequencies ranging from visible light (the rainbow colors you can see), infrared, microwave, and radio waves have long waves unable to penetrate molecules. Indeed, microwave wavelengths are so long that microwave ovens employ a simple viewing screen that can block these long waves and yet allow visible light through. As a result, we can watch our popcorn pop without feeling any heat. Keep in mind that visible light consists of radiation frequencies closer to the danger end of the spectrum than microwave light.

Lower radiation frequencies can cause damage only if the *intensity* is strong enough, and that damage is limited to common burns. Microwave ovens cook food by drawing 800 or more watts and converting them into a very intense (bright) microwave light. Cellular telephones, by comparison, draw a very tiny amount of current from the phone's battery and use the resulting microwaves to transmit a signal. In fact, the heat you feel from the cell phone is not from the microwaves but rather from its discharging battery. It is extremely unlikely that either device can give the user cancer, though a microwave oven could cause serious burns if the operator disables its safety features.

a. Use an Internet search engine and report back what the World Health Organization (WHO) has had to say about microwave radiation or nonionizing radiation.

b. Use an Internet search engine to identify the various complaints posed by stakeholders regarding cell phone towers. Write a one-page paper describing an alternative to cell phone towers that would enable cell phone use and yet mitigate all or most of these complaints.

4. **Maximizing Communications**
Human Networking
Ms. Sapper, this year's annual partner meeting coordinator for a global accounting firm, faced an interesting challenge. With 400 high-powered partners gathering from all around the world, she wanted to arrange meal seating in a way that maximized diversity at each table. She hoped that this seating would encourage partners to open up new lines of communication and discourage old cliques from re-forming. The banquet facility included 50 tables, each seating eight guests. Sapper had all the necessary partner data, but she found herself stumped about how to maximize diversity at each table. Let's walk her through the process.

Download and save "partners.xls" from the MIS 9e OLC. Open the file and note that in addition to partners' names, it also contains industry, region, and gender information. The Table No. column has been left blank.

a. In Excel's menu, select "Data" and then "Sort" and then press the "F1" key for help. Read through each of the topics. How would an *ascending* sort arrange the list "Smith; Jones; Zimmerman"?

b. What feature allows users to sort month lists so *January* appears before *April*?

c. Sort the partner data first on Gender, then by Industry, and then by Region, and save the file.

d. Examine the sorted results from the previous step. Notice that assigning the first eight partners to the *same* table would minimize diversity. This result should also provide a clue about how to *maximize* diversity. Using this insight, assign a table number in the range from 1 to 50 to each partner in your sorted list so to maximize diversity. Save the file as "partners_sorted.xls" and explain your logic.

Metric & Multistandard Components Corp.: The Business Value of a Secure Self-Managed Network for a Small-to-Medium Business

With 22,000 customers, 48,800 cataloged parts, and 150 employees working in five U.S. locations and an office in Germany, the last thing John Bellnier needs is an unreliable network.

Yet that's exactly what he contended with for years as IT manager at Metric & Multistandard Components Corp. (MMCC). MMCC may still be classified as a small business by some standards, but this small-to-medium business (SMB) definitely has been a big-time success story in its industry.

MMCC was founded in 1963 by three Czech immigrants in Yonkers, New York, and has grown into one of the largest U.S. distributors of metric industrial fasteners. In the last 10 years business has doubled, reaching $20 million in sales in 2005, and growing just as fast in 2006. However, the company's growth overwhelmed its telecommunications network, which was managed by an outside telecom network management company. The network crashed frequently, interrupting e-mail communications and leaving customer service representatives unable to fulfill orders promptly.

"We had locked ourselves into a three-year contract with our provider," Bellnier says. "It was a managed system and therefore we didn't have passwords to the routers. I experienced dozens of episodes of spending days on the phone trying to escalate job tickets to get the problems solved. It was a nightmare."

He recalls a particular challenge that occurred when the provider denied that its router had gone down: "Their network was broken, and we had to deal with the downtime consequences on top of spending time trying to convince someone 2,000 miles away that one of their routers needed repair."

Several months before MMCC's contract with the provider was to expire, Bellnier began to seek a better network solution. He outlined five key requirements for a new network for the company:

- **Reliability.** Provide maximum network uptime to sustain business operations.
- **Scalability.** Grow with MMCC's increasing business demands.
- **Security.** Ensure confidentiality and integrity of company data.
- **Economy.** Reduce costs for both initial outlay and ongoing administrative and maintenance overhead.
- **Responsibility.** "I wanted all the hardware from one vendor so when issues come up, I know who to turn to," Bellnier adds.

Bellnier met with MMCC executives in 2004 and told them that he believed he could manage a new companywide network internally, on a limited budget, and could recoup the upfront investment by lowering operating expenses. Company executives agreed that the current network situation was intolerable and gave Bellnier the go-ahead to research and select an experienced local IT consulting firm that was certified to build telecom networks by one of the top telecom hardware and software vendors.

Bellnier selected Hi-Link Computer Corp., a Cisco Systems Premier Certified Partner that had earned Cisco specializations in wireless local area networks (LANs) and virtual private network (VPN) security. As a first step, Hi-Link audited MMCC's existing network and interviewed management about business goals and requirements. Company management was impressed with Hi-Link and agreed that Bellnier should seek a formal project proposal from the consultants.

Hi-Link's consulting engineers, led by Business Development Manager Jim Gartner, proposed to Bellnier that MMCC build a secure network foundation consisting of virtual private network links between sites. Using Cisco integrated services routers and security appliances, the network blueprint was designed to give Bellnier transparent remote access to all necessary devices, increase his control over the network, and improve network performance. Hi-Link showed Bellnier how a secure network foundation works to automate routine maintenance, monitor the network, and alert IT staff of security or performance issues. Bellnier accepted Hi-Link's network plan and made a formal presentation outlining the proposal to company management.

After discussing the business costs, risks, and benefits of Hi-Link's plan, MMCC executives agreed to the proposal and the following key project objectives:

Goal. Create a business network for MMCC with higher reliability, security, and scalability, but lower costs, than the existing externally managed network.

Strategy. Design an IP (Internet Protocol) network with advanced technologies for high availability and efficient network and security management, which can be operated by a very small IT department.

Technology. Use virtual private network technologies to connect remote offices and users securely and facilitate company expansion.

Support. After designing and quickly implementing a secure network foundation based on Cisco products, Hi-Link will help MMCC with technical support whenever needed.

Once the consulting contract was signed. Hi-Link began working with Cisco and the local telecom company to install the telecommunications lines needed for the new network. When those were in place, it took less than a week to deploy the Cisco routers, switches, and other telecommunications hardware preconfigured by Hi-Link. "Hi-Link made this implementation effortless by working efficiently at the best times for us," Bellnier says. "They handled all the details associated with the local telecom company, Internet providers, and project management."

After the secure, internally managed network was up and running, the following benefits soon became apparent:

- The new network eliminated MMCC's network congestion almost immediately.

- Network bandwidth, reliability, and security were significantly improved.

- The sophisticated network monitoring system greatly improved network management.

- Network downtime was reduced to nearly zero.

- The new network is saving MMCC a significant amount of money.

"The previous network had cost us just under $11,000 a month; the new high-bandwidth telecommunications lines we lease cost $4,400 per month," Bellnier explains. "We've calculated an annual savings of $77,000, which means we got our return on investment in our first six months."

Best of all, the network is transparent and easy to manage. "We can access all our Cisco routers. We can view the errors and logs. All our telecommunications lines are contracted directly with the local exchange carrier, which gives us a direct communications link to resolve troubles," Bellnier says.

Hi-Link's Gartner says of MMCC's network: "Every remote office is configured in exactly the same way, and we can easily duplicate it to bring up any new location. We can easily add extra bandwidth to meet additional demands." Thus, Hi-Link is helping MMCC add wireless capability to all its warehouses, knowing that additional capacity can be provided if needed.

Gartner emphasizes that as it did for MMCC, a secure network foundation can improve a small company's operational efficiency, secure sensitive data, contain costs, and enhance employee connectivity and customer responsiveness. For example, companies with such network capabilities allow customers to track their orders securely in real time over the Web, empower customer service agents with detailed account information even before they answer the customer's phone call, and provide easy, inexpensive videoconferencing for remote workers, vendors, and customers.

Bellnier offers advice to other IT managers in small companies that may be considering building and managing their own network: "Do not limit company expansion by thinking you cannot support or afford a self-managed system with limited resources," he says.

He adds that MMCC's experience with Hi-Link shows just how quickly an SMB can "recoup the cost and implement a self-managed system with far superior performance and a lot fewer problems."

Source: Adapted from Eric J. Adams, "Creating a Foundation for Growth," *iQ Magazine*, Second Quarter 2006.

CASE STUDY QUESTIONS

1. What were the most important factors contributing to MMCC's success with its new, secure, self-managed network? Explain the reasons for your choices.

2. What are some of the business benefits and challenges of self-managed and externally managed networks?

3. Which type of network management would you advise small-to-medium business firms to use? Explain the reasons for your recommendation.

REAL WORLD ACTIVITIES

1. Use the Internet to discover more about the telecommunications products and services, and the current business performance and prospects, of Cisco Systems and Hi-Link and some of their many competitors in the telecom industry. Which telecom hardware and software company and IT consulting firm would you recommend to a small-to-medium business with which you are familiar? Explain your reasons to the class.

2. In telecommunications network installation and management, as in many other business situations, the choice between "do it yourself" and "let the experts handle it" is a crucial business decision for many companies. Break into small groups with your classmates to debate this choice for small-to-medium businesses. See if you can agree on several key criteria that should be considered in making this decision, and report your conclusions to the class.

MODULE III

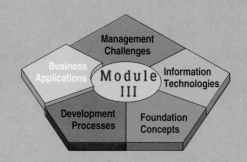

BUSINESS APPLICATIONS

How do Internet technologies and other forms of IT support business processes, e-commerce, and business decision making? The four chapters of this module show you how such business applications of information systems are accomplished in today's networked enterprises.

- **Chapter 7: e-Business Systems** describes how information systems integrate and support enterprisewide business processes, especially customer relationship management, enterprise resource planning, and supply chain management, as well as the business functions of marketing, manufacturing, human resource management, accounting, and finance, and discusses the benefits and challenges of these major enterprise applications.

- **Chapter 8: e-Commerce Systems** introduces the basic process components of e-commerce systems, and discusses important trends, applications, and issues in e-commerce.

- **Chapter 9: Decision Support Systems** shows how management information systems, decision support systems, executive information systems, expert systems, and artificial intelligence technologies can be applied to decision-making situations faced by business managers and professionals in today's dynamic business environment.

CHAPTER 7

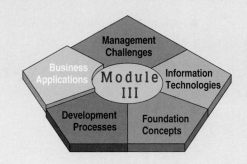

e-BUSINESS SYSTEMS

Chapter Highlights

Learning Objectives

1. Identify the following cross-functional enterprise systems, and give examples of how they can provide significant business value to a company:

   a. Enterprise resource planning.

   b. Customer relationship management.

   c. Supply chain management.

   d. Enterprise application integration.

   e. Transaction processing systems.

   f. Enterprise collaboration systems.

2. Give examples of how the Internet and other information technologies support business processes within the business functions of accounting, finance, human resource management, marketing, and production and operations management.

3. Understand the need for enterprise application integration to improve the support of business interactions across multiple e-business applications.

SECTION I   Enterprise Business Systems

Introduction

Contrary to popular opinion, e-business is not synonymous with e-commerce. E-business is much broader in scope, going beyond transactions to signify use of the Net, in combination with other technologies and forms of electronic communication, to enable any type of business activity.

This chapter introduces the fast-changing world of business applications of information technology, which increasingly consists of what are popularly called *e-business* applications. Remember that e-business, a term originally coined by Lou Gerstner, CEO of IBM, is the use of the Internet and other networks and information technologies to support e-commerce, enterprise communications and collaboration, and Web-enabled business processes, both within a networked enterprise and with its customers and business partners. E-business includes *e-commerce*, which involves the buying, selling, marketing, and servicing of products, services, and information over the Internet and other networks. We will cover e-commerce in greater depth in Chapter 8.

In this chapter, we explore some of the major concepts and applications of e-business. We begin by focusing in Section I on examples of cross-functional enterprise systems, especially customer relationship management, enterprise resource planning, and supply chain management. In Section II, we explore examples of information systems that support essential processes in the functional areas of business. See Figure 7.1.

Read the Real World Case on the next page. We can learn a lot from this case about the challenges and benefits of customer relationship management systems.

Cross-Functional Enterprise Applications

Many companies today are using information technology to develop integrated cross-functional enterprise systems that cross the boundaries of traditional business functions to reengineer and improve vital business processes all across the enterprise. These organizations view cross-functional enterprise systems as a strategic way to use IT to share information resources and improve the efficiency and effectiveness of business processes, as well as to develop strategic relationships with customers, suppliers, and business partners. Figure 7.2 illustrates a cross-functional business process.

Many companies first moved from functional, mainframe-based *legacy systems* to integrated, cross-functional *client/server* applications. This move typically involved installing *enterprise resource planning, supply chain management,* or *customer relationship management* software from SAP America, Oracle, or others. Instead of focusing on the information processing requirements of business functions, such enterprise software focuses on supporting integrated clusters of business processes involved in the operations of a business.

Now, as we see continually in the Real World Cases in this text, business firms are using Internet technologies to help them reengineer and integrate the flow of information among their internal business processes and their customers and suppliers. Companies all across the globe are using the World Wide Web and their intranets and extranets as technology platforms for their cross-functional and interenterprise information systems.

Enterprise Application Architecture

Figure 7.3 presents an enterprise application architecture, which illustrates the interrelationships of the major cross-functional enterprise applications that many companies have or are installing today. This architecture is not intended as a detailed or exhaustive application blueprint but rather as a conceptual framework to help you visualize the basic components, processes, and interfaces of these major e-business applications, along with their interrelationships. This application architecture also spotlights the roles these business systems play in supporting the customers, suppliers, partners, and employees of a business.

REAL WORLD CASE 1

NetSuite Inc., Berlin Packaging, Churchill Downs, and Others: The Secret to CRM Is in the Data

Zach Nelson sits in a Silicon Valley coffeehouse, sipping a latte, nibbling a pastry, and drawing IT architecture diagrams. His mission: to illustrate what he believes is the biggest reason that the software category known as customer relationship management (CRM) has been unable to shake the black marks of too many failed multimillion-dollar deployments.

CRM is easier to implement when a company is young, he says. "The elephant in the room with CRM systems is that there's no customer data native in them," says Nelson, CEO of NetSuite Inc., which sells a suite of Web-based, on-demand business applications, including CRM. "That's why they fail."

When CRM came onto the market in the mid-1990s, driven largely by Siebel Systems, the software typically came bundled with proprietary databases, which then had to be populated with customer data housed in disparate enterprise systems. The result? "Customer records are scattered and there's often overlap and inconsistency," Nelson contends.

By the time he's finished with his morning snack, Nelson has also made a convincing case as to why small and midsize companies are primed to get CRM right. CRM is a lot easier to do early in a company's history than it is later. Also, Web-based subscription software, such as the kind that Nelson's company offers, has given them access to IT applications that in the past might have been too costly or too complex. Designs for Health Inc., a $10 million-a-year maker of prescription nutritional supplements, isn't ready to invest millions in a big CRM package, but it did need a more sophisticated accounting system than Intuit Corp.'s Quick-Books. So it turned to NetSuite to host a general-ledger

application that would let the company automate its accounting processes and easily share the data with other NetSuite applications, such as the CRM module it would add later.

Perhaps the most crucial factor to the CRM success of small and midsize businesses is that most aren't yet paralyzed by data silos and disparate systems, and they've learned from those that have had to spend lots of time and energy bridging the silos. "The biggest problem I have with having disparate systems is determining what is your source of the truth," says Steve Canter, CIO at Berlin Packaging LLC, a $200 million-a-year maker of cans and bottles used to package everything from makeup to jelly. "I have a customer-relationship-management system that has a customer master file. I have an order-management system that has a customer master. If the information between those systems doesn't agree, which one is true? Having a single instance of the customer master, we know what the truth is."

In theory, customer data integration provides a universal view of a customer by resolving discrepancies in names and addresses, as well as summarizing customer interaction data from multiple systems. Customer data in many IT companies remain balkanized as CRM, enterprise resource planning, and supply chain management systems have proliferated. That means the IT behind customer-facing operations such as call centers often can't provide employees with a single view of a customer.

Berlin considered adding a PeopleSoft CRM application to the company's existing PeopleSoft enterprise resource planning and supply chain management system, but it decided such an effort might prove too distracting. So Berlin opted to use the PeopleTools programming code in the ERP system to build bolt-on applications that convert financial and supply chain management functions into CRM processes. Including housing records on more than 27,000 customers acquired since the mid-1990s, the ERP database now serves as a clearinghouse of customer data that lets any part of the company access definitive and wide-ranging information. The knowledge that there are no other collections of customer data elsewhere in the company provides significant peace of mind.

What's more, Canter not only has accomplished this without absorbing any hard costs, but employees have quickly adopted every tool he's introduced, something any big-company CIO will tell you is the most elusive part of a CRM deployment. The key, Canter says, has been a combination of incremental changes and interfaces salespeople already are familiar with. "It's not like implementing a CRM system where overnight their lives are changed," he says. "Little by little, they're getting a CRM system without even realizing it."

Creating de facto CRM systems out of other applications isn't for everyone, says Barton Goldenberg, president of CRM consulting firm ISM. Goldenberg is a firm believer that CRM software can provide data intelligence and support for front-end business processes that even the most carefully tweaked

FIGURE 7.1

CRM software enables sales and marketing professionals to increase sales revenue by providing more and better services to customers and prospects.

Source: © Simon Dearden/Corbis.

ERP system can't match. "Data in its own right is useless unless it's put into context," he says. "I can serve data up via pigeons, but it's the CRM application that adds the value."

A CRM deployment that's carefully thought out has done just that for Churchill Downs Inc., the $500 million-a-year operator of six horse-racing tracks, including its namesake, the famed home of the Kentucky Derby. It's also converting its mass-market advertising to a more one-to-one approach.

Before Atique Shah joined the company in late 2003 as vice president of CRM and technology solutions, Churchill Downs had just assumed that the aggregate data culled from its Twin Spires loyalty club could be broken into four distinct buckets of customers. Shah wasn't so sure. So he got budget approval to obtain a range of technologies, starting with Epiphany Inc.'s CRM software and supported by SPSS Inc.'s Clementine data-mining tool and IBM's Ascential data-extraction and transformation software. Shah then ran the data through Clementine and discovered that there were actually nine aggregate customer types, which was an indication that its previous marketing efforts probably weren't as useful or relevant as they should have been. Asked how close he is to achieving a 360-degree view of his customers, he laughs and says, "I believe we're probably at about 190 degrees." Churchill Downs has 27 sources of customer information, and refereeing among them is a constant problem, Shah says.

To reflect the more-detailed profiles that emerged, Shah transitioned from generic labels for the old buckets—platinum, gold, silver, and bronze—to descriptions that hinted at the personalities of each segment. So a female customer who only visits the track a few times a year and is there more for the social spectacle than for the betting is now known as a "Seldom Sally," and a wealthy man in his fifties who spends more than $100,000 a year at the track and is confident in his racing knowledge is a "Smarty Steve."

Shah published the new intelligence to the company's various tracks and engineered a test campaign with Arlington Park near Chicago. Arlington's staff selected 55,000 households out of its database and then broke them into the nine customer segments Clementine had spit out. Each distinct group of customers then received direct-mail advertisements that reflected its profile, with information and offers that jibed with its attributes. The response rate was impressive, with nearly 10 percent of those who received the mailing coming to the park during the following season.

"What was more amazing was that the group of customers they had segmented generated $1.6 million in the first two weeks," Shah says. "A year earlier, the same customers generated $950,000."

The success of that campaign underscored the value of the data that Churchill Downs had, in many ways, been sitting on.

However small and midsize companies implement CRM, it's clear that data can translate into increased sales.

ISM's Goldenberg reiterates, though, that companies need to make sure data are in order before they launch any major CRM initiative. Even though he believes that in most cases, it's the CRM application, not the data, that's providing the real business value, it's also clear that one can't thrive without the other. "Without accurate, complete, and comprehensive data, any CRM effort will be less than optimal," he says.

Which brings us back to the prediction that NetSuite's Nelson makes: A few years from now, today's small companies will be running circles around their larger competitors, primarily because establishing a master record of customer data will prove to be a less-daunting task for them. The way Nelson sees it, the decision to jump on establishing unified sources of customer data will pay off for the emerging companies that do so. "Once you get your data in place, things that were very complex before become quite trivial," he says.

Maybe not as trivial as sipping coffee and nibbling on a Danish pastry, but wouldn't it be great if it were pretty darn close?

Source: Adapted from Tony Kontzer, "CRM's Secret Is in the Data," *InformationWeek*, August 15, 2005; and Charles Babcock, "Looking for a Clearer View of the Customer," *InformationWeek*, August 8, 2005.

CASE STUDY QUESTIONS

1. What are the business benefits of CRM implementations for organizations such as Berlin Packaging and Churchill Downs? What other uses of CRM would you recommend to the latter? Provide several alternatives.

2. Do you agree with the idea that smaller organizations are better positioned to be more effective users of CRM than larger ones? Why or why not? Justify your answer.

3. One of the main issues noted in the case is the importance of "good" data for the success of CRM implementations. We discussed many of these in Chapter 5, when we compared the file processing and database management approaches to data resource management. Which of the problems discussed there do you see present in this case? How do CRM applications attempt to address them? Use examples from the case to illustrate your answer.

REAL WORLD ACTIVITIES

1. NetSuite Inc. is a leading provider of on-demand enterprise applications, including CRM as featured in the case. Other important players in this market include Salesforce.com and Siebel On Demand. Use the Internet to research all three product offerings and discover how these companies are faring in this increasingly competitive industry. Compare and contrast their product features to understand whether offerings are becoming differentiated or more alike as a result.

2. The CRM implementations in this case highlight the critical importance of information about customers, their preferences and activities, and how to use it to understand and develop better marketing solutions. On the other hand, the degree to which these companies are able to target customers individually may be of concern to some people. Break into small groups with your classmates to discuss these concerns, as well as ways for both companies and their customers to benefit from CRM systems, and still protect customer privacy.

FIGURE 7.2 The new product development process in a manufacturing company. This is an example of a business process that must be supported by cross-functional information systems that cross the boundaries of several business functions.

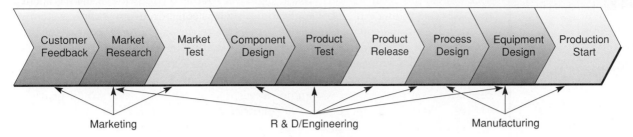

Notice that instead of concentrating on traditional business functions, or only supporting the internal business processes of a company, enterprise applications are focused on accomplishing fundamental business processes in concert with a company's customer, supplier, partner, and employee stakeholders. Thus, enterprise resource planning (ERP) concentrates on the efficiency of a firm's internal production, distribution, and financial processes. Customer relationship management (CRM) focuses on acquiring and retaining profitable customers via marketing, sales, and service processes. Partner relationship management (PRM) aims at acquiring and retaining partners who can enhance the selling and distribution of a firm's products and services. Supply chain management (SCM) focuses on developing the most efficient and effective sourcing and procurement processes with suppliers for the products and services needed by a business. Knowledge management (KM) applications focus on providing a firm's employees with tools that support group collaboration and decision support.

We will discuss CRM, ERP, and SCM applications in detail in this section and cover knowledge management applications in Chapter 9. Now let's look at a real-world example of some of the challenges involved in rolling out global, cross-functional systems.

FIGURE 7.3

This enterprise application architecture presents an overview of the major cross-functional enterprise applications and their interrelationships.

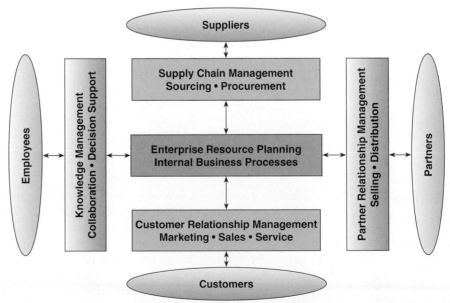

Source: Adapted from Mohan Sawhney and Jeff Zabin, *Seven Steps to Nirvana: Strategic Insights into e-Business Transformation* (New York: McGraw-Hill, 2001), p. 175.

Ogilvy & Mather and MetLife: The Interpersonal Challenges of Implementing Global Applications

Atefeh Riazi's quarter-million frequent-flier miles are testament to the fact that it's not such a small planet after all. As CIO at Ogilvy & Mather Worldwide, Riazi has spent the past years rolling out global applications, such as collaborative workflow systems, creative asset management, knowledge management, messaging, and security for the New York City–based marketing giant. Most recently, Riazi has been trying to convince the Asian, European, and Latin American offices to replace their legacy systems with North America's SAP enterprise resource planning system for finance, human resources, and production. A common enterprise system, she says, would provide Ogilvy's 400 offices in more than 100 countries with access to real-time information so they can make quick decisions, better respond to market changes, and cut costs.

The fact is that globalization adds new dynamics to the workplace, and CIOs who stick to the true-blue American business formula will fail. They must abandon the idea of force-fitting their visions into worldwide offices and move toward a global infrastructure built collaboratively by staff from around the world.

Take the company that rolls out a global system with high-bandwidth requirements. That system might not be feasible for IT directors in the Middle East or parts of Asia, where the cost of bandwidth is higher than in New York. Is the standardized system multilingual? Can it convert different currencies? Can it accommodate complex national tax laws?

For global projects, working virtually is critical, but it's also one of the biggest challenges. "You're dealing with different languages, different cultures, different time zones," says George Savarese, vice president of operations and technology services at New York City–based MetLife. His 6 p.m. Monday meeting, for instance, falls at 8 a.m. in South Korea and 9 p.m. in Brazil. Savarese adds, however, that telephone and e-mail alone won't cut it. "You really have to be there, in their space, understanding where it's at," he says, adding that he spends about half of each month abroad.

"Globalization challenges your people skills every day," says Ogilvy's Riazi. For example, workers in the United Kingdom often rely heavily on qualitative research; they take their time in making decisions, as opposed to Americans, who tend to be action-oriented. So, in a recent attempt to get offices in the United States and the United Kingdom to collaborate on a common system rollout, Riazi hit a wall of resistance because she didn't spend enough time going over analytical arguments with the people in the U.K. office.

Having international teams run global projects goes a long way toward mending fences. Ogilvy, for instance, manages a financial reporting project out of Ireland. "The IT director there has a European point of view, so we're not going to be blindsided by something that isn't a workable solution," she says.

"We have let control go," she says of Ogilvy's New York headquarters. "A lot of global companies cannot let go of that control. They're holding so tight. It's destructive."

Source: Adapted from Melissa Solomon, "Collaboratively Building a Global Infrastructure," *CIO Magazine*, June 1, 2003.

Getting All the Geese Lined Up: Managing at the Enterprise Level

Here's a question you probably never expected to find in your information system text: Have you ever noticed how geese fly? They start out as a seemingly chaotic flock of birds but very quickly end up flying in a V-shape or echelon pattern like that shown in Figure 7.4. As you might imagine, this consistency in flying formation is not an accident. By flying in this manner, each bird receives a slight, but measurable, benefit in reduced drag from the bird in front. This makes it easier for all of the birds to fly long distances than if they just took up whatever portion of the sky they happened to find. Of course, the lead bird has the toughest job, but geese have figured out a way to help there, as well. Systematically, one of the birds from the formation will fly up to relieve

FIGURE 7.4

Geese fly in a highly organized and efficient V-shaped formation—much like a well-run business.

Source: © Warren Jacobi/Corbis.

the current lead bird. In this way, the entire flock shares the load as they all head in the same direction.

Okay, so what does this have to do with information systems? This chapter will focus on systems that span the enterprise and that are intended to support three enterprisewide operations: customer relationships, resource planning, and supply chain.

Each operation requires a unique focus and, thus, a unique system to support it, but they all share one common goal: to get the entire organization to line up and head in the same direction, just as the geese do.

We could cover these important enterprise systems in any order, and if we asked three people how to do it, we would likely get three different approaches. For our purposes, we will start with the focus of every business: the customer. From there, we will expand our view to the back-office operations and finally to systems that manage the movement of raw materials and finished goods. The end result, of course, is that we get all the "geese" in the business to fly in the same direction in as efficient a manner as possible.

Customer Relationship Management: The Business Focus

Today, customers are in charge. It is easier than ever for customers to comparison shop and, with a click of the mouse, to switch companies. As a result, customer relationships have become a company's most valued asset. These relationships are worth more than the company's products, stores, factories, Web addresses, and even employees. Every company's strategy should address how to find and retain the most profitable customers possible.

The primary business value of customer relationships today is indisputable. That's why we emphasized in Chapter 2 that becoming a customer-focused business was one of the top business strategies that can be supported by information technology. Thus, many companies are implementing customer relationship management (CRM) business initiatives and information systems as part of a customer-focused or customer-centric strategy to improve their chances for success in today's competitive business environment. In this section, we will explore basic CRM concepts and technologies, as well as examples of the benefits and challenges faced by companies that have implemented CRM systems as part of their customer-focused business strategy.

What Is CRM?

Managing the full range of the customer relationship involves two related objectives: one, to provide the organization and all of its customer-facing employees with a single, complete view of every customer at every touch point and across all channels; and, two, to provide the customer with a single, complete view of the company and its extended channels.

This quote is why companies are turning to customer relationship management (CRM) to improve their customer focus. CRM uses information technology to create a cross-functional enterprise system that integrates and automates many of the *customer-serving* processes in sales, marketing, and customer services that interact with a company's customers. CRM systems also create an IT framework of Web-enabled software and databases that integrates these processes with the rest of a company's business operations. CRM systems include a family of software modules that provides the tools that enable a business and its employees to provide fast, convenient, dependable, and consistent service to its customers. Siebel Systems, Oracle, SAP AG, IBM, and Epiphany are some of the leading vendors of CRM software. Figure 7.5 illustrates some of the major application components of a CRM system. Let's take a look at each of them.

Contact and Account Management

CRM software helps sales, marketing, and service professionals capture and track relevant data about every past and planned contact with prospects and customers, as well as other business and life cycle events of customers. Information is captured from all customer *touchpoints*, such as telephone, fax, e-mail, the company's Web site, retail stores, kiosks, and personal contact. CRM systems store the data in a common customer database that integrates all customer account information and makes it available throughout the company via Internet, intranet, or other network links for sales, marketing, service, and other CRM applications.

Sales

A CRM system provides sales representatives with the software tools and company data sources they need to support and manage their sales activities and optimize *cross-selling* and *up-selling*. Cross-selling is an approach in which a customer of one product or service, say, auto insurance, might also be interested in purchasing a related product or service, say, homeowner's insurance. By using a cross-selling technique, sales representatives can better serve their customers while simultaneously improving their sales. Up-selling refers to the process of finding ways to sell

FIGURE 7.5

The major application clusters in customer relationship management.

a new or existing customer a better product than they are currently seeking. Examples include sales prospect and product information, product configuration, and sales quote generation capabilities. CRM also provides real-time access to a single common view of the customer, enabling sales representatives to check on all aspects of a customer's account status and history before scheduling their sales calls. For example, a CRM system would alert a bank sales representative to call customers who make large deposits to sell them premier credit or investment services. Or it would alert a salesperson of unresolved service, delivery, or payment problems that could be resolved through a personal contact with a customer.

Marketing and Fulfillment

CRM systems help marketing professionals accomplish direct marketing campaigns by automating such tasks as qualifying leads for targeted marketing and scheduling and tracking direct marketing mailings. Then the CRM software helps marketing professionals capture and manage prospect and customer response data in the CRM database and analyze the customer and business value of a company's direct marketing campaigns. CRM also assists in the fulfillment of prospect and customer responses and requests by quickly scheduling sales contacts and providing appropriate information about products and services to them, while capturing relevant information for the CRM database.

Customer Service and Support

A CRM system provides service representatives with software tools and real-time access to the common customer database shared by sales and marketing professionals. CRM helps customer service managers create, assign, and manage requests for service by customers. *Call center* software routes calls to customer support agents on the basis of their skills and authority to handle specific kinds of service requests. *Help desk* software provides relevant service data and suggestions for resolving problems for customer service reps who assist customers with problems with a product or service. Web-based self-service enables customers to easily access personalized support information at the company Web site, while giving them an option to receive further assistance online or by phone from customer service personnel.

Retention and Loyalty Programs

Consider the following:

- It costs six times more to sell to a new customer than to sell to an existing one.
- A typical dissatisfied customer will tell eight to ten people about his or her experience.
- A company can boost its profits 85 percent by increasing its annual customer retention by only 5 percent.
- The odds of selling a product to a new customer are 15 percent, whereas the odds of selling a product to an existing customer are 50 percent.
- Seventy percent of complaining customers will do business with the company again if it quickly takes care of a service problem.

That's why enhancing and optimizing customer retention and loyalty is a major business strategy and primary objective of customer relationship management. CRM systems try to help a company identify, reward, and market to their most loyal and profitable customers. CRM analytical software includes data mining tools and other analytical marketing software, and CRM databases may consist of a customer data warehouse and CRM data marts. These tools are used to identify profitable and loyal customers and to direct and evaluate a company's targeted marketing and relationship marketing programs toward them. Figure 7.6 is an example of part of a proposed Web-based report format for evaluating Charles Schwab & Co.'s customer retention performance.

FIGURE 7.6   Proposed report format for evaluating the customer retention performance of Charles Schwab & Co.

	Navigation	Performance	Operations	Environment
Customer Retention	Customer retention rate Household retention rate Average customer tenure	Retention rate by customer cohort Retention rate by customer segment Customer loyalty rating	Percentage of customers who are active Web users Percentage of customers who interact via e-mail Decline in customer activity Propensity to defect	Competitors' offers Share of portfolio Comparative retention Comparative customer tenure
Customer Experience	Satisfaction by customer segment Satisfaction by cohort Satisfaction by customer scenario	Customer satisfaction by: • Task • Touchpoint • Channel partner End-to-end performance by scenario Customer satisfaction with quality of information provided	Elapsed time for commonly performed tasks Accuracy of Web search results Percentage of trades executed with price improvement Percentage of e-mails answered accurately in one hour	Comparative satisfaction: Competitors: • Other online brokers • Other financial service firms • All products and services
Customer Spending	Average revenue per customer Average profitability per customer Growth in customer assets Customer lifetime value	Revenues per customer segment Profits per customer segment Growth in customer assets per segment	Daily log-ins at market opening Revenue trades per day Percentage increase in customer assets Cost to serve by touchpoint	Total brokerage assets Growth in brokerage assets

The Three Phases of CRM

Figure 7.7 illustrates another way to think about the customer and business value and components of customer relationship management. We can view CRM as an integrated system of Web-enabled software tools and databases that accomplish a variety of customer-focused business processes that support the three phases of the relationship between a business and its customers.

FIGURE 7.7
How CRM supports the three phases of the relationship between a business and its customers.

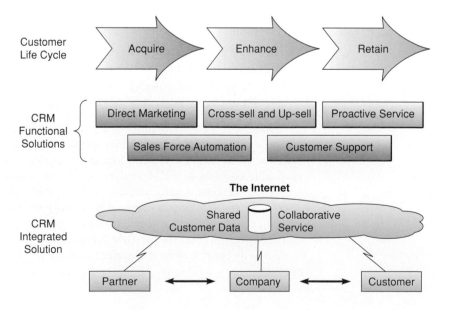

- **Acquire.** A business relies on CRM software tools and databases to help it acquire new customers by doing a superior job of contact management, sales prospecting, selling, direct marketing, and fulfillment. The goal of these CRM functions is to help customers perceive the value of a superior product offered by an outstanding company.

- **Enhance.** Web-enabled CRM account management and customer service and support tools help keep customers happy by supporting superior service from a responsive, networked team of sales and service specialists and business partners. And CRM sales force automation and direct marketing and fulfillment tools help companies cross-sell and up-sell to their customers, thus increasing their profitability to the business. The value perceived by customers is the convenience of one-stop shopping at attractive prices.

- **Retain.** CRM analytical software and databases help a company proactively identify and reward its most loyal and profitable customers to retain and expand their business via targeted marketing and relationship marketing programs. The value perceived by customers is of a rewarding personalized business relationship with "their company."

Benefits and Challenges of CRM

The potential business benefits of customer relationship management are many. For example, CRM allows a business to identify and target its best customers—those who are the most profitable to the business—so they can be retained as lifelong customers for greater and more profitable services. It makes possible real-time customization and personalization of products and services based on customer wants, needs, buying habits, and life cycles. CRM can also keep track of when a customer contacts the company, regardless of the contact point. In addition, CRM systems can enable a company to provide a consistent customer experience and superior service and support across all the contact points a customer chooses. All of these benefits would provide strategic business value to a company and major customer value to its customers.

Continental Airlines: Getting to Know Your Customers

Wouldn't it be nice if just once, one of those surly airline employees offered a sincere and unequivocal apology for losing your luggage or for a delayed flight? If you fly first class with Continental Airlines, you may finally get that apology.

Since 2001, the Houston-based carrier has been enhancing the in-flight reports it provides to flight attendants just before takeoff with more detailed information on passengers. For example, in addition to indicating which passengers ordered special meals, the expanded reports flag the airline's high-value customers and detail such things as whether they've had their luggage lost in the recent past or experienced a delayed flight. Armed with this information, flight attendants can now approach these customers during the flight to apologize for the inconveniences. Such high-touch, personalized service increases customer loyalty, particularly among Continental's most valuable patrons, and that loyalty in turn drives revenue.

Continental breaks customers into different levels of profitability: Since building its new system, the airline reports earning an average of $200 in revenue on each of its 400,000 valuable customers and an additional $800 in revenue from each of the 35,000 customers it places in its most profitable tier—all because it accords them better service.

Continental's desire to improve its ranking in a competitive industry drove it to build a real-time enterprise data warehouse (EDW). When the EDW was first being developed in 1998, its initial purpose was to bring data from some 27 systems together so that the company could more accurately forecast revenue. Since then, the company has used it to determine if customer loyalty initiatives really affect revenue. By testing a sample of 30,000 customers who experienced delays, Continental found that those individuals to whom the airline sent a letter of apology and some sort of compensation (either in the form of a free cocktail on their next flight or extra frequent flier miles) forgot the event and didn't hold a grudge. In fact, Continental says that revenue from those passengers who received letters jumped 8 percent.

Using operational and customer data in the EDW, the data warehousing team developed a solution to one of the biggest headaches gate agents face: accommodating passengers inconvenienced by a cancellation or delay. The team created a program that automates the rebooking process. Before the program was developed, gate agents had to figure out on their own how to reroute passengers. Now, when a cancellation or delay occurs, the system does the work for them. For example, when the system identifies a high-value customer whose flight has been cancelled, the gate agent may decide to put that traveler on a competitor's flight just to make the individual happy and to get him on his way as fast as possible.

"Before the data warehouse, the person who yelled the loudest got the best service. Now our most valuable customers get the best service," says Alicia Acebo, Continental's data warehousing director.

Source: Adapted from Meridith Levinson, "Getting to Know Them," *CIO Magazine*, May 9, 2007.

CRM Failures

The business benefits of customer relationship management are not guaranteed but instead have proven elusive for many companies. Surveys by industry research groups include a report that over 50 percent of CRM projects did not produce the results that were promised. In another research report, 20 percent of businesses surveyed reported that CRM implementations had actually damaged long-standing customer relationships. And in a survey of senior management satisfaction with 25 management tools, CRM ranked near the bottom in user satisfaction, even though 72 percent expected to have CRM systems implemented shortly.

What is the reason for such a high rate of failure or dissatisfaction with CRM initiatives? Research shows that the major reason is a familiar one: lack of understanding and preparation. That is, too often business managers rely on a major new application of information technology (like CRM) to solve a business problem without first developing the business process changes and change management programs that are required. For example, in many cases, failed CRM projects were implemented without the participation of the business stakeholders involved. Therefore, employees and customers were not prepared for the new processes or challenges that were part of the new CRM implementation. We will discuss the topic of failures in information technology management, system implementation, and change management further in subsequent chapters.

Unum Group: The Long Road to CRM

The multiple mergers that formed insurer Unum Group in the late 1990s aggregated billions in revenue, assembled thousands of employees—and created a quagmire of customer data systems that couldn't talk to each other. In all, between Provident, Colonial, Paul Revere, and Unum there were 34 disconnected policy and claims back-office systems, all loaded with critical customer data. As a result, "it was very difficult to get your hands around the information," understates Bob Dolmovich, Unum Group's VP of business integration and data architecture. One Unum Group customer's account, for instance, might exist in multiple places within the newly combined company, leading, of course, to a great deal of waste.

For the first couple of years after the mergers, Unum Group used a homegrown data-store solution as a band aid. But by 2004 the $10 billion disability insurer felt compelled to embark on a new master data management strategy aimed at uniting the company's disparate pockets of customer data, including account activity, premiums, and payments.

Core to Unum Group's strategy would be a customer data integration (CDI) hub, built on service-oriented architecture using a standard set of protocols for connecting applications via the Web (in effect, Web services). The project, begun in early 2005, has already improved data quality, soothed the multiple customer records headaches, and created the possibility for a companywide, in-depth customer analysis. But as Dolmovich acknowledges, there's still a long way to go. Of those original 34 systems, he has been able to get rid of only four to date. But he's still optimistic.

Despite the long, slow slog, Dolmovich is hoping that the new CDI approach will ultimately give his company the 360-degree view of the customer that has been promised by vendors since the dawn of CRM. In the late 1990s, enterprise software vendors like Oracle, PeopleSoft, and Siebel sold the single-customer view as CRM's holy grail. But implementation flameouts and legacy integration nightmares soured many CIOs on these expensive enterprisewide rollouts.

A CDI hub differs from a traditional CRM solution in that a CDI hub allows a company to automatically integrate all of its customer data into one database while ensuring the quality and accuracy of the data before it is sent to the hub's central store for safekeeping. A standalone CRM system can't do that because it can't be integrated with the billing, marketing, ERP, and supply chain systems that house customer data, and it has no way to address inconsistent data across platforms.

Dolmovich says the first data loaded into the CDI hub in late 2005 came from business customers and brokers.

With the new system, Dolmovich says, "We are now able to assimilate and display a broker's entire block of business and create some statistics and a profile of our relationship with that broker." Unum Group is now working to create individual profiles of employer customers so that every time a new customer account is created or accessed—perhaps to change an address or add new customer information—all employees of the insurance company, regardless of what system they are using, will see that change at the same time. "The desired end state is a CDI hub that has information about all customers across all products," he says.

Source: Adapted from Thomas Wailgum, "The Quest for Customer Data Integration," *CIO Magazine*, August 1, 2006.

Enterprise Resource Planning: The Business Backbone

What do Microsoft, Coca-Cola, Cisco, Eli Lilly, Alcoa, and Nokia have in common? Unlike most businesses, which operate on 25-year-old back-office systems, these market leaders reengineered their businesses to run at breakneck speed by implementing a transactional backbone called enterprise resource planning (ERP). These companies credit their ERP systems with having helped them reduce inventories, shorten cycle times, lower costs, and improve overall operations.

Businesses of all kinds have now implemented enterprise resource planning (ERP) systems. ERP serves as a cross-functional enterprise backbone that integrates and automates many internal business processes and information systems within the manufacturing, logistics, distribution, accounting, finance, and human resource functions of a company. Large companies throughout the world began to install ERP systems in the 1990s as a conceptual framework and catalyst for reengineering their business processes. ERP also served as the vital software engine needed to integrate and accomplish the cross-functional processes that resulted. Now, ERP is recognized as a necessary ingredient that many companies need in order to gain the efficiency, agility, and responsiveness required to succeed in today's dynamic business environment.

What Is ERP?

ERP is the technological backbone of e-business, an enterprisewide transaction framework with links into sales order processing, inventory management and control, production and distribution planning, and finance.

FIGURE 7.8

The major application components of enterprise resource planning demonstrate the cross-functional approach of ERP systems.

Enterprise resource planning (ERP) is a cross-functional enterprise system driven by an integrated suite of software modules that supports the basic internal business processes of a company. For example, ERP software for a manufacturing company will typically process the data from, and track the status of, sales, inventory, shipping, and invoicing, as well as forecast raw material and human resource requirements. Figure 7.8 presents the major application components of an ERP system.

ERP gives a company an integrated real-time view of its core business processes, such as production, order processing, and inventory management, tied together by the ERP application software and a common database maintained by a database management system. ERP systems track business resources (e.g., cash, raw materials, production capacity) and the status of commitments made by the business (e.g., customer orders, purchase orders, employee payroll), no matter which department (e.g., manufacturing, purchasing sales, accounting) has entered the data into the system.

ERP software suites typically consist of integrated modules of manufacturing, distribution, sales, accounting, and human resource applications. Examples of manufacturing processes supported are material requirements planning, production planning, and capacity planning. Some of the sales and marketing processes supported by ERP are sales analysis, sales planning, and pricing analysis, while typical distribution applications include order management, purchasing, and logistics planning. ERP systems support many vital human resource processes, from personnel requirements planning to salary and benefits administration, and accomplish most required financial record keeping and managerial accounting applications. Figure 7.9 illustrates the processes

FIGURE 7.9   The business processes and functions supported by the ERP system implemented by Colgate-Palmolive Co.

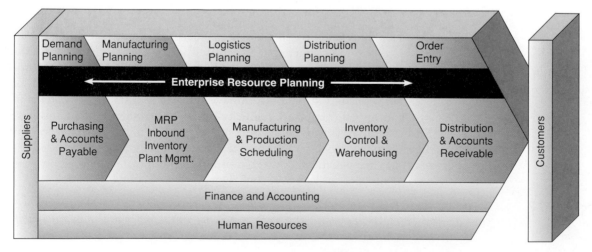

supported by the ERP system installed by Colgate-Palmolive Co. Let's take a closer look at its experience with ERP.

Colgate-Palmolive: The Business Value of ERP	Colgate-Palmolive is a global consumer products company that implemented the SAP R/3 enterprise resource planning system. Colgate embarked on an implementation of SAP R/3 to allow the company to access more timely and accurate data, get the most out of working capital, and reduce manufacturing costs. An important factor for Colgate was whether it could use the software across the entire spectrum of its business. Colgate needed the ability to coordinate globally and act locally. The implementation of SAP across the Colgate supply chain contributed to increased profitability. Now installed in operations that produce most of Colgate's worldwide sales, SAP was expanded to all Colgate divisions worldwide. Global efficiencies in purchasing—combined with product and packaging standardization—also produced large savings.

• Before ERP, it took Colgate U.S. anywhere from one to five days to acquire an order and another one to two days to process the order. Now, order acquisition and processing combined take four hours, not up to seven days. Distribution planning and picking used to take up to four days; today, they take 14 hours. In total, the order-to-delivery time has been cut in half.

• Before ERP, on-time deliveries used to occur only 91.5 percent of the time, and cases ordered were delivered correctly 97.5 percent of the time. After R/3, the figures are 97.5 percent and 99.0 percent, respectively.

• After ERP, domestic inventories have dropped by one-third and receivables outstanding have dropped to 22.4 days from 31.4. Working capital as a percentage of sales has plummeted to 6.3 percent from 11.3 percent. Total delivered cost per case has been reduced by nearly 10 percent. |

Benefits and Challenges of ERP

As the example of Colgate-Palmolive illustrates, ERP systems can generate significant business benefits for a company. Many other companies have found major business value in their use of ERP in several basic ways.

• **Quality and Efficiency.** ERP creates a framework for integrating and improving a company's internal business processes that results in significant improvements in the quality and efficiency of customer service, production, and distribution.

• **Decreased Costs.** Many companies report significant reductions in transaction processing costs and hardware, software, and IT support staff compared with the nonintegrated legacy systems that were replaced by their new ERP systems.

• **Decision Support.** ERP quickly provides vital, cross-functional information on business performance to managers, which significantly improves their ability to make better decisions in a timely manner across the entire business enterprise.

• **Enterprise Agility.** Implementing ERP systems breaks down many former departmental and functional walls or "silos" of business processes, information systems, and information resources. This agility results in more flexible organizational structures, managerial responsibilities, and work roles and therefore a more agile and adaptive organization and workforce that can more easily capitalize on new business opportunities.

The Costs of ERP

An ERP implementation is like the corporate equivalent of a brain transplant. We pulled the plug on every company application and moved to PeopleSoft software. The risk was certainly disruption of business, because if you do not do ERP properly, you can kill your company, guaranteed.

FIGURE 7.10

Typical costs of implementing a new ERP system.

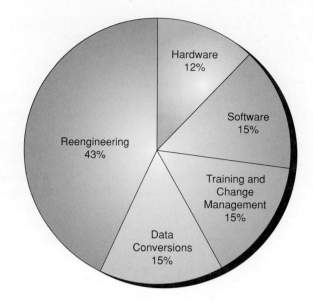

So says Jim Prevo, CIO of Green Mountain Coffee Roasters in Vermont, commenting on its successful implementation of an ERP system. Although the benefits of ERP are many, the costs and risks are also considerable, as we will continue to see in some of the real-world cases and examples in the text. Figure 7.10 illustrates the relative size and types of costs of implementing an ERP system in a company. Notice that hardware and software costs are a small part of total costs, and the costs of developing new business processes (reengineering) and preparing employees for the new system (training and change management) make up the bulk of implementing a new ERP system. Converting data from previous legacy systems to the new cross-functional ERP system is another major category of ERP implementation costs.

The costs and risks of failure in implementing a new ERP system are substantial. Most companies have had successful ERP implementations, but a sizable minority of firms experienced spectacular and costly failures that heavily damaged their overall business. Big losses in revenue, profits, and market share resulted when core business processes and information systems failed or did not work properly. In many cases, orders and shipments were lost, inventory changes were not recorded correctly, and unreliable inventory levels caused major stockouts to occur for weeks or months. Companies like Hershey Foods, Nike, A-DEC, and Connecticut General sustained losses running into hundreds of millions of dollars in some instances. In the case of FoxMeyer Drugs, a $5 billion pharmaceutical wholesaler, the company had to file for bankruptcy protection and then was bought out by its arch competitor McKesson Drugs.

American LaFrance: Botched ERP Implementation Leads to Failure (and Bankruptcy)	American LaFrance (ALF), a maker of emergency vehicles such as fire trucks and ambulances, filed for bankruptcy protection on January 28, 2008; in court papers, it is claiming that their software vendor's work installing and transitioning to a new ERP system contributed to inventory and production problems. Officials at American LaFrance, which has been in business making fire and emergency response equipment since 1832, stated that "this is a legal 'reorganization' process to make the company stronger."

The bankruptcy filing was due to "operational disruptions caused by the installation of a new ERP system," as well as obsolete inventory that American LaFrance's previous owner, Freightliner, did not properly disclose. A New York–based investment company, Patriarch Partners, bought American LaFrance in late 2005 for an undisclosed sum.

"As a result of the unanticipated obsolescence of inventory and the ongoing ERP problems, American LaFrance has incurred approximately $100 million in secured debt since it purchased its business," company officials said in a statement. "These problems have resulted in slowed production, a large unfulfilled backlog, and a lack of sufficient funds to continue operating."

ALF had purchased Freightliner's business in 2005. As part of the purchase agreement, Freightliner had managed inventory, payroll, and manufacturing processes until June 2007, according to news reports. "But American LaFrance, which was preparing to take over those functions by creating its own in-house system, fumbled the changeover," wrote *The Post and Courier* of Charleston, South Carolina.

Citing company statements, the newspaper added: "The two systems were not entirely compatible, and a wide range of financial information was lost in the changeover. Inventory was in disarray, and workers were unable to find the parts they needed." According to U.S. Bankruptcy Court documents, the new system ALF set up with the help of a software vendor had "serious deficiencies" that had "a crippling impact" on the company's operations.

The multitude of business and IT problems "forced American LaFrance to seek protection from its more than 1,000 creditors, who collectively are owed more than $200 million," the paper reported. Results from a recent CIO survey on ERP systems and their importance to twenty-first-century businesses explain how and why technology disasters like American LaFrance's can happen. More than 85 percent of survey respondents agreed or strongly agreed that their ERP systems were essential to the core of their businesses, and that they "could not live without them."

Source: Adapted from Jennifer Zaino, "Modern Workforce: Capital One Puts ERP at Core of Work," *InformationWeek*, July 11, 2005.

Causes of ERP Failures

What have been the major causes of failure in ERP projects? In almost every case, the business managers and IT professionals of these companies underestimated the complexity of the planning, development, and training that were needed to prepare for a new ERP system that would radically change their business processes and information systems. Failure to involve affected employees in the planning and development phases and to change management programs, or trying to do too much too fast in the conversion process, also were typical causes of failed ERP projects. Insufficient training in the new work tasks required by the ERP system and failure to do enough data conversion and testing were other causes of failure. In many cases, ERP failures were also due to overreliance by company or IT management on the claims of ERP software vendors or on the assistance of prestigious consulting firms hired to lead the implementation. The following experience of a company that did it right give us a helpful look at what is needed for a successful ERP implementation.

Capital One Financial: Success with ERP Systems

Just a few years ago at Capital One Financial Corp., it took 10 human-resources (HR) specialists to sign off on one change-of-address form. With thousands of employees worldwide, that's a lot of paper-pushing. Today, address changes are done via a self-service application that has freed HR to devote time to strategic staffing, program planning, and change management.

This example illustrates a big change that has taken place at the $2.6 billion-a-year financial services company since it began to roll out PeopleSoft applications. "It's a cultural change that has freed people to not deal with minutiae but to deal with business value," says Gregor Bailar, executive VP and CIO.

"It really has been transformative." Bailar envisions more automation ahead, with financials following in the footsteps of HR's "lean-process" design to deal with the mountain of data requests the financials team receives and processes within the group.

The PeopleSoft ERP system, which serves as Capital One's backbone for financials, HR, asset management, and supply chain processes, supports about 18,000 users, including Capital One's 15,000 associates and some business partners. The applications are accessible via a Web portal based on BEA Systems Inc.'s technology.

Capital One is exploring the possibility of partnering with ERP application service providers, now that the hard work of correcting data and linking processes is done. Running the applications may be more of a commodity job at this point, but the applications themselves serve as a pillar for the company's future-of-work initiative. Bailar describes this as "a very mobile, interactive, collaborative environment" designed to support the requirements of the company's biggest asset, its knowledge workers. It's characterized not only by extensive Wi-Fi access, VoIP-enabled laptops, instant messaging, and BlackBerrys, but also by workflows that, for the most part, come to users electronically. Says Bailar, "Everyone's daily life is kind of drawn back to this suite of apps."

Source: Adapted from Jennifer Zaino, "Modern Workforce: Capital One Puts ERP at Core of Work," *InformationWeek*, July 11, 2005.

Supply Chain Management: The Business Network

Starting an e-business takes ideas, capital, and technical savvy. Operating one, however, takes supply chain management (SCM) skills. A successful SCM strategy is based on accurate order processing, just-in-time inventory management, and timely order fulfillment. SCM's increasing importance illustrates how a tool that was a theoretical process 10 years ago is now a hot competitive weapon.

That's why many companies today are making supply chain management a top strategic objective and major e-business application development initiative. Fundamentally, supply chain management helps a company get the right products to the right place at the right time, in the proper quantity and at an acceptable cost. The goal of SCM is to manage this process efficiently by forecasting demand; controlling inventory; enhancing the network of business relationships a company has with customers, suppliers, distributors, and others; and receiving feedback on the status of every link in the supply chain. To achieve this goal, many companies today are turning to Internet technologies to Web-enable their supply chain processes, decision making, and information flows.

What Is SCM?

Legacy supply chains are clogged with unnecessary steps and redundant stockpiles. For instance, a typical box of breakfast cereal spends an incredible 104 days getting from factory to supermarket, struggling its way through an unbelievable maze of wholesalers, distributors, brokers, and consolidators, each of which has a warehouse. The e-commerce opportunity lies in the fusing of each company's internal systems to those of its suppliers, partners, and customers. This fusion forces companies to better integrate interenterprise supply chain processes to improve manufacturing efficiency and distribution effectiveness.

Supply chain management (SCM) is a cross-functional interenterprise system that uses information technology to help support and manage the links between some of a company's key business processes and those of its suppliers, customers, and business partners. The goal of SCM is to create a fast, efficient, and low-cost network of business relationships, or supply chain, to get a company's products from concept to market (see Figure 7.11).

What exactly is a company's supply chain? Let's suppose a company wants to build and sell a product to other businesses. To accomplish this, it must buy raw materials and a variety of contracted services from other companies. The interrelationships with suppliers, customers, distributors, and other businesses that are needed to design, build, and sell a product make up the network of business entities, relationships, and

FIGURE 7.11

Computer-based supply chain management systems are enabling reduced cycle times, increased revenues, and a competitive edge in fast-paced retail markets.

Source: Gary Gladstone Studio Inc./ Getty Images.

processes that is called a supply chain. And because each supply chain process should add value to the products or services a company produces, a supply chain is frequently called a *value chain*, a different but related concept we discussed in Chapter 2. In any event, many companies today are using Internet technologies to create interenterprise e-business systems for supply chain management that help a company streamline its traditional supply chain processes.

Figure 7.12 illustrates the basic business processes in the supply chain life cycle and the functional SCM processes that support them. It also emphasizes how many companies today are reengineering their supply chain processes, aided by Internet technologies and supply chain management software. For example, the demands of today's competitive business environment are pushing manufacturers to use their

FIGURE 7.12

Supply chain management software and Internet technologies can help companies reengineer and integrate the functional SCM processes that support the supply chain life cycle.

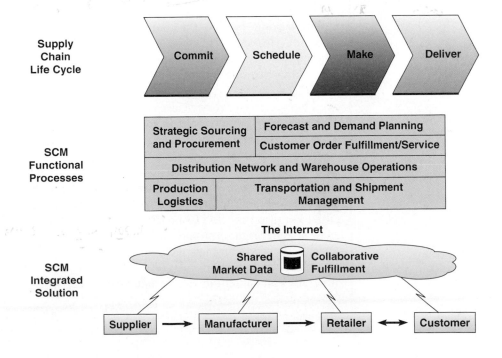

intranets, extranets, and e-commerce Web portals to help them reengineer their relationships with their suppliers, distributors, and retailers. The objective is to significantly reduce costs, increase efficiency, and improve their supply chain cycle times. SCM software can also help improve interenterprise coordination among supply chain process players. The result is much more effective distribution and channel networks among business partners. The Web initiatives of PC Connection illustrate these developments.

PC Connection: Learning to Stop, Drop, and Ship

PC Connection has razor-thin margins. To stay healthy, the $1.8 billion-a-year tech reseller has slashed inefficiencies wherever possible in recent years. Yet despite tight financial circumstances, PC Connection invested substantially to overhaul its supply chain, building Web services modules in front of its ERP system to more efficiently integrate with partners and suppliers. The upgrades will help the company take on new business opportunities, such as selling software licenses, that promise higher margins than hardware.

Although the company has grown significantly over the years, the growth hasn't been without pain. While PC Connection now offers goods and services from more than 1,400 manufacturers, its core ERP system hadn't changed much from the days when the company sold directly to customers. "It was built for the days of pick, pack, and ship," Jack Ferguson, PC Connection's treasurer and CFO, says of the company's Oracle JD Edwards ERP system. That became a growing problem as the company over the last several years expanded its catalog and extended its fulfillment network to include more than a dozen external partners to handle increasingly complex drop-ship orders. "We were faced with a growing number of products, and we also had a desire to cut inventory," Ferguson says.

It soon became apparent that the system wasn't built to handle such a multitiered fulfillment network. "Once you move to drop-ship it gets more complicated," says Ferguson, who notes that even basic requirements, like the calculation of sales tax on an order, were affected by the new drop-ship arrangements. Before long, managers from various departments within PC Connection were requesting ad hoc changes to the company's ERP system to meet new requirements as they evolved. But the process was becoming unmanageable. As a result, PC Connection last year decided to embark on a thorough overhaul of its fulfillment system.

IT staffers looked at numerous off-the-shelf E-commerce packages, but all were found lacking. Instead, the company launched a labor-intensive campaign to internally develop new front-end modules for the existing JD Edwards system. These modules were built using both Web services and traditional EDI to deal with the company's growing web of fulfillment partners.

The first set of enhancements to the JD Edwards system went online recently, and Ferguson says they're already paying off in terms of time and cost savings. "In the past, much of what our buyers did was very manual and time consuming, with lots of order entry across multiple systems," he says. "This takes 90% of the manual part out of their day."

Among other things, there are now modules that can automatically determine the quickest, most economical way to fulfill an order, whether directly from one of the company's warehouses or through a partner in a particular geographic location. Still, Ferguson says PC Connection is investing for future growth, and adds that the new system means customer orders will continue to be filled with greater speed and accuracy, even as business picks up.

"It's a customer satisfaction issue," he says. "To stay in the game you have to upgrade your system to handle increased requests."

Source: Adapted from Paul McDougall, "PC Connection Learns to Stop, Drop, and Ship," *InformationWeek*, September 15, 2008.

FIGURE 7.13 A typical example of electronic data interchange activities, an important form of business-to-business electronic commerce. EDI over the Internet is a major B2B e-commerce application.

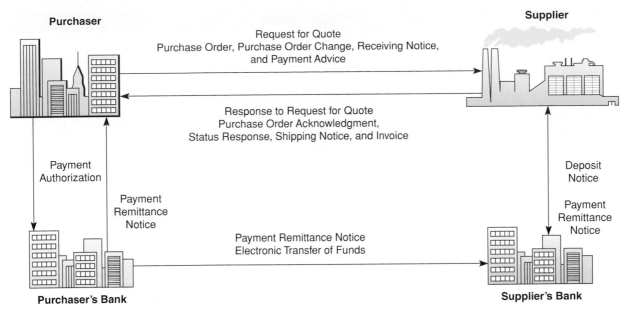

Electronic Data Interchange

Electronic data interchange (EDI) was one of the earliest uses of information technology for supply chain management. EDI involves the electronic exchange of business transaction documents over the Internet and other networks between supply chain trading partners (organizations and their customers and suppliers). Data representing a variety of business transaction documents (e.g., purchase orders, invoices, requests for quotations, shipping notices) are automatically exchanged between computers using standard document message formats. Typically, EDI software is used to convert a company's own document formats into standardized EDI formats specified by various industry and international protocols. Thus, EDI is an example of the almost complete automation of an e-commerce supply chain process. And EDI over the Internet, using secure *virtual private networks*, is a growing B2B e-commerce application.

Formatted transaction data are transmitted over network links directly between computers without paper documents or human intervention. In addition to direct network links between the computers of trading partners, third-party services are widely used. Value-added network companies like GE Global Exchange Services and Computer Associates offer a variety of EDI services for relatively high fees. But many EDI service providers now offer secure, lower cost EDI services over the Internet. Figure 7.13 illustrates a typical EDI system.

EDI is still a popular data-transmission format among major trading partners, primarily to automate repetitive transactions, though it is increasingly being replaced by XML-based Web services. EDI automatically tracks inventory changes; triggers orders, invoices, and other documents related to transactions; and schedules and confirms delivery and payment. By digitally integrating the supply chain, EDI streamlines processes, saves time, and increases accuracy. And by using Internet technologies, lower-cost Internet-based EDI services are now available to smaller businesses.

The Role of SCM

Figure 7.14 helps us understand the role and activities of supply chain management in business more clearly. The top three levels of Figure 7.14 show the strategic, tactical, and operational objectives and outcomes of SCM planning, which are then accomplished by the business partners in a supply chain at the execution level of SCM. The role of information technology in SCM is to support these objectives with interenterprise

FIGURE 7.14   The objectives and outcomes of supply chain management are accomplished for a business with the help of interenterprise SCM information systems.

SCM Objectives		SCM Outcomes
What? Establish objectives, policies, and operating footprint	**Strategic**	• Objectives • Supply policies (service levels) • Network design
How much? Deploy resources to match supply to demand	**Tactical**	• Demand forecast • Production, procurement, logistics plan • Inventory targets
When? Where? Schedule, monitor, control, and adjust production	**Operational**	• Work center scheduling • Order/inventory tracking
Do Build and transport	**Execution**	• Order cycle • Material movement

Source: Adapted from Keith Oliver, Anne Chung, and Nick Samanach, "Beyond Utopia: The Realist's Guide to Internet-Enabled Supply Chain Management," *Strategy and Business,* Second Quarter, 2001, p. 99.

information systems that produce many of the outcomes a business needs to effectively manage its supply chain. That's why many companies today are installing SCM software and developing Web-based SCM information systems.

Until recently, SCM software products typically were developed for either supply chain planning or execution applications. SCM planning software from vendors such as i2 and Manugistics supports a variety of applications for supply and demand forecasting. SCM execution software from vendors such as EXE Technologies and Manhattan Associates supports applications like order management, logistics management, and warehouse management. However, big ERP vendors like Oracle and SAP are now offering Web-enabled software suites of e-business applications that include SCM modules. Examples include Oracle's e-Business Suite and SAP AG's mySAP.

Benefits and Challenges of SCM

Creating a real-time SCM infrastructure is a daunting and ongoing issue and quite often a point of failure for several reasons. The chief reason is that the planning, selection, and implementation of SCM solutions is becoming more complex as the pace of technological change accelerates and the number of a company's partners increases.

The promised outcomes that are outlined in Figure 7.15 emphasize the major business benefits that are possible with effective supply chain management systems. Companies know that SCM systems can provide them with key business benefits such as faster, more accurate order processing, reductions in inventory levels, quicker times to market, lower transaction and materials costs, and strategic relationships with their suppliers. All of these benefits of SCM are aimed at helping a company achieve agility and responsiveness in meeting the demands of its customers and the needs of its business partners.

However, developing effective SCM systems has proven to be a complex and difficult application of information technology to business operations. So achieving the business value and customer value goals and objectives of supply chain management, as illustrated in Figure 7.16, has been a major challenge for most companies.

What are the causes of problems in supply chain management? Several reasons stand out. A lack of proper demand-planning knowledge, tools, and guidelines is a major source of SCM failure. Inaccurate or overoptimistic demand forecasts will cause major production, inventory, and other business problems, no matter how efficient the

FIGURE 7.15   The supply chain management functions and potential benefits offered by the SCM module in the mySAP e-business software suite.

SCM Functions	SCM Outcomes
Planning	
Supply Chain Design	● Optimize network of suppliers, plants, and distribution centers.
Collaborative Demand and Supply Planning	● Develop an accurate forecast of customer demand by sharing demand and supply forecasts instantaneously across multiple tiers. ● Internet-enable collaborative scenarios, such as collaborative planning, forecasting, and replenishment (CPFR), and vendor-managed inventory.
Execution	
Materials Management	● Share accurate inventory and procurement order information. ● Ensure materials required for production are available in the right place at the right time. ● Reduce raw material spending, procurement costs, safety stocks, and raw material and finished goods inventory.
Collaborative Fulfillment	● Commit to delivery dates in real time. ● Fulfill orders from all channels on time with order management, transportation planning, and vehicle scheduling. ● Support the entire logistics process, including picking, packing, shipping, and delivery in foreign countries.
Supply Chain Event Management	● Monitor every stage of the supply chain process, from price quotation to the moment the customer receives the product, and receive alerts when problems arise.
Supply Chain Performance Management	● Report key measurements in the supply chain, such as filling rates, order cycle times, and capacity utilization.

rest of the supply chain management process. Inaccurate production, inventory, and other business data provided by a company's other information systems are a frequent cause of SCM problems. And the lack of adequate collaboration among marketing, production, and inventory management departments within a company, and with suppliers, distributors, and others, will sabotage any SCM system. Even the SCM software tools themselves are considered to be immature, incomplete, and hard to implement by many companies that are installing SCM systems.

FIGURE 7.16

Achieving the goals and objectives of supply chain management is a major challenge for many companies today.

Objectives of Supply Chain Management

FIGURE 7.17
Enterprise application integration software connects front-office and back-office applications.

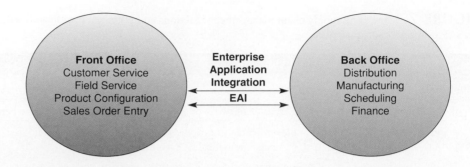

Enterprise Application Integration

How does a business interconnect its cross-functional enterprise systems? **Enterprise application integration (EAI)** software is being used by many companies to connect their major e-business applications. See Figure 7.17. EAI software enables users to model the business processes involved in the interactions that should occur between business applications. EAI also provides *middleware* that performs data conversion and coordination, application communication and messaging services, and access to the application interfaces involved. Thus, EAI software can integrate a variety of enterprise application clusters by letting them exchange data according to rules derived from the business process models developed by users. For example, a typical rule might be:

> *When an order is complete, have the order application tell the accounting system to send a bill and alert shipping to send out the product.*

Thus, as Figure 7.17 illustrates, EAI software can integrate the front-office and back-office applications of a business so that they work together in a seamless, integrated way. This vital capability provides real business value to a business enterprise that must respond quickly and effectively to business events and customer demands. For example, the integration of enterprise application clusters has been shown to dramatically improve customer call center responsiveness and effectiveness. That's because EAI integrates access to everything the customer and product data customer

FIGURE 7.18   An example of a new customer order process showing how EAI middleware connects several business information systems within a company.

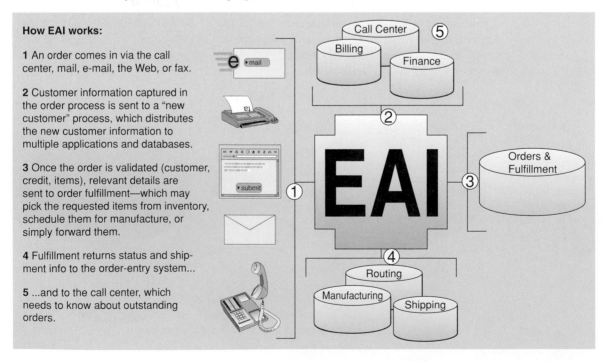

reps need to serve customers quickly. EAI also streamlines sales order processing so that products and services can be delivered faster. Thus, EAI improves customer and supplier experience with the business because of its responsiveness. See Figure 7.18.

EAI: Costly, Painful, and Worth It	If you order speakers from Bose, your order goes into a system CIO Robert Ramrath calls the Common Order Interface.

Ramrath's group knit this custom framework together about three years ago. Two legacy call center applications, plus a Web commerce application built mostly with Microsoft tools, are all linked to an underlying database and connected to the corporate back-office ERP system, so your order winds up in SAP regardless of how it was placed.

That's the kind of setup for which enterprise application integration (EAI) tools were born. EAI software connects applications through a central message-routing hub; EAI tools are also equipped to parse and translate data, as well as automatically route information according to business processes.

Make no mistake: EAI systems are expensive.

Top-end EAI covers a lot of turf: a stack of functions from basic messaging up through business process management. On top of this central engine, EAI customers buy "adapters" to connect to their applications (such as an SAP or Siebel adapter) and custom adapters for idiosyncratic legacy applications. There's more to the total cost than just the software.

EAI projects carry three red flags: consulting costs, maintenance costs, and data definition problems that can drive up the first two costs. Those are classic IT project expenditures, but they're worth flagging with EAI because early vendor marketing efforts suggested the idea that EAI stuff is off-the-shelf, once-and-done, plug-and-play. Not so, say practitioners.

Detroit-based General Motors is the poster child for EAI because of the sheer size of its application portfolio.

GM standardized on SeeBeyond's EAI toolset. The vast array of applications includes all of GM's consumer-facing Web activity, a Siebel CRM system, dealer support systems, and portal software from iPlanet. GM's supply chain application infrastructure includes connections to Covisint, a custom vehicle order management system, planning and logistics applications, and inventory management. Some GM units (those in smaller geographical regions) use SAP as their foundation; others don't. There is also an i2 Technologies supply chain management package rollout under way. That package will replace older planning applications as part of an ambitious reengineering of GM's entire order-to-delivery process.

Big companies such as General Motors report concrete savings of as much as 80 percent on certain integration projects once the messaging hub is in place and reuse of interfaces starts to kick in. Smaller companies have a tougher decision to make, but those with multiple or business-critical integration needs can also experience benefits from EAI. EAI is infrastructure, and cost justification is always a tough sell for infrastructure projects. Taking a long-term view, however, the only thing more expensive is not using these tools.

Source: Adapted from Derek Slater, "INTEGRATION—Costly, Painful, and Worth It," *CIO Magazine*, January 15, 2002.

Transaction Processing Systems

Transaction processing systems (TPS) are cross-functional information systems that process data resulting from the occurrence of business transactions. We introduced transaction processing systems in Chapter 1 as one of the major application categories of information systems in business.

Transactions are events that occur as part of doing business, such as sales, purchases, deposits, withdrawals, refunds, and payments. Think, for example, of the data generated whenever a business sells something to a customer on credit, whether in a retail store or at an e-commerce site on the Web. Data about the customer, product, salesperson, store, and so on must be captured and processed. This need prompts additional transactions, such as credit checks, customer billing, inventory changes, and increases in accounts receivable balances, which generate even more data. Thus, transaction processing activities are needed to capture and process such data, or the operations of a business would grind to a halt. Therefore, transaction processing systems play a vital role in supporting the vital operations of most companies today.

Online transaction processing systems play a strategic role in Web-enabled business processes and electronic commerce. Many firms are using the Internet and other networks that tie them electronically to their customers or suppliers for online transaction processing (OLTP). Such *real-time* systems, which capture and process transactions immediately, can help firms provide superior service to customers and other trading partners. This capability adds value to their products and services and thus gives them an important way to differentiate themselves from their competitors.

Syntellect's Online Transaction Processing

Figure 7.19 illustrates an online transaction processing system for cable pay-per-view systems developed by Syntellect Interactive Services. Cable TV viewers can select pay-per-view events offered by their cable companies using the phone or the World Wide Web. The pay-per-view order is captured by Syntellect's interactive voice response system or Web server, and then transported to Syntellect database application servers. There the order is processed, customer and sales databases are updated, and the approved order is relayed back to the cable company's video server, which transmits the video of the pay-per-view event to the customer. Thus, Syntellect teams with over 700 cable companies to offer a very popular and very profitable service.

FIGURE 7.19   The Syntellect pay-per-view online transaction processing system.

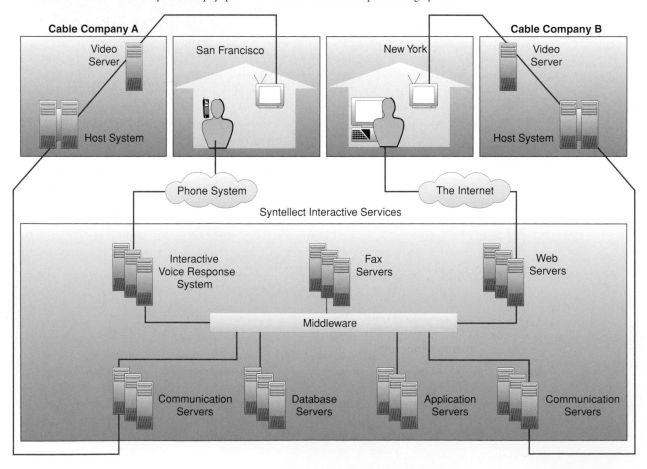

FIGURE 7.20

The transaction processing cycle. Note that transaction processing systems use a five-stage cycle of data entry, transaction processing, database maintenance, document and report generation, and inquiry processing activities.

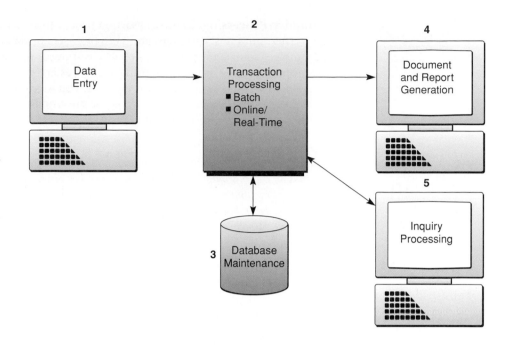

The Transaction Processing Cycle

Transaction processing systems, such as Syntellect's, capture and process data describing business transactions, update organizational databases, and produce a variety of information products. You should understand this as a transaction processing cycle of several basic activities, as illustrated in Figure 7.20.

● **Data Entry.** The first step of the transaction processing cycle is the capture of business data. For example, transaction data may be collected by point-of-sale terminals using optical scanning of bar codes and credit card readers at a retail store or other business. Or transaction data can be captured at an electronic commerce Web site on the Internet. The proper recording and editing of data so they are quickly and correctly captured for processing is one of the major design challenges of information systems discussed in Chapter 12.

● **Transaction Processing.** Transaction processing systems process data in two basic ways: (1) batch processing, where transaction data are accumulated over a period of time and processed periodically; and (2) real-time processing (also called online processing), where data are processed immediately after a transaction occurs. All online transaction processing systems incorporate real–time processing capabilities. Many online systems also depend on the capabilities of *fault tolerant* computer systems that can continue to operate even if parts of the system fail. We will discuss this fault tolerant concept in Chapter 11.

● **Database Maintenance.** An organization's databases must be maintained by its transaction processing systems so that they are always correct and up-to-date. Therefore, transaction processing systems update the corporate databases of an organization to reflect changes resulting from day-to-day business transactions. For example, credit sales made to customers will cause customer account balances to be increased and the amount of inventory on hand to be decreased. Database maintenance ensures that these and other changes are reflected in the data records stored in the company's databases.

● **Document and Report Generation.** Transaction processing systems produce a variety of documents and reports. Examples of transaction documents include purchase orders, paychecks, sales receipts, invoices, and customer statements. Transaction reports might take the form of a transaction listing such as a payroll register or edit reports that describe errors detected during processing.

- **Inquiry Processing.** Many transaction processing systems allow you to use the Internet, intranets, extranets, and Web browsers or database management query languages to make inquiries and receive responses regarding the results of transaction processing activity. Typically, responses are displayed in a variety of prespecified formats or screens. For example, you might check on the status of a sales order, the balance in an account, or the amount of stock in inventory and receive immediate responses at your PC.

Enterprise Collaboration Systems

Really difficult business problems always have many aspects. Often a major decision depends on an impromptu search for one or two key pieces of auxiliary information and a quick ad hoc analysis of several possible scenarios. You need software tools that easily combine and recombine data from many sources. You need Internet access for all kinds of research. Widely scattered people need to be able to collaborate and work the data in different ways.

Enterprise collaboration systems (ECS) are cross-functional information systems that enhance communication, coordination, and collaboration among the members of business teams and workgroups. Information technology, especially Internet technologies, provides tools to help us collaborate—to communicate ideas, share resources, and coordinate our work efforts as members of the many formal and informal process and project teams and workgroups that make up many of today's organizations. Thus, the goal of ECS is to enable us to work together more easily and effectively by helping us:

- **Communicate.** Sharing information with each other.
- **Coordinate.** Coordinating our individual work efforts and use of resources with each other.
- **Collaborate.** Working together cooperatively on joint projects and assignments.

For example, engineers, business specialists, and external consultants may form a virtual team for a project. The team may rely on intranets and extranets to collaborate via e-mail, videoconferencing, discussion forums, and a multimedia database of work-in-progress information at a project Web site. The enterprise collaboration system may use PC workstations networked to a variety of servers on which project, corporate, and other databases are stored. In addition, network servers may provide a variety of software resources, such as Web browsers, groupware, and application packages, to assist the team's collaboration until the project is completed.

Tools for Enterprise Collaboration

The capabilities and potential of the Internet as well as intranets and extranets are driving the demand for better enterprise collaboration tools in business. However, it is Internet technologies like Web browsers and servers, hypermedia documents and databases, and intranets and extranets that provide the hardware, software, data, and network platforms for many of the groupware tools for enterprise collaboration that business users want. Figure 7.21 provides an overview of some of the software tools for electronic communication, electronic conferencing, and collaborative work management.

Electronic communication tools include electronic mail, voice mail, faxing, Web publishing, bulletin board systems, paging, and Internet phone systems. These tools enable you to electronically send messages, documents, and files in data, text, voice, or multimedia over computer networks. This capability helps you share everything from voice and text messages to copies of project documents and data files with your team members, wherever they may be. The ease and efficiency of such communications are major contributors to the collaboration process.

Electronic conferencing tools help people communicate and collaborate while working together. A variety of conferencing methods enables the members of teams and workgroups at different locations to exchange ideas interactively at the same time

FIGURE 7.21

Electronic communications, conferencing, and collaborative work software tools enhance enterprise collaboration.

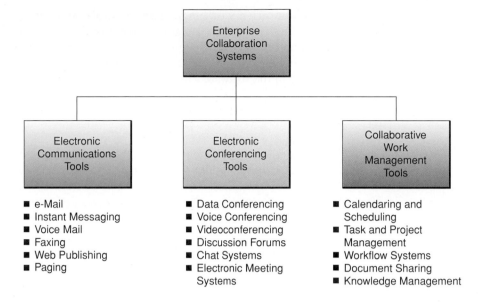

or at different times at their convenience. These methods include data and voice conferencing, videoconferencing, chat systems, and discussion forums. Electronic conferencing options also include *electronic meeting systems* and other *group support systems* where team members can meet at the same time and place in a *decision room* setting or use the Internet to work collaboratively anywhere in the world. See Figure 7.22.

FIGURE 7.22

QuickPlace by Lotus Development helps virtual workgroups set up Web-based work spaces for collaborative work assignments.

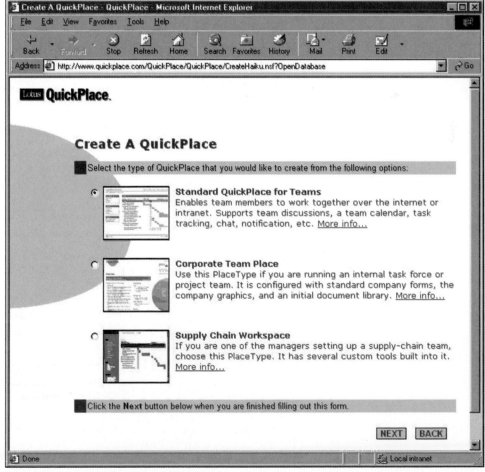

Source: ©Reproduced with permission of Yahoo! Inc.

Collaborative work management tools help people accomplish or manage group work activities. This category of software includes calendaring and scheduling tools, task and project management, workflow systems, and knowledge management tools. Other tools for joint work, such as joint document creation, editing, and revision, are found in the software suites discussed in Chapter 4.

Exploring Virtual Worlds as Collaboration Tools

For emergency responders working along Interstate 95, accidents aren't a game; they're a way of life (and death). So it seemed odd to a group of firefighters, cops, and medics when researchers from the University of Maryland suggested it use a virtual world to collaborate on training for rollovers, multicar pileups, and life-threatening injuries.

The phrase *virtual world* is often associated with Second Life, the much-hyped 3-D environment hosted by Linden Lab that allows users to talk to friends, sell T-shirts, fly around on carpets, and even build amusement parks—in other words, to play. "It wasn't until we started to do elaborate demos that the first responders started to realize the true potential," says Michael Pack, director of research with the University of Maryland's Center for Advanced Transportation Technology, who has since begun rolling out a virtual world pilot project that could accommodate training for hundreds of emergency workers.

Industry analysts and developers of virtual worlds believe that by immersing users in an interactive environment that allows for social interactions, virtual worlds have the potential to succeed where other collaborative technologies, like teleconferencing, have failed. Phone-based meetings begin and end abruptly at the mercy of the person or service administering it. In a virtual world, conversations between employees can continue within the virtual space—just as they do in company hallways after a meeting ends.

However, businesses must overcome many technical and cultural obstacles before they adopt virtual worlds on a major scale. Perhaps even more important than the technical challenges, companies must tackle the issue of workers' online identities. People's 3-D representations, known as avatars, must be constructed in such a way that allows users of virtual worlds to have faith that they're talking to the right colleague. Security challenges abound; most companies using virtual worlds today do so on a public or externally hosted platform with limited options to protect corporate data.

Pack says training in a virtual world presents a desirable alternative to real-life exercises, which can be pricey and inefficient. "You'd go out in a field and flip a car over and have people act as victims," he says. Trainers couldn't introduce many variables (such as mounting traffic). "It's supposed to be as human as possible, so anything goes," he says. "We've put together lots of scenarios, from fender benders to 20-car pileups. We put [the participants] in dangerous situations to see how they will respond." In virtual worlds, Pack and his team can program multiple scenarios into the software. For example, if a first responder gets out of his car and fails to put on a reflective jacket, the system might respond with a car hitting that person's avatar.

"You want people to be so comfortable in the virtual world that they're not concentrating on how to use them," Pack says. "They can't be worried about how to turn left or talk to someone. They need to be worried about how to do their jobs, just like they would in the real world."

Source: Adapted from C.G. Lynch. "Companies Explore Virtual Worlds as Collaboration Tools," *CIO Magazine*, February 6, 2008.

SECTION II Functional Business Systems

Business managers are moving from a tradition where they could avoid, delegate, or ignore decisions about IT to one where they cannot create a marketing, product, international, organization, or financial plan that does not involve such decisions.

There are as many ways to use information technology in business as there are business activities to be performed, business problems to be solved, and business opportunities to be pursued. As a business professional, you should have a basic understanding and appreciation of the major ways information systems are used to support each of the functions of business that must be accomplished in any company that wants to succeed. Thus, in this section, we discuss functional business systems, that is, a variety of types of information systems (transaction processing, management information, decision support, etc.) that support the business functions of accounting, finance, marketing, operations management, and human resource management.

Read the Real World Case below. We can learn a lot about the impact of IT on the HR function from this case. See Figure 7.23.

IT in Business

It is also important that you, as a business professional, have a specific understanding of how information systems affect a particular business function (e.g., marketing) or a particular industry (e.g., banking) that is directly related to your career objectives. For example, someone whose career objective is a marketing position in banking should have a basic understanding of how information systems are used in banking and how they support the marketing activities of banks and other firms.

Figure 7.24 illustrates how information systems can be grouped into business function categories. Thus, information systems in this section will be analyzed according to the business function they support by looking at a few key examples in each functional area. This approach should give you an appreciation of the variety of functional business systems that both small and large business firms may use.

Marketing Systems

The business function of marketing is concerned with the pricing, promotion, and sale of existing products in existing markets, as well as the development of new products and new markets to better attract and serve present and potential customers. Thus, marketing performs a vital function in the operation of a business enterprise. Business firms have increasingly turned to information technology to help them perform vital marketing functions in the face of the rapid changes of today's environment.

Figure 7.25 illustrates how marketing information systems provide information technologies that support major components of the marketing function. For example, Internet/intranet Web sites and services make an *interactive marketing* process possible, in which customers can become partners in creating, marketing, purchasing, and improving products and services. *Sales force automation* systems use mobile computing and Internet technologies to automate many information-processing activities for sales support and management. Other marketing information systems assist marketing managers in customer relationship management, product planning, pricing and other product management decisions, advertising, sales promotion, targeted marketing strategies, and market research and forecasting. Let's take a closer look at three of these marketing applications.

Interactive Marketing

The term interactive marketing has been coined to describe a customer-focused marketing process that is based on using the Internet, intranets, and extranets to establish two-way transactions between a business and its customers or potential customers. The goal of interactive marketing is to enable a company to use those networks

REAL WORLD CASE 2

OHSU, Sony, Novartis, and Others: Strategic Information Systems—It's HR's Turn

"Our people are our most valuable asset." How many times have you heard that company slogan? In recent years, HR departments have focused their technology efforts on driving down costs by automating or outsourcing nonstrategic, transaction-oriented processes such as benefits enrollment and payroll. As a result, many employees can now do a number of things online that used to require the intervention of HR staff, such as viewing pay stubs, changing personal information, or enrolling for benefits.

Increasingly, however, HR is being urged not only to reduce the cost of hiring, retaining, and compensating employees but also to optimize the corporate talent pool. After all, if your workforce is your biggest expense, shouldn't you shape it to support in the best way possible the strategic goals of the business?

Imagine placing an electronic order to hire an employee the same way a factory manager uses ERP software to order more parts for the assembly line. That's roughly what's happening at Oregon Health & Science University (OHSU). "More and more, HR is being called upon to be a strategic partner," says Joe Tonn, manager of HR management systems at OHSU in Portland.

The payoff is significant: The university is filling job openings two weeks faster than it once did and saving at least $1,500 per job now that it's using Oracle Corp.'s iRecruitment software. The iRecruitment application, part of Oracle's E-Business Human Resources Management System (HRMS) suite, enables managers to request a new employee and process applications electronically. The software handles most of the time-consuming administrative work, including routing requisition forms to the appropriate managers and posting the job on the Web site. "We wanted to be able to

open a job requisition in the morning and have qualified candidates in the afternoon," says Tonn.

In fact, OHSU now has access to applicants only minutes after a job opening is posted to the university's Web site, and it fills those jobs in just four weeks instead of six or more. The university also recently added Oracle's Manager Self-Service module for logging changes to employee status (e.g., promotions or use of family leave) and uses the Oracle Employee Self-Service application for benefits management.

Tonn expects to add software for performance reviews, succession planning, and learning management over the next couple of years.

Large and midsize organizations such as OHSU are increasingly turning to these new types of employee management applications—commonly called human capital management (HCM) or workforce optimization software—to automate HR processes that used to be done manually, on paper, or by e-mail.

"Human capital management covers the whole discipline of managing the workforce, bringing them in and tracking them over time," says Christa Manning, an analyst at AMR Research Inc. in Boston. AMR forecasts a 10 percent compound annual growth rate through 2010 for the $6 billion HCM market. Much of the market growth can be attributed to the upcoming retirement of baby boomers, which will shrink the pool of available workers. Companies need to automate their systems so that they can better identify employees they want to retain and then provide a career path for them.

Sony Computer Entertainment America Inc. uses recruitment software from WorkforceLogic to automate its process for hiring contract workers. Sally Buchanan, director of human resources, says the software is particularly useful for ensuring that hiring managers understand and comply with the legal distinctions between contract and salaried employees.

"When they requisition a contractor, they must answer a series of questions through the WorkforceLogic interface, and the application renders a recommendation on whether the position is best filled by a contractor or by someone on the payroll," says Buchanan.

Employee performance management, career development, and succession planning are all functions that can be automated with HCM applications. For example, Tyco International Ltd. uses Kenexa's CareerTracker to track employee performance and promotions. The software, which is configured with Tyco's performance standards and rating system, can plot employee performance on a graph to identify the top performers, both in terms of job achievement and in meeting Tyco's leadership behavior standards.

Using the database of employee credentials and expertise, Tyco can also locate the best people to fill key job openings and analyze what types of training they'll need. "We can identify who we have and how they fit," says Shaun Zitting, director of organizational development at the Princeton, New Jersey–based company.

According to AMR's Manning, most corporate executives like having a tool that helps them evaluate and promote people on purely objective criteria. "They know it's not based on, 'I like Joe because we go to lunch every day.' It brings some real

FIGURE 7.23

More and more HR is being called to be a strategic business partner, and professionals in this area are turning to IT for innovative solutions.

©Jack Hollingsworth/Corbis

science to the process and allows you to not only identify your top performers but also to know why they're top performers," she says. Career development and succession planning applications have also become more important as baby boomers retire and organizations have to find qualified replacements.

Succession planning isn't just for CEOs and other top executives anymore. "It's starting to cascade down into the organization as the collecting and associating of employee information become easier," says Manning.

Managers can associate key characteristics with specific jobs and analyze the traits of successful employees. Employees themselves can use the data to see their most likely career paths in an organization. Compensation management, another function often found in HCM tools, enables organizations to create incentive programs, tie compensation to performance goals, and analyze pay packages and trends.

Scheduling work shifts for 27,000 health care professionals in a wide range of specialties and at multiple locations is a formidable task. At Banner Health, a large hospital system based in Phoenix, however, the implementation of the Kronos scheduling application has automated much of the process. Banner uses the Kronos application to log hours worked and to plan schedules, says Kathy Schultz, director of IT at Banner Health.

Integrating data about hours worked with future scheduling helps to ensure that employees aren't expected to work if they've just put in a lot of overtime. "What hours you work isn't always what you were scheduled to work," notes Schultz. "Having scheduling integrated with live time-and-attendance information is extremely critical."

At pharmaceutical giant Novartis AG, sales and research and development professionals are expected to take various classes to keep them up to date on the latest products and trends. With about 550 Web-based and classroom-based courses available, the old paper- and Excel-based process for administering training had become cumbersome and time-consuming. Yet by using Saba Software Inc.'s Learning Suite, administrative work has been reduced by 50 percent, according to John Talanca, head of learning technologies at Novartis. "It's allowed the administrators to be more efficient and take on other work. In the past, they would spend hours and hours each day managing this," says Talanca.

HR applications often contain a variety of employee data, including salaries, experience, education, performance reviews, and benefits selections. Analysis tools can enable HR managers to leverage those data for strategic decision making. They can, for instance, track employee performance against company benchmarks, forecast the skills that will be needed for future projects, analyze salary increases by geographic region or professional field, or predict trends in benefits selection and costs.

For example, OHSU's Tonn hopes eventually to use analysis tools to evaluate recruiting practices more efficiently.

Honing the school's recruiting campaigns could produce better candidates as well as lower costs. "We can see how many applications a particular source gives us, and whether we ever hire applicants from that source. If we do hire them, do they become successful employees? Running an ad in *The Oregonian* might produce a thousand applications. But if we didn't hire any of them, then that was a whole lot of administrative work that didn't bear any fruit."

Organizations such as Tyco are increasingly viewing employees as assets, to be acquired, cultivated, and deployed strategically—not unlike product inventory or IT systems. The very name of the software category, human capital management, conveys the notion that a worker is an investment that should be optimized. "Managers want to see how the people they hired are doing," says Manning. "It's taking the organization's people assets and leveraging them to reach business goals, such as increased sales, profitability, and customer satisfaction."

Individually, the various HCM tools are helpful, but to get optimal value, they need to be integrated, with the data stored in a common repository. Organizational issues may be in the way, such as if the various HCM functions are split between different corporate departments, or if the HCM suite has to be implemented across multiple business units running disparate ERP and HR applications.

Changing your HR system from transactional to strategic can take three to five years, but the important thing is to get started. As we move from an industrial to a knowledge economy, it's not what you manufacture but what your people know that gives you competitive advantage.

Source: Adapted from Sue Hildreth, "HR Gets a Dose of Science," *Computerworld*, February 5, 2007; and Mary Brandel, "HR Gets Strategic," *Computerworld*, January 24, 2005.

CASE STUDY QUESTIONS

1. What are some of the business benefits of the technologies described in the case? Provide several examples beyond the mere automation of transaction-oriented processes.

2. Do you think the business value of these strategic HRM applications depends on the type of business a company is in, for instance, consulting, manufacturing, or professional services? Why or why not? Explain.

3. What are some of the challenges and obstacles in developing and implementing HRM systems? Are these unique to this type of system? What strategies would you recommend for companies to meet those challenges? Provide several specific recommendations.

REAL WORLD ACTIVITIES

1. The case refers to a view of employees as "assets, to be acquired, cultivated, and deployed strategically—not unlike product inventory or IT systems." It also mentions these systems allow managers to evaluate and promote people on objective criteria. Do you believe extensive adoption of these technologies may lead to a depersonalization of the employment relationship? Why or why not? Break into small groups to discuss these issues and then summarize your ideas.

2. What are some of the HR trends that seem to be operating behind this renewed emphasis on strategic applications of technology to this functional area? What new developments have recently arisen in this domain? Search the Internet for innovative applications of IT in HRM and write a report to summarize your findings.

FIGURE 7.24   Examples of functional information systems. Note how they support the major functional areas of business.

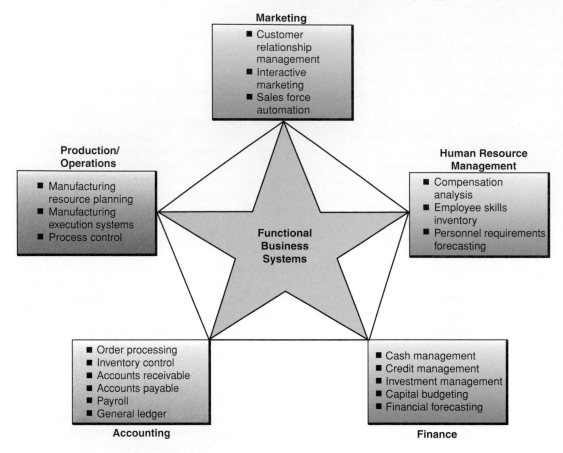

profitably to attract and keep customers who will become partners with the business in creating, purchasing, and improving products and services.

In interactive marketing, customers are not just passive participants who receive media advertising prior to purchase but are actively engaged in network-enabled proactive and interactive processes. Interactive marketing encourages customers to become involved in product development, delivery, and service issues. This involvement is enabled

FIGURE 7.25

Marketing information systems provide information technologies to support major components of the marketing function.

FIGURE 7.26

The five major components of targeted marketing for electronic commerce.

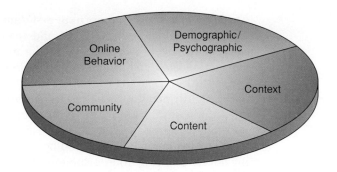

by various Internet technologies, including chat and discussion groups, Web forms and questionnaires, instant messaging, and e-mail correspondence. Finally, the expected outcomes of interactive marketing are a rich mixture of vital marketing data, new product ideas, volume sales, and strong customer relationships.

Targeted Marketing

Targeted marketing has become an important tool in developing advertising and promotion strategies to strengthen a company's e-commerce initiatives, as well as its traditional business venues. As illustrated in Figure 7.26, targeted marketing is an advertising and promotion management concept that includes five targeting components.

- **Community.** Companies can customize their Web advertising messages and promotion methods to appeal to people in specific communities. They can be *communities of interest*, such as *virtual communities* of online sporting enthusiasts or arts and crafts hobbyists, or geographic communities formed by the Web sites of a city or other local organization.

- **Content.** Advertising such as electronic billboards or banners can be placed on a variety of selected Web sites, in addition to a company's Web site. The content of these messages is aimed at the targeted audience. An ad for a product campaign on the opening page of an Internet search engine is a typical example.

- **Context.** Advertising appears only in Web pages that are relevant to the content of a product or service. So advertising is targeted only at people who are already looking for information about a subject (e.g., vacation travel) that is related to a company's products (e.g., car rental services).

- **Demographic/Psychographic.** Web marketing efforts can be aimed at specific types or classes of people—unmarried, twenty-something, middle income, male college graduates, for example.

- **Online Behavior.** Advertising and promotion efforts can be tailored to each visit to a site by an individual. This strategy is based on a variety of tracking techniques, such as Web "cookie" files recorded on the visitor's disk drive from previous visits. This technique enables a company to track a person's online behavior at a Web site so that it can target marketing efforts (e.g., coupons redeemable at retail stores or e-commerce Web sites) to that individual during each visit to its Web site.

An interesting and effective marriage between e-business and target marketing is the emergence of the digital billboard. It is estimated that approximately 450,000 billboard faces exist in the United States. While only a tiny fraction of them are digital, the new billboards are making a huge impact on markets all over the country.

The concept behind the digital billboard is elegantly simple. A billboard is constructed using hundreds of thousands of small LEDs which are controlled via a computer interface that can be accessed via the Web. Advertisers can change their messages quickly, including multiple times in one day. For example, a restaurant can feature breakfast specials in the morning and dinner specials in the evening. A realtor can feature individual houses for sale and change the creative content when the house sells. Print and broadcast news media use digital billboards to deliver headlines, weather updates, and programming information. WCPO-TV credits their meteoric rise in the ratings to the use of digital billboards to deliver breaking news and updates to the nightly newscast. The television station went from the bottom of the ratings in 2002 to the third largest ABC affiliate in the nation. When the I-35 bridge collapse occurred in Minneapolis in 2007, a dangerous situation for unsuspecting drivers existed. Within minutes, a digital billboard network in the area had switched from showing advertising copy to informing drivers about the collapse. Later that evening, the digital billboards advised motorists to take alternate routes. Target marketing is in the digital arena, with a new way of doing something old.

Sales Force Automation

Increasingly, computers and the Internet are providing the basis for **sales force automation**. In many companies, the sales force is being outfitted with notebook computers, Web browsers, and sales contact management software that connect them to marketing Web sites on the Internet, extranets, and their company intranets. This connectivity not only increases the personal productivity of salespeople but dramatically speeds up the capture and analysis of sales data from the field to marketing managers at company headquarters. In return, it allows marketing and sales management to improve the delivery of information and the support they provide to their salespeople. Therefore, many companies are viewing sales force automation as a way to gain a strategic advantage in sales productivity and marketing responsiveness. See Figure 7.27.

For example, salespeople use their PCs to record sales data as they make their calls on customers and prospects during the day. Then each night, sales reps in the field can connect their computers by modem and telephone links to the Internet and extranets, which can access intranet or other network servers at their company. They can upload information about sales orders, sales calls, and other sales statistics, as well as send electronic mail messages and access Web site sales support information. In return, the network servers may download product availability data, lists of information about good sales prospects, and e-mail messages.

FIGURE 7.27

This Web-based sales force automation package supports sales lead management of qualified prospects and the management of current customer accounts.

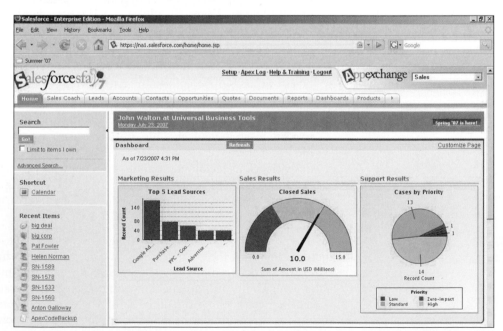

Source: Courtesy of Salesforce.com.

Baker Tanks: Web-Based Sales Force Automation

Baker Tanks, a nationwide leader in rentals of industrial containment and transfer equipment, serves customers throughout the country in industries ranging from construction to aerospace. Because of this varied client base, it's especially important—and challenging—for salespeople to be aware of the specifics of each account every time they speak to customers. The company's 50 sales professionals are on the road four days a week visiting customers on location. That creates additional challenges when it comes to keeping track of customer information and accessing it when needed.

In the past, salespeople filled out paper forms to track customer information, which was later entered into an electronic database. This process left the reps with less time to do what they do best—selling. Even worse, the traveling representatives had no way of connecting to the electronic database from the customer's location. They were collecting plenty of information, but they couldn't access and use it effectively.

"They were recording everything on paper, and that's a very unproductive way of getting things done," says Scott Whitford, systems administrator and lead on the wireless Salesforce.com solution. "We were looking for a solution that would improve our communications, not only between corporate and field people, but between field people and our customers." Adds Darrell Yoshinaga, marketing manager at Baker Tanks, "We were looking for a tool we could implement quickly, but that would still give us the flexibility we needed to become more efficient."

Baker Tanks was immediately drawn to the Web-based functionality, quick implementation time, and low capital investment of a sales force automation system. The ability to connect to sales information anywhere at any time was also an attractive feature. So Baker Tanks moved from a paper-based system to a Web-based system, eliminating the extra step of transferring information from paper documents to the database. Next, sales reps were outfitted with personal digital assistants (PDAs) enabled with the Salesforce.com service. "Our salespeople are real road warriors, and we needed to extend the system to them rather than make them come to the system," Whitford reflects.

Each PDA is equipped with a wireless modem that allows the salesperson to connect to Salesforce.com for customer contact information, as well as sales history and anecdotal notes on the customer—all with read and write access. Salespeople can also use the PDAs to e-mail responses to customers more promptly and improve time management by integrating appointment scheduling and calendar viewing. Says Yoshinaga: "We have achieved our main objective of communicating better with our customers. And our salespeople have become more productive because they have instant access to information and electronic reporting capabilities."

Source: Adapted from "Baker Tanks Leverages Salesforce.com's Wireless Access to Extend Range of Customer Service," salesforce.com, 2002.

Manufacturing Systems

Manufacturing information systems support the *production/operations* function that includes all activities associated with the planning and control of the processes that produce goods or services. Thus, the production/operations function is concerned with the management of the operational processes and systems of all business firms. Information systems used for operations management and transaction processing support all firms that must plan, monitor, and control inventories, purchases, and the flow of goods and services. Therefore, firms such as transportation companies, wholesalers, retailers, financial institutions, and service companies must use production/operations information systems to plan and control their operations. In this section, we will concentrate on computer-based manufacturing applications to illustrate information systems that support the production/operations function.

Computer-Integrated Manufacturing

Once upon a time, manufacturers operated on a simple build-to-stock model. They built 100 or 100,000 of an item and sold them via distribution networks. They kept track of the stock of inventory and made more of the item once inventory levels dipped below a threshold. Rush jobs were both rare and expensive, and configuration options limited. Things have changed. Concepts like just-in-time inventory, build-to-order (BTO) manufacturing, end-to-end supply chain visibility, the explosion in contract manufacturing, and the development of Web-based e-business tools for collaborative manufacturing have revolutionized plant management.

Various manufacturing information systems, many of them Web enabled, are used to support computer-integrated manufacturing (CIM). See Figure 7.28. CIM is an overall concept that stresses that the objectives of computer-based systems in manufacturing must be to:

- **Simplify** (reengineer) production processes, product designs, and factory organization as a vital foundation to automation and integration.

- **Automate** production processes and the business functions that support them with computers, machines, and robots.

- **Integrate** all production and support processes using computer networks, cross-functional business software, and other information technologies.

The overall goal of CIM and other such manufacturing information systems is to create flexible, agile, manufacturing processes that efficiently produce products of the highest quality. Thus, CIM supports the concepts of *flexible manufacturing systems, agile manufacturing*, and *total quality management*. Implementing such manufacturing concepts enables a company to respond quickly to and fulfill customer requirements with high-quality products and services.

Manufacturing information systems help companies simplify, automate, and integrate many of the activities needed to produce products of all kinds. For example, computers are used to help engineers design better products using both *computer-aided engineering* (CAE) and *computer-aided design* (CAD) systems and achieve better production processes with *computer-aided process planning*. They are also used to help plan the types of material needed in the production process, which is called *material requirements*

FIGURE 7.28

Manufacturing information systems support computer-integrated manufacturing. Note that manufacturing resources planning systems are one of the application clusters in an ERP system.

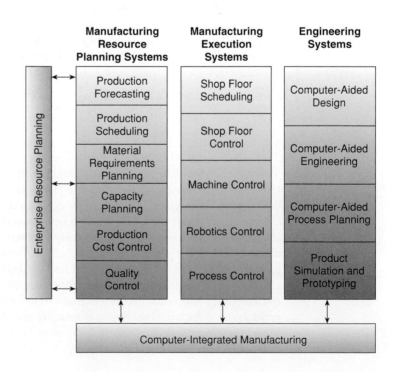

planning (MRP), and to integrate MRP with production scheduling and shop floor operations, which is known as *manufacturing resource planning*. Many of the processes within manufacturing resource planning systems are included in the manufacturing modules of enterprise resource planning (ERP) software, as discussed in the first section of this chapter.

Computer-aided manufacturing (CAM) systems are those that automate the production process. For example, this automation could be accomplished by monitoring and controlling the production process in a factory (manufacturing execution systems) or by directly controlling a physical process (process control), a machine tool (machine control), or machines with some humanlike work capabilities (robots).

Manufacturing execution systems (MES) are performance-monitoring information systems for factory floor operations. They monitor, track, and control the five essential components involved in a production process: materials, equipment, personnel, instructions and specifications, and production facilities. MES includes shop floor scheduling and control, machine control, robotics control, and process control systems. These manufacturing systems monitor, report, and adjust the status and performance of production components to help a company achieve a flexible, high-quality manufacturing process.

Process control is the use of computers to control an ongoing physical process. Process control computers control physical processes in petroleum refineries, cement plants, steel mills, chemical plants, food product manufacturing plants, pulp and paper mills, electric power plants, and so on. A process control computer system requires the use of special sensing devices that measure physical phenomena such as temperature or pressure changes. These continuous physical measurements are converted to digital form by analog-to-digital converters and relayed to computers for processing.

Machine control is the use of computers to control the actions of machines, also popularly called *numerical control*. The computer-based control of machine tools to manufacture products of all kinds is a typical numerical control application used by many factories throughout the world.

Human Resource Systems

The human resource management (HRM) function involves the recruitment, placement, evaluation, compensation, and development of the employees of an organization. The goal of human resource management is the effective and efficient use of the human resources of a company. Thus, human resource information systems are designed to support (1) planning to meet the personnel needs of the business, (2) development of employees to their full potential, and (3) control of all personnel policies and programs. Originally, businesses used computer-based information systems to (1) produce paychecks and payroll reports, (2) maintain personnel records, and (3) analyze the use of personnel in business operations. Many firms have gone beyond these traditional *personnel management* functions and developed human resource information systems (HRIS) that also support (1) recruitment, selection, and hiring; (2) job placement; (3) performance appraisals; (4) employee benefits analysis; (5) training and development; and (6) health, safety, and security. See Figure 7.29.

HRM and the Internet

The Internet has become a major force for change in human resource management. For example, online HRM systems may involve recruiting employees through recruitment sections of corporate Web sites. Companies are also using commercial recruiting services and databases on the World Wide Web, posting messages in selected Internet newsgroups, and communicating with job applicants via e-mail.

The Internet has a wealth of information and contacts for both employers and job hunters. Top Web sites for job hunters and employers on the World Wide Web include Monster.com, HotJobs.com, and CareerBuilder.com. These Web sites are full of reports, statistics, and other useful HRM information, such as job reports by industry or listings of the top recruiting markets by industry and profession.

FIGURE 7.29   Human resource information systems support the strategic, tactical, and operational use of the human resources of an organization.

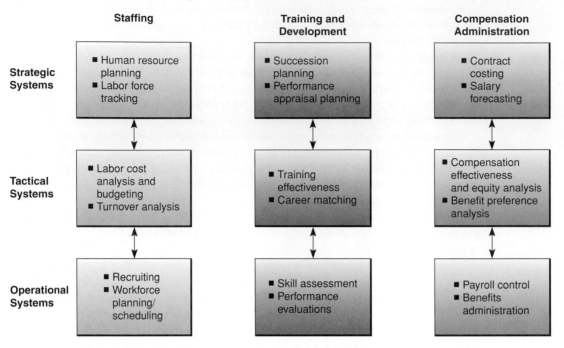

HRM and Corporate Intranets

Intranet technologies allow companies to process most common HRM applications over their corporate intranets. Intranets allow the HRM department to provide around-the-clock services to their customers: the employees. They can also disseminate valuable information faster than through previous company channels. Intranets can collect information online from employees for input to their HRM files, and they can enable managers and other employees to perform HRM tasks with little intervention by the HRM department. See Figure 7.30.

FIGURE 7.30

An example of an employee hiring review system.

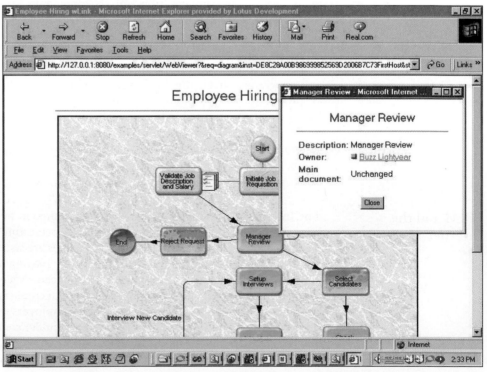

Source: Courtesy of IBM.

For example, *employee self-service* (ESS) intranet applications allow employees to view benefits, enter travel and expense reports, verify employment and salary information, access and update their personal information, and enter data that has a time constraint. Through this completely electronic process, employees can use their Web browsers to look up individual payroll and benefits information online, right from their desktop PCs, mobile computers, or intranet kiosks located around a worksite.

Another benefit of the intranet is that it can serve as a superior training tool. Employees can easily download instructions and processes to get the information or education they need. In addition, employees using new technology can view training videos over the intranet on demand. Thus, the intranet eliminates the need to loan out and track training videos. Employees can also use their corporate intranets to produce automated paysheets, the online alternative to time cards. These electronic forms have made viewing, entering, and adjusting payroll information easy for both employees and HRM professionals.

Chiquita Brands: Finding Out How Many Employees They Have	It seems like a straightforward and simple question that your typical HR application and corporate ERP system should be able to answer: How many employees are working for our company today?

At Chiquita Brands, the Fortune 500 company best known for its blue-stickered bananas, "We couldn't answer that question," recalls Manjit Singh, Chiquita's CIO since September 2006. "It would take us a couple of weeks to get the answer pulled together and by that time, of course, it was all incorrect."

Chiquita boasts a global workforce of 23,000 employees in 70 countries on six continents, though most of the workers are predominantly in Central America. Up until 2008, the Cincinnati-based food manufacturer had employed a hodgepodge of legacy HR systems that were inadequate at managing the complex demands of its decentralized workforce. Manual, inefficient workarounds (Excel spreadsheets and paper-based processes) were frequently used.

When Chiquita hired a new employee, for instance, the HR paper-trail process could contain 20 to 30 steps, Singh notes.

"At any point, if that paper gets lost, things are going to fall through the cracks," he says. "Many times new employees have shown up and haven't had an office, a PC or a phone. Obviously that causes pain to the employee, it doesn't make the employer look good, and you've lost productivity from the moment the employee walks through the door."

In October 2008, Chiquita went live on Workday HCM with 5,000 U.S.-based employees and 500 managers across 42 countries. Singh took advantage of customization options Workday offered when necessary. But he and his team tried to minimize customization as much as possible, so that they could shorten implementation time lines as they continue phased rollouts to 18,000 Latin America–based employees and nearly 3,000 employees throughout Europe.

Today, Chiquita's North American operations enjoy the fruits of the new system, including core HR functions such as employee hiring, job changes, compensation tracking and more. "We can see exactly where in the process the employee is, or how the hiring is going, who is holding it up and why it's being held up, so that we can guarantee when an employee walks through the door, they have an office, a phone, a PC, and they've been given access to all of the systems they need to have access to," says Singh.

"That's big, when you talk about the number of employees we hire in a given month," Singh continues. "That drops dollars back down to the bottom line."

Lastly, the new HR system has freed up many of Chiquita's 200 IT staffers to focus on higher-value projects. "I want my folks sitting arm and arm with business folks, talking about process transformation and trying to figure out how to bring products to market even quicker," Singh says, "not keeping the lights on running a system."

Source: Adapted from Thomas Wailgum, "Why Chiquita Said 'No' to Tier 1 ERP Providers and 'Yes' to SaaS Apps from Upstart Workday," *CIO Magazine*, April 7, 2009.

Accounting Systems

Accounting information systems are the oldest and most widely used information systems in business. Computer-based accounting systems record and report the flow of funds through an organization on a historical basis and produce important financial statements such as balance sheets and income statements. Such systems also produce forecasts of future conditions, including projected financial statements and financial budgets. A firm's financial performance is measured against such forecasts by other analytical accounting reports.

Operational accounting systems emphasize legal and historical record keeping and the production of accurate financial statements. Typically, these systems include transaction processing systems such as order processing, inventory control, accounts receivable, accounts payable, payroll, and general ledger systems. Management accounting systems focus on the planning and control of business operations. They emphasize cost accounting reports, the development of financial budgets and projected financial statements, and analytical reports comparing actual to forecasted performance.

Figure 7.31 illustrates the interrelationships of several important accounting information systems commonly computerized by both large and small businesses. Many accounting software packages are available for these applications. Figure 7.32 summarizes the essential purpose of six common, but important, accounting information systems used by both large and small business firms.

Online Accounting Systems

It should come as no surprise that the accounting information systems illustrated in Figures 7.31 and 7.32 are being transformed by Internet technologies. Using the Internet and other networks changes how accounting information systems monitor and track business activity. The online, interactive nature of such networks calls for new forms of transaction documents, procedures, and controls. This demand particularly

FIGURE 7.31 Important accounting information systems for transaction processing and financial reporting. Note how they are related to each other in terms of input and output flows.

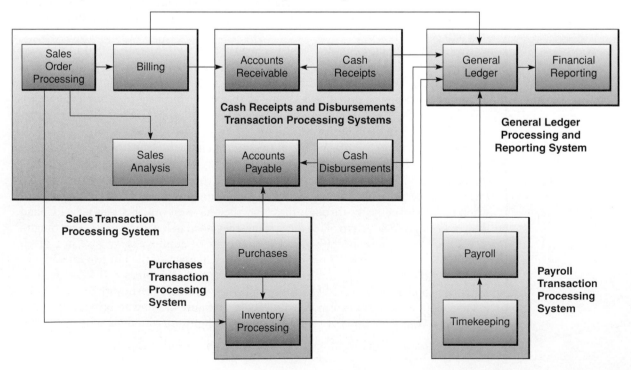

FIGURE 7.32   A summary of six essential accounting information systems used in business.

Common Business Accounting Systems
● **Order Processing** Captures and processes customer orders and produces data for inventory control and accounts receivable.
● **Inventory Control** Processes data reflecting changes in inventory and provides shipping and reorder information.
● **Accounts Receivable** Records amounts owed by customers and produces customer invoices, monthly customer statements, and credit management reports.
● **Accounts Payable** Records purchases from, amounts owed to, and payments to suppliers, and produces cash management reports.
● **Payroll** Records employee work and compensation data and produces paychecks and other payroll documents and reports.
● **General Ledger** Consolidates data from other accounting systems and produces the periodic financial statements and reports of the business.

applies to systems like order processing, inventory control, accounts receivable, and accounts payable. As outlined in Figure 7.32, these systems are directly involved in the processing of transactions between a business and its customers and suppliers. So naturally, many companies are using Internet and other network links to these trading partners for such online transaction processing systems, as discussed in Section I. Figure 7.33 is an example of an online accounting report.

FIGURE 7.33

An example of an online accounting report.

Source: Hyperion.

FIGURE 7.34

Examples of important financial management systems.

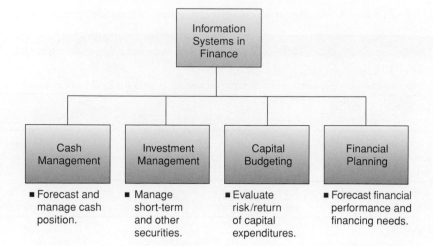

Financial Management Systems

Computer-based financial management systems support business managers and professionals in decisions regarding (1) the financing of a business and (2) the allocation and control of financial resources within a business. Major financial management system categories include cash and investment management, capital budgeting, financial forecasting, and financial planning. See Figure 7.34.

For example, the **capital budgeting** process involves evaluating the profitability and financial impact of proposed capital expenditures. Long-term expenditure proposals for facilities and equipment can be analyzed using a variety of return on investment (ROI) evaluation techniques. This application makes heavy use of spreadsheet models that incorporate present value analysis of expected cash flows and probability analysis of risk to determine the optimum mix of capital projects for a business.

Financial analysts also typically use electronic spreadsheets and other **financial planning** software to evaluate the present and projected financial performance of a business. They also help determine the financing needs of a business and analyze alternative methods of financing. Financial analysts use financial forecasts of the economic situation, business operations, types of financing available, interest rates, and stock and bond prices to develop an optimal financing plan for the business. Electronic spreadsheet packages, DSS software, and Web-based groupware can be used to build and manipulate financial models. Answers to what-if and goal-seeking questions can be explored as financial analysts and managers evaluate their financing and investment alternatives. We will discuss such applications further in Chapter 9.

Summary

- **Cross-Functional Enterprise Systems.** Major e-business applications and their interrelationships are summarized in the enterprise application architecture of Figure 7.3. These applications include integrated cross-functional enterprise systems such as enterprise resource planning (ERP), customer relationship management (CRM), and supply chain management (SCM). These applications may be interconnected by enterprise application integration (EAI) systems so that business professionals can more easily access the information resources they need to support the demands of customers, suppliers, and business partners. Enterprise collaboration systems (ECS) are cross-functional systems that support and enhance communication and collaboration among the teams and

  workgroups in an organization. Refer to Figures 7.17 and 7.20 for summary views of the business applications in EAI systems and enterprise collaboration systems.

- **Transaction Processing Systems.** Online transaction processing systems play a vital role in business. Transaction processing involves the basic activities of (1) data entry, (2) transaction processing, (3) database maintenance, (4) document and report generation, and (5) inquiry processing. Many firms are using the Internet, intranets, extranets, and other networks for online transaction processing to provide superior service to their customers and suppliers. Figure 7.20 illustrates the basic activities of transaction processing systems.

- **Customer Relationship Management: The Business Focus.** Customer relationship management is a cross-functional enterprise system that integrates and automates many of the customer-serving processes in sales, marketing, and customer services that interact with a company's customers. CRM systems use information technology to support the many companies who are reorienting themselves into customer-focused businesses as a top business strategy. The major application components of CRM include contact and account management, sales, marketing and fulfillment, customer service and support, and retention and loyalty programs, all aimed at helping a company acquire, enhance, and retain profitable relationships with its customers as a primary business goal. However, many companies have found CRM systems difficult to implement properly due to lack of adequate understanding and preparation by management and affected employees. Finally, many companies are moving toward collaborative CRM systems that support the collaboration of employees, business partners, and the customers themselves in enhancing profitable customer relationships.

- **Enterprise Resource Planning: The Business Backbone.** Enterprise resource planning is a cross-functional enterprise system that integrates and automates many of the internal business processes of a company, particularly those within the manufacturing, logistics, distribution, accounting, finance, and human resource functions of the business. Thus, ERP serves as the vital backbone information system of the enterprise, helping a company achieve the efficiency, agility, and responsiveness required to succeed in a dynamic business environment. ERP software typically consists of integrated modules that give a company a real-time cross-functional view of its core business processes, such as production, order processing, and sales, and its resources, such as cash, raw materials, production capacity, and people. However, properly implementing ERP systems is a difficult and costly process that has caused serious business losses for some companies that underestimated the planning, development, and training that were necessary to reengineer their business processes to accommodate their new ERP systems. However, continuing developments in ERP software, including Web-enabled modules and e-business software suites, have made ERP more flexible and user-friendly, as well as extending it outward to a company's business partners.

- **Supply Chain Management: The Business Network.** Supply chain management is a cross-functional inter-enterprise system that integrates and automates the network of business processes and relationships between a company and its suppliers, customers, distributors, and other business partners. The goal of SCM is to help a company achieve agility and responsiveness in meeting the demands of their customers and needs of their suppliers by enabling it to design, build, and sell its products using a fast, efficient, and low-cost network of business partners, processes, and relationships, or supply chain. SCM is frequently subdivided into supply chain planning applications, such as demand and supply forecasting, and supply chain execution applications, such as inventory management, logistics management, and warehouse management. Developing effective supply chain systems and achieving the business goals of SCM has proven to be a complex and difficult challenge for many firms. But SCM continues to be a major concern and top e-business initiative as companies increase their use of Internet technologies to enhance integration and collaboration with their business partners and improve the operational efficiency and business effectiveness of their supply chains.

- **Functional Business Systems.** Functional business information systems support the business functions of marketing, production/operations, accounting, finance, and human resource management through a variety of e-business operational and management information systems summarized in Figure 7.24.

- **Marketing.** Marketing information systems support traditional and e-commerce processes and management of the marketing function. Major types of marketing information systems include interactive marketing on e-commerce Web sites, sales force automation, customer relationship management, sales management, product management, targeted marketing, advertising and promotion, and market research. Thus, marketing information systems assist marketing managers in electronic commerce product development and customer relationship decisions, as well as in planning advertising and sales promotion strategies and developing the e-commerce potential of new and present products, and new channels of distribution.

- **Manufacturing.** Computer-based manufacturing information systems help a company achieve computer-integrated manufacturing (CIM) and thus simplify, automate, and integrate many of the activities needed to quickly produce high-quality products to meet changing customer demands. For example, computer-aided design using collaborative manufacturing networks helps engineers collaborate on the design of new products and processes. Then manufacturing resource planning systems help plan the types of resources needed in the production process. Finally, manufacturing execution systems monitor and control the manufacture of products on the factory floor through shop floor scheduling and control systems, controlling a physical process (process control), a machine tool (numerical control), or machines with some humanlike work capabilities (robotics).

- **Human Resource Management.** Human resource information systems support human resource management in organizations. They include information systems for staffing the organization, training and development, and compensation administration. HRM Web sites on the Internet or corporate intranets have become important tools for providing HR services to present and prospective employees.

● **Accounting and Finance.** Accounting information systems record, report, and analyze business transactions and events for the management of the business enterprise. Figure 7.32 summarizes six essential accounting systems: order processing, inventory control, accounts receivable, accounts payable, payroll, and general ledger. Information systems in finance support managers in decisions regarding the financing of a business and the allocation of financial resources within a business. Financial information systems include cash management, online investment management, capital budgeting, and financial forecasting and planning.

Key Terms and Concepts

These are the key terms and concepts of this chapter. The page number of their first explanation is in parentheses.

1. Accounting information systems (300)
2. Batch processing (285)
3. Computer-aided manufacturing (CAM) (297)
4. Computer-integrated manufacturing (CIM) (296)
5. Cross-functional enterprise systems (260)
6. Customer relationship management (CRM) (266)
7. E-business (260)
8. Electronic data interchange (EDI) (279)
9. Enterprise application architecture (260)

10. Enterprise application integration (EAI) (282)
11. Enterprise collaboration systems (ECS) (286)
12. Enterprise resource planning (ERP) (272)
13. Financial management systems (302)
14. Functional business systems (289)
15. Human resource information systems (297)
16. Interactive marketing (289)
17. Machine control (297)
18. Manufacturing execution systems (MES) (297)

19. Manufacturing information systems (295)
20. Marketing information systems (289)
21. Online transaction processing systems (284)
22. Process control (297)
23. Real-time processing (285)
24. Sales force automation (294)
25. Supply chain (276)
26. Supply chain management (SCM) (276)
27. Targeted marketing (293)
28. Transaction processing cycle (285)
29. Transaction processing systems (TPS) (283)

Review Quiz

Match one of the key terms and concepts listed previously with one of the brief examples or definitions that follow. Try to find the best fit for the answers that seem to fit more than one term or concept. Defend your choices.

_____ 1. Using the Internet and other networks for e-commerce, enterprise collaboration, and Web-enabled business processes.

_____ 2. Information systems that cross the boundaries of the functional areas of a business to integrate and automate business processes.

_____ 3. Information systems that support marketing, production, accounting, finance, and human resource management.

_____ 4. Many business applications of IT today fit into a framework of interrelated cross-functional enterprise applications.

_____ 5. Software that interconnects enterprise application systems.

_____ 6. Information systems for customer relationship management, sales management, and promotion management.

_____ 7. Collaborating interactively with customers in creating, purchasing, servicing, and improving products and services.

_____ 8. Using mobile computing networks to support salespeople in the field.

_____ 9. Information systems that support manufacturing operations and management.

_____ 10. A conceptual framework for simplifying and integrating all aspects of manufacturing automation.

_____ 11. Using computers in a variety of ways to help manufacture products.

_____ 12. Use electronic communications, conferencing, and collaborative work tools to support and enhance collaboration among teams and workgroups.

_____ 13. Using computers to operate a petroleum refinery.

_____ 14. Using computers to help operate machine tools.

____ 15. Information systems to support staffing, training and development, and compensation administration.

____ 16. The automatic exchange of electronic business documents between the networked computers of business partners.

____ 17. Accomplishes legal and historical record keeping and gathers information for the planning and control of business operations.

____ 18. Information systems for cash management, investment management, capital budgeting, and financial forecasting.

____ 19. Performance monitoring and control systems for factory floor operations.

____ 20. Customizing advertising and promotion methods to fit their intended audience.

____ 21. A cross-functional system that helps a business develop and manage its customer-facing business processes.

____ 22. A cross-functional enterprise system that helps a business integrate and automate many of its internal business processes and information systems.

____ 23. A cross-functional interenterprise system that helps a business manage its network of relationships and processes with its business partners.

____ 24. A network of business partners, processes, and relationships that supports the design, manufacture, distribution, and sale of a company's products.

____ 25. Collecting and periodically processing transaction data.

____ 26. Processing transaction data immediately after they are captured.

____ 27. A sequence of data entry, transaction processing, database maintenance, document and report generation, and inquiry processing activities.

____ 28. Systems that immediately capture and process transaction data and update corporate databases.

____ 29. A cross-functional information system designed to process data arising from business transactions.

Discussion Questions

1. Refer to the Real World Case on NetSuite, Berlin Packaging, and Churchill Downs in the chapter. In this case, how could CRM systems like those reviewed help a business that you know or deal with provide you with better service? Provide some examples other than those discussed in the case.

2. Why is there a strong trend toward cross-functional integrated enterprise systems in the business use of information technology?

3. Which of the 13 tools for accounting information systems summarized in Figure 7.29 do you feel are essential for any business to have today? Which of them do you feel are optional, depending on the type of business or another factor? Explain.

4. Refer to the example about Enterprise Application Integration in the chapter. What other solutions could there be for the problem of information systems incompatibility in business besides EAI systems?

5. Refer to the example about Chiquita Brands in the chapter. What are the most important HR applications a company should offer to its employees? Why?

6. How could sales force automation affect salesperson productivity, marketing management, and competitive advantage?

7. How can Internet technologies be involved in improving a process in one of the functions of business? Choose one example and evaluate its business value.

8. Refer to the Real World Case on strategic HRM technologies in the chapter. What are some of the most important HR applications a company should offer its employees? Why? Are any of them missing from the examples included in the case?

9. What are several e-business applications that you might recommend to a small company to help it survive and succeed in challenging economic times? Why?

10. Refer to the example about virtual worlds in the chapter. Do these type of systems contribute to bottom-line profits for a business? Discuss the reasons for your answer.

Analysis Exercises

1. **Application Service Provider Marketplace**
   The traditional ASP definition includes Web interface (or thin client) and external, Internet-based, server-side processing and data storage. However, the business world hasn't always felt constrained by these definitions. Microsoft, McAfee, QuickBooks, and others are providing Internet-based application services without meeting these exact criteria.

   Microsoft provides automatic Internet-based application maintenance as part of its one-time licensing fee. Through "automatic updates," Microsoft provides updates, fixes, and security patches to its software without IT staff involvement and minimal end-user inconvenience.

McAfee, in contrast, charges an annual maintenance fee that includes daily application and virus definition updates. McAfee provides it for one year as part of its license. After the first year, license holders may continue to use the software, but they must pay a subscription fee if they want updates. Customers tend to pay for this subscription service to protect themselves from new virus threats.

a. Would you use or recommend any of Intuit's online application services (www.intuit.com) to a small business? Why or why not?

b. America Online provides a free instant messaging service (AIM, for AOL Instant Messenger). This service enables instant messaging, file sharing, and voice and video conferencing through a free application anyone can download and install. Is AOL operating as an ASP? How so?

c. Visit AOL's "Enterprise AIM services" Web site (www.aimatwork.com). What additional features does AOL provide to enterprises? Why do you suppose AOL moved away from the ASP model for its enterprise solution?

2. eWork Exchange and eLance.com: Online Job Matching and Auctions

Many opportunities await those who troll the big job boards, the free-agent sites, the auction services where applicants bid for projects, and the niche sites for specialized jobs and skills. Examples of top job matching and auction sites are eWorkExchange and eLance.com.

eWork Exchange (www.ework.com). No more sifting through irrelevant search results; fill out a list of your skills and let eWork Exchange's proprietary technology find the most suitable projects for you—no bidding required.

eLance.com (www.elance.com). This global auction marketplace covers more than just IT jobs; it runs the gamut from astrology and medicine to corporate work and cooking projects. Register a description of your services, or go straight to browsing the listings of open projects—and then start bidding. A feedback section lets both employers and freelancers rate one another.

a. Check out eWork Exchange, eLance, and other online job sites on the Web.

b. Evaluate several sites on the basis of their ease of use and their value to job seekers and employers.

c. Which Web site was your favorite? Why?

3. Job Search Database

Visit Web sites like Monster.com and others mentioned in this chapter to gather information about available jobs. Look up and record the relevant data for at least 10 current job openings that are of interest to you or that meet criteria provided by your instructor.

a. Create a database table to store key characteristics of these job opportunities. Include all of the job characteristics shown in the list that follows as fields in

your table, but feel free to add fields of interest to you. If data are not available for some fields (e.g., salary range) for a particular job, leave that field blank.

b. Write a query that sorts jobs by region and then business function.

c. Create a report that groups jobs by region and sorts jobs within each region by business function.

Table: Jobs

Field	Sample Data (find your own field for this exercise)
Employer	Techtron Inc.
Job Title	Systems Analyst
Region	North East
Location	Springfield, MA
Business Function	Information Technology
Description	Work with team to analyze, design, and develop e-commerce systems. Skills in systems analysis, relational database design, and programming in Java are required
Qualifications	Bachelors degree in Information Systems or Computer Science, two years' Java programming experience
Salary Range	$48,000–60,000 depending on experience

4. Performing an Industry Financial Analysis

Employees apply their skills for the benefit of their organization. In addition to skills specific to their business function, employees need a keen understanding of their business environment. This environment includes their organization's business and financial structure as well as its relationships with competitors, customers, and relevant regulatory agencies.

Interviewers expect job candidates to have basic knowledge in of each of these areas. Developing such an understanding demonstrates the candidate's interest in the position and helps assure the interviewer that the candidate knows what he or she is getting into. Indeed, after a modest amount of research, job hunters may rule out certain opportunities based on what they discover. The Internet combined with good database skills can help simplify these tasks.

a. Go to the Web sites of at least three firms you identified in Problem 3. Obtain information about their financial operations, including net sales (or net revenue), after-tax income, and any current information affecting the organization or industry.

b. Using the same database you created in Problem 3, create a new table that includes the fields described next. Add fields that may interest you as well.

c. Add a field called OrganizationID to the Jobs table you created in the previous exercise. Make its field type Number (long integer). Write an update query that populates this new field with the appropriate values from the Organizations table's Organization ID field. To do this, join the Jobs table and the Organizations table using the Employer/Organization Name fields. This join will only work if the names used are identical, so be sure you've typed them in that way. Execute the query to complete the update. The tables already join using the Employer/Organization Name fields, so why might you want to also join them on the OrganizationID field? Is the Employer field in the Jobs table still necessary?

d. Create a report that shows job opportunities by industry. Within each industry, sort the records by the organization's name. Include Job Title, Globalization, Net Income, and Competitors in each record. Be sure to join the Jobs table and the Organizations table using the OrganizationID field.

Table: Organizations

Field	Sample Data (find your own field for this exercise)
OrganizationID	Set this as your primary key and let the database automatically generate the value
Organization Name	Be sure to spell the name exactly as you did in the job opportunity table (copy and paste works best for this)
Industry	Legal, medical, consulting, education, etc.
Globalization	Local, regional, national, international
Revenue	Net sales or revenue from the most current financial reports
Net Income (after tax)	From the most current financial reports
Competitors	Names of key competitors
Employees	Number of employees

Perdue Farms and Others: Supply Chain Management Meets the Holiday Season

Although you've got only one turkey to handle at Thanksgiving, in 2003 the folks at Perdue Farms managed to move roughly one million turkeys, each within 24 hours of processing, to reach holiday tables across the nation. The task isn't as tricky as it was before the food and agricultural products company invested $20 million in supply chain management technology five years ago.

Using Manugistics forecasting software and supply chain planning tools, Perdue has become more adept at delivering the right number of turkeys to the right customers at the right time, says CIO Don Taylor. "As we get to November, we have live information at our fingertips," he says. Before investing in supply chain management and forecasting software, Perdue's managers went by the "gut feel" of its suppliers and customers, as well as the seasonal history of past consumption.

It worked well enough; the company Arthur W. Perdue founded in 1920 has grown to reach annual sales of $2.7 billion. With the forecasting and supply chain systems, Taylor says the privately held company monitors its products year-round, checking in more frequently as Thanksgiving approaches. Although the third week of November is Perdue's busiest time of year, the company's output doesn't change radically. The big difference is the form the turkeys take. Most of the year, it's more food parts and deli meats, while this time of year it's whole birds.

Getting turkeys from farm to table is a race against time, so Perdue has turned to technology to make sure its products arrive fresh. Each of its delivery trucks is equipped with a global positioning system that allows dispatchers to keep tabs on the turkeys en route from each of the company's four distribution centers to their destinations. If a truck breaks down, a replacement is sent to rescue the palettes of poultry. "We know where our trucks are exactly at all times," says Dan DiGrazio, Perdue's director of logistics.

Perdue uses everything but smoke signals to communicate with customers, staying in touch via telephone, e-mail, and videoconferencing. "We're always looking at new technologies as they come along to see what makes sense for us," says Taylor.

Black Friday and Cyber Monday sound nothing like the joyous season that's supposed to follow. They're more ominous and scary. To many retailers and manufacturers those two pivotal days—and the month or so that follows—are just that.

These two days are ominous because the holiday shopping crush that happens just after Thanksgiving is a make-or-break time for retailers and consumer goods companies looking to bolster their fourth-quarter revenues with loads of sales. They're scary because what sells and what doesn't is just so unpredictable.

Nowhere is that uncertainty and accompanying pressure more intense than inside supply chain departments, where seasonal good cheer is replaced with gut-churning anxiety.

"The holiday season is a completely difficult time for manufacturers and retailers," says Brian Tomlin, an assistant professor of operations, technology, and innovation management at the University of North Carolina's Kenan-Flagler Business School. "They're making educated guesses and bets on what demand is going to be, and they're not going to get it right every single time."

Indeed, the period from just before Thanksgiving all the way into the New Year is usually the "moment of truth" for retail and manufacturing supply chain and e-commerce systems. Not all of them are successful. Tomlin says that retailers and manufacturers face a delicate balancing act. "If they're overly optimistic, they can have too much inventory, have to mark down everything and do fire sale prices," he says. "If they're overly pessimistic, they'll have unsatisfied customers and leave a lot of money on the table."

There are a number of reasons for this.

The first is that consumers' tastes can change overnight, especially with toys, consumer electronics, and apparel. "The product cycles are so short; what's cool today isn't what's going to be cool tomorrow," says Dave Haskins, CTO of Kinaxis, a vendor that offers on-demand response management for supply chains. Talking about his daughter's recent cell phone purchase, he notes: "She's buying a cell phone for reasons of fashion and not function. The consumer today is unbelievably fickle."

Another challenge is that sometimes one Christmas gift grabs more worldwide attention than any marketing or operations manager could have ever predicted even in his wildest dreams. The resulting mass hysteria feeds on itself (remember the late 1990s Furby craze?) and becomes wonderful fodder for holiday news. It also leads the general public to think that "someone made a mistake," says Tomlin, even though the situation was too difficult to foresee. Although it may seem like a nice problem to have, it's a frustrating situation for manufacturers who try to keep up inventory and retailers who try to keep their shelves stocked.

So while speed and flexibility are paramount to respond to volatile demand, many retailers and suppliers are stuck because of one big self-inflicted wound: "Half of their supply chain is sitting in Asia," Haskins says. "Now suppliers have to deal with the fact that their product has to sit five weeks on a boat because the boardroom said, 'We want it cheaper.'" The result is that longer travel distances lead to elongated supply chains.

That critical cost-versus-flexibility trade-off can rear its ugly head during the holidays, when marketing plans and inventory strategies have to be made far in advance. "The challenge is that suppliers need to make sourcing decisions early, and when they do that, demand uncertainty is high," Tomlin says. Yet just overstocking inventory is a mistake companies are typically not foolish enough to make.

"What smart companies do is figure out how best to use information as a substitute for inventory," he says, "because inventory is an expensive strategy."

Haskins, whose company sells supply chain demand software, notes that many manufacturers' supply chain systems work on monthly planning cycles, which don't give enough information. There can also be a vast gap between the retailers' systems and the point of sale (POS) data that they can send to their suppliers and what the suppliers can actually do with it. "The distribution signals—meaning what's actually selling and the actual inventory—need to be coordinated on a continuous basis. Most organizations are still struggling to do that," he says.

The holiday shopping season will expose any supply chain weaknesses. "That's because the window to respond to fluctuations is so much shorter," Haskins says, adding that companies with better systems typically perform better during the holidays, and do better throughout the year.

Haskins advises retailers and their suppliers to ask themselves these questions right now: How quickly can I respond to something that happens in my supply chain? Am I providing good, actionable information to my suppliers and filling in any gaps in the data? Am I acting on up-to-date point-of-sale data that I'm getting from my retailer? Do I understand exactly what is being sold every day?

The first question—flexible, fast response to supply chain events—is a key tactic that can help both retailers and manufacturers move more product. For example, if demand for a manufacturer's product is hot in the eastern part of the United States but not the West, companies have to make sure they have the right systems in place to see that, detect the trend, and share that information, and the right processes and logistics to adjust and remedy the situation.

"Companies have to err on the side of flexibility rather than forcing in rigidity," Haskins says. Of course, picking up on the supply chain signals, interpreting them, and reacting is still a monumental personnel and technical challenge for many manufacturers and retailers.

"If you're waiting for the store to tell you there's a stock out, you're way too late," he says.

Another trend that retailers and manufacturers need to be aware of is the exploding financial girth of the "gift-card season," which has seen multibillion-dollar gains in the last several years. A 2006 report from AMR Research noted the trend and its substantial effect on inventory and staffing decisions for the months of January and February, when many people who received gift cards redeem them.

Data from Ellen Davis, a communications director at the National Retail Federation, back that up: Only 20 percent of all gift cards are redeemed within the week after Christmas; the remaining 80 percent is spread over January and February.

To match the spirit of the holiday season, Haskins offers a practical piece of advice for retailers and manufacturers that need each other more during the holidays than ever. "Remember," he says, "you're only as good as your suppliers' supply chain and your suppliers' ability to have a quick, integrated view of total demand and supply."

Source: Adapted from Sharron Luttrell, "Perdue CIO Talks Supply Chain Management," *CIO Magazine*, November 1, 2003; and Thomas Wailgum, "The High-Stakes Search for Supply Chain Excellence during the Holiday Rush," *CIOMagazine*, November 16, 2007.

CASE STUDY QUESTIONS

1. What are the key factors that determine the success or failure of supply chains during the holiday season? Which of these are or could be under the control of companies, and which are inherent in the end-consumer business? Provide several examples.

2. Consider the increasing use of gift cards in lieu of gifts during the holiday season. What effects does this new practice introduce into demand planning and supply chain management? Consider the fact that virtually nothing is known about the recipients of gift cards. What strategies can retailers and their suppliers consider to accommodate these effects?

3. Prof. Brian Tomlin says that smart companies substitute information for inventory. What do you think he means by this statement? How do you think companies can take advantage of more extensive and accurate information to improve their inventory and logistic practices? Provide some examples.

REAL WORLD ACTIVITIES

1. Search the Internet for news stories about stocking (either over or under) problems that happened during recent holiday seasons. How can you relate your findings to the issues discussed in the case? Do you think the affected companies could have done something differently? Why or why not? Justify your answer.

2. How do your holiday shopping practices compare to those discussed in the text? How early do you decide how much money you are going to spend and what you are going to purchase? Break into small groups to compare your experiences and how those feed into the issues identified in the case: demand uncertainty and planning.

CHAPTER 8

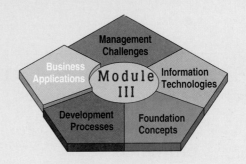

e-COMMERCE SYSTEMS

Chapter Highlights

Learning Objectives

1. Identify the major categories and trends of e-commerce applications.

2. Identify the essential processes of an e-commerce system and give examples of how it is implemented in e-commerce applications.

3. Identify and give examples of several key factors and Web store requirements needed to succeed in e-commerce.

4. Identify and explain the business value of several types of e-commerce marketplaces.

5. Discuss the benefits and trade-offs of several e-commerce clicks-and-bricks alternatives.

SECTION I   e-Commerce Fundamentals

Introduction to e-Commerce

E-commerce is changing the shape of competition, the speed of action, and the streamlining of interactions, products, and payments from customers to companies and from companies to suppliers.

For most companies today, electronic commerce is more than just buying and selling products online. Instead, it encompasses the entire online process of developing, marketing, selling, delivering, servicing, and paying for products and services transacted on internetworked, global marketplaces of customers, with the support of a worldwide network of business partners. In fact, many consider the term "e-commerce" to be somewhat antiquated. Given that many young businesspeople have grown up in a world in which online commerce has always been available, it may soon be time to eliminate the distinction between e-commerce and e-business and accept that it is all just "business as usual." Until then, we will retain the term "e-commerce" because it allows for a clearer picture of the differences between online and more traditional business transactions.

As we will see in this chapter, e-commerce systems rely on the resources of the Internet and many other information technologies to support every step of this process. We will also see that most companies, large and small, are engaged in some form of e-commerce activities. Therefore, developing an e-commerce capability has become a competitive necessity for most businesses in today's marketplace.

Read the Real World Case below. We can learn a lot about the challenges companies face in the online world from this example. See Figure 8.1.

The Scope of e-Commerce

Figure 8.2 illustrates the range of business processes involved in the marketing, buying, selling, and servicing of products and services in companies that engage in e-commerce. Companies involved in e-commerce as either buyers or sellers rely on Internet-based technologies and e-commerce applications and services to accomplish marketing, discovery, transaction processing, and product and customer service processes. For example, e-commerce can include interactive marketing, ordering, payment, and customer support processes at e-commerce catalog and auction sites on the World Wide Web. However, e-commerce also includes e-business processes such as extranet access of inventory databases by customers and suppliers (transaction processing), intranet access of customer relationship management systems by sales and customer service reps (service and support), and customer collaboration in product development via e-mail exchanges and Internet newsgroups (marketing/discovery).

The advantages of e-commerce allow a business of virtually any size that is located virtually anywhere on the planet to conduct business with just about anyone, anywhere. Imagine a small olive oil manufacturer in a remote village in Italy selling its wares to major department stores and specialty food shops in New York, London, Tokyo, and other large metropolitan markets. The power of e-commerce allows geophysical barriers to disappear, making all consumers and businesses on Earth potential customers and suppliers.

e-Commerce Technologies

What technologies are necessary for e-commerce? The short answer is that most information technologies and Internet technologies that we discuss in this text are, in some form, involved in e-commerce systems. A more specific answer is illustrated in Figure 8.3, which gives an example of the technology resources required by many e-commerce systems. The figure illustrates some of the hardware, software, data, and network components used by FreeMarkets Inc. to provide business-to-business (B2B) online auction e-commerce services.

REAL WORLD CASE 1

KitchenAid and the Royal Bank of Canada: Do You Let Your Brand Go Online All by Itself?

A reputation is a fragile thing—especially on the Internet, where trademarked images are easily borrowed, corporate secrets can be divulged anonymously in chat rooms, and idle speculation and malicious commentary on a blog can affect a company's stock price. Brands are under constant attack, but companies such as BrandProtect, MarkMonitor, and NameProtect (now part of Corporation Services Company) are stepping in to offer companies some artillery in the fight for control of their brands and reputations.

Brian Maynard, director of marketing for KitchenAid, a division of Whirlpool, had a rather unique problem. Like the classic Coke bottle and Disney's Mickey Mouse ears, the silhouette of the KitchenAid mixer, that colorful and distinctively rounded wedding registry staple, is a registered trademark. Although the KitchenAid stand mixer silhouette has been a registered trademark since the mid-1990s, it has been a well-recognized symbol since the current design was introduced in the 1930s. "The KitchenAid mixer is an incredible asset so it is important for us to protect both the name and the image from becoming generic," says Maynard, who reports that the equity of the brand has been estimated to be in the tens of millions of dollars. Any kind of violations that go unnoticed can quickly erode that precious equity.

KitchenAid had experienced some problems on the Web with knockoffs and unauthorized uses of the mixer's image, but getting a handle on the many and varied online trademark infringements seemed daunting. Maynard knew that historically, corporate brands that were not well-protected and policed by their owners had been ruled generic by the courts—aspirin and escalator are two examples. "Throughout history terms like escalator and aspirin have become generic simply because people did not do the work to protect them," says Maynard. "To avoid that fate, you have to show the courts that you have put every effort into protecting your brand. If you don't police your brand, courts will typically rule that the mark is no longer meaningful and has become ubiquitous." So when he received a cold-call from Brand-Protect, he was intrigued.

Criminals hijacking online corporate brands and masquerading for profit, however, are ramping up their efforts. Dubbed "brandjacking" by MarkMonitor Inc., a San Francisco–based brand protection service provider, the practice is becoming a major threat to household names. "Not only is the volume of these abuses significant, but abusers are becoming alarmingly savvy marketers," says Frederick Felman, MarkMonitor's chief marketing officer. In its first Brandjacking Index report, MarkMonitor tracked 25 of the top 100 brands for three weeks by monitoring illegal or unethical tactics that ranged from cybersquatting to pay-per-click fraud. Media companies made up the greatest percentage of targeted brands.

Cybersquatting, which usually means registering a URL that includes a real brand's name, easily took the prize for the most threats. MarkMonitor tracked more than 286,000 instances in the three-week span. "When I heard about the solution I didn't even realize there was anything like that out there," says Maynard. "I saw right away that it solved a problem I didn't even realize existed."

BrandProtect uses a technology platform that functions like a giant spider, mapping the Web and identifying what's going on in its darkest recesses. The mapping technology is combined with a filter and human analysis component that identifies and returns to its clients actionable data on illicit activities that may adversely affect their corporate identity. Depending on the client's chosen service level, those activities can include any of 22 categories of infractions—from phishing to counterfeiting, misuse of corporate logos and trademarked product images, domain infractions, and employees blogging about corporate trade secrets. Staying ahead of the many ways that a company's brand can be compromised or diluted online is a challenge that Kevin Joy, vice president of marketing for BrandProtect, compares to a never-ending game of Whack-a-Mole.

The challenge of brand protection, however, has grown exponentially for companies operating in the online world. "With the advent of the Internet a few things happened," explains Maynard. "Everyone in the world could now see the mixer so the potential for misuse of our trademark became greater. Because it is so well known, there was more risk of companies creating knock-off products and marketing them under other names. So it was even more important than ever to prove that we were putting every effort into protecting the brand and our trademarks."

FIGURE 8.1

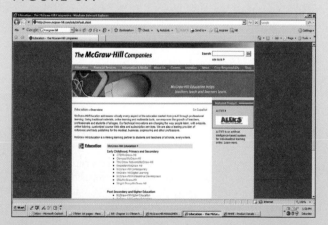

Companies that do business online must police unauthorized use of their brand names, logos, and other trademarks to protect their investments.

Source: Courtesy of Microsoft®.

Other types of violations also surfaced as KitchenAid's online policing activities grew. Some, such as sites using the logo without permission, were minor and could be easily fixed with a warning letter. Others were not so innocent, such as using the logo to create links to illegal sites. "We spent a lot of time training people and policing online activities," says Maynard.

The many successes have made the relationship worthwhile. Recently, Maynard was impressed by how quickly he was able to resolve a case of domain infraction. A small vendor that works with KitchenAid was experimenting with registering URLs such as shopkitchenaid.com and buykitchenaid.com for marketing purposes. That Friday when Maynard received his report, he noticed the new URLs, recognized the name of the owner, and called his contact at the company to explain that any URLs containing the name KitchenAid had to be owned by the company. Maynard says his contact was shocked by how quickly KitchenAid had gotten on top of the issue. "He didn't even know he couldn't have ownership of that URL and was stunned that we knew about it so quickly."

Given the strategic importance of the KitchenAid brand, Maynard says BD-BrandProtect has played a major role in bringing him peace of mind. "It is my responsibility to protect this brand and I am not going to allow any loss of equity on my watch. In fact, the value of the stand mixer silhouette continues to increase year after year. Before BD-BrandProtect, however, I thought I was out there doing it on my own. Now I know I can leave the brand in better condition than when I started."

As Manager of Brand Standards for the Royal Bank of Canada, Lise Buisson knows that the job of protecting the bank's brand online involves a lot more than finding out when someone has cut and pasted a logo onto their site without permission. "As brands become more valued, any improper use of your brand can become a reputational risk. When someone displays your logo, for example, it becomes a de facto endorsement, whether we have approved it or not. We have to be careful about things like that." Royal Bank of Canada and its subsidiaries operate under the master brand name of RBC.

With 70,000 full- and part-time employees serving 15 million clients through offices in North America and 34 countries around the world, RBC is the largest bank in Canada.

"We didn't expect to see what we saw. We were inundated. No one realized how easy it was for someone to come to our site, grab a logo, and put it somewhere else. It forced us to sit down as a group and figure out what we could do," says Buisson. She quickly discovered that a majority of the infractions noted were harmless and did not require a second thought. "In most cases the users were well meaning," she says. "It could be a charity site or mortgage partner using our logo. I would say that 90 percent of these incidents were quite harmless."

"BD-BrandProtect immediately flagged and dealt with a bank in the North Sea region that had used our logo and positioned themselves with another name. When anyone misrepresents themselves as an affiliate of ours, it makes us very nervous," notes Buisson. Where concerns are raised, RBC will take the appropriate measures, from issuing a polite request to the user to cease using their brand to initiating legal action. "In the vast majority of cases a polite letter is enough." Once a year, RBC reviews its branding policies to ensure that the reports continue to reflect their top priorities. It has also established a number of policies to ensure that the appropriate follow-up measures are used when required. "If, for example, we find advertising of our logo on a gambling site, we now have a policy about that," she says.

Buisson says that as Internet activities continue to escalate, she has come to realize that the job of monitoring online brand activities properly would just have been too much for departmental staff to handle. "I'm a big proponent of going to the experts and sitting down and working with them. It's very reassuring to work with a company that's looking out for us. It certainly helps some of us sleep at night."

Source: Adapted from Daintry Duffy, "Brand Aid for a Manufacturer's Online Property," *CIO Magazine*, September 17, 2007; *Royal Bank of Canada Case Study* and *KitchenAid Case Study*, www.bdbrandprotect.com, accessed April 22, 2008; and Gregg Ketzer, "Brandjackers' Make Millions Feeding Off Internet Brand Names," *Computerworld*, April 30, 2007.

CASE STUDY QUESTIONS

1. Consider your own online shopping patterns. How much weight do you place on the presence of a name or logo or other trademark (such as the KitchenAid silhouette) on a Web site when purchasing goods or services? Do you ever stop to consider whether you may have been misled? How could you tell the difference?

2. Brian Maynard of KitchenAid notes that the development of the Internet changed the problem of brand policing. What are some of these changes? What new challenges can you think of that did not exist in the pre-online world? Provide several examples.

3. The companies mentioned in the case (e.g., KitchenAid, RBC, Disney, and Coke) were well established and enjoyed strong brand recognition well before the advent of the Internet. Do you think online-only companies face the same problems as they do? Why or why not? Justify the rationale for your answer.

REAL WORLD ACTIVITIES

1. Online trust providers such as eTrust (www.etrust.org) and others review privacy policies, including information collection and use, sharing and disclosure, and security, and then certify Web sites as meeting their standards. Companies that achieve this can then display a logo to that effect. Search the Internet to discover how these providers prevent unauthorized lifting and use of their certification logos by Web sites that have not gone through the process. Prepare a report to summarize your findings. Have you ever noticed these logos? Does it make any difference to you as a consumer whether a Web site displays them or not?

2. The case features technology developed by BrandProtect (www.brandprotect.com); competitors include MarkMonitor (www.markmonitor.com) and NameProtect (www.cscprotectbrands.com). Visit their Web sites to compare and contrast their offerings. Then break into small groups to compare your findings and discuss new features that you believe are lacking, as well as why you think these vendors should include these features.

FIGURE 8.2 E-commerce involves accomplishing a range of business processes to support the electronic buying and selling of goods and services.

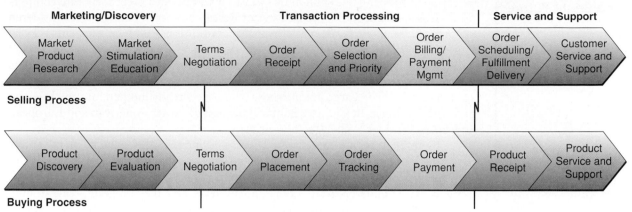

Marketing/Discovery		Transaction Processing				Service and Support	
Market/ Product Research	Market Stimulation/ Education	Terms Negotiation	Order Receipt	Order Selection and Priority	Order Billing/ Payment Mgmt	Order Scheduling/ Fulfillment Delivery	Customer Service and Support

Selling Process

Product Discovery	Product Evaluation	Terms Negotiation	Order Placement	Order Tracking	Order Payment	Product Receipt	Product Service and Support

Buying Process

FIGURE 8.3

The hardware, software, network, and database components and IT architecture of B2B online auctions provider FreeMarkets Inc. are illustrated in this example of its Internet-based QuickSource auction service.

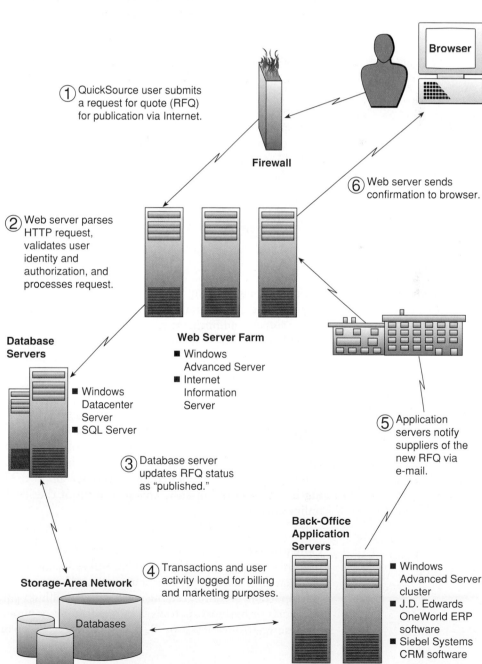

① QuickSource user submits a request for quote (RFQ) for publication via Internet.

Browser

Firewall

⑥ Web server sends confirmation to browser.

② Web server parses HTTP request, validates user identity and authorization, and processes request.

Web Server Farm
■ Windows Advanced Server
■ Internet Information Server

Database Servers
■ Windows Datacenter Server
■ SQL Server

③ Database server updates RFQ status as "published."

⑤ Application servers notify suppliers of the new RFQ via e-mail.

④ Transactions and user activity logged for billing and marketing purposes.

Storage-Area Network

Databases

Back-Office Application Servers
■ Windows Advanced Server cluster
■ J.D. Edwards OneWorld ERP software
■ Siebel Systems CRM software

Forrester: Web 2.0 Has a Bright Future	As a standard enterprise tool, Web 2.0 has a bright future, one for which companies are expected to spend $4.6 billion by 2013 to integrate into their corporate computing environments, according to a Forrester Research report. Though still considered an upstart technology, Forrester believes that conventional Web 2.0 elements—social networking, RSS, blogs, wikis, mashups, podcasting, and widgets—are fast becoming the norm for communicating with employees and customers. The report highlights megacompanies such as General Motors, McDonald's, Northwestern Mutual Life Insurance, and Wells Fargo among those who have already jumped into the Web 2.0 pool with both feet. In addition, some 56 percent of North American and European enterprises consider Web 2.0 to be a priority.

"If I wanted to be anywhere in the Web 2.0 economy, I'd want to be on the enterprise side," says report author and Forrester Research analyst Oliver Young. "We're seeing enterprise-class software coming from startups, but we're seeing them through very low price points . . . so it [Web 2.0] will never be a mega market," says Young. "It will eventually disappear into the fabric of the enterprise, despite the major effects the technology will have on how businesses market their products and optimize their workforces."

The consumer-facing ad-funded Web 2.0 sites like Facebook, MySpace, and Delicious will also have difficulty as similar technologies are incorporated into the enterprise. "Even Google is having a hard time selling the advertising," Young said. Still, start-ups have much to gain in pursuing the Web 2.0 world, such as understanding how companies are adopting their technology. Small groups within a company are more likely to adopt blogs, wikis, mashups, and widgets. The key to adoption, he adds, is to show how there is a business value in using the Web 2.0 tools. "Web 2.0 is not a critical 'must have' for any company at this point, but it's more than likely that your competition is using it and is showing faster results because of it."

Source: Adapted from Michael Singer, "Web 2.0: Companies Will Spend $4.6 Billion by 2013, Forrester Predicts," *InformationWeek*, April 21, 2008.

Categories of e-Commerce

Many companies today are participating in or sponsoring four basic categories of e-commerce applications: business-to-consumer, business-to-business, consumer-to-consumer, and business-to-government e-commerce. Note: We do not explicitly cover business-to-government (B2G) and *e-government* applications because they are beyond the scope of this text, but many e-commerce concepts apply to such applications.

Business-to-Consumer (B2C) e-Commerce. In this form of e-commerce, businesses must develop attractive electronic marketplaces to sell products and services to consumers. For example, many companies offer e-commerce Web sites that provide virtual storefronts and multimedia catalogs, interactive order processing, secure electronic payment systems, and online customer support. The B2C marketplace is growing like a wildfire but still remains the tip of the iceberg when compared with all online commerce.

Consumer-to-Consumer (C2C) e-Commerce. The huge success of online auctions like eBay, where consumers (as well as businesses) can buy from and sell to one another in an auction process at an auction Web site, makes this e-commerce model an important e-commerce business strategy. Thus, participating in or sponsoring consumer or business auctions is an important e-commerce alternative for B2C, C2B (consumer-to-business), or B2B e-commerce. Electronic personal advertising of products or services to buy or sell by consumers at electronic newspaper sites, consumer e-commerce portals, or personal Web sites is also an important form of C2C e-commerce.

Business-to-Business (B2B) e-Commerce. If B2C activities are the tip of the iceberg, B2B represents the part of the iceberg that is under the water—the biggest part. This category of e-commerce involves both e-business marketplaces and direct market links between businesses. For example, many companies offer secure Internet or extranet e-commerce catalog Web sites for their business customers and suppliers. Also very important are B2B e-commerce portals that provide auction and exchange marketplaces for businesses. Others may rely on electronic data interchange (EDI) via the Internet or extranets for computer-to-computer exchange of e-commerce documents with their larger business customers and suppliers.

Essential e-Commerce Processes

The essential e-commerce processes required for the successful operation and management of e-commerce activities are illustrated in Figure 8.4. This figure outlines the nine key components of an *e-commerce process architecture* that is the foundation of the e-commerce initiatives of many companies today. We concentrate on the role these processes play in e-commerce systems, but you should recognize that many of these components may also be used in internal, noncommerce e-business applications. An example would be an intranet-based human resource system used by a company's employees, which might use all but the catalog management and product payment processes shown in Figure 8.4. Let's take a brief look at each essential process category.

FIGURE 8.4   This e-commerce process architecture highlights nine essential categories of e-commerce processes.

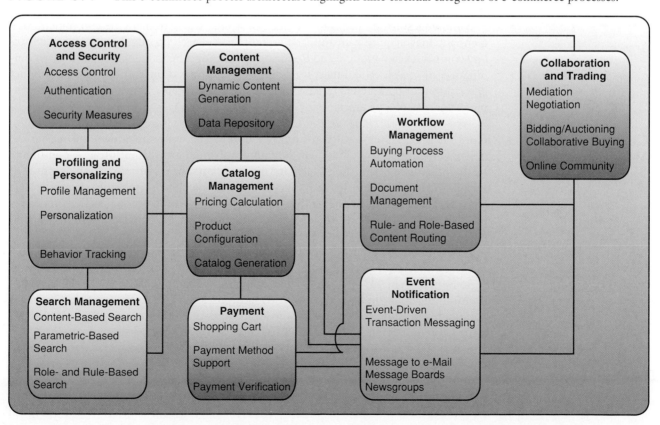

Access Control and Security

E-commerce processes must establish mutual trust and secure access between the parties in an e-commerce transaction by authenticating users, authorizing access, and enforcing security features. For example, these processes establish that a customer and e-commerce site are who they say they are through user names and passwords, encryption keys, or digital certificates and signatures. The e-commerce site must then authorize access to only those parts of the site that an individual user needs to accomplish his or her particular transactions. Thus, you usually will be given access to all resources of an e-commerce site except for other people's accounts, restricted company data, and Web master administration areas. Companies engaged in B2B e-commerce may rely on secure industry exchanges for procuring goods and services or Web trading portals that allow only registered customers to access trading information and applications. Other security processes protect the resources of e-commerce sites from threats such as hacker attacks, theft of passwords or credit card numbers, and system failures. We discuss many of these security threats and features in Chapter 11.

Profiling and Personalizing

Once you have gained access to an e-commerce site, profiling processes can occur that gather data on you and your Web site behavior and choices, as well as build electronic profiles of your characteristics and preferences. User profiles are developed using profiling tools such as user registration, cookie files, Web site behavior tracking software, and user feedback. These profiles are then used to recognize you as an individual user and provide you with a personalized view of the contents of the site, as well as product recommendations and personalized Web advertising as part of a *one-to-one marketing* strategy. Profiling processes are also used to help authenticate your identity for account management and payment purposes and gather data for customer relationship management, marketing planning, and Web site management. Some of the ethical issues in user profiling are discussed in Chapter 11.

Search Management

Efficient and effective search processes provide a top e-commerce Web site capability that helps customers find the specific product or service they want to evaluate or buy. E-commerce software packages can include a Web site search engine component, or a company may acquire a customized e-commerce search engine from search technology companies like Google and Requisite Technology. Search engines may use a combination of search techniques, including searches based on content (e.g., a product description) or parameters (e.g., above, below, or between a range of values for multiple properties of a product).

Content and Catalog Management

Content management software helps e-commerce companies develop, generate, deliver, update, and archive text data and multimedia information at e-commerce Web sites. For example, German media giant Bertelsmann, part owner of BarnesandNoble.com, uses StoryServer content manager software to generate Web page templates that enable online editors from six international offices to easily publish and update book reviews and other product information, which are sold (syndicated) to other e-commerce sites.

E-commerce content frequently takes the form of multimedia catalogs of product information. As such, generating and managing catalog content is a major subset of content management, or catalog management. For example, W.W. Grainger & Co., a multibillion-dollar industrial parts distributor, uses the CenterStage catalog management software suite to retrieve data from more than 2,000 supplier databases, standardize the data, translate it into HTML or XML for Web use, and organize and enhance the data for speedy delivery as multimedia Web pages at its www.grainger.com Web site.

Content and catalog management software works with the profiling tools we mentioned previously to personalize the content of Web pages seen by individual users. For example, Travelocity.com uses OnDisplay content manager software to push personalized promotional information about other travel opportunities to users while they are involved in an online travel-related transaction.

Finally, content and catalog management may be expanded to include *product configuration* processes that support Web-based customer self-service and the *mass customization* of a company's products. Configuration software helps online customers select the optimum feasible set of product features that can be included in a finished product. For example, both Dell Computer and Cisco Systems use configuration software to sell built-to-order computers and network processors to their online customers.

e-Commerce Tools to Close the Deal	Nothing is as heart-wrenching to an e-tailer as watching a customer abandon a full cart just seconds before consummating the deal. To be so close yet so cashless is more than frustrating; it's harmful to an e-tailer's health. A virtual armory of tools are in use to woo, cajole, prompt, and push consumers to make the buy—but are they working, or are they turning even more customers away?

"Most fall woefully short," says Matthew Brown, senior director of e-commerce and interactive marketing at MarketNet. "Instead of focusing on using tools and technologies to help the customer, much more thought and time needs to go into Web site architecture in the first place."

Many theories are being tossed about as to why consumers turn fickle a hair short of the finish line. For each theory, there are a multitude of technological solutions. "Retailers continue to launch and test technologies and features aimed at reducing abandonment or increasing online conversion," says Jessica Ried, a director of retail strategy at Resource Interactive. "In our experience, it is difficult to know for sure if any particular one is going to be effective for a given retailer without testing it with that retailer's customer base, or at least having a solid understanding of existing customer behaviors on the site through site analytics and surveys."

Once an e-tailer understands the true obstacles to closing the deal, there are a range of tools available to clear the way to bigger profits. The most commonly deployed are live chat, pop-up discounts, and follow-up email programs; some are achieved through the standard use of cookies, others via pixel-based triggers. Third-person endorsements are also frequently used. "Hosting consumer-generated content such as ratings and reviews has typically allowed retailers to improve conversions," explains Ried, "as customers are more confident with their selections. That's because they have access to an 'unbiased' opinion, building trust rather than having to rely solely on the marketing copy on the retailer's site."

"We use Liveperson chat extensively. It has been an incredible tool for answering any last-minute doubts during the last few states of the transaction," notes Adrian Salamunovic, cofounder of DNA 11, a multimillion-dollar e-commerce art retailer. "Our average transaction is over US$500, so this is very important to us."

"It pays for itself many times over each month," he adds. "For us, interrupting the client with pop-ups or invitations to chat really doesn't work—in fact, it does the opposite. We've watched customers bounce (exit) quite quickly after being interrupted with pop-ups."

Therein lies the conundrum. No two customers are identical. At least some personalized customization is essential. There is a point, however, at which actions considered helpful by the retailer are perceived as intrusive by the consumer. "Some customers welcome the help; others are unnerved by the Big Brother effect it can suggest," says Resource Interactive's Ried. "Start by considering what is known about consumer behavior in evaluating which technologies, features, and functionalities to explore first."

Source: Adapted from Pam Baker, "Rescuing the e-Commerce Deal When the Customer's Walking Way," *E-Commerce Times*, April 24, 2009.

FIGURE 8.5

The role of catalog/content management and workflow management in a Web-based procurement process: the MS Market system used by Microsoft Corp.

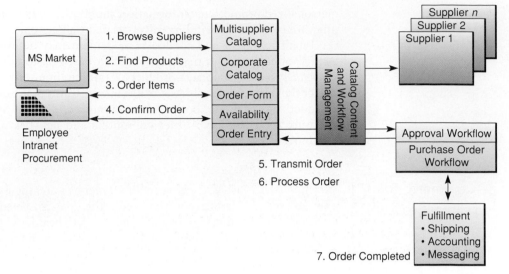

Workflow Management

Many of the business processes in e-commerce applications can be managed and partially automated with the help of workflow management software. E-business workflow systems for enterprise collaboration help employees electronically collaborate to accomplish structured work tasks within knowledge-based business processes. Workflow management in both e-business and e-commerce depends on a *workflow software engine* containing software models of the business processes to be accomplished. The workflow models express the predefined sets of business rules, roles of stakeholders, authorization requirements, routing alternatives, databases used, and sequence of tasks required for each e-commerce process. Thus, workflow systems ensure that the proper transactions, decisions, and work activities are performed, and the correct data and documents are routed to the right employees, customers, suppliers, and other business stakeholders.

As many of you begin your business careers, you will be charged with the responsibility of driving cost out of existing business processes while maintaining or improving the effectiveness of those processes. As you continue to acquire a greater appreciation for, and understanding of, how technology can benefit business, you will explore workflow management as the key to this optimization of cost and effectiveness throughout the business.

For example, Figure 8.5 illustrates the e-commerce procurement processes of the MS Market system of Microsoft Corp. Microsoft employees use its global intranet and the catalog/content management and workflow management software engines built into MS Market to purchase electronically more than $3 billion annually of business supplies and materials from approved suppliers connected to the MS Market system by their corporate extranets.

Microsoft Corporation: e-Commerce Purchasing Processes

MS Market is an internal e-commerce purchasing system that works on Microsoft's intranet. MS Market has drastically reduced the personnel required to manage low-cost requisitions and gives employees a quick, easy way to order materials without being burdened with paperwork and bureaucratic processes. These high-volume, low-dollar transactions represent about 70 percent of total volume but only 3 percent of Microsoft's accounts payable. Employees were wasting time turning requisitions into purchase orders (POs) and trying to follow business rules and processes. Managers wanted to streamline this process, so the decision was made to create a requisitioning tool that would take all the controls and validations used by requisition personnel and push them onto the Web. Employees wanted an easy-to-use online form for ordering supplies that included extranet interfaces to procurement partners, such as Boise Cascade and Marriott.

How does this system work? Let's say a Microsoft employee wants a technical book. He goes to the MS Market site on Microsoft's intranet, and MS Market immediately identifies his preferences and approval code through his log-on ID. The employee selects the Barnes & Noble link, which brings up a catalog, order form, and a list of hundreds of books with titles and prices that have been negotiated between Microsoft buyers and Barnes & Noble. He selects a book, puts it in the order form, and completes the order by verifying his group's cost center number and manager's name.

The order is transmitted immediately to the supplier, cutting down on delivery time, as well as accounting for the payment of the supplies. Upon submission of the order, MS Market generates an order tracking number for reference, sends notification via e-mail to the employee's manager, and transmits the order over the Internet to Barnes & Noble for fulfillment. In this case, since the purchase total is only $40, the manager's specific approval is not required. Two days later, the book arrives at the employee's office. Thus, MS Market lets employees easily order low-cost items in a controlled fashion at a low cost, without going through a complicated PO approval process.

Source: Adapted from Microsoft IT Showcase, "MS Market: Business Case Study," 2002.

Event Notification

Most e-commerce applications are *event-driven* systems that respond to a multitude of events—from a new customer's first Web site access, to payment and delivery processes, to innumerable customer relationship and supply chain management activities. That is why event notification processes play an important role in e-commerce systems; customers, suppliers, employees, and other stakeholders must be notified of all events that might affect their status in a transaction. **Event notification** software works with workflow management software to monitor all e-commerce processes and record all relevant events, including unexpected changes or problem situations. Then it works with user-profiling software to notify all involved stakeholders automatically of important transaction events using appropriate user-preferred methods of electronic messaging, such as e-mail, newsgroup, pager, and fax communications. This notification includes a company's management, who then can monitor their employees' responsiveness to e-commerce events and customer and supplier feedback.

For example, when you purchase a product at a retail e-commerce Web site like Amazon.com, you automatically receive an e-mail record of your order. Then you may receive e-mail notifications of any change in product availability or shipment status and, finally, an e-mail message notifying you that your order has been shipped and is complete.

Collaboration and Trading

This major category of e-commerce processes consists of those that support the vital collaboration arrangements and trading services needed by customers, suppliers, and other stakeholders to accomplish e-commerce transactions. Thus, in Chapter 2, we discussed how a customer-focused e-business uses tools such as e-mail, chat systems, and discussion groups to nurture online *communities of interest* among employees and customers to enhance customer service and build customer loyalty in e-commerce. The essential collaboration among business trading partners in e-commerce may also be provided by Internet-based trading services. For example, B2B e-commerce Web portals provided by companies like Ariba and Commerce One support matchmaking, negotiation, and mediation processes among business buyers and sellers. In addition, B2B e-commerce is heavily dependent on Internet-based trading platforms and portals that provide online exchange and auctions for e-business enterprises. Therefore, the online auctions and exchanges developed by companies like FreeMarkets are revolutionizing the procurement processes of many major corporations. We will discuss these and other e-commerce applications in Section II.

Electronic Payment Processes

Payment for the products and services purchased is an obvious and vital set of processes in e-commerce transactions. Payment processes, however, are not simple because of the nearly anonymous electronic nature of transactions taking place between the networked computer systems of buyers and sellers and the many security issues involved. E-commerce payment processes are also complex because of the wide variety of debit and credit alternatives, as well as the financial institutions and intermediaries that may be part of the process. Therefore, a variety of electronic payment systems have evolved over time. In addition, new payment systems are being developed and tested to meet the security and technical challenges of e-commerce over the Internet.

Web Payment Processes

Most e-commerce systems on the Web involving businesses and consumers (B2C) depend on credit card payment processes, but many B2B e-commerce systems rely on more complex payment processes based on the use of purchase orders, as was illustrated in Figure 8.5. However, both types of e-commerce typically use an electronic *shopping cart* process, which enables customers to select products from Web site catalog displays and put them temporarily in a virtual shopping basket for later checkout and processing. Figure 8.6 illustrates and summarizes a B2C electronic payment system with several payment alternatives.

Electronic Funds Transfer

Electronic funds transfer (EFT) systems are a major form of electronic payment systems in banking and retailing industries. EFT systems use a variety of information technologies to capture and process money and credit transfers between banks and businesses and their customers. For example, banking networks support teller terminals at all bank offices and automated teller machines (ATMs) at locations throughout the world. Banks, credit card companies, and other businesses may support pay-by-phone services. Very popular also are Web-based payment services, such as PayPal and BillPoint for cash transfers, and CheckFree and Paytrust for automatic bill payment,

FIGURE 8.6

An example of a secure electronic payment system with many payment alternatives.

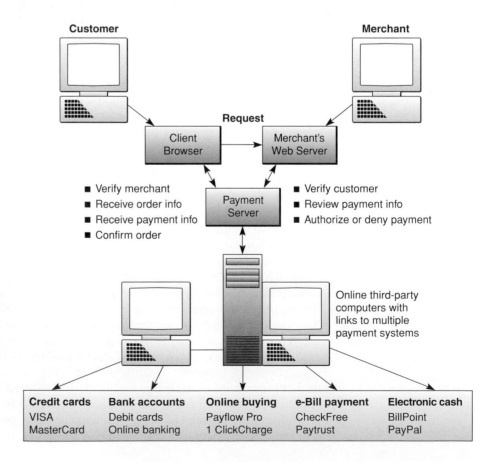

that enable the customers of banks and other bill payment services to use the Internet to pay bills electronically. In addition, most point-of-sale terminals in retail stores are networked to bank EFT systems, which makes it possible for you to use a credit card or debit card to pay instantly for gas, groceries, or other purchases at participating retail outlets.

Secure Electronic Payments

When you make an online purchase on the Internet, your credit card information is vulnerable to interception by *network sniffers*, software that easily recognizes credit card number formats. Several basic security measures are being used to solve this security problem: (1) encrypt (code and scramble) the data passing between the customer and merchant, (2) encrypt the data passing between the customer and the company authorizing the credit card transaction, or (3) take sensitive information offline. Note: Because encryption and other security issues are discussed in Chapter 11, we will not explain how they work in this section.

For example, many companies use the Secure Socket Layer (SSL) security method developed by Netscape Communications that automatically encrypts data passing between your Web browser and a merchant's server. However, sensitive information is still vulnerable to misuse once it's decrypted (decoded and unscrambled) and stored on a merchant's server, so a digital wallet payment system was developed. In this method, you add security software add-on modules to your Web browser. That enables your browser to encrypt your credit card data in such a way that only the bank that authorizes credit card transactions for the merchant gets to see it. All the merchant is told is whether your credit card transaction is approved or not.

The Secure Electronic Transaction (SET) standard for electronic payment security extends this digital wallet approach. In this method, software encrypts a digital envelope of digital certificates specifying the payment details for each transaction. VISA, MasterCard, IBM, Microsoft, Netscape, and most other industry players have agreed to SET. Therefore, a system like SET may become the standard for secure electronic payments on the Internet. See Figure 8.7.

FIGURE 8.7

VeriSign provides electronic payment, security, and many other e-commerce services.

Source: Courtesy of VeriSign Inc.

SECTION II e-Commerce Applications and Issues

E-commerce is here to stay. The Web and e-commerce are key industry drivers. It's changed how many companies do business. It's created new channels for our customers. Companies are at the e-commerce crossroads and there are many ways to go.

Thus, e-commerce is changing how companies do business both internally and externally with their customers, suppliers, and other business partners. As managers confront a variety of e-commerce alternatives, the way companies apply e-commerce to their businesses is also subject to change. The applications of e-commerce by many companies have gone through several major stages as e-commerce matures in the world of business. For example, e-commerce between businesses and consumers (B2C) moved from merely offering multimedia company information at corporate Web sites (*brochureware*) to offering products and services at Web storefront sites via electronic catalogs and online sales transactions. B2B e-commerce, in contrast, started with Web site support to help business customers serve themselves, and then moved toward automating intranet and extranet procurement systems.

Read the Real World Case below. We can learn a lot from this example about the challenges and opportunities faced by companies attempting to conduct online marketing campaigns. See Figure 8.8.

e-Commerce Trends

Figure 8.9 illustrates some of the trends taking place in the e-commerce applications that we introduced at the beginning of this section. Notice how B2C e-commerce moves from simple Web storefronts to interactive marketing capabilities that provide a personalized shopping experience for customers, and then toward a totally integrated Web store that supports a variety of customer shopping experiences. B2C e-commerce is also moving toward a self-service model in which customers configure and customize the products and services they wish to buy, aided by configuration software and online customer support as needed.

B2B e-commerce participants moved quickly from self-service on the Web to configuration and customization capabilities and extranets connecting trading partners. As B2C e-commerce moves toward full-service and wide-selection retail Web portals, B2B is also trending toward the use of e-commerce portals that provide catalog, exchange, and auction markets for business customers within or across industries. Of course, both of these trends are enabled by e-business capabilities like customer relationship management and supply chain management, which are the hallmarks of the customer-focused and internetworked supply chains of a fully e-business–enabled company.

Business-to-Consumer e-Commerce

E-commerce applications that focus on the consumer share an important goal: to attract potential buyers, transact goods and services, and build customer loyalty through individual courteous treatment and engaging community features.

What does it take to create a successful B2C e-commerce business venture? That's the question that many are asking in the wake of the failures of many pure B2C *dot-com* companies. One obvious answer would be to create a Web business initiative that offers attractive products or services of great customer value, with a business plan based on realistic forecasts of profitability within the first year or two of operation—a condition that was lacking in many failed dot-coms. Such failures, however, have not stemmed the tide of millions of businesses, both large and small, that are moving at least part of their business to the Web. So let's take a look at

REAL WORLD CASE 2

LinkedIn, Umbria, Mattel, and Others: Driving the "Buzz" on the Web

David Hahn has spotted a trend. As director of advertising for the popular online business networking site LinkedIn, he's being asked pointed questions by large advertisers about his ability to help them find "influentials"—those people within the LinkedIn community who are the most likely to go out and spread the word about a particular product or experience. "Some of them are requesting it specifically, while others are more implying it, but it comes down to the same thing," Hahn says. "Marketers are very interested in the value of online social networks, and how leaders in those networks can be used to drive proactive behaviors in the population."

Hahn isn't alone in his observations.

"The notion of the online influencer is quite the thing today in the marketing world," says Janet Edan-Harris, CEO of Umbria, which monitors chatter in cyberspace communities for corporations wanting to know what's being discussed online about their brands and products. "Companies are incredibly eager to get to those people. Do that—or so the conventional wisdom says—and you'll be in marketing heaven."

But new research, as well as growing business experience, suggests that such thinking may be overly simplistic. The effectiveness of using online word-of-mouth campaigns—or using individuals rather than traditional media advertising to spread the word about products or—is increasingly viewed as an effective way to reach consumers.

But the popular notion that frequently accompanies this, that there are special individuals who hold the key to the hearts of entire online communities, is coming under fire.

Dave Balter certainly thinks so. As CEO of BzzAgent, a word-of-mouth marketing firm, Balter three years ago had a

FIGURE 8.8

Online opinion leaders may be tapping into underlying trends that are critical to marketers.

Source: © Digital Vision/PunchStock.

revelation: The so-called "influentials," or opinion leaders, in online communities can't be influenced in a way that accelerates the success of a word-of-mouth campaign. "We actually believed in the idea that influentials drove market trends at that point," says Balter. "But upon closer look, we found out it didn't add up. The sales data of our campaigns didn't match the profiles of the opinion leaders we had targeted, and it really caused us to re-evaluate some of our core assumptions." Today, when a client comes in with the goal of influencing the influentials, "we tell them that's fools' gold," says Balter.

"It sounds really great, it sounds really sexy, but the results simply don't fly."

This indeed is what Edan-Harris has concluded from her experiences working with online communities. "We say [*sic*], 'Wait a minute, is this really a correct assumption, that there are individuals on the Internet that have that much influence?" she says.

Her conclusion: "Not nearly as much as everyone seems to think."

Despite this, companies are putting significant dollars into efforts to find these online opinion leaders, whether they're bloggers, contributors to discussion boards, or members of online social networks. Indeed, a whole cottage industry has sprung up based upon the notion that all marketers need to kick off a successful marketing strategy with a list of Internet opinion leaders. And with the expanding universe of blogs, online communities, and social networks such as MySpace, FaceBook, and LinkedIn, the appeal of this idea has become even more entrenched. There's a growing perception that the increasingly ubiquitous availability of broadband coupled with the rise in popularity of blogs and online communities make "influentials" even more influential.

It's critical to understand, however, that all these proponents of opinion leaders as drivers of social and commercial trends aren't talking about media stars or personalities, but about otherwise seemingly ordinary members of a community who, through accumulation of knowledge or number of connections with others, act as catalysts for change. Not surprisingly, marketers of all stripes almost at once began trying to take advantage of this—at first off-line, and now increasingly within the online social networks rising in popularity.

"The largest companies had already established influence-based programs and are now extending that model into the online social networking space," says Matthew Hurst, a scientist at Microsoft LiveLabs who follows online marketing trends. "It's not the notion of influence that's new, it's the technology that is now enabling it to a greater degree." Not surprisingly, a rapidly increasing number of companies have leaped into the fray to help firms identify the influentials in cyberspace.

Buzzlogic is one of them. Launched in 2007, Buzzlogic is dedicated to this idea that opinion leaders in online social networks can be identified, and their influence measured.

An early Buzzlogic beta customer is Protuo.com, a Web-based career management portfolio service that provides matchmaking between employers and potential employees. Not having the funds to buy expensive marketing spots in TV, radio, or mainstream print media, Jennifer Gerlach, VP of marketing, hired Buzzlogic to find the people who are the most influential in the human resource/employee professional space, contact them, and get them to buzz about the product. "We noticed that once one blogger wrote about our service, then suddenly a bunch of other people were writing about it. All at once, there were reviewers everywhere," says Gerlach, who just snagged a major feature in Inc. that she attributes to the online "influentials" campaign. She says she can map increases in site traffic precisely to blog mentions, and views the campaign as a huge success.

But despite this apparent triumph, a steadily growing number of online marketing experts would argue that rather than being responsible for the deluge of publicity that Protuo.com is experiencing, the bloggers targeted by Buzzlogic were simply tapping into a sort of zeitgeist waiting to happen—in this case, intense interest in how the Internet could be used to bring employers and candidates together more efficiently than traditional job boards are capable of doing.

Indeed, a growing school of thought is that "influentials" aren't so much leading trends as acting as mouthpieces for underlying social movements that are either already in progress or lying fallow waiting to be triggered. Thus successful marketing doesn't depend so much on finding influential people and seeding them with ideas so much as doing the kind of research that exposes embryo trends, and then helping "influentials" discover them.

This in fact is what Umbria does by focusing on tracking online conversations taking place in discussion boards and social networks as well as blogs. "It's much more important to identify those themes that are gaining momentum than try to find opinion leaders," says Edan-Harris. "You want to ride the wave rather than trying to start one on your own." By listening first to the conversations and being nimble enough to use the Internet to craft campaigns that jump on an existing trend, "you get much better results than attempting to generate your own little epicenter," she says.

Protuo.com's Gerlach agreed with some aspects of that. "There has to be a story around your product, and that story has to resonate in the world for the opinion leader strategy to work," she says.

Herein lies the problem with swallowing the 'influentials' theory whole cloth. Much of the so-called evidence of how the process works is a matter of reverse engineering. Once something happens—if there's a best-selling book coming out of nowhere, or a surprise political upset—you can always go back to the beginning and find the event or person that seems to have triggered it. You can always tell a causal story in retrospect.

Michael Shore, VP of worldwide consumer insights for Mattel, directs an organization that increasingly monitors blogs, social networks, discussion boards, and forums to figure out what the market might want from toys in general and Mattel products in particular. But unlike many other global consumer-brands companies, Mattel isn't interested in simply smoking out those individuals who are inordinately influential in their online communities and pushing top-down marketing messages onto them.

Despite the fact that this has become the strategy du jour in the online world, Shore's philosophy is a more holistic one.

"We're not just interested in opinion leaders. We'd consider that too narrow a focus," says Shore, who hired MarketTools.com to help him develop and get involved with online communities. Instead, he uses the online universe to do what he calls "cultural assessments" that involve analyzing language, behavioral patterns, and values. Armed with that information, Shore says, Mattel gets valuable information from the Internet that it uses to shape future product development as well as marketing campaigns.

If there's one thing that everyone agrees on, it's that marketers need to invest a great deal more effort into how online social networks and Internet communities actually work with respect to selling products and services at the grassroots level.

"It's an emerging medium, and the rules haven't yet been established," says Umbria's Edan-Harris. "We're still learning what does and doesn't work."

Source: Adapted from Alice LaPlante, "Online Influencers: How The New Opinion Leaders Drive Buzz on the Web," *InformationWeek*, May 5, 2007.

CASE STUDY QUESTIONS

1. How can companies benefit from the "cultural assessments" regularly performed by Mattel? How could the information obtained be used to create business value for those organizations? Provide multiple examples.

2. The case notes that, in spite of disconfirming evidence as to the effectiveness of targeting online opinion leaders, companies are nonetheless increasing their efforts to identify and contact them. Why do you think this is the case?

3. One of the participants in the case states that "you want to ride the wave rather than trying to start one of your own." What does she mean by that? If companies are not starting these "waves," where are they coming from?

REAL WORLD ACTIVITIES

1. A number of technological and cultural developments in recent years has resulted in the emergence of extensive social networks and a large number of avidly followed blogs. Go online to research how companies are tapping into these trends and what new marketing practices have arisen as a result. Prepare a report to summarize your findings.

2. Reflect on your own purchasing behavior. How much do you rely on blogs, feedbacks, and recommendations from past customers to make your own purchase decisions? Why do you (or not) rely on these sources of information? Do you believe they are largely unbiased? Break into small groups to discuss these issues with your classmates and compare perspectives on them.

University of Chester, Seaborne Library

Title: Information systems today :
managing in the digital world / Joseph S.
Valacich and Christoph Schneid
ID: 36103295
Due: 15-05-15

Title: Management information systems /
James A. O'Brien, George M. Marakas
ID: 36170210
Due: 15-05-15

Title: Introduction to information systems /
James A. O'Brien, George M. Marakas
ID: 36102776
Due: 15-05-15

Total items: 3
24/04/2015 17:30

Renew online at:
http://libcat.chester.ac.uk/patroninfo

Thank you for using Self Check

4

FIGURE 8.9   Trends in B2C and B2B e-commerce, and the business strategies and value driving these trends.

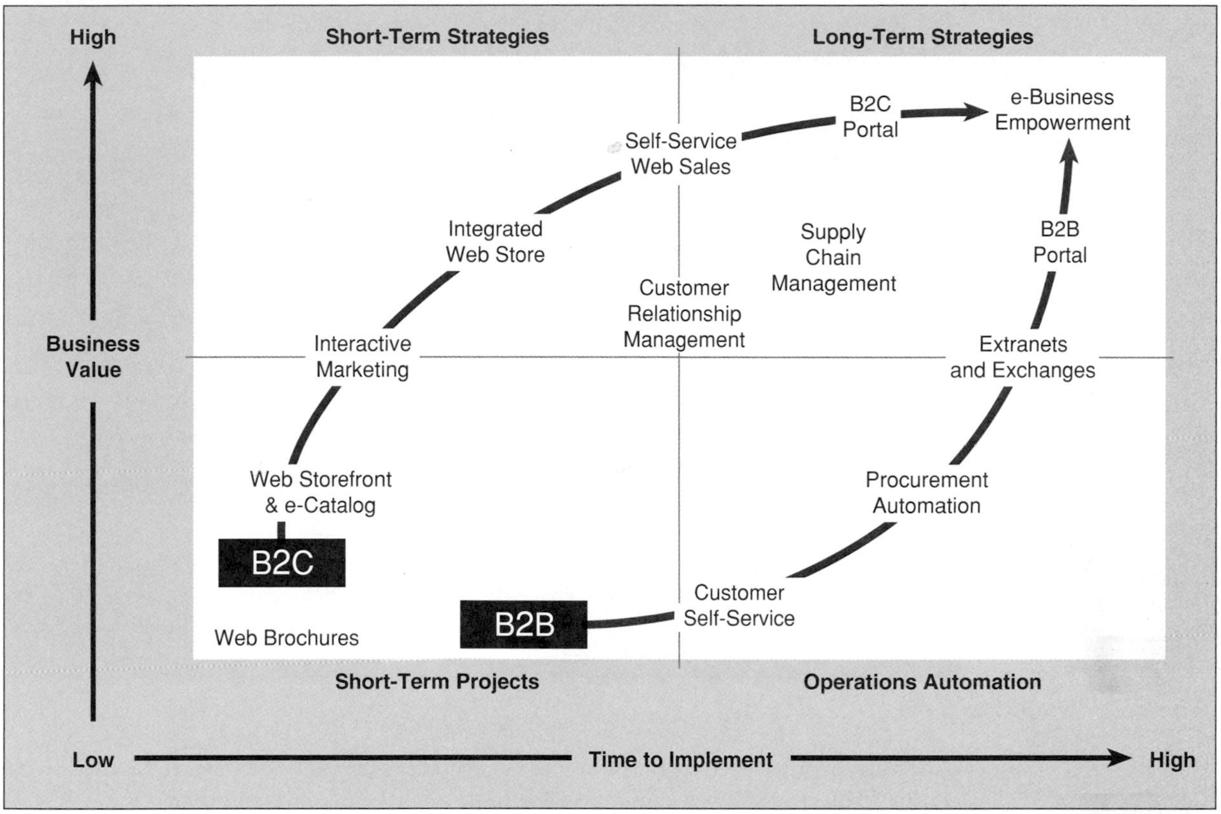

Source: Adapted from Jonathan Rosenoer, Douglas Armstrong, and J. Russell Gates, *The Clickable Corporation: Successful Strategies for Capturing the Internet Advantage* (New York: The Free Press, 1999), p. 24.

some essential success factors and Web site capabilities for companies engaged in either B2C or B2B e-commerce. Figure 8.10 provides examples of a few top-rated retail Web companies.

e-Commerce Success Factors

On the Internet, the barriers of time, distance, and form are broken down, and businesses are able to transact the sale of goods and services 24 hours a day, 7 days a week, 365 days a year with consumers all over the world. In certain cases, it is even possible to convert a physical good (CDs, packaged software, a newspaper) to a virtual good (MP3 audio, downloadable software, information in HTML format).

A basic fact of Internet retailing is that all retail Web sites are created equal as far as the "location, location, location" imperative of success in retailing is concerned. No site is any closer to its Web customers, and competitors offering similar goods and services may be only a mouse click away. This scenario makes it vital that businesses find ways to build customer satisfaction, loyalty, and relationships so that customers keep coming back to their Web stores. Thus, the key to e-tail (retail business conducted online) success is to optimize several key factors such as selection and value, performance and service efficiency, the look and feel of the site, advertising and incentives to purchase, personal attention, community relationships, and security and reliability. Let's briefly examine each of these factors that are essential to the success of a B2C Web business. See Figure 8.11.

Selection and Value. Obviously, a business must offer Web shoppers a good selection of attractive products and services at competitive prices, or the shoppers will quickly

FIGURE 8.10

Examples of a few top-rated retail Web sites.

Top Retail Web Sites
● **Amazon.com** $14.8B Web sales volume   www.amazon.com Amazon.com is the exception to the rule that consumers prefer to shop "real world" retailers online. The mother of all shopping sites, Amazon features a vast selection of books, videos, DVDs, CDs, toys, kitchen items, electronics, and even home and garden goods sold to millions of loyal customers.
● **Staples, Inc.** $5.6B Web sales volume   www.staples.com Staples tops the "Big 3" office supply giants in terms of Internet sales, although Office Depot and OfficeMax are also members of the top 10 retail Web sites list. Consumers can access the entire catalog online and can have their purchases delivered to their home or office within 24 hours and often within the same business day.
● **Apple, Inc.** $2.7B Web sales volume   www.apple.com Apple created a boutique atmosphere in their brick and mortar outlets and have successfully recreated that same feel in their online store. Literally every Apple product can be viewed, sampled, and configured online and then shipped directly to the consumer.
● **Sears** $2.6B Web sales volume   www.sears.com The Internet has become a transforming force for Sears and their Web sales have increased every year since they first launched their Web site in 1999. Today, customers can order any product online and can have their purchase delivered directly to their home or business with applicable freight charges or can pick up their purchase at their local Sears store with no additional shipping charges.

click away from a Web store. However, a company's prices don't have to be the lowest on the Web if it builds a reputation for high quality, guaranteed satisfaction, and top customer support while shopping and after the sale. For example, top-rated e-tailer REI.com helps you select quality outdoor gear for hiking and other activities with a "How to Choose" section and gives a money-back guarantee on your purchases.

Performance and Service. People don't want to be kept waiting when browsing, selecting, or paying in a Web store. A site must be efficiently designed for ease of

FIGURE 8.11

Some of the key factors for success in e-commerce.

e-Commerce Success Factors
● **Selection and Value.** Attractive product selections, competitive prices, satisfaction guarantees, and customer support after the sale.
● **Performance and Service.** Fast, easy navigation, shopping, and purchasing, and prompt shipping and delivery.
● **Look and Feel.** Attractive Web storefront, Web site shopping areas, multimedia product catalog pages, and shopping features.
● **Advertising and Incentives.** Targeted Web page advertising and e-mail promotions, discounts, and special offers, including advertising at affiliate sites.
● **Personal Attention.** Personal Web pages, personalized product recommendations, Web advertising and e-mail notices, and interactive support for all customers.
● **Community Relationships.** Virtual communities of customers, suppliers, company representatives, and others via newsgroups, chat rooms, and links to related sites.
● **Security and Reliability.** Security of customer information and Web site transactions, trustworthy product information, and reliable order fulfillment.
● **Great Customer Communication.** Easy-to-find contact information, online order status, product support specialists.

access, shopping, and buying, with sufficient server power and network capacity to support Web site traffic. Web shopping and customer service must also be friendly and helpful, as well as quick and easy. In addition, products offered should be available in inventory for prompt shipment to the customer.

Look and Feel. B2C sites can offer customers an attractive Web storefront, shopping areas, and multimedia product catalogs. These could range from an exciting shopping experience with audio, video, and moving graphics to a more simple and comfortable look and feel. Thus, most retail e-commerce sites let customers browse product sections, select products, drop them into a virtual shopping cart, and go to a virtual checkout station when they are ready to pay for their order.

Advertising and Incentives. Some Web stores may advertise in traditional media, but most advertise on the Web with targeted and personalized banner ads and other Web page and e-mail promotions. Most B2C sites also offer shoppers incentives to buy and return. Typically, these incentives mean coupons, discounts, special offers, and vouchers for other Web services, sometimes with other e-tailers at cross-linked Web sites. Many Web stores also increase their market reach by being part of Web banner advertising exchange programs with thousands of other Web retailers. Figure 8.12 compares major marketing communications choices in traditional and e-commerce marketing to support each step of the buying process.

Personal Attention. Personalizing your shopping experience encourages you to buy and make return visits. Thus, e-commerce software can automatically record details of your visits and build user profiles of you and other Web shoppers. Many sites also encourage you to register with them and fill out a personal interest profile. Then, whenever you return, you are welcomed by name or with a personal Web page, greeted with special offers, and guided to those parts of the site in which you are most interested. This *one-to-one marketing* and relationship building power is one of the major advantages of personalized Web retailing.

Community Relationships. Giving online customers with special interests a feeling of belonging to a unique group of like-minded individuals helps build customer loyalty and value. Thus, Web site relationship and affinity marketing programs build and promote virtual communities of customers, suppliers, company representatives, and others via a variety of Web-based collaboration tools. Examples include discussion forums or newsgroups, chat rooms, message board systems, and cross-links to related Web site communities.

Security and Reliability. As a customer of a successful Web store, you must feel confident that your credit card, personal information, and details of your transactions are secure from unauthorized use. You must also feel that you are dealing with a

FIGURE 8.12 How traditional and Web marketing communications differ in supporting each step of the buying process.

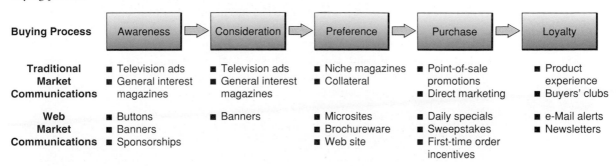

trustworthy business whose products and other Web site information you can trust to be as advertised. Having your orders filled and shipped as you requested, in the time frame promised, and with good customer support are other measures of an e-tailer's reliability.

Great Customer Communications. As more consumers shift their habits from the traditional bricks and mortar approach to an online shopping experience, one thing becomes even more important than ever: the need for constant and informative communication channels with the customer. Despite the conveniences associated with online shopping, consumers still have questions that need to be answered by a human being. Issues ranging from product information to order status or modification are often still handled the "old fashioned way." Land's End, the famous outdoor clothing retailer, provides telephone and chat space access to customer representatives that will even help you pick out your purchases in real time.

Amazon.com: Partnering and Leveraging Infrastructure

Amazon.com has just launched an application on Facebook that enables members of the social network to buy gifts for each other based on wish lists registered with the online retailer. *Amazon Giver* also provides Facebook members with the option of viewing suggested items for friends based on interests listed on their profile pages. A second Facebook application, *Amazon Grapevine*, provides a news feed of friends' activity on Amazon, such as when they update their wish lists, write reviews, or tag products. Both applications only share information between Facebook members who have opted in to the service.

"By combining Amazon's vast selection of products with Facebook's millions of users, we are able to make activities like giftgiving more efficient and rewarding for Facebook users," says Eva Manolis, VP of Amazon.

By adding the *Amazon Giver* application to their profile, Facebook members get the option of clicking directly to a secure Amazon checkout page. If the recipient has a wish list, then Amazon can ship the item without the buyer entering a shipping address, which would already be on file. In order for people to view a wish list, it would have to be set as "public." With *Amazon Grapevine*, people have the option to choose what type of activity they would be willing to share with friends through the news feed. Activity updates are entirely opt-in.

Amazon.com has also introduced a new way for online merchants to leverage Amazon's infrastructure to ship physical products. "The *Amazon Fulfillment Web Service* (Amazon FWS) allows merchants to tap in to Amazon's network of fulfillment centers and our expertise in logistics," says Amazon Web Services evangelist Jeff Barr. "Merchants can store their own products to our fulfillment centers and then, using a simple Web service interface, fulfill orders for the products."

Amazon FWS is designed to complement *Fulfillment By Amazon* (FBA), the fulfillment service Amazon has offered since 2006, by making the fulfillment process accessible programmatically. Amazon also maintains a separate fulfillment program called *Amazon Advantage*, which allows content publishers to send Amazon music, books, and videos for sale on consignment, with a 55 percent fee.

The idea, Barr explains, is to be able to ship a product with a simple Web service call. By making it possible for merchants to further automate their e-commerce and fulfillment efforts, Amazon is demonstrating its commitment to selling "muck," as CEO Jeff Bezos has referred to his company's e-commerce infrastructure.

Source: Adapted from Antone Gonsalves, "Amazon.com Launches Shopping Apps on Facebook," *InformationWeek*, March 13, 2008; and Thomas Claburn, "Amazon Introduces Fulfillment Web Service," *InformationWeek*, March 20, 2008.

Web Store Requirements

Most business-to-consumer e-commerce ventures take the form of retail business sites on the World Wide Web. Whether a huge retail Web portal like Amazon.com or a small specialty Web retailer, the primary focus of such e-tailers is to develop, operate, and manage their Web sites so they become high-priority destinations for consumers who will repeatedly choose to go there to buy products and services. Thus, these Web sites must be able to demonstrate the key factors for e-commerce success that we have just covered. In this section, let's discuss the essential Web store requirements that you would have to implement to support a successful retail business on the Web, as summarized and illustrated in Figure 8.13.

Developing a Web Store

Before you can launch your own retail store on the Internet, you must build an e-commerce Web site. Many companies use simple Web site design software tools and predesigned templates provided by their Web site hosting service to construct their Web retail store. That includes building your Web storefront and product catalog Web pages, as well as tools to provide shopping cart features, process orders, handle credit card payments, and so forth. Of course, larger companies can use their own software developers or hire an outside Web site development contractor to build a custom-designed e-commerce site. Also, like most companies, you can contract with your ISP (Internet service provider) or a specialized Web hosting company to operate and maintain your B2C Web site.

Once you build your Web site, it must be developed as a retail Web business by marketing it in a variety of ways that attract visitors to your site and transform them into loyal Web customers. So, your Web site should include Web page and e-mail advertising and promotions for Web visitors and customers, as well as Web advertising

FIGURE 8.13 To develop a successful e-commerce business, these Web store requirements must be implemented by a company or its Web site hosting service.

Developing a Web Store		
● **Build**	● **Market**	
Web site design tools	Web page advertising	
Site design templates	E-mail promotions	
Custom design services	Web advertising exchanges with affiliate sites	
Web site hosting	Search engine registrations and optimization	
Serving Your Customers		
● **Serve**	● **Transact**	● **Support**
Personalized Web pages	Flexible order process	Web site online help
Dynamic multimedia catalog	Credit card processing	Customer service e-mail
Catalog search engine	Shipping and tax calculations	Discussion groups and chat rooms
Integrated shopping cart	E-mail order notifications	Links to related sites
Managing a Web Store		
● **Manage**	● **Operate**	● **Protect**
Web site usage statistics	24×7 Web site hosting	User password protection
Sales and inventory reports	Online tech support	Encrypted order processing
Customer account management	Scalable network capacity	Encrypted Web site administration
Links to accounting system	Redundant servers and power	Network firewalls and security monitors

exchange programs with other Web stores. Also, you can register your Web business with its own domain name (e.g., yourstore.com), as well as registering your Web site with the major Web search engines and directories to help Web surfers find your site more easily. In addition, you might consider affiliating as a small business partner with large Web portals like Yahoo! and Netscape, large e-tailers and auction sites like Amazon and eBay, and small business e-commerce portals like Microsoft's Small Business Center.

Spamming Web Searches 	A new market for writing has arisen online, and it's targeted at search engines. Content optimized for successful search results ranges from informative articles to incoherent copy stuffed with keywords, a plague that's been labeled search-engine spam. Popular keywords generate significant traffic for Web sites with related content, giving Web site owners a financial incentive to host content that ranks near the top of search results. As traffic rises, ad revenue tends to follow, often through ad-delivery services for Web sites like Google's AdSense. A cottage industry has formed to help people tailor content for search engines, such as rewriting copy by substituting synonyms for certain words so that text can be repurposed to score well on search engines. The rephrased text looks different to a search engine, contributing to the host site's rank and traffic. Google's Webmaster Guidelines warns against the practice of crafting copy for its search engine: "Make pages for users, not for search engines." But that hasn't stopped many from trying. Creating content for search engines is one aspect of what's called "search-engine optimization" or SEO, part of a broader business known as "search-engine marketing," or SEM. In sufficient quantity, and absent sufficient quality, SEO content is a form of spam that's aimed at search engines rather than people. And like product-oriented spam, it's controversial. Chris Winfield, president and cofounder of SEM company 10e20 LLC, says one of the biggest problems for Google, MSN, and Yahoo is search-engine spam. "That spam consists of pages that are created for the search engines or pages that otherwise trick the end user," he says. Ani Kortikar, CEO of SEM company Netramind Technologies Pvt. Ltd., says that while search engines may require businesses to employ certain tactics to show up in search results, the tactics should be used to support good content rather than simply to drive traffic. But just as legitimate e-mail marketers have felt the backlash against spammers, well-intentioned search-engine marketers—and search engines as well—may suffer if the tricksters continue to thrive. Says Winfield of 10e20, "One of the most important things for any search engine is people having confidence and becoming repeat users." Source: Adapted from Thomas Claburn, "The Spamming of Web Search," *InformationWeek*, April 1, 2005.

Getting Customers to Find You

Just because your Web store has been launched does not mean customers will come flocking to your cyber front door. Your Web store needs to be discovered by your customers and this means getting listed in the popular search engines.

You can submit your Web site to search engines such as Yahoo, Google, Live, and others and each will begin looking at your Web pages and listing you when appropriate search terms are entered. Waiting for your site to show up competitively ranked with all the other similar site could take weeks and even months. There is a science to search engine ranking and it is an essential element in Web store success.

Search engine optimization (SEO) is considered a subset of search engine marketing, and focuses on improving the number and/or quality of visitors to a Web site over "natural" (aka "organic" or "algorithmic" search engine) listings. The term SEO can also refer to "search engine optimizers," an industry of consultants who carry out optimization projects on behalf of clients.

Search engines display different kinds of listings on a results page, including paid advertising in the form of pay-per-click (PPC) advertisements and paid inclusion listings, as well as unpaid organic search results and keywords specific listings, such as news stories, definitions, map locations, and images. As an Internet marketing strategy, SEO considers how search engines work and what people search for.

Optimizing a Web site primarily involves editing its content and HTML coding to both increase its relevance to specific keywords and to remove barriers to the indexing activities of search engines. Because SEO requires making changes to the source code of a site, it is often most effective when incorporated into the initial development and design of a site, leading to the use of the term "search engine friendly" to describe designs, menus, content management systems, and shopping carts that can be optimized easily and effectively.

A range of strategies and techniques are employed in SEO, including changes to a site's code (referred to as "on page factors") and getting links from other sites (referred to as "off page factors"). These techniques include two broad categories: techniques that search engines recommend as part of good design, and those techniques that search engines do not approve of and attempt to minimize the effect of, referred to as spamdexing. Methods such as *link farms*, where a group of Web sites is set up such that all hyperlink to every other Web site in the group, and *keyword stuffing*, where a Web page is loaded with keywords in the meta tags or in content, are examples of techniques considered "black hat" SEO. Such techniques serve only to degrade both the relevance of search results and the user experience of search engines.

SEO, as a marketing strategy, can often generate a good return. However, as the search engines are not paid for the traffic they send from organic search, the algorithms used can and do change, and there are many problems that can cause Search Engine problems when crawling or ranking a site's pages, there are no guarantees of success, either in the short or long term. Due to this lack of guarantees and certainty, SEO is often compared to traditional public relations (PR), with PPC advertising closer to traditional advertising.

Serving Your Customers

Once your retail store is on the Web and receiving visitors, the Web site must help you welcome and serve them personally and efficiently so that they become loyal customers. So most e-tailers use several Web site tools to create user profiles, customer files, and personal Web pages and promotions that help them develop a one-to-one relationship with their customers. This effort includes creating incentives to encourage visitors to register, developing *Web cookie files* to identify returning visitors automatically, or contracting with Web site tracking companies like DoubleClick and others for software to record and analyze the details of the Web site behavior and preferences of Web shoppers automatically.

Of course, your Web site should have the look and feel of an attractive, friendly, and efficient Web store. That means having e-commerce features like a dynamically changing and updated multimedia catalog, a fast catalog search engine, and a convenient shopping cart system that is integrated with Web shopping, promotions, payment, shipping, and customer account information. Your e-commerce order processing software should be fast and able to adjust to personalized promotions and customer options like gift handling, special discounts, credit card or other payments, and shipping and tax alternatives. Also, automatically sending your customers e-mail notices to document when orders are processed and shipped is a top customer service feature of e-tail transaction processing.

Providing customer support for your Web store is an essential Web site capability. Thus, many e-tail sites offer help menus, tutorials, and lists of FAQs (frequently asked questions) to provide self-help features for Web shoppers. Of course, e-mail correspondence with customer service representatives of your Web store offers more personal assistance to customers. Establishing Web site discussion groups and chat rooms for your customers and store personnel to interact helps create a more personal community that can provide invaluable support to customers, as well as build customer loyalty. Providing links to related Web sites from your Web store can help customers find additional information and resources, as well as earning commission income from the affiliate marketing programs of other Web retailers. For example, the Amazon. com affiliate program pays commissions of up to 15 percent for purchases made by Web shoppers clicking to its Web store from your site.

Managing a Web Store

A Web retail store must be managed as both a business and a Web site, and most e-commerce hosting companies offer software and services to help you do just that. For example, companies like FreeMerchant, Prodigy Biz, and Verio provide their hosting clients with a variety of management reports that record and analyze Web store traffic, inventory, and sales results. Other services build customer lists for e-mail and Web page promotions or provide customer relationship management features to help retain Web customers. Also, some e-commerce software includes links to download inventory and sales data into accounting packages like QuickBooks for bookkeeping and preparation of financial statements and reports.

Of course, Web-hosting companies must enable their Web store clients to be available online 24 hours a day and seven days a week all year. This availability requires them to build or contract for sufficient network capacity to handle peak Web traffic loads and redundant network servers and power sources to respond to system or power failures. Most hosting companies provide e-commerce software that uses passwords and encryption to protect Web store transactions and customer records, as well as to employ network firewalls and security monitors to repel hacker attacks and other security threats. Many hosting services also offer their clients 24-hour tech support to help them with any technical problems that arise. We will discuss these and other e-commerce security management issues in Chapter 11.

Online Shopping: How to Get the Impulse Purchase

You see it, you want it, you buy it. That's what e-commerce sites are banking on each holiday shopping season. Having blocked and tackled basics such as shopping carts and credit card approvals, online retailers know a significant chunk of their future sales will be in the up-sell and cross-sell—impulse buys, in other words. Yet striking a shopper's fancy is harder to do electronically than in the physical world of sounds, smells, and ambiance.

E-mail marketing as well as on-screen suggestions, pop-up boxes, and live chat are the most common ways of sparking shoppers to buy more than they anticipated, but not all retailers handle these tools well. Shipping promotions are always a grabber. Sixty-one percent of those polled by Forrester Research said they are more likely to shop with an online retailer that offers free shipping.

Another too frequent mistake is making too many product offers as soon as shoppers land on the site, says Jared Spool, CEO of User Interface Engineering, an online consulting firm in Bradford, Massachusetts. Macys.com does this. If you search for "men's jeans," you will find 422 items, dozens and dozens of which are not men's jeans. "You have to work really hard to get to products you're interested in. They're always thrusting things at you," Spool says. "It's department-store thinking," he says. "They think of their Web site as a Sunday flier."

Instead, e-commerce sites should offer suggestions after a shopper has placed items in the cart. That's a "seducible moment"—after the shopper has found what she wants and before she's checked out, he says. Then suggest a sweater for the skirt, a picture frame along with the locket. Landsend.com does this with pop-ups, while Anntaylorloft.com runs clickable images down the right-hand side of the screen. Either way works, says Spool.

If you've ever shopped online, your inbox is getting filled now because e-mail is the most cost-effective and successful tool for customer retention, according to Forrester. Seventy-three percent of retailers send e-mails about new products to customers. Still, for e-commerce companies, e-mail come-ons can be more effective than the direct mailings the U.S. Postal Service delivers. Although response rates to paper mailings are 2 percent or 3 percent, response rates for e-mail pitches can range from 5 percent to 30 percent, Spool says. In part that's because the mail goes to interested people who have, presumably, opted in or at least didn't opt out for them. The attitude among marketers is, "Hey, it's not spam if you sign up for it!"

Source: Adapted from Kim Nash, "Online Shopping: How to Get the Impulse Purchase," *CIO Magazine*, November 16, 2007.

Business-to-Business e-Commerce

Business-to-business e-commerce is the wholesale and supply side of the commercial process, where businesses buy, sell, or trade with other businesses. B2B e-commerce relies on many different information technologies, most of which are implemented at e-commerce Web sites on the World Wide Web and corporate intranets and extranets. B2B applications include electronic catalog systems, electronic trading systems such as exchange and auction portals, electronic data interchange, electronic funds transfers, and so on. All of the factors for building a successful retail Web site that we discussed previously also apply to wholesale Web sites for business-to-business e-commerce.

In addition, many businesses are integrating their Web-based e-commerce systems with their e-business systems for supply chain management, customer relationship management, and online transaction processing, as well as with their traditional, or legacy, computer-based accounting and business information systems. This integration ensures that all e-commerce activities are integrated with e-business processes and supported by up-to-date corporate inventory and other databases, which in turn are automatically updated by Web sales activities.

SpecEx.com: B2B Trading of Wireless Spectrum

Trading of Wireless Spectrum Online marketplaces like Craigslist and Freecycle allow consumers to make low-cost sales—or even exchange goods for free—through sophisticated technological systems that make such transactions efficient.

Some companies are attempting to apply a similar model to online business-to-business marketplaces.

The FCC holds auctions to grant licenses for radio spectrums, and most of these are used by cell phone carriers, or for first responders and their communication gear. But some of these spectrums aren't being used for a variety of reasons.

Spectrum Bridge's Web site, SpecEx.com, aims to create a secondary market for these unused spectrum. The company says the site can provide an easy and effective way to connect buyers and sellers. The market could potentially be large, as public-safety agencies, and major wireless carriers like Verizon Wireless and AT&T routinely purchase spectrum on the secondary market. The cable companies could also become potential buyers, especially as some are eyeing the wireless voice space. Spectrum Bridge makes money by taking a percentage of the transaction.

All transfers of spectrum would have to be approved by the FCC, but the agency has been supportive of spectrum trading in the past.

The idea of organizing the secondary spectrum market isn't a new one, but previous attempts have not been successful because they couldn't get enough buyers and sellers. "The spectrum world is almost tribal," says Peter Stanforth, chief technology officer for Spectrum Bridge. "It consists of small groups of people who know each other—and do everything manually." That is not an efficient system for smaller parcels—SpecEx's sweet spot. "By automating a lot of functions and bringing in a wider audience of buyers and sellers, we are making these smaller pieces more liquid and valuable," explains Stanforth.

Rick Rotondo, chief marketing officer of Spectrum Bridge, compares the SpecEx service to Craigslist, a favorite site for consumer bargains. With its launch several years ago, Craigslist made the sale of small consumer items efficient, which is what SpecEx aims to do with respect to the sale of wireless spectrum parcels. "Let's say you had used sunglasses you wanted to sell, for maybe $25. Before online classifieds were introduced, it would not have been cost-efficient to try to sell them to a huge audience in a paper, because the ad probably would have cost you $20." Same thing with wireless spectrum, he says. "Transaction costs are eating up most of the value for small buyers and sellers."

E-commerce technology can standardize much of the process, notes Stanforth. "What we are trying to do is be the eBay of the wireless spectrum world—a one-stop shop where companies can go to monetize excess or idle spectrum, and spectrum seekers can go to find reasonably priced unused spectrums."

Source: Adapted from Erika Morphy, "The Corporate Bargain Hunters' Quest for a Business Model," *E-Commerce Times*, January 20, 2009; and Marin Perez, "Spectrum Bridge Launches Online Secondary Market," *InformationWeek*, September 5, 2008.

e-Commerce Marketplaces

The latest e-commerce transaction systems are scaled and customized to allow buyers and sellers to meet in a variety of high-speed trading platforms: auctions, catalogs, and exchanges.

Businesses of any size can now buy everything from chemicals to electronic components, excess electrical energy, construction materials, or paper products at business-to-business e-commerce marketplaces. Figure 8.14 outlines five major types of e-commerce marketplaces used by businesses today. However, many B2B portals provide several types of marketplaces. Thus, they may offer an electronic catalog shopping and ordering site for products from many suppliers in an industry. Or they may serve as an exchange for buying and selling via a bid-ask process or at negotiated prices. Very popular are electronic auction Web sites for B2B auctions of products and services. Figure 8.15 illustrates a B2B trading system that offers exchange, auction, and reverse auction (where sellers bid for the business of a buyer) electronic markets.

FIGURE 8.14

Types of e-commerce marketplaces.

e-Commerce Marketplaces
● **One to Many.** Sell-side marketplaces. Host one major supplier, who dictates product catalog offerings and prices. Examples: Cisco.com and Dell.com.
● **Many to One.** Buy-side marketplaces. Attract many suppliers that flock to these exchanges to bid on the business of a major buyer like GE or AT&T.
● **Some to Many.** Distribution marketplaces. Unite major suppliers who combine their product catalogs to attract a larger audience of buyers. Examples: VerticalNet and Works.com.
● **Many to Some.** Procurement marketplaces. Unite major buyers who combine their purchasing catalogs to attract more suppliers and thus more competition and lower prices. Examples: the auto industry.
● **Many to Many.** Auction marketplaces used by many buyers and sellers that can create a variety of buyers' or eBay and FreeMarkets.

FIGURE 8.15

An example of a B2B e-commerce Web portal that offers exchange, auction, and reverse auction electronic markets.

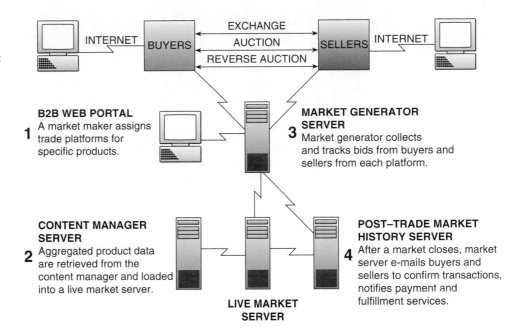

B2B WEB PORTAL
1 A market maker assigns trade platforms for specific products.

MARKET GENERATOR SERVER
3 Market generator collects and tracks bids from buyers and sellers from each platform.

CONTENT MANAGER SERVER
2 Aggregated product data are retrieved from the content manager and loaded into a live market server.

POST–TRADE MARKET HISTORY SERVER
4 After a market closes, market server e-mails buyers and sellers to confirm transactions, notifies payment and fulfillment services.

LIVE MARKET SERVER

Many of these B2B **e-commerce portals** are developed and hosted by third-party *market-maker* companies who serve as infomediaries that bring buyers and sellers together in catalog, exchange, and auction markets. Infomediaries are companies that serve as intermediaries in e-business and e-commerce transactions. Examples are Ariba, Commerce One, and VerticalNet, to name a few successful companies. All provide e-commerce marketplace software products and services to power business Web portals for e-commerce transactions.

These B2B e-commerce sites make business purchasing decisions faster, simpler, and more cost-effective because companies can use Web systems to research and transact with many vendors. Business buyers get one-stop shopping and accurate purchasing information. They also get impartial advice from infomediaries that they can't get from the sites hosted by suppliers and distributors. Thus, companies can negotiate or bid for better prices from a larger pool of vendors. Of course, suppliers benefit from easy access to customers from all over the globe. Now, let's look at a real world example.

ChemConnect and Heritage Services: Public and Private B2B Exchanges

Public B2B Exchanges. The pricing was becoming cutthroat in the closing minutes of the online auction. A North American chemical producer offered to sell a plastics stabilizer to a Fortune 20 firm for $4.35 per kilogram. With two minutes left, however, a lower price from a Chinese company flashed across the computer screens at ChemConnect (www.chemconnect.com), the San Francisco operator of a public online marketplace for the chemical industry. The North American producer lowered its price. Back and forth the two firms went as ChemConnect officials saw the price drop penny by penny. The Chinese offered $4.23. Finally, the North American company won the $500,000 contract with an offer of $4.20. The auction was just one of 20 taking place on ChemConnect's Web site one August morning, as companies from North America, Europe, and Asia bid on the lucrative six-month contracts.

ChemConnect hosted the event during several hours on a recent Monday morning. The same bidding process without the online auction would have taken at least three months, according to the company that held the event—even using e-mail. In the past, this company sent e-mails to all the suppliers it wanted to bid on its business. Then, in a few days, those companies would respond with their opening bids. The buyer would counter. Up to a week elapsed between every round.

Not only does ChemConnect help save companies time when they're buying, but it offers a central hub in a fragmented industry. More than 89,000 companies around the world produce chemicals, according to the American Chemical Council. Chem-Connect, housed on one floor of a San Francisco high-rise, allows many of them to find suppliers or buyers they did not know existed.

Private B2B Exchanges. Heritage Environmental Services President Ken Price agreed to enter two B2B Web public auctions, hosted by FreeMarkets (now owned by Ariba), to bid on contracts in 2001. Yet Heritage did not win. Not only that, the online auction process emphasized price, which meant that Heritage had to lower its fees to compete.

Heritage managers quickly concluded that this flavor of Net commerce wasn't for them. Instead, they decided on a different strategy: building their own online portal to link Heritage with existing customers. Heritage's B2B Web-based exchange lets customers order hazardous-waste management services and keep tabs on their accounts. It also speeds up the billing process because it accepts payment for services online. "What we've got is a nice central focal point where everyone in the process can see what's going on," says Price, who expects his company to book up to 15 percent of its business this year through the private portal.

Heritage is at the forefront of business-to-business e-commerce: private exchanges. This form of online link appeals to a growing number of large and small companies disappointed by public Internet markets intended to facilitate auctions and group purchasing. Like Heritage, many suppliers have been unhappy with the downward price pressures they encounter in public Internet markets.

Businesses concerned that participating in public B2B exchanges would put sales information and other critical data in the hands of customers and competitors are also turning to private exchanges. Smaller companies such as Heritage, as well as giants like Dell Computer, Intel, and Wal-Mart, have set up private online exchanges to link to suppliers and customers, help streamline the business, and boost sales. Private exchanges offer more control, say executives at these companies, and permit easier customization—allowing automation of processes, such as sending purchase orders or checking delivery schedules.

Source: Adapted from Eric Young, "Web Marketplaces That Really Work," *Fortune/CNET Tech Review*, Winter 2002.

Clicks and Bricks in e-Commerce

Companies are recognizing that success will go to those who can execute clicks-and-mortar strategies that bridge the physical and virtual worlds. Different companies will need to follow very different paths when deciding how closely—or loosely—to integrate their Internet initiatives with their traditional operations.

Figure 8.16 illustrates the spectrum of alternatives and benefit trade-offs that e-business enterprises face when choosing an e-commerce clicks-and-bricks strategy. E-business managers must answer this question: Should we integrate our e-commerce virtual business operations with our traditional physical business operations or keep them separate? As Figure 8.16 shows, companies have implemented a range of integration/separation strategies and made key benefit trade-offs in answering that question. Let's take a look at several alternatives.

e-Commerce Integrtion

The Internet is just another channel that gets plugged into the business architecture.

So says CIO Bill Seltzer of the office supply retailer Office Depot, which fully integrates its OfficeDepot.com e-commerce sales channel into its traditional business operations. Thus, Office Depot is a prime example of why many companies have chosen integrated clicks-and-bricks strategies, where their e-commerce business is integrated in some major ways into the traditional business operations of a company. The business case for such strategies rests on:

FIGURE 8.16 Companies have a spectrum of alternatives and benefit trade-offs when deciding on an integrated or separate e-commerce business.

- Capitalizing on any unique strategic capabilities that may exist in a company's traditional business operations that could be used to support an e-commerce business.
- Gaining several strategic benefits of integrating e-commerce into a company's traditional business, such as sharing established brands and key business information, joint buying power, and distribution efficiencies.

For example, Office Depot already had a successful catalog sales business with a professional call center and a fleet of over 2,000 delivery trucks. Its 1,825 stores and 30 warehouses were networked by a sophisticated information system that provided complete customer, vendor, order, and product inventory data in real time. These business resources made an invaluable foundation for coordinating Office Depot's e-commerce activities and customer services with its catalog business and physical stores. Thus, customers can shop at OfficeDepot.com at their home or business or at in-store kiosks. Then they can choose to pick up their purchases at the stores or have them delivered. In addition, the integration of Web-enabled e-commerce applications within Office Depot's traditional store and catalog operations has helped increase the traffic at their physical stores and improved the catalog operation's productivity and average order size.

Borders and Amazon.com: Splitting Up Is Never Easy	Borders.com has always been run by Amazon.com. It features Amazon's inventory, site content, fulfillment, and customer service capabilities. The sales even belong to Amazon, with a percentage going to Borders. The new Borders site marks a major juncture in Borders' business and e-commerce strategy and the end of what will be a seven-year relationship with Amazon.com at a time when the Ann Arbor, Michigan–based bookseller is in the midst of a turnaround.
	In 2001, when the retailing rivals inked this deal to develop a cobranded Web site, it was mutually beneficial. Amazon.com, which had gone public in 1997, was under pressure to turn its first profit. Extending the e-commerce infrastructure into which it had invested millions of dollars to third parties such as Borders injected much-needed cash into Amazon.com's business. Borders, which like many traditional brick-and-mortar stores at the time, was struggling to make the e-commerce game work for

them, got a tried and tested, user-friendly e-commerce site powered by a company that consumers trusted. Never mind the fact that Amazon was a competitor.

"The relationship with Amazon.com allowed us at the time to focus on our brick-and-mortar stores while still having an online channel that was branded Borders," says Anne Roman, a spokeswoman for Borders. She notes that the company had its own e-commerce site before it partnered with Amazon but that the costs associated with operating and marketing it outweighed the revenue it generated at the time.

Roman says the existing relationship with Amazon doesn't allow Borders to do all the things it wants to do to move forward to create a more integrated, cross-channel experience for customers, such as give Borders' customers access to author readings and concerts at the company's flagship store in Ann Arbor via online video. Borders also wants customers to be able to earn points toward the Borders Rewards loyalty program when they shop online. Currently, customers can't earn points when they use the cobranded site because it exists as a separate silo of Borders's business. "Once we launch the proprietary site, that loyalty program will be fully integrated into it," says Roman.

However, Borders has to give customers a compelling reason to buy books, movies, and music from Borders.com instead of Amazon.com. That's not going to be easy when Amazon.com has customer loyalty locked up and is so competitive on pricing. Gartner Research analyst Adam Sarner notes that the Web influences 40 percent of commerce in the off-line world. If Borders can take advantage of that dynamic, he adds, they'll be better able to compete with Amazon. "If their site can become a lead management tool that gets more people to visit the store and pick up more books or visit three times instead of two, that might be a better model for them," says Sarner. "Borders has the benefit of the physical stores. That's where they can differentiate themselves from Amazon."

Source: Adapted from Meridith Levinson, "Borders Tries to Open New Chapter with Web Site Relaunch Separate from Amazon.com," *CIO Magazine*, October 2, 2007.

Other Clicks-and-Bricks Strategies

As Figure 8.16 illustrates, other clicks-and-bricks strategies range from partial e-commerce integration using joint ventures and strategic partnerships to complete separation via the spin-off of an independent e-commerce company.

For example, KBtoys.com is an e-commerce joint venture of KB Online Holdings LLC, created by toy retailer KB Toys, and BrainPlay.com, formerly an e-tailer of children's products. The company is 80 percent owned by KB Toys but has independent management teams and separate distribution systems. However, KBtoys.com has successfully capitalized on the shared brand name and buying power of KB Toys, as well as the ability of its customers to return purchases to over 1,300 KB Toys stores, which also heavily promote the e-commerce site.

The strategic partnership of the Rite Aid retail drugstore chain and Drugstore.com is a good example of a less integrated e-commerce venture. Rite Aid only owns about 25 percent of Drugstore.com, which has an independent management team and a separate business brand. However, both companies share the decreased costs and increased revenue benefits of joint buying power, an integrated distribution center, cobranded pharmacy products, and joint prescription fulfillment at Rite Aid stores.

Finally, let's look at an example of the benefits and challenges of a completely separate clicks-and-bricks strategy. Barnesandnoble.com was created as an independent e-commerce company that was spun off by the Barnes & Noble book retail chain. This status enabled it to gain several hundred million dollars in venture capital funding, create an entrepreneurial culture, attract quality management, maintain a high degree of business flexibility, and accelerate decision making. However, the book e-retailer has done poorly since its founding and failed to gain market share from Amazon.com, its leading competitor. Many business analysts say that the failure of

FIGURE 8.17

Key questions for developing an e-commerce channel strategy.

A Checklist for Channel Development
1. What audiences are we attempting to reach?
2. What action do we want those audiences to take? To learn about us, to give us information about themselves, to make an inquiry, to buy something from our site, to buy something through another channel?
3. Who owns the e-commerce channel within the organization?
4. Is the e-commerce channel planned alongside other channels?
5. Do we have a process for generating, approving, releasing, and withdrawing content?
6. Will our brands translate to the new channel or will they require modification?
7. How will we market the channel itself?

Barnes & Noble to integrate some of the marketing and operations of Barnesandnoble.com within their thousands of bookstores meant it forfeited a key strategic business opportunity.

e-Commerce Channel Choices

Some of the key questions that the management of companies must answer in making a clicks-and-bricks decision and developing the resulting e-commerce channel are outlined in Figure 8.17. An e-commerce channel is the marketing or sales channel created by a company to conduct and manage its chosen e-commerce activities. How this e-commerce channel is integrated with a company's traditional sales channels (e.g., retail/wholesale outlets, catalog sales, and direct sales) is a major consideration in developing its e-commerce strategy.

Thus, the examples in this section emphasize that there is no universal clicks-and-bricks e-commerce strategy or e-commerce channel choice for every company, industry, or type of business. Both e-commerce integration and separation have major business benefits and shortcomings. Deciding on a clicks-and-bricks strategy and e-commerce channel depends heavily on whether a company's unique business operations provide strategic capabilities and resources to support a profitable business model successfully for its e-commerce channel. As these examples show, most companies are implementing some measure of clicks-and-bricks integration because "the benefits of integration are almost always too great to abandon entirely."

REI: Scaling e-Commerce Mountain

When outdoor equipment retailer REI wanted to boost in-store sales, the company looked to its Web site. In June 2003, REI.com launched free in-store pickup for customers who ordered online. The logic behind that thinking: People who visit stores to collect their online purchases might be swayed to spend more money upon seeing the colorful displays of clothing, climbing gear, bikes, and camping equipment.

REI's hunch paid off. "One out of every three people who buy something online will spend an additional $90 in the store when they come to pick something up," says Joan Broughton, REI's vice president of multichannel programs. That tendency translates into a healthy 1 percent increase in store sales.

As Broughton sees it, the mantra for any multichannel retailer should be "a sale is a sale is a sale, whether online, in stores or through catalogs." The Web is simply not an isolated channel with its own operational metrics or exclusive group of customers.

As the Web has matured as a retail channel, consumers have turned to online shopping as an additional place to interact with a retailer rather than a replacement for existing channels such as stores or catalogs.

And to make that strategy as cost-efficient as possible, the company uses the same trucks that restock its stores to fulfill online orders slated for in-store pickup. To make this work, REI had to integrate order information from the Web site and replenishment orders from stores at its distribution warehouse in Washington state.

In and of itself, integrating the two types of order information wasn't complex, says Brad Brown, REI's vice president of information services. What was difficult, however, was coordinating fulfillment of both online and replenishment orders because "orders placed on the Web by customers are nothing like replenishment orders that stores place," he says. Online orders are picked from the warehouse at the time of the order and then put in a queue until the appropriate truck is loaded, whereas store orders are picked by an automated replenishment system that typically picks orders at one time based on either a weekly or biweekly replenishment schedule.

To make in-store pickup a reality, Brown's group wrote a "promise algorithm" that informs customers of a delivery date when they place an online order. Timing can get tricky when orders are placed the day before a truck is scheduled to depart the warehouse with a store-replenishment delivery. For example, if an online order is placed on a Monday night and a truck is scheduled to depart Tuesday morning, the system promises the customer a pickup date of a week later, as if the order would be placed on the following week's truck. However, REI will shoot for fulfilling the order that night; if it can do it, REI (and, ultimately, the customer) is happy because the order arrives sooner than was promised.

Creating effective business-to-consumer retail Web sites entails more than simply calculating sales figures. It's about delivering the functionality that users expect and using the site to drive sales through other channels. And only IT integration can make this happen.

Source: Adapted from Megan Santosus, "Channel Integration—How REI Scaled e-Commerce Mountain," *CIO Magazine*, May 15, 2004.

Summary

- **e-Commerce.** E-commerce encompasses the entire online process of developing, marketing, selling, delivering, servicing, and paying for products and services. The Internet and related technologies and e-commerce Web sites on the World Wide Web and corporate intranets and extranets serve as the business and technology platforms for e-commerce marketplaces for consumers and businesses in the basic categories of business-to-consumer (B2C), business-to-business (B2B), and consumer-to-consumer (C2C) e-commerce. The essential processes that should be implemented in all e-commerce applications—access control and security, personalizing and profiling, search management, content management, catalog management, payment systems, workflow management, event notification, and collaboration and trading—are summarized in Figure 8.4.

- **e-Commerce Issues.** Many e-business enterprises are moving toward offering full-service B2C and B2B e-commerce portals supported by integrated customer-focused processes and internetworked supply chains, as illustrated in Figure 8.9. In addition, companies must evaluate a variety of e-commerce integration or separation alternatives and benefit trade-offs when choosing a clicks-and-bricks strategy and e-commerce channel, as summarized in Figures 8.16 and 8.17.

- **B2C e-Commerce.** Businesses typically sell products and services to consumers at e-commerce Web sites that provide attractive Web pages, multimedia catalogs, interactive order processing, secure electronic payment systems, and online customer support. However, successful e-tailers build customer satisfaction and loyalty by optimizing factors outlined in Figure 8.11, such as selection and value, performance and service efficiency, the look and feel of the site, advertising and incentives to purchase, personal attention, community relationships, and security and reliability. In addition, a Web store has several key business requirements, including building and marketing a Web business, serving and supporting customers, and managing a Web store, as summarized in Figure 8.13.

- **B2B e-Commerce.** Business-to-business applications of e-commerce involve electronic catalog, exchange, and auction marketplaces that use Internet, intranet, and extranet Web sites and portals to unite buyers and sellers, as summarized in Figure 8.14 and illustrated in Figure 8.15. Many B2B e-commerce portals are developed and operated for a variety of industries by third-party market-maker companies called infomediaries, which may represent consortiums of major corporations.

Key Terms and Concepts

These are the key terms and concepts of this chapter. The page number of their first explanation is in parentheses.

1. Clicks-and-bricks strategy (338)
2. E-commerce channel (341)
3. E-commerce marketplaces (336)
   a. Auction (336)
   b. Catalog (336)
   c. Exchange (336)
   d. Portal (334)
4. E-commerce processes (317)
   a. Access control and security (318)

   b. Collaboration and trading (321)
   c. Content and catalog management (318)
   d. Electronic payment systems (322)
   e. Event notification (321)
   f. Profiling and personalizing (318)
   g. Search management (318)
   h. Workflow management (320)

5. Electronic commerce (312)
   a. Business-to-business (B2B) (316)
   b. Business-to-consumer (B2C) (316)
   c. Consumer-to-consumer (C2C) (316)
6. Electronic funds transfer (EFT) (322)
7. Infomediaries (337)
8. Search engine optimization (332)

Review Quiz

Match one of the key terms and concepts listed previously with each of the brief examples or definitions that follow. Try to find the best fit for the answers that seem to fit more than one term or concept. Defend your choices.

____ 1. The online process of developing, marketing, selling, delivering, servicing, and paying for products and services.

____ 2. Business selling to consumers at retail Web stores is an example.

____ 3. Using an e-commerce portal for auctions by business customers and their suppliers is an example.

____ 4. Using an e-commerce Web site for auctions among consumers is an example.

____ 5. E-commerce applications must implement several major categories of interrelated processes, such as search and catalog management, in order to be effective.

____ 6. Helps to establish mutual trust between you and an e-tailer at an e-commerce site.

____ 7. Tracks your Web site behavior to provide you with an individualized Web store experience.

____ 8. Develops, generates, delivers, and updates information to you at a Web site.

____ 9. Ensures that proper e-commerce transactions, decisions, and activities are performed to serve you more efficiently.

____ 10. Sends you an e-mail when your e-commerce order has been shipped.

____ 11. Includes matchmaking, negotiation, and mediation processes among buyers and sellers.

____ 12. Companies that serve as intermediaries in e-commerce transactions.

____ 13. A process aimed at improving the volume and/or quality of traffic to a Web site.

____ 14. An e-commerce marketplace that may provide catalog, exchange, or auction service for businesses or consumers.

____ 15. Buyers bidding for the business of a seller.

____ 16. Marketplace for bid (buy) and ask (sell) transactions.

____ 17. The most widely used type of marketplace in B2C e-commerce.

____ 18. The marketing or sales channel created by a company to conduct and manage its e-commerce activities.

____ 19. The processing of money and credit transfers between businesses and financial institutions.

____ 20. Ways to provide efficient, convenient, and secure payments in e-commerce.

____ 21. Companies can evaluate and choose from several e-commerce integration alternatives.

____ 22. Web sites and portals hosted by individual companies, consortiums, or intermediaries that bring together buyers and sellers to accomplish e-commerce transactions.

____ 23. A component of e-commerce sites that helps customers find what they are looking for.

Discussion Questions

1. Most businesses should engage in e-commerce on the Internet. Do you agree or disagree with this statement? Explain your position.

2. Are you interested in investing in, owning, managing, or working for a business that is primarily engaged in e-commerce on the Internet? Explain your position.

3. Refer to the Real World Case on KitchenAid and the Royal Bank of Canada in the chapter. What recent uses of the Internet may these companies be overlooking in their quest to protect the equity of their brands? About those that you identified, what strategies would be adequate to face them?

4. Why do you think there have been so many business failures among "dot-com" companies that were devoted only to retail e-commerce?

5. Do the e-commerce success factors listed in Figure 8.11 guarantee success for an e-commerce business venture? Give a few examples of what else could go wrong and how you would confront such challenges.

6. If personalizing a customer's Web site experience is a key success factor, then electronic profiling processes to track visitor Web site behavior are necessary. Do you agree or disagree with this statement? Explain your position.

7. All corporate procurement should be accomplished in e-commerce auction marketplaces, instead of using B2B Web sites that feature fixed-price catalogs or negotiated prices. Explain your position on this proposal.

8. Refer to the Real World Case on LinkedIn, Umbria, Mattel and Others in the chapter. What is your take on the debate as to whether these 'influential' individuals do really have an effect on others, or they are representative of an underlying cultural trend? How would a company react based on their position on the issue?

9. If you were starting an e-commerce Web store, which of the business requirements summarized in Figure 8.13 would you primarily do yourself, and which would you outsource to a Web development or hosting company? Why?

Analysis Exercises

Complete the following exercises as individual or group projects that apply chapter concepts to real-world business situations.

1. Small Business e-Commerce Portals
On the Internet, small businesses have become big business, and a really big business, Microsoft, wants a piece of the action. The company's Small Business Center (www.microsoft.com/smallbusiness) is one of many sites offering advice and services for small businesses moving online. Most features, whether free or paid, are what you'd expect: lots of links and information along the lines established by Prodigy Biz (www.prodigybiz.com) or Entrabase.com. Small Business Center, however, stands out for its affordable advertising and marketing services. See Figure 8.18.

One program helps businesses create banner ads and places them on a collection of Web sites that it claims are visited by 60 percent of the Web surfing community. With its "Banner Network Ads" program,

FIGURE 8.18

Microsoft's Small Business Center is a small business e-commerce portal.

Source: Courtesy of Microsoft®.

buyers don't pay a huge fee upfront, and they don't run the risk that a huge number of visitors will unexpectedly drive up clickthrough commissions. Instead, this program allows small business to pay a small, fixed fee for a guaranteed number of clickthroughs (people who click on your banner ad to visit your Web site). Small Business Center rotates these banner ads around a network of participating Web sites and removes the ad as soon as it has received the guaranteed number of clickthrough visitors. This action eliminates the guesswork regarding both traffic and fees. The three packages—100, 250, and 1,000 visitors—break down to 50 cents per visitor.

a. Check out Small Business Center and the other e-commerce portals mentioned. Identify several benefits and limitations for a business using these Web sites.

b. Which Web site is your favorite? Why?

c. Which site would you recommend or use to help a small business wanting to get into e-commerce? Why?

2. e-Commerce Web Sites for Car Buying

Nowadays new car buyers can configure the car of their dreams on Microsoft's MSN Autos Web site, as well as those of Ford, GM, and other auto giants. Many independent online car purchase and research companies offer similar services. See Figure 8.19. Car buying information

provided by manufacturers, brokerage sites, car dealers, financial institutions, and consumer advocate Web sites has exploded in the past few years.

Yet in the age of the Internet, the auto industry remains a steadfast holdout to innovations that might threaten the well-established and well-connected supply chain, the car dealership. American new car buyers simply cannot skip the middleperson and purchase an automobile directly from the manufacturer. That's not just a business decision by the manufacturers; that's the law.

Even so, many car buyers use the Internet as a place to research their purchases. Instead of selling new cars directly, Web sites such as Autobytel.com of Irvine, California, just put consumers in touch with a local dealer where they test-drive a vehicle and negotiate a price. Autobytel.com has been referring buyers to new and used car dealers since 1995. It also offers online financing and insurance.

Online car-buying sites on the Web make consumers less dependent on what cars a dealer has on the lot. At online sites, buyers can customize a car—or van, truck, or sport utility vehicle—by selecting trim, paint, color, and other options before purchase. They can also use Web sites such as CarBuyingTips.com to help prepare for the final negotiating process.

FIGURE 8.19
Table for Problem 2.

Top Car-Buying Web Sites
• **Autobytel.com**   www.autobytel.com Enter make and model, and a local dealer will contact you with a price offer. Home delivery is an option.
• **AutoNation**   www.autonation.com Every make and model available, as well as financing and insurance information, home delivery, and test drives.
• **Microsoft MSN Autos**   www.autos.msn.com Auto reviews, detailed vehicle specifications, safety ratings, and buying services for new and used cars, including customizing your very own Ford.
• **cars.com**   www.cars.com Research tools include automotive reviews, model reports, dealer locators, and financing information.
• **CarsDirect.com**   www.carsdirect.com Research price and design, and then order your car. CarsDirect will deliver it to your home. A top-rated site.
• **Edmunds.com**   www.edmunds.com For an objective opinion, Edmunds.com provides reviews, safety updates, and rebate news for car buyers.
• **FordVehicles.com**   www.fordvehicles.com Research, configure, price, and order your new Ford car, minivan, truck, or SUV at this Web site.
• **GM BuyPower**   www.gmbuypower.com With access to nearly 6,000 GM dealerships, car shoppers can get a price quote, schedule a test drive, and buy.

a. Check out several of the Web sites shown in Figure 8.19. Evaluate them based on ease of use, relevance of information provided, and other criteria you feel are important. Don't forget the classic: "Did they make you want to buy?"

b. Which sites would you use or recommend if you or a friend actually wanted to buy a car? Why?

c. Check out the Consumer Federation of America's study on anticompetitive new car-buying state laws or similar studies online. How much does it estimate consumers would save if they could purchase cars directly from manufacturers online?

3. Comparing e-Commerce Sites
In this exercise, you will experiment with electronic shopping and compare alternative e-commerce sites. First, select a category of product widely available on the Web, such as books, CDs, or toys. Second, select five specific products to price on the Internet, for example, five specific CDs you might be interested in buying. Third, search three prominent e-commerce sites selling this type of product and record the price charged for each product by each site.

a. Using a spreadsheet, record a set of information similar to that shown for each product. (Categories describing the product will vary depending on the type of product you select—CDs might require the title of the CD and the performer[s], whereas toys or similar products would require the name of the product and its description.) See Figure 8.20.

b. For each product, rank each company on the basis of the price charged. Give a rating of 1 for the lowest price and 3 for the highest, and split the ratings for ties—two sites tying for the lowest price would each receive a 1.5. If a site does not have one of the products available for sale, give that site a rating of 4 for that product. Add the ratings across your products to produce an overall price/availability rating for each site.

c. Based on your experience with these sites, rate them on their ease of use, completeness of information, and order-filling and shipping options. As in Part (b), give a rating of 1 to the site you feel is best in each category, a 2 to the second best, and a 3 to the poorest site.

d. Prepare a set of PowerPoint slides or similar presentation materials summarizing the key results and including an overall assessment of the sites you compared.

4. e-Commerce: The Dark Side
Anonymous transactions on the Internet can have a dark side. Research each of the terms below on the Web. Prepare a one-page report for each term researched. Your paper should describe the problem and provide examples and illustrations where possible. Conclude each paper with recommendations on how to guard against each type of fraud.

a. Search using the terms "Ponzi Scheme" or "Pyramid Scheme." To find current examples in action, try searching for "plasma TV $50," "cash matrix," "e-books" and "matrix," or "gifting" through a search engine or action site.

b. Search using the terms "phishing" and "identity." If possible, include a printout of a real-world example that you or an acquaintance may have received via e-mail.

c. Search using the term "third-party escrow." What legitimate function does this serve? Provide an example of a legitimate third-party escrow service for Internet transactions. How has the third-party escrow system been used to commit fraud on the Internet?

d. Prepare a one-page paper describing a type of online fraud not covered in the previous questions. Prepare presentation materials and present your findings to the class. Be sure to include a description of the fraud, how to detect it, and how to avoid it. Use real-world illustrations if possible.

FIGURE 8.20   Table for Problem 3.

Title of Book	Author	Price Site A	Site B	Site C	Rating A	B	C
The Return of Little Big Man	Berger, T.	15.00	16.95	14.50	2	3	1
Learning Perl/Tk	Walsh, N. & Mui, L.	26.36	25.95	25.95	3	1.5	1.5
Business at the Speed of Thought	Gates, W.	21.00	22.95	21.00	1.5	3	1.5
Murders for the Holidays	Smith, G.		8.25	7.95	4	2	1
Designs for Dullards	Jones	17.95	18.50	18.50	1	2.5	2.5
Sum of ratings (low score represents most favorable rating)					11.5	12	7.5

REAL WORLD CASE 3

Entellium, Digg, Peerflix, Zappos, and Jigsaw: Success for Second Movers in e-Commerce

Anyone who has watched short-track speed skating during the Winter Olympics knows that skating with the lead is no easy task.

The No. 2 skater gets to conserve precious energy by drafting behind the leader. No. 2 watches the frontrunner's every move, gauging when and where to make a bid for the gold. Now corporate America and speed skating have much in common.

There are no safe leads.

For companies that use the Internet as the home base for their businesses, the second-mover advantage seems even more substantial. That's why Paul Johnston is deeply grateful to Marc Benioff.

Johnston's Seattle-based start-up, Entellium, has won hundreds of contracts against Benioff's Salesforce.com and other competitors since it moved from Malaysia in 2004, and its revenues grew fivefold in 2005. What Johnston really likes, though, is not having to sell companies on the concept of letting an outsider host their customer relationship management software.

What makes fast-following the hot strategy of the moment is the relative ease with which founders can get a start-up out on the track and send it chasing the competition. Cheap open-source tools can help you deploy new business software quickly.

Offshore manufacturers can quickly churn out anything from semiconductors to engine parts. The Web connects marketers to a vast pool of beta testers, while angel investors and venture capitalists, flush with new funds, stand at the ready.

Of course, fast-following isn't as simple as saying "Me too." To battle established leaders, you need the right product and strategy, as well as a big dose of savvy. Here's how to show up after the starting gun and still come out on top.

Number 1: Be better, faster, cheaper, easier

To steal business from Benioff, Johnston knew that Entellium had to offer something different. "This is true for any follower," he says.

It's what Johnston calls the "awesome, awesome, not totally ****-ed up" approach. The first "awesome" is how Entellium's software works. Johnston, formerly an Apple sales exec, aims to bring to the stodgy world of enterprise software the ease of use of consumer-directed offerings like Google Maps and the role-playing game Everquest. He even hired developers from the gaming industry to borrow interface tricks.

After appealing to customers on usability, Johnston hits them with the price: about 40 percent less than the competition. That's the second "awesome." The last part is making Entellium a less risky decision.

Who wants to put their job on the line for a start-up the boss has never heard of? Johnston offers free 24×7 service to make it easier for new customers to stick their necks out.

Number 2: Trip up incumbents with tactics from other fields

Common wisdom would say that the last thing the world needs is another technology news Web site, but Digg founders Jay Adelson and Kevin Rose are uncommonly wise.

A year ago, inspired by social-networking sites like MySpace—whose users rank everything from people to music—Adelson and Rose decided to use the same approach to build a better version of tech news site Slashdot.

Digg lets readers submit news stories and vote for the ones they think are most important. The top 15 vote-getters make it to the front page. The formula is working. Between May and November, the number of monthly unique visitors to Digg surged 284 percent to 404,000, eclipsing Slashdot's 367,000, according to ComScore Media Metrix. In addition, Adelson and Rose recently landed $2.8 million from investors, including eBay founder Pierre Omidyar and Netscape cofounder Marc Andreessen.

Moving forward, Adelson and Rose won't be shy about borrowing even more from seemingly unrelated companies. Soon they'll start tracking what members read and offering story recommendations à la Amazon. Digg is also set to branch out into nontechnology stories, which readers will be able to categorize with Delicious-style social bookmarking tags.

"A lot of companies are afraid to touch their original technology, to reconsider the premise on which they started the business," Adelson notes. "But when you stop doing that, that's when you get lapped [overtaken]."

Number 3: Swipe their business models and start your own race

When Billy McNair and Danny Robinson were hatching the idea for a new DVD company, Netflix handed them part of their business plan. Consumers had already learned that renting by mail was easy. McNair and Robinson believed they could do better than rentals. After all, eBay had shown them how.

By mixing together the best of two worlds, the founders came up with Peerflix, a Web site on which people exchange DVDs for a 99-cent transaction fee. Like eBay, Peerflix sits in the middle, linking movie fans and taking a piece of the action. Eager to avoid going head-to-head with eBay, however, McNair and Robinson are starting with lower-ticket items—those that sell for less than $25—for which auctions may not be worth the hassle.

"We've married the best of online rental services and online secondary markets," McNair claims. Since it launched in September, Peerflix has helped trade nearly 200,000 DVDs, and the founders are now talking about extending the idea to video games and other items.

Number 4: Follow the biggest leader you can find

When he hatched Zappos six years ago, Nick Swinmum put other online shoe sellers in his cross-hairs. Web-based competitors typically carried a limited number of brands and catered to small niches—say, women's dress shoes or men's outdoor boots. Zappos would crush them, Swinmum reasoned, with an online store that offered every conceivable make and model.

That was the right idea, but it focused on the wrong competitors. The online shoe market was so tiny that even if Zappos dominated it, there wouldn't be enough business for the company to thrive. To grow, it had to steal customers from bricks-and-mortar stores. Before 2001, Zappos didn't carry inventory; rather, the company asked distributors to "drop-ship" directly to consumers.

It was an easy, cheap arrangement, but the problem was that Zappos couldn't guarantee service; 8 percent of the time customers tried to buy shoes, the desired pair was out of stock. In other words, the experience was nothing like walking into a shoe store. "We realized then who our real competition was, and that we had to find a way to make an inventory model work," Swinmum says.

So Zappos began to cozy up to suppliers.

Contrary to industry practice, Swinmum shared data with manufacturers on exactly how well their shoes were selling. "Traditionally the vendor–retail relationship was adversarial," he recognizes. "We thought, 'Instead of trying to hide this information from the brands, let's open every-thing up. They can help us build the business.'" Did they ever! Grateful shoe reps helped Zappos craft promotions to spur sales.

Since targeting traditional shoe stores, Zappos has thrived. In 2001, the company did $8.6 million in sales; the next year it did $32 million. In 2005, Zappos posted more than $300 million in revenues from an expanding line of shoes, handbags, and other leather goods.

Number 5: Aim for the leader's Achilles' heel

When he was VP for sales at online marketing shop Digital Impact, Jim Fowler watched his field reps fail with a growing sense of frustration. Their problem? The leading online databases of corporate information, such as Dun & Bradstreet subsidiary Hoover's, didn't offer the deep, up-to-date contact lists that salespeople need to close deals.

Rather than complain about those vendors, Fowler decided to improve on them.

His company, Jigsaw, is a new kind of contact subscription service: All of the names and addresses in Jigsaw's database come from its users. Sales reps pay a minimum of $25 per month to access contacts at thousands of companies, or they pay nothing if they contribute 25 contacts per month themselves. Users police the listings to ensure they're current.

Since Jigsaw's launch in December 2004, its database has surged from 200,000 contacts to more than 2 million; some 38,000 subscribers are adding 10,000 new contacts a day. Through Jigsaw you can find more than 16,000 contacts at Medtronic, for example; Hoover's, meanwhile, offers extensive research on the company but only about 30 contacts. According to Fowler, "It's never too late if you are smarter and better than everyone else."

CASE STUDY QUESTIONS

1. Is the second-mover advantage always a good business strategy? Defend your answer with examples of the companies in this case.

2. What can a front-runner business do to foil the assaults of second movers? Defend your answer using the examples of the front-runner companies in the case.

3. Do second movers always have the advantage in Web-based business success? Why or why not? Evaluate the five strategies given in the case and the companies that used them to help defend your answer.

REAL WORLD ACTIVITIES

1. Use the Internet to research the current business status of all of the many companies in this case. Are the second movers still successfully using their strategies, or have the first movers foiled their attempts? Have new strong players entered the markets of the first and second movers, or have business, economic, or societal developments occurred to change the nature of competition in these markets?

2. Assume you will start an Internet-based business similar to one of those mentioned in this case or another one of your choice. Would you be a first, second, or later mover in the market you select? How would you differentiate yourself from other competitors or prospective new entrants? Break into small groups to share your ideas and attempt to agree on the best Web-based business opportunity of the group.

CHAPTER 9

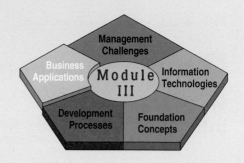

Management Challenges

Business Applications

Module III

Information Technologies

Development Processes

Foundation Concepts

DECISION SUPPORT SYSTEMS

Chapter Highlights

Learning Objectives

1. Identify the changes taking place in the form and use of decision support in business.

2. Identify the role and reporting alternatives of management information systems.

3. Describe how online analytical processing can meet key information needs of managers.

4. Explain the decision support system concept and how it differs from traditional management information systems.

5. Explain how the following information systems can support the information needs of executives, managers, and business professionals:

   a. Executive information systems

   b. Enterprise information portals

   c. Knowledge management systems

6. Identify how neural networks, fuzzy logic, genetic algorithms, virtual reality, and intelligent agents can be used in business.

7. Give examples of several ways expert systems can be used in business decision-making situations.

SECTION I   Decision Support in Business

Introduction

As companies migrate toward responsive e-business models, they are investing in new data-driven decision support application frameworks that help them respond rapidly to changing market conditions and customer needs.

To succeed in business today, companies need information systems that can support the diverse information and decision-making needs of their managers and business professionals. In this section, we will explore in more detail how this is accomplished by several types of management information, decision support, and other information systems. We concentrate our attention on how the Internet, intranets, and other Web-enabled information technologies have significantly strengthened the role that information systems play in supporting the decision-making activities of every manager and knowledge worker in business.

Read the Real World Case below. We can learn a lot from this case about the value of business intelligence projects. See Figure 9.1.

Information, Decisions, and Management

Figure 9.2 emphasizes that the type of information required by decision makers in a company is directly related to the **level of management decision making** and the amount of structure in the decision situations they face. It is important to understand that the framework of the classic *managerial pyramid* shown in Figure 9.2 applies even in today's *downsized organizations* and *flattened* or nonhierarchical organizational structures. Levels of management decision making still exist, but their size, shape, and participants continue to change as today's fluid organizational structures evolve. Thus, the levels of managerial decision making that must be supported by information technology in a successful organization are:

- **Strategic Management.** Typically, a board of directors and an executive committee of the CEO and top executives develop overall organizational goals, strategies, policies, and objectives as part of a strategic planning process. They also monitor the strategic performance of the organization and its overall direction in the political, economic, and competitive business environment.

- **Tactical Management.** Increasingly, business professionals in self-directed teams as well as business unit managers develop short- and medium-range plans, schedules, and budgets and specify the policies, procedures, and business objectives for their subunits of the company. They also allocate resources and monitor the performance of their organizational subunits, including departments, divisions, process teams, project teams, and other workgroups.

- **Operational Management.** The members of self-directed teams or operating managers develop short-range plans such as weekly production schedules. They direct the use of resources and the performance of tasks according to procedures and within budgets and schedules they establish for the teams and other workgroups of the organization.

Information Quality

What characteristics of information products make them valuable and useful to you? To answer this important question, we must first examine the characteristics or attributes of **information quality.** Information that is outdated, inaccurate, or hard to understand is not very meaningful, useful, or valuable to you or other business professionals. People need information of high quality, that is, information products whose characteristics, attributes, or qualities make the information more valuable to them. It is useful to think of information as having the three dimensions of time, content, and form. Figure 9.3 summarizes the important attributes of information quality and groups them into these three dimensions.

CASE 1

Hillman Group, Avnet, and Quaker Chemical: Process Transformation through Business Intelligence Deployments

Jim Honerkamp, CIO of Hillman Group, is proud of his new business intelligence (BI) system. Why not? It's much better than what came before. In the bad old days, executives looking for sales information, for example, had to ask one of Honerkamp's programmers to make a manual database query to pull the numbers from the company's legacy systems. The lag time made the charts "stale the minute they came out," according to Honerkamp, whose company is a $380 million manufacturer and distributor of engraving technologies and hardware, such as keys and signs.

With Hillman Group's new BI system, curious business executives can query the system themselves and get instant answers about such critical questions as the number of un-filled customer orders, which is tracked by the system in real time. There's just one problem: The new system hasn't made the business better—at least not yet—only better informed.

That's generally the problem with BI, the umbrella term that refers to a variety of software applications used to analyze an organization's raw data (e.g., sales transactions) and extract useful insights from them. Most CIOs still think of it as a reporting and decision support tool. Though the tools haven't changed much recently, there is a small revolution going on in the ways BI tools are being deployed by some CIOs. Done right, BI projects can transform business processes—and the businesses that depend on those processes—into lean, mean machines.

FIGURE 9.1

Business intelligence tools, coupled with changes to business processes, can have a significant impact on the bottom line.

It isn't easy to take BI to the next level; it requires a change in thinking about the value of information inside organizations from the CEO down. Information is power, and some people don't like to share it. Yet sharing is vital to this new vision of BI because everyone involved in the process must have full access to information to be able to change the ways that they work.

The other major impediment to using BI to transform business processes is that most companies don't understand their business processes well enough to determine how to improve them. Companies also need to be careful about the processes they choose. If the process does not have a direct impact on revenue, or the business isn't behind standardizing the process across the company, the entire BI effort could disintegrate. Companies need to understand all the activities that make up a particular business process, how information and data flow across various processes, how data are passed between business users, and how people use it to execute their particular part of the process. They need to understand all this before they start a BI project—if they hope to improve how people do their jobs.

The new, greater scope of these BI projects gives CIOs a strong justification for working with the business to study processes and determine how these tools and the insights they provide can support and improve them. Companies that use BI to uncover flawed business processes are in a much better position to successfully compete than those companies that use BI merely to monitor what's happening. Indeed, CIOs who don't use BI to transform business operations put their companies at a disadvantage. For CIOs who have carried out this difficult strategy successfully, there is no looking back.

Avnet, a computer systems, component, and embedded subsystems manufacturer, took the new process-oriented BI strategy directly to the processes that matter most: selling and serving customers. The company has put together a system from three BI vendors—Informatica, Business Objects, and InfoBurst—to generate reports on orders, shipment schedules, and dates by which Avnet will no longer manufacture certain products. Reports, however, were just the beginning. To transform the sales and customer service processes, CIO Steve Phillips rolled out the system to 2,000 salespeople so that they could actively incorporate that information into their day-to-day workflows and interactions with customers.

Employees use the information to modify their individual and team work practices, which leads to improved performance among the sales teams. When sales executives see a big difference in performance from one team to another, they work to bring the laggard teams up to the level of the leaders. "We try to identify, using our reporting tools, where best practices exist inside our work teams and then extend those best practices across the company," says Phillips.

One of those best practices is to alert customers if a product they have purchased in the past is about to be discontinued. Salespeople can ensure that customers have ordered enough for all of their future needs or identify a new component to replace the one that's being phased out. Those kinds of conversations boost sales and convince customers that Avnet's salespeople are looking out for their needs and interests.

It helps that Avnet's sales team is flexible and willing to adapt to the information. "Because our sales team is so flexible, they'll take this information from BI reports and change processes when they see a benefit to it," says Phillips. Sometimes, they don't even realize they are changing the ways they work—a kind of organic reengineering. Indeed, salespeople benefit so directly from better information and have such a big impact on revenue that they can be the best advocates for transformative BI in the company.

Yet this kind of effortless link between information and processes doesn't happen by magic. Phillips says his company has been able to use BI effectively because IT and business users have worked closely and steadily. "We needed to know how things really happen day to day, over and above the documented processes so that we could anticipate some of the business's information needs as we built out the warehouse," says Phillips.

Now that the BI system matches up with the way the company conducts its business, improving those processes and sharing the improvements are that much easier. "This is not just about reporting," says Phillips. "It's about using BI to make us smarter."

Quaker Chemical used its BI system to change completely the way it manages accounts receivable. In the past, the process of keeping track of whether customers paid their bills, and if they paid them on time, was primarily the purview of employees in the accounting department. Collection managers used the company's accounting system to identify which accounts were overdue, but they had limited information about the details of overdue balances. As a result, they had visibility only into glaring payment problems—customers who hadn't paid their bills at all in 60 days or more—and couldn't proactively identify which customers were at risk for not paying in full. Occasionally, they asked a sales manager to get involved, but the whole process for identifying which customers weren't paying and why they weren't paying and putting salespeople on the case was ad hoc.

To improve accounts receivable, Quaker Chemical decided in early 2005 that salespeople needed to play a larger, more formal role in the collections process. After all, they were the ones who had the primary relationship with the customers and had opportunities to speak with them more often, more proactively, and more sympathetically about their outstanding payments.

To get the salespeople involved, the IT department created a data mart that extracted accounts receivable information from transaction systems: It analyzed historical payments and historical balances by customer and by transaction and then loaded it into the data warehouse. By using its BI tools from SAS to analyze factors such as the amount of time it took Quaker Chemical to collect payment from a customer on a given invoice, as well as the number of times a customer paid part, but not all, of what he or she owed, the company was able to identify which customers were consistently paying late and which customers weren't paying at all. The IT department programmed the data warehouse to run reports automatically on which customers still owed money to Quaker Chemical. The system would then send those reports directly to the sales manager in charge of those accounts several times a month so that they could follow up with those customers. Collections managers no longer have to keep tabs on this information manually.

Quaker CIO Irving Tyler says this business process change was successful in part because IT was careful to deliver only the most specific, relevant information in these reports to salespeople. "If you don't focus the information and deliver it intelligently, people won't understand how to incorporate it into their workflows," says Tyler. This kind of dramatic change in process needs to be linked to the overall business strategy, according to Tyler. "Information doesn't necessarily change anything. You have to have a strategy to drive any change," he says.

Avnet and Quaker Chemical demonstrate that BI is about more than decision support. As a result of improvements in the technology and the way CIOs are implementing it, BI now has the potential to transform organizations. CIOs like Avnet's Phillips and Quaker Chemical's Tyler who successfully use BI to improve business processes contribute to their organizations in more far-reaching ways than by implementing basic reporting tools. "Our BI system provides information that helps us seek out greater efficiency," says Avnet's Phillips.

Source: Adapted from Meridith Levinson, "Business Intelligence: Not Just for Bosses Anymore," *CIO Magazine*, January 15, 2006; and Diann Daniel, "Five Ways to Get Your Employees Better Information More Quickly," *CIO Magazine*, January 10, 2008.

CASE STUDY QUESTIONS

1. What are the business benefits of BI deployments such as those implemented by Avnet and Quaker Chemical? What roles do data and business processes play in achieving those benefits?

2. What are the main challenges to the change of mindset required to extend BI tools beyond mere reporting? What can companies do to overcome them? Use examples from the case to illustrate your answer.

3. Both Avnet and Quaker Chemical implemented systems and processes that affect the practices of their salespeople. In which ways did the latter benefit from these new implementations? How important was their buy-in to the success of these projects? Discuss alternative strategies for companies to foster adoption of new systems like these.

REAL WORLD ACTIVITIES

1. Search the Internet for other examples of both "mere reporting" and transformational implementations of business intelligence tools. In which ways are these similar to the ones discussed in the case? In which ways are these different? What seem to be the main distinction between reporting and process-transformation BI rollouts? Prepare a report to summarize your findings.

2. How do you think the possession or access to certain information shapes the political dynamics of organizations? Do you believe companies should be open about widespread access to information, or will they be better off by restricting it? Why? Break into small groups with your classmates to discuss these issues, and take turns advocating the two alternative positions.

FIGURE 9.2 Information requirements of decision makers. The type of information required by directors, executives, managers, and members of self-directed teams is directly related to the level of management decision making involved and the structure of decision situations they face.

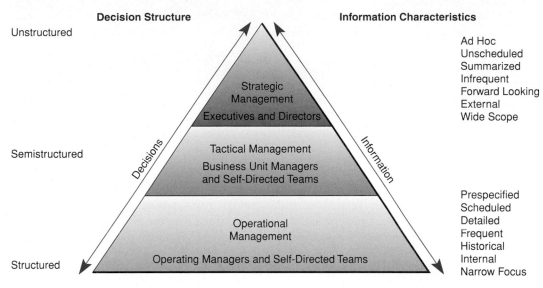

FIGURE 9.3

A summary of the attributes of information quality. This figure outlines the attributes that should be present in high-quality information products.

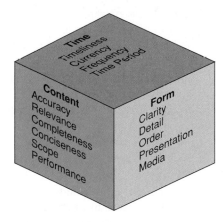

Time Dimension

Timeliness	Information should be provided when it is needed.
Currency	Information should be up-to-date when it is provided.
Frequency	Information should be provided as often as needed.
Time Period	Information can be provided about past, present, and future time periods.

Content Dimension

Accuracy	Information should be free from errors.
Relevance	Information should be related to the information needs of a specific recipient for a specific situation.
Completeness	All the information that is needed should be provided.
Conciseness	Only the information that is needed should be provided.
Scope	Information can have a broad or narrow scope, or an internal or external focus.
Performance	Information can reveal performance by measuring activities accomplished, progress made, or resources accumulated.

Form Dimension

Clarity	Information should be provided in a form that is easy to understand.
Detail	Information can be provided in detail or summary form.
Order	Information can be arranged in a predetermined sequence.
Presentation	Information can be presented in narrative, numeric, graphic, or other forms.
Media	Information can be provided in the form of printed paper documents, video displays, or other media.

FIGURE 9.4   Examples of decisions by the type of decision structure and level of management.

Decision Structure	Operational Management	Tactical Management	Strategic Management
Unstructured	Cash management	Business process reengineering Workgroup performance analysis	New e-business initiatives Company reorganization
Semistructured	Credit management Production scheduling Daily work assignment	Employee performance appraisal Capital budgeting Program budgeting	Product planning Mergers and acquisitions Site location
Structured	Inventory control	Program control	

Decision Structure

One way to understand decision making is to look at decision structure. Decisions made at the operational management level tend to be more *structured*, those at the tactical level are more *semistructured*, and those at the strategic management level are more *unstructured*. Structured decisions involve situations in which the procedures to follow, when a decision is needed, can be specified in advance. The inventory reorder decisions that most businesses face are a typical example. Unstructured decisions involve decision situations in which it is not possible to specify in advance most of the decision procedures to follow. Most decisions related to long-term strategy can be thought of as unstructured (e.g., "What product lines should we develop over the next five years?"). Most business decision situations are semistructured; that is, some decision procedures can be prespecified but not enough to lead to a definite recommended decision. For example, decisions involved in starting a new line of e-commerce services or making major changes to employee benefits would probably range from unstructured to semistructured. Finally, decisions that are unstructured are those for which no procedures or rules exist to guide the decision makers toward the correct decision. In these types of decisions, many sources of information must be accessed, and the decision often rests on experience and "gut feeling." One example of an unstructured decision might be the answer to the question, "What business should we be in 10 years from now?" Figure 9.4 provides a variety of examples of business decisions by type of decision structure and level of management.

Therefore, information systems must be designed to produce a variety of information products to meet the changing needs of decision makers throughout an organization. For example, decision makers at the strategic management level may look to *decision support systems* to provide them with more summarized, ad hoc, unscheduled reports, forecasts, and external intelligence to support their more unstructured planning and policymaking responsibilities. Decision makers at the operational management level, in contrast, may depend on *management information systems* to supply more prespecified internal reports emphasizing detailed current and historical data comparisons that support their more structured responsibilities in day-to-day operations. Figure 9.5 compares the information and decision support capabilities of management information systems and decision support systems, which we will explore in this chapter.

Decision Support Trends

The emerging class of applications focuses on personalized decision support, modeling, information retrieval, data warehousing, what-if scenarios, and reporting.

As we discussed in Chapter 1, using information systems to support business decision making has been one of the primary thrusts of the business use of information technology. During the 1990s, however, both academic researchers and business practitioners began to report that the traditional managerial focus originating in classic management information systems (1960s), decision support systems (1970s), and executive information systems (1980s) was expanding. The fast pace of new information technologies like PC hardware and software suites, client/server networks, and networked PC versions of DSS software made decision support available to lower levels of management, as well as to nonmanagerial individuals and self-directed teams of business professionals.

FIGURE 9.5
Comparing the major differences in the information and decision support capabilities of management information systems and decision support systems.

	Management Information Systems	Decision Support Systems
● Decision support provided	Provide information about the performance of the organization	Provide information and decision support techniques to analyze specific problems or opportunities
● Information form and frequency	Periodic, exception, demand, and push reports and responses	Interactive inquiries and responses
● Information format	Prespecified, fixed format	Ad hoc, flexible, and adaptable format
● Information processing methodology	Information produced by extraction and manipulation of business data	Information produced by analytical modeling of business data

This trend has accelerated with the dramatic growth of the Internet, as well as of intranets and extranets that internetwork companies and their stakeholders. The e-business and e-commerce initiatives that are being implemented by many companies are also expanding the information and decision support uses and the expectations of a company's employees, managers, customers, suppliers, and other business partners. Figure 9.6 illustrates that all business stakeholders expect easy and instant access to information and Web-enabled self-service data analysis. Today's businesses are responding with a variety of personalized and proactive Web-based analytical techniques to support the decision-making requirements of all of their constituents.

Thus, the growth of corporate intranets and extranets, as well as the Web, has accelerated the development and use of "executive-class" information delivery and decision support software tools by lower levels of management and by individuals and teams of business professionals. In addition, this dramatic expansion has opened the door to the use of such business intelligence (BI) tools by the suppliers, customers, and other business stakeholders of a company for customer relationship management, supply chain management, and other e-business applications.

In 1989, Howard Dresner (later a Gartner Group analyst) proposed BI as an umbrella term to describe "concepts and methods to improve business decision making by using fact-based support systems." It was not until the late 1990s that this usage became widespread. Today, BI is considered a necessary and mission critical element in crafting and executing a firm's strategy. Consider the following findings from a 2009 Gartner Group study:

- Because of lack of information, processes, and tools, through 2012, more than 35 percent of the top 5,000 global companies will regularly fail to make insightful decisions about significant changes in their business and markets.

- By 2012, business units will control at least 40 percent of the total budget for business intelligence.

FIGURE 9.6
A business must meet the information and data analysis requirements of its stakeholders with more personalized and proactive Web-based decision support.

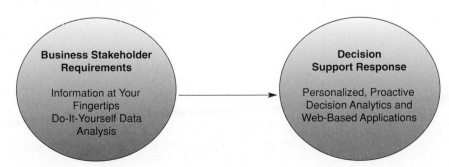

FIGURE 9.7

Business intelligence applications are based on personalized and Web-enabled information analysis, knowledge management, and decision support technologies.

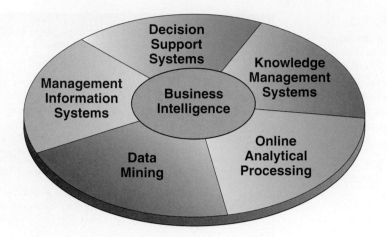

- By 2010, 20 percent of organizations will have an industry-specific analytic application, delivered via software as a service, as a standard component of their business intelligence portfolio.
- In 2009, collaborative decision making will emerge as a new product category that combines social software with business intelligence platform capabilities.

When you consider some of these findings, it becomes easy to see that BI is rapidly becoming the mainstay for business decision making in the modern organization. Before long, it will evolve into a competitive necessity for many industries.

Figure 9.7 highlights several major information technologies that are being customized, personalized, and Web-enabled to provide key business information and analytical tools for managers, business professionals, and business stakeholders. We highlight the trends toward such business intelligence applications in the various types of information and decision support systems that are discussed in this chapter.

Hyatt Hotels: Dashboards Integrate Financial and Operational Information

A few years ago, executives at Chicago-based Hyatt Hotels decided the company needed a way to consolidate its disparate financial data so that it could more easily forecast future sales and plan its business accordingly. In other words, the company wanted to install a typical financial performance management layer, with dashboards and scorecards for top-level managers. But after some discussion on the matter, the installation grew not-so-typical.

Gebhard Rainer, Hyatt's vice president of hotel finance and systems, wanted to combine these financial elements—budgeting, planning, modeling, and reporting—with operational data from the hotels themselves. The idea was that a complete picture of the company's business, available on a daily basis to executives as well as hotel managers, was not possible without having the two together in the same dashboard.

Motivating the concept was a changing world, with terrorist risks and natural disasters causing an ever-shifting array of business variables. Rainer, in a Middle Eastern country in the aftermath of a terrorist attack several years ago, confronted these issues first-hand—as did the company, which owns hotels in New Orleans and along the hurricane-ravaged Gulf Coast. The first line of business is the safety of hotel guests. But in terms of the big picture, hotel companies must re-forecast their business goals from the ground up based on a set of entirely new metrics dealing with issues from resource allocation to skittish tourists rethinking their travel plans. It wasn't a job for spreadsheets.

Hyatt was among the first of Hyperion's customers to adopt System 9. The company selected Hyperion based on its "integrateability" with its source systems, as well as its user-friendliness. At first, Hyatt wanted a small-scale installation, delivering the

System 9 dashboards to about 40 executive users. "This phase was a 'show-me-what-you-can-do' thing," says Sufel Barkat, Hyatt's assistant vice president for financial systems. "We simply wanted to understand the capability of the tools. The next stage will have a much bigger impact." The ultimate plan is to spread the system throughout the Hyatt organization to its many subsidiaries, in the United States and abroad, and to its individual properties—full-blown operational BI. Eventually, hotel managers will have access to dashboards so that everyone is on the same page, and so that local employees can make local decisions based on the same information viewed at headquarters.

Hyatt ended up using a data warehouse from Teradata to cleanse operational information coming from the decentralized ERP systems of Hyatt's individual hotels around the world. The company also uses the warehouse to store and cleanse external marketing data, such as what the competition is up to, or market share in each region.

On the financial side, other sources include the proprietary company's general ledger system and an Oracle database—systems already consolidated and unified through Hyatt's original performance management outlay.

The next step will be to deliver the dashboards to between 500 and 600 users at Hyatt—all the way down to the regional manager level. The full-blown operational BI roll-out will target around 3,000 users. So far, in these early stages, Barkat hasn't been able to quantify the results of System 9 with any real figures. But, he says, users have been providing feedback on metrics, which, to him, indicates a strong "cultural and business adaptation" among Hyatt's executive class.

Source: Adapted from Scott Eden, "Hyatt Merges Financial, Ops Data," *InformationWeek*, January 17, 2006.

Decision Support Systems

Decision support systems are computer-based information systems that provide interactive information support to managers and business professionals during the decision-making process. Decision support systems use (1) analytical models, (2) specialized databases, (3) a decision maker's own insights and judgments, and (4) an interactive, computer-based modeling process to support semistructured business decisions.

Example

An example might help at this point. Sales managers typically rely on management information systems to produce sales analysis reports. These reports contain sales performance figures by product line, salesperson, sales region, and so on. A decision support system (DSS), however, would also interactively show a sales manager the effects on sales performance of changes in a variety of factors (e.g., promotion expense and salesperson compensation). The DSS could then use several criteria (e.g., expected gross margin and market share) to evaluate and rank alternative combinations of sales performance factors.

Therefore, DSS are designed to be ad hoc, quick-response systems that are initiated and controlled by business decision makers. Decision support systems are thus able to support directly the specific types of decisions and the personal decision-making styles and needs of individual executives, managers, and business professionals.

DSS Components

Unlike management information systems, decision support systems rely on **model bases** as well as databases as vital system resources. A DSS model base is a software component that consists of models used in computational and analytical routines that mathematically express relationships among variables. For example, a spreadsheet program might contain models that express simple accounting relationships among variables, such as Revenue − Expenses = Profit. A DSS model base could also include models and analytical techniques used to express much more complex relationships. For example, it might contain linear programming models, multiple regression forecasting models, and capital budgeting present value models. Such models may be stored in the form of spreadsheet models or templates, or statistical and mathematical programs and program modules. See Figure 9.8.

FIGURE 9.8
Components of a Web-enabled marketing decision support system. Note the hardware, software, model, data, and network resources involved.

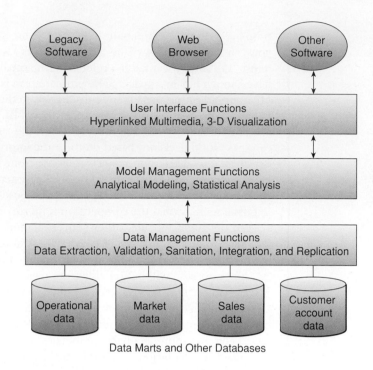

In addition, DSS software packages can combine model components to create integrated models that support specific types of decisions. DSS software typically contains built-in analytical modeling routines and also enables you to build your own models. Many DSS packages are now available in microcomputer and Web-enabled versions. Of course, electronic spreadsheet packages also provide some of the model building (spreadsheet models) and analytical modeling (what-if and goal-seeking analysis) offered by more powerful DSS software. As businesses become more aware of the power of decision support systems, they are using them in ever-increasing areas of the business. See Figure 9.9.

FIGURE 9.9 Many businesses are turning to decision support systems and their underlying models to improve a wide variety of business functions.

Analytics competitors make expert use of statistics and modeling to improve a wide variety of functions. Here are some common applications:		
Function	**Description**	**Exemplars**
Supply chain	Simulate and optimize supply chain flows; reduce inventory and stockouts.	Dell, Wal-Mart, Amazon
Customer selection, loyalty, and service	Identify customers with the greatest profit potential; increase likelihood that they will want the product or service offering; retain their loyalty.	Harrah's, Capital One, Barclays
Pricing	Identify the price that will maximize yield or profit.	Progressive, Marriott
Human capital	Select the best employees for particular tasks or jobs at particular compensation levels.	New England Patriots, Oakland A's, Boston Red Sox
Product and service quality	Detect quality problems early and minimize them.	Honda, Intel
Financial performance	Better understand the drivers of financial performance and the effects of nonfinancial factors.	MCI, Verizon
Research and development	Improve quality, efficacy, and, where applicable, safety of products and services.	Novartis, Amazon, Yahoo

Source: Adapted from Thomas H. Davenport, "Competing on Analytics," *Harvard Business Review*, January 2006.

Rolling the Dice: Technology for Better Decision Making	New economic research affirms what most executives suspect: Even when given good data, people make bad decisions. We misunderstand, misinterpret, and mismanage important problems. It's not that we're stupid; our thought processes have bugs. There are technologies emerging now to help us fix those bugs. Decision support software has been around for years, but its latest incarnations tap pervasive computing power to generate thousands of scenarios covering all conceivable real-world contingencies. Products such as @risk and XL Sim allow people to test their assumptions through what is essentially repeated rolls of the dice: random number generation. The technique, known as Monte Carlo simulation, can turn ordinary spreadsheets into probabilistic wind tunnels for designing good decisions.

"With any luck, the rise of cheap, easy Monte Carlo simulations will reduce the number of stupid decisions managers make by relying on simplistic averages," says Sam Savage, the creator of XL Sim and a pioneer in spreadsheet-based statistical literacy, as well as a consulting professor at Stanford University.

Consider the case of a Silicon Valley product manager who has just been asked to forecast demand for a next-generation microchip. "The guy typically will offer a forecast range between, say, 50,000 and 150,000 units," he says. The problem, says Savage, is that the boss doesn't want a range. He wants a number. So the manager says, "100,000," the average. So the boss plugs that figure and the cost of building a 100,000-chip–capacity plant into a spreadsheet. The bottom line is a healthy $10 million, which he reports to his board as the average expected profit. Assuming that demand is the only uncertainty and that 100,000 is the correct average, then $10 million must be the best guess for profit. Right? Wrong.

What Savage calls "the flaw of averages" ensures that average profit has to be less than the profit associated with the predicted average demand. If demand is less than 100,000, then profits will be lower than $10 million. Yet the profits can never be higher than $10 million because the maximum capacity of the plant is based on a flawed average. Consequently, the product manager's correct forecast of average demand leads to an inflated forecast of average profit.

Savage predicts that, one day, every executive who manages plant capacity, every investor with a stock portfolio, and every employee with a retirement fund will be running Monte Carlo simulations to test their intuitive assumptions about average returns and average losses.

Source: Adapted from Michael Schrage, "Decision Support Software Shows You the Scenarios," *CIO Magazine*, January 1, 2003.

Management Information Systems

Recall from Chapter 1 that management information systems were the original type of information system developed to support managerial decision making. An MIS produces information products that support many of the day-to-day decision-making needs of managers and business professionals. Reports, displays, and responses produced by management information systems provide information that these decision makers have specified in advance as adequately meeting their information needs. Such predefined information products satisfy the information needs of decision makers at the operational and tactical levels of the organization who are faced with more structured types of decision situations. For example, sales managers rely heavily on sales analysis reports to evaluate differences in performance among salespeople who sell the same types of products to the same types of customers. They have a pretty good idea of the kinds of information about sales results (by product line, sales territory, customer, salesperson, and so on) that they need to manage sales performance effectively.

Managers and other decision makers use an MIS to request information at their networked workstations that supports their decision-making activities. This information takes the form of periodic, exception, and demand reports and immediate responses to inquiries. Web browsers, application programs, and database management software provide access to information in the intranet and other operational databases of the organization. Remember, operational databases are maintained by transaction processing systems. Data about the business environment are obtained from Internet or extranet databases when necessary.

Management Reporting Alternatives

Management information systems provide a variety of information products to managers. Four major **reporting alternatives** are provided by such systems.

- **Periodic Scheduled Reports.** This traditional form of providing information to managers uses a prespecified format designed to provide managers with information on a regular basis. Typical examples of such periodic scheduled reports are daily or weekly sales analysis reports and monthly financial statements.

- **Exception Reports.** In some cases, reports are produced only when exceptional conditions occur. In other cases, reports are produced periodically but contain information only about these exceptional conditions. For example, a credit manager can be provided with a report that contains only information on customers who have exceeded their credit limits. Exception reporting reduces *information overload* instead of overwhelming decision makers with periodic detailed reports of business activity.

- **Demand Reports and Responses.** Information is available whenever a manager demands it. For example, Web browsers, DBMS query languages, and report generators enable managers at PC workstations to get immediate responses or to find and obtain customized reports as a result of their requests for the information they need. Thus, managers do not have to wait for periodic reports to arrive as scheduled.

- **Push Reporting.** Information is *pushed* to a manager's networked workstation. Thus, many companies are using Webcasting software to broadcast selectively reports and other information to the networked PCs of managers and specialists over their corporate intranets. See Figure 9.10.

FIGURE 9.10   An example of the components in a marketing intelligence system that uses the Internet and a corporate intranet system to "push" information to employees.

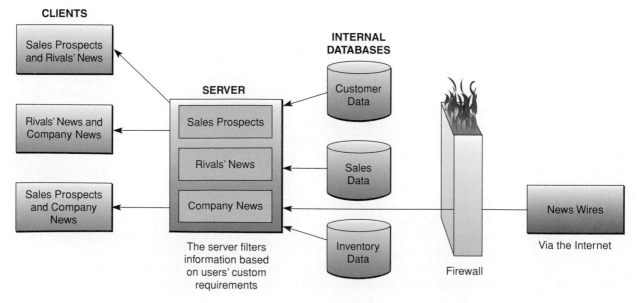

Online Analytical Processing

At a stockholder meeting, the former CEO of PepsiCo, D. Wayne Calloway, said: "Ten years ago I could have told you how Doritos were selling west of the Mississippi. Today, not only can I tell you how well Doritos sell west of the Mississippi, I can also tell you how well they are selling in California, in Orange County, in the town of Irvine, in the local Vons supermarket, in the special promotion, at the end of Aisle 4, on Thursdays."

The competitive and dynamic nature of today's global business environment is driving demands by business managers and analysts for information systems that can provide fast answers to complex business queries. The IS industry has responded to these demands with developments like analytical databases, data marts, data warehouses, data mining techniques, and multidimensional database structures (discussed in Chapter 5), and with specialized servers and Web-enabled software products that support online analytical processing (OLAP).

Online analytical processing enables managers and analysts to interactively examine and manipulate large amounts of detailed and consolidated data from many perspectives. OLAP involves analyzing complex relationships among thousands or even millions of data items stored in data marts, data warehouses, and other multidimensional databases to discover patterns, trends, and exception conditions. An OLAP session takes place online in real time, with rapid responses to a manager's or analyst's queries, so that the analytical or decision-making process is undisturbed. See Figure 9.11.

Online analytical processing involves several basic analytical operations, including consolidation, "drill-down," and "slicing and dicing." See Figure 9.12.

- **Consolidation.** Consolidation involves the aggregation of data, which can involve simple roll-ups or complex groupings involving interrelated data. For example, data about sales offices can be rolled up to the district level, and the district-level data can be rolled up to provide a regional-level perspective.

- **Drill-down.** OLAP can also go in the reverse direction and automatically display detailed data that comprise consolidated data. This process is called drill-down. For example, the sales by individual products or sales reps that make up a region's sales totals could be easily accessed.

- **Slicing and Dicing.** Slicing and dicing refers to the ability to look at the database from different viewpoints. One slice of the sales database might show all sales of a product type within regions. Another slice might show all sales by sales channel within each product type. Slicing and dicing is often performed along a time axis to analyze trends and find time-based patterns in the data.

FIGURE 9.11

Online analytical processing may involve the use of specialized servers and multidimensional databases. OLAP provides fast answers to complex queries posed by managers and analysts using traditional and Web-enabled OLAP software.

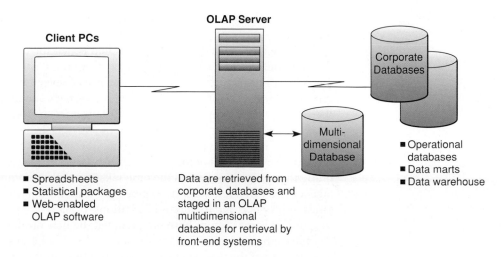

FIGURE 9.12

Comshare's Management Planning and Control software enables business professionals to use Microsoft Excel as their user interface for Web-enabled online analytical processing.

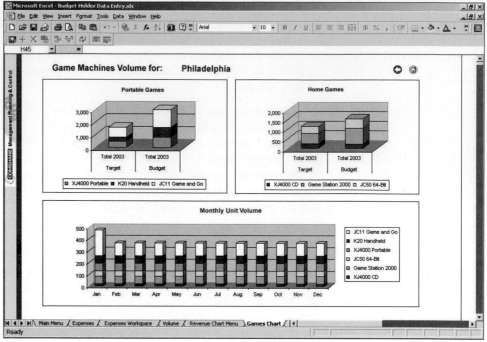

Source: Courtesy of Microsoft®.

OLAP Examples

Probably the best way to understand the power of OLAP fully is to look at common business applications of the technique. The real power of OLAP comes from the marriage of data and models on a large scale. Through this marriage, managers can solve a variety of problems that previously would be considered too complex to tackle effectively. Common business areas where OLAP can solve complex problems include:

- Marketing and sales analysis
- Clickstream data
- Database marketing
- Budgeting
- Financial reporting and consolidation
- Profitability analysis
- Quality analysis

Let's look at one or two examples of how OLAP can be used in the modern business setting.

It is near the end of a business quarter, and senior management is worried about the market acceptance of several new products. A marketing analyst is asked to provide an update to senior management. The problem is that the update must be delivered in less than an hour due to a last-minute request from the CEO. The analyst really only has a few minutes to analyze the market acceptance of several new products, so she decides to group 20 products that were introduced between six and nine months ago and compare their sales with a comparable group of 50 products introduced between two and three years ago. The analyst just defines two new, on-the-fly, product groupings and creates a ratio of the new group to the older group. She can then track this ratio of sales revenue or volume by any level of location, over time, by customer sector or by sales group. Defining the new groupings and the ratio takes a couple of minutes, and any of the analyses take a matter of a few seconds to generate, even though the database has tens of thousands of products and hundreds of locations. It takes no more than a total of 15 minutes to spot that some regions have not accepted the new products as fast as others.

Then, the analyst investigates whether this was because of inadequate promotion, unsuitability of the new products, lack of briefings of the sales force in the slow areas, or whether some areas always accept new products more slowly than others. Looking at other new product introductions by creating new groupings of products of different ages, she finds that the same areas are always conservative when introducing expensive new products. She then uses this information to see if the growth in the slow areas is in line with history and finds that some areas have taken off even more slowly than previously. Given the results of this analysis, senior management decides it is premature in its concern and tables further discussion until the next quarterly sales data can be assessed.

In another example, let's consider a general merchandise retailer who has joined the e-tailing ranks, wants the company Web site to be as "sticky" as possible, and has begun to analyze clickstream data to surmise why customers might leave the site prematurely. The company sharpened its analysis to determine the value of abandoned shopping carts. When a customer leaves the site in the middle of a shopping trip, for whatever reason, the company looks to see what products were in the abandoned cart. The data are then compared with similar data from other carts to examine:

- How much revenue the abandoned carts represented (in other words, the amount of revenue that was lost because of the customer's early departure).
- Whether the products in the cart were high-profit items or loss leaders.
- Whether the same products were found in other abandoned carts.
- The volume of products and the number of different product categories in the cart.
- Whether the total bill for the abandoned carts consistently fell within a certain dollar range.
- How the average and total bills for abandoned carts compared with unabandoned carts (those that made it through the checkout process).

The results of using OLAP to conduct this analysis trigger some interesting theories. For instance, it is possible that none of the products in the cart was appealing enough to a particular customer to keep that customer shopping. The customer might have been annoyed by frequent inquiries, such as "Are you ready to check out?" At a particular dollar total, the customer might have changed his or her mind about the entire shopping trip and left. It's also possible that a number or mix of products in a cart reminded the customer of another site that might offer a steeper discount for similar purchases.

Admittedly, some of these theories are mere guesses. After all, maybe the customer's Internet connection was on the fritz, or the site had a bug that abruptly booted the user. When examined regularly and with consistent metrics, however, clickstreams can reveal interesting patterns. After several analyses, the e-tailer decides to make some changes to the Web site.

First, the e-tailer tweaks the site to show a rolling total as items are added to the cart, thereby allowing the customer to see the total charge during the shopping time and to check out once the magic budget limit is reached. In addition, rather than requiring the customer to go to another page for specific product information, the site now invites the customer to see pop-up product information with a click of the right mouse button, keeping the buy mode alive. Finally, the vendor decides to integrate the clickstream data with more specific customer behavior information, including information from the CRM system.

Rather than just examining a customer's navigation patterns and guessing about which actions to take, the e-tailer can combine those patterns with more specific customer data (such as previous purchases in that product category, key demographic and psychographic data, or lifetime value score) to provide a complete view of that customer's value and interests. That kind of analysis will show you whether the lost customer was a one-time-only shopper or a high-value customer. A tailored e-mail message or electronic coupon—perhaps targeting one of the products left behind on a prior trip—could make all the difference the next time that high-value customer logs on.

Here's a real-world example of how OLAP can help solve complex business problems.

Direct Energy: Mining BI to Keep Its Customers

Even before bad debt shook the mortgage industry, Direct Energy was feeling its effects, including eroding revenue streams due to customer churn. Until then, the company effectively mined its way out in the best fashion: business intelligence. "Various groups were pulling data from various systems and not having integrated information," explains John Katsinos, vice president of IS for Direct Energy's mass markets operations. "There was no way to tie together a customer's end-to-end lifecycle."

Without that holistic view of customer records, it was difficult for Direct Energy analysts to understand, let alone prevent, customer churn. So began BI Jumpstart, the company's initiative to give its analysts insight into customer actions that precipitate into the dropping of Direct Energy services, as well as tools for forecasting bad debt. The result has been savings of tens of millions of dollars and a more proactive approach to customer retention via more accurate pricing, forecasting, and targeted marketing.

"We wanted to mitigate the risk to our business and customer base, and to grow our customer base and revenue," Katsinos adds.

"That meant being able to understand customer data at a level where we can forecast and predict behavior." Katsinos kicked off BI Jumpstart by assembling a crack analytics team consisting of an IS project manager, a data modeler, a pair of ETL developers, an analytic developer, a BI architect, and a BI administrator. That group then implemented a "multilayered business intelligence" strategy that, Katsinos explains, comprises data warehousing, data marts, OLAP repositories, and ETL.

The result is a data miner's dream: Direct Energy analysts can use the integrated BI program to predict what customers in which areas are likely to turn over, and then adjust the company's services, pricing, and marketing campaigns accordingly.

For example, with BI Jumpstart in place, Direct Energy can now determine why one of its offerings experiences a 2 percent churn while another sees 20 percent of its customers dropping the service.

More than an initiative geared toward new revenue streams, BI Jumpstart helps Direct Energy make the most of what it already has. "Now, we can slice and dice any way we want," Katsinos says.

Source: Adapted from Tom Sullivan, "Direct Energy Mines BI to Conserve Revenue Streams," *InfoWorld*, November 17, 2008.

Geographic Information and Data Visualization Systems

Geographic information systems (GIS) and data visualization systems (DVS) are special categories of DSS that integrate computer graphics with other DSS features. A geographic information system is a DSS that uses *geographic databases* to construct and display maps, as well as other graphics displays that support decisions affecting the geographic distribution of people and other resources. Many companies are using GIS technology along with *global positioning system* (GPS) devices to help them choose new retail store locations, optimize distribution routes, or analyze the demographics of their target audiences. For example, companies like Levi Strauss, Arby's, Consolidated Rail, and Federal Express use GIS packages to integrate maps, graphics, and other geographic data with business data from spreadsheets and statistical packages. GIS software such as MapInfo and Atlas GIS is used for most business GIS applications. See Figure 9.13.

Data visualization systems represent complex data using interactive, three-dimensional, graphical forms such as charts, graphs, and maps. DVS tools help users interactively sort, subdivide, combine, and organize data while the data are in their graphical form. This assistance helps users discover patterns, links, and anomalies in business or scientific data in an interactive knowledge discovery and decision support process. Business applications like data mining typically use interactive graphs that let users drill down in real time and manipulate the underlying data of a business model to help clarify their meaning for business decision making. Figure 9.14 is an example of airline flight analysis by a data visualization system.

FIGURE 9.13

Geographic information systems facilitate the mining and visualization of data associated with a geophysical location.

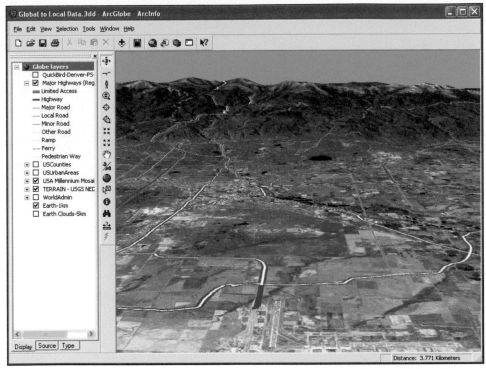

Source: Courtesy of Rockware Inc.

The concept of the geographic information system and data visualization is not a new one. One of the first recorded uses of the concept occurred in September 1854. During a 10-day period, 500 people, all from the same section of London, England, died of cholera. Dr. John Snow, a local physician, had been studying this cholera epidemic for some time. In trying to determine the source of the cholera, Dr. Snow located every cholera death in the Soho district of London by marking the location of the home of each victim with a dot on a map he had drawn. Figure 9.15 contains a replica of his original map.

FIGURE 9.14

Using a data visualization system to analyze airplane flights by segment and average delay, with drill down to details.

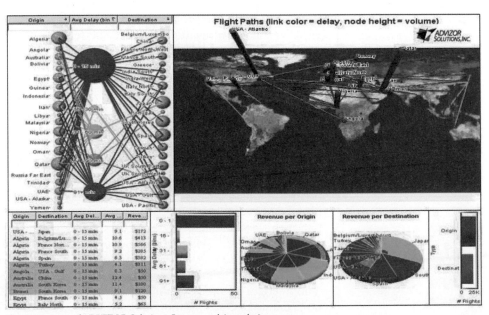

Source: Courtesy of ADVIZOR Solutions, Inc. www.advisorsolutions.com.

FIGURE 9.15

Replica of Dr. John Snow's cholera epidemic map.

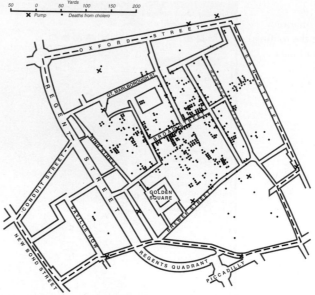

Source: E.R. Tufte, *The Visual Display of Quantitative Information,* 2nd ed. (Cheshire, Connecticut; Graphics Press, 2001), p. 24.

As can be seen on the map, Dr. Snow marked the deaths with dots, and the 11 Xs represent water pumps. By examining the scattering and clustering of the dots, Dr. Snow observed that the victims of the cholera shared one common attribute: They all lived near—and drank from—the Broad Street water pump. To test his hypothesis, Dr. Snow requested that the handle of the pump be removed, thus rendering it inoperable. Within a very short time, the cholera epidemic, which claimed more than 500 lives, was over.

JPMorgan and Panopticon: Data Visualization Helps Fixed Income Traders

Visualizing and understanding vast quantities of credit market data can be overwhelming using traditional techniques such as charts and tables. Navigating through this data to find specific reports and analytical information can also prove daunting and traditional information delivery mechanisms have tended to provide unruly volumes of data.

The Internet is today the obvious delivery mechanism for such market data and proprietary analyses, yet the providers of such services must deliver more intuitive visualization and navigation to provide better value to their customers.

Fixed income research and analytics providers are looking at new means of visualizing data to provide more valuable and intuitive services to their users by going beyond simple online tables, charts, and document repositories.

JPMorgan created their CreditMap application using Panopticon Developer in order to provide their customers with a graphical representation of real-time activity in the corporate bond market. JPMorgan blurred the lines between providing informative research and valuable analytics, which has enabled them to win the Euromoney award for "Best Online Fixed Income Research."

JPMorgan was able to provide their users with quicker access to their existing online information using new visualization and navigation tools. To do this they implemented Panopticon's interactive treemap visualization as a presentation layer and navigation system that provides a bird's-eye view of the data at the same time allowing the user to drill-down to specific reports and analytics.

JPMorgan's CreditMap allows users to visualize information through the use of color, size and proximity in any way they desire with an easily customizable interface. This interface acts as a catalyst enabling users to recognize patterns, analyze information, and make decisions more quickly and more accurately than ever before. Before

CreditMap, the brokerage firm's customers could read text reports on the corporate bond market and view various tables of statistical information. But the market is so extensive that it could be difficult to keep things in perspective or to be aware of many of the investment opportunities.

CreditMap presents the corporate bond universe as a quilt of rectangles on a computer screen. The quilt is divided into industry sectors, and the rectangles within each sector represent bond issues. The size of the rectangle indicates the size of the issue, and the color indicates the issue's performance. So at a glance, investors can see which sectors and which individual issues are hot, and whether an issue's size fits their investment needs. Clicking on a rectangle opens a window that gives basic information on the issue—including its ratings and the name and phone number of the analyst who covers the issue—along with a drop-down menu offering detailed research.

"Panopticon treemaps have greatly enhanced our users' ability to visualize the credit markets and utilize analytics—it was an important contributing factor to us winning the Euromoney award," says Lee McGinty, head of European Portfolio & Index Strategy at JPMorgan.

Source: Adapted from *Case Study: JPMorgan CreditMap*, www.panopticon.com, March 2008.

Using Decision Support Systems

A decision support system involves an interactive analytical modeling process. For example, using a DSS software package for decision support may result in a series of displays in response to alternative what-if changes entered by a manager. This differs from the demand responses of management information systems because decision makers are not demanding prespecified information; rather, they are exploring possible alternatives. Thus, they do not have to specify their information needs in advance. Instead, they use the DSS to find the information they need to help them make a decision. This is the essence of the decision support system concept.

Four basic types of analytical modeling activities are involved in using a decision support system: (1) what-if analysis, (2) sensitivity analysis, (3) goal-seeking analysis, and (4) optimization analysis. Let's briefly look at each type of analytical modeling that can be used for decision support. See Figure 9.16.

What-If Analysis

In what-if analysis, a user makes changes to variables, or relationships among variables, and observes the resulting changes in the values of other variables. For example, if you were using a spreadsheet, you might change a revenue amount (a variable) or a tax rate

FIGURE 9.16

Activities and examples of the major types of analytical modeling.

Type of Analytical Modeling	Activities and Examples
What-if analysis	Observing how changes to selected variables affect other variables. *Example:* What if we cut advertising by 10 percent? What would happen to sales?
Sensitivity analysis	Observing how repeated changes to a single variable affect other variables. *Example:* Let's cut advertising by $100 repeatedly so we can see its relationship to sales.
Goal-seeking analysis	Making repeated changes to selected variables until a chosen variable reaches a target value. *Example:* Let's try increases in advertising until sales reach $1 million.
Optimization analysis	Finding an optimum value for selected variables, given certain constraints. *Example:* What's the best amount of advertising to have, given our budget and choice of media?

FIGURE 9.17

This what-if analysis involves the evaluation of probability distributions of net income and net present value (NPV) generated by changes to values for sales, competitors, product development, and capital expenses.

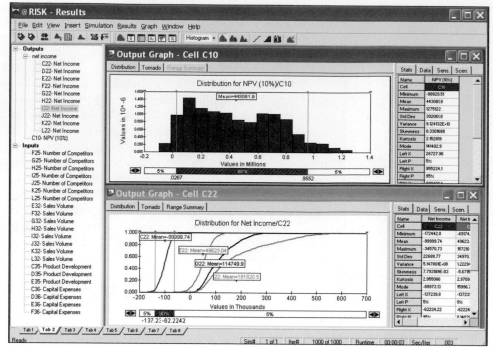

Source: Courtesy of Palisade Software.

formula (a relationship among variables) in a simple financial spreadsheet model. Then you could command the spreadsheet program to recalculate all affected variables in the spreadsheet instantly. A managerial user would be able to observe and evaluate any changes that occurred to the values in the spreadsheet, especially to a variable such as net profit after taxes. To many managers, net profit after taxes is an example of the *bottom line*, that is, a key factor in making many types of decisions. This type of analysis would be repeated until the manager was satisfied with what the results revealed about the effects of various possible decisions. Figure 9.17 is an example of what-if analysis.

Sensitivity Analysis

Sensitivity analysis is a special case of what-if analysis. Typically, the value of only one variable is changed repeatedly, and the resulting changes on other variables are observed. As such, sensitivity analysis is really a case of what-if analysis that involves repeated changes to only one variable at a time. Some DSS packages automatically make repeated small changes to a variable when asked to perform sensitivity analysis. Typically, decision makers use sensitivity analysis when they are uncertain about the assumptions made in estimating the value of certain key variables. In our previous spreadsheet example, the value of revenue could be changed repeatedly in small increments, and the effects on other spreadsheet variables observed and evaluated. This process would help a manager understand the impact of various revenue levels on other factors involved in decisions being considered.

Goal-Seeking Analysis

Goal-seeking analysis reverses the direction of the analysis done in what-if and sensitivity analyses. Instead of observing how changes in a variable affect other variables, goal-seeking analysis (also called *how-can* analysis) sets a target value (goal) for a variable and then repeatedly changes other variables until the target value is achieved. For example, you could specify a target value (goal) of $2 million in net profit after taxes for a business venture. Then you could repeatedly change the value of revenue or expenses in a spreadsheet model until you achieve a result of $2 million. Thus, you would discover the amount of revenue or level of expenses the business venture needs to reach the goal of $2 million in after-tax profits. Therefore, this form of analytical modeling would help answer the question, "How can we achieve $2 million in net profit after taxes?" instead of the question, "What happens if we change revenue or expenses?" So, goal-seeking analysis is another important method of decision support.

Optimization Analysis

Optimization analysis is a more complex extension of goal-seeking analysis. Instead of setting a specific target value for a variable, the goal is to find the optimum value for one or more target variables, given certain constraints. Then one or more other variables are changed repeatedly, subject to the specified constraints, until you discover the best values for the target variables. For example, you could try to determine the highest possible level of profits that could be achieved by varying the values for selected revenue sources and expense categories. Changes to such variables could be subject to constraints, such as the limited capacity of a production process or limits to available financing. Optimization typically is accomplished using software like the Solver tool in Microsoft Excel and other software packages for optimization techniques, such as linear programming.

Casual Male Retail Group: On-Demand Business Intelligence

Ask Dennis Hernreich, COO and CFO of Casual Male Retail Group, what his life was like before he switched to an on-demand business intelligence reporting application, and he remembers the frustration all too easily.

Casual Male Retail Group, a specialty retailer of big and tall men's apparel with $464 million in annual sales, was using a legacy on-premise reporting application for its catalog operations. (The company also has 520 retail outlets and e-commerce operations.) Yet the reporting features built into the system were "extremely poor," as Hernreich describes them: "Visibility to the business? Terrible. Real-time information? Doesn't exist. How are we doing with certain styles by size? Don't know."

"It was unacceptable," Hernreich says. In addition, you could only view those "canned" reports (which lacked features such as exception reporting) by making a trip to the printer for a stack of printouts. "It was hundreds of pages," he recalls. "That's just not how you operate today."

It's not as though Casual Male didn't have all this information; it just didn't have an intuitive and easy way to see the sales and inventory trends for its catalog business in real time. That changed in 2004, when Casual Male began to use a on-demand BI tool from vendor Oco (www.oco-inc.com), which takes all of Casual Male's data, builds and maintains a data warehouse for it off-site, and creates "responsive, real-time reporting dashboards that give us and our business users information at their fingertips," Hernreich says.

Today, Hernreich and Casual Male's merchandise planners and buyers have access to easy-to-consume dashboards full of catalog data: "What styles are selling today? How much inventory are we selling today? Where are we short? Where do we need to order? How are we selling by size? What are we out of stock in?" he says. "All of these basic questions, in terms of running the business—that's what we're learning every day from these reports."

Best of all, those annoying trips to the printer have ended.

Source: Adapted from Thomas Wailgum, "Business Intelligence and On-Demand: The Perfect Marriage?" *CIO Magazine*, March 27, 2008.

Data Mining for Decision Support

We discussed data mining and data warehouses in Chapter 5 as vital tools for organizing and exploiting the data resources of a company. Thus, data mining's main purpose is to provide decision support to managers and business professionals through a process referred to as *knowledge discovery*. Data mining software analyzes the vast stores of historical business data that have been prepared for analysis in corporate data warehouses and tries to discover patterns, trends, and correlations hidden in the data that can help a company improve its business performance.

Data mining software may perform regression, decision tree, neural network, cluster detection, or market basket analysis for a business. See Figure 9.18. The data mining process can highlight buying patterns, reveal customer tendencies, cut redundant

FIGURE 9.18

Data mining software helps discover patterns in business data, like this analysis of customer demographic information.

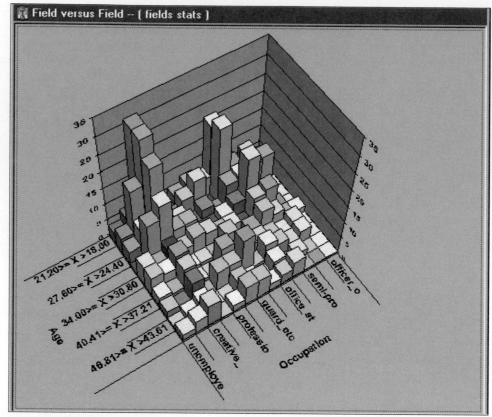

Source: Courtesy of XpertRule Software.

costs, or uncover unseen profitable relationships and opportunities. For example, many companies use data mining to find more profitable ways to perform successful direct mailings, including e-mailings, or discover better ways to display products in a store, design a better e-commerce Web site, reach untapped profitable customers, or recognize customers or products that are unprofitable or marginal.

Market basket analysis (MBA) is one of the most common and useful types of data mining for marketing. The purpose of market basket analysis is to determine what products customers purchase together with other products. MBA takes its name from the concept of customers throwing all their purchases into a shopping cart (a market basket) during grocery shopping. It can be very helpful to a retailer or any other company to know what products people purchase as a group. A store could use this information to place products frequently sold together into the same area, and a catalog or World Wide Web merchant could use it to determine the layouts of a catalog and order form. Direct marketers could use the basket analysis results to determine what new products to offer their prior customers.

In some cases, the fact that items are sold together is obvious; every fast-food restaurant asks their customers "Would you like fries with that?" whenever a customer orders a sandwich. Sometimes, however, the fact that certain items would be sold together is far from obvious. A well-known example is the relationship between beer and diapers. A supermarket performing a basket analysis discovered that diapers and beer sell well together on Thursdays. Although the result makes some sense—couples stock up on supplies for themselves and for their children before the weekend starts—it's far from intuitive. The strength of market basket analysis is as follows: By using computer data mining tools, it's not necessary for a person to think of what products consumers would logically buy together; instead, the customers' sales data speak for themselves. This is a good example of data-driven marketing.

Consider some of the typical applications of MBA:

- **Cross Selling.** Offer the associated items when customer buy any items from your store

- **Product Placement.** Items that are associated (such as bread and butter, tissues and cold medicine, potato chips and beer) can be put near to each other. If the customers see them, it has higher probability that they will purchase them together.

- **Affinity Promotion.** Design the promotional events based on associated products.

- **Survey Analysis.** The fact that both independent and dependent variables of market basket analysis are nominal (categorical) data type makes MBA very useful to analyze questionnaire data.

- **Fraud Detection.** Based on credit card usage data, we may be able to detect certain purchase behaviors that can be associated with fraud.

- **Customer Behavior.** Associating purchase with demographic, and socioeconomic data (such as age, gender, and preference) may produce very useful results for marketing.

Once it is known that customers who buy one product are likely to buy another, it is possible for a company to market the products together or make the purchasers of one product target prospects for another. If customers who purchase diapers are already likely to purchase beer, they'll be even more likely to buy beer if there happens to be a beer display just outside the diaper aisle. Likewise, if it's known that customers who buy a sweater from a certain mail-order catalog have a propensity toward buying a jacket from the same catalog, sales of jackets can be increased by having the telephone representatives describe and offer the jacket to anyone who calls in to order the sweater. By targeting customers who are already known to be likely buyers, the effectiveness of a given marketing effort is significantly increased—regardless of whether the marketing takes the form of in-store displays, catalog layout design, or direct offers to customers.

| Boston Celtics: Using Data Analytics to Price Tickets | Boston Celtics executives are taking advantage of a data analytics tool in their annual January task of setting prices for the 18,600 seats in TD Banknorth Garden. The NBA team installed the StratBridge.net tool from StratBridge Inc. to monitor consumer demand through real-time displays of sold and available seats in its home arena. Now team officials are also using the tool during the month-long project to set base ticket prices for the next season.

The new tool has helped the organization quickly develop promotions and sales strategies to fill available seats and to analyze revenue based on long-term sales trends, says Daryl Morey, senior vice president of operations and information for the Celtics. "Until we had this tool, it was very difficult to create dynamic packages because our ticket providers didn't have a rapid way to see which seats were open," Morey says. "Now we can actually see in real time every single seat and how much it is sold for."

The basketball team has already seen a "seven figure" return on investment fueled by five-figure revenue boosts every one to two weeks since it began to use StratBridge.net in 2006, according to Morey. Before using data analytics, sales executives used Excel spreadsheets to adjust pricing. In that system, pricing could be adjusted only for all the seats within each of 12 large sections in the arena. "It was a leap of faith looking at the data at that level," says Morey. |

Using the analytics tool, for example, planners found that ticket buyers tended to favor aisle seating in certain sections; as a result, the team now focuses on marketing the inner seats. Now, in the ticket office, group- and individual-ticket sellers can see an image of the arena seating chart on a plasma TV screen with different color blocks indicating real-time availability and revenue for home games. Sales executives can access this information from their desktops to study buying trends and design new promotions.

StratBridge.net extracts data from internal and external sources and displays it visually in Internet browsers and Microsoft Office applications. The analysis can be presented to users in Word, Excel, PowerPoint, and Adobe PDF files. Bill Hostmann, an analyst at Gartner Inc., said companies trying to market "perishable" products like basketball games, hotel rooms, or live television broadcasts are beginning to turn to this type of data analysis, which was first perfected in the airline industry. "You're seeing more and more of this kind of analytical functionality being embedded in the application itself as a part of the process, as opposed to being done on a quarterly or weekly basis," Hostmann said. "The ROI is very fast on these types of applications."

Source: Adapted from Heather Havenstein, "Celtics Turn to Data Analytics Tool for Help Pricing Tickets," *Computerworld*, January 6, 2006.

Executive Information Systems

Executive information systems (EIS) are information systems that combine many of the features of management information systems and decision support systems. When they were first developed, their focus was on meeting the strategic information needs of top management. Thus, the first goal of executive information systems was to provide top executives with immediate and easy access to information about a firm's *critical success factors* (CSFs), that is, key factors that are critical to accomplishing an organization's strategic objectives. For example, the executives of a retail store chain would probably consider factors such as its e-commerce versus traditional sales results or its product line mix to be critical to its survival and success.

Yet managers, analysts, and other knowledge workers use executive information systems so widely that they are sometimes humorously called "everyone's information systems." More popular alternative names are enterprise information systems (EIS) and executive support systems (ESS). These names also reflect the fact that more features, such as Web browsing, e-mail, groupware tools, and DSS and expert system capabilities, are being added to many systems to make them more useful to managers and business professionals.

Features of an EIS

In an EIS, information is presented in forms tailored to the preferences of the executives using the system. For example, most executive information systems emphasize the use of a graphical user interface, as well as graphics displays that can be customized to the information preferences of executives using the EIS. Other information presentation methods used by an EIS include exception reporting and trend analysis. The ability to *drill down*, which allows executives to retrieve displays of related information quickly at lower levels of detail, is another important capability.

Figure 9.19 shows one of the displays provided by the Web-enabled Hyperion executive information system. Notice that this display is simple and brief, and note how it provides users of the system with the ability to drill down quickly to lower levels of detail in areas of particular interest to them. In addition to the drill-down capability, the Hyperion EIS emphasizes trend analysis and exception reporting. Thus, a business user can quickly discover the direction in which key factors are heading and the extent to which critical factors are deviating from expected results.

FIGURE 9.19

This Web-based executive information system provides managers and business professionals with a variety of personalized information and analytical tools for decision support.

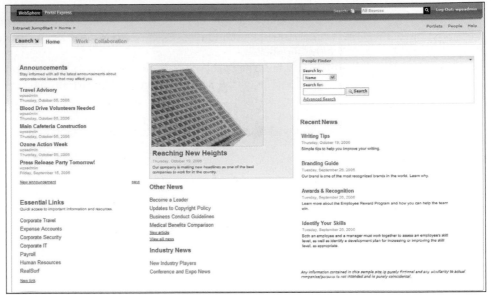

Source: Courtesy of IBM.

Executive information systems have spread into the ranks of middle management and business professionals as their feasibility and benefits have been recognized and as less expensive systems for client/server networks and corporate intranets became available. For example, one popular EIS software package reports that only 3 percent of its users are top executives.

Southwest Airlines and Motorola Inc.: The Value of EIS for Everyone	The executive information systems (EIS) of the 1980s stayed in the executive suite and provided fancy pie charts of financial data. Now these business intelligence tools have found a new home in the cubicles. Dashboards aren't just for financial data anymore. "We are now seeing them all over the enterprise, and for a variety of reasons," says John Hagerty, an analyst at AMR Research Inc. in Boston. More than half of the 135 companies he recently surveyed are implementing dashboards, which are also spreading into various nonfinancial departments.

"At Southwest Airlines, they call them 'cockpits,' and they're specialized so that the guy in charge of putting peanuts on airplanes gets a different view than the guy who's in charge of purchasing jet fuel," says John Kopcke, chief technology officer at software vendor Hyperion Solutions Corp.

The payoff is that delivering dashboard data to frontline workers puts business intelligence in the hands of people who can exploit it to make money-saving decisions on a daily basis. Motorola Inc., for example, deployed business intelligence software from Informatica Corp. in Redwood City, California, to about 200 desktops in various purchasing offices. Falgun Patel, senior manager for sourcing systems at Schaumburg, Illinois–based Motorola, says his dashboard gives him unprecedented access to purchasing information.

"We got the system up and running in mid-2002," says Patel. "Prior to that, we had to pull information from a variety of spreadsheets and custom databases from locations all over the globe." In fact, this is still the case, but now Informatica's software does the pulling, and sourcing officers like Patel can get instant access to sophisticated metrics.

"It used to take 20 days for one of our indirect purchasing officers to collect global stats," says Chet Phillips, IT director for business intelligence at Motorola. "Now it takes minutes." Patel says the result is smarter, faster decisions. "On my dashboard, I can immediately see our global spend with a particular supplier," he explains. "I can slice the data in a number of ways—various charts, historical records, purchases by departments, etc. This gives me exactly what I need to negotiate a better deal with the supplier."

He says the dashboard also allows him to be more proactive. "By combining the purchasing analytics on my desktop with current market conditions, I can determine whether it is better to negotiate for a commodity or go ahead and lock in a supply," Patel says. The result is a fabulous return on investment. "We estimate that this system saved us about $15 million a month in 2002," says Phillips.

Source: Adapted from Mark Leon, "Business-Intelligence Dashboards Get Democratic," *Computerworld*, June 16, 2003.

Enterprise Portals and Decision Support

Don't confuse portals with the executive information systems that have been used in some industries for many years. Portals are for everyone in the company, and not just for executives. You want people on the front lines making decisions using browsers and portals rather than just executives using specialized executive information system software.

We mentioned previously in this chapter that major changes and expansions are taking place in traditional MIS, DSS, and EIS tools for providing the information and modeling managers need to support their decision making. Decision support in business is changing, driven by rapid developments in end-user computing and networking; Internet and Web technologies; and Web-enabled business applications. One of the key changes taking place in management information and decision support systems in business is the rapid growth of enterprise information portals.

Enterprise Information Portals

A user checks his e-mail, looks up the current company stock price, checks his available vacation days, and receives an order from a customer—all from the browser on his desktop. That is the next-generation intranet, also known as a corporate or enterprise information portal. With it, the browser becomes the dashboard to daily business tasks.

An **enterprise information portal (EIP)** is a Web-based interface and integration of MIS, DSS, EIS, and other technologies that give all intranet users and selected extranet users access to a variety of internal and external business applications and services. For example, internal applications might include access to e-mail, project Web sites, and discussion groups; human resources Web self-services; customer, inventory, and other corporate databases; decision support systems; and knowledge management systems. External applications might include industry, financial, and other Internet news services; links to industry discussion groups; and links to customer and supplier Internet and extranet Web sites. Enterprise information portals are typically tailored or personalized to the needs of individual business users or groups of users, giving them a personalized *digital dashboard* of information sources and applications. See Figure 9.20.

The business benefits of enterprise information portals include providing more specific and selective information to business users, providing easy access to key corporate intranet Web site resources, delivering industry and business news, and providing better access to company data for selected customers, suppliers, or business partners. Enterprise information portals can also help avoid excessive surfing by employees across company and Internet Web sites by making it easier for them to receive or find the information and services they need, thus improving the productivity of a company's workforce.

Figure 9.21 illustrates how companies are developing enterprise information portals as a way to provide Web-enabled information, knowledge, and decision support to their executives, managers, employees, suppliers, customers, and other

FIGURE 9.20

An enterprise information portal can provide a business professional with a personalized workplace of information sources, administrative and analytical tools, and relevant business applications.

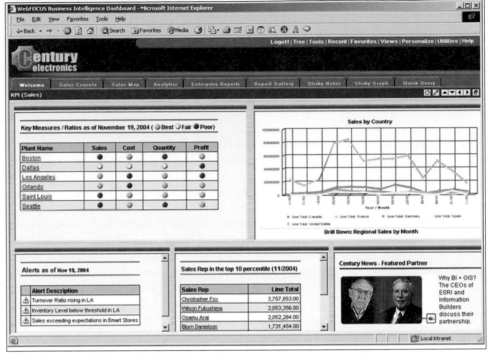

Source: Courtesy of Information Builders.

FIGURE 9.21

The components of this enterprise information portal identify it as a Web-enabled decision support system that can be personalized for executives, managers, employees, suppliers, customers, and other business partners.

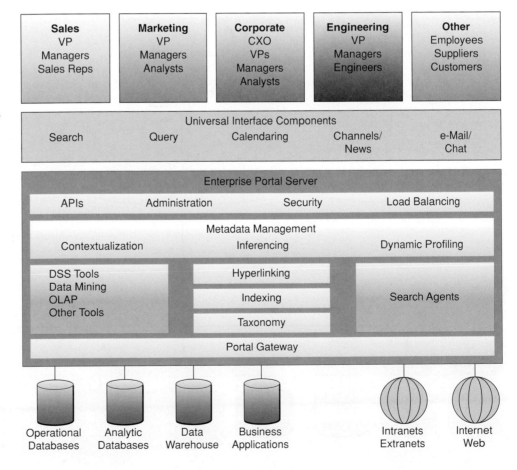

business partners. The enterprise information portal is a customized and personalized Web-based interface for corporate intranets, which gives users easy access to a variety of internal and external business applications, databases, and services. For example, the EIP in Figure 9.20 might give a qualified user secure access to DSS, data mining, and OLAP tools; the Internet and the Web; the corporate intranet; supplier or customer extranets; operational and analytical databases; a data warehouse; and a variety of business applications.

Knowledge Management Systems

We introduced knowledge management systems in Chapter 2 as the use of information technology to help gather, organize, and share business knowledge within an organization. In many organizations, hypermedia databases at corporate intranet Web sites have become the *knowledge bases* for storage and dissemination of business knowledge. This knowledge frequently takes the form of best practices, policies, and business solutions at the project, team, business unit, and enterprise levels of the company.

For many companies, enterprise information portals are the entry to corporate intranets that serve as their knowledge management systems. That's why such portals are called enterprise knowledge portals by their vendors. Thus, enterprise knowledge portals play an essential role in helping companies use their intranets as knowledge management systems to share and disseminate knowledge in support of business decision making by managers and business professionals. See Figure 9.22. Now let's look at an example of a knowledge management system in business.

FIGURE 9.22   This example of the capabilities and components of an enterprise knowledge portal emphasizes its use as a Web-based knowledge management system.

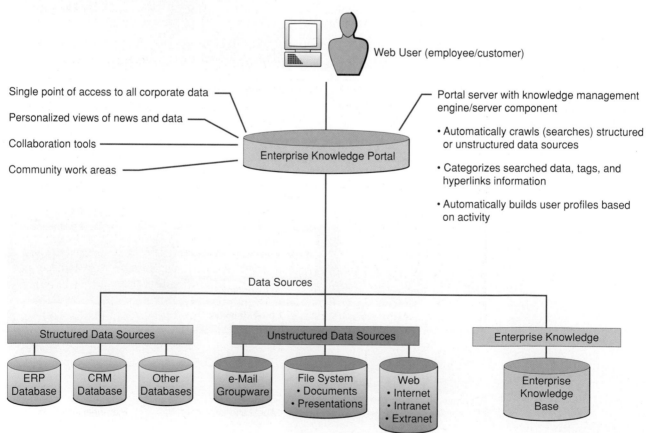

Northrop Grumman: Passing Knowledge Down through Generations

In 1997, with the Cold War well behind them, thousand of engineers who had helped design and maintain the B-2 bomber were asked to leave the integrated systems sector of Northrop Grumman. As the nearly 12,000 workers filed out the door, leaving only 1,200 from a staff of 13,000, they took with them years of experience and in-depth knowledge about what was considered at the time to be the most complex aircraft ever built.

Northrop Grumman knew it had to keep enough of that know-how to support the division's long-term maintenance of the B-2 bomber, so a newly formed knowledge management team identified top experts and videotaped interviews with them before they left. But it was hard to get everything in a single interview, says Scott Shaffar, Northrop Grumman's director of knowledge management for the Western region of the integrated systems sector. "We did lose some of that knowledge," says Shaffar. "In an exit interview, you can capture certain things, but not a lifetime of experience."

Several years later, the company uses a variety of tools to retain and transfer knowledge from its engineers—well before they retire. Shaffar and his team have put in place document management systems and common work spaces that record how an engineer did his job for future reference. They have started programs that bring together older and younger engineers across the country to exchange information via e-mail or in person about technical problems, and they are using software that helps people find experts within the company.

While most companies won't face the sudden departure of thousands of skilled workers, as Northrop Grumman did in the late 1990s, they and government agencies alike will need to prepare for the loss of important experience and technical knowledge as the baby boomer generation gets ready to retire over the coming decade. By 2010, more than half of all workers in the United States will be over 40. While most top managers are aware that they'll soon have a lot of workers retiring, few are doing much to prepare for the event. That's often because it's hard to quantify the cost of losing knowledge.

At Northrop Grumman, times have changed since its massive downsizing in the 1990s. Although a large percentage of its workforce is nearing retirement, the average age of employees has dropped from the high 40s to the mid 40s in the past four years since the company started hiring more college grads. Shaffar says he is now working on balancing the more gradual transfer of knowledge from older to younger workers, with the need to capture some crucial expertise quickly before it's too late. For example, Northrop Grumman engineers who are competing on a proposal for a "crew exploration vehicle," which is being designed to replace the space shuttle and travel to the moon (and eventually to Mars), met with a group of retirees who worked on the Apollo program that sent men to the moon more than 35 years ago.

Using a PC program called Quindi and a camera attached to a laptop, a facilitator recorded retirees telling stories about how they grappled with the technical problems of sending a man to the moon. These tales will be available as Web pages for engineers working on this project. Shaffar acknowledges that employees would rather go to another person than a system for advice, but he says the exercise helped capture knowledge that otherwise soon would be gone.

Most important, Shaffar has learned that the problem goes beyond looking at what skills you have right now. "There have always been new generations, and we're not any different in that way," he says. "Mentoring, training and passing on knowledge is not something you can do at the last minute. You have to plan ahead."

Source: Adapted from Susannah Patton, "How to Beat the Baby Boomer Retirement Blues," *CIO Magazine*, January 15, 2006.

SECTION II | Artificial Intelligence Technologies in Business

Business and AI

Artificial intelligence (AI) technologies are being used in a variety of ways to improve the decision support provided to managers and business professionals in many companies. See Figure 9.23. For example:

> *AI-enabled applications are at work in information distribution and retrieval, database mining, product design, manufacturing, inspection, training, user support, surgical planning, resource scheduling, and complex resource management.*
>
> *Indeed, for anyone who schedules, plans, allocates resources, designs new products, uses the Internet, develops software, is responsible for product quality, is an investment professional, heads up IT, uses IT, or operates in any of a score of other capacities and arenas, AI technologies already may be in place and providing competitive advantage.*

Read the Real World Case on the next page. We can learn a lot about artificial intelligence applications in business from this example.

An Overview of Artificial Intelligence

What is artificial intelligence? Artificial intelligence (AI) is a field of science and technology based on disciplines such as computer science, biology, psychology, linguistics, mathematics, and engineering. The goal of AI is to develop computers that can simulate the ability to think, as well as see, hear, walk, talk, and feel. A major thrust of artificial intelligence is the simulation of computer functions normally associated with human intelligence, such as reasoning, learning, and problem solving, as summarized in Figure 9.24.

Debate has raged about artificial intelligence since serious work in the field began in the 1950s. Technological, moral, and philosophical questions about the possibility of intelligent, thinking machines are numerous. For example, British AI pioneer Alan Turing in 1950 proposed a test to determine whether machines could think. According to the Turing test, a computer could demonstrate intelligence if a human interviewer, conversing with an unseen human and an unseen computer, could not tell which was which. Although much work has been done in many of the subgroups that fall under the AI umbrella, critics believe that no computer can truly pass the Turing test. They claim that it is just not possible to develop intelligence to impart true humanlike capabilities to computers, but progress continues. Only time will tell whether we will achieve the ambitious goals of artificial intelligence and equal the popular images found in science fiction.

One derivative of the Turing test that is providing real value to the online community is a CAPTCHA. A **CAPTCHA** (Completely Automated Public Turing test to tell Computers and Humans Apart) is a type of challenge-response test used in a wide variety of computing applications to determine that the user is really a human and not a computer posing as one. A CAPTCHA is sometimes described as a reverse Turing test because it is administered by a machine and targeted to a human, in contrast to the standard Turing test that is typically administered by a human and targeted to a machine. The process involves one computer (such as a server for a retail Web site) asking a user to complete a simple test that the computer is able to generate and grade. Because other computers are unable to solve the CAPTCHA, any user entering a correct solution is presumed to be human. A common type of CAPTCHA requires that the user type the letters of a distorted image, sometimes with the addition of an obscured sequence of letters or digits that appears on the screen. No doubt you have seen this when registering for a new account with a merchant or checking out from an online purchase. Figure 9.25 shows several common examples of CAPTCHA patterns.

REAL WORLD CASE 2

Goodyear, JEA, OSUMC, and Monsanto: Cool Technologies Driving Competitive Advantage

If necessity is the mother of invention, then capitalism is surely the mother of innovation. Companies are being driven to develop unique applications of undeniably cool technologies by the drive to create a sustainable competitive advantage. "At the end of the day, as cool as this thing we've developed is, it's a tool," says Stephanie Wernet, Goodyear's CIO. "It is meant to serve a business end. In our case, this tool lets us put out new, more innovative products faster than the competition."

Working with Sandia National Labs, Goodyear's IT department developed software to design and test tires virtually. In the past, the company built physical prototypes and tested them by driving thousands of miles on tracks. Using a mathematical model, the software simulates tire behavior in different driving conditions so that the designer can see how the tire gets pushed, pulled, and stretched as it rolls down a road, hits bumps, turns corners, screeches to a halt, and grips the road in wet, dry, and icy conditions. Goodyear wanted to shorten that time to get its products to market more quickly. Three research and development employees advanced the idea of testing prototypes using computer simulations, which could do the job faster.

The company had never done simulations but figured initial investments and subsequent maintenance costs were worth the payoff. Goodyear's cost of goods sold as well as its sales decreased by 2.6 percent from 2003 to 2004, the year its first fully simulated tires hit the market. Meanwhile, the research and development (R&D) budget for tire testing and design decreased by 25 percent.

Custom-built software runs on hundreds of processors on hundreds of Linux computers in a massively parallel computing environment. Goodyear invested more than $6 million to build this high-powered computing environment. It plans to expand and upgrade its Linux clusters to meet business demands for new tires and to improve the fidelity of its virtual tests. The company believes it is the first tire maker to use computers to design and test its wheels. Although the auto industry has done computer-assisted design work since the 1980s, the technology had not been applied to tires because their malleable materials made simulation difficult.

Designers can perform 10 times more tests, reducing a new tire's time to market from two years to as little as nine months. Goodyear attributes its sales growth from $15 billion in 2003 to $20 billion in 2005 to new products introduced as a result of this change.

Public utility JEA uses neural network technology to create an artificial intelligence system it has recently implemented. The system automatically determines the optimal combinations of oil and natural gas the utility's boilers need to produce electricity cost-effectively, given fuel prices and the amount of electricity required. It also ensures that the amount of nitrous oxide (N_2O) emitted during the generation process does not exceed government regulations.

JEA needed to decrease operating expenses, in particular fuel costs, as oil and gas prices began their precipitous ascent in 2002. Forty percent of JEA's $1.3 billion budget goes to the purchase of oil and gas to power its boilers, so a small change in the way electricity is produced could add millions of dollars to the bottom line. Neural network technology models the process of producing electricity. Optimization software from NeuCo determines the right combinations of oil and gas to produce electricity at low cost while minimizing emissions.

JEA, which serves more than 360,000 customers in Jacksonville and three neighboring Florida counties, is the first utility in the world to apply neural network technology to the production of electricity in circulating fluidized-bed boilers. It built a system that makes decisions based on historical operating data and as many as 100 inputs associated with the combustion process, including air flows and megawatt outputs. The system learns which fuel combinations are optimal by making adjustments to the boiler in real time; it also forecasts what to do in the future based on specific fuel cost assumptions. "We had issues with oil prices. At the same time, gas prices went from $4 a BTU to over $14. We need to use gas because it decreases emissions. This solution helped us balance all of those items," says Wanyonyi Kendrick, JEA's CIO.

The project, which IT drove, cost $800,000 and paid for itself in eight weeks. The system reduced the quantity of natural gas that is used to control N_2O emissions by 15 percent, an estimated annual savings of $4.8 million. With natural gas prices at $11 per BTU, JEA expects to save $13 million on fuel in 2006. What's more, JEA has discovered it can use the new technology applications for its water business.

The Ohio State University Medical Center (OSUMC) replaced its overhead rail transport system with 46 self-guided

FIGURE 9.23

Advanced technologies such as artificial intelligence, mathematical simulations, and robotics can have dramatic impacts on both business processes and financial results.

Source: © Charles Smith/Corbis.

robotic vehicles to move linens, meals, trash, and medical supplies throughout the 1,000-bed hospital. The robots do not interact with patients; they carry out routine tasks that hospital staff used to do. Faced with declining revenue and rising costs, OSUMC needed to save money while improving patient care. A steering committee comprising IT, other hospital departments, consultants, and vendors drove this project. They convinced medical staff of its value by demonstrating the technology and communicating how it improved working conditions and patient care. Materials transport was identified as a place to cut costs since the hospital needed to upgrade the existing system.

The robots, made by FMC Technologies, are guided by a wireless infrared network from Cisco Systems. The network is embedded in corridor walls and elevators designed for the robots' use. Three Windows servers linked to the network maintain a database of robot jobs and traffic patterns. OSUMC is the first hospital in the United States to implement an infrared-guided automated system for transporting materials. Hospital staff use a touch-screen computer connected to a server to call a robot when, for example, a linen cart needs to go to the laundry room. To get from point A to point B, the robots rely on a digital map of the medical center programmed into their memory; they also track their movements against the number of times their wheels rotate in a full circle. So if it takes a robot 1,000 wheel revolutions to get from a building's kitchen to the sixth floor, and its wheels have moved in 500 revolutions, the robot knows it is halfway there. If a robot loses network contact, it shuts down.

The $18 million system is expected to save the hospital approximately $1 million a year over the next 25 years. Since it went live in 2004, OSUMC has saved $27,375 annually on linen delivery alone. OSUMC's CIO Detlev Smaltz says the system improves patient care by freeing up personnel: "If we can take mundane jobs like taking out the trash off of our employees and give them more time to do the things they came into the health-care profession to do, then that's an added benefit of the system."

Monsanto's IT department created software to identify genes that indicate a plant's resistance to drought, herbicides, and pests; those genetic traits are used to predict which plants breeders should reproduce to yield the healthiest, most bountiful crops. The software crunches data from breeders worldwide and presents them in a colorful, easy-to-comprehend fashion. By pinpointing the best breeding stock, it increases breeders' odds of finding a commercially viable combination of genetic traits from one in a trillion to one in five. Monsanto's global breeding organization drove the project.

When the patent expired for Roundup, Monsanto's signature weed killer, the St. Louis company invested in growing its business involving seeds and genetic traits, which comprises more than half of its $6.3 billion revenue and $255 million profits in 2005. Monsanto believes it can sell more corn, soybean, and cotton seeds if farmers know its seeds will produce heartier crops and require fewer sprays of insecticide and herbicide, thus reducing costs.

Monsanto's scientists use the software to engineer seeds that effectively resist drought and pests and to produce plants that are healthier for humans and animals to eat. They do it by implanting those seeds with the genetic material that makes a plant resist insects or produce more protein. What would Gregor Mendel, the father of genetics, think of this? "This is really different from the way breeders bred their crops," says Monsanto CIO Mark Showers. "They didn't have this level of molecular detail to determine and select plants they wanted to move forward from year to year."

Monsanto reaps the benefit of its software but wouldn't reveal development costs. Earnings per share (EPS) on an ongoing basis grew from $1.59 to $2.08, or 30 percent, from 2004 to 2005. Its EPS is expected to grow by 20 percent more in 2006. "In the last four or five years, we've had a marked improvement in taking market share from our competition. We've grown our share at a couple of points per year," says Showers.

Source: Adapted from Meridith Levinson, "IT Innovation: Robots, Supercomputers, AI and More," *CIO Magazine*, August 15, 2006.

CASE STUDY QUESTIONS

1. Consider the outcomes of the projects discussed in the case. In all of them, the payoffs are both larger and achieved more rapidly than in more traditional system implementations. Why do you think this is the case? How are these projects different from others you have come across in the past? What are those differences? Provide several examples.

2. How do these technologies create business value for the implementing organizations? In which ways are these implementations similar in how they accomplish this, and how are they different? Use examples from the case to support your answer.

3. In all of these examples, companies had an urgent need that prompted them to investigate these radical, new technologies. Do you think the story would have been different had the companies been performing well already? Why or why not? To what extent are these innovations dependent on the presence of a problem or crisis?

REAL WORLD ACTIVITIES

1. Choose one of the companies introduced in the case and search the Internet to update the current status of their project. Also take a look at their competitors, and discover how they have responded to the introduction of the developments mentioned in the case. Have they attempted to imitate them?

2. As these technologies go beyond the capacity and abilities of human beings, what is the role of people in the processes they affect? Do you think these technologies empower us by allowing us to overcome our limitations and expand our range of possibilities? Instead, do they relegate people to the role of uncritically accepting the outcomes of these processes? Break into small groups to discuss these issues, and note which arguments that support one or the other position arise as a result.

FIGURE 9.24

Some of the attributes of intelligent behavior. AI is attempting to duplicate these capabilities in computer-based systems.

Attributes of Intelligent Behavior
● Think and reason.
● Use reason to solve problems.
● Learn or understand from experience.
● Acquire and apply knowledge.
● Exhibit creativity and imagination.
● Deal with complex or perplexing situations.
● Respond quickly and successfully to new situations.
● Recognize the relative importance of elements in a situation.
● Handle ambiguous, incomplete, or erroneous information.

The Domains of Artificial Intelligence

Figure 9.26 illustrates the major **domains** of AI research and development. Note that AI **applications** can be grouped under three major areas—cognitive science, robotics, and natural interfaces—though these classifications do overlap, and other classifications can be used. Also note that expert systems are just one of many important AI applications. Let's briefly review each of these major areas of AI and some of their current technologies. Figure 9.27 outlines some of the latest developments in commercial applications of artificial intelligence.

Cognitive Science. This area of artificial intelligence is based on research in biology, neurology, psychology, mathematics, and many allied disciplines. It focuses on researching how the human brain works and how humans think and learn. The results of such research in *human information processing* are the basis for the development of a variety of computer-based applications in artificial intelligence.

Applications in the cognitive science area of AI include the development of *expert systems* and other *knowledge-based systems* that add a knowledge base and some reasoning capability to information systems. Also included are *adaptive learning systems* that can modify their behaviors on the basis of information they acquire as they operate. Chess-playing systems are primitive examples of such applications, though many more

FIGURE 9.25

Examples of typical CAPTCHA patterns that can be easily solved by humans but prove difficult to detect by a computer.

FIGURE 9.26

The major application areas of artificial intelligence. Note that the many applications of AI can be grouped into the three major areas of cognitive science, robotics, and natural interfaces.

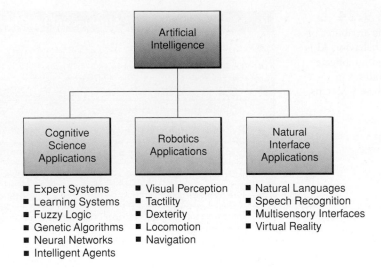

applications are being implemented. *Fuzzy logic* systems can process data that are incomplete or ambiguous, that is, *fuzzy data*. Thus, they can solve semistructured problems with incomplete knowledge by developing approximate inferences and answers, as humans do. *Neural network* software can learn by processing sample problems and

FIGURE 9.27

Examples of some of the latest commercial applications of AI.

Commercial Applications of AI
Decision Support
• Intelligent work environment that will help you capture the *why* as well as the *what* of engineered design and decision making.
• Intelligent human–computer interface (HCI) systems that can understand spoken language and gestures, and facilitate problem solving by supporting organizationwide collaborations to solve particular problems.
• Situation assessment and resource allocation software for uses that range from airlines and airports to logistics centers.
Information Retrieval
• AI-based intranet and Internet systems that distill tidal waves of information into simple presentations.
• Natural language technology to retrieve any sort of online information, from text to pictures, videos, maps, and audio clips, in response to English questions.
• Database mining for marketing trend analysis, financial forecasting, maintenance cost reduction, and more.
Virtual Reality
• X-ray–like vision enabled by enhanced-reality visualization that allows brain surgeons to "see through" intervening tissue to operate, monitor, and evaluate disease progression.
• Automated animation interfaces that allow users to interact with virtual objects via touch (e.g., medical students can "feel" what it's like to suture severed aortas).
Robotics
• Machine-vision inspections systems for gauging, guiding, identifying, and inspecting products and providing competitive advantage in manufacturing.
• Cutting-edge robotics systems, from microrobots and hands and legs to cognitive robotic and trainable modular vision systems.

their solutions. As neural nets start to recognize patterns, they can begin to program themselves to solve such problems on their own. *Genetic algorithm* software uses Darwinian (survival of the fittest), randomizing, and other mathematics functions to simulate evolutionary processes that can generate increasingly better solutions to problems. In addition, *intelligent agents* use expert system and other AI technologies to serve as software surrogates for a variety of end-user applications.

Robotics. AI, engineering, and physiology are the basic disciplines of robotics. This technology produces robot machines with computer intelligence and computer-controlled, humanlike physical capabilities. This area thus includes applications designed to give robots the powers of sight, or visual perception; touch, or tactile capabilities; dexterity, or skill in handling and manipulation; locomotion, or the physical ability to move over any terrain; and navigation, or the intelligence to find one's way to a destination.

Natural Interfaces. The development of natural interfaces is considered a major area of AI applications and is essential to the natural use of computers by humans. For example, the development of *natural languages* and speech recognition are major thrusts of this area of AI. Being able to talk to computers and robots in conversational human languages and have them "understand" us as easily as we understand each other is a goal of AI research. This goal involves research and development in linguistics, psychology, computer science, and other disciplines. Other natural interface research applications include the development of multisensory devices that use a variety of body movements to operate computers, which is related to the emerging application area of *virtual reality*. Virtual reality involves using multisensory human–computer interfaces that enable human users to experience computer-simulated objects, spaces, activities, and "worlds" as if they actually exist. Now, let's look at some examples of how AI is becoming increasingly more relevant in the business world.

Artificial Intelligence Gets Down to Business	Today, AI systems can perform useful work in "a very large and complex world," says Eric Horvitz, an AI researcher at Microsoft Research (MSR). "Because these small software agents don't have a complete representation of the world, they are uncertain about their actions. So they learn to understand the probabilities of various things happening, they learn the preferences of users and costs of outcomes and, perhaps most important, they are becoming self-aware."

These abilities derive from something called machine learning, which is at the heart of many modern AI applications. In essence, a programmer starts with a crude model of the problem he's trying to solve but builds in the ability for the software to adapt and improve with experience.

Speech recognition software gets better as it learns the nuances of your voice, for example, and over time Amazon.com more accurately predicts your preferences as you shop online. Machine learning is enabled by clever algorithms, of course, but what has driven it to prominence in recent years is the availability of huge amounts of data, both from the Internet and, more recently, from a proliferation of physical sensors.

For instance, Microsoft Research has combined sensors, machine learning, and analysis of human behavior in a road traffic prediction model. Predicting traffic bottlenecks would seem to be an obvious and not very difficult application of sensors and computer forecasting. But MSR realized that most drivers hardly need to be warned that the interstate heading out of town will be jammed at 5 p.m. on Monday. What they really need to know is where and when anomalies, or "surprises," are occurring and, perhaps more important, where they will occur. So MSR built a "surprise forecasting" model that learns from traffic history to predict surprises 30 minutes in advance based on actual traffic flows captured by sensors. In tests, it has been able to predict about 50% of the surprises on roads in the Seattle area, and it is in use now by several thousand drivers who receive alerts on their Windows Mobile devices.

Few organizations need to make sense of as much data as search engine companies do. For example, if a user searches Google for "toy car" and then clicks on a Wal-Mart ad that appears at the top of the results, what's that worth to Wal-Mart, and how much should Google charge for that click? The answers lie in an AI specialty that employs "digital trading agents," which companies like Wal-Mart and Google use in automated online auctions.

Michael Wellman, a University of Michigan professor and an expert in these markets, explains: "There are millions of keywords, and one advertiser may be interested in hundreds or thousands of them. They have to monitor the prices of the keywords and decide how to allocate their budget, and it's too hard for Google or Yahoo to figure out what a certain keyword is worth. They let the market decide that through an auction process."

When the "toy car" query is submitted, in a fraction of a second Google looks up which advertisers are interested in those keywords, then looks at their bids and decides whose ads to display and where to put them on the page. "The problem I'm especially interested in," Wellman says, "is how should an advertiser decide which keywords to bid on, how much to bid and how to learn over time—based on how effective their ads are—how much competition there is for each keyword."

Source: Adapted from Gary Anthes, "Future Watch: A.I. Comes of Age," *Computerworld*, January 26, 2009.

Expert Systems

One of the most practical and widely implemented applications of artificial intelligence in business is the development of expert systems and other knowledge-based information systems. A knowledge-based information system (KBIS) adds a knowledge base to the major components found in other types of computer-based information systems. An expert system (ES) is a knowledge-based information system that uses its knowledge about a specific, complex application area to act as an expert consultant to end users. Expert systems provide answers to questions in a very specific problem area by making humanlike inferences about knowledge contained in a specialized knowledge base. They must also be able to explain their reasoning process and conclusions to a user, so expert systems can provide decision support to end users in the form of advice from an expert consultant in a specific problem area.

Components of an Expert System

The components of an expert system include a knowledge base and software modules that perform inferences on the knowledge in the knowledge base and communicate answers to a user's questions. Figure 9.28 illustrates the interrelated components of an expert system. Note the following components:

FIGURE 9.28

A summary of four ways that knowledge can be represented in an expert system's knowledge base.

Methods of Knowledge Representation
● **Case-Based Reasoning.** Representing knowledge in an expert system's knowledge base in the form of cases, that is, examples of past performance, occurrences, and experiences.
● **Frame-Based Knowledge.** Knowledge represented in the form of a hierarchy or network of *frames*. A frame is a collection of knowledge about an entity consisting of a complex package of data values describing its attributes.
● **Object-Based Knowledge.** Knowledge represented as a network of objects. An object is a data element that includes both data and the methods or processes that act on those data.
● **Rule-Based Knowledge.** Knowledge represented in the form of rules and statements of fact. Rules are statements that typically take the form of a premise and a conclusion, such as If (condition), Then (conclusion).

FIGURE 9.29   Components of an expert system. The software modules perform inferences on a knowledge base built by an expert and/or knowledge engineer. This provides expert answers to an end user's questions in an interactive process.

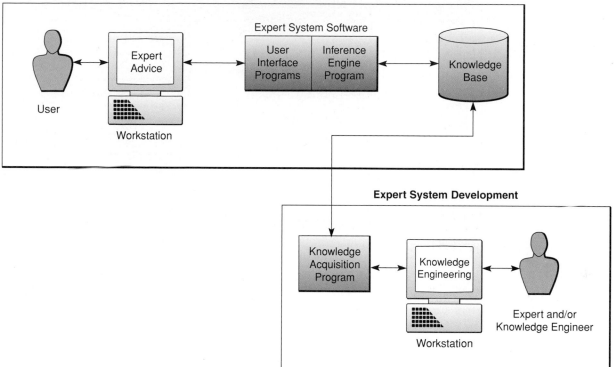

- **Knowledge Base.** The knowledge base of an expert system contains (1) facts about a specific subject area (e.g., *John is an analyst*) and (2) heuristics (rules of thumb) that express the reasoning procedures of an expert on the subject (e.g., *IF John is an analyst, THEN he needs a workstation*). There are many ways that such knowledge is represented in expert systems. Examples are *rule-based*, *frame-based*, *object-based*, and *case-based* methods of knowledge representation. See Figure 9.29.

- **Software Resources.** An expert system software package contains an inference engine and other programs for refining knowledge and communicating with users. The inference engine program processes the knowledge (such as rules and facts) related to a specific problem. It then makes associations and inferences resulting in recommended courses of action for a user. User interface programs for communicating with end users are also needed, including an explanation program to explain the reasoning process to a user if requested. Knowledge acquisition programs are not part of an expert system but are software tools for knowledge base development, as are *expert system shells*, which are used for developing expert systems.

Expert System Applications

Using an expert system involves an interactive computer-based session in which the solution to a problem is explored, with the expert system acting as a consultant to an end user. The expert system asks questions of the user, searches its knowledge base for facts and rules or other knowledge, explains its reasoning process when asked, and gives expert advice to the user in the subject area being explored. For example, Figure 9.30 illustrates an expert system application.

FIGURE 9.30

Tivoli Business Systems Manager by IBM automatically monitors and manages the computers in a network with proactive expert system software components based on IBM's extensive mainframe systems management expertise.

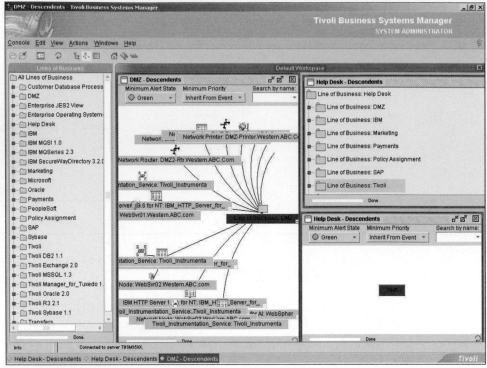

Source: Courtesy of IBM.

Expert systems are being used for many different types of applications, and the variety of applications is expected to continue to increase. You should realize, however, that expert systems typically accomplish one or more generic uses. Figure 9.31 outlines five generic categories of expert system activities, with specific examples of actual expert system applications. As you can see, expert systems are being used in many different fields, including medicine, engineering, the physical sciences, and business. Expert systems now help diagnose illnesses, search for minerals, analyze compounds, recommend repairs, and do financial planning. So from a strategic business standpoint, expert systems can be and are being used to improve every step of the product cycle of a business, from finding customers to shipping products to providing customer service.

Benefits of Expert Systems

An expert system captures the expertise of an expert or group of experts in a computer-based information system. Thus, it can outperform a single human expert in many problem situations. That's because an expert system is faster and more consistent, can have the knowledge of several experts, and does not get tired or distracted by overwork or stress. Expert systems also help preserve and reproduce the knowledge of experts. They allow a company to preserve the expertise of an expert before she leaves the organization. This expertise can then be shared by reproducing the software and knowledge base of the expert system.

Limitations of Expert Systems

The major limitations of expert systems arise from their limited focus, inability to learn, maintenance problems, and developmental cost. Expert systems excel only in solving specific types of problems in a limited domain of knowledge. They fail miserably in solving problems requiring a broad knowledge base and subjective problem solving. They do well with specific types of operational or analytical tasks but falter at subjective managerial decision making.

Expert systems may also be difficult and costly to develop and maintain. The costs of knowledge engineers, lost expert time, and hardware and software resources may be too high to offset the benefits expected from some applications. Also, expert systems can't maintain themselves; that is, they can't learn from experience but instead must be

FIGURE 9.31

Major application categories and examples of typical expert systems. Note the variety of applications that can be supported by such systems.

Application Categories of Expert Systems
● **Decision Management.** Systems that appraise situations or consider alternatives and make recommendations based on criteria supplied during the discovery process: Loan portfolio analysis Employee performance evaluation Insurance underwriting Demographic forecasts
● **Diagnostic/Troubleshooting.** Systems that infer underlying causes from reported symptoms and history: Equipment calibration Help desk operations Software debugging Medical diagnosis
● **Design/Configuration.** Systems that help configure equipment components, given existing constraints: Computer option installation Manufacturability studies Communications networks Optimum assembly plan
● **Selection/Classification.** Systems that help users choose products or processes, often from among large or complex sets of alternatives: Material selection Delinquent account identification Information classification Suspect identification
● **Process Monitoring/Control.** Systems that monitor and control procedures or processes: Machine control (including robotics) Inventory control Production monitoring Chemical testing

taught new knowledge and modified as new expertise is needed to match developments in their subject areas.

Although there are practical applications for expert systems, applications have been limited and specific because, as discussed, expert systems are narrow in their domain of knowledge. An amusing example of this is the user who used an expert system designed to diagnose skin diseases to conclude that his rusty old car had likely developed measles. In addition, once some of the novelty had worn off, most programmers and developers realized that common expert systems were just more elaborate versions of the same decision logic used in most computer programs. Today, many of the techniques used to develop expert systems can now be found in most complex programs without any fuss about them.

Healthways: Applying Expert Systems to Healthcare

Healthways, the US leader in health and care support for well and chronically ill populations, relies on SAS to identify high-risk patients and implement preventative actions. The company knows that a key to successful disease management is the correct identification of those members in greatest need of care. Using SAS, Healthways reduces costs and helps to improve member health outcomes by predicting who is at most risk for developing specific health problems. In doing so, it is able to coordinate intervention plans that address care designed to avoid complications down the road.

Healthways provides disease and care management to more than two million health-plan members in all 50 states, the District of Columbia, Guam, and Puerto Rico. The company provides its services on behalf of the nation's leading health plans. It employs thousands of nurses at call centers throughout the country who collect data and provide clinical support to health-plan members and their physicians.

At Healthways, the goal is to empower health-plan members to manage their health effectively. The company achieves its objective using SAS for data mining and a group of robust artificial intelligence neural networks. To support predictive analytics, Healthways accesses hundreds of data points involving care for millions of health-plan members.

"We want to develop predictive models that not only identify and classify patients who are at risk, but also anticipate who is at the highest risk for specific diseases and complications and then determine which of those are most likely to comply with recommended standards of care," says Adam Hobgood, Director of Statistics at Healthways' Center for Health Research. "Most of all we want to predict their likelihood of success with our support programs. By identifying high-risk patients and implementing preventative actions against future conditions, we hope to head off the increased costs of care before they occur."

With SAS, Healthways builds predictive models that assess patient risk for certain outcomes and establishes starting points for providing services. Once Healthways loads patient risk-stratification levels into its own "clinical expert system," the system evaluates clinical information from hospitals, data that nurses collect by phone and information that employer groups and health-plan members report.

Finally, the clinical expert system adjusts the initial risk-stratification levels based on the new inputs and expert clinical judgment. The resulting approach to member stratification is a hybrid solution that incorporates sophisticated artificial intelligence neural network predictive models, clinically relevant rule-based models and expert clinician judgment.

"It's a very powerful hybrid solution, and we have worked closely with clinical experts in the company to integrate the neural network predictive model with our world-class clinical expert system," says Matthew McGinnis, Senior Director of Healthways' Center for Health Research. "The ability of our highly experienced clinicians to use their expert clinical judgment further complements the model and rounds out our hybrid approach to stratification. We believe that sophisticated statistical models are necessary to help risk-stratify our significant member populations, and by coupling this with the expertly trained clinical mind, we have created a hybrid solution that is unrivaled in the industry."

Source: Adapted from "Healthways Heads Off Increased Costs with SAS®," www.sas.com, accessed April 25, 2009.

Developing Expert Systems

What types of problems are most suitable to expert system solutions? One way to answer this question is to look at examples of the applications of current expert systems, including the generic tasks they can accomplish, as were summarized in Figure 9.31. Another way is to identify criteria that make a problem situation suitable for an expert system. Figure 9.32 outlines some important criteria.

Figure 9.32 emphasizes that many real-world situations do not fit the suitability criteria for expert system solutions. Hundreds of rules may be required to capture the assumptions, facts, and reasoning that are involved in even simple problem situations. For example, a task that might take an expert a few minutes to accomplish might require an expert system with hundreds of rules and take several months to develop.

The easiest way to develop an expert system is to use an expert system shell as a developmental tool. An expert system shell is a software package consisting of an expert system without its kernel, that is, its knowledge base. This leaves a *shell* of

FIGURE 9.32

Criteria for applications that are suitable for expert systems development.

Suitability Criteria for Expert Systems
● **Domain.** The domain, or subject area, of the problem is relatively small and limited to a well-defined problem area.
● **Expertise.** Solutions to the problem require the efforts of an expert. That is, a body of knowledge, techniques, and intuition is needed that only a few people possess.
● **Complexity.** Solution of the problem is a complex task that requires logical inference processing, which would not be handled as well by conventional information processing.
● **Structure.** The solution process must be able to cope with ill-structured, uncertain, missing, and conflicting data, and a problem situation that changes with the passage of time.
● **Availability.** An expert exists who is articulate and cooperative, and who has the support of the management and end users involved in the development of the proposed system.

software (the inference engine and user interface programs) with generic inferencing and user interface capabilities. Other development tools (e.g., rule editors, user interface generators) are added in making the shell a powerful expert system development tool.

Expert system shells are now available as relatively low-cost software packages that help users develop their own expert systems on microcomputers. They allow trained users to develop the knowledge base for a specific expert system application. For example, one shell uses a spreadsheet format to help end users develop IF–THEN rules, automatically generating rules based on examples furnished by a user. Once a knowledge base is constructed, it is used with the shell's inference engine and user interface modules as a complete expert system on a specific subject area. Other software tools may require an IT specialist to develop expert systems. See Figure 9.33.

Knowledge Engineering

A knowledge engineer is a professional who works with experts to capture the knowledge (facts and rules of thumb) they possess. The knowledge engineer then builds the knowledge base (and the rest of the expert system if necessary), using an iterative, prototyping process until the expert system is acceptable. Thus, knowledge engineers perform a role similar to that of systems analysts in conventional information systems development.

FIGURE 9.33

Using the Visual Rule Studio and Visual Basic to develop rules for a credit management expert system.

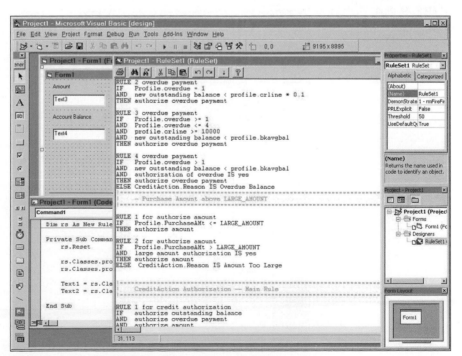

Source: Courtesy of Trading Solutions.

Once the decision is made to develop an expert system, a team of one or more domain experts and a knowledge engineer may be formed. Experts skilled in the use of expert system shells could also develop their own expert systems. If a shell is used, facts and rules of thumb about a specific domain can be defined and entered into a knowledge base with the help of a rule editor or other knowledge acquisition tool. A limited working prototype of the knowledge base is then constructed, tested, and evaluated using the inference engine and user interface programs of the shell. The knowledge engineer and domain experts can modify the knowledge base, and then retest the system and evaluate the results. This process is repeated until the knowledge base and the shell result in an acceptable expert system.

Neural Networks

Neural networks are computing systems modeled after the brain's meshlike network of interconnected processing elements, called *neurons*. Of course, neural networks are a lot simpler in architecture (the human brain is estimated to have more than 100 billion neuron brain cells!). Like the brain, however, the interconnected processors in a neural network operate in parallel and interact dynamically. This interaction enables the network to "learn" from data it processes. That is, it learns to recognize patterns and relationships in these data. The more data examples it receives as input, the better it can learn to duplicate the results of the examples it processes. Thus, the neural network will change the strengths of the interconnections between the processing elements in response to changing patterns in the data it receives and the results that occur. See Figure 9.34.

Modern Neurosurgery: Neural Nets Help Save Lives

Neurosurgery, surgery performed on the brain and spinal cord, has advanced to extraordinary levels of skill and success in just the last decade. One of the most common applications of neurosurgical techniques is the removal of brain tumors. Currently, surgeons search for tumors manually using a metal biopsy needle inserted into the brain. Guided by ultrasound and modern imaging techniques such as MRI/CT scans, they primarily use tactile feedback to localize the tumor. This method,

---

FIGURE 9.34

Evaluating the training status of a neural network application.

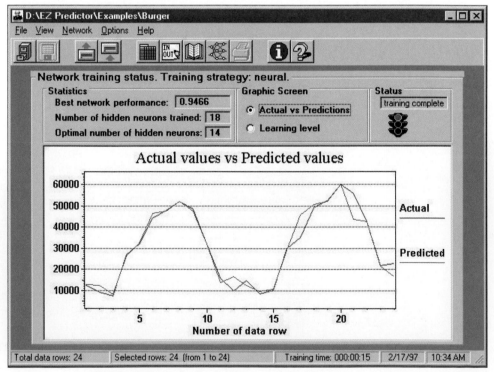

Source: Courtesy of Trading Solutions.

however, can be imprecise, as the tumors can easily shift during surgery, causing healthy tissue to be mistakenly treated as tumorous tissue. This inaccuracy can increase the risk of a stroke should a needle accidentally sever an artery.

A new technique, which is a combination of hardware and software, has been developed that gives neurosurgeons the ability to find their way through the brain while doing less damage as they operate. The primary piece of the hardware is a robotic probe that has on its tip several miniature sensors: an endoscope that transmits images and instruments that measure tissue density and blood flow. This probe is inserted into the brain and guided through it by a robotic mechanism that is more precise and accurate than human hands.

The real power in this miracle technique, however, is the sophisticated, adaptable neural network software that provides an instant in-depth analysis of the data gathered by the probe. Surgeons are able to look at a computer screen in the operating room and see a vast array of useful real-time information about what is going on in the patient's brain, such as whether the probe is encountering healthy tissue, blood vessels, or a tumor. The neural net software is adaptable in that it learns from experience the difference between normal tissue and tumorous tissue. Laboratory biopsy test results are used to validate the data used for training the neural net software. Once trained, the neural net can be used to identify in real time abnormal tissues encountered during surgical operations. Once learned, the probe is robotically advanced and stops immediately when it detects a signature significantly different from what was learned to be normal tissue. At this point, tissue identification is performed automatically, and the results presented to the surgeon. The surgeon can then treat the abnormal tissue appropriately and without delay.

This new technique gives surgeons finer control of surgical instruments during delicate brain operations. Overall, the new technique will increase the safety, accuracy, and efficiency of surgical procedures.

Source: Adapted from Bioluminate Inc., Press Release, "Bioluminate to Develop 'Smart Probe' for Early Breast Cancer Detection," December 5, 2002; and "NASA Ames Research Center Report," Smart Surgical Probe, Bioluminate Inc., 2003.

For example, a neural network can be trained to learn which credit characteristics result in good or bad loans. Developers of a credit evaluation neural network could provide it with data from many examples of credit applications and loan results to process, with opportunities to adjust the signal strengths between its neurons. The neural network would continue to be trained until it demonstrated a high degree of accuracy in correctly duplicating the results of recent cases. At that point it would be trained enough to begin making credit evaluations of its own.

Fuzzy Logic Systems

In spite of their funny name, fuzzy logic systems represent a small, but serious, application of AI in business. Fuzzy logic is a method of reasoning that resembles human reasoning, in that it allows for approximate values and inferences (fuzzy logic) and incomplete or ambiguous data (fuzzy data) instead of relying only on *crisp data*, such as binary (yes/no) choices. For example, Figure 9.35 illustrates a partial set of rules (fuzzy rules) and a fuzzy SQL query for analyzing and extracting credit risk information on businesses that are being evaluated for selection as investments.

Notice how fuzzy logic uses terminology that is deliberately imprecise, such as *very high, increasing, somewhat decreased, reasonable,* and *very low.* This language enables fuzzy systems to process incomplete data and quickly provide approximate, but acceptable, solutions to problems that are difficult for other methods to solve. Thus, fuzzy logic queries of a database, such as the SQL query shown in Figure 9.35, promise to improve the extraction of data from business databases. It is important to note that fuzzy logic isn't fuzzy or imprecise thinking. Fuzzy logic actually brings precision to decision scenarios where it previously didn't exist.

FIGURE 9.35 An example of fuzzy logic rules and a fuzzy logic SQL query in a credit risk analysis application.

```
Fuzzy Logic Rules

Risk should be acceptable
If debt-equity is very high
    then risk is positively increased
If income is increasing
    then risk is somewhat decreased
If cash reserves are low to very low
    then risk is very increased
If PE ratio is good
    then risk is generally decreased
```

```
Fuzzy Logic SQL Query

Select companies
    from financials
        where revenues are very large
        and pe_ratio is acceptable
        and profits are high to very high
        and (income/employee_tot) is reasonable
```

Fuzzy Logic in Business

Examples of applications of fuzzy logic are numerous in Japan but rare in the United States. The United States has preferred to use AI solutions like expert systems or neural networks, but Japan has implemented many fuzzy logic applications, especially the use of special-purpose fuzzy logic microprocessor chips, called fuzzy process controllers. Thus, the Japanese ride on subway trains, use elevators, and drive cars that are guided or supported by fuzzy process controllers made by Hitachi and Toshiba. Many models of Japanese-made products also feature fuzzy logic microprocessors. The list is growing and includes autofocus cameras, autostabilizing camcorders, energy-efficient air conditioners, self-adjusting washing machines, and automatic transmissions.

Genetic Algorithms

The use of **genetic algorithms** is a growing application of artificial intelligence. Genetic algorithm software uses Darwinian (survival of the fittest), randomizing, and other mathematical functions to simulate an evolutionary process that can yield increasingly better solutions to a problem. Genetic algorithms were first used to simulate millions of years in biological, geological, and ecosystem evolution in just a few minutes on a computer. Genetic algorithm software is being used to model a variety of scientific, technical, and business processes.

Genetic algorithms are especially useful for situations in which thousands of solutions are possible and must be evaluated to produce an optimal solution. Genetic algorithm software uses sets of mathematical process rules (*algorithms*) that specify how combinations of process components or steps are to be formed. This process may involve trying random process combinations (*mutation*), combining parts of several good processes (*crossover*), and selecting good sets of processes and discarding poor ones (*selection*) to generate increasingly better solutions. Figure 9.36 illustrates a business use of genetic algorithm software.

United Distillers: Moving Casks Around with Genetic Algorithms

United Distillers (now part of Diageo PLC) is the largest and most profitable spirits company in the world. United Distillers' two grain distilleries account for more than one-third of total grain whiskey production, and the company's Johnnie Walker brand is the world's top whiskey, achieving sales of up to 120 million bottles a year.

Nevertheless, Christine Wright, Inventory and Supply Manager at United Distillers, points out that some parts of the business attract less attention than others: "Each week, 20,000 casks are moved in and out of our 49 warehouses throughout Scotland to provide the whiskey needed for the blending program. Warehousing is a physical and laborious process and has tended to be the forgotten side of the business." The introduction of genetic algorithm computer technology, however, during the past year has given a fillip to the blend selection process at United Distillers.

"We want to maximize our operational efficiency without compromising the quality," states Christine Wright. United Distillers' Blackgrange warehouse site alone houses approximately 3 million casks, indicating the scale of the challenge. Of the

20,000 casks that are moved each week, 10,000 are not used but are moved only to allow access to those identified by the selection process. "Although we had 100 percent accurate positional information about all the stock, casks had to be selected numerically. Given the practical challenges involved in warehouse management, casks are seldom stored numerically."

Information held on the system about recipes, site constraints, and the blending program is given to the XpertRule package, which works out the best combinations of stocks to produce the blends. This information is supplemented with positional information about the casks. The system then optimizes the selection of required casks, keeping to a minimum the number of "doors" (warehouse sections) from which the casks must be taken and the number of casks that need to be moved to clear the way. Other constraints must be satisfied, such as the current working capacity of each warehouse and the maintenance and restocking work that may be in progress. Lancashire-based expert systems specialist XpertRule Software Limited has worked closely with United Distillers to develop the software application using XpertRule. The system is based on the use of genetic algorithms and adopts the Darwinian principle of natural selection to optimize the selection process.

"The incidence of non-productive cask movements has plummeted from a high of around 50 percent to a negligible level of around 4 percent and our cask handling rates have almost doubled." She adds: "The new technology enables staff to concentrate on what they want to achieve, rather than the mechanism of how to go about it. They can concentrate on the constraints that they wish to impose and get the system to do the leg work of finding the best scenario within those constraints. It means that the business can be driven by primary objectives." "Not only does the lack of wasted effort allow warehouse staff to get on with their work, but it enables them to plan ahead and organize long-term maintenance programs. It encourages a mind-set that is strategic, rather than reactive, and empowers managers to manage their own sites."

Source: Adapted from XpertRule Case Study, "A Break from Tradition in Blend Selection at United Distillers & Vintners," http://www.xpertrule.com/pages/case_ud.htm, accessed April 23, 2008.

FIGURE 9.36

Risk Optimizer software combines genetic algorithms with a risk simulation function in this airline yield optimization application.

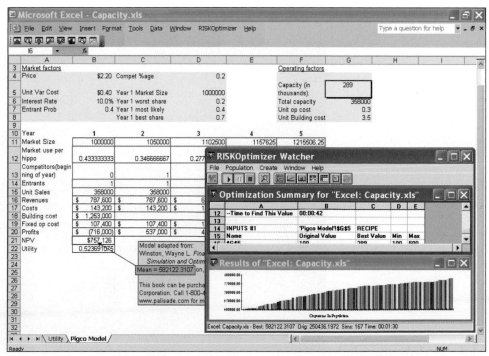

Source: Courtesy of Palisade Software.

Virtual Reality

Virtual reality (VR) is computer-simulated reality. Virtual reality is a fast-growing area of artificial intelligence that had its origins in efforts to build more natural, realistic, multisensory human–computer interfaces. So virtual reality relies on multisensory input/output devices such as a tracking headset with video goggles and stereo earphones, a *data glove* or jumpsuit with fiber-optic sensors that track your body movements, and a *walker* that monitors the movement of your feet. Then you can experience computer-simulated "virtual worlds" three-dimensionally through sight, sound, and touch. Virtual reality is also called *telepresence*. For example, you can enter a computer-generated virtual world, look around and observe its contents, pick up and move objects, and move around in it at will. Thus, virtual reality allows you to interact with computer-simulated objects, entities, and environments as if they actually exist. See Figure 9.37.

VR Applications

Current applications of virtual reality are wide-ranging and include computer-aided design (CAD), medical diagnostics and treatment, scientific experimentation in many physical and biological sciences, flight simulation for training pilots and astronauts, product demonstrations, employee training, and entertainment, especially 3D video arcade games. CAD is the most widely used industrial VR application. It enables architects and other designers to design and test electronic 3D models of products and structures by entering the models themselves and examining, touching, and manipulating sections and parts from all angles. This scientific-visualization capability is also used by pharmaceutical and biotechnology firms to develop and observe the behavior of computerized models of new drugs and materials and by medical researchers to develop ways for physicians to enter and examine a virtual reality of a patient's body.

VR becomes *telepresence* when users, who can be anywhere in the world, use VR systems to work alone or together at a remote site. Typically, this involves using a VR system to enhance the sight and touch of a human who is remotely manipulating equipment to accomplish a task. Examples range from virtual surgery, where surgeon and patient may be on either side of the globe, to the remote use of equipment in hazardous environments such as chemical plants or nuclear reactors.

The hottest VR application today is Linden Lab's *Second Life*. Here, users can create avatars to represent them, teleport to any of the thousands of locations in *Second Life*, build personal domains, "buy" land, and live out their wildest fantasies. *Second Life* has grown to enormous proportions although actual statistics regarding size and

FIGURE 9.37

This landscape architect uses a virtual reality system to view and move through the design of the Seattle Commons, an urban design proposal for downtown Seattle.

Source: © George Steinmetz/Corbis.

number of users are constantly in dispute. Today, *Second Life* is home to individuals, commercial organizations, universities, governments (the Maldives was the first country to open an embassy in *Second Life*), churches, sports entertainment, art exhibits, live music, and theater. Just about anything goes in *Second Life* and, as technologies advance, the lines between your first life and your second one may begin to blur—stay tuned.

Norsk Hydro: Drilling Decisions Made in a Virtual Oil Field 	Norsk Hydro, based in Oslo, Norway, is a *Fortune* 500 energy and aluminum supplier operating in more than 40 countries worldwide. It is a leading offshore producer of oil and gas, the world's third-largest aluminum supplier, and a leader in the development of renewable energy sources. Norsk Hydro is also an innovator in the use of virtual reality technology. It uses VR to make decisions that, if wrong, could cost the company millions in lost revenues and, more important, could harm the environment. One example of its successful use of VR is the Troll Oil Field project. The Troll Oil Field is located in the North Sea. The eastern part of the field has an oil column only 39–46 feet wide, but with in-place reserves of approximately 2.2 billion barrels. The oil is produced by horizontal wells located 1.5–5 feet above the point where the oil and seawater make contact. During one drilling of a horizontal well, the drill bit was in sand of relatively low quality. No further good-quality reservoir sands were predicted from the geological model along the planned well track. Approximately 820 feet remained to the planned total depth, so a major decision to terminate the well required confirmation. If the decision to terminate the well was the right decision, the cost of drilling to that date would be lost, but no further loss or damage to the environment would occur. If, however, the decision to terminate the well was the wrong decision, valuable oil reserves would be lost forever. Virtual reality technology was fundamental in deciding whether to terminate the well. All relevant data were loaded into the system for review. During a virtual reality session, the well team discovered a mismatch between the seismic data and the geological model. Based on this observation, they made a quick reinterpretation of some key seismic horizons and updated the geological model locally around the well. The updated model changed the prognosis for the remaining section of the well from poor-quality sand to high-quality sand. It was decided to continue drilling, and the new prognosis was proven correct. As a result, 175 meters of extra-high-quality sand with an estimated production volume of 100,000 standard cubic meters of oil were drilled in the last section of the well. Source: Adapted from Norsk Hydro Corporate Background, www.hydro.com, 2004; and Schlumberger Information Solutions, "Norsk Hydro Makes a Valuable Drilling Decision," Schlumberger Technical Report GMP-5911, 2002.

Intelligent Agents

Intelligent agents are growing in popularity as a way to use artificial intelligence routines in software to help users accomplish many kinds of tasks in e-business and e-commerce. An intelligent agent is a *software surrogate* for an end user or a process that fulfills a stated need or activity. An intelligent agent uses its built-in and learned knowledge base about a person or process to make decisions and accomplish tasks in a way that fulfills the intentions of a user. Sometimes an intelligent agent is given a graphic representation or persona, such as Einstein for a science advisor, Sherlock Holmes for an information search agent, and so on. Thus, intelligent agents (also called *software robots* or "bots") are special-purpose, knowledge-based information systems that accomplish specific tasks for users. Figure 9.38 summarizes major types of intelligent agents.

The wizards found in Microsoft Office and other software suites are among the most well-known examples of intelligent agents. These wizards are built-in capabilities that can analyze how an end user is using a software package and offer suggestions on how to complete various tasks. Thus, wizards might help you change document

FIGURE 9.38

Examples of different types of intelligent agents.

Types of Intelligent Agents
User Interface Agents
● **Interface Tutors.** Observe user computer operations, correct user mistakes, and provide hints and advice on efficient software use.
● **Presentation Agents.** Show information in a variety of reporting and presentation forms and media based on user preferences.
● **Network Navigation Agents.** Discover paths to information and provide ways to view information that are preferred by a user.
● **Role-Playing Agents.** Play what-if games and other roles to help users understand information and make better decisions.
Information Management Agents
● **Search Agents.** Help users find files and databases, search for desired information, and suggest and find new types of information products, media, and resources.
● **Information Brokers.** Provide commercial services to discover and develop information resources that fit the business or personal needs of a user.
● **Information Filters.** Receive, find, filter, discard, save, forward, and notify users about products received or desired, including e-mail, voice mail, and all other information media.

margins, format spreadsheet cells, query a database, or construct a graph. Wizards and other software agents are also designed to adjust to your way of using a software package so that they can anticipate when you will need their assistance. See Figure 9.39.

The use of intelligent agents is growing rapidly as a way to simplify software use, search Web sites on the Internet and corporate intranets, and help customers do comparison shopping among the many e-commerce sites on the Web. Intelligent agents are becoming necessary as software packages become more sophisticated and powerful, as the Internet and the World Wide Web become more vast and complex, and as information sources and e-commerce alternatives proliferate exponentially. In fact, some commentators forecast that much of the future of computing will consist of intelligent agents performing their work for users.

FIGURE 9.39

Intelligent agent software such as Copernic can help you access information from a variety of categories and from a variety of sources.

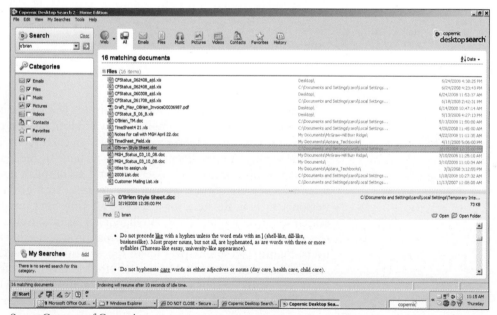

Source: Courtesy of Copernic.

Security Uses of Intelligent Software Agents	In 2002, the Army began to use intelligent software agents instead of people to route the background files of soldiers who required security clearance to the proper authorities for review. *The result*: A process that once took days now takes 24 hours. The Army reduced its year-long backlog, and the Army Central Clearance Facility in Fort Meade, Maryland, can now handle 30 percent more requests a year. The intelligent agent retrieves the necessary background information from existing records and builds an electronic folder for each case. It then examines the file to determine whether it's a clean case or there are warning signs, such as financial problems, arrests, or anything to indicate that a person might be susceptible to improper influence. Human investigators take closer looks at the tough cases.

Intelligent agents are semiautonomous, proactive, and adaptive software systems that can act on a user's behalf. Give an intelligent agent a goal, such as to help a U.S. ambassador pick a safe evacuation route following a terrorist attack in a foreign country, and it creates the best plan after gathering weather information, news reports, airplane schedules, road information, and police reports.

Such agents can also help investigators identify unusual patterns of activity, says Henry Lieberman, research scientist and leader of the Software Agents Group at the MIT Media Lab in Cambridge, Massachusetts. "Law enforcement can say to an intelligent agent, 'Let me know when any person arrived from a sensitive Middle Eastern country that was recently involved in a large bank transfer.' Or government agencies like the Securities and Exchange Commission can use them to monitor financial statements for fraud. Maybe they could have caught the whole Enron thing earlier."

Nevertheless, the issue of trust may deter their widespread adoption in business. "People just aren't used to using these kinds of things yet," says Lieberman. "When you first start using one of these agents, you have to watch it closely to make sure it's doing what you want. But performance improves over time. And the agent just makes a proposal. Then it's up to you."

Source: Adapted from Stephanie Overby, "Security Strategy Includes Intelligent Software Agents," *CIO Magazine*, January 1, 2003.

Summary

- **Information, Decisions, and Management.** Information systems can support a variety of management decision-making levels and decisions. These include the three levels of management activity (strategic, tactical, and operational decision making) and three types of decision structures (structured, semistructured, and unstructured). Information systems provide a wide range of information products to support these types of decisions at all levels of the organization.

- **Decision Support Trends.** Major changes are taking place in traditional MIS, DSS, and EIS tools for providing the information, and modeling managers need to support their decision making. Decision support in business is changing, driven by rapid developments in end-user computing and networking; Internet and Web technologies; and Web-enabled business applications. The growth of corporate intranets and extranets, as well

as the Web, has accelerated the development of "executive-class" interfaces like enterprise information portals and Web-enabled business intelligence software tools, as well as their use by lower levels of management and individuals and teams of business professionals. In addition, the growth of e-commerce and e-business applications has expanded the use of enterprise portals and DSS tools by the suppliers, customers, and other business stakeholders of a company.

- **Management Information Systems.** Management information systems provide prespecified reports and responses to managers on a periodic, exception, demand, or push reporting basis to meet their need for information to support decision making.

- **OLAP and Data Mining.** Online analytical processing interactively analyzes complex relationships among large amounts of data stored in multidimensional databases. Data mining analyzes the vast amounts of historical data that have been prepared for analysis in data warehouses. Both technologies discover patterns, trends, and exception conditions in a company's data that support business analysis and decision making.

● **Decision Support Systems.** Decision support systems are interactive, computer-based information systems that use DSS software and a model base and database to provide information tailored to support semistructured and unstructured decisions faced by individual managers. They are designed to use a decision maker's own insights and judgments in an ad hoc, interactive, analytical modeling process leading to a specific decision.

● **Executive Information Systems.** Executive information systems are information systems originally designed to support the strategic information needs of top management; however, their use is spreading to lower levels of management and business professionals. EIS are easy to use and enable executives to retrieve information tailored to their needs and preferences. Thus, EIS can provide information about a company's critical success factors to executives to support their planning and control responsibilities.

● **Enterprise Information and Knowledge Portals.** Enterprise information portals provide a customized and personalized Web-based interface for corporate intranets to give their users easy access to a variety of internal and external business applications, databases, and information services that are tailored to their individual preferences and information needs. Thus, an EIP can supply personalized Web-enabled information, knowledge, and decision support to executives, managers, and business professionals, as well as to customers, suppliers, and other business partners. An enterprise knowledge portal is a corporate intranet portal that extends the use of an EIP to include knowledge management functions and knowledge base resources so that it becomes a major form of knowledge management system for a company.

● **Artificial Intelligence.** The major application domains of artificial intelligence (AI) include a variety of applications in cognitive science, robotics, and natural interfaces. The goal of AI is the development of computer functions normally associated with human physical and mental capabilities, such as robots that see, hear, talk, feel, and move, and software capable of reasoning, learning, and problem solving. Thus, AI is being applied to many applications in business operations and managerial decision making, as well as in many other fields.

● **AI Technologies.** The many application areas of AI are summarized in Figure 9.26, including neural networks, fuzzy logic, genetic algorithms, virtual reality, and intelligent agents. Neural nets are hardware or software systems based on simple models of the brain's neuron structure that can learn to recognize patterns in data. Fuzzy logic systems use rules of approximate reasoning to solve problems when data are incomplete or ambiguous. Genetic algorithms use selection, randomizing, and other mathematic functions to simulate an evolutionary process that can yield increasingly better solutions to problems. Virtual reality systems are multisensory systems that enable human users to experience computer-simulated environments as if they actually existed. Intelligent agents are knowledge-based software surrogates for a user or process in the accomplishment of selected tasks.

● **Expert Systems.** Expert systems are knowledge-based information systems that use software and a knowledge base about a specific, complex application area to act as expert consultants to users in many business and technical applications. Software includes an inference engine program that makes inferences based on the facts and rules stored in the knowledge base. A knowledge base consists of facts about a specific subject area and heuristics (rules of thumb) that express the reasoning procedures of an expert. The benefits of expert systems (such as preservation and replication of expertise) must be balanced with their limited applicability in many problem situations.

Key Terms and Concepts

These are the key terms and concepts of this chapter. The page number of their first explanation is in parentheses.

1. Analytical modeling (367)
   a. Goal-seeking analysis (368)
   b. Optimization analysis (369)
   c. Sensitivity analysis (368)
   d. What-if analysis (367)
2. Artificial intelligence (378)
3. Business intelligence (355)
4. Data mining (369)
5. Data visualization system (364)
6. Decision structure (354)
7. Decision support system (357)

8. Enterprise information portal (374)
9. Enterprise knowledge portal (376)
10. Executive information system (372)
11. Expert system (384)
12. Expert system shell (388)
13. Fuzzy logic (391)
14. Genetic algorithms (392)
15. Geographic information system (364)
16. Inference engine (385)
17. Intelligent agent (395)

18. Knowledge base (385)
19. Knowledge engineer (389)
20. Knowledge management system (376)
21. Management information system (359)
22. Model base (357)
23. Neural network (390)
24. Online analytical processing (361)
25. Robotics (383)
26. Virtual reality (394)

Review Quiz

Match one of the key terms and concepts listed previously with one of the brief examples or definitions that follow. Try to find the best fit for answers that seem to fit more than one term or concept. Defend your choices.

_____ 1. Decision-making procedures cannot be specified in advance for some complex decision situations.

_____ 2. Information systems for the strategic information needs of top and middle managers.

_____ 3. Systems that produce predefined reports for management.

_____ 4. Provide an interactive modeling capability tailored to the specific information needs of managers.

_____ 5. Provides business information and analytical tools for managers, business professionals, and business stakeholders.

_____ 6. A collection of mathematical models and analytical techniques.

_____ 7. Analyzing the effect of changing variables and relationships and manipulating a mathematical model.

_____ 8. Changing revenues and tax rates to see the effect on net profit after taxes.

_____ 9. Changing revenues in many small increments to see revenue's effect on net profit after taxes.

_____ 10. Changing revenues and expenses to find how you could achieve a specific amount of net profit after taxes.

_____ 11. Changing revenues and expenses subject to certain constraints to achieve the highest profit after taxes.

_____ 12. Real-time analysis of complex business data.

_____ 13. Attempts to find patterns hidden in business data in a data warehouse.

_____ 14. Represents complex data using three-dimensional graphical forms.

_____ 15. A customized and personalized Web interface to internal and external information resources available through a corporate intranet.

_____ 16. Using intranets to gather, store, and share a company's best practices among employees.

_____ 17. An enterprise information portal that can access knowledge management functions and company knowledge bases.

_____ 18. Information technology that focuses on the development of computer functions normally associated with human physical and mental capabilities.

_____ 19. Development of computer-based machines that possess capabilities such as sight, hearing, dexterity, and movement.

_____ 20. Computers that can provide you with computer-simulated experiences.

_____ 21. An information system that integrates computer graphics, geographic databases, and DSS capabilities.

_____ 22. A knowledge-based information system that acts as an expert consultant to users in a specific application area.

_____ 23. A collection of facts and reasoning procedures in a specific subject area.

_____ 24. A software package that manipulates a knowledge base and makes associations and inferences leading to a recommended course of action.

_____ 25. A software package consisting of an inference engine and user interface programs used as an expert system development tool.

_____ 26. An analyst who interviews experts to develop a knowledge base about a specific application area.

_____ 27. AI systems that use neuron structures to recognize patterns in data.

_____ 28. AI systems that use approximate reasoning to process ambiguous data.

_____ 29. Knowledge-based software surrogates that do things for you.

_____ 30. Software that uses mathematical functions to simulate an evolutionary process.

Discussion Questions

1. Are the form and use of information and decision support systems for managers and business professionals changing and expanding? Why or why not?

2. Has the growth of self-directed teams to manage work in organizations changed the need for strategic, tactical, and operational decision making in business?

3. What is the difference between the ability of a manager to retrieve information instantly on demand using an MIS and the capabilities provided by a DSS?

4. Refer to the Real World Case on Business Intelligence rollouts in the chapter. How do companies know when they need these types of systems? How do they make a decision on which projects to tackle? Discuss the role of political dynamics in the latter.

5. In what ways does using an electronic spreadsheet package provide you with the capabilities of a decision support system?

6. Are enterprise information portals making executive information systems unnecessary? Explain your reasoning.

7. Refer to the Real World Case on Goodyear, JEA, OSUMC, and Monsanto in the chapter. Given the large a priori uncertainties associated with these technologies, how do you make a business case for investing in them in the first place? Provide several ideas.

8. Can computers think? Will they ever be able to? Explain why or why not.

9. Which applications of AI have the most potential value for use in the operations and management of a business? Defend your choices.

10. What are some of the limitations or dangers you see in the use of AI technologies such as expert systems, virtual reality, and intelligent agents? What could be done to minimize such effects?

Analysis Exercises

1. e-Commerce Web Site Reviews
BizRate.com
BizRate (www.bizrate.com) instantly provides information about hundreds of online stores. Supported product lines include books, music, electronics, clothes, hardware, gifts, and more. Customer reviews help shoppers select products and retailers with confidence. BizRate also features a "Smart Choice" tag that balances retailer reviews, price, and other variables to recommend a "best buy."

  a. Use BizRate.com to check out a product of interest. How thorough, valid, and valuable were the product and retailer reviews to you? Explain.

  b. How could nonretail businesses use a similar Web-enabled review system? Give an example.

  c. How is BizRate's Web site functionality similar to a decision support system (DSS)?

2. Enterprise Application Integration
Digital Desktops
Information coming from a variety of business systems can appear on the executive desktop as a consolidated whole. Often referred to as a "digital dashboard," the information contained in such a view might include the executive's schedule, current e-mail, a brief list of production delays, major accounts past due, current sales summaries, and a financial market summary. Although it isn't possible to fit all of an organization's information on a single screen, it is possible to summarize data in ways specified by the executive and then act as a launching point or portal for further point-and-click enquiries.

How might such a system look? Portals such as my.Excite.com, my.MSN.com, iGoogle (www.google.com/ig), and my.Yahoo.com make good general-purpose information portals. These Web sites contain characteristics in common with their business-oriented brethren. They provide information from many different sources such as e-mail, instant messages, calendars, tasks lists, stock quotes, weather, and news. They allow users to determine what information sources they see; for example, a user may choose to list only business-related news and omit sports, lottery results, and horoscopes. They also allow users to filter the information they see; for example, a user may choose to view only local weather,

news containing specific keywords, or market results only for stocks the user owns. They allow users to arrange their own information space so that information a user finds most important appears in the right place. Finally, they allow users to drill down into the information they find important to receive more detail.

Once a user has set up an account and identified his or her preferences, these public portals remember the user's preferences and deliver only what the user has requested. Users may change their preferences as often as they wish, and the controls to make these changes require only point-and-click programming skills.

  a. Visit one of the portal sites listed above. Configure the site to meet your own information needs. Provide a printout of the result.

  b. Look up Digital Dashboard on the 20/20 Software Web site (www.2020software), read about products with this feature, and describe these products in your own words.

3. Case-Based Marketing
Selling on Amazon.com
A case-based reasoning system is a type of expert system. It attempts to match the facts on hand to a database of prior cases. When a case-based reasoning system finds one or more cases in its database that closely match the facts at hand, it then evaluates and reports the most common outcomes. Given enough cases, such a system can prove very useful. Even better, if a case-based system automatically captures cases as they occur, then it will become a powerful tool that continually fine-tunes its results as it gains "experience."

Amazon.com relies on just such a system to refer books to its customers. Like many e-commerce sites, Amazon allows visitors to search for, buy, and review books. Amazon.com takes its database interactivity a step further. Given a particular book title, its case-based reasoning engine examines all past sales of that book to see if the customers who bought that book shared other book purchases in common. It then produces a short list and presents that list to the user. The overall effect approaches that of a sales clerk who says, "Oh! If you like this book, then you'll really like reading these as well." Amazon's system has the experience of hundreds of millions more transactions than even the most wizened and well-read sales clerk.

Equipped with this information, customers may consider purchasing additional books, or the information may increase customers' confidence that they have selected the right book. Better information increases customers' confidence in their purchases and encourages additional sales.

a. What is the source of expertise behind Amazon's online book recommendations?

b. How do you feel about online merchants tracking your purchases and using this information to recommend additional purchases?

c. What measures protect consumers from the government's obtaining their personal shopping histories maintained by Amazon?

d. Although Amazon doesn't share personal information, it still capitalizes on its customers' shopping data. Is this ethical? Should Amazon offer its customers the right to opt out of this information gathering?

4. Palm City Police Department
Goal Seeking

The Palm City Police Department has eight defined precincts. The police station in each precinct has primary responsibility for all activities in its precinct area. The table lists the current population of each precinct, the number of violent crimes committed in each precinct, and the number of officers assigned to each precinct. The department has established a goal of equalizing access to police services. Ratios of population per police officer and violent crimes per police officer should be calculated for each precinct. These ratios for the city as a whole are shown at right.

a. Build a spreadsheet to perform this analysis and print it out.

b. Currently, no funds are available to hire additional officers. On the basis of the citywide ratios, the department has decided to develop a plan to shift resources as needed to ensure that no precinct has more than 1,100 residents per police officer and no precinct has more than seven violent crimes per police officer. The department will transfer officers from precincts that easily meet these goals to precincts that violate one or both of these ratios. Use "goal seeking" on your spreadsheet to move police officers between precincts until the goals are met. You can use the goal seek tool to see how many officers would be required to bring each precinct into compliance and then judgmentally reduce officers in precincts that are substantially within the criteria. Print out a set of results that allow the departments to comply with these ratios and a memorandum to your instructor summarizing your results and the process you used to develop them.

Precinct	Population	Violent Crimes	Police Officers
Shea Blvd.	96,552	318	85
Lakeland Heights	99,223	582	108
Sunnydale	68,432	206	77
Old Town	47,732	496	55
Mountainview	101,233	359	82
Financial District	58,102	511	70
Riverdale	78,903	537	70
Cole Memorial	75,801	306	82
Total	**625,978**	**3,315**	**629**
Per Officer	**995.196**	**5.270**	

CASE 3

Harrah's Entertainment, LendingTree, DeepGreen Financial, and Cisco Systems: Successes and Challenges of Automated Decision Making

For over half a century, the field of artificial intelligence (AI) has promised that computers would relieve managers and professionals of the need to make certain types of decisions. Computer programs would analyze data and make sound judgments, whether it be to configure a complex computer, diagnose and treat a patient's illness, or determine when to stir a big vat of soup, with little or no human help.

Automated decision making has been slow to materialize. Many early artificial intelligence applications were just solutions looking for problems, contributing little to improved organizational performance. In medicine, for example, doctors showed little interest in having machines diagnose their patients' diseases. In the business sector, even when expert systems were directed at real issues, extracting the right kind of specialized knowledge from seasoned decision makers and maintaining it over time proved to be more difficult than anticipated.

Now, automated decision making is finally coming of age. The new generation of applications, however, differs from prior AI-based decision support systems in several important respects. To begin with, the new systems are easier to create and manage than earlier ones, which leaned heavily on the expertise of knowledge engineers. What's more, the new applications do not require anyone to identify the problems or to initiate the analysis. Indeed, decision-making capabilities are embedded into the normal flow of work, and they are typically triggered without human intervention: They sense online data or conditions, apply codified knowledge or logic, and make decisions—all with minimal amounts of human intervention. Finally, unlike earlier systems, the new ones are designed to translate decisions into action quickly, accurately, and efficiently.

Of course, there is still a role for people. Managers still need to be involved in reviewing and confirming decisions and, in exceptional cases, in making the actual decisions. Also, even the most automated systems rely on experts and managers to create and maintain rules and monitor the results.

Today's automated decision systems are best suited for decisions that must be made frequently and rapidly, using information that is available electronically. The knowledge and decision criteria used in these systems need to be highly structured, and the factors that must be taken into account must be well understood. If experts can readily codify the decision rules and if high-quality data are available, the conditions are ripe for automating the decision.

Bank credit decisions are a good example: They are repetitive, are susceptible to uniform criteria, and can be made by drawing on the vast supply of consumer credit data that are available. A decision about whom to hire as CEO, by contrast, would be a poor choice. It occurs only rarely, and different observers are apt to apply their own criteria, such

as personal chemistry, which cannot be easily captured in a computer model.

The transportation industry was one of the first to employ automated decision making on a large scale. After being used initially by airlines to optimize seat pricing, decision-making technology has since been applied to a variety of areas, including flight scheduling and crew and airport staff scheduling.

Yield-management programs have also been adopted in related businesses, such as lodging. For example, Harrah's Entertainment, the world's largest casino operator, makes several million dollars a month in incremental revenue by optimizing room rates at its hotels and offering different rates to members of its loyalty program based on projected demand. The use of yield-management systems for hotel room pricing is common, but combining it with loyalty management programs is unusual. The combination ensures that the best customers get the best prices and, in turn, these customers will reward the company with their loyalty.

Investment firms have relied upon AI-based decision-making technology extensively for program trading and arbitrage. Yet much of the recent activity within the financial industry has revolved around creating new applications aimed at finding good banking and insurance customers and serving their needs. The widespread availability of online credit information and financial history, the need for differentiation through rapid customer service, and the rapid growth of online financial services providers have led to increases in automated decisions.

To compete in the same arena as LendingTree, lenders are forced to be more highly automated and are implementing automated decision engines to help them remain competitive. For example, DeepGreen Financial in Cleveland, Ohio, was created from the ground up to make use of automated decision technology. DeepGreen originates loans in 46 states through its Web site and through partnerships with LendingTree, priceline.com, and MortgageIT.com, based in New York City. It also offers home equity lending services for mortgage brokers and private-label or cobranded home equity lending technology and fulfillment services. Since its inception in 2000, DeepGreen's Internet technology has been used to process more than 325,000 applications and originate more than $4.4 billion of home equity lines of credit, according to Jerry Selitto, the bank's founding chief executive officer.

DeepGreen created an Internet-based system that makes credit decisions within minutes by skimming off the customers with the best credit, enabling just eight employees to process some 400 applications a day. Instead of competing on the basis of interest rates, DeepGreen's drawing card is ease of application and speedy approval. The company provides almost instantaneous, unconditional decisions without requiring traditional appraisals or upfront paperwork from borrowers.

Customers can complete the application within five minutes, at which point the automated process begins: A credit report is pulled, the credit is scored, a property valuation is completed using online data, confirmations are made concerning fraud and flood insurance, and a final decision is made on the loan. In about 80 percent of the cases, customers receive a final decision within two minutes. (In some cases, DeepGreen is only able to offer a conditional commitment because some of the information—usually the valuation—is not available online.) After approval, the system selects a notary public located near the customer's home and the customer chooses a closing date. All the loan documents are automatically generated and express-mailed to the notary.

DeepGreen's competitive strategy is driven by the convergence of several factors. At its core, it relies on the advancement of analytic and rule-based AI technologies without which the business would not be possible. It also leverages the bank's deep understanding of changing market conditions and pricing dynamics. Together with DeepGreen's extensive use of online information, these factors enable the company to tailor loan terms to the needs of individual borrowers. Moreover, the company's focus on high-end customers makes it possible to offer speed, service, and convenience. Credit decisions involving affluent, low-risk borrowers are relatively easy to make. Finally, high-end borrowers tend to be Internet-savvy; if you build an online service that meets their specific needs, they will come.

The consequences of not defining limits can be huge. Several years ago, during the e-commerce boom, Cisco Systems, based in San Jose, California, belatedly found out that it was relying too heavily on its automated ordering and supply chain systems. Management realized that many of the orders that had been entered on the books were not as firm as they assumed and, in all likelihood, would never be shipped. This glitch eventually forced Cisco to write off more than $2 billion in excess inventory.

Over and above their close monitoring of risk levels, managers in charge of automated decision systems must also develop processes for managing exceptions. Among other things, they need to determine in advance what happens when the computer has too little data on which to make a decision (a frequent reason for allowing exceptions). Companies should have clear criteria for determining when cases cannot be addressed through automation and who should deal with the exceptions. They should also ensure that exceptions are viewed internally as opportunities to learn, rather than as failures of the system.

Source: Adapted from Thomas H. Davenport and Jeanne G. Harris, "Automated Decision Making Comes of Age," *MIT Sloan Management Review*, Summer 2005; Thomas H. Davenport, "Competing on Analytics," *Harvard Business Review*, January 2006.

CASE STUDY QUESTIONS

1. Why did some previous attempts to use artificial intelligence technologies fail? What key differences of the new AI-based applications versus the old cause the authors to declare that automated decision making is finally coming of age?

2. What types of decisions are best suited for automated decision making? Provide several examples of successful applications from the companies in this case to illustrate your answer.

3. What role do humans play in automated decision-making applications? What are some of the challenges faced by managers where automated decision-making systems are being used? What solutions are needed to meet such challenges?

REAL WORLD ACTIVITIES

1. Use the Internet to find examples of companies that are using automated decision making or other business applications of artificial intelligence. You might begin by looking for such information on the companies mentioned in this case and their main competitors, and then widen your search to encompass other companies. What business benefits or challenges do you discover?

2. Artificial intelligence applications in business, such as automated decision making, pose potential business risks, as evidenced by the Cisco Systems experience, and have the potential for other risks to business and human security and safety, for example. Break into small groups with your classmates to discuss such risks and propose controls and safeguards to lessen the possibility of such occurrences.

MODULE IV

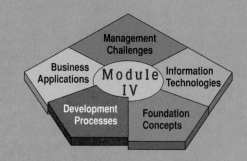

DEVELOPMENT PROCESSES

How can business professionals plan, develop, and implement strategies and solutions that use information technologies to help meet the challenges and opportunities faced in today's business environment? Answering that question is the goal of the chapter of this module, which concentrates on the processes for planning, developing, and implementing IT-based business strategies and applications.

- **Chapter 10: Developing Business/IT Solutions** introduces the traditional, prototyping, and end-user approaches to the development of information systems and discusses the processes and managerial issues in the implementation of new business applications of information technology, including the topics of user resistance and involvement and change management.

CHAPTER 10

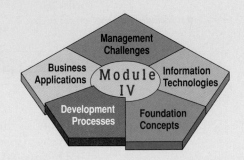

DEVELOPING BUSINESS/IT SOLUTIONS

Chapter Highlights

Section I
Developing Business Systems

IS Development

The Systems Approach

Real World Case: PayPal: Going Global All Languages
at a Time

Systems Analysis and Design

The Systems Development Life Cycle

Starting the Systems Development Process

Systems Analysis

Systems Design

End-User Development

Technical Note: Overview of Object-Oriented Analysis
and Design

Section II
Implementing Business Systems

Implementation

Implementing New Systems

Real World Case: Blue Cross and Blue Shield and
Others: Understanding the Science behind Change

Project Management

Evaluating Hardware, Software, and Services

Other Implementation Activities

Implementation Challenges

User Resistance and Involvement

Change Management

Real World Case: Infosys Technologies: The
Implementation Challenges of Knowledge Management
Initiatives

Learning Objectives

1. Use the systems development process outlined
   in this chapter and the model of IS components
   from Chapter 1 as problem-solving frameworks
   to help you propose information systems solutions
   to simple business problems.

2. Describe and give examples to illustrate how you
   might use each of the steps of the information
   systems development cycle to develop and implement a business information system.

3. Explain how prototyping can be used as an effective technique to improve the process of systems
   development for end users and IS specialists.

4. Understand the basics of project management and
   their importance to a successful system development effort.

5. Identify the activities involved in the implementation of new information systems.

6. Compare and contrast the four basic system conversion strategies.

7. Describe several evaluation factors that should be
   considered in evaluating the acquisition of hardware, software, and IS services.

8. Identify several change management solutions
   for user resistance to the implementation of new
   information systems.

SECTION I	# Developing Business Systems

IS Development

Suppose the chief executive of the company where you work asks you to find a Web-enabled way to get information to and from the salespeople in your company. How would you start? What would you do? Would you just plunge ahead and hope you could come up with a reasonable solution? How would you know whether your solution was a good one for your company? Do you think there might be a systematic way to help you develop a good solution to the CEO's request? There is. It's a problem-solving process called *the systems approach*.

When the systems approach to problem solving is applied to the development of information systems solutions to business problems, it is called *information systems development* or *application development*. This section will show you how the systems approach can be used to develop business systems and applications that meet the business needs of a company and its employees and stakeholders.

Refer to the Real World Case on the next page. We can learn a lot about the development challenges faced by global organizations from this example. See Figure 10.1.

The Systems Approach

The systems approach to problem solving uses a systems orientation to define problems and opportunities and then develop appropriate, feasible solutions in response. Analyzing a problem and formulating a solution involves the following interrelated activities:

1. Recognize and define a problem or opportunity using *systems thinking*.
2. Develop and evaluate alternative system solutions.
3. Select the system solution that best meets your requirements.
4. Design the selected system solution.
5. Implement and evaluate the success of the designed system.

Systems Thinking

Using systems thinking to understand a problem or opportunity is one of the most important aspects of the systems approach. Management consultant and author Peter Senge calls systems thinking *the fifth discipline*. Senge argues that mastering systems thinking (along with the disciplines of personal mastery, mental models, shared vision, and team learning) is vital to personal fulfillment and business success in a world of constant change. The essence of the discipline of systems thinking is "seeing the forest *and* the trees" in any situation by:

- Seeing *interrelationships* among *systems* rather than linear cause-and-effect chains whenever events occur.
- Seeing *processes* of change among *systems* rather than discrete "snapshots" of change, whenever changes occur.

One way of practicing systems thinking is to try to find systems, subsystems, and components of systems in any situation you are studying. This approach is also known as using a *systems context* or having a *systemic view* of a situation. For example, the business organization or business process in which a problem or opportunity arises could be viewed as a system of input, processing, output, feedback, and control components. Then to understand a problem and solve it, you would determine if these basic systems functions are being properly performed. See Figure 10.2.

Example. The sales process of a business can be viewed as a system. You could then ask: Is poor sales performance (output) caused by inadequate selling effort (input), out-of-date sales procedures (processing), incorrect sales information (feedback), or inadequate sales management (control)? Figure 10.2 illustrates this concept.

REAL WORLD CASE 1

PayPal: Going Global All Languages at a Time

When you're a global company that keeps expanding into new countries, how do you keep all of your consumer sites updated in the local language—without spending a ton of time and money?

PayPal realized five years ago that if it didn't solve this problem it would hinder the e-commerce payment company's ability to grow, says Matthew Mengerink, the company's vice president of core technologies; his IT responsibilities include PayPal's architecture and payment system infrastructure. Today, PayPal has rearchitected the software code for its site to allow simultaneous refreshes for 15 locales ranging from France to Poland. In the development community, they call this unusual achievement "polylingual simultaneous shipping" or "SimShip."

"This is a big problem that's been around a long time," says Ron Rogowski, a principal analyst for Forrester Research, who specializes in globalization issues. "For the most part, companies really do a poor job localizing content," he says, noting that technology solutions in this area aren't plentiful, and companies also must conquer organizational battles over who controls what content. "Companies would like to manage their translations better," Rogowski says, "to realize internal and external cost savings. But the real benefit is the potential for revenue growth, the ability to roll into markets quickly."

That ability today translates into a large portion of PayPal's bottom line: For PayPal, international business now represents 44 percent of net revenue, which was $582 million for the first quarter of 2008, a 32 percent increase year-over-year. As of late 2007, PayPal handles about $1,806 in payment volume per second; the company's re-architected code played a key role in this increase.

FIGURE 10.1

PayPal has successfully overcome the challenge of being a global company that speaks the local language

PayPal, now part of online auction giant eBay, had to go global to support customer desire, Mengerink says. People outside of the United States were demanding that eBay let them use PayPal (the primary purchase mechanism on eBay) and that PayPal be presented to them as seamlessly as it had been presented in English, he says. The company had to do more than present a stilted translation of English into, say, French or German, he adds.

"Imagine you're going into a bank and you want to speak French," Mengerink says. "The teller can speak French. But that's not enough. You want to feel you're in France. You want to see the French flag on the wall. Especially in the banking industry, it was very important to express something that people trust, in such a way that it is natural and native for them," he says.

Traditionally, companies solve the localization issue by working with third-party translation companies, whose staffers convert an English-based site into multiple languages, says Mengerink. The problem: "If you can't send them the smallest amount of text, it gets fantastically expensive," Mengerink says. "Here at PayPal you have a full site experience, you have to translate it, and we're an Internet company; we update the site every six weeks. How do you not slow the company down with the process of translation?"

PayPal's decision to custom-develop a solution is unusual and interesting. Few software vendors compete in the translation tools arena. Also, many companies can't even overcome the organizational hurdles related to translation. "There's a whole organizational issue that has to be looked at, who's in charge of what," says Rogowski.

For example, he notes that a consumer electronics company may not even have similar-looking content, never mind identical content, on Web sites in multiple countries. "A lot of times Web content springs up without any plan for centralization," he says. "Before your company can translate all of its sites efficiently, you may get embroiled in organizational messes," Rogowski warns, which is why some companies are tackling the problem silo by silo.

Not Paypal. Five years ago, Mengerink and a team of localization experts inside of IT began their project to fix the problem in a very centralized way. Often, Mengerink says, companies facing this problem try to cut and paste code, and then translate it into different languages; this can lead to trouble because it's not simple to keep compressing and unifying the code. "It's far easier to manipulate text than code," he says.

PayPal decided that it had to rearchitect its code to accommodate the language localization issue—purely for reasons of business speed, he says: "If you get the architecture right, you can get into new countries faster." No commercial tools existed that fit the bill, Mengerink says, so all the development was done in-house with a small IT team; PayPal will not disclose the exact size of the team, or the cost metrics.

"There's this notion of a country code and a language code," Mengerink says. "Your software has to understand two things: What country am I in and what language is being read? This is extremely important because there are countries outside the United States where customers cannot imagine not having multiple languages, Canada for example. The first thing we said is put both codes everywhere," Mengerink says. Then his developers had to create a code base with much more flexibility than the original; it had to convince the software, for instance, that strings of information such as e-mail addresses, customer support phone numbers, and time of day would change depending on the country code.

The second key to the project's success for PayPal: Ghassan Haddad, PayPal's director of localization, and the development team created a tool that color codes text in the software code base to note newly added strings of text that will need translating. "People just program as if it's in English," Mengerink says. "At the same time, the software extracts the new pieces." Then PayPal can send only the new pieces, instead of whole paragraphs, to the translation house. "This can take 5, 10 days depending on the size of the release," Mengerink says. "Then off we go to the races, releasing simultaneously in all locales."

So what's the next challenge for Mengerink and his developer team at PayPal? "We got very good at managing content with engineering," he says. "Now the question is, how we put that content management in the hands of business. They want to change it themselves without an intermediary. The business folks are saying 'we respect you but pretty please can we do it ourselves?'" That's a challenge, he says, given that the development toolset will continue to grow.

By the way, PayPal isn't looking to license the technology it developed. "Our tools are built for PayPal," Mengerink says. "We're encouraging others to build it for themselves." Although his team worked primarily in HTML, the programming language is not the important choice, he says. "Think about the methodology. That's a really critical part. We built custom tools and they literally change every six

months. This is a nascent industry. When you start looking at the publishing tools and content tools, most are appropriate for preview and publish," he says.

That's a simpler model than what PayPal does, for example, frequently linking new content with new features, he notes. "There was a lot of fear, a lot of people saying, 'Why aren't we being industry standard?' Leverage what you can, but you have to be good at creating your own tools. In the beginning, there was a lot of healthy skepticism, even internally," Mengerink says. "Some of your execs and developers will note that their last company tried to do simultaneous shipping and failed," he says. "Some people in the developer community still don't think it's possible," he adds. "Once it was done, we saw that it's not just manageable, it's a core advantage."

The sooner your company can start working on a SimShip project, the better: "Once you get too big, you can't afford the interrupt to the cycle," he notes.

"Very early on, you have to create the generic structures for the code," he says. "Build every next thing correct."

What's the bottom line for PayPal from Mengerink's team's work? "Today, we have 15 languages, 17 currencies, 190 markets," he says. "Our code base has grown a lot. All of the new code is being built using the right structure. You have to build internationalized." PayPal's re-architected code base now keeps e-commerce humming as the company continues to expand: PayPal's net total payment volume for 2007, the total value of transactions, was $47 billion, a gain of 33 percent over the previous year.

To put that in context, PayPal's net total payment volume for fourth quarter 2007, $14 billion, represented almost 12 percent of U.S. e-commerce, and almost 8 percent of global e-commerce.

Source: Adapted from Laurianne McLaughlin, "How PayPal Keeps e-Commerce Humming in 15 Languages at Once," *CIO Magazine*, March 14, 2008.

CASE STUDY QUESTIONS

1. One of the challenges that PayPal faces now that they have managed to overcome the polylingual obstacle is finding the best way to put this functionality in the hands of the business, so that they do not have to go through IT each time. How do you balance this need for responsiveness and flexibility versus IT's need to keep some degree of control to make sure everything keeps working with everything else? Provide some recommendations to managers who find themselves in this situation.

2. PayPal opted to deviate from industry standards and build their own custom technology that would better suit their needs. When is it a good idea for companies to take this alternative? What issues factor into that decision? Provide a discussion and some examples.

3. Although the new system has been quite successful, PayPal has chosen not to license this technology to others, forgoing a potentially important revenue stream given the lack of good solutions to this problem. Why do you think PayPal chose not to sell this technology? Do you really think this can be made into a strategic advantage over their competitors? How easy would it be for their competitors to imitate this accomplishment?

REAL WORLD ACTIVITIES

1. Choose two or three companies with global operations that interest you and visit their Web sites for countries other than the United States. Even if you are not familiar with the language, do the Web sites have the same look and feel of the U.S. site? In which ways are they similar, and in which ways are they different? If you did not know, would you have guessed it was the same company? Prepare a presentation with screenshots to share your findings with the rest of the class.

2. Although PayPal opted for a centralized approach to keep consistency across Web site appearance and content, other companies let both of these vary for each of the countries in which they operate. When would you use one or the other approach? Would it depend on the company, products offered, markets, countries, or on another factor? Break into small groups with your classmates to discuss these issues.

FIGURE 10.2

An example of systems thinking. You can better understand a sales problem or opportunity by identifying and evaluating the components of a sales system.

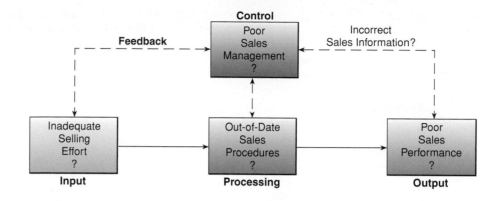

Systems Analysis and Design

The overall process by which information systems are designed and implemented within organizations is referred to as systems analysis and design (SA&D). Within this process are contained activities that include the identification of business problems; the proposed solution, in the form of an information system (IS), to one or more of the problems identified; and the design and implementation of that proposed solution to achieve the desired and stated goals of the organization.

Today, there are many approaches to SA&D. The two most common approaches are **object-oriented analysis and design** and the **life cycle approach.** Although each has its advantages and disadvantages, and the two approaches differ in many respects, they both are concerned with the analysis and design of a successful information system. In most cases, the choice of approach will depend on the type of system under study and the degree to which users are able to specify their needs and requirements clearly. A thorough discussion of both approaches is beyond the scope of this text, but we provide a brief overview of the object-oriented approach, with a focus on the most common method: the life cycle approach.

Along with an overview of the two most common approaches, it is important to note that a wide variety of approaches have been developed over the years to address shortcomings in previous methods. Some claim to shorten cycle time or project length. Others claim to create a parallel tasking environment where multiple steps can be executed simultaneously. Still others focus on improving defect rates in the programming phase of a project. To pay adequate attention to this wide variety of development approaches would take many volumes and is clearly beyond the scope of this text. The good news is that if you understand the basic concepts of the two main development approaches, you can easily understand the nuances in all other approaches. No matter what the name or the approach, the fundamental issues remain the same. This is why we have chosen to focus our attention on the life cycle approach as it lays the foundation for all other approaches.

The Systems Development Life Cycle

One method of using the systems approach to develop information system solutions, and the one that is most prevalent in organization systems analysis and design, can be viewed as a multistep, iterative process called the systems development life cycle (SDLC). Figure 10.3 illustrates what goes on in each stage of this process: (1) investigation, (2) analysis, (3) design, (4) implementation, and (5) maintenance.

It is important to realize, however, that all of the activities involved in the SDLC are highly related and interdependent. Therefore, in actual practice, several developmental activities may be occurring at the same time, and certain activities within a given step may be repeated. Therefore, both users and systems analysts may recycle back at any time to repeat previous activities to modify and improve a system under development. We discuss the activities and products of each step of the systems development cycle in this chapter.

FIGURE 10.3

The traditional information systems development life cycle. Note how the five steps of the cycle are based on the stages of the systems approach. Also note the products that result from each step in the cycle and that you can recycle back to any previous step if more work is needed.

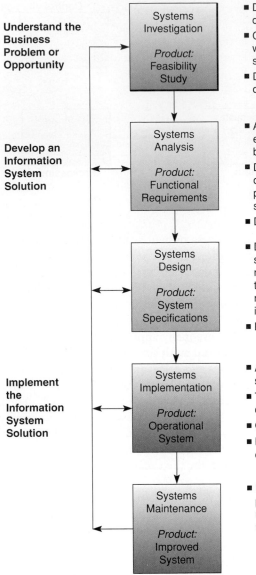

Understand the Business Problem or Opportunity

Systems Investigation

Product: Feasibility Study

- Determine how to address business opportunities and priorities.
- Conduct a feasibility study to determine whether a new or improved business system is a feasible solution.
- Develop a project management plan and obtain management approval.

Develop an Information System Solution

Systems Analysis

Product: Functional Requirements

- Analyze the information needs of employees, customers, and other business stakeholders.
- Develop the functional requirements of a system that can meet business priorities and the needs of all stakeholders.
- Develop logical models of current system.

Systems Design

Product: System Specifications

- Develop specifications for the hardware, software, people, network, and data resources, and the information products that will satisfy the functional requirements of the proposed business information system.
- Develop logical models of new system.

Implement the Information System Solution

Systems Implementation

Product: Operational System

- Acquire (or develop) hardware and software.
- Test the system, and train people to operate and use it.
- Convert to the new business system.
- Manage the effects of system changes on end users.

Systems Maintenance

Product: Improved System

- Use a postimplementation review process to monitor, evaluate, and modify the business system as needed.

Starting the Systems Development Process

Do we have business opportunities? What are our business priorities? How can information technologies provide information system solutions that address our business priorities? These are the questions that have to be answered in the **systems investigation stage**—the first step in the systems development process. This stage may involve consideration of proposals generated by a company's business/IT planning process, which we will discuss in Chapter 12. Typically, the IT function performs feasibility studies to evaluate proposed information system solutions to meet a company's business priorities and opportunities, as identified in its strategic planning process.

Feasibility Studies

Because the process of development can be costly, the systems investigation stage typically requires the development of a feasibility study. At this stage, the feasibility study is a preliminary study that determines the information needs of prospective users and the resource requirements, costs, benefits, and feasibility of a proposed project. Then a team of business professionals and IS specialists might formalize the findings of this study in a written report that includes preliminary specifications and a developmental plan for a proposed business application. If the management of the company approves the recommendations of the feasibility study, the development process can continue.

By design, the preliminary feasibility study of a project is a very rough analysis of its viability that must be continually refined over time. It is, nonetheless, a necessary first step in making the final commitment of organizational resources to the development of the proposed system. In some cases, however, the preliminary feasibility assessment is unnecessary. For extremely small or obvious projects, it may actually represent a waste of valuable time. Also, certain changes in the business environment may dictate the need for change, regardless of the assessed feasibility of such change. If the government changes the tax structure for employee income, an organization has no choice but to make the necessary changes to its payroll system. If a critical program has a major bug in it, the organization has no choice but to address and resolve it. In other words, there is little point in assessing the feasibility of a problem that must be solved. In these cases, the feasibility assessment may be better directed to the analysis of alternative approaches to the solution rather than the problem itself. Regardless, however, the conduct of a thorough preliminary feasibility study should be the default standard in the organization, and a decision to eliminate this first step in the process should always be carefully scrutinized and justified.

Thus, the goal of the preliminary feasibility study is to evaluate alternative system solutions and propose the most feasible and desirable business application for development. The feasibility of a proposed business system can be evaluated in terms of five major categories, as illustrated in Figure 10.4.

Operational Feasibility

The operational feasibility assessment focuses on the degree to which the proposed development project fits with the existing business environment and objectives with regard to development schedule, delivery date, corporate culture, and existing business processes. Furthermore, this assessment determines the degree to which the project meets the specific business objectives set forth during the proposal phase. In the early stages of operational feasibility assessment, we are primarily interested in determining whether the identified problem is worth solving or the proposed solution actually solves the problem at hand. In addition, we must concern ourselves with an initial assessment of **schedule feasibility**—can we identify and solve the problem at

FIGURE 10.4

Operational, economic, technical, human, and legal/political factors. Note that there is more to feasibility than cost savings or the availability of hardware and software.

Operational Feasibility	Economic Feasibility
• How well the proposed system supports the business priorities of the organization • How well the proposed system will solve the identified problem • How well the proposed system will fit with the existing organizational structure	• Cost savings • Increased revenue • Decreased investment requirements • Increased profits • Cost/benefit analysis
Technical Feasibility	**Human Factors Feasibility**
• Hardware, software, and network capability, reliability, and availability	• Employee, customer, supplier acceptance • Management support • Determining the right people for the various new or revised roles
Legal/Political Feasibility	
• Patent, copyright, and licensing • Governmental restrictions • Affected stakeholders and reporting authority	

hand within a reasonable time period? In the latter stages of operational feasibility assessment, such as during the physical design phase of the SDLC, we shift focus to one of strategic fit and organizational impact, such as determining to what degree the proposed physical system will require changes in the organizational structure or what changes in the current spans of authority need to be made to accommodate the new system.

Economic Feasibility

The purpose of the economic feasibility assessment is to determine the extent to which the proposed system will provide positive economic benefits to the organization. This determination involves the identification and quantification of all benefits expected from the system, as well as the explicit identification of all expected costs of the project. In the early stages of the project, it is impossible to define and assess accurately all of the benefits and costs associated with the new system. Thus, the economic feasibility assessment is an ongoing process in which the definable short-term costs are constantly being weighed against the definable long-term benefits. If a project cannot be accurately judged as economically feasible using hard costs, then the project should not proceed, regardless of the other assessment category outcomes.

The assessment of economic feasibility typically involves the preparation of a cost/benefit analysis. If costs and benefits can be quantified with a high degree of certainty, they are referred to as *tangible*; if not, they are called *intangible*. Examples of tangible costs are the costs of hardware and software, employee salaries, and other quantifiable costs needed to develop and implement an IS solution. Intangible costs are difficult to quantify; they include the loss of customer goodwill or employee morale caused by errors and disruptions arising from the installation of a new system.

Tangible benefits are favorable results, such as the decrease in payroll costs caused by a reduction in personnel or a decrease in inventory carrying costs caused by reduction in inventory. Intangible benefits are harder to estimate. Such benefits as better customer service or faster and more accurate information for management fall into this category. Figure 10.5 lists typical tangible and intangible benefits with examples. Possible tangible and intangible costs would be the opposite of each benefit shown.

Technical Feasibility

The assessment of technical feasibility is focused on gaining an understanding of the present technical resources of the organization and their applicability to the expected needs of the proposed system. The analyst must assess the degree to which the current technical resources, including hardware, software, and operating environments, can be upgraded or added to, such that the needs of the proposed system can be met. If the

FIGURE 10.5

Possible benefits of new information systems, with examples. Note that an opposite result for each of these benefits would be a cost or disadvantage of new systems.

Tangible Benefits	Example
• Increase in sales or profits	• Development of IT-based products
• Decrease in information processing costs	• Elimination of unnecessary documents
• Decrease in operating costs	• Reduction in inventory carrying costs
• Decrease in required investment	• Decrease in inventory investment required
• Increased operational efficiency	• Less spoilage, waste, and idle time
Intangible Benefits	**Example**
• Improved information availability	• More timely and accurate information
• Improved abilities in analysis	• OLAP and data mining
• Improved customer service	• More timely service response
• Improved employee morale	• Elimination of burdensome job tasks
• Improved management decision making	• Better information and decision analysis
• Improved competitive position	• Systems that lock in customers
• Improved business image	• Progressive image as perceived by customers, suppliers, and investors

FIGURE 10.6

Examples of how a feasibility study might measure the feasibility of a proposed e-commerce system for a business.

Operational Feasibility	Economic Feasibility
● How well a proposed e-commerce system fits the company's plans for developing Web-based sales, marketing, and financial systems	● Savings in labor costs ● Increased sales revenue ● Decreased investment in inventory ● Increased profits ● Acceptable return on investment

Technical Feasibility	Human Factors Feasibility
● Capability, reliability, and availability of Web store hardware, software, and management services	● Acceptance of employees ● Management support ● Customer and supplier acceptance ● Staff developers have necessary skills

Legal/Political Feasibility

● No patent or copyright violations
● Software licensing for developer side only
● No governmental restrictions
● No changes to existing reporting authority

current technology is deemed sufficient, then the technical feasibility of the project is clear. If this is not the case, however, the analyst must determine whether the technology necessary to meet the stated specifications exists. The danger here is that the project may require technology that does not yet exist in a stable form. Despite the claims of vendors that they can supply whatever is required, the analyst must be able to accurately assess the degree to which the needed technology exists in a form suitable for the proposed project. See Figure 10.6.

Human Factors Feasibility

It is one thing to assess the degree to which a proposed system can work and quite another to evaluate whether the system will work. The human factors feasibility assessment focuses on the most important components of a successful system implementation: the managers and end users. No matter how elegant the technology, the system will not work if the end users and managers do not perceive it to be relevant and therefore do not support it. In this category, we assess the degree of resistance to the proposed system, the perceived role of end users in the development process, the degree of change to the end users' working environment as a result of the new system, and the current state of human resources available to conduct the project and manage and use the system on completion.

Legal/Political Feasibility

This category of assessment is often overlooked during the early stages of project initiation and analysis. The legal/political feasibility of a proposed project includes a thorough analysis of any potential legal ramifications resulting from the construction and implementation of the new system. Such legal issues include copyright or patent infringements, violation of existing antitrust laws (e.g., the antitrust suit brought against Microsoft Corporation over Windows and Internet Explorer by the U.S. Justice Department in 1998), foreign trade restrictions, or any existing contractual obligations of the organization.

The political side of the assessment focuses on gaining an understanding of who the key stakeholders within the organization are and the degree to which the proposed system may positively or negatively affect the distribution of power. Such distribution can have major political repercussions and may cause disruption or failure of an otherwise relevant development effort.

Systems Analysis

What is **systems analysis?** Whether you want to develop a new application quickly or are involved in a long-term project, you will need to perform several basic activities of systems analysis. Many of these activities are extensions of those used in conducting a feasibility study. However, systems analysis is not a preliminary study. It is an in-depth study of end-user information needs that produces *functional requirements* that are used as the basis for the design of a new information system. Systems analysis traditionally involves a detailed study of:

- The information needs of a company and end users like yourself.
- The activities, resources, and products of one or more of the present information systems being used.
- The information system capabilities required to meet your information needs and those of other business stakeholders that may use the system.

Organizational Analysis

An organizational analysis is an important first step in systems analysis. How can people improve an information system if they know very little about the organizational environment in which that system is located? They can't. That's why the members of a development team have to know something about the organization, its management structure, its people, its business activities, the environmental systems it must deal with, and its current information systems. Someone on the team must know this information in more detail for the specific business units or end-user workgroups that will be affected by the new or improved information system being proposed. For example, a new inventory control system for a chain of department stores cannot be designed unless someone on a development team understands a great deal about the company and the types of business activities that affect its inventory. That's why business end users are frequently added to systems development teams.

Analysis of the Present System

Before you design a new system, it is important to study the system that will be improved or replaced (assuming there is one). You need to analyze how this system uses hardware, software, network, and people resources to convert data resources, such as transactions data, into information products, such as reports and displays. Then you should document how the information system activities of input, processing, output, storage, and control are accomplished.

For example, you might evaluate the format, timing, volume, and quality of input and output activities. Such *user interface* activities are vital to effective interaction between end users and a computer-based system. Then, in the systems design stage, you can specify what the resources, products, and activities should be to support the user interface in the system you are designing.

Wal-Mart and Others: Stress-Testing Web Sites for the Holiday Season

What if, in the days leading up to Christmas, a crush of shoppers forced a retailer to lock its doors during peak business hours? Unimaginable—but that's exactly what happened to varying degrees at the Web stores for Wal-Mart, Macy's, and other retailers as the 2006 holiday season got off to a blazing start.

Wal-Mart's failure on Black Friday, the day after Thanksgiving, was the most stunning. Walmart.com was down for a total of about 10 hours that day, according to Internet monitoring firm Keynote Systems, forcing it to greet shoppers at times with a "come back later" notice. "I'm afraid it was too much of a good thing on Friday," a Wal-Mart spokesman said. Wal-Mart expected order activity to be double the level on the previous year's Black Friday, but it came in at seven times the previous year's volume. Wal-Mart had set big online goals for that holiday season, having spent 13 months adding faster checkouts and an interactive toy section, the kind of features it hoped will lure about 300 million visitors. Not if the door's closed they won't.

Macy's site performed poorly for about nine hours on that Black Friday, according to Keynote, and was down for about an hour that day and then again part of the following Tuesday. Zappos' and Foot Locker's sites also had some performance problems. Keynote says most sites, including Wal-Mart's, recovered Monday and didn't have major problems that day.

With the Web bringing in increasingly significant sales, why would retailers drop the ball on site performance? In most cases, they aren't. Many conduct load testing, forecasting, and monitoring using tools from companies such as Keynote and Gomez, and they use content distribution networks to speed performance. They build their e-commerce infrastructures with an eye on performance, with redundancy at common failure points. But sites can still fail.

One reason is that the various teams—marketing, site designers, QA testers—too often aren't watching or sharing the same metrics, says Matthew Poepsel, VP of professional services at Gomez. If groups worry only about their metrics—marketing pushes a promotion, for instance, without being sure site design and capacity can handle it—you have "individual success but collective failure," he says. When a problem hits, Poepsel says, 80% of the recovery time is spent identifying the problem. "Once you know what the problem is, you can get it fixed pretty quickly, unless it's a sheer bandwidth issue and you need to cut a new contract," he says.

Customers are ruthlessly unforgiving of poor performance. In a Gomez survey of 1,173 online shoppers, 53% say they'll switch to a competitor if a site takes too long to load, and 21% will call customer service. When testing their systems for load capacity in preparation for Black Friday, retailers typically used twice the capacity their sites had on the same day last year, says Keynote, which equates that level to a 600% increase over an average shopping day outside of the holidays.

Stores that kept their sites up did blockbuster business. However, when a major competitor's site fails, others pick up a rush of new customers that stresses their sites. There's less time than ever to react to shifts in traffic, too.

Source: Adapted from Mary Hayes Weier, "Opening Holiday Weeks Show Uptime Isn't Easy For Online Retailers," *InformationWeek*, December 4, 2006.

Logical Analysis

One of the primary activities that occurs during the analysis phase is the construction of a logical model of the current system. The logical model can be thought of as a blueprint of the current system that displays only *what* the current system does without regard to *how* it does it. By constructing and analyzing a logical model of the current system, a systems analyst can more easily understand the various processes, functions, and data associated with the system without getting bogged down with all the issues surrounding the hardware or the software. Also, by creating a logical model, the various noncomputer components of a system can be incorporated, analyzed, and understood. For example, in the physical version of a system, a person's inbox may be the location where new orders are stored until they have been entered into the computer. In the logical model, that inbox is treated just like a computer hard drive or other electronic storage media. In a logical sense, it is just another place to store data.

Functional Requirements Analysis and Determination

This step of systems analysis is one of the most difficult. You may need to work as a team with IS analysts and other end users to determine your specific business information needs. For example, first you need to determine what type of information each business activity requires; what its format, volume, and frequency should be; and what response times are necessary. Second, you must try to determine the information processing capabilities required for each system activity (input, processing, output, storage, control) to meet these information needs. *As with the construction of the logical model, your main goal is to identify what should be done, not how to do it.*

FIGURE 10.7

Examples of functional requirements for a proposed e-commerce system for a business.

Examples of Functional Requirements
● **User Interface Requirements** Automatic entry of product data and easy-to-use data entry screens for Web customers.
● **Processing Requirements** Fast, automatic calculation of sales totals and shipping costs.
● **Storage Requirements** Fast retrieval and update of data from product, pricing, and customer databases.
● **Control Requirements** Signals for data entry errors and quick e-mail confirmation for customers.

When this step of the life cycle is complete, a set of functional requirements for the proposed new system will exist. Functional requirements are end-user information requirements that are not tied to the hardware, software, network, data, and people resources that end users presently use or might use in the new system. That is left to the design stage to determine. For example, Figure 10.7 shows examples of functional requirements for a proposed e-commerce application for a business.

Systems Design

Once the analysis portion of the life cycle is complete, the process of **systems design** can begin. Here is where the logical model of the current system is modified until it represents the blueprint for the new system. This version of the logical model represents what the new system will do. During the **physical design** portion of this step, users and analysts focus on determining *how* the system will accomplish its objectives. This point is where issues related to hardware, software, networking, data storage, security, and many others will be discussed and determined. As such, systems design consists of design activities that ultimately produce physical system specifications satisfying the functional requirements that were developed in the systems analysis process.

A useful way to look at systems design is illustrated in Figure 10.8. This concept focuses on three major products, or *deliverables*, that should result from the design stage. In this framework, systems design consists of three activities: user interface, data, and process design. This framework results in specifications for user interface methods and products, database structures, and processing and control procedures.

Prototyping

During the design phase, the development process frequently takes the form of, or includes, a *prototyping* approach. Prototyping is the rapid development and testing of working models, or **prototypes,** of new applications in an interactive, iterative

FIGURE 10.8 Systems design can be viewed as the design of user interfaces, data, and processes.

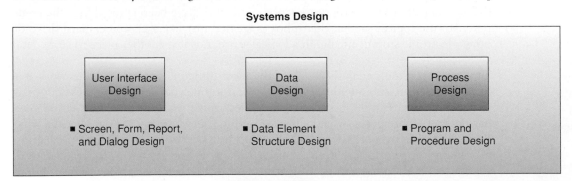

Systems Design

- User Interface Design
  - ■ Screen, Form, Report, and Dialog Design
- Data Design
  - ■ Data Element Structure Design
- Process Design
  - ■ Program and Procedure Design

process that can be used by both IS specialists and business professionals. Prototyping, as a development tool, makes the development process faster and easier, especially for projects for which end-user requirements are hard to define. Prototyping has also opened up the application development process to end users because it simplifies and accelerates systems design. Thus prototyping has enlarged the role of the business stakeholders affected by a proposed system and helps enable a quicker and more responsive development process called *agile systems development* (ASD). See Figure 10.9.

The Prototyping Process

Prototyping can be used for both large and small applications. Typically, large business systems still require using a traditional systems development approach, but parts of such systems can frequently be prototyped. A prototype of a business application needed by an end user is developed quickly using a variety of application development software tools. The prototype system is then repeatedly refined until it is acceptable.

As Figure 10.9 illustrates, prototyping is an iterative, interactive process. End users with sufficient experience with application development tools can do prototyping themselves. Alternatively, you could work with an IS specialist to develop a prototype system in a series of interactive sessions. For example, you could develop, test, and refine prototypes of management reports, data entry screens, or output displays.

Usually, a prototype is modified several times before end users find it acceptable. Program modules are then generated by application development software using conventional programming languages. The final version of the application system is turned over to its end users for operational use. Although prototyping is a useful method of allowing an end user to develop small software applications, its real power is as a development tool, within a life cycle project, to assist analysts and users in finalizing the

FIGURE 10.9

Application development using prototyping. Note how prototyping combines the steps of the systems development cycle and changes the traditional roles of IS specialists and end users.

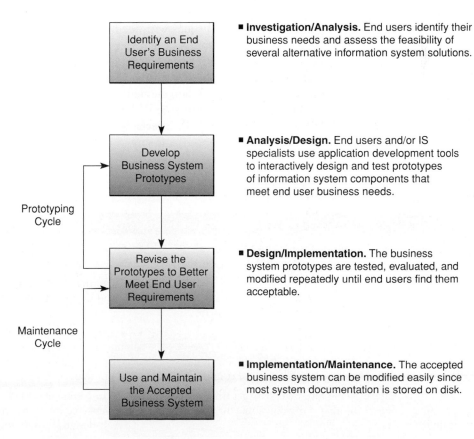

FIGURE 10.10

An example of a typical application of prototyping during a software development project.

Example of Prototyping Development
● **Team.** A few end users and IS developers form a team to develop a business application.
● **Schematic.** The initial prototype schematic design is developed.
● **Prototype.** The schematic is converted into a simple point-and-click prototype using prototyping tools.
● **Presentation.** A few screens and routine linkages are presented to users.
● **Feedback.** After the team gets feedback from users, the prototype is reiterated.
● **Reiteration.** Further presentations and reiterations are made.
● **Consultation.** Consultations are held with IT consultants to identify potential improvements and conformance to existing standards.
● **Completion.** The prototype is used as a model to create a finished application.
● **Acceptance.** Users review and sign off on their acceptance of the new business system.
● **Installation.** The new business software is installed on network servers.

various interfaces and functions of a large business system. Figure 10.10 outlines a typical prototyping-based systems development process for a business application.

User Interface Design

Let's take a closer look at user interface design, because it is the system component closest to business end users and the one they will most likely help design. The user interface design activity focuses on supporting the interactions between end users and their computer-based applications. Designers concentrate on the design of attractive and efficient forms of user input and output, such as easy-to-use Internet or intranet Web pages.

As we mentioned previously, user interface design is frequently a *prototyping* process, in which working models or prototypes of user interface methods are designed and modified several times with feedback from end users. The user interface design process produces detailed design specifications for information products such as display screens, interactive user/computer dialogues (including the sequence or flow of dialogue), audio responses, forms, documents, and reports. Figure 10.11 gives examples of user interface design elements and other guidelines suggested for the multimedia Web pages of e-commerce Web sites. Figure 10.12 presents actual before and after screen displays of the user interface design process for a work scheduling application of State Farm Insurance Company.

FIGURE 10.11   Useful guidelines for the design of business Web sites.

Checklist for Corporate Web Sites	
● **Remember the Customer.** Successful Web sites are built solely for the customer, not to make company vice presidents happy.	● **Searchability.** Many sites have their own search engines; very few are actually useful. Make sure yours is.
● **Aesthetics.** Successful designs combine fast-loading graphics and simple color palettes for pages that are easy to read.	● **Incompatibilities.** A site that looks great on a PC using Internet Explorer can often look miserable on an iBook running Netscape.
● **Broadband Content.** The Web's coolest stuff can't be accessed by most Web surfers. Including a little streaming video isn't bad, but don't make it the focus of your site.	● **Registration Forms.** Registration forms are a useful way to gather customer data. But make your customers fill out a three-page form, and watch them flee.
● **Easy to Navigate.** Make sure it's easy to get from one part of your site to another. Providing a site map, accessible from every page, helps.	● **Dead Links.** Dead links are the bane of all Web surfers—be sure to keep your links updated. Many Web-design software tools can now do this for you.

FIGURE 10.12   An example of the user interface design process. State Farm developers changed this work scheduling and assignment application's interface after usability testing showed that end users working with the old interface (at left) didn't realize that they had to follow a six-step process. If users jumped to a new page out of order, they would lose their work. The new interface (at right) made it clearer that a process had to be followed.

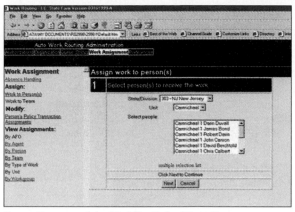

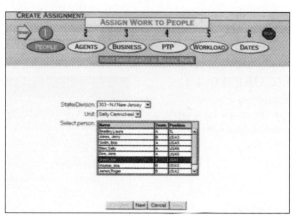

Source: Courtesy of the Usability Lab of State Farm.

Google's Interface: Balancing Freedom and Consistency	For most people, including its own executives, Google still means search. On both the query page and the results pages, design flourishes have been legendarily kept to a minimum, with layout decisions based on what will provide the user with the fastest, most efficient service. Nonetheless, engineers and analysts pore over streams of data to assess the impact of experiments with colors, shading, and the position of every element on the page. Even changes at the pixel level can affect revenue.

But as Google products proliferate beyond search, design decisions become more critical if the company wants a coherent brand image. "More than anything, Google prefers to make design decisions based on what performs well. And as a company, Google cares about being fast, so we want our user experience to be fast," says Irene Au, Google's director of user experience. That's not just in terms of front-end latency—how long it takes the page to download—it's also about making people use their computers more efficiently. "A lot of our design decisions are really driven by cognitive psychology research that shows that, say, people online read black text against a white background much faster than white against black, or that sans serif fonts are more easily read than serif fonts online," says Au.

Google has a big culture of being bottom-up and that can make it difficult to get a coherent design experience. There's a federation of people doing whatever they think is best for their product and not looking out for the bigger picture. "We don't want everything to be dictated and top-down, but we do want to find a balance," says Au. "For example, Google apps all look different from each other. As you move from one app to another, the keyboard shortcuts are different, the save model is different.

The interaction consistency is not there. For good reason: "These were all different startups using different backends. But we're trying to pull all that together. More and more, these experiences are going to get integrated with each other, or there'll be reusable components that might be built for applications but also appear in a search experience. It's becoming increasingly critical for us to have common UIs [user interfaces] and common infrastructure," she notes.

At Google, there's top-down support for consistency, but not a mandate. But middle layers of management are hearing loud and clear from Larry Page and Sergey Brin and the executives that there should be one way to do things.

"Inconsistency drives Larry and Sergey crazy. So there's growing appreciation and awareness and with that comes motivation. As a group, we're trying to be very opportunistic and pragmatic. The design team has to be a few steps out—we're designing the target for all the different products to converge towards," says Au.

Source: Adapted from Helen Walters, "Google's Irene Au: On Design Challenges," *BusinessWeek Online*, March 18, 2009.

FIGURE 10.13

Examples of system specifications for a new e-commerce system for a business.

Examples of System Specifications
● **User Interface Specifications** Use personalized screens that welcome repeat Web customers and make product recommendations.
● **Database Specifications** Develop databases that use object/relational database management software to organize access to all customer and inventory data and to multimedia product information.
● **Software Specifications** Acquire an e-commerce software engine to process all e-commerce transactions with fast responses—that is, retrieve necessary product data and compute all sales amounts in less than one second.
● **Hardware and Network Specifications** Install redundant networked Web servers and sufficient high-bandwidth telecommunications lines to host the company e-commerce Web site.
● **Personnel Specifications** Hire an e-commerce manager and specialists and a Webmaster and Web designer to plan, develop, and manage e-commerce operations.

System Specifications

System specifications formalize the design of an application's user interface methods and products, database structures, and processing and control procedures. Therefore, systems designers frequently develop hardware, software, network, data, and personnel specifications for a proposed system. Figure 10.13 shows examples of system specifications that could be developed for an e-commerce system of a company.

End-User Development

In a traditional systems development cycle, your role as a business end user is similar to that of a customer or a client. Typically, you make a request for a new or improved system, answer questions about your specific information needs and information processing problems, and provide background information on your existing business systems. Then IS professionals work with you to analyze your problem and suggest alternative solutions. When you approve the best alternative, it is designed and implemented. Here again, you may be involved in a prototyping design process or be on an implementation team with IS specialists.

However, in end-user development, IS professionals play a consulting role while you do your own application development. Sometimes a staff of user consultants may be available to help you and other end users with your application development efforts. This help may include training in the use of application packages; selection of hardware and software; assistance in gaining access to organization databases; and, of course, assistance in analysis, design, and implementing the business application of IT that you need.

Focus on IS Activities

It is important to remember that end-user development should focus on the fundamental activities of any information system: input, processing, output, storage, and control, as we described in Chapter 1. Figure 10.14 illustrates these system components and the questions they address.

FIGURE 10.14   End-user development should focus on the basic information processing activity components of an information system.

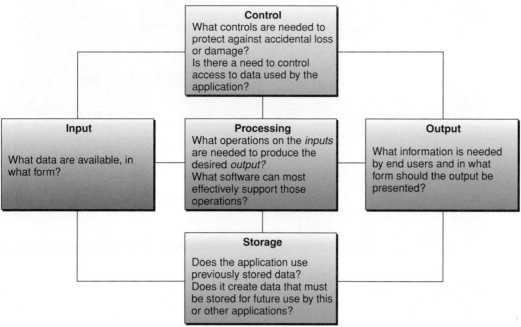

Source: Adapted from James N. Morgan, *Application Cases in MIS*, 4th ed. (New York: Irwin/McGraw-Hill, 2002), p. 31.

In analyzing a potential application, you should focus first on the *output* to be produced by the application. What information is needed, and in what form should it be presented? Next, look at the *input* data to be supplied to the application. What data are available? From what sources? In what form? Then you should examine the *processing* requirements. What operations or transformation processes will be required to convert the available inputs into the desired output? Among software packages the developer is able to use, which package can best perform the operations required?

You may find that the desired output cannot be produced from the inputs that are available. If this is the case, you must either make adjustments to the output expected or find additional sources of input data, including data stored in files and databases from external sources. The *storage* component will vary in importance in end-user applications. For example, some applications require extensive use of stored data or the creation of data that must be stored for future use. These are better suited for database management development projects than for spreadsheet applications.

Necessary *control* measures for end-user applications vary greatly depending on the scope and duration of the application, the number and nature of the users of the application, and the nature of the data involved. For example, control measures are needed to protect against accidental loss or damage to end-user files. The most basic protection against this type of loss is simply to make backup copies of application files on a frequent and systematic basis. Another example is the cell protection feature of spreadsheets that protects key cells from accidental erasure by users.

Doing End-User Development

In end-user development, you and other business professionals can develop new or improved ways to perform your jobs without the direct involvement of IS specialists. The application development capabilities built into a variety of end-user software packages have made it easier for many users to develop their own computer-based solutions. For example, Figure 10.15 illustrates a Web site development tool you could use to help you develop, update, and manage an intranet Web site for your business

FIGURE 10.15
Microsoft FrontPage is an example of an easy-to-use end-user Web site development tool.

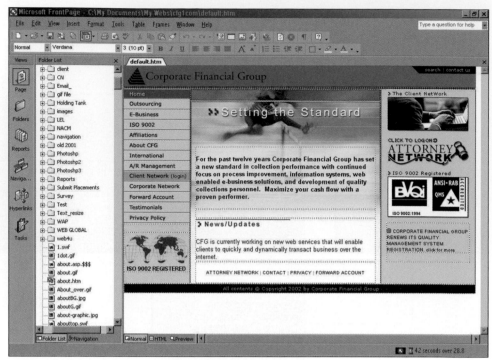

Source: Courtesy of Microsoft®.

unit. Or you might use an electronic spreadsheet package as a tool to develop an easy way to analyze weekly sales results for the sales managers in a company. Or you could use a Web site development package to design Web pages for a small business Web store or a departmental intranet Web site. Many companies are encouraging business end users to do their own Web site development. See Figure 10.16.

Blue Prism: "Shadow" IT is Becoming More Pervasive	Businesses increasingly accept the existence of a "shadow" IT culture, in which end users install uncontrolled rogue technology to make good the shortcomings of over-stretched IT departments. Rogue IT includes users who install software or tamper with existing software or macros without the IT department's consent, according to a survey by integration specialist Blue Prism. Budget and resource constraints often lead to elements of rogue behavior, reported by 67 percent of respondents to the survey. Twenty-four percent believed that rogue IT isn't used in their organizations, and 10 percent admitted that they didn't know.

These systems are not necessarily simple variations on the Excel spreadsheet. On the contrary, they can be very sophisticated—rivaling and even exceeding any technological solution produced by IT departments. Such systems range from consumer solutions like Google Apps to highly tailored ones. It seems that end users are increasingly aware nowadays that their IT department cannot always deliver a practical solution for their needs, which can lead to the creation of a shadow IT culture within an organization, whereby users actively install their own applications or find their own workaround solutions in order to do their day-to-day job.

This is often because IT departments have to manage business-critical projects, sometimes at the expense of helping business users with tactical change requests.

Indeed, more than 52 percent reported that working on strategic projects was the main focus for their department, with 40 percent saying that delivering day-to-day business change requests was their priority.

The Blue Prism survey, however, also challenges the traditional perception that IT departments frown upon rogue behavior by users. The survey concludes that many IT departments fully understand why pockets of rogue behavior exist, and it reveals that these departments were equally pragmatic when asked for the best way of dealing with it.

With this change in the relationship between end users and technology, the IT department's singular claim to technology knowledge is disappearing, and with it, its position of power. The more technologists try to counter this effect by enforcing the old ways, the more defunct and isolated they will become; their decisions will be ignored and their solutions will be unused.

One of the primary reasons shadow systems succeed is that people at the front-lines of organizations need them.

They know that when they have a problem and when they find a solution that works well for them, their needs are met. IT departments, on the other hand, focus too strongly on the technology to solve a problem rather than on the problem itself—to the extent that when end users do not use officially sanctioned solutions, IT may proceed on radical search-and-destroy missions of user-created systems. In doing so, it ignores why the user did not use its solutions in the first place and, in effect, it destroys one of the few sources of IT strategic and competitive advantage an organization has.

Source: Adapted from Tom Jowitt, "'Shadow IT Culture' on the Rise for Businesses," *CIO Magazine*, July 5, 2007; and Sandy Behrens, "Time to Rethink Your Relationship with End Users," *CIO Magazine*, July 24, 2007.

FIGURE 10.16

How companies are encouraging and managing intranet Web site development by business end users.

Encouraging End-User Web Development
● **Look for Tools that Make Sense** Some Web development tools may be more powerful and more costly than what your business end users really need.
● **Spur Creativity** Consider a competition among business departments for the best Web site to help spur users to more creative uses of their intranet sites.
● **Set Some Limits** Yes, you have to keep some control. Consider putting limits on exactly what parts of a Web page users can change and who can change what pages. You still want some consistency across the organization.
● **Give Managers Responsibility** Make business unit managers sign off on who will be Web publishing from their groups, and make the managers personally responsible for the content that goes on their Web sites. That will help prevent the publishing of inappropriate content by some users.
● **Make Users Comfortable** Training users well on the tools will help them become confident in their ability to properly manage and update their sites—and save IT the trouble of fixing problems later on or providing continuous support for minor problems.

Technical Note: Overview of Object-Oriented Analysis and Design

As stated at the beginning of this chapter, there are two common approaches to analysis and design: SDLC and object-oriented. Whereas the SDLC remains the predominant approach to software development, the object-oriented approach is gaining favor, particularly among programmers focusing on complex systems that require handling a wide variety of complex data structures, such as audio, video, images, documents, Web pages, and other types of data.

We introduced the concepts of objects and object oriented databases in Chapter 5. Thorough coverage of the object-oriented approach to analysis and design is beyond the scope of this text, but a brief overview is presented here. Let's begin with a simple definition of anything object-oriented.

An **object-oriented system** is composed of *objects*. An object can be anything a programmer wants to manage or manipulate—cars, people, animals, savings accounts, food products, business units, organizations, customers—literally anything. Once an object is defined by a programmer, its characteristics can be used to allow one object to interact with another object or pass information to another object. The behavior of an object-oriented system entails collaboration between these objects, and the state of the system is the combined state of all the objects in it.

Collaboration between objects requires them to send messages or information to one another. The exact semantics of message sending between objects varies, depending on the kind of system being modeled. In some systems, "sending a message" is the same as "invoking a method." In others, "sending a message" might involve sending data using a pre-prescribed media. The three areas of interest to us in an object-oriented system are object-oriented programming, object-oriented analysis, and object-oriented design.

Object-oriented programming (OOP) is the programming paradigm that uses "objects" to design applications and computer programs. It employs several techniques from previously established paradigms, including

- **Inheritance.** The ability of one object to inherit the characteristics of a higher-order object. For example, all cars have wheels; therefore, an object defined as a *sports car* and as a special type of the object *cars* must also have wheels.

- **Modularity.** The extent to which a program is designed as series of interlinked yet stand-alone modules.

- **Polymorphism.** The ability of an object to behave differently depending on the conditions in which its behavior is invoked. For example, two objects that inherit the behavior *speak* from an object class *animal* might be a dog object and a cat object. Both have a behavior defined as *speak*. When the dog object is commanded to speak, it will *bark*, whereas when the cat object is commanded to speak, it will *meow*.

- **Encapsulation.** Concealing all of the characteristics associated with a particular object inside the object itself. This paradigm allows objects to inherit characteristics simply by defining a subobject. For example, the object *airplane* contains all of the characteristics of an airplane: wings, tail, rudder, pilot, speed, altitude, and so forth.

Even though it originated in the 1960s, OOP was not commonly used in mainstream software application development until the 1990s. Today, many popular programming languages (e.g., ActionScript, Ada 95/2005, C#, C++, Delphi, Java, JavaScript, Lisp, Objective-C, Perl, PHP, Python, RealBasic, Ruby, Squeak, VB.Net, Visual FoxPro, and Visual Prolog) support OOP.

Object-oriented analysis (OOA) aims to model *the problem domain*, that is, the problem we want to solve, by developing an object-oriented (OO) system. The source of the analysis is a set of written requirement statements and/or diagrams that illustrates the statements.

Similar to the SDLC-developed model, an object-oriented analysis model does not take into account implementation constraints, such as concurrency, distribution, persistence, or inheritance, nor how the system will be built. Because object-oriented systems are modular, the model of a system can be divided into multiple domains, each of which are separately analyzed and represent separate business, technological, or conceptual areas of interest. The result of object-oriented analysis is a description of what is to be built, using concepts and relationships between concepts, often expressed as a conceptual model. Any other documentation needed to describe what is to be built is also included in the result of the analysis.

Object-oriented design (OOD) describes the activity when designers look for logical solutions to solve a problem using objects. Object-oriented design takes the conceptual model that results from the object-oriented analysis and adds implementation constraints imposed by the environment, the programming language, and the chosen tools, as well as architectural assumptions chosen as the basis of the design.

The concepts in the conceptual model are mapped to concrete classes, abstract interfaces, and roles that the objects take in various situations. The interfaces and their implementations for stable concepts can be made available as reusable services. Concepts identified as unstable in object-oriented analysis will form the basis for policy classes that make decisions and implement environment or situation-specific logics or algorithms. The result of the object-oriented design is a detailed description of how the system can be built, using objects.

Thus, the object-oriented world bears many similarities to the more conventional SDLC approach. This approach simply takes a different view of the programming domain and thus approaches the problem-solving activities inherent in system development from a different direction.

In the next section, we will continue looking at systems development by changing our focus from design to implementation.

SECTION II Implementing Business Systems

Implementation

Once a new information system has been designed, it must be implemented as a working system and maintained to keep it operating properly. The implementation process we will cover in this section follows the investigation, analysis, and design stages of the systems development cycle we discussed in Section I. Implementation is a vital step in the deployment of information technology to support the employees, customers, and other business stakeholders of a company.

Read the Real World Case on the next page. We can learn a lot from this case about the challenges companies face in implementing the changes needed for new IT-based business initiatives. See Figure 10.17.

Implementing New Systems

Figure 10.18 illustrates that the systems implementation stage involves hardware and software acquisition, software development, testing of programs and procedures, conversion of data resources, and a variety of conversion alternatives. It also involves the education and training of end users and specialists who will operate a new system.

Implementation can be a difficult and time-consuming process. However, it is vital in ensuring the success of any newly developed system, for even a well-designed system will fail if it is not properly implemented. That is why the implementation process typically requires a **project management** effort on the part of IT and business unit managers. They must enforce a project plan that includes job responsibilities, timelines for major stages of development, and financial budgets. This plan is necessary if a project is to be completed on time and within its established budget while still meeting its design objectives. Figure 10.19 illustrates the activities and timelines that might be required to implement an intranet for a new employee benefits system in the human resource department of a company.

Project Portfolio Management: Shoot the Bad Projects, Keep the Good Ones

IT departments are either the darlings or the despised of corporate America, and some practitioners would debate which extreme causes the most pain. Let's face it; nowadays the reward for doing a great job is more work. Once an IT group earns the trust of business units, it must then survive the onslaught of new projects. Good organizations, like good bosses, don't want you to take on more than you can handle and collapse in the process.

Smart organizations have a grip on project portfolio management (PPM) and are willing to prioritize and, when needed, end projects when they turn bad. Like risk management, PPM is nothing new for mature disciplines. "We've picked up where construction and engineers have been for years," says John Nahm, an IT project manager for the state of Virginia.

The highest performers in the IT world, as defined in a recent study by the IT Process Institute, are those most likely to cancel projects—at a rate double that of their lower-performing counterparts, in fact. "It's counterintuitive until you think about it," says Kurt Milne, managing director of the institute. The business world is accustomed to trying new initiatives but being willing to move on if they don't work. But, as Milne points out, in IT there's value in stability, so we're hesitant to pull the trigger. "I don't know that that's a skill that IT folks think they need to have, but logically, it makes sense to shoot your bad projects and move on."

Line-of-business executives understand capacity planning and prioritization, Milne says, but they expect these choices to be presented in business language.

(text continues on page 429)

REAL WORLD CASE 2

Blue Cross and Blue Shield and Others: Understanding the Science behind Change

Kevin Sparks has been trying to get his staff to change the way it monitors and supports the data center for the past year, but he hasn't been getting anywhere.

Not that he's getting resistance—at least not overtly. His staffers at Blue Cross and Blue Shield of Kansas City agree that installing automated monitoring software, along with a centralized control room and a set of standard processes for responding to problems, would be more efficient than the way they deal with things now, which is mostly through ad hoc heroism.

"Logic always prevails and everyone will agree—at the intellectual level—that we need to change things," says Sparks, who is vice president and CIO. Then he finds himself surrounded by empty chairs at meetings while the people who should be sitting there are off fighting the latest fire.

"I tell them I need them at the meetings and if we changed things they'd have the time to be there. But things always break down when we talk about taking monitoring out of their hands through automation," Sparks says.

To help his staff accept the new processes, Sparks says he's taken layoffs off the table, even though the proposed automation and process efficiencies could reduce the need for bodies. The change is part of a larger effort to implement the IT Infrastructure Library (ITIL) process framework to improve overall productivity. "I don't want fewer people; I want the ones I have to do more things," he says, sighing with frustration.

In other words, Sparks's staff doesn't seem to have any logical reason for resisting the changes; but before you dismiss them as a bunch of inflexible, fearful losers, know this: They are you, and you are them.

FIGURE 10.17

Understanding the science behind change and resistance can lead to more effective approaches to foster involvement and smooth out transitions to new systems.

Maybe your resistance to change manifests itself in a different way or in a different setting; for example, it might be a refusal to throw away that old slide rule, to look while the nurse draws your blood, or to dance at weddings. We all refuse to change our ways. This happens for reasons that are often hard to articulate, until you begin to look at it from a scientific perspective. In the past few years, improvements in brain analysis technology have allowed researchers to track the energy of a thought coursing through the brain in much the same way that they can track blood flowing through the circulatory system.

These advances are bringing a much-needed hard foundation of science to a leadership challenge that to CIOs has long seemed hopelessly soft and poorly defined: change management. Pictures of the brain show that our responses to change are predictable and universal.

From a neurological perspective, we all respond to change in the same way: We try to avoid it. Yet understanding the brain's chemistry and mechanics has led to insights that can help CIOs ameliorate the pain of change and improve people's abilities to adapt to new ways of doing things.

Change hurts. Not the boo-hoo, woe-is-me kind of hurt that executives tend to dismiss as an affliction of the weak and sentimental, but actual physical and psychological discomfort.

The brain pictures actually prove it. Change lights up an area of the brain, the prefrontal cortex, which is like RAM memory in a PC. The prefrontal cortex is fast and agile, able to hold multiple threads of logic at once to enable quick calculations. Like RAM, the prefrontal cortex's capacity is finite; it can deal comfortably with only a handful of concepts before bumping up against limits. That bump generates a palpable sense of discomfort, producing fatigue and even anger.

Resistance to change is not inevitable. The prefrontal cortex has its limitations, but it is also capable of insight and self-control. The ability to be aware of our habitual impulses and do something about them is what makes us human.

"The prefrontal cortex is extremely influential in our behavior, but it does not have to be completely determinative," says Jeffrey M. Schwartz, research psychiatrist at the School of Medicine at the University of California at Los Angeles. "We can make decisions about how much we want to be influenced by our animal biology."

Unfortunately, traditional change management tactics are based more in animal training than in human psychology. Leaders promise bonuses and promotions to those who go along with the change (the carrot), and they punish those who don't with less important work and the potential loss of their jobs (the stick). "The carrot-and-stick approach works at the systemwide level—offering cash bonuses to the sales department to increase the number of customers in Latin America will get you more customers there, for example—but at a personal level it doesn't work," says David Rock, founder and CEO of Results Coaching Systems, a consulting firm. "Our personal motivations are too complex, and you can only offer so many raises."

Patience is critical, says Rock. "You have to paint a broad picture of change and resist the urge to fill in all the gaps for people," he says.

"They have to fill them in on their own. If you get too detailed, it prevents people from making the connections on their own." Leaving holes in any plan is especially hard for CIOs, who tend to be ambitious and process-oriented, which means they have thought out all the details involved in a strategy or systems change and believe they know all the steps required to get there. In general, they're bursting with the need to tell everyone exactly how to do it.

"When I put out change proposals, it's obvious to me why we should be changing, so when people resist I tend to get more aggressive in trying to convince them," says Matt Miszewski, CIO of the state of Wisconsin. "But we lose people in that situation. The more we try to explain things, the more dug in they get."

To try to focus people's attention on personal insight and change their behavior, Rock uses the same technique that psychoanalysts have used since the profession began: He asks questions. "When you ask someone questions, you are getting them to focus on an idea," he says. "When you pay more attention to something, you make more connections in the brain." Rock also says that asking questions gets people to voice their ideas. "The best way to get people to change is to lay out the objective in basic terms and then ask them how they would go about getting there," Rock says.

One of the biggest mistakes that leaders, like CIOs, make in trying to win over the skeptical middle is assuming that everyone is motivated by ambition, as many CIOs are. Many people, especially IT professionals, are motivated as much or more by the work they do (e.g., the craft of software development) as they are by the opportunity to move up in the hierarchy. "There are a lot of people who don't want to be king or queen," says Michael Wakefield, senior enterprise associate at the Center for Creative Leadership, a consulting firm. "That's difficult for people to reveal because they fear their bosses will start to question their courage and commitment." If these people don't see an opportunity to maintain their allegiance to the work they love as part of a change, they won't see the benefit of going along. They will remain skeptical or, worse, move into the camp of active resisters.

One of the best ways to bring the skeptics around is through learning.

At the New York State Workers' Compensation Board, a change readiness survey of employees at the beginning of an effort to shift compensation cases from paper folders to electronic files found that employees' number-one demand was for training. "They wanted reassurance that we weren't going to ask them to do something new without giving them the support they needed to do it," says Nancy Mulholland, who is deputy executive director and CIO of the Workers' Compensation Board.

Change management is time-consuming and hard to quantify for process-oriented CIOs. Yet avoiding the challenge leads to failure. "Anybody can stick $2,000 in someone's face to get them to finish a job, but it's the people who can inspire others to follow them that are the most successful in the long run," says Richard Toole, who is CIO for PharMerica, a pharmacy services company. "The soft stuff is important," but inspiring others to change isn't a matter of charisma or charm, say the experts.

Sparks's latest tactic for engaging his staff's prefrontal cortexes was to bring in an outside consultant to discuss the IT Infrastructure Library program and to field concerns. "We had an outstanding instructor, and she was able to address many of the questions people had," recalls Sparks. "I could begin to see the lights come on in some of the skeptics. After a long meeting, one of my people stood up and said, 'You know, we should have started working on this [automated monitoring] six months ago.'"

Source: Adapted from Christopher Koch, "Change Management—Understanding the Science of Change," *CIO Magazine*, September 15, 2006.

CASE STUDY QUESTIONS

1. Although a very detailed change proposal may prevent people from making their own connections, as discussed in the case, it may lead others to consider the proposal to be vague and unfinished. How do you balance these two concerns? What guidelines would you use to ensure that you are not veering too far off in either direction?

2. Kevin Sparks of Blue Cross and Blue Shield of Kansas City had a difficult time convincing his people of the need for change. What would you have suggested that he should do before you read the case? What about afterward? How did your recommendations change as a result?

3. Organizational change goes beyond promotions and the threat of layoffs. What ways other than those discussed in the case would you use to entice people to embrace proposed changes? Provide several suggestions and justify their rationale.

REAL WORLD ACTIVITIES

1. Search the Internet for examples of recent successful and failed IT implementations. What was the role of employee involvement and resistance in each one of those? What strategies did companies use to manage the change process, and how much success did they have in doing so? Prepare a report to share your findings with the class.

2. Break into small groups to discuss what change management strategies and tactics you would use to ensure a smooth transition, either at a company you are familiar with or at one you know about from previous research for this or another class. How would you achieve a good balance between positive and negative consequences, as well as involvement in the process? Choose one of your members to share your insights with the rest of the class.

FIGURE 10.18 An overview of the implementation process. Implementation activities are needed to transform a newly developed information system into an operational system for end users.

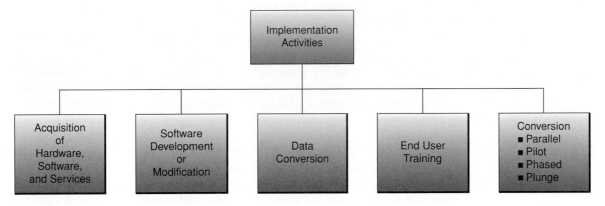

What they don't understand is when IT overpromises and then underdelivers, failing to meet deadlines or not completing a project. Unless IT becomes skilled at PPM, we'll never close this credibility gap.

Once you put a process in place, the other P-word—politics—will inevitably appear. The magic behind PPM is that, when you do it right, it becomes clear why a given project shouldn't get done in the context of your overall IT governance strategy. Consider the following situation: Your portfolio management process comes up with a "not now" or a "no" for a business unit's project, but the business unit (which has its own budget and a degree of autonomy) moves ahead without IT's approval; this rogue project then creates urgent unplanned work for IT as the improperly planned technology spirals out of control or fails to integrate with enterprise systems. What do you do in this case?

ITPI's Milne answers this question with a question: "How do you handle it when your corporate strategy says, 'We're not going into the Latin America market,' and a line business does it anyway?" If your PPM process is sufficiently integrated into executive corporate strategy, units that are totally out of line will not need to be nailed by IT; the organization will rein them in, with or without IT's participation.

Source: Adapted from Jonathan Feldman, "Project Management Keeps IT from Being a Victim of Success," *InformationWeek*, April 5, 2008.

FIGURE 10.19

An example of the implementation process activities and timelines for a company installing an intranet-based employee benefits system in its human resource management department.

Intranet Implementation Activities	Month 1	Month 2	Month 3	Month 4
Acquire and install server hardware and software	■			
Train administrators	■			
Acquire and install browser software	■	■		
Acquire and install publishing software	■			
Train benefits employees on publishing software	■			
Convert benefits manuals and add revisions	■			
Create Web-based tutorials for the intranet		■	■	
Hold rollout meetings				■

Project Management

Any discussion of information systems design and development would be incomplete without including a discussion of basic project management concepts, techniques, and tools. So, before we progress any further into our discussion of implementation, we need to understand how our project got to this point, hopefully on time and on budget. Although a thorough discussion of project management is far beyond the scope of this text, we can nonetheless look at the big picture and acquaint ourselves with the necessary steps in the process. It is important to note that the skills and knowledge necessary to be a good project manager will translate into virtually any project environment, and people who have acquired them are regularly sought after by most organizations.

What Is a Project?

A **project** is a special set of activities with a clear beginning and end. Every project has a set of *goals*, *objectives*, and *tasks*. Also, every project must deal with a set of *limitations* or *constraints*. Finally, though the content can vary from one project to the next, there are many important similarities in the process. The first, and probably the greatest, contribution of the modern project management approach is to identify the project as a series of steps or phases. The SDLC is a project management approach tailored toward the design and development of information systems. Before we return our focus to a specific project management approach such as the SDLC, let's look at a more generic picture of project management and see how it compares. No matter what the project, three elements will be necessary to manage it effectively and efficiently: *process*, *tools*, and *techniques*.

The Process of Project Management

The modern project management approach has identified five phases in the process. Figure 10.20 illustrates the five phases.

FIGURE 10.20

The five phases of project management.

Project Management Phase	Example Activities
Initiating/Defining	• State the problem(s)/goal(s). • Identify the objectives. • Secure resources. • Explore costs/benefits in feasibility study.
Planning	• Identify and sequence activities. • Identify the "critical path." • Estimate time and resources needed for completion. • Write a detailed project plan.
Executing	• Commit resources to specific tasks. • Add additional resources/personnel if necessary. • Initiate project work.
Controlling	• Establish reporting obligations. • Create reporting tools. • Compare actual progress with a baseline. • Initiate control interventions if necessary.
Closing	• Install all deliverables. • Finalize all obligations/commitments. • Meet with stakeholders. • Release project resources. • Document the project. • Issue final report.

Initiating and Defining. The first phase of the project management process serves as a foundation for all that follows. The most important objective to achieve during this phase is the clear and succinct statement of the problem that the project is to solve or the goals that the project is to achieve. Any ambiguity at this point often spells doom for even the best executed projects. Also during this phase, it is necessary to identify and secure the resources necessary to execute the project, explore the costs and benefits, and identify any risks. As you have probably recognized, this is exactly what happens during the systems investigation phase of the SDLC.

Planning. The next phase in the project management process involves planning the project. Here, every project objective and every activity associated with that objective must be identified and sequenced. Several tools have been created to assist in the sequencing of these activities, including simple *dependence diagrams, program evaluation and review* (PERT), *critical path method* (CPM), and a commonly used timeline diagram known as a *Gantt chart*. All of these tools have a particular use in project management, but their common goal is to assist in the planning and sequencing of activities associated with the objectives of the project, such that nothing is left out, performed out of logical order, or done twice. These same tools also assist the project manager in determining how long each activity is going to take and thus how long the project is going to take. Finally, later in the project process, the tools will be used to see if the project is on schedule and, if not, where the delays occurred and what might be done to remedy the delay.

Executing. Once all of the activities in the planning phase are complete and all detailed plans have been created and approved, the execution phase of the project can begin. It is here that all of the plans are put into motion. Resources, tasks, and schedules are brought together, and the necessary work teams are created and set forth on their assigned paths. In many respects, this is the most exciting part of the project management process. The phases of systems analysis and system design are the primary phases associated with project execution in the SDLC.

Controlling. Some project management experts suggest that controlling is simply an integral part of the execution phase of project management. Others suggest it must be viewed as a separate set of activities that, admittedly, occur simultaneous to the execution phase. In either case, it is important to give sufficient attention to the controlling activities to ensure the project objectives and deadlines are met.

Probably the single most important tool for project control is the report. Three common types of reports are generated to assist with project control. The *variance report* contains information related to the difference between actual and planned project progress. It is useful in identifying when a project is off track but provides little evidence as to what is causing the delay.

The second and third types of reports are more helpful in determining the cause of delays and the appropriate corrections. The *status report* is an open-ended report that details the process that led to the current project state. By analyzing this report, a project manager can pinpoint where the delay began and create a plan to get past it and possibly make up for lost time. This is where the *resource allocation* report becomes useful. This report identifies the various resources (e.g., people, equipment) that are being applied to specific project activities and where currently unused, or *slack*, resources may be available.

Closing. This last phase of the project management process focuses on bringing a project to a successful end. The beginning of the end of a project is the implementation and installation of all of the project deliverables. The next step is the formal release of the project resources so they can be redeployed into other projects or job roles. The final step in this phase is to review the final documentation and publish the final project report. Here is where the good, and bad, news concerning the project is documented, and the elements necessary for a postproject review are identified.

Many airline pilots (and passengers, for that matter) identify the final approach and landing as one of the most critical elements of any flight. It is during those remaining moments that even the smoothest of flights can come to an undesirable conclusion. Projects are quite similar in this regard. The most beautifully planned, executed, and controlled project can be deemed a failure if it is poorly implemented. As such, we must turn our attention back to the issues of systems implementation, hopefully with a clearer understanding of how we arrived at this point and the process we will follow to do it again in another project.

Evaluating Hardware, Software, and Services

A major activity during the implementation phase of the SDLC is the acquisition of the hardware and software necessary to implement the new system. How do companies evaluate and select hardware, software, and IT services, such as those shown in Figure 10.21? Large companies may require suppliers to present bids and proposals based on system specifications developed during the design stage of systems development. Minimum acceptable physical and performance characteristics for all hardware and software requirements are established. Most large business firms and all government agencies formalize these requirements by listing them in a document called an RFP (request for proposal) or RFQ (request for quotation). Then they send the RFP or RFQ to appropriate vendors, which use it as the basis for preparing a proposed purchase agreement.

Companies may use a *scoring* system of evaluation when there are several competing proposals for a hardware or software acquisition. They give each **evaluation factor** a certain number of maximum possible points. Then they assign each competing proposal points for each factor, depending on how well it meets the user's specifications. Scoring evaluation factors for several proposals helps organize and document the evaluation process. It also spotlights the strengths and weaknesses of each proposal.

Whatever the claims of hardware manufacturers and software suppliers, the performance of hardware and software must be demonstrated and evaluated. Independent hardware and software information services (e.g., Datapro, Auerbach) may be used to gain detailed specification information and evaluations. Other users are frequently the best source of information needed to evaluate the claims of manufacturers

FIGURE 10.21

Examples from IBM Corporation of the kinds of hardware, software, and IS services that many companies are evaluating and acquiring to support their e-commerce initiatives.

Hardware
Full range of offerings, including xSeries servers, iSeries midrange servers for small and midsize businesses, RS/6000 servers for UNIX customers and z900 mainframes for large enterprises. Also has full range of storage options.

Software
Web server. Lotus DominoGo Web server.
Storefront. WebSphere Commerce Suite (formerly known as Net.Commerce) for storefront and catalog creation, relationship marketing, and order management. Can add Commerce Integrator to integrate with back-end systems and Catalog Architect for content management.
Middleware/Transaction Services. WebSphere application server manages transactions. MQ Series queues messages and manages connections. CICS processes transactions.
Database. DB2 Universal Database.
Tools. WebSphere Studio includes set of predefined templates and common business logic.
Other Applications. IBM Payment Suite for handling credit cards and managing digital certificates.

Services
IBM Global Services, which includes groups organized by each major industry, including retail and financial. Can design, build, and host e-commerce applications.

and suppliers. That's why Internet newsgroups and Weblogs established to exchange information about specific software or hardware vendors and their products have become one of the best sources for obtaining up-to-date information about the experiences of users of the products.

Large companies frequently evaluate proposed hardware and software by requiring the processing of special *benchmark* test programs and test data. Benchmarking simulates the processing of typical jobs on several computers and evaluates their performances. Users can then evaluate test results to determine which hardware device or software package display the best performance characteristics.

Hardware Evaluation Factors

When you evaluate the hardware needed by a new business application, you should investigate specific physical and performance characteristics for each computer system or peripheral component to be acquired. Specific questions must be answered concerning many important factors. Ten of these **hardware evaluation factors** and questions are summarized in Figure 10.22.

Notice that there is much more to evaluating hardware than determining the fastest and cheapest computing device. For example, the question of obsolescence must be addressed by making a technology evaluation. The factor of ergonomics is also very important. Ergonomic factors ensure that computer hardware and software are user friendly, that is, safe, comfortable, and easy to use. Connectivity is another important evaluation factor, because so many network technologies and bandwidth alternatives are available to connect computer systems to the Internet, intranet, and extranet networks.

FIGURE 10.22

A summary of 10 major hardware evaluation factors. Notice how you can use this to evaluate a computer system or a peripheral device.

Hardware Evaluation Factors	Rating
Performance What is its speed, capacity, and throughput?	
Cost What is its lease or purchase price? What will be its cost of operation and maintenance?	
Reliability What are the risks of malfunction and its maintenance requirements? What are its error control and diagnostic features?	
Compatibility Is it compatible with existing hardware and software? Is it compatible with hardware and software provided by competing suppliers?	
Technology In what year of its product life cycle is it? Does it use a new untested technology, or does it run the risk of obsolescence?	
Ergonomics Has it been "human factors engineered" with the user in mind? Is it user-friendly, designed to be safe, comfortable, and easy to use?	
Connectivity Can it be easily connected to wide area and local area networks that use different types of network technologies and bandwidth alternatives?	
Scalability Can it handle the processing demands of a wide range of end users, transactions, queries, and other information processing requirements?	
Software Is system and application software available that can best use this hardware?	
Support Are the services required to support and maintain it available?	
Overall Rating	

FIGURE 10.23
A summary of selected software evaluation factors. Note that most of the hardware evaluation factors in Figure 10.22 can also be used to evaluate software packages.

Software Evaluation Factors	Rating
Quality Is it bug free, or does it have many errors in its program code?	
Efficiency Is the software a well-developed system of program code that does not use much CPU time, memory capacity, or disk space?	
Flexibility Can it handle our business processes easily, without major modification?	
Security Does it provide control procedures for errors, malfunctions, and improper use?	
Connectivity Is it Web-enabled so it can easily access the Internet, intranets, and extranets on its own or by working with Web browsers or other network software?	
Maintenance Will new features and bug fixes be easily implemented by our own software developers?	
Documentation Is the software well documented? Does it include help screens and helpful software agents?	
Hardware Does existing hardware have the features required to best use this software?	
Other Factors What are its performance, cost, reliability, availability, compatibility, modularity, technology, ergonomics, scalability, and support characteristics? (Use the hardware evaluation factor questions in Figure 10.22.)	
Overall Rating	

Software Evaluation Factors

You should evaluate software according to many factors that are similar to those used for hardware evaluation. Thus, the factors of performance, cost, reliability, availability, compatibility, modularity, technology, ergonomics, and support should be used to evaluate proposed software acquisitions. In addition, however, the **software evaluation factors** summarized in Figure 10.23 must also be considered. You should answer the questions they generate to evaluate software purchases properly. For example, some software packages are notoriously slow, hard to use, bug-filled, or poorly documented. They are not a good choice, even if offered at attractive prices.

Evaluating IS Services

Most suppliers of hardware and software products and many other firms offer a variety of **IS services** to end users and organizations. Examples include assistance in developing a company Web site, installation or conversion of new hardware and software, employee training, and hardware maintenance. Some of these services are provided without cost by hardware manufacturers and software suppliers.

Other types of IS services needed by a business can be outsourced to an outside company for a negotiated price. For example, *systems integrators* take over complete responsibility for an organization's computer facilities when an organization outsources its computer operations. They may also assume responsibility for developing and implementing large systems development projects that involve many vendors and subcontractors. Value-added resellers (VARs) specialize in providing industry-specific hardware, software, and services from selected manufacturers. Many other services are available to end users, including systems design, contract programming, and consulting services. Evaluation factors and questions for IS services are summarized in Figure 10.24.

FIGURE 10.24

Evaluation factors for IS services. These factors focus on the quality of support services business users may need.

Evaluation Factors for IS Services	Rating
Performance What has been their past performance in view of their past promises?	
Systems Development Are Web site and other e-business developers available? What are their quality and cost?	
Maintenance Is equipment maintenance provided? What are its quality and cost?	
Conversion What systems development and installation services will they provide during the conversion period?	
Training Is the necessary training of personnel provided? What are its quality and cost?	
Backup Are similar computer facilities available nearby for emergency backup purposes?	
Accessibility Does the vendor provide local or regional sites that offer sales, systems development, and hardware maintenance services? Is a customer support center at the vendor's Web site available? Is a customer hotline provided?	
Business Position Is the vendor financially strong, with good industry market prospects?	
Hardware Do they provide a wide selection of compatible hardware devices and accessories?	
Software Do they offer a variety of useful e-business software and application packages?	
Overall Rating	

Other Implementation Activities

Testing, data conversion, documentation, and training are keys to successful implementation of a new business system.

Testing

System testing may involve testing and debugging software, testing Web site performance, and testing new hardware. An important part of testing is the review of prototypes of displays, reports, and other output. Prototypes should be reviewed by end users of the proposed systems for possible errors. Of course, testing should not occur only during the system's implementation stage but throughout the system's development process. For example, you might examine and critique prototypes of input documents, screen displays, and processing procedures during the systems design stage. Immediate end-user testing is one of the benefits of a prototyping process.

Data Conversion

Implementing new information systems for many organizations today frequently involves replacing a previous system and its software and databases. One of the most important implementation activities required when installing new software in such cases is called data conversion. For example, installing new software packages may require converting the data elements in databases that are affected by a new application into new data formats. Other data conversion activities that are typically required include correcting incorrect data, filtering out unwanted data, consolidating data from several databases, and organizing data into new data subsets, such as databases, data marts, and data warehouses. A good data conversion process is essential, because improperly organized and formatted data are frequently reported to be one of the major causes of failures in implementing new systems.

During the design phase, the analysts create a data dictionary that not only describes the various data elements contained in the new system but also specifies any necessary conversions from the old system. In some cases, only the name of the data element is changed, such as the old system field CUST_ID becomes CLIENT_ID in the new system. In other cases, the actual format of the data is changed, thus requiring some conversion application to be written to filter the old data and put them into the new format. An example of this might be the creation of a new CUSTOMER_ID format to allow for expansion or make two merged systems compatible with each other. This type of data element conversion requires additional time to occur, because each element must pass through the conversion filter before being written into the new data files.

Yet another issue is the time necessary to transfer the data from the old data files into the files for the new system. Although it is possible that the new system may have been designed to use the existing data files, this is not normally the case, especially in situations when a new system is replacing a legacy system that is fairly old. The time necessary to transfer the old data can have a material impact on the conversion process and on the strategy that is ultimately selected. Consider the following situation.

Suppose the conversion to the new system requires the transfer of data from 10 different data files. The average record length across the 10 files is 1,780 bytes, and the total number of records contained in the 10 files is 120 million. With this information and an estimate of the transfer time in bytes per minute, the total transfer time can be easily calculated as follows: Assume a transfer rate of 10.5 megabytes per second (Mbps) (Fast Ethernet) with no conversion algorithm. Then,

$$\text{1,780 bytes} \times \text{120 million records} = \text{213,600,000,000 bytes.}$$
$$\text{213,600,000,000 bytes/10.5 Mbps} = \text{20,343 seconds.}$$
$$\text{20,343 seconds} = \text{5.65 hours.}$$

Although the preceding calculations appear to be such that the conversion process does not take an inordinate amount of time, we must also be aware that they assume an error-free transfer, no format conversion, and 100 percent use of available network bandwidth. If the transfer is done using a slower communication medium, say 1.25 Mbps, the time jumps to 47.47 hours (just under two days).

The important consideration here is not simply the time necessary to effect the transfer but the preservation of the integrity of the current system data files during the process. If the transfer turns out to be around 4.5 hours, then it could theoretically occur after business hours and be easily accomplished by the opening of the next day's business. If, however, the process takes two full days, then it would need to begin at the close of business on Friday and would not be complete until late Sunday afternoon. Should any glitches show up in the process, either the transfer would have to wait a week to be rerun or the possibility of disrupting daily operations or losing new data would be very real. As you can see, careful thought about the logistics associated with data transfer must be given when recommending the most appropriate conversion strategy for the new system.

Documentation

Developing good user documentation is an important part of the implementation process. Sample data entry display screens, forms, and reports are good examples of documentation. When *computer-aided systems engineering* methods are used, documentation can be created and changed easily because it is stored and accessible on disk in a *system repository*. Documentation serves as a method of communication among the people responsible for developing, implementing, and maintaining a computer-based system. Installing and operating a newly designed system or modifying an established application requires a detailed record of that system's design. Documentation is extremely important in diagnosing errors and making changes, especially if the end users or systems analysts who developed a system are no longer with the organization.

FIGURE 10.25 How one company developed training programs for the implementation of an e-commerce Web site and intranet access for its employees.

Training

Training is a vital implementation activity. IS personnel, such as user consultants, must be sure that end users are trained to operate a new business system, or its implementation will fail. Training may involve only activities like data entry, or it may involve all aspects of the proper use of a new system. In addition, managers and end users must be educated in how the new technology affects the company's business operations and management. This knowledge should be supplemented by training programs for any new hardware devices, software packages, and their use for specific work activities. Figure 10.25 illustrates how one business coordinated its end-user training program with each stage of its implementation process for developing intranet and Internet access within the company.

System Conversion Strategies

The initial operation of a new business system can be a difficult task. It typically requires a conversion process from the use of a present system to the operation of a new or improved application. Conversion methods can soften the impact of introducing new information technologies into an organization. Four major forms of system conversion are illustrated in Figure 10.26. They include:

- Parallel conversion
- Pilot conversion
- Phased conversion
- Direct conversion

Direct Conversion. The simplest conversion strategy, and probably the most disruptive to the organization, is the **direct cutover** approach. This method, sometimes referred

FIGURE 10.26

The four major forms of conversion to a new system.

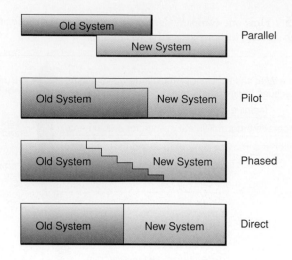

to as the **slam dunk** or **cold-turkey strategy,** is as abrupt as its name implies. Using this approach, the old system is simply turned off, and the new system is turned on in its place. Although this method is the least expensive of all available strategies and may be the only viable solution in situations in which activating the new system is an emergency or when the two systems cannot coexist under any conditions, it is also the one that poses the greatest risk of failure. Once the new system becomes operational, the end users must cope with any errors or dysfunctions, and depending on the severity of the problem, this approach can have a significant effect on the quality of the work performed. Direct conversion should be considered only in extreme circumstances, when no other conversion strategy is viable.

Parallel Conversion. At the opposite end of the risk spectrum is the **parallel conversion** strategy. Here, the old and new systems are run simultaneously until the end users and project coordinators are fully satisfied that the new system is functioning correctly and the old system is no longer necessary. Using this approach, a parallel conversion can be effected with either a **single cutover,** with a set, predetermined date for stopping the parallel operation, or a **phased cutover,** which uses some predetermined method of phasing in each piece of the new system and turning off a similar piece of the old system.

Although clearly having the advantage of low risk, the parallel approach also brings with it the highest cost. To execute a parallel approach properly, the end users must literally perform all daily functions with both systems, thus creating a massive redundancy in activities and literally double the work. In fact, unless the operational costs of the new system are significantly less than the old system, the cost of parallel operation can be as much as three to four times greater than the old system alone. During a parallel conversion, all outputs from both systems are compared for concurrency and accuracy, until it is determined that the new system is functioning at least as well as the one it is replacing. Parallel conversion may be the best choice in situations in which an automated system is replacing a manual one. In certain circumstances when end users cannot cope with the often confusing redundancy of two systems, the parallel conversion strategy may not be viable. Also, parallel conversion may not be possible if the organization does not have the available computing resources to operate two systems at the same time.

Pilot Conversion. In some situations, the new system may be installed in multiple locations, such as a series of bank branches or retail outlets. In other cases, the conversion may be able to be planned from a geographic perspective. When these types of scenarios exist, the possibility for using a **pilot conversion** strategy exists. This approach allows for the conversion to the new system, using either a direct or parallel method, at a single location. The advantage to this approach is that a location can be selected that best represents the conditions across the organization but also may be less risky in terms of any loss of time or delays in processing. Once the installation is complete at the pilot site, the process can be evaluated and any changes to the system made to prevent problems encountered at the pilot site from reoccurring at the remaining installations. This approach may also be required if the individual sites or locations have certain unique characteristics or idiosyncrasies that make either a direct or parallel approach infeasible.

Phased Conversion. A **phased** or **gradual conversion** strategy attempts to take advantage of the best features of both the direct and parallel approaches while minimizing the risks involved. This incremental approach to conversion allows for the new system to be brought online as a series of functional components that are logically ordered to minimize disruption to end users and the flow of business.

Phased conversion is analogous to the release of multiple versions of an application by a software developer. Each version of the software should correct any known bugs and allow for 100 percent compatibility with data entered into or processed by the previous version. Although having the advantage of lower risk, the phased approach takes the most time and thus creates the most disruption to the organization over time.

Postimplementation Activities

When all is said and done, the single most costly activity occurs after the system implementation is complete: the **postimplementation** maintenance phase. The primary objectives associated with systems maintenance are to correct errors or faults in the system, provide changes to effect performance improvement, or adapt the system to changes in the operating or business environment. In a typical organization, more programmers and analysts are assigned to application maintenance activities than to application development. Furthermore, though a new system can take several months or years to design and build and cost hundreds of thousands or millions of dollars, the resulting system can operate around the clock and last for five to ten years, or longer. One major activity in postimplementation involves making changes to the system as a result of the users finally having an opportunity to use it. These are called **change requests.** Such requests can range from fixing a software bug not found during testing to designing an enhancement to an existing process or function.

Systems Maintenance

Managing and implementing change requests is only one aspect of the systems maintenance phase activities. In some ways, once the maintenance phase begins, the life cycle starts over again. New requirements are articulated, analyzed, designed, checked for feasibility, tested, and implemented. Although the range and nature of specific maintenance requests vary from system to system, four basic categories of maintenance can be identified: (1) corrective, (2) adaptive, (3) perfective, and (4) preventive.

The activities associated with **corrective maintenance** are focused on fixing bugs and logic errors not detected during the implementation testing period. **Adaptive maintenance** refers to those activities associated with modifying existing functions or adding new functionality to accommodate changes in the business or operating environments. **Perfective maintenance** activities involve changes made to an existing system that are intended to improve the performance of a function or interface. The final category of maintenance activities, **preventive maintenance,** involves those activities intended to reduce the chances of a system failure or extend the capacity of a current system's useful life. Although often the lowest-priority maintenance activity, preventive maintenance is nonetheless a high value-adding function and vital to an organization's ability to realize the full value of its investment in the system.

Postimplementation Review

The maintenance activity also includes a postimplementation review process to ensure that newly implemented systems meet the business objectives established for them. Errors in the development or use of a system must be corrected by the maintenance process. This process includes a periodic review or audit of a system to ensure that it is operating properly and meeting its objectives. This audit occurs in addition to continually monitoring a new system for potential problems or necessary changes.

Project Success (or Failure): What We Know But Choose to Ignore

There is no mystery as to why most projects succeed or fail; people have been writing about effective project management for millennia.

More than 2,000 years ago, Sun Tzu described how to organize a successful, highly complex project (a military campaign) in *The Art of War*. Fred Brooks' classic book, *The Mythical Man-Month*, offers management advice targeted at running large IT projects.

The U.K. National Audit Office recently published an excellent guide to delivering successful IT-enabled business change. Over the past 10 years, virtually every major IT publication has printed articles on why large projects succeed or fail.

Despite all the excellent advice available, more than half of the major projects undertaken by IT departments still fail or get canceled. We know what works. We just don't do it.

- **An ineffective executive sponsor.** A weak or, even worse, nonexistent executive sponsor almost guarantees business project failure. Under weak executive leadership, all projects become IT projects rather than business initiatives with IT components.

- **A poor business case.** An incomplete business case allows incorrect expectations to be set—and missed.

- **The business case is no longer valid.** Marketplace changes frequently invalidate original business assumptions. But teams often become so invested in a project that they ignore warning signs and continue as planned.

- **The project is too big.** Bigger projects require more discipline.

- **A lack of dedicated resources.** Large projects require concentration and dedication for the duration. But key people are frequently required to support critical projects while continuing to perform their existing full-time jobs.

- **Out of sight, out of mind.** If your suppliers fail, you fail, and you own it. Don't take your eyes off them.

- **Unnecessary complexity.** Projects that attempt to be all things to all people usually result in systems that are difficult to use, and they eventually fail.

- **Cultural conflict.** Projects that violate cultural norms of the organization seldom have a chance.

- **No contingency.** Stuff happens. Projects need flexibility to address the inevitable surprises.

- **Too long without deliverables.** Most organizations expect visible progress in six to nine months. Long projects without intermediate products risk losing executive interest, support, and resources.

- **Betting on a new, unproven technology.** Enough said.

- **An arbitrary release date.** Date-driven projects have little chance of success. Companies should learn to plan the project before picking a release date, not the other way around.

Anything here that doesn't make sense? *That's exactly* the point.

Source: Adapted from Bart Perkins, "12 Things You Know About Projects But Choose to Ignore," *Computerworld*, March 12, 2007.

FIGURE 10.27

The 10 greatest challenges of developing and implementing intranet enterprise portals and enterprise resource planning systems reported by 100 companies.

Intranet Enterprise Portal Challenges	Enterprise Resource Planning Challenges
• Security, security, security	• Getting end user buy-in
• Defining the scope and purpose of the portal	• Scheduling/planning
• Finding the time and the money	• Integrating legacy systems/data
• Ensuring consistent data quality	• Getting management buy-in
• Getting employees to use it	• Dealing with multiple/international sites and partners
• Organizing the data	• Changing culture/mindsets
• Finding technical expertise	• IT training
• Integrating the pieces	• Getting, keeping IT staff
• Making it easy to use	• Moving to a new platform
• Providing all users with access	• Performance/system upgrades

Implementation Challenges

Implementing new business/IT strategies, particularly when they involve large-scale innovative technologies, involves major organizational change. For many organizations, moving into e-business represents the fourth or fifth major change they have experienced, and endured, since the early 1980s. Successful implementation of these new strategies and applications requires managing the effects of changes in key organizational dimensions such as business processes, organizational structures, managerial roles, work assignments, and stakeholder relationships. Figure 10.27 emphasizes the variety and extent of the challenges reported by 100 companies that developed and implemented new enterprise information portals and ERP systems.

User Resistance and Involvement

Any new way of doing things generates some resistance from the people affected. For example, the implementation of new work support technologies can generate fear and resistance to change in employees. One of the keys to solving problems of user resistance to new information technologies is proper education and training. Even more important is user involvement in organizational changes and the development of new information systems. Organizations have a variety of strategies to help manage business change, and one basic requirement is the involvement and commitment of top management and all business stakeholders affected by the new system.

Direct end-user participation in business planning and application development projects before a new system is implemented is especially important in reducing the potential for end-user resistance. That is why end users frequently are members of systems development teams or do their own development work. Such involvement helps ensure that end users assume ownership of a system and that its design meets their needs. Systems that tend to inconvenience or frustrate users cannot be effective systems, no matter how technically elegant they are or how efficiently they process data. For example, Figure 10.28 illustrates some of the major obstacles to

FIGURE 10.28

Obstacles to knowledge management systems. Note that end-user resistance to knowledge sharing is the biggest obstacle.

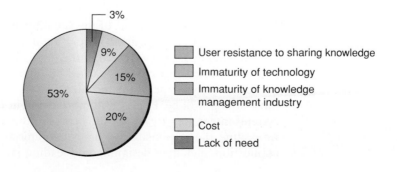

- 3%
- 9%
- 15%
- 53%
- 20%

■ User resistance to sharing knowledge
■ Immaturity of technology
■ Immaturity of knowledge management industry
☐ Cost
■ Lack of need

knowledge management systems in business. Notice that end-user resistance to sharing knowledge is the biggest obstacle to the implementation of knowledge management applications. Let's look at a real-world example that spotlights end-user resistance and some of its solutions.

Société de Transport de Montréal: Smooth Ride after a Bumpy Start

Suburban sprawl might make a great business case for a transit agency, but when it came to servers, Canada's Société de Transport de Montréal (STM) drew the line. Mike Stefanakis, senior systems engineer at STM, says that the main reason he started looking at virtualization technology was to prevent server sprawl. He wanted consolidation, particularly for development servers at the agency, which provides over 360 million bus and metro rides each year.

"We crunched the numbers and realized that our growth was going to cause a few problems in the near future," he says. If things kept going as they had, the agency would need an additional 20–30 servers each year, on top of its existing base of 180 primarily Wintel machines. "Too many servers were going to be needed to feed the needs of our users and clients," Stefanakis says.

But even though staffers were convinced of virtualization's benefits pretty early on, the agency's end users didn't necessarily feel the same way. Several factors contributed to the initial resistance. For starters, there was a fear of the unknown. There were questions like "How stable is this new technology?" and "What do you mean I will be sharing my resources with other servers?" Potential users thought the new technology might slow them down.

To help users get over their fears, Stefanakis focused on giving people the information they needed, while explaining the advantages of the new technology. Among them: great response time for business applications and baked-in disaster recovery. If anything does fail, restoration is just a quickly restored image away. Stefanakis and his staff kept "talking up" the technology and its benefits. "Virtualization came up in every budget, strategy and development meeting we had," he recalls. "We made sure the information was conveyed to the proper people so that everyone in our department knew that virtualization was coming."

STM has been staging production servers in its virtual environment since December 2005.

The first virtual machine was staged in STM's testing center as a means of quickly recovering a downed production server. Once the first few applications were implemented, user resistance quickly became history. "After people see the advantages, stability and performance available to them on a virtual platform, they tend to lose any inhibitions they previously may have had. The psychological barrier for virtualization has been broken," Stefanakis says, "and now users will ask for a new server as if they are ordering a coffee and danish."

Source: Adapted from Mary Ryan Garcia, "After Bumpy Start, Transit Agency Finds Virtualization a Smooth Ride," *Computerworld*, March 8, 2007.

Change Management

Figure 10.29 illustrates some of the key dimensions of change management and the level of difficulty and business impact involved. Notice some of the people, process, and technology factors involved in the implementation of business/IT strategies and applications or other changes caused by introducing new information technologies into a company. Some of the technical factors listed, such as systems integrators and outsourcing, will be discussed in more detail in the next few chapters. For example, systems integrators are consulting firms or other outside contractors that may be paid to assume the responsibility for developing and implementing a new e-business application, including designing and leading its change management activities. And

FIGURE 10.29 Some of the key dimensions of change management. Examples of the people, process, and technology factors involved in managing the implementation of IT-based changes to an organization.

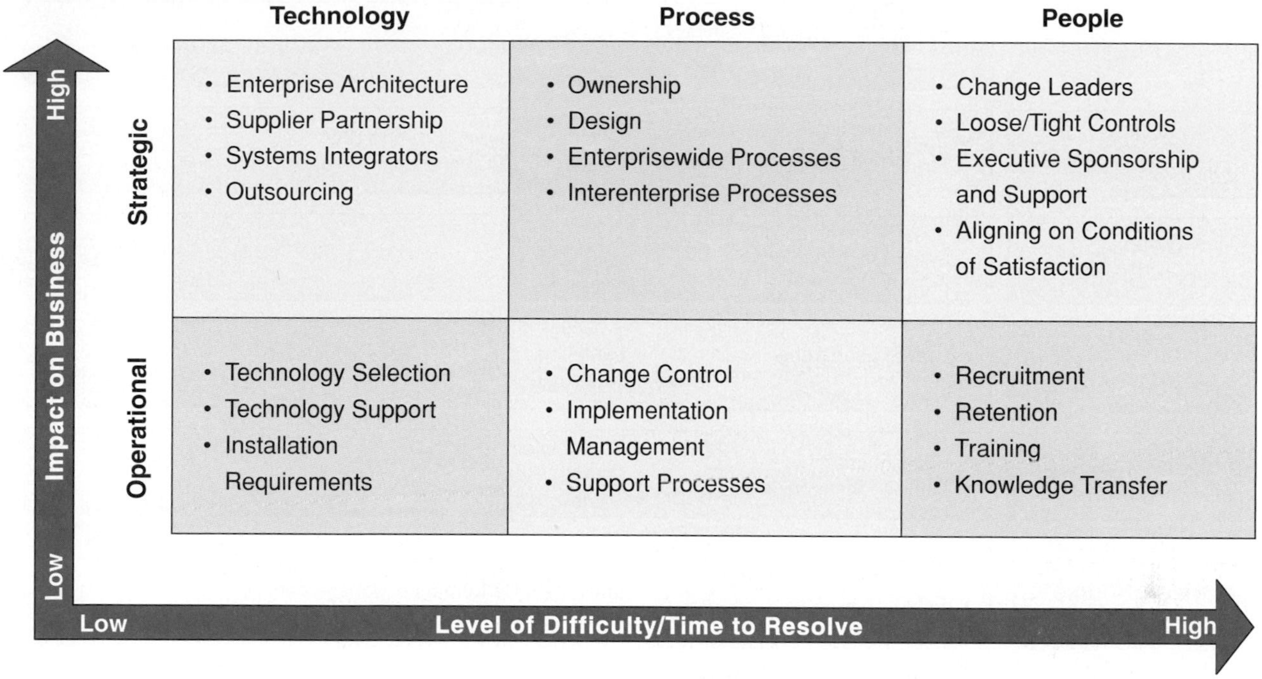

Source: Adapted from Grant Norris, James Hurley, Kenneth Hartley, John Dunleavy, and John Balls, *E-Business and ERP: Transforming the Enterprise* (New York, John Wiley & Sons, 2000), p. 120. Reprinted by permission.

notice that people factors have the highest level of difficulty and longest time to resolve of any dimension of change management.

Thus, people are a major focus of organizational change management. This focus includes activities such as developing innovative ways to measure, motivate, and reward performance, as well as designing programs to recruit and train employees in the core competencies required in a changing workplace. Change management also involves analyzing and defining all changes facing the organization and developing programs to reduce the risks and costs and maximize the benefits of change. For example, implementing a new e-business application such as customer relationship management might involve developing a *change action plan*, assigning selected managers as *change sponsors*, developing employee *change teams*, and encouraging open communications and feedback about organizational changes. Some key tactics change experts recommend include:

● Involve as many people as possible in e-business planning and application development.

● Make constant change an expected part of the culture.

● Tell everyone as much as possible about everything as often as possible, preferably in person.

● Make liberal use of financial incentives and recognition.

● Work within the company culture, not around it.

A Change Management Process

An eight-level process of change management for organizations is illustrated in Figure 10.30. This change management model is only one of many that could be applied to manage organizational changes caused by new business/IT strategies and applications and other changes in business processes. For example, this model suggests

FIGURE 10.30 A process of change management. Examples of the activities involved in successfully managing organizational change caused by the implementation of new business processes.

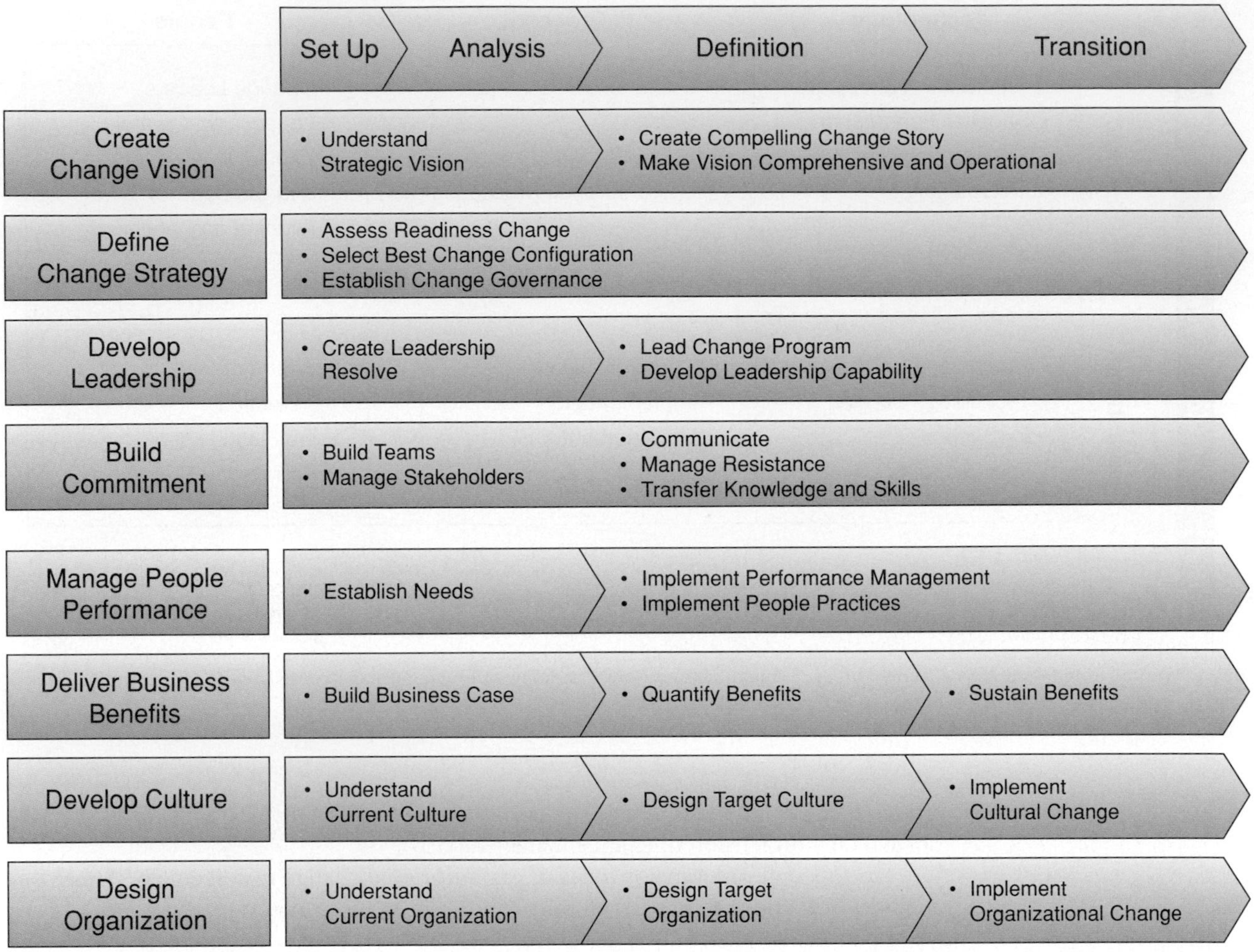

	Set Up	Analysis	Definition	Transition
Create Change Vision	• Understand Strategic Vision	• Create Compelling Change Story • Make Vision Comprehensive and Operational		
Define Change Strategy	• Assess Readiness Change • Select Best Change Configuration • Establish Change Governance			
Develop Leadership	• Create Leadership Resolve	• Lead Change Program • Develop Leadership Capability		
Build Commitment	• Build Teams • Manage Stakeholders	• Communicate • Manage Resistance • Transfer Knowledge and Skills		
Manage People Performance	• Establish Needs	• Implement Performance Management • Implement People Practices		
Deliver Business Benefits	• Build Business Case	• Quantify Benefits	• Sustain Benefits	
Develop Culture	• Understand Current Culture	• Design Target Culture	• Implement Cultural Change	
Design Organization	• Understand Current Organization	• Design Target Organization	• Implement Organizational Change	

Source: Adapted from Martin Diese, Conrad Nowikow, Patric King, and Amy Wright, *Executive's Guide to E-Business: From Tactics to Strategy,* p. 190. Copyright © 2000 by John Wiley & Sons Inc. Reprinted by permission.

that the business vision created in the strategic planning phase should be communicated in a compelling *change story* to the people in the organization. Evaluating the readiness for changes within an organization and then developing change strategies and choosing and training change leaders and champions based on that assessment could be the next steps in the process.

These change leaders are the change agents who then are able to lead change teams of employees and other business stakeholders in building a business case for changes in technology, business processes, job content, and organizational structures. They also communicate the benefits of these changes and lead training programs on the details of new business applications. Of course, many change management models include methods for performance measurement and rewards to provide financial incentives for employees and stakeholders to cooperate with changes that may be required. In addition, fostering a new e-business culture within an organization by establishing communities of interest for employees and other business stakeholders via Internet, intranet, and extranet discussion groups could be a valuable change management strategy. Such groups encourage stakeholder involvement and buy-in for the changes brought about by implementing new e-business applications of information technology.

Summary

- **The Systems Development Cycle.** Business end users and IS specialists may use a systems approach to help them develop information system solutions to meet business opportunities. This approach frequently involves a systems development cycle in which IS specialists and end users conceive, design, and implement business systems. The stages, activities, and products of the information systems development cycle are summarized in Figure 10.3.

- **Prototyping.** Prototyping is a major alternative methodology to the traditional information systems development cycle. It includes the use of prototyping tools and methodologies, which promote an iterative, interactive process that develops prototypes of user interfaces and other information system components. See Figure 10.9.

- **End-User Development.** The application development capabilities built into many end-user software packages have made it easier for end users to develop their own business applications. End users should focus their development efforts on the system components of business processes that can benefit from the use of information technology, as summarized in Figure 10.14.

- **Implementing IS.** The implementation process for information system projects is summarized in Figure 10.27.

Implementation involves acquisition, testing, documentation, training, installation, and conversion activities that transform a newly designed business system into an operational system for end users.

- **Evaluating Hardware, Software, and Services.** Business professionals should know how to evaluate the acquisition of information system resources. IT vendors' proposals should be based on specifications developed during the design stage of systems development. A formal evaluation process reduces the possibility of incorrect or unnecessary purchases of hardware or software. Several major evaluation factors, summarized in Figures 10.22, 10.23, and 10.24, can be used to evaluate hardware, software, and IS services.

- **Implementing Business Change.** Implementation activities include managing the introduction and implementation of changes in business processes, organizational structures, job assignments, and work relationships resulting from business/IT strategies and applications such as e-business initiatives, reengineering projects, supply chain alliances, and the introduction of new technologies. Companies use change management tactics such as user involvement in business/IT planning and development to reduce end-user resistance and maximize acceptance of business changes by all stakeholders.

FIGURE 10.31

An overview of the implementation process. Implementation activities are needed to transform a newly developed information system into an operational system for end users.

Implementing New Systems
● **Acquisition** Evaluate and acquire necessary hardware and software resources and information system services. Screen vendor proposals.
● **Software Development** Develop any software that will not be acquired externally as software packages. Make any necessary modifications to software packages that are acquired.
● **Data Conversion** Convert data in company databases to new data formats and subsets required by newly installed software.
● **Training** Educate and train management, end users, customers, and other business stakeholders. Use consultants or training programs to develop user competencies.
● **Testing** Test and make necessary corrections to the programs, procedures, and hardware used by a new system.
● **Documentation** Record and communicate detailed system specifications, including procedures for end users and IS personnel and examples of input screens and output displays and reports.
● **Conversion** Convert from the use of a present system to the operation of a new or improved system. This conversion may involve operating both new and old systems in *parallel* for a trial period, operation of a *pilot* system on a trial basis at one location, *phasing* in the new system one location at a time, or a *direct cutover* to the new system.

Key Terms and Concepts

These are the key terms and concepts of this chapter. The page number of their first explanation is in parentheses.

1. Change management (442)
2. Conversion (437)
3. Cost/benefit analysis (412)
4. Data conversion (435)
5. Documentation (436)
6. Economic feasibility (412)
7. End-user development (420)
8. Feasibility study (410)
9. Functional requirements (416)
10. Human factors feasibility (413)
11. Implementation process (426)
12. Intangible (412)
    a. Benefits (412)
    b. Costs (412)
13. Legal/political feasibility (413)
14. Logical model (415)
15. Operational feasibility (411)
16. Organizational analysis (414)
17. Postimplementation review (440)
18. Project management (430)
19. Prototyping (416)
20. Systems analysis and design (409)
21. Systems approach (406)
22. Systems development life cycle (409)
23. Systems implementation (426)
24. Systems maintenance (439)
25. Systems specifications (420)
26. System testing (435)
27. Systems thinking (406)
28. Tangible (412)
    a. Benefits (412)
    b. Costs (412)
29. Technical feasibility (412)
30. User interface design (418)
31. User involvement (441)
32. User resistance (441)

Review Quiz

Match one of the key terms and concepts listed previously with each of the brief examples or definitions that follow. Try to find the best fit for answers that seem to fit more than one term or concept. Defend your choices.

____ 1. Using an organized sequence of activities to study a problem or opportunity using systems thinking.

____ 2. Trying to recognize systems and the new interrelationships and components of systems in any situation.

____ 3. Evaluating the success of a solution after it has been implemented.

____ 4. Your evaluation shows that benefits outweigh costs for a proposed system.

____ 5. The costs of acquiring computer hardware, software, and specialists.

____ 6. Loss of customer goodwill caused by errors in a new system.

____ 7. Increases in profits caused by a new system.

____ 8. Improved employee morale caused by efficiency and effectiveness of a new system.

____ 9. A multistep process to conceive, design, and implement an information system.

____ 10. A diagram or blueprint of a system that shows what it does without regard to how it does it.

____ 11. Determines the organizational, economic, technical, and operational feasibility of a proposed information system.

____ 12. Analyzing whether cost savings and additional profits will exceed the investment required.

____ 13. Reliable hardware and software are available to implement a proposed system.

____ 14. Determining whether any copyright or patent infringements exist as the result of a new system.

____ 15. Do we have the right people to operate the new system?

____ 16. Studying in detail the information needs of users and any information systems presently used and then developing a system to correct a problem or improve operations.

____ 17. A detailed description of user information needs and the input, processing, output, storage, and control capabilities required to meet those needs.

____ 18. Systems design should focus on developing user-friendly input and output methods for a system.

____ 19. A detailed description of the hardware, software, people, network, and data resources and information products required by a proposed system.

____ 20. Acquiring hardware and software, testing and documenting a proposed system, and training people to use it.

____ 21. Making improvements to an operational system.

____ 22. An interactive and iterative process of developing and refining information system prototypes.

____ 23. Managers and business specialists can develop their own e-business applications.

____ 24. Includes acquisition, testing, training, and conversion to a new system.

____ 25. Operate in parallel with the old system, use a test site, switch in stages, or cut over immediately to a new system.

____ 26. Checking whether hardware and software work properly for end users.

____ 27. A user manual communicates the design and operating procedures of a system.

____ 28. Keeping an IS project on time and within its budget would be a major goal.

____ 29. Common response to major changes in organizational structures, roles, and stakeholder relationships.

____ 30. Participation in business planning and application development projects before a new system is implemented is one example.

____ 31. Among other things, it involves analyzing and defining all changes facing an organization and developing programs to reduce risks and maximize benefits.

____ 32. Transferring and converting data from old systems to the new one being implemented.

____ 33. Cost and benefits that can be quantified with a high degree of certainty.

____ 34. The degree to which a proposed system fits with the business environment and organizational objectives.

____ 35. Costs and benefits of a new system that are hard to quantify.

____ 36. A phase within systems analysis focused on understanding the organization and its environment.

Discussion Questions

1. Why has prototyping become a popular way to develop business applications? What are prototyping's advantages and disadvantages?

2. Refer to the Real World Case on PayPal in the chapter. Matthew Mengerink of PayPal notes that is not enough for a bank teller to speak French to feel you are in France, and he highlights the value customers place in expressions of trust and comfort, such as feeling that you are there. Why do you think people place value on these issues? How much difference would this make to you over and above the functionality of the Web site?

3. Review the real-world example about Wal-Mart and Others in the chapter. How could these companies prepare for the unexpected changes in demand that brought down their sites? Explain your reasoning.

4. What are the three most important factors you would use in evaluating computer hardware? Computer software? Explain why.

5. Assume that in your first week on a new job you are asked to use a type of business software that you have never used before. What kind of user training should your company provide to you before you start?

6. Refer to the Real World Case on Blue Cross and Blue Shield and others about organizational change in the chapter. What is the value of the strategy followed by Kevin Sparks of bringing an outsider to discuss the change program? Why do you think it was successful? Explain.

7. What is the difference among the parallel, direct, phased, and pilot forms of IS conversion? Which conversion strategy is best? Explain why.

8. Review the Google real-world example in the chapter. How might you change the user interface of Google's search pages and those of some of its other products on the Web? Defend your proposals.

9. Review the real-world example discussing the factors involved in project failure in the chapter. If these are well-known, why would companies choose to ignore them over and over again? What could be the reasons behind such behavior?

10. Pick a business task you would like to computerize. How could you use the steps of the information systems development cycle, as illustrated in Figure 10.3, to help you? Use examples to illustrate your answer.

Analysis Exercises

1. **SDLC in Practice**
   Community Action
   The Systems Development Life Cycle (SDLC) provides a structured problem-solving software development methodology. However, what works for information system–related problems also works for many business problems too. The SDLC provides a

framework that requires adherents to follow a logical sequence. This sequence promotes careful analysis and helps ensure you are doing the right thing as well as doing the thing right.

You can apply the SDLC to address many business problems. Think about a problem in your community. Your community may include your campus, your work, or your neighborhood. Your instructor may provide additional guidelines. Select a problem, complete each step in turn, and prepare a report detailing each step. Due to the location-specific nature of this exercise, expect to conduct first-hand research and interviews.

a. Select a problem and quantify its effects.

b. Identify the cause or causes of the problem.

c. Describe various solutions to this problem. Include estimated costs and benefits for each solution.

d. Select a solution and prepare a plan for its implementation.

e. Identify the parties responsible for monitoring and maintaining the solution. What metrics should they use to monitor the results?

2. **Planning for Success**
Project Planning
Projects have many dependencies, any of which could become points of failure. Without the cooperation or input from even one vital resource, a project may fail to meet its objectives. Effective project planning helps project managers think through a project before it starts and prepare communication strategies in advance.

a. Read the article "How to Create a Clear Project Plan," *Darwin Magazine*, August 2004 (www.darwinmag.com/read/080104/project.html), and summarize its main points.

b. Read through the "SDLC in Practice" exercise and select a problem as directed by your professor.

c. Prepare a project plan for the problem you selected.

d. Present your project plan to your class. Solicit your peers' suggestions for improvement.

3. **Americans with Disabilities Act**
Enabling Technologies
The Americans with Disabilities Act prohibits discrimination on the basis of disability in public accommodations and commercial facilities. This act has been interpreted to include certain information systems as well. All information systems development projects should take ADA issues into consideration during development. Accommodating disabled employees and customers must never become an afterthought.

Even if you do not presently experience physical limitations, you may in the future, or you may have employees under your supervision who require special tools to enable access to information systems. Research information systems access solutions. Be sure to include a detailed description of the hardware or software solution, solution provider, and cost of accommodating each limitation listed next.

a. Partial visual impairment.

b. Total visual impairment.

c. Manual dexterity impairment.

4. **Central London Congestion Charging Scheme**
Conversion Strategies
The city of London is well-known for its many historic sites, live theater, and heavy traffic. Despite a sophisticated underground subway system known locally as the "tube," traffic delays, car exhaust, noise pollution, and vehicle–pedestrian accidents have plagued Londoners for decades. After long deliberation, London's city government adopted the Central London Congestion Charging Scheme. This plan involved establishing a toll perimeter around London's center. Rather than stopping cars to collect tolls, however, London set up video cameras at each toll zone crossing. These cameras link to a billing system that charges each vehicle's registered owner a one-day access toll with same-day reentrance privileges. The steep toll, approximately $8, discourages vehicle traffic into London's city center.

Londoners who live within the toll zone receive a special discount, as do residents living near the toll zone boundary, certain government workers, and businesses operating fleets of vehicles. Tolls remain in effect during working hours on workdays. Car owners have until the end of the day to pay their toll through e-mail, SMS messaging, telephone, Web site, or kiosk.

The tolls have resulted in a significant decrease in automobile traffic, increased use of mass transit, fewer accidents, and faster driving times. The tolls have had a negligible effect on business operations and most residents. They have also generated significant revenue that London uses to maintain the system and enhance public transportation.

Consider the massive work involved in educating the public, marking all streets entering the toll zone, setting up cameras, and building the information systems. The information systems alone must process the raw images, match license plates to a payment database, receive payments, send out nonpayment notices, and process appeals. Police also use the system's databases for a variety of law enforcement–related work.

a. Briefly describe the advantages and disadvantages of each conversion strategy (parallel, pilot, phased, and plunge) as they apply to the Central London Congestion Charging Scheme project.

b. Which conversion strategy would you recommend for this project?

c. Defend your recommendation in detail.

REAL WORLD CASE 3

Infosys Technologies: The Implementation Challenges of Knowledge Management Initiatives

Infosys Technologies, headquartered in Bangalore, India, is one of the world's largest software development contractors, with revenue of $1.6 billion in fiscal 2005 and employing over 50,000 software engineers and other staff in early 2006. The company has a long history of trying to leverage knowledge created by its employees for corporate advantage. Its adage "learn once, use anywhere" reinforces the continual learning and reflection required for knowledge accumulation and reuse.

It also draws attention to a core belief that knowledge belongs not only to those employees who create it but to the entire company.

Infosys began efforts to transform its employees' knowledge into an organizationwide resource in the early 1990s. In 1999, a central knowledge management (KM) group was created to facilitate a companywide KM program, including the creation of an intranet knowledge portal called KShop for the accumulation and reuse of organizational knowledge.

But by early 2000, patronage of KShop by employees remained low. Employees within various project teams and practice communities continued to use their informal networks to access knowledge in times of need. Local repositories of specialized knowledge continued to proliferate within project teams and practice communities. In other words, processes at different levels of the knowledge system were not coupling and reinforcing one another.

In response, during the first quarter of 2001, the KM group implemented a major initiative called "the knowledge currency unit (KCU) incentive" scheme to jump-start contributions to KShop.

According to the scheme, Infosys employees who contributed or reviewed contributions to KShop would be awarded KCUs, which they could accumulate and exchange for monetary rewards or prizes. In addition, employees' cumulative KCU scores would be displayed on a scoreboard on KShop, thereby increasing the visibility and standing of prolific contributors.

These initiatives began yielding results, especially after the KCU incentive scheme was introduced. For instance, within a year of introduction of the KCU scheme, more than 2,400 new knowledge assets project proposals, case studies, and reusable software codes were contributed to KShop, with nearly 20 percent of Infosys employees contributing at least one knowledge asset. Over 130,000 KCUs were generated by the KM group and distributed among contributing and reviewing employees.

Even as these events unfolded, the KM group began wondering if the KCU incentive scheme had become too successful. One concern had to do with employees experiencing information overload and, consequently, higher search costs for reusable knowledge. As a member of the KM team commented: "Some people have told us informally that they are finding it faster to do things on their own or to ask someone they know instead of searching the repository for reusable content."

Complicating matters, the explosive growth in the number of contributions began placing a heavy burden on the limited number of volunteer reviewers. A shortage of reviewers made it difficult for the KM group to ensure that contributions were reviewed for quality and relevance before being published on KShop. With review processes still struggling to keep pace with the accelerating pace of contributions, assets of uncertain quality began appearing on KShop. When even contributions of questionable quality began receiving high-quality ratings from colleagues, the rating scheme itself came under scrutiny.

Concerns also began emerging about the possible impacts of the KCU scheme on knowledge processes at the other levels of the organization.

One such concern was the potential for the KCU incentive scheme to destroy the spirit of community and the asking culture within the company. What employees would have given freely to one another previously was now being monetized through the KCU incentive scheme. "Why not gain some rewards and recognition for my knowledge contributions, especially when others are doing so?" was the question being asked by employees who had shared their knowledge earlier for free. An additional concern was the real possibility that some project teams and practice groups, disappointed with KShop, could revert to building and relying on their own local repositories instead of contributing to the central portal.

Sensing the potential of the KCU incentive scheme to compromise the companywide KM program, the KM group took several actions. First, it intervened to decouple knowledge sharing from the economic incentives that threatened the spirit of community and the perceived utility of KShop. Specifically, in April 2002, the KM group modified the KCU incentive scheme to emphasize recognition and personal visibility for knowledge-sharing contributions more than monetary rewards. It formulated a new composite KCU score that emphasized the usefulness and benefit of contributions to Infosys as rated not just by volunteer reviewers or colleagues but also by actual users. Moreover, to increase the accountability of reviewers and users who rated contributions to KShop, the KM group began demanding tangible proof to justify any high ratings.

Finally, the KM group significantly reduced the number of KCUs awarded for reviewing contributions to KShop and raised the bar for cashing in the KCU incentive points for monetary rewards. The KM group hoped that these steps would shift the motivation to share knowledge away from monetary rewards.

A second set of initiatives focused on improving KM practices within project teams and practice communities.

Intense time pressure in completing projects within stringent deadlines reduced knowledge codification efforts within teams. To address this issue, the KM group modified forms and project templates to facilitate extraction of knowledge using automated tools. The group also implemented a project-tracking tool on KShop to log details and deliverables pertaining to every project within Infosys. The objective of these initiatives was to enable the codification and extraction of knowledge even as teams carried out their routine project-related tasks.

Despite these attempts, knowledge codification continued to vary across project teams. To address this shortcoming, the KM group introduced a hierarchy of roles to broker knowledge sharing among project teams, practice communities, and the wider organization.

Within each project team, one volunteer member would be designated as the KM prime. The KM prime would be responsible for identifying and facilitating the fulfillment of the team's knowledge needs for each project. The KM prime would also ensure that, after the completion of each project, the team codified and shared critical knowledge gained during the project with the rest of the company. At the practice community and wider organizational levels, the KM group created the role of knowledge champions to spearhead and facilitate knowledge sharing and reuse in critical or emerging technologies and methodologies. Furthermore, the KM group encouraged employees to swap stories on KShop with the view of promoting widespread sharing of tacit individual and team-level knowledge and experiences.

After the modified KCU scheme was introduced, those who had contributed to KShop just to secure monetary rewards reduced their participation. For instance, in the two quarters immediately following the introduction of the modified KCU scheme, the number of new contributors per quarter declined by nearly 37 percent, whereas the number of new knowledge assets contributed to KShop per quarter declined by approximately 26 percent. After this significant initial decline, however, the number of new knowledge assets contributed to KShop slowly stabilized and then increased at a more manageable pace. Finally, users of KShop reported lower search costs and significant increases in the quality and utility of knowledge assets available through the portal.

Looking into the future, the KM group was optimistic that the KM prime and knowledge champion roles in project groups and development communities would yield positive outcomes. A manager who had been associated with the KM initiative from the beginning reflected on the challenges faced in the implementation process at Infosys:

We are coming to realize that knowledge management requires much more than just technology. We have to pay attention to the cultural and social facets of knowledge management as well. We have to continually campaign and evangelize besides investing the time and resources to manage the content. Knowledge management initially appears to be a deceptively simple task. But, make just one wrong move, and it is difficult to convince people to come back.

Source: Adapted from Raghu Garud and Arun Kumaraswamy, "Vicious and Virtuous Circles in the Management of Knowledge: The Case of Infosy," *MIS Quarterly*, March 2005; and Julie Schlosser, "Infosys U.," *Fortune*, March 20, 2006.

CASE STUDY QUESTIONS

1. Why do you think the knowledge management system at Infosys faced such serious implementation challenges? Defend your answer with examples from the case.

2. What steps did the KM group at Infosys take to improve participation in the KM system? Why were some of these initiatives counterproductive? The KM group responded with corrective initiatives. Do you think these will succeed? Why or why not?

3. What change management initiatives should the KM group have initiated at Infosys before attempting to develop and implement knowledge management at the company? Defend your proposals, paying particular attention to the final quote in the case by a longtime KM manager at Infosys.

REAL WORLD ACTIVITIES

1. Research the Internet to find examples of successful implementations of knowledge management systems. What successes do these companies claim, and what reasons do they give for their successful KM initiatives?

2. If knowledge management would succeed anywhere, one would think it would be a smashing success at a progressive successful IT company like Infosys. Break into small groups with your classmates to discuss what change management and other implementation strategies and tactics you would use to ensure a successful KM initiative at Infosys, one of the companies you found in your previous Internet research, or a company of your choice.

MODULE V

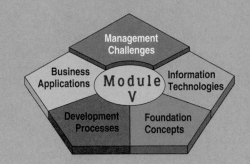

MANAGEMENT CHALLENGES

What managerial challenges do information systems pose for today's business enterprises? The two chapters of this module emphasize how managers and business professionals can manage the successful use of information technologies in a global economy.

- **Chapter 11: Security and Ethical Challenges** discusses the threats against and defenses needed for the performance and security of business information systems, as well as societal impact and ethical implications of information technology.

- **Chapter 12: Enterprise and Global Management of Information Technology** discusses the major challenges that information technology presents to business managers, the components of information systems management, and the managerial implications of the use of information technology in global business.

CHAPTER 11

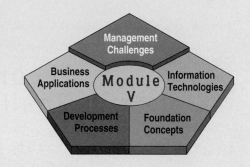

Management Challenges · Business Applications · Module V · Information Technologies · Development Processes · Foundation Concepts

SECURITY AND ETHICAL CHALLENGES

Chapter Highlights

Learning Objectives

1. Identify several ethical issues regarding how the use of information technologies in business affects employment, individuality, working conditions, privacy, crime, health, and solutions to societal problems.

2. Identify several types of security management strategies and defenses and explain how they can be used to ensure the security of business applications of information technology.

3. Propose several ways that business managers and professionals can help lessen the harmful effects and increase the beneficial effects of the use of information technology.

SECTION I	# Security, Ethical, and Societal Challenges of IT

Introduction

There is no question that the use of information technology in business presents major security challenges, poses serious ethical questions, and affects society in significant ways. Therefore, in this section, we explore the threats to businesses and individuals as a result of many types of computer crime and unethical behavior. In Section II, we will examine a variety of methods that companies use to manage the security and integrity of their business systems. Now let's look at a real-world example.

Read the Real World Case on the next page. We can learn a lot from this case about the security and ethical issues that result from the pervasive use of IT in organizations and society today. See Figure 11.1.

Business/IT Security, Ethics, and Society

The use of information technologies in business has had a major impact on society and thus raises ethical issues in the areas of crime, privacy, individuality, employment, health, and working conditions. See Figure 11.2.

It is important to understand that information technology has had beneficial results, as well as detrimental effects, on society and people in each of these areas. For example, computerizing a manufacturing process may have the beneficial result of improving working conditions and producing products of higher quality at lower cost, but it also has the adverse effect of eliminating people's jobs. So your job as a manager or business professional should involve managing your work activities and those of others to minimize the detrimental effects of business applications of information technology and optimize their beneficial effects. That would represent an ethically responsible use of information technology.

Ethical Responsibility of Business Professionals

As a business professional, you have a responsibility to promote ethical uses of information technology in the workplace. Whether or not you have managerial responsibilities, you should accept the ethical responsibilities that come with your work activities. That includes properly performing your role as a vital human resource in the business systems you help develop and use in your organization. As a manager or business professional, it will be your responsibility to make decisions about business activities and the use of information technologies that may have an ethical dimension that must be considered.

For example, should you electronically monitor your employees' work activities and e-mail? Should you let employees use their work computers for private business or take home copies of software for their personal use? Should you electronically access your employees' personnel records or workstation files? Should you sell customer information extracted from transaction processing systems to other companies? These are a few examples of the types of decisions you will have to make that have an ethical dimension. So let's take a closer look at several **ethical foundations** in business and information technology.

Business Ethics

Business ethics is concerned with the numerous ethical questions that managers must confront as part of their daily business decision making. For example, Figure 11.3 outlines some of the basic categories of ethical issues and specific business practices that have serious ethical consequences. Notice that the issues of intellectual property rights, customer and employee privacy, security of company records, and workplace safety are highlighted because they have been major areas of ethical controversy in information technology.

How can managers make ethical decisions when confronted with business issues such as those listed in Figure 11.3? Several important alternatives based on theories of

REAL WORLD CASE 1

Ethics, Moral Dilemmas, and Tough Decisions: The Many Challenges of Working in IT

What Bryan found on an executive's computer six years ago still weighs heavily on his mind. He's particularly troubled that the man he discovered using a company PC to view pornography of Asian women and of children was subsequently promoted and moved to China to run a manufacturing plant. "To this day, I regret not taking that stuff to the FBI." It happened when Bryan, who asked that his last name not be published, was IT director at the U.S. division of a $500 million multinational corporation based in Germany.

The company's Internet usage policy, which Bryan helped develop with input from senior management, prohibited the use of company computers to access pornographic or adult-content Web sites. One of Bryan's duties was to use products from SurfControl PLC to monitor employee Web surfing and to report any violations to management.

Bryan knew that the executive, who was a level above him in another department, was popular within both the U.S. division and the German parent. Yet when the tools turned up dozens of pornographic Web sites visited by the exec's computer, Bryan followed the policy. "That's what it's there for. I wasn't going to get into trouble for following the policy," he reasoned.

Bryan's case is a good example of the ethical dilemmas that IT workers may encounter on the job. IT employees have privileged access to digital information, both personal and professional, throughout the company, and they have the technical prowess to manipulate that information. That gives them both the power and responsibility to monitor and report employees who break company rules. IT professionals may also uncover evidence that a coworker is, say, embezzling funds, or they could be tempted to peek at private salary information or personal e-mails. There's little guidance, however, on what to do in these uncomfortable situations.

In the case of the porn-viewing executive, Bryan didn't get into trouble, but neither did the executive, who came up with "a pretty outlandish explanation" that the company accepted, Bryan says. He considered going to the FBI, but the Internet bubble had just burst, and jobs were hard to come by. "It was a tough choice," Bryan says. "But I had a family to feed."

Perhaps it would ease Bryan's conscience to know that he did just what labor attorney Linn Hynds, a senior partner at Honigman Miller Schwartz and Cohn LLP, would have advised in his case. "Let the company handle it," she says. "Make sure you report violations to the right person in your company, and show them the evidence. After that, leave it to the people who are supposed to be making that decision." Ideally, corporate policy takes over where the law stops, governing workplace ethics to clear up gray areas and remove personal judgment from the equation as much as possible.

"If you don't set out your policy and your guidelines, if you don't make sure that people know what they are and understand them, you're in no position to hold workers accountable," says John Reece, a former CIO at the Internal Revenue Service and Time Warner Inc. Having clear ethical guidelines also lets employees off the hook emotionally if the person they discover breaking the policy is a friend, someone who reports to them directly, or a supervisor, says Reece, who is now head of consultancy at John C. Reece and Associates LLC. Organizations that have policies in place often focus on areas where they had trouble in the past or emphasize whatever they are most worried about. When Reece was at the IRS, for example, the biggest emphasis was on protecting the confidentiality of taxpayer information.

At the U.S. Department of Defense, policies usually emphasize procurement rules, notes Stephen Northcutt, president of the SANS Technology Institute and author of *IT Ethics Handbook: Right and Wrong for IT Professionals*. Adding to the complexity, an organization that depends on highly skilled workers might be more lenient. When Northcutt worked in IT security at the Naval Surface Warfare Center in Virginia, it was a rarefied atmosphere of highly sought-after PhDs. "I was told pretty clearly that if I made a whole lot of PhDs very unhappy so that they left, the organization wouldn't need me anymore," says Northcutt.

Of course, that wasn't written in any policy manual, so Northcutt had to read between the lines. "The way I interpreted it was: Child pornography, turn that in," he says. "But if the leading mathematician wants to download some pictures of naked girls, they didn't want to hear from me."

Northcutt says that he did find child porn on two occasions and that both events led to prosecution. As for other offensive

FIGURE 11.1

The pervasive use of information technology in organizations and society presents individuals with new ethical challenges and dilemmas.

Source: ©Courtesy of Punchstock.

photos that he encountered, Northcutt pointed out to his superiors that there might be a legal liability, citing a Supreme Court decision that found that similar pictures at a military installation indicated a pervasive atmosphere of sexual harassment. That did the trick. "Once they saw that law was involved, they were more willing to change culture and policy," Northcutt says.

When policies aren't clear, ethical decisions are left to the judgment of IT employees, which varies by person and the particular circumstances. For example, Gary, a director of technology at a nonprofit organization in the Midwest, flat-out refused when the assistant CEO wanted to use a mailing list that a new employee had stolen from her former employer. Yet Gary, who asked that his last name not be used, didn't stop his boss from installing unlicensed software on PCs for a short time, although he refused to do it himself. "The question is, how much was it really going to hurt anybody? We were still going to have 99.5% compliant software. I was OK with that." He says he uninstalled it, with his boss's approval, as soon as he could, which was about a week later.

Northcutt argues that the IT profession should have two things that professions such as law or accounting have had for years: a code of ethics and standards of practice. That way, when company policy is nonexistent or unclear, IT professionals still have standards to follow.

That might be useful for Tim, a systems administrator who works at a Fortune 500 agricultural business. When Tim, who asked that his last name not be published, happened across an unencrypted spreadsheet of salary information on a manager's PC, he copied it. He didn't share the information with anyone or use it to his advantage. It was an impulsive act, he admits, that stemmed from frustration with his employer. "I didn't take it for nefarious reasons; I just took it to prove that I could," he says.

Tim's actions point to a disturbing trend: IT workers are justifying their ethically questionable behavior. That path can end in criminal activity, says fraud investigator Chuck Martell. "We started seeing a few cases about seven or eight years ago," says Martell, managing director of investigative services at Veritas Global LLC, a security firm in Southfield, Michigan. "Now we're investigating a tremendous amount of them."

Whole Foods Market Chairman and CEO John Mackey spent years earning a positive reputation as a corporate leader who was not afraid to take a stand on ethics issues. Before other companies figured out that it pays to be environmentally friendly, Whole Foods led by setting standards for humane animal treatment. In 2006, Mackey took the bold step of reducing his own annual salary to one dollar, pledging money instead for an emergency fund for his staff. Not shy about expressing his views, Mackey challenged leading thinkers, like Nobel Prize–winner Milton Friedman, on business ethics issues. Like many leaders, Mackey seemed to relish the public spotlight.

On July 20, 2007, however, Mackey got more than he bargained for in terms of publicity. The *Wall Street Journal* reported that Mackey had long used the pseudonym "Rahodeb" to make postings in Yahoo Finance forums that flattered his own company and leveled criticisms against the competition. Serious financial and possibly legal repercussions continue to unfold from this incident, and the final consequences may not be known for some time.

Amid the furor that followed this disclosure of Mackey's secret online alias, it is vital that we not lose sight of the critical issues it raises about ethics and leadership in a rapidly evolving business world. There is no question that the current climate has prompted many more companies to tackle ethics issues.

By now, "business ethics" is an established part of doing business, not just in the United States, but also increasingly around the world. People no longer joke that "business ethics is an oxymoron," as society has come not merely to expect, but to demand, that business conduct itself according to basic rules of ethics and integrity. Business will always need to pay attention to ethics and leadership, but these lessons are continually challenged by new developments, including technological advances that promote new kinds of communication online. Business leaders cannot afford to overlook these challenges, as even a single misstep can be enough to undo a reputation for ethical leadership.

Source: Adapted from Tam Harbert, "Ethics in IT: Dark Secrets, Ugly Truths—and Little Guidance," *Computerworld*, October 29, 2007; and David Schmidt, "What Is the Moral Responsibility of a Business Leader?" *CIO Magazine*, September 12, 2007.

CASE STUDY QUESTIONS

1. Companies are developing ethical policies and guidelines for legal reasons, but also to clarify what is acceptable and what is not. Do you think any of the issues raised in the case required clarification? Would you take exception to any of them being classified as inappropriate behavior? Why do you think these things happen anyway?

2. In the first example (Bryan's), it is apparent that he did not believe justice had been ultimately served by the decision his company made. Should he have taken the issue to the authorities? Or was it enough that he reported the problem through the proper channels and let the organization handle it, as was the recommendation of Linn Hynds? Provide a rationale for the position you are willing to take on this matter.

3. In the case, Gary chose not to stop his boss from installing unlicensed software, although he refused to do it himself. If installing unlicensed software is wrong, is there any difference between refusing to do it versus not stopping somebody else? Do you buy his argument that it was not really going to hurt anybody? Why or why not?

REAL WORLD ACTIVITIES

1. Go online to follow up on John Mackey's story and search for other instances of debatable behavior where IT has been an important factor. Are the ones featured in the case exceptions, or are these occurrences becoming more and more common? How do organizations seem to be coping with these issues? What type of responses did you find? Prepare a report to summarize your findings.

2. The case features many examples of what is arguably unethical behavior, including child pornography, accessing adult content on company-owned equipment, installing unlicensed software, and so on. Are some of these practices "more wrong" than others? Is there any one that you would not consider problematic? Break into small groups to discuss these questions and make a list of other ethical problems involving IT that were not mentioned in the case.

FIGURE 11.2

Important aspects of the security, ethical, and societal dimensions of the use of information technology in business. Remember that information technologies can support both beneficial and detrimental effects on society in each of the areas shown.

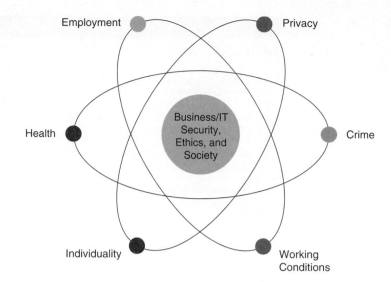

corporate social responsibility can be used. For example, in business ethics, the *stockholder theory* holds that managers are agents of the stockholders, and their only ethical responsibility is to increase the profits of the business without violating the law or engaging in fraudulent practices.

However, the *social contract theory* states that companies have ethical responsibilities to all members of society, which allows corporations to exist according to a social contract. The first condition of the contract requires companies to enhance the economic satisfaction of consumers and employees. They must do that without polluting the environment or depleting natural resources, misusing political power, or subjecting their employees to dehumanizing working conditions. The second condition requires companies to avoid fraudulent practices, show respect for their employees as human beings, and avoid practices that systematically worsen the position of any group in society.

The *stakeholder theory* of business ethics maintains that managers have an ethical responsibility to manage a firm for the benefit of all its stakeholders, that is, all individuals and groups that have a stake in, or claim on, a company. These stakeholders usually include the corporation's stockholders, employees, customers, suppliers, and

FIGURE 11.3   Basic categories of ethical business issues. Information technology has caused ethical controversy in the areas of intellectual property rights, customer and employee privacy, security of company information, and workplace safety.

Equity	Rights	Honesty	Exercise of Corporate Power
Executive salaries	Corporate due process	Employee conflicts	Product safety
Comparable worth	Employee health	of interest	Environmental issues
Product pricing	screening	**Security of company**	Disinvestment
Intellectual	**Customer privacy**	**information**	Corporate contributions
property rights	**Employee privacy**	Inappropriate gifts	Social issues raised by
Noncompetitive	Sexual harassment	Advertising content	religious organizations
agreements	Affirmative action	Government contract issues	Plant/facility closures and
	Equal employment	Financial and cash	downsizing
	opportunity	management procedures	Political action committees
	Shareholder interests	Questionable business	**Workplace safety**
	Employment at will	practices in foreign	
	Whistle-blowing	countries	

FIGURE 11.4

Ethical principles to help evaluate the potential harms or risks of the use of new technologies.

Principles of Technology Ethics
● **Proportionality.** The good achieved by the technology must outweigh the harm or risk. Moreover, there must be no alternative that achieves the same or comparable benefits with less harm or risk.
● **Informed Consent.** Those affected by the technology should understand and accept the risks.
● **Justice.** The benefits and burdens of the technology should be distributed fairly. Those who benefit should bear their fair share of the risks, and those who do not benefit should not suffer a significant increase in risk.
● **Minimized Risk.** Even if judged acceptable by the other three guidelines, the technology must be implemented so as to avoid all unnecessary risk.

the local community. Sometimes the term is broadened to include all groups who can affect or be affected by the corporation, such as competitors, government agencies, and special-interest groups. Balancing the claims of conflicting stakeholders is obviously not an easy task for managers.

Technology Ethics

Another important ethical dimension deals specifically with the ethics of the use of any form of technology. For example, Figure 11.4 outlines four principles of technology ethics. These principles can serve as basic ethical requirements that companies should meet to help ensure the ethical implementation of information technologies and information systems in business.

One common example of technology ethics involves some of the health risks of using computer workstations for extended periods in high-volume data entry job positions. Many organizations display ethical behavior by scheduling work breaks and limiting the exposure of data entry workers to staring at a computer monitor to minimize their risk of developing a variety of work-related health disorders, such as hand or eye injuries. The health impact of information technology is discussed later in this chapter.

Ethical Guidelines

We have outlined a few ethical principles that can serve as the basis for ethical conduct by managers, end users, and IS professionals. But what more specific guidelines might help your ethical use of information technology? Many companies and organizations answer that question today with detailed policies for ethical computer and Internet usage by their employees. For example, most policies specify that company computer workstations and networks are company resources that must be used only for work-related uses, whether using internal networks or the Internet.

Another way to answer this question is to examine statements of responsibilities contained in codes of professional conduct for IS professionals. A good example is the code of professional conduct of the Association of Information Technology Professionals (AITP), an organization of professionals in the computing field. Its code of conduct outlines the ethical considerations inherent in the major responsibilities of an IS professional. Figure 11.5 is a portion of the AITP code of conduct.

Business and IS professionals can live up to their ethical responsibilities by voluntarily following such guidelines. For example, you can be a **responsible professional** by (1) acting with integrity, (2) increasing your professional competence, (3) setting high standards of personal performance, (4) accepting responsibility for your work, and (5) advancing the health, privacy, and general welfare of the public. Then you would be demonstrating ethical conduct, avoiding computer crime, and increasing the security of any information system you develop or use.

FIGURE 11.5

Part of the AITP standards of professional conduct. This code can serve as a model for ethical conduct by business end users as well as IS professionals.

AITP Standards of Professional Conduct
In recognition of my obligation to my employer I shall:

- Avoid conflicts of interest and ensure that my employer is aware of any potential conflicts.
- Protect the privacy and confidentiality of all information entrusted to me.
- Not misrepresent or withhold information that is germane to the situation.
- Not attempt to use the resources of my employer for personal gain or for any purpose without proper approval.
- Not exploit the weakness of a computer system for personal gain or personal satisfaction.

In recognition of my obligation to society I shall:

- Use my skill and knowledge to inform the public in all areas of my expertise.
- To the best of my ability, ensure that the products of my work are used in a socially responsible way.
- Support, respect, and abide by the appropriate local, state, provincial, and federal laws.
- Never misrepresent or withhold information that is germane to a problem or a situation of public concern, nor will I allow any such known information to remain unchallenged.
- Not use knowledge of a confidential or personal nature in any unauthorized manner to achieve personal gain.

Source: 2007 PricewaterhouseCoopers Global Security Survey.

Enron Corporation: Failure in Business Ethics

Much has been said about the driven, cultlike ethos of the organization that styled itself "the world's leading company." Truth be told, for all its razzle-dazzle use of Internet technology, a lot of the things Enron did weren't so very exceptional: paying insanely large bonuses to executives, for example, often in the form of stock options (a practice that not only hid true compensation costs but also encouraged managers to keep the stock price up by any means necessary); promising outlandish growth, year after year, and making absurdly confident predictions about every new market it entered, however untested; scarcely ever admitting a weakness to the outside world; and showing scant interest in the questions or doubts of some in its own ranks about its questionable, unethical, and even illegal business and accounting practices.

Credibility comes hard in business. You earn it slowly by conducting yourself with integrity year in and year out, or by showing exceptional leadership in exceptional circumstances, such as on September 11, 2001. The surest way to lose it, short of being caught in an outright lie, is to promise much and deliver little. Those, at least, are two conclusions suggested by an exclusive survey of executives that Clark, Martire, and Bartolomeo conducted for *Business 2.0.*

Executives rated Enron Chairman and CEO Ken Lay least credible of the business figures in the survey. Perhaps it had something to do with statements like:

- "Our performance has never been stronger; our business model has never been more robust; our growth has never been more certain . . . I have never felt better about the prospects for the company."—E-mail to employees, August 14, 2001
- "The company is probably in the strongest and best shape that it has ever been in."—Interview in *BusinessWeek*, August 24, 2001
- "Our 26 percent increase in [profits] shows the very strong results of our core wholesale and retail energy businesses and our natural gas pipelines."—Press release, October 16, 2001

Yet three weeks later, Enron admitted that it had overstated earnings by $586 million since 1997. Within a few more weeks, Enron also disclosed a stunning $638 million third-quarter loss and then filed for Chapter 11 bankruptcy.

Dick Hudson, former CIO of Houston-based oil drilling company Global Marine Inc. and now president of Hudson & Associates, an executive IT consulting firm in Katy, Texas, thinks Enron started with a good business strategy and that if it hadn't pushed the envelope, it could well have been a successful Fortune 1000 firm. Instead, it aimed for the Fortune 10, so it got into markets such as broadband, which is a tough nut to crack even for the industry's leaders. "Those good old boys in Houston, they had to walk with the big dogs," accuses Hudson. "They are a textbook case of greed and mismanagement."

On May 25, 2006, Kenneth Lay was convicted on six counts of securities and wire fraud and faced a total of 45 years in prison. Lay died on July 5, 2006, before sentencing could be passed. His protege, Jeffrey K. Skilling, was convicted of 19 of 28 counts, and was sentenced to 24 years in prison. Andrew S. Fastow, the former chief financial officer, was sentenced to six years in prison for his role in the conspiracy that led to the collapse of Enron. His former lieutenant, Michael Kopper, received a reduced sentence of 37 months for cooperating with the investigation.

Source: Adapted from Melissa Solomon and Michael Meehan, "Enron Lesson: Tech Is for Support," *Computerworld*, February 18, 2002.

Computer Crime

Cyber crime is becoming one of the Net's growth businesses. Today, criminals are doing everything from stealing intellectual property and committing fraud to unleashing viruses and committing acts of cyberterrorism.

Computer crime, a growing threat to society, is caused by the criminal or irresponsible actions of individuals who are taking advantage of the widespread use and vulnerability of computers and the Internet and other networks. It presents a major challenge to the ethical use of information technologies. Computer crime also poses serious threats to the integrity, safety, and survival of most business systems and thus makes the development of effective security methods a top priority. See Figure 11.6.

Computer crime is defined by the Association of Information Technology Professionals (AITP) as including (1) the unauthorized use, access, modification, and destruction of hardware, software, data, or network resources; (2) the unauthorized release of information; (3) the unauthorized copying of software; (4) denying an end user access to his or her own hardware, software, data, or network resources; and (5) using or conspiring to use computer or network resources to obtain information or tangible property illegally. This definition was promoted by the AITP in a Model Computer Crime Act and is reflected in many computer crime laws.

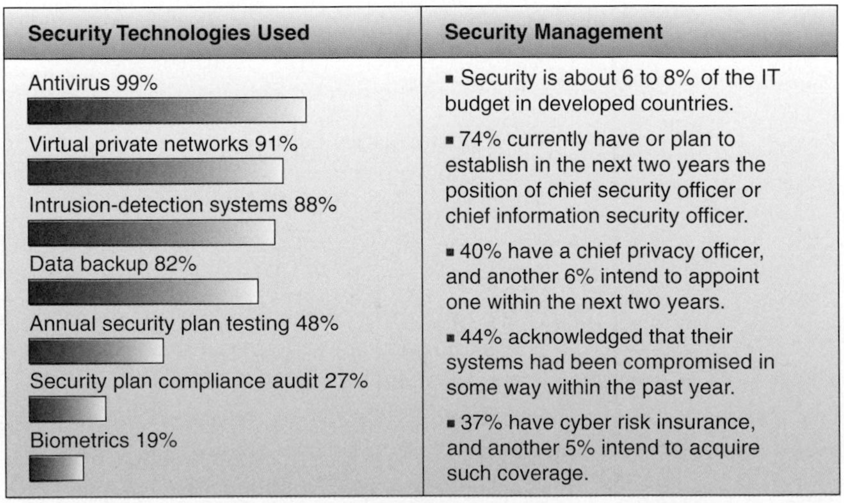

FIGURE 11.6

How large companies are protecting themselves from cyber crime.

Security Technologies Used	Security Management
Antivirus 99%	■ Security is about 6 to 8% of the IT budget in developed countries.
Virtual private networks 91%	■ 74% currently have or plan to establish in the next two years the position of chief security officer or chief information security officer.
Intrusion-detection systems 88%	
Data backup 82%	■ 40% have a chief privacy officer, and another 6% intend to appoint one within the next two years.
Annual security plan testing 48%	■ 44% acknowledged that their systems had been compromised in some way within the past year.
Security plan compliance audit 27%	
Biometrics 19%	■ 37% have cyber risk insurance, and another 5% intend to acquire such coverage.

Source: 2007 PricewaterhouseCoopers Global Security Survey.

The Online Crusade against Phishing

Until just a few years ago, Gary Warner did not have the kind of day job you'd expect from an antiphishing crusader. He didn't work for a security vendor or a bank, or any kind of company you'd expect to care about phishing. Warner's career as a cyber-sleuth began on Halloween 2000. That's when his company's Web site was defaced by an entity named Pimpshiz as part of a pro-Napster Internet graffiti campaign.

"My boss came to me and said, 'Find out who did this and put them in jail,'" said Warner, who was at the time an IT staffer with Energen, a Birmingham, Alabama oil and gas company. It was an eye-opening experience. "I called the police and they were like, 'What do you want us to do?'" he said. Months later, when Pimpshiz struck servers at NASA, Warner reached out, calling staff there and saying "Hey, we know who this guy is. Here's his name and address."

Since then, Warner has quietly become one of the most-respected authorities on phishing in the United States—the kind of guy that federal agents and banking IT staff call when they want to know how to catch the bad guys and shut down their credit-card-stealing Web sites.

With Warner's help, authorities eventually arrested Pimpshiz, whose real name is Robert Lyttle, in connection with the defacements.

Warner said that the Pimpshiz case was formative, underlining how hard it is for law enforcement to catch the bad guys on the Internet. "The experience showed me that it's not that they don't care," Warner said. "Their hands are tied by the legal process."

In July of 2007, with recommendations from FBI and Secret Service agents, Warner took a job as Director of Research in Computer Forensics with the University of Alabama at Birmingham (UAB). He also began working with law enforcement, not only educating FBI and Secret Service agents on how crimes were committed, but also helping to track down the criminals and helping with take-downs.

For Warner, the work isn't so much a job, as it is his moral responsibility as a computer scientist. "One of the things that really bothered me from the very beginning was people who were using my field to attack other people," he said. "The way I see it, this is our Internet. I'm going to stand at the end of my driveway and protect what's mine."

Warner is now focusing on fighting cyber-crime full-time and on training a new generation of network forensics investigators.

"You wouldn't believe the looks on their eyes the first time they got an e-mail back from a Webmaster saying, 'Thanks for letting me know. I just shut that down.'" Five days after final exams at the University of Alabama at Birmingham and though it would have no effect on their marks, four students were still coming into the labs to help shut down phishers.

"That idea that as a private citizen, you can help, that's the kind of thing we're trying to inspire," he says.

Source: Adapted from Robert McMillan, "Crime and Punishment: The White Knight of Phish-Busting," *Computerworld*, December 31, 2007.

Hacking and Cracking

Cyber thieves have at their fingertips a dozen dangerous tools, from "scans" that ferret out weaknesses in Web site software programs to "sniffers" that snatch passwords.

Hacking, in computerese, is the obsessive use of computers or the unauthorized access and use of networked computer systems. Hackers can be outsiders or company employees who use the Internet and other networks to steal or damage data and programs. One of the issues in hacking is what to do about a hacker who commits only *electronic breaking and entering*, that is, gets access to a computer system and reads some files but neither steals nor damages anything. This situation is common in computer crime cases that are prosecuted. In most cases, courts have found that the typical computer crime statute language prohibiting malicious access to a computer system did apply to anyone gaining unauthorized access to another's computer networks. See Figure 11.7.

FIGURE 11.7

Examples of common hacking tactics to assault companies through the Internet and other networks.

Common Hacking Tactics

Denial of Service. This is becoming a common networking prank. By hammering a Web site's equipment with too many requests for information, an attacker can effectively clog the system, slowing performance or even crashing the site. This method of overloading computers is sometimes used to cover up an attack.

Scans. Widespread probes of the Internet to determine types of computers, services, and connections. That way the bad guys can take advantage of weaknesses in a particular make of computer or software program.

Sniffer. Programs that covertly search individual packets of data as they pass through the Internet, capturing passwords or the entire contents.

Spoofing. Faking an e-mail address or Web page to trick users into passing along critical information like passwords or credit card numbers.

Trojan Horse. A program that, unknown to the user, contains instructions that exploit a known vulnerability in some software.

Back Doors. In case the original entry point has been detected, having a few hidden ways back makes reentry easy—and difficult to detect.

Malicious Applets. Tiny programs, sometimes written in the popular Java computer language, that misuse your computer's resources, modify files on the hard disk, send fake e-mail, or steal passwords.

War Dialing. Programs that automatically dial thousands of telephone numbers in search of a way in through a modem connection.

Logic Bombs. An instruction in a computer program that triggers a malicious act.

Buffer Overflow. A technique for crashing or gaining control of a computer by sending too much data to the buffer in a computer's memory.

Password Crackers. Software that can guess passwords.

Social Engineering. A tactic used to gain access to computer systems by talking unsuspecting company employees out of valuable information such as passwords.

Dumpster Diving. Sifting through a company's garbage to find information to help break into their computers. Sometimes the information is used to make a stab at social engineering more credible.

Hackers can monitor e-mail, Web server access, or file transfers to extract passwords, steal network files, or plant data that will cause a system to welcome intruders. A hacker may also use remote services that allow one computer on a network to execute programs on another computer to gain privileged access within a network. Telnet, an Internet tool for interactive use of remote computers, can help hackers discover information to plan other attacks. Hackers have used Telnet to access a computer's e-mail port, for example, to monitor e-mail messages for passwords and other information about privileged user accounts and network resources. These are just some of the typical types of computer crimes that hackers commit on the Internet on a regular basis. That's why Internet security measures like encryption and firewalls, as discussed in the next section, are so vital to the success of e-commerce and other e-business applications.

The hacking community is quick to make the distinction between hacking and cracking. A cracker (also called a black hat or darkside hacker) is a malicious or criminal hacker. This term is seldom used outside of the security industry and by some modern programmers. The general public uses the term *hacker* to refer to the same thing. In computer jargon, the meaning of *hacker* can be much more broad. The name comes from the opposite of white hat hackers.

Usually a cracker is a person who maintains knowledge of the vulnerabilities he or she finds and exploits them for private advantage, not revealing them to either the general public or the manufacturer for correction. Many crackers promote individual freedom and accessibility over privacy and security. Crackers may seek to expand holes in systems; any attempts made to patch software are generally to prevent others from also compromising a system over which they have already obtained secure control. In the most extreme cases, a cracker may work to cause damage maliciously or make threats to do so for blackmail purposes.

The term *cracker* was coined by Richard Stallman to provide an alternative to abusing the existing word *hacker* for this meaning. This term's use is limited (as is "black hat") mostly to some areas of the computer and security field and, even there, is considered controversial. One group that refers to themselves as hackers consists of skilled computer enthusiasts. The other, and more common usage, refers to people who attempt to gain unauthorized access to computer systems. Many members of the first group attempt to convince people that intruders should be called crackers rather than hackers, but the common usage remains ingrained.

Cyber Theft

Many computer crimes involve the theft of money. In the majority of cases, they are inside jobs that involve unauthorized network entry and fraudulent alteration of computer databases to cover the tracks of the employees involved. Of course, many computer crimes involve the use of the Internet. One early example was the theft of $11 million from Citibank in late 1994. Russian hacker Vladimir Levin and his accomplices in St. Petersburg used the Internet for an electronic break-in of Citibank's mainframe systems in New York. They then succeeded in transferring the funds from several Citibank accounts to their own accounts at banks in Finland, Israel, and California.

In most cases, the scope of such financial losses is much larger than the incidents reported. Companies don't usually reveal that they have been targets or victims of computer crime. They fear scaring customers and provoking complaints by shareholders. In fact, several British banks, including the Bank of London, paid hackers more than a half million dollars not to reveal information about electronic break-ins.

Cyberterrorism

Cyberterrorism is the leveraging of an organization's or government's computers and information, particularly via the Internet, to cause physical, real-world harm or severe disruption of infrastructure. There are some that argue cyberterrorism is really a form of hacking or information warfare. They disagree with labeling it terrorism because of the unlikelihood of the creation of fear, significant physical harm, or death in a population using electronic means, considering current attack and protective technologies.

The National Conference of State Legislatures (NCSL) puts a much finer point on the definition of the term:

> *the use of information technology by terrorist groups and individuals to further their agenda. This can include use of information technology to organize and execute attacks against networks, computer systems and telecommunications infrastructures, or for exchanging information or making threats electronically.*

Cyberterrorism can have a serious large-scale influence on significant numbers of people. It can significantly weaken a country's economy, thereby denying it access to vital resources and making it more vulnerable to military attack. Cyberterror can also affect Internet-based businesses. Like bricks and mortar retailers and service providers, most Web sites that produce income (whether by advertising, monetary exchange for goods, or paid services) could stand to lose money in the event of downtime created by cyber criminals. As Internet-businesses have increasing economic importance to countries, what is normally cyber crime becomes more political and therefore "terror" related.

To date, there have been no reported cyber attacks on the United States. There have, however, been several large-scale examples of cyberterrorism in other countries. One such example occurred in Romania when cyberterrorists illegally gained access to the computers controlling the life-support systems at an Antarctic research station, endangering the 58 scientists involved. However, the culprits were stopped before damage actually occurred. Mostly nonpolitical acts of sabotage have caused financial and other damage, as in a case where a disgruntled employee caused the release of untreated sewage into water in Maroochy Shire, Australia. Computer viruses have degraded or shut down some nonessential systems in nuclear power plants, but this is not believed to have been a deliberate attack.

More recently, in May 2007 Estonia was subjected to a mass cyber attack in the wake of the removal of a Russian World War II war memorial from downtown Talinn. The attack was a distributed denial of service attack in which selected sites were bombarded with traffic in order to force them off-line; nearly all Estonian government ministry networks as well as two major Estonian bank networks were knocked off-line; in addition, the political party Web site of Estonia's current Prime Minister Andrus Ansip featured a counterfeit letter of apology from Ansip for removing the memorial statue. Despite speculation that the attack had been coordinated by the Russian government, Estonia's defense minister admitted he had no evidence linking cyber attacks to Russian authorities. Russia called accusations of its involvement "unfounded," and neither NATO nor European Commission experts were able to find any proof of official Russian government participation. In January 2008 a man from Estonia was convicted for launching the attacks against the Estonian Reform Party Web site and fined.

Leaving Your Job? Don't Take Anything with You

Employees who sign a noncompete agreement when hired, then break the agreement by leaving to work for a competitor, might want to exercise a little extra caution. Ex-employers might be able to use the Computer Fraud and Abuse Act to prosecute those suspected of stealing company intellectual property. The Act, designed to protect government computers and punish hackers, has been amended and now applies to any computer connected to the Internet, says Gregory Trimarche, a partner at the influential law and lobbying firm Greenberg Traurig.

Sensitive data can range from detailed customer and employee contact lists to internal marketing material. Trimarche considers intellectual property and trade secrets to be information that derives "independent economic value" that's not "generally known or available to the general public or competitors." An employee's know-how or talent doesn't fall into this category, but the company phone list with extensions could.

It's Sergio Kopelev's job to collect the evidence. Kopelev, a computer forensic specialist at LECG, which provides independent testimony, analysis, and consulting services to resolve disputes, said, "70 percent of people have stolen key information from work." By looking at the metadata, employers can determine when a document was printed. "You can secure the file's metadata by right-clicking on files running Microsoft Windows within the properties, for example," he says. "You also can tell when documents are copied to a thumb or flash drive. When you look at the drive forensically, the fact that someone has copied documents to a thumb drive is seen."

There is operating system metadata, software-dependent metadata, some collected by the machine and others by the user. "The most pilfered items include e-mail, address books and contact lists and customer databases," notes Kopelev.

Aside from taking the ex-employee to court, what's the recourse for companies that have executives who leave to work at a competitor? Vengeful employers can start yanking back stock options. John Giovannone, corporate attorney and partner at Greenberg Traurig, said there's a growing trend to include a "claw-back provision" giving employers the right to terminate stock options under certain circumstances, or make the employee pay back the difference between the exercised option price and fair-market stock price.

Lawyers at Greenberg Traurig "routinely" include the Computer Fraud and Abuse Act in lawsuits brought against ex-employees who jump ship to a competitor, says Trimarche. In the past several years, he's used the statute a handful of times. "It's a new tool and just now coming into common use. When you have a new statute that gives you a powerful tool, it takes time for the legal community, including judges, to get comfortable with it."

Source: Adapted from Laurie Sullivan, "Companies Urged to Prosecute Ex-Employees for Bringing Info to Competitors," *InformationWeek*, May 29, 2006.

Unauthorized Use at Work

The unauthorized use of computer systems and networks can be called *time and resource theft*. A common example is unauthorized use of company-owned computer networks by employees. This use may range from doing private consulting or personal finances to playing video games to unauthorized use of the Internet on company networks. Network monitoring software, called *sniffers*, is frequently used to monitor network traffic to evaluate network capacity, as well as to reveal evidence of improper use. See Figure 11.8.

According to one survey, 90 percent of U.S. workers admit to surfing recreational sites during office hours, and 84 percent say they send personal e-mail from work. So this kind of activity alone may not get you fired from your job; however, other Internet activities at work can bring instant dismissal. For example, *The New York Times* fired 23 workers because they were distributing racist and sexually offensive jokes on the company's e-mail system.

Xerox Corp. fired more than 40 workers for spending up to eight hours a day on pornography sites on the Web. Several employees even downloaded pornographic videos, which took so much network bandwidth that it choked the company network and prevented coworkers from sending or receiving e-mail. Xerox instituted an eight-member SWAT team on computer abuse that uses software to review every Web site its 40,000 computer users view each day. Other companies clamp down even harder by installing software like SurfWatch, which enables them to block and monitor access to off-limit Web sites.

FIGURE 11.8

Internet abuses in the workplace.

Internet Abuses	Activity
General E-mail Abuses	Include spamming, harassments, chain letters, solicitations, spoofing, propagations of viruses/worms, and defamatory statements.
Unauthorized Usage and Access	Sharing of passwords and access into networks without permission.
Copyright Infringement/ Plagiarism	Using illegal or pirated software that costs organizations millions of dollars because of copyright infringements. Copying of Web sites and copyrighted logos.
Newsgroup Postings	Posting of messages on various non-work–related topics from sex to lawn care advice.
Transmission of Confidential Data	Using the Internet to display or transmit trade secrets.
Pornography	Accessing sexually explicit sites from workplace as well as the display, distribution, and surfing of these offensive sites.
Hacking	Hacking of Web sites, ranging from denial of service attacks to accessing organizational databases.
Non-Work–Related Download/Upload	Propagation of software that ties up office bandwidth. Use of programs that allow the transmission of movies, music, and graphical materials.
Leisure Use of the Internet	Loafing around the Internet, which includes shopping, sending e-cards and personal e-mail, gambling online, chatting, game playing, auctioning, stock trading, and doing other personal activities.
Usage of External ISPs	Using an external ISP to connect to the Internet to avoid detection.
Moonlighting	Using office resources such as networks and computers to organize and conduct personal business (side jobs).

Source: Adapted from Keng Siau, Fiona Fui-Hoon Nah, and Limei Teng, "Acceptable Internet Use Policy," *Communications of the ACM*, January 2002, p. 76.

Survey: E-mail and Internet Abuse Can Get You Fired

Think you can get away with using e-mail and the Internet in violation of company policy? *Think again*. A new survey found that more than one-quarter of employers have fired workers for misusing e-mail, and one-third have fired workers for misusing the Internet on the job. The study, conducted by the American Management Association and the ePolicy Institute, surveyed 304 U.S. companies of all sizes.

The vast majority of bosses who fired workers for Internet misuse, 84 percent, said the employee was accessing porn or other inappropriate content. Although it is obviously wrong to look at inappropriate content on company time, a surprising number of people were fired just for surfing the Web. As many as 34 percent of managers in the study said they let go of workers for excessive personal use of the Internet, according to the survey.

Among managers who fired workers for e-mail misuse, 64 percent did so because the employee violated company policy and 62 percent said the workers' e-mail contained inappropriate or offensive language. More than a quarter of bosses said they fired workers for excessive personal use of e-mail, and 22 percent said their workers were fired for breaching confidentiality rules in e-mail.

Companies are worried about the inappropriate use of the Internet, and so 66 percent of those in the study said they monitor Internet connections. As many as 65 percent of them use software to block inappropriate Web sites. Eighteen percent of the companies block URLs (uniform resource locators) to prevent workers from visiting external blogs.

Companies use different methods to monitor workers' computers, with 45 percent of those participating in the survey tracking content, keystrokes, and time spent at the keyboard. An additional 43 percent store and review computer files. Twelve percent monitor blogs to track content about the company, and 10 percent monitor social-networking sites.

The researchers found that even though only two states require companies to notify their workers that they're monitoring them, most tell employees of their monitoring activities. Of the companies that monitor workers in the survey, 83 percent said they tell employees that they are monitoring content, keystrokes, and time spent at the keyboard. As many as 84 percent tell employees that they review computer activity, and 71 percent alert workers that they monitor their e-mails.

Source: Adapted from Nancy Gohring, "Over 50% of Companies Fire Workers for E-Mail, 'Net Abuse," *CIO Magazine*, February 28, 2008.

Software Piracy

Computer programs are valuable property and thus the subject of theft from computer systems. However, unauthorized copying of software, or software piracy, is also a major form of software theft. Software piracy by company employees is widespread, which has resulted in lawsuits by the Software Publishers Association, an industry association of software developers, against major corporations that allowed unauthorized copying of their programs.

Unauthorized copying is illegal because software is intellectual property that is protected by copyright law and user licensing agreements. For example, in the United States, commercial software packages are protected by the Computer Software Piracy and Counterfeiting Amendment to the Federal Copyright Act. In most cases, the purchase of a commercial software package is really a payment to license its fair use by an individual end user. Therefore, many companies sign *site licenses* that legally allow them to make a certain number of copies for use by their employees at a particular location. Other alternatives are *shareware*, which allows you to make copies of software for others, and *public domain software*, which is not copyrighted.

The most recent study by the Business Software Alliance, an antipiracy group whose members include Apple Computer, IBM, Intel, and Microsoft, shows that in 2007, pirated software accounts for 38 percent of software in use worldwide. Reported losses from software piracy in 2007 were almost $48 billion—up $8 billion from the year before. "That's over a third of the industry's revenue," says Bob Kruger, the group's vice president for enforcement. According to the findings, only $50 billion of the $100 billion in software purchased in 2007 was legally acquired. In other words, for every dollar spent on software purchased legitimately worldwide, there was 50 cents' worth of software that was obtained illegally.

Theft of Intellectual Property

Software is not the only property that is subject to computer-based piracy. Other intellectual property theft occurs in the form of infringements of copyrighted material, such as music, videos, images, articles, books, and other written works, which most courts have deemed illegal. Digitized versions can easily be captured by computer systems and made available for people to access or download at Internet Web sites or can be readily disseminated by e-mail as file attachments. The development of peer-to-peer (P2P) networking technologies (discussed in Chapter 6) has made digital versions of copyrighted material even more vulnerable to unauthorized use. For example, P2P file-sharing software enables direct MP3 audio file transfers of specified tracks of music between your PC and those of other users on the Internet. Thus, such software creates a *peer-to-peer network* of millions of Internet users who electronically trade digital versions of copyrighted or public domain music stored on their PC's hard drives. More recently, music publishers and manufacturers are offering legal, and relatively inexpensive, methods to access online music in a variety of formats. Because of this proactive posture, the music industry reports that illegal downloading of music and video properties is down and continuing to drop significantly. Let's look at the ongoing debate in this controversial area more closely with a real-world example that emphasizes the threat of developments in IT to intellectual property rights.

Music Piracy: The Long War

"Canadian pirates" is what the music dealers call publishing houses across the line who are flooding this country, they say, with spurious editions of the latest copyrighted popular songs. They use the mails [sic] to reach purchasers, so members of the American Music Publishers' Association assert, and as a result the legitimate music publishing business of the United States has fallen off 50 percent in the past twelve months. Their investigation has revealed that all of the most popular pieces have been counterfeited, despite the fact that they are copyrighted, and by unknown publishers are sold at from 2 cents to 5 cents per copy, though the original compositions sell at from 20 to 40 cents per copy.

Sounds somewhat familiar? You may be a little too young to remember, but it was published in *The New York Times* sometime ago—June 13, 1897 to be exact. As you can see, music piracy is hardly a recent phenomenon. It has, however, reached staggering proportions in the last two decades or so, from Napster to torrents, and including the less sophisticated but widely available CD burners.

However, only a few years after Napster's launch, online song-swapping took a big hit from a dogged legal campaign by the Recording Industry Association of America (RIAA) to shut down the top services, Napster and Audiogalaxy. Others—like Kazaa and Morpheus—went on the run, as their users were being sued by the RIAA.

Other networks, like Gnutella, had been built to withstand legal assault. By avoiding centralized servers and spreading the goods around the globe, the free-music hackers hoped their networks would be impossible to shut down. Too bad they also became impossible to use. Shawn Fanning (the creator of Napster) had a hit because Napster provided quick and easy access to a huge trove of music. His deservedly nameless imitators required far more work to find far fewer tunes.

At times, the attention moved to the pirating and copying of physical CDs. Look at the numbers: Industry estimates say that more than 6 billion blank CDs were sold worldwide in 2003—that's one for every person alive today—along with 44 million drives on which to burn them. By 2004, worldwide sales of CD-Audio, CD-ROM, and CD-R all together surpassed 30 billion units. In addition, millions of people now own writable drives—far more than the most optimistic membership claims made by Napster or any of its heirs. "You'll find one on nearly every consumer PC," cites Gartner analyst Mary Craig, one of the more bearish forecasters in the business. "They're not using them for backups."

Today, peer-to-peer (P2P) torrent clients have spread broadly. LimeWire, a grizzled veteran of the peer-to-peer (P2P) file-sharing scene, remains the most popular software for exchanging music, video, and software—much of it pirated—through the Internet, with μTorrent a not-too-close second. LimeWire was used on 17.8% of PCs in September of 2007, according to a Digital Media Desktop Report. Since about half of surveyed PCs have at least one peer-to-peer sharing application installed, that gives LimeWire a 36.4% share—more than three times the 11.3% share of the next-most-popular client, μTorrent.

Source: Adapted from Paul Boutin, "Burn Baby Burn," *Wired*, December 2002; and Eric Lai, "Study: LimeWire Remains Top P2P Software; μTorrent Fast-Rising No. 2," *Computerworld*, April 17, 2008.

Computer Viruses and Worms

One of the most destructive examples of computer crime involves the creation of a computer virus or *worm*. *Virus* is the more popular term, but technically, a virus is a program code that cannot work without being inserted into another program. A worm is a distinct program that can run unaided. In either case, these programs copy annoying or destructive routines into the networked computer systems of anyone who accesses computers infected with the virus or who uses copies of magnetic disks taken from infected computers. Thus, a computer virus or worm can spread destruction among many users. Although they sometimes display only humorous messages, they more often destroy the contents of memory, hard disks, and other storage devices. See Figure 11.9.

Computer viruses typically enter a computer system through e-mail and file attachments via the Internet and online services or through illegal or borrowed copies of software. Copies of *shareware* software downloaded from the Internet can be another source of viruses. A virus usually copies itself into the files of a computer's operating system. Then the virus spreads to the main memory and copies itself onto the computer's hard disk and any inserted floppy disks. The virus spreads to other computers through e-mail, file transfers, other telecommunications activities, or floppy disks from infected computers. Thus, as a good practice, you should avoid using software from questionable sources without checking for viruses. You should also regularly use *antivirus programs* that can help diagnose and remove computer viruses from infected files on your hard disk. We will discuss defense against viruses further in Section II.

Oldies but Goodies: Old Threats That Just Won't Go Away

Worried about the virulent Storm worm that has been buffeting the Internet with mass mailings? Symantec Corp. researchers said that the "Storm Trojan," aka "Peacomm," is now spreading via AOL Instant Messenger (AIM), Google Talk, and Yahoo Messenger.

An alert to some Symantec customers pegged the new infection vector as "insidious" because the message—such as the cryptic "LOL;)"—and the included URL can be dynamically updated by the attacker. Even worse, according to Alfred Huger, senior director of Symantec's security response team, "it injects a message and URL only into already open windows. It's not just some random message that

(text continues on page 470)

FIGURE 11.9   The top five virus families of all time. Note that three of the five occurred during 2004.

Top Five Virus Families of All Time

MyDoom   **First Discovered: 1/26/2004**

- Spreads both by e-mail and over the Kazaa file-sharing network. It appears to install some form of backdoor component on compromised machines, as well as effecting a denial of service attack on the SCO Group's Web site.
- The e-mail poses either as a returned message, or as a Unicode message that can't be rendered properly, and urges the target to click on the attachment to see the message.
- This worm also has a backdoor component, which opens up two TCP ports—that stay open even after the worm's termination date (February 12, 2004).
- Upon executing the virus, a copy of Notepad is opened, filled with lots of nonsense characters.

Netsky   **First Discovered: 3/3/2004**

- A mass-mailing worm that spreads by e-mailing itself to all e-mail addresses found in files on all local and mapped network drives.
- It also tries to spread via peer-to-peer file-sharing applications by copying itself into the shared folder used by the file-sharing applications (it searches for folders whose name contains the string "share" or "sharing"), renaming itself to pose as one of 26 other common files along the way.

SoBig   **First Discovered: 6/25/2003**

- A mass-mailing e-mail worm that arrives in the form of an e-mail attachment named either "Movie_0074.mpeg.pif," "Document003.pif," "Untitled1.pif," or "Sample.pif." The message subject title will read either "Re: Movies," "Re: Sample," "Re: Document," or "Re: Here is that sample," and it will appear to originate from big@boss.com.
- The worm will scan all .WAB, .DBX, .HTML, .HTM, .EML, and .TXT files on the victim's machine looking for e-mail addresses to which it can send itself and attempts to spread over the local network.
- It will also attempt to download updates for itself.

Klez   **First Discovered: 4/17/2002**

- A mass-mailing e-mail worm that arrives in the form of an e-mail attachment with a random file name. The worm exploits a known vulnerability in MS Outlook to autoexecute on unpatched clients. Once run, the worm will try to disable a selection of security applications—specifically virus scanners—and tries to copy itself to all local and networked drives, renaming itself with a random file name.
- Virus has a very damaging payload: It drops the W32/Elkern virus, which will delete all files it can find on the infected machine and any mapped network drives on the 13th of all even-numbered months.

Sasser   **First Discovered: 8/24/2004**

- Spreads by exploiting a recent Microsoft vulnerability, spreading from machine to machine with no user intervention required.
- The worm spawns multiple threads, some of which scan the local class A subnet, others the class B subnet, and others completely random subnets. The worm scans public ranges like 10.0.0.0 and 192.168.0.0 only if they are part of the local subnet.

The Cost of All This...

- Nearly 115 million computers across 200 countries were infected at one time or another in 2004 by rapidly proliferating software agents including Trojans, viruses, and worms.
- As many as 11 million computers worldwide—mostly within homes and small organizations—are now believed to be permanently infected and are used by criminal syndicates or malevolents to send out spam; mount distributed denial of service (DDoS) attacks; carry out extortion, identity theft, and phishing scams; or disseminate new viruses.
- The total economic damage worldwide from virus proliferation—with an additional 480 new species in 2004 alone—is now estimated to lie between $166 billion and $202 billion for 2004 by the mi2g Intelligence Unit.
- With an installed base of around 600 million Windows-based computers worldwide, average damage per installed machine is between $277 and $336.

Source: Mi2g.com, "2004: Year of the Global Malware Epidemic—Top Ten lesson," November 21, 2004.

pops up, but it appears only to people you are already talking to. That makes the approach very effective."

Well, you should be concerned about the Storm worm, but Gunter Ollmann, director of security strategy at IBM's Internet Security Systems, says the most common malware attack today is coming from the Slammer worm. *No, you didn't misread that last sentence.* The Slammer worm, which hit in January 2003, is still working its way around the Internet and within corporate networks, according to Ollmann. And it's still spreading in a big way. Slammer isn't the only piece of old-time malware that is still wreaking havoc.

"The stuff malware authors wrote a while ago is still out there and still propagating and still infecting machines," he said. "Some have more infections now than they did when they were headline news. All those old vulnerabilities haven't all gone away." Slammer, the worm that brought many networks to their knees by attacking Microsoft's SQL Server, is at the top of Ollmann's list of current malware problems.

"When we hear about the latest worm and zero-day, Slammer still beats them by a long shot," he added. "Slammer is still out there on a large number of infected hosts and it's still sending out malicious network traffic—malicious packets. . . . When people restore data after a crash, it probably is from an old system and it may not have the patches so it can easily be re-infected."

Another problem is that some users just don't do the patching they should, while other users aren't even aware that Microsoft SQL Server is running on their desktop because it's common to several other applications. If they don't know it's there, they don't know to take care of it.

"All these old viruses are never going to go away," said Ollmann.

Source: Adapted from Sharon Gaudin, "Oldies but Goodies: Slammer Worm Still Attacking," *InformationWeek*, August 24, 2007; and Gregg Keizer, "'Storm Trojan' Ignites Worm War," *Computerworld*, February 12, 2007.

Adware and Spyware

Two more recent entries into the computer vulnerabilities arena are adware and spyware. By definition, adware is software that, while purporting to serve some useful function and often fulfilling that function, also allows Internet advertisers to display advertisements as banners and pop-up ads without the consent of the computer user. In the extreme, adware can also collect information about the user of its host computer and send it over the Internet to its owner. This special class of adware is called **spyware** and is defined as any software that employs users' Internet connection in the background without their knowledge or explicit permission. Spyware programs collect specific information about you, ranging from general demographics like name, address, and Internet surfing habits to credit card, Social Security number, user names, passwords, or other personal information. It is important to understand that not all adware programs are spyware. Proper adware represents a viable, albeit sometimes irritating, revenue model for many software companies that allows you to get products for free and, when used correctly, does not pose any significant privacy threat. In contrast, spyware is and should be considered a clear threat to your privacy.

Whereas proper adware generally allows the computer user to opt in to its use in exchange for free use of a piece of software, spyware operates under a rather bizarre ethical model. Consider the following:

● You illegally enter a bank's computer system and place a stealth piece of software in their system. If you are detected or caught, you might be prosecuted and may go to jail.

● You write a worm or virus and spread it around the Internet or other networks. If you are detected or caught, you might be prosecuted and may go to jail.

- You write a program that spreads a spyware agent across computer systems connected to the Internet that steals the private information of the users it infects, manipulates their Internet experience, and uses other people's Web sites and browsers to display your advertising. If you are detected or caught, you may get rich, you don't go to jail, and the computer users are left with possibly rebuilding their computer system to get rid of your spyware.

Spyware has a variety of characteristics, beyond its potential for stealing valuable private information, which make it undesirable to most computer users. At the very least, it plagues the user of the infected machine with unwanted advertising. More often, it watches everything a user does online and sends that information back to the marketing company that created the spyware. Often, spyware applications add advertising links to Web pages owned by other people, for which the Web page owner does not get paid, and may even redirect the payments from legitimate affiliate-fee advertisers to the makers of the spyware. Other undesirable characteristics include setting an infected system's browser home page and search settings to point to the spyware owner's Web sites (generally loaded with advertising), often in a manner that prevents you from changing back the settings (referred to as home-page hijacking). In the extremes, spyware can make a dial-up modem continually call premium-rate phone numbers, thus causing large telephone charges (and usually fees to the spyware owner) or leave security holes in an infected system allowing the makers of the spyware—or, in particularly bad cases, anyone at all—to download and run software on the infected machine (such downloads are called *Trojans*). In almost all cases, spyware severely degrades system performance. As you can see, spyware doesn't have any redeeming features except for the benefits to its owner. Its use is pervasive, and failing to protect against it virtually ensures that your system will eventually become infected.

Protecting against adware and spyware generally requires the purchase and installation of one of a variety of programs designed to prevent the software from being downloaded and installed. Once a computer is infected, however, removal programs are often not completely successful in eliminating the nuisance.

| Commtouch: Trends in Virus, Spam, and Phishing | Commtouch, a developer of technology for real-time antispam and virus protection, reports on a variety of spam and computer virus statistics on a periodic basis. Although new threats arise daily by the hundreds (if not thousands), just looking at a single quarter will provide you with an idea of what is constantly going on in this world.

So here are some of the highlights from the first quarter of 2009.

The major news of the quarter was the rapid propagation of the Conficker worm. Research indicates its three variations infected more than 15 million computers, weaving a massive zombie botnet, since appearing on the scene in November 2008. The botnet lay dormant for weeks, leaving computer users nervous and vulnerable; and only later did it begin to be activated for malicious purposes.

Another growing trend was the use of social networking sites (e.g., Facebook, Twitter) for phishing schemes. One scam targeted Twitter users via direct messages proclaiming that a blog post had been written about them or that funny pictures of them had been located online. If a user clicked on the link provided in suspect messages, he or she was directed to a landing page that looks exactly like the Twitter home page—but, of course, it isn't. Upon closer inspection, however, the URL appeared to be a variation on the real Twitter URL, for example, http://twitter.access-logins.com.

During the first quarter of 2009, Commtouch analyzed which categories of Web sites were most likely to contain malware or phishing. As expected, pornographic and sexually explicit sites topped the list of sites infected with malware, but the less expected job search sites also made an appearance, albeit further down the list. Criminal activity sites fell from first to sixth place that quarter. |

Spammers continued to exploit legitimate sites to host their materials. They also masked their e-mail addresses and, most recently, have "borrowed" images from legitimate, well-known hosts to use in e-mails in hopes of bypassing spam filters. A January outbreak included a "News Summary" image in the header—that particular image is actually hosted on the legitimate CBS News site. Although boasting different URLs within the messages, the sites they linked to were all for a pharmaceutical spammer site. Another example involved stealing the "Order Now" and "Find Exclusive Deals Online!" image buttons from PizzaHut. By including links to legitimate sites within their spam messages, the perpetrators hope to confuse traditional spam filters.

Loan spam jumped from 3% of all spam messages in Q4 2008 to first place, with 28% of all spam messages in Q1 2009, possibly reflective of the global economic situation. Pharmacy spam fell from the number one spot at 42% last quarter to third place with 19% that quarter. The following table shows the most popular spam topics in Q1 2009:

Category of Spam	% of Spam
Loans	28
Replicas	20
Pharmacy	19
Enhancers	11
Weight Loss	7
Dating	6
Degrees	4
Software	1
Other	4.6

Spam levels averaged 72% of all e-mail traffic throughout the quarter and peaked at 96% (*96% of all e-mail!*) in early January, and bottomed out at 65% in February.

Source: Commtouch, "Q1 2009 Internet Threats Trend Report," April 14, 2009.

Privacy Issues

Information technology makes it technically and economically feasible to collect, store, integrate, interchange, and retrieve data and information quickly and easily. This characteristic has an important beneficial effect on the efficiency and effectiveness of computer-based information systems. The power of information technology to store and retrieve information, however, can have a negative effect on the **right to privacy** of every individual. For example, confidential e-mail messages by employees are monitored by many companies. Personal information is being collected about individuals every time they visit a site on the World Wide Web. Confidential information on individuals contained in centralized computer databases by credit bureaus, government agencies, and private business firms has been stolen or misused, resulting in the invasion of privacy, fraud, and other injustices. The unauthorized use of such information has badly damaged the privacy of individuals. Errors in such databases could seriously hurt the credit standing or reputation of an individual.

Governments around the world, but none more than in the United States, are debating privacy issues and considering various forms of legislation. With regard to the Internet, opt-in versus opt-out is central to the debate over privacy legislation. Consumer protection groups typically endorse an opt-in standard, making privacy the default. An opt-in system automatically protects consumers who do not specifically allow data to be compiled about them. Most business interests back opt-out, arguing it doesn't disrupt the flow of e-commerce. Interestingly, current laws in this regard differ between the

United States and Europe. In the United States, opt-out is the default position, whereas in Europe, consumers must opt-in or their information cannot be used.

Additional privacy issues under debate include:

- Accessing private e-mail conversations and computer records and collecting and sharing information about individuals gained from their visits to Internet Web sites and newsgroups (violation of privacy).

- Always knowing where a person is, especially as mobile and paging services become more closely associated with people rather than places (computer monitoring).

- Using customer information gained from many sources to market additional business services (computer matching).

- Collecting telephone numbers, e-mail addresses, credit card numbers, and other personal information to build individual customer profiles (unauthorized personal files).

Privacy on Internet

If you don't take the proper precautions, any time you send an e-mail, access a Web site, post a message to a newsgroup, or use the Internet for banking and shopping . . . whether you're online for business or pleasure, you're vulnerable to anyone bent on collecting data about you without your knowledge. Fortunately, by using tools like encryption and anonymous remailers—and by being selective about the sites you visit and the information you provide—you can minimize, if not completely eliminate, the risk of your privacy being violated.

The Internet is notorious for giving its users a feeling of anonymity when in reality they are highly visible and open to violations of their privacy. Most of the Internet and its World Wide Web, e-mail, chat, and newsgroups are still a wide open, unsecured electronic frontier, with no tough rules on what information is personal and private. Information about Internet users is captured legitimately and automatically each time you visit a Web site or newsgroup and is recorded as a "cookie file" on your hard disk. Then the Web site owners or online auditing services like DoubleClick may sell the information from cookie files and other records of your Internet use to third parties. To make matters worse, much of the Net and Web is an easy target for the interception or theft by hackers of private information furnished to Web sites by Internet users.

Of course, you can protect your privacy in several ways. For example, sensitive e-mail can be protected by encryption, if both e-mail parties use compatible encryption software built into their e-mail programs. Newsgroup postings can be made privately by sending them through *anonymous remailers* that protect your identity when you add your comments to a discussion. You can ask your Internet service provider not to sell your name and personal information to mailing list providers and other marketers. Finally, you can decline to reveal personal data and interests on online service and Web site user profiles to limit your exposure to electronic snooping.

Identity Theft: As Easy as Stealing a Check

Frank W. Abagnale Jr. was a check forger for five years in the 1960s. Currently he runs Abagnale and Associates, a financial fraud consultancy company. His life story provided the inspiration for the feature film *Catch Me If You Can*, starring Leonardo DiCaprio as Frank Abagnale Jr., as well as Tom Hanks.

Forty years ago, few people could have predicted that identity theft would become as big an epidemic as it is today. Few could have imagined protecting your ID would mean taking mail to the post office instead of leaving it in our mailboxes for pickup, shredding documents before throwing them in the trash, or that a $2 pen could help prevent a crime.

"We need to find ways to protect ourselves before identity theft strikes. We can make drastic improvements toward diminishing this crime, but it will never disappear altogether. If you haven't been a victim of identity theft, it is because thieves haven't gotten to you yet. If things fail to change, your turn will come. Prevention is not simply a matter of following a checklist of tips, it is about education—the primary factor in protecting ourselves," says Frank W. Abagnale Jr.—and he should know.

While more and more people are using online banking, America's 78 million baby boomers, who make up 15 percent of the U.S. population, continue to be a paper-driven majority. This group also accounts for 30 percent of fraud victims, as estimated by Consumer Action, a consumer-advocacy group.

"A check holds all of the information needed to steal your identity: name, address, bank account, routing number. If written with a ball point pen, information can easily be removed by a process called check washing, a common form of identity theft. It is the process of taking a check or document that has already been filled out, removing the ink with a regular household chemical, then re-writing in a new dollar amount and recipient," says Abagnale. If you are careless, your personal check could contribute to the 1.2 million fraudulent checks written every day. That's more than 13 per second.

The American Bankers Association states that check fraud is growing 25 percent per year. To slow this growth, it is important to understand how it works. "I know firsthand how easy it is to perform check fraud. About 40 years ago, I cashed $2.5 million in fraudulent checks in every state and 26 foreign countries over a five-year period. I was involved in a high-stakes game of stolen identities. And to know how easy it can be to perform, I know it is just as easy to prevent," he notes.

Criminals rely on our mistakes to make their job easier. Taking a few precautions will make you less attractive to predators. Don't leave mail in your mailbox overnight or over the weekend. When writing checks and filling out important documents, use a gel pen, so thieves can't remove the ink and change the information. In addition, shred or tear up unwanted documents that contain personal information before discarding them. The cost of a high-quality shredder is far less than the cost of having your identity stolen.

"Let's face it; we can't always control what is happening in our world, so we must take steps to control what we can. Technology is here to stay, but there are still simple and inexpensive ways to prevent identity theft when writing checks. Remember that a crook always looks for the easiest route to riches. Don't hand him a map. Be proactive and start protecting yourself today," says Abagnale.

Source: Adapted from Frank Abagnale, "Abagnale: Top Tips to Prevent Identity Theft and Fraud," *CIO Magazine*, May 24, 2007.

Computer Matching

Computer profiling and mistakes in the computer matching of personal data are other controversial threats to privacy. Individuals have been mistakenly arrested and jailed and people have been denied credit because their physical profiles or personal data have been used by profiling software to match them incorrectly or improperly with the wrong individuals. Another threat is the unauthorized matching of computerized information about you extracted from the databases of sales transaction processing systems and sold to information brokers or other companies. A more recent threat is the unauthorized matching and sale of information about you collected from Internet Web sites and newsgroups you visit, as we discussed previously. You are then subjected to a barrage of unsolicited promotional material and sales contacts as well as having your privacy violated.

Privacy Laws

Many countries strictly regulate the collection and use of personal data by business corporations and government agencies. Many government *privacy laws* attempt to enforce the privacy of computer-based files and communications. For example, in the

United States, the Electronic Communications Privacy Act and the Computer Fraud and Abuse Act prohibit intercepting data communications messages, stealing or destroying data, or trespassing in federal-related computer systems. Because the Internet includes federal-related computer systems, privacy attorneys argue that the laws also require notifying employees if a company intends to monitor Internet usage. Another example is the U.S. Computer Matching and Privacy Act, which regulates the matching of data held in federal agency files to verify eligibility for federal programs.

More recently, new legislation intended to protect individual privacy has created some new challenges for organizations. Sarbanes-Oxley, the Health Insurance Portability and Accountability Act (HIPAA), Gramm-Leach-Bliley, the USA PATRIOT Act, the California Security Breach Law, and Securities and Exchange Commission rule 17a-4 are but a few of the compliance challenges facing organizations. In an effort to comply with these new privacy laws, it is estimated that a typical company will spend 3–4 percent of its IT budget on compliance applications and projects.

HIPAA. The Health Insurance Portability and Accountability Act (HIPAA) was enacted by the U.S. Congress in 1996. It is a broad piece of legislation intended to address a wide variety of issues related to individual health insurance. Two important sections of HIPAA include the privacy rules and the security rules. Both of these portions of the law are intended to create safeguards against the unauthorized use, disclosure, or distribution of an individual's health-related information without their specific consent or authorization. While the privacy rules pertain to all Protected Health Information (PHI) including paper and electronic, the security rules deal specifically with Electronic Protected Health Information (EPHI). These rules lay out three types of security safeguards required for compliance: *administrative*, *physical*, and *technical*. For each of these types, the rules identify various security standards, and for each standard, name both required and addressable implementation specifications. Required specifications must be adopted and administered as dictated by the HIPAA regulation. Addressable specifications are more flexible. Individual covered entities can evaluate their own situation and determine the best way to implement addressable specifications.

Sarbanes-Oxley. The Sarbanes-Oxley Act of 2002, also known as the Public Company Accounting Reform and Investor Protection Act of 2002 and commonly called Sarbanes-Oxley, Sarbox, or SOX, is a U.S. federal law enacted on July 30, 2002, as a reaction to a number of major corporate and accounting scandals, including those affecting Enron, Tyco International, Adelphia, Peregrine Systems, and WorldCom. These scandals, which cost investors billions of dollars when the share prices of affected companies collapsed, shook public confidence in the nation's securities markets. Named after sponsors U.S. Senator Paul Sarbanes and U.S. Representative Michael G. Oxley, the act was approved by the House by a vote of 334-90 and by the Senate 99-0. President George W. Bush signed it into law, stating it included "the most far-reaching reforms of American business practices since the time of Franklin D. Roosevelt."

The legislation set new or enhanced standards for all U.S. public company boards, management, and public accounting firms. It does not, however, apply to privately held companies. The act contains 11 sections, ranging from additional corporate board responsibilities to criminal penalties, and requires the Securities and Exchange Commission (SEC) to implement rulings on requirements to comply with the new law.

Debate continues over the perceived benefits and costs of SOX. Supporters contend the legislation was necessary and has played a useful role in restoring public confidence in the nation's capital markets by, among other things, strengthening corporate accounting controls. Opponents of the bill claim it has reduced America's international competitive edge against foreign financial service providers, saying SOX has introduced an overly complex and regulatory environment into U.S. financial markets.

Computer Libel and Censorship

The opposite side of the privacy debate is the right of people to know about matters others may want to keep private (freedom of information), the right of people to express their opinions about such matters (freedom of speech), and the right of people to publish those opinions (freedom of the press). Some of the biggest battlegrounds in the debate are the bulletin boards, e-mail boxes, and online files of the Internet and public information networks such as America Online and the Microsoft Network. The weapons being used in this battle include *spamming*, *flame mail*, libel laws, and censorship.

Spamming is the indiscriminate sending of unsolicited e-mail messages (*spam*) to many Internet users. Spamming is the favorite tactic of mass mailers of unsolicited advertisements, or *junk e-mail*. Spamming has also been used by cyber criminals to spread computer viruses or infiltrate many computer systems.

Flaming is the practice of sending extremely critical, derogatory, and often vulgar e-mail messages (*flame mail*) or newsgroup postings to other users on the Internet or online services. Flaming is especially prevalent on some of the Internet's special-interest newsgroups.

There have been many incidents of racist or defamatory messages on the Web that have led to calls for censorship and lawsuits for libel. In addition, the presence of sexually explicit material at many World Wide Web locations has triggered lawsuits and censorship actions by various groups and governments.

The Current State of Cyber Law

Cyber law is the term used to describe laws intended to regulate activities over the Internet or via the use of electronic data communications. Cyber law encompasses a wide variety of legal and political issues related to the Internet and other communications technologies, including intellectual property, privacy, freedom of expression, and jurisdiction.

The intersection of technology and the law is often controversial. Some feel that the Internet should not (or possibly cannot) be regulated in any form. Furthermore, the development of sophisticated technologies, such as encryption and cryptography, make traditional forms of regulation extremely difficult. Finally, the fundamental end-to-end nature of the Internet means that if one mode of communication is regulated or shut down, another method will be devised and spring up in its place. In the words of John Gilmore, founder of the Electronic Frontier Foundation, "the Internet treats censorship as damage and simply routes around it."

One example of advancements in cyber law is found in the Federal Trade Commission's (FTC) Consumer Sentinel Project. Consumer Sentinel is a unique investigative cyber tool that provides members of the Consumer Sentinel Network with access to data from millions of consumer complaints. Consumer Sentinel includes complaints about identity theft, do-not-call registry violations, computers, the Internet, and on-line auctions, telemarketing scams, advance-fee loans, and credit scams, sweepstakes, lotteries, and prizes, business opportunities and work-at-home schemes, health and weight loss products, debt collection, credit reports, and other financial matters.

Consumer Sentinel is based on the premise that sharing information can make law enforcement even more effective. To that end, the Consumer Sentinel Network provides law enforcement members with access to complaints provided directly to the Federal Trade Commission by consumers, as well as providing members with access to complaints shared by data contributors.

According to the FTC Sentinel Report for 2007, over 800,000 complaints were processed through Sentinel with Internet-related offenses representing 11 percent of the total complaints and computer-related identity theft representing 23 percent. While many of these complaints are difficult, if not impossible to prosecute, we are beginning to see more resources being committed to addressing cyber-related crime.

Cyber law is a new phenomenon, having emerged after the onset of the Internet. As we know, the Internet grew in a relatively unplanned and unregulated manner. Even the early pioneers of the Internet could not have anticipated the scope and far-reaching consequences of the cyberspace of today and tomorrow. Although major legal disputes related to cyber activities certainly arose in the early 1990s, it was not until 1996 and 1997 that an actual body of law began to emerge. The area, clearly in its infancy, remains largely unsettled. The debate continues regarding the applicability of analogous legal principles derived from prior controversies that had nothing to do with cyberspace. As we progress in our understanding of the complex issues in cyberspace, new and better laws, regulations, and policies will likely be adopted and enacted.

Other Challenges

Let's now explore some other important challenges that arise from the use of information technologies in business, as illustrated in Figure 11.2. These challenges include the potential ethical and societal impact of business applications of IT in the areas of employment, individuality, working conditions, and health.

Employment Challenges

The impact of information technologies on employment is a major ethical concern that is directly related to the use of computers to achieve automation of work activities. There can be no doubt that the use of information technologies has created new jobs and increased productivity while also causing a significant reduction in some types of job opportunities. For example, when computers are used for accounting systems or the automated control of machine tools, they are accomplishing tasks formerly performed by many clerks and machinists. Also, jobs created by information technology may require different types of skills and education than do the jobs that are eliminated. Therefore, people may become unemployed unless they can be retrained for new positions or new responsibilities.

However, there can be no doubt that Internet technologies have created a host of new job opportunities. Many new jobs, including Internet Webmasters, e-commerce directors, systems analysts, and user consultants, have been created to support e-business and e-commerce applications. Additional jobs have been created because information technologies make possible the production of complex industrial and technical goods and services that would otherwise be impossible to produce. Thus, jobs have been created by activities that are heavily dependent on information technology, in such areas as space exploration, microelectronic technology, and telecommunications.

Computer Monitoring

One of the most explosive ethical issues concerning workplace privacy and the quality of working conditions in business is computer monitoring. That is, computers are being used to monitor the productivity and behavior of millions of employees while they work. Supposedly, computer monitoring occurs so employers can collect productivity data about their employees to increase the efficiency and quality of service. However, computer monitoring has been criticized as unethical because it monitors individuals, not just work, and is done continually, which violates workers' privacy and personal freedom. For example, when you call to make a reservation, an airline reservation agent may be timed on the exact number of seconds he or she took per caller, the time between calls, and the number and length of breaks taken. In addition, your conversation may be monitored. See Figure 11.10.

Computer monitoring has been criticized as an invasion of the privacy of employees because, in many cases, they do not know that they are being monitored or don't know how the information is being used. Critics also say that an employee's right of due process may be harmed by the improper use of collected data to make personnel decisions. Because computer monitoring increases the stress on employees who must work under constant electronic surveillance, it has also been blamed for causing health problems among monitored workers. Finally, computer monitoring has been blamed for robbing workers of the dignity of their work. In its extremes, computer monitoring can create an "electronic sweatshop," in which workers are forced to work at a hectic pace under poor working conditions.

FIGURE 11.10

Computer monitoring can be used to record the productivity and behavior of people while they work.

Source: © LWA-JDC/Corbis.

Political pressure is building to outlaw or regulate computer monitoring in the workplace. For example, public advocacy groups, labor unions, and many legislators are pushing for action at the state and federal level in the United States. The proposed laws would regulate computer monitoring and protect the worker's right to know and right to privacy. In the meantime, lawsuits by monitored workers against employers are increasing. So computer monitoring of workers is one ethical issue in business that won't go away.

Challenges in Working Conditions

Information technology has eliminated monotonous or obnoxious tasks in the office and the factory that formerly had to be performed by people. For example, word processing and desktop publishing make producing office documents a lot easier to do, and robots have taken over repetitive welding and spray painting jobs in the automotive industry. In many instances, this shift allows people to concentrate on more challenging and interesting assignments, upgrades the skill level of the work to be performed, and creates challenging jobs requiring highly developed skills in the computer industry and computer-using organizations. Thus, information technology can be said to upgrade the quality of work because it can upgrade the quality of working conditions and the content of work activities.

Of course, some jobs in information technology—data entry, for example—are quite repetitive and routine. Also, to the extent that computers are used in some types of automation, IT must take some responsibility for the criticism of assembly-line operations that require the continual repetition of elementary tasks, thus forcing a worker to work like a machine instead of like a skilled craftsperson. Many automated operations are also criticized for relegating people to a "do-nothing" standby role, where workers spend most of their time waiting for infrequent opportunities to push some buttons. Such effects do have a detrimental effect on the quality of work, but they must be compared against the less burdensome and more creative jobs created by information technology.

Challenges of Individuality

A frequent criticism of information systems centers on their negative effect on the individuality of people. Computer-based systems are criticized as impersonal systems that dehumanize and depersonalize activities that have been computerized because they eliminate the human relationships present in noncomputer systems.

Another aspect of the loss of individuality is the regimentation that seems required by some computer-based systems. These systems do not appear to possess any flexibility. They demand strict adherence to detailed procedures if the system is to work. The negative impact of IT on individuality is reinforced by horror stories that describe how inflexible and uncaring some organizations with computer-based processes are when it comes to rectifying their own mistakes. Many of us are familiar with stories of how computerized customer billing and accounting systems continued to demand payment and send warning notices to a customer whose account had already been paid, despite repeated attempts by the customer to have the error corrected.

However, many business applications of IT are designed to minimize depersonalization and regimentation. For example, many e-commerce systems stress personalization and community features to encourage repeated visits to e-commerce Web sites. Thus, the widespread use of personal computers and the Internet has dramatically improved the development of people-oriented and personalized information systems.

Health Issues

The use of information technology in the workplace raises a variety of health issues. Heavy use of computers is reportedly causing health problems like job stress, damaged arm and neck muscles, eyestrain, radiation exposure, and even death by computer-caused accidents. For example, computer monitoring is blamed as a major cause of computer-related job stress. Workers, unions, and government officials criticize computer monitoring as putting so much stress on employees that it leads to health problems.

People who sit at PC workstations or visual display terminals (VDTs) in fast-paced, repetitive keystroke jobs can suffer a variety of health problems known collectively as *cumulative trauma disorders* (CTDs). Their fingers, wrists, arms, necks, and backs may become so weak and painful that they cannot work. Strained muscles, back pain, and nerve damage may result. In particular, some computer workers may suffer from *carpal tunnel syndrome*, a painful, crippling ailment of the hand and wrist that typically requires surgery to cure.

Prolonged viewing of video displays causes eyestrain and other health problems in employees who must do this all day. Radiation caused by the cathode ray tubes (CRTs) that produce video displays is another health concern. CRTs produce an electromagnetic field that may cause harmful radiation of employees who work too close for too long in front of video monitors. Some pregnant workers have reported miscarriages and fetal deformities due to prolonged exposure to CRTs at work. Studies have failed to find conclusive evidence concerning this problem; still, several organizations recommend that female workers minimize their use of CRTs during pregnancy.

Ergonomics

Solutions to some of these health problems are based on the science of ergonomics, sometimes called *human factors engineering*. See Figure 11.11. The goal of ergonomics is to design healthy work environments that are safe, comfortable, and pleasant for people to work in, thus increasing employee morale and productivity. Ergonomics emphasizes the healthy design of the workplace, workstations, computers and other machines, and even software packages. Other health issues may require ergonomic solutions emphasizing job design rather than workplace design. For example, this approach may require policies providing for work breaks from heavy video monitor use every few hours, while limiting the CRT exposure of pregnant workers. Ergonomic job design can also provide more variety in job tasks for those workers who spend most of their workday at computer workstations.

Societal Solutions

As we noted at the beginning of the chapter, the Internet and other information technologies can have many beneficial effects on society. We can use information technologies to solve human and social problems through societal solutions such as medical diagnosis, computer-assisted instruction, governmental program planning, environmental quality control, and law enforcement. For example, computers can help diagnose an illness,

FIGURE 11.11
Ergonomic factors in the workplace. Note that good ergonomic design considers tools, tasks, the workstation, and the environment.

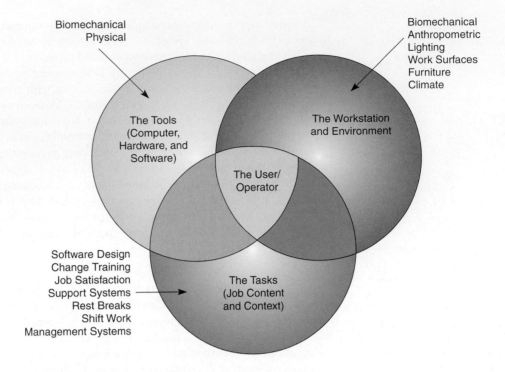

prescribe necessary treatment, and monitor the progress of hospital patients. Computer-assisted instruction (CAI) and computer-based training (CBT) enable interactive instruction tailored to the needs of students. Distance learning is supported by telecommunications networks, videoconferencing, e-mail, and other technologies.

Information technologies can be used for crime control through various law enforcement applications. For example, computerized alarm systems allow police to identify and respond quickly to evidence of criminal activity. Computers have been used to monitor the level of pollution in the air and in bodies of water, detect the sources of pollution, and issue early warnings when dangerous levels are reached. Computers are also used for the program planning of many government agencies in such areas as urban planning, population density and land use studies, highway planning, and urban transit studies. Computers are being used in job placement systems to help match unemployed persons with available jobs. These and other applications illustrate that information technology can be used to help solve the problems of society.

Obviously, individuals or organizations that do not accept ethical responsibility for their actions cause many of the detrimental effects of information technology. Like other powerful technologies, information technology possesses the potential for great harm or great good for all humankind. If managers, business professionals, and IS specialists accept their ethical responsibilities, then information technology can help improve living and working conditions for all of society.

SECTION II Security Management of Information Technology

Introduction

With Internet access proliferating rapidly, one might think that the biggest obstacle to e-commerce would be bandwidth. But it's not; the number one problem is security. And part of the problem is that the Internet was developed for interoperability, not impenetrability.

As we saw in Section I, there are many significant threats to the security of information systems in business. That's why this section is dedicated to exploring the methods that companies can use to manage their security. Business managers and professionals alike are responsible for the security, quality, and performance of the business information systems in their business units. Like any other vital business assets, hardware, software, networks, and data resources need to be protected by a variety of security measures to ensure their quality and beneficial use. That's the business value of security management.

Read the Real World Case on the next page. We can learn a lot about why IT managers are increasingly concerned about keeping their sensitive data from getting out, and how they are facing this challenge. See Figure 11.12.

Tools of Security Management

The goal of security management is the accuracy, integrity, and safety of all information system processes and resources. Thus, effective security management can minimize errors, fraud, and losses in the information systems that interconnect today's companies and their customers, suppliers, and other stakeholders. As Figure 11.13 illustrates, security management is a complex task. As you can see, security managers must acquire and integrate a variety of security tools and methods to protect a company's information system resources. We discuss many of these security measures in this section.

Top Executives Agree, Information Security Is a Top Priority

What do CXOs and other business leaders really think about information security? A recent survey and interviews conducted by *InformationWeek* reveal they're more aligned with "infosec" [information security] teams than you might think—when comes to information security, non-IT execs just might get it. The results suggest that C-level executives not only recognize the importance of information security, but actively support their IT organizations' efforts to protect corporate assets and reduce risk.

At times, that comes as a surprise. The rants from IT pros about stingy executives who are ignorant of critical security issues and regard security as an impediment to doing business are quite common. Indeed, conflicts between executives and IT organizations are still common. Moneymaking opportunities that present considerable security risks still go forward over the objections of information security teams. Conversely, security teams don't always appreciate that risk can't be entirely eliminated, or that some security measures go so far as to make information and technology too cumbersome to be useful.

Among the more security-minded executives is William McNabb, CEO of investment firm Vanguard Group. He sums up his company's information security responsibility this way: "We manage more than a trillion dollars of other people's money. That's important trust they've placed with us, and we have to do everything in our power to protect it." Seventy-five percent of survey respondents say information security is among the highest of corporate priorities.

There are four major reasons for this high level of executive support. First is the rise of high-volume theft of credit card information, Social Security numbers, and other personal data. Such attacks began to make headlines in 2005, when DSW Shoe

(text continues on page 484)

It's not what's coming into the corporate network that concerns Gene Fredriksen. It's what's going out. For the chief security officer at securities brokerage Raymond James Financial Inc. in St. Petersburg, Florida, leakage of sensitive customer data or proprietary information is the new priority. The problem isn't just content within e-mail messages, but the explosion of alternative communication mechanisms that employees are using, including instant messaging, blogs, FTP transfers, Web mail, and message boards. It's not enough to just monitor e-mail, Fredriksen says. "We have to evolve and change at the same pace as the business," he explains. "Things are coming much faster."

So Fredriksen is rolling out a network-based outbound content monitoring and control system. The software, from San Francisco–based Vontu Inc., sits on the network and monitors traffic in much the same way that a network-based intrusion-detection system would. Rather than focusing on inbound traffic, however, Vontu monitors the network activity that originates from Raymond James' 16,000 users. It examines the contents of each network packet in real time and issues alerts when policy violations are found.

Network-based systems do more than just rule-based scanning for Social Security numbers and other easily

FIGURE 11.12

Companies are starting to focus on keeping sensitive information within their boundaries. Outbound content management tools are being deployed to monitor outgoing traffic.

Source: Courtesy of Getty Images.

identifiable content. They typically analyze sensitive documents and content types and generate a unique fingerprint for each. Administrators then establish policies that relate to that content, and the system uses linguistic analysis to identify sensitive data and enforce those policies as information moves across the corporate LAN. The systems can detect both complete documents and "derivative documents," such as an IM exchange in which a user has pasted a document fragment.

When BCD Travel began to investigate what it would take to get Payment Card Industry (PCI) certification for handling customer credit card data, Senior Vice President of Technology Brian Flynn realized that he didn't really know how his employees were handling such information. Not only could PCI certification be denied, but the travel agency's reputation and business could also be harmed. At the National Football League's Houston Texans, IT Director Nick Ignatiev came to the same realization as he investigated PCI certification.

In both cases, vendors they'd been working with suggested a new technology: outbound content management tools that look for proprietary information that might be leaving the company via e-mail, instant messaging, or other avenues. Flynn started to use Reconnex's iGuard network appliance, with vivid results. "It was a shock to see what was going out, and that gave us the insight to take action," he says. After Ignatiev examined his message flow using Palisade Systems' PacketSure appliance, he too realized that his employees needed to do a better job protecting critical data, including customer credit cards, scouting reports, and team rosters.

How does the technology work? Basically, the tools filter outgoing communication across a variety of channels, such as e-mail and IM, to identify sensitive information. They're based on some of the same technologies—like pattern matching and contextual text search—that help antivirus and antispam tools block incoming threats.

Tools typically come with basic patterns already defined for personally identifiable information, such as Social Security and credit card numbers, as well as templates for commonly private information, such as legal filings, personnel data, and product testing results.

Companies typically look for three types of information using these tools, notes Paul Kocher, president of the Cryptography Research consultancy. The first—and easiest—type is personally identifiable information, such as Social Security numbers and credit card information. The second type is confidential company information, such as product specifications, payroll information, legal files, or supplier contracts. Although this information is harder to identify, most tools can uncover patterns of language and presentation when given enough samples, Kocher notes. The third category is inappropriate use of company resources, such as potentially offensive communications involving race.

The traditional security methods may restrict sensitive data to legitimate users, but Flynn and Ignatiev found that even legitimate users were putting the data, and their companies, at risk. At BCD Travel, a corporate travel service, nearly 80 percent of its 10,000 employees work in call centers and thus have legitimate access to sensitive customer information. BCD and the Texans did not find malicious activity; instead, they found people who were unaware of security risks, such as sending a customer's credit card number by e-mail to book a flight or room from a vendor that didn't have an online reservations system.

Fidelity Bancshares Inc. in West Palm Beach, Florida, is using the message-blocking feature in PortAuthority from PortAuthority Technologies Inc. in Palo Alto, California. Outbound e-mail messages that contain Social Security numbers, account numbers, loan numbers, or other personal financial data are intercepted and returned to the user, along with instructions on how to send the e-mail securely.

Joe Cormier, vice president of network services, says he also uses PortAuthority to catch careless replies. Customers often send in questions and include their account information. "The customer service rep would reply back without modifying the e-mail," he says.

"The challenge with any system like this is they're only as valuable as the mitigation procedures you have on the back end," notes Fredriksen. Another key to success is educating users about monitoring to avoid "Big Brother" implications. "We are making sure that the users understand why we implement systems like this and what they're being used for," he says.

Mark Rizzo, vice president of operations and platform engineering at Perpetual Entertainment Inc. in San Francisco, learned in a previous job the consequences of not protecting intellectual property. "I have been on the side of things disappearing and showing up at competitors," he says. The start-up online game developer deployed Tablus's Content Alarm to remedy the problem. Rizzo uses it to look for suspicious activity, such as large files that are moving outside the corporate LAN. Now that the basic policies and rules have been set, the system doesn't require much ongoing maintenance, he says. Still, Rizzo doesn't use blocking because he would need to spend significant amounts of time to create more policies in order to avoid false positives.

Although companies in highly regulated industries can justify investing in outbound content monitoring and blocking tools, other organizations may have to sharpen their pencils to justify the cost. These are very expensive solutions to deploy. Fredriksen, who built a system to support 16,000 users, says that for a setup with about 20,000 users, "you're in the $200,000 range, easily."

With outbound content management tools, "you can build very sophisticated concept filters," says Cliff Shnier, vice president for the financial advisory and litigation practice at Aon Consulting. Typically, the tools come with templates for types of data that most enterprises want to filter, and they can analyze contents of servers and databases to derive filters for company-specific information, he says. (Consulting firms can improve these filters using linguists and subject matter experts.)

As any user of an antispam tool knows, no filter is perfect. "A big mistake is to have too much faith in the tools. They can't replace trust and education," says consultant Kocher. They also won't stop a determined thief, he says. Even when appropriately deployed, these tools don't create an ironclad perimeter around the enterprise. For example, they can't detect information that flows through Skype voice over IP (VoIP) service or SSL (Secure Sockets Layer) connections, Kocher notes. They can also flood logs with false positives, which makes it hard for IT security staff to identify real problems.

That's why CIOs should look at outbound content management as a supplemental tool to limit accidental or unknowing communication of sensitive data, not as the primary defense. Fredriksen says that although Vontu is important, it's still just one piece of a larger strategy that includes an overlapping set of controls that Raymond James uses to combat insider threats. "This augments the intrusion–detection and firewall systems we have that control and block specific ports," he says. "It's just a piece. It's not the Holy Grail."

Source: Adapted from Galen Gruman, "Boost Security with Outbound Content Management," *CIO Magazine*, April 9, 2007; and Robert Mitchell, "Border Patrol: Content Monitoring Systems Inspect Outbound Communications," *Computerworld*, March 6, 2006.

CASE STUDY QUESTIONS

1. Barring illegal activities, why do you think that employees in the organizations featured in the case do not realize themselves the dangers of loosely managing proprietary and sensitive information? Would you have thought of these issues?

2. How should organizations strike the right balance between monitoring and invading their employees' privacy, even if it would be legal for them to do so? Why is it important that companies achieve this balance? What would be the consequences of being too biased to one side?

3. The IT executives in the case all note that outbound monitoring and management technologies are only part of an overall strategy, and not their primary defense. What should be the other components of this strategy? Which weight would you give to human and technological factors? Why?

REAL WORLD ACTIVITIES

1. Technologies such as VoIP used by Skype and similar products make it more difficult to monitor outgoing information. Search the Internet to help you understand these technologies and why these problems arise. Other than banning them, what alternatives would you suggest to companies facing this problem? Prepare a presentation to deliver your recommendations.

2. As a customer of many of the companies noted in the case, or others in the same industries, what is your expectation about the measures and safeguards that these organizations have implemented to protect inappropriate leaking of your personal information? After reading the case, has your expectation changed? Break into small groups with your classmates to discuss these issues.

FIGURE 11.13

Examples of important security measures that are part of the security management of information systems.

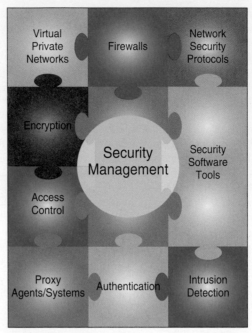

Source: Courtesy of Wang Global.

Warehouse and ChoicePoint were hit. In the DSW case, thieves stole 1.4 million credit card numbers from stores in 25 states. Meanwhile, poor controls at Choice-Point enabled scam artists posing as legitimate businesses to access consumer records and perpetrate identity theft. Since then, a string of larger information thefts from the likes of the Hannaford Bros, grocery chain, job site Monster.com, retailer TJX, and, most recently, Heartland Payment Systems has put executives on notice: Such breaches can no longer be dismissed as merely isolated incidents.

Second, the high-profile thefts have triggered a number of state breach-disclosure laws, which compel companies to publicize the theft or loss of personally identifiable information. Companies also face industry data-protection standards, the most prominent of which is the Payment Card Industry Data Security Standard, which requires a variety of security measures for businesses that accept and process credit cards.

The third trend changing executives' attitudes about security is the rising cost of information breaches.

From lawsuit payouts to fines to the expense of setting up credit-monitoring services for victimized customers, executives can see exactly how much a security failure costs. U.S. companies paid an average of $202 per exposed record in 2008, up from $197 in 2007, according to a report by the Ponemon Institute, a privacy management researcher. The report also says the average total cost per breach for each company was $6.6 million in 2008, up from $6.3 million in 2007 and $4.7 million in 2006.

The fourth major trend is the damage to a company's brand and reputation. While it's hard to put a price on the loss of customer trust or efforts to repair a brand, no CEO wants to have to try to do that math.

Source: Adapted from Andrew Conry-Murray, "A Unified Front," *InformationWeek*, February 16, 2009.

Internetworked Security Defenses

Few professionals today face greater challenges than those IT managers who are developing Internet security policies for rapidly changing network infrastructures. How can they balance the need for Internet security and Internet access? Are the budgets for Internet security adequate? What impact will intranet, extranet, and Web application development have on security architectures? How can they come up with best practices for developing Internet security policy?

The security of today's networked business enterprises is a major management challenge. Many companies are still in the process of getting fully connected to the Web and the Internet for e-commerce and are reengineering their internal business processes with intranets, e-business software, and extranet links to customers, suppliers, and other business partners. Vital network links and business flows need to be protected from external attack by cyber criminals and from subversion by the criminal or irresponsible acts of insiders. This protection requires a variety of security tools and defensive measures and a coordinated security management program. Let's take a look at some of these important security defenses.

Encryption

Encryption of data has become an important way to protect data and other computer network resources, especially on the Internet, intranets, and extranets. Passwords, messages, files, and other data can be transmitted in scrambled form and unscrambled by computer systems for authorized users only. Encryption involves using special mathematical algorithms, or keys, to transform digital data into a scrambled code before they are transmitted, and then to decode the data when they are received. The most widely used encryption method uses a pair of public and private keys unique to each individual. For example, e-mail could be scrambled and encoded using a unique *public key* for the recipient that is known to the sender. After the e-mail is transmitted, only the recipient's secret *private key* could unscramble the message. See Figure 11.14.

Encryption programs are sold as separate products or built into other software used for the encryption process. There are several competing software encryption standards, but the top two are RSA (by RSA Data Security) and PGP (which stands for "pretty good privacy"), a popular encryption program available on the Internet. Software products including Microsoft Windows XP, Novell NetWare, and Lotus Notes offer encryption features using RSA software.

FIGURE 11.14   How public key/private key encryption works.

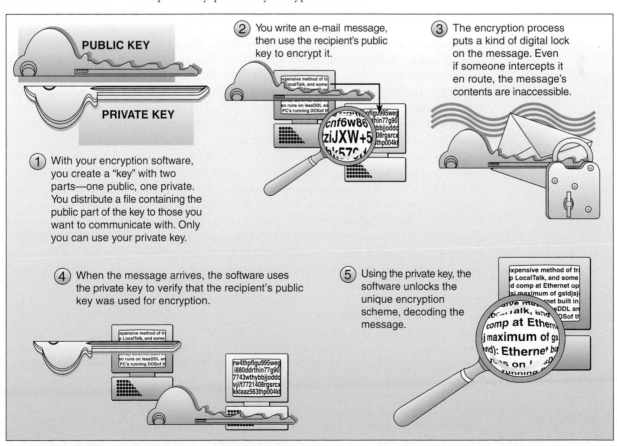

FIGURE 11.15 An example of the Internet and intranet firewalls in a company's networks.

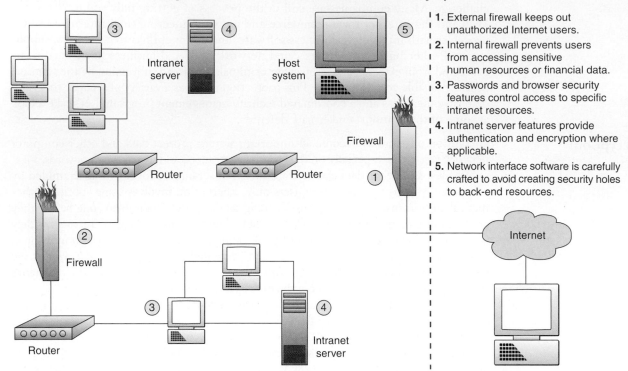

1. External firewall keeps out unauthorized Internet users.
2. Internal firewall prevents users from accessing sensitive human resources or financial data.
3. Passwords and browser security features control access to specific intranet resources.
4. Intranet server features provide authentication and encryption where applicable.
5. Network interface software is carefully crafted to avoid creating security holes to back-end resources.

Firewalls

Another important method for control and security on the Internet and other networks is the use of firewall computers and software. A network firewall can be a communications processor, typically a *router*, or a dedicated server, along with firewall software. A firewall serves as a gatekeeper system that protects a company's intranets and other computer networks from intrusion by providing a filter and safe transfer point for access to and from the Internet and other networks. It screens all network traffic for proper passwords or other security codes and only allows authorized transmissions in and out of the network. Firewall software has also become an essential computer system component for individuals connecting to the Internet with DSL or cable modems because of their vulnerable, "always-on" connection status. Figure 11.15 illustrates an Internet/intranet firewall system for a company.

Firewalls can deter, but not completely prevent, unauthorized access (hacking) into computer networks. In some cases, a firewall may allow access only from trusted locations on the Internet to particular computers inside the firewall, or it may allow only "safe" information to pass. For example, a firewall may permit users to read e-mail from remote locations but not run certain programs. In other cases, it is impossible to distinguish the safe use of a particular network service from unsafe use, so all requests must be blocked. The firewall may then provide substitutes for some network services (such as e-mail or file transfers) that perform most of the same functions but are not as vulnerable to penetration.

WhiteHat Security: "Black Box Testing" Mimics Hackers to Discover Vulnerabilities	Jeremiah Grossman wants you to know that firewalls and SSL encryption won't prevent a hacker from breaking into your e-commerce Web site, compromising your customers' data, and possibly stealing your money. That's because most Web site attacks these days exploit bugs in the Web application itself, rather than in the operating system on which the application is running. Grossman is the founder and chief technology officer of WhiteHat Security, a Silicon Valley firm that offers an outsourced Web site vulnerability management service. Using a combination of proprietary scanning and so-called ethical hacking, WhiteHat assesses the security of its clients' Web sites, looking for exploitable vulnerabilities.

WhiteHat does its scanning without access to the client's source code and from outside the client's firewall using the standard HTTP Web protocol. This approach is sometimes called "black box testing" because the Web site's contents are opaque to the security assessors. The problem with black box testing, of course, is that it is sure to miss many vulnerabilities and back doors that are hidden in the source code. Black box testing can only find vulnerabilities that are visible to someone who is using your Web site, but the advantage of this approach is that it precisely mimics how a hacker would most likely conduct his reconnaissance and break-in.

From his vantage point at WhiteHat, Grossman has seen several organizations migrate Web sites from Microsoft's original ASP to ASP.NET. "ASP classic, the first generation of ASP websites, are generally riddled with vulnerabilities," he says. Yet when these organizations rewrote their applications using ASP.NET, suddenly their applications improved tremendously security-wise. "Same developers, two different frameworks. It wasn't an education problem; it was a technology problem."

At another company—a financial institution—WhiteHat discovered an easily exploited vulnerability that would have let customers steal money. WhiteHat called up the company, and the problem was hot-fixed within 24 hours. A few months later, the vulnerability came back. "The developers were working on the next release, set to come out in two to three months. Some developer did not back-port the hot-fix from the production server to the development server. So when the push occurred three months later, they pushed the vulnerability again." Ugh!

You may not be a big fan of this approach to security, but if you talk to Grossman for a couple of hours, he will convince you that it's a necessary part of today's e-commerce Web sites. Yes, it would be nice to eliminate these well-known bugs with better coding practices, but we live in the real world. It's better to look for the bugs and fix them than to just cross your fingers and hope that they aren't there.

Source: Adapted from Simson Garfinkel, "An Introduction to the Murky Science of Web Application Security," *CIO Magazine*, May 11, 2007.

Denial of Service Attacks

Major attacks against e-commerce and corporate Web sites in the past few years have demonstrated that the Internet is extremely vulnerable to a variety of assaults by criminal hackers, especially **distributed denial of service (DDOS)** attacks. Figure 11.16 outlines the steps organizations can take to protect themselves from DDOS attacks.

Denial of service assaults via the Internet depend on three layers of networked computer systems: (1) the victim's Web site, (2) the victim's Internet service provider (ISP), and (3) the sites of "zombie" or slave computers that the cyber criminals commandeered. For example, in early 2000, hackers broke into hundreds of servers, mostly poorly protected servers at universities, and planted Trojan horse.exe programs, which were then used to launch a barrage of service requests in a concerted attack on e-commerce Web sites like Yahoo! and eBay.

As Figure 11.16 shows, defensive measures and security precautions must be taken at all three levels of the computer networks involved. These are the basic steps

FIGURE 11.16

How to defend against denial of service attacks.

Defending against Denial of Service
● **At the zombie machines:** Set and enforce security policies. Scan regularly for Trojan horse programs and vulnerabilities. Close unused ports. Remind users not to open .exe mail attachments.
● **At the ISP:** Monitor and block traffic spikes. Filter spoofed IP addresses. Coordinate security with network providers.
● **At the victim's Web site:** Create backup servers and network connections. Limit connections to each server. Install multiple intrusion-detection systems and multiple routers for incoming traffic to reduce choke points.

companies and other organizations can take to protect their Web sites from denial of service and other hacking attacks. Now let's take a look at a real-world example of a more sophisticated defense technology.

As If Phishing Wasn't Enough: Denial of Service Attacks

Kevin Dougherty has seen his share of spam and phishing scams, as has any IT leader in the financial services industry. But the sender's name on this particular e-mail sent a shudder down his spine: It was from one of his board members at the Central Florida Educators' Federal Credit Union (CFEFCU). The e-mail claimed in convincing detail that there was a problem with the migration to a new Visa credit card that the board member was promoting to the credit union's customers. The fraudulent message urged customers to click on a link—to a phony Web site set up by criminals—and enter their account information to fix the problem.

But what happened later that Friday afternoon—after Dougherty, who is senior vice president of IT and marketing, had wiped the credit card migration information off the Web site and put up an alert warning customers of the scam—really scared him.

Around 2 p.m., the site suddenly went dark, like someone had hit it with a baseball bat. That's when Dougherty realized that he was dealing with something he hadn't seen before. And he couldn't describe it with conventional terms like phishing or spamming. This was an organized criminal conspiracy targeting his bank. "This wasn't random," he says. "They saw what we were doing with the credit card and came at us hard."

Dougherty's Web site lay in a coma from a devastating distributed denial of service (DDOS) attack that, at its peak, shot more than 600,000 packets per second of bogus service requests at his servers from a coordinated firing squad of compromised computers around the globe. That the criminals had the skill and foresight to launch a two-pronged attack against Dougherty and his customers was a clear indication of how far online crime, which is now a $2.8 billion business according to research company Gartner, has come in the past few years.

Obviously, the first thing Dougherty had to do was stop the attack. He had to hurriedly assemble a coalition of vendors and consultants to help him, and then he had to convince his CEO that drastic steps were needed—steps that would temporarily cut off customers from any possibility of getting to their accounts online until the problems were completely eradicated. Dougherty wanted to have the site temporarily blacklisted with his telecom provider, BellSouth, to deflect the attack, thereby reducing pressure on the site and giving him the time and flexibility to make protective changes. But his CEO resisted—as might anyone who has not experienced an attack. "He wanted to keep it up so we could service the members," says Dougherty.

At 11 p.m., after a long night of battling the attackers and plotting strategy, Dougherty finally convinced his CEO to have the site blacklisted and to take a break until morning.

Continuing in a tired and emotional state would have played into the attackers' hands. "It's a mind game," says Dougherty.

By Saturday morning, Dougherty had RSA, a security vendor he called in when the attacks began, working to set up a "take-down" service that seeks out and dispatches criminal Web sites (in this case, more than 30) with its own cyber baseball bat. Meanwhile, BellSouth began beefing up security around the credit union site to try to thwart attacks.

The site was back up by Saturday evening. In the end, 22 customers gave up their information to the thieves and the total losses were "less than five figures," says Dougherty. Though the credit union had averted disaster, "it was a rude awakening," he says.

Source: Adapted from Nancy Weil, "Your Plan to Fight Cyber Crime," *CIO Magazine*, June 15, 2007.

E-mail Monitoring

Spot checks just aren't good enough anymore. The tide is turning toward systematic monitoring of corporate e-mail traffic using content-monitoring software that scans for troublesome words that might compromise corporate security. The reason: Users of monitoring software said they're concerned about protecting their intellectual property and guarding themselves against litigation.

As we mentioned in Section I, Internet and other online e-mail systems are one of the favorite avenues of attack by hackers for spreading computer viruses or breaking into networked computers. E-mail is also the battleground for attempts by companies to enforce policies against illegal, personal, or damaging messages by employees versus the demands of some employees and others who see such policies as violations of privacy rights.

Employee Monitoring: Who's Watching Now?

Just the mention of employee monitoring raises concerns about Big Brother and privacy, as well as issues of trust, loyalty, and respect. Yet monitoring employee use of e-mail, the Internet, and telephones in the workplace has become more common than gatherings at the office watercooler. Ten years ago, employee monitoring meant that the supervisor would walk the floor and watch the activities of workers. Today, businesses increasingly use automated tools to ensure that workers are completing tasks, not wasting resources, and complying with a growing list of government regulations.

A report by the Privacy Rights Clearinghouse says there's little that employees can do to limit monitoring by their employers. Bosses have the right to listen to workers' phone calls in most instances, obtain records of those calls, use software to see what's being displayed on computer screens, check what information is stored on hard disks, and track and record e-mail. Some companies have little choice but to monitor employees.

Presidio Financial Partners provides investment consulting services, controlling approximately $3 billion in assets for 150 clients. It falls under the scrutiny of the Securities and Exchange Commission and the National Association of Securities Dealers, and it must provide regulators with access to e-mail and other correspondence between the company and its clients, as well as maintain an archive of the information.

"We have to have this information at our disposal," says Jeff Zlot, managing director for Presidio. "But our clients are high-profile individuals, and the last thing we need is information getting into the wrong hands."

Presidio began to use Fortiva Supervision software from Fortiva to monitor, track, and archive the e-mail of its consultants, and it was pleased that Fortiva keeps archived material encrypted. Fortiva Supervision is used to track e-mail between Presidio salespeople and clients, specifically looking for keywords that could pose problems. "We can show the regulators that we set up guidelines and that we are enforcing those guidelines from a sales supervision standpoint," Zlot says.

Phrases that will be flagged by the software include such things as guaranteed return or guaranteed performance, or any time the word *complaint* is used. If the keywords are spotted, supervisors must review the e-mail. As many as 50 e-mails a day get queued for review. "This forces the sales supervisors to look and approve the work the employees are doing," Zlot says.

The growing number of automated monitoring tools makes it easier for employers to keep an eye on what employees are doing than in the old days—when you really had to keep an eye on them.

Source: Adapted from Darrell Dunn, "Who's Watching Now?" *InformationWeek*, February 27, 2006.

Virus Defenses

Is your PC protected from the latest viruses, worms, Trojan horses, and other malicious programs that can wreak havoc on your PC? Chances are it is, if it's periodically linked to the corporate network. These days, corporate antivirus protection is a centralized function of information technology. Someone installs it for you on your PC and notebook or, increasingly, distributes it over the network. The antivirus software runs in the background, popping up every so often to reassure you. The trend right now is to automate the process entirely.

FIGURE 11.17

An example of security suite PC software that includes antivirus and firewall protection.

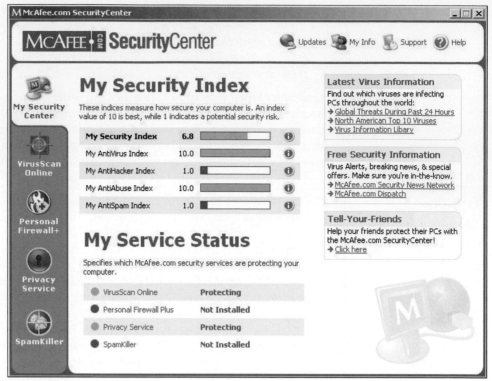

Source: Courtesy of McAfee.

Many companies are building defenses against the spread of viruses by centralizing the distribution and updating of antivirus software as a responsibility of their IS departments. Other companies are outsourcing the virus protection responsibility to their Internet service providers or telecommunications or security management companies.

One reason for this trend is that the major antivirus software companies like McAfee (VirusScan) and Symantec (Norton Antivirus) have developed network versions of their programs, which they are marketing to ISPs and others as a service they should offer to all their customers. The antivirus companies are also marketing *security suites* of software that integrate virus protection with firewalls, Web security, and content-blocking features. See Figure 11.17.

The Future of Antivirus

Antivirus software makes Greg Shipley so mad he has to laugh. "The relationship between signature-based antivirus companies and the virus writers is almost comical. One releases something and then the other reacts, and they go back and forth. It's a silly little arms race that has no end."

Shipley, chief technology officer at Neohapsis, a security consulting firm in Chicago, says the worst part is that the arms race isn't helpful either to him or to his clients. "I want to get off of signature-based antivirus as rapidly as possible. I think it's a broken model, and I think it's an incredible CPU hog."

Antivirus as an industry has modeled itself on the human immune system, which slaps a label on things like viruses so it knows to attack them when it sees that same label, or signature, again. Signature-based antivirus has moved well beyond that simple type of signature usage (although, at the beginning, it did look for specific lines of code). The number of malware signatures that security software company F-Secure tracked doubled in 2007, and while you might cynically expect such a company to say there's more malware out there, 2007's total doubled the number of signatures F-Secure had built up over the previous 20 years.

Antivirus firms think that reports of their death are greatly exaggerated, thank you very much—even those that aren't overly reliant on signatures, like BitDefender, which says that signature-based techniques account for only 20 percent of the malware it catches. Corporate CISOs (chief information security officers) certainly don't expect to find one answer to their problems. "If you rely on signatures for security, you're pretty much dead in the water," says Ken Pfeil, head of information security for the Americas region of WestLB, a German bank. Pfeil thinks signatures are useful and his firm uses them, but when new malware appears, he often finds it faster to try to break it down himself to understand its potential effects, rather than wait for his vendor to give him an update. His firm has also adopted tools that use heuristics techniques and anomaly testing, to add oomph to its antivirus approach.

That kind of layered approach to software fits with where Natalie Lambert, an analyst at Forrester Research, thinks the market is going. She says that signature-based antivirus is "table stakes" for security software, and techniques like heuristic information processing systems, or HIPS, which look for suspicious actions by software, is like an application opening itself from the Temp folder. The downside to these technologies is that none is as simple and alluring as the old signature-based antivirus, which she called a "set it and forget it" technology. She notes that HIPS technologies are difficult to manage and will never be as simple as the old model, although she expects they will get easier over time.

Antivirus firms agree that they are becoming something different; however, David Harley, administrator of Avien, the antivirus information exchange network, thinks that there are psychological reasons that antivirus software is unlikely to go away. "The idea of a solution that stops real threats and doesn't hamper nonmalicious objects and processes is very attractive. People (at any rate, those who aren't security specialists) like the idea of threat-specific software, as long it catches all incoming malware and doesn't generate any false positives, because then they can just install it and forget about it. Unfortunately, that's an unattainable ideal."

Note to Greg Shipley: Don't hold your breath on getting rid of your antivirus software.

Source: Adapted from Michael Fitzgerald, "The Future of Antivirus," *Computerworld*, April 14, 2008.

Other Security Measures

Let's now briefly examine a variety of security measures that are commonly used to protect business systems and networks. These include both hardware and software tools, like fault-tolerant computers and security monitors, and security policies and procedures, like passwords and backup files. All are part of an integrated security management effort at many companies today.

Security Codes

Typically, a multilevel **password** system is used for security management. First, an end user logs on to the computer system by entering his or her unique identification code, or user ID. Second, the end user is asked to enter a password to gain access into the system. (Passwords should be changed frequently and consist of unusual combinations of upper- and lowercase letters and numbers.) Third, to access an individual file, a unique file name must be entered. In some systems, the password to read the contents of a file is different from that required to write to a file (change its contents). This feature adds another level of protection to stored data resources. For even stricter security, however, passwords can be scrambled, or *encrypted*, to avoid their theft or improper use, as we will discuss shortly. In addition, *smart cards*, which contain microprocessors that generate random numbers to add to an end user's password, are used in some secure systems.

Backup Files

Backup files, which are duplicate files of data or programs, are another important security measure. Files can also be protected by *file retention* measures that involve storing copies of files from previous periods. If current files are destroyed, the files from previous

FIGURE 11.18

The eTrust security monitor manages a variety of security functions for major corporate networks, including monitoring the status of Web-based applications throughout a network.

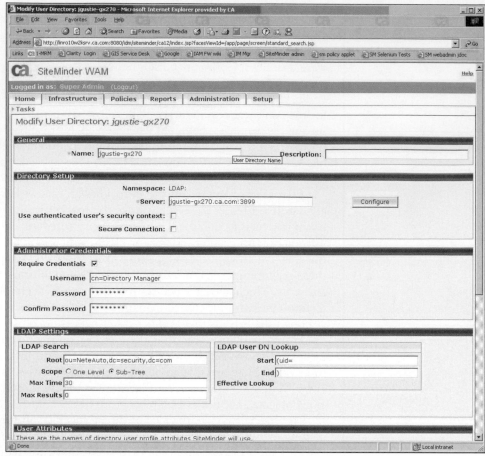

Source: Courtesy of McAfee.

periods can be used to reconstruct new current files. Sometimes, several generations of files are kept for control purposes. Thus, master files from several recent periods of processing (known as *child*, *parent*, and *grandparent* files) may be kept for backup purposes. Such files may be stored off-premises, that is, in a location away from a company's data center, sometimes in special storage vaults in remote locations.

Security Monitors

Security of a network may be provided by specialized system software packages known as **system security monitors**. See Figure 11.18. System security monitors are programs that monitor the use of computer systems and networks and protect them from unauthorized use, fraud, and destruction. Such programs provide the security measures needed to allow only authorized users to access the networks. For example, identification codes and passwords are frequently used for this purpose. Security monitors also control the use of the hardware, software, and data resources of a computer system. For example, even authorized users may be restricted to the use of certain devices, programs, and data files. In addition, security programs monitor the use of computer networks and collect statistics on any attempts at improper use. They then produce reports to assist in maintaining the security of the network.

Biometric Security

Biometric security is a fast-growing area of computer security. These are security measures provided by computer devices that measure physical traits that make each individual unique, such as voice verification, fingerprints, hand geometry, signature dynamics, keystroke analysis, retina scanning, face recognition, and genetic pattern analysis. Biometric control devices use special-purpose sensors to measure and digitize a biometric profile of a person's fingerprints, voice, or other physical trait. The digitized signal is processed and compared to a previously processed profile of the individual

FIGURE 11.19

An evaluation of common biometric security techniques based on user requirements, accuracy, and cost.

Evaluation of Biometric Techniques				
	User Criteria		System Criteria	
	Intrusiveness	Effort	Accuracy	Cost
Dynamic signature verification	Excellent	Fair	Fair	Excellent
Face geometry	Good	Good	Fair	Good
Finger scan	Fair	Good	Good	Good
Hand geometry	Fair	Good	Fair	Fair
Passive iris scan	Poor	Excellent	Excellent	Poor
Retina scan	Poor	Poor	Very good	Fair
Voice print	Very good	Poor	Fair	Very good

stored on magnetic disk. If the profiles match, the individual is allowed entry into a computer network and given access to secure system resources. See Figure 11.19.

Notice that the examples of biometric security listed in Figure 11.19 are rated according to the degree of intrusiveness (how much the technique interrupts a user) and the relative amount of effort required by the user to authenticate. Also, the relative accuracy and cost of each are assessed. As you can see, trade-offs in these four areas exist in every example. Whereas face geometry is judged easy on the user in terms of intrusiveness and effort, its accuracy is not considered as high as that of other methods. Biometrics is still in its infancy, and many new technologies are being developed to improve on accuracy while minimizing user effort.

Computer Failure Controls

"Sorry, our computer systems are down" is a well-known phrase to many end users. A variety of controls can prevent such computer failure or minimize its effects. Computer systems fail for several reasons—power failures, electronic circuitry malfunctions, telecommunications network problems, hidden programming errors, computer viruses, computer operator errors, and electronic vandalism. For example, computers are available with automatic and remote maintenance capabilities. Programs of preventive maintenance of hardware and management of software updates are commonplace. A backup computer system capability can be arranged with *disaster recovery organizations*. Major hardware or software changes are usually carefully scheduled and implemented to avoid problems. Finally, highly trained data center personnel and the use of performance and security management software help keep a company's computer system and networks working properly.

Fault-Tolerant Systems

Many firms also use **fault-tolerant** computer systems that have redundant processors, peripherals, and software that provide a *fail-over* capability to back up components in the event of system failure. This system may provide a *fail-safe* capability so that the computer system continues to operate at the same level even if there is a major hardware or software failure. Many fault-tolerant computer systems, however, offer a *fail-soft* capability so that the computer system can continue to operate at a reduced but acceptable level in the event of a major system failure. Figure 11.20 outlines some of the fault-tolerant capabilities used in many computer systems and networks.

ETrade Financial Corp.: 24/7 Data Center

ETrade Financial Corp. and other online stock brokerages are at war over how fast they can execute a trade. ETrade has 3.5 million customer accounts and completes more than 100,000 trades each day, on average. The company says most of its trades are completed in less than a second, a remarkable achievement for a complex operation that spans multiple computers, routers, and applications, not all of them controlled by ETrade.

In 2001, the cost of proprietary systems was rising while the cost of open systems running on Intel processors was falling, says Joshua S. Levine, ETrade's chief technology and administrative officer. With the savings from open-source products came the luxury of being able to overprovision by buying spare capacity for every conceivable hardware failure and spike in demand. "When you are buying servers so cheaply, the concept of 'capacity' drops away," Levine says. "We buy a machine for $3,900, and we don't even buy maintenance on it. When it fails, we throw it away."

Performance and reliability aren't just about computer hardware and software: IT assets must be protected. That was one of the priorities when ETrade built its regional operations center (ROC) during the stock market boom of 1999. Speed was another. "Those were heady days for companies like ETrade," says Greg Framke, an executive vice president and head of IT at ETrade. "Companies could barely keep up with demand. The ROC was built in less than 12 months."

ETrade's main data center, the $70 million (excluding the computer gear) regional operations center, is an unmarked, windowless concrete fortress in Alpharetta, Georgia. The facility is classified as a "Tier IV—Fault Tolerant" data center, with two independent electrical systems, multiple power and cooling distribution paths, redundant components, and 99.995 percent availability.

Six telecommunications carriers have pipes into the building, and there are three electrical feeds to the data center. Two rooms each houses a pair of 600-ton chillers, and a million-gallon tank of cold water can supply cooling if a chiller fails. The center has four enormous rooms housing uninterruptible power supply units, any one of which can fail with no operational impact. Two other rooms each houses a pair of redundant, 2-megawatt diesel generators. Nearby is a 220,000-gallon tank of diesel fuel, which is enough to power the data center for two weeks. Security is tight. There are closed-circuit television monitors, doors are equipped with badge readers, and a fingerprint-recognition system controls access to the computer room.

Says Levine, "What I'm most proud of is that we operate at 100% every day, 24 hours a day. And it's out there for everyone to see if you have a failure. I mean, my career could end right now with a three-hour outage."

Source: Adapted from Gary Anthes, "Sidebar: Inside ETrade's Data Center," *Computerworld*, September 27, 2004; and Gary Anthes, "ETrade Beats the Clock," *Computerworld*, September 27, 2004.

FIGURE 11.20

Methods of fault tolerance in computer-based information systems.

Layer	Threats	Fault-Tolerant Methods
Applications	Environment, hardware, and software faults	Application-specific redundancy and rollback to previous checkpoint
Systems	Outages	System isolation, data security, system integrity
Databases	Data errors	Separation of transactions and safe updates, complete transaction histories, backup files
Networks	Transmission errors	Reliable controllers; safe asynchrony and handshaking; alternative routing; error-detecting and error-correcting codes
Processes	Hardware and software faults	Alternative computations, rollback to checkpoints
Files	Media errors	Replication of critical data on different media and sites; archiving, backup, retrieval
Processors	Hardware faults	Instruction retry; error-correcting codes in memory and processing; replication; multiple processors and memories

Disaster Recovery

Natural and human-made disasters do happen. Hurricanes, earthquakes, fires, floods, criminal and terrorist acts, and human error can all severely damage an organization's computing resources and thus the health of the organization itself. Many companies, especially online e-commerce retailers and wholesalers, airlines, banks, and Internet service providers, for example, are crippled by losing even a few hours of computing power. Many firms could survive only a few days without computing facilities. That's why organizations develop **disaster recovery** procedures and formalize them in a *disaster recovery plan*. It specifies which employees will participate in disaster recovery and what their duties will be; what hardware, software, and facilities will be used; and the priority of applications that will be processed. Arrangements with other companies for use of alternative facilities as a disaster recovery site and off-site storage of an organization's databases are also part of an effective disaster recovery effort.

System Control and Audits

Two final security management requirements that need to be mentioned are the development of information system controls and auditing business systems. Let's take a brief look at these two security measures.

Information System Controls

Information system controls are methods and devices that attempt to ensure the accuracy, validity, and propriety of information system activities. Information system (IS) controls must be developed to ensure proper data entry, processing techniques, storage methods, and information output. Thus, IS controls are designed to monitor and maintain the quality and security of the input, processing, output, and storage activities of any information system. See Figure 11.21.

For example, IS controls are needed to ensure the proper entry of data into a business system and thus avoid the garbage in, garbage out (GIGO) syndrome. Examples include passwords and other security codes, formatted data entry screens, and audible error signals. Computer software can include instructions to identify incorrect, invalid, or improper input data as it enters the computer system. For example, a data entry program can check for invalid codes, data fields, and transactions, and conduct "reasonableness checks" to determine if input data exceed specified limits or are out of sequence.

FIGURE 11.21

Examples of information system controls. Note that they are designed to monitor and maintain the quality and security of the input, processing, output, and storage activities of an information system.

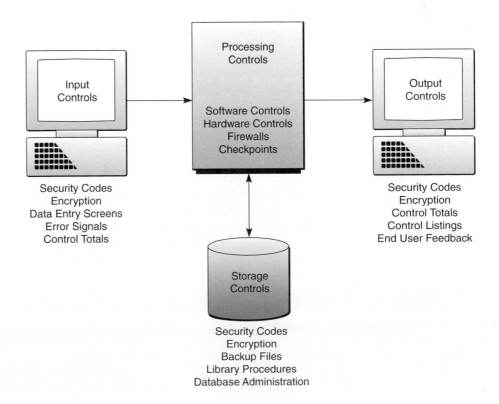

FIGURE 11.22

How to protect yourself from cyber crime and other computer security threats.

Security Management for Internet Users
1. Use antivirus and firewall software and update it often to keep destructive programs off your computer.
2. Don't allow online merchants to store your credit card information for future purchases.
3. Use a hard-to-guess password that contains a mix of numbers and letters, and change it frequently.
4. Use different passwords for different Web sites and applications to keep hackers guessing.
5. Install all operating system patches and upgrades.
6. Use the most up-to-date version of your Web browser, e-mail software, and other programs.
7. Send credit card numbers only to secure sites; look for a padlock or key icons at the bottom of the browser.
8. Use a security program that gives you control over "cookies" that send information back to Web sites.
9. Install firewall software to screen traffic if you use DSL or a cable modem to connect to the Net.
10. Don't open e-mail attachments unless you know the source of the incoming message.

Auditing IT Security

IT security management should be periodically examined, or audited, by a company's internal auditing staff or external auditors from professional accounting firms. Such audits review and evaluate whether proper and adequate security measures and management policies have been developed and implemented. This process typically involves verifying the accuracy and integrity of the software used, as well as the input of data and output produced by business applications. Some firms employ special computer security auditors for this assignment. They may use special test data to check processing accuracy and the control procedures built into the software. The auditors may develop special test programs or use audit software packages.

Another important objective of business system audits is testing the integrity of an application's *audit trail*. An audit trail can be defined as the presence of documentation that allows a transaction to be traced through all stages of its information processing. This journey may begin with a transaction's appearance on a source document and end with its transformation into information in a final output document or report. The audit trail of manual information systems is quite visible and easy to trace. However, computer-based information systems have changed the form of the audit trail. Now auditors must know how to search electronically through disk and tape files of past activity to follow the audit trail of today's networked computer systems.

Many times, this *electronic audit trail* takes the form of *control logs* that automatically record all computer network activity on magnetic disk or tape devices. This audit feature can be found on many online transaction processing systems, performance and security monitors, operating systems, and network control programs. Software that records all network activity is also widely used on the Internet, especially the World Wide Web, as well as on corporate intranets and extranets. Such an audit trail helps auditors check for errors or fraud, but also helps IS security specialists trace and evaluate the trail of hacker attacks on computer networks.

Figure 11.22 summarizes 10 security management steps you can take to protect your computer system resources from hacking and other forms of cyber crime.

Summary

- **Ethical and Societal Dimensions.** The vital role of information technologies and systems in society raises serious ethical and societal issues in terms of their impact on employment, individuality, working conditions, privacy, health, and computer crime, as illustrated in Figure 11.2.

  Employment issues include the loss of jobs—a result of computerization and automation of work—versus the jobs created to supply and support new information technologies and the business applications they make possible. The impact on working conditions involves the issues of computer monitoring of employees and the quality of the working conditions of the jobs that use information technologies heavily. The effect of IT on individuality addresses the issues of the depersonalization, regimentation, and inflexibility of some computerized business systems.

Employees' heavy use of computer workstations for long periods raises issues about and may cause work-related health disorders. The use of IT to access or collect private information without authorization, as well as for computer profiling, computer matching, computer monitoring, and computer libel and censorship, raises serious privacy issues. Computer crime issues surround activities such as hacking, computer viruses and worms, cyber theft, unauthorized use at work, software piracy, and piracy of intellectual property.

Managers, business professionals, and IS specialists can help solve the problems of improper use of IT by assuming their ethical responsibilities for the ergonomic design, beneficial use, and enlightened management of information technologies in our society.

- **Ethical Responsibility in Business.** Business and IT activities involve many ethical considerations. Basic principles of technology and business ethics can serve as guidelines for business professionals when dealing with ethical business issues that may arise in the widespread use of information technology in business and society. Examples include theories of corporate social responsibility, which outline the ethical responsibility of management and employees to a company's stockholders, stakeholders, and society, and the four principles of technology ethics summarized in Figure 11.4.

- **Security Management.** One of the most important responsibilities of the management of a company is to ensure the security and quality of its IT-enabled business activities. Security management tools and policies can ensure the accuracy, integrity, and safety of the information systems and resources of a company and thus minimize errors, fraud, and security losses in its business activities. Examples mentioned in the chapter include the use of encryption of confidential business data, firewalls, e-mail monitoring, antivirus software, security codes, backup files, security monitors, biometric security measures, computer failure controls, fault-tolerant systems, disaster recovery measures, information system controls, and security audits of business systems.

Key Terms and Concepts

These are the key terms and concepts of this chapter. The page number of their first explanation is in parentheses.

1. Antivirus software (490)
2. Audit trail (496)
3. Backup files (491)
4. Biometric security (492)
5. Business ethics (454)
6. Computer crime (460)
7. Computer matching (474)
8. Computer monitoring (477)
9. Computer virus (468)
10. Cyber law (476)
11. Disaster recovery (495)
12. Distributed denial of service (487)
13. Encryption (485)
14. Ergonomics (479)
15. Ethical foundations (454)
16. Fault tolerant (493)
17. Firewall (486)
18. Flaming (476)
19. Hacking (461)
20. Information system controls (495)
21. Intellectual property theft (467)
22. Opt-in/Opt-out (472)
23. Passwords (491)
24. Security management (481)
25. Societal solutions (479)
26. Software piracy (466)
27. Spamming (476)
28. Spyware/Adware (470)
29. System security monitor (492)
30. Unauthorized use (465)

Review Quiz

Match one of the key terms and concepts listed previously with one of the brief examples or definitions that follow. Try to find the best fit for the answers that seem to fit more than one term or concept. Defend your choices.

_____ 1. Ensuring the accuracy, integrity, and safety of business/IT activities and resources.

_____ 2. Control totals, error signals, backup files, and security codes are examples.

_____ 3. Software that can control access and use of a computer system.

_____ 4. A computer system can continue to operate even after a major system failure if it has this capability.

_____ 5. A computer system that serves as a filter for access to and from other networks by a company's networked computers.

____ 6. Laws and regulations focused on issues related to the Internet and other forms of networked communications.

____ 7. The presence of documentation that allows a transaction to be traced through all stages of information processing.

____ 8. Using your voice or fingerprints to identify yourself electronically.

____ 9. A plan to continue IS operations during an emergency.

____ 10. Scrambling data during its transmission.

____ 11. Ethical choices may result from decision-making processes, cultural values, or behavioral stages.

____ 12. Managers must confront numerous ethical questions in their businesses.

____ 13. Sending unsolicited e-mail indiscriminately.

____ 14. Software that can infect a machine and transmit private information back to its owner.

____ 15. Two different perspectives on the use of private information.

____ 16. Using computers to identify individuals that fit a certain profile.

____ 17. Using computers to monitor the activities of workers.

____ 18. Overwhelming a Web site with requests for service from captive computers.

____ 19. Using computers and networks to steal money, services, software, or data.

____ 20. Using company computers to access the Internet during work hours for personal business.

____ 21. Unauthorized copying of software.

____ 22. Unauthorized copying of copyrighted material.

____ 23. Electronic breaking and entering into a computer system.

____ 24. A program that makes copies of itself and destroys data and programs.

____ 25. Finds and eliminates computer viruses.

____ 26. Sending extremely critical, derogatory, and vulgar e-mail messages.

____ 27. Designing computer hardware, software, and workstations that are safe, comfortable, and easy to use.

____ 28. Applications of information technology that have beneficial effects for society at large.

____ 29. Duplicate files of programs or data that are periodically copied and stored elsewhere in case the original is damaged and needs to be restored.

____ 30. A piece of data, known only to an authorized user, that is used to gain access to a system.

Discussion Questions

1. What can be done to improve the security of business uses of the Internet? Give several examples of security measures and technologies you would use.

2. What potential security problems do you see in the increasing use of intranets and extranets in business? What might be done to solve such problems? Give several examples.

3. Refer to the Real World example about copying CDs and music downloading in the chapter. Is copying music CDs an ethical practice? How about Internet music downloading? Explain.

4. What are your major concerns about computer crime and privacy on the Internet? What can you do about it? Explain.

5. What is disaster recovery? How could it be implemented at your school or work?

6. Refer to the Real World Case on ethics and moral dilemmas in the case. Although John Mackey's actions may be debatable from an ethical standpoint, they were likely not illegal. Is it inappropriate for an employee to blog or emit opinions about his or her own company or its competitors? Why or why not? What if it had been an analyst, as opposed to the CEO?

7. Is there an ethical crisis in business today? What role does information technology play in unethical business practices?

8. What are several business decisions that you will have to make as a manager that have both ethical and IT dimensions? Give examples to illustrate your answer.

9. Refer to the Real World Case on outbound content management in the chapter. The case notes that although companies in highly regulated industries can more easily justify their investment in these technologies, others may have some challenges in doing this. How can these companies present a business case for acquiring or developing these technologies? What factors would need to be taken into account? Provide several examples.

10. What would be examples of one positive and one negative effect of the use of information technologies in each of the ethical and societal dimensions illustrated in Figure 11.2? Explain several of your choices.

FIGURE 11.23

Network monitoring software (sniffers) are used to monitor the use of the Internet by employees at work. They can also block access to unauthorized Web sites.

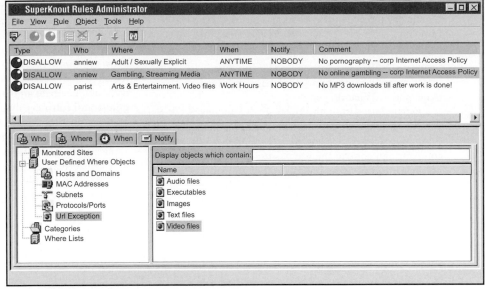

Source: Courtesy of Aptara.

Analysis Exercises

1. **Problems with Passwords**
   Authentication
   Network and application managers need to know who is accessing their systems to determine appropriate access levels. Typically, they require that users create secret passwords. A secret password, known only to the user, allows an administrator to feel confident that a user is who the user says he or she is. Systems administrators even have the authority to determine the characteristics of passwords. For example, they may set a minimum length and require that a password include numbers, symbols, or mixed letter case. They may also require that a user change his or her password every few weeks or months. These approaches have numerous problems:

   - Users often forget complicated or frequently changing passwords, resulting in frequent calls to a help desk. The help-desk employee then faces the burden of identifying the employee by some other means and resetting the password. This process takes time and is subject to social engineering.

   - Users may write down their passwords. However, this leaves passwords subject to discovery and theft.

   - Users often pick the same password for many different accounts, which means that someone who discovers one of these passwords then has the "keys" to all the accounts.

   - Users may pick an easy-to-remember password, which is easy to anticipate and therefore easy to guess. Password-cracking programs cycle through entire dictionaries of English language words and common word/number combinations such as "smart1" or "2smart4U."

   - Users may give away their passwords over the phone (social engineering) or via e-mail (phishing, a type of social engineering) to individuals representing themselves as a system administrator. Perhaps you have already received e-mails purportedly from a financial institution claiming identity or account difficulties and asking you to "reconfirm" your account information on their authentic-looking Web site.

   As you can see, using passwords to identify a person is fraught with problems. Here are some alternatives to explore. Look up each authentication approach listed below on the Internet, describe the method in your own words (be sure to cite your sources), and briefly list the advantages and disadvantages.

   a. Biometrics (biological measuring)
   b. Smart cards
   c. Biochips

2. **Your Internet Job Rights**
   Three Ethical Scenarios
   Whether you're an employer or an employee, you should know what your rights are when it comes to Internet use in the workplace. Mark Grossman, a Florida attorney who specializes in computer and Internet law, gives answers to some basic questions.

   - **Scenario 1:** Nobody told you that your Internet use in the office was being monitored. Now you've been warned you'll be fired if you use the Internet for recreational surfing again. What are your rights?
     Bottom line: When you're using your office computer, you essentially have no rights. You'd have

a tough time convincing a court that the boss invaded your privacy by monitoring your use of the company PC on company time. You should probably be grateful you got a warning.

- **Scenario 2:** Your employees are abusing their Internet privileges, but you don't have an Internet usage policy. What do you do?

    Bottom line: Although the law isn't fully developed in this area, courts are taking a straightforward approach: If it's a company computer, the company can control the way it's used. You don't need an Internet usage policy to prevent inappropriate use of your company computers. To protect yourself in the future, distribute an Internet policy to your employees as soon as possible.

- **Scenario 3:** Employee John Doe downloads adult material to his PC at work, and employee Jane Smith sees it. Smith then proceeds to sue the company for sexual harassment. As the employer, are you liable?

    Bottom line: Whether it comes from the Internet or from a magazine, adult material has no place in the office. So Smith could certainly sue the company for allowing a sexually hostile environment. The best defense is for the company to have an Internet usage policy that prohibits visits to adult sites. Of course, you have to follow through. If someone is looking at adult material in the office, you must at least send the offending employee a written reprimand. If the company lacks a strict Internet policy, though, Smith could prevail in court.

a. Do you agree with the advice of attorney Mark Grossman in each of the scenarios? Why or why not?
b. What would your advice be? Explain your positions.
c. Identify any ethical principles you may be using to explain your position in each of the scenarios.

3. Exploiting Security Weaknesses
Social Engineering

An employee who needs permission to access an electronic workspace, database, or other information systems resource typically fills in a request form and obtains approval from the responsible manager. The manager then routes the request to one of the system's administrators.

Highly trusted and well-trained systems administrators spend a significant amount of time doing nothing more technical than adding or removing names from access control lists. In large organizations, it's not unusual for systems administrators to have never met any of the people involved in a specific request. The administrators may not even work in the same office.

Hackers have learned to take advantage of this approach to access authorization. They begin by probing an organization. The hacker doesn't expect to compromise the system during this initial probe. He or she just starts by making a few phone calls to learn who is responsible for granting access and how to apply. A little

more probing helps the hacker learn who's who within the organization's structure. Some organizations even post this information online in the form of employee directories. With this information in hand, the hacker knows whom to talk to, what to ask for, and what names to use to sound convincing. The hacker is now ready to try to impersonate an employee and trick a systems administrator into revealing a password and unwittingly granting unauthorized access.

Organizations determine who needs access to which applications. They also need a system through which they can authenticate the identity of an individual making a request. Finally, they need to manage this process both effectively and inexpensively.

a. Describe the business problems that this exercise presents.
b. Suggest several ways to reduce an organization's exposure to social engineering.
c. Prepare an orientation memo to new hires in your IT department describing "social engineering." Suggest several ways employees can avoid being tricked by hackers.

4. Privacy Statements
The Spyware Problem

Web surfers may feel anonymous as they use the Internet, but that feeling isn't always justified. IP addresses, cookies, site log-in procedures, and credit card purchases all help track how often users visit a site and what pages they view. Some companies go further.

Some free screensaver software and peer-to-peer file sharing come with "spyware" embedded within their applications. Once loaded, these applications run in the background. What they actually track depends on the specific software. To stay on the "right side" of U.S. law, these companies outline their software's functions in general terms and include this information in the small print within their end-user licensing agreement (EULA) and/or privacy policy. In fact, these agreements may even include a stipulation that users not disable any part of their software as a condition for free use.

Because most users don't read these policies, they have no idea what privacy rights they may have given up. They indeed get their free file-sharing program or screen saver, but they may be getting a lot more. Some spyware programs even remain on hard drives and stay active after users have uninstalled their "free" software.

a. Use a search engine to search for "spyware," "spyware removal," "adware," or other related terms. Prepare a one-page summary of your results. Include URLs for online sources.
b. Select three of your favorite Web sites and print out their privacy policies. What do they share in common? How do they differ?
c. Write your own Web site privacy policy, striking a balance between customer and business needs.

REAL WORLD CASE 3

Cyber Scams: Four Top Cyber Criminals—Who They Are and What They Do

Cyber scams are today's fastest-growing criminal niche. Scores of banks and e-commerce giants, from JPMorgan Chase & Co. to Wal-Mart.com, have been hit, sometimes repeatedly, by hackers and online fraud schemes. The 2005 FBI Computer Crime Survey estimated annual losses to all types of computer crime—including attacks of viruses and other malware, financial fraud, and network intrusions—at $67 billion a year. Of the 2,066 companies responding to the survey, 87 percent reported a security incident. In addition, the U.S. Federal Trade Commission says identity theft is its top complaint.

To track cyber crime, law enforcement officers work with companies such as eBay or Microsoft, as well as with legal authorities around the globe. eBay has 60 people that combat fraud, while Microsoft's Internet Safety Enforcement team has 65 operatives, including former law enforcement agents and federal prosecutors. To document the extent of the activity, *BusinessWeek* reporters scoured underground Web sites where stolen data are swapped like so many baseball cards on eBay.

Consider this e-mail promoting the launch of an online crime trading bazaar, vendorsname.ws, last year: "During the battle with US Secret Service, we !@# &! all those bastards and now are running a brand new, improved and the biggest carders' forum you ever seen." The message brags about its array of stolen goods: U.S. and European credit card data, "active and wealthy" PayPal accounts, and Social Security numbers. Those who "register today" get a "bonus" choice of "one Citybank account with online access with 3K on board" or "25 credit cards with PINs for online carding."

What follows is a look at four individuals who have been identified by multiple law enforcement authorities as high-priority targets in their investigations. It's no coincidence that all are Russian. Strong technical universities, comparatively low incomes, and an unstable legal system make the former Soviet Union an ideal breeding ground for cyber scams. Also, tense political relations sometimes complicate efforts to obtain cooperation with local law enforcement. "The low standard of living and high savviness is a bad combination," argues Robert C. Chesnut, a former federal prosecutor who is a senior vice president directing antifraud efforts at eBay.

Among the most pernicious scams to emerge in the last few years are so-called reshipping rings. The king of these rings is a Russian-born hacker who goes by the name Shtirlitz—a sly reference to a fictional Soviet secret agent who spied on the Nazis. In real life, Shtirlitz is being investigated by the U.S. Postal Inspection Service in connection with tens of millions of dollars' worth of fraud in which Americans signed up to serve as unwitting collaborators in converting stolen credit card data into tangible goods that can be sold for cash. "We think he is involved in the recruitment of hundreds of people," says William A. Schambura, an analyst with the U.S. Postal Inspection Service.

Investigators believe that people like Shtirlitz use stolen credit cards to purchase goods they send to Americans whose homes serve as drop-off points. The Americans send the goods overseas, before either the credit card owner or the online merchant catches on. Then the goods are fenced on the black market.

BusinessWeek found that reshipping groups take out advertisements in newspapers and spoof ads from online job sites. "We have a promotional job offer for you!!" beckons one e-mail for a "shipping-receiving position" from UHM Cargo that appeared to come from Monster.com. It states that "starting salary is $70–$80 per processed shipment. Health and life benefits after 90 days."

Officials do not know Shtirlitz's real name but believe he is 25–27 years old and lived in the San Francisco area at one time after his parents emigrated. They do not know where he is now but believe he is active. In one forum of Carding-World.cc, a person with the alias iNFERNis, posted this request on December 23, 2005: "Hi, I need eBay logins with mail access, please icq 271-365-234." A few hours later, Shtirlitz replied: "I know good vendor. ICQ me: 80–911."

Once equipped, someone could log into those eBay accounts and use them to buy goods with the owners' money while emptying the money out of their PayPal accounts. "The Web sites are more like a dating service," notes Yohai Einav, an analyst at RSA Security Inc. "Then you can conduct transactions in private chat rooms. I can click on someone's name and start doing business with them."

The technical tools to steal credit card numbers and online bank account log-in data are often just as valuable as the stolen goods themselves. A cyber criminal known as Smash is being investigated by the Postal Inspection Service on the suspicion that he helps hackers hack. The picture, or avatar, that accompanies Smash's posts in online chat rooms shows a fallen angel. Around 25–30 years old and based in Moscow, he is believed to be an expert in building spyware programs, malicious code that can track Web surfers' keystrokes and is often hidden in corrupted Web sites and spam e-mail.

The U.S. enforcement officials say Smash's Russia-based company, RAT Systems, openly hawks spyware on the Web at www.ratsystems.org. On its home page, RAT Systems denies any malicious intent: "In general, we're against destructive payloads and the spreading of viruses. Coding spyware is not a crime." Yet the "terms of service" guarantee that its spyware products will be undetectable by the antivirus software made by security companies such as McAfee Inc. and Symantec Corp. One product, called the TAN Systems Security Leak, created to attack German companies, sells for $834.

Postal Inspection Service officials are also investigating Smash's activity as a senior member of the International Association for the Advancement of Criminal Activity, which they describe as a loose-knit network of hackers, identity thieves, and financial fraudsters. Smash and another sought-after hacker named Zoomer jointly operate IAAcA's Web site, www. theftservices.com, one of the most popular and virulent stolen-data trading sites, according to U.S. officials.

On May 11, 2005, Massachusetts Attorney General Tom Reilly filed a lawsuit against Leo Kuvayev and six accomplices, accusing them of sending millions of spam e-mails to peddle counterfeit drugs, pirated software, fake watches, and pornography. Kuvayev, a 34-year-old native of Russia who uses the nickname BadCow, is one of the world's top three spammers, according to antispam group Spamhaus. State officials allege that Kuvayev and his associates used a number of Web-hosting services from the United States and around the world to launch attacks.

Massachusetts was able to go after Kuvayev because he listed a Massachusetts address on his driver's license and conducted business using a Boston post office box. On October 11, 2005, after none of the defendants appeared to answer the charges, a Superior Court judge issued a default judgment against them. The judge found the spammers in violation of state and federal consumer protection laws and ordered a permanent shutdown of dozens of illegal Web sites. Kuvayev and his codefendants were ordered to pay $37 million in civil penalties for sending nearly 150,000 illegal e-mails.

Federal law enforcement officials believe Kuvayev's operation was pulling in more than $30 million a year. State officials suspect Kuvayev fled to Russia before he was sued. "The problem is, Russia does not have any anti-spamming laws at the moment," says U.S. Postal Inspection Service senior investigator Gregory Crabb. "It's hard to catch someone who isn't breaking the law."

Bank robbers rob banks because that's where the money is. For cyber criminals, the best loot is often found inside the networks of credit card processors, the middlemen that handle card transactions for merchants and banks. Postal Inspection Service officials say they are investigating Roman Khoda, aka MyO, on the strong suspicion that he is connected to the theft of a million credit card numbers in recent years.

A 26-year-old Russian with a university degree in physics, Khoda once worked with the leading members of carderplanet, one of the largest online marketplaces used to buy and sell pilfered bank account and card data, until it was broken up by U.S. and foreign officials in August 2004. Yet Khoda is unlike some cocky hackers who often write their own digital signatures into malicious code, says Crabb; Khoda operates with stealth. At carderplanet and successor Web sites, he has not left a detailed trail connecting him directly to stolen data.

Still, Crabb says that officials know that Khoda and two accomplices conducted extensive due diligence on the computer networks of recent targets they intended to break into, even setting up fake companies with accounts at the credit card processors to test for holes in their systems. Then they lugged PCs to a rented apartment on the Mediterranean island of Malta, according to Crabb. Using proxy servers in the United States, China, and Ukraine to hide their Internet connection, Khoda & Co. then unleashed their break-in attacks.

Source: Adapted from Spencer Ante and Brian Grow, "Meet the Hackers," *BusinessWeek*, May 29, 2006.

CASE STUDY QUESTIONS

1. List several reasons "cyber scams are today's fastest-growing criminal niche." Explain why the reasons you give contribute to the growth of cyber scams.

2. What are several security measures that could be implemented to combat the spread of cyber scams? Explain why your suggestions would be effective.

3. Which of the four top cyber criminals described in this case poses the biggest threat to businesses? To consumers? Explain the reasons for your choices, and describe how businesses and consumers can protect themselves from these cyber scammers.

REAL WORLD ACTIVITIES

1. Note: It is not advisable to visit any of the cyber scam Web sites mentioned in this case or any others you discover. To do so could make you, your computer, and your network vulnerable to various forms of cyber crime. Search other sites on the Internet for the latest information on cyber scams, the cyber criminals mentioned in this case, and ways to combat cyber scams. What are some of the new developments you find in each of these areas?

2. How can you protect yourself from cyber scams and other forms of cyber crime? Break into small groups with your classmates to discuss this issue and formulate some key protective recommendations. Include all forms of cyber crime mentioned in this case in your recommendations, as well as those you uncover in your Internet research.

CHAPTER 12

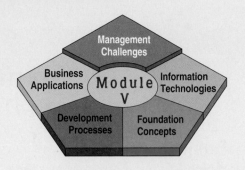

ENTERPRISE AND GLOBAL MANAGEMENT OF INFORMATION TECHNOLOGY

Chapter Highlights

Learning Objectives

1. Identify each of the three components of IT management and use examples to illustrate how they might be implemented in a business.

2. Explain how failures in IT management can be reduced by the involvement of business managers in IT planning and management.

3. Identify several cultural, political, and geoeconomic challenges that confront managers in the management of global information technologies.

4. Explain the effect on global business/IT strategy of the trend toward a transnational business strategy by international business organizations.

5. Identify several considerations that affect the choice of IT applications, IT platforms, data access policies, and systems development methods by a global business enterprise.

6. Understand the fundamental concepts of outsourcing and offshoring, as well as the primary reasons for selecting such an approach to IS/IT management.

| SECTION I | # Managing Information Technology |

Business and IT

The strategic and operational importance of information technology in business is no longer questioned. As the 21st century unfolds, many companies throughout the world are intent on transforming themselves into global business powerhouses through major investments in global e-business, e-commerce, and other IT initiatives. Thus, there is a real need for business managers and professionals to understand how to manage this vital organizational function. In this section, we explore how the IS function can be organized and managed, and we emphasize the importance of a customer and business value focus for the management of information technologies. Whether you plan to be an entrepreneur and run your own business, a manager in a corporation, or a business professional, managing information systems and technologies will be one of your major responsibilities. See Figure 12.1.

Read the Real World Case on the next page. We can learn a lot from this case about the many challenges faced by retiring IT executives and different approaches to mentoring and developing the IT leaders of the future.

Managing Information Technology

As we have seen throughout this text, information technology is an essential component of business success for companies today; however, information technology is also a vital business resource that must be properly managed. Thus, we have also seen many real world examples in which the management of information technologies plays a pivotal role in ensuring the success or contributing to the failure of a company's strategic business initiatives. Therefore, managing the information systems and technologies that support the modern business processes of companies today is a major challenge for both business and IT managers and professionals.

How should information technology be managed? Figure 12.2 illustrates one popular approach to managing information technology in a large company. This managerial approach has three major components:

- **Managing the Joint Development and Implementation of Business/IT Strategies.** Led by the CEO (chief executive officer) and CIO (chief information officer), proposals are developed by business and IT managers and professionals regarding the use of IT to support the strategic business priorities of the company. This business/IT planning process *aligns* IT with strategic business goals. The process also includes evaluating the business case for investing in the development and implementation of each proposed business/IT project.

- **Managing the Development and Implementation of New Business/IT Applications and Technologies.** This step is the primary responsibility of the CIO and CTO (chief technology officer). This area of IT management involves managing the processes for information systems development and implementation we discussed in Chapter 12, as well as the responsibility for research into the strategic business uses of new information technologies.

- **Managing the IT Organization and the IT Infrastructure.** The CIO and IT managers share responsibility for managing the work of IT professionals who are typically organized into a variety of project teams and other organizational subunits. In addition, they are responsible for managing the IT infrastructure of hardware, software, databases, telecommunications networks, and other IT resources, which must be acquired, operated, monitored, and maintained.

Let's look at a real-world example.

Toyota, Procter & Gamble, Hess Corporation, and Others: Retiring CIOs and the Need for Succession Planning

Barbra Cooper started as a CIO when the position was still called "VP of IS." In her more than 30 years in IT, she's seen the role become ever more strategic. Until now, the CIO is in the unique position of being the C-level officer who can "see across the entire enterprise."

As the CIO for Toyota Motor Sales USA, Cooper thinks tomorrow's CIOs will be even more strategic and influential, but she also worries about the future business and technology changes they face. "The next 10 to 20 years are going to be challenging," she says. As she talks about the challenges that lie ahead, the question arises: Where will the IT leaders come from to tackle them?

It's a question more and more IT executives are asking themselves. CIOs are moving up and out. The first full-career CIO generation is beginning to retire. Others are increasingly taking on broader responsibilities or moving out of IT and into other business leadership roles as the position evolves beyond its technology roots. In fact, *CIO*'s 2008 *State of the CIO* report found that 56 percent of CIOs surveyed say long-term strategic thinking and planning is the executive leadership skill most critical in their current role, followed by collaboration and influence (47 percent) and expertise running IT (39 percent). At the same time, many CIOs don't know who would lead IT if they left tomorrow. When you consider that just 17 percent of respondents to the *State of the CIO* survey cited people development as a critical leadership competency, that's not surprising.

The skills to be CIO have also changed as the role has shifted from technologist to business strategist. It used to be that "we could afford to let the business tell us what they wanted us to do, be good at delivering it and keep our

jobs," says Cooper. "Now, the physics and velocity of business and its demands mean you can't afford to wait until something happens."

Indeed, CEOs now look to the CIO to act more as a strategic business leader and less as a function head. TAC Worldwide CEO Robert Badavas says he seldom speaks about technology with his CIO; instead, the two talk about "shaping the business value to our clients," he says. To be successful, he notes, the CIO needs to understand the value proposition of the business. "By staying in the silo of technology, HR, accounting or any other," says Badavas, "you're not going to be as valuable to the business." Or to the CEO.

With all that in mind, CIOs today must groom not only competent replacements for themselves but also next-generation IT leaders who are "business ready" and able to succeed in a more IT-intense and integral business environment. The shift in business expectations means that CIOs have better job security than in the past. It also takes longer to find good ones with the right mix of business and technical know-how. For example, Pete Walton is in his second stint as CIO at Hess Corp. The petroleum products company coaxed him out of retirement in 2005 when its CIO at that time left. Hess wanted someone who could take its Information Services "to the next level," says Walton.

"CEOs want someone who's business savvy and can figure out how you can use technology for the business. Trying to find that hybrid person is hard," says Diane S. Wallace, CIO for the state of Connecticut. It will only get harder to find them, just for demographic reasons. "We have this triple threat of labor shortage: The Boomers are retiring, young people are not going into IT and fewer people are getting degrees," says Robert D. Scott, who in February retired as Procter & Gamble's vice president of Global Business Services. Scott says he noticed a drop in IT interest during the technology bubble of the late 1990s. Then the rush to outsourcing created a cloud around U.S. IT jobs. That pall persists despite strong job growth in IT, which is expected to add more than 200,000 jobs by 2016, according to the Bureau of Labor Statistics.

Procter & Gamble (P&G) is a case in point. It outsourced about half of its IT staff in 2003, but IT employment is now back to the level it was five years ago. Scott says that this is because the company outsourced its commodity IT, and "internal IT moved up the food chain, and is creating more and more business value."

Scott says P&G continues to attract strong candidates for IT jobs, but the hiring pool is not as deep as in years past. Plus, P&G believes strongly in promoting people steeped in its culture. It worries about keeping its Generation Y employees. The triple threat is already creating an IT brain drain. Wallace says 40 percent of her staff of 518 will be eligible for retirement in the next two to three years. Barbara A. White, CIO and associate provost at the University of Georgia, says that when three staff members retired in April,

FIGURE 12.1

Developing and mentoring their successors is one of the key responsibilities of IT leaders in an environment that includes the changing role of the CIO and a shortage of qualified managers.

Source: ©DigitalVision/Getty Images.

505

she lost their combined 90 years of experience, and has a lot of staff likely to retire in the next 10 years.

Toyota's Cooper is dedicating time to prepare her organization for the future, which includes being as proactive as possible and staying ahead of the business needs. It also means a commitment to active succession planning. Two years ago, Cooper sat down for 90 minutes with 27 team members who reported either directly to her or directly to another team member. Each meeting was an open coaching session structured around her ideas of what IT leaders will need to be in 10 years. She then crafted a three- to four-page letter for each team member, detailing the capabilities she wanted them to develop and a plan for showing how they were achieving them. Those who reported directly to her received a summary of what she sent to their team members.

Procter & Gamble has a corporate culture that promotes from within. It saw, however, that good technical talent was getting harder to keep, and it also understood that Gen Y employees expect to change companies frequently. To combat both challenges, it blazed a new, faster IT career path for its younger workers. IT leadership adopted an accelerated development program, as a part of the career path, says Scott. It would place a new set of top performers in a Career Executive Development Program, designed to provide them exposure to high-level IT executives and assignments to help accelerate their growth. It comes with one caveat: If you don't perform, you'll be looking for another employer. It's a modified version of what's in place in the company's fabled brand management department.

"We wanted to signal that we were very serious about growing people, and were willing to invest extra time and energy" in them, he says. The program is only two years old and is too new to have clear results (no one, for instance, has been asked to leave yet).

P&G also created what it calls "The CIO Circle," which rewards long-time IT people who have mastered an area of technical expertise. This "master's" designation allows P&G to acknowledge their status as knowledge leaders even if they are not on the management track. Rewards programs encourage employee loyalty, says Laurie Orlov, a consultant and principal of LMO Insight. Fast-track development in particular should help companies cultivate Gen Y leaders. With so much training and management exposure, they have every reason to stay, she says.

CIOs who are serious about developing leaders in their group have to be willing to invest time in their people and to give them opportunities to grow, even if that means sometimes letting them fail. It might also mean getting out of their way when the time comes. Hess Corp.'s Walton says that his goal at all of his jobs has been to identify and develop replacements for himself. "You do that by creating opportunities for them, you make them look like leadership heroes in the eyes of their business and let them take all the glory," says Walton, who is 63 and retired from Hess for the second time last month after the company named Jeff Steinhorn, who served under Walton, as its new CIO.

Like most CIOs who aim to develop their staff, Walton has used a multipronged strategy for helping people along: He mentors, he provides role models, he moves staff into new opportunities, and he invests heavily in education. In fact, he sent selected top managers to a Harvard Business School executive program, and IT has two memberships to the BSG Concours Group, a strategy and executive education firm.

Walton sees the coming leadership challenge as a plus, not a minus. "There is a gap, but it's an exciting one to fill," he says. For one thing, Walton thinks the blend of experience and technical savvy available when you mix Baby Boomers and Gen Y is a powerful one for companies that work to bring these generations together. He is talking with Hess about how to do it, and he may want to take on such a role in the future. Now that a new IT leader is in place at Hess, however, Walton can relax for a bit. "I'm going to get my handicap down," he says.

Source: Adapted from Michael Fitzgerald, "How to Develop the Next Generation of IT Leaders," *CIO Magazine*, May 2, 2008.

CASE STUDY QUESTIONS

1. Several comments in the case note that CIOs are in a unique position for companywide leadership, extending beyond their primary technological concerns. Why do you think this is the case? How are CIOs different in this regard from other chief officers, for example, in finance, HR, or marketing?

2. After reading the case, what do you think are the most important competencies for the successful CIO of tomorrow? How do you rate yourself in those? Have you considered the importance of these skills and abilities before?

3. How can CIOs prepare their successors for an uncertain future that will most likely require skills different from those possessed by the successful CIOs of today? Which key competencies are enduring, and which ones are a function of the current technological environment? How can CIOs prepare for the latter?

REAL WORLD ACTIVITIES

1. Go online to research the topic of executive succession planning and the different approaches in use by companies today. Are there any differences for those in information technology, as opposed to other functional areas, because of the dynamics of technology change and evolution? Which competencies are being targeted for IT executives? Prepare a report to summarize your findings.

2. The case mentions several strategies used by companies to mentor and develop their next generation of IT leaders: career planning, leadership development exercises, coaching, and so on. As a Gen Y member discussed in the chapter, how do these fit in with your expectations for the future? Break into small groups with your classmates to discuss these issues, in particular, to what extent you believe these approaches match well with your culture and personality.

FIGURE 12.2

The major components of information technology management. Note the executives with primary responsibilities in each area.

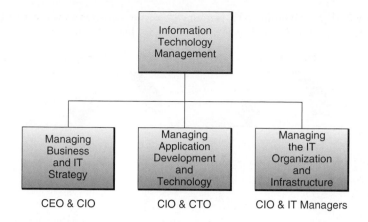

Avnet Marshall: Managing IT

Figure 12.3 contrasts how Avnet Marshall's information technology management differs from conventional IT management. Notice that it uses the model of IT management illustrated in Figure 12.2. For example, in technology management, Avnet Marshall uses a best-of-breed approach that supports business needs instead of enforcing a standardized and homogeneous choice of hardware, software, database, and networking technologies. In managing its IT organization, Avnet Marshall hires IS professionals who can integrate IT with business. These IS professionals are organized in workgroups around business/IT initiatives that focus on building IT-enabled business services for customers.

Business/IT Planning

Figure 12.4 illustrates the business/IT planning process, which focuses on discovering innovative approaches to satisfying a company's customer value and business value goals. This planning process leads to the development of strategies and business models for new business applications, processes, products, and services. Then a company can

FIGURE 12.3

Comparing conventional and e-business-driven IT management approaches.

IT Management	Conventional Practices	Avnet Marshall's Business/IT Practices
Technology Management	• Approach to IT infrastructure may sacrifice match with business needs for vendor homogeneity and technology platform choices.	• Best-of-breed approach to IT infrastructure in which effective match with business needs takes precedence over commitment to technology platform choices and vendor homogeneity.
Managing the IT Organization	• Hire "best by position" who can bring specific IT expertise. • Departments organized around IT expertise with business liaisons and explicit delegation of tasks. • IT projects have separable cost/value considerations. Funding typically allocated within constraints of yearly budget for IT function.	• Hire "best athletes" IS professionals who can flexibly integrate new IT and business competencies. • Evolving workgroups organized around emerging IT-intensive business initiatives with little explicit delegation of tasks. • IT funding typically based on value proposition around business opportunity related to building services for customers. IT project inseparable part of business initiative.

Source: Adapted from Omar El Sawy, Arvind Malhotra, Sanjay Gosain, and Kerry Young, "IT-Intensive Value Innovation in the Electronic Economy: Insights from Marshall Industries," *MIS Quarterly*, September 1999.

FIGURE 12.4   The business/IT planning process emphasizes a customer and business value focus for developing business strategies and models and an IT architecture for business applications.

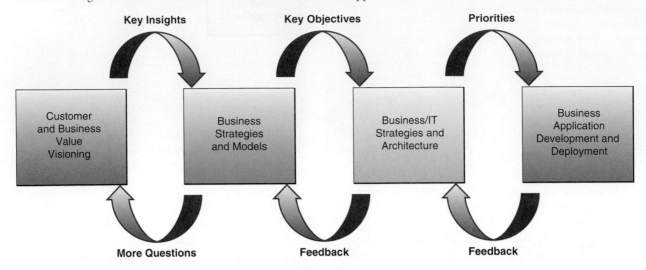

develop IT strategies and an IT architecture that supports building and implementing its newly planned business applications.

Both the CEO and the CIO of a company must manage the development of complementary business and IT strategies to meet its customer value and business value vision. This *coadaptation* process is necessary because, as we have seen so often in this text, information technologies are a fast-changing but vital component in many strategic business initiatives. The business/IT planning process has three major components:

- **Strategy Development.** Developing business strategies that support a company's business vision. For example, using information technology to create innovative e-business systems that focus on customer and business value. We will discuss this process in more detail shortly.

- **Resource Management.** Developing strategic plans for managing or outsourcing a company's IT resources, including IS personnel, hardware, software, data, and network resources.

- **Technology Architecture.** Making strategic IT choices that reflect an information technology architecture designed to support a company's business/IT initiatives.

Information Technology Architecture

The IT architecture created by the strategic business/IT planning process is a conceptual design, or blueprint, that includes the following major components:

- **Technology Platform.** The Internet, intranets, extranets, and other networks, computer systems, system software, and integrated enterprise application software provide a computing and communications infrastructure, or platform, that supports the strategic use of information technology for e-business, e-commerce, and other business/IT applications.

- **Data Resources.** Many types of operational and specialized databases, including data warehouses and Internet/intranet databases (as reviewed in Chapter 5), store and provide data and information for business processes and decision support.

- **Applications Architecture.** Business applications of information technology are designed as an integrated architecture *or portfolio* of enterprise systems that support strategic business initiatives, as well as cross-functional business processes. For example, an applications architecture should include support for developing and maintaining the interenterprise supply chain applications and integrated

FIGURE 12.5
Comparing business/IT
strategic and application
planning approaches.

Conventional IT Planning	Avnet Marshall's Business/IT Planning
● Strategic alignment: IT strategy tracks specified enterprise strategy.	● Strategic improvisation: IT strategy and enterprise business strategy coadaptively unfold based on the clear guidance of a focus on customer value.
● CEO endorses IT vision shaped through CIO.	● CEO proactively shapes IT vision jointly with CIO as part of e-business strategy.
● IT application development projects functionally organized as technological solutions to business issues.	● IT application development projects colocated with e-business initiatives to form centers of IT-intensive business expertise.
● Phased application development based on learning from pilot projects.	● Perpetual application development based on continuous learning from rapid deployment and prototyping with end-user involvement.

enterprise resource planning and customer relationship management applications discussed in Chapters 7 and 8.

● **IT Organization.** The organizational structure of the IS function within a company and the distribution of IS specialists are designed to meet the changing strategies of a business. The form of the IT organization depends on the managerial philosophy and business/IT strategies formulated during the strategic planning process.

Avnet Marshall: Business/IT Planning

Figure 12.5 outlines Avnet Marshall's planning process for business/IT initiatives and compares it with conventional IT planning approaches. Avnet Marshall weaves both business and IT strategic planning together *coadaptively* under the guidance of the CEO and the CIO, instead of developing IT strategy by just tracking and supporting business strategies. Avnet Marshall also locates IT application development projects within the business units that are involved in an e-business initiative to form centers of business/IT expertise throughout the company. Finally, Avnet Marshall uses a prototyping application development process with rapid deployment of new business applications instead of a traditional systems development approach. This application development strategy trades the risk of implementing incomplete applications with the benefits of gaining competitive advantages from early deployment of new e-business services to employees, customers, and other stakeholders and of involving them in the "fine-tuning" phase of application development.

Source: Adapted from Omar El Sawy, Arvind Malhotra, Sanjay Gosain, and Kerry Young, "IT-Intensive Value Innovation in the Electronic Economy: Insights from Marshall Industries," *MIS Quarterly*, September 1999.

Managing the IT Function

A radical shift is occurring in corporate computing—think of it as the recentralization of management. It's a step back toward the 1970s, when a data processing manager could sit at a console and track all the technology assets of the corporation. Then came the 1980s and early 1990s. Departments got their own PCs and software; client/server networks sprang up all across companies.

Three things have happened in the past few years: The Internet boom inspired businesses to connect all those networks; companies put on their intranets essential applications without which their businesses could not function; and it became apparent that maintaining PCs on a network is very, very expensive. Such changes create an urgent need for centralization.

Organizing IT

In the early years of computing, the development of large mainframe computers and telecommunications networks and terminals caused a centralization of computer hardware and software, databases, and information specialists at the corporate level of organizations. Next, the development of minicomputers and microcomputers accelerated a downsizing trend, which prompted a move back toward decentralization by many business firms. Distributed client/server networks at the corporate, department, workgroup, and team levels came into being, which promoted a shift of databases and information specialists to some departments and the creation of *information centers* to support end-user and workgroup computing.

Lately, the trend is to establish more centralized control over the management of the IT resources of a company while still serving the strategic needs of its business units, especially their e-business and e-commerce initiatives. This trend has resulted in the development of hybrid structures with both centralized and decentralized components. See Figure 12.6. For example, the IT function at Avnet Marshall is organized into several business-focused development groups, as well as operations management and planning groups.

Some companies spin off their information systems function into IS *subsidiaries* that offer IS services to external organizations, as well as to their parent company. Other companies create or spin off their e-commerce and Internet-related business units or IT groups into separate companies or business units. Corporations also **outsource,** that is, turn over all or parts of their IS operations to outside contractors known as *systems integrators*. In addition, some companies are outsourcing software procurement and support to *application service providers* (ASPs), which provide and support business application and other software via the Internet and intranets to all of a company's employee workstations. We will discuss outsourcing in greater detail later in this section. In the meantime, let's take a few minutes to review, and expand on, what we know about managing the various functions and activities in IS.

Managing Application Development

Application development management involves managing activities such as systems analysis and design, prototyping, applications programming, project management, quality assurance, and system maintenance for all major business/IT development projects. Managing application development requires managing the activities of teams of systems analysts, software developers, and other IS professionals working on a variety of information systems development projects. Thus, project management is a key IT management responsibility if business/IT projects are to be completed on time, within their budgets, and meet their design objectives. In addition, some systems

FIGURE 12.6

The organizational components of the IT function at Avnet Marshall.

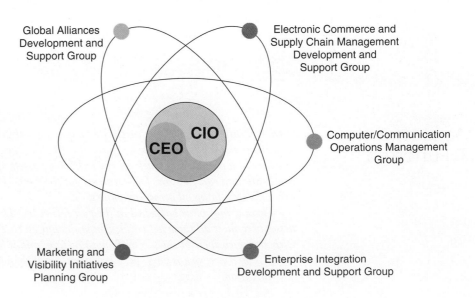

development groups have established *development centers* staffed with IS professionals. Their role is to evaluate new application development tools and help information systems specialists use them to improve their application development efforts.

Managing IS Operations

IS operations management is concerned with the use of hardware, software, network, and personnel resources in the corporate or business unit data centers (computer centers) of an organization. Operational activities that must be managed include computer system operations, network management, production control, and production support.

Most operations management activities are being automated by the use of software packages for computer system performance management. These system performance monitors look after the processing of computer jobs, help develop a planned schedule of computer operations that can optimize computer system performance, and produce detailed statistics that are invaluable for effective planning and control of computing capacity. Such information evaluates computer system utilization, costs, and performance. This evaluation provides information for capacity planning, production planning and control, and hardware/software acquisition planning. It is also used in quality assurance programs, which stress the quality of services to business end users. See Figure 12.7.

System performance monitors also supply information needed by chargeback systems that allocate costs to users on the basis of the information services rendered. All costs incurred are recorded, reported, allocated, and charged back to specific end-user business units, depending on their use of system resources. When companies use this arrangement, the information services department becomes a service center whose costs are charged directly to business units rather than being lumped with other administrative service costs and treated as overhead costs.

Many performance monitors also feature **process control** capabilities. Such packages not only monitor but also automatically control computer operations at large data centers. Some use built-in expert system modules that are based on knowledge gleaned from experts in the operations of specific computer systems and operating systems. These performance monitors provide more efficient computer operations than human-operated systems. They also enable "lights out" data centers at some companies, where computer systems are operated unattended, especially after normal business hours.

FIGURE 12.7

The CA-Unicenter TNG system performance monitor includes an Enterprise Management Portal module that helps IT specialists monitor and manage a variety of networked computer systems and operating systems.

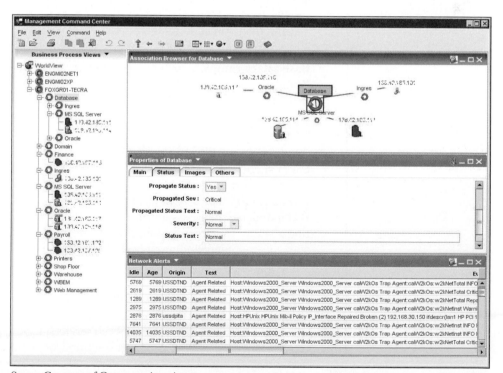

Source: Courtesy of Computer Associates.

IT Staff Planning

The success or failure of an information services organization rests primarily on the quality of its people. Many firms consider IT staff planning, or recruiting, training, and retaining qualified IS personnel, as one of their greatest challenges. Managing information services functions involves the management of managerial, technical, and clerical personnel. One of the most important jobs of information services managers is to recruit qualified personnel and develop, organize, and direct the capabilities of existing personnel. Employees must be continually trained to keep up with the latest developments in a fast-moving and highly technical field. Employee job performances must be continually evaluated, and outstanding performances must be rewarded with salary increases or promotions. Salary and wage levels must be set, and career paths must be designed so that individuals can move to new jobs through promotion and transfer as they gain seniority and expertise.

The CIO and Other IT Executives

The chief information officer (CIO) oversees all use of information technology in many companies and brings it into alignment with strategic business goals. Thus, all traditional computer services, Internet technology, telecommunications network services, and other IS technology support services are the responsibility of this executive. The CIO does not direct day-to-day information services activities; instead, CIOs concentrate on business/IT planning and strategy. They also work with the CEO and other top executives to develop strategic uses of information technology in e-business and e-commerce that help make the firm more competitive in the marketplace. Many companies have also filled the CIO position with executives from the business functions or units outside the IS field. Such CIOs emphasize that the chief role of information technology is to help a company meet its strategic business objectives.

Top IT Jobs: Requirements and Compensation

- **Chief information officer**
  Base salary range: $194,000–$303,000+; varies by location
  Bonus range: Up to 40 percent of salary
  The top position in IT isn't all about technology. To land this job, you need to be a Business Technologist with a big "B" and a big "T." If you understand the business, the organization's strategy, and the broad spectrum of technologies, systems, applications, and people necessary to execute it, you will be in great demand by organizations.

- **Chief technology officer**
  Base salary range: $162,000–$245,000+; varies by location
  Bonus range: Up to 40 percent of salary
  If you're second-in-command to the CIO or chief technology officer and you have years of applications development experience, your next move should be into the chief technology officer's spot. To land this job, you'll need to be a passionate problem solver with a demonstrated record of reducing development time.

- **Chief security officer**
  Base salary range: $142,000–$205,000+; varies by location
  Bonus range: Up to 40 percent of salary
  If you understand the issues related to securing the data resources and information assets of the organization, then this is the job for you. Strong candidates with a deep understanding of both the technical and managerial sides of the field are in great demand.

- **E-commerce architect**
  Base salary range: $115,000–$170,000+; varies by location
  Bonus range: Up to 15 percent of salary
  If you know Java, Perl, C++, and Web services; have experience in systems architecture; and can design an Internet solution from concept through implementation, many companies want you to plan and develop their e-commerce sites.

- **Technical team leader**
  Base salary range: $75,000–$100,000+; varies by location
  Bonus range: Up to 20 percent of salary
  Senior technical team leaders with good communication, project management, and leadership skills, as well as knowledge of Web languages and databases, are still in great demand.

- **Practice manager**
  Base salary range: $70,000–$100,000+; varies by location
  Bonus range: Up to 20 percent of salary
  If you've got a background in IT assessment and a pedigree in business development (MBA preferred), you can land a job as a point person for big projects. You'll need skills in IT operations and software assessment, as well as in marketing, staffing, budgeting, and building customer relationships.

- **Systems analyst**
  Base salary range: $56,000–$100,000+; varies by location
  Bonus range: Up to 25 percent of salary
  If you have problem-solving skills and a degree in information systems (BS or MBA), you can be assured of finding a good job as a systems analyst. You'll need to have excellent interpersonal skills, good technical skills, and an ability to apply your problem-solving and critical-thinking skills to the design of new systems.

Source: www.salary.com.

Technology Management

The management of rapidly changing technology is important to any organization. Changes in information technology, like the rise of the PC, client/server networks, and the Internet and intranets, have come swiftly and dramatically and are expected to continue into the future. Developments in information systems technology have had, and will continue to have, a major impact on the operations, costs, management work environment, and competitive position of many organizations.

Thus, all information technologies must be managed as a technology platform for integrating internally focused or externally facing business applications. Such technologies include the Internet, intranets, and a variety of e-commerce and collaboration technologies, as well as integrated enterprise software for customer relationship management, enterprise resource planning, and supply chain management. In many companies, **technology management** is the primary responsibility of a **chief technology officer (CTO)**, who is in charge of all information technology planning and deployment.

Managing User Services

Teams and workgroups of business professionals commonly use PC workstations, software packages, and the Internet, intranets, and other networks to develop and apply information technology to their work activities. Thus, many companies have responded by creating **user services**, or *client services*, functions to support and manage end-user and workgroup computing.

End-user services provide both opportunities and problems for business unit managers. For example, some firms create an *information center* group staffed with user liaison specialists or Web-enabled intranet help desks. IS specialists with titles such as user consultant, account executive, or business analyst may also be assigned to end-user workgroups. These specialists perform a vital role by troubleshooting problems, gathering and communicating information, coordinating educational efforts, and helping business professionals with application development.

In addition to these measures, most organizations still establish and enforce policies for the acquisition of hardware and software by end users and business units. This process ensures their compatibility with company standards for hardware, software, and network connectivity. Also important is the development of applications with proper security and quality controls to promote correct performance and safeguard the integrity of corporate and departmental networks and databases.

Outsourcing and Offshoring IT and IS

An increasingly popular approach to managing the IS and IT functions of the organization is to adopt an outsourcing strategy. Outsourcing, in broad terms, is the purchase of goods or services that were previously provided internally from third-party partners. Outsourcing is a generic term used for a broad range of information technology functions that are selectively contracted to an external service provider.

Outsourcing

A commonly outsourced IS function is software application development. This process includes contracting (or subcontracting) with an external organization for the development of complete or partial software products/projects, the purchase of packaged or customized package software products, or activities and/or resources that aid in the software development life cycle. Figure 12.8 lists the functions typically outsourced, the reasons behind the decision to outsource, and several aspects associated with successful vendor selection and a successful outsourcing effort.

Although companies can, theoretically, choose to outsource any organization function for any reason, there are five main reasons behind a decision to outsource:

FIGURE 12.8   Outsourcing's Top 10. Notice, despite all of the media coverage, application development is No. 3.

Top 10 Reasons Companies Outsource	Top 10 Factors in Vendor Selection
1. Reduce and control operating costs	1. Commitment to quality
2. Improve company focus	2. Price
3. Gain access to world-class capabilities	3. References/reputation
4. Free internal resources for other purposes	4. Flexible contract terms
5. Necessary resources are not available internally	5. Scope of resources
6. Accelerate reengineering benefits	6. Additional value-added capability
7. Function is difficult to manage internally or is out of control	7. Cultural match
8. Make capital funds available	8. Existing relationship
9. Share risks	9. Location
10. Cash infusion	10. Other

Top 10 Factors for Successful Outsourcing	Top 10 IT Areas Being Outsourced
1. Understand company goals and objectives	1. Maintenance and repair
2. A strategic vision and plan	2. Training
3. Select the right vendor	3. Applications development
4. Ongoing management of the relationships	4. Consulting and reengineering
5. A properly structured contract	5. Mainframe data centers
6. Open communication with affected individuals/groups	6. Client/server services and administration
7. Senior executive support and involvement	7. Network administration
8. Careful attention to personnel issues	8. Desktop services
9. Near-term financial justification	9. End-user support
10. Use of outside expertise	10. Total IT outsourcing

Source: The Outsourcing Institute.

Save Money—Achieve Greater Return on Investment (ROI)

- Outsourcing IS/IT functions to skilled service providers is often a strategic approach to stretching strained budgets. Companies that take a well-managed approach to outsourcing can gain cost savings of upwards of 40–80 percent.

Focus on Core Competencies

- Outsourced professionals allow an organization and its employees to focus on the business they are in rather than a business in which they are not. By using an outsourcing strategy for application development, an organization can focus its IS professionals on identifying and solving business problems rather than on programming and prototyping new applications.

Achieve Flexible Staffing Levels

- Strategic use of an outsourcing approach to IS/IT functions can result in business growth without increasing overhead. Outsourcing provides a pool of qualified professionals available for unique, niche, or overflow projects. If the unique skill set required by an organization is difficult to find or expensive to maintain in-house, outsourcing can allow for the acquisition of the needed expertise.

Gain Access to Global Resources

- The Outsourcing Institute asserts that the rules for successfully growing a business have changed: "It's no longer about what you own or build. . . . [Instead] success is hinged to resources and talent you can access." Using global expertise allows an organization to gain the advantage of skilled labor, regardless of location, and significantly increase the quality of its deliverables. As such, outsourcing can create opportunities for smaller businesses that might not otherwise be possible due to costs or geophysical constraints.

Decrease Time to Market

- Outsourcing extends the traditional small business benefits of flexibility and responsiveness, allowing smaller organizations to compete effectively against bigger firms. Supplementing an existing workforce with offshore support could allow for productivity 24 hours a day. Having access to resources able to work on key projects even while local employees are asleep can serve to accelerate time to market and provide a key competitive advantage.

Offshoring

Although often confused with outsourcing, offshoring is also increasingly becoming part of a strategic approach to IS/IT management. Offshoring can be defined as a relocation of an organization's business processes (including production/manufacturing) to a lower-cost location, usually overseas. Offshoring can be considered in the context of either *production* offshoring or *services* offshoring. After its accession to the World Trade Organization (WTO), China emerged as a prominent destination for production offshoring. After technical progress in telecommunications improved the possibilities of trade in services, India became a country that chose to focus on this domain.

The growth of services offshoring in information systems is linked to the availability of large amounts of reliable and affordable communication infrastructure following the telecom bust of the late 1990s. Coupled with the digitization of many services, it became possible to shift the actual delivery location of services to low-cost locations in a manner theoretically transparent to end users.

India, the Philippines, Ireland, and Eastern European countries benefited greatly from this trend due to their large pool of English-speaking and technically qualified workers. India's offshoring industry took root in IT functions in the 1990s and has since moved to back-office processes, such as call centers and transaction processing, as well as high-end jobs such as application development.

Offshoring is often enabled by the transfer of valuable information to the offshore site. Such information and training allows the remote workers to produce results of comparable value previously produced by internal employees. When such transfer includes proprietary materials, such as confidential documents and trade secrets, protected by nondisclosure agreements, then intellectual property has been transferred or exported. The documentation and valuation of such exports is quite difficult but should be considered because it comprises items that may be regulated or taxable.

Offshoring has been a controversial issue with heated debates. On one hand, it is seen as benefiting both the origin and destination country through free trade. On the other hand, job losses in developed countries have sparked opposition to offshoring. Some critics agree that both sides will benefit in terms of overall production and numbers of jobs created but that the subjective quality of the new jobs will be less than the previous ones. While this debate continues, companies continue to use offshoring as a viable IS/IT management approach. Let's look at a real-world example of global outsourcing.

Royal Dutch Shell: Multisupplier Global Outsourcing Deal

Royal Dutch Shell has signed a five-year, $4 billion outsourcing deal with three global IT and telecommunications suppliers. The value of the contracts for the three suppliers is $1.6 billion with AT&T, $1 billion for EDS, and $1.6 billion with T-Systems.

Shell announced that it has contracted T-Systems, AT&T, and EDS under a master service agreement (MSA), for "significant improvements" to its efficiency and productivity that will see an axing of some tech jobs and a transfer of 3,000 IT staff to the service providers. Under the MSA, Shell will outsource its IT infrastructure in three service bundles: "AT&T for network and telecommunications, T-Systems for hosting and storage, and EDS for end user computing services and for integration of the infrastructure services."

The suppliers will provide integrated services to more than 1,500 sites worldwide. "Shell's approach combines all the advantages of decentralised service provision with the benefits and efficiency of a centralised governance structure," says Elesh Khakhar, a partner at consultant firm TPI, which is an advisor to Shell. Khakar added that the multisupplier deal has been designed to "encourage collaborative behavior" between suppliers, while it allows Shell to "retain full control of strategy and service integration. In addition to all of the usual business benefits, Shell will be able to exploit emerging commoditized services designed for the consumer market, such as email or internet phone services, and integrate them within their services when they become robust enough for commercial use."

Shell CIO Alan Matula said: "This deal is a major strategic choice for Shell. Partnering with EDS, T-Systems and AT&T gives us greater ability to respond to the growing demands of our businesses. It allows Shell IT to focus on Information Technology that drives competitive position in the oil and gas market, whilst suppliers focus on improving essential IT capability."

Source: Adapted from Siobhan Chapman, "Shell Signs $4 Billion, Multi-Supplier Outsourcing Deal," *CIO Magazine*, April 3, 2008.

Trends in Outsourcing and Offshoring

While in the past much of the motivation to outsource and offshore various portions of the IT/IS operation of a firm were driven primarily by cost, a more recent and troubling trend is the increasing motivation to find highly qualified IT/IS talent. Jobs are plentiful in the United States for today's IS graduate but enrollments in United States. IS programs remain down. This results in a decreasing supply of qualified labor for the best paying jobs in the field. To combat this, firms are looking at the science and engineering graduate of other countries to fill their needs. As we discussed in Chapter 2, the jobs that were outsourced and offshored in the late 1990s and early 2000 were not the ones typically benchmarked by university-level IS programs. As such, no real job opportunities were lost to qualified graduates. Today, however, the lack of qualified IS graduates means companies have to turn elsewhere to fill these jobs. The jobs are staying here, but the labor is being imported. The single most effective method to counter this trend is for more young people to seek a career in the information systems field. IS/IT is one of the hottest fields on the planet for job opportunities and the word needs to get out. Many organizations are focusing on outreach programs that extend down to the pre-high school levels to begin educating, or reeducating, the public with regard to these vast opportunities.

Failures in IT Management

Managing information technology is not an easy task. The information systems function often has performance problems in many organizations. The promised benefits of information technology have not occurred in many documented cases. Studies by management consulting firms and university researchers have shown that many businesses have not been successful in managing their use of information technology. Thus, it is evident that in many organizations, information technology is not being used effectively and efficiently, and there have been **failures in IT management.** For example:

- Information technology is not being used *effectively* by companies that use IT primarily to computerize traditional business processes instead of developing innovative e-business processes involving customers, suppliers, and other business partners, e-commerce, and Web-enabled decision support.

- Information technology is not being used *efficiently* by information systems that provide poor response times and frequent downtimes, or by IS professionals and consultants who do not properly manage application development projects.

Let's look more closely, using a real-world example.

Risk without Reward: Weak IT Controls at Société Générale

It's a lethal combination of process oversights and system failures that is the stuff of CIO nightmares: An investigation into rogue trader Jerome Kerviel's fraudulent actions at Société Générale bank uncovered an apparent breakdown in financial and internal IT controls subverted by an employee with IT know-how and authorized systems access. IT experts say the case should serve as a warning that businesses can do better to manage IT-related risk.

"Much time is spent on protecting the external threat," says J.R. Reagan, managing director and global solution leader for risk, compliance and security at BearingPoint. "But the internal threat can be even larger in terms of risk to the company." In the case of Société Générale, not only were IT security controls insufficient, but the bank's staff did not fully investigate red flags that arose. Recent research by the Ponemon Institute concludes that "insider threats represent one of the most significant information security risks." In a survey of 700 IT practitioners, 78 percent said they believe individuals have too much access to information that isn't pertinent to their jobs, while 59 percent said such access presents business risks. What's more, IT professionals see a disconnect with business leaders: 74 percent said senior management does not view governance of access to information as a strategic issue.

One of Société Générale's primary business lines is derivatives—financial instruments that allow traders to make contracts on a wide range of assets (such as equities, bonds, or commodities) and attempts to reduce (or hedge) the financial risk for one party in the deal. Trading derivatives, however, necessitates some aggressiveness and can be fraught with risk.

Reagan observes that in the case of Société Générale, "their activities deal with high volume, high velocity and quick tempo trading of stock," and it's likely business leaders "wouldn't put up with" security measures that would slow them down. For example, Société Générale employed single-factor authentication (using one method, such as passwords, to grant access to its systems) rather than stronger dual-factor authentication (requiring that individuals employ two methods of identifying themselves to gain access). "The security team needs to explain the risk exposure and the possibility of losing billions in fraudulent trades if security is not adequately addressed," Reagan says. "But most security guys aren't well enough in tune with the business to be able to articulate a business case like that."

That disconnect can be enormously destructive, as the Société Générale incident shows. "The Société Générale case brings to the fore the fact that business risk can be directly exposed through IT," says Scott Crawford, a security expert and research director at Enterprise Management Associates. "Kerviel allegedly manipulated the IT controls on the business systems based on his midoffice experience and back-office knowledge and expertise."

"Businesses are just now beginning to awaken to the controls within the IT environment," Crawford says. "If you're betting the farm and strategy on the IT controls, it behooves the organization to ensure that those controls are reasonably resistant to subversion."

Source: Adapted from Nancy Weil, "Risk without Reward," *CIO Magazine*, May 1, 2008.

Management Involvement

What is the solution to failures in the information systems function? There are no quick and easy answers. However, the experiences of successful organizations reveal that extensive and meaningful **managerial and end-user involvement** is the key ingredient of high-quality information systems performance. Involving business managers in the governance of the IS function and business professionals in the development of IS applications should thus shape the response of management to the challenge of improving the business value of information technology. See Figure 12.9.

Involving managers in the management of IT (from the CEO to the managers of business units) requires the development of *governance structures* (e.g., executive councils, steering committees) that encourage their active participation in planning and controlling the business uses of IT. Thus, many organizations have policies that require managers to be involved in IT decisions that affect their business units. This requirement helps managers avoid IS performance problems in their business units and development projects. With this high degree of involvement, managers can improve the strategic business value of information technology. Also, as we noted in Chapter 10, only direct end-user participation in system development projects can solve the problems of employee resistance and poor user interface design. Overseeing such involvement is another vital management task.

IT Governance

Information technology governance (ITG), is a subset discipline of corporate governance focused on the information technologies (IT), information systems (IS), their performance, use, and associated risks. The rising interest in IT governance is due, in part, to governmental compliance initiatives such as Sarbanes-Oxley in the United States and its counterpart in Europe, Basel II. Additional motivation comes from the acknowledgment that IT projects can easily get out of control and profoundly affect the performance of an organization.

A characteristic theme of IT governance discussions is that the IT capability can no longer be thought of as a mythical black box, the contents of which are known only to the IT personnel. This traditional handling of IT management by board-level executives is due to limited technical experience and the perceived complexity of IT. Historically, key

FIGURE 12.9 Senior management needs to be involved in critical business/IT decisions to optimize the business value and performance of the IT function.

IT Decision	Senior Management's Role	Consequences of Abdicating the Decision
● **How much should we spend on IT?**	Define the strategic role that IT will play in the company, and then determine the level of funding needed to achieve that objective.	The company fails to develop an IT platform that furthers its strategy, despite high IT spending.
● **Which business processes should receive our IT dollars?**	Make clear decisions about which IT initiatives will and will not be funded.	A lack of focus overwhelms the IT unit, which tries to deliver many projects that may have little companywide value or can't be implemented well simultaneously.
● **Which IT capabilities need to be companywide?**	Decide which IT capabilities should be provided centrally and which should be developed by individual businesses.	Excessive technical and process standardization limit the flexibility of business units, or frequent exceptions to the standards increase costs and limit business synergies.
● **How good do our IT services really need to be?**	Decide which features—for example, enhanced reliability or response time—are needed on the basis of their costs and benefits.	The company may pay for service options that, given its priorities, aren't worth their costs.
● **What security and privacy risks will we accept?**	Lead the decision making on the trade-offs between security and privacy on one hand and convenience on the other.	An overemphasis on security and privacy may inconvenience customers, employees, and suppliers; an underemphasis may make data vulnerable.
● **Whom do we blame if an IT initiative fails?**	Assign a business executive to be accountable for every IT project; monitor business metrics.	The business value of systems is never realized.

Source: Jeanne W. Ross and Peter Weill, "Six IT Decisions Your IT People Shouldn't Make," *Harvard Business Review*, November 2002, p. 87.

decisions were often deferred to IT professionals. IT governance implies a system in which all stakeholders, including the board, internal customers, and related areas such as finance, have the necessary input into the decision-making process. This prevents a single stakeholder, typically IT, from being blamed for poor decisions. It also prevents users from later complaining that the system does not behave or perform as expected.

The focus of ITG is specifying decision inputs and rights along with an accountability framework such that desirable behaviors toward and in the use of IT are developed. It highlights the importance of IT-related matters in contemporary organizations and ensures that strategic IT decisions are owned by the corporate board, rather than by the CIO or other IT managers. The primary goals for information technology governance are to (1) assure that the significant organizational investments in IT and IS generate their maximum business value and (2) mitigate the risks that are associated with IT. This is accomplished by implementing an organizational structure with well-defined roles for the responsibility of the decisions related to the management and use of IT such as infrastructure, architecture, investment, and use.

One very popular approach to IT governance is COBIT (Control Objectives for Information and related Technology). COBIT is a framework of best practices for IT management created by the Information Systems Audit and Control Association (ISACA) and the IT Governance Institute (ITGI). COBIT provides all members of the organization with a set of generally accepted measures, indicators, processes, and best practices to help them maximize the benefits derived through the use of information technology and in developing appropriate IT governance and control structures in a company.

COBIT has 34 high-level processes covering 210 control objectives categorized in four domains: (1) Planning and Organization, (2) Acquisition and Implementation,

(3) Delivery and Support, and (4) Monitoring. Managers benefit from COBIT because it provides them with a foundation upon which IT-related decisions and investments can be based. Decision making is more effective because COBIT helps management define a strategic IT plan, define the information architecture, acquire the necessary IT hardware and software to execute an IT strategy, ensure continuous service, and monitor the performance of the IT system. IT users benefit from COBIT because of the assurance provided to them by COBIT's defined controls, security, and process governance. COBIT also benefits auditors because it helps them identify IT control issues within a company's IT infrastructure, and it helps them corroborate their audit findings. Figure 12.10 illustrates the relationships between the four domains in COBIT and categorizes both the high-level processes and control objectives associated with them.

Let's look at a real-world example of COBIT in action.

FIGURE 12.10 COBIT is a popular IT governance approach that focuses on all aspects of the IT function throughout the organization.

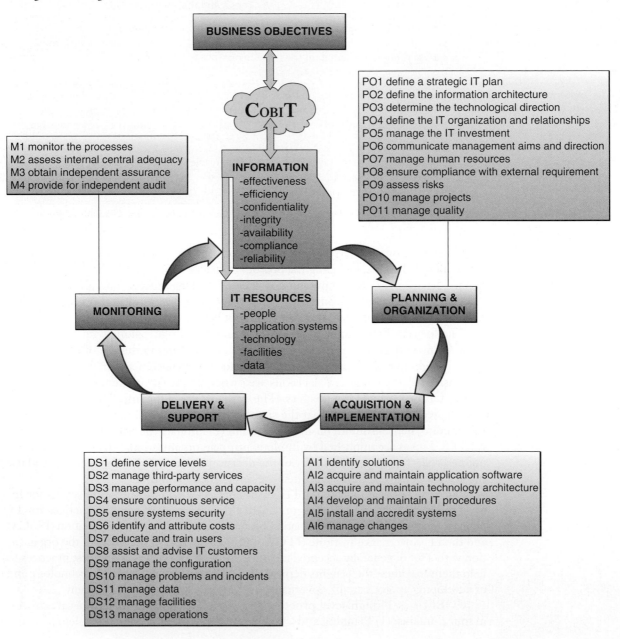

Harley-Davidson Motor Company: Adopting COBIT as an Umbrella for All Control and Compliance Activities

Harley-Davidson Motor Company was founded in 1903 in Milwaukee, Wisconsin. It is the oldest producer of motorcycles in the United States and has enjoyed 20 consecutive years of record revenue. For the year ended December 31, 2005, Harley-Davidson shipped 329,000 motorcycles (a 3.7 percent increase), had revenue of $5.3 billion, and experienced worldwide growth of 6.2 percent.

In 2003, Harley-Davidson had limited IT controls in place and its staff had limited control knowledge. There was no standardized user access process, no defined and documented change management process, and no rigor on backup and recovery processes, and there were minimal organizational standards. Although the company had been able to operate this way for more than a hundred years, the need to get up to speed on compliance and control was looming in the horizon: SOX, the Sarbanes-Oxley Act.

To jump-start IT governance and Sarbanes-Oxley activities, Harley-Davidson created an IS compliance department and began to implement a vendor's general computer controls model. After attending a COBIT User Convention, a Harley-Davidson risk specialist recommended COBIT to management and then converted the control framework to COBIT, published by the IT Governance Institute. Concurrently, the internal audit department was driving IT to move beyond pure compliance. The company realized it needed a broad control framework, which helped eliminate the constantly changing "bar" used as a benchmark.

Key to introducing COBIT was ensuring that all of IT and management understood why they needed to care about effective, value-focused controls. Getting them to realize that there are many important business reasons for this was the first key hurdle to be successfully addressed. COBIT's business-focused language allowed management, IT, and internal audit to ensure that they were on the same road.

Harley-Davidson's COBIT migration process needed to go beyond questions such as "Do you have a systems development life cycle process (SDLC)?" to stimulate internal conversations on what an SDLC really is and which skills were required. The team started by mapping implemented controls to COBIT and compared the results to a previously accepted Big 4 accounting firm's COBIT mapping. Gaps were identified and plans were developed to close these gaps.

One of the major benefits of using COBIT as its overall internal control and compliance model was getting everyone—especially nontechnical motorcycle experts—revved up about control activities and why controls are important. Harley-Davidson is subject to many regulations, including HIPAA and Gramm-Leach-Bliley, and COBIT serves as an umbrella framework that helps the company zero in on appropriate control and compliance activities.

Driving internal change was also a key goal of this highly competitive company, and COBIT benchmarking was an invaluable tool for independent comparison. It put the information in the right perspective for management and to obtain overall buy-in. The framework shows peer comparison in an unbiased format and is used as part of every IT audit. Best of all, it invites discussion about where the company would like to be.

Source: Adapted from ISACA, *COBIT and IT Governance Case Study: Harley-Davidson*, May 2006.

SECTION II Managing Global IT

The International Dimension

Whether they are in Berlin or Bombay, Kuala Lumpur or Kansas, San Francisco or Seoul, companies around the globe are developing new models to operate competitively in a digital economy. These models are structured, yet agile; global, yet local; and they concentrate on maximizing the risk-adjusted return from both knowledge and technology assets.

International dimensions have become a vital part of managing a business enterprise in the internetworked global economies and markets of today. Whether you become a manager in a large corporation or the owner of a small business, you will be affected by international business developments and deal in some way with people, products, or services whose origin is not your home country.

Read the Real World Case on the next page. We can learn a lot about approaches to successfully develop and roll out worldwide system implementations from this case. See Figure 12.11.

Global IT Management

Figure 12.12 illustrates the major dimensions of the job of managing global information technology that we cover in this section. Notice that all global IT activities must be adjusted to take into account the cultural, political, and geoeconomic challenges that exist in the international business community. Developing appropriate business and IT strategies for the global marketplace should be the first step in global information technology management. Once that is done, end users and IS managers can move on to developing the portfolio of business applications needed to support business/IT strategies; the hardware, software, and Internet-based technology platforms to support those applications; the data resource management methods to provide necessary databases; and finally the systems development projects that will produce the global information systems required.

Global Teams: It's Still a Small World

We seem to have reached a point where virtually every CIO is a global CIO—a leader whose sphere of influence (and headaches) spans continents. The global CIO's most common challenge, according to CIO Executive Council members, is managing global virtual teams. In an ideal world, HR policies across the global IT team should be consistent, fair, and responsive. Titles and reporting structures (if not compensation) should be equalized.

The council's European members, representing Royal Dutch Shell, Galderma, Olympus, and others, commissioned a globalization playbook that collects and codifies best practices in this and other globalization challenges.

Obtain local HR expertise. Companies must have a local HR person in each country to deal with local laws. "Hiring, firing, and training obligations must be managed very differently in each location, and you need someone with local expertise on the laws and processes," says Michael Pilkington, former CIO of Euroclear, the Brussels-based provider of domestic and cross-border settlement for bond, equity, and fund transactions.

Create job grade consistency across regions. Euroclear is moving toward a job evaluation methodology that organizes job types into vertical categories, such as managing people/process, product development, business support, and project management. This provides a basis for comparing and managing roles and people across locations. Grade level is not the same thing as a title; people's titles are much more subject to local conventions.

(text continues on page 525)

REAL WORLD CASE 2

Reinsurance Group of America and Fonterra: Going for Unified Global Operations

The reinsurance industry isn't for the faint of heart. The business processes that enable reinsurance firms to form agreements with other insurance companies to accept all or part of their risk can get mighty complex, mighty quickly.

Now imagine developing a single system that manages reinsurance business processes for numerous offices around the world—offices whose staffs speak different languages, are in different time zones, and just might be stuck in their ways as to how they manage their business. It's a challenge that could overwhelm you if you tried to tackle it all at once instead of breaking it into small pieces.

When workers in the global software group at Reinsurance Group of America Inc. (RGA) in Chesterfield, Missouri, first took on this mammoth project, they would have been the first to tell you they were unprepared for the obstacles that lay ahead.

"This whole system required so much communication and teamwork, and I'm not sure we understood at first what we needed to contribute to make it a success," says Mike Ring, project manager at RGA. Yet by engaging the business and adapting its own practices to the demands of the situation, the group is successfully rolling out an integrated, multicurrency, multilanguage life reinsurance administration system, dubbed CybeRe, for its international division.

Before CybeRe, workers in RGA's global offices mainly relied on a mix of spreadsheets and databases to manage clients. Now, with information stored in one location, workers can analyze data by client, contract, and product and find client errors more easily. "People can stop worrying about, 'If I sell this business, how am I going to manage it?'" says

FIGURE 12.11

Consistency across the different business functions, countries, languages, and processes involved in worldwide implementations is one of the most important challenges faced by global organizations today.

Source: Getty Images.

Azam Mirza, vice president of global software and head of the CybeRe effort.

The system also strengthens data validation and data quality, Ring adds, which will enable better risk analysis and retention analysis, resulting in better profitability. Ultimately, return on investment will reach over 15 percent, "which compares very favorably to the average ROI for RGA's products, which are normally in the range of 12 percent to 15 percent," Mirza says.

The picture wasn't always this rosy. When the project began six years ago, IT began to gather business requirements from the global offices, planning to emerge a couple of years later with a full-blown system. By late 2001, however, it became apparent that a phased approach was more practical. "The different units all do things slightly differently, and getting everyone to agree became very contentious," Chan explains. So the group embarked on a plan to build a pilot system in one office (South Africa) and gradually implement it in the remaining ones, with as few customizations as possible.

It wasn't always smooth sailing. For one thing, converting all the historical data and loading it into the CybeRe system required a significant data cleansing and migration effort. Other factors, such as differences in the terminologies used in various offices, also caused delays. For example, while it gathered requirements, IT asked whether the South African office used compound benefits. Although it said it did not, it turned out that the office just used a different term: acceleration of benefits.

"The change in scope delayed us four or five months," Mirza says. Probably the biggest challenge—which continues today—is getting people to accept common practices as defined by the system. "That's where we're the bad guys," Mirza says. "If they really need it, they have to prove it. We challenge everything. We don't want to create a product that's convoluted because it tries to be everything to everybody."

Despite the local customizations, RGA still maintains just one version of CybeRe. Local units can just "turn on" the options or customizations that are relevant to their businesses. "Not maintaining 13 different versions is very important," Mirza says. "It's critical to our success."

"Given the life reinsurance market's consolidation of recent years, CybeRe should provide RGA with an important competitive weapon. RGA aims to 'reinvent reinsurance.' That is an ambitious goal. CybeRe is an important step along the way."

Greg James is chief information officer and general manager of global business processes at Fonterra. It is a unique role, instrumental in ensuring that the only silos at the dairy group are of the giant stainless steel variety. James was on sabbatical following a year-long assignment in Europe with the New Zealand Dairy Board when he was offered to head what he describes as a "small business initiative" called Jedi.

The call came from an executive of Fonterra, which had just been formed, and the job was director of the dairy group's biggest business transformation program to date.

Jedi, which was rolled out in 2.5 years, entailed moving Fonterra's commodity business to a common ERP platform and "a single global way of doing things." James says the Jedi program aimed to look at the supply chain of the dairy giant "from cow to manufacturing to storage to happy customers."

The change involved was massive, for Fonterra's supply chain covers four million cows that produce 20 billion liters of milk each year. It has offices in 70 countries and employs nearly 19,000 staff. Fonterra, says James, would be recognized as New Zealand's largest company if it were listed in the Stock Exchange. In order to implement the new environment, "We had to reinvent ourselves; analyze every part of the business, all processes, all organizational structure," says James.

In effect, the Jedi program dismantled traditional silos in the organization and standardized global processes. "It has enabled us to effectively bring all components that previously existed in each group, in other business units, bring them all together and get commonality in terms of the way we do things. It has driven consistency of processes, and has enabled us to draw consistency in approaching framework in terms of how we operate."

Today, he notes, "We do the things the same way in Germany, Mexico and New Zealand." As James explains, Fonterra was set up in 2000 as an amalgamation of the old dairy industry, with self-contained business functions. Fonterra consolidated its back-office functions globally within New Zealand, into a business transactional services activity based in Hamilton. James says the Hamilton operations fared well when benchmarked against BPO organizations locally and overseas. "Our model is better than most international models."

Instead of having disparate sales offices for various business units, a customer service center was set up at the Auckland's Princes Street headquarters. This center operates round the clock, providing multilingual support for customers across the globe.

For Fonterra's 200-member IS team, the new system means being exposed to areas of the business they traditionally would not have been. "If they worked in this part of the business under the old structure, they tended to stay in that part of the business. But now we pool the resources together so it means they could be working on X, Y, or Z within any given period. They are given a lot more flexibility and ability to learn the various parts of the business in the new model."

He believes this setup also helps in staff retention. "It does give us the ability to retain staff as opposed to having staff leave to go to other organizations to experience different types of skill sets." If there is another thing James is emphatic about, it is that these days at Fonterra, "There is no such thing as an IT project by itself."

"We sit down with the business in terms of our planning, and we align our plans to their plans." He says there is now an "enterprise road map" that consists of all the activities the business wants to undertake over the next 18 months up to three years.

What is his primary advice for IT professionals who wish to move on to chief information officer and other C-level roles? "Make sure that you understand the business that you work with." He adds, "Keep a watchful eye on very, very competent people that you might need to hire one day to be part of a bigger team." They could be people in your current organization or people you meet outside, in industry functions.

Lastly, he says, "Never ever fear hiring someone in your organization that is smarter than you. You actually need a lot of smart people working around you."

Source: Adapted from Mary Brandel, "Reinsurance Group Simplifies on Global Scale with Administration System," *Computerworld*, March 14, 2005; and Divina Paredes, "Unifying Global Operations," *CIO Magazine*, March 27, 2007.

CASE STUDY QUESTIONS

1. What is the business value of these global system developments for the companies mentioned in the case? How did they achieve these benefits? What were the major obstacles they had to overcome?

2. What are the advantages and disadvantages of a full-blown versus a phased approach for system implementations in general, and global ones in particular? How do you make the decision on which road to take?

3. How important is it that all units in global organization speak the same business language, and use the same functions and business processes? How do you balance the competing needs for flexibility and consistency across operations?

REAL WORLD ACTIVITIES

1. Both organizations featured in the case have been quite successful with their global rollouts. Search the Internet for examples of less-than-thriving global or international system implementations. How do they compare to the ones in the case? What differences in the approaches taken by the successful and unsuccessful cases do you think could account for the differences in outcome? Prepare a report and a presentation to share your findings with the rest of the class.

2. Implementing major systems in global organizations, particularly when development is concentrated in headquarters or a powerful country subsidiary, can cause a lot of resentment and frustration for the other units in the organization. Break into small groups with your classmates to discuss which approaches companies can take to ease these issues and incorporate all their units into the process.

FIGURE 12.12

The major dimensions of global e-business technology management.

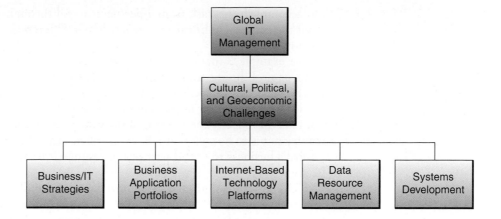

Manage dispersed staff as portfolio teams. ON Semiconductor has IT staff that support sales in Slovakia, where ON has a factory; in Hong Kong, where ON has a major sales office; in Shenzhen, China, where a customer service center is located; and in Kuala Lumpur, Malaysia, at its regional development center. ON overcomes potential disconnects by having a single sales IT portfolio owner, based at headquarters in Phoenix, who sets objectives and distributes work to the members of that team no matter where they reside.

Make the work meaningful. To keep morale high and turnover low, be sure that each remote location contributes to important projects. Don't send remote workers a steady diet of maintenance. Pilkington suggests building a center of excellence in each remote location.

Clearly defining the roles of remote groups can also help knit them together. For example, global company leaders can hold meetings at all levels to discuss the distinct purposes of corporate headquarters, the regions, and the local units. Knowing what their roles are in the larger picture and what they can expect from others "creates a sense of identity and purpose," says Nariman Karimi, senior VP and CIO of DHL Asia Pacific.

Bring remote staff to headquarters. ON Semiconductor brings its foreign-based employees to the United States to work on key initiatives and interact with other business units at corporate headquarters. This may not be a monetary reward, but in many cultures it represents an endorsement and source of pride.

Foster communication across regional boundaries. Videoconferencing is an obvious tool to enhance global team communication, but it's important to have in-person meetings as well. At DHL, Karimi, together with the regional board members, visits one of the top 10 sites around the Asia Pacific region each month; each gets at least one personal visit a year. The visits include time for the local unit to showcase itself, and there is also unstructured time for informal and personal interaction.

Source: Adapted from Richard Pastore, "Global Team Management: It's a Small World After All," *CIO Magazine*, January 23, 2008.

Cultural, Political, and Geoeconomic Challenges

"Business as usual" is not good enough in global business operations. The same holds true for global e-business technology management. There are too many cultural, political, and geoeconomic (geographic and economic) realities that must be confronted for a business to succeed in global markets. As we have just mentioned, global information technology management must focus on developing global business IT strategies and managing global e-business application portfolios, Internet technologies, platforms, databases, and systems development projects. Managers, however, must also accomplish this task from a perspective and through methods that take into account the cultural, political, and geoeconomic differences that exist when doing business internationally.

For example, a major **political challenge** is that many countries have rules regulating or prohibiting transfer of data across their national boundaries (transborder data flows), especially personal information such as personnel records. Others severely restrict, tax, or prohibit imports of hardware and software. Still others have local content laws that specify the portion of the value of a product that must be added in that country if it is to be sold there. Some countries have reciprocal trade agreements that require a business to spend part of the revenue it earns in a country in that nation's economy.

Geoeconomic challenges in global business and IT refer to the effects of geography on the economic realities of international business activities. The sheer physical distances involved are still a major problem, even in this day of Internet telecommunications and jet travel. For example, it may still take too long to fly in specialists when IT problems occur in a remote site. It is still difficult to communicate in real time across the world's 24 time zones. It is still difficult to get good-quality telephone and telecommunications service in many countries. There are still problems finding the job skills required in some countries or enticing specialists from other countries to live and work there. Finally, there are still problems (and opportunities) in the great differences in the cost of living and labor costs in various countries. All of these geoeconomic challenges must be addressed when developing a company's global business and IT strategies.

Cultural challenges facing global business and IT managers include differences in languages, cultural interests, religions, customs, social attitudes, and political philosophies. Obviously, global IT managers must be trained and sensitized to such cultural differences before they are sent abroad or brought into a corporation's home country. Other cultural challenges include differences in work styles and business relationships. For example, should you take your time to avoid mistakes or hurry to get something done early? Should you go it alone or work cooperatively? Should the most experienced person lead, or should leadership be shared? The answers to such questions depend on the culture you are in and highlight the cultural differences that might exist in the global workplace. Let's take a look at a real world example involving the global IT talent pool.

Swimming in the Global Talent Pool

When he was a 16-year-old student, Jeff Kiiza would never have imagined that 10 years later he'd be writing code in Perl, PHP/MySQL, and AJAX for companies in the United States, Canada, Australia, and Spain—and that he'd be doing it from his home in Cordoba, Argentina. "Back then, it would have been a dream or science fiction," he says. "But the availability of greater free-flowing bandwidth and companies turning to the Internet have allowed it."

Hemang Dani is pretty amazed that in the past six months, he has boosted his income to $5,000 per month by working for companies in the United States, the United Kingdom, Germany, and Australia. Not bad, considering the low cost of living in his home city of Mumbai, India. Dani's projects range from coding "shopping carts" and enabling credit card processing on Web sites to managing portals as a Web master.

Dani and Kiiza have jumped with both feet into the global talent pool. Both worked for overseas organizations even before they joined Menlo Park, California–based oDesk Corp.'s online marketplace, which links programmers with businesses that need their services. Kiiza coded for a university in Tanzania, and Dani picked up work through GetaFreelancer.com, which is owned by a Swedish company called Innovate IT.

Because there are more programmers like them every day in developing parts of the world, IT professionals in the United States are now competing in the global talent pool as well. While many U.S. companies today are still hiring globally only when their need is short-lived, or skills are scarce or too high-priced in the local or domestic labor pool, some are going global just to find the best of the best, no matter where they're located, according to Kevin Wheeler, president of Global Learning Resources Inc., a recruiting consulting firm in Fremont, California. "Cisco, Microsoft, Google—these companies have clearly taken the position that they're going where the talent is," he says.

Source: Adapted from Mary Brandel, "Swimming in the Global Talent Pool," *Computerworld*, January 15, 2007.

Global Business/IT Strategies

Businesses are moving away from *international* strategies in which foreign subsidiaries are autonomous but depend on headquarters for new processes, products, and ideas, or *global* strategies, in which a company's worldwide operations are closely managed by corporate headquarters. Instead, companies are moving toward a transnational strategy, where the company's business depends heavily on its information systems and Internet technologies to help it integrate its global business activities. Instead of having independent IS units at its subsidiaries, or even a centralized IS operation directed from its headquarters, a transnational business tries to develop an integrated and cooperative worldwide hardware, software, and Internet-based architecture for its IT platform. Figure 12.13 compares the three approaches to global business/IT strategy. Figure 12.14 illustrates how transnational business and IT strategies have been implemented by global companies.

FIGURE 12.13 Companies operating internationally are moving toward transnational business and IT strategies. Note some of the chief differences among international, global, and transnational business and IT strategies.

Comparing Global Business/IT Strategies

International	Global	Transnational
• Autonomous operations • Region specific • Vertical integration • Specific customers • Captive manufacturing • Customer segmentation and dedication by region and plant	• Global sourcing • Multiregional • Horizontal integration • Some transparency of customers and production • Some cross regionalization	• Virtual business operations via global alliances • World markets and mass customization • Global e-commerce and customer service • Transparent manufacturing • Global supply chain and logistics • Dynamic resource management

Information Technology Characteristics

International	Global	Transnational
• Stand-alone systems • Decentralized/no standards • Heavy reliance on interfaces • Multiple systems, high redundancy, and duplication of services and operations • Lack of common systems and data	• Regional decentralization • Interface dependent • Some consolidation of applications and use of common systems • Reduced duplication of operations • Some worldwide IT standards	• Logically consolidated, physically distributed, Internet connected • Common global data resources • Integrated global enterprise systems • Internet, intranet, extranet, and Web-based applications • Transnational IT policies and standards

FIGURE 12.14 Examples of how transnational business and IT strategies were implemented by global companies.

Tactic	Global Alliances	Global Sourcing and Logistics	Global Customer Service
Examples	British Airways/US Airways KLM/Northwest Qantas/ American	Benetton	American Express
IT Environment	Global network (online reservation system).	Global network, EPOS terminals in 4,000 stores, CAD/CAM in central manufacturing, robots and laser scanner in automated warehouse.	Global network linked from local branches and local merchants to the customer database and medical or legal referrals database.
Results	• Coordination of schedules • Code sharing • Coordination of flights • Co-ownership	• Produce 2,000 sweaters per hour using CAD/CAM • Quick response (in stores in 10 days) • Reduced inventories (just-in-time)	• Worldwide access to funds • "Global Assist" hotline • Emergency credit card replacement • 24-hour customer service

Global Business/IT Applications

The applications of information technology developed by global companies depend on their **global business/IT strategies** and their expertise and experience in IT. Their IT applications, however, also depend on a variety of global business drivers, that is, business requirements caused by the nature of the industry and its competitive or environmental forces. One example would be companies like airlines or hotel chains that have global customers who travel widely or have global operations. Such companies need global IT capabilities for online transaction processing so that they can provide fast, convenient service to their customers—or face losing them to their competitors. The economies of scale provided by global business operations are other business drivers that require the support of global IT applications. Figure 12.15 summarizes some of the business requirements that make global IT a competitive necessity.

Of course, many global IT applications, particularly finance, accounting, and office applications, have been in operation for many years. For example, most multinational

FIGURE 12.15

Some of the business reasons driving global business applications.

Business Drivers of Global IT
• **Global Customers.** Customers are people who may travel anywhere or companies with global operations. Global IT can help provide fast, convenient service.
• **Global Products.** Products are the same throughout the world or are assembled by subsidiaries throughout the world. Global IT can help manage worldwide marketing and quality control.
• **Global Operations.** Parts of a production or assembly process are assigned to subsidiaries based on changing economic or other conditions. Only global IT can support such geographic flexibility.
• **Global Resources.** The use and cost of common equipment, facilities, and people are shared by subsidiaries of a global company. Global IT can keep track of such shared resources.
• **Global Collaboration.** The knowledge and expertise of colleagues in a global company can be quickly accessed, shared, and organized to support individual or group efforts. Only global IT can support such enterprise collaboration.

companies have global financial budgeting, cash management systems, and office auto-mation applications such as fax and e-mail systems. As global operations expand and global competition heats up, however, there is increasing pressure for companies to install global e-commerce and e-business applications for their customers and suppliers. Examples include global e-commerce Web sites and customer service systems for cus-tomers, and global supply chain management systems for suppliers. In the past, such systems relied almost exclusively on privately constructed or government-owned tele-communications networks; now the explosive business use of the Internet, intranets, and extranets for e-commerce has made such applications much more feasible for global companies.

Colorcon Inc.: **Benefits and** **Challenges of** **Global ERPs** 	Since Colorcon Inc. consolidated all of its global offices and seven manufacturing sites onto one ERP system in 2001, the benefits have been indisputable. The spe-cialty chemicals manufacturer has increased its annual inventory turns by 40 percent, closes its books each quarter more than 50 percent faster than it once did, and has improved its production lead times. "It was a significant improvement," says CIO Perry Cozzone.

Yet getting to a single, global instance has also been fraught with challenges for the West Point, Pennsylvania–based company. Those included cleansing and verify-ing data from legacy systems, standardizing business processes globally, and getting buy-in from business leaders in locales as disparate as Brazil, Singapore, and the United Kingdom.

"It was hard work," says Cozzone, who oversaw the final stages of the system implementation. Transitioning to a single, global instance of an ERP system is a heady challenge for large and midsize multinationals alike. For many organizations, the toughest challenge in moving to one ERP system is change management. "It's a real struggle for many companies to have consistency around their business proc-esses" because of differences in regional business requirements, says Rob Karel, an analyst at Forrester Research Inc.

Still, companies that have achieved a single instance say it's worth the struggle to streamline financial reporting and increase the visibility of operations around the world because doing so allows executives to make decisions faster.

The most common technical challenge that project teams face is verifying the integrity of legacy data and moving it to the ERP environment. "One of the lessons learned is that you can never spend enough time on ensuring data quality," says Cozzone. Early in Colorcon's project, when there were questions about the quality of a set of data, team members and executives didn't always agree on what needed to be done. "There was inconsistency about how to measure quality and manage it," says Cozzone.

So the project team developed a data-quality dashboard to illustrate to busi-ness leaders why compromised data needed to be fixed before being entered into the new environment. The dashboard demonstrates, for instance, how poor-quality customer contact information could lead to an increase in erroneous orders. The dashboard includes steps that business users can take to correct faulty data, and it quantifies monthly business improvements achieved by reducing bad data. They also had to work through minor issues in retiring legacy systems and so-called ghost systems—those used in various business units but unknown to corpo-rate IT.

"We're not a multibillion-dollar company, but we still had ghost systems," says Cozzone. "We made these a high priority and got rid of them quickly." |

Source: Adapted from Thomas Hoffman, "Global ERP: You Can Get There from Here, but Should You?" *Computer-world*, October 15, 2007.

Global IT Platforms

The management of technology platforms (also called the technology infrastructure) is another major dimension of global IT management—that is, managing the hardware, software, data resources, telecommunications networks, and computing facilities that support global business operations. The management of a global IT platform not only is technically complex but also has major political and cultural implications.

For example, hardware choices are difficult in some countries because of high prices, high tariffs, import restrictions, long lead times for government approvals, lack of local service or spare parts, and lack of documentation tailored to local conditions. Software choices can also present unique problems. Software packages developed in Europe may be incompatible with American or Asian versions, even when purchased from the same hardware vendor. Well-known U.S. software packages may be unavailable because there is no local distributor or because the software publisher refuses to supply markets that disregard software licensing and copyright agreements.

Managing international data communications networks, including Internet, intranet, extranet, and other networks, is a key global IT challenge. Figure 12.16 outlines the top 10 international data communications issues as reported by IS executives at 300 Fortune 500 multinational companies. Notice how political issues dominate the top 10 listing over technology issues, clearly emphasizing their importance in the management of global telecommunications.

Establishing computing facilities internationally is another global challenge. Companies with global business operations usually establish or contract with systems integrators for additional data centers in their subsidiaries in other countries. These data centers meet local and regional computing needs and even help balance global computing workloads through communications satellite links. Offshore data centers, however, can pose major problems in headquarters' support, hardware and software acquisition, maintenance, and security. That's why many global companies turn to application service providers or systems integrators like EDS or IBM to manage their overseas operations.

FIGURE 12.16

The top 10 issues in managing international data communications.

International Data Communications Issues
Network Management Issues
• Improving the operational efficiency of networks
• Dealing with different networks
• Controlling data communication security
Regulatory Issues
• Dealing with transborder data flow restrictions
• Managing international telecommunication regulations
• Handling international politics
Technology Issues
• Managing network infrastructure across countries
• Managing international integration of technologies
Country-Oriented Issues
• Reconciling national differences
• Dealing with international tariff structures

Source: Adapted from Vincent S. Lai and Wingyan Chung, "Managing International Data Communications," *Communications of the ACM*, March 2002, p. 91.

Fidelity and Unisys: Working in a Worldwide Campus

Once upon a time, companies boasted of having offices in Manhattan, Munich, Madrid, Mumbai, and Manila. Each office managed its set of customers and suppliers, with a lot of "good advice" coming in from the head office. There was precious little governance or standardization. Paradoxically, the use of third-party service providers has catalyzed better governance and standards in captive or shared-services centers scattered in distant parts of the world.

Boston-based Fidelity, the world's largest mutual fund company, for example, has subsidiary offices in most countries, which service local markets; has captive centers in India to service its global operations; has outsourced to almost half a dozen third-party IT service providers; and itself functions as a human resources and benefits administration provider to companies such as General Motors and Novartis.

There are multiple ways to implement the concept of a worldwide campus. Regardless of the company having globally dispersed teams working on disparate pieces of work, what binds these offices together is a defined, common architecture and a shared-enterprise objective.

Such complexity in operations is nothing new; it has been happening in other industries for decades. In manufacturing, for instance, components may be produced in China and Taiwan, assembled in Malaysia, and packaged in and shipped from China. All of these activities may be coordinated from the United States. "The services industry, and business process outsourcing (BPO) in general, is just starting to catch up with its manufacturing brethren," says Brian Maloney, recently appointed as president of the newly formed Unisys Global Industries. Maloney has been CEO of AT&T Solutions and COO of Perot Systems.

"In a worldwide campus communication is not as simple as having everybody in the same room and saying 'this is what we will do today, tomorrow or next week.' Now you have to deal with the distance, time differences and cultural differences—when you and I have a conversation, we may be using the same language but we may have different nuances to the words," he says.

"You need to have somebody who is close to the customer and the customer's business processes. In day-to-day problems, you need somebody who can understand what the CIO and business unit head are wrestling with and translate that back to the people who are doing the system-designing code work in India," notes Maloney. "This has to be an ongoing collaboration, on a day-to-day basis. The good news is that technology allows that. At AT&T Solutions, which offers IT services to internal and external customers, we took engineers from Asia, Europe and the U.S.A. and put them in the customer's premises for a couple of weeks."

Source: Adapted from Juhi Bhambal, "Worldwide Campus," *InformationWeek*, May 29, 2006.

The Internet as a Global IT Platform

What makes the Internet and the World Wide Web so important for international business? This interconnected matrix of computers, information, and networks that reaches tens of millions of users in over one hundred countries is a business environment free of traditional boundaries and limits. Linking to an online global infrastructure offers companies unprecedented potential for expanding markets, reducing costs, and improving profit margins at a price that is typically a small percentage of the corporate communications budget. The Internet provides an interactive channel for direct communication and data exchange with customers, suppliers, distributors, manufacturers, product developers, financial backers, information providers—in fact, with all parties involved in a given business venture.

So the Internet and the World Wide Web have now become vital components in international business and commerce. Within a few years, the Internet, with its

FIGURE 12.17
Key questions for
companies establishing
global Internet Web sites.

Key Questions
● Will you have to develop a new navigational logic to accommodate cultural preferences?
● What content will you translate, and what content will you create from scratch to address regional competitors or products that differ from those in the United States?
● Should your multilingual effort be an adjunct to your main site, or will you make it a separate site, perhaps with a country-specific domain name?
● What kinds of traditional and new media advertising will you have to do in each country to draw traffic to your site?
● Will your site get so many hits that you'll need to set up a server in a local country?
● What are the legal ramifications of having your Web site targeted at a particular country, such as laws on competitive behavior, treatment of children, or privacy?

interconnected network of thousands of networks of computers and databases, has established itself as a technology platform free of many traditional international boundaries and limits. By connecting their businesses to this online global infrastructure, companies can expand their markets, reduce communications and distribution costs, and improve their profit margins without massive cost outlays for new telecommunications facilities. Figure 12.17 outlines key considerations for global e-commerce Web sites.

The Internet, along with its related intranet and extranet technologies, provides a low-cost interactive channel for communications and data exchange with employees, customers, suppliers, distributors, manufacturers, product developers, financial backers, information providers, and so on. In fact, all parties involved can use the Internet and other related networks to communicate and collaborate to bring a business venture to its successful completion. As Figure 12.18 illustrates, however, much work needs to be done to bring secure Internet access and e-commerce to more people in more countries, but the trend is clearly toward continued expansion of the Internet as it becomes a pervasive IT platform for global business.

Global Data Access Issues

Global data access issues have been a subject of political controversy and technology barriers in global business operations for many years but have become more visible with the growth of the Internet and the pressures of e-commerce. A major example is the issue of

FIGURE 12.18 Current numbers of Internet users by world region. Note: Internet usage and population statistics, updated on March 24, 2005.

World Internet Usage and Population Statistics					
World Regions	Population (2005 Est.)	Population (% of World)	Internet Usage, Latest Data	Usage Growth 2000–2005 (%)	Penetration (% Population)	World Users (%)
Africa	900,465,411	14.0	13,468,600	198.3	1.5	1.5
Asia	3,612,363,165	56.3	302,257,003	164.4	8.4	34.0
Europe	730,991,138	11.4	259,653,144	151.9	35.5	29.2
Middle East	259,499,772	4.0	19,370,700	266.5	7.5	2.2
North America	328,387,059	5.1	221,437,647	104.9	67.4	24.9
Latin America/Caribbean	546,917,192	8.5	56,224,957	211.2	10.3	6.3
Oceania/Australia	33,443,448	0.5	16,269,080	113.5	48.6	1.8
WORLD TOTAL	6,412,067,185	100.0	888,681,131	146.2	13.9	100.0

Source: www.internetworldstats.com.

FIGURE 12.19

Key data privacy provisions of the agreement to protect the privacy of consumers in e-commerce transactions between the United States and the European Union.

U.S.–E.U. Data Privacy Requirements
● Notice of purpose and use of data collected
● Ability to opt out of third-party distribution of data
● Access for consumers to their information
● Adequate security, data integrity, and enforcement provisions

transborder data flows (TDF), in which business data flow across international borders over the telecommunications networks of global information systems. Many countries view TDF as a violation of their national sovereignty because these data flows avoid customs duties and regulations for the import or export of goods and services. Others view TDF as a violation of their laws to protect the local IT industry from competition or their labor regulations for protecting local jobs. In many cases, the data flow business issues that seem especially politically sensitive are those that affect the movement out of a country of personal data in e-commerce and human resource applications.

Many countries, especially those in the European Union (E.U.), may view transborder data flows as a violation of their privacy legislation because, in many cases, data about individuals are being moved out of the country without stringent privacy safeguards. For example, Figure 12.19 outlines the key provisions of a data privacy agreement between the United States and the European Union. The agreement exempts U.S. companies engaging in international e-commerce from E.U. data privacy sanctions if they join a self-regulatory program that provides E.U. consumers with basic information about, and control over, how their personal data are used. Thus, the agreement is said to provide a "safe harbor" for such companies from the requirements of the E.U.'s Data Privacy Directive, which bans the transfer of personal information on E.U. citizens to countries that do not have adequate data privacy protection.

Europe: Tighter Laws Worry Security Professionals

Moves by several European countries to tighten laws against computer hacking worry security professionals who often use the same tools as hackers but for legitimate purposes. The United Kingdom and Germany are among the countries that are considering revisions to their computer crime laws in line with the 2001 Convention on Cybercrime, a Europe-wide treaty, and with a similar European Union measure passed in early 2005.

But security professionals are scrutinizing those revisions out of concern for how prosecutors and judges could apply the laws. Security professionals are especially concerned about cases where the revisions apply to programs that could be used for bad or good. Companies often use hacking programs to test the mettle of their own systems.

"One useful utility in the wrong hands is a potentially malicious hacking tool," says Graham Cluley, senior technology consultant at Sophos in Abingdon, England. The proposed revisions would make it illegal to create or supply a tool to someone who intends to use it for unauthorized computer access or modification. Likewise, the proposed changes to German law would also criminalize making and distributing hacking tools. The German government said the changes will bring it into compliance with the 2001 Convention on Cybercrime. Several German security companies are planning to lobby against the law, as they fear it could hamper those who test security systems, says Alexander Kornbrust, founder and chief executive officer of Red-Database-Security in Neunkirchen, Germany. For example, tools to check the strength of passwords, often freely distributed, could also be used by malicious hackers, he says.

"The security community is very unhappy with this approach," Kornbrust says. "The concern is that the usage and possession of so-called hacker tools will become illegal."

The United Kingdom and Germany are trying to align their laws with Article 6 of the convention, which bans the creation of computer programs for the purpose of committing cybercrime. So far, 43 countries have signed the convention, which indicates their willingness to revise their laws to comply. Fifteen have ratified the convention. After a country changes its laws, it can ratify the convention and put it into force.

Source: Adapted from Dave Gradijan, "Euro Computer Crime Laws Have Security Pros Worried," *CSO Magazine*, September 29, 2006.

Internet Access Issues

The Paris-based organization Reporters Without Borders (RSF) reports that there are 45 countries that "restrict their citizens' access to the Internet." At its most fundamental, the struggle between Internet censorship and openness at the national level revolves around three main means: controlling the conduits, filtering the flows, and punishing the purveyors. In countries such as Burma, Libya, North Korea, Syria, and the countries of Central Asia and the Caucasus, Internet access is either banned or subject to tight limitations through government-controlled ISPs, says the RSF.

Figure 12.20 outlines the restrictions to public **Internet access** by the governments of the 20 countries deemed most restrictive by the Paris-based Reporters Without Borders (RSF). See their Web site at www.rsf.fr.

So the Internet has become a global battleground over public access to data and information at business and private sites on the World Wide Web. Of course, this becomes a business issue because restrictive access policies severely inhibit the growth of e-commerce with such countries. Most of the rest of the world has decided that restricting Internet access is not a viable policy but in fact would hurt their countries' opportunities for economic growth and prosperity. Instead, national and international efforts are being made to rate and filter Internet content deemed inappropriate or criminal, such as Web sites for child pornography or terrorism. In any event, countries that significantly restrict Internet access are also choosing to restrict their participation in the growth of e-commerce.

To RSF and others, these countries' rulers face a losing battle against the Information Age. By denying or limiting Internet access, they stymie a major engine of economic growth. By easing access, however, they expose their citizenry to ideas that potentially might destabilize to the status quo. Either way, many people will get access to the electronic information they want. "In Syria, for example, people go to Lebanon for the weekend to retrieve their e-mail," says Virginie Locussol, RSF's desk officer for the Middle East and North Africa.

FIGURE 12.20

Countries that restrict or forbid Internet access by their citizens.

Global Government Restrictions on Internet Access
● **High Government Access Fees** Kazakhstan, Kyrgyzstan
● **Government-Monitored Access** China, Iran, Saudi Arabia, Azerbaijan, Uzbekistan
● **Government-Filtered Access** Belarus, Cuba, Iraq, Tunisia, Sierra Leone, Tajikistan, Turkmenistan, Vietnam
● **No Public Access Allowed** Burma, Libya, North Korea

Global Systems Development

Just imagine the challenges of developing efficient, effective, and responsive applications for business end users domestically. Then, multiply that by the number of countries and cultures that may use a global e-business system. That's the challenge of managing global systems development. Naturally, there are conflicts over local versus global system requirements, as well as difficulties agreeing on common system features such as multilingual user interfaces and flexible design standards. All of this effort must take place in an environment that promotes involvement and "ownership" of a system by local end users.

Other systems development issues arise from disturbances caused by systems implementation and maintenance activities. For example, "An interruption during a third shift in New York City will present midday service interruptions in Tokyo." Another major development issue relates to the trade-offs between developing one system that can run on multiple computer and operating system platforms or letting each local site customize the software for its own platform.

Other important global systems development issues are concerned with global standardization of data definitions. Common data definitions are necessary for sharing data among the parts of an international business. Differences in language, culture, and technology platforms can make global data standardization quite difficult. For example, a sale may be called an "order booked" in the United Kingdom, an "order scheduled" in Germany, and an "order produced" in France. Yet, businesses are moving ahead to standardize data definitions and structures. By moving their subsidiaries into data modeling and database design, they hope to develop a global data architecture that supports their global business objectives.

Systems Development Strategies

Several strategies can be used to solve some of the systems development problems that arise in global IT. The first strategy is to transform an application used in the home office into a global application. Often, the system that has the best version of an application will be chosen for global use. Another approach is to set up a *multinational development team* with key people from several subsidiaries to ensure that the system design meets the needs of local sites, as well as corporate headquarters.

A third approach is called *parallel development*. That's because parts of the system are assigned to different subsidiaries and the home office to develop at the same time, based on the expertise and experience at each site. Another approach is the concept of *centers of excellence*. In this approach, an entire system may be assigned for development to a particular subsidiary based on its expertise in the business or technical dimensions needed for successful development. A final approach that has rapidly become a major development option is to outsource the development work to global or *offshore* development companies that have the skills and experience required to develop global business/IT applications. Obviously, all of these approaches require development team collaboration and managerial oversight to meet the global needs of a business. So, global systems development teams are making heavy use of the Internet, intranets, groupware, and other electronic collaboration technologies. See Figure 12.21.

Invensys PLC: Drawing Talent from Around the World for Software Development

It's great being able to draw upon your best programmers from throughout the world. SimSci-Esscor, the industrial process simulation and control unit of Invensys PLC, will assign personnel from any of its offices to assemble the right team. "Our development projects operate in a virtual mode and gather people from multiple sites based on project needs," says Joe Ayers, director of development services at SimSci-Esscor in Lake Forest, California. "It is common for projects to utilize developers from three different time zones in a 'follow the sun' development mode."

The approach allows Invensys to find the right talent for the project, and work is done in an efficient way. But managing those far-flung developers can be a nightmare. "Invensys had brought together multiple companies with different cultures and processes," Ayers explains. "Some of the issues we have had to address include

FIGURE 12.21   An example of Internet-enabled collaboration in global IT systems development. Note the roles played by the client company, offshore outsource developer, global open-source community, and just-in-time development team.

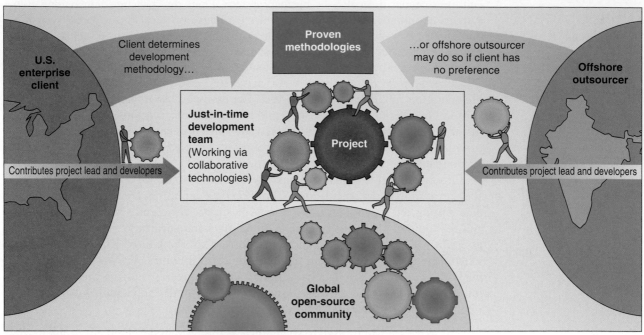

Source: Adapted from Jon Udell, "Leveraging a Global Advantage," *Infoworld*, April 21, 2003, p. 35.

duplication of source code, multiple tools and processes in use, and limited network connectivity and reliability."

To tackle these issues, Invensys created a virtual development infrastructure for 135 developers in five locations. To facilitate communication, it incorporated desktop-sharing tools, instant messaging, conference calling, and voice-over-IP technology.

For working on the code itself, the company deployed three products from Telelogic AB in Malmo, Sweden: Synergy/CM for controlling project configuration items, Synergy/Change for controlling change requests, and Synergy/Distributed CM for synchronizing change requests and source code between databases at multiple sites. It also implemented a wide-area file-sharing system from Availl Inc. in Andover, Massachusetts, for other documents. "With this development structure, we have the ability to add or remove changes to software builds at the last minute, with no project-delivery slips attributed to distributed development complexity over the last year," says Ayers. "We've been able to lower project start-up time and project costs."

Experts say managing distributed development teams requires a mix of processes and tools. "Rarely is it a problem with the technology, though that used to be a major hurdle in the past," says Dale Karolak, vice president of product development at Intier Automotive Inc. in Novi, Michigan, and author of *Global Software Development: Managing Virtual Teams and Environments*. "Most problems now are with communications, documentation and alignment." Karolak says managers need to exert more discipline when it comes to scheduling and holding meetings and tracking project targets and spend more time visiting off-site locations for face-to-face meetings. Proper management also requires a greater awareness of potential problems.

"Jump on problems right away. Don't wait," Karolak says. "Longer distances will cause longer delays in solving the issues if they are not addressed quickly."

Source: Adapted from Drew Robb, "Global Workgroups," *Computerworld*, August 15, 2005.

Summary

- **Managing Information Technology.** This can be viewed as managing three major components: (1) the joint development and implementation of e-business and IT strategies, (2) the development of e-business applications and the research and implementation of new information technologies, and (3) IT processes, professionals, and subunits within a company's IT organization and IS function.

- **Failures in IT Management.** Information systems are not being used effectively or efficiently by many organizations. The experiences of successful organizations reveal that the basic ingredient of high-quality information system performance is extensive and meaningful management, as well as user involvement in the governance and development of IT applications. Thus, managers may serve on executive IT groups and create IS management functions within their business units.

- **Managing Global IT.** The international dimensions of managing global information technologies include dealing with cultural, political, and geoeconomic challenges posed by various countries; developing appropriate business and IT strategies for the global marketplace; and developing a portfolio of global e-business

and e-commerce applications and an Internet-based technology platform to support them. In addition, data access methods have to be developed and systems development projects managed to produce the global e-business applications that are required to compete successfully in the global marketplace.

- **Global Business and IT Strategies and Issues.** Many businesses are becoming global companies and moving toward transnational business strategies in which they integrate the global business activities of their subsidiaries and headquarters. This transition requires that they develop a global IT platform—that is, an integrated worldwide hardware, software, and Internet-based network architecture. Global companies are increasingly using the Internet and related technologies as a major component of this IT platform to develop and deliver global IT applications that meet their unique global business requirements. Global IT and end-user managers must deal with limitations to the availability of hardware and software; restrictions on transborder data flows, Internet access, and movement of personal data; and difficulties with developing common data definitions and system requirements.

Key Terms and Concepts

These are the key terms and concepts of this chapter. The page number of their first explanation is in parentheses.

1. Application development management (510)
2. Business/IT planning process (507)
3. Centralization or decentralization of IT (510)
4. Chargeback systems (511)
5. Chief information officer (512)
6. Chief technology officer (513)
7. Data center (511)
8. Downsizing (510)

9. Global business drivers (528)
10. Global information technology management (522)
    a. Data access issues (532)
    b. Systems development issues (535)
11. IS operations management (511)
12. IT architecture (508)
13. IT staff planning (512)
14. Management involvement (518)

15. Managing information technology (504)
16. Offshoring (515)
17. Outsourcing (514)
18. System performance monitor (511)
19. Technology management (513)
20. Transborder data flows (533)
21. Transnational strategy (527)
22. User services (513)

Review Quiz

Match one of the key terms and concepts listed previously with one of the brief examples or definitions that follow. Try to find the best answer, even though some seem to fit more than one term or concept. Defend your choices.

_____ 1. Focuses on discovering innovative approaches to satisfying a company's customer value and business value goals with the support of IT.

_____ 2. Concerned with the use of hardware, software, network, and IS personnel resources within the corporate or business unit.

_____ 3. Managing business/IT planning and the IS function within a company.

_____ 4. A conceptual design, or blueprint, of an organization's IS/IT functions, hardware, and software created by a strategic business/IT planning process.

_____ 5. Many organizations have both centralized and decentralized IT units.

_____ 6. Managing the creation and implementation of new business applications.

_____ 7. End users need liaison, consulting, and training services.

_____ 8. Involves recruiting, training, and retaining qualified IS personnel.

_____ 9. Corporate locations for computer system operations.

_____ 10. Rapidly changing technological developments must be anticipated, identified, and implemented.

_____ 11. A relocation of an organization's business processes (including production/manufacturing) to a lower-cost location, usually overseas.

_____ 12. The executive responsible for strategic business/ IT planning and IT management.

_____ 13. The executive in charge of researching and implementing new information technologies.

_____ 14. Software that helps monitor and control computer systems in a data center.

_____ 15. The cost of IS services may be allocated back to end users.

_____ 16. Many business firms are replacing their mainframe systems with networked PCs and servers.

_____ 17. The purchase of goods or services from third-party partners that were previously provided internally.

_____ 18. Managing IT to support a company's international business operations.

_____ 19. A business depends heavily on its information systems and Internet technologies to help it integrate its global business activities.

_____ 20. Global customers, products, operations, resources, and collaboration.

_____ 21. Global telecommunications networks like the Internet move data across national boundaries.

_____ 22. Agreement is needed on common user interfaces and Web site design features in global IT.

_____ 23. Security requirements for personal information in corporate databases within a host country are a top concern.

_____ 24. Business managers should oversee IT decision making and projects that are critical to their business units' success.

Discussion Questions

1. What has been the impact of information technologies on the work relationships, activities, and resources of managers?

2. What can business unit managers do about performance problems in the use of information technology and the development and operation of information systems in their business units?

3. Refer to the Real World Case about retiring CIOs and succession planning in the chapter. How would you balance the development and mentoring of your executives and managers with your own job security and career planning? How would you make the decision that it is "time to move on"?

4. How are Internet technologies affecting the structure and work roles of modern organizations? For example, will middle management wither away? Will companies consist primarily of self-directed project teams of knowledge workers? Explain your answers.

5. Should the IS function in a business be centralized or decentralized? Use the Internet to find recent developments to support your answer.

6. Refer to the Real World Case on Reinsurance Group of America and Fonterra in the chapter. Fonterra's approach to global development exposes IT professionals to a variety of business areas, functions, and processes. What are the advantages of this exposure for them? What are the challenges?

7. How might cultural, political, or geoeconomic challenges affect a global company's use of the Internet? Give several examples.

8. Will the increasing use of the Internet by firms with global business operations change their move toward a transnational business strategy? Explain.

9. How might the Internet, intranets, and extranets affect the business drivers or requirements responsible for a company's use of global IT, as shown in Figure 12.13? Give several examples to illustrate your answer.

Analysis Exercises

1. **Top-Rated Web Sites for Executives**
   CEO Express
   Check out CEO Express (www.ceoexpress.com), a top-rated Web portal for busy executives. See Figure 12.22.

The site provides links to top U.S. and international newspapers, business and technology magazines, and news services. Hundreds of links to business and technology research sources and references are provided,

FIGURE 12.22
The CEO Express Web site.

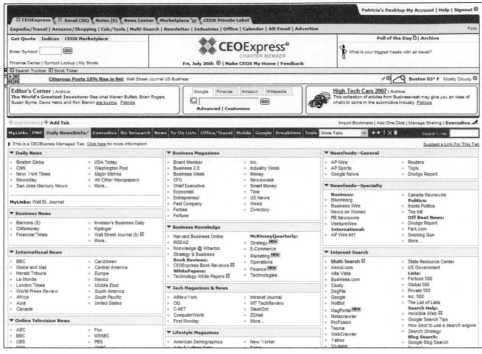

Source: Courtesy of CEO Express.

as well as travel services, online shopping, and recreational Web sites. Premium services include e-mail, contact management, calendaring and scheduling, community networking, and powerful information organizing and sharing tools.

a. Evaluate the CEO Express Web site as a source of useful links to business and technology news, analysis, and research sources for business executives and professionals.

b. Compare CEO Express with Google News (news.google.com) and Google IG (www.google.com/ig). What advantages does CEO Express provide?

c. Select the featured article from the "Editor's Corner." What was the source? Summarize the article. Was it useful to you?

2. **Information and Communications for Development**
Assessing Global Capabilities
Over one billion people take their electrical and telecommunications systems for granted. However, for billions more, the service-on-demand mentality remains a distant dream and Internet access only a rumor. Recognizing the need to promote global information and communications technologies (GICT), the World Bank has undertaken numerous technology infrastructure assessment and development projects.

a. What is the World Bank (www.worldbank.org) doing to address third-world computer literacy needs?

b. What is MIT (www.mit.edu) doing to help increase global computer literacy?

3. **Overseas Assignments**
Incompatible Electricity?
Business travelers who need to remain connected face special challenges outside their home country, especially those who work out of their hotel rooms. Electricity varies by voltage, cycles, and electric-plug shape. Likewise, telephone jacks may vary from country to country and, for the most part, American cell phones work only in America.

If you find yourself on an overseas assignment, how will you keep your laptop computer charged? How will you access the Internet? Can you free yourself from expensive hotel telephone surcharges?

Pick a country to "visit" (your professor may assign one instead), and report on specific solutions to each question. Be sure to include the manufacturer and model number of any hardware you may require. Cite all your sources.

a. What do you need to bring with you to keep your laptop computer charged?

b. What do you need to bring with you to connect your laptop's modem to the local telephone network?

c. What will you use in place of your handy cell phone?

d. Use a collaboration-enabled system such as Blackboard, Web CT, Dreamweaver, or Front Page to merge, organize, and publish your results with the rest of your class to create an online resource.

4. **Knowledge Work on the Move**
Business Process Outsourcing
As a result of the location independence of knowledge work, many organizations seek to lower their labor

costs by moving their digital operations overseas. When managers evaluate such opportunities, they must consider the following regional attributes:

- Political and regulatory environment
- Infrastructure (electrical, telecommunications)
- Professionally skilled labor force
- Information systems skilled labor force

All prospective locations must have a supportive political and regulatory environment; however, variations within the other three attributes will pose special limitations. For example, India has millions of well-educated workers but notoriously unreliable telecommunications and electrical grids. Organizations that set up outsourcing operations in India build their own islands of stability with backup power and satellite telecommunications systems. A region with a shortage of profes-

sionally skilled labor may offer labor-intensive activities such as call centers or data entry instead, yet even these jobs require basic computer literacy.

The value of services provided depends primarily on the expertise or creativity involved in its performance. List suitable job titles for each work characteristic below. Rank each item in order of the value provided.

a. Digitize: Convert data or information into a digital form.
b. Distribute: Process information in one direction or another based on strict rules and nondigital inputs (if the inputs were digital, a computer could probably do the job).
c. Analyze: Process information based on human expertise.
d. Create: Create new information or products based on human expertise.

REAL WORLD CASE 3

IBM Corporation: Competing Globally by Offshoring IT Workers and Giving Away Technology

It's IBM's nightmare. In a conference room in Bangalore, a team of retail experts at software company Wipro are redesigning the consumer experience for a major U.S. retail chain. They're methodically evaluating the checkout area. The client wants state-of-the-art processes, and Srikant Shankaranarayana, Wipro's brainy, intense, 44-year-old general manager for retail solutions, is pushing his consultants and engineers to ask tough questions: Should salesclerks carry handheld transaction devices or stand at cash registers? Which merchandise should be tracked electronically? How much information needs to be in the database to ensure that discount promotions don't last longer than necessary?

Those are exactly the kinds of questions that IBM wants to ask its retail customers, and the fact that such companies as Louis Vuitton and Target are turning to India for answers is not a good thing for IBM. Almost half of IBM's revenues now come from such business/IT services, and only services promise to provide growth on the massive scale that IBM needs to make shareholders happy. Luckily for IBM, Wipro has only 100 retail consultants—so far.

Meanwhile, IBM's costs remain those of a mature First World corporation. It has approximately 260,000 expensive employees in the United States and other developed countries (the other 60,000 are in lower-cost regions) and 164,000 pensioned retirees, all quarterbacked from a gleaming modern headquarters on 432 acres of pricey Westchester County real estate.

Although they don't put it quite this boldly, CEO Sam Palmisano and other top IBMers think they're well on the way to solving the problem. Interviews with the CEO's lieutenants reveal their strategy: It will not only challenge upstarts like Wipro directly by taking the low-cost model right back at them, but it also includes a dimension that is so original and so bold that it will either reenergize Big Blue's profits or undermine its vaunted status as the biggest company in IT.

Simply put, IBM is gambling that it can win by giving away crown jewels—precious intellectual property in the form of software, patents, and ideas. Spread enough of those riches around, the theory goes, and the entire industry will grow faster, opening new frontiers. That, in turn, should create opportunities for IBM to sell high-value products and services that meet the new demand.

IBM's response to the India threat has been swift. In April 2005, after first-quarter revenues from services came in unexpectedly weak and IBM disappointed Wall Street's earnings expectations, the company eliminated 14,500 jobs, mostly in Europe. It was the biggest job cut in three years: The company shut its European headquarters and moved most of the surviving employees out to the field, to what Palmisano calls "client-facing positions."

Next, *The New York Times* reported that it obtained an internal IBM memo that said the company would hire 14,000 people in India this year. IBM calls the figure "exaggerated,"

but newcomers in any number would add to an already surprisingly large roster in developing countries. Of the programmers who write custom code for IBM's services group, about half—26,000 or so—are in India, Brazil, or China. "Strategic low-cost geographies" is the IBM lingo for such places.

India already accounts for the largest number of IBMers outside the United States (it recently surpassed Japan). In 2004, Big Blue acquired India's Daksh eServices, whose 6,000 employees operate call centers for companies like Amazon.com and Citicorp. Goldman Sachs calculates that by the end of next year, IBM Services' head count in India will top 52,000. That would be more than one-fourth of all its services personnel and about one-sixth of IBMers worldwide. It would put IBM in India on a par with Wipro, the largest local software company, and it would make it bigger than Infosys and Tata Consultancy Services.

Growth in the developing world is a natural part of implementing a "global delivery model" for services, says senior vice president Bob Moffat. In July, Palmisano reorganized services, naming the 49-year-old Moffat as one of three executives who will run it jointly. Although the other two will oversee the delivery of services to clients, Moffat's job is to find efficiencies. He spent the past three years taking billions of dollars in costs out of IBM's physical supply chain—the delivery of parts and goods to and from factories and then on to the customer. His mission now is to cut the cost of delivering services, even high-value ones, by tightening the "services supply chain." Mostly, that means people; he must get the right ones to the right place at the right time. He has to extract every last penny of value from IBM's 260,000 developed-country employees if they're going to stay on the payroll.

Palmisano certainly sounds confident. In an e-mail to *Fortune*, he makes a remarkable claim: that by adopting the strategy that he calls, simply, "openness," IBM has tapped a major new "spur to innovation itself." The company lavishes some $5.7 billion a year on R&D. By sharing its discoveries wisely, Palmisano says, IBM will "make the pie bigger," and the entire industry will grow faster.

Collaborating with customers, and even rivals, to invent new technologies is a big part of this sharing plan, and the first fruits are already apparent. In hardware, IBM, Sony, and Toshiba have codeveloped a breakthrough chip called the Cell, which could eventually help transform all of IBM's computers. In software, embracing Linux and other open-source technology has given IBM new platforms on which it is building almost all of its high-growth applications.

The idea that giving things away makes the pie bigger for everybody is not IBM's invention, of course. The open-source software movement that developed Linux is a good example. Says Palmisano: "This isn't theory for us. Collaborative innovation today is crucial to every aspect of our business. We've learned how to deliver value within this kind of business system and how to make money."

A walking, talking embodiment of that is Jim Stallings, Palmisano's vice president for intellectual property and standards—a job Palmisano invented when he tapped Stallings for it last September. Stallings, 49, used to manage IBM's work with the Linux community; now he's the guy who figures out what Big Blue should give away and what it should keep. A buttoned-down former Marine Corps captain and 14-year IBM veteran, he's not the most likely high-tech Santa. Yet he's almost hypnotically good at explaining how IBM's plan works. The giveaways to open-source software groups, customer groups, universities, and other IT companies are surprisingly extensive and diverse.

IBM says there's no way to attach a precise dollar value to its giveaways, but *Fortune* calculates they're worth at least $150 million a year. Although sharing is not yet a universal part of its culture, the company has come a long way from the arrogant, standoffish, monopolistic IBM of yore.

What's in it for IBM? Big Blue seldom gives away a technology unless it has intellectual property and expertise that will enable it to make money if the technology is widely adopted. When IBM hands out tools to retailers, it often sells them additional software and consulting services. What's more, freebies themselves can be a potent weapon. Application-related software from Microsoft can be costly. An open-source version like Apache Geronimo is free and is the latest salvo in IBM's open-source challenge to Microsoft. It has also embraced the Linux operating system, a formidable rival to Windows, as well as Firefox, a popular challenger to the Internet Explorer Web browser.

IBM has also found giveaways to be a potent door opener abroad, where the company derives 63 percent of its revenues. Stallings has been to China four times this year and plans to go two more times in September. He's working to convince policymakers and business leaders that using open-source software makes more sense than buying Microsoft's. This IBMer bearing gifts has found a receptive audience. Now IBM is helping build a giant network based largely on Linux to connect all of China's libraries.

All this sounds well and good, but the outcome is far from certain. IBM is in a brutally competitive marketplace with a long list of rivals going after the same customer dollar, but Palmisano argues that IBM will be able to create products and services that capitalize on new markets as they emerge.

Yet even his own executives need to be convinced from time to time. Two years ago, some insiders fretted that IBM might be "shooting itself in the foot" by giving its ideas away. In the end, however, company researchers concluded that as long as IT remains hard to use, expensive, and labor-intensive, with customers continuing to need help solving business problems, IBM will have the opportunity to thrive. Any business computer user would guess that means forever.

Source: Adapted from David Kirkpatrick, "IBM Shares Its Secrets," *Fortune*, September 5, 2005.

CASE STUDY QUESTIONS

1. Do you agree with IBM's employment response to competition from software development contractors in India, like Wipro, that are expanding into IT consulting services? Why or why not?

2. Will IBM's plan to give away some of its IT assets and intellectual property, as well as increase its support of open-source software products like Linux, be a successful growth strategy in the "brutally competitive marketplace" in which it operates? Why or why not?

3. Do you agree with IBM researchers' assumption that IT will remain "hard to use, expensive, and labor-intensive, with customers continuing to need help solving business problems" for a long time to come? Should IBM bet its business on that assumption? Defend your answers to both questions.

REAL WORLD ACTIVITIES

1. Use the Internet to research news on the latest developments in the competition to provide IT consulting services to businesses and governments. Check out IBM's performance, as well as major players like HP and Accenture, new entrants like Dell, and international competitors like Wipro. Who appears to be winning or losing in this arena? What reasons can you uncover for the results you find?

2. IBM eliminated 14,500 jobs, mostly in Europe, and then reportedly hired thousands of additional IT workers in India. Cutting high-cost jobs and then offshoring jobs to a subsidiary in a lower-cost country is a controversial business strategy being used by other global companies. Break into small groups with your classmates to discuss the implications of this issue for your current or future career choices and the kinds of companies or organizations you would want to work for.

Review Quiz Answers

Chapter 1

1. 20	8. 1	15. 2	22. 13*b*	29. 16*c*	36. 19	43. 22
2. 18	9. 23*b*	16. 3	23. 25	30. 16*d*	37. 11	44. 23*a*
3. 24	10. 8	17. 14	24. 25*a*	31. 16*e*	38. 7	45. 4
4. 24*a*	11. 9	18. 16	25. 25*b*	32. 27	39. 27*d*	46. 27*f*
5. 24*b*	12. 10	19. 17	26. 23	33. 27*c*	40. 5	47. 21
6. 24*c*	13. 26	20. 13	27. 16*a*	34. 27*b*	41. 6	48. 27*e*
7. 15	14. 12	21. 13*a*	28. 16*b*	35. 27*a*	42. 14*a*	49. 27*g*

Chapter 2

1. 3	4. 11	7. 6	10. 2	13. 8
2. 4	5. 5	8. 14	11. 1	14. 9
3. 12	6. 13	9. 10	12. 15	15. 7

Chapter 3

1. 3	9. 21	17. 9*c*	25. 15	33. 34*c*	41. 36	49. 28*d*
2. 2	10. 1	18. 20	26. 12	34. 4	42. 6	50. 34*b*
3. 5	11. 7	19. 19	27. 16	35. 34	43. 32	51. 29
4. 8	12. 13	20. 35	28. 17	36. 37	44. 31	52. 34*d*
5. 27	13. 14	21. 10	29. 33	37. 34*a*	45. 9	53. 34*g*
6. 30	14. 9*a*	22. 28*c*	30. 24	38. 34*f*	46. 11	
7. 25	15. 9*b*	23. 34*e*	31. 28	39. 31*b*	47. 23	
8. 22	16. 18	24. 26	32. 28*a*	40. 31*a*	48. 28*b*	

Chapter 4

1. 5	7. 32	13. 33	19. 37	25. 20	31. 28	37. 16
2. 2	8. 6	14. 12	20. 8	26. 3	32. 15	38. 36
3. 31	9. 34	15. 11	21. 26	27. 14	33. 38	
4. 1	10. 22	16. 35	22. 17	28. 10	34. 18	
5. 4	11. 27	17. 9	23. 29	29. 24	35. 25	
6. 7	12. 19	18. 30	24. 13	30. 23	36. 21	

Chapter 5

1. 11	7. 12	13. 6	19. 13*a*	25. 1	31. 16*a*	36. 13*c*
2. 3	8. 20*b*	14. 16*e*	20. 13*e*	26. 13	32. 20	37. 16
3. 9	9. 13*d*	15. 16*g*	21. 13*b*	27. 16*b*	33. 7	
4. 19	10. 20*d*	16. 16*f*	22. 20*e*	28. 18	34. 14	
5. 2	11. 8	17. 16*c*	23. 20*a*	29. 4	35. 16*d*	
6. 10	12. 5	18. 15	24. 20*c*	30. 17		

Chapter 6

1. 34	7. 8	13. 9	19. 24	25. 21*a*	31. 22	37. 21
2. 23	8. 10	14. 3	20. 1	26. 21*b*	32. 26	38. 30
3. 20	9. 35	15. 31	21. 2	27. 25	33. 6	39. 37
4. 17	10. 15	16. 32	22. 33	28. 12	34. 14	
5. 16	11. 7	17. 18	23. 5	29. 11	35. 28	
6. 13	12. 29	18. 19	24. 27	30. 4	36. 36	

Chapter 7

1. 7	6. 20	11. 3	16. 8	21. 6	26. 23
2. 5	7. 16	12. 11	17. 1	22. 12	27. 28
3. 14	8. 24	13. 22	18. 13	23. 26	28. 21
4. 9	9. 19	14. 17	19. 18	24. 25	29. 29
5. 10	10. 4	15. 15	20. 27	25. 2	

Chapter 8

1. 5	5. 4	9. 4*h*	13. 8	17. 3*b*	21. 1
2. 5*b*	6. 4*a*	10. 4*e*	14. 3*d*	18. 2	22. 3
3. 5*a*	7. 4*f*	11. 4*b*	15. 3*a*	19. 6	23. 4*g*
4. 5*c*	8. 4*c*	12. 7	16. 3*c*	20. 4*d*	

Chapter 9

1. 6	6. 22	11. 1*b*	16. 20	21. 15	26. 19
2. 10	7. 1	12. 24	17. 9	22. 11	27. 23
3. 21	8. 1*d*	13. 4	18. 2	23. 18	28. 13
4. 7	9. 1*c*	14. 5	19. 25	24. 16	29. 17
5. 3	10. 1*a*	15. 8	20. 26	25. 12	30. 14

Chapter 10

1. 21	7. 28*b*	13. 29	19. 25	25. 2	31. 1
2. 27	8. 12*a*	14. 13	20. 23	26. 26	32. 4
3. 17	9. 22	15. 10	21. 24	27. 5	33. 28
4. 3	10. 14	16. 20	22. 19	28. 18	34. 15
5. 28*b*	11. 8	17. 9	23. 7	29. 32	35. 12
6. 12*b*	12. 6	18. 30	24. 11	30. 31	36. 16

Chapter 11

1. 24	6. 10	11. 15	16. 7	21. 26	26. 18
2. 20	7. 2	12. 5	17. 8	22. 21	27. 14
3. 29	8. 4	13. 27	18. 12	23. 19	28. 25
4. 16	9. 11	14. 28	19. 6	24. 9	29. 3
5. 17	10. 13	15. 22	20. 30	25. 1	30. 23

Chapter 12

1. 2	5. 3	9. 7	13. 6	17. 17	21. 20
2. 11	6. 1	10. 19	14. 18	18. 10	22. 10*b*
3. 15	7. 22	11. 16	15. 4	19. 21	23. 10*a*
4. 12	8. 13	12. 5	16. 8	20. 9	24. 14

Selected References

Preface

Sawhney, Mohan; and Jeff Zabin. *The Seven Steps to Nirvana: Strategic Insights into e-Business Transformation.* New York: McGraw-Hill, 2001.

Chapter 1—Foundations of Information Systems in Business

1. Melymuka, Kathleen. "Profiting from Mistakes." *Computerworld*, April 20, 2001.

2. Kalakota, Ravi; and Marcia Robinson. *E-Business 2.0: Roadmap for Success.* Reading, MA: Addison-Wesley, 2001.

3. Institute for Development Policy and Management, http://www.egov4dev.org/home.htm and http://www.e-devexchange.org/eGov/home.htm, March 2004.

4. "Citibank E-Mail Hoax and Webpage Scam," http://www.millersmiles.co.uk/identitytheft/citibank-email-verification-hoax.htm, November 2003.

5. Lee, Allen. "Inaugural Editor's Comments." *MIS Quarterly*, March 1999.

6. Norris, Grant; James Hurley; Kenneth Hartley; John Dunleavy; and John Balls. *E-Business and ERP: Transforming the Enterprise.* New York: John Wiley & Sons, 2000.

7. Radcliff, Deborah. "Aligning Marriott." *Computerworld*, April 20, 2000.

8. Rosencrance, L. "Citibank Customers Hit with E-Mail Scam." *Computerworld*, October 24, 2003.

9. Steadman, Craig. "Failed ERP Gamble Haunts Hershey." *Computerworld*, November 1, 1999.

10. Weiss, Todd. "Hershey Upgrades R/3 ERP System without Hitches." *Computerworld*, September 9, 2002.

11. Williams, Lisa. "EMC Keeps Red Sox in the Game." *ITworldcanada.com*. 2006.

12. Thibodeau, Patrick. "Want to Win in Vegas? Bet on an IT Job, Not the Super Bowl." *Computerworld*, February 2, 2007.

Chapter 2—Competing with Information Technology

1. "Agilent Technologies ERP Information for Customers," http://www.tmintl.agilent.com/model/index.shtml, n.d.

2. Applegate, Lynda; Robert D. Austin; and F. Warren McFarlan. *Corporate Information Systems Management: Text and Cases.* 6th ed. Burr Ridge, IL: Irwin/McGraw-Hill, 2003.

3. Bowles, Jerry. "Best Practices for Global Competitiveness." *Fortune*, Special Advertising Section, November 24, 1997.

4. Caron, J. Raymond; Sirkka Jarvenpaa; and Donna Stoddard. "Business Reengineering at CIGNA Corporation: Experiences and Lessons from the First Five Years." *MIS Quarterly*, September 1994.

5. Christensen, Clayton. *The Innovators Dilemma: When New Technologies Cause Great Firms to Fail.* Boston: Harvard Business School Press, 1997.

6. Cronin, Mary. *The Internet Strategy Handbook.* Boston: Harvard Business School Press, 1996.

7. Davenport, Thomas H. *Process Innovation: Reengineering Work through Information Technology.* Boston: Harvard Business School Press, 1993.

8. El Sawy, Omar; and Gene Bowles. "Redesigning the Customer Support Process for the Electronic Economy: Insights from Storage Dimensions." *MIS Quarterly*, December 1997.

9. El Sawy, Omar; Arvind Malhotra; Sanjay Gosain; and Kerry Young. "IT-Intensive Value Innovation in the Electronic Economy: Insights from Marshall Industries." *MIS Quarterly*, September 1999.

10. Frye, Colleen. "Imaging Proves Catalyst for Reengineering." *Client/Server Computing*, November 1994.

11. Garner, Rochelle. "Please Don't Call IT Knowledge Management!" *Computerworld*, August 9, 1999.

12. Goldman, Steven; Roger Nagel; and Kenneth Preis. *Agile Competitors and Virtual Organizations: Strategies for Enriching the Customer.* New York: Van Nostrand Reinhold, 1995.

13. Grover, Varun; and Pradipkumar Ramanlal. "Six Myths of Information and Markets: Information Technology Networks, Electronic Commerce, and the Battle for Consumer Surplus." *MIS Quarterly*, December 1999.

14. Hamm, Steve; and Marcia Stepaneck. "From Reengineering to E-Engineering." *BusinessWeek e.biz*, March 22, 1999.

15. Hoffman, T. "In the Know: Knowledge Management Case Study Pays Off for BAE Systems." *Computerworld*, October 14, 2002.

16. "Intel Telecom Case Studies, Best Known Call Center Practices," http://www.intel.com/network/csp/resources/case_studies/enterprise/7867web.htm, n.d.

17. Kalakota, Ravi; and Marcia Robinson. *E-Business 2.0: Roadmap for Success*. Reading, MA: Addison-Wesley, 2001.

18. Kettinger, William; Varun Grover; and Albert Segars. "Do Strategic Systems Really Pay Off? An Analysis of Classic Strategic IT Cases." *Information Systems Management*, Winter 1995.

19. Kettinger, William; James Teng; and Subashish Guha. "Business Process Change: A Study of Methodologies, Techniques, and Tools." *MIS Quarterly*, March 1997.

20. Nonaka, Ikujiro. "The Knowledge Creating Company." *Harvard Business Review*, November–December 1991.

21. Porter, Michael, and Victor Millar. "How Information Gives You Competitive Advantage." *Harvard Business Review*, July–August 1985.

22. Prokesch, Steven. "Unleashing the Power of Learning: An Interview with British Petroleum's John Browne." *Harvard Business Review*, September–October 1997.

23. Sambamurthy, V.; Anandhi Bharadwaj; and Varun Grover. "Shaping Agility through Digital Options: Reconceptualizing the Role of Information Technology in Contemporary Firms." *MIS Quarterly*, June 2003.

24. Seybold, Patricia. *Customers.com: How to Create a Profitable Business Strategy for the Internet and Beyond*. New York: Times Books, 1998.

25. Shapiro, Carl; and Hal Varian. *Information Rules: A Strategic Guide to the Network Economy*. Boston: Harvard Business School Press, 1999.

26. Siekman, Philip. "Why Infotech Loves Its Giant Job Shops." *Fortune*, May 12, 1997.

27. Songini, Marc. "ERP Effort Sinks Agilent Revenue." *Computerworld*, August 26, 2002.

28. Strategy Works, "Retrieval Is the Key to the New Economy," http://www.thestrategyworks.com/articles/knowledge2.htm, August 31, 2000.

29. Babcock, Charles. "Evolve Business Processes, Don't Reengineer Them." *InformationWeek*, November 11, 2004.

30. Weill, Peter; and Michael Vitale. *Place to Space: Migrating to E-Business Models*. Boston: Harvard Business School Press, 2001.

Chapter 3—Computer Hardware

1. *Computerworld, PC Week, PC Magazine*, and *PC World* are just a few examples of many good magazines for current information on computer systems hardware and its use in end-user and enterprise applications.

2. The World Wide Web sites of computer manufacturers such as Apple Computer, Dell Computer, Gateway, IBM, Hewlett-Packard, Compaq, and Sun Microsystems are good sources of information about computer hardware developments.

3. Alexander, Steve. "Speech Recognition." *Computerworld*, November 8, 1999.

4. "Computing in the New Millennium." *Fortune*, Technology Buyers Guide, Winter 2000.

5. Guyon, Janet. "Smart Plastic." *Fortune*, October 13, 1997.

6. "Hardware." *Fortune*, Technology Buyer's Guide, Winter 1999.

7. Hecht, Jeff. "Casino Chips to Carry RFID Tags." *New Scientist*, January 2004.

8. Joch, Alan. "Fewer Servers, Better Service." *Computerworld*, June 4, 2001.

9. Kennedy, Ken, et al. "A Nationwide Parallel Computing Environment." *Communications of the ACM*, November 1997.

10. Messerschmitt, David. *Networked Applications: A Guide to the New Computing Infrastructure*. San Francisco: Morgan Kaufmann, 1999.

11. Ouellette, Tim. "Goodbye to the Glass House." *Computerworld*, May 26, 1997.

12. Ouellette, Tim. "Tape Storage Put to New Enterprise Uses." *Computerworld*, November 10, 1997.

13. Reimers, Barbara. "Blades Spin ROI Potential." *Computerworld*, February 11, 2002.

14. Simpson, David. "The Datamation 100." *Datamation*, July 1997.

15. "Top 500 Supercomputer Sites: ASCII White," www.top500.org, May 18, 2003.

16. Gaudin, Sharon. "Kurzweil: Computers Will Enable People to Live Forever." *Informationweek*, November 21, 2006.

Chapter 4—Computer Software

1. Examples of many good magazines for current information and reviews of computer software for business applications can be found at ZD Net, the Web site for ZD Publications (www.zdnet.com), including *PC Magazine*, *PC Week*, *PC Computing*, *Macworld*, *Inter@ctive week*, and *Computer Shopper*.

2. The Web sites of companies like Microsoft, Sun Microsystems, Lotus, IBM, Apple Computer, and Oracle are good sources of information about computer software developments.

3. Ascent Solutions Inc., http://www.ascentsolutionsus.com/erp.htm.

4. Citrix i-Business Report. "Achieving Business Transformation through Application Service Providers." *Business Communications Review*, May 3, 2002.

5. Iyer, Bala; Jim Freedman; Mark Gaynor; and George Wyner. "Web Services: Enabling Dynamic Business Networks." *Communications of the Association for Information Systems* 11, 2003.

6. Gonsalves, A. "At Orbitz, Linux Delivers Double the Performance at One-Tenth the Cost." *InternetWeek.com*, July 1, 2003.

7. Mearian, Lucas. "Fidelity Makes Big XML Conversion." *Computerworld*, October 1, 2001.

8. Microsoft Corporation, "Introducing the Windows 2003 Family," www.microsoft.com, July 1, 2003.

9. Oracle Corporation, "Visa to Save Millions a Year by Automating Back-Office Processes with Oracle E-Business Suite," Customer Profile, www.oracle.com, September 13, 2002.

10. Orbitz Corporate, http://www.orbitz.com/App/about/about.jsp?z=63z0&r=42.

11. Sliwa, Carol. ".Net vs. Java." *Computerworld*, May 20, 2002.

12. Smith, T. "How Web Services Help Wells Fargo Customers." *InternetWeek*, May 13, 2003.

13. Transchannel, LLC., "Transchannel Announces ie2 for People-Soft," http://www.prnewswire.com/, 2002.

14. Vogelstein, Fred. "Servers with a Smile." *Fortune*, September 30, 2002.

15. Wainewright, Ivan. "An Introduction to Application Service Providers (ASPs)." *TechSoup*, May 1, 2000.

Chapter 5—Data Resource Management

1. Amato-McCoy, D. "Enterprise Data Solution Finds a Home at BofA." *Financial Technology Network*, http://www.financetech.com/story/BNK/BNK20021210S0030, December 10, 2002.

2. Fox, Pimm. "Extracting Dollars from Data." *Computerworld*, April 15, 2002.

3. Jacobsen, Ivar; Maria Ericsson; and Ageneta Jacobsen. *The Object Advantage: Business Process Reengineering with Object Technology*. New York: ACM Press, 1995.

4. Weiss, Todd. "IBM to Play Lead Role in Creation of Global Film Database," *Computerworld*, September 3, 2003.

5. IBM Corporation, "DB2 Business Intelligence," www.ibm.com, July 27, 2003.

6. Kalakota, Ravi; and Marcia Robinson. *E-Business 2.0: Roadmap for Success*. Reading, MA: Addison-Wesley, 2002.

7. Sullivan, Laurie. "Lucasfilm Linking Movies, Games, Animation with IT," *InformationWeek*, August 7, 2006.

8. Lorents, Alden; and James Morgan. *Database Systems: Concepts, Management and Applications*. Fort Worth, TX: Dryden Press, 1998.

9. MacSweeney, G. "Aetna Mines Ethnic Health Data." *InsuranceTech*, April 1, 2003.

10. Mannino, Michael. *Database Application Development and Design*. Burr Ridge, IL: McGraw-Hill/Irwin, 2001.

11. Nance, Barry. "Managing Tons of Data." *Computerworld*, April 23, 2001.

12. Whiting, Rick. "The Data-Warehouse Advantage," *InformationWeek*, July 28, 2003.

Chapter 6—Telecommunications and Networks

1. Armor, Daniel. *The E-Business (R)Evolution: Living and Working in an Interconnected World*. Upper Saddle River, NJ: Prentice Hall, 2000.

2. Barksdale, Jim. "The Next Step: Extranets." *Netscape Columns: The Main Thing*, December 3, 1996.

3. "Boeing 777: A Case Study," http://www.eweek.org/2002/nbm/collaborate/collab01.html, n.d.

4. Bresnick, Alan. "Verizon Turns Up Heat in Online Data Wars." *Cable Datacom News*, June 1, 2003.

5. "Cable Modem Info Center," www.cabledatacomnews.com, July 26, 2003.

6. McGee, Marianne Kolbasuk. "Constellation Energy Use IT to Get Employees Working Together and More Productively." *InformationWeek*, September 12, 2006.

7. Chatterjee, Samir. "Requirements for Success in Gigabit Networking." *Communications of the ACM*, July 1997.

8. "Countrywide Home Loans Uses Netscape Platform to Develop Extensive Internet and Intranet Solutions." Netscape Corporate Public Relations Press Release, August 15, 1996.

9. Cronin, Mary. *Doing More Business on the Internet*. New York: Van Nostrand Reinhold, 1995.

10. www.internetworldstats.com, February 19, 2007.

11. Friedman, Matthew. "SSL VPNs Will Grow 54% a Year, Become Defacto Access Standard: Report. *InformationWeek*, January 5, 2005.

12. Housel, Thomas; and Eric Skopec. *Global Telecommunications Revolution: The Business Perspective*. New York: McGraw-Hill/Irwin, 2001.

13. Garevy, Martin J. "Threats Bring IT and Operations Together." *InformationWeek*, September 19, 2005.

14. Kalakota, Ravi; and Marcia Robinson. *E-Business 2.0: Roadmap for Success*. Reading, MA: Addison-Wesley, 2001.

15. Lais, Sami. "Satellites Link Bob Evans Farms." *Computerworld*, July 2, 2001.

16. Messerschmitt, David. *Network Applications: A Guide to the New Computing Infrastructure*. San Francisco: Morgan Kaufmann, 1999.

17. Murphy, Kate. "Cruising the Net in Hyperdrive." *BusinessWeek*, January 24, 2000.

18. Norris, G., "Boeing's Seventh Wonder," *IEEE Spectrum*, http://www.spectrum.ieee.org/publicaccess/1095b777.html, 1995.

19. O'Brien, Atiye. "Friday Intranet Focus." Upside.com: Hot Private Companies. Upside, 1996.

20. Orenstein, David. "Price, Speed, Location All Part of Broadband Choice." *Computerworld*, July 26, 1999.

21. Papows, Jeff. "Endquotes." NetReady Adviser, Winter 1997.

22. "Snap-On Tools Company Uses Netscape Software for Extranet Solution." Netscape Corporate Public Relations Press Release, March 6, 1997.

23. Hamblen, Matthew. "Carriers See Big Growth in IP-based VPN Services." *Computerworld*, January 6, 2005.

24. Stuart, Anne. "Cutting the Cord." *Inc. Tech*, March 2001.

25. UPS corporate Web site, "About UPS," http://www.ups.com/content/us/en/about/index.html, n.d.

26. Farber, Dan. "UPS Takes Wireless to the Next Level." ZDNet Tech Update, http://techupdate.zdnet.com/techupdate/stories/main/0,14179,2913461,00.html, February 19, 2007.

27. Gonsalves, Antone. "Seaport Hotel In-Room Portal Converges Voice, Web Services." *InformationWeek*, January 24, 2007.

Chapter 7—Electronic Business Systems

1. "Baker Tanks Leverages salesforce.com's Wireless Access to Extend Range of Customer Service." Salesforce.com, 2002.

2. Afuah, Allan; and Christopher Tucci. *Internet Business Models and Strategies*. New York: McGraw-Hill/Irwin, 2001.

3. Clark, Charles; Nancy Cavanaugh; Carol Brown; and V. Sambamurthy. "Building Change-Readiness Capabilities in the IS Organization: Insights from the Bell Atlantic Experience." *MIS Quarterly*, December 1997.

4. Cole-Gomolski, Barb. "Users Loath to Share Their Know-How." *Computerworld*, November 17, 1997.

5. Collett, S. "SAP: Whirlpool's Rush to Go Live Leads to Shipping Snafus." *Computerworld*, November 4, 1999.

6. "Communications Leader Becomes Customer-Focused E-Business," *Siebel.com*, March 12, 2001.

7. Cronin, Mary. *The Internet Strategy Handbook*. Boston: Harvard Business School Press, 1996.

8. Cross, John; Michael Earl; and Jeffrey Sampler. "Transformation of the IT Function at British Petroleum." *MIS Quarterly*, December 1997.

9. Das, Sidhartha; Shaker Zahra; and Merrill Warkentin. "Integrating the Content and Process of Strategic MIS Planning with Competitive Strategy." *Decision Sciences Journal*, November–December 1991.

10. De Geus, Arie. "Planning as Learning." *Harvard Business Review*, March–April 1988.

11. Earl, Michael. "Experiences in Strategic Information Systems Planning." *MIS Quarterly*, March 1993.

12. El Sawy, Omar; and Gene Bowles. "Redesigning the Customer Support Process for the Electronic Economy: Insights from Storage Dimensions." *MIS Quarterly*, December 1997.

13. Gates, Bill. *Business @ the Speed of Thought*. New York: Warner Books, 1999.

14. Grover, Varun; James Teng; and Kirk Fiedler. "IS Investment Priorities in Contemporary Organizations." *Communications of the ACM*, February 1998.

15. Hawson, James; and Jesse Beeler. "Effects of User Participation in Systems Development: A Longitudinal Field Experiment." *MIS Quarterly*, December 1997.

16. Hoffman, Thomas. "Intranet Helps Workers Navigate Corporate Maze." *Computerworld*, June 4, 2001.

17. Kettinger, William; James Teng; and Subashish Guha. "Business Process Change: A Study of Methodologies, Techniques, and Tools." *MIS Quarterly*, March 1997.

18. Kalakota, Ravi; and Marcia Robinson, *E-Business 2.0: Roadmap for Success*. Reading, MA: Addison-Wesley, 2001.

19. Keen, Peter; and Craigg Ballance. *Online Profits: A Manager's Guide to Electronic Commerce*. Boston: Harvard Business School Press, 1997.

20. Koudsi, Suzanne. "Actually, It Is Like Brain Surgery." *Fortune*, March 20, 2000.

21. KPMG Case Study. "Think Different: Apple Americas Transforms Its US Business with SAP/R3 in Just Twelve Months." 1999.

22. Levinson, M. "Cleared for Takeoff." *CIO*, April 1, 2002.

23. Martin, Chuck. *The Digital Estate: Strategies for Competing, Surviving, and Thriving in an Internetworked World*. New York: McGraw-Hill, 1997.

24. Orenstein, David. "Enterprise Application Integration." *Computerworld*, October 4, 1999.

25. Robb, Drew. "Rediscovering Efficiency." *Computerworld*, July 16, 2001.

26. Sawhney, Mohan, and Jeff Zabin. *The Seven Steps to Nirvana: Strategic Insights into e-Business Transformation*. New York: McGraw-Hill, 2001.

Chapter 8—Electronic Commerce Systems

1. Armor, Daniel. The *E-Business (R)Evolution: Living and Working in an Interconnected World*. Upper Saddle River, NJ: Prentice Hall, 2000.

2. Cross, Kim. "Need Options? Go Configure." *Business 2.0*, February 2000.

3. Davis, Jeffrey. "How IT Works." *Business 2.0*, February 2000.

4. Davis, Jeffrey. "Mall Rats." *Business 2.0*, January 1999.

5. Essex, David. "Betting on Win 2K." *Computerworld*, February 26, 2001.

6. Enterasys Company Info., http://www.enterasys.com/corporate, n.d.

7. Fellenstein, Craig; and Ron Wood. *Exploring E-Commerce, Global E-Business, and E-Societies*. Upper Saddle River, NJ: Prentice Hall, 2000.

8. Fingar, Peter; Harsha Kumar; and Tarun Sharma. *Enterprise E-Commerce*. Tampa, FL: Meghan-Kiffer Press, 2000.

9. Georgia, Bonnie. "Give Your E-Store an Edge." *Smart Business*, October 2001.

10. Gulati, Ranjay; and Jason Garino. "Get the Right Mix of Clicks and Bricks." *Harvard Business Review*, May–June 2000.

11. Hoque, Faisal. *E-Enterprise: Business Models, Architecture and Components*. Cambridge, UK: Cambridge University Press, 2000.

12. Kalakota, Ravi; and Marcia Robinson. *E-Business 2.0: Roadmap for Success*. Reading, MA: Addison-Wesley, 2001.

13. Kalakota, Ravi; and Andrew Whinston. *Electronic Commerce: A Manager's Guide*. Reading, MA: Addison-Wesley, 1997.

14. Keenan, Faith; and Timothy Mullaney. "Let's Get Back to Basics." *BusinessWeek e.biz*, October 29, 2001.

15. Leon, Mark. "Trading Spaces." *Business 2.0*, February 2000.

16. May, Paul. *The Business of E-Commerce: From Corporate Strategy to Technology*. Cambridge, UK: Cambridge University Press, 2001.

17. Microsoft IT Showcase, "MS Market: Business Case Study," http://download.microsoft.com/download/6/5/9/659955d7-0cb7-42b6-8e78-daf1e9c49a75/MSMarketBCS.doc, 2002.

18. Morgan, Cynthia. "Dead Set against SET?" *Computerworld*, March 29, 1999.

19. Nesdore, P., "Customer Relationship Management: Getting Personal," *e-commerceIQ.com*, http://www.ecommerceiq.com/special_interests/crm/80-eCommerceIQ_crm.html, 2003.

20. "Pay-Per-Click Marketing," http://www.pay-per-click-adwords.com/pay-per-click-adwords.html, n.d.

21. Rayport, Jeffrey; and Bernard Jaworski. *Introduction to e-Commerce*. New York: McGraw-Hill/Irwin, 2001.

22. Riley, M.; S. Laiken; and J. Williams; "Digital Business Designs in Financial Services," Mercer Management Consulting Commentary, http://www.mercermc.com/Perspectives/WhitePapers/Commentaries/Comm00DBDinFinancialServices.pdf, 2002.

23. Rosenoer, Jonathan; Douglas Armstrong; and J. Russell Gates. *The Clickable Corporation: Successful Strategies for Capturing the Internet Advantage*. New York: The Free Press, 1999.

24. "Servers with a Smile." *Fortune*, Technology Buyers Guide, Summer 2000.

25. Seybold, Patricia; with Ronnie Marshak. *Customers. Com: How to Create a Profitable Business Strategy for the Internet and Beyond*. New York: Times Business, 1998.

26. Sliwa, Carol. "Users Cling to EDI for Critical Transactions." *Computerworld*, March 15, 1999.

27. "Tech Lifestyles: Shopping." *Fortune*, Technology Buyers Guide, Winter 2001.

28. "Telefónica Servicios Avanzados De Informació Leads Spain's Retail Industry into Global Electronic Commerce," www.netscape.com/solutions/business/profiles, March 1999.

29. Young, Eric. "Web Marketplaces That Really Work." *Fortune/CNET Tech Review*, Winter 2002.

Chapter 9—Decision Support Systems

1. "AmeriKing," Customer Profile, Plumtree.com, October 25, 2002.

2. Ashline, Peter; and Vincent Lai. "Virtual Reality: An Emerging User-Interface Technology." *Information Systems Management*, Winter 1995.

3. Beacon Analytics Case Study, "Analyzing Key Measures in a Retail Environment," http://www.beaconus.com/downloads/Beacon%20Case%20Study-The%20GAP.pdf, 2003.

4. Begley, Sharon. "Software au Naturel." *Newsweek*, May 8, 1995.

5. Belcher, Lloyd; and Hugh Watson. "Assessing the Value of Conoco's EIS." *MIS Quarterly*, September 1993.

6. Bioluminate Inc. Press Release, "Bioluminate to Develop 'Smart Probe' for Early Breast Cancer Detection," http://www.bioluminate.com/press_rel1.html, December 5, 2000.

7. Bose, Ranjit; and Vijayan Sugumaran. "Application of Intelligent Agent Technology for Managerial Data Analysis and Mining." *The Data Base for Advances in Information Systems*, Winter 1999.

8. Botchner, Ed. "Data Mining: Plumbing the Depths of Corporate Databases." *Computerworld*, Special Advertising Supplement, April 21, 1997.

9. Brown, Eryn. "Slow Road to Fast Data." *Fortune*, March 18, 2002.

10. Brown, Stuart. "Making Decisions in a Flood of Data." *Fortune*, August 13, 2001.

11. Bylinsky, Gene. "The e-Factory Catches On." *Fortune*, August 13, 2001.

12. Cox, Earl. "Relational Database Queries Using Fuzzy Logic." *AI Expert*, January 1995.

13. Darling, Charles. "Ease Implementation Woes with Packaged Datamarts." *Datamation*, March 1997.

14. Deck, Stewart. "Data Visualization." *Computerworld*, October 11, 1999.

15. Deck, Stewart. "Data Warehouse Project Starts Simply." *Computerworld*, February 15, 1999.

16. Deck, Stewart. "Early Users Give Nod to Analysis Package." *Computerworld*, February 22, 1999.

17. Freeman, Eva. "Desktop Reporting Tools." *Datamation*, June 1997.

18. Gantz, John. "The New World of Enterprise Reporting Is Here." *Computerworld*, February 1, 1999.

19. "GAP, Inc. at a Glance," http://www.gapinc.com/about/At_A_Glance.pdf, Summer 2004.

20. Glode, M. "Scans: Most Valuable Player." *Wired Magazine*, July 22, 1997.

21. Goldberg, David. "Genetic and Evolutionary Algorithms Come of Age." *Communications of the ACM*, March 1994.

22. Gorry, G. Anthony; and Michael Scott Morton. "A Framework for Management Information Systems." *Sloan Management Review*, Fall 1971; republished Spring 1989.

23. Hall, Mark. "Get Real." *Computerworld*, April 1, 2002.

24. Hall, Mark. "Supercomputing: From R&D to P&L." *Computerworld*, December 13, 1999.

25. Hoffman, Thomas. "In the Know." *Computerworld*, October 14, 2002.

26. Jablonowski, Mark. "Fuzzy Risk Analysis: Using AI Systems." *AI Expert*, December 1994.

27. Kalakota, Ravi; and Marcia Robinson. *E-Business 2.0: Roadmap for Success*. Reading, MA: Addison-Wesley, 2001.

28. Kalakota, Ravi; and Andrew Whinston. *Electronic Commerce: A Manager's Guide*. Reading, MA: Addison-Wesley, 1997.

29. King, Julia. "Sharing GIS Talent with the World." *Computerworld*, October 6, 1997.

30. Kurszweil, Raymond. *The Age of Intelligent Machines*. Cambridge, MA: The MIT Press, 1992.

31. Lundquist, Christopher. "Personalization in E-Commerce." *Computerworld*, March 22, 1999.

32. Machlis, Sharon. "Agent Technology." *Computerworld*, March 22, 1999.

33. Mailoux, Jacquiline. "New Menu at PepsiCo." *Computerworld*, May 6, 1996.

34. McNeill, F. Martin; and Ellen Thro. *Fuzzy Logic: A Practical Approach*. Boston: AP Professional, 1994.

35. Mitchell, Lori. "Enterprise Knowledge Portals Wise Up Your Business." *Infoworld.com*, December 2000.

36. Murray, Gerry. "Making Connections with Enterprise Knowledge Portals." White Paper. *Computerworld*, September 6, 1999.

37. "NASA Ames Research Center Report," Smart Surgical Probe, Bioluminate Inc., http://technology.arc.nasa.gov/success/probe.html, 2003.

38. Norsk Hydro Corporate Background, http://www.hydro.com/en/about/index.html, 2004.

39. Orenstein, David. "Corporate Portals." *Computerworld*, June 28, 1999.

40. Ouellette, Tim. "Opening Your Own Portal." *Computerworld*, August 9, 1999.

41. Pimentel, Ken; and Kevin Teixeira. *Virtual Reality through the New Looking Glass*. 2nd ed. New York: Intel/McGraw-Hill, 1995.

42. Rosenberg, Marc. *e-Learning: Strategies for Delivering Knowledge in the Digital Age*. New York: McGraw-Hill, 2001.

43. Schlumberger Information Solutions, "Norsk Hydro Makes a Valuable Drilling Decision," Schlumberger Technical Report GMP-5911, http://www.sis.slb.com/media/software/success/ir_drillingdecision.pdf, 2002.

44. Shay, S. "Trendlines." *CIO Magazine*, February 1, 1998.

45. Turban, Efraim; and Jay Aronson. *Decision Support Systems and Intelligent Systems*. Upper Saddle River, NJ: Prentice Hall, 1998.

46. Vandenbosch, Betty; and Sid Huff. "Searching and Scanning: How Executives Obtain Information from Executive Information Systems." *MIS Quarterly*, March 1997.

47. Wagner, Mitch. "Reality Check." *Computerworld*, February 26, 1997.

48. Watson, Hugh; and John Satzinger. "Guidelines for Designing EIS Interfaces." *Information Systems Management*, Fall 1994.

49. Watterson, Karen. "Parallel Tracks." *Datamation*, May 1997.

50. Winston, Patrick. "Rethinking Artificial Intelligence." Program Announcement, Massachusetts Institute of Technology, September 1997.

51. Wreden, Nick. "Enterprise Portals: Integrating Information to Drive Productivity." *Beyond Computing*, March 2000.

Chapter 10—Developing Business/IT Solutions

1. Anthes, Gary. "The Quest for IT E-Quality." *Computerworld*, December 13, 1999.

2. Clark, Charles; Nancy Cavanaugh; Carol Brown; and V. Sambamurthy. "Building Change-Readiness Capabilities in the IS Organization: Insights from the Bell Atlantic Experience." *MIS Quarterly*, December 1997.

3. Cole-Gomolski, Barbara. "Companies Turn to Web for ERP Training." *Computerworld*, February 8, 1999.

4. Cole-Gomolski, Barbara. "Users Loath to Share Their Know-How." *Computerworld*, November 17, 1997.

5. Cronin, Mary. *The Internet Strategy Handbook*. Boston: Harvard Business School Press, 1996.

6. Diese, Martin; Conrad Nowikow; Patrick King; and Amy Wright. *Executive's Guide to E-Business: From Tactics to Strategy*. New York: John Wiley & Sons, 2000.

7. "Design Matters." *Fortune*, Technology Buyers Guide, Winter 2001.

8. Casey, Susan. "On the Hot Seat." *Fortune*, January 22, 2007.

9. Hawson, James; and Jesse Beeler. "Effects of User Participation in Systems Development: A Longitudinal Field Experiment." *MIS Quarterly*, December 1997.

10. Hills, Melanie. *Intranet Business Strategies*. New York: John Wiley & Sons, 1997.

11. Kalakota, Ravi; and Marcia Robinson. *E-Business 2.0: Roadmap for Success*. Reading, MA: Addison-Wesley, 2001.

12. King, Julia. "Back to Basics." *Computerworld*, April 22, 2002.

13. Lazar, Jonathan. *User-Centered Web Development*. Sudbury, MA: Jones and Bartlett, 2001.

14. McDonnel, Sharon. "Putting CRM to Work." *Computerworld*, March 12, 2001.

15. Melymuka, Kathleen. "An Expanding Universe." *Computerworld*, September 14, 1998.

16. Melymuka, Kathleen. "Energizing the Company." *Computerworld*, August 13, 2001.

17. Melymuka, Kathleen. "Profiting from Mistakes." *Computerworld*, April 20, 2001.

18. Morgan, James N. *Application Cases in MIS*. 4th ed. New York: Irwin/McGraw-Hill, 2002.

19. Neilsen, Jakob. "Better Data Brings Better Sales." *Business 2.0*, May 15, 2001.

20. Nielsen, Jakob. "Design for Process, Not for Products." *Business 2.0*, July 10, 2001.

21. Orenstein, David. "Software Is Too Hard to Use." *Computerworld*, August 23, 1999.

22. Ouellette, Tim. "Giving Users the Key to Their Web Content." *Computerworld*, July 26, 1999.

23. Ouellette, Tim. "Opening Your Own Portal." *Computerworld*, August 9, 1999.

24. Panko, R. "Application Development: Finding Spreadsheet Errors." *InformationWeek*, May 29, 1995.

25. Panko, R. "What We Know about Spreadsheet Errors." *Journal of End-User Computing* 10, no. 2, 1998, pp. 15–21.

26. Schwartz, Matthew. "Time for a Makeover." *Computerworld*, August 19, 2002.

27. Senge, Peter. *The Fifth Discipline: The Art and Practice of the Learning Organization*. New York: Currency Doubleday, 1994.

28. Sliwa, Carol. "E-Commerce Solutions: How Real?" *Computerworld*, February 28, 2000.

29. Solomon, Melissa. "Filtering Out the Noise." *Computerworld*, February 25, 2002.

30. Songini, Marc. "GM Locomotive Unit Puts ERP Rollout Back on Track." *Computerworld*, February 11, 2002.

31. Steinert-Thelkeld, Tom. "Aviall Thinks Outside the Box." *Baseline*, January 17, 2003.

32. Whitten, Jeffrey, and Lonnie Bentley. *Systems Analysis and Design Methods*. 5th ed. New York: McGraw-Hill/Irwin, 2000.

Chapter 11—Security and Ethical Challenges

1. Alexander, Steve, and Matt Hamblen. "Top-Flight Technology." *Computerworld*, September 23, 2002.

2. Anthes, Gary. "Biometrics." *Computerworld*, October 12, 1998.

3. Anthes, Gary. "When Five 9s Aren't Enough." *Computerworld*, October 8, 2001.

4. Berniker, M., "Study: ID Theft Often Goes Unrecognized," *Internetnews.com*, http://www.internetnews.com/ecnews/article.php/3081881, 2003.

5. Boutin, Paul. "Burn Baby Burn." *Wired*, December 2002.

6. Deckmyn, Dominique. "More Managers Monitor E-Mail." *Computerworld*, October 18, 1999.

7. Dejoie, Roy; George Fowler; and David Paradice, eds. *Ethical Issues in Information Systems*. Boston: Boyd & Fraser, 1991.

8. Donaldson, Thomas. "Values in Tension: Ethics Away from Home." *Harvard Business Review*, September–October 1996.

9. Dunlop, Charles; and Rob Kling, eds. *Computerization and Controversy: Value Conflicts and Social Choices*. San Diego: Academic Press, 1991.

10. Elias, Paul. "Paid Informant." *Red Herring*, January 16, 2001.

11. Harrison, Ann. "Virus Scanning Moving to ISPs." *Computerworld*, September 20, 1999.

12. "In Depth: Security." *Computerworld*, July 9, 2001.

13. Joy, Bill. "Report from the Cyberfront." *Newsweek*, February 21, 2000.

14. Johnson, Deborah. "Ethics Online." *Communications of the ACM*, January 1997.

15. Lardner, James. "Why Should Anyone Believe You?" *Business 2.0*, March 2002.

16. Levy, Stephen; and Brad Stone. "Hunting the Hackers." *Newsweek*, February 21, 2000.

17. Madsen, Peter; and Jay Shafritz. *Essentials of Business Ethics*. New York: Meridian, 1990.

18. McCarthy, Michael. "Keystroke Cops." *The Wall Street Journal*, March 7, 2000.

19. Nance, Barry. "Sending Firewalls Home." *Computerworld*, May 28, 2001.

20. Naughton, Keith. "CyberSlacking." *Newsweek*, November 29, 1999.

21. Neumann, Peter. *Computer-Related Risks*. New York: ACM Press, 1995.

22. Phillips, Robert. *Stakeholder Theory and Organizational Ethics*. San Francisco: Berrett-Koehler, 2003.

23. Radcliff, Deborah. "Cybersleuthing Solves the Case." *Computerworld*, January 14, 2002.

24. Robinson, Lori. "How It Works: Viruses." *Smart Computing*, March 2000.

25. Rothfeder, Jeffrey. "Hacked! Are Your Company Files Safe?" *PC World*, November 1996.

26. Rothfeder, Jeffrey. "No Privacy on the Net." *PC World*, February 1997.

27. Sager, Ira; Steve Hamm; Neil Gross; John Carey; and Robert Hoff. "Cyber Crime." *BusinessWeek*, February 21, 2000.

28. Schoepke, P., and G. Milner, "Phishing Scams Increase 180% in April Alone!" *BankersOnline.com*, http://www.bankersonline.com/technology/tech_phishing052404.html, 2004.

29. Smith, H. Jefferson; and John Hasnas. "Debating the Stakeholder Theory." *Beyond Computing*, March–April 1994.

30. Smith, H. Jefferson; and John Hasnas. "Establishing an Ethical Framework." *Beyond Computing*, January–February 1994.

31. Solomon, Melissa; and Michael Meehan. "Enron Lesson: Tech Is for Support." *Computerworld*, February 18, 2002.

32. Spinello, Richard. *Cyberethics: Morality and Law in Cyberspace*. 2nd ed. Sudbury, MA: Jones and Bartlett, 2003.

33. Sullivan, B. "ID Theft Victims Face Tough Bank Fights." MSNBC.com, http://msnbc.msn.com/id/4264051/, 2004.

34. Verton, Dan. "Insider Monitoring Seen as Next Wave in IT Security." *Computerworld*, March 19, 2001.

35. VanScoy, Kayte. "What Your Workers Are Really Up To." *Ziff Davis Smart Business*, September 2001.

36. Vijayan, Jaikumar. "Nimda Needs Harsh Disinfectant." *Computerworld*, September 24, 2001.

37. Vijayan, Jaikumar. "Securing the Center." *Computerworld*, May 13, 2002.

38. Willard, Nancy. *The Cyberethics Reader*. Burr Ridge, IL: Irwin/McGraw-Hill, 1997.

39. York, Thomas. "Invasion of Privacy? E-Mail Monitoring Is on the Rise." *InformationWeek Online*, February 21, 2000.

40. Youl, T. "Phishing Scams: Understanding the Latest Trends." *FraudWatch International*, White Paper, 2004.

41. Commtouch Press Release, February 15, 2006. http://www.commtouch.com/Site/News_Events/pr_content.asp? news_id=602&cat_id=1.

Chapter 12—Enterprise and Global Management of Information Technology

1. Bryan, Lowell; Jane Fraser; Jeremy Oppenheim; and Wilhelm Rall. *Race for the World: Strategies to Build a Great Global Firm*. Boston: Harvard Business School Press, 1999.

2. Christensen, Clayton. *The Innovators Dilemma: When New Technologies Cause Great Firms to Fail*. Boston: Harvard Business School Press, 1997.

3. Cronin, Mary. *Global Advantage on the Internet*. New York: Van Nostrand Reinhold, 1996.

4. "Delta Signs Offshore Call Center Agreement." *South Florida Business Journal*, October 7, 2002.

5. El Sawy, Omar; Arvind Malhotra; Sanjay Gosain; and Kerry Young. "IT-Intensive Value Innovation in the Electronic Economy: Insights from Marshall Industries." *MIS Quarterly*, September 1999.

6. Gilhooly, Kym. "The Staff That Never Sleeps." *Computerworld*, June 25, 2001.

7. Grover, Varun; James Teng; and Kirk Fiedler. "IS Investment Opportunities in Contemporary Organizations." *Communications of the ACM*, February 1998.

8. Hall, Mark. "Service Providers Give Users More IT Options." *Computerworld*, February 7, 2000.

9. Ives, Blake, and Sirkka Jarvenpaa. "Applications of Global Information Technology: Key Issues for Management." *MIS Quarterly*, March 1991.

10. Kalakota, Ravi, and Marcia Robinson. *E-Business 2.0: Roadmap for Success*. Reading, MA: Addison-Wesley, 2001.

11. Kalin, Sari. "The Importance of Being Multiculturally Correct." Global Innovators Series, *Computerworld*, October 6, 1997.

12. Kirkpatrick, David. "Back to the Future with Centralized Computing." *Fortune*, November 10, 1997.

13. LaPlante, Alice. "Global Boundaries.com." Global Innovators Series, *Computerworld*, October 6, 1997.

14. Leinfuss, Emily. "Blend It, Mix It, Unify It." *Computerworld*, March 26, 2001.

15. McDougall, P. "Opportunity on the Line." *InformationWeek*, October 20, 2003.

16. Mearian, Lucas. "Citibank Overhauls Overseas Systems." *Computerworld*, February 4, 2002.

17. Mische, Michael. "Transnational Architecture: A Reengineering Approach." *Information Systems Management*, Winter 1995.

18. Palvia, Prashant; Shailendra Palvia; and Edward Roche, eds. *Global Information Technology and Systems Management*. Marietta, GA: Ivy League, 1996.

19. Radcliff, Deborah. "Playing by Europe's Rules." *Computerworld*, July 9, 2001.

20. Ross, Jeanne; and Peter Weill. "Six IT Decisions Your IT People Shouldn't Make." *Harvard Business Review*, November 2002.

21. Songini, Marc; and Kim Nash. "Try, Try Again." *Computerworld*, February 18, 2002.

22. Thibodeau, Patrick. "Europe and U.S. Agree on Data Rules." *Computerworld*, March 20, 2000.

23. Vitalari, Nicholas; and James Wetherbe. "Emerging Best Practices in Global Systems Development." In *Global Information Technology and Systems Management*, ed. Prashant Palvia et al. Marietta, GA: Ivy League, 1996.

24. West, Lawrence; and Walter Bogumil. "Immigration and the Global IT Workforce." *Communications of the ACM*, July 2001.

25. Reporters Without Borders. "The 15 Enemies of the Internet and Other Countries to Watch." www.rsf.org. November, 17, 2005.

Accounting Information Systems Information systems that record and report business transactions and the flow of funds through an organization, and then produce financial statements. These statements provide information for the planning and control of business operations, as well as for legal and historical recordkeeping.

Ada A programming language named after Augusta Ada Byron, considered the world's first computer programmer. Developed for the U.S. Department of Defense as a standard high-order language.

Ad Hoc Inquiries Unique, unscheduled, situation-specific information requests.

Agile Competition The ability of a company to operate profitably in a competitive environment of continual and unpredictable changes in customer preferences, market conditions, and business opportunities.

Algorithm A set of well-defined rules or processes for solving a problem in a finite number of steps.

Analog Computer A computer that operates on data by measuring changes in continuous physical variables such as voltage, resistance, and rotation. Contrast with Digital Computer.

Analytical Database A database of data extracted from operational and external databases to provide data tailored to online analytical processing, decision support, and executive information systems.

Analytical Modeling Interactive use of computer-based mathematical models to explore decision alternatives using what-if analysis, sensitivity analysis, goal-seeking analysis, and optimization analysis.

Applet A small, limited-purpose application program or small, independent module of a larger application program.

Application Development See Systems Development.

Application Generator A software package that supports the development of an application through an interactive terminal dialogue, where the programmer/analyst defines screens, reports, computations, and data structures.

Application Portfolio A planning tool used to evaluate present and proposed information systems applications in terms of the amount of revenue or assets invested in information systems that support major business functions and processes.

Applications Architecture A conceptual planning framework in which business applications of information technology are designed as an integrated architecture of enterprise systems that support strategic business initiatives and cross-functional business processes.

Application Server System software that provides a middleware interface between an operating system and the application programs of users.

Application Software Programs that specify the information processing activities required for the completion of specific tasks of computer users. Examples are electronic spreadsheet and word processing programs or inventory or payroll programs.

Application-Specific Programs Application software packages that support specific applications of end users in business, science and engineering, and other areas.

Arithmetic-Logic Unit (ALU) The unit of a computing system containing the circuits that perform arithmetic and logical operations.

Artificial Intelligence (AI) A science and technology whose goal is to develop computers that can think, as well as see, hear, walk, talk, and feel. A major thrust is the development of computer functions normally associated with human intelligence, for example, reasoning, inference, learning, and problem solving.

ASCII: American Standard Code for Information Interchange A standard code used for information interchange among data processing systems, communication systems, and associated equipment.

Assembler A computer program that translates an assembler language into machine language.

Assembler Language A programming language that utilizes symbols to represent operation codes and storage locations.

Asynchronous A sequence of operations without a regular or predictable time relationship. Thus, operations do not happen at regular timed intervals, but an operation will begin only after a previous operation is completed. The data transmission involves the use of start and stop bits with each character to indicate the beginning and end of the character being transmitted. Contrast with Synchronous.

Audit Trail The presence of media and procedures that allow a transaction to be traced through all stages of information processing, beginning with its appearance on a source document and ending with its transformation into information in a final output document.

Automated Teller Machine (ATM) A special-purpose transaction terminal used to provide remote banking services.

Back-End Processor Typically, a smaller, general-purpose computer dedicated to database processing using a database management system (DBMS). Also called a database machine or server.

Background Processing The automatic execution of lower-priority computer programs when higher-priority programs are not using the resources of the computer system. Contrast with Foreground Processing.

Backward-Chaining An inference process that justifies a proposed conclusion by determining if it will result when rules are applied to the facts in a given situation.

Bandwidth The frequency range of a telecommunications channel, which determines its maximum transmission rate. The speed and capacity of transmission rates are typically measured in bits per second (bps). Bandwidth is a function of the telecommunications hardware, software, and media used by the telecommunications channel.

Bar Codes   Vertical marks or bars placed on merchandise tags or packaging that can be sensed and read by optical character-reading devices. The width and combination of vertical lines are used to represent data.

Barriers to Entry   Technological, financial, or legal requirements that deter firms from entering an industry.

BASIC: Beginner's All-Purpose Symbolic Instruction Code   A programming language developed at Dartmouth College and designed for programming by end users.

Batch Processing   A category of data processing in which data are accumulated into batches and processed periodically. Contrast with Real-Time Processing.

Baud   A unit of measurement used to specify data transmission speeds. It is a unit of signaling speed equal to the number of discrete conditions or signal events per second. In many data communications applications, it represents one bit per second.

Binary   Pertaining to a characteristic or property involving a selection, choice, or condition in which there are two possibilities, or pertaining to the number system that utilizes a base of 2.

Biometric Controls   Computer-based security methods that measure physical traits and characteristics such as fingerprints, voice prints, and retina scans.

Bit   A contraction of "binary digit." It can have the value of either 0 or 1.

Block   A grouping of contiguous data records or other data elements that are handled as a unit.

Branch   A transfer of control from one instruction to another in a computer program that is not part of the normal sequential execution of the instructions of the program.

Browser   See Web Browser.

Buffer   Temporary storage used when transmitting data from one device to another to compensate for a difference in rate of flow of data or time of occurrence of events.

Bug   A mistake or malfunction.

Bulletin Board System (BBS)   A service of online computer networks in which electronic messages, data files, or programs can be stored for other subscribers to read or copy.

Bundling   The inclusion of software, maintenance, training, and other products or services in the price of a computer system.

Bus   A set of conducting paths for movement of data and instructions that interconnects the various components of the CPU.

Business Ethics   An area of philosophy concerned with developing ethical principles and promoting ethical behavior and practices in the accomplishment of business tasks and decision making.

Business Intelligence (BI)   A term primarily used in industry that incorporates a range of analytical and decision support applications in business including data mining, decision support systems, knowledge management systems, and online analytical processing.

Business/IT Planning   The process of developing a company's business vision, strategies, and goals, as well as how they will be supported by the company's information technology architecture and implemented by its business application development process.

Business Process Reengineering (BPR)   Restructuring and transforming a business process by a fundamental rethinking and redesign to achieve dramatic improvements in cost, quality, speed, and so on.

Byte   A sequence of adjacent binary digits operated on as a unit and usually shorter than a computer word. In many computer systems, a byte is a grouping of eight bits that can represent one alphabetic or special character or that can be packed with two decimal digits.

C   A low-level structured programming language that resembles a machine-independent assembler language.

C++   An object-oriented version of C that is widely used for software package development.

Cache Memory   A high-speed temporary storage area in the CPU for storing parts of a program or data during processing.

Capacity Management   The use of planning and control methods to forecast and control information processing job loads, hardware and software usage, and other computer system resource requirements.

Case-Based Reasoning   Representing knowledge in an expert system's knowledge base in the form of cases, that is, examples of past performance, occurrences, and experiences.

Cathode Ray Tube (CRT)   An electronic vacuum tube (television picture tube) that displays the output of a computer system.

CD-ROM   An optical disk technology for microcomputers featuring compact disks with a storage capacity of over 500 megabytes.

Cellular Phone Systems   A radio communications technology that divides a metropolitan area into a honeycomb of cells to greatly increase the number of frequencies and thus the users that can take advantage of mobile phone service.

Central Processing Unit (CPU)   The unit of a computer system that includes the circuits that control the interpretation and execution of instructions. In many computer systems, the CPU includes the arithmetic-logic unit, the control unit, and the primary storage unit.

Change Management   Managing the process of implementing major changes in information technology, business processes, organizational structures, and job assignments to reduce the risks and costs of change and optimize its benefits.

Channel   (1) A path along which signals can be sent. (2) A small special-purpose processor that controls the movement of data between the CPU and input/output devices.

Chargeback Systems   Methods of allocating costs to end-user departments on the basis of the information services rendered and information system resources utilized.

Chat Systems   Software that enables two or more users at networked PCs to carry on online, real-time text conversations.

Check Bit   A binary check digit: for example, a parity bit.

Check Digit   A digit in a data field that is utilized to check for errors or loss of characters in the data field as a result of data transfer operations.

Checkpoint A place in a program where a check or a recording of data for restart purposes is performed.

Chief Information Officer A senior management position that oversees all information technology for a firm concentrating on long-range information system planning and strategy.

Client (1) An end user. (2) The end user's networked microcomputer in client/server networks. (3) The version of a software package designed to run on an end user's networked microcomputer, such as a Web browser client and a groupware client.

Client/Server Network A computer network where end-user workstations (clients) are connected via telecommunications links to network servers and possibly to mainframe superservers.

Clock A device that generates periodic signals utilized to control the timing of a computer. Also, a register whose contents change at regular intervals in such a way as to measure time.

Coaxial Cable A sturdy copper or aluminum wire wrapped with spacers to insulate and protect it. Groups of coaxial cables may also be bundled together in a bigger cable for ease of installation.

COBOL: COmmon Business Oriented Language A widely used business data processing programming language.

Code Computer instructions.

Cognitive Science An area of artificial intelligence that focuses on researching how the human brain works and how humans think and learn, to apply such findings to the design of computer-based systems.

Cognitive Styles Basic patterns in how people handle information and confront problems.

Cognitive Theory Theories about how the human brain works and how humans think and learn.

Collaborative Work Management Tools Software that helps people accomplish or manage joint work activities.

Communications Satellite Earth satellites placed in stationary orbits above the equator that serve as relay stations for communications signals transmitted from earth stations.

Competitive Advantage Developing products, services, processes, or capabilities that give a company a superior business position relative to its competitors and other competitive forces.

Competitive Forces A firm must confront (1) rivalry of competitors within its industry, (2) threats of new entrants, (3) threats of substitutes, (4) the bargaining power of customers, and (5) the bargaining power of suppliers.

Competitive Strategies A firm can develop cost leadership, product differentiation, and business innovation strategies to confront its competitive forces.

Compiler A program that translates a high-level programming language into a machine-language program.

Computer A device that has the ability to accept data; internally store and execute a program of instructions; perform mathematical, logical, and manipulative operations on data; and report the results.

Computer-Aided Design (CAD) The use of computers and advanced graphics hardware and software to provide interactive design assistance for engineering and architectural design.

Computer-Aided Engineering (CAE) The use of computers to simulate, analyze, and evaluate models of product designs and production processes developed using computer-aided design methods.

Computer-Aided Manufacturing (CAM) The use of computers to automate the production process and operations of a manufacturing plant. Also called factory automation.

Computer-Aided Planning (CAP) The use of software packages as tools to support the planning process.

Computer-Aided Software Engineering (CASE) Same as Computer-Aided Systems Engineering, but emphasizing the importance of software development.

Computer-Aided Systems Engineering (CASE) Using software packages to accomplish and automate many of the activities of information systems development, including software development or programming.

Computer Application The use of a computer to solve a specific problem or accomplish a particular job for an end user. For example, common business computer applications include sales order processing, inventory control, and payroll.

Computer-Assisted Instruction (CAI) The use of computers to provide drills, practice exercises, and tutorial sequences to students.

Computer-Based Information System An information system that uses computer hardware and software to perform its information processing activities.

Computer Crime Criminal actions accomplished through the use of computer systems, especially with intent to defraud, destroy, or make unauthorized use of computer system resources.

Computer Ethics A system of principles governing the legal, professional, social, and moral responsibilities of computer specialists and end users.

Computer Generations Major stages in the historical development of computing.

Computer Graphics Using computer-generated images to analyze and interpret data, present information, and create computer-aided design and art.

Computer Industry The industry composed of firms that supply computer hardware, software, and services.

Computer-Integrated Manufacturing (CIM) An overall concept that stresses that the goals of computer use in factory automation should be to simplify, automate, and integrate production processes and other aspects of manufacturing.

Computer Matching Using computers to screen and match data about individual characteristics provided by a variety of computer-based information systems and databases to identify individuals for business, government, or other purposes.

Computer Monitoring Using computers to monitor the behavior and productivity of workers on the job and in the workplace.

Computer Program A series of instructions or statements in a form acceptable to a computer, prepared to achieve a certain result.

Computer System Computer hardware as a system of input, processing, output, storage, and control components. Thus, a computer system consists of input and output devices, primary and secondary storage devices, the central processing unit, the control unit within the CPU, and other peripheral devices.

Computer Terminal   Any input/output device connected by telecommunications links to a computer.

Computer Virus or Worm   Program code that copies its destructive program routines into the computer systems of anyone who accesses computer systems that have used the program, or anyone who uses copies of data or programs taken from such computers. This spreads the destruction of data and programs among many computer users. Technically, a virus will not run unaided but must be inserted into another program, whereas a worm is a distinct program that can run unaided.

Concurrent Processing   The generic term for the capability of computers to work on several tasks at the same time, that is, concurrently. This may involve specific capabilities such as overlapped processing, multiprocessing, multiprogramming, multitasking, and parallel processing.

Connectivity   The degree to which hardware, software, and databases can be easily linked together in a telecommunications network.

Control   (1) The systems component that evaluates feedback to determine whether the system is moving toward the achievement of its goal and then makes any necessary adjustments to the input and processing components of the system to ensure that proper output is produced. (2) A management function that involves observing and measuring organizational performance and environmental activities and modifying the plans and activities of the organization when necessary.

Control Listing   A detailed report that describes each transaction occurring during a period.

Control Totals   Accumulating totals of data at multiple points in an information system to ensure correct information processing.

Control Unit   A subunit of the central processing unit that controls and directs the operations of the computer system. The control unit retrieves computer instructions in proper sequence, interprets each instruction, and then directs the other parts of the computer system in their implementation.

Conversion   The process in which the hardware, software, people, network, and data resources of an old information system must be converted to the requirements of a new information system. This usually involves a parallel, phased, pilot, or plunge conversion process from the old to the new system.

Cooperative Processing   Information processing that allows the computers in a distributed processing network to share the processing of parts of an end user's application.

Cost/Benefit Analysis   Identifying the advantages or benefits and the disadvantages or costs of a proposed solution.

Critical Success Factors   A small number of key factors that executives consider critical to the success of the enterprise. These are key areas in which successful performance will assure the success of the organization and attainment of its goals.

Cross-Functional Information Systems   Information systems that are integrated combinations of business information systems, thus sharing information resources across the functional units of an organization.

Cursor   A movable point of light displayed on most video display screens to assist the user in the input of data.

Customer Relationship Management (CRM)   A cross-functional e-business application that integrates and automates many customer serving processes in sales, direct marketing, account and order management, and customer service and support.

Cybernetic System   A system that uses feedback and control components to achieve a self-regulating capability.

Cylinder   An imaginary vertical cylinder consisting of the vertical alignment of tracks on each surface of magnetic disks that are accessed simultaneously by the read/write heads of a disk drive.

Data   Facts or observations about physical phenomena or business transactions. More specifically, data are objective measurements of the attributes (characteristics) of entities such as people, places, things, and events.

Data Administration   A data resource management function that involves the establishment and enforcement of policies and procedures for managing data as a strategic corporate resource.

Database   An integrated collection of logically related data elements. A database consolidates many records previously stored in separate files so that a common pool of data serves many applications.

Database Administration   A data resource management function that includes responsibility for developing and maintaining the organization's data dictionary, designing and monitoring the performance of databases, and enforcing standards for database use and security.

Database Administrator   A specialist responsible for maintaining standards for the development, maintenance, and security of an organization's databases.

Database Maintenance   The activity of keeping a database up to date by adding, changing, or deleting data.

Database Management Approach   An approach to the storage and processing of data in which independent files are consolidated into a common pool, or database, of records available to different application programs and end users for processing and data retrieval.

Database Management System (DBMS)   A set of computer programs that controls the creation, maintenance, and utilization of the databases of an organization.

Database Processing   Utilizing a database for data processing activities such as maintenance, information retrieval, or report generation.

Data Center   An organizational unit that uses centralized computing resources to perform information processing activities for an organization. Also known as a computer center.

Data Conferencing   Users at networked PCs can view, mark up, revise, and save changes to a shared whiteboard of drawings, documents, and other material.

Data Conversion   Converting data into new data formats required by a new business application and its software and databases. Also includes correcting incorrect data, filtering out unwanted data, and consolidating data into new databases and other data subsets.

Data Design   The design of the logical structure of databases and files to be used by a proposed information system. This design produces detailed descriptions of the entities, relationships, data elements, and integrity rules for system files and databases.

Data Dictionary   A software module and database containing descriptions and definitions concerning the structure, data elements, interrelationships, and other characteristics of a database.

Data Entry   The process of converting data into a form suitable for entry into a computer system. Also called data capture or input preparation.

Data Flow Diagram   A graphic diagramming tool that uses a few simple symbols to illustrate the flow of data among external entities, processing activities, and data storage elements.

Data Management   Control program functions that provide access to data sets, enforce data storage conventions, and regulate the use of input/output devices.

Data Mining   Using special purpose software to analyze data from a data warehouse to find hidden patterns and trends.

Data Model   A conceptual framework that defines the logical relationships among the data elements needed to support a basic business or other process.

Data Modeling   A process in which the relationships between data elements are identified and defined to develop data models.

Data Planning   A corporate planning and analysis function that focuses on data resource management. It includes the responsibility for developing an overall information policy and data architecture for the firm's data resources.

Data Processing   The execution of a systematic sequence of operations performed on data to transform them into information.

Data Resource Management   A managerial activity that applies information systems technology and management tools to the task of managing an organization's data resources. Its three major components are database administration, data administration, and data planning.

Data Warehouse   An integrated collection of data extracted from operational, historical, and external databases and cleaned, transformed, and cataloged for retrieval and analysis (*data mining*) to provide business intelligence for business decision making.

Debug   To detect, locate, and remove errors from a program or malfunctions from a computer.

Decision Support System (DSS)   An information system that utilizes decision models, a database, and a decision maker's own insights in an ad hoc, interactive analytical modeling process to reach a specific decision by a specific decision maker.

Demand Reports and Responses   Information provided whenever a manager or end user demands it.

Desktop Publishing   The use of microcomputers, laser printers, and page makeup software to produce a variety of printed materials that were formerly produced only by professional printers.

Desktop Videoconferencing   The use of end-user computer workstations to conduct two-way interactive video conferences.

Development Centers   Systems development consultant groups formed to serve as consultants to the professional programmers and systems analysts of an organization to improve their application development efforts.

Digital Computer   A computer that operates on digital data by performing arithmetic and logical operations on the data. Contrast with Analog Computer.

Digitizer   A device that is used to convert drawings and other graphic images on paper or other materials into digital data that are entered into a computer system.

Direct Access   A method of storage in which each storage position has a unique address and can be individually accessed in approximately the same period without having to search through other storage positions. Same as Random Access. Contrast with Sequential Access.

Direct Access Storage Device (DASD)   A storage device that can directly access data to be stored or retrieved, for example, a magnetic disk unit.

Direct Data Organization   A method of data organization in which logical data elements are distributed randomly on or within the physical data medium. For example, logical data records distributed randomly on the surfaces of a magnetic disk file. Also called direct organization.

Direct Input/Output   Methods such as keyboard entry, voice input/output, and video displays that allow data to be input into or output from a computer system without the use of machine-readable media.

Disaster Recovery   Methods for ensuring that an organization recovers from natural and human-caused disasters that have affected its computer-based operations.

Discussion Forum   An online network discussion platform to encourage and manage online text discussions over a period among members of special interest groups or project teams.

Distributed Databases   The concept of distributing databases or portions of a database at remote sites where the data are most frequently referenced. Sharing of data is made possible through a network that interconnects the distributed databases.

Distributed Processing   A form of decentralization of information processing made possible by a network of computers dispersed throughout an organization. Processing of user applications is accomplished by several computers interconnected by a telecommunications network, rather than relying on one large centralized computer facility or on the decentralized operation of several independent computers.

Document   (1) A medium on which data have been recorded for human use, such as a report or invoice. (2) In word processing, a generic term for text material such as letters, memos, and reports.

Documentation   A collection of documents or information that describes a computer program, information system, or required data processing operations.

Downsizing   Moving to smaller computing platforms, such as from mainframe systems to networks of personal computers and servers.

Downtime   The time interval during which a device is malfunctioning or inoperative.

DSS Generator   A software package for a decision support system that contains modules for database, model, and dialogue management.

Duplex In communications, pertains to a simultaneous two-way independent transmission in both directions.

EBCDIC: Extended Binary Coded Decimal Interchange Code An eight-bit code that is widely used by mainframe computers.

Echo Check A method of checking the accuracy of data transmission in which the received data are returned to the sending device for comparison with the original data.

e-Commerce Marketplaces Internet, intranet, and extranet Web sites and portals hosted by individual companies, consortiums of organizations, or third-party intermediaries providing electronic catalog, exchange, and auction markets to unite buyers and sellers to accomplish e-commerce transactions.

Economic Feasibility Whether expected cost savings, increased revenue, increased profits, and reductions in required investment exceed the costs of developing and operating a proposed system.

EDI: Electronic Data Interchange The automatic electronic exchange of business documents between the computers of different organizations.

Edit To modify the form or format of data. For example, to insert or delete characters such as page numbers or decimal points.

Edit Report A report that describes errors detected during processing.

EFT: Electronic Funds Transfer The development of banking and payment systems that transfer funds electronically instead of using cash or paper documents such as checks.

Electronic Business (e-Business) The use of Internet technologies to internetwork and empower business processes, electronic commerce, and enterprise communication and collaboration within a company and with its customers, suppliers, and other business stakeholders.

Electronic Commerce (e-Commerce) The buying and selling, marketing and servicing, and delivery and payment of products, services, and information over the Internet, intranets, extranets, and other networks, between an internetworked enterprise and its prospects, customers, suppliers, and other business partners. Includes business-to-consumer (B2C), business-to-business (B2B), and consumer-to-consumer (C2C) e-commerce.

Electronic Communications Tools Software that helps communicate and collaborate with others by electronically sending messages, documents, and files in data, text, voice, or multimedia over the Internet, intranets, extranets, and other computer networks.

Electronic Conferencing Tools Software that helps networked computer users share information and collaborate while working together on joint assignments, no matter where they are located.

Electronic Data Processing (EDP) The use of electronic computers to process data automatically.

Electronic Document Management An image processing technology in which an electronic document may consist of digitized voice notes and electronic graphics images, as well as digitized images of traditional documents.

Electronic Mail Sending and receiving text messages between networked PCs over telecommunications networks. E-mail can also include data files, software, and multimedia messages and documents as attachments.

Electronic Meeting Systems (EMS) Using a meeting room with networked PCs, a large-screen projector, and EMS software to facilitate communication, collaboration, and group decision making in business meetings.

Electronic Payment Systems Alternative cash or credit payment methods using various electronic technologies to pay for products and services in electronic commerce.

Electronic Spreadsheet Package An application program used as a computerized tool for analysis, planning, and modeling that allows users to enter and manipulate data into an electronic worksheet of rows and columns.

Emulation To imitate one system with another so that the imitating system accepts the same data, executes the same programs, and achieves the same results as the imitated system.

Encryption To scramble data or convert them, prior to transmission, to a secret code that masks the meaning of the data to unauthorized recipients. Similar to enciphering.

End User Anyone who uses an information system or the information it produces.

End-User Computing Systems Computer-based information systems that directly support both the operational and managerial applications of end users.

Enterprise Application Integration (EAI) A cross-functional e-business application that integrates front-office applications like customer relationship management with back-office applications like enterprise resource management.

Enterprise Collaboration Systems The use of groupware tools and the Internet, intranets, extranets, and other computer networks to support and enhance communication, coordination, collaboration, and resource sharing among teams and workgroups in an internetworked enterprise.

Enterprise Information Portal A customized and personalized Web-based interface for corporate intranets and extranets that gives qualified users access to a variety of internal and external e-business and e-commerce applications, databases, software tools, and information services.

Enterprise Knowledge Portal An enterprise information portal that serves as a knowledge management system by providing users with access to enterprise knowledge bases.

Enterprise Model A conceptual framework that defines the structures and relationships of business processes and data elements, as well as other planning structures, such as critical success factors and organizational units.

Enterprise Resource Planning (ERP) Integrated cross-functional software that reengineers manufacturing, distribution, finance, human resources, and other basic business processes of a company to improve its efficiency, agility, and profitability.

Entity Relationship Diagram (ERD) A data planning and systems development diagramming tool that models the relationships among the entities in a business process.

Entropy The tendency of a system to lose a relatively stable state of equilibrium.

Ergonomics The science and technology emphasizing the safety, comfort, and ease of use of human-operated machines such as computers. The goal of ergonomics is to produce systems that are user-friendly: safe, comfortable, and easy to use. Ergonomics is also called human factors engineering.

Exception Reports   Reports produced only when exceptional conditions occur, or reports produced periodically that contain information only about exceptional conditions.

Executive Information System (EIS)   An information system that provides strategic information tailored to the needs of executives and other decision makers.

Executive Support System (ESS)   An executive information system with additional capabilities, including data analysis, decision support, electronic mail, and personal productivity tools.

Expert System (ES)   A computer-based information system that uses its knowledge about a specific complex application area to act as an expert consultant to users. The system consists of a knowledge base and software modules that perform inferences on the knowledge and communicate answers to a user's questions.

Extranet   A network that links selected resources of a company with its customers, suppliers, and other business partners, using the Internet or private networks to link the organizations' intranets.

Facilities Management   The use of an external service organization to operate and manage the information processing facilities of an organization.

Fault Tolerant Systems   Computers that have multiple central processors, peripherals, and system software and that are able to continue operations even if there is a major hardware or software failure.

Faxing (Facsimile)   Transmitting and receiving images of documents over the telephone or computer networks using PCs or fax machines.

Feasibility Study   A preliminary study that investigates the information needs of end users and the objectives, constraints, basic resource requirements, cost/benefits, and feasibility of proposed projects.

Feedback   (1) Data or information concerning the components and operations of a system. (2) The use of part of the output of a system as input to the system.

Fiber Optics   The technology that uses cables consisting of very thin filaments of glass fibers that can conduct the light generated by lasers for high-speed telecommunications.

Field   A data element that consists of a grouping of characters that describe a particular attribute of an entity. For example, the name field or salary field of an employee.

Fifth Generation   The next generation of computers. Major advances in parallel processing, user interfaces, and artificial intelligence may provide computers that will be able to see, hear, talk, and think.

File   A collection of related data records treated as a unit. Sometimes called a data set.

File Management   Controlling the creation, deletion, access, and use of files of data and programs.

File Processing   Organizing data into specialized files of data records designed for processing only by specific application programs. Contrast with Database Management Approach.

Financial Management Systems   Information systems that support financial managers in the financing of a business and the allocation and control of financial resources. These include cash and securities management, capital budgeting, financial forecasting, and financial planning.

Firewall   Computers, communications processors, and software that protect computer networks from intrusion by screening all network traffic and serving as a safe transfer point for access to and from other networks.

Firmware   The use of microprogrammed read-only memory circuits in place of hard-wired logic circuitry. See also Microprogramming.

Floating Point   Pertaining to a number representation system in which each number is represented by two sets of digits. One set represents the significant digits or fixed-point "base" of the number, while the other set of digits represents the "exponent," which indicates the precision of the number.

Floppy Disk   A small plastic disk coated with iron oxide that resembles a small phonograph record enclosed in a protective envelope. It is a widely used form of magnetic disk media that provides a direct access storage capability for microcomputer systems.

Flowchart   A graphical representation in which symbols are used to represent operations, data, flow, logic, equipment, and so on. A program flowchart illustrates the structure and sequence of operations of a program, whereas a system flowchart illustrates the components and flows of information systems.

Foreground Processing   The automatic execution of the computer programs that have been designed to preempt the use of computing facilities. Contrast with Background Processing.

Format   The arrangement of data on a medium.

FORTRAN: FORmula TRANslation   A high-level programming language widely utilized to develop computer programs that perform mathematical computations for scientific, engineering, and selected business applications.

Forward Chaining   An inference strategy that reaches a conclusion by applying rules to facts to determine if any facts satisfy a rule's conditions in a particular situation.

Fourth-Generation Languages (4GL)   Programming languages that are easier to use than high-level languages such as BASIC, COBOL, or FORTRAN. They are also known as nonprocedural, natural, or very high-level languages.

Frame   A collection of knowledge about an entity or other concept consisting of a complex package of slots, that is, data values describing the characteristics or attributes of an entity.

Frame-Based Knowledge   Knowledge represented in the form of a hierarchy or network of frames.

Front-End Processor   Typically a smaller, general-purpose computer that is dedicated to handling data communications control functions in a communications network, thus relieving the host computer of these functions.

Functional Business Systems   Information systems within a business organization that support one of the traditional functions of business such as marketing, finance, or production. Functional business systems can be either operations or management information systems.

Functional Requirements The information system capabilities required to meet the information needs of end users. Also called system requirements.

Fuzzy Logic Systems Computer-based systems that can process data that are incomplete or only partially correct, that is, fuzzy data. Such systems can solve unstructured problems with incomplete knowledge, as humans do.

General-Purpose Application Programs Programs that can perform information processing jobs for users from all application areas. For example, word processing programs, electronic spreadsheet programs, and graphics programs can be used by individuals for home, education, business, scientific, and many other purposes.

General-Purpose Computer A computer that is designed to handle a wide variety of problems. Contrast with Special-Purpose Computer.

Generate To produce a machine-language program for performing a specific data processing task based on parameters supplied by a programmer or user.

Genetic Algorithm An application of artificial intelligence software that uses Darwinian (survival of the fittest) randomizing and other functions to simulate an evolutionary process that can yield increasingly better solutions to a problem.

Gigabyte One billion bytes. More accurately, 2 to the 30th power, or 1,073,741,824 in decimal notation.

GIGO An acronym of "Garbage In, Garbage Out," which emphasizes that information systems will produce erroneous and invalid output when provided with erroneous and invalid input data or instructions.

Global Company A business that is driven by a global strategy so that all its activities are planned and implemented in the context of a whole-world system.

Global e-Business Technology Management Managing information technologies in a global e-business enterprise, amid the cultural, political, and geoeconomic challenges involved in developing e-business/IT strategies, global e-business and e-commerce applications portfolios, Internet-based technology platforms, and global data resource management policies.

Global Information Technology The use of computer-based information systems and telecommunications networks using a variety of information technologies to support global business operations and management.

Globalization Becoming a global enterprise by expanding into global markets, using global production facilities, forming alliances with global partners, and so on.

Goal-Seeking Analysis Making repeated changes to selected variables until a chosen variable reaches a target value.

Graphical User Interface A software interface that relies on icons, bars, buttons, boxes, and other images to initiate computer-based tasks for users.

Graphics Pertaining to symbolic input or output from a computer system, such as lines, curves, and geometric shapes, using video display units or graphics plotters and printers.

Graphics Pen and Tablet A device that allows an end user to draw or write on a pressure-sensitive tablet and have

the handwriting or graphics digitized by the computer and accepted as input.

Graphics Software A program that helps users generate graphics displays.

Group Decision Making Decisions made by groups of people coming to an agreement on a particular issue.

Group Decision Support System (GDSS) A decision support system that provides support for decision making by groups of people.

Group Support Systems (GSS) An information system that enhances communication, coordination, collaboration, decision making, and group work activities of teams and workgroups.

Groupware Software to support and enhance the communication, coordination, and collaboration among networked teams and workgroups, including software tools for electronic communications, electronic conferencing, and cooperative work management.

Hacking (1) Obsessive use of a computer. (2) The unauthorized access and use of computer systems.

Handshaking Exchange of predetermined signals when a connection is established between two communications terminals.

Hard Copy A data medium or data record that has a degree of permanence and that can be read by people or machines.

Hardware (1) Machines and media. (2) Physical equipment, as opposed to computer programs or methods of use. (3) Mechanical, magnetic, electrical, electronic, or optical devices. Contrast with Software.

Hash Total The sum of numbers in a data field that are not normally added, such as account numbers or other identification numbers. It is utilized as a control total, especially during input/output operations of batch processing systems.

Header Label A machine-readable record at the beginning of a file containing data for file identification and control.

Heuristic Pertaining to exploratory methods of problem solving in which solutions are discovered by evaluation of the progress made toward the final result. It is an exploratory trial-and-error approach guided by rules of thumb. Opposite of algorithmic.

Hierarchical Data Structure A logical data structure in which the relationships between records form a hierarchy or tree structure. The relationships among records are one to many, because each data element is related only to one element above it.

High-Level Language A programming language that utilizes macro instructions and statements that closely resemble human language or mathematical notation to describe the problem to be solved or the procedure to be used. Also called a compiler language.

Homeostasis A relatively stable state of equilibrium of a system.

Host Computer Typically a larger central computer that performs the major data processing tasks in a computer network.

Human Factors Hardware and software capabilities that can affect the comfort, safety, ease of use, and user customization of computer-based information systems.

Human Information Processing A conceptual framework about the human cognitive process that uses an information processing context to explain how humans capture, process, and use information.

Human Resource Information Systems (HRIS) Information systems that support human resource management activities such as recruitment, selection and hiring, job placement and performance appraisals, and training and development.

Hybrid AI Systems Systems that integrate several AI technologies, such as expert systems and neural networks.

Hypermedia Documents containing multiple forms of media, including text, graphics, video, and sound, that can be interactively searched, like Hypertext.

Hypertext Text in electronic form that has been indexed and linked (hyperlinks) by software in a variety of ways so that it can be randomly and interactively searched by a user.

Hypertext Markup Language (HTML) A popular page description language for creating hypertext and hypermedia documents for World Wide Web and intranet Web sites.

Icon A small figure on a video display that looks like a familiar office or other device such as a file folder (for storing a file) or a wastebasket (for deleting a file).

Image Processing A computer-based technology that allows end users to electronically capture, store, process, and retrieve images that may include numeric data, text, handwriting, graphics, documents, and photographs. Image processing makes heavy use of optical scanning and optical disk technologies.

Impact Printers Printers that form images on paper through the pressing of a printing element and an inked ribbon or roller against the face of a sheet of paper.

Index An ordered reference list of the contents of a file or document together with keys or reference notations for identification or location of those contents.

Index Sequential A method of data organization in which records are organized in sequential order and also referenced by an index. When utilized with direct access file devices, it is known as index sequential access method, or ISAM.

Inference Engine The software component of an expert system, which processes the rules and facts related to a specific problem and makes associations and inferences resulting in recommended courses of action.

Infomediaries Third-party market-maker companies that serve as intermediaries to bring buyers and sellers together by developing and hosting electronic catalog, exchange, and auction markets to accomplish e-commerce transactions.

Information Data placed in a meaningful and useful context for an end user.

Information Appliances Small Web-enabled microcomputer devices with specialized functions, such as handheld PDAs, TV set-top boxes, game consoles, cellular and PCS phones, wired telephone appliances, and other Web-enabled home appliances.

Information Architecture A conceptual framework that defines the basic structure, content, and relationships of the organizational databases that provide the data needed to support the basic business processes of an organization.

Information Center A support facility for the end users of an organization. It allows users to learn to develop their own application programs and accomplish their own information processing tasks. End users are provided with hardware support, software support, and people support (trained user consultants).

Information Float The time that a document is in transit between the sender and receiver and thus unavailable for any action or response.

Information Processing A concept that covers both the traditional concept of processing numeric and alphabetic data and the processing of text, images, and voices. It emphasizes that the production of information products for users should be the focus of processing activities.

Information Quality The degree to which information has content, form, and time characteristics that give it value for specific end users.

Information Resource Management (IRM) A management concept that views data, information, and computer resources (computer hardware, software, networks, and personnel) as valuable organizational resources that should be efficiently, economically, and effectively managed for the benefit of the entire organization.

Information Retrieval The methods and procedures for recovering specific information from stored data.

Information Superhighway An advanced high-speed Internet-like network that connects individuals, households, businesses, government agencies, libraries, schools, universities, and other institutions with interactive voice, video, data, and multimedia communications.

Information System (1) A set of people, procedures, and resources that collects, transforms, and disseminates information in an organization. (2) A system that accepts data resources as input and processes them into information products as output.

Information System Model A conceptual framework that views an information system as a system that uses the resources of hardware (machines and media), software (programs and procedures), people (users and specialists), and networks (communications media and network support) to perform input, processing, output, storage, and control activities that transform data resources (databases and knowledge bases) into information products.

Information Systems Development See Systems Development.

Information System Specialist A person whose occupation is related to the providing of information system services. For example, a systems analyst, programmer, or computer operator.

Information Technology (IT) Hardware, software, telecommunications, database management, and other information processing technologies used in computer-based information systems.

Information Technology Architecture A conceptual blueprint that specifies the components and interrelationships of a company's technology infrastructure, data resources, applications architecture, and IT organization.

Information Technology Management Managing information technologies by (1) the joint development and implementation of business and IT strategies by business and IT executives, (2) managing the research and implementation of new information technologies and the development of business applications, and (3) managing the IT processes, professionals, subunits, and infrastructure within a company.

Information Theory   The branch of learning concerned with the likelihood of accurate transmission or communication of messages subject to transmission failure, distortion, and noise.

Input   Pertaining to a device, process, or channel involved in the insertion of data into a data processing system. Opposite of Output.

Input/Output (I/O)   Pertaining to either input or output, or both.

Input/Output Interface Hardware   Devices such as I/O ports, I/O buses, buffers, channels, and I/O control units, which assist the CPU in its input/output assignments. These devices make it possible for modern computer systems to perform input, output, and processing functions simultaneously.

Inquiry Processing   Computer processing that supports the real-time interrogation of online files and databases by end users.

Instruction   A grouping of characters that specifies the computer operation to be performed.

Intangible Benefits and Costs   The nonquantifiable benefits and costs of a proposed solution or system.

Integrated Circuit   A complex microelectronic circuit consisting of interconnected circuit elements that cannot be disassembled because they are placed on or within a "continuous substrate" such as a silicon chip.

Integrated Packages   Software that combines the ability to do several general-purpose applications (such as word processing, electronic spreadsheet, and graphics) into one program.

Intelligent Agent   A special-purpose knowledge-based system that serves as a software surrogate to accomplish specific tasks for end users.

Intelligent Terminal   A terminal with the capabilities of a microcomputer that can thus perform many data processing and other functions without accessing a larger computer.

Interactive Marketing   A dynamic collaborative process of creating, purchasing, and improving products and services that builds close relationships between a business and its customers, using a variety of services on the Internet, intranets, and extranets.

Interactive Processing   A type of real-time processing in which users can interact with a computer on a real-time basis.

Interactive Video   Computer-based systems that integrate image processing with text, audio, and video processing technologies, which makes interactive multimedia presentations possible.

Interface   A shared boundary, such as the boundary between two systems. For example, the boundary between a computer and its peripheral devices.

Internet   A rapidly growing computer network of millions of business, educational, and governmental networks connecting hundreds of millions of computers and their users in over 200 countries.

Internetwork Processor   Communications processors used by local area networks to interconnect them with other local area and wide area networks. Examples include switches, routers, hubs, and gateways.

Internetworks   Interconnected local area and wide area networks.

Interoperability   Being able to accomplish end-user applications using different types of computer systems, operating systems, and application software, interconnected by different types of local and wide area networks.

Interorganizational Information Systems   Information systems that interconnect an organization with other organizations, such as a business and its customers and suppliers.

Interpreter   A computer program that translates and executes each source language statement before translating and executing the next one.

Interrupt   A condition that causes an interruption in a processing operation during which another task is performed. At the conclusion of this new assignment, control may be transferred back to the point at which the original processing operation was interrupted or to other tasks with a higher priority.

Intranet   An Internet-like network within an organization. Web browser software provides easy access to internal Web sites established by business units, teams, and individuals, and other network resources and applications.

Inverted File   A file that references entities by their attributes.

IT Architecture   A conceptual design for the implementation of information technology in an organization, including its hardware, software, and network technology platforms, data resources, application portfolio, and IS organization.

Iterative   Pertaining to the repeated execution of a series of steps.

Java   An object-oriented programming language designed for programming real-time, interactive, Web-based applications in the form of applets for use on clients and servers on the Internet, intranets, and extranets.

Job   A specified group of tasks prescribed as a unit of work for a computer.

Job Control Language (JCL)   A language for communicating with the operating system of a computer to identify a job and describe its requirements.

Joystick   A small lever set in a box used to move the cursor on the computer's display screen.

K   An abbreviation for the prefix *kilo*, which is 1,000 in decimal notation. When referring to storage capacity, it is equivalent to 2 to the 10th power, or 1,024 in decimal notation.

Key   One or more fields within a data record that are used to identify it or control its use.

Keyboarding   Using the keyboard of a microcomputer or computer terminal.

Knowledge Base   A computer-accessible collection of knowledge about a subject in a variety of forms, such as facts and rules of inference, frames, and objects.

Knowledge-Based Information System   An information system that adds a knowledge base to the database and other components found in other types of computer-based information systems.

Knowledge Engineer   A specialist who works with experts to capture the knowledge they possess to develop a knowledge base for expert systems and other knowledge-based systems.

Knowledge Management   Organizing and sharing the diverse forms of business information created within an organization. Includes managing project and enterprise document libraries, discussion databases, intranet Web site databases, and other types of knowledge bases.

Knowledge Workers   People whose primary work activities include creating, using, and distributing information.

Language Translator Program   A program that converts the programming language instructions in a computer program into machine language code. Major types include assemblers, compilers, and interpreters.

Large-Scale Integration (LSI)   A method of constructing electronic circuits in which thousands of circuits can be placed on a single semiconductor chip.

Legacy Systems   The older, traditional, mainframe-based business information systems of an organization.

Light Pen   A photoelectronic device that allows data to be entered or altered on the face of a video display terminal.

Liquid Crystal Displays (LCDs)   Electronic visual displays that form characters by applying an electrical charge to selected silicon crystals.

List Organization   A method of data organization that uses indexes and pointers to allow for nonsequential retrieval.

List Processing   A method of processing data in the form of lists.

Local Area Network (LAN)   A communications network that typically connects computers, terminals, and other computerized devices within a limited physical area such as an office, building, manufacturing plant, or other worksite.

Locking In Customers and Suppliers   Building valuable relationships with customers and suppliers that deter them from abandoning a firm for its competitors or intimidating it into accepting less profitable relationships.

Logical Data Elements   Data elements that are independent of the physical data media on which they are recorded.

Logical System Design   Developing general specifications for how basic information systems activities can meet end-user requirements.

Loop   A sequence of instructions in a computer program that is executed repeatedly until a terminal condition prevails.

Machine Cycle   The timing of a basic CPU operation as determined by a fixed number of electrical pulses emitted by the CPU's timing circuitry or internal clock.

Machine Language   A programming language in which instructions are expressed in the binary code of the computer.

Macro Instruction   An instruction in a source language that is equivalent to a specified sequence of machine instructions.

Magnetic Disk   A flat, circular plate with a magnetic surface on which data can be stored by selective magnetization of portions of the curved surface.

Magnetic Ink   An ink that contains particles of iron oxide that can be magnetized and detected by magnetic sensors.

Magnetic Ink Character Recognition (MICR)   The machine recognition of characters printed with magnetic ink. Primarily used for check processing by the banking industry.

Magnetic Tape   A plastic tape with a magnetic surface on which data can be stored by selective magnetization of portions of the surface.

Mag Stripe Card   A plastic, wallet-size card with a strip of magnetic tape on one surface; widely used for credit/debit cards.

Mainframe   A larger computer system, typically with a separate central processing unit, as distinguished from microcomputer and minicomputer systems.

Management Information System (MIS)   A management support system that produces prespecified reports, displays, and responses on a periodic, exception, demand, or push reporting basis.

Management Support System (MSS)   An information system that provides information to support managerial decision making. More specifically, an information-reporting system, executive information system, or decision support system.

Managerial End User   A manager, entrepreneur, or managerial-level professional who personally uses information systems. Also, the manager of the department or other organizational unit that relies on information systems.

Managerial Roles   Management of the performance of a variety of interpersonal, information, and decision roles.

Manual Data Processing   Data processing that requires continual human operation and intervention and that utilizes simple data processing tools such as paper forms, pencils, and filing cabinets.

Manufacturing Information Systems   Information systems that support the planning, control, and accomplishment of manufacturing processes. This includes concepts such as computer-integrated manufacturing (CIM) and technologies such as computer-aided manufacturing (CAM) or computeraided design (CAD).

Marketing Information Systems   Information systems that support the planning, control, and transaction processing required for the accomplishment of marketing activities, such as sales management, advertising, and promotion.

Mass Storage   Secondary storage devices with extra-large storage capacities, such as magnetic or optical disks.

Master File   A data file containing relatively permanent information that is utilized as an authoritative reference and is usually updated periodically. Contrast with Transaction File.

Mathematical Model   A mathematical representation of a process, device, or concept.

Media   All tangible objects on which data are recorded.

Megabyte   One million bytes. More accurately, 2 to the 20th power, or 1,048,576 in decimal notation.

Memory   See Storage.

Menu   A displayed list of items (usually the names of alternative applications, files, or activities) from which an end user makes a selection.

Menu Driven   A characteristic of interactive computing systems that provides menu displays and operator prompting to assist an end user in performing a particular job.

Metadata   Data about data; data describing the structure, data elements, interrelationships, and other characteristics of a database.

Microcomputer   A very small computer, ranging in size from a "computer on a chip" to handheld, laptop, and desktop units, and servers.

Micrographics   The use of microfilm, microfiche, and other microforms to record data in greatly reduced form.

Microprocessor   A microcomputer central processing unit (CPU) on a chip. Without input/output or primary storage capabilities in most types.

Microprogram   A small set of elementary control instructions called microinstructions or microcode.

Microprogramming   The use of special software (microprograms) to perform the functions of special hardware (electronic control circuitry). Microprograms stored in a read-only storage module of the control unit interpret the machine language instructions of a computer program and decode them into elementary microinstructions, which are then executed.

Microsecond   A millionth of a second.

Middleware   Software that helps diverse software programs and networked computer systems work together, thus promoting their interoperability.

Midrange Computer   A computer category between microcomputers and mainframes. Examples include minicomputers, network servers, and technical workstations.

Millisecond   A thousandth of a second.

Minicomputer   A type of midrange computer.

Model Base   An organized software collection of conceptual, mathematical, and logical models that express business relationships, computational routines, or analytical techniques.

Modem   (MOdulator-DEModulator) A device that converts the digital signals from input/output devices into appropriate frequencies at a transmission terminal and converts them back into digital signals at a receiving terminal.

Monitor   Software or hardware that observes, supervises, controls, or verifies the operations of a system.

Mouse   A small device that is electronically connected to a computer and is moved by hand on a flat surface to move the cursor on a video screen in the same direction. Buttons on the mouse allow users to issue commands and make responses or selections.

Multidimensional Structure   A database model that uses multidimensional structures (such as cubes or cubes within cubes) to store data and relationships between data.

Multimedia Presentations   Providing information using a variety of media, including text and graphics displays, voice and other audio, photographs, and video segments.

Multiplex   To interleave or simultaneously transmit two or more messages on a single channel.

Multiplexer   An electronic device that allows a single communications channel to carry simultaneous data transmissions from many terminals.

Multiprocessing   Pertaining to the simultaneous execution of two or more instructions by a computer or computer network.

Multiprocessor Computer Systems   Computer systems that use a multiprocessor architecture in the design of their central processing units. This includes the use of support microprocessors and multiple instruction processors, including parallel processor designs.

Multiprogramming   Pertaining to the concurrent execution of two or more programs by a computer by interleaving their execution.

Multitasking   The concurrent use of the same computer to accomplish several different information processing tasks. Each task may require the use of a different program or the concurrent use of the same copy of a program by several users.

Nanosecond   One billionth of a second.

Natural Language   A programming language that is very close to human language. Also called very high-level language.

Network   An interconnected system of computers, terminals, and communications channels and devices.

Network Architecture   A master plan designed to promote an open, simple, flexible, and efficient telecommunications environment through the use of standard protocols, standard communications hardware and software interfaces, and the design of a standard multilevel telecommunications interface between end users and computer systems.

Network Computer   A low-cost networked microcomputer with no or minimal disk storage, which depends on Internet or intranet servers for its operating system and Web browser, Java-enabled application software, and data access and storage.

Network Computing   A network-centric view of computing in which "the network is the computer," that is, the view that computer networks are the central computing resource of any computing environment.

Network Data Structure   A logical data structure that allows many-to-many relationships among data records. It allows entry into a database at multiple points, because any data element or record can be related to many other data elements.

Neural Networks   Computer processors or software whose architecture is based on the human brain's meshlike neuron structure. Neural networks can process many pieces of information simultaneously and learn to recognize patterns and programs to solve related problems on their own.

Node   A terminal point in a communications network.

Nonprocedural Languages   Programming languages that allow users and professional programmers to specify the results they want without specifying how to solve the problem.

Numerical Control   Automatic control of a machine process by a computer that makes use of numerical data, generally introduced as the operation is in process. Also called machine control.

Object   A data element that includes both data and the methods or processes that act on those data.

Object-Based Knowledge Knowledge represented as a network of objects.

Object-Oriented Language An object-oriented programming (OOP) language used to develop programs that create and use objects to perform information processing tasks.

Object Program A compiled or assembled program composed of executable machine instructions. Contrast with Source Program.

OEM: Original Equipment Manufacturer A firm that manufactures and sells computers by assembling components produced by other hardware manufacturers.

Office Automation (OA) The use of computer-based information systems that collect, process, store, and transmit electronic messages, documents, and other forms of office communications among individuals, workgroups, and organizations.

Offline Pertaining to equipment or devices not under control of the central processing unit.

Offshoring A relocation of an organization's business processes to a lower cost location overseas.

Online Pertaining to equipment or devices under control of the central processing unit.

Online Analytical Processing (OLAP) A capability of some management, decision support, and executive information systems that supports interactive examination and manipulation of large amounts of data from many perspectives.

Online Transaction Processing (OLTP) A real-time transaction processing system.

Open Systems Information systems that use common standards for hardware, software, applications, and networking to create a computing environment that allows easy access by end users and their networked computer systems.

Operand That which is operated upon. That part of a computer instruction that is identified by the address part of the instruction.

Operating Environment Software packages or modules that add a graphics-based interface among end users, the operating system, and their application programs and that may also provide multitasking capability.

Operating System The main control program of a computer system. It is a system of programs that controls the execution of computer programs and may provide scheduling, debugging, input/output control, system accounting, compilation, storage assignment, data management, and related services.

Operational Feasibility The willingness and ability of management, employees, customers, and suppliers to operate, use, and support a proposed system.

Operation Code A code that represents specific operations to be performed upon the operands in a computer instruction.

Operations Support System (OSS) An information system that collects, processes, and stores data generated by the operations systems of an organization and produces data and information for input into a management information system or for the control of an operations system.

Operations System A basic subsystem of the business firm that constitutes its input, processing, and output components. Also called a physical system.

Optical Character Recognition (OCR) The machine identification of printed characters through the use of light-sensitive devices.

Optical Disks A secondary storage medium using CD (compact disk) and DVD (digital versatile disk) technologies to read tiny spots on plastic disks. The disks are currently capable of storing billions of characters of information.

Optical Scanner A device that optically scans characters or images and generates their digital representations.

Optimization Analysis Finding an optimum value for selected variables in a mathematical model, given certain constraints.

Organizational Feasibility How well a proposed information system supports the objectives of an organization's strategic plan for information systems.

Output Pertaining to a device, process, or channel involved with the transfer of data or information out of an information processing system. Opposite of Input.

Outsourcing Turning over all or part of an organization's information systems operation to outside contractors, known as systems integrators or service providers.

Packet A group of data and control information in a specified format that is transmitted as an entity.

Packet Switching A data transmission process that transmits addressed packets such that a channel is occupied only for the duration of transmission of the packet.

Page A segment of a program or data, usually of fixed length.

Paging A process that automatically and continually transfers pages of programs and data between primary storage and direct access storage devices. It provides computers with multiprogramming and virtual memory capabilities.

Parallel Processing Executing many instructions at the same time, that is, in parallel. Performed by advanced computers using many instruction processors organized in clusters or networks.

Parity Bit A check bit appended to an array of binary digits to make the sum of all the binary digits, including the check bit, always odd or always even.

Pascal A high-level, general-purpose, structured programming language named after Blaise Pascal. It was developed by Niklaus Wirth of Zurich in 1968.

Pattern Recognition The identification of shapes, forms, or configurations by automatic means.

PCM: Plug-Compatible Manufacturer A firm that manufactures computer equipment that can be plugged into existing computer systems without requiring additional hardware or software interfaces.

Peer-to-Peer Network (P2P) A computing environment in which end-user computers connect, communicate, and collaborate directly with one another via the Internet or other telecommunications network links.

Pen-Based Computers Tablet-style microcomputers that recognize handwriting and hand drawing done by a pen-shaped device on their pressure-sensitive display screens.

Performance Monitor   A software package that monitors the processing of computer system jobs, helps develop a planned schedule of computer operations that can optimize computer system performance, and produces detailed statistics that are used for computer system capacity planning and control.

Periodic Reports   Providing information to managers using a prespecified format designed to provide information on a regularly scheduled basis.

Peripheral Devices   In a computer system, any unit of equipment, distinct from the central processing unit, that provides the system with input, output, or storage capabilities.

Personal Digital Assistant (PDA)   Handheld microcomputer devices that enable you to manage information such as appointments, to-do lists, and sales contacts, send and receive e-mail, access the Web, and exchange such information with your desktop PC or network server.

Personal Information Manager (PIM)   A software package that helps end users store, organize, and retrieve text and numerical data in the form of notes, lists, memos, and a variety of other forms.

Physical System Design   Design of the user interface methods and products, database structures, and processing and control procedures for a proposed information system, including hardware, software, and personnel specifications.

Picosecond   One trillionth of a second.

Plasma Display   Output devices that generate a visual display with electrically charged particles of gas trapped between glass plates.

Plotter   A hard-copy output device that produces drawings and graphical displays on paper or other materials.

Pointer   A data element associated with an index, a record, or other set of data that contains the address of a related record.

Pointing Devices   Devices that allow end users to issue commands or make choices by moving a cursor on the display screen.

Pointing Stick   A small buttonlike device on a keyboard that moves the cursor on the screen in the direction of the pressure placed upon it.

Point-of-Sale (POS) Terminal   A computer terminal used in retail stores that serves the function of a cash register as well as collecting sales data and performing other data processing functions.

Port   (1) Electronic circuitry that provides a connection point between the CPU and input/output devices. (2) A connection point for a communications line on a CPU or other front-end device.

Postimplementation Review   Monitoring and evaluating the results of an implemented solution or system.

Presentation Graphics   Using computer-generated graphics to enhance the information presented in reports and other types of presentations.

Prespecified Reports   Reports whose format is specified in advance to provide managers with information periodically, on an exception basis, or on demand.

Private Branch Exchange (PBX)   A switching device that serves as an interface between the many telephone lines within a work area and the local telephone company's main telephone lines or trunks. Computerized PBXs can handle the switching of both voices and data.

Procedure-Oriented Language   A programming language designed for the convenient expression of procedures used in the solution of a wide class of problems.

Procedures   Sets of instructions used by people to complete a task.

Process Control   The use of a computer to control an ongoing physical process, such as petrochemical production.

Process Design   The design of the programs and procedures needed by a proposed information system, including detailed program specifications and procedures.

Processor   A hardware device or software system capable of performing operations on data.

Program   A set of instructions that causes a computer to perform a particular task.

Programmed Decision   A decision that can be automated by basing it on a decision rule that outlines the steps to take when confronted with the need for a specific decision.

Programmer   A person mainly involved in designing, writing, and testing computer programs.

Programming   The designing, writing, and testing of a program.

Programming Language   A language used to develop the instructions in computer programs.

Programming Tools   Software packages or modules that provide editing and diagnostic capabilities and other support facilities to assist the programming process.

Project Management   Managing the accomplishment of an information system development project according to a specific project plan, in order that a project is completed on time and within its budget and meets its design objectives.

Prompt   Messages that assist a user in performing a particular job. This would include error messages, correction suggestions, questions, and other messages that guide an end user.

Protocol   A set of rules and procedures for the control of communications in a communications network.

Prototype   A working model. In particular, a working model of an information system that includes tentative versions of user input and output, databases and files, control methods, and processing routines.

Prototyping   The rapid development and testing of working models, or prototypes, of new information system applications in an interactive, iterative process involving both systems analysts and end users.

Pseudocode   An informal design language of structured programming that expresses the processing logic of a program module in ordinary human language phrases.

Pull Marketing   Marketing methods that rely on the use of Web browsers by end users to access marketing materials and resources at Internet, intranet, and extranet Web sites.

Push Marketing   Marketing methods that rely on Web broadcasting software to push marketing information and other marketing materials to end users' computers.

Quality Assurance   Methods for ensuring that information systems are free from errors and fraud and provide information products of high quality.

Query Language A high-level, humanlike language provided by a database management system that enables users to easily extract data and information from a database.

Queue (1) A waiting line formed by items in a system waiting for service. (2) To arrange in or form a queue.

RAID Redundant array of independent disks. Magnetic disk units that house many interconnected microcomputer hard disk drives, thus providing large, fault-tolerant storage capacities.

Random Access Same as Direct Access. Contrast with Sequential Access.

Random-Access Memory (RAM) One of the basic types of semiconductor memory used for temporary storage of data or programs during processing. Each memory position can be directly sensed (read) or changed (written) in the same length of time, regardless of its location on the storage medium.

Reach and Range Analysis A planning framework that contrasts a firm's ability to use its IT platform to reach its stakeholders with the range of information products and services that can be provided or shared through IT.

Read-Only Memory (ROM) A basic type of semiconductor memory used for permanent storage. Can only be read, not "written," that is, changed. Variations are Programmable Read-Only Memory (PROM) and Erasable Programmable Read-Only Memory (EPROM).

Real Time Pertaining to the performance of data processing during the actual time a business or physical process transpires, in order that results of the data processing can be used to support the completion of the process.

Real-Time Processing Data processing in which data are processed immediately rather than periodically. Also called online processing. Contrast with Batch Processing.

Record A collection of related data fields treated as a unit.

Reduced Instruction Set Computer (RISC) A CPU architecture that optimizes processing speed by the use of a smaller number of basic machine instructions than traditional CPU designs.

Redundancy In information processing, the repetition of part or all of a message to increase the chance that the correct information will be understood by the recipient.

Register A device capable of storing a specified amount of data, such as one word.

Relational Data Structure A logical data structure in which all data elements within the database are viewed as being stored in the form of simple tables. DBMS packages based on the relational model can link data elements from various tables as long as the tables share common data elements.

Remote Access Pertaining to communication with the data processing facility by one or more stations that are distant from that facility.

Remote Job Entry (RJE) Entering jobs into a batch processing system from a remote facility.

Report Generator A feature of database management system packages that allows an end user to quickly specify a report format for the display of information retrieved from a database.

Reprographics Copying and duplicating technology and methods.

Resource Management An operating system function that controls the use of computer system resources such as primary storage, secondary storage, CPU processing time, and input/output devices by other system software and application software packages.

Robotics The technology of building machines (robots) with computer intelligence and humanlike physical capabilities.

Routine An ordered set of instructions that may have some general or frequent use.

RPG: Report Program Generator A problem-oriented language that utilizes a generator to construct programs that produce reports and perform other data processing tasks.

Rule Statements that typically take the form of a premise and a conclusion, such as if–then rules: If (condition), Then (conclusion).

Rule-Based Knowledge Knowledge represented in the form of rules and statements of fact.

Scalability The ability of hardware or software to handle the processing demands of a wide range of end users, transactions, queries, and other information processing requirements.

Scenario Approach A planning approach in which managers, employees, and planners create scenarios of what an organization will be like three to five years or more into the future and identify the role IT can play in those scenarios.

Schema An overall conceptual or logical view of the relationships between the data in a database.

Scientific Method An analytical methodology that involves (1) recognizing phenomena, (2) formulating a hypothesis about the causes or effects of the phenomena, (3) testing the hypothesis through experimentation, (4) evaluating the results of such experiments, and (5) drawing conclusions about the hypothesis.

Secondary Storage Storage that supplements the primary storage of a computer. Synonymous with auxiliary storage.

Sector A subdivision of a track on a magnetic disk surface.

Security Codes Passwords, identification codes, account codes, and other codes that limit the access and use of computer-based system resources to authorized users.

Security Management Protecting the accuracy, integrity, and safety of the processes and resources of an internetworked e-business enterprise against computer crime, accidental or malicious destruction, and natural disasters, using security measures such as encryption, firewalls, antivirus software, fault tolerant computers, and security monitors.

Security Monitor A software package that monitors the use of a computer system and protects its resources from unauthorized use, fraud, and vandalism.

Semiconductor Memory Microelectronic storage circuitry etched on tiny chips of silicon or other semiconducting material. The primary storage of most modern computers consists of microelectronic semiconductor storage chips for random-access memory (RAM) and read-only memory (ROM).

Semistructured Decisions   Decisions involving procedures that can be partially prespecified but not enough to lead to a definite recommended decision.

Sensitivity Analysis   Observing how repeated changes to a single variable affect other variables in a mathematical model.

Sequential Access   A sequential method of storing and retrieving data from a file. Contrast with Random Access and Direct Access.

Sequential Data Organization   Organizing logical data elements according to a prescribed sequence.

Serial   Pertaining to the sequential or consecutive occurrence of two or more related activities in a single device or channel.

Server   (1) A computer that supports applications and telecommunications in a network, as well as the sharing of peripheral devices, software, and databases among the workstations in the network. (2) Versions of software for installation on network servers designed to control and support applications on client microcomputers in client/server networks. Examples include multiuser network operating systems and specialized software for running Internet, intranet, and extranet Web applications, such as electronic commerce and enterprise collaboration.

Service Bureau   A firm offering computer and data processing services. Also called a computer service center.

Smart Products   Industrial and consumer products, with "intelligence" provided by built-in microcomputers or microprocessors that significantly improve the performance and capabilities of such products.

Software   Computer programs and procedures concerned with the operation of an information system. Contrast with Hardware.

Software Package   A computer program supplied by computer manufacturers, independent software companies, or other computer users. Also known as canned programs, proprietary software, or packaged programs.

Software Piracy   Unauthorized copying of software.

Software Suites   A combination of individual software packages that share a common graphical user interface and are designed for easy transfer of data between applications.

Solid State   Pertaining to devices such as transistors and diodes whose operation depends on the control of electric or magnetic phenomena in solid materials.

Source Data Automation   The use of automated methods of data entry that attempt to reduce or eliminate many of the activities, people, and data media required by traditional data entry methods.

Source Document   A document that is the original formal record of a transaction, such as a purchase order or sales invoice.

Source Program   A computer program written in a language that is subject to a translation process. Contrast with Object Program.

Special-Purpose Computer   A computer designed to handle a restricted class of problems. Contrast with General-Purpose Computer.

Speech Recognition   Direct conversion of spoken data into electronic form suitable for entry into a computer system. Also called voice data entry.

Spooling   Simultaneous peripheral operation online. Storing input data from low-speed devices temporarily on high-speed secondary storage units, which can be quickly accessed by the CPU. Also, writing output data at high speeds onto magnetic tape or disk units from which it can be transferred to slow-speed devices such as a printer.

Stage Analysis   A planning process in which the information system's needs of an organization are based on an analysis of its current stage in the growth cycle of the organization and its use of information systems technology.

Standards   Measures of performance developed to evaluate the progress of a system toward its objectives.

Storage   Pertaining to a device into which data can be entered, in which they can be held, and from which they can be retrieved at a later time. Same as Memory.

Strategic Information Systems   Information systems that provide a firm with competitive products and services that give it a strategic advantage over its competitors in the marketplace. Also, information systems that promote business innovation, improve business processes, and build strategic information resources for a firm.

Strategic Opportunities Matrix   A planning framework that uses a matrix to help identify opportunities with strategic business potential, as well as a firm's ability to exploit such opportunities with IT.

Structure Chart   A design and documentation technique to show the purpose and relationships of the various modules in a program.

Structured Decisions   Decisions that are structured by the decision procedures or decision rules developed for them. They involve situations in which the procedures to follow when a decision is needed can be specified in advance.

Structured Programming   A programming methodology that uses a top-down program design and a limited number of control structures in a program to create highly structured modules of program code.

Structured Query Language (SQL)   A query language that is becoming a standard for advanced database management system packages. A query's basic form is SELECT . . . FROM . . . WHERE.

Subroutine   A routine that can be part of another program routine.

Subschema   A subset or transformation of the logical view of the database schema that is required by a particular user application program.

Subsystem   A system that is a component of a larger system.

Supercomputer   A special category of large computer systems that are the most powerful available. They are designed to solve massive computational problems.

Superconductor   Materials that can conduct electricity with almost no resistance. This allows the development of extremely fast and small electronic circuits. Formerly only possible at supercold temperatures near absolute zero. Recent developments promise superconducting materials near room temperature.

Supply Chain   The network of business processes and interrelationships among businesses that are needed to build, sell, and deliver a product to its final customer.

Supply Chain Management Integrating management practices and information technology to optimize information and product flows among the processes and business partners within a supply chain.

Switch (1) A device or programming technique for making a selection. (2) A computer that controls message switching among the computers and terminals in a telecommunications network.

Switching Costs The costs in time, money, effort, and inconvenience that it would take a customer or supplier to switch its business to a firm's competitors.

Synchronous A characteristic in which each event, or the performance of any basic operation, is constrained to start on, and usually to keep in step with, signals from a timing clock. Contrast with Asynchronous.

System (1) A group of interrelated or interacting elements forming a unified whole. (2) A group of interrelated components working together toward a common goal by accepting inputs and producing outputs in an organized transformation process. (3) An assembly of methods, procedures, or techniques unified by regulated interaction to form an organized whole. (4) An organized collection of people, machines, and methods required to accomplish a set of specific functions.

System Flowchart A graphic diagramming tool used to show the flow of information processing activities as data are processed by people and devices.

Systems Analysis (1) Analyzing in detail the components and requirements of a system. (2) Analyzing in detail the information needs of an organization, the characteristics and components of presently utilized information systems, and the functional requirements of proposed information systems.

Systems Approach A systematic process of problem solving that defines problems and opportunities in a systems context. Data are gathered describing the problem or opportunity, and alternative solutions are identified and evaluated. Then the best solution is selected and implemented, and its success is evaluated.

Systems Design Deciding how a proposed information system will meet the information needs of end users. Includes logical and physical design activities and user interface, data, and process design activities that produce system specifications that satisfy the system requirements developed in the systems analysis stage.

Systems Development (1) Conceiving, designing, and implementing a system. (2) Developing information systems by a process of investigation, analysis, design, implementation, and maintenance. Also called the systems development life cycle (SDLC), information systems development, or application development.

Systems Development Tools Graphical, textual, and computer-aided tools and techniques used to help analyze, design, and document the development of an information system. Typically used to represent (1) the components and flows of a system, (2) the user interface, (3) data attributes and relationships, and (4) detailed system processes.

Systems Implementation The stage of systems development in which hardware and software are acquired, developed, and installed; the system is tested and documented; people are trained to operate and use the system; and an organization converts to the use of a newly developed system.

Systems Investigation The screening, selection, and preliminary study of a proposed information system solution to a business problem.

Systems Maintenance The monitoring, evaluating, and modifying of a system to make desirable or necessary improvements.

System Software Programs that control and support operations of a computer system. System software includes a variety of programs, such as operating systems, database management systems, communications control programs, service and utility programs, and programming language translators.

System Specifications The product of the systems design stage. It consists of specifications for the hardware, software, facilities, personnel, databases, and the user interface of a proposed information system.

Systems Thinking Recognizing systems, subsystems, components of systems, and system interrelationships in a situation. Also known as a systems context or a systemic view of a situation.

System Support Programs Programs that support the operations, management, and users of a computer system by providing a variety of support services. Examples are system utilities and performance monitors.

Tangible Benefits and Costs The quantifiable benefits and costs of a proposed solution or system.

Task and Project Management Managing team and workgroup projects by scheduling, tracking, and charting the completion status of tasks within a project.

Task Management A basic operating system function that manages the accomplishment of the computing tasks of users by a computer system.

TCP/IP Transmission control protocol/Internet protocol. A suite of telecommunications network protocols used by the Internet, intranets, and extranets that has become a de facto network architecture standard for many companies.

Technical Feasibility Whether reliable hardware and software capable of meeting the needs of a proposed system can be acquired or developed by an organization in the required time.

Technology Management The organizational responsibility to identify, introduce, and monitor the assimilation of new information system technologies into organizations.

Telecommunications Pertaining to the transmission of signals over long distances, including not only data communications but also the transmission of images and voices using radio, television, and other communications technologies.

Telecommunications Channel The part of a telecommunications network that connects the message source with the message receiver. It includes the hardware, software, and media used to connect one network location to another for the purpose of transmitting and receiving information.

Telecommunications Controller A data communications interface device (frequently a special-purpose mini- or microcomputer) that can control a telecommunications network containing many terminals.

Telecommunications Control Program A computer program that controls and supports the communications between the computers and terminals in a telecommunications network.

Telecommunications Monitors Computer programs that control and support the communications between the computers and terminals in a telecommunications network.

Telecommunications Processors Internetwork processors such as switches and routers and other devices such as multiplexers and communications controllers that allow a communications channel to carry simultaneous data transmissions from many terminals. They may also perform error monitoring, diagnostics and correction, modulation-demodulation, data compression, data coding and decoding, message switching, port contention, and buffer storage.

Telecommuting The use of telecommunications to replace commuting to work from one's home.

Teleconferencing The use of video communications to allow business conferences to be held with participants who are scattered across a country, continent, or the world.

Telephone Tag The process that occurs when two people who wish to contact each other by telephone repeatedly miss each other's phone calls.

Teleprocessing Using telecommunications for computer-based information processing.

Terabyte One trillion bytes. More accurately, 2 to the 40th power, or 1,009,511,627,776 in decimal notation.

Text Data Words, phrases, sentences, and paragraphs used in documents and other forms of communication.

Throughput The total amount of useful work performed by a data processing system during a given period.

Time Sharing Providing computer services to many users simultaneously while providing rapid responses to each.

Total Quality Management Planning and implementing programs of continuous quality improvement, where quality is defined as meeting or exceeding the requirements and expectations of customers for a product or service.

Touch-Sensitive Screen An input device that accepts data input by the placement of a finger on or close to the CRT screen.

Track The portion of a moving storage medium, such as a drum, tape, or disk, that is accessible to a given reading head position.

Trackball A rollerball device set in a case used to move the cursor on a computer's display screen.

Transaction An event that occurs as part of doing business, such as a sale, purchase, deposit, withdrawal, refund, transfer, or payment.

Transaction Document A document produced as part of a business transaction: for example, a purchase order, paycheck, sales receipt, or customer invoice.

Transaction File A data file containing relatively transient data to be processed in combination with a master file. Contrast with Master File.

Transaction Processing Cycle A cycle of basic transaction processing activities including data entry, transaction processing, database maintenance, document and report generation, and inquiry processing.

Transaction Processing System (TPS) An information system that processes data arising from the occurrence of business transactions.

Transaction Terminals Terminals used in banks, retail stores, factories, and other worksites to capture transaction data at their point of origin. Examples are point-of-sale (POS) terminals and automated teller machines (ATMs).

Transborder Data Flows (TDF) The flow of business data over telecommunications networks across international borders.

Transform Algorithm Performing an arithmetic computation on a record key and using the result of the calculation as an address for that record. Also known as key transformation or hashing.

Transnational Strategy A management approach in which an organization integrates its global business activities through close cooperation and interdependence among its headquarters, operations, and international subsidiaries and its use of appropriate global information technologies.

Turnaround Document Output of a computer system (such as customer invoices and statements) that is designed to be returned to the organization as machine-readable input.

Turnaround Time The elapsed time between submission of a job to a computing center and the return of the results.

Turnkey Systems Computer systems in which all of the hardware, software, and systems development needed by a user are provided.

Unbundling The separate pricing of hardware, software, and other related services.

Uniform Resource Locator (URL) An access code (such as http://www.sun.com) for identifying and locating hypermedia document files, databases, and other resources at Web sites and other locations on the Internet, intranets, and extranets.

Universal Product Code (UPC) A standard identification code using bar coding printed on products that can be read by optical scanners such as those found at a supermarket checkout.

Unstructured Decisions Decisions that must be made in situations in which it is not possible to specify in advance most of the decision procedures to follow.

User Friendly A characteristic of human-operated equipment and systems that makes them safe, comfortable, and easy to use.

User Interface That part of an operating system or other program that allows users to communicate with it to load programs, access files, and accomplish other computing tasks.

User Interface Design Designing the interactions between end users and computer systems, including input/output methods and the conversion of data between human-readable and machine-readable forms.

Utility Program A standard set of routines that assists in the operation of a computer system by performing some frequently required process such as copying, sorting, or merging.

Value-Added Carriers Third-party vendors who lease telecommunications lines from common carriers and offer a variety of telecommunications services to customers.

Value-Added Resellers (VARs) Companies that provide industry-specific software for use with the computer systems of selected manufacturers.

Value Chain Viewing a firm as a series, chain, or network of basic activities that adds value to its products and services and thus adds a margin of value to the firm.

Videoconferencing Real-time video and audio conferencing (1) among users at networked PCs (desktop videoconferencing) or (2) among participants in conference rooms or auditoriums in different locations (teleconferencing). Videoconferencing can also include whiteboarding and document sharing.

Virtual Communities Groups of people with similar interests who meet and share ideas on the Internet and online services and develop a feeling of belonging to a community.

Virtual Company A form of organization that uses telecommunications networks and other information technologies to link the people, assets, and ideas of a variety of business partners, no matter where they may be, to exploit a business opportunity.

Virtual Machine Pertaining to the simulation of one type of computer system by another computer system.

Virtual Mall An online multimedia simulation of a shopping mall with many different interlinked retail Web sites.

Virtual Memory The use of secondary storage devices as an extension of the primary storage of the computer, thus giving the appearance of a larger main memory than actually exists.

Virtual Private Network A secure network that uses the Internet as its main backbone network to connect the intranets of a company's different locations or to establish extranet links between a company and its customers, suppliers, or other business partners.

Virtual Reality The use of multisensory human/ computer interfaces that enable human users to experience computer-simulated objects, entities, spaces, and "worlds" as if they actually existed.

Virtual Storefront An online multimedia simulation of a retail store shopping experience on the Web.

Virtual Team A team whose members use the Internet, intranets, extranets, and other networks to communicate, coordinate, and collaborate with one another on tasks and projects, even though they may work in different geographic locations and for different organizations.

VLSI: Very-Large-Scale Integration Semiconductor chips containing hundreds of thousands of circuits.

Voice Conferencing Telephone conversations shared among several participants via speaker phones or networked PCs with Internet telephone software.

Voice Mail Unanswered telephone messages that are digitized, stored, and played back to the recipient by a voice messaging computer.

Volatile Memory Memory (such as electronic semiconductor memory) that loses its contents when electrical power is interrupted.

Wand A handheld optical character recognition device used for data entry by many transaction terminals.

Web Browser A software package that provides the user interface for accessing Internet, intranet, and extranet Web sites. Browsers are becoming multifunction universal clients for sending and receiving e-mail, downloading files, accessing Java applets, participating in discussion groups, developing Web pages, and other Internet, intranet, and extranet applications.

Web Publishing Creating, converting, and storing hyperlinked documents and other material on Internet or intranet Web servers so that they can be easily shared via Web browsers with teams, workgroups, or the enterprise.

Web Services A collection of Web and object-oriented technologies for linking Web-based applications running on different hardware, software, database, or network platforms. For example, Web services could link key business functions within the applications a business shares with its customers, suppliers, and business partners.

What-If Analysis Observing how changes to selected variables affect other variables in a mathematical model.

Whiteboarding See Data Conferencing.

Wide Area Network (WAN) A data communications network covering a large geographic area.

Window One section of a computer's multiple-section display screen, each section of which can have a different display.

Wireless LANs Using radio or infrared transmissions to link devices in a local area network.

Wireless Technologies Using radio wave, microwave, infrared, and laser technologies to transport digital communications without wires between communications devices. Examples include terrestrial microwave, communications satellites, cellular and PCS phone and pager systems, mobile data radio, and various wireless Internet technologies.

Word (1) A string of characters considered as unit. (2) An ordered set of bits (usually larger than a byte) handled as a unit by the central processing unit.

Word Processing The automation of the transformation of ideas and information into a readable form of communication. It involves the use of computers to manipulate text data to produce office communications in the form of documents.

Workgroup Computing Members of a networked workgroup may use groupware tools to communicate, coordinate, and collaborate and to share hardware, software, and databases to accomplish group assignments.

Workstation (1) A computer system designed to support the work of one person. (2) A high-powered computer to support the work of professionals in engineering, science, and other areas that require extensive computing power and graphics capabilities.

World Wide Web (WWW) A global network of multimedia Internet sites for information, education, entertainment, e-business, and e-commerce.

XML (Extensible Markup Language) A Web document content description language that describes the content of Web pages by applying hidden identifying tags or contextual labels to the data in Web documents. By categorizing and classifying Web data this way, XML makes Web content easier to identify, search, analyze, and selectively exchange between computers.

Name Index

Subject Index